# Mexico City Metro

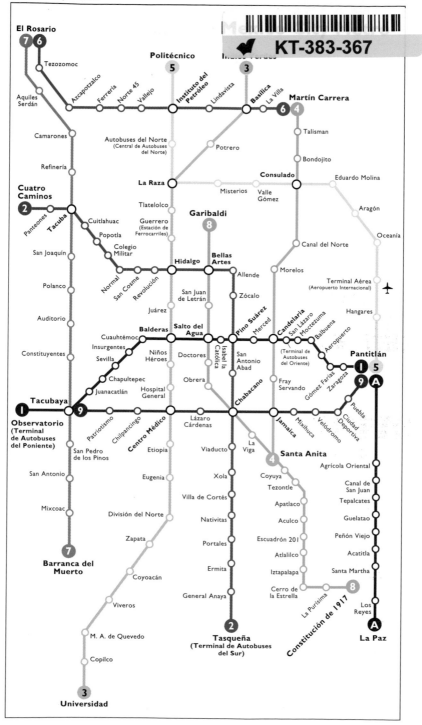

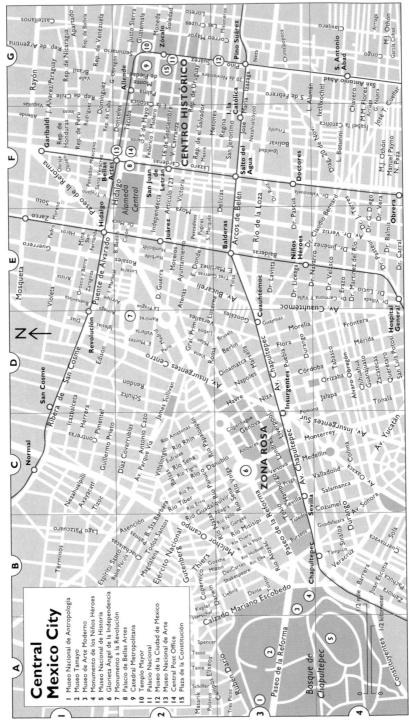

## Central Mexico City

1  Museo Nacional de Antropología
2  Museo Tamayo
3  Museo de Arte Moderno
4  Monumento de los Niños Héroes
5  Museo Nacional de Historia
6  Glorieta Ángel de la Independencia
7  Monumento a la Revolución
8  Palacio de Bellas Artes
9  Catedral Metropolitana
10 Templo Mayor
11 Palacio Nacional
13 Museo de la Ciudad de Mexico
13 Museo Nacional de Arte
14 Central Post Office
15 Plaza de la Constitución

### Central Mexico City

# LET'S GO:

# MEXICO

**is the best book for anyone traveling on a budget. Here's why:**

### ▧ No other guidebook has as many budget listings.

In Mexico we list over 5,000 budget travel bargains. We tell you the cheapest way to get around, and where to get an inexpensive and satisfying meal once you've arrived. We give hundreds of money-saving tips that anyone can use, plus invaluable advice on discounts and deals for students, children, families, and senior travelers.

### ▧ Let's Go researchers have to make it on their own.

Our Harvard-Radcliffe researcher-writers travel on budgets as tight as your own—no expense accounts, no free hotel rooms.

### ▧ Let's Go is completely revised each year.

We don't just update the prices, we go back to the place. If a charming café has become an overpriced tourist trap, we'll replace the listing with a new and better one.

### ▧ No other guidebook includes all this:

Honest, engaging coverage of both the cities and the countryside; up-to-the-minute prices, directions, addresses, phone numbers, and opening hours; in-depth essays on local culture, history, and politics; comprehensive listings on transportation between and within regions and cities; straight advice on work and study, budget accommodations, sights, nightlife, and food; detailed city and regional maps; and much more.

### ▧ Let's Go is for anyone who wants to see Mexico on a budget.

# LET'S GO PUBLICATIONS

*Let's Go: Alaska & The Pacific Northwest*
*Let's Go: Britain & Ireland*
*Let's Go: California*
*Let's Go: Central America*
*Let's Go: Eastern Europe*
*Let's Go: Europe*
*Let's Go: France*
*Let's Go: Germany*
*Let's Go: Greece & Turkey*
*Let's Go: Ireland*
*Let's Go: Israel & Egypt*
*Let's Go: Italy*
*Let's Go: London*
*Let's Go: Mexico*
*Let's Go: New York City*
*Let's Go: Paris*
*Let's Go: Rome*
*Let's Go: Southeast Asia*
*Let's Go: Spain & Portugal*
*Let's Go: Switzerland & Austria*
*Let's Go: USA*
*Let's Go: Washington, D.C.*

## Map Guides (coming March 1996)

*Let's Go: Boston*
*Let's Go: London*
*Let's Go: New York City*
*Let's Go: Paris*
*Let's Go: San Francisco*
*Let's Go: Washington, D.C.*

# LET'S GO

The Budget Guide to

## MEXICO

# 1996

**Jayesh M. Rathod**
Editor

**Fabian Giraldo**
Associate Editor

Macmillan

# HELPING LET'S GO

If you want to share your discoveries, suggestions, or corrections, please drop us a line. We read every piece of correspondence, whether a postcard, a 10-page e-mail, or a coconut. All suggestions are passed along to our researcher-writers. Please note that mail received after May 1996 may be too late for the 1997 book, but will be retained for the following edition.

Address mail to:

**Let's Go: Mexico**
**Let's Go, Inc.**
**One Story Street**
**Cambridge, MA 02138**
**USA**

Send e-mail to:

**LetsGo@delphi.com**
**Subject: "Let's Go: Mexico"**
Visit Let's Go in the travel section of:
**http://www.americanexpress.com/
student/**

In addition to the invaluable travel advice our readers share with us, many are kind enough to offer their services as researchers or editors. Unfortunately, the charter of Let's Go, Inc. enables us to employ only currently enrolled Harvard-Radcliffe students.

---

# About Let's Go

## THIRTY-SIX YEARS OF WISDOM

Back in 1960, a few students at Harvard University banded together to produce a 20-page pamphlet offering a collection of tips on budget travel in Europe. This modest, mimeographed packet was offered to passengers as an extra on their student charter flights to Europe. The following year, students traveling to Europe researched the first full-fledged edition of *Let's Go: Europe*, a pocket-sized book featuring irreverent write-ups of sights and a decidedly youthful slant. Throughout the 60s, our guides reflected the times; one section of the 1968 *Let's Go: Europe* discussed "Street Singing in Europe on No Dollars a Day," which we said "has very little to do with music." The 1969 guide to America led off with sound advice on San Francisco's Haight-Ashbury ("dig the scene"). During the 70s and 80s, we gradually added regional and city guides, and expanded coverage into the Middle East, Central America, and Asia.

We've seen a lot in 36 years. *Let's Go: Europe* is now the world's best-selling international guide, translated into seven languages. And our guides are still researched, written, and produced entirely by students who know first-hand how to see the world on the cheap. As the budget travel world expands, so does Let's Go. The first editions of *Let's Go: Central America* and *Let's Go: Southeast Asia* hit the shelves this year, and *Let's Go: India & Nepal* is right on their heels. Our useful new series of map guides combine concise city coverage with vivid fold-out maps. Our new guides bring our total number of titles, with their spirit of adventure and their honesty, accuracy, and editorial integrity, to 28.

## HOW WE DO IT

Each guide is completely revised and updated every year by a well-traveled set of 200 students, who work on all aspects of each guide's development. Every winter, we recruit over 110 researchers and 50 editors to write our books anew. After several months of training, Researcher-Writers hit the road for seven weeks of exploration, from Anchorage to Ankara, Estonia to El Salvador, Iceland to Indonesia. Those hired possess a rare combination of budget travel sense, writing ability, stamina, and courage. Train strikes, stolen luggage, food poisoning, and irate tourist officials are all part of a day's work. Editors work from spring to fall, massaging copy written on Himalayan bus rides into witty yet informative prose. A student staff of typesetters, cartographers, publicists, and managers keeps our lively and sophisticated team together. In September, the collected efforts of the summer are delivered to our printer, who turns them into books in record time. And even as you read this, work on next year's editions is well underway.

## WHY WE DO IT

At Let's Go, our goal is to give you a great vacation. We don't think of budget travel as the last recourse of the destitute; we believe that it's the only way to travel. Living cheaply and simply brings you closer to the real people and places you've been saving up to visit. Our book will ease your anxieties and answer your questions about the basics—to help you get off the beaten track and explore. Once you learn the ropes, we encourage you to put Let's Go away now and then to strike out on your own. As any seasoned traveler will tell you, the best discoveries are often those you make yourself. When you find something worth sharing, drop us a line. We're Let's Go Publications, One Story Street, Cambridge, MA 02138, USA (e-mail: LetsGo@delphi.com).

## HAPPY TRAVELS!

# Contents

# Maps

# Color Maps

# ■ Acknowledgments

And so, the journey of 1,000 miles has come to an end; and six months of work have finally come to a cadence. Thanks first and foremost to the five truly amazing R-Ws whose efforts have created a remarkable work. And my friend Fabian, whose pen brought life to our book, and whose humor (blip) had me *chorreando* with laughter amidst the drudgery of copyflow: we did it, finding a spoonful or two of warm salvation along the way. Tim: your patience, calm, and wisdom have seen us through to the very end; *hombres* of the Hot Room: Mama Mía, what a summer it's been; and Adam, my fellow Chicagoan: endless gratitude for help when it hurt. Thanks to Emil, Julian, and Max for forcing this job upon me, and Adam and Nat for summertime sanity. And to Mami, Papa, Madhavi, Preeti, and Ba: my love. Thank you for understanding my prolonged absences. This book is dedicated to you.**—JMR**

What a wonderfully torturous publishing trial this has been! And as it continually dawns on me that Mexico *is* a big country, I want to thank and express gratitude with every cell in my rattled body to five "I-still-can't-believe-how-great-they-are" R-Ws. Chris, Clay, Leondra, Robin, and Sam—it has been *my* pleasure to work with you. And then there was Jay. Jay, Jay, Jay: Editor, Jefe, Chief, Expert, and best of all, Friend. A walking panacea, he cured moments of anxiety, boredom, and direction-less-ness. A word of thanks to: Bernie, for memorable crisis lunch-breaks; Tim, for M.E. kindness and knowledge; Dave Tannenbaum, for a witty Pop Culture section; ABBA and the men of the Hot Room, a combination that could never go wrong at 4pm *every* day. My love to friends far and near, but above all and especially to Remy. To Mom, Dad, Juan Carlos, and Ana Maria, love always, of course.**—FG**

| | |
|---|---|
| **Editor** | Jayesh M. Rathod |
| **Associate Editor** | Fabian Giraldo |
| **Managing Editor** | Timothy S. Perlstein |
| | |
| **Publishing Director** | Sean Fitzpatrick |
| **Production Manager** | Michael L. Cisneros |
| **Associate Production Manager** | Eunice C. Park |
| **Cartography Manager** | Samuel P. Trumbull |
| **Associate Cartography Manager** | Amanda K. Bean |
| **Editorial Manager** | Timothy S. Perlstein |
| **Editorial Manager** | Haneen M. Rabie |
| **Financial Manager** | Katarzyna Drozd |
| **Personnel Manager** | Sean K. Desmond |
| **Publicity Manager** | Timur Okay Harry Hiçyılmaz |
| **Associate Publicity Manager** | Eleni N. Gage |
| | |
| **General Manager** | Richard Olken |
| **Assistant General Manager** | Anne E. Chisholm |
| **Office Coordinator** | Jennifer L. Schuberth |
| **Director of Advertising and Sales** | Jean C. Anderson |
| **Sales Assistant Manager** | Sammy Lai |
| **Sales Representatives** | Matthew S. Abramson |
| | Delphine Gabbay, Godfffrey Williams |

# Researcher-Writers

**Chris Baker**                              *Yucatán Peninsula, Chiapas, Tabasco*
Chris sent back page after page of absolutely irreproachable copy, choc-a-bloc full of
witty descriptions and incisive cultural insights. After conquering the *costa
torquesa* in grand, yet cheap, style, Chris breezed through the Mayan route and into
Chiapas, revitalizing our coverage with a politically attuned perspective. Both original and frank, his thorough copy made us laugh uncontrollably at times and raised
more than a few jealous editorial eyebrows around the office. How could anyone
write so much, so well, so consistently, and have so much energy to spare? We've
yet to figure it out. Be sure to compliment this incredible, globe-trotting Brit on his
Mexican-grown goatee—he earned it, as well as our utmost respect and admiration.

**Robin S. Goldstein**                        *Baja California, Northwest Mexico*
From the wilderness of Northampton, Mass., to the "wild"erness of Tijuana, not
even 5,400 miles of inhumane desert terrain or Mexico's unpredictable transportation system could deter Robin from completing his itinerary with high-flying colors
and steadfastness—nor from making spectacular off-the-beaten-path discoveries.
With an intensely perceptive eye, he uncovered the region's duality, heaping
exquisite imagery upon informed social analysis. As the eloquent advocate of the
budget traveler, Robin was devoted to cultivating the fine art of the cheap find—and
a taste for just about anything *al mojo de ajo*. Without a doubt, travelers to Baja and
the Northwest will be the fortunate heirs to the Goldstein legacy for years to come.

**Leondra Reid Kruger**            *Puebla, Tlaxcala, Veracruz, Oaxaca, Guerrero*
Leondra's highly evocative writing somehow conveyed both the seemingly incom-
municable grandeur of colonial Mexico and the beauty of the country's Gulf and
Pacific coasts. As she wove between the interior and the shore, Leondra unearthed
a bounty of budget gems, from unique eateries to charming cafés; she also ventured
into new towns, rendering write-ups so perfect we scarcely altered a word. Her
flawless copy, good cheer, and amazing linguistic resources made for an ideal
Researcher-Writer—small surprise that her application was a hot commodity during
the hiring process. We could never run out of positive things to say about our southern Mexico correspondent extraordinaire. Go, Leondra. You're one-in-a-million.

**Samuel Mario Rosaldo**            *Western Mexico, El Bajío, Central Mexico*
A veteran of Latin America with unflappable calm and an unrelenting pen (which
often ran out of ink), Sam steamrolled through Mexico's western coast before diving
into the colonial heartland, and emerged, naturally, with prose as sharp and revealing as that of any investigative reporter. He faced a grueling itinerary that mysteriously rendered the words "rest day" obsolete, yet Sam never failed to entertain with
his deadpan humor and tales of *huero* life, and always wowed us with simply
impeccable copybatches. To each place he visited, Sam brought both an acute
awareness of Mexican character and an intuitive gift for seeing past the surface, and
his assets translated into remarkably in-depth coverage. Sam, *Let's Go* salutes you.

**Clay West**        *NE Mexico, Mexico City, Morelos, San Luis Potosí, N. Veracruz*
With enthusiasm running in torrents, and reportage as extensive and efficient as
Mexico City's subway system, Clay's performance in the world's second-largest city
will be hard to repeat. Both his effortless synthesis of history and culture, and his
penetrating observations of Mexican life created copy that brought into vivid color
the country's vibrant character. He managed the unruly megalopolis and the more
sedate environs along the way, tackling a diverse array of terrain with disarming agil-
ity and a keen eye that never lacked for originality or scope. A couple of smog-free,
deep breaths later—home is southern Illinois—and nary a complaint, Clay was suddenly off again, this time off the backpackers' trail, and onto the Presidential one.

# How To Use This Book

Let's Go: Mexico is written for the adventurous budget traveler. In the long, hot, and humid Cambridge summer of 1995, we sent five roving researchers out on a shoe-string budget with your concerns in mind: how to get from place to place, find salvation in local cuisine, enjoy the evenings, and get some sleep, all in the most economical way possible. Ultimately, we have tried to produce a book deeply infused with a sense of place, to present the distinctive history, culture, and ways of life which mark the remarkable country of Mexico.

The first chapter of this book, **Mexico: An Introduction** is chock full of information you'll want to have a look at before leaving. Turn to this chapter for information on anything and everything—booking a flight, enrolling in a language school, procuring a passport, changing money, packing, securing car insurance, and, perhaps most imporant of all, phoning home. Subsections focus on women and travel, older travelers, travelers with disabilities, and gay and lesbian travelers. Our introduction concludes with a series of essays on Mexican history, culture, and character, in its wonderfully various forms—read it before you go to Mexico and you'll have a better, deeper sense of what life is like there.

Coverage of Mexico begins in Mexico City; from there, coverage generally proceeds in a northwest-southeast direction, starting with Baja California and rounding out with the Yucatán peninsula. Each city or town is sub-divided into care-packages. Introductions focus on culture and history, and aim to answer a simple question: why should I go there? Introductions are followed by **Orientation,** which describes the layout of the city, and **Practical Information,** which lists essential schedules, addresses, and numbers. **Accommodations, Food, Sights,** and **Entertainment** are fairly self-explanatory. In researching and writing the book, we have tried to accommodate the diverse backgrounds and tastes of our readers. That said, we wish you an exciting and enjoyable trip. *Ándale, pues,* and happy travels.

---

## A NOTE TO OUR READERS

The information for this book is gathered by Let's Go researchers during the summer months. Each listing is derived from the assigned researcher's opinion based upon his or her visit at a particular time. The opinions are expressed in a candid and forthright manner. Other travelers might disagree. Those traveling at a different time may have different experiences since prices, dates, hours, and conditions are always subject to change. You are urged to check beforehand to avoid inconvenience and surprises. Travel always involves a certain degree of risk, especially in low-cost areas. When traveling, especially on a budget, you should always take particular care to ensure your safety.

# ■ Mexico:
# An Introduction

## PLANNING YOUR TRIP

### ■■■ CLIMATE

The Tropic of Cancer bisects Mexico into a temperate north and tropical south, but the climate varies considerably even within these belts. For each of the geographic divisions used in this book, very general climate conditions hold true. **Northwest Mexico,** including Baja California, is the driest area of the country, but still offers a unique array of desert flora and fauna, while the **Northeast** is a bit more temperate. Pleasant beaches are scattered on the **Gulf Coast,** although they can't compare with the beauty of those elsewhere in Mexico. The central region north of Mexico City, known as the **Bajío,** and **South Central Mexico** both experience the cooler climates of the highlands as well as coastal warmth. Natural beauty extends from world-famous beaches to inland forests. Lush, green jungles obscure ruins of the ancient civilizations of the **Yucatán Peninsula.**

The rainy season lasts from May until October (with a hurricane season in the south Aug.-Oct.). The southern half of the country averages over 250cm per year (75% of that during the rainy season), so a summer vacation is likely to be on the damp side. Exhaustive statistics on climate are available in a chart compiled by the International Association for Medical Assistance to Travelers (see Health, below).

### ■■■ AT-HOME RESOURCES

#### GOVERNMENT AGENCIES

**Embassy of Mexico,** 1911 Pennsylvania Ave. NW, Washington, DC 20006 (tel. (202) 728-1600); in the **U.K.,** 42 Hertford St., Mayfair, London W1 (tel. (0171) 495-4024; fax 495-4035); in **Canada,** 45 O'Connor St. #1500, Ottawa, Ont. K1P 1A4 (tel. (613) 233-8988; fax 235-9123); in **Australia,** 14 Perth Ave., Yarralumla, 2600 Canberra (tel. 273-3905 or 273-3947; fax 273-1190).

**Consulate of Mexico,** 2827 16th St. NW, Washington, DC 20036 (tel. (202) 736-1000); in **Canada,** 199 Bay St., Commerce Court West, Toronto, Ont. M5L1E9 (tel. (416) 368-2875); in the **U.K.,** 8 Halkin St., London SW1 X7DW (tel. (0171) 235-6393); in **Australia,** 135-153 New South Head Rd., Edgecliff, Sydney 2027 NSW (tel. (2) 326-1311 or 326-1292; fax +61 (2) 327-1110).

**Mexican Government Tourism Office (Secretaría de Turismo or SECTUR),** In the **U.S.,** 405 Park Ave. #1402, New York, NY 10022 (tel. (212) 838-2949 or 755-4756; fax 753-2874; 24-hr. information tel. (800) 262-8900); 10100 Santa Monica Blvd. #224, Los Angeles, CA 90067 (tel. (310) 203-8191; fax 203-8316); 128 Aragon Ave., Coral Gables, FL 33134 (tel. (305) 443-9160; fax 443-1186); 70 E. Lake St. #1413, Chicago, IL 60601-5977 (tel. (312) 606-9015; fax 606-9012); 2707 N. Loop W. #450, Houston, TX 77008 (tel. (713) 880-5153; fax 880-1833); 1911 Pennsylvania Ave., Washington, DC 20036 (tel. (202) 728-1750; fax 728-1758); in **Canada,** 2 Floor St. W #1801, Toronto, Ontario M4W 3E2 (tel. (416) 925-0704; fax 925-6061) or 1 Place Ville Marie #2409, Montreal, Quebec H3B 3M9 (tel. (514) 871-1052; fax 871-3825) or 1610-999 West Hastings Ave., Vancouver, B.C. V6C 2W2; in **Germany,** Wiessenhuttenplatz 26, D 6000 Frankfurt Am Main 1 (tel. (4969) 25-3413 or 25-3541; fax 25-3755); in the **U.K.,** 60/61

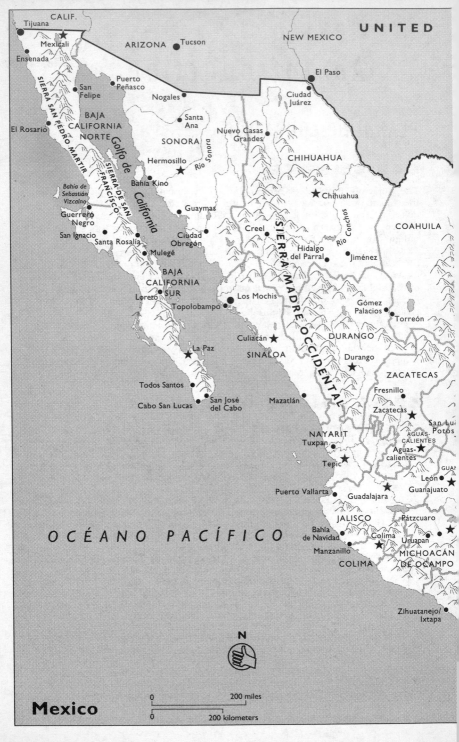

UNITED

CALIF.

Tijuana

Mexicali

Ensenada

ARIZONA

Tucson

NEW MEXICO

El Paso

Puerto
Peñasco

San
Felipe

Nogales

Ciudad
Juárez

El Rosario

BAJA
CALIFORNIA
NORTE

SIERRA SAN PEDRO MARTIR

Golfo de California

Santa
Ana

Nuevo Casas
Grandes

SONORA

CHIHUAHUA

COAHUILA

Hermosillo

Río Sonora

Chihuahua

Bahía Kino

SIERRA DE SAN FRANCISCO

Bahía de
Sebastián
Vizcaíno

Guerrero
Negro

San Ignacio

Santa Rosalía

Mulegé

Guaymas

Creel

Río Conchos

SIERRA MADRE OCCIDENTAL

Hidalgo
del Parral

Jiménez

BAJA
CALIFORNIA
SUR

Loreto

Topolobampo

Ciudad
Obregón

Los Mochis

Gómez
Palacios

Torreón

La Paz

Culiacán

DURANGO

SINALOA

Durango

ZACATECAS

Todos Santos

Cabo San Lucas

San José
del Cabo

Mazatlán

Fresnillo

Zacatecas

San Luis
Potosí

AGUAS
CALIENTES

NAYARIT

Tuxpan

Aguas-
calientes

Tepic

León

Guanajuato

GUA

Puerto Vallarta

Guadalajara

JALISCO

Pátzcuaro

Bahía
de Navidad

Colima

Uruapan

Manzanillo

COLIMA

MICHOACÁN
DE OCAMPO

OCÉANO PACÍFICO

Zihuatanejo/
Ixtapa

N

Mexico

0                    200 miles

0

200 kilometers

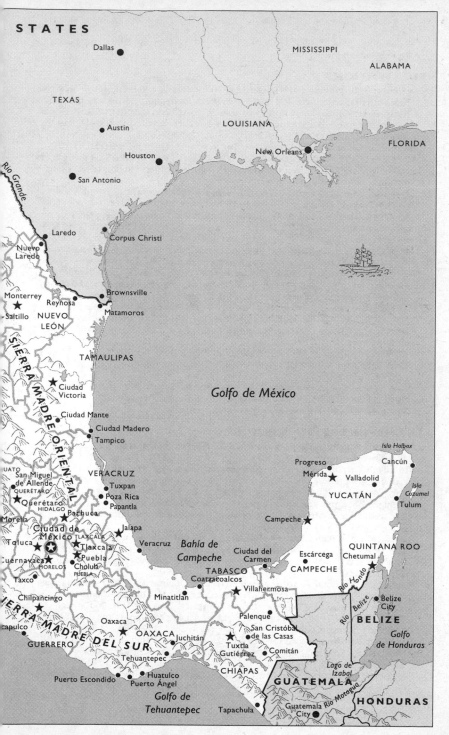

Trafalgar Sq., London WC2N 5DS (tel. (0171) 839-3177). Provides maps, information and tourist cards. Check your phone book for local offices. Also operates a 24-hr. hotline out of Mexico City (tel. (5) 250-01-23) for complaints, emergencies, and less urgent information

## PUBLICATIONS

**Adventures in Mexico (AIM),** Apdo. 31-70, Guadalajara, Jalisco, 45050 Mexico. Newsletter on retirement and travel in Mexico. Endearing approach to the country's quirks. Annual subscription (6 issues) costs US$16 or CDN$23. Personal checks accepted. Back issues, most of which are devoted to a single city or region, available for US$2.50 each, or 3 issues for US$6.

**Animal and Plant Health Inspection Service,** Attn.: Quarantines/Traveler's Tips, P.O. Box 96464, Washington, D.C. 20090-6464 (tel. (301) 734-8645). A division of the USDA, APHIS publishes the *Traveler's Tips* pamphlet, which provides information on which plant and animal products you can safely bring home from other countries. Consult your local Blue Pages for the number of the nearest branch.

**Forsyth Travel Library,** P.O. Box 2975, Shawnee Mission, KS 66201 (tel. (800) 367-7984; fax (913) 384-3553). Mail-order maps and travel guides for Mexico.

**Hippocrene Books, Inc.,** 171 Madison Ave., New York, NY 10016 (tel. (212) 685-4371, orders (718) 454-2366; fax (718) 454-1391). Publishes travel reference books, travel guides, maps, and foreign language dictionaries. Free catalog.

**John Muir Publications,** P.O. Box 613, Santa Fe, NM 87504 (tel. (800) 888-7504 or (505) 982-4078; fax 988-1680). Publishes the *People's Guide to RV Camping in Mexico* (US$13.95), plus general guides to Mexico, Belize, Costa Rica, and Guatemala. Shipping fees range from US$4.25-6.25 depending on order size.

**México Desconocido,** Monte Pelvoux 110-104, Lomas de Chapultepec, México, D.F. 11000 (tel. (5) 202-65-85 or 259-09-39; fax 540-17-71). Monthly travel magazines in Spanish and English describing little-known areas and customs of Mexico.

**Superintendent of Documents,** U.S. Government Printing Office, P.O. Box 371954, Pittsburgh, PA 15250-7954 (tel. (202) 512-1800; fax 512-2250). Publishes *Your Trip Abroad* (US$1.25), *Health Information for International Travel* (US$7), and "Background Notes" on all countries (US$1). Postage included.

**Wide World Books and Maps,** 1911 N. 45th St., Seattle, WA 98103 (tel. (206) 634-3453; fax 634-0558, email travelbk@nwlink.com). Wide selection of books about Mexico and hard-to-find maps of the country.

## TRANSPORTATION SERVICES

**American Automobile Association (AAA) Travel Related Services,** 1000 AAA Drive, Heathrow, FL, 32746 (tel. (407) 444-7000). Road maps and guides free to members; *1994: Mexico* includes information on gas, oil, repairs, and border crossings. Members eligible to receive Mexican auto insurance (see Getting There: By Car, below) and can buy AmEx traveler's checks commission-free. Dues average US$52 per year (US$40 per year renewal). AAA members needing roadside assistance in Mexico should contact the Mexican Automobile Association (tel. (5) 588-70-55 or 588-93-55).

**Asociación Mexicana Automovilística, A.C. (AMA),** Av. Orizaba 7, Mexico, D.F. 06700 (tel. (5) 208-88-69; fax 511-62-85). Members receive information about car travel in Mexico, up-to-date road maps, emergency road assistance, and other services.

**Asociación Nacional Automovilística (ANA),** Oficinas ANA, José María Iglesias 59, México, D.F. 06470 (tel. (5) 705-05-01 or 705-10-01); emergency services Lerdo 361, Entre San Timor y Manuel González, México, D.F. 06470 (tel. (5) 597-42-83 or 597-19-62). Offers AAA-type services in Mexico, but is not affiliated with the U.S. organization.

**Canadian Automobile Association,** 60 Commerce Valley Dr. E., Thorn Hill, Ontario. L3T 7P9 (tel. (905) 771-3170). Maps of Mexico for members. Will highlight routes directly on the maps.

**Ferrocarriles Nacionales de México (National Railways of Mexico),** Buenavista Gran Central Estación, Departamento de Tráfico de Pasajeros, México,

D.F. 06358 (tel. (5) 547-89-72). Write for timetables and information about Mexican railways.

# ■■■ PAPERWORK

## TOURIST CARDS

All visitors to Mexico must carry a **tourist card** (FMT, Spanish for *folleto de migración turística*) in addition to proof of citizenship. U.S. and Canadian citizens can skip the FMT if they don't expect to travel past border towns or stay anywhere in the country for more than 72 hours. U.S. and Canadian citizens traveling to Baja California will need a card only if they plan to venture beyond Maneadero on the Pacific Coast, south of Mexicali on Rte. 5, or if they stay anywhere for more than 72 hours.

Tourist cards, like all entry documents, are free of charge. Many people get their cards when they cross the border or when they check in at the airline ticket counter for their flight into Mexico; however, you can avoid delays by obtaining one from a Mexican embassy, consulate, or tourist office before you leave (see Useful Organizations). You will have to present proof of citizenship, and if your financial condition looks suspect, officials will ask you to flash your return ticket. Travelers from outside North America must present a passport. U.S. and Canadian citizens can obtain a tourist card with an original birth certificate or naturalization papers, plus some type of photo ID (with the exception of naturalized Canadians, who must carry a passport). But be forewarned: traveling in Mexico without a passport is asking for trouble. A passport carries much more authority with local officials than does a birth certificate. Returning home by air is particularly difficult with only a birth certificate. Finally, a passport is mandatory for anyone who is driving through Mexico to Central America.

On the FMT, you must indicate your intended destination and expected length of stay. Tourist cards are valid for 90 days and must be returned to border officials upon leaving the country. If you stay in Mexico past your 90-day limit, you will be slapped with a fine. Request a special, 180-day multiple-entry permit at your point of entry if you plan to leave and re-enter the country several times within a short time period. Otherwise, you must get a new FMT every time you re-enter the country, even if your old one has not expired. Try to get a card that will be valid longer than your projected stay, since obtaining an extension on a 90-day FMT is a huge hassle: you'll need a physician's authorization stating that you are too ill to travel. If you do need an extension, visit a local office of the Delegación de Servicios Migratorios several weeks before your card expires. They also take care of lost cards.

Special regulations apply if you are entering Mexico on a business trip, or if you expect to study in the country for more than six months; contact a Mexican consulate several months before you leave home. Steep fines face any business travelers caught with only a tourist card. If you're crossing Mexico *en route* to Guatemala or Belize, ask for a **transmigrant form,** which will allow you to remain in Mexico for up to 30 days; you'll need a passport or current photo ID, a Guatemalan or Belizean visa, and proof of sufficient funds for your trip.

While in Mexico, you are required by law to carry your tourist card at all times. Make a photocopy and keep it in a separate place. Although it won't replace a lost or stolen tourist card, a copy should facilitate replacement. If you do lose your card, expect hours of delay and bureaucratic inconvenience while immigration verifies your record of entrance.

## PASSPORTS

As a precaution in case your passport is lost or stolen, be sure *before you leave* to photocopy the page of your passport that contains your photograph and identifying information. Especially important is your passport number. Carry this photocopy in a safe place apart from your passport, perhaps with a traveling companion, and

PAPERWORK

leave another copy at home. Better yet, carry a photocopy of all the pages of the passport, including all visa stamps, apart from your actual passport, and leave a duplicate copy with a relative or friend. These measures will help prove your citizenship and facilitate the issuing of a new passport. Consulates also recommend that you carry an expired passport or an *official* copy of your birth certificate in a part of your baggage separate from other documents. You can request a duplicate birth certificate from the Bureau of Vital Records and Statistics in your state or province of birth.

If your passport is lost or stolen, immediately notify the local police and the nearest embassy or consulate of your home government. To expedite the replacement of your passport, you will need to know *all the information that you had previously recorded and photocopied* and to show identification and proof of citizenship. Some consulates can issue new passports within two days if you give them proof of citizenship. In an emergency, ask for immediate temporary traveling papers that will permit you to return to your home country.

**U.S. citizens** may apply for a passport, valid for 10 years (5 years if under 18) at any one of several thousand federal or state courthouses or post offices authorized to accept passport applications, or at a U.S. Passport Agency. Refer to the "U.S. Government, State Department" section of the telephone directory or call your local post office for addresses. Parents must apply in person for children under 13. You must apply in person if this is your first passport, if you are under age 18, or if your current passport is more than 12 years old or was issued before your 18th birthday.

Processing usually takes three to four weeks, more in spring and summer. Passports are processed according to the departure date indicated on the application form. *File your application as early as possible.* If you fail to indicate a departure date, the agency will assume you are not planning any immediate travel. Your passport will be mailed to you; you may pay for express mail return of your passport. Passport Agencies offer rush service: if you have proof that you are departing within five working days (e.g. an airplane ticket), a Passport Agency will issue a passport while you wait.

Abroad, a U.S. embassy or consulate can usually issue a new passport, given proof of citizenship. For Passport Agency locations and more information, contact the U.S. Passport Information's 24-hour recorded message (tel. (202) 647-0518). For inquiries regarding the processing of your passport write the National Passport Center, 31 Rochester Avenue, Portsmouth, NH 03801 or call (603) 334-0500.

**Canadian application** forms in English and French are available at all passport offices, post offices, and most travel agencies. Citizens may apply in person at any one of 28 regional Passport Offices across Canada. Citizens who reside in the U.S. can contact a Canadian diplomatic mission; those outside Canada and the U.S. should contact the nearest embassy or consulate. You can apply by mail by sending a completed application form with appropriate documentation and fee to Passport Office, Foreign Affairs, Ottawa, Ontario, K1A 0G3. The processing time is approximately five business days for in-person applications and three weeks for mailed ones. Keep in mind that some countries require that a child carry his or her own passport. A passport is valid for five years and is not renewable. For additional **information,** call the 24-hour number (tel. (800) 567-6868 from Canada only). Refer to the booklet *Bon Voyage, But...* for further help and a list of Canadian embassies and consulates abroad. It is available free of charge from any passport office or from: Info-Export (BPTE), External Affairs, Ottawa, Ontario, K1A 0G2.

**British citizens,** British Dependent Territories citizens, and British Overseas citizens can obtain a full passport valid for 10 years (5 years if under 16) by applying in person or by mail to the London Passport Office or by mail to a passport office located in Liverpool, Newport, Peterborough, Glasgow, or Belfast. Applications are available at post offices. Processing usually takes four to six weeks. The London office offers same-day walk-in rush service; arrive early.

**Australian citizens** must apply for a passport in person at a local post office, a passport office, an Australian diplomatic mission overseas, or one of nine passport offices. A parent may file an application for a child who is under 18 and unmarried. Application fees are adjusted frequently; call the toll-free information service for current details (tel. 13-12-32).

New Zealand citizens can obtain an application from their local Link Centre, travel agent, or New Zealand Representative. Questions should be addressed to the New Zealand Passport Office, Documents of National Identity Division, Department of Internal Affairs, Box 10-526, Wellington (tel. (04) 474 81 00). Standard processing time is 10 working days from receipt of completed application. Overseas citizens should send the passport application to the nearest embassy, high commission, or consulate that is authorized to issue passports.

## VISAS

A **visa** is an endorsement that a foreign government stamps into your passport; it allows the bearer to stay in that country for a specified purpose and period of time. Visas are not necessary for U.S., Canadian, or British citizens unless they will be in Mexico for more than six months. Holders of European Community passports need only their **permanent resident cards ("green cards").** Australians and New Zealanders, however, do need visas, regardless of the length of stay. Businesspeople, missionaries, and students who expect to earn a diploma in Mexico must also obtain a visa. Applications require a valid passport, six frontal photos and five profile photos. Consulates claim to have 24-hour visa service if you apply in person; by mail they may take weeks.

## STUDENT AND YOUTH IDENTIFICATION

You might consider spending your hard-earned money on an **International Student Identity Card (ISIC),** available at many student travel offices (see Useful Organizations: Travel Organizations, above) and administered by the **International Student Travel Confederation (ISTC),** Store Kongensgade 40H, 1264 Copenhagen K, Denmark (tel. 33-93-93-03). The ISIC card provides access to Council student airfares, US$3000 of accident-related coverage with no daily limit, and access to a toll-free Traveler's Assistance hotline whose multilingual staff can provide help in medical, legal, and financial emergencies overseas. Many student travel offices issue ISICs, including Council, Let's Go Travel, and STA Travel in the U.S.; Travel CUTS in Canada; and any of the organizations under the auspices of the ISTC around the world. The card is valid from September to December of the following year. The fee is US$15. Applicants must be at least 12 years old and must be a degree-seeking student of a secondary or post-secondary school. Because of the proliferation of phony ISICs, many airlines and some other services now require other proof of student identity. To obtain a card by using a credit card, please call (800) 255-1000, extension 425.

If you are ineligible for the ISIC but are under 26, you can take advantage of the **GO 25 Card,** issued by the **Federation of International Youth Travel Organizations (FIYTO),** Bredgade 25H, DK-1260 Copenhagen K, Denmark (tel. (33) 33 96 00). The GO 25 card entitles you to some price reductions in Mexico. To get the card, you must submit proof of birthdate, a passport-sized photo with your name printed on the back, and US$16. The card is offered by most of the travel organizations listed above.

## DRIVER'S LICENSE AND VEHICLE PERMITS

An international driver's license is not necessary for driving in Mexico; any valid driver's license is acceptable. You will, however, need a Mexican **vehicle permit,** issued as you cross the border. Requirements for these permits have changed rapidly; contact a Mexican consulate or tourist office for the most up-to-date information. As of July 1995, to complete the necessary paperwork at the border, you need two copies (the original and a photocopy) of the following: your state vehicle registration certificate **and** vehicle title, a valid driver's license, and a birth certificate, or passport, or resident card. Those leasing a vehicle must provide their contract (also

CUSTOMS

in duplicate), which must be in their name. You will also be asked to make a financial guarantee for temporary importation. Having a credit card (AmEx, MC, or Visa) makes the process easiest—you can charge the US$10 fee. Without a credit card, you must make a cash deposit calculated according to the value of your vehicle, plus a US$10 deposit. In return, you'll receive two punched stickers bearing the expiration date of your permit. Regulations change frequently; the Mexican government has a hotline for info at tel. (800) 446-8277. To extend a vehicle permit beyond its original expiration date, contact the temporary importation department of Mexican customs. Permits are not required within the **Free Zone** (see Getting There: By Car below).

Resist the temptation to abandon, sell, or give away your car in Mexico. Once you enter the country with a car, your tourist card will be marked such that you will not be allowed to collect the bond or to leave without the vehicle. Even if your car disintegrates somewhere in Mexico, you must get permission to leave without it; permission can be obtained (for a fee) at either the federal registry of automobiles in Mexico City or a local office of the treasury department.

A vehicle permit is valid only for the person to whom it was issued unless another driver is approved by the federal registry. A temporarily imported vehicle may be driven by another foreigner or Mexican national, as long as the spouse or any descendant or ascendant of the permit holder is present in the automobile. Other drivers are allowed only if the permit holder is in the vehicle. Violation of this law can result in confiscation of the vehicle or heavy fines. Furthermore, only legitimate drivers may purchase car-ferry tickets.

### PHOTOGRAPHY PERMITS

To use a **video camera** at archaeological sites, you must pay 25 pesos to obtain a permit. The use of flashes or tripods at archaeological sites is not permitted except for commercial purposes, and you must obtain a permit. Contact the Instituto Nacional de Antropología e História, Director de Asuntos Jurídicos, Cordoba No. 45, 2o piso, Col. Roma, México, D.F. 06700 (tel. (5) 511-08-44).

# ■■■ CUSTOMS

### ENTERING MEXICO

Crossing into Mexico can be as uneventful as driving from Illinois to Indiana. Sometimes, however, you'll by confronted by border guards. They will direct travelers to the immigration office, where a new batch of officials will issue a tourist card to those who don't have one already and a car permit to auto drivers. Customs officials will then inspect luggage and stamp papers. If there is anything amiss when you reach the immigration checkpoint 22km into the interior, you'll have to turn back.

A clean, neat appearance will help upon your arrival. Don't pass out *mordidas* (bribes; literally, "little bites"); they may do more harm than good. Border officials may still request a tip, but they're not authorized to do so. Above all, do not attempt to carry drugs across the border as the German shepherds will not be amused. Indeed, don't even think of buying or using in Mexico—you could spend some serious time in jail, and your embassy and consulate will be powerless to help you. If you are a resident alien of the United States or simply have a Latino surname you may receive a lot of hassling from immigration upon your return. You must make up your own mind as to how to react to racist harassment. Pragmatists answer as straighforwardly as possible any questions the border patrol might ask (they have been known to ask "who won the Civil War" and other "prove-it" puzzles).

Entering Mexico by air is easier. Agents process forms and examine luggage right in the airport. Because air passengers are rarely penniless, immigration officials are less strict than at the border. If your papers are out of order at any official location, however, count on a long wait. Keep some form of picture ID with you at all times, since customs officials stop buses all over Mexico, not just at the border.

## LEAVING MEXICO

Crossing the border can take five minutes or five hours; the better your paperwork, the shorter your ordeal with customs should be. When reentering your home country, you must declare all articles acquired abroad and pay a duty on those which exceed your country's customs allowance. To establish value when you return home, keep receipts for items purchased abroad. Since you pay no duty on goods brought from home, record the serial numbers of any expensive items (cameras, computers, radios, etc.) you are taking on vacation before you leave. Check with your country's customs office to see if it has a special form for registering these valuables and turn in your list to the airport customs office before you depart.

Most countries object to the importation of firearms, explosives, ammunition, obscene literature and films, fireworks, and lottery tickets. Do not try to take illegal drugs out of Mexico. Label prescription drugs clearly and have the prescription or a doctor's certificate ready to show the customs officer.

Crossing the border (on your return) with live animals is usually prohibited. For information on wildlife and wildlife products, contact TRAFFIC USA, World Wildlife Fund, 1250 24th St. NW, Washington, DC 20037 (tel. (202) 293-4800), or the Animal and Plant Health Inspection Service (see Useful Addresses: Publications).

**United States citizens** returning home must declare all merchandise acquired abroad, including gifts, purchases, and articles bought in duty-free shops. Remember to have sales slips ready, since customs officials may ask for them. The first US$400 worth merchandise is duty-free; the next US$1000 worth is subject to a 10% tax. Goods are considered duty-free if they are for personal or household use (this includes gifts) and cannot include more than 100 cigars, 200 cigarettes, and one liter of alcoholic beverages. You must be over 21 to bring liquor into the U.S. To be eligible for the duty-free allowance, you must have remained abroad for at least 48 hours and cannot have used this exemption or any part of it within the preceding 30 days.

You can mail unsolicited gifts duty-free if they are worth less than US$100 (as of October 1994), though you may not mail alcohol, tobacco, or perfume. Officials occasionally spot check parcels, so mark the price and nature of the gift and the words "Unsolicited Gift" on the package. If you send back a non-gift parcel or a gift worth more than US$100, the Postal Service will collect a duty for its value plus a handling charge to deliver it. If you mail home personal goods of U.S. origin, you can avoid duty charges by marking the package "American goods returned." For more information, consult the brochure *Know Before You Go,* available from the U.S. Customs Service, P.O. Box 7407, Washington, DC 20044 (tel. (202) 927-6724). Foreign nationals living in the U.S. are subject to different regulations and should ask for the leaflet *Customs Hints for Visitors (Nonresidents)*; both are free.

**Canadian citizens** who remain abroad for at least one week may bring back up to CDN$300 worth of goods duty-free once every calendar year; this amount can't be combined from various trips. Canadian citizens or residents who travel for a period between 48 hours and six days can bring back up to CDN$100 with the exception of tobacco and alcohol. You are permitted to ship goods except tobacco and alcohol home under this exemption as long as you declare them when you arrive. Citizens of legal age (which varies by province) may import in-person up to 200 cigarettes, 50 cigars, 400g of loose tobacco or sticks, 1.14L of wine or alcohol, and 24 355ml cans/bottles of beer; the value of these products is included in the CDN$300. For more information, contact Canadian Customs, 2265 St. Laurent Blvd., Ottawa, Ontario, K1G 4K3 (tel. (613) 993-0534). From Canada, call (800) 461-9999.

## ■■■ MONEY

In January of 1993 new currency was introduced by the Mexican Treasury Department in an effort to stabilize the currency. The new bills are worth 1000 times the old peso. As the old currency is gradually removed from circulation, prices in some areas may be listed in the old peso, or in both the old and new peso. *All prices in this book are listed in new pesos; simply multiply by 1000 to derive the price in old pesos.* The prices given in the book were accurate in the summer of 1995; if you find that *Let's Go* prices are consistently high or low by a certain amount, use that figure to anticipate other recent changes.

| | |
|---|---|
| US$1 = 6.24 pesos | 1 peso = US$0.16 |
| CDN$1 = 4.59 pesos | 1 peso= CDN$0.22 |
| UK£1 = 9.61 pesos | 1 peso = UK£0.10 |
| IR£1 = 9.84 pesos | 1 peso = IR£0.10 |
| AUS$1 = 4.59 pesos | 1 peso = AUS$0.22 |
| NZ$1 = 4.06 pesos | 1 peso = NZ$0.25 |
| SARand = 1.71 pesos | 1 peso = SARand$0.59 |

### CURRENCY AND EXCHANGE

Be sure to buy approximately US$50 worth of pesos before leaving home, especially if you will arrive in the afternoon or on a weekend, including the equivalent of US$1 in change. This will save you time at the airport and help you avoid the predicament of having no cash after bank hours. It's sometimes very difficult to get change for large Mexican bills in rural areas. Therefore, it's wise to obtain (and hoard) change when you're in a big city. The symbol for pesos is the same as for U.S. dollars (although an "S" with *two* bars is always a dollar-sign). The common abbreviation for *Moneda Nacional* **"M.N."** (or, more frequently, "N") also stands for the peso.

Changing money in Mexico can be inconvenient. Some banks won't exchange until noon, when the daily peso quotes come out, and then stay open only until 1:30pm. You can switch U.S. dollars for pesos anywhere, but some banks refuse to deal with other foreign currencies; non-American travelers would be wise to keep some U.S. dollars on hand. Banks use the official exchange rates, but they sometimes extract a flat commission as well. Therefore, the more money you change at one time, the less you will lose in the transaction. The lineup of national banks in Mexico includes **Bánamex, Bancomer, Comermex,** and **Serfin.**

*Casas de cambio* (currency exchange booths) may offer better exchange rates than banks and are usually open as long as the stores near which they do business. In most towns, the exchange rates at restaurants, hotels, and airports are extremely unfavorable; avoid them unless it's an emergency.

### TRAVELER'S CHECKS

Traveler's checks are probably the safest way to hold money; if they get lost or stolen, you will be reimbursed by the checks' issuers. Many banks and companies sell traveler's checks, usually for the face value of the checks plus a 1-2% commission. To avoid problems when cashing your checks, always have your passport with you (not just the number); it often means the difference between apologetic refusal and grudging acceptance. Remember that some places (especially in northern Mexico) are accustomed to the real, green dollar and will accept no substitute. Carry traveler's checks in busy towns and cities, but stick to cash, risky though it may be, when traveling through the less touristed spots.

The following toll-free numbers provide information about purchasing traveler's checks and obtaining refunds:

**American Express,** in the **U.S.** and **Canada,** tel. (800) 221-7282; in the **U.K.,** tel. (0800) 52 13 13; from elsewhere, call U.S. collect (801) 964-6665 for referral to offices in individual countries. AmEx traveler's checks are easy to replace if lost or stolen. Checks can be purchased for a small fee at American Express Travel Service Offices, banks, and American Automobile Association Offices (AAA members can buy the checks commission-free). AmEx offices cash their own checks commission-free (except where prohibited by national governments) and sell checks which can be signed by either of two people traveling together. Holding AmEx checks allows you to use their offices to receive mail, even if you don't have a card. Soon, traveler's checks will be available over America OnLine. Call (800) 673-3782 to find out more, or check ExpressNet on America OnLine.

**Citicorp,** in the **U.S.** and **Canada,** tel. (800) 645-6556; in the U.K., tel. (0171) 982 40 40; elsewhere call collect (813) 623-1709. Sells Citicorp and Citicorp Visa traveler's checks in U.S. and Canadian dollars, British pounds, German marks, Swiss francs, and Japanese yen for a 1-2% commission. Checkholders are automatically enrolled for 45 days in Travel Assist Hotline (tel. (800) 523-1199), which provides check refund assistance and referrals to English-speaking doctors and lawyers. World Courier Service delivers traveler's checks anywhere in the world.

**Thomas Cook MasterCard,** in the **U.S., Canada,** and **Mexico,** tel. (800) 223-9920; in the **U.K.,** toll-free tel. (0800) 622 101 or collect tel. (1733) 502 995; elsewhere, call collect (609) 987-7300. Checks available in 11 currencies. Participating banks (look for the MasterCard logo in the window) will charge a 1-2% commission. For potentially lower commissions (0-2%), try buying the checks at a **Thomas Cook** office.

**Visa,** in the **U.S.** and **Canada,** tel. (800) 227-6811; in the **U.K.,** tel. (0171) 937-8091; from anywhere else in the world call the U.S. collect (212) 858-8500. Sells its traveler's checks by mail; call (800) 235-7366 to order them. Any kind of Visa traveler's checks can be reported lost at the Visa number.

Each agency refunds lost or stolen traveler's checks, but expect hassles if you lose track of them. When buying checks, get a list of refund centers. To expedite the refund process, separate your check receipts and keep them in a safe place. Record check numbers as you cash them to help identify exactly which checks might be missing. As an additional precaution, leave a list of the numbers with someone at home. Even with the check numbers in hand, you will probably find that getting a refund involves hours of waiting and spools of red tape.

It's best to buy most of your checks in small denominations (US$20) to minimize your losses at times when you need cash fast and can't avoid a bad exchange rate. Don't keep all your money in the same place: split it up among pockets and bags, or better yet, use a money belt. If possible, purchase checks in U.S. dollars, since many *casas de cambio* refuse to change other currencies.

## CREDIT CARDS AND CASH CARDS

Most of the banks that cash traveler's checks will make cash advances on a credit card. Be prepared to flash your passport. Major credit cards can prove invaluable in a financial emergency; **Visa** and **MasterCard** are accepted by many Mexican businesses, **American Express** to a lesser degree. Major credit cards can also work in some **automated teller machines** (ATMs). And if you lose your airline ticket, you can charge a new one.

All major credit card companies have some form of worldwide lost card protection service, and most offer a variety of additional travel services to cardholders—make sure to inquire before you leave home. Students and other travelers who may have difficulty procuring a credit card should know that family members can sometimes obtain a joint-account card.

Cirrus now has international cash machines in 60 countries, including Mexico; call (800) 424-7787 for current ATM availability information. ATMs offer low, "wholesale" exchange rates, but Cirrus charges US$5 to withdraw outside the U.S., so it's only worthwhile if you withdraw large amounts of money. The PLUS network can also be accessed in 51 countries; call (800) 843-7587 to see if there's a machine near you. Foreign ATM machines often have keypads with numbers only. If you remember your ATM password by letters, be sure to jot down its numeric equiva-

SAFETY AND SECURITY

lent before leaving the U.S. Also, four-digit PINs are standard in most countries. If you don't have a four-digit PIN, contact your bank or credit card company so they can assign you one before you leave.

Some Mexican ATM machines have been known to withdraw money from an account without issuing any money. If you attempt to withdraw money and are turned down, write down the time, location and amount of the transaction, and check this against bank statements.

## SENDING MONEY

The cheapest way to receive emergency money in Mexico is to have it sent through a large commercial bank that has associated banks within Mexico. The sender must either have an account with the bank or bring in cash or a money order, and some banks cable money only for regular customers. The service costs US$25-80, depending on the amount sent. Cabled money should arrive in one to three days if the sender can furnish exact information (i.e. recipient's passport number and the Mexican bank's name and address); otherwise, there will be significant delays. To pick up money, you must show some form of positive identification, such as a passport.

**Western Union** (tel. (800) 325-6000) offers a convenient service for cabling money. Visa or MasterCard holders can call (800) 225-5227, recite their card number, and send up to US$10000. If the sender has no credit card, he or she must go in person to one of Western Union's offices with cash—no money orders accepted, and cashier's checks are not always accepted. The money will arrive at the central telegram office or post office of the designated city. If you are in a major city, the money should arrive within 24 hours or less. In a smaller town, it could take 48 hours. The money will arrive in pesos and will be held for 30 days. Cabling costs run up to US$50 for sending as much as US$1000.

Finally, if you are a U.S. citizen and suddenly find yourself in an extreme emergency, you can have money sent via the State Department's **Citizen Emergency Center** (tel. (202) 647-5225, open Mon.-Fri. 8:15am-10pm, Sat. 9am-3pm; after hours and Sundays call (202) 647-4000). The quickest way to get the money (preferably less than US$500) to the State Department is to cable it through Western Union or else to drop off cash, certified check, bank draft, or money order at the center itself. It takes longer to send the money through your own bank. Once they receive it, the State Department will cable the money, for a fee of US$15, to the nearest embassy or consulate, which will then release the cash according to the sender's instructions. The money should arrive within 24 hours. If you want to, you can send a short telegraphic message along with the money. The center's address is: State Department Citizen Emergency Center, U.S. Dept. of State, 2201 C St. NW, Washington, DC 20520.

## ■■■ SAFETY AND SECURITY

Mexico is relatively safe, although large cities (especially Mexico City) demand extra caution. For up-to-date information on any current travel advisories on Mexico, call the U.S. State Department's Citizens Emergency Hotline at (202) 647-5225.

After dark, keep away from bus and train stations, subways, and public parks. Shun empty train compartments; many travelers avoid the theft-ridden Mexican train system altogether. When on foot, stay out of trouble by sticking to busy, well-lit streets. Act as if you know exactly where you are going: an obviously bewildered bodybuilder is more likely to be harassed than a stern and confident 98-pound human stick figure. Ask the manager of your hotel for advice on specific areas. In small, cheap, and dark accommodations, check to make sure your door locks.

Keep your money and valuables near you at all times–under the pillow at night and in the bathroom while you shower. A **money belt** is probably the best way to carry cash; you can buy one at most camping supply stores or through the Forsyth Travel Library; see Useful Organizations: Publications, above). The best combination of convenience and invulnerability is the nylon, zippered pouch with belt that should sit *inside* the waist of your pants or skirt. A **neck pouch,** although less accessible, is equally safe. Do avoid keeping anything precious in a fanny-pack (even if it's worn on your stomach): your valuables will be highly visible and easy to steal In city crowds and especially on public transportation, pickpockets are amazingly deft at their craft. Hold your bags tightly. *Ladrones* have been known to surgically remove valuables by slitting the underside of bags as unsuspecting travelers hold on to them. Make two photocopies of all important documents; keep one copy with you (separated from the original) and leave one with someone at home.

## DRINKING AND DRUGS

Drinking in Mexico is not for amateurs; bars and *cantinas* are strongholds of Mexican *machismo*. When someone calls you *amigo* and orders you a beer, bow out quickly unless you want to match him glass for glass in a challenge that could last several days.

Note that a minimum jail sentence awaits anyone found guilty of possessing more than a token amount of any drug, and that Mexican law does not distinguish between marijuana and other narcotics. Even if you aren't convicted, arrest and trial might just ruin your day. Derived from Roman and Napoleonic law, the Mexican judicial process does *not* assume that you are innocent until proven guilty, and it is not uncommon to be detained for a year before a verdict is even reached. Foreigners and suspected drug traffickers are not released on bail. Ignorance of Mexican law is no protection whatsoever—"I didn't know it was illegal" won't get you out of jail. Furthermore, there is little your consulate can do to help you out (except inform your relatives and bring care packages to you in jail).

Finally, don't even think about bringing drugs back into the U.S. Customs agents and their perceptive K-9s are not to be taken lightly. On the northern highways, especially along the Pacific coast, expect to be stopped repeatedly by burly, humorless troopers looking for contraband. That innocent-looking hitchhiker you were kind enough to pick up may be a drug peddler with a stash of illegal substances. If the police catch it in your car, the drug possession charges will extend to you, and your car may be confiscated.

For the free pamphlet *Travel Warning on Drugs Abroad,* send a self-addressed, stamped envelope to the Bureau of Consular Affairs, Public Affairs #6831, Dept. of State, Washington, DC 20520-4818 (tel. (202) 647-1488).

# ■■■ HEALTH

Before you can say "pass the *jalapeños*," a long-anticipated vacation can turn into an unpleasant study of the wonders of the Mexican health care system. Local pharmacists can give shots and dispense other remedies for mild illnesses. Wherever possible, *Let's Go* lists a pharmacy open for extended hours. If not listed, you can ask a policeman or cab driver where the pharmacy is. If you have an emergency and the door is locked, knock loudly; someone is probably sleeping inside.

Anyone with a chronic condition requiring medication should see a doctor before leaving. Allergy sufferers should find out if their conditions are likely to be aggravated in the regions they plan to visit. Obtain a full supply of any necessary medication before your trip, since matching your prescription to a foreign equivalent is not always easy, safe, or possible. Always carry up-to-date, legible prescriptions or a statement from your doctor, especially if you use insulin, a syringe, or a narcotic.

Contact lens wearers should bring an adequate supply of cleaning solutions and lubricating drops from home. Mexican equivalents can be hard to find and could irritate your eyes, although almost all pharmacies will carry saline solution.

Those with medical conditions that cannot be immediately recognized (e.g. diabetes, allergies to antibiotics, epilepsy, heart conditions) should obtain a steel **Medic Alert identification tag** (US$35), which identifies the disease and gives a toll-free number to call for information. Contact Medic Alert Foundation International, P.O. Box 1009, Turlock, CA 95381-1009, or call their 24-hour hotline at (800) 432-5378.

For additional information before you go, you may wish to contact the **International Association for Medical Assistance to Travelers (IAMAT)**. IAMAT will supply you with a free directory of English-speaking doctors around the world who have agreed to treat members for a set fee schedule. Also available are brochures describing immunization requirements, various tropical diseases, climate, and sanitation. Membership to the organization is free (although donations are welcome) and doctors are on call 24 hours a day for IAMAT members. Contact chapters in the **U.S.,** 417 Center St., Lewiston, NY 14092, (tel. (716) 754-4883); in **Canada,** 40 Regal Rd., Guelph, Ontario, N1K 1B5 (tel. (519) 836-0102), and 1287 St. Clair Ave. West, Toronto, Ontario M6E 1B8 (tel. (416) 652-0137; fax (519) 836-3412).

## PREVENTING DISEASE

Take a look at your **immunization records** before you go. Visitors to Mexico do not need to carry vaccination certificates (though anyone entering Mexico from South America or Africa may be asked to show proof of vaccination for yellow fever). However, a few medical precautions can make your trip a safer one. **Typhoid fever** is common in Mexico, especially in rural areas. Transmitted through contaminated food and water and by direct contact, typhoid produces fever, headaches, fatigue, and constipation in its victims. Vaccinations are 70-90% effective and last for three years. **Cholera,** caused by bacteria in contaminated food, has recently reached epidemic stages in parts of Mexico. Cholera's symptoms are diarrhea, dehydration, vomiting, and cramps, and can be fatal if untreated. Vaccines are recommended for those planning travel to rural areas and persons with stomach problems. Gamma globulin shots are strongly recommended before traveling to these areas. **Hepatitis A** is a risk in rural parts of the country; vaccines are available in the U.S.

**Malaria,** transmitted by mosquitoes, is a risk in many rural regions of Mexico (Oaxaca, Chiapas, Guerrero, Campeche, Quintana Roo, Sinaloa, Michoacan, Nayarit, Colima, and Tabasco). Flu-like symptoms can strike up to a year after returning home; visit a doctor if you're in doubt, since untreated malaria can cause anemia, kidney failure, coma, and death. Your best protection is to wear long pants and long sleeves, and to use mosquito repellent with DEET. If you're hiking or camping, tuck long pants into socks and use a bednet at night. You can also take weekly anti-malarial tablets; ask for some well in advance of your trip. **Dengue** is just one more reason to arm yourself against dive-bombing mosquitoes. Transmitted by blood-sucking insects, dengue produces flu-like symptoms and a rash. Recent epidemics have been reported in parts of Mexico. No vaccine or treatment is available.

## TRAVELER'S DIARRHEA

One of the biggest health threats in Mexico is the water. **Traveler's diarrhea,** known in Mexico as *turista,* is the dastardly consequence of ignoring this advice. *Turista* often lasts two or three days; symptoms include cramps, nausea, vomiting, chills, and a fever as high as 103°F (39°C). Consult a doctor if symptoms persist.

To avoid *turista,* never drink unbottled water; ask for *agua purificada* in restaurants and hotels. If you must purify your own water, bring it to a rolling boil (simmering isn't enough), or treat it with iodine drops or tablets. Don't brush your teeth with tap water, and don't even rinse your toothbrush under the faucet. Keep your mouth closed in the shower. Many a sorry traveler has been fooled by the clever disguise of impure water—the ice-cube. Stay away from those tasty-looking salads: uncooked vegetables (including lettuce and coleslaw) are a great way to get *turista*. Other culprits are raw shellfish, unpasteurized milk, and sauces containing raw eggs. Peel fruits and vegetables before eating them, and beware of watermelon, which is often injected with impure water. Beware of food from markets or street vendors that may have been "washed" in dirty water or fried in rancid oil; juices, peeled fruits, and exposed coconut slices are common culprits. Also beware of ice or frozen treats that may have been made with bad water. A golden rule in Mexico: boil it, peel it, cook it, or forget it. Otherwise, your stomach will not forgive you.

## HEAT

Common sense goes a long way in preventing **heat exhaustion:** relax in hot weather, drink lots of non-alcoholic fluids, and lie down inside if you feel awful. Continuous heat stress can eventually lead to **heatstroke,** characterized by rising body temperature, severe headache, and cessation of sweating. The victim must be cooled off with wet towels and taken to a doctor immediately. Though you may not consider it a serious malady, consider the fact that thousands die each year due to heat related sickness.

Finally, be sure to drink plenty of liquids—much more than you're accustomed to drinking. Heat and high altitudes will dehydrate you more swiftly than you expect, and you can avoid many health problems if you drink enough fluid to keep your urine clear. Alcoholic beverages are dehydrating, as are coffee, strong tea, and caffeinated sodas. You'll be sweating a lot, so be sure to eat enough salty food to prevent electrolyte depletion—otherwise, you may be stricken with headaches.

Less debilitating, but still dangerous, is sunburn, which in serious cases can produce painful blistering, fever, and unsightly peeling. If you're prone to sunburn, carry sunscreen with you and apply it liberally and often—when it comes to your health, don't be cheap. If you do get sunburn (despite all the warnings!), drink even more water and non-alcoholic fluids than you normally would; it'll cool you down and help your poor, overdone skin recover faster.

## WOMEN'S HEALTH

Women traveling in unsanitary conditions are vulnerable to urinary tract and bladder infections, uncomfortable bacterial diseases which cause a burning sensation during painful and sometimes frequent urination. Untreated, these infections can lead to kidney infections. To minimize their risk, women should drink plenty of liquids, especially juice rich in vitamin C (such as cranberry), and urinate frequently, particularly right after intercourse. Women prone to vaginal yeast infections should pack a reliable brand of over-the-counter medication, as treatment may not be readily available elsewhere. Women also need to be aware that tampons and pads are sometimes hard to find overseas; certainly your preferred brands may not be available in Cholula (though you'll find the world's biggest pyramid there), so it may be advisable to take supplies along. O.b.© brand tampons (available in the U.S.) have very little packaging and take up less space in a backpack or suitcase.

## ALL YOU WANTED TO KNOW BUT COULDN'T ASK

Reliable **contraception** may be difficult to come by when traveling. Women on the pill should bring enough to allow for possible loss, and anyone planning to use a diaphragm should stock up on contraceptive jelly. Although **condoms** are widely available in Mexico, quality is variable, so stock up before you leave.

**Abortion** is illegal in Mexico. The U.S. **National Abortion Federation's hotline** (tel. (800) 772-9100, Mon.-Fri. 9:30am-5:30pm) can direct you to organizations which provide information on abortion in other countries. Your embassy may also be able to provide a list of doctors who perform abortions. The **International Planned Parenthood Federation,** European Regional Office, Regent's College Inner Circle, Regent's Park, London NW1 4NS (tel. 44 (0171) 486-0741; fax 487-7950) is a source of general information on contraception and abortion worldwide.

All travelers should be concerned about **Acquired Immune Deficiency Syndrome (AIDS),** transmitted through the exchange of body fluids with an individual who is HIV-positive. *Do not* share syringes, intravenous or tattooing needles, and *never* have vaginal, oral, or anal sex without using a condom, preferably one lubricated with spermicide. Latex condoms are safer than lambskin ones, which have virus-permeable pores. Avoid oil-based lubricants like Vaseline, which destroy the integrity of the latex, rendering them useless in the prevention of HIV transmission.

## EXPERIENCE LANGUAGE AND CULTURE IN COLONIAL MEXICO

Baden-Powell Institute invites you to come and study Spanish in the friendly setting of our school in Morelia, one of the most beautiful colonial cities in Mexico.

With us, you may form your own study plan, which may start any Monday year-round, with the option of flexible schedules and various subjects. W e offer ONE-ON-ONE Lessons or group classes (3 to 5 students).

At Baden-Powell you can enjoy Mexican culture your way. We can help you in choosing a local family to live with or any other accomodation to suit you.

We feel confident that our experience and qualified faculty will get you the results you want.

If you'd like to receive further information, we'll be happy to provide it.

**...Live the Mexico experience!!!**

Baden-Powell Institute
Eugenio Cortés, Director
Antonio Alzate 565
Morelia, Michoacán
Mexico 58000
Phone (43) 12-40-70

The U.S. Center for Disease Control's 24-hour **AIDS Hotline** provides information on AIDS in the U.S. and can refer you to other organizations with information on Mexico (tel. (800) 342-2437; TTD (800) 243-7889, Mon.-Fri. 10am-10pm; Spanish tel. (800) 344-7332, daily 8am-2am). Call the **U.S. State Department** for country-specific restrictions for HIV-positive travelers (tel. (202) 647-1488; fax 647-3000) or write the Bureau of Consular Affairs, #6831, U.S. Dept. of State, Washington, DC 20520. The **World Health Organization** provides written material on AIDS internationally (tel. (202) 861-3200 in the U.S.). Those travelers who are HIV-positive should thoroughly check possible immigration restrictions in the country which they wish to visit.

# ■■■ INSURANCE

Beware of unnecessary coverage—your current policies might well extend to many travel-related accidents. **Medical insurance** (especially university policies) often cover costs incurred abroad, although **Medicare's** foreign travel coverage is valid only in Canada and Mexico. Canadians are protected by their home province's health insurance plan for up to 90 days after leaving the country; check with the provincial Ministry of Health or Health Plan Headquarters. Your **homeowners' insurance** (or your family's coverage) often covers theft during travel. Homeowners are generally covered against loss of travel documents (passport, plane ticket, railpass, etc.) for up to $500.

**ISIC,** International Student or Teacher ID Cards provide US$3000 worth of accident and illness insurance and US$100 per day up to 60 days of hospitalization, and give you access to a toll-free Traveler's Assistance hotline whose multilingual staff can provide help in medical, legal, and financial emergencies overseas (see Documents and Formalities below). **Council** and **STA** both offer comprehensive insurance plans (see Useful Organizations). American Express cardholders receive automatic car-rental and flight insurance on purchases made with the card.

**ARM Coverage, Inc./Carefree Travel Insurance,** 100 Garden City Plaza, P.O. Box 9366, Garden City, NY 11530-9366 (tel. (800) 323-3149 or (516) 294-0220; fax (516) 294-1821). Offers two comprehensive packages including coverage for trip delay, accident and sickness, medical, baggage loss, bag delay, accidental death and dismemberment, travel supplier insolvency. Trip cancellation/interruption may be purchased separately at a rate of US$5.50 per US$100 of coverage. 24-hr. hotline.

**Travel Assistance International,** by Worldwide Assistance Services, Inc., 1133 15th St., NW, Suite 400, Washington, DC 20005-2710 (tel. (800) 821-2828 or (202) 828-5894; fax (202) 331-1530). TAI provides its members with a 24-hr. hotline for emergencies and referrals. Their year-long frequent traveler package ($226) includes medical and travel insurance, financial assistance, and help in replacing lost documents.

**Travel Insured International,** 52-S Oakland Ave., P.O. Box 280568, East Hartford, CT 06128-0568 (tel. (800) 243-3174; fax 528-8005). Insurance against accident, baggage loss, sickness, trip cancellation/interruption, travel delay, and default. Covers emergency medical evacuation and automatic flight insurance.

# ■■■ ALTERNATIVES TO TOURISM

## WORK AND VOLUNTEERING

Volunteering is an excellent way to immerse yourself in Mexican culture and Spanish language while improving the lives of others. There are plenty of volunteer opportunities available, and a little research will pay off in locating worthwhile and interesting positions. Paid work, on the other hand, is difficult to obtain. Just as the U.S. spends billions of dollars every year to safeguard jobs for its own citizens, the Mexican government isn't about to give up precious jobs to traveling *gringos* when

many of its own people are unemployed. It used to be that only 10% of the employees of foreign firms located in Mexico could have non-Mexican citizenship; now, as "development" has become a priority, the limit depends on the sector. Hotels, for instance, are often eager to hire English-speaking personnel for prestige and the convenience of their patrons, and are allowed as many legal work permits as they wish. It is no longer the case that to get a job you must have some specialized skill that cannot be found in Mexico; but attitudes are in flux, and you might still be unwelcome even as an English teacher. If you manage to secure a position with a Mexican business, your employer must get you a work permit. It is possible, but illegal, to work without a permit. You risk deportation if caught.

Adventurous job-hunters can arm themselves with a battery of books; a few are published by the following organizations.

**Council,** 205 E. 42nd St., New York, NY 10017 (tel. (212) 661-1414). A private, not-for-profit organization that can help students secure work visas and find employment through work-exchange programs. Publishes *Work, Study, Travel Abroad: The Whole World Handbook* (US$13.95 plus $1.50 shipping), *Volunteer! The Comprehensive Guide to Voluntary Service in the U.S. and Abroad* (US$12.95 plus $1.50 shipping), and *The High School Student's Guide to Study, Travel, and Adventure Abroad* (US$13.95 plus $1.50 shipping).

**Addison-Wesley,** Order Department, Jacob Way, Reading, MA 01867 (tel. (800) 322-1377 for college students, (800) 552-2259 for high school students). Publishes *International Jobs: Where They Are, How to Get Them* (US$14.95); also available at many bookstores.

**Peterson's,** P.O. Box 2123, Princeton, NJ 08543 (tel. (800) 338-3282). Their *Directory of Overseas Summer Jobs* lists 50,000 openings worldwide, volunteer and paid (US$14.95 plus $4.75 shipping; available in January 1995).

The following organizations may be able to arrange volunteer opportunities, paid positions, or internships in Mexico and Central America.

**American Friends Service Committee,** 1501 Cherry St., Philadelphia, PA 19102-1479 (tel. (215) 241-7295). Runs volunteer work camps in Mexican villages for 18- to 26-year-olds. Work has included construction, gardening, reforestation, health and nutrition, and education. Programs run each summer from late June to mid-August (participation fee US$1900). Fluency in Spanish required. Limited financial aid available. Address inquiries to the Human Resources Dept.

**IAESTE Training Program,** 10400 Little Patuxent Pkwy., #250, Columbia, MD 21044-33510 (tel. (410) 997-3068 or 3069). The International Association for the Exchange of Students for Technical Experience runs an internship exchange for science, architecture, engineering, agriculture, and math students who have completed at least two years at an accredited four-year institution. Opportunities are generally available in Mexico. There is a non-refundable application fee of US$75; apply by December 10 for summer placement.

**International Schools Services,** P.O. Box 5910, Princeton, NJ 08543 (tel. (609) 452-0990). Coordinates the placement of teachers in schools in Mexico, Costa Rica, Guatemala, Nicaragua, and Honduras.

**Los Niños,** 287 "G" Street, Chula Vista, CA 91910 (tel. (619) 426-9110; fax 426-6664). Accepts short-term volunteers to a variety of programs to work near the U.S.-Mexico border in a combination of community projects and education programs. US$190 for a week, US$900 for the summer.

**WorldLearning,** Summer Abroad Leadership, Kipling Rd., P.O. Box 676, Brattleboro, VT 05302 (tel. (800) 345-2929 or (802) 257-7751). WorldLearning (formerly the Experiment in International Living) runs summer programs in Mexico and Costa Rica for high school students; program leaders are paid for all expenses and receive an honorarium. Leaders must be at least 24 years old, have lived in Mexico or Costa Rica, and speak fluent Spanish.

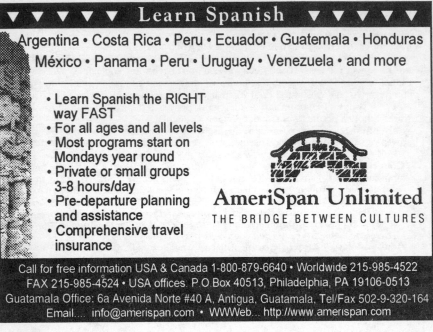
100%

## STUDY

A number of organizations publish useful resources for those wishing to study abroad. **UNIPUB,** 4611-F Assembly Dr., Lanham, MD 20706-4391 (in U.S., tel. (800) 274-4888; in Canada, (800) 233-0504) distributes UNESCO's unwieldy but fascinating book *Study Abroad* (US$25.95 plus $3 shipping). Programs which take place in Mexico are described in Spanish. **Institute of International Education Books (IIE Books),** 809 United Nations Pl., New York, NY 10017-3580 (tel. (212) 984-5412; fax 984-5458) publishes and *Vacation Study Abroad* (US$36.95 plus $4 shipping), which has information on courses, costs, and accommodations for programs in Mexico. **Council** (see Work and Volunteering, above) administers education exchange programs all over the world and can provide general information on academic opportunities abroad. They publish *Smart Vacations: The Traveler's Guide to Learning Adventures Abroad* (US$14.95 plus $1.50 postage) in addition to the work/study guides listed above.

If you're already fluent in Spanish, consider enrolling in the regular programs of a Mexican university. Applications to Mexican state universities are due in early spring. For information contact the Secretaría de Relaciones Exteriores, Homero 213, P.B., Colonia Chapultepec Morales, 11560, México, D.F. (tel. (5) 255-09-88, ext. 2006 or 2013, ask for the *"beca"* office). Don't expect to receive credit at your home institution, however. The only Mexican university accredited in the U.S. is the **Universidad de las Américas,** Santa Catarina Martír, Cholula, Puebla 72820 (tel. (22) 29-20-00 or 29-20-17), ask for the *decanatura de asuntos internacionales*).

Many U.S. universities offer students the opportunity to study in Mexico for a semester or a year, and some Mexican universities organize programs specifically designed for foreign students. The **Universidad Nacional Autónoma de México (UNAM)** has a school in Mexico City for foreign students that operates semester, intensive, and summer programs in Spanish, art, history, literature, and Chicano studies. The program is open to both undergraduates and graduates. The school also has a campus in Taxco, a colonial mining town located on the road between Mexico City and Acapulco. Write to: UNAM, Centro de Enseñanza para Extranjeros, Apdo. 70-391, Ciudad Universitaria, Delegación Coyoacán, México, D.F. 04510 (tel. (5) 622-24-70; fax 616-26-72).

Many cities in Mexico host language schools; Cuernavaca is one center for language instruction (see Cuernavaca: Practical Information: Academic Programs for more information). San Miguel de Allende hosts a number of schools offering cultural and artistic classes (see San Miguel: Academic Institutions). Smaller local schools are generally cheaper, but international organizations may be better able to arrange academic credit at your home institution.

**School for International Training (SIT),** College Semester Abroad Admissions, Kipling Rd., P.O. Box 676, Brattleboro, VT 05302 (tel. (800) 336-1616 or (802) 258-3279). Runs semester-long programs in Mexico that include cross-cultural orientation, intensive language study, homestay, field study, and independent study projects. Semester programs US$8200-10300, including tuition, room and board, round-trip international airfare, and insurance. But take heart: U.S. Federal financial aid can be applied to SIT programs. SIT offers limited scholarships, and some home institutions will provide additional aid and often accept SIT transfer credits.
**American Institute for Foreign Study,** College Division, 102 Greenwich Avenue, Greenwich, CT 06830 (tel. (800) 727-2437). Organizes academic year and/or summer programs in Merida. Minority and merit scholarships available. High-school programs also available; call (800) 888-2247.
**American Field Service Intercultural Programs,** 220 E. 42nd St., 3rd Floor, New York, NY 10017 (tel. (212) 949-4242). AFS administers summer, semester, and year-long homestay exchange programs for high school students in many countries including Mexico.
**Language Link Incorporated,** P.O. Box 3006, Peoria, IL (tel. (800) 552-2051). Runs the Spanish Language Institute-Center for Latin American Studies in Cuernavaca, Morelos. Program offers beginning, intermediate, and advanced level lan-

ALTERNATIVES TO TOURISM

guage courses. Students live with Mexican families (private and shared rooms available). To contact the Institute directly call (73) 11-00-63.

# ■■■ WOMEN AND TRAVEL

Women travelers to Mexico are often surprised by the unwanted attention they receive. If you look like an *extranjera* (foreigner), you will find it difficult to remain alone except when locked in a hotel room. Persistent men will insist on joining you; walking down the street, you will hear whistles and propositions. If you're fair-skinned, "*güera, güera, güera*" will follow you everywhere. Offer no response and no eye contact; any kind of answer could be interpreted as a come-on. In real emergencies, scream for help. Don't consider yourself safe just because people in uniform are around.

Awareness of Mexican social standards can also prevent unpleasant and dangerous confrontations. Women wearing short shorts or halter tops (or not wearing bras) will suffer more harassment than usual. It's best to wear knee-length shorts, and women should bring a lightweight long skirt to wear in churches or in conservative regions like Chiapas. *Cantinas* are all-male institutions; the only women who ever enter are working, either as servers or as prostitutes.

Northern Mexico is less congenial to women travelers than anywhere else in Mexico; Oaxaca, Chiapas, and the Yucatán are the most congenial. If you are traveling with a male friend, it may help to pose as a couple. This will assuage any misgivings hotel proprietors have about letting you share rooms and may serve to chill the blood of your Mexican admirer. Some women wear a "wedding ring" on their left hand to discourage unwanted attention.

Women travelers to Mexico may want to consult *Women Going Places,* a women's travel and resource guide emphasizing women-owned enterprises. Geared toward lesbians, but offers advice appropriate for all women (US$14). Order from Inland Book Company, PO Box 12061, East Haven, CT 06512 (tel. (203) 467-4257). Another helpful resource is *Wander Women,* 136 N. Grand Ave. #237, West Covina, CA 91791 (tel. (818) 966-8857).

# ■■■ SENIOR TRAVELERS

Senior travelers should bring a medical record that includes an update on conditions and prescriptions; the name, phone number, and address of a regular doctor; and a summary of their recent medical history. Find out if you have insurance that will cover costs you may incur in Mexico.

*Unbelievably Good Deals and Great Adventures That You Absolutely Can't Get Unless You're Over 50,* by Joan Rattner Heilman (US$7.95, Contemporary Books). After you finish reading the title, check inside for some great tips on senior discounts and the like. The *International Health Guide for Senior Travelers* (US$4.95 plus US$1.50 postage) is available from Pilot Books, 103 Cooper St., Babylon, NY 11702 (tel. (516) 422-2225).

For more information, write to a Mexican Government Tourism Office (see Useful Organizations). The following organizations and publications can also be helpful:

**American Association of Retired Persons (AARP),** 601 E St. NW, Washington, DC 20049 (tel. (202) 434-2277). Members 50 and over receive benefits and services including the AARP Motoring Plan from Amoco (tel. (800) 334-3300) as well as discounts on lodging, car rental, and sight-seeing. Annual fee: US$8 per couple, US$75 for lifetime membership.

**Elderhostel,** 75 Federal St., 3rd floor, Boston, MA 02110-1941 (tel. (617) 426-8056). You must be 55 or over and may bring a spouse of any age. Programs at colleges and universities in over 50 countries focus on varied subjects and generally last one to four weeks.

**DISABLED TRAVELERS**

**Gateway Books,** 2023 Clemens Rd., Oakland CA 94602 (tel. (510) 530-0299; fax 530-0497). Publishes *Get Up and Go: A Guide for the Mature Traveler* (US$10.95), *Adventures Abroad* (US$12.95), which offer general hints for the budget senior traveler who is considering a long stay or even retiring abroad. For credit card orders (800) 669-0773.

## ■■■ DISABLED TRAVELERS

Mexico is becoming increasingly accessible to travelers with disabilities, especially in popular resorts such as Acapulco and Cancún. Money talks—the more you are willing to spend, the less difficult it is to find accessible facilities. Most public and long-distance modes of transportation and most of the non-luxury hotels don't accommodate wheelchairs. Public bathrooms are almost all inaccessible, as are many ruins, parks, historic buildings, and museums. Still, with some advance planning, an affordable Mexican vacation is not impossible. Air travel in general is gradually becoming less restrictive. Give prior notice of your needs to the airline, which may require a traveling companion or doctor's letter allowing you to fly. Cruises are a costly alternative to flying. If you intend to bring a seeing-eye dog to Mexico, you must have a veterinarian's certificate of health (see Documents and Formalities: Pet Health certificates). The following organizations provide useful information and can help plan your vacation:

**American Foundation for the Blind,** 11 Penn Plaza, New York, NY 10011 (tel. (212) 502-7600), open Mon.-Fri. 8:30am-4:30pm. Provides information and services for the visually impaired. For a catalogue of products, contact **Lighthouse Low-Vision Products** at (800) 829-0500.

**Mobility International, USA (MIUSA),** P.O. Box 10767, Eugene, OR 97440 (tel. (503) 343-1284 voice and TDD; fax 343-6812). International headquarters in Britain, 228 Borough High St., London SE1 1JX (tel. +44 (0171) 403-5688). Contacts

in 30 countries. Information on travel programs, international work camps, accommodations, access guides, and organized tours. Membership US$20 per year, newsletter US$10. Sells updated *A World of Options: A Guide to International Educational Exchange, Community Service, and Travel for Persons with Disabilities* (US$14 for members, US$16 for non-members, postpaid). In addition, MIUSA offers a series of courses that teach strategies helpful for travelers with disabilities. Call for details.

**The Guided Tour, Inc.,** Elkins Park House #114B, 7900 Old York Rd., Elkins Park, PA 19027-2339 (tel. (215) 782-1370 or (800) 783-5841; fax 635-2637). Organizes year-round travel and vacation programs, domestic and international, for persons with developmental and physical challenges as well as those geared to the needs of persons requiring renal analysis. Call, fax, or write for a free brochure.

**Twin Peaks Press,** P.O. Box 129, Vancouver, WA 98666-0129 (tel. (360) 694-2462 or (800) 637-2256 for MC and Visa orders; fax 696-3210). Publishes *Wheelchair Vagabond* (US$14.95), *Directory for Travel Agencies of the Disabled* (US$19.95), and *Directory of Accessible Van Rentals* (US$9.95). Add US$3 shipping for the first book, $1 each additional book.

# ■■■ GAY AND LESBIAN TRAVELERS

In Mexico, the legal age for consensual homosexual intercourse is 18. Police often ignore the legal status of homosexual activity and Mexicans generally disapprove of public displays of gay affection, but there is a gay rights movement in Mexico and discreet homosexuality is tolerated in most areas.

**Giovanni's Room,** 345 S. 12th St., Philadelphia, PA 19107 (tel. (215) 923-2960; fax 923-0813). An international feminist, lesbian, and gay bookstore and mail-order house with resources and information for tourists. Free catalog.

**Damron Travel Guides,** P.O. Box 422458, San Francisco, CA 94142 (tel. (800) 462-6654 or (415) 255-0404). Publishers of the *Damron Address Book* (US$13.95), which lists over 800 bars, restaurants, guest houses, and services catering to the gay male. Covers the U.S., Canada, and Mexico.

**Ferrari Publications,** P.O. Box 37887, Phoenix, AZ 85069 (tel. (602) 863-2408). Publishes *Ferrari's Places of Interest* (US$16), *Ferrari's Places for Men* (US$15), *Ferrari's Places for Women* (US$13), and *Inn Places: USA and Worldwide Gay Accommodations* (US$14.95). Available in bookstores or by mail-order. For postage, add US$4.50 for 1st item, $1 for each additional title.

**Spartacus International Gay Guide,** published by Bruno Gmünder, Postfach 110729, D-10837 Berlin, Germany (tel. +49 (30) 615 00 30). Lists of bars, restaurants, hotels, and bookstores around the world catering to gay men. Most importantly, Spartacus provides homosexuality laws for each country it covers. However, laws sometimes change faster than the book. Available in the U.S. by mail order from Giovanni's Room (see listing above) as well as in other bookstores (US$29.95).

# ■■■ PACKING

Pack light. That means you.

Set out everything you'll need, and then take half of that plus more money. One *New York Times* correspondent recommends that you "take no more than you can carry for half a mile at a dead run." This advice may be extreme (unless you expect to be pursued by *federales*), but the gist is clear.

If you will be riding a lot of buses or covering a lot of ground by foot, a **backpack** may be the best choice for toting your loot. An internal-frame model is less bulky and can't be broken as easily by baggage handlers. For hiking, an external frame lifts weight off the back and distributes it more evenly, allows for some ventilation, and is more pleasant to carry over uneven terrain; internal frames mold to the back bet-

ter, keep a lower center of gravity, and are more comfortable for long-distance hiking on the level. If you're taking a sleeping bag, keep in mind that you can strap it onto the outside of an external frame, while you usually must allow room for bedding inside an internal frame pack. Remember that zippers and flaps make easy targets for pickpockets. Decent packs start at about US$120.

**Footwear** is not the place to cut costs. Comfortable walking shoes or a good pair of running shoes is essential; save your sandals for short walks and evenings out. If you plan to hike or climb over pyramids and ruins, bring a pair of sturdy hiking shoes. Shorts, on either sex, are not appropriate in rural areas, in churches, in the more traditional southern states, or in more cosmopolitan cities like Guadalajara and Puerto Vallarta. Pack a rain poncho if you're traveling between May and October, and bring a sweater for chilly nights if you're going to the mountains.

Most toiletries such as aspirin and razor blades are available in Mexican pharmacies, but some items—tampons, prescription drugs and contraceptives—are best brought from home. Even when these items are available over the counter, their ingredients may differ from the same-named product in the U.S. Cities sometimes carry U.S. brands of saline solution for contact lens wearers, but no stores stock comparable cleaners. Toilet paper is often elusive; always carry some for those out-of-the way places and extra, extra cheap hotels.

# GETTING THERE

# ■■■ TRAVEL ORGANIZATIONS

**Council,** 205 E. 42nd St., New York, NY 10017 (tel. (212) 661-1414). A private, not-for-profit organization. Administers academic, volunteer, work, and professional programs around the world. Issues ISICs, ITICs, and GO 25 cards. Council's biannual travel magazine for college students, *Student Travels,* is available free. They also publish *Work, Study, and Travel Abroad: The Whole World Handbook* ($13.95, postage $1.50); *The High School Student's Guide to Study, Travel, and Adventure Abroad* ($13.95, postage $1.50); *Volunteer! The Comprehensive Guide to Voluntary Service in the U.S. and Abroad* ($12.95, postage $1.50); and *Smart Vacations: The Traveler's Guide to Learning Adventures Abroad* ($14.95, postage $1.50).

**Council Travel,** the travel division of Council, specializes in student and budget travel. Over 50 offices worldwide. Sells charter flight tickets, guidebooks (including *Let's Go*), ISICs, ITICs, GO 25 cards, hostel cards, and gear. **Atlanta,** Emory Village, 1561 N. Decatur Rd., GA 30307 (tel. (404) 377-9997). **Austin,** 2000 Guadalupe, TX 78705 (tel. (512) 472-4931). **Boston,** 729 Boylston St., Suite #201, MA 02116 (tel. (617) 266-1926). **Chicago,** 1153 N. Dearborn St., 2nd floor, IL 60610 (tel. (312) 951-0585). **Dallas,** 6715 Hillcrest, TX 75205 (tel. (214) 363-9941). **Los Angeles,** 10904 Lindbrook Dr., CA 90024 (tel. (310) 208-3551). **Miami,** One Datran Center, 9100 S. Dadeland Blvd., FL 33156 (tel. (305) 670-9261). **New York,** 205 E. 42nd St., NY 10017 (tel. (212) 661-1450). **San Francisco,** 530 Bush St., Ground Floor, CA 94108 (tel. (415) 421-3473). **Seattle,** 1314 N.E. 43rd St., Suite # 210, WA 98105 (tel. (206) 632-2448). **Britain,** 28A Poland St., Oxford Circus, London WIV 3DB (tel. (0171) 437-7767). **France,** 22, rue des Pyramides, 75001 Paris (tel. (1) 44 55 55 65). For US cities not listed, call 1-800-226-8624.

**STA Travel:** Over 100 offices worldwide. Call (213) 937-1150 for general information or (800) 777-0112 for travel sales. Discount airfares for travelers under 26 and full-time students under 32; sells ISICs, rail passes, accommodations, tours, and insurance. Eleven **U.S.** offices include: **Boston,** 297 Newbury St., MA 02116 (tel. (617) 266-6014). **New York,** 48 E. 11th St., NY 10003 (tel. (212) 477-7166). **San Francisco,** 51 Grant Ave., CA 94108 (tel. (415) 391-8407). In **Britain,** 86 Old Brompton Rd., London SW7 3LQ and 117 Euston Rd., London NW1 2SX (tel. (0171) 937-9971 for North American travel, or (0171) 937-9962 for long-haul travel). In

**Australia,** 220 Faraday St., Melbourne, VIC 3053 (tel. (03) 349-2411). In **New Zealand,** 10 High St., Auckland (tel. (09) 398-9995).

**Let's Go Travel,** Harvard Student Agencies, 53A Church St., Cambridge, MA 02138 (tel. (800) 553-8746 or (617) 495-9649). Let's Go Travel offers railpasses, HI-AYH memberships, ISICs, International Teacher ID cards, GO 25 cards, guide-books, maps, bargain flights, and a complete line of budget travel gear. All items available by mail; call or write for a catalog (or see catalog in center of this publi-cation).

**International Student Exchange Flights (ISE),** 5010 E. Shea Blvd., #A104, Scottsdale, AZ 85254 (tel. (602) 951-1177). Budget student flights to Europe and Asia, Eurail, HI-AYH memberships, the International Student Exchange Identity Card, and travel guides. Free catalog.

**Servicio Educativo de Turismo de los Estudiantes y la Juventud de México (SETEJ),** Hamburgo 305, Col. Juárez, México, D.F. 06000 (tel. (5) 211-07-43 or 211-66-36; fax 211-13-28). Sells ISIC and GO 25 cards. Arranges group tours with Mexican students. Has information about hostels and budget hotels. Offers lan-guage courses and helps with domestic and international flights. See Accommoda-tions below for hostel information.

**Travel CUTS (Canadian Universities Travel Services, Ltd.),** 187 College St., Toronto, Ontario M5T 1P7 (tel. (416) 798-2887; fax 979-8167). In **Britain,** 295-A Regent St., London W1R 7YA (tel. (0171) 637-3161). The Canadian equivalent of Council. 40 offices across Canada. Discounted European, South Pacific, and domestic flights; special student fares to all destinations with valid ISIC. Issues ISIC, FIYTO, HI hostel cards, and discount travel passes. Special fares with valid ISIC or FIYTO cards. Offers free *Student Traveller* magazine, and info on Student Work Abroad Program (SWAP).

# ■■■ BY PLANE

A little research can pay off with discounts or cheaper flights. A travel agent is often a good source of information on scheduled flights and fares, and student travel orga-nizations provide leads on airfare discounts (see Useful Organizations, Travel Orga-nizations). If you're coming from Europe, it's cheapest to fly first to a U.S. city, then connect to Mexico City or some other Mexican airport.

**Mexicana** (tel. (800) 531-7921) and **Aeroméxico** (tel. (800) 237-6639), are the two major national airlines. Together, they cover most of Mexico; regional airlines also provide service in many areas. Be aware of the **departure tax** levied at Mexican international airports (US$12). These taxes are included in the ticket price.

The availability of standby flights is declining on many airlines, but if you can find them, their advantage is flexibility. The disadvantage is that flying standby can ran-domize your vacation more than you would like. Call individual carriers for availabil-ity and prices. Tickets are usually sold at the airport on the day of departure.

Travelers who agree to serve as **couriers** receive a considerable discount (often 50%) on their airfare; in return, they surrender luggage space and must have a flexi-ble itinerary. Couriers must be at least 18 years old and possess a valid passport. **Now Voyager,** 74 Varick St. #307, New York, NY 10013 (tel. (212) 431-1616) and **Halbart Express,** 147-05 176th St., Jamaica, NY 11434 (tel. (718) 656-5000), among other firms, mediate such transactions.

Discount clearing houses also offer savings on charter flights, commercial flights, tour packages, and cruises. These clubs make unsold tickets available from three weeks up to a few days before departure. Annual dues run US$25-50, but the fares offered can be extremely cheap. Places to investigate include:

**Last Minute Travel Club,** 1249 Boylston St., Boston, MA 02215 (tel. (800) 527-8646 or (617) 267-9800). No membership fee.

**Discount Travel International,** 169 W. 81st St., New York, NY 10024 (tel. (212) 362-3636; fax (212) 362-3236). No membership fee. Monthly newsletter is US$12 for a quarter year.

**Moment's Notice,** 425 Madison Ave., Suite 702, New York, NY 10017 (tel. (212) 486-0500). US$25 annual fee per family. World-wide service.

**Travel Avenue,** 10 S. Riverside Plaza, Suite 1404, Chicago, IL 60606 (tel. (800) 333-3335). For a ticketing fee of 5-12%, depending on the number of travelers and the itinerary, Travel Avenue will search for the lowest international airfare available, and then take 7% off the base price.

An even more adventurous option is to register for a flexible flight. Flying with these carriers is sort of like hitchhiking on the road: they will simply get you *near* your destination. Vacationers will be frustrated, but the rugged traveler could save a lot of money. Typically, travelers register with a company, specify a preferred destination, and give a two- to five-day travel window. If there isn't a flight within your window, you get a refund. Two companies offer this service:

**AirTech Unlimited,** 584 Broadway #1007, New York, NY 10012 (tel. (212) 219-7000). Handles flexible, couriers, and confirmed/reserved flights. Flights from the U.S. to Mexico as low as US$139 each way. Reachable by e-mail at dirtcheap@aerotech.com. *Let's Go* has received complaints about delays, false information, and bad service associated with Airtech. Days-long waits for flights could incur costs that outweigh initial savings.

**Airhitch,** 2641 Broadway, 3rd. Floor, New York, NY 10025 (tel. (212) 864-2000 or (800) 326-2009). New York City to Los Angeles as low as US$129 one way. The Better Business Bureau of New York and *Let's Go* have received complaints about Airhitch; the company has recently changed ownership, but customers should be careful. Days-long waits for flights could incur costs that outweigh initial savings.

# ■■■ BY BUS OR TRAIN

Greyhound serves many border towns, including El Paso and Brownsville. Smaller lines serve other destinations. Buses tend not to cross the border, but at each of these stops you can pick up Mexican bus lines on the other side. Tres Estrellas de Oro, Estrella Blanca, and Transportes Del Norte provide service from the border.

By train, you can take Amtrak to El Paso (US$254-494 round-trip from New York), walk across the border to Ciudad Juárez and from there use other forms of transportation to reach points within Mexico. Amtrak also serves San Diego (US$278-436 round-trip from New York). It is also possible to travel by Amtrak to San Antonio (US$279 round-trip from New York) and take a bus from there to the border towns.

# ■■■ BY CAR

Driving entails no bureaucratic complications within the Zona Libre (Free Zone). The Zona Libre extends from the U.S. border 22km into Mexico; it also includes all of Baja California. You will encounter checkpoints as soon as you reach the end of the Zona Libre; see Planning Your Trip: Documents and Formalities: Driver's License and Vehicle Permits for details about driving past the checkpoints.

On the U.S. side of the border, several **auto clubs** provide routing services and protection against breakdowns. Your auto club may be affiliated with the **Asociación Mexicana Automovilística (AMA)** through international motoring agreements. The **Asociación Nacional Automovilística (ANA)** is not associated with U.S. clubs and requires separate membership. Both organizations can provide you with travel services and information (see Useful Organizations: Transportation Services). Both the AMA and the ANA sell road maps. The Mexican consulate or nearest tourist office also provides free road maps.

All non-Mexican car insurance is invalid in Mexico, no matter what your policy says. Make sure you arrange to have your car insured in Mexico if you plan to drive it there. You will probably be able to buy insurance at the border at one of the many small insurance offices located next door to the Mexico immigration offices. **San-**

**born's,** Home Office, P.O. Box 310, McAllen, TX 78505-0310 (tel. (210) 686-0711; fax 686-0732) offers Mexico and Central American Insurance through each of its 21 U.S. agencies located at major border cities in California, Texas, and Arizona. Along with insurance, you get all the trimmings including road maps, newsletters, a ride board, mile-by-mile guides to all the highways in Mexico called the Travelog, and "Mexico" Mike Nelson (write him at Dept. N at the McAllen address for up-to-date information on driving in Mexico). Remember, in Mexico the law code is Napoleonic (guilty until proven innocent). If you do not purchase a separate Legal Aid policy, and you are involved in an accident, the police might hold you in jail until everything is sorted out and all claims are settled.

# ONCE THERE

## ■■■ EMBASSIES AND CONSULATES

**Embassies** and **consulates** provide a variety of services for citizens away from home. They can refer you to an English-speaking doctor or lawyer, help you replace a lost tourist card, and wire family or friends if you need money and have no other means of obtaining it. They cannot, however, cash checks, act as a postal service, get you out of trouble, supply counsel, or interfere in any way with the legal process in Mexico. Once in jail, you're on your own. (For a list of embassies, see Mexico City Practical Information below.)

Mexico has many tourist offices. Branches of the **Mexican Government Tourism Office** (Secretaría de Turismo or SECTUR) are located in the capital city of each state and wherever else tourists gather. The address in Mexico City is Mariano Escobedo 726, Delegación Miguel Hidalgo, C.P. 11590, Mexico, D.F. (tel. (5) 211-00-99).

## ■■■ GETTING AROUND

### BY PLANE

Flying within Mexico is more expensive than taking a bus or train, but it is considerably cheaper than comparable flights between U.S. cities. In the summer of 1995, you could fly from Guadalajara to Manzanillo for US$56, or from La Paz to Mexico City for US$218. Check with Mexican airlines for special rates (see telephone numbers in Getting There: By Plane).

### BY BUS

Mexico's extensive, astoundingly cheap bus service is truly amazing. A first-class ticket from Tijuana all the way to Mexico City costs roughly 261 pesos. First-class buses are relatively comfortable and efficient; they occasionally even have bathrooms and functioning air-conditioners (ask at the ticket window). Second- and third-class buses, which are only slightly cheaper than first class, are often overcrowded, hot, and uncomfortable.

When you buy your ticket the agent will ask where you want to sit. At night, the right side of the bus won't face the constant glare of oncoming headlights. During the day, the shady side of the bus will be a lot cooler. Mexicans usually refuse to open the windows when the bus is moving.

Buses are either *de local* or *de paso*. *De local* originate at the station from which you leave. Buy your ticket a day (or at least a few hours) in advance because only a few *de locales* leave per day. Once you get on the bus, keep your ticket stub, as you may be asked to show it at a later stop (occasionally, bus drivers will conduct inspections in order to thwart free-loaders).

*De paso* buses originate elsewhere and pass through your station. First-class *de pasos* sell only as many tickets as there are available seats—when the bus arrives, the driver disembarks to give this information to the ticket seller. When these tickets go on sale, forget civility, chivalry, and anything which might possibly stand between you and a ticket, or plan to spend the greater portion of your vacation in bus stations. Second-class *de paso* buses sell tickets based on the number of people with assigned seats who have gotten off the bus. This system does not, unfortunately, take into account the people and packages jammed into the aisle. You may find someone (or something) already in your assigned seat when you reach it; in this case, enlist the bus driver's help. Hold your ground and try to keep calm. It is proper to offer to hold someone's heavy equipment (such as children or chickens), but if you feel the urge to give up your seat to someone who looks more in need of a rest than you, just envision how much you'll need it in ten hours.

If you know when boarding the bus that no seats are available, it's best to wait and board last. That way, while all other passengers without seats have to stand in the aisle, you are able to sit semi-comfortably on the step between the driver's compartment and the aisle.

Food and drinks at terminal restaurants are generally overpriced and unappetizing. Bring your own grub whenever possible. Drinking alcoholic beverages during bus rides is prohibited. Do not bring drugs or guns on board; federal law enforcement officials regularly stop buses and search riders' belongings. Keep your tourist card handy during baggage inspection.

---

### Busing It: Words of Advice

When boarding your bus, try to carry on everything you may need. Because no matter how much you may need that security blanket or Newsweek, once bags have been checked you can't retrieve anything from them—not even at rest stops. The driver is not allowed to break the inspection sticker. Buses generally make rest stops every couple of hours, and 5-10 minutes is usually allotted for bathroom and snack breaks. While feeding on potato chips or the twinkie-like Tía María processed pastry snacks, keep your eye on the bus. The drivers aren't always aware that you're intending to get back on. Many horror stories have resulted from buses leaving behind unsuspecting rest-stoppers. Verbally informing the driver of your existence and travel plans is always a good idea.

---

## BY TRAIN

The Mexican railroads are all government-owned, with most lines operating under the name of **Ferrocarriles Nacionales de Mexico** (National Railways of Mexico). Trains run from the border at Nogales, Piedras Negras, Nuevo Laredo, Matamoros, and Mexicali. Write to Ferrocarriles Nacionales de Mexico for a complete rail schedule (see Useful Organizations: Transportation Services). The train system is not as extensive nor as punctual as the bus system. Even when they are on time, trains can take twice as long as buses to reach their destination. Typically, only very poor Mexicans ride trains; you probably won't rely on trains unless you're nearly broke, or unless you crave scenic, leisurely travel in very picturesque areas.

There are several train options: *rápido* trains, which cost more than *locales*, cut travel time in half by chugging past smaller towns without stopping. *Rápido* trains are almost always cleaner and more comfortable. *Primera clase* (first class) or, better yet, *primera clase especial* (comparable to "business" or "ambassador" class), cost significantly more than *segunda clase* (second class), but you get cleanliness and comfort for your money. *Segunda clase* may be the cheapest form of transportation in the world—a ticket from Guadalajara to Mexico city costs just around 24 pesos—but expect to stand for 20 hours in a hot, dirty, crowded car, with pickpockets and animals for company, and a hole cut in the floor for a toilet.

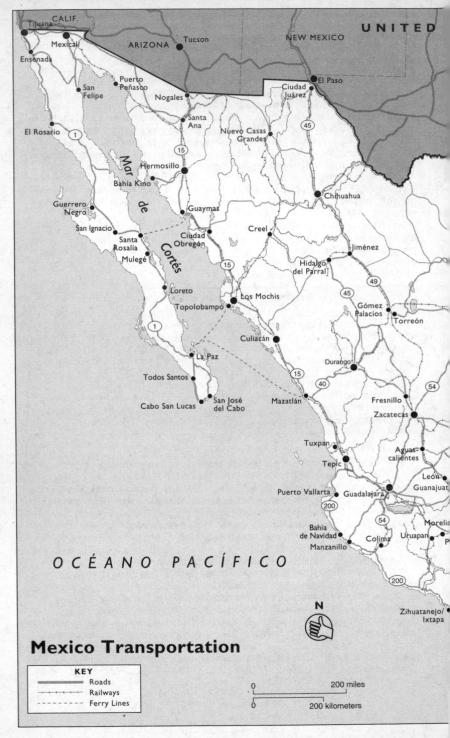

# Mexico Transportation

**KEY**

| | |
|---|---|
| ▬▬▬ | Roads |
| ┼┼┼┼ | Railways |
| ‒ ‒ ‒ | Ferry Lines |

| | 0 | | 200 miles |
|---|---|---|---|
| | 0 | | 200 kilometers |

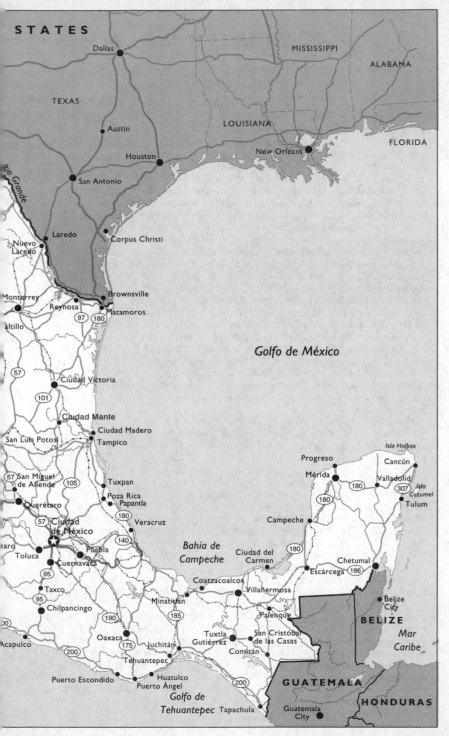

## BY CAR

The maximum speed on Mexican highways is 100km per hour (62mph) unless otherwise posted. Speed limits can be frustratingly low. In most small towns, you'll come across speed bumps. Usually one slows traffic on each side of town, and another perches right in the middle. Roadwork is continually in progress across Mexico; you will regularly drive by construction workers making utterly incomprehensible but codified signals, at which point you should slow down until you figure out what is going on. One particularly confusing signal looks like a plea for you to back up. In fact, it is a request to move forward. In general, take it easy until you master the sign language of Mexican roads.

Be especially careful driving during the rainy season (May-Oct.), when roads are often in poor condition, potholes become craters, and landslides are common. At night, pedestrians and livestock pop up on the roadway at the darndest times. This doesn't seem to bother the locals, many of whom drive without headlights. If you can help it, don't drive at night. (And whatever you do, never spend the night on the side of the road.) When approaching a one-lane bridge, labeled *puente angosto* or *solo carril,* the first driver to flash headlights has the right of way. Lanes are narrow, so if a truck tries to pass your car on a two-lane road, you might need to pull off onto the gravel or graded dirt in order to give the vehicle enough room. (But be careful: the shoulder is often nonexistent or covered with vegetation.)

Exercise particular caution when driving along: Rte. 15 in the state of Sinaloa; Rte. 2 in the vicinity of Carborca, Sonora; Rte. 57 between Matehuala and San Luis Potosí; the highway between Palomares and Tuxtepec, Oaxaca; and Rte. 40. A number of assaults have occurred on these stretches of pavement. Check with local authorities or the nearest U.S. consulate to update the situation and to identify other areas of potential danger. When driving on roads near the capital, watch out for fog. A sign warning *Maneje despacio* (Drive slowly) should be taken seriously.

To help reduce the heinous pollution in Mexico City, tourist traffic in the metropolis is restricted (see Mexico City: Transportation Within Mexico City for details).

In Baja California, if you want to leave your car and go somewhere by public transportation for a few days, you must pay to park in an authorized lot; otherwise, the car will be towed or confiscated. The Motor Vehicle Office will tell you where to leave your car legally.

**PEMEX** (Petroleos Mexicanos) sells two types of gas: Nova (regular) and Extra (unleaded). Nova (*no va* in Spanish means "doesn't go") is appropriately named, and one whiff of a Nova-burning car will make you realize why emissions controls are so important. Unless your car is old, rugged, and satisfied with low-quality leaded gas, driving it through Mexico is not the brightest idea. Unleaded gas, no longer as hard to get as in years past, is making its presence felt in Mexico. You will find it throughout the Baja as well as in Guadalajara, Monterrey, Mexico City, most border towns, and all major metropolitan areas. But beware: even if you do find a silver Extra pump, it may be filled with Nova gasoline. The Mexican government has introduced two new types of gas, Nova Plus and Extra Plus, but the gasoline situation remains unpredictable. Mechanically inclined drivers might want to order a "test" pipe from a specialty parts house to replace the catalytic converter so the car can process Nova upon its arrival in Mexico.

Both Nova and Extra are extremely cheap by all but Saudi Arabian standards. Don't get overcharged: know how much gas you'll need before you pull in and make sure the register is rung back to zero before pumping begins. PEMEX accepts cash and checks only. When you pull into a PEMEX station to check the tires, remember that pumps in Mexico are calibrated in kilograms (1kg = 2.2 lb.).

The heat, bumpy roads, and fair-to-middling gas may well take a toll on your car. Mexican mechanics are good and charge very reasonable rates, but if they've never seen your model, reconcile yourself to a lengthy stay. Oil is scarce, and parts are available only for those models that Mexicans drive; all the various VWs are in plentiful supply, especially the Beetle (known as the *Vochito*), as are Datsun/Nissans and 1970s Detroit boat-cars. No matter what kind of car you sport, bring spare oil, spark plugs, fan belts and air, and fuel filters—these should take care of all but the biggest problems. If you break down on one of the major highways between 8am and 8pm, pull completely off the road, raise the hood, and wait for the **Ángeles Verdes** (Green Angel) to come to the rescue. Green Angels are the Mexican Government Tourism Office's innovation—green-and-white emergency trucks dispatched by radio, staffed by almost a thousand English-speaking mechanics, and equipped for performing common repair jobs, towing, changing tires, and addressing minor medical problems. If you're near a phone, you can speed things up by calling the radio communications office at (5) 250-48-17. Your green saviors may take a while to show up, but the service (except for parts, gas and oil) is free. Tipping is optional but polite. Green Angels go everywhere but the *Distrito Federal.*

While on the road in Mexico, you'll probably be stopped at least once by agents of the Federal Public Ministry and the Federal Judicial Police for a search of your car and its contents. To avoid being detained or arrested, be as cooperative as possible. Do *not* carry drugs or firearms in your car.

---

### Taxi Tips

If you've had it with riding next to unfriendly chickens on Mexican buses and don't feel up to walking to your intended destination, taxis are always a practical and fairly economical alternative, provided you know what you're getting into when you step into the vehicle. Taxi drivers can be ruthless opportunists, experts at spotting green tourists and their greenbacks—don't be taken for a ride! Be sure to ask the driver what the fare is expected to be, and act like you know the route; consulting with tourist officials or hotel staff about distance and routes beforehand is very helpful in this situation. If the meter works, require that it be used (don't trust the driver's interesting calculating methods). Some taxis offer hourly and daily rates with fares that become miraculously un"fixed" with aggressive haggling. So look smart, be wary, and as David Horowitz would say, "don't let anyone rip you off"—the chickens back on the *segunda clase* Malinalco bus would be proud.

---

## ■■■ BY THUMB

*Let's Go* urges you to use common sense if you decide to hitch, and to seriously consider all possible risks before you make that decision. The information listed below and throughout the book is not intended to recommend hitchhiking; *Let's Go* does not recommend hitchhiking as a means of transportation.

The Mexicans who pick up tourists are often friendly, often offering meals, tours, or other extras, but suspicion is warranted. Those who hitch should find out where the driver is going before they get in, and think twice if he or she opens the door quickly and offers to drive anywhere. Do not accept a ride if any cause for concern arises; make an excuse and wait for another car to come along. Women should never hitchhike alone. Never accept a ride without sizing up the driver. On many highways (the Mexico City-Acapulco road, for example), *bandidos* are common.

Before getting in, make sure the passenger window or door opens from inside. If there are several people in the car, do not sit in the middle. Assume a quick-exit position, which rules out the back seat of a two-door car. Keep backpacks and other baggage where they are easily accessible—don't let the driver store them in the trunk. If you have trouble getting out for any reason, affecting the pose of someone about to vomit works wonders.

Every city and every road has a best and worst spot for hitchhiking. Hitchers recommend stretches near a major intersection where many cars converge or PEMEX stations. They also recommend that hitchers should be cautious when standing on the shoulders of highways, since they are not considered off-limits to drivers, and that they should bring along something to drink and some sort of protection from the sun and rain. Furthermore, it is said that those who appear neat and travel light have a better chance of getting a ride.

# ■■■ ACCOMMODATIONS

## HOTELS

Though hotels in Mexico include some of the world's most overpriced, the majority are shockingly affordable. All hotels, ranging from luxury resorts in Cancún to dumps in Monterrey, are controlled by the government's **Secretaria de Turismo** (SECTUR). SECTUR ensures that hotels of similar quality charge similar prices and requires that all hotels display the official tariff sheet. You should always ask to see this sheet if you doubt the quoted price; make sure it is up-to-date. Although hotel prices are regulated, proprietors are not prohibited from charging *less* than the official rate. If the hotel looks like it hasn't seen a customer in several days, a little bargaining may work wonders, especially if you offer to stay a number of days. For a room with one bed, request *un cuarto con una cama*. If bedding down with a fellow wayfarer, ask for one *con dos camas* (with two beds).

Usually located within a block or two of the *zócalo,* the cheapest hotels (20-30 pesos) rarely provide private bathrooms or other amenities. Slightly higher-priced hotels (30-50 pesos) usually reside in the same district but are much better equipped, including rooms with private bathrooms. Before accepting any room, ask to see it, and always ask if the price includes any meals.

If the hotels listed in *Let's Go* are full or don't appeal to you, ask cab drivers or vendors in the market for a good recommendation. Also, hotel people in one town are often a good source for hotel leads in the next town on your itinerary. For the bare-bones budget traveler, the hammock is the way to go. If you plan to travel on a shoestring, buy one. Most towns in Mexico are dotted with *palapas*. For a small fee, these open-air restaurants double as places to hang your hat and hammock when the sun goes down. In small *yucateco* towns, locals often let travelers use hammock hooks for a pittance.

Hotels in Mexico often lock their doors at night, and small-town establishments may do so surprisingly early. A locked door doesn't necessarily mean "closed for the night," as someone usually is on duty. By arriving early in small towns or calling ahead if you can't avoid arriving late, and by checking with the hotel desk before going out for a late night on the town, you'll help dispel the Mexican myth of the obnoxious foreigner.

Reservations are not absolutely necessary (except during Christmas, *Semana Santa,* and other festivals), but if you're exhausted upon arrival, they make life much easier. You can just about always find a bed somewhere, but without reservations you may waste money and time.

## HOSTELS

Mexican hostels are often run-down, far from town, and not much cheaper than local hotels (15-20 pesos per night). The only people who should consider hosteling are younger travelers who want the security and discipline of an orderly establishment with regular meals and nighttime supervision. Their ban on alcohol, smoking restrictions, and limited hours (most are open from 7-9am and 5-10pm) also deter many budget travelers.

Most Mexican hostels will give you a bed even if you don't have a hostel card. They may, however, charge you more for it. If you plan to stay in hostels regularly, get a **Hosteling International** (HI, formerly International Youth Hostel Federation, IYHF) card (see Useful Organizations: Travel Organizations). For more information, write the Agencia Nacional de Turismo Juvenil, Glorieta del Metro Insurgentes, Local CC-11, Col. Juárez, México, D.F.06600 (tel. (5) 525-26-99, 525-29-16, 533-12-91, or 525-29-74).

For addresses and telephone numbers of **YMCAs** in Mexico, call or write Y's Way International, 224 E. 47th St., New York, NY 10017 (tel. (212) 308-2899).

## CAMPING

For the budget travel experience par excellence, try camping in Mexico—it eliminates hotel costs, and if you bring fishing gear to the beach, it can also save you money on food. Campers accustomed to prim and proper campgrounds will be taken aback, however. Mexican national parks often exist only in theory; many are indistinguishable from the surrounding cities. Trails, campgrounds, and rangers are strictly *norteamericano* concepts.

Privately owned **trailer parks** are relatively common on major highways—look for signs with a picture of a trailer, or the words *parque de trailer, campamento,* or *remolques.* These places may or may not allow campers to pitch tents. Don't set up camp next to a well-traveled road, or screeching brakes and the shattering glass of your car may shake you from that peaceful slumber.

The best guide for campers is *The People's Guide to RV Camping in Mexico* (see John Muir in Useful Organizations: Publications). The **Sierra Club Bookstore,** 730 Polk St., San Francisco, CA 94109 (tel. (415) 923-5500) offers useful publications for those planning to camp in Mexico. For adventure narratives or *Mexico's Volcanoes, A Climbing Guide* (US$14.95), which contains maps, photos, and a bilingual mountaineering glossary, write or call **Mountaineers Books,** 1011 SW Klickitat Way, Suite 107, Seattle, WA 98134 (tel. (800) 553-4453 or (206) 223-6303; fax (206) 223-6306). **Wilderness Press** (see address in Planning Your Trip: Specific Concerns: Traveling With Children) disseminates general backpacking information and publishes outdoor guides which include information on Mexico.

For information on hostel-affiliated campgrounds, write to Agencia Nacional de Turismo Juvenil (see Hostels).

## ■■■ KEEPING IN TOUCH

### MAIL

Mexican mail service can be slow, but it is generally dependable. Airmail often reaches the U.S. in as few as six days, but can just as easily take a month or more. It takes even longer (at least two weeks) to Europe and other destinations. Official estimates average 40 days by boat, but in reality may take months. Postage for letters costs about three pesos, or two pesos for *tarjetas postales* (postcards). Anything important should be sent registered mail, or else duplicates should be sent. There is no size limitation for packages, but parcels cannot weigh more than 25kg. Never deposit anything important in the black holes Mexicans call mailboxes. *La estampilla* or *el timbre* is "the stamp" in Spanish, and *la carta* is "the letter."

You can have letters sent to you in Mexico through **Lista de Correos,** a letter-holding service similar to General Delivery in the U.S. When picking up mail sent to you via *Lista de Correos,* look for a list posted in the post office. Check it carefully for any possible misspellings. If there is no list posted, ask the attendant, "*¿Está la lista de hoy?*" (Is today's list here?). If it is, give your name. Letters and packages will be held no more than 15 days (sometimes fewer). If you have friends or family in Mexico, using their address may be better. Hotels where you have reserved a room will usually hold mail for you. **American Express offices** will hold mail for 30 days before returning it; just write "Client's Mail" on the envelope. You don't need to be a cardholder to receive the service as long as you purchase traveler's checks from AmEx. Call American Express customer service at (800) 528-4800 for information and ask for the free *Directory of Traveler Service Offices.*

Mail sent to *Lista de Correos* should be addressed to a first and last name only, capitalizing and underlining the name under which the item should be filed alphabetically. Keep names as simple as possible. Because Mexican *apellidos* (paternal last names) fall in the middle of the written name, confusion arises for foreigners with more than a simple first and last name, or in the case of mail addressed to more than one person. A letter could be filed under any misspelled permutation of the recipient's names. If possible, go through the *Lista de Correos* yourself. If not, watch the person who does and ask for the mail under both your first and your last name, just to make sure. Address letters as follows:

Leondra <u>KRUGER</u>
a/c Lista de Correos
Catemaco [city], Veracruz [state]
95870 [postal code, if you know it], MEXICO

The letter should also be marked *Favor de retener hasta la llegada* ("Please hold until arrival").

It's wise to use the Spanish abbreviations or names for countries (EEUU or EUA for the U.S.). Write *Por Avión* on all postcards and letters not otherwise marked, unless you don't mind it arriving sometime in the next millennium.

Regulations for mailing parcels may vary from state to state. While it is often possible to send packages from smaller towns, post offices in large cities (especially ports or trade centers such as Mérida and Acapulco) provide more reliable service. Mailing a package involves locating a box, tape, string, wrapping paper, and the correct forms to be stamped and signed by the appropriate officials. Before attempting to send anything, go to the post office and note the weight limitations, necessary documentation, addresses and hours of the customs and trade offices in the city, and whether the box should be brought open or sealed. After the contents have been inspected at the post office and at customs, you can wrap your package (usually on the post office floor). All packages are reopened and inspected by customs at the border, so closing the box with string rather than tape is recommended.

In some cases, customs and the post office are under the same roof. In others, the two lie at opposite ends of town and have conflicting schedules. In general, in order to send packages you must provide the following: tourist card data (number, duration of validity, date of issue, place of issue), list of contents including estimated value and nature of the package ("Gift" works best), address and return address. It is customary for those mailing parcels to use their home address, or at least some address in the same country as the parcel's destination, as a return address to ensure eventual delivery. In a trade office, you may need to show receipts for each item purchased in Mexico. Postal officials usually record the information from the customs form on the front of the package as well.

## TELEPHONES

When trying to reach Mexico from another country, patience is the key to success. If you are calling Mexican information, don't be surprised if the phone is not answered right away. To reach Mexico from the U.S., dial 011-52, then the city code (5 for Mexico City), and then the phone number.

Getting lines to foreign countries is very difficult. Many public phones don't have access to international lines. If you speak Spanish fluently and can't reach the international operator, call the national operator, who will connect you (sometimes even a local operator can help). The term for a collect call is a *llamada por cobrar* or *llamada con cobro revertido*. Calling from hotels is usually faster.

Calling abroad from Mexico is extremely expensive thanks to taxes and surcharges. Long-distance charges vary from city to city; calls to the U.S. usually set you back about eight pesos per minute, and can run as high as 14 pesos per minute. Call collect if you can; not only is it cheaper (about half the price of direct), but you will avoid the enormous surcharges that hotel switchboards impose if you call direct. Remember, however, that there can be a fee of one to five pesos for collect calls that are not accepted, depending on where you place the call. Using a U.S. operator to call collect or with a calling card will let you pay U.S. rates (around $5-6 per min. depending on distance between cities).

**LADATEL** phones, increasingly prevalent, take coins or LADATEL phone cards. International calls using these phones are cheaper and involve less waiting than any of the alternatives. LADATEL **phone cards,** available at Teléfonos Mexicanos offices and various stores, eliminate the need for coins. Without them, the challenge is to find enough coins of large denominations, because these phones take no more than 10 coins at a time and some calls require a minimum initial deposit. When dialing, use the station-to-station prefixes. The blue push-button phones do direct dial while the orange old-fashioned ones do not. Dial 95-800-462-4240 from LADATEL phones to reach an **AT&T USADirect** operator; dial 95-800-674-7000 from LADATEL phones to reach an **MCI WorldPhone** operator; dial 95-800-877-8000 to reach a **Sprint Express** operator in Mexico City only.

To reach the English-speaking international operator on a plain old phone, dial 09 and wait until the operator answers (sometimes immediately, but be prepared to wait 30min. or more). For direct calls, dial 01; national operator 02; local assistance 04 (restricted to numbers not in the directory); for bilingual (Spanish and English) emergency operators 06. To make long-distance phone calls within Mexico, dial 91 plus the telephone code and number (station to station), or 92 plus the telephone code and number (person to person). The prefixes for calling the U.S. or Canada are 95 for station to station and 96 for person to person; for all other countries the prefixes are 98 and 99, respectively.

# ANNALS OF CIVILIZATION

## ■ PRE-COLUMBIAN SOCIETIES

### The Mysterious Olmecs: Mexico's First Civilization

Little is known about the first settled peoples of Mexico, the Olmecs (Náhuatl for "People from the Land of Rubber"). The Olmecs inhabited the cities now known as La Venta, San Lorenzo and Tres Zapotes from 1200-100 BCE, yet no skeletal remains have ever been discovered. Archaeologists didn't even recognize their existence as a distinct civilization until someone stumbled on an immense basalt head in the jungles of southern Mexico. The Olmecs apparently lived in socially stratified communities concentrated in what is now Tabasco and southern Veracruz, though their cultural influence can be traced as far south as Costa Rica. It was among the Olmecs that the feathered serpent—a figure ubiquitous in pre-Hispanic Mexico—had its origins. Among their most notable developments were a glyphic writing system and recorded dates. The jaguar was a symbol of utmost importance in Olmec mythology; sculpted human figures often have feline forms and mouths curled into jaguar-like snarls. San Lorenzo was violently destroyed around 900 BCE, and La Venta suffered a similar fate before another four centuries had elapsed. While the Olmecs perished, many of their cultural achievements were transmitted to other Mesoamerican peoples, including the Maya.

### The Mayan Dominion

The genius of the Maya can be seen in the remains of their ancient cities—most notably Palenque, Chichén Itzá, Uxmal, Tulum, and Bonampak—scattered about the Yucatán Peninsula and modern-day Chiapas. During the first 300 years of the Mexican Classic Period (300-900 CE), the Maya became proficient in engineering, mathematics, architecture, creative arts, calendrical calculations, and astronomy, devising a method to predict the movement of celestial bodies with startling precision. Strangely, however, this sophisticated society never used the wheel other than for children's playthings.

Around 900 CE, the Mayan empire mysteriously collapsed; apparently, the Mayans had farmed the land into exhaustion, causing food shortages and perhaps peasant revolts. A Mayan renaissance occurred in the northern Yucatán after 1200 CE, but with a new influence from the west—Teotihuacán culture, as elaborated by the Toltecs. (See Near Mexico City: Teotihuacán). Parallel Maya-Toltec legends tell how Quetzalcóatl (The Feathered Serpent, also known as Kukulcán), a great Toltec king, broke away from the Toltec empire and made his way to the Yucatán with his people; the myths predict his eventual return.

The Toltec empire dominated most of central Mexico during the Post-Classic Period (900-1540 CE) with Xochicalco (See Near Cuernavaca), Cholula, and Tula serving as their most prominent cities. The bellicose Toltecs practiced human sacrifice and, like the Olmecs, placed the jaguar at the center of their iconography. This violent and powerful culture would provide the framework for the Aztec civilization, next to forge an empire.

### The Aztecs: An Age of Violence

After the fall of Toltec civilization, the Aztecs, or Mexica, wandered nomadically from the end of the 12th century until 1325. Legend has it, in that year, the Aztec peoples had arrived at the southwestern border of Lake Texcoco, an unappealing swamp that no other group had claimed. There, they beheld an eagle perched upon a cactus with a serpent in its talons: the vision was taken as a sign to build the legendary floating city Tenochtitlán on this sacred site.

The Aztecs practiced a religion derived from their Toltec predecessors; they worshipped a supreme being, the aggregate force of numerous deities. The chief Aztec god was the young warrior Huitzilopochtli, the personification of the sun. According to legend, he perished red and sated every evening only to be reborn anemic the following dawn, craving the blood of human victims. In contrast to this solar vampire, Quetzalcóatl, the god of the air, instructed the natives in the use of metals, in agriculture, and in the art of government. He was thought to have been light-skinned with dark hair and a long flowing beard.

The Aztec civilization was as bloody and hierarchical as any that followed it in Mexican history. At the height of their power, Aztec priests practiced human sacrifice on a large scale. In the yearly offering to Tezcatlipoca, the god of honor, the most attractive youth in the land was selected to live like a king for eleven months and then, stripped of his lavish accoutrements, to part with his heart at the hands of the head-priest and master of ceremonies.

Motivated by a literal need for human blood, the Aztecs built Mexico's largest *indígena* empire, with about five million people inhabiting a dominion that stretched from the Atlantic to the Pacific and all the way to Guatemala and Nicaragua. The beauty and architectural sophistication of the island city Tenochtitlán, connected to the mainland by a network of canals and causeways, led Western chroniclers to compare it to the fabulous cities of their chivalric romance tales and to dub it the Venice of the New World. *Chinampas*, or "floating gardens," enabled the Aztecs to cultivate the swamp efficiently. Tenochtitlán developed into one of the world's largest cities.

# ■ CONQUEST AND COLONIZATION

### The Arrival of Cortés

Then, suddenly, history ended and began again. When Hernán Cortés landed on the island of Cozumel in 1519 in search of slaves and gold, he turned the old world upside down. Arriving in enormous ships and wearing shiny shells of armor, Cortés and his men resembled nothing the *indígenas* had ever seen. The Spaniards carried "fire-breathing" guns, sat atop armored horses—which the *indígenas* believed to be immortal—and rode with packs of huge, vicious war-dogs. Some communities capitulated instantly, showering the Spaniards with fruit, flowers, gold, and women; other towns fought the invaders tooth and nail. But Cortés, heavily in debt and fleeing arrest by the Spanish governor of Cuba, had no choice but to press ahead. He sunk his own ships to prevent his men from turning back, cut off the feet of those who attempted mutiny, and marched on toward the great Aztec capital of Tenochtitlán with the assistance of Jerónimo de Aguilar, a Spaniard who had been shipwrecked there several years earlier and spoke the native language. As they moved westward through Tabasco, the Spaniards acquired a second interpreter, La Malinche, a native who became Cortés's mistress and adviser. Along the way to the capital, Cortés recruited about 6000 warriors from the Totonacs and Tlaxcalans—enemies of the Aztecs—and massacred 6000 of the Aztecs' allies at Cholula.

The Aztec emperor Moctezuma II (1502-1520) received word of Cortés's approach, and politely sent a message to the Spaniards, discouraging them from traveling to the capital. Moctezuma, however, also grappled with rumors that Cortés was the light-skinned, bearded god Quetzalcóatl, who had sailed away after incurring the wrath of the gods, declaring that he and his descendants would one day return. Plagued by conflicting advice, Moctezuma finally welcomed the Spaniards into the city. An initial period of peaceful, if tense, relations quickly soured when Moctezuma was kidnapped by the Spanish, and Cortés was driven from the city in a rout. An incredible string of lucky coincidences let Cortés regroup quickly, and two years later, on August 13, 1521, the Aztecs, though valiantly led by their new emperor Cuauhtémoc, were soundly defeated at Tlatelolco. The capital had fallen for good.

## The Great Death

The Spaniards' arrival triggered what may be the most devastating biological holocaust in world history. Geographically isolated for millennia, the indigenous peoples of the Americas lacked natural resistance to European diseases. Smallpox, typhoid, yellow fever, and dysentery spread ravenously through Mesoamerica. The mild childhood diseases of Europe—measles, mumps, influenza, and chicken pox—proved fatal to *indígenas*. Within 100 years of Cortés' landing, a silent viral bomb had wiped out as much as 96% of the indigenous population—about 24 million people. Smallpox was by far the biggest killer: encrusted with running sores, victims vomited dried black blood as their skin gradually sloughed off their bodies. Those who lived were sometimes left blind or hideously scarred. Entire villages disappeared from the map, and Spaniards simply moved onto the empty lands, called *tierras baldías,* or bought deserted acreage at bargain prices. Settlers quickly grabbed huge estates; by 1618, one family had acquired over 11 million acres on the northern frontier.

## Land and Power

Epidemics meant, from the Spaniards' point of view, chronic labor shortages. For a time, *conquistadores* enslaved prisoners captured in battle, but due to rampant disease and maltreatment, *indígena* slavery was abolished in 1542. (Owning black slaves, however, was legal in Mexico until 1829.) Instead, royal officials gave Spanish settlers *encomiendas* (labor grants): *indígena* villages had to send a quota of workers to labor on the Spaniards' farms, and in return, the *encomendero* was supposed to educate and defend the village. In practice, *indígena* workers were overworked, abused, and segregated from their families.

Afraid that maverick *encomenderos* would challenge royal authority, the crown tried to restrict faraway *encomiendas*. But the crown had its own concerns at stake, not those of natives: regulations protecting *indígenas* were rarely enforced—"do little and do it slowly" was the motto of New Spain's first viceroy. After the Church and crown began imposing taxes on villagers, *encomenderos* had an easier time recruiting *indígena* labor: since *indígenas* needed the once-useless colonial currency to pay taxes, they were forced to work for inadequate wages in Spanish farms.

Abuses were worst where wealth was greatest—in the mines. Rich veins of silver were discovered in central Mexico in the 1540s, and mining camps proliferated overnight, fueling the growth of colonial boom towns. Miners climbed out of the shafts on ladders made of notched logs, and at night they slept on the same pieces of cloth they used to haul their loads of ore. *Indígenas* forced to work in the mines died in the pits by the thousands, felled by floods, explosions, and noxious gases.

## The Church

Christianization was central to the Conquest—even Cortés took every opportunity to lecture indigenous villages on their salvation. When the Spaniards took Tenochtitlán, they razed the Aztecs' central temple and built a cathedral atop the rubble. Such bombastic tactics often backfired, and some communities, like the tenacious Lancandóns, fiercely defended their native religions.

Later missionaries were more successful; many *indígenas* were especially impressed by the arrival of the first 12 Franciscan friars, who walked barefoot all the way from Veracruz to the capital. While the Franciscans concentrated their efforts in the center of the country, the Jesuits pushed northwards and the Dominicans moved into the southern regions. Religious services and holidays were the only sanctioned days of rest for many villagers, and by the mid-1500s missionaries had won millions of converts. But Catholic ritual and belief mixed with traditional practices, creating a vibrant and often peculiar brand of religious syncretism that persists today in many rural areas.

Many clergymen tried to protect *indígenas* against exploitation, often locking horns with local *encomenderos* and crown officials. The militant Dominican Bartolomé de Las Casas, a vocal critic of the *encomienda* system, was largely responsible for early crown laws protecting *indígenas*. The Franciscan Juan de Zumárraga, Mexico's first archbishop, personified the best and worst of colonial Catholicism. Zumárraga bravely condemned corrupt judges and lobbied for *indígena* rights—yet burned native nobles at the stake on charges of heresy, and regularly boasted that he had razed 500 temples and crushed 20,000 idols.

## Race and Class

When the Spanish built a new city on the ruins of Tenochtitlán, they tried to establish clear racial boundaries. Only whites could live in the city's core; *indígenas* were confined to the fringes and had to commute into the city each day, rowing through narrow canals in dugout canoes. But complete segregation was impossible, and within a few generations, a new racial group had emerged—*mestizos,* children of mixed Spanish and *indígena* parentage. African slaves—permitted to live as domestic servants in the city center—added to the genetic soup.

At the top of the heap were *peninsulares,* whites born in Spain. Just below them were *criollos,* whites born in the Americas. Many whites born in the New World bitterly resented the gulf between *peninsulares* and *criollos.* All *peninsulares* expected to be addressed as "Don" or "Doña," regardless or their actual rank. Certain professions were closed to *criollos,* and Spanish-born settlers typically refused to marry outside their class. Though indignant, *criollos* were hardly interested in leveling social barriers—they simply wanted to join the aristocracy. *Mestizos* were the great, amorphous class of colonial Mexico, outnumbering *criollos* by the end of the colonial period. Some lived in white districts, while others were absorbed into the *indígena* villages of their mothers. Still others wandered the countryside or made their living on the streets, rejected by both cultures. *Indígenas* formed the bottom rung of the socio-economic ladder, vastly outnumbering all other racial groups. Physically isolated from whites, most *indígenas* spoke no Spanish, and were barred from almost all occupations. Spaniards were loath to hire them as domestic servants. Though the Spanish brought horses to the Americas, they used *indígenas* to haul all sorts of loads—even employing dark-skinned porters to carry their dogs. Clothing was restricted as a mark of race and class: an *indígena* caught wearing European garb was punished with 100 lashes and a month in jail.

# ■ INDEPENDENCE AND REFORM

### The First Calls for Freedom

Enter Miguel Hidalgo y Costilla, an iconoclastic priest in the small parish of Dolores. Always rebellious, Hidalgo had been tried by the Inquisition on charges of gambling, dancing, reading forbidden books, fornicating, questioning the immaculate conception, and denouncing the king of Spain. (He was acquitted on insufficient evidence.) Hidalgo spent little time proselytizing; instead, he tried to improve parishioners' economic lot by introducing new trades and crafts to the village of Dolores. He also stockpiled guns. When Spanish officials discovered his hidden reserve, Hidalgo ran to Dolores' church and rang the bells to summon the parishioners. As stunned villagers listened, Hidalgo delivered a ringing call to arms—*El Grito de Dolores*—and verbally whipped his congregation into an instant army. *Indígena* resentment was high; the summer of 1809 had been so dry that corn withered in the fields, and shortages had sparked 400% inflation in some regions. Hidalgo's army quickly swelled, capturing several major cities before Hidalgo was killed in an ambush by Spanish troops in March 1811.

Another parish priest, José María Morelos y Pavón, rose to lead the Independence movement after Hidalgo's death. Under his command the rebels captured Mexico City, but the tide soon turned and Spanish troops took the capital once again. But history plays funny tricks: after Napoleon's troops invaded Spain and forced a liberal constitution on the king, many conservative colonists decided to cut their ties to Spain. Frightened by the spectre of a revolutionary French government, wealthy *criollos* swallowed their pride and joined the liberal Independence movement. The most famous turncoat was Agustín de Iturbide, a *criollo* loyalist who had led Spanish troops into battle against Hidalgo. In 1820, he suddenly defected, uniting forces with rebel leader Vincente Guerrero. Reassuringly conservative—Iturbide and Guerrero proclaimed Mexico an independent monarchy and endorsed the Catholic church—the compromise won wide support and by September 1821, Spain had been thoroughly defeated.

### The First Empire

"He is prompt, bold, and decisive, and not scrupulous about the means he employs to obtain his ends." So wrote a U.S. visitor of Iturbide, who had promptly crowned himself emperor of Mexico. As the uneasy compromise between liberals and conservatives crumbled, Iturbide simply dissolved the legislature—setting a dangerous precedent. Anticlericalists, *indígenas,* and *criollos* of modest means rebelled against Iturbide, led by the *criollo* military commander Antonio López de Santa Anna. In 1823, Iturbide finally resigned, but his legacy of despotism endured.

Mexico was in shambles. In the fighting between 1810 and 1823, half a million people—one in 12 Mexicans—had died. War had dislocated the entire colonial economy as trade with Spain dried up. Battles had left mines flooded and fields fallow. Idle ex-soldiers roamed the country, and unemployment was rampant. The fledgling government was flat-out broke.

### The Era of Santa Anna

Into the void stepped Santa Anna. Though the presidency of Mexico officially changed hands 36 times between May 1833 and August 1855, Santa Anna dominated the political scene. Initially elected on a liberal, mildly anticlerical platform, Santa Anna quickly abandoned his duties and retired to his personal estate. When his vice-president implemented promised reforms, Santa Anna led a conservative uprising and recaptured the presidency, this time as a conservative and a supporter of the church. Irony piled upon injustice, and the megalomaniac Santa Anna eventually occupied the presidency no fewer than 11 times.

As his cronies grew rich on graft and bribery, Santa Anna drained the state coffers, desperately levying taxes on gutters, dogs, and wheels to build a huge standing army. Sure enough, Mexico was soon at war again. In 1838, France attacked Veracruz, demanding reparations for property damaged during the war. The conflict was dubbed "The Pastry War" in honor of a French pastry cook whose wares had been gobbled by marauding Mexican troops. The attacking French ships were driven back to sea, but Santa Anna lost his leg in the bombardment. Four years later, Santa Anna had his severed leg removed from its grave, carried to the capital in a huge procession, and entombed in an urn atop a towering pillar as the Congress, cabinet, diplomatic corps, and army serenaded the decayed limb.

Meanwhile, the Mexican army was fighting a losing battle on its northern frontier. Angered by Mexico's abolition of slavery in 1829, and under-represented in the legislature, Texan settlers demanded independence from Mexico in 1830. Santa Anna's troops overwhelmed Texan rebels holed up in an old Franciscan monastery called the Alamo. But when the U.S. annexed Texas in 1845, Mexico found itself up against a more formidable adversary. U.S. forces closed in on Mexico City from the north and east. Young cadets, the Niños Héroes (Boy Heroes), valiantly fought off U.S. troops from their military school in Chapultepec Castle, then (according to legend) wrapped themselves in the Mexican flag and leapt off the tower when all hope was lost. Under the terms of the Treaty of Guadalupe Hidalgo, the U.S. bought Texas, New Mexico, and California for a paltry sum. Two thousand Mexicans had died in the battle for Mexico City—only to lose half the nation's territory in the war. Five years later, Santa Anna sold off in the Gadsden Purchase what today is Arizona and southern New Mexico.

## Daily Life in the Mid-19th Century

"The Mexican population presents the most striking contrasts," wrote a German immigrant in Veracruz in the mid-1800s. "On one side splendour and luxury, elegant carriages, and Parisian toilette, on the other dirt and indigence." While Iturbide commissioned a French baroness to design the costumes for his lavish coronation, and Santa Anna made himself a millionaire, most Mexicans lived as they had for centuries—poor and isolated. Over one-third of the population lived in remote *indígena* villages. Though *pueblos* were largely self-governed, most villagers lived in grinding poverty. Rural *indígenas* lived in dirt-floored huts furnished mainly with grass mats, which served as tables, chairs, and beds. *Puebleros* grew their own corn, beans, squash, and chiles, with women working alongside men in the fields. In a male-dominated society, hard-working *indígena* women earned a reputation for frugality. According to a common saying, "*Donde las mujeres comen, las hormigas lloran.*" (Where the women eat, the ants cry.)

Despite economic chaos, provincial capitals grew quickly during the early 19th century. The traditional Spanish pattern of these larger towns is still visible today: major streets enclosed a *zócalo* (central plaza) bordered on four sides by the town cathedral, governmental offices, and sometimes a string of stone *portales* (arcades). Inhabitants of these mid-sized towns enjoyed more amenities than residents of small *pueblos,* yet *indígenas* who relocated to larger cities to live among *mestizos* fared little better than their rural cousins. In order to fill the ranks of the army, the government forcibly conscripted urban males into the military; military scouts would ambush unsuspecting revelers outside bars and bullfights, tearing conscripts from their families and leaving them vagrant and jobless at the end of their service.

Education was a luxury enjoyed only by the *criollo* elite; only 1% of the total population was enrolled in school. There were just 1300 schools in the entire nation in 1842 and of these, only one-third were free. But even wealthy families neglected to educate their daughters. A typical case was the rich and powerful Gordoa family: one son became a senator and a college administrator, while another son was sent to study languages, drawing, and music in Europe. The daughters of the family, however, were barely literate: "*No boi boi a verte,*" wrote one of the Gordoas to her sister.

## Juárez and Reform

Eventually, the façade of Santa Anna's regime cracked under enormous opposition. The emerging leader of the reform movement was Benito Juárez, who has become one of the most revered presidents in Mexican history. His childhood was the stuff of legend: born in a tiny Zapotec *pueblo* in Oaxaca, at age 12 Juárez walked 66km to the state capital (today known as Oaxaca de Juárez), where he apprenticed himself to a book-binder and earned a law degree. Elected governor of Oaxaca, Juárez expanded the school system while reducing state debt. Exiled to New Orleans by Santa Anna, Juárez joined other liberal politicians and journalists in whipping up opposition to Santa Anna abroad, while dissidents in Mexico raised rebel armies. In 1855, Santa Anna was forced to resign.

The new government's policies reflected the ideology of 19th-century liberalism. The reformers abolished the old *fueros,* special regulations protecting the military and church from prosecution under civil laws. Juárez pushed through a new law prohibiting any institution from owning property not directly used in its day-to-day operations. Intended to weaken the church, which owned vast rural and urban properties, the new law ended up stripping *indígenas* of their lands and livelihood, since *ejidos* (indigenous communal lands) had to be auctioned off as well.

Conservatives reacted violently, provoking the War of the Reform, Mexico's bloodiest civil war to date. The church joined the military and dispossessed *pueblos* in fighting the liberal government. Meanwhile, the liberals were aided by *mestizo* reformers and many *indígenas* who supported Juárez, Mexico's first *indígena* president. Both sides committed atrocities: conservatives shot doctors who treated liberal casualties, while liberals defaced churches and executed priests who refused to give the sacrament to their troops.

## French Intervention

After the liberals finally regained the upper hand in 1861, Juárez faced a massive federal budget deficit. He declared a moratorium on payment of Mexico's foreign debts—prompting Spain, Britain, and France to attack Veracruz once again. Spain and Britain soon pulled out, but Napoleon III sent his troops inland. On May 5, 1862, outnumbered Mexican troops successfully repelled diarrhea-plagued French soldiers from the city of Puebla. Cinco de Mayo is now a huge national holiday—but the invaders captured the capital anyway a year later.

When Napoleon selected Austrian archduke Ferdinand Maximilian of Hapsburg as emperor of Mexico, he made a poor choice. Maximilian was naive to an extreme: he insisted that the Mexican people approve his ascension in a national plebiscite (Napoleon saw to it that Maximilian "won" overwhelmingly), then immediately hired a Spanish tutor for his wife Carlota. Maximilian and Carlota landed in Veracruz expecting a grand welcome, but *veracruzanos* refused to leave their houses. The royal couple drove through silent streets in a delicate Viennese carriage, which soon became mired in the muddy roads leading to Mexico City. Carlota cried.

"The so-called entertainments of Europe, such as evening receptions, the gossip of tea parties, etc. are quite unknown here," Maximilian wrote, "and we shall take good care not to introduce them." Weirdly idealistic, Maximilian felt a duty to shelter Mexico from the decadence of the Old World—not realizing he was the puppet of European imperialism. The new emperor was moderately liberal and anti-Catholic; instead of rescinding Juárez's anticlerical laws, Maximilian imposed forced loans on the church to shore up the collapsing treasury. Mexican conservatives were predictably infuriated; Maximilian's modest popularity evaporated. Meanwhile, liberals stockpiled weapons and hired thousands of U.S. Civil War veterans to fight against the French. Napoleon belatedly withdrew his troops in 1867, abandoning Maximilian despite Carlotta's wild pleas. After Carlotta went mad, Maximilian surrendered himself to Juárez, who had him promptly shot. But the human toll of the war was far higher on the Mexican side: 50,000 had died fighting the French.

INDEPENDENCE AND REFORM

## Struggling to Rebuild

Juárez returned to the capital in a solemn black carriage—a stark contrast to Maximilian's flimsy Viennese vehicle. Juárez's characteristically dour appearance seemed appropriate, since the Mexican economy was once again in tatters. Unemployment was rampant: to assert the executive's control over the military, Juárez had slashed the size of the Mexican army by two-thirds, so thousands of decommissioned soldiers wandered through the countryside, raiding *haciendas* and rural villages for food. *Léperos* (beggars) roamed the streets of Mexico City. Even the small middle class—merchants, bureaucrats, prosperous shopkeepers—lived in modest homes without running water. There were only enough schools for 10% of Mexican children to attend classes; of these students, just 22% were girls. When Juárez died in office in July of 1872, Mexico enjoyed peace but not prosperity.

## The Porfiriato

The regime of José de la Cruz Porfirio Díaz, which lasted from 1876 to 1911, is one of the most colorful and brutal chapters in Mexican history. In the 55 years since Independence, the Mexican presidency had changed hands 75 times; now stability was vital. Díaz's official motto was "Liberty, Order, and Progress"—but for the dictator, the price of order and progress was liberty itself. Elections were rigged, dissident journalists were jailed (one more than 30 times), and Díaz's most strident critics were assassinated. The provinces were controlled by retired generals and *jefes políticos* (political bosses). When uprisings erupted, they were swiftly smothered by bands of *rurales* (rural police).

Díaz's wealthy, European-trained, *criollo* advisors believed that the nation's problems could be solved with scientific techniques. Under Díaz, Mexico was mechanized, paved, and electrified. Ironically, the regime that brought prosperity to Mexico harbored deeply anti-Mexican prejudices. The Positivist *científicos*—as Díaz's advisors were called—believed that *indígenas* were weak, immoral, and ineducable. Few of the new schools built during the Porfiriato were located in indigenous *pueblos*. When the Fifth Pan-American Congress was held in Mexico City just after the turn of the century, *indígenas* and *mestizos* were prohibited from serving foreign dignitaries; only whites could work as waiters and porters during the congress. French, not Mexican, culture was the rage among the upper classes. French furniture, food, dance, opera, and fashion were *de rigueur* among the *criollo* elite.

Díaz brought in French and British firms to build a vast infrastructure of railroads linking agricultural areas to urban factories. As a result, industry prospered and land values skyrocketed. But few poor Mexicans profited from the economic boom. Under a new law, indigenous *ejidos* could be forced to sell their public lands if they couldn't show a legal title to the plots they farmed. By the turn of the century, most villages saw their *ejidos* taken by wealthy individuals and private companies. In one case, a town was so entirely stripped of its communal lands that it no longer had space to bury its dead. Meanwhile, *científicos* made millions speculating in the volatile land market, manipulating railroad contracts to their own advantage.

Vast *haciendas* sprung up in the north, some as large as seven million acres, fed by cheap land prices. Half of Mexico's rural population worked as *peones* on such *haciendas*, and were typically paid only with coupons redeemable at the company store, where prices were artificially inflated. *Hacendados* charged *peones* for funerals, weddings, and fiestas—even for the privilege of patronizing the company store. Driven into debt, *peones* were legally bound to work on their *haciendas* until the money was repaid. The price of corn and chile more than doubled during the 19th century, and the price of beans rose by 500%—but the average daily wage for a farm worker remained stagnant, at about 35 centavos per day. Meanwhile, generals, cabinet ministers, and the president paid 700 pesos per month for membership at the Jockey Club in Mexico City, where they whiled away evenings at baccarat.

# ■ REVOLUTION

## Challenges From All Sides

Unlike the war for Independence, which was ignited by *criollo* discontent, the Revolution began smoldering in the lowest levels of Mexican society. In 1906, copper miners in Sonora went on strike, citing low wages and the discriminatory policies of the mine's U.S. owners. The protest was quashed when Díaz permitted U.S. mercenaries to cross the border and kill strikers in order to protect the interests of U.S. investors. But a similar strike erupted seven months later in the textile mills of Río Blanco, fueling a growing sense of instability.

In the 1910 presidential election, Díaz faced a vocal opponent. Francisco Madero, a wealthy *hacienda* owner from Coahuila, was no social revolutionary, but his calls for liberty and democracy were enough for Díaz to throw him into jail. Escaping to the U.S., Madero orchestrated a series of grass-roots rebellions in northern states from his base in San Antonio. Meanwhile, Emiliano Zapata led the revolt against Díaz in the southern state of Morelos. Unlike Madero, Zapata believed the rebels' first priority was to restore communal lands to the indigenous *pueblos*. Zapata quickly raised an army of angry *indígenas*, traveling to remote pueblos and addressing villagers in Nahuatl when necessary.

After Madero's troops captured Ciudad Juárez, the 81-year-old Díaz fled to Paris. But once in power, the cautious Morelos hesitated to restore any land to the Zapatistas, and ordered the rebels in the south to disband. Zapata resisted the order, and the Zapatistas tangled with General Victoriano Huerta's troops. A pattern for the Revolution had been set.

## The Coalition Collapses

After fending off rebellions from radical factions, Madero's government finally fell to a conservative uprising led by Huerta and Díaz's nephew. Venustiano Carranza, the governor of Coahuila, urged state governors to revolt against the federal government. Guerrilla armies sprung up, led by Pancho Villa in Chihuahua and Álvaro Obregón in Sonora. Provisional governments proliferated; by late 1913, there were more than 25 different types of paper money in circulation. After U.S. troops bombed Veracruz in 1914, Huerta resigned.

Now Obregón seized the capital; Carranza controlled Veracruz; Villa ruled the north; Zapata held the south. When Villa's troops attacked Obregón's forces at the bloody battle of Celaya, 4000 Villistas were shredded on barbed wire entrenchments; 5000 more were wounded. As Villistas wreaked havoc on Texas border towns, Carranza's own government found itself hopelessly divided between old-style liberals and radical land reformists. The fighting in the south was the most vicious of all. Thousands of civilians were executed as alleged Zapatista sympathizers, and Zapata responded by blowing up a train and killing some 400 innocent passengers. In 1919, Carranza's men assassinated Zapata in an ambush, and Carranza assumed the presidency, inaugurating a period of relative calm.

One in eight Mexicans had died in the wars of 1910-1920. Civilian casualties were high, and many of those killed in battle were unwilling victims of forced conscription. Soldiers on every side took advantage of helpless villagers, stealing livestock and food, trampling crops, and torching homes. As all the rebel governments had printed their own money, the economy was in ruins. Inflation slashed the real wages of urban laborers; flooding and sabotage put miners out of work. Many Mexicans were on the brink of starvation.

## Institutionalized Revolution

In 1917, Carranza gathered delegates to draft a new constitution; the document they produced still governs the Republic. Zapatistas, Villistas, and Huertistas were barred from the convention, yet delegates outlined a thoroughly radical agenda for the nation. Present was the familiar liberal anticlericalism of the 19th century; more startling were the socialistic articles of the new constitution. Private ownership of land was declared to be a privilege, not a right, and the state was supposed to redistribute lands seized from *pueblos* during the Porfiriato. Workers were guaranteed an eight-hour day, a six-day week, and a minimum wage; the right to strike was protected. But the moderate Carranza failed to implement most of the radical document, and the Revolution drifted to the right as successive presidents reversed modest gains in land reform and workers' rights.

The Constitution of 1917 codified the Revolution; the machine politics of the 1920s institutionalized it. Plutarco Calles, elected president in 1924, ruled the country for a decade though a series of puppet presidents. Calles, known as the "Jefe Máximo," consolidated the government's support in the new Partido Nacional Revolucionario (PNR), which has ruled Mexico unopposed in the 65 years since.

# ■ MODERN MEXICO

## A Return to Redistribution

The Great Depression hit Mexico in the gut: as the value of the peso plummeted, wages dropped by 10%, and many Mexicans began to question the direction of the Revolution. Reacting to the mood of the times, Mexico's new president, Lázaro Cárdenas, seized the reins from his PNR handlers and steered the Revolution sharply to the left. Cárdenas redistributed 49 million acres—twice as much as all his predecessors combined—to thousands of indigenous *ejidos,* where lands were farmed in common as they had been for hundreds of years before the Porfiriato. Economically, most *ejidos* were a failure, and agricultural productivity dropped drastically. But the *ejido* program won an enormous symbolic goal: no longer a peon, the rural *indígena* had regained some of the political and social autonomy that disappeared with the loss of communal lands in the late 19th century.

## Industrial Capitalism and the Problem of Liberty

By drawing labor groups and agrarian reformers into the government, Cárdenas immeasurably strengthened the ruling party, now called the Partido Revolucionario Institucional (PRI). At the same time, however, land reform stalled and the government limited the right to strike. Meanwhile, WWII speeded the pace of Mexican development, accelerating the shift from socialism to industrial capitalism. But the working class didn't share proportionately in the new prosperity. Policy-makers believed that some measure of inequity was necessary in order to increase the size of the economic pie. Mexican industrialists were urged to keep costs down—and, by implication, to keep wages low. When oil workers went on strike in the early 1950s, the army was called in and dozens of union leaders were fired.

Clearly, the way to get ahead was to play by the rules. The PRI has been likened to a floating log: if you want to stay afloat, you have to grab on. Lured by the promise of cushy government jobs, union officials and peasant leaders joined the PRI's swelling political machine. Enjoying wide institutional support, the PRI has not yet lost a presidential election since its inception in 1929. But the stability of single-party rule has come at the price of liberty. Even under president Adolfo López Mateos, who between 1958 and 1964 expanded social security coverage and redoubled efforts at land reform, Mexicans were not free to speak their minds. López Mateos removed the Communist leadership of the teachers' and railroad unions and sent in the army to break a railroad-workers' strike in 1959. When the head of the PRI tried to reform the party's nomination process, he was fired by the president under pressure from state political bosses. Student unrest and worker dissatisfaction culminated in 1968 at Mexico City's Tlatelolco Plaza, where police killed an estimated 300 to 400 peaceful demonstrators and jailed another 2000 protesters just 10 days before the Olympic Games were to open.

## Salinas: Towards Democracy

"The era of one-party rule in Mexico is over," declared PRI presidential candidate Carlos Salinas de Gortari during the tense week following the 1988 presidential elections. Salinas officially (and conveniently) received 50.4% of the vote when the final contested results were announced, but many interpreted his remarks and the election itself as a fresh start for Mexican politics.

Mexico's ruling party did not lose a single presidential, senatorial, or gubernatorial race from 1929 to 1988; in the few local elections that it did lose, the PRI often installed its own candidates anyway. Through a combination of patronage, fraud and ineffectual opposition, the party ran Mexico like a political machine. But in the 1982 election, the murmurs of dissent were heard, and the right-of-center National Action Party (PAN) won 14% of the vote, most of it in the northern states. In 1983, when the PRI experimented with fraud-free elections, the PAN picked up three mayorships in the state of Chihuahua alone.

When Salinas, a Harvard graduate, began his six-year term as president on December 1, 1988, he had to confront high unemployment, a US$105 billion foreign debt, the domestic production and transport of drugs, and a skeptical nation. Salinas instituted wage and price controls to keep inflation down, then boosted his popularity with several prominent arrests of a union boss, a fraudulent businessman, and a drug trafficker.

On February 4, 1990, representatives of the Mexican government and its 450 foreign commercial creditors signed a debt reduction agreement designed to ease the U.S. banking crisis and deflect outlandishly high interest payments. This reprieve, along with Salinas's austerity program, has led to growing foreign investment and steady growth (3% a year) in Mexico's gross domestic product. Inflation has stuck at 16-22%, however, and unemployment remains near 20%. Reduced or not, foreign debt has continued to suck capital out of the country, and a blossoming trade deficit is squeezing out small and medium businesses as foreign franchises muscled in.

The fate of these smaller firms was at the center of the controversial North American Free Trade Agreement (NAFTA). The treaty eliminated the tariffs, quotas, and subsidies that had protected Mexican industry and agriculture since the 1940s. Smaller Mexican-owned businesses are being driven out of business by *maquiladoras,* U.S.-owned assembly and automotive-sector factories. On the other hand, freer trade means cheaper consumer goods for financially strapped Mexicans—a blessing in a nation plagued by constant inflation. Increased competition may eventually reap profits for the Mexican economy, but development is now exacting high human and environmental costs.

In 1991, PRI technocrats dismantled the *ejido* system, which ostensibly guaranteed communal land rights for rural campesinos. With this constitutional reform and other changes, including rapid privatization, an agrarian culture thousands of years old is being phased out to pave the way for industrialism. Traditional support systems are lost in urbanization while government safety nets are eliminated, all part of an economic streamlining backed by the U.S. and international lenders. The costs of this structural adjustment program (centered around NAFTA) have yet to be determined, but fall heavily on the lower classes in the meantime, while the benefits loom on the long-term horizon.

## 1994 to the Present: Mexico at a Crossroads

On January 1, 1994, the day that NAFTA took effect, Mayan rebels rose up and captured San Cristóbal de Las Casas, the capital of Chiapas state. Within days, government troops had driven the rebels back into the highlands and the Lacandón rainforest, leaving about 150 dead. Months of negotiations followed, during which the government's top negotiator resigned after accusing the PRI of sabotaging his efforts. The rebels rejected the government's peace plan, and threatened to shatter the fragile cease-fire unless upcoming presidential elections were free and fair.

In an election year that was supposed to express Mexico's material progress and fledgling democracy, the rebels drew attention to the vast inequities that still exist within the Republic. The Zapatistas, as the rebels call themselves, demanded land, food, housing, education, and health care. Chiapas is Mexico's poorest state: four out of five homes have dirt floors without drains, and illiteracy rates in some areas top 45%. President Salinas de Gortari had poured more anti-poverty money into the state than any other—but to little avail. The price of coffee, the state's major crop, had dropped on the world market, and the labor market was glutted with refugees from Guatemala and El Salvador. Furthermore, *indígena* rebels clearly harbored deep resentments that no amount of PRI money could assuage. "We are the product of 500 years of struggle," read a statement posted in San Cristóbal by the Zapatistas. Memories of the Conquest are still fresh in a state where, as late as the 1950s, *indígenas* were expected to step off a narrow sidewalk when a white person passed.

The Zapatista uprising foreshadowed turmoil to come. On March 23, the PRI presidential candidate, Luis Donaldo Colosio, was assassinated as he left a rally in Tijuana. It is a measure of Mexicans' political cynicism that many believed the PRI had killed its own candidate; the subsequent killing of the Tijuana police chief investigating the assassination simply fueled the rumors. Meanwhile, the PRI closed ranks, tapping Budget and Planning minister Ernesto Zedillo Ponce de León to replace the slain candidate, and rebuild the campaign from scratch. The PRI used to win elections by fraud, recruiting union officials and peasant leaders to twist voters' arms. Such tactics are no longer acceptable; instead, the PRI relied on more than 800,000 grass-roots organizers to comb the country door-to-door, building on an old network of patronage and pork-belly politics. Sure enough, the PRI won handily, faring especially well among Mexico's poorest voters.

But it is hard to disprove allegations of subtle coercion; for example, many Mexicans are afraid to admit over the phone that they oppose the PRI. If the government knows your number, Mexicans believe, you could be targeted for reprisals—and so the Mexico City phone book is called "The Book of the Dead" because many people choose to list their number under the name of the line's original owner.

Just months into his presidency, on December 20, Zedillo confronted a precipitous drop in the peso. Spurred by the assassination of Colosio and the unsettling events in Chiapas, foreign investors had dumped US$25 billion of Mexican government peso bonds, heralding the imminent monetary devaluation. Aided by the International Monetary Fund (IMF) and the U.S. government, Mexico was salvaged from the depths of economic crisis. Still, severe economic difficulties persisted: in March 1995, interest rates skyrocketed to above 90 percent, bringing the banking system to a near collapse. The growing legions of middle-class professionals and entrepreneurs that relied on foreign dollars were left frustrated and frightened. Mexicans have laid the blame squarely on Zedillos's shoulders, citing his delay in appointing key cabinet posts and in instituting promised economic initiatives.

Though the prospect of successfully taming the economy seemed distant, Zedillo sought to pacify the anxious masses with further political reforms. Whereas the PRI used to control all state governorships, several state governors, including that of Jalisco, now belong to the opposition Partido de Acción Nacional (PAN). Zedillo has attacked corruption in other realms, arresting high-level officials—including Salinas's brother—on charges of conspiracy and murder.

Despite attempts to tranquilize the nation, unrelenting economic woes continue to court political instability. Revelations that the 1993 assassination of the Cardinal of Guadalajara might have been planned by drug traffickers struck fear in a nation that had worked diligently to control the trade of narcotics. And the situation in Chiapas continues to smolder: in February 1995, Zedillo deployed over one thousand troops into the region to stamp out any lingering rebellious elements. Negotiations between the Zapatistas and government representatives have continued, though progress is slow.

Still, Mexico seems to be inching toward democracy. The PRI has loosened its grip on the media, and independent observers enjoyed unprecedented latitude in supervising the 1994 elections. As shown by the events of the past two years, perhaps Mexico's most tumultuous time since the Revolution, even an entrenched political machine can be shocked into change without the full-scale violence that has plagued much of the nation's history.

# CULTURE AND CHARACTER

## ■ ART AND ARCHITECTURE

The art of Mexico has always been deeply rooted in the spiritual, political, and environmental interactions of its people. Though this might easily be said of all cultures, it would be very difficult, if not impossible, to find another people whose tools, techniques, materials, and models have varied to such a remarkable degree. For instance, temples like those found at Palenque in Chiapas state attest to the mathematical aptitude of the Maya. The temples' striking symmetry and elaborate ornamentation inspire even today's seen-it done-that tourist as they must have the *indígenas* when they were first erected. Much of what archaeologists have been able to piece together about the daily life and beliefs of Mexico's ancient peoples stems mainly from the artifacts—both functional and purely decorative—they left behind. Early Mexican art, like Western art, was devoted to the sacred. The colonial period favored stilted European imitation, but the Revolution instilled a sense of nationalism and resuscitated native styles, now informed by modern themes. Art historians tend to classify works within three periods: the Indian (6000 BCE-1525 CE), the Colonial (1525-1810), and the Modern (1810-present). While such timeframes are helpful in organizing an extraordinary amount of artistic works, it is important to note that stylistic continuities from one period to another do exist.

### Art on a Grand Scale: The Olmecs

The colossal heads found at La Venta, San Lorenzo, and Tres Zapotes, stone monuments thought to represent human-like deities, are the best-known creations of the Olmec civilization (1200-100 BCE). Incredibly, the Olmecs imported the massive basalt stones—some weighing as much as twenty tons—from other areas by floating them across waterways on highly effective rafts (see La Venta and La Venta Parque Museo, Tabasco).

Not all Olmec artistry was this large in size. Olmecs were also fine potters and expert jade carvers; their handicrafts were esteemed and emulated later by the Maya. Tending away from idealization, many Olmec figurines take as their subjects plump children, child-men, hunchbacks, and half-man half-jaguar beings in various positions of repose, reverence, and agitation. The fluid lines of the numerous acrobat and contortionist figures that have been unearthed provide further evidence of Olmec skill as well as the value they placed on performance and entertainment. The eventual demise of the Olmec culture marked a transition from the Pre-Classic period (2000-100 BCE) to the Classic (100 BCE-900 CE), and the dawn of other powerful cultures, most notably, Teotihuacán and the Maya.

### An Artistic Metropolis: Teotihuacán

Located in the Valley of Mexico about 50km northeast of Mexico City, Teotihuacán was the Americas' first metropolis, a great commercial and artistic center with over 25,000 inhabitants (see Near Mexico City: Teotihuacán). The achievements in architecture are obvious: a number of pyramids, temples, and dwelling units, where Teotihuacanos worshipped, transacted business, slept, ate, and celebrated still stand to this day and are arguably Mexico's main draw to tourists worldwide. In order to maintain a harmonic balance with the heavens, pyramids were built according to specific geomantic positions in relation to the sun. The Pyramid of the Sun, for instance, aligns with the sunset point at the summer solstice. In general, the pyramids were constructed by setting down layers of clay on an earth or masonry foundation; the main structural features are the *talud* (sloping wall) and the *tablero* (entablature). This type of architectural design lend the pyramids their characteristic severe and ponderous quality.

Temples and pyramids were both a source of civic pride and a religious necessity. The structures were ornamented in relief with images of serpents, jaguars, gods,

ART AND ARCHITECTURE

and, though not as evident today, were also often decorated with vibrant colors. Frescoes on interior walls of buildings depict, among other subjects, paradise scenes, floral arrangements, religious rituals, and athletic events.

It says something about the Teotihuacanos' level of organization and technological savvy that they were able to "mass-produce" figurines; from clay molds, copies were made, remnants of which have been discovered throughout the region. The people of Teotihuacán even left behind statuettes with moveable appendages. Precursors of the modern-day G.I. Joe or Barbie? Archaeologists and scientists have yet to come to a definitive conclusion.

## The Origins of Glamour

Heirs to the artistic and scientific achievements of the Olmecs, the Maya, undisputed representatives of Mexico's golden age, reached their cultural pinnacle in the period between 300 and 600 CE. The Maya flourished in areas of the Chiapas highlands, northern Yucatán, and Guatemala—impressive ruins can be found at Chichén Itzá, Palenque, Uxmal, Tikal, Bonampak, and Copán. Despite the fact they had no metal tools or use of the wheel, the Maya built temples, palaces, altars, stelae (pillar-shaped monuments), calculated a 365-day calendar, and developed a mathematical system, based on the number twenty, which used zero as a value.

A brief glimpse at the characters populating Mayan artifacts—in colorful frescoes, pottery decoration, and stelae—reveals their unflagging devotion to fashion and accessories. Gods and nobility (of both genders) adorn themselves with massive headdresses replete with lengthy feathers, necklaces with beads the size of eggs, and gold and copper bracelets to match the enormous bangles hanging from their earlobes. An unapologetic Mayan get-up would give most participants of Wigstock (the annual New York City drag festival) a run for their money.

The materials of choice from Mayan artisans were limestone, sandstone, and to a lesser degree, wood and jade. Using only stone tools they modeled figurines, vessels, and architectural frieze. A masterwork in bas-relief, the Temple of Inscriptions at Palenque, in one of its scenes, documents pictorially two nobles making offerings to a king sitting on the backs of slaves. Above the figures are numerous glyphs conveying religious and calendrical information. Characteristic of Mayan relief, contour is predominate and facial features are stylized.

## The Aztecs: The Sunset of Indígena Art

The art of the Mexica (1300-1521), or the Aztecs as they are better known, points to the culture's paradoxical nature: the great sensitivity and unassailable skill consistently applied to creative endeavor seem to belie their inclination toward violence and warfare.

Founders of Tenochtitlán (modern-day Mexico City), the Aztecs built a truly remarkable city, sprawling, yet highly organized according to a rectangular grid-plan. In the central area, where important religious events such as human sacrifices were held, pyramids and temples stood majestically as symbols of technological achievement and spiritual devotion. Proof that the Aztecs weren't slaves to work and art—certainly there were more than a few veritable jocks among them—remnants of ball courts have been discovered in numerous dwellings and public buildings. Known for its athletic and crowd-pleasing appeal, the ball games also served serious religious functions.

The clearly stratified society of Tenochtitlán produced an organized labor force that undoubtedly contributed much to the city's marketplace, a center that drew crowds of up to 30,000. From this milieu of expert craftsmanship resulted two of the Aztec's most recognizable and famous creations: the Stone of the Sun ("Aztec Calendar"), measuring nearly twelve feet in diameter, and Tenochtitlán's great Coatlicue sculpture, a monumental statue over eight feet tall representing the Goddess of the Earth. The Stone of the Suns' narrative is a tragic one: within its concentric rings are contained the four symbols of previous suns, rain, tiger, water, and wind, the elements responsible for the destruction of earlier populations; Aztecs believed they were living in the period of the fifth sun, thus, they expected to be obliterated by an earthquake, the symbol for which also ominously appears on the stone. But it wasn't a pernicious earthquake that irreversibly altered the Aztec culture, it was the landing of the *conquistadores* in 1521 led by Hernán Cortés—the force that would change the world as the Aztecs knew it, and consequently, their art as well.

## The Architecture of New Spain

Not surprisingly, the first examples of colonial art were created specifically to facilitate religious indoctrination. Churches were often constructed on top of Indian temples and pyramids, obviously causing serious and irreparable damage to ancient sites. Volcanic stone, plentiful in most areas, was the main building material. In general, colonial architecture, much of it recalling Romanesque and Gothic stylistic elements, is characterized by the use of huge buttresses, arches, and crenelations (indented or embattled moldings). An architectural phenomenon that developed early on was the open chapel (*capilla abierta*), a group of arches "enclosing" an atrium. The open chapels were a sort of architectural ideal for they could be built quickly (a good thing in the eyes of the clergy, lest the *indígenas* die heathens), and could accommodate large numbers of worshippers.

The monasteries and churches under the direction of Franciscan, Dominican, and Augustinian missionaries were built according to climactic and geographic limitations. The Franciscan style tended to be functional and economic, the Dominican ascetic and harsh, due to earthquake danger and warm weather. The Augustinian style was clearly the most free-spirited and grandiose, indulging in sumptuous decoration whenever and wherever possible. Remarkable Augustinian buildings include the Monastery of St. Augustin of Acolmán near Mexico City and the Monastery of Actopán in Hidalgo state.

## A Blossoming of the Baroque

The steady growth and spread of the Catholic church throughout the 17th and 18th centuries necessitated the construction of cathedrals, parochial chapels, and convents; moreover, this period produced the birth and eventual nadir of the Baroque style in New Spain. By turns elegant and garish—but always luxurious—Baroque façades teem (at times grotesquely) with dynamic images of angels and saints. The role of art in colonial Mexico, as in the Middle Ages and much of the Renaissance, was to produce a feeling of awe and respect in the hearts of the converted *indígenas*. The narratives set in stone were accessible to the illiterate and easily committed to memory. A look at the cathedrals of Zacatecas and Chihuahua reveals the degree of artistry Baroque ideals encouraged.

Baroque painting found its expression in the works of Alonso López de Herrera, Baltazar de Echave Orío (the elder), Baltazar de Echave Ibía, and Alonso Vázquez. In Herrera's the *Assumption of the Virgin,* the holy mother, surrounded by angels, hovers over an enthralled crowd while a sunburst in the background casts a luminous aura about her figure. Similarly, the *Martyrdom of San Ponciano* by Orío expresses a dramatic religious event through the use of Renaissance conventions, particularly in the figures' gestures and by their hierarchical arrangement on the canvas.

Sumptuosness, frivolity, ornamentation—it appears as though late 18th century artists and builders couldn't have too much of a good thing, and so came the *Churrigueresque* style, or, Mexican High Baroque carried to the extreme. The hallmarks of the *Churrigueresque* are excessively and intricately decorated *estípites* (pilasters); at times these were installed merely for looks and not support. The Church of Santa Prisca and San Sebastián in Taxco is a mind-boggling example of the potential the style could achieve.

## 20th Century Murals: The Political Aesthetic

As the Revolution reduced their land to shambles, Mexican painters developed an unapologetic national style. This success was made possible by José Vasconcelos's Ministry of Education program, which commissioned murals for public buildings and sent artists into the countryside to teach and participate in rural life.

The Mexican mural, unequivocally nationalistic in its current form, ironically dates back to the early days of the conquest when Catholic evangelists, fighting the language barrier, used allegorical murals to impart the rudiments of Christian iconography. Among the famous muralists to have worked during the formative years of the Revolution, Diego Rivera has achieved the most renown. His murals at the Rockefeller Center in New York City and the Palacio Nacional in Mexico City exposed his political themes—land reform, Marxism, the marginalization of *indigena* life—to a wide audience and embroiled him international controversy. The others in the "Big Four" pantheon were David Alfaro Siqueiros, who brought new materials and dramatic revolutionary themes to his murals; the Cubism-influenced Rufino Tomayo, arguably the most abstract of the four; and José Clemente Orozco. The anguished, dynamic figures in a number of Siqueiros's formally innovative works appear to threaten the boundaries of the picture plane. Orozco focused on the violence and brutality of the Revolution, but was less explicitly political than his colleagues. In his work, the mythic dimension of human history and existence prevails. "Good murals are really painted bibles," Orozco said, "and the people need them as much as written bibles."

But many Mexican artists have since turned against the didacticism of Rivera's era. "Diego Rivera created a completely bureaucratic art," the Mexican abstract painter Juan Soriano once grumbled. "He made himself a propagandist of the victorious revolution... I reproach him for having completely prostituted the pictoral language, reducing it to little more than a caricature, vulgarizing it."

## Frida Kahlo and the Woman Artist

And where are the woman artists? Respected feminist art critic and historian Linda Nochlin—author of the ground-breaking article "Why Have There Been No Great Women Artists?" (1970)—suggests that the exclusionary modernist canon has been largely responsible for limiting female artists from gaining international recognition, as did "The Big Four" led by Rivera. In a culture anchored by misogyny and machismo, within an art world unabashedly biased toward the United States and Western Europe, it is not surprising that the art of Mexican women wasn't dealt with seriously until the latter half of this century. Among the celebrated Mexican women artists of the 20th century are the painters María Izquierdo (she had a lengthy relationship with Rufino Tomayo), Lilia Carrillo, and the photographer Lola Álvarez Bravo.

Due in part to her appalling talent and Hayden Herrera's landmark biography, Frida Kahlo (1907-54) surpasses all other Mexican artists—men included—in terms of current worldwide recognition. Partially paralyzed in a traumatic bus accident at the age of 18, Kahlo married Diego Rivera and was welcomed by Andre Breton into the Surrealist fold of the 1930s. Her paintings and self-portraits are icons of pain: red smudges on the frame of *Unos Cuantos Piquetitos* (A Few Small Nips) project the bed-ridden, writhing body from the canvas into the realm of the viewer. In *La Columna Rota* (The Broken Column), a weeping Kahlo appears in a desolate landscape, her body riddled with nails, a cracking Greek column enmeshed in her body where her spinal chord should be—again, the viewer is forced to confront the artist's self-obsession in its most violent and extreme manifestations. The Museo Frida Kahlo is in her childhood home, Coyoacán, a suburb of Mexico City.

# ■ LITERATURE

### Pre-Conquest Writing: A Multi-Media Affair

As far as linguists and archaeologists have been able to tell, three languages were dominant in Mexico before the arrival of the Spanish: the Nahuatl, Maya, and Cakchiquel. The earliest examples of writing are thought to be the glyphs inscribed at Monte Albán in Oaxaca, a site containing astounding figural reliefs dating back to 600 BCE. The Spaniards' destructive rampage, particularly in the initial years of the Conquest, took with it invaluable information relating to *indígena* language, both oral and written; the imposition of the Spanish language all but extinguished what was left of what had been Mexico's rich linguistic life. Considered a dangerous affront to Christian teachings, Maya and Aztec codices (unbound "books" or manuscripts) were, naturally, fed to the flames, but due either to the grace of God or less than scrupulous destruction, a number of Maya codices did survive. The Dresden, Paris, and Madrid codices convey important information about divination and the Mayan calendar.

The *Popol-Vuh* (Book of Advice), a pre-eminent example of Nahuatl poetry which was kept alive through oral transmission then recorded in Latin characters, imparts moral counsel and different versions of the Mayan creation myth. Along with the *Popol-Vuh,* works such as the *Libros de Chilam Balam* (Books of the Speaker of the Jaguar), transcribed into Maya in 1782, and the Annals of the Cakchiquel cover a range of topics, yet they are not exclusively historical, but narrative and poetic, laden with symbolism and lofty metaphor. The *Rabinal Achí* (Knight of Achí), the story of a sacrificed warrior, is considered to be the only surviving example of pre-Columbian drama. A production even Andrew Lloyd Webber and Tommy Tune would be proud of, the *Rabinal Achí* was originally performed with elaborate costumes and song and dance routines. The friars were not ones to let a good proselytizing tool get away, and it was no time until they adopted the methods of *indígena* ritual drama to widely disperse Christian teachings.

### A Move Toward Historiography

Like astronauts on a new planet, the Spanish were eager to send news home about the new land they had conquered and the ways of life of Mexico's indigenous population. These letters home, famous among them Cortes's *Cartas de relación* (Letters of Relation), were mainly Crown- and Church-flattering documents detailing the exhaustive efforts being undertaken to educate and Christianize *indígenas.* Other chronicles such as the *Nuevo Mundo y conquista* (New World and Conquest) by Francisco de Terrazas and *Grandeza Mexicana* (Mexican Grandeur) by Bernardo de Balbuena were rhymed in order to take the edge off the monotonous melange of factoid stew.

In the harsh and brutal society of New Spain, only religious orders enjoyed the luxury of genuine intellectual freedom. Many clergymen worked to preserve indigenous languages and texts, and a handful of universities sprung up. The Jesuits' 23 colleges were the best in the colony—until the crown expelled the Jesuits from the Americas in 1767 because of their growing influence.

Though historical texts dominated Mexico's literary output throughout much of the 16th and 17th centuries, substantial achievements in poetry were made. Sor Juana Inés (1648-1695), the Mexican equivalent of our Emily Dickinson, became a master lyricist known for her razor-sharp wit. A *criolla* of illegitimate birth, Sor Juana turned to the cloistered life and married God, instead of the numerous suitors she undoubtedly had—her beauty was legendary. In the Church she found a moral and physical haven where she produced her most famous works, *Respuesta a Sor Filotea* (Response to Sor Filotea) and *Hombres Necios* (Injudicious Men). Her love poems display a passionate, almost erotic sensibility, and many verses display a witty feminism ahead of their time:

LITERATURE

¿Cuál es más de culpar,　　　　Which deserves the sterner blame,
aunque cualquiera mal haga:　　Though each will be a sinner:
la que peca por la paga　　　　She who becomes a whore for pay,
o el que paga por pecar?　　　　Or he who pays to win her?

## Struggling for a Literary Identity

During the 18th century, the Inquisition vied with the French Enlightenment to distract Mexican writers from anything that could be described as innovative. The establishment of the Spanish *Academia de Lengua* (Academy of Language) in 1713 grew out of a desire to regulate Spanish where it was spoken, including colonies. An explosion of writing focusing on science occurred about this time. Studies of Mexican geography, weather, flora and fauna swept away scientists and writers on a wave of rational and analytical thought.

The literary impetus of philosophical movements eventually gave way to political ones. The struggle toward independence, by the end of the 18th century, became the singular social fact from which many Mexican texts grew. In 1816, Jose Fernández de Lizardi, a prominent Mexican journalist, wrote the first Latin American novel: *El periquillo sarniento* (The Itching Parrot), a picaresque tale which revealed Mexican society's displeasure with the status quo. His ideological, moralizing angle on fiction has been very influential. With the Spanish-American modernists of the 19th century, poetry reached an affective level it had not achieved since Sor Juana. At the same time, Manuel Gutierrez Najera composed the poem *De Blanco* (On Whiteness), linguistic representation at its most distilled and self-contained.

Many romantic novels of the period used historical themes to introduce sweeping indictments of the military and clergy. Novelists sought to define Mexico's national identity, glorifying strength, secularism, progress, and education. Artists were similarly didactic, producing works with such inspirational titles as *Triumph and Study Over Ignorance*. Whereas European romanticism was an aesthetic challenge to neoclassicism, Mexican romanticism was an artistic response to the country's political and social realities. Shortly after the heyday of the romantic novel came the popular novel of manners, significant among them being *El fistol del diablo* by Manuel Payno, *Juanita Sousa* and *Antón Pérez* by Manuel Sánchez Mármol.

Literature during the Porfiriato (1876-1911) abandoned romanticism for realism, and most writers expressed little sympathy with the poor. Wrote José López Portillo y Rojas, the preeminent realist of the period, "Our workers will come out of their abject condition when they aspire to eat well, to dress decently, and to acquire the comforts of life." Others adopted a modernist style, emphasizing language and imagery, and replacing didactic social themes with psychological topics. Visual artists, by contrast, had begun to reject the creed of the *científicos*. Many favored experimental techniques, and chose to depict slums, brothels, and scenes from indigenous life. Their iconoclasm foreshadowed a growing dissatisfaction with the Díaz regime.

## 20th Century Global Perspectives

Mexican literature in the post-Revolutionary era is marked by a frustrated desire to forge a national tradition from the vestiges of pre-colonial culture. Nobel prize winner Octavio Paz, in such works as *El laberinto de la soledad* (The Labyrinth of Solitude), draws on Marxism, romanticism and post-Modernism to explore the making and unmaking of a national archetype. Paz, like his equally famous successor Carlos Fuentes, concerns himself with myth and legend in an effort to come to terms with Spanish cultural dominance. Fuentes, Mexico's most celebrated author (and onetime Harvard professor) published his first novel, *La region más transparente,* in 1958. His latest novel, *Cristobal nonato* (Christopher Unborn), chronicles the lengthy search for a god-head who will accurately and unproblematically personify the true spirit of the Mexican people. Juan Rulfo's *Pedro Páramo*, set in rural Jalisco, blurs the line between life and death and between past and present as it relates one man's search for his father. This work is seen as the beginning of the magical realism movement which would later hit the continent.

Since the 1960s Mexican literature has become even more pluralistic and serves an ever-growing pool of readers. Western prototypes retain their fascination for writers and readers alike, as is evidenced by the wildly popular work of Gustavo Sainz and Jose Agustín, the instigators of *literatura de la honda* ("hip" literature). On the other hand, Luis Spota, one of Mexico's most widely read authors, restricts himself to Mexican themes and boasts, as a result, international anonymity.

---

### The Rise of the Revista

If one genre could be said to define Mexico's pop literary scene, it would have to be that of the *revista*. *Revistas* are most easily likened to American comic books directed towards a more mature audience. Filled with colorful pictures, bonehead language, and shallow plot lines, the short "novels" are clearly targeted at the masses. The *revistas* cover a whole range of subject matter, including adventure, romance, politics, science fiction, humor, and religion. The romance theme is probably the most popular, and while from the cover of most *revistas* one would expect a pornographic slant, the stories tend to be relatively tame. *Revistas* have become ingrained into Mexican culture, as some series, such as *Kalimán: El hombre increíble* (since 1965), have been running for decades.

---

# ■ POPULAR CULTURE

## Music

Like most other components of its culture, Mexican music is an eclectic stew of styles and flavors borrowed from all across the continent and overseas. Mexico's traditional music is mostly regional, making for a rich and varied collage of styles and artists. Up north, one will hear groups such as Los Bukis, Bronco, and Los Tigres del Norte sing in the style aptly labeled *norteña*. Further south, you'll be treated to *chicana*, a style that is primarily heard in and around Mexico City. One of the most popular and well-known styles of traditional Mexican music is *mariachi*, which is especially popular in Jalisco, but heard all over the country. *Mariachi* is usually played live (though a slightly "jazzed up" variation can be heard over the airwaves), and the world-famous tradition of being serenaded by a group performing *mariachi*-style music in traditional Mexican garb is seen as an almost obligatory supplement to a romantic evening; foreplay, if you will. Listen for José Alfaro Jimenez, Vicente Fernandez, and Lucero, three well-known *mariachi* group leaders.

The Mexican music scene is adorned with both Spanish and American influences. The former is apparent with young artists such as the pop group Garibaldi, whose scantily clad bods perennially grace (disgrace?) music and teen fanzines. Travelers from up north won't feel too far from home, as American music in all forms is ubiquitous both on the radio and in bars and *discotecas*. Always striving to Mexicanize imports in some way, Mexican artists will often take an American piece and make it their "own" with altered lyrics or a slightly more Latin beat. At last glance, Michael Jackson, Madonna, Aerosmith, Nirvana, The Cranberries, and Whitney Houston all mirrored the popularity they enjoy in the U.S.

Pop rock native to Mexico is sung by such artists as Luis Miguel, Lucero, Selena, Millionario, Diramos, Mafia, and Timbiriche. Love songs tend to dominate this scene, even more so than in the U.S. Luis Miguel is lusted after for his romantic songs and good looks, though his popularity seems to have recently dwindled. The recent murder of Selena just as she was about to break into English-language music market, shocked both the U.S. and Mexico, and she is now described with biting frankness by many as "more popular dead than alive." Sadly, the amorphous teenage group Menudo is noticeably absent from the pop scene, having *desintegrado* over the past few years.

### Television and Movies

Television in Mexico can mostly be broken into four categories: *telenovelas* (known in the U.S. as soap operas), weekly dramas, sit-coms, and imported American shows. *Telenovelas* are the most popular and widely aired of this collective. Occupying a huge block of air time from noon to early evening, these hour-long shameless examples of dramaturgy tend to run for 2-4 months before being ousted for a fresh group of characters and convoluted conflicts. Don't be surprised if you witness Erik Estrada (yes, that's Frank "Ponch" Poncherello of CHiPs) embroiled in a Spanish-language love triangle. Some of the most popular actors include Veronica Castro, Alejandro Guzmán, Ana Cochero, and Juan Gabriel.

The half-hour sitcoms that dominate American TV don't seem to be as popular in Mexico, though there are a few. One very popular show that seems to fit the niche occupied in the U.S. by The Price is Right is *Siempre el Domingo,* which runs for two hours every Sunday night. Other popular shows include *Papá Soltero, Chespirito,* and just about anything on the *Canal de las Estrellas.*

American shows are often dubbed, though they can be found in their original English forms on cable television, which, incidentally, is out of the financial reach of many Mexicans. As in the U.S., shows such as Melrose Place (featuring Heather Locklear's boundless treachery) and Baywatch (showcasing Pamela Anderson's truly amazing life saving techniques) are very popular. Cartoons are imported from both the U.S. and Japan, though the apparent obscurity of *Los* Simpsons leads one to question their popularity.

One interesting phenomena to note is the predominance of European-looking, light-skinned people who dominate nearly all Mexican broadcasts. Perhaps this tendency is indicative of Mexico's general association between race and class, and/or the significant American influence on Mexican culture.

Most movies in Mexico are subtitled Hollywood imports, though occasionally a Mexican-made gem will surface—*Like Water for Chocolate* is a recent Mexican hit which has also been very successful as an import in the U.S. Travelers may be caught unawares by the interruption of a movie in the many theaters which have only one projector and must rewind and replace reels midway through a flick.

# ■ FOOD AND DRINK

Devoting only two pages to food and drink in Mexico is the equivalent of...well, of devoting only twelve pages to all of Mexican history. Mexican food is probably emulated more than that of any other developing country, and the existence of Americanized fast-food versions of it (read: Taco Bell) are merely a testimony to Mexican food's popularity. Although you will find a Taco Bell billboard on the border at Nogales, real Mexican food (like most foreign cuisines) bears little resemblance to its counterpart across the border.

Mexicans usually choose to have their big meal of the day—the *comida*—between 2pm and 4pm. The *comida corrida* at restaurants is a fixed price meal with several courses, for which several choices are offered. The meat dish is often a *guisado*—a soup or stew with meat—although a *caldo* (broth-like soup) and a regular plate of meat are also common; rice (sometimes *arroz con huevo,* rice with chopped egg), beans, and tortillas are always included; dessert is usually included as well. Breakfasts (*desayunos*) range from the continental-style *café con leche* (thick coffee with steamed milk) and pastry to a full meal with steak or other meat. Dinner (*cena*) is usually a light meal served relatively late in the evening, usually after 8pm

### The Staples

From tacos slapped together at a roadside *taquería* to a magnificent plate full of garlic shrimp or chicken with mole sauce, Mexican food is broad yet invariably maintains one common link: the *tortilla.* This most ubiquitous staple of Mexican cuisine is a flat, round, thin pancake made from either wheat flour (*harina*), or corn flour (*maíz*). You will surely develop a preference for one or the other—wheat or corn—early on, and most restaurants will let you choose which kind you want with your *antojito* or full meal. Even if a choice isn't offered, either is usually available upon your request. Cuisine in southern Mexico leans heavily towards corn flour.

The other two staples of Mexican food are the always cheap, always filling, and mostly nutritious pair—rice and beans. Rice (*arroz*) is usually standard fare; yellow Spanish or Mexican rice prepared with oil is a special treat. Beans (*frijoles*) are soft and range from pasty to soupy. These three foods will be served in various forms with just about every full plate of food you order, be it breakfast, lunch, or dinner.

---

### How Will You Have Your Eggs?

Aside from the standard *café con leche* or *pan dulce* (sweetened bread), the most common breakfast served at Mexican restaurants is similar to an American breakfast. *Huevos al gusto* (eggs any style) almost always includes eggs and a choice of *jamón* (ham), *tocino* (bacon), or *machaca* (dried, shredded beef). *Tortillas, frijoles,* and sometimes *papas fritas* (french fries) and/or rice are served on the side. The eggs themselves are usually *revueltos* (scrambled) with the meat mixed in, but you can ask for the meat fried on the side or the eggs *estrellados* (fried) instead. Also falling under the *huevos al gusto* category are *huevos rancheros,* that classic Mexican breakfast specialty of two fried eggs served on corn tortillas and covered with a spicy red salsa. More expensive Mexican breakfasts include omelettes with any of the above meats or seafood such as camarones (*shrimp*) or even *langosta* (lobster) and *pan francés* (french toast).

---

## Ah, Antojitos

*Antojito* might be roughly translated as "any Mexican dish in which one food (meat, chicken, fish, or cheese) is stuffed or wrapped inside another (usually a tortilla but sometimes a piece of bread or chile)." There are eight major types of *antojitos* (listed here in order of how common they are). *Tacos* are small, grilled chunks of meat (sometimes chicken, fried fish, or fried shellfish are used) placed on an open, warm tortilla, left for you to top yourself with a row of condiments ranging from lettuce and tomato to guacamole and hot sauce. *Burritos* are thin, rolled flour tortillas filled with meat (often *machaca*, chicken, or beans) and a few cooked vegetables such as green peppers and onions. Occasionally you will see tex-mex-style *super burritos* filled with everything but the kitchen sink. *Burritos* in general are not very common in the southern parts of Mexico. *Enchiladas* are corn tortillas filled with meat or chicken, topped with red or green enchilada sauce, baked or fried, then topped with shredded cheese. Some variations exist, such as *enchiladas suizas* (topped with sour cream) or *enchiladas de mole* (see below for description of mole sauce). *Quesadillas* are filled with melted cheddar cheese. Sometimes other things are added—such as ham or other meats—to make a *sincronizada* or *quesotaco*. *Tostadas* consist of a deep-fried tortilla garnished with vegetables, cheese, and almost anything else, from meat or chicken to exotic seafood like *pulpo* (octopus). *Tostadas* are the only *antojito* to which raw vegetables are always added; prudent travelers should beware of uncooked vegetables, especially lettuce, while in Mexico. A *chile relleno,* a unique and wonderful Mexican creation, consists of a large, green chile pepper stuffed with cheese (and occasionally meat), dipped in a batter, fried, and topped with red *salsa.* They are not particularly *picante* (spicy-hot)—the frying process rids the chile of most of its potency. *Tamales,* also unique, are ground-corn dough packed with meat or chicken in corn husks; they have the consistency of thick dumplings. Finally, *chimichangas* are essentially the same as *burritos,* but deep fried to produce a rich, crunchy, artery-hardening shell.

## Meats, Poultry, and Seafood

Meat platters are usually either *bistek* (derived from the little-used English term "beefsteak"), which is a standard fried cut of beef, *carne asada,* thin slices of beef fried until crispy, or a pricier cut of steak such as T-bone, fillet mignon, or New York strip (English names are used). The meat can be prepared normally (it's usually served fairly well-done), *empanizado* or *milanesa* (breaded or fried), or *a la mexicana* which means served charred up and topped with a Mexican red *salsa*. *Cebellado* means served with grilled onions. In any case, meat dishes are accompanied by *arroz, frijoles, tortillas,* and sometimes *papas fritas.*

Chicken (*pollo*), if by itself or included in a platter, is either *rostizado* (spit-roasted over an open fire, "rotisserie"-style) or *asado* (grilled), served with the same side dishes mentioned above.

Seafood dishes include *pescado* (generic fish fillet, usually a local catch), *camarones* (shrimp), *langosta* (lobster), *calamar* (fillet of squid), and *huachinango* (the exceedingly tasty red snapper, with the name that's as fun to pronounce—wa-chee-NAAN-go—as it is to eat). Seafood is usually served either *empanizado* (breaded and fried), *ranchero,* or *al mojo de ajo* (in garlic butter). *A la veracruzana* is a special preparation, native to Veracruz, in which the fish is decked out in olives, capers, and olive oil.

## When You Get Thirsty

*Cerveza* (beer) ranks only slightly below tortillas and beans on the list of Mexican staples. It is impossible to drive through a Mexican town, anywhere, without coming across a double-digit number of Tecate (and, only slightly less so, *Corona*) billboards, painted buildings, and *agencias,* cheap beer stores, selling anywhere from one beer to several cases at a time. *Tecate* is Mexico's version of Budweiser—it's cheap and none too good. Popular pilsner beers in Mexico (listed in order of quality) are *Bohemia* (a world-famous, outstanding beer), *Pacífico, Dos Equis, Corona Extra, Carta Blanca, Modelo,* and the unfortunate *Tecate.*

*Tequila* is king when it comes to Mexican liquor. It is the quintessential Mexican drink, a famous version of *mezcal* (distilled from the *maguey* cactus). *Herradura, Tres Generaciones,* and *Jose Cuervo 1800* are among the most famous, most expensive, and best brands of *tequila.* Cheap *tequila* can be bought for prices you wouldn't believe: one Hermosillo supermarket frequently advertises a liter of tequila for US$.80! Non-*tequila mezcal,* found mainly in Oaxaca, is sometimes served with the worm native to the plant—upon downing the shot, you are expected to ingest the worm. Some say it induces hallucination; however, evidence is to the contrary. If you get a chance to sample *pulque,* the fermented juice of the *maguey,* don't hesitate—it was the sacred drink of the Aztec nobility.

Fear not, there are non-alcoholic drinks in México. Coca-Cola ("Coca") is perhaps even more universal in Mexico than in the U.S. Pepsi, Sprite, 7-Up, and orange sodas are also available, as expected, but some unique Mexican sodas, *Vita* being the most common, also make an appearance. *Soda de fresa* (strawberry soda) is delicious; also try *toronja* (grapefruit soda), *soda de piña* (pineapple soda), *manzanilla* (apple soda), and *sangría* (a non-alcoholic, carbonated version of wine with fruit juice). *ToniCol* is a dark, vanilla soda that is also quite tasty. Soda rarely costs more than 4 pesos (US$.65), even at fancy restaurants, and usually costs between 2 and 3 pesos (US$.32-.48) for a bottle or can. *Aguas frescas,* including *limonada* (lemonade) are fruit-based drinks with sugar—don't drink them unless you're sure they're purified. Often they contain *hielo* (ice) made from tap water.

# Mexico City

"City" is not the word for it: the 1,480 square kilometers of urban settlement that line the Valley of Mexico constitute far more than one city. The high-efficiency bustle of the executive areas on Reforma, the impoverished neighborhoods on the northern outskirts, the commercial coagulation of the *centro,* and the wealthy southern ultra-suburbs of Coyoacán and San Ángel cohabitate in the omnipresent smog. Shantytowns sprawl out bereft of public support, themselves as large as cities; a sleek slab of boutiques rises above the city in the tallest tower in the Republic. Mexico City is a breeding ground for staggering statistics: 2000 new residents and 700 million gallons of water go in every day—12,000 tons of air pollution come out.

With the simultaneous rising and falling of *indígena* and colonial civilizations, this phoenix-like metropolis contains a plurality of cities, and no one can decide upon a single significance for any single structure. The massive Templo Mayor is simultaneously a paean to the magnificent Aztec empire of which it was once the capital, and a memorial of the carnal sacrifices the Aztecs staged for the sake of their hungry god Huitzilopochtli. The awe and faith inspired by the grand Catedral Metropolitana struggle eternally with bitter resentment at the economic and cultural imperialism of those who forced the indigenous peoples to build it. A few blocks away stands the Palacio de Bellas Artes, a glorious symbol of modern Mexico built by the dictator Porfirio Díaz, whose grand projects also sapped the money of a struggling nation. Less than a mile to the west, the Monumento a la Revolución, originally intended by Díaz as the spectacular seat of his regime's legislature, reaffirms the democratic freedom of a "new" Mexico, transmogrified by ten long years of bloody battle.

Mexicans call this oxymoronic conglomeration **el D.F.,** short for *Distrito Federal* (Federal District), or simply *México.* It's the second largest population center in the world with more than 20 million people in over 220 *colonias* (neighborhoods). Virtually the entire federal bureaucracy inhabits the *Distrito Federal,* including the Ministry of the Navy (2240m above sea level). The principal national collections of art, ethnography, and archaeology are also found here; the gargantuan Museo Nacional de Antropología is reason enough for a visit. The Aztec Templo Mayor, though prostrated on the altar of the majestic Catedral Metropolitana, still inspires awe. Spectacular mosaics and murals by Rivera, Orozco, Siqueiros, and Tamayo adorn the walls of the city.

While more people are arriving (to climb the stairs of the narrowest apartment building in the world and to pray in the smallest church), Mexico City's denizens are uncomfortably aware of bad tidings to come. The 1985 quake cast citizens as extras in a geological nightmare that may not be over. As water shortages become increasingly serious, citizens curse the topography of their metropolis: landlocked and ringed by mountains, it lets neither water in nor sewage out. Mexico City's infamous demographic crisis becomes daily more difficult to ignore. Within time the capital will merge with Puebla, Cuernavaca, Tlaxcala, Pachuca, and Querétaro to form a sprawling megalopolis of 35 million. As formerly food-producing rural migrants flock to the shantytowns on the city's edge and the city expands to engulf their abandoned plots, the prospect of feeding everyone becomes decreasingly realistic.

One-quarter of Mexico's population lives in the D.F., and one-quarter of those are employed as *comerciantes,* the independent vendors who crowd the streets. Both the commerce and life of the city are unabashedly displayed as such—Mexico City has neither the space nor the desire to hide its history, culture, and manic vitality. Even art takes on this massive and external character in the immense and awesome murals that celebrate Mexican life. Here, no one buries the ruined triumphs and fiascoes of the past, nor apologizes for the excesses of the present.

# ■■■ GETTING THERE

All roads lead to Mexico City. Buses, trains, and planes haul passengers from every town in the republic into the smoggy hyperactivity of the city's many temples of transport—the expanding Benito Juárez International Airport, four crowded bus stations, a desolate train station, and a network of freeways. Fortuitously, airports and stations in Mexico City nearly always have information booths for frazzled tourists equipped with quasi-English-speaking personnel, free or cheap maps, some sort of referral service to lead you into the *centro,* and heaps of advice.

## BY AIR

Flying into Mexico City from abroad entails the usual customs and immigration procedures. Tourist cards are distributed on the plane and stamped at the airport. Although many border officials are lax about enforcement, the "stoplight" system at the airport ensures that a certain percentage of passengers are inspected—after a certain period of time, the light comes on, and that passenger is searched. Be prepared to allow an agent to pick through your silky intimates.

The **Benito Juárez International Airport** (tel. 571-32-95) lies 6.5km east of the *zócalo,* the formal center of the city. Blvd. Capitán Juan Sarabio heads northeast to the airport from Blvd. Puerto Aéreo, one of the major roads circling the city. The airport is jam-packed with facilities:

**Tourist Office: INFOTUR,** *Sala* A and *Sala* F (tel. 762-67-63 or -73). Invaluable information and free maps of the city and the Metro. Pick up a copy of the *Mini-Guía Roji* here. Open daily 9am-9pm, and often after hours.

**Cultural Information: Instituto Nacional de Antropología y Historia,** *Sala* A. Information about archaeological sites and museums throughout the country. Open Mon.-Sat. 8am-10pm, Sun. 8am-3pm.

**Post Office:** In *Sala* A. Open Mon.-Fri. 8am-7pm, Sat.-Sun. 9am-5pm.

**Telephones: LADATELs** around the airport accept phonecards sold at nearby magazine stands. Some phones take international credit cards.

**Telegrams:** In *Sala* A. Open Mon.-Fri. 9am-8pm, Sat. 9am-noon.

**Currency Exchange: Bánamex, Banco Internacional,** and **Bancomer** have branches in different *salas.* Exchange international currency and traveler's check here. **ATMs** in *Sala* A and directly under the *Sala* B sign. *Casas de cambio* in *Salas* B, D, and E. Open 6am-10pm.

**Car Rental:** In *Sala* F (see page 76).

**Storage Lockers:** Next to the snack bar to the left of the arrival gate in *Sala* A. Storage 16 pesos per 24 hrs., 18-45 pesos for larger bags.

**Bookstore:** In *Sala* C. Novels in Spanish and English. Maps available. Open Mon.-Sat. 7am-9:30pm, Sun. 8am-8pm.

**Pharmacy:** In *Sala* C. Open daily 6am-10pm.

**Hotel Reservations:** In *Sala* E. Designate an area and they'll make the reservation for you. No charge, but be prepared to pay for the first night on the spot. English spoken. Open daily 7am-midnight.

**Restaurants** and **cafeterias** are open 24 hrs.

For information on flights out of Benito Juárez International Airport, first dial 571-36-00 or 571-44-00, and then ask for domestic or international flights.

**Domestic Flights:** Flight schedules and prices change frequently. Prices are roughly the same from airline to airline. There are usually no discounts for students, but always ask about *tarifas promocionales* (some of which may be available to students only) that can save you up to 50% on flights. **Aeroméxico,** Paseo de la Reforma 445 (tel. 327-40-00), close to Misisipi. Also at Reforma 80 (tel. 566-1078). Both open Mon.-Sat. 9am-6:15pm. At the airport, *Sala* A (tel. 762-18-18). Open daily 5am-10pm. The following information is only a partial listing; prices given are the most economical one-way coach fare on a given weekday; round-trip is approximately double. To Acapulco (10 per day, 1hr., 297 pesos),

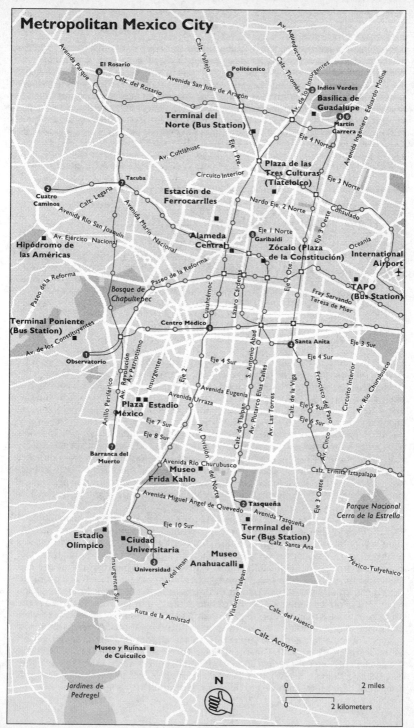

# Metropolitan Mexico City

Avenida Parque
El Rosario **6**
Calz. del Rosario
Av. Aqueducto
Calz. Vallejo
Calz. Ticomán
Av. de los Insurgentes
Avenida San Juan de Aragón
Politécnico **5**
Indios Verdes **3**
**Basílica de Guadalupe**
**Martín Carrera** **6**
**Terminal del Norte (Bus Station)** ■
Av. Cuitláhuac
Eje 4 Norte
Avenida Ingeniero Eduardo Molina
Circuito Interior
**Plaza de las Tres Culturas (Tlatelolco)**
Eje 1 Pte.
Eje 3 Norte
Tacuba **7**
Cuatro Caminos **2**
Calz. Legaria
Avenida Río San Joaquín
Avenida Marín Nacional
**Estación de Ferrocarriles**
Nardo Eje. 2 Norte
Eje 3 Oeste
Consulado
Av. Ejército Nacional
**Hipódromo de las Américas**
Eje 1 Norte
Garibaldi **8**
**Alameda Central**
**Zócalo (Plaza de la Constitución)**
Oceanía
**International Airport** ✈
Paseo de la Reforma
Paseo de la Reforma
**Bosque de Chapultepec**
Cuauhtémoc
Lázaro Cárdenas
Eje Ote.
Fray Servando Teresa de Mier
**TAPO (Bus Station)**
**Terminal Poniente (Bus Station)**
Av. de los Constituyentes
**Centro Médico** **9**
Av. Revolución
Av. Patriotismo
Cuauhtémoc
S. Antonio Abad
Eje Ote.
**Santa Anita** **4**
Eje 3 Sur
Observatorio **1**
Insurgentes
Eje 2
Eje 4 Sur
Calz. de Tlalpan
Av. Plutarco Elías Calles
Av. Las Torres
Calz. de la Viga
Eje 4 Sur
Circuito Interior
Av. Río Churubusco
Avenida Eugenia
Avenida Urraza
Francisco
Av. Cinco
**Plaza México**
**Estadio**
Eje 7 Sur
Av. División del Norte
Eje 5 Sur
Eje 6 Sur
Av. Cinco
Eje 8 Sur
**Barranca del Muerto** **7**
Avenida Río Churubusco
**Museo Frida Kahlo** ■
Eje 3 Oeste
Calz. Ermita Iztapalapa
**Parque Nacional Cerro de la Estrella**
Avenida Miguel Ángel de Quevedo
**Tasqueña** **2**
Avenida Tasqueña
**Terminal del Sur (Bus Station)**
Eje 10 Sur
Calz. Santa Ana
**Estadio Olímpico**
**Ciudad Universitaria** ■
**Museo Anahuacalli** ■
Insurgentes Sur
Anillo Periférico
Universidad **3**
Av. del Imán
México-Tulyehaico
Viaducto Tlalpan
Calz. del Huesco
Calz. Acoxpa
**Museo y Ruínas de Cuicuilco** ■
Ruta de la Amistad
**Jardines de Pedregal**

N

0 _____ 2 miles

0 _____ 2 kilometers

Aguascalientes (2 per day, 1hr., 459 pesos), Cancún (12 per day, 2hrs., 496 pesos), Chihuahua (8 per day, 2hrs., 822 pesos), Guadalajara (18 per day, 1hr., 376 pesos), Hermosillo (7 per day, 3½hrs., 810 pesos), Ixtapa-Zihuatanejo (5 per day, 1hr., 431 pesos), La Paz (4 per day, 2hrs., 862 pesos), Los Mochis (2 per day, 2hrs., 940 pesos), Mazatlán (5 per day, 1½hrs., 829 pesos), Mérida (6 per day, 2hrs., 650 pesos), Oaxaca (2 per day, 1hr., 305 pesos), Puerto Vallarta (5 per day, 2hrs., 466 pesos), and Villahermosa (4 per day, 1½hrs., 329 pesos). **Mexicana,** Amberes and Reforma 312 (tel. 511-04-24), in the Zona Rosa. Also at Reforma 51 (tel. 592-17-71) at Lafragua. Both open Mon.-Fri. 9am-6pm. A third location at airport *Sala* B (tel. 227-02-61, for reservations 325-09-90). Open daily 6am-11:30pm. To Acapulco (9 per day, 1hr., 296 pesos), Cancún (10 per day, 2hrs., 496 pesos), Cozumel (2 per day, 3hrs., 724 pesos), Guadalajara (12 per day, 1hr., 365 pesos), Ixtapa-Zihuatanejo (6 per day, 1hr., 301 pesos), Los Cabos (3 per day, 2hrs., 822 pesos), Manzanillo (2 per day, 1hr., 585 pesos), Mazatlán (1 and 2:15pm, 1hr., 815 pesos), Mérida (7 per day, 2hrs., 648 pesos), Monterrey (10 per day, 1½hrs., 510 pesos), Oaxaca (6 per day, 1hr., 308 pesos), Puerto Vallarta (7 per day, 2hrs., 465 pesos), Tijuana (5 per day, 2½hrs., 864 pesos), Villahermosa (3 per day, 1hr., 322 pesos), and Veracruz (5 per day, 1hr., 419 pesos).

**International Flights: Air Canada,** Hamburgo 108, 5th floor (tel. 511-20-94 or 514-75-16). **Air France,** Reforma 404, 15th floor (tel. 627-60-60 or 566-00-66), at airport (tel. 571-61-50). **American,** Reforma 300, 1st floor (tel. 208-63-96 or 203-94-44), at airport (tel. 571-32-19). **British Airways,** Reforma 10, 14th floor (tel. 628-0500). **Canadian Airlines,** Reforma 390-1402 (tel. 208-18-83). **Continental,** Andrés Bello 45 (tel. 280-34-34), at airport (tel. 571-36-65). **United,** Hamburgo 213, ground floor (tel. 627-02-22). **Delta,** Reforma 381 (tel. 202-16-08 or 207-34-11), at airport (tel. 571-32-37). **KLM,** Paseo de Palmas 735, 7th floor (tel. 202-44-44), and at airport (tel. 571-32-46). **Lufthansa,** Las Palmas 239 (tel. 202-88-66), at airport (tel. 571-27-13). **Swissair,** Hamburgo 66, 3rd floor (tel. 207-24-55). **Aeroméxico** and **Mexicana** have flights to Central America and the U.S.

Transportation into the city is uncomplicated. From the *venta de boletos* desk in *Sala* A, buy a ticket; this ticket is presentable to any of the white-and-yellow taxis labeled *transporte terrestre* that wait outside. The price is set by which zone of the city you're traveling to (35 pesos to the center, more after-hours). Ask to see the map—just because it's an official-looking booth does not mean you won't be overcharged. *Don't* pay cash for a ride from the airport; you'll pay heavily for the convenience. Unauthorized taxis will try to rip you off; the authorized cabs (labeled *transporte terrestre* at the airport) are clearly marked and await in a specified area. Call 784-48-11 or 571-36-00 (24 hrs.) to get a taxi back to the airport from the city. Whenever you hop into a taxi anywhere else in the city, make sure there's a functioning meter—and that it functions consistently the entire trip—or else negotiate a price beforehand. If the meter suddenly jumps into a high price range, threaten to get out or not pay at all until the actual price returns.

The airport **subway** station, **Terminal Aérea** (Line 5), located at the junction of Capitán Juan Sarabío and Blvd. Puerto Aéreo, is only a five-minute walk from *Sala* A. Signs will point you in the right direction (see Getting Around below, for the scoop on the Metro). Large bags are officially prohibited, but it's not uncommon for somebody to waltz aboard with bulky items. Provided you avoid rush hours and can maneuver through the turnstile, a typical pack should not pose much of a problem. For your own safety and the comfort of others, remove the pack from your back when you're on the subway. Also, try to ride in the first or last cars, as these are the least crowded. If a train appears frighteningly jam-packed, simply let it pass; another will arrive within minutes. The Metro is by far the cheapest (0.40 pesos) and most convenient route to the city. **If you return to the airport by Metro, do not get off at the Aeropuerto stop. The correct stop is Terminal Aérea.**

Travelers **driving** to *el centro* should take Blvd. Puerto Aéreo north to Eje 2 Nte. (see Getting Around, below), then head west on Eje 2 Nte. to Paseo de la Reforma. A left turn here leads southwest to Juárez or, farther down, to Insurgentes.

## BY TRAIN

**Estación Buenavista** of the **Ferrocarriles Nacionales de México** (tel. 547-10-97; open daily 6am-10pm) is located due north of the **Monumento de la Revolución** at the corner of Insurgentes and Mosqueta (Eje 1 Alzate), five long blocks from the nearest Metro station, Revolución (Line 2). Mosqueta is currently undergoing a major face-lift; if construction still blocks access to the station, walk east a bit for a pedestrian bridge. Taxis leave from the parking lot on the Mosqueta side of the main building. Be sure to check the meter and the official fare chart in the cab before you pay, as abuses are par for the course.

An **information booth** (tel. 547-10-84, -97, or 91-800-90-392 for tourist info) to the left of the ticket windows does little more than dispense train schedules. Both the information booth and the ticket windows are open daily 6:30am to 9:30pm. The station has a **fax/long distance service** (open Mon.-Sat. 8am-9:30pm, Sun. 9am-3pm) and a 24-hour Cirrus **ATM**. Located in the second-class area, down the walkway from the main *sala*, is a **luggage storage** service that will hold your *equipaje* for five pesos per day (open daily 6:30am-9:30pm). There are also a few 24-hour restaurants of questionable hygienic integrity.

There are four classes of trains: *primera especial* (first-class reserved, without bed), *dormitorio camarín* (reserved with two separate beds per compartment), *alcoba* (reserved, with bunk bed), *primera general* (unreserved). First-class tickets can be purchased up to a month in advance. Other than *Semana Santa*, spots are usually available up to one hour before departure. Buying second class tickets is as wholly unpleasant as riding second-class trains; for popular routes arrive at the station five hours before departure. Regardless of their class, trains tend to be excruciatingly slow, except for those to Guadalajara, Veracruz, Monterrey (without 2nd-class service), and Piedras Negras. Other immensely popular routes are from the D.F. to Oaxaca, Yucatán, Ciudad Juárez, and Nuevo Laredo. Get train information in English from the **Departamento de Tráfico de Pasajeros** hidden off to the right of long-distance booth #6 in the main station lobby (tel. 547-86-55; fax 547-89-72; open Mon.-Fri. 6am-10pm).

**First-class Primera Especial service:** Daily to Guadalajara (8:30pm, 12hrs., 65.80 pesos), Monterrey (6pm, 14hrs., 100.10 pesos or 9am, 17¼hrs., 105.45 pesos), Morelia (9pm, 8½hrs., 39.90 pesos), Oaxaca (7pm, 14½hrs., 62.25 pesos), Puebla (7pm, 5hrs., 22.90 pesos), Saltillo (6pm, 12hrs., 88.45 pesos), San Luis Potosí (6pm, 6hrs., 47 pesos or 9am, 8hrs., 52.40 pesos), Uruapan (9pm, 12hrs., 54.70 pesos), and Veracruz (9:15pm, 10hrs., 49.90 pesos).

**Second-class service:** Daily to Guadalajara (9pm, 12hrs., 36.65 pesos), Monterrey (9am, 17hrs., 58.75 pesos), Morelia (9pm, 8¼hrs., 22.20 pesos), Oaxaca (7pm, 14½hrs., 34.70 pesos), Puebla (7pm, 5hrs., 12.65 pesos), Saltillo (9am, 15hrs., 52.30 pesos), San Luis Potosí (9am, 8hrs., 29.15 pesos), Uruapan (9pm, 12hrs., 30.50 pesos), and Veracruz (9:15pm, 10hrs., 27.80 pesos).

## BY BUS

Mexico City's four main bus stations correspond to the points of the compass. **Central de Autobuses del Norte** (North Station) serves the Bajío, northern Veracruz, Jalisco, and most of northern Mexico; **Terminal Central de Autobuses del Sur** (South Station) launches buses to Morelos and Guerrero; **Terminal de Autobuses de Pasajeros de Oriente (TAPO)** (East Station) sends buses to Puebla, southern Veracruz, Oaxaca, Chiapas, and the Yucatán Peninsula; and the **Terminal de Autobuses del Poniente** (West Station) serves the states of México and Michoacán.

All stations are served by the Metro and offer an official 24-hour taxi service that charges fixed rates for a ride to any point in the city (rates set by zones) or adjacent parts of Mexico state. Buy your ticket inside to avoid a rip-off, but be wary of being charged for an extra zone—if you can find it, consult the zone map. *Peseros* (a.k.a. *colectivos*) also serve the four stations. Quality budget hotels near the bus stations (see Accommodations on page 83) are rare—it's a much safer bet to head toward the city center. The following listings are by no means comprehensive; given the extensive network, it is possible to go almost anywhere at any time. All ticket sales are final and all seats reserved.

## Central de Autobuses del Norte

The Central de Autobuses del Norte (tel. 587-15-52) is on Cien Metros, Metro station Autobuses del Norte (Line 5). Bánamex **ATM**, restaurant, and luggage storage (per 24hrs., small 12 pesos, big 20 pesos) are all open around the clock. A *casa de cambio* near the main entrance offers poor rates (open Mon.-Fri. 8am-9pm, Sat.-Sun. 9am-4pm). The post office and telegram office are nearby (open Mon.-Fri. 8am-5pm, Sat. 8am-1pm). A booth of the **Hoteles Asociados** (hotel reservations service) is occasionally open near the main entrance (supposedly open 8am-9pm).

More companies than those listed below operate out of this terminal/zoo. They are listed in the order they appear from waiting room 1 to 8.

**Primera Plus** (tel. 587-52-22 or 587-52-00). First class to Aguascalientes (12 per day, 6½hrs., 104 pesos), Guadalajara (29 per day, 8hrs., 127 pesos), León (every ½hr., 5hrs., 78 pesos), Manzanillo (8:30 and 9pm, 13hrs., 153 pesos), Querétaro (every 20min., 3hrs., 42 pesos), and San Luis Potosí (8 per day, 6hrs., 82 pesos).

**ETN** (tel. 368-11-88). First class pampering to Aguascalientes (7 per day, 6½hrs., 125 pesos), Guadalajara (18 per day, 8hrs., 165 pesos), Morelia (1 and 11:30pm, 4½hrs., 95 pesos), Puerto Vallarata (2 per day, 255 pesos), Querétaro (30 per day, 3hrs., 60 pesos), and San Luis Potosí (15 per day, 6hrs., 105 pesos).

**Transportes del Norte** (tel. 587-54-00). To Matamoros (2 per day, 15hrs., 193 pesos), Monterrey (every hr. from 8am, 12hrs., 173 pesos), Querétaro (4 per day, 3hrs., 41 pesos), and Reynosa (2 per day, 15hrs., 194 pesos).

**Estrella Blanca** (tel. 587-54-00). To Ciudad Juárez (8:30pm, 23½hrs., 295 pesos), Durango (4 per day, 12hrs., 146 pesos), and Fresnillo (8 per day, 109 pesos).

**Omnibus de México** (tel. 567-67-58 or 567-72-87). To Aguascalientes (14 per day, 6½hrs., 100 pesos), Chihuahua (6 per day, 18hrs., 272 pesos), Guadalajara (13 per day, 8hrs., 121 pesos), Guanajuato (3 per day, 5hrs., 70 pesos), San Luis Potosí (15 per day, 6hrs., 78 pesos), Tampico (8 per day, 8hrs., 95 pesos), Tuxpan, Veracruz (5 per day, 7hrs., 57 pesos), and Zacatecas (16 per day, 8hrs., 118 pesos).

**Autobuses del Oriente (ADO)** (tel. 587-66-88). To Jalapa (4 per day, 4½hrs., 57.50 pesos), Papantla (6 per day, 6hrs., 51 pesos), Tampico (11 per day, 9hrs., 95 pesos), and Tuxpan (9 per day, 5hrs., 57 pesos).

**Tres Estrellas de Oro** (tel. 587-57-77). To Hermosillo (11 per day, 21hrs., 385 pesos), Ixtlán del Río (7:30am, 140 pesos), La Peñita (7:15pm, 185 pesos), Manzanillo (3 per day, 12hrs., 142 pesos), and Mexicali (6 per day, 38hrs., 407 pesos).

**Flecha Amarilla** (tel. 587-52-00). Second-class service to many nearby towns.

**Transportes México-Pachuca** (tel. 567-64-39). To Ixmiquilpan (4 per day, 19 pesos) and Pachuca (every 5 min., 5am-midnight, 13 pesos).

## Terminal de Autobuses de Pasajeros de Oriente (TAPO)

The TAPO (tel. 762-59-77) is on General Ignacio Zaragoza 200, Metro station San Lázaro (Line 1). Ticket counters await in a rotunda at the end of a long, store-lined passageway. Police booths are scattered throughout the station. A tourist information kiosk (supposedly open daily 9am-9pm) and taxi ticket booths are located near the entrance to the Metro. The station also contains a 24-hour MC/Cirrus/Plus **ATM,** restaurant, pharmacy, and currency exchange services (open daily 7am-11pm).

**Autobuses Unidos (AU)** (tel. 542-42-10, ext. 19). To Córdoba (38 per day, 5hrs., 55.50 pesos), Jalapa (28 per day, 5hrs., 58.50 pesos), Oaxaca (13 per day, 9hrs., 77 pesos), San Andrés Tuxtla (2 per day, 9½hrs., 97 pesos), Santa Cruz (14 per day, hrs., 74.50 pesos), Tuxtepec (11 per day, 8hrs., 79 pesos), Veracruz (24 per day, 7hrs., 66.50 pesos), and Villahermosa (3 per day, 14hrs., 136.50 pesos).

**ADO** (tel. 542-71-92). 1st class to Campeche (4 per day, 20hrs., 239.50 pesos), Cancún (3 per day, 26hrs., 286 pesos), Jalapa (30 per day, 5hrs., 57.50 pesos), Oaxaca (22 per day, 9hrs., 91 pesos), Palenque (4 and 6:10pm, 14hrs., 189

pesos), Tuxtepec (6 per day, 8hrs., 90 pesos), Tuxtla Gutiérrez (5:15 and 8pm, 15hrs., 198 pesos), and Villahermosa (7 per day, 14hrs., 165 pesos).
**Estrella Roja** (tel. 522-72-00). To Puebla (every 15 min. from 4am-10pm, every ½ hr. from 10pm-midnight, 1¾hrs., 22 pesos).
**Autobuses Cristóbal Colón** (tel. 542-72-63). 1st class to Oaxaca (8 per day, 9hrs., 104 pesos), San Cristóbal de las Casas (4 per day, 17hrs., 204 pesos), Tapachula (3 per day, 12hrs., 212 pesos), Tonalá (7pm, 13hrs., 179 pesos), Tuxtla Gutiérrez (3 per day, 16hrs., 191 pesos), and service to Central America.
**UNO** (tel. 522-11-11). Only if you must live in the lap of luxury.

## Terminal de Autobuses del Poniente

The Terminal de Autobuses del Poniente (tel. 271-00-38) is on Av. Sur 122, Metro station Observatorio (Line 1). Take a left as you exit the metro station; a bridge leads to the terminal. Operates mainly second-class routes; brace for slow, indirect service. The station is built in the shape of a "V" with most important services clustered at the "V"ertex. Round-the-clock station services include a restaurant, long distance *caseta*, and luggage storage (8 pesos for 24hrs., 12 pesos for subjectively "extra large" luggage). The following services sleep at night: a pharmacy (open daily 7am-10pm), post and telegram offices (open Mon.-Fri. 8am-5pm, Sat. 8am-1pm), food-stands, shops, and newspaper stands.

**Turismos México-Toluca** (tel. 271-03-44). To Altacomulco (every 15min., 6am-8pm, 2hrs., 20 pesos) and Toluca (every 5 min., 6am-10:30pm, 1½hrs., 11 pesos).
**ETN** (tel. 273-02-51). 1st-class service to Morelia (22 per day, 4hrs., 95 pesos), Toluca (22 per day, 1½hrs., 17 pesos), and Uruapan (6 per day, 6hrs., 118 pesos).
**Vía 2000** (tel. 271-01-06). To Guadalajara (1 and 8:15pm, 12hrs., 112 pesos), Morelia (7 per day, 4hrs., 50 pesos), and Zamora (1 and 10:35pm, 9hrs., 85 pesos).
**Autobuses de Occidente** (tel. 271-01-06). To Guadalajara (9 per day, 12hrs., 99 pesos), Manzanillo (5 per day, 15hrs., 124 pesos), Morelia (every 20min., 4hrs., 50 pesos), and Zamora (9 per day, 9hrs., 72 pesos).
**Herradura de Plata** (tel. 271-03-25). To Morelia (12 per day, 4hrs., 63 pesos) and Pátzcuaro (7 per day, 5¼hrs., 80 pesos).

## Terminal de Autobuses del Sur (Taxqueña)

The Taxqueña terminal (tel. 689-97-45) is on Taxqueña 1320, Metro station Taxqueña (Line 2). The station has a post office (open Mon.-Sat. 8am-5pm), telegram office (open Mon.-Fri. 8am-6pm, Sat. 9am-5pm), long-distance *caseta* with fax service (open daily 7am-9:30pm), and LADATELs scattered about. There is also a mini-travel agency for hotel reservations in Mexico City, Acapulco, and Mazatlán (open Mon.-Fri. 9am-7pm, Sat. 9am-3pm), a 24-hour pharmacy, and a round-the-clock cafeteria. Luggage lockers (small 10 pesos, large 18 pesos for 24 hrs.) are near exit #3.

**Pullman de Morelos** (tel. 549-35-05). 1st class to Cuautla (every 20min., 6am-11pm, 2hrs., 18.50 pesos), Cuernavaca (every 10min., 5:30am-midnight, 1¼hrs., 18 pesos), Oaxtepec (every 30min., 6am-11pm, 1¼hrs., 18 pesos), and Tepotzlán (every hr., 6:30am-8:30pm, 1½hrs., 15 pesos).
**Estrella de Oro** (tel. 549-85-20, ext. 29). 1st class to Acapulco (8 per day, 7hrs., 89 pesos), Chilpancingo (11 per day, 4½hrs., 60 pesos), Iguala (10 per day, 3hrs., 37 pesos), Taxco (3 per day, 3½hrs., 29 pesos), and Zihuatanejo (3 per day, 11hrs., 118 pesos), and Iguala (9 per day, 3hrs., 28 pesos).
**Servicio Coordinado (Turi-Star, Estrella Blanca,** and more, tel. 689-80-00). 1st class to Acapulco (every ½hr., 5:15am-10pm, 1¼hrs., 89 pesos) and Chilpancingo (4 per day, 7hrs., 80 pesos).

## BY CAR

No other vehicular endeavor matches the experience of driving into Mexico City. Serene mountain roads slowly metamorphose into blaring, multi-lane highways. Soon, any semblance of defensive driving goes out the window—welcome to the city where the stoplights are perpetually green.

Several major highways lead into the D.F. and intersect with the **Circuito Interior,** the highway that rings the city, at which point they continue under assumed names. **Route 57,** from Querétaro and Tepotzotlán, becomes Manuel Ávila Camacho just outside the Circuito. **Route 15,** from Toluca, turns into Reforma as it enters the city. **Route 95,** from Cuernavaca and Acapulco, becomes Insurgentes, which plugs into the Circuito on the south side. **Route 150,** from Puebla and Texcoco, becomes Ignacio Zaragoza, which connects to the Circuito on the east side. **Route 85,** from Pachuca, Teotihuacán, and Texcoco, becomes Insurgentes in the city.

# ■■■ ORIENTATION

## CIRCUITO INTERIOR AND EJES VIALES

The **Circuito Interior** is a roughly rectangular artery made up of several smaller, connected highways. **Boulevard Puerto Aéreo** forms the upper east side of the box, running north from the airport. As it bends left at the northeast corner of the box and heads west, it becomes **Avenida Río Consulado.** Río Consulado turns south and becomes **Calzada Melchor Ocampo.** Ocampo heads south until it intersects Paseo de la Reforma at Bosque de Chapultepec, after which it continues as **Avenida Vasconcelos.** From Vasconcelos, two roads run to the southwest corner of the Circuito, **Av. Patriotismo** and **Av. Revolución,** either of which could be considered the Circuito at this point. At that point they turn into Av. Río Mixcoac, which becomes **Avenida Río Churubusco,** running east-west. Río Churubusco is the longest and sneakiest of the highways that constitute the Circuito. It continues east, turns north for a while, heads east again, then turns north once more to connect with Blvd. Puerto Aéreo south of the airport to complete the Circuito.

Aside from the large thoroughfares—Insurgentes, Reforma, and Miguel Alemán—a system of **Ejes Viales** (axis roads) conducts the majority of traffic within the Circuito. *Ejes* run one way (except for the bus lanes, which go against traffic). Running east-west, Eje 1 Nte. and Eje 2 Nte. are north of the *zócalo,* while Ejes 2 through 8 Sur run south of it. The numbers increase heading away from the *zócalo.* **Eje Central Lázaro Cárdenas** runs north-south and bisects the box formed by the Circuito. East of it and parallel lie Ejes 1 through 3 Ote., which veer off to the northwest; west of it are Ejes 1 through 3 Pte. Using the Ejes together with the Circuito, you can theoretically reach any general area of the city without much delay. The **Guía Roji** street atlas (about 40 pesos), *Ciudad de México,* is available at many newsstands, bookstores, and at the airport; this comprehensive guide is a valuable aid for anyone planning to travel in the city for an extended period of time. A **mini-Guía Roji** (15 pesos) that provides a quick overview of the major thoroughfares is also available at the airport.

## CITY CENTER

Huge as Mexico City is, almost everything of interest to visitors lies within the northern half of the area circumscribed by the Circuito Interior. Moreover, many attractions are within easy reach of **Paseo de la Reforma,** the broad thoroughfare that runs southwest-northeast, or **Av. Insurgentes,** the boulevard running north-south through the city; these streets constitute the heart of the Federal District. The **Bosque de Chapultepec,** home to the principal museums of the city, marks the western limit of tourists' wanderings. From Chapultepec, Reforma proceeds northeast, punctuated by *glorietas* (traffic circles), each with a monument in the center. Moving up Reforma from Chapultepec, the Zona Rosa is followed by Buenavista (near the Monumento a la Revolucíon), then the Alameda and the Centro.

The accommodations and food listings for Mexico City are divided according to the four areas which are of most interest to tourists. The area termed the **Centro** contains most of the historic sights and museums, extensive budget accommodations, and lively inexpensive restaurants. This area is bounded by Cárdenas to the west, Uruguay to the south, Pino Suárez to the east, and Rep. de Peru to the north.

The area called the **Alameda** contains budget accommodations and many restaurants, and is bounded by Eje 1 Pte. (known as Rosales, Guerrero, and Bucareli) to the west, Arcos de Belén to the south, Cárdenas to the east, and Violeta to the north. The **Monumento a la Revolución/Buenavista** area, like the Alameda, contains many inexpensive hotels and eateries. It is bounded by Insurgentes Norte to the west, Reforma to the south and east, and Mosqueta to the north. The **Zona Rosa** (Pink Zone) is the capital's most affluent commercial district. This neighborhood is contained within Reforma to the north and west, Av. Chapultepec to the south, and Insurgentes to the east. (Note: a few *Let's Go* listings for this area lie just east of Insurgentes, as well as a gaggle of bars and clubs which spill south past Chapultepec along Insurgentes Sur).

Unlike the streets themselves, names in Mexico City are systematic. **Streets** in a given area generally carry names that are generically related. For example, streets in the Zona Rosa are all named after European cities, while the streets directly across Reforma are named after large rivers of the world. North of Chapultepec, streets are named after famous people. One point to remember when looking for street numbers is that they start from zero at the end of the street nearest the main post office (on Parque Alameda's northeast corner) and continue to the border of the next *colonia* (neighborhood), where the street name changes and the addresses start at zero again. Note that different neighborhoods can use the same street name; the 300 Benito Juárez streets in the Mexico City area attest to this tradition of redundancy.

## OUTLYING DISTRICTS

Mexico City reaches outward from the Centro roughly 20km to the south, 10km to the north, 10km to the west, and 8km to the east. Year after year, the city's boundaries extend hungrily into neighboring cities. Because of the central location of most sights, few travelers venture past the Bosque de Chapultepec to the west, La Basílica de Guadalupe to the north, the *zócalo* or la Merced marketplace to the east side of the Centro, or south past San Ángel and the Universidad Nacional Autónoma de México. The major southern thoroughfare is **Insurgentes Sur,** which extends to the southern limit of the city. Metro Line 3 parallels Insurgentes on Cuauhtémoc and then Universidad, ending at Ciudad Universitaria, well before the city's edge. Most sights to the south, including **San Ángel, Coyoacán, Ciudad Universitaria,** and the **Pyramid of Cuicuilco,** lie near or along Insurgentes. Metro Line 2 runs east of Line 3 and is closer to **Xochimilco,** one of the few southern sights not along Insurgentes.

# ■■■ TRANSPORTATION WITHIN MEXICO CITY

If walking is not your thing, your chief obstacle to getting around in Mexico City will be congestion. Streets are crowded with the municipal gray with green and blue buses (.40 pesos), the thousands of mini-buses (white and green) known as *peseros, micros, colectivos,* or *camiones* (1-2.50 pesos), and the considerably more expensive and omnipresent taxis. While the Metro is usually the fastest and most efficient method of transportation, it is inhumanly crowded at peak commuting hours. Most transportation depots in Mexico City are large, clean, well-lit, well-policed, and well-marked. Public transportation—whether by bus, Metro, or *pesero*—is easy to use and economical.

Travelers who plan to make frequent use of the Metro and bus systems should purchase an *abono de ahorro de transporte* (14 pesos) at a subway ticket window. *Abonos* (each is a pair of cards), available at all subway stations, Lotería Nacional stands, and Conasupo markets, entitle the bearer to unlimited use of the Metro (the blue card) and city buses (the purple card) for 15 days following the purchase date. *Abonos* are sold at the beginning and in the middle of every month. Be sure to go early—the cards disappear faster than you can say peso devaluation.

# Central Mexico City

## BY METRO

The Metro always amazes—trains come quickly and regularly, the fare is insanely cheap, the crowds are enormous and bizarre, the ride is smooth, the service is extensive, and the stations are immaculate and marmoreal. Built in the late 1960s, the Metro transports five million people daily. Its tracks and stations are in continual pursuit of Mexico City's ever-expanding perimeter. What is not covered by the regular Metro service can often be reached via the smaller *tren ligero,* which interconnects many lines at the city's edge and offers service to outlying suburbs.

The 0.40-peso fare includes transfers. Gates operate by inserting a magnetically coded ticket, which must be bought at the booths marked *taquilla.* Transfer gates are marked *correspondencia* and exits are marked *salida;* passing through the turnstiles leaves you outside the station, and you must pay again to re-enter. While some of the connections are difficult to locate, most transfer stations have information booths to help clueless travelers. Just remember that passing through the turnstile is the *wrong* direction if getting to another line is the goal. If you have an *abono,* be sure to enter only through the blue turnstiles. If you use a white turnstile your ticket will be swallowed. Color-coded subway guides are available at the tourist office or at the Metro information booths.

Metro tickets are sold in booths at every station. Buy in bulk, or else come prepared with exact change, since the *taquillas* are often short of small denominations. For lines 1, 2, 3, and A, the first train runs Monday through Friday at 5am, Saturday at 6am, and Sunday at 7am. For lines 4-9, the first train runs Monday through Saturday at 6am, Sunday at 7am. For all lines the last train runs at 11:30pm from Sunday through Friday, and on Saturday as late as 2:30am. Try to avoid using the Metro from 7:30 to 9am, 7 to 9pm on weekdays, and during the city's 2-4pm lunchbreak; huge crowds during these hours attract pickpockets. Cars at either end of the train tend to be slightly less crowded, *ergo* safer and less uncomfortable.

Directions are stated in terms of the station at the end of a given line. Each of the two *andenes* (platforms) has signs indicating the terminus toward which trains are heading. (For example, if you are on Line 3 between Indios Verdes and Universidad, you can go "Dirección Indios Verdes" or "Dirección Universidad.") If you realize you are headed in the wrong direction, fear not; simply get off and walk under (or sometimes over) to the other side.

As in many parts of Mexico, being single and having two X chromosomes is just not a convenient combination while using the Metro. Lewd remarks and stares are a given, and the horrible experience of being groped is a very distinct possibility when the train is crowded or if the train stops mid-tunnel between stations. Do not be afraid to call attention to the offender. During rush hours many lines have cars reserved for women and children. If you are female, use them. They are usually located at the front of the train and designated by a partition labeled "Mujeres"; often you will see women and children gathering on a separate part of the platform for the reserved car.

Theft is a chronic problem on the Metro. Carry bags in front of you or on your lap; simply closing the bag does little good, because thieves use razors to slit the bag open from the bottom. Subway thieves often work in pairs—one will distract you while the other pulls your wallet. Rear pockets are easy to pick; front pockets are safer, empty pockets are best. If you ride with a backpack on your back, the small pocket is likely to be violated. The safest place in a crowded car is with your back against the wall and your backpack (if you have one) in front of you. Because of overcrowding, large bags or suitcases are not allowed on the Metro. Some travelers have bags slipped past the gate, but on a crowded train, luggage will make fellow passengers uncomfortable and will attract thieves. If you are intent on making it on the Metro with that overstuffed pack, come very early or after 10:30pm, when the Metro is fairly empty and guards are more likely to look the other way.

For Metro and bus information, ask at any information booth or contact **COVITUR (Comisión de Vialidad y Transporte Urbano del D.F.),** Public Relations, Universidad 800 on the 14th floor (tel. 512-01-12 or 627-48-61), at the corner of

Félix Cuervas just outside the Zapata Metro station. To complain about the Metro dial 709-11-33, ext. 5051 or 5052. Nearly all stations have guards and security offices; immediately report any problems or incidents that occur on the Metro. Further, all trains have an emergency red handle, to be pulled in the event of severe harrassment or any emergency. If you lose something on the Metro, call the **Oficina de Objetos Extraviados** (tel. 709-11-33, ext. 4643), located in the Fray Servando station (Line 4). Keep hope alive, but don't hold your breath.

> ### Station Education
> Some Metro stops are sights in their own right. Pino Suárez houses a small Aztec building located at mid-transfer. The science tunnel in the marathon transfer at La Raza is an educational experience: wear your whites and glow in the dark under a map of the constellations. The *zócalo* stop has scale models of the plaza as it has appeared throughout its history, the *andenes* at Copilco are lined with murals, and the Bellas Artes stop houses Aztec statuettes. In fact, nearly every Metro transfer stop has some kind of exhibit, from elementary school drawings of the subway system to a re-creation of a London theatre.

## BY BUS

While the public bus system extends much farther than the Metro, there is no published information about routes and schedules available to the tourist; unless you stick to the major thoroughfares you might find it difficult to navigate the city by bus. Moreover, buses are usually slower than the Metro, particularly during rush hours. Buses come in two flavors (brown and yellow or blue and gray) and run 0.50-1 peso; have change ready when you board. They run daily from 5am to midnight, but are scarce after 10pm. They pass bus stops every 20-30 minutes.

Buses are required to stop only at the bus stops along Ejes Viales and the following major streets: Reforma, Insurgentes, Calzada de Tlalpan, and Viaducto Miguel Alemán. Otherwise, hundreds of north-south or east-west routes are scattered along most major thoroughfares. Keep in mind that each one-way Eje has a single bus lane running in the *opposite* direction to traffic. Anywhere, flag down the bus by holding out your arm and pointing at the street in front of you. To get off the bus, press the button above the exit door at the rear of the bus. If you don't hear a buzz, bang once on the wall or bark *¡Bajo!* to let the driver know you want out.

In an effort to meet the growing demand for efficient transportation, the city is slowly incorporating "Express" buses into the system. These swift steeds stop only on major avenues such as Insurgentes, Reforma, and Mazaryk.

Like the Metro, buses are crowded and seats are hot items. The popular routes along Paseo de la Reforma are notorious for robbery and are plagued by organized gangs of thieves. Leave your valuables at the hotel; don't keep money in your pockets; put your bag in front of you, and keep your fingers crossed. Avoid buses that run down Paseo altogether.

## BY PESERO (MINIBUS)

*Peseros,* a.k.a. *colectivos, combis,* or *micros,* are white-and-green minibuses, often with a "Magna Sin" gasoline logo on the side. Priced economically between cabs and buses, they cruise the streets on set routes. Though no printed information is available, destinations are either painted on or posted on the front window. To hail a *pesero,* wave your hand or hold out as many fingers as there are people in your group. Drivers will typically honk (horns are often rigged to play an annoying melody) at virtually every pedestrian to signal availability.

Fares vary according to distance; expect to fork over 1-2.50 peso for cross-city rides, 4 pesos for long-distance trips over 17km. Fares are 10% higher between 10pm and 6am. To prevent a missed stop, pay when you get on and tell the driver your destination. Some *peseros* run only until midnight, but the major routes—on Reforma, between Chapultepec and San Ángel, and along Insurgentes—run 24 hours. Other well-traveled *pesero* routes include: Metro Hidalgo to Ciudad Universitaria (via Reforma, Bucareli, and Av. Cuauhtémoc); La Villa to Chapultepec (via Reforma); Reforma to Auditorio (via Reforma and Juárez); *zócalo* to Chapultepec (via 5 de Mayo and Reforma); San Ángel to Izazaga (via 5 de Mayo and Reforma); Bolívar to Ciudad Universitaria/Coyoacán (via Bolívar in the *Centro*); and San Ángel to Metro Insurgentes (via Av. de la Paz and Insurgentes Sur). Many depart from the Chapultepec Metro station to San Ángel, La Merced, and the airport. Central routes are indicated by Metro stops, while suburban *peseros* may also have numbers.

The beauty of the *pesero* is its convenience; *peseros* will pick you up and drop you off at virtually any corner along their routes. If you're heading for a specific address, consider hailing a *pesero*.

## BY TAXI

Cabs constantly cruise the major avenues. Most taxis are equipped with meters; base fares typically begin at two pesos. Be certain that the meter is functioning as soon as you plop onto the cushion; at night, meters are often conveniently *descompuesto*. If a meter is out of order, insist on setting the price before the driver goes anywhere. Another commonly used trick is for a normally functioning meter to suddenly jump into the triple digits—watch the meter at all times and immediately threaten a driver with non-payment if the price instantaneously skyrockets. Some taxis have meters that display reference numbers for the driver's price conversion table instead of prices. Ask to see it before you pay, to insure that the price you're given matches the meter number. Hotel cabs and *turismo* taxis have no meters and charge up to three times more than regular taxis; the ubiquitous green VW bugs are the cheapest but must be hailed; larger, orange taxis have digital meters that require no conversion. Tips are unnecessary unless you are granted some sort of special service—if the cabbie helps carry your luggage or gives you a previously agreed-to tour, hand over a *propina.*

At the airport and at all bus terminals, purchase a taxi ticket for a set fee (according to destination) at a registered booth. In the rare instance that no taxi is in sight, call **Servi-taxi** (tel. 516-60-20) or **Taxi Radio Mexicana** (tel. 574-45-96). VW bug taxis should display the driver's photo, credentials, and license over the glove compartment. Taxis commonly prey on the easy tourist victim. At the airport or bus terminals, try to consult a zone map before buying your ticket and always count your change. On the street, ask a local what the fare should be and insist on paying that and no more; there'll always be a driver who will accept.

## BY CAR

Be forewarned that driving is the craziest and least economical way to get around the Federal District. Central Mexico City is encircled by a number of connected highways that together make up the **Circuito Interior.** This system is supposed to allow motorists to get fairly close to their destination before hitting the gridlocked streets of the center. Unfortunately, the Circuito itself is frequently jammed, especially during rush hour (Mon.-Fri. 7-9am and 6-9pm).

Mexico City's drivers are notoriously evil; they became that way in large measure because highway engineers did not design city roads with them in mind. Highway dividers are often absent and stop signs are planted midstream. Is it any wonder that red lights are routinely defied? Even angels fear to tread in the D.F.: the fast and free *Ángeles Verdes* do *not* serve the Distrito Federal. If your car should break down within city boundaries, call **Asociación Automovilística Mexicana** (tel. 519-34-36) and request assistance. Wait for them beside your car, with the hood raised. If you leave your car alone, give it a good-bye kiss before you go.

Parking within the city is seldom a problem: parking lots are everywhere (approx. 1-8 pesos per hr., depending on the location and condition of the lot). Street parking in Mexico City is rare, and vandalism is extremely common. Never leave anything valuable inside your car. Police will remove your license plate if you park illegally; should this happen, wait near your car with some cash in your pocket until they return. If anything else was missing from your car and you suspect that the police were tampering with it, call the English-speaking LOCATEL (tel. 658-11-11).

All vehicles, even those of non-Mexican registration, must follow Mexico City's anti-smog regulations. Depending on the last digit of the license plate, cars are forbidden from driving one day a week, according to this schedule: Monday final digits: 5 or 6; Tuesday: 7 or 8; Wednesday: 3 or 4; Thursday: 1 or 2; Friday: 9 or 0. Restrictions apply from 5am-10pm, and penalties for violations are stiff. (No limitations on weekends and between 10pm and 5am daily.)

Car rental rates are exorbitant, driving a hassle, and the entire process draining. Requirements to rent vary, but nearly all require the renter to be at least 21 years old; some require the renter to be 26, have a major credit card, and show a passport or tourist card. Any driver's license is valid in Mexico. Prices for rentals tend to be similar; try the Zona Rosa or *Sala* F in the airport. **Dollar,** Av. Chapultepec 322 (tel. 207-38-38), in the airport, will rent a VW sedan for 220 pesos per or 1366 pesos per week, with free mileage. Renter must be 25 and have a valid driver's license and major credit card (open daily 7am-8pm). **Budget,** Hamburgo 71 (tel. 533-04-50), in the Zona Rosa and at the airport, charges 223 pesos, with similar conditions as Dollar (open Mon.-Fri. 7am-9pm, Sat. 8am-6pm). **Global Rent-a-Car** (tel. 726-03-98), in the Zona Rosa and in Sala F at the airport, charges 363.40 pesos per day for a mid-size car, but will rent to those 21 and over (open daily 8am-11pm).

# ■■■ SAFETY

Like all large cities, Mexico City presents safety problems to the traveler. However, misconceptions about the magnitude of these problems can easily prevent an enjoyable visit. In general, the downtown area, where most sights and accommodations are located, tends to be safer, although the backstreets near Buenavista and the Alameda are significantly less so. Try to avoid carrying large amounts of cash, and use a money belt or similar security device. Ignore strangers who seem even slightly suspicious, no matter how friendly their chatter or smile may seem. Never follow a vendor or shoeshiner out of public view.

Women are, unfortunately, at higher risk of attack. Stick with other people, especially at night or in an isolated area. Light hair and North American-style shorts will attract undesirable stares and propositions. A loud clear *¡Déjame!* (stop it, DEH-ha-meh) will make your intentions clear. If in trouble, do not be shy about screaming *¡Ayúdame!* (help me; ah-YOO-dah-may).

Transportation presents its own safety concerns (see Getting Around for more info). Mexico City's drivers are notoriously aggressive and often ignore traffic signals. Insist on seeing a taxi driver's photo license. Locals warn of late-night attacks by *bandidos* posing as police officers.

The city's notoriously smoggy air may cause problems for contact lens wearers and people with allergies, though the summer rainy season does wonders in cleaning the air. *The News* publishes a detailed smog report daily.

# ■■■ PRACTICAL INFORMATION

Navigating the city will be easier if you pick up a few current publications. The *Mexico City Daily Bulletin,* which includes news, information on tourist sights, and a helpful map of Mexico City is available free at the City Tourism Office and all over the Zona Rosa. To locate performances and show times, pick up a copy of *The News* (4 pesos), an English-language daily, or look for *Tiempo Libre* (Free Time; 5 pesos), published every Thursday, and on sale at most corner newsstands. *The News* has film and theater listings; *Tiempo Libre* covers galleries, restaurants, dances, museums, and most cultural events. *La Jornada* (3 pesos), a top national newspaper, lists art films showing at the university and elsewhere. *Macho Tips,* available at newsstands along Reforma, has information on gay events in the city. *Ser Gay,* available at newsstands and many gay bars, is less widely distributed but has a more complete listing of gay nightlife options.

Be sure to keep a light rain poncho or umbrella handy; Mexico City's rainy season lasts from May to October and features a daily, hour-long rain storm anywhere from 4-6pm. Otherwise, sunny and moderate weather prevails year-round.

**Federal Tourist Office: Infotur,** Amberes 54 (tel. 525-93-80 or 525-93-82), at Londres in the Zona Rosa. Metro: Insurgentes. Helpful and friendly. Some officials speak English. Maps of the city and Metro on request. Lists of hotels grouped by region and price range. Open daily 9am-9pm. During the same hours, the office operates information booths in *Salas* A and F (tel. 762-67-73) at the airport, and at the TAPO bus station.

**Ministry of Tourism:** Presidente Masaryk 172 (tel. 250-85-55, ext. 11), at Hegel in Col. Polanco. From Metro Polanco (line 7), go south one block down Arquimedes, take a left on Masaryk, and walk 3½ blocks—the building is to your right and easy to miss. Not as well staffed as the Zona Rosa location, but brochures are available on virtually every area of Mexico. Make hotel reservations here. Open Mon.-Fri. 8am-7pm (24-hr. phone lines).

**Department of Tourist Security:** Presidente Masaryk 172 (tel. 250-01-51 or 250-04-93), in Col. Polanco. Calls answered by employees of the Ministry of Tourism, who will respond to complaints, suspected abuses, emergencies, and questions. Report all problems with tourist establishments here. Some English. A very good place to start after a mishap. Open 24 hrs. for phone calls; staffed 8am-8pm.

**Legal Advice: Supervisión General de Servicios a la Comunidad,** Florencia 20 (tel. 625-87-61), in the Zona Rosa, nearest the Metro: Insurgentes (line 1). Call the 24-hr. **hotline** (tel. 625-86-64) if you are the victim of a robbery or accident and need legal advice. Some employees speak English.

**Tourist Card Information: Secretaría de Gobernación, Dirección General de Servicios Migratorios,** Av. Chapultepec 284, 5th floor (tel. 626-72-00 or 206-05-06), in Col. Juárez. Metro Insurgentes (Line 1). Come here to extend the date on your FMT and/or clear up any immigration problems. Open Mon.-Fri. 8am-2pm.

**Police: Secretaría General de Protección y Vialidad** (tel. 256-06-06 or 768-80-44). Dial 08 for the Policía Judicial to report assaults, robberies, crashes, abandoned vehicles, or other emergencies. No English spoken.

**Central Post Office:** Lázaro Cárdenas (tel. 521-73-94), at Tacuba across from Bellas Artes. Open for stamps Mon.-Fri. 8am-6pm, Sat. 9am-8pm, for registered mail Mon.-Fri. 8am-5:30pm, Sat. 9am-4:30pm. For *Lista de Correos* Mon.-Fri. 8am-9pm, Sat. 9am-5pm. Postal museum upstairs. **Postal Code:** 06002.

**Courier Services: DHL,** Reforma 76 (tel. 566-80-28, 24-hr. service at 227-02-99), also at Insurgentes Sur 859 (tel. 592-60-11), in Col. Nápoles. **Federal Express,** Estocolmo 4-2 (tel. 208-67-68 or 208-96-70). Send before 3:30pm for overnight service. Open Mon.-Fri. 8am-6pm.

**Telephones:** Look for glorious **LADATELs** at the airport, bus stations, Metro stations, VIPs Restaurant, and on the street in the Zona Rosa or the Centro.. LADATELs can be used for international collect and credit card calls, and also with a LADATEL card (20 pesos). For those who miss the golden days of the Mexican phone system, long-distance *casetas* are at Airport *Sala* D (open daily 6am-8:30pm), the train station (open Mon.-Sat. 8am-9:30pm, Sun. 9am-3pm), or Central Camionera del Norte (open daily 8am-9pm). **Telephone Code:** 5.

**Telegrams:** Tacuba 8 (tel. 512-21-95), at the Museo Nacional de Arte in the right wing of the building, behind the central post office. Domestic and international service. From the U.S., send through Western Union to **México Central Telégrafos.** Open Mon.-Fri. 8am-midnight, Sat. 9am-12:45pm. To send telegrams by phone, call 709-8500 domestic, 709-8625 international.

**Accommodations Service: Hoteles Asociados,** Airport *Sala* E (tel. 571-59-02 or 571-63-82) and the Central de Autobuses del Norte. Up-to-date information on prices and locations of Mexico City hotels. Give 'em a price range and an area, they'll get you a reservation free of charge. For budget lodgings, be sure to ask for rock-bottom prices. English spoken.

**Embassies:** Will replace lost passports, issue visas, and provide legal assistance. Visa processing can take up to 24 hrs.; bring plenty of ID. If you find yourself in an emergency after hours, try contacting the embassy anyway—you could be in luck. **Australia,** Jaime Balmes 11, 10th floor (tel. 395-99-88), between Ejército Nacional and Homero. Open Mon.-Wed. 8am-5pm, Thurs.-Fri. 8am-2pm. **Austria,** Sierra Tarahumara 420 (tel. 251-16-06). Open Mon.-Fri. 9am-noon. **Belize,** Bernardo de Galvez 215 (tel. 520-12-74). Open Mon.-Fri. 9am-1:30pm. **Canada,** Schiller 529 (tel. 724-79-00), behind the Museum of Anthro. Open Mon.-Fri. 8:30am-2pm. **Costa Rica,** Río Po 113 (tel. 525-77-64 through -66), between Río Lerma and Río Panuco, behind the U.S. embassy. Open Mon.-Fri. 9:30am-4:30pm. **Denmark,** Tres Picos 43 (tel. 255-34-05), north of Bosque de Chapultepec. Open Mon.-Thurs. 9am-3pm, Fri. 9am-12:30pm. **France,** Havre 15 (tel. 533-13-60 through -64), between Hamburgo and Reforma. Open Mon.-Fri. 8:30am-12:30pm. For visas, consulate at Alejandro Dumas 16 (tel. 281-04-47), close to the corner of Campos Eliseos. Open Mon.-Fri. 9am-noon. **Germany,** Byron 737 (tel. 280-54-09 or 280-55-34). Open Mon.-Fri. 9am-noon. **Guatemala,** 1025 Av. Explanada (tel. 540-75-20). Open Mon.-Fri. 10am-1pm. **Honduras,** Alfonso Reyes 220 (tel. 211-57-47), between Saltillo and Ometusco. Open Mon.-Fri. 10am-2pm. **New Zealand,** Homero 229, 8th floor (tel. 250-59-99). Open Mon.-Fri. 9:30am-5:30pm. **Nicaragua,** Payo de Rivera 120 (tel. 540-56-25 or -26), between Virreyes and Monte Atos. Open Mon.-Fri. 9am-3pm. **Norway,** Av. Virreyes 1460 (tel. 540-34-86 or 540-52-20), between Apalachis and Montes Auberne. Open Mon.-Fri. 9am-2pm. **Panama,** Campos Eliseos 111-1 (tel. 250-42-29), between Hegel and Lope de Vega. Open Mon.-Fri. 8:30am-2pm. **Sweden,** Ávila Camacho 1, 6th floor (tel. 540-63-93), at Plaza Comermex. Open Mon.-Fri. 10am-1pm. **Switzerland,** Hamburgo 66, 4th floor (tel. 207-48-20 or 207-11-58). Open 9am-1pm. **U.K.,** Río Lerma 71 (tel. 207-21-49), at Cuauhtémoc. Open 9am-2pm. **U.S.,** Reforma 305 (tel. 211-00-42), at Glorieta Ángel de la Independencia. Open Mon.-Fri. 8:30am-12:45pm for passports and visas, Mon.-Fri. 8:30am-5:30pm for general business. Call after hours and on weekends for emergencies only.

**Currency Exchange:** All banks offer the same exchange rate and usually charge commissions. All banks exchange from 9am-1:30pm, but the wait may be considerable. The nation-wide **ATM** network, **Red Cajeros Compartidos,** takes MC and Visa for cash advances, and many ATMs work with other U.S. system cards. Scores of ATMs are located along Reforma, in the Zona Rosa and Polanco, and in the Centro. Lost or stolen cards can be reported 24 hrs. to 227-27-77. **Citibank,** Reforma 390 (tel. 211-30-30, open 24 hrs.), and **Bank of America,** Reforma 116, 10th-12th floors (tel. 591-00-11), can also help in an emergency. *Casas de cambio* keep longer hours than banks, give better exchange rates, and typically stay open on Saturday. They are concentrated along Reforma and in the Zona Rosa. Most in the Zona Rosa can change a number of non-U.S. currencies. The downtown area, where most sights, restaurants, and accommodations are located, has *casas de cambio* within a short distance of everything. Call the **Asociación Mexicana de Casas de Cambio** (tel. 264-08-84 or 264-08-41) to locate an exchange bureau near you. In the Centro: **Casa de Cambio Euromex,** Venustiano Carranza 64, 3rd floor (tel. 518-41-99), **Casa de Cambio Velasco Sucesores,** Gante 12, local B (tel. 521-50-28). Open Mon.-Fri. 9am-4:30pm. On the south side of the Alameda: **Casa de Cambio Plus,** Juárez 38 (tel. 510-89-53). Open Mon.-Fri. 9am-4pm, Sat. 10am-2pm. On Reforma, near the Monumento a la Revolución/Buenavista: **Casa de Cambio Catorce,** Reforma 51 (tel. 705-24-60).

**American Express:** Reforma 234 (tel. 207-72-82), at Havre in the Zona Rosa. Cashes personal checks and accepts mail for customers only. Money can be wired here. Travel service available. Report lost credit cards to the branch at Patriotismo 635 (tel. 326-26-66), lost traveler's checks to either branch. Open Mon.-Fri. 9am-6pm, Sat. 9am-1pm. In case of a lost **Visa** card, call 625-21-88.

**English Bookstores: American Bookstore,** Madero 25 (tel. 512-72-84), in the Centro with an extensive selection of fiction, guide books, and a matchless Latin American history and politics section. Also a branch at Revolución 1570 (tel. 661-1916) in San Ángel. Both branches open Mon.-Sat. 10am-7pm. **Portico de la Ciudad de México,** Central 124 (tel. 510-96-83 or 280-54-72), at Carranza. Sells

PRACTICAL INFORMATION

English and Spanish books on Mexican history and guides to archaeological sites. Open Mon.-Sat. 10am-7pm. For magazines and newspapers in Spanish, English, French, and German try **La Casa de la Prensa Internacional,** Florencia 57 in the Zona Rosa. Open Mon.-Sat. 8am-9pm. Also popular is the **Librería Gandhi,** M.A. de Quevedo 128 in San Ángel. The **Museo Nacional de Antropología** has a selection of archaeological guides in English (see Sights). The English-language newspaper, *The News,* is sold at most newsstands.

**Supermarket:** Most supermarkets are far from the city center at residential Metro stops. **Bodega,** Serapio Rendón 117, just south of Antonio Caso. Open Mon.-Sat. 8am-9pm, Sun. 9am-8pm. **Aurrera,** 5 blocks north of Puente de Alvaro on Insurgentes. Open daily 9am-9pm. **Comercial Mexicana,** at Corregidora and Correo Mayor, on the southeast side of the Palacio Nacional in the Centro. Open daily 8am-8pm.

**Laundromats:** Near the Monumento a la Revolución: **Lavandería Automática,** Edison 91. Wash or dry 12 pesos per 2¼kg. Full service 25 pesos. Soap 5 pesos. Open Mon.-Sat. 10am-6pm. In the Zona Rosa: **Lavanderet,** Chapultepec 463 (tel. 514-01-06), at Toledo. Wash or dry 12 pesos. Full service 25 pesos. Open Mon.-Sat. 9am-7pm. Most hotels have laundry service or can tell you where to find the nearest facility.

**Ben Franklin Library:** Londres 16 (tel. 211-00-42, ask for the library), at Berlin, 2 blocks southeast of the Cuauhtémoc monument. 75% of the books are in English, including a large variety of newspapers and periodicals. Open Tues.-Thurs. 10am-3pm, Mon. and Fri. 3-7:30pm.

**Cultural and Arts Information: Palacio Nacional de Bellas Artes** (tel. 709-31-113), Juárez and Eje Central, for info. and reservations for Bellas Artes events. Check *Tiempo Libre* and other newsstand publications for city-wide events.

**Rape Crisis: Hospital de Traumatología de Balbuena,** Cecilio Robelo 103 (tel. 552-16-02 or 764-03-39), near Calle Sur, east of Alameda. **Hospital de la Mujer** (tel. 541-46-61). Also call 06 or LOCATEL.

**Gay, Lesbian, and Bisexual Information: Colectivo Sol.** Address inquiries care of Apdo. 13-320 Av. México 13, D.F. 03500. A mainly political group that offers information on upcoming political and social events. Events for gays are publicized at gay bars and clubs and in *Tiempo Libre* and *Ser Gay.*

**Sexually Transmitted Disease Information: Secretaría de Salud** (tel. 277-63-11 or 533-72-04). Open Mon.-Fri. 8am-2pm and 3:30-7pm, Sat. 9am-1pm.

**AIDS Hotline: TELSIDA/CONASIDA,** Florencia 8 (tel. 207-41-43 or 207-40-77), Col. Roma, Metro Cuauhtémoc. Information and help center.

**LOCATEL:** (tel. 658-11-11.) City's official lost-and-found hotline. Call if your car (or friend) is missing. Also information and directions in cases of medical emergencies and information about sports events, etc. Limited English spoken.

**Red Cross:** Ejército Nacional 1032 (tel. 557-57-58 or 557-57-57), in the Col. Polanco. Open 24 hrs. Fastest and most efficient ambulance service.

**Pharmacies: VYR,** San Jerónimo 630 (tel. 595-59-83 or 595-59-98), near Periférico Sur shopping center. Open 24 hrs. More convenient during the day might be **Farmacia El Fénix,** Isabel La Católica 15 (tel. 585-04-55), at 5 de Mayo. Some English spoken. Well-stocked, but will take Spanish prescriptions only. Open Mon.-Sat. 9am-10pm. All big markets have well-stocked pharmacy counters.

**Medical Care:** The **U.S. Embassy** (see above) has a list of doctors in the city, with their specialties, addresses, telephone numbers, and languages spoken. **Dirección General de Servicios Médicos** (tel. 518-51-00) has information on all city hospitals. Open Mon.-Fri. 9am-6pm. Free emergency medical assistance is available at **Procuraduría General de Justicia del D.F.,** Florencia 20 (tel. 525-62-22 or 625-87-61), in the Zona Rosa. For tourists, the **American British Cowdray (ABC) Hospital,** Calle Sur 136 (tel. 227-50-00 or 515-83-59 in an emergency) at Observatorio, Col. Las Américas. No foreign health plans valid, but all major credit cards accepted. Open 24 hrs. **Torre Médica,** José Maria Iglesias 21 (tel. 546-24-85), at Metro Revolución near Monumento de la Revolución.

**Emergency Shelter: Casa de Protección Social** (tel. 530-85-36).

# ■■■ ACCOMMODATIONS

Rooms abound in the Centro (between Alameda and the *zócalo*) and near the Alameda Central, and are sprinkled throughout the area surrounding the Monumento a la Revolución on the Pl. de la República. Rooms priced at 55-65 pesos for one bed and 75-85 pesos for two beds should be clean, have carpeting, a TV, and a telephone (with free local calls). Most budget hotels charge according to the number of beds needed and not per person; beds tend to be large enough for two people. If you don't mind, snuggling is a potential source of substantial savings.

Avoid the filthier sections of the Alameda and any area that makes you feel uncomfortable—there are plenty more from which to choose. Don't be put off by the mid- to high-priced hotels around Insurgentes Sur and Reforma, just northeast of the Zona Rosa tourist belt; they are still inexpensive by U.S. standards. In an attempt to cut down on problems with prostitution, many budget establishments have adopted "No Guests Allowed" policies. Beware of any place where the hotel itself (and not the parking lot) is marked "Hotel Garage." These rooms are frequented by businessfolk "working late at the office" and are designed to allow entry directly from the garage to the room—thus bypassing the lobby altogether in exchange for a sky-high hourly rate. Always ask to look at a room before you accept it; rooms are most likely to be free after check-out time (between noon and 2pm). Hotels whose prices are higher than 65 pesos per single and 75 pesos per double usually accept MC and Visa. AmEx is rarely taken, except at the more expensive Zona Rosa hotels.

For hostel information, call **Villa Deportiva Juvenil** (tel. 525-26-99), which operates the city's lone hostel on the Plaza de la Independencia, near the Zona Rosa (25 pesos per night). They can't guarantee you a spot and often fill up with visiting sports teams competing in the city.

## CENTRO

Situated between the *zócalo* and Alameda Central, this *colonia* is the historic colonial heart of Mexico City. Its hotels are reasonably priced and feel fairly safe, though the throngs disappear as they head home for the night, leaving the streets relatively empty. Nonetheless, the Centro remains the most exciting place to stay and the best base from which to explore the traditional core of one of the world's magnificent cities. Of course, with action inevitably come noise and congestion. If you crave quiet, consider moving west to the Buenavista or Alameda areas.

Many of the hotels listed below are north of Madero and 5 de Mayo, the parallel east-west streets that connect the Alameda with the *zócalo,* and east of Lázaro Cárdenas, the north-south Eje Central that runs one block east of Alameda. Metro stations Bellas Artes and Allende (both Line 2) serve these hotels. The hotels on 5 de Mayo, Isabel la Católica, and Uruguay are better served by Metro stations *zócalo* and Isabel la Católica. Keep in mind that street names change north of Tacuba; Isabel la Católica becomes República de Chile, and Bolívar turns into Allende. Except for Hotel Principal, Hotel Juárez, and Hotel Congreso, the hotels listed below accept MasterCard and Visa.

**Hotel Antillas,** Belisario Domínguez 34 (tel. 526-56-74 through -79), between Allende and República de Chile. The colonial exterior promises a history-drenched grandeur: the dim interior does not disappoint. The eager staff and clean bathrooms promise a relaxing stay, complete with TVs, bottled water, and lounge areas. Singles 80 pesos. Doubles 115 pesos.

**Hotel Atlanta,** Belisario Domínguez 31 (tel. 518-12-00 and 518-12-03), at Allende. The wood-paneled lobby leads into carpeted and homey rooms. Enjoy the southern hospitality: TV, phone, and refreshingly uncramped bathrooms. Singles 60 pesos. Doubles 85 pesos.

**Hotel Principal,** Bolívar 29 (tel. 521-13-33), by the Parilla Leonesa restaurant. Friendly staff bustles about under the arched brick ceiling. Tan rooms have a balcony, mirror, TV, telephone, and bottled water. Singles with communal bath 35 pesos, with private bath 65 pesos. Doubles 75 pesos.

**Hotel Monte Carlo,** Uruguay 69 (tel. 521-25-59), between Metro Isabel la Católica and Metro Allende. The relaxing lounge areas and the top-floor skylight are popular with guests. Large, colorful rooms with wooden doors sometimes offer balconies with street views. Clean bathrooms. Singles 70 pesos. Doubles 75 pesos.

**Hotel Florida,** Belisario Domínguez 57 (tel. 521-77-64 or 521-76-04), between Allende and República de Chile. Receptionists are hard to catch. Clean, blue-green rooms have TV, radio, phone, and (wow!) a bidet. Some noise can be heard from the street below. Singles 55 pesos. Doubles 60 pesos.

**Hotel Isabel,** Isabel la Católica 63 (tel. 518-12-13 through -17), between El Salvador and Uruguay. With dull gray-and-brown carpets, neither the large foyer nor the king-sized rooms are particularly attractive. On the up side: a bathtub, huge chest of drawers, TV, bottled water, and cleanliness. Singles 75 pesos. Double 90 pesos.

**Hotel Juárez,** Cerrada de 5 de Mayo 17 (tel. 512-69-29), between Isabel la Católica and Palma. Location, location, location—you can't get much closer to the action. Rooms have a drab color scheme, but the carpeting, private bathroom, telephone, and TV make for an enjoyable stay. Good ole' Benito would be proud. Singles 65 pesos. Doubles 75 pesos.

## ALAMEDA CENTRAL

Although the painfully protracted construction of Metro Line 8 is virtually at an end, scaffolding, clouds of dust, and somewhat seedy activity have enshrouded the Alameda in the ever-present problems of big city life. The expansive park itself is always throbbing with activity, and should present no problem to either men or women. But the greenery fades over the course of a few blocks, making way for dirt and danger. Women will feel safer in other parts of the city.

**Hotel Hidalgo,** Santa Veracruz 37 (tel. 521-87-71 through -77), just north of the Alameda. Metro: Bellas Artes (line 3). Located up the 2 de Abril walkway to the left of Teatro Hidalgo. The art deco cushions throughout the hallways could easily serve double duty as earthquake pads; this place survived the '85 earthquake. Wood trim, carpet, and monogrammed sheets top off the clean rooms, while artwork makes up for the lack of a view. Adjoining restaurant, TVs, phones, and laundry service. Singles 105 pesos. Doubles 130 pesos.

**Hotel Manolo Primero,** Luis Moya 111 (tel. 521-77-09), just north of Arcos de Belén, three blocks west of the Salto del Agua Metro stop (line 1). Spacious blue hallways and the cavernous lobby lead into large bathrooms with enormous full-length mirrors. The big blue carpets and paintings of the wide-open fields add a small touch of class to an otherwise huge experience. Rooms include (what else?) big-screen TVs. Singles and doubles 80 pesos.

**Hotel Conde,** Pescaditos 15 (tel. 521-10-84), at Revillagigedo. Exit the Metro at Juárez (Line 1), follow Artículo 123 to Revillagigedo, then take a right and walk 3 blocks. Sure, you're not near any awe-inspiring sights, four-star restaurants, or historical monuments. But despite the location and the slightly worn stairways, the blue-green color scheme nearly matches, bathrooms boast both toilets and bidets, and the bottled water promises a healthy stay. Singles and doubles 70 pesos.

## NEAR THE MONUMENTO A LA REVOLUCIÓN/ BUENAVISTA

Rooms near the Monumento a la Revolución offer more peace and quiet and cost less than their counterparts in the Centro or the Alameda, mainly because there are few historical sites here of interest to tourists, and because few people have moved back since the area was heavily damaged in the 1985 quake. As a result, budget travelers tend to congregate here, particularly in the hotels on Mariscal and Edison. Metro Revolución serves those hotels south of Puente de Alvarado/Hidalgo, while Metro Guerrero serves those to the north near the train station.

**Casa de Los Amigos,** Ignacio Mariscal 132 (tel. 705-05-21 or 705-06-46), across from Gran Hotel Texas. Metro: Revolución. Originally the home and studio of Mexican painter José Clemente Orozco, the House of Friends is a Quaker-run guest house for both tourists and social activists. Not a hostel but a place with its own character, international atmosphere, and reasonable requirements. The staff will give you an information sheet when you arrive so that you understand the purpose of the *casa* and agree to respect their cooperative atmosphere. Friendly, helpful, bilingual staff. Kitchen facilities. Will hold mail. 2-day minimum stay, 15-day maximum stay. Key deposit 10 pesos. Breakfast 7 pesos. Dorm rooms 30 pesos. Private rooms 45 pesos. Doubles 65-70 pesos.

**Hotel Oxford,** Ignacio Mariscal 67 (tel. 566-05-00), at Alcázar, next to the small park. Metro: Revolución. Beyond the dark lounge are bright hallways and large rooms, many of which offer a great view of the nearby park. Clean and inviting bathrooms with huge sinks to do laundry in. TV, telephone, and bottled water included. Singles 50 pesos. Doubles 80 pesos.

**Hotel Londres,** Plaza Buenavista 5 (tel. 705-09-10 or 705-07-85), off Buenavista, three blocks south of the train station, two blocks north of Puente de Alvarado. Metro: Guerrero. Rooms are simple and clean, with small bathrooms. Friendly staff. Lush greenery and a fountain—a veritable garden—occupy a beautifully tiled central courtyard. Singles 48 pesos. Doubles 94 pesos. Visa, MC accepted.

**Hotel Yale,** Mosqueta 200 (tel. 591-15-45 or 591-14-88), between Zaragoza and Guerrero, to the left as you exit the train station. Metro: Guerrero. This New Haven of a hotel has a bubbling fountain to comfort the blue traveler. Provides a welcome refuge from the heavy construction on Mosqueta, with recently remodeled rooms, full-length mirrors, TVs, and (surprise) orange furniture that doesn't quite match. Ask for Jorge Herbert Walker. Singles 60 pesos. Doubles 95 pesos. No new taxes.

## NEAR THE BUS STATIONS

Few good budget accommodations are located in the vicinity of any of Mexico City's four principal bus stations. For travelers just passing through Mexico City who arrive at the **Central de Autobuses del Norte** (northern station), **Hotel Acuario,** Poniente 112 #100 (tel. 587-26-77), offers medium-quality rooms in a very low-quality neighborhood. Use the subway tunnel to pass under the road, walk left for two blocks, make a right onto Poniente, and go west for half a block. A strict "no guest" policy ensures a good night's sleep (singles 60 pesos; doubles 90 pesos). For a pricier but definitely more comfy option, **Hotel Brasilia,** Av. de los 100 Mts. 4823 (tel. 587-85-77), is three blocks to the left along the main thoroughfare as you exit the bus station. It's all you could possibly expect in a major U.S. chain, and more (singles 110 pesos; doubles 150 pesos). Near the **Terminal de Autobuses Sur** (southern station), the closest place is **Hotel Montreal,** Calzada de Tlalpán 2073 (tel. 689-00-11), at the corner of Quevedo. Exit the bus station to the right, follow the train tracks up three blocks, and cross the highway on the pedestrian bridge. Rooms, the cheapest in the general area, are the ultimate honeymoon spot, complete with mirrors galore, complimentary condoms, and the adult channel (singles 120 pesos; doubles 170 pesos). If you're arriving at the **Terminal de Autobuses de Pasajeros de Oriente** (eastern station), head to the *centro* via the Metro. And if you find yourself at the **Terminal del Autobuses del Poniete** (western station), swing over to the Tacubaya Metro stop for the nearest hotels.

# ■■■ FOOD

The teeming masses that inhabit Mexico City demand an unparalleled quantity and diversity of edibles, a demand readily met by the apparently equal number of stores, stands, restaurants, and vendors. The wide range of choices is matched only by the disparity in cleanliness; as always, no matter how delicious that beef tongue in vinegar dressing looks, inspect it carefully before popping it into your mouth.

Culinary options fall into six basic categories: the very cheap (and very risky) vendor stalls scattered about the streets; fast, inexpensive, and generally safe *taquerías;* slightly more formal *cafeterías;* more pricey and decorous Mexican restaurants; locally popular North-Americanized diners; and expensive international fare. In addition, U.S. fast-food chains mass-produce predictable fare for the timid palate. **VIPs** offers 60 commercialized Denny's-like eateries throughout the D.F. If you're preparing your own food, **Conasupos** supermarkets stock almost anything you could need; if you can't find what you want, head to **La Merced** (the market). With all of the above, exercise caution when dealing with ice and freshly washed fruits and vegetables. Likewise, a taste for well-done meat is not a bad thing to acquire.

Soda is sold at every corner. *Agua mineral* means mineral water, *sidral* is a great carbonated apple drink, and *refrescos* are your standard soda pops. Cans and bottles are customarily recycled, and patrons pay extra for the privilege of keeping them. Avoid a deposit, however, by imitating the locals and taking your drink in a plastic bag (*bolsa*) with straw (*popote*), to go.

## CENTRO

When it comes to eats, the historic downtown area of Mexico City offers a wide selection and super-low prices. Scattered between the colonial structures are slick U.S. fast-food establishments, expansive *cafeterías*, and countless small eateries offering inexpensive tacos, *tortas*, and other staples. If you're in search of a cheap, filling *comida corrida*, the Centro will not disappoint.

**Café Tacuba,** Tacuba 28 (tel. 518-49-50), at Allende Metro stop. Mexican cuisine and murals depicting scenes of the colonial aristocracy. A bastion of serenity in the heart of downtown since 1912. Beef tongue with vinegar dressing 36 pesos. *Comida corrida* 35 pesos. MC, Visa accepted. Open daily 8am-11:30pm.

**Comedor Vegetariano,** Motolina 315, 2nd floor (tel. 512-65-75). A true find. Since 1937, this yellow Quixote-themed restaurant has welcomed patrons to its balcony tables. The fruit buffet table looks scrumptious, and the filling *comida corrida* (16 pesos) does wonders for an empty stomach. Open Mon.-Fri. 1-6pm.

**Restaurante El Vegetariano,** Filomeno Mata 13 (tel. 510-01-13), between 5 de Mayo and Madero. The sunshine-yellow decor and nature photographs are appropriate for this happy, healthy eatery. Spaghetti with mushroom sauce 15 pesos, spinach salad 23 pesos. MC, Visa accepted. Open Mon.-Sat. 8am-8pm.

**Pastelería La Ideal,** 16 de Septiembre 14, 1 block east of Cárdenas. Lovers of all that is baked and good come for the food and stay for the fun. 4 huge sections, one each for plain bread, cakes, pies, and pastries. A battalion of towering wedding cakes, some of which tower over 10 feet high. Open daily 7am-10pm.

**Restaurant Danubio,** Uruguay 3, just east of Lázaro Cárdenas. Stately seafood joint boasts its own coat-of-arms and hefty price tags. Famous artsy types have left their scribbling framed on the walls. Pricey entrees big enough to feed 2—stick to the 5-course *comida corrida* 45 pesos. Open daily 1-10pm for a la carte.

**Super Soya,** Tacuba 40. A wildly colorful conglomeration of a grocery store, café, diner, and yogurt stand that has it all—for under 7 pesos. Vegetarian pizzas 5 pesos, *tacos de guisado* 3.50 pesos. Open daily 9am-9pm.

## ZONA ROSA

The myth: only moneyed tourists eat in the Zona Rosa. The reality: many area eateries cater chiefly to clerks from the scores of surrounding office buildings. Source of the misconception: the city's most expensive restaurants, serving everything from international cuisine to traditional Mexican cooking, are located in the Zona Rosa.

The street vendors which are crammed into every other inch of Mexican sidewalk are sparse, but the Zona Rosa also has more fast-food joints than any other area of the city. If you're more interested in the Zona Rosa's slick party atmosphere than in filling your stomach, skip dinner and settle for a drawn-out evening appetizer.

**La Bonne Cuisine,** Londres 49B (tel. 511-19-18), at Nopales, east of Insurgentes. This quasi-French-style café and its milieu of old U.S. movie posters make for an enchanting escape from the bustling Zona Rosa. Daily special 16 pesos, *crepas de pollo a la poblana* 16.50 pesos. Pay at the cashier. Open Mon.-Sat. 1-6pm.

FOOD

**La Luna,** Oslo 11, on the narrow walkway between Niza and Copenhagne. Fresh flowers grace every table in this intimate, stark-white restaurant. At odd times, the restaurant converts to a drinks-only café. The 10-peso *comida corrida* includes soup, 2 entrees (one small, one large), and beverage. Open daily 8am-10pm.

**Kobá-ich,** Londres 136A (tel. 208-57-91). Yucateca cuisine in pleasant wooden sur-roundings. The owner heads back to the Yucatán every year to maintain his dishes' authenticity. The house specialty, *chamorro horneado al pibil* runs 27 pesos. Other dishes 17-23-pesos. Open Mon.-Sat. 8am-10pm.

**Restaurante Vegetariano Las Fuentes,** Río Panuco 127 (tel. 207-64-14). Follow Río Tiber north past Reforma for two blocks. Lush with greenery and complete with murals depicting pre-colonial Mexican history. International vegetarian fare; *jitomate relleno* 16 pesos. Credit cards accepted. Open daily 8am-6pm.

**Fonda Don Lucas,** Londres 178-C (tel. 511-20-67), after the crossing with Floren-cia. Young executives network and preen in the mirrors that line the walls. Come early for more space and faster service. *Económica* menu 12 pesos, *ejecutivo* 15 pesos. Both include 3 dishes and dessert. Beer 3-4 pesos. Open Mon.-Fri. 1-5pm.

**Restaurant Vegetariano "Karl"** (tel. 525-26-15), Amberes near Londres. Even the grains of wheat are colorful pastel shades. A trendy option for Mexican yuppies. Try the *Arnold Schwarzenegger* (it's not a tumor, it's bananas and rum), 12 pesos. Breakfast 8am-12:30pm. All-you-can-eat buffet 1-8pm, 22 pesos.

**Salón de Té Auseba,** Hamburgo 159-B (tel. 511-37-69), near Florencia. Comfort-able tea-room pushes calories on a quiet, upper-class clientele. A glass case shows off pastries, cakes, and pies (10-14 pesos). A great place to sit out a rainshower. 13 varieties of tea 5.50 pesos. Open Mon.-Sat. 9am-10pm, Sun. 11am-10:30pm.

## ALAMEDA CENTRAL

The convivial atmosphere that permeates the Alameda carries over to the various restaurants that pepper the area. Gone is the stuffy elitism of the Zona Rosa and the frenetic pace of the Centro. Instead, you'll find plenty of good, cheap, back-to-basics eateries in the Alameda, each offering a hearty meal, a hearty handshake, and a big ole' platter of food.

**Fonda Santa Anita,** Humboldt 48 (tel. 518-46-09). From the Hidalgo Metro stop (Line 2), go one block south to Juárez, then two blocks west to the unlabeled Humboldt. It's 2 blocks south down Humboldt. Friendly service and tasty por-tions; this restaurant has represented Mexico in 5 World's Fairs. Mexican handi-crafts draped across the ceiling add a touch of home. Enormous *comida corrida* 18.50 pesos. Most credit cards. Open Mon.-Fri. 1:30-9pm.

**Taquería Tlaquepaque,** Independencia 4 (tel. 521-30-82), just west of Cárdenas. Watch the row of chefs behind the grill brandish their sharpened knives under blinding heat lamps and rapidly churn out *ricos tacos*. Three tacos 4.50-7.50 pesos; most specialties (steak, etc.) under 15 pesos. Open daily 9am-3am.

**Centro Naturista de México,** Dolores 10 (tel. 512-53-77), ½ block south of Juárez near the southeast corner of the park, under the big yin 'n' yang. Devour hearty portions in a cafeteria-style vegetarian/egalitarian utopia. Don't be afraid to squeeze in at the table—there's room for all, my sister. *Comida corrida* 12-14 pesos. Open daily 12:30-5:30pm. Adjoining store open daily 11am-7pm.

## NEAR THE MONUMENTO A LA REVOLUCIÓN

Without many affluent residents or big tourist draws, this area lacks the snazzy inter-national cuisine of other areas. Instead, homey cafés, *torterías,* and *taquerías* abound. For hearty portions and low prices, this is your spot.

**La Taberna,** Arriaga at Ignacio Mariscal, next to Hotel Pennsylvania. Below street level, this restaurant delivers that cozy Italian feel. The service is fast, the tables checkered, and the *comida corrida* cheap. 3 daily menus (14, 17, and 22 pesos) include 5 courses, pizza, and dessert. Visa, MC accepted. Open Mon.-Sat. 1-10pm.

**Restaurant Samy's,** Ignacio Mariscal 42 (tel. 591-11-00). A cool and casual restau-rant tucked behind the colorless façades. The tie-wielding business-class clientele

FOOD

is soothed by soft rock (Elton John) and even softer prices (Italian spaghetti for 9 pesos). 5-course *comida corrida* 14 pesos. Open Mon.-Fri. 8am-6pm.

**Restaurant La Pizza** (tel. 535-55-01), Puente de Alvarado at Buenavista. Look past the iron grating; the interior is vibrant and colorful. Decorating the wood panel-ing are pictures of dozens of mouth-watering entrees. The 2nd-floor balcony offers a relaxing place for a conversation. Small pizzas start at 19 pesos. *Menú del día* (16 pesos) includes two slices, pasta, and salad. Open Mon.-Fri. 1-11pm.

## NEAR CHAPULTEPEC

The immediate vicinity of the Bosque de Chapultepec is cluttered with vendors and small restaurants offering the remarkably popular and remarkably mundane *torta*. A bit farther east, however, one can find a slew of restaurants guaranteed to please even the most fickle palate. The eateries on Cozumel are within walking distance of the Sevilla Metro station; Cozumel is just around the corner from the southern *sal-ida*. The entrance to the park lies five long blocks west along Av. Chapultepec.

**Las Palomas Fonda,** Cozumel 37 (tel. 286-30-54), in Col. Roma just north of Durango. As if the *mariachis* were not entertaining enough, the food is delicious and the prices reasonable. Exotic plants and flowers add that chic touch. *Carne asada* 31 pesos. Open Mon.-Fri. 1:30-11pm, Sat.-Sun. 1:30-6:30pm.

**Centro Macrobiótico Tao,** Cozumel 76 (tel. 211-46-41), in Col. Roma south of Colima on the east side of the street. No steak and potatoes here. Everything is all natural, and the adjoining store is a haven for the utterly health-conscious: diet books, spices, and breads line the walls. The New Age music and floor seating are perfect for the latent hippie in all of us. Most vegetarian entrees run 17-24 pesos. Open daily 1:30-4:30pm. Store open 10am-6pm.

**Los Sauces,** Avenida Chapultepec 530, at the corner of Acapulco Roma, 1½ blocks east of the Chapultepec Metro stop. Unique tiled bar/grill and walls cluttered with pictures of Mexican politicians and stars. 3.50-peso taco special, 11.50-peso house specialties—try the *alambre con queso*. Open daily 10am-10pm.

## COYOACÁN

The southern suburb of Coyoacán attracts students, young couples, and literati to its complement of elegant restaurants and fine dining. Coyoacán is the birthplace of many Mexican politicians and presidents, and its restaurants cater to an upper-class clientele. Outdoor cafés and ice cream shops fill the colonial buildings that line the cobbled streets. You'll find menu items you don't usually see in downtown Mexico City: if you crave brie, cheesecake, or pesto, spend the afternoon in these 'burbs.

**Café El Parnaso,** Carrillo Puerto 2, at Jardín Centenario across from the cathedral. Outdoor café, book and record store, and art gallery—all in one prime locale on the plaza's edge. Sip coffee and compose free verse in tribute to the mocha cake, or cheesecake with strawberries (12-16 pesos). Open daily 8:30am-10:30pm.

**Restaurante los Balcones,** Allende 15-A (tel. 554-79-61), across from the north-east corner of Pl. Hidalgo. A less stuffy atmosphere than Coyoacán's other offer-ings. Red-and-white checkered tablecloths and hanging plants valiantly try to lend credibility to the semi-Italian theme. Great pizza (18-26 pesos). Open 8am-11pm.

**El Morral,** Allende 2 (tel. 554-02-98), diagonally across the street from Los Bal-cones. Wins points for aesthetics—beautifully tiled walls, artwork, and a glass roof, though the flashing cross almost goes over the top. Somewhat upscale, but the clientele likes it that way. Glamorous five-course *comida corrida* 38 pesos, but many items still hover in the teens. Open daily 7:30am-8:30pm.

## SAN ÁNGEL

The chic restaurants and *típico* taco stands of San Ángel pack 'em in, especially on Saturdays, when crowds of well-to-do tourists and Mexicans flock to the booths of overpriced art in the Bazaar Sábado. If you want to dine in style, and don't mind dropping lots of pesos, the restaurants on the Plaza San Jacinto won't disappoint.

**Restaurante Hasti Bhawan: La Casona del Elefante,** Pl. San Jacinto 9 (tel. 616-22-08). Hindustani ambiance: swaying palm trees, authentic sculpture and paintings, kingly South Asian chairs, and elephant-shaped planters. Scrumptious Indo-Thai chicken 26 pesos, vegetarian platter 24 pesos. Treat yourself to a *lassi,* a thick yogurt drink (7 pesos) or *pakoras* or *samosas* 7 pesos. Live jazz Thurs. 9pm-midnight, Fri.-Sat. until 1am. Open Tues.-Sat. noon-midnight, Sun. 1-6pm.

**El Rincón de La Lechuza,** Miguel Ángel de Quevedo 34 (tel. 661-59-11), straight down Quevedo from the same Metro stop, just before the Parque de la Bombilla. Joyfully crowded. Clay owls dot the western walls in a bright yellow interior. Tasty tacos 6.50-15.50 pesos, casseroles prepared with meat imported from New Zealand, 20-27 pesos, *menú del día* 17.50 pesos. Open Mon.-Thurs. 1pm-1am, Fri.-Sat. 1pm-2am, Sun. 1pm-midnight.

# ■■■ SIGHTS

It would be impossible to find an appetite which can't be satiated by Mexico City's incredibly diverse range of sights and attractions. While there are no beaches or intact Mayan temples here, there's a little bit of just about everything else. For a well-rounded picture of Mexico City's sights, you'll need to spend at least 10 days in the metropolis. If you like exploring with a guide, **Promoción Social del Centro Historic,** Chile 8 (tel. 510-25-41, ext. 1499), sponsors free walking tours in English, a different one each Sunday. Call for the week's destination and meeting spot.

## CENTRO

The heart of Mexico City, the Centro is, at least in some ways, at the heart of the Republic as well. The Centro's most impressive structures—the Palacio Nacional and the Catedral Metropolitana—lord over the national consciousness and highlight the uneasy truce that has been struck throughout the country between indigenous and European ways of life. Note, for instance, the proximity of the Aztec pyramids to the cathedral, which has attracted the faith of so many *indígenas,* and the Palacio Nacional, from which the modern state is run.

The sights described in this section are divided into those east, north, and south of the *zócalo.* To reach the *zócalo* by Metro, take Line 2 to Zócalo. The station's entrance sits on the east side of the square, in front of the Palacio Nacional. The Catedral Metropolitana lies to the north, the Federal District offices to the south, and the Suprema Corte de Justicia to the southeast. For an intelligently annotated checklist of every sight in the *Centro,* get a copy of the *Historic Center of the City of Mexico* from the map's publisher, SAC BE, Apdo. 22-315, 14000 México, D.F. *The Official Guide to Mexico City's Historic Center,* available in the shops of the Museum of Anthropology, Palacio de Bellas Artes, and major English-language bookstores (35-45 pesos) is another excellent and detailed source of information.

### The Zócalo

Officially the **Plaza de la Constitución,** the *zócalo* is the principal square of Mexico City. Now surrounded by imposing colonial monuments, the square was once the nucleus of the Aztec capital **Tenochtitlán.** Cortés's men razed the city; atop the ruins they built the power center from which they would rule New Spain. Stones from the destroyed city were used to construct Spanish churches and government buildings. To the southwest of the Templo Mayor (the Aztecs' principal place of worship, which they called Teocalli) was the Aztec marketplace and major square. Cortés paved this expanse with stones from the main pyramid, calling it Plaza de Armas or Plaza Real. The Plaza went up in flames during the riots of 1692; it was leveled and reorganized in 1790 in accord with Moorish design principles, which stressed the importance of fountains to a structure's appearance. During rebuilding, two important objects were unearthed: a statue of Coatlicue (deity of life and death) and Piedra del Sol ("Stone of the Sun," the Aztec calendar). This second stone spent nearly a century leaning quietly against the cathedral's west side before the old Museo Nacional claimed it in 1885.

The square became the Plaza de la Constitución in 1812 when the representative assembly of the viceroyalty adopted the liberal Constitución de Cádiz here to protest Napoleon Bonaparte's occupation of Spain. This act of rebellion fueled the turmoil that eventually led to Mexico's independence. In 1843, the dictator Santa Ana destroyed the Mercado del Parián and ordered that a monument to independence be constructed in the center of the square. Only the monument's *zócalo* (pedestal) was in place when the project was abandoned. The citizens of Mexico began to refer to the square as *el zócalo,* which has become the generic name for the central plazas which mark the Republic's cities and towns.

These days, the *zócalo* is filled with protesting groups, *artesanías,* street artists, and gaping tourists. Labor rallies and the booming megaphones of quasi-political organizations electrify the plaza. Street vendors, selling everything from hard liquor to holy water line the outskirts of the square. Just east of the Catedral Metropolitana, a group of Mexican youth recreates their indigenous heritage by performing a traditional Aztec dance—yet upon taking a break, they crank up the Pearl Jam on their boomboxes, just like teenagers 'round the world. Above all the politics, commerce, and culture, the Mexican flag, lowered in a solemn and interesting ceremony every day at 6pm, looms large.

## East of the Zócalo

### Palacio Nacional

Aztec ruler Moctezuma II built a new palace, called the "New Houses," just south of the Teocalli. The Spaniards obliterated it, and in 1529 the King of Spain granted the land to Fernando Cortés, who proceeded to erect a home for himself there. Designed by architects Rodrigo de Pontecillas and Juan Rodríguez, the building was constructed by *indígena* slave laborers using stones from Moctezuma's palace. In 1562, the King of Spain bought back the house from Don Martín Cortés (illegitimate son of the conquistador) so as to make it the palace of the king's viceroys. The palace was destroyed during the Riot of 1692 and rebuilt a year later with stones from the original building. Subsequent modifications have given the building a Baroque character, although vestiges of earlier styles remain.

Now called the **Palacio Nacional de México** (tel. 512-20-60), the building occupies the entire east side of the *zócalo,* and is bounded on the north and south by Moneda and Corregidora respectively. Chief executive center of the Republic, the Palacio houses monumental murals and a museum in honor of Benito Juárez.

It took Diego Rivera from 1929 to 1951 to sketch and paint the **frescoes** on the Palacio's western and northern walls. *Mexico Through the Centuries,* one of his most famous works, is on the west wall of the Palacio at the top of the grand staircase. The mural is divided into eight smaller scenes, each of which depicts an event in the social history of Mexico. Each of the five arches at the top of the mural deals with the Mexican nation—from its independence in 1810 up to the Mexican Revolution in 1910. Near the bottom of the mural are portrayed scenes of the founding of Tenochtitlán in 1325 through its fall and rule by the Spanish colonists. To the left and right of this grand central mural are two other famous works by Rivera. Covering the southern portion of the palace's western wall, *La Lucha de las Clases* (The Class Struggle) depicts Mexican *campesinos* next to workers from around the world. Opposite it on the northern wall is a work entitled *La Leyenda de Quetzalcóatl,* which illustrates the life of the legendary Toltec priest-king who conquered the Mayan people, and ruled over the Yucatán Peninsula before fleeing his kingdom. The murals on the second floor of the palace continue the dramatic history lesson. On the east wall, *El Desembarco en Veracruz* graphically depicts the injustices of the slave trade. Three murals relate the achievements of the Tarascan, Zapotec, and Totonac civilizations. Other murals depict the evolution of corn, the harvesting of cacao, and the processes by which *maguey* is harvested and used in tequila production. *La Gran Tenochtitlán* is dominated by the Mercado de Tlatelolco and filled out with the Temple of Tlatelolco, the center of Tenochtitlán, and the volcanoes Popocatépetl (Smoking Mountain) and Itzaccíhuatl (Sleeping Woman). These murals remain unfinished to this day—a result of Rivera's age and pressing political agendas. Guides to the murals and postcards are sold at the base of the central staircase (20 pesos), but are sometimes unavailable. Guided tours (Mon.-Fri. 10am-4pm) are available for 45 pesos. Exercise your budget-travel savvy and discreetly join (for free) a tour that has already begun.

The Palacio also contains the **Bell of Dolores,** which was brought to the capital in 1896 from Dolores Hidalgo in Guanajuato state. It can be seen from outside, at the top of the Palacio's Baroque façade. Miguel Hidalgo rang this bell on September 16, 1810, calling Mexicans to fight for their independence. Every year on that date it rings in memory of the occasion, when the Mexican President repeats the words once shouted by the father of independence (Palacio open daily 8am-6pm).

The museum dedicated to Mexico's most revered president, Benito Juárez, has been closed for the past three years for renovations, but is expected to reopen sometime in the late fall of 1995. At the entrance to the **Museo Recinto Homenaje a Benito Juárez** (tel. 522-56-46), on the first floor, is a statue of Juárez that is supposedly cast from the bronze of enemy ammunition used in the War of Reform. The museum, located in the very room in which he died on the Palacio's second floor, contains furniture from Juárez's house, some personal belongings, and a chilling death mask cast before his body had even cooled. In the back room is Juárez's personal library, which houses more than 3000 documents from the reform years. To reach the museum, enter through the northern door of the palace, or walk north through the palace's central court (open Tues.-Fri. 9am-7:30pm; free). While the museum is still closed, a temporary display housing many of these articles is located at Hidalgo 79, near the Alameda.

On the east side of the Palacio's second floor is the **Cámara de Dipuestos,** which served as a legislative chamber for a few years after the drafting of the 1857 constitution. The dark ante-chamber displays an original 1857 constitution and is graced by the stern faces of politicians who have been important to the history of the Republic. You'll hear these names again and again in every city in the nation; try matching the faces to street names (open Mon.-Fri. 9am-8pm).

Connected to the palace is the **Museo Nacional de las Culturas,** Moneda 13 (tel. 512-74-52 or 542-01-87), housed in Mexico City's former mint. The museum takes a serious look at the lives of various ethnic groups from around the world—peruse the impressive collection of utensils and masks from African countries. In the main lobby sits the enrapturing mural *Revolución* by Rufino Tamayo, which depicts the Mexican Revolution (open Tues.-Sat. 9:30am-5:45pm, Sun. 9am-3:45pm).

### Other Sights

**La Merced,** Circunvalación at Anaya east of the *zócalo,* or at Metro Merced on Line 2 (turn left out of the subway's eastern exit), is the largest food market of its kind in the world. Farmers from all over Mexico sell their goods here. The fruit section alone covers a large fraction of the 600 square blocks. Here you'll find fruits of every sort imaginable—papayas, homegrown litchi nuts, *mameyes* from Tabasco, mangos, nine different kinds of *plátanos,* hot tamales, and two full blocks of assorted chiles. Indigenous foods such as fried turtles, steamed chicken intestines, *charales*—corn husks stuffed with shiners—and steamed crayfish abound. Die of happiness among displays of *dulces* (candies) that stretch for five blocks; each vendor's stall displays over 300 kinds.

Near the market, on the corner of Manzanares and Circunvalación, is **El Señor de la Humilidad,** which measures 6m by 9m, seats 20 thin people, and is reputed to be the smallest church in the world. With a bright pink exterior and an interior altar inlaid with gold and silver, this symbol of humility (however small it is) provides quite a bit of bang for the buck (open daily 9am-8pm). On the corner of Calle de la Santísima and Zapata is the exquisitely ornamented **Templo de la Santísima.** Finished in 1783, the church is one of Mexico City's most important examples of the Churrigueresque style. Avoid the church after dusk; the *templo* is lit but not well-patrolled (open daily 7am-1pm and 5-8pm).

## North of the Zócalo

### Catedral Metropolitana

In the wake of Cortés's military triumphs, a land devoted to Quetzalcóatl, Tlaloc, and Huitzilopochtli became a New World stronghold of Christianity. Cortés built Mexico's first cathedral in 1524; the third cathedral in the land was the **Catedral Metropolitana** (tel. 521-76-37), the massive structure on the north side of the *zócalo,* begun in 1544. The 109m-long and 54m-wide cruciform cathedral encompasses the architectural styles of three centuries. Between 1544 and 1573, architect Claudio Arciniega directed the construction of the cathedral, modeling it after the one in Sevilla, Spain. Though it was dedicated in the middle of the 17th century, the Catedral Metropolitana wasn't finished until 1813. In that year, Manuel Tolsá completed the great central dome, the façade, and the statues of Faith, Hope, and Charity which crown the clock tower.

The cathedral has several attached annexes. The main annex, with its door to the left of the cathedral, holds the **Altar de Perdón** (Forgiveness), a replica of a Churrigueresque altarpiece built by Jerónimo de Balbás between 1731 and 1736 and destroyed by fire in 1967. The cedar interior of the choir gallery, constructed in 1695 by Juan de Rojas, is decorated with an elegant grille of gold, silver, and bronze. Juan Correa's murals of the coronation of Mary, St. Michael's slaying of the dragon, and the triumphant entrance of Jesus into Jerusalem cover the sacristy's walls. Cristóbal de Villalpando painted the two other grand murals in this section, *La Concepción Imaculada* and *El Triunfo de la Iglesia.* Of the cathedral's many altars, one of the most magnificent is Balbás's Churrigueresque **Altar de los Reyes** (Kings), which is dedicated to those kings who were also saints. In the annex holding the Altar de Perdón, there are 14 *capillas* (chapels) dedicated to saints. Two chapels near the entrance honor Mexico's patron, the Virgin of Guadalupe.

The eastern annex holds the **Sagrario Metropolitano** (sanctuary), closed to the public as of the summer of 1995 because its floor is heavily damaged from sinking into the ground. Primarily reserved for baptisms and confirmations, the Sagrario holds six chapels, with one main and two lateral altars. Designed by the great Churrigueresque architect Lorenzo Rodríguez, the Sagrario was built between 1749 and 1768. Since then, its façades have been copied in thousands of Mexican churches. Left of center are statues of the 12 apostles; to the right, the 12 prophets. In the center, above the door, are statues of St. John and, above him, St. Joseph. Elaborate reliefs decorate the whole façade, and the Virtues crown the structure.

Unfortunately, the splendor of the cathedral is occluded by the green support structures constructed to stem the sinking of the temple into the ground. To make matters worse, ongoing renovations mean scaffolding and partitions occasionally obscure parts of the exterior. Just outside the church doors are vendors hawking every sort of religious paraphenalia imaginable, as well as post cards, toy airplanes, and bottles of orange juice (open daily 8:30am-8pm; the schedule for mass is posted on the door farthest west).

### Templo Mayor (Teocalli)

North of the *zócalo*'s northeast corner, a pool of water laps at a brass model of the Aztec capital, Tenochtitlán. At the center of this city was a great square surrounded by walls 550m long. According to myth, the city was the first place the Aztecs could call home, arriving at this spot after wandering for hundreds of years, driven by the hummingbird god Huitzilopochtli. When Tenoch, the high-priest, spied an eagle perched on a cactus, he took it as a sign that the Aztecs' wandering was over; the Templo Mayor, or Teocalli, was built on the spot where Tenoch saw the eagle. On the corner of Seminario and República de Guatemala, and a few meters north of the brass model, Teocalli is the major excavated archaeological site in Mexico City.

On February 28, 1978, workers digging east of the cathedral struck a massive rock. They eventually unearthed an eight-ton stone on which the Aztecs had carved the dismembered figure of the moon goddess Coyolxauhqui, sister of Huitzilopochtli. The stone identified the area as the site of Teocalli, earlier believed to be buried under the Catedral Metropolitana to the southwest.

According to Aztec legend, Coatlicue, the goddess of earth and death (whose monolithic statue now sits in the Museo Nacional de Antropología) became pregnant while sweeping out the temple. Her daughter Coyolxauqui grew jealous of her and plotted with her 400 brothers to kill their mother. When they reached her, however, they discovered that Huitzilopochtli had already been born, full-grown. He beheaded his sister; his brothers he turned into the planets and stars—all this with a withered foot. By any standard, Huitzilopochotli was a great Aztec warrior; after his death, he came to be associated with war and the sun in its passage across the sky. The stone that the diggers found had been part of the base of a great pyramid. At the pyramid's summit were two temples, one of which was dedicated to the almighty god Huitzilopochtli. The practice of ritually sacrificing humans to Huitzilopochtli was popularized by Moctezuma I, who ruled from 1440-1468. The Aztecs believed that Huitzilopochtli craved gallons of warm, beating human hearts. As sacrifice (and some cannibalism) claimed 10,000-20,000 lives each year, the supply of local victims ran low and Montezuma I devised the "Flower Wars"—the Aztecs demanded sacrificial victims from their neighbors, threatening to attack their cowed neighbors if their bloody demands were not met.

When the conquistadors arrived, Teocalli measured 103m by 79.5m at its base and was 61m high. Moctezuma II led Cortés on the grand tour of the temple, proudly pointing out the caked walls and sacrificial stones. Instead of lauding the Aztecs' blood-spilling, Cortés requested that Montezuma clear a small place in the temple for an altar to the Virgin Mary. The Emperor's refusal to do so marked the first rift in a relationship that soon deteriorated into war.

Today, the ruins are just east of the cathedral and north of the Palacio Nacional. At first, the huge site appears to be little more than the foundation of a demolished modern complex. Before making any judgments, however, have a look inside. The excavated ruins reveal five layers of pyramids, built one on top of the other as the Aztec empire grew. Signs along the paths help explain which layer belongs to which temple. Over 7000 artifacts, including sculpture, jewelry, and pottery, have been found amidst the ruins. Many of the pieces have been traced to distant societies dominated by the long arm of the Aztec Empire. The extraordinary **Museo del Templo Mayor** (tel. 542-06-06), now part of the archaeological complex, houses this unique collection. This museum is a *de rigeur* stop even for visitors on a whirlwind tour of Mexico City. The exhibit is divided into eight *salas* (halls): antecedents and the settling of the Aztecs at the site of Tenochtitlán, war and sacrifice, tribute and commerce, Huitzilopochtli, Tlaloc, fauna, religion, and the fall of Tenochtitlán. The museum was designed to imitate the layout of the original temple, and is constructed so that the artifacts found in the excavation are accompanied by excerpts from the ancient Aztec texts which describe them. Highlights of this exhibit are a scale model of Tenochtitlán at the height of its power, along with the stone of Coyolxauqui and the *tzompantli* (skull rack), a platform where the freshly picked skulls of sacrificial victims were displayed to the public and the gods above. Along with the silent and decapitated ruins adjacent to it, the museum bears witness to the glories of México-Tenochtitlán and makes the arrogant pride of their *cantares mexicanos* more understandable: "Oh giver of life! Bear it in mind, oh princes. Forget it not. Who can siege Tenochtitlán? Who can disturb the foundations of the sky? With our arrows, with our shields, the city exists. México-Tenochtitlán persists! Proud of herself rises the city of México-Tenochtitlán. No one fears death in combat here. This is our glory. This is your mandate." (Museums and ruins open Tues.-Sun. 9am-5pm. Guided tours in Spanish free, in English 10 pesos per person. Admission 16 pesos, 10-peso fee to take pictures, free Sun.)

## South of the Zócalo

In 1691, a heavy rainfall destroyed the wheat crop, causing a famine among the working classes the following year. The viceroy, Count de Gálvez, initiated rationing, but when rumors of nearly exhausted grain supplies spread, a group of *indígenas* was sent to investigate. De Gálvez turned them away, bringing on the Riot of 1692, the most violent Mexico has ever seen. Several buildings were burned, including part of the palace and much of the Casas del Cabildo, which had sheltered the city government offices and archives. These are now located in the two buildings that compose the offices of the **Departamento del Distrito Federal** (tel. 518-11-00). The older of the buildings, located on the southwest end of the *zócalo,* was built according to the same plan as the pre-riot structure; on the exterior of this building are tiled mosaic shields that chronicle scenes from the history of Mexico. The newer building, on the southeast end of the *zócalo,* was built between 1940 and 1948, 400 years after its twin.

### Suprema Corte de Justicia

The Suprema Corte de Justicia, built in 1929, stands on the corner of Pino Suárez and Corregidora, on the spot where the southern half of Moctezuma's royal palace once stood. After the palace was leveled, Spanish colonists turned the area into a garbage dump. Cortés claimed the property, had it cleared, and designated it the site of city festivities, including a maypole dance, in which men suspended by ropes swung in circles from a pole. Four rather ferocious murals by José Clemente Orozco cover the second-floor walls of the present day Supreme Court. On the west wall hangs *Riquezas Nacionales,* in which a giant tiger, representing the national conscience, defends the mineral riches of the Republic. The mural on the east wall, *El Trabajo* (Work), symbolizes Article 123 of the Mexican Constitution, which guarantees workers' rights. The two remaining murals are called *La Justicia.* The one on the north wall shows a bolt of fire taking human form; the apparition wields a huge axe, with which it threatens a group of masked evildoers. On the south wall, Justice sleeps on a pedestal, holding a sword and the law (open Mon.-Fri. 9am-2pm).

### Museo de la Ciudad de México

The Museo de la Ciudad de México, Pino Suárez 30 (tel. 542-04-87), at República de El Salvador, three blocks south of the *zócalo's* southeast corner, houses maps, photographs, lithographs, and murals charting the lives and achievements of Mexico City's founders. Since it has just re-opened after major renovations, many of the exhibits are still being set up and may be closed to the public. The exhibits start on the ground floor and chronologically illustrate pre-Conquest development in the Valley of Mexico. The first exhibit showcases the geological formation of the Valley of Mexico and Lake Texcoco. Other rooms detail the rise of the Aztec Empire in the 15th and 16th centuries, with models of Tenochtitlán and diagrams of its social structure. An upstairs exhibit chronicles the evolution of "New Spain," from the 16th century to the usurpations, betrayals, and victories of 1910. The final exhibit is in the south wing of the second story; it portrays contemporary Mexico City, highlighting the construction of the Metro and showcasing a gigantic model of the Torre Latinoamericana. A photo of modern Mexico City center fills an entire wall, successfully communicating the metropolis's immensity. As the Museo de la Ciudad offers a solid account of Mexican history and culture, it provides a broad background for other sight-seeing in the city, and is an ideal place to begin your exploration of the city (open Tues.-Sun.10am-6pm; free).

### Other Sights

Across the street from the cathedral's west side on Calle Monte de Piedad is the **Monte Nacional de Piedad** (tel. 521-19-46), or the National Pawn Shop. In pre-Conquest times the building was part of the Palace of Axayacatl; today it houses a state-controlled flea market where dealers sell reasonably priced jewelry and astonishingly expensive gift items (market open Mon.-Fri. 10am-5pm, Sat. 10am-3pm).

**Calle Corregidora,** the street between the Suprema Corte and Palacio Nacional, skirts part of an ancient **canal system** that once connected the Aztec capital to the *pueblos* around Xochimilco. After the conquest of Tenochtitlán, Cortés ordered that the remains of the buildings he destroyed be dumped into the canals, and they fell into disuse. But as late as 1945, canals still connected some parts of the city. Today, both sides of the ancient canal system are paved as a pedestrian thoroughfare and the canal itself is covered by shrubs and small flower bushes.

Southwest of the *zócalo,* just west of the corner of 5 de Febrero and 16 de Septiembre, is the famous **Gran Hotel de la Ciudad de México.** Visit at midday to see the light shine through the Tiffany stained-glass ceiling with three flower-shaped central domes. Every detail is pure art nouveau; even the parakeets live in elaborate brass cages with stained glass ceilings.

Directly above Restaurante El Malecón, three blocks west of the plaza at Carranza 9, is what was once considered the **skinniest apartment building in the world.** Its four stories measure 11m high and only 3m wide; Mexicans see this as just another example of the extremes necessitated by living in the largest city in the world.

## ALAMEDA

The area around the Alameda Central is doubly blessed, filled with must-see sights and easily accessible by public transportation. Near the park are two Metro stations, Hidalgo (Lines 2 and 3), at the intersection of Hidalgo and Paseo de la Reforma, just one block west of the park's northwest corner, and Bellas Artes (Line 2), one block east of the park's northeast corner, between the park and Bellas Artes itself.

### Alameda Central

Amidst the howling sprawl that is downtown Mexico City, the Alameda is a verdant oasis of sanity and photosynthetic oxygen production. But while the green Alameda can feel like an island, it is not impervious to the urban life which bustles all around it—three major thoroughfares flank the Alameda and the park is packed with mimes, young lovers, protesters, and *comerciantes* hawking their wares.

The Alameda was designed several hundred years ago by Don Luis de Velasco II, who intended it as a place for the wealthy to relax and stroll. The park takes its name from the rows of shady *alamos* (poplars) which flood it. Since it was opened to the public in this century, Mexico City has fallen in love with the park. Mexicans of all sorts flock to the Alameda, and even in a city where real-estate values have soared and over-crowding is endemic, no one even considers paving over the park.

At the center of the Alameda's southern side is the **Monumento a Juárez,** a semicircular marble monument constructed to honor the revered former president in 1910, on the 10th anniversary of Mexican Independence. A somber-faced Juárez sits on a central pedestal among 12 doric columns. On July 19th of each year, a civic ceremony commemorates the anniversary of Juárez's death.

### Palacio de Bellas Artes

This impressive white palace, located at Juárez and Eje Central, at the northeast corner of Alameda Central (tel. 709-31-11 ext. 133), is but one result of the "capitalization" plan established during the dictatorship of Porfirio Díaz (1876-1911). Apart from its role as a repository of important works by 20th-century Mexican artists, the Palacio de Bellas Artes is a fascinating artifact of the Porfiriato. Soon after construction began, the theater started to sink into the city's soft ground. (It has sunk 5m to date; the sinking is not widely held to be part of the symbolism.)

The bulk of the museum's collection is 19th-century Mexican art; José María Velasco, Eugenio Langesio, Julio Ruelasa, and Joaquín Clausell are prominently featured. Most tourists, however, come to the palace to see the second and third floors, where the walls have been painted by the most celebrated Mexican muralists of the 20th century. On the east wall of the third floor, murals by the leftist José Clemente Orozco depict the supposed tension between natural human characteristics and industrialization. In addition to Orozco's work, the Palacio displays the frescoes of

David Alfaro Siqueiros, the 20th-century Mexican muralist, Stalinist, nationalist, and would-be assassin of Leon Trotsky. Siqueiros experimented with lighting, colors, and surfaces, but he is best known as a *típico* muralist. Look for his work on the third floor of the Palacio. Like his contemporary Diego Rivera, Siqueiros favored themes of class struggle and social injustice, and like Rivera he flaunted a cavalier disregard for topical subtlety. One example of the latter is *Tormento de Cuauhtémoc*, which describes Cortés's attack on the last vestiges of the Aztec nation. Beyond the cruelty exhibited by the *conquistadores*, Siqueiros plays upon the theme of new technology encountering the old, represented by the armor of the Spanish. Another mural, *Víctimas del Fascismo*, decries the horrible outcomes caused by fascism in Germany and throughout the world. Many of Siqueiros's paintings are layered with masonite, giving them a three-dimensional effect. A good example of this technique is *Explosión en la Ciudad*, in which the smoke from an explosion seems to stream toward the viewer.

If you have time for only one mural, see the one by Diego Rivera on the west wall of the third floor. Intended for a North American audience, the original was to be painted in New York City's Rockefeller Center with Rockefeller's chosen theme: "Man at Crossroads Looking with Hope and High Vision to the Choosing of a New and Better Future." Rivera was prohibited from finishing the mural, however, when Rockefeller noticed Lenin in the foreground. When an angry Rivera petitioned the Mexican government to allow him to duplicate the work, he was given this space in the Palacio. This second, more vehement rendering is entitled *El Hombre, Contralor del Universo, 1934,* and includes an unflattering portrayal of John D. Rockefeller (open daily 10am-8pm).

On the fourth floor of the palace is the **Museo Nacional de Arquitectura** (National Museum of Architecture). The exhibit is of early sketches and blueprints for the most architecturally distinctive buildings in Mexico City, including the *Teatro Nacional*, the monument to the Revolution, and the Hotel Del Prado. A bookstore on the first floor of the museum sells numerous books about the history of art and Mexican artists, as well as guides to museums in Mexico City. (Palacio de Bellas Artes open Tues.-Sun. 10am-6pm. Admission 10 pesos to see the murals and art exhibits on the upper floor, free for students and teachers with ID. Temporary exhibits on the first floor are generally free.)

The **Ballet Folklórico de México** performs regional dances in the **Palacio de Bellas Artes** and the **Teatro Ferrocarrilero** (tel. 529-17-01), near the Revolución Metro stop. Their two companies, one resident and one traveling, are world-renowned for their choreographic and theatrical skill. (Performances Wed. at 9pm, Sun. at 9:30am and 9pm. Tickets 100, 135, or 150 pesos, sold 3 or 4 days in advance at Bellas Artes but usually available Mon.-Sat. 11am-3pm and 5-7pm, Sun. 9am-1pm and 4-7pm.) Travel agencies snatch up lots of tickets during Christmas, *Semana Santa,* and summer; check first at Bellas Artes, then try along Reforma or in the Zona Rosa. These performances are the only way to see the crystal curtain designed by Gerardo Murelli, one of Mexico's greatest painters. It consists of almost one million pieces of multicolored crystal which, when illuminated from behind, represent the Valley of Mexico in twilight.

### Museo Nacional de Arte

The **Museo Nacional de Arte**, Tacuba 8 (tel. 512-32-24 or 512-06-84), half a block east of the Palacio's north side, was built during the Porfiriato to house the Secretary of Communications. The building's architect, Silvio Conti, designed the Museo's pre-Cambrian façade and paid particular attention to the central staircase—its sculpted baroque handrails were crafted by artists in Florence. The design leaves the museum with an empty feel, and footsteps echo through the lonely galleries.

The museum contains works from the stylistic and ideological schools of every era in Mexican history. Look for Guerra's *Monumento a José Martí*, a celebration not only of the young revolutionary's life, but also of color and space. The upper floors exhibit art ranging from Greek and biblical themes to 17th- and 18th-century historical depictions. José María Velasco's panoramic landscapes of the Valley of Mexico take up an entire *sala* and are excellent fodder for a picture. "No Flash!" three guards will simultaneously chime (museum open Tues.-Sun. 10am-5:30pm; admission 10 pesos, free Sun. and for students and teachers with ID, adults over 60, and children under 13).

## Near Alameda Central

A poet, José Martí was a leader of the Cuban independence movement in the late 19th century. He dreamed of a united and free Latin America with Mexico as a leader in the region, and repeatedly warned of the dangers of North American imperialism. Martí's acerbic poetry figures prominently at the **Centro Cultural José Martí,** Dr. Mora 2 (tel. 521-21-15), at Hidalgo on Alameda's west end. In a small library graced by both a colossal bust of Martí and his words, *"De America soy hijo...a ella me debo"* ("Of the Americas I am a son, to her I am indebted"), the center preserves a collection of writing by Martí and other anti-interventionists. Covering three walls of the building is a rainbow-colored mural depicting Martí and the people of Latin America. A tally sheet in the corner of the mural records Spanish, British, French, and U.S. interventions in Latin America from 1800-1969; the grand total is a staggering 784 (open Mon.-Fri. 9am-9pm, Sat. 9am-2pm; free).

The **Pinacoteca Virreinal de San Diego,** Dr. Mora 7 (tel. 510-27-93), next door to Centro Cultural José Martí, was once a monastery inhabited by the order of San Diego. The building was originally constructed in the Baroque style, but Neoclassical elements were added in the 19th century. Now the monastery's rooms with high, decorated ceilings and wooden floors contain an extensive collection of Baroque and Mannerist paintings, generally of religious themes. No photos allowed (open Tues.-Sun. 9am-5pm; admission 7 pesos, free Sun. and for students with ID).

The **Museo de la Alameda** (tel. 512-07-54), on Calzada Colón and Balderas, facing the small park at the west end of the Alameda, holds Diego Rivera's *Sueño de un Tarde Dominical en la Alameda Central* (Dream of a Sunday Afternoon at the Alameda Central), originally commissioned by the Hotel del Prado in 1946. Rivera finished the masterpiece in 1948, but when the Hotel Del Prado proudly hung the just-finished work, a national controversy ensued over the figure of Ignacio Ramírez, who is shown holding up a pad of paper that reads "God does not exist," an excerpt from a speech he gave in 1836. The archbishop of Mexico refused to bless the hotel, and on June 4th at dawn, more than 100 angry students broke into the hotel, erased the "does not exist" fragment from the original phrase and damaged the face of the young Diego Rivera in the center of the mural. The Hotel del Prado partially collapsed during the 1985 quake, and the mural was moved to the museum, which was constructed solely to hold this piece. The key in front of the mural points out the portrayal of historical figures woven into the crowd: Frida Kahlo, José Martí, and a chubby young Rivera, among others. José Guadalupe Posada's *La Calavera Catrina,* the central figure in the mural, mocks the aristocratic pretentions under the Díaz presidency (museum open daily 10am-2pm and 3-5pm; admission 7 pesos, free Sun. and for students and teachers with ID).

The tallest building in the Republic, the **Torre Latinoamericana** (Latin American Tower), 181m and 42 stories high, touches the sky over the corner of Lázaro Cárdenas and Madero (the continuation of Juárez), one block east of Alameda Central's southeast corner. Its 44th-floor observatory, a good 2422m above sea level, commands a startling view of the city. (Top-floor observatory open daily 10am-11pm. Admission 15 pesos for adults, 12 pesos for children under 12. Telescope fee 1 peso.) If you're interested in seeing the natural order inverted, visit the 38th floor of the tower which holds "the highest **aquarium** in the world." While their gimmicky boast is probably correct, the place seems more like a neighborhood pet store than a real aquarium (open daily 10am-10pm; admission 10 pesos, children 8 pesos).

Built in 1716, **La Iglesia de San Francisco** rests in the shadow of the Torre Latinoamericana just to the east on Madero. It was once a vast Franciscan complex that included several churches, a school, and a hospital. Two fragments of the original cloisters can be seen at Gante 5, on the east side of the church, and Lázaro Cárdenas 8, behind a vacant lot. The Franciscans were the first order to arrive in Mexico; the first 12 Franciscan friars in the country landed in Veracruz and walked barefoot to the capital—today a seven-hour bus ride. The church is open daily 7am to 8:45pm, but avoid visiting Saturday morning and afternoon and all day Sunday during mass hours (open Mon.-Fri. 9am-1pm and 5-7pm, Sat. 9am-1pm).

Across the street from San Francisco shimmers the **Casa de Azulejos,** an early 17th-century building covered with *azulejos* (blue-and-white tiles) from Puebla. To be able to afford even a token few of these tiles was a mark of considerable status. This mansion was festooned by an insulted son who set out to prove his worth to his father. There is an Orozco mural on the staircase wall, and a great view of the building can be had from the second-floor balcony, but you have to pass through Sanborn's restaurant to view them (open daily 7:30am-10pm).

**Palacio Iturbide** (tel. 521-57-97), at Madero 17 between Bolívar and Gante, 1½ blocks east of Lázaro Cárdenas and near the Iglesia de San Francisco, is a grand 18th-century palace with an impressive colonnaded courtyard. The Count of San Mateo Valparaíso lived here, but in 1821 Emperor Agustín de Iturbide took over the residence. Bánamex took over the building from the Emperor—a case of capitalism succeeding nationalism succeeding aristocracy. There is a gallery on the ground floor; exhibits change every three months (open daily 9am-2pm and 4-6pm).

Just north of the Alameda is the **Museo Franz Mayer,** Hidalgo 45 (tel. 518-22-65), at Pl. de Santa Veracruz. Formerly the Hospital de San Juan de Dios, the building has been expertly restored and now houses an extensive collection of ceramics, colonial furniture, and religious paintings. The first-floor exhibit of colonial processional and ceremonial crosses is neat-o (open Tues.-Sun. 10am-5pm; admission 8 pesos, 4 pesos for students with ID, free Sun.; guided tours Tues.-Sat. in the early afternoon).

Next door to the Franz Mayer museum in the pink building at Hidalgo 39 (tel. 521-22-24) is the **Museo Nacional de la Estampa.** Here lies the National Institute of Fine Arts's graphic arts and engraving collection, tracing the art of printmaking from pre-Hispanic seals to contemporary engravers. The highlight of the museum is the work of the acclaimed José Guadalupe Posada, Mexico's foremost engraver and print-maker. His woodcuts depict skeletons dancing, singing, and generally cavorting in ridiculous costumes—a graphic indictment of the Porfiriato's excesses (open Tues.-Sun. 10am-6pm; admission 8 pesos, free Sun.).

At the Plaza de la República under the **Monumento a la Revolución** is the **Museo Nacional de la Revolución** (tel. 546-21-15). Díaz originally planned the site as the seat of Congress, but as revolutionary fighting entered the city streets, progress was halted, and the dome was left only half-completed. It wasn't until the 1930s that the monument and space below were finally dedicated to the memory of the revolution. Today 32 flag poles representing the Mexican states line the pathway to this marmoreal dome. The entrance to the museum's subterranean exhibition is just northeast of the monument, in a black-stone park. Just inside the doors, a thorough chronology (in Spanish) of the revolution unfolds (museum open Tues.-Sat. 9am-5pm, Sun. 9am-3pm; free; call to arrange for a tour).

At the corner of Arranza and Puente del Alvarado, three blocks north of the Monumento a la Revolución, the **Museo San Carlos** houses an old art school and an)

---

### Of Angels and Human Remains

A kilometer east of Chapultepec Park is the **Ángel de la Independencia.** Situated at the fourth traffic circle on the Paseo de la Reforma, the Angel soars 50m above passing cars. Designed by Antonio Rivas Mercado, the monument is a stone column capped by a golden angel; its round-terraced base holds the remains of Hidalgo, Allende, and other national heroes. Crowds often converge here after major *fútbol* victories. The view at night, when the angel is embraced by the surrounding lights and skyline of the city, is simply magnificent.

impressive collection of European painting spanning the 16th through the 19th centuries, including works by Rubens and Goya (open Tues.-Sun. 10am-5pm; admission 13 pesos; free Sun.

## BOSQUE DE CHAPULTEPEC

Literally "Forest of Grasshoppers," this is the area on the western side of the city center where the Aztecs, new and unwelcome arrivals to the Valley of Mexico, first settled. Today, this 2100-acre expanse is one of the oldest natural parks in the New World. With its manifold museums, hiking paths, and modern sports facilities, one could easily spend several days in the Bosque. Mexico's most famous museum, the **Museo Nacional de Antropología,** sits among the hills of the park.

Although signs warn visitors about the stiff penalties for littering (three months' salary), the park is hardly elysian. Stray garbage and scraggly patches of browned grass pepper the lawn. The area is relatively safe during the day, but women should remain alert and should avoid the more remote areas of the park. Despite these detractions, on the right sort of day the Bosque can seem downright wonderful.

All the museums listed are in Old Chapultepec, the eastern half of the park, which fans out to the west of the Zona Rosa. Take the Metro to Auditorio (Line 7) or to Chapultepec (Line 1) to reach the park. The Auditorio stop is closer to the zoo, while the Chapultepec stop is closer to the **Niños Héroes** monument, closer to most of the museums, and much more convenient.

Try to visit the Bosque on Sunday, when families flock here for cheap entertainment. Musical spectacles and open-air concerts enliven the park, and voices fill the air promoting foods and trinkets. Best of all, the zoo and most of the museums in the area are **free** on Sundays (open daily 5am-5pm).

## Museo Nacional de Antropología

Some journey to Mexico just to consult this magnificent and massive mega-museum, located at Paseo de la Reforma and Gandhi (tel. 553-62-66). It is 4km of Mexico's finest archaeological and ethnographic treasures and the yardstick by which all other Mexican museums are measured.

Constructed of volcanic rock, wood, and marble, the museum opened in 1964. Pedro Ramírez Vásquez and his team of 42 engineers and 52 architects designed and built the structure in 18 months; meanwhile, archaeologists, buyers, and 20 teams of ethnographers scrambled to enlarge the museum's collection. After the huge stone image of the rain-god Tláloc greets you outside, 23 exhibition halls await within. Poetry from ancient texts and epics graces the entrances from the main courtyard. In the center of the courtyard, a stout column covered with symbolic carvings supports a vast, water-spouting aluminum pavilion.

You'll need about three days to pay homage to the entire museum, though many are afflicted with pottery overload after a few hours. *Salas* (halls), each devoted to a specific culture or region, occupy the ground floor. On the north side of the ground floor, a general introduction to anthropology precedes a series of chronologically arranged galleries. These trace the histories of many central Mexican groups, from the first migrations to the Americas up to the Spanish Conquest. The Oaxacan, Mayan, Gulf Coast, Northern, and Western displays are on the southern side—keep an eye out for the massive Aztec stone calendar featured in carvings and on t-shirts throughout the country. Upper-level rooms contain modern ethnographic displays (museum open Tues.-Sat. 9am-7pm, Sun. 10am-6pm; admission 16 pesos, free Sun.).

The museum also contains a **restaurant** (open Tues.-Sun. 9am-6pm) and a large **bookshop** that sells English guides to archaeological sites around the country as well as histories and ethnographies of Mexico's indigenous populations. Some of these guides are not available at the sites themselves, so plan ahead. To reach the museum, take bus #55 or 76 southwest on Reforma and signal the driver to let you off at the second stop after entering the park. On the Metro, take Line 1 to the Auditorio station; the museum is just east down Reforma. Take the first left on Gandhi for the main entrance. For a more scenic route, take Line 1 to Chapultepec station.

At the end of the long walkway just inside stands the **Monumento a los Niños Héroes,** six white pillars capped with monoliths and teased by small fountains. The monument is dedicated to the young cadets of the 19th-century military academy (then at Castillo de Chapultepec). In 1847, during the last major battle of the war with the U.S., the Niños Héroes fought the invading army of General Winfield Scott. Refusing to surrender, the last six boys are said to have wrapped themselves in the Mexican flag before throwing themselves from the castle wall. To the side of the monument is the **Tree of Moctezuma,** boasting a circumference of 44 feet and reputed to have been around since the time of the Aztecs. Behind the monument, Gran Avenida cuts through the park. Walk west on this street and take the *second* right on Gandhi. A five-minute stroll north takes you to Reforma and the museum.

## Museo Tamayo and Museo de Arte Moderno

Just to the east of the Museo Nacional de Antropología is the **Museo Tamayo de Arte Contemporáneo Internacional** (tel. 286-65-19), on the corner of Reforma and Gandhi. The museum is easy to miss: take the first right on Gandhi from the Chapultepec Metro stop. After a five-minute walk on Gandhi, the museum lies to the left down a small, almost hidden, path through the trees. Alternatively, walk due east from the entrance of the anthropology museum down the path into the woods; Tamayo is 100m straight ahead. The Mexican government created the nine halls of the museum after Rufino and Olga Tamayo donated their international collection to the Mexican people. The murals of Rufino Tamayo, born in 1889 in Oaxaca, were much criticized in the wake of the Revolution of 1910 for not being sufficiently nationalistic. Recently, however, his reputation has been rehabilitated and he has taken his place with Rivera, Siqueiros, and Orozco among the key figures of modern Mexican art. The museum, opened in 1981, houses important works by de Kooning and Surrealists Miró, Ernst, and Masson. The main *sala* holds photos from various press organizations depicting life around the world, while smaller rooms are dedicated to Hotoro Koyama and experimental photography techniques in Japan (open Tues.-Sun. 10am-5:45pm; admission 10 pesos, free for students and teachers with ID; call to arrange guided tours).

The **Museo de Arte Moderno,** at Reforma and Gandhi (tel. 553-62-11), north of the Monumento a los Niños Héroes, houses a collection of contemporary paintings by artists such as Kahlo, Siqueiros, José Luis Cuevas, Rivera, Orozco, and Velasco. The museum is linked to the Galería Fernando Camboa—a very modern assemblage of sculptures and exhibits—by an outdoor sculpture garden (open Tues.-Sun. 10am-6pm; admission 10 pesos, free Sun. and for students and teachers with ID).

## Museo Nacional de Historia

Inside the Castillo de Chapultepec, on top of the hill behind the Monumento a los Niños Héroes, is the Museo Nacional de Historia (tel. 553-72-02), which narrates the history of Mexico from before the time of the Conquest. An immense portrait of King Ferdinand and Queen Isabella of Spain greets visitors in the first *sala*. Galleries contain displays on Mexican economic and social structure during the war for independence, the Porfiriato, and the Revolution. The upper level exhibits Mexican art and dress from the viceroyalty through the 20th century. Other galleries exhibit carriages used by Maximilian (the elaborate ones) and Juárez (the basic black ones), and a Juan O'Gorman mural depicting the revolution, from the cruelties of the aristocracy to the triumph of the constitution. The walls of *sala* 13 are completely covered by Siqueiros's *Del Porfirismo a la Revolución.* (Open Tues.-Sun. 9am-5pm, tickets sold until 4pm. Admission about 15 pesos. Free Sun., but all 2nd-floor *salas* are closed. Video 10 pesos. Camera 5 pesos.)

## Museo del Caracol

The **Museo Galería de la Lucha del Pueblo Mexicano por su Libertad** (The Museum of the Struggle of the Mexican People for Liberty, tel. 553-62-85), is on the southern side of Chapultepec hill. Designed by Pedro Vásquez, the museum is often listed as **Galería de Historia** or even more commonly as **Museo del Caracol** (Conch) because of its spiral design. The gallery consists of 12 halls dedicated to the greatest hits of Mexican history from the early 19th to the early 20th century. A lengthy quote at the entrance urges visiting Mexicans to live up to the legacy embodied in the museum. From the start of your downward spiral, the gist of the museum's message is clear: foreign intervention has made Mexico's fight for its liberty an uphill battle. Especially interesting are exhibits on the executions of Hidalgo and Morelos, the flight of Benito Juárez, the execution of Maximilian, and the battles of Villa, Zapata, and Obregón. The museum's exhibits consist of amazingly life-like mini-dioramas, scores of paintings, and various other historical artifacts. However, visitors unfamiliar with the contours of Mexican history will be bewildered by the Spanish-only explanations. The staircase leads to a beautiful round skylit hall, the sides of which form the inner wall of the spiral you have been ascending. Also inside is a copy of the Constitution of 1917 in Venustiano Carranza's hand (open Tues.-Sat. 9am-4:30pm, Sun. 10am-3:30pm; admission 7 pesos; free Sun.).

### Elsewhere in Chapultepec

Twenty-five days before his death in January of 1974, David Alfaro Siqueiros donated his house and studio to the people of Mexico. In compliance with his will, the government created the **Museo Sala de Arte Público David Alfaro Siqueiros,** Tres Picos 29 (tel. 531-33-94), at Hegel just outside the park. Walk north from the Museo Nacional de Antropología to Rubén Darío. The street Tres Picos forks off to the northwest on the left; follow it for one block. The museum is on the right. Siqueiros was not only an artist, but also a revolutionary soldier, propagandist, communist, republican, Stalinist, and anti-fascist. Fifteen thousand murals, lithographs, photographs, drawings, and documents recount the story of Siqueiros's life. Call before visiting to arrange a guided tour in English or Spanish (open Mon.-Fri. 10am-2pm and 5-7pm, Sat. 10am-2pm; admission 7 pesos, students with ID 3 pesos, free Sun.).

West of the Siqueiros museum along Rubén Darío, at the intersection with Reforma, is the **Jardín Escultórico,** a sculpture park containing realist and symbolist statues. To the south and east of the sculpture garden, at Reforma and Av. Heróico Colegio Militar, flourishes the **Jardín Botánico,** a botanical garden whose lake contains a variety of fish (open daily 9am-5pm; free). The **Lago de Chapultepec,** situated at the heart of the park, has rowboats for rent from 7:30am-4:30pm (9 pesos per hour). Or, make a bee line for **Parque Zoológico de Chapultepec,** just east of the Jardín Botánico. Though the zoo's collection is quite impressive, animal lovers may shed a tear for the proud beasts restricted to humble habitats and subjected to the city's smog. There is hope, however: renovations are underway at the zoo (temporarily closed; usually open Wed.-Sun. 9am-4:45pm; free).

### TLATELOLCO

Archaeological work has shown that the city of Tlatelolco ("Mound of Sand" in Nahuatl) existed long before the great Aztec capital of Tenochtitlán. The first king of Tlatelolco, Teutlehuac, began his rule in 1375. He and his warriors distinguished themselves in battle, conquering enemy territory near Tepeyac on the outskirts of Tenochtitlán. By 1463, the Tlatelolco king, Moquihuix, had built his city into a busy trading center coveted by the Aztec ruler, Axayacatl. Tension mounted over territorial and fishing boundaries, and soon Moquihuix learned that the Aztecs were preparing to attack his city. Even forewarned, Moquihuix couldn't handle the Aztec war machine, and Tlatelolco was absorbed into the huge empire. Ironically, it was here that the Aztec nation made its own last stand against Cortés.

Today, a state low-income housing project surrounds the 17th-century church that stands on the grounds of Tlatelolco's ancient temple. Three cultures—ancient Aztec, colonial Spanish, and modern Mexican—have left their mark on this square, giving rise to the name **Plaza de las Tres Culturas,** at the corner of Lázaro Cárdenas and Ricardo Flores Magón, 13 blocks north of the Palacio de Bellas Artes.

The plaza's history has been extremely bloody, beginning in 1521, when the last Aztec emperor Cuauhtémoc made his last stand here. With stoic optimism, a plaque in the southwest corner of the plaza asserts: "On August 13, 1521, heroically defended by Cuauhtémoc, Tlatelolco fell to Hernán Cortés. It was neither a triumph nor a defeat, but the birth of the *mestizo* city that is the México of today."

More than 400 years later, the plaza was the site of the Tlatelolco Massacre of October 2, 1968. An adolescent rivalry between two secondary schools led to fighting in the streets; with the Mexico City Olympic games just a few months away, the government thought it necessary to forcefully quell all disturbances. Fueled by anger at the PRI's economic policies, the street fighting gave way to protests, and in September the city's universities were occupied by soldiers. On October 2, after a cancelled protest march, students and their families gathered in the Plaza de Las Tres Culturas for a peaceful rally. Toward the end of the rally, government troops descended on the plaza, shooting and killing hundreds of protesters.

In memory of the victims of the massacre, a simple sandstone monument was erected in the plaza and dedicated in 1993, on the 25th anniversary of the incident. The humble monument lists the names of the dead and bitterly expresses outrage at the lack of attention paid to the horrific shootings. A small plaque on the back of the monolith explains that the present monument, already dirtied and chipped, is but a temporary construction, and that a more fitting memorial will be built when more funds are collected. At times, the plaza can feel eerie and desolate, as if it has been abandoned to slow decay. Unlike most of Mexico City's public spaces, the plaza is rarely filled with lingering couples, *comerciantes,* or prolific conversationalists. Litter and faded vandalism mar the plaza. The Republic's red, white, and green flag is rarely raised here, as if a feeling of shame and hollowness still lingered.

In the plaza, parts of the **Pyramid of Tlatelolco** (also known as the **Templo Mayor**) and its ceremonial square remain. Enter from the southwest corner, in front of the Iglesia de Santiago, and walk alongside the ruins, down a steel and concrete path which overlooks the eight building stages of the main pyramid. At the time of the Conquest, the base of the pyramid extended from what is now Insurgentes to the current site of Iglesia de Santiago. The pyramid was second in importance to the great Teocalli of the Aztec capital, and its summit reached nearly as high as the modern skyscraper just to the south (the **Relaciones Exteriores** building). During the Spanish blockade of Tenochtitlán, the Aztecs heaved the freshly sacrificed bodies of Cortés's forces down the temple steps, within sight of the *conquistadors* camped to the west at Tacuba. Aztec priests would collect the leftover body parts at the foot of the steps; food was scarce during the siege and all meat was valuable.

Another notable structure is the **Templo Calendárico "M,"** an M-shaped building used by the Aztecs to keep time. Near its base, scores of skeletons were discovered; a male and female pair that were found facing each other upon excavation have been dubbed "The Lovers of Tlatelolco."

On the east side of the plaza is the simple **Iglesia de Santiago,** an enormous, fortress-like church named after the patron saint of Spain. The church was erected in 1609 to replace a structure built in 1543. Continue past the church towards the skyscraper for two blocks, right through the parking lot, to reach the **Museo de Siqueiros,** a white building housing a lone three-dimensional mural (open Tues.-Sun. 9am-5pm; free).

To get to Tlatelolco, take the Metro Line 3 to the Tlatelolco stop (Line 3) and exit through the González *salida.* From the exit, turn right on González, walk three blocks east until you reach Cárdenas, turn right at the small park, and walk one very long block south until you see the plaza on your left. 200m further south is a yellow pedestrian bridge that makes crossing Cárdenas feasible.

## LA BASÍLICA DE GUADALUPE

According to a variation on the legend that has become central to Mexicans' religious identity, the Virgin appeared on a mountain before a poor peasant named Juan Diego, entreating him to have a church built in her honor at that site. In order to convince the Mexican bishop of his vision, Diego laid a sheet full of fresh roses cut during the cold of December in front of the bishop. Both in awe, they watched the Virgin's portrait emerge on the sheet. Our Lady of Guadalupe has since become the patron of Mexico, an icon of the nation's religious culture. Diego's mantle can be seen in **La Basílica de Guadalupe,** north of the city center. Designed by the venerated Pedro Ramírez Vásquez in the 1970s, the new Basílica is an immense, aggressively modern structure that bears an uncanny resemblance to Disney World's Space Mountain. The Basílica draws crowds of thousands daily to the Virgin's miraculous likeness; the devout and the curious alike flock around the central altar and impressive organ to catch a glimpse of Diego's holy cloak. Just outside, a huge statue of Pope John Paul II stands watch (open daily 5am-9pm).

Next to the new Basílica is the old Basílica, built at the end of the 17th century. These days, the old Basílica houses the **Museo de la Basílica de Guadalupe,** Pl. Hidalgo 1 (tel. 577-60-22), in the Villa de Guadalupe. The colonial paintings dedicated to the virgin pale beside the intensely emotional collection of *retablos,* small paintings made by the devout to express their thanks to the Virgin of Guadalupe for coming to their assistance. A large room at the base of the staircase contains a pair of golden soccer shoes offered to the Virgin before the 1994 World Cup by the Mexican star Hugo Sánchez (museum open Tues.-Sun. 10am-6pm; admission 2 pesos).

Behind the Basílica, winding steps lead up the side of a small hill, past lush gardens, crowds of the faithful, and cascading waterfalls. A small chapel dedicated to the Virgin of Guadalupe, the **Panteón del Tepeyac,** surmounts the hill. The bronze and polished wood interior of the chapel depicts the apparitions witnessed by Juan Diego. From the steps beside the church, one can absorb a breathtaking panoramic view of the city framed by the hillsides and distant mountains. Descending the other side of the hill, past the spouting gargoyles bearing a surprising resemblance to Quetzalcóatl, statues of Juan Diego and a group of *indígenas* kneel before a gleaming Virgin doused with the spray from a rushing waterfall. On the other side of the hill, another waterfall drenches a bed of flowers. Vendors, both in and around the Basílica's grounds, hawk religious paraphernalia: holy water, holy shoes, holy t-shirts, holy jeans, and more. You'd be wise, however, to heed the signs and ignore those selling stamps and other allegedly consecrated doo-dads.

To get to the Villa de Guadalupe, take the Metro to La Villa (Line 6), go past the vendor stands, and make a right onto Calzada de Guadalupe. A small walkway between the two lanes of traffic leads directly to the Basílica. Alternatively, take the Metro to Basílica (Line 3). Walk along Insurgentes in the direction of traffic. At Montiel, turn right and head 500m east straight to the plaza.

## COYOACÁN

The Toltecs founded Coyoacán ("Place of the Coyotes" in Nahuatl) between the 10th and 12th centuries. Cortés later established the seat of the colonial government here, and, after the fall of Tlatelolco, had Cuauhtémoc tortured here in the hope that he would reveal the hiding place of the legendary Aztec treasure.

South of the center, Coyoacán is Mexico City's most attractive suburb, worth visiting for its museums or simply for a stroll in peaceful **Plaza Hidalgo** (also called **Placita de la Conchita**) or among the sculpted hedges of the **Jardín Centenario,** just southwest of the Plaza Hidalgo. Come to Coyoacán for a respite from downtown Mexico City; the pace is slower here. Coyoacán is centered on the Pl. Hidalgo, which is bounded by the cathedral and the Casa de Cortés. The two parks are split by Calle Cabrillo Puerto which runs north-south just west of the church.

Near Plaza Hidalgo's northeast corner is a bronze statue of Miguel Hidalgo. The **Casa de Cortés** (tel. 544-78-22), the one-story, reddish structure at the north end of the plaza, now the Palacio Municipal of Coyoacán, was Cortés's administrative building. On the porch sits the coat of arms given to Coyoacán by the King of Spain; inside are murals by local hero Diego Rivera showing scenes from the Conquest. Public access to the building is sporadic (open Mon.-Fri. 9am-9pm).

South of the plaza, beyond the Hidalgo statue, is the 16th-century **Parroquia de San Juan Bautista,** bordered by Pl. Hidalgo on the north and Jardín Centenario on the west. The church interior is elaborately decorated with gold and bronze. Enter south of the church's main door (open Tues.-Sat. 5:30am-8:30pm, Mon. 5:30am-7:30pm). A few blocks southeast of Pl. Hidalgo, facing the Placita de la Conchita and marked by the gardened plaza at the end of Higuera, is the **Casa Colorada,** Higuera 57, which Cortés built for Malinche, his Aztec lover. When Cortés's wife arrived from Spain, she stayed here briefly with her husband, but soon disappeared without a trace. It is believed that Cortés murdered his spouse because of his passion for Malinche, although he later gave her away as loot to one of his *conquistador* cronies. On the street running east from the northeast corner of Plaza Hidalgo is the **Museo Nacional de Culturas Populares,** Hidalgo 289 (tel. 658-12-65). Temporary exhibits on the history of popular culture in Mexico are the mainstay here; past exhibits include Karl Lumholtz's *Two Worlds, Two Visions,* which explores the duality of life in Mexico—rural vs. urban, modern vs. the eighteenth century (museum open Tues.-Sat. 10am-6pm, Sun. 10am-5pm; free).

After Leon Trotsky was expelled from the U.S.S.R. by Stalin in 1927, he wandered in exile until Mexico's President Lázaro Cárdenas granted him political asylum at the suggestion of muralist Diego Rivera, a friend of the Russian revolutionary. Trotsky arrived in Mexico in 1937 with his wife Natalia Sedova and settled into the house that is now the **Museo y Casa de Leon Trotsky** (tel. 658-87-32), Viena 45, seven blocks north of Pl. Hidalgo's northeast corner up Allende, then three blocks east on Viena to the corner of Morelos. The entrance is around back at Río Churubusco 410.

The house was outfitted with lookout towers and thick steel doors, and bullet holes riddle the walls—relics of an attack on Trotsky's life led by the Stalinist muralist David Alfaro Siqueiros on May 24, 1940. Trotsky and Sedova survived the attack, but Siqueiros's group abducted Trotsky's secretary, Robert Sheldon Harte, whose body was found a few days later on the road to Toluca. A marble plaque just inside the entrance to the house is dedicated to Harte. A monument in the center of the garden holds Trotsky's and Sedova's ashes. Trotsky died on August 20, 1940, stabbed through the skull with an ice pick by Ramón Mercader, a Stalinist agent posing as the boyfriend of Trotsky's assistant.

The interior remains as it was when Trotsky lived here. The rooms are stark, decorated only by Mexican rugs. Notice that the library is filled with books in Spanish, English, and Russian, and that a book about Stalin is open on Trotsky's desk, in the study where he was assassinated. The rooms display many of the couple's belongings, including a turn-of-the-century Russian dictionary and the complete works of Lenin, Marx, and Engels. In the guardhouse outside is a detailed chronology of Trotsky's life, along with a photo exhibit illustrating his childhood and youth in Russia and his later years in Mexico. There is also a touching letter from Trotsky's wife to President Cárdenas, dated a month after Trotsky's assassination, thanking him for his kindness in allowing them to enter Mexico (museum open Tues.-Sun. 10am-5pm; admission 10 pesos, students with ID 5 pesos; Free Sun.).

One of Coyoacán's more affecting sights is the **Museo Frida Kahlo,** Londres 247 (tel. 554-59-99), at Allende five blocks north of Pl. Hidalgo's northeast corner, in the blue and brown building at the northeast corner of the intersection. Works by Rivera, Orozco, Duchamp, and Klee hang in this well-restored colonial house, the birthplace and home of Frida Kahlo (1907-1954), whose work has gained a great deal of popularity in the U.S. Having suffered a debilitating accident as a young woman, Kahlo was confined to a wheelchair and bed for most of her life. While married to Diego Rivera, she began painting and became a celebrated artist. Her chronic health problems, together with her devotion to an adulterous husband (she, by the way, was also quite adulterous), inspired the fantastic and shocking subject matter of her works. During Rivera's absences she became emotionally attached to Leon Trotsky, but after a personal and political break between Rivera and Trotsky, a bust of Stalin replaced the pictures of Trotsky that she once hung in her home. Her wheelchair, crutches, and the cast that covered her entire upper torso are still in the house. The cast is covered with patterns and figures painted by Kahlo and her husband. Display cases also show the couple's personal possessions (included shelves of Marxist tracts), and a death mask of Kahlo along with her ashes wrapped up in the clothes she died in. As testament to Kahlo's interest in *indígena* culture, the rooms contain pottery, ceramics, and cookware and other native-produced pieces. Kahlo died at age 42 in the upper-story studio that Rivera built for her. Embroidered on Kahlo's pillowcase are the words *"No me olvides, amor mío"* ("Don't forget me, my love"). (Open Tues.-Sun. 10am–6pm. Admission 10 pesos, students 5 pesos.)

The **Convento de Nuestra Señora de Los Ángeles de Churubusco,** 20 de Agosto and General Anaya, was built in 1524 over the ruins of a pyramid dedicated to the Aztec war god Huitzilopochtli. The convent was originally Franciscan, but the Franciscans soon abandoned it, and in 1580 a group of Diegans moved in. The present structure was built in 1668. It was here that, on August 20, 1847, 800 Mexicans halted ten times as many advancing U.S. soldiers. When the U.S. General Twiggs asked General Pedro Anaya to turn over his remaining munitions, Anaya responded, "If we had munitions you would not be here." Still guarding the convent's main entrance are two of the original seven cannon that defended the convent during the 1847 invasion. Two more cannon and a monument to Anaya flank the western side of the structure. Inside, an old garden grows, its walls scratched with indecipherable inscriptions (convent open Mon.-Fri. 7am-10pm, Sat. noon-2pm and 6-8:30pm, Sun. 8am-2pm and 5:30-8pm).

Mexico has been invaded more than 100 times, most often by the U.S. Inside the Convento de Churubusco is a museum dedicated to the history of the invasions, the **Museo Nacional de Las Intervenciones** (tel. 604-06-99). The museum's halls cover four eras, from the late 18th century to 1917. A few halls are also dedicated to exhibits on North American expansionism and cruelty to *indígenas,* U.S. slavery and its significance for Mexico, and European imperialism (museum open Tues.-Sun. 9am-6pm; admission 14 pesos, free Sun. and for students and teachers with ID). To get to the convent and museum from Coyoacán, walk four blocks down Hidalgo and then follow Anaya as it branches left, four blocks farther to the convent grounds. Far easier is to take the Metro, get off at General Anaya (line 2), and walk two blocks west on 20 de Agosto.

Atop a hill is the **Museo Anahuacalli** (tel. 677-29-84), on Calle Museo. Designed by Diego Rivera with Aztec and Mayan architectural influences in mind, Museo Anahuacalli houses the artist's huge collection of pre-Conquest art. Anahuacalli commands one of the best views in Mexico, comparable to those of the Torre Latinoamericana and Castillo de Chapultepec (open Tues.-Sun. 10am-2pm and 3-6pm). To reach the museum from Pl. Hidalgo or Churubusco, go by *pesero* 5km south on Av. División del Nte. to Calle Museo.

To reach Coyoacán from downtown, take the Metro directly to the Coyoacán station (line 3). *Pesero* "Coyoacán" (every 20min., 1 peso) at the station stops within two blocks of Pl. Hidalgo. Taxis cost about 6 pesos. One can also walk; it's a pleasant route. You might want to ask the driver to point out the stop as it is not visible immediately. Turn right onto Museo and soon you'll reach the place.

## La Heroína del Dolor

Depending on who you talk to, many residents of Coyoacán would say their town's most cherished product was *la heroína del dolor* (the heroine of pain), the artist Frida Kahlo. Famously self-obsessed, famously morbid, and famously shocking, Kahlo's work, in recent years, has been riding a wave of unprecedented popularity and critical success. *Self-Portrait with Monkey and Parrot* (1942) recently sold for 3.2 million dollars. The Frida Files are about to be burdened once again with the publishing of a facsimile of the diary Kahlo kept in the last ten years of her life. The colorful, idiosyncratic journal, filled with frantic drawings and cryptic phrases may well add to the ever-growing Kahlo mythology rather than shed a clarifying light on the artist's life and body of work.

## SAN ÁNGEL

South of Mexico City is the wealthy, suburban community of San Ángel. Dotted with churches and exquisite colonial homes, San Ángel is a great place for a stroll. To reach the area, 10km south of the Centro along Insurgentes, take the Metro to the M.A. Quevedo station (line 3). Turn left out of the Metro station and left at the intersection, then head west on Quevedo for three blocks to the romantic and wonderfully verdant **Parque de la Bombilla,** at the intersection of Insurgentes and Miguel Ángel de Quevedo. Quevedo forms the northern boundary of the park, but Avenida de la Paz forks off of it just before the park and runs right into the heart of the greenery before exiting through the southwest side. The centerpiece of this lovely park is the shaft-like concrete **Monumento al General Álvaro Obregón,** at Insurgentes Sur, best reached by taking the Av. de la Paz fork from Quevedo between Arenal and Abasolo. Obregón was one of the revolutionary leaders who united against Huerta, the usurper who seized power and executed Madero in 1913. Obregón allied with Venustiano Carranza and helped to construct the 1917 constitution. With Carranza's death in 1920, Obregón became the first president of the post-revolutionary era. Reliefs on the four sides of the monument represent peace, agriculture, industry, and the people in arms. The inscription on the far wall of the chamber reads, "I die blessing the revolution." In the main hall of the monument is a shiny green statue of the one-armed Obregón and a plaque that reads "in place of your sacrifice." The lower-level contains a small jail cell which houses a wooden replica of Obregón's arm (open daily 7am-3pm; free).

Walking two blocks along La Paz and through the big Insurgentes intersection, you finally come to the intersection with Revolución. One block to the south (left) are the three tiled domes of **Iglesia del Carmen,** Revolución at Monasterio. Designed and built between 1615 and 1626 by Fray Andrés de San Miguel of the Carmelite order, the church and adjacent ex-convent are decorated with tiles and paintings. An outstanding statue of Christ the Nazarene is located in the Capilla del Señor Contreras (open daily 7am-1pm and 4:30-9pm). The ex-convent has been converted into the **Museo del Carmen** (tel. 616-28-16). The museum displays colonial art, tons of crucifixes, and portraits of various saints and nuns. Also exhibited are typical convent rooms—look out for the flat wooden bed and oh-so-comfy log pillow. Most tourists come to see the mummies; located in an underground crypt, the grotesque cadavers were originally disturbed in 1916 when the Zapatistas arrived in search of treasure (open Tues.-Sun. 10am-5pm; admission 14 pesos, free Sun.).

The Plaza del Carmen is across the street from the the church. The large building on its southern side is the **Centro Cultural,** which hosts changing art exhibits and dispenses much-needed maps of the area. One block up the southwest corner of the Plaza de Carmen on Madero (the street right beside the Centro Cultural) is the Plaza de San Jacinto, at San Francisco, Benito Juárez, and Frontera. Every Saturday, the plaza fills up with ritzy shoppers scoping pricey arts and crafts at the **Bazaar Sábado.** Although many pieces are beyond the budget travelers' economic grasp, there are plenty of bargains and shady places to relax. On the north side of the plaza is the **Casa de Risco,** Plaza San Jacinto 15 (tel. 550-92-86), a well-preserved 17th-century house donated by Isidro Fabela. The house holds Fabela's collection of European art spanning the 14th through the 18th centuries. The whitewashed inner courtyard contains an exquisitely tiled fountain made out of pieces of bowls and plates (called *riscos*) that were collected from around the world. Also look out for *Crisol de Razas,* a painted chart that lists racial combinations and colonial verdicts on the mixing of races; some racial mixtures were dubbed *lobo* (wolf), while others were called *salto atrás* (a step backwards). To reach the **Iglesia de San Jacinto,** continue from the plaza one block west on Juárez. Sit in the tranquil garden of this 16th-century church and take in its ancient orange façade and beautifully carved wooden doors. This neighborhood, the oldest in San Ángel, contains some swanky modern mansions as well (church open daily 8am-8pm).

Three blocks north on Revolución from the intersection of La Paz and Madero, to the right if coming for the Parque de la Bombilla, is the **Museo Carrillo Gil,** Revolución 1608 (tel. 548-74-67), a modern building housing the contemporary art collection of the late Carillo Gil. The small museum contains paintings by Siqueiros as well as a whole floor of Orozcos and some works by the young Rivera. Siqueiros's famous *Cain en los Estados Unidos* is on the third floor (open Tues.-Sun. 10am-6pm; admission 7 pesos, students with ID 3 pesos, free Sun.).

## CIUDAD UNIVERSITARIA

The **Universidad Nacional Autónoma de México** (National Autonomous University of Mexico—UNAM) is the Republic's largest public university, boasting an enrollment that now surpasses the 300,000 mark. Immediately after the new colonial regime was established, the religious orders that arrived in Mexico built elementary and secondary schools to indoctrinate new converts and to educate young men who had come over from Spain. After petitioning the king of Spain, the first university was established in 1553 in the building at the corner of Moneda and Seminario, just off the *zócalo*. As the university grew, classes were moved to the building that now houses the Monte de Piedad, on the west side of the *zócalo*, and then to a building at the east end of the Pl. del Volador, where the Suprema Corte now stands. On July 5th, 1950, construction began on the present site; the 7.3 million square meters on which the modern university stands was donated by then President Miguel Alemán. Most of the buildings were completed by 1954; the area now boasts 26km of paved roads, 39 bridges, 430,000 square meters of greenery, and 4,000,000 planted trees. Today's ultramodern buildings belie UNAM's status as one of the three oldest universities in the Americas.

Despite the rock-bottom tuition, the university is still able to support an amazingly varied collection of student groups, activities, and social and cultural events. Few dormitories exist on the campus itself, and the university city is noticeably empty during the weekend, but films, shows, and club meetings abound on Saturday and Sunday. You name it, it's here—from a Tae Kwon Do club, to a film about young gay Mexicans to tribal dances that explore Mexico's indigenous heritage.

Pick up a copy of the leaflet **Cartelera** or **Los Universitarios,** both of which list all scheduled events for the month (some of also appear in Tiempo Libre) during your visit at the Centro Cultural Universitario, two bus stops south along Insurgentes Sur from the Olympic stadium; get off at the yellow pedestrian crossing. This pleasant, modern complex houses the **Teatro Juan Ruíz de Alarcón** (tel. 662-71-66), a few concert halls—the biggest is **Netzahualcóyotl** (tel. 622-70-21)—and two movie theatres: **Salas José Revueltas** and **Julío Braucho** (tel. 665-28-50). Many of the performances and movies are excellent, and you can get a 50% discount with a student ID. Hundreds of other events are also posted on bulletin boards in the area.

The **Estadio Olímpico 1968** is located on the west side of Insurgentes Sur, just past the entrance to Ciudad Universitaria. The stadium was built in the 1950s, designed to resemble a volcano with a huge crater—an appropriate motif since lava coats the ground on which it is built. The impressive mosaic that covers the stadium was made by the indefatigable Rivera using large colored rocks; it depicts a man and a woman holding two torches, symbolic of the 1968 Olympics held in the stadium. Unfortunately, the gates to the stadium are usually locked.

Although the university's architecture is impressive, most visitors come to see the murals which meditate upon academic subjects. From the stadium, cross Insurgentes (a pedestrian tunnel under the thoroughfare leads to the main part of campus) and continue east (straight ahead); west of the Jardín Central's southern half, the university's administrative building is distinguished by a 3-D Siqueiros mosaic on the south wall, which shows students studying at desks supported by society. One of the world's largest mosaics, the work of Juan O'Gorman, wraps around the university library, a windowless box next to the rectory tower. A pre-Hispanic eagle and Aztec warriors peer out from the side facing the philosophy department. The side facing the esplanade shows the Spaniards' first encounter with the natives; the opposite side depicts a huge atom and its whirling components. Farther east is the expansive Jardín Central; this vast, tree-lined quadrangle is popular with students looking to relax or start a pick-up game of *fútbol.*

To get to Ciudad Universitaria, take the C.U. Metro (Line 3) to Universidad. Free shuttle service, though limited and irregular after classes end, is available to all campus areas. From Metro Universidad, take line #1 to both the stadium and esplanade/museum areas (about 5 stops). Many *peseros* will be waiting just below the station, but follow the students past the vendors to the free buses. The free university buses run along the circular streets around the main campus. For transportation along Insurgentes Sur, the *peseros* (1 peso) are generally the best option. The university can also be reached by taking the Metro to Copilco (Line 3) and follow the collegiate crowd the short distance to campus. Take the first left as you exit the station and walk two blocks, crossing Av. Copilco. Turn right at the dead end and then left to reach the edge of campus, the Paseo de las Facultades. A right on this main street will lead eventually to the junction with Insurgentes near the Estadio Olímpico.

Near the end of the pre-Classic Period, the tiny volcano **Xitle** erupted, leaving eight square kilometers covered with several meters of hardened lava. The lava flow preserved one of the first pyramids constructed in the Valley of Mexico and formed what is now the **Cuicuilco Archaeological Zone** (tel. 553-22-63) on the southeast corner of the intersection of Insurgentes Sur and Anillo Periférico. Take bus #130 ("San Fernando Huipulco", 1 peso) to the entrance on the west side of Insurgentes Sur, south of the Periférico. The **Pyramid of Cuicuilco,** which means "Place of the Many-Colored Jasper," was built between 600 and 200 BCE by the early inhabitants of the Valley of Mexico, about when ceremonial centers first began to spring up in Mesoamerica and priests gained extraordinary powers. Measuring 125m across at its base and 20m in height, Cuicuilco consists of five layers, with an altar to the god of fire at its summit. The lava rock around the base has been removed, allowing visitors to walk along it and up to the altar. From here, on less smoggy days, you can see Xitle to the south and Popocatépetl to the east (zone open daily 9am-4pm; free). Next to the pyramid is a museum with exhibits on volcanology, the geology and ecology of the area, and the eruption of Xitle. It takes about 15 minutes to stroll through (open Tues.-Sun. 9am-4pm; free).

South of the university on Insurgentes is a sculpture park known as the **Espacio Escultórico,** just west of the Biblioteca y Hemeroteca Nacional. Out of a huge lava bed and surrounding cave formations rises a pan-chromatic collection of Herculean sculptures constructed in the early 1980s of metal, cement, and wood. The artists wanted to revive, through modern techniques, the architectural traditions of pre-Conquest ceremonial centers. The Espacio Escultórico is best visited during the day, since it is located on the outskirts of the campus in a secluded area. From the center of the university, take bus #17 or #130 ("San Fernando") from the stadium and get off at the first designated stop (at the yellow pedestrian overpass).

---

### Higher Learning—On a Budget, Of Course

Part of UNAM's mandate is fulfilling Mexico's constitutional guarantee of universal education to all citizens. The sacred power of this right was evidenced by the student strikes which shut down the school in the summer of 1992, in response to proposals to raise tuition from a virtually nonexistent 0.20 pesos to 20 pesos per anum. These days, classes still cost less than US$5 per semester for nationals and roughly US$10 for foreign students.

---

## XOCHIMILCO

Centuries ago, the Aztecs cultivated floating gardens to feed the inhabitants of Tenochtitlán, a tradition which is celebrated daily in a vastly different form in the southern district of Xochimilco. Today, multicolored *chalupa* boats crowd the maze of canals, ferrying passengers past a floating market offering food, flowers, and music. The market is especially popular on Sundays, when hordes of city dwellers and tourists relax in the hand-poled *chalupas.* They lounge and listen to the water-borne *mariachis,* celebrating Mexico City's aquatic past as they munch tacos from the floating taco bars which tie up pirate-style to the passenger boats. Delicate orchids and bubbly beer are also on sale.

The keyword for almost anything you do in Xochimilco is bargaining. From the markets to the boats, this is the only way to get around in this overly-popular tourist spot. Be aware that if you come earlier, you'll find a much emptier Xochimilco, with far fewer boats and much higher prices. For a private boat for six people, expect to pay about 40 pesos per hour; consult the official diagram for prices, as boat owners will try to charge eight or 10 times as much. If confronted with inflation, wait for more people to arrive and begin bargaining. *Colectivo* boats cost only three pesos per person and are usually more fun than the private boats; *colectivos* run only on weekends after noon. The standardized rates price *mariachis* at 25 pesos per song.

To get to Xochimilco, take the Metro to Taxqueña (Line 2) and then use the *tren ligero* service (0.40 pesos; follow the *correspondencia* signs inside the station) in the direction of Xochimilco and get off at the Xochimilco stop. The boats are three blocks east of the station—exit to your left. *Peseros* below the station will also take you there; ask to be let off at *las canoas* (the canoes). To reach the central marketplace, walk south down Embarcadero, turn right onto Violeta, and then left onto Nuevo León. The market is just beyond the **Iglesia de San Bernandino de Cera.**

If you wish to stay in this area, a clean and new hotel, **Hotel Xochimilco,** Nezahualcóyotl 7 (tel. 676-08-00), at the corner of Morelos, is one block south of the central market. The rooms are clean and carpeted, with TVs (singles and 1-bed doubles 60 pesos; 2-bed doubles 110 pesos). For more information, call the Director of Tourism at 676-08-10 (open Mon.-Fri. 9am-9pm, Sat.-Sun. 10am-5pm).

# ■■■ SHOPPING

While most Mexican cities have a single central market, Mexico City has a central market for every retail good. These markets are relatively cheap, since the city usually takes care of overhead. Each *colonia* has its own market, but the major marketplaces are all in the center of town.

**La Merced,** Circunvalación at Anaya, east of the *zócalo.* Merced Metro stop (Line 2). Primarily food, shipped from all over the country. Huge selection of fresh produce at rock bottom prices. Locals claim that La Merced moves as much money daily as the entire city of Monterrey. Open daily 8am-7pm. (See Sights: Centro.)

**Sonora,** Teresa de Mier and Cabaña, 2 blocks south of Merced. If you want to turn your significant other into a toad, head for Sonora. Specializes in witchcraft, medicinal teas and spices, ceramic pottery, figurines, and ceremonial figures. Search no further for lucky cows' feet, shrunken heads, eagle claws, aphrodisiacs, black salt (for nosy neighbors), talismans to ward off the evil eye, poison antidotes, powdered skull (for the domination of one's enemies), amber, patchouli incense, energy pills, courage powder, bath oil (for success in business), black candle figurines, and dead butterflies, among other things. Tell them your problems—they'll give you a remedy for it. Outside the market are caged birds, spiders, ducks, and turtles. Rare species sometimes appear. Open daily 8am-7pm.

**Mercado de La Ciudadela,** just north of Metro Balderas. One of the largest and cheapest markets in the city. An incredible array of crafts and traditional clothing. Bargaining is appropriate, but often unnecessary. Open daily 8am-7pm.

**Tepito,** between Metro stops Revolución and San Cosme, accessible by a *pesero* called "Tepito" along Reforma, and often called the "Thieves Market." Blocks of outdoor clothing stalls and rows upon rows of shoes—it's like Imelda Marcos's closet writ large. Tepito is the national clearinghouse for gray-market imports from the U.S. and South Asia; come here for counterfeit watches. Neat-o police raids occur daily. Watch your wallet. Open daily 9am-9pm.

**San Juan,** Pl. El Buen Tono, 4 blocks south of Alameda Central, 2 blocks west of Lázaro Cárdenas. Bounded by Ayuntamiento, Aranda, Pugibet, and Dolores. Follow the painted footprints indoors. Targets tourist pesos. An incredible variety of baskets, furniture, blankets, traditional clothing, keychains, T-shirts, dolls, *sombreros,* wall hangings, and fake parrots. Open Mon.-Sat. 9am-7pm, Sun. 9am-4pm.

**La Lagunilla,** Comonfort at Rayón, east of the intersection of Lázaro Cárdenas and Reforma. Two large yellow buildings on either side of the street. Although famous for the antiques and old books sold here on Sundays, the market has metamorphosed into a daily vending site for practical goods. Open daily 8am-7pm.

**Buenavista,** Aldama 187 (tel. 529-12-54), at Degollado in Col. Guerréro. Giant blue and pink crafts warehouse. Like San Juan, it is geared almost exclusively to the tourist. It's overpriced, but offers a wide selection. Somewhat pricey merchandise includes stuffed bulls' heads, "genuine" obsidian blades, and videos about traditional Mexico. Open Mon.-Sat. 9am-6pm, Sun. 9am-2pm.

**Bazaar Sábado,** Pl. San Jacinto 11, in San Ángel. Open on Sat. only, as the name suggests. A good excuse to voyage out to San Ángel. High quality folk crafts: dolls, paintings, rugs, papier-mâché, jewelry, and much more. A great place to browse, but bring lots of cash if you plan to buy. Slightly cheaper bazaar in the plaza just outside. Open Sat. 10am-7pm.

**FONART.** There's a FONART near you: Patriotismo 691; Juárez 89; Insurgentes 1630 Sur; Londres 6 at the Museo de Cera; Londres 136, in San Ángel at Av. de La Paz 37; and Ciudad Satélite on Manuel Izaguirre 10. Stores selling regional crafts from all over the Republic. Giant tapestries, Oaxacan rugs, silver jewelry, glassware, pottery, colorful embroidery, and folk art. Open Mon.-Sat. 10am-7pm.

**Museo Nacional de Artes del Instituto Nacional Indigenista,** Juárez 44, across from the Alameda. A shop as well as a museum. A map on the wall shows regional crafts from all areas of Mexico. The store stocks many of these crafts and lots of jewelry. Open Mon.-Fri. 9am-6pm, Sat.-Sun. 10am-6pm.

# ■■■ ENTERTAINMENT

Fear not the monotonous discos that dominate the nightlife in small towns throughout the Republic—you're in Mexico City. The chameleon that is entertainment in the nation's capital can turn any color you choose. Be it the Ballet Folklórico at Bellas Artes, an old film at an art cinema, a bullfight in the Plaza México, or blues in a smoke-filled bar, the city has something for everyone.

At many large nightclubs, dates of the opposite sex are sometimes prerequisites for admission. Cover charges range from 15 to 80 pesos, but women are sometimes admitted free. Those places without a cover often have minimum consumption requirements and high drink prices. Covers magically drop during the week when business is scarce, especially for those *norteamericanos* thought to have hearty appetites and deep pockets. If prices are not listed, be sure to ask before ordering, lest you be charged exorbitant *gringo* prices. Be aware that Mexican-made drinks, from Kahlúa to *sangría,* are considerably cheaper than imported ones. Watch out for ice-cubes—avoid at all costs these secret agents of *turista.* Bars with dimly lit interiors, no windows, or swinging doors are called *cantinas;* women are not welcome in these bastions of *machismo.*

The Zona Rosa and the strip along Insurgentes Sur offer the most variety for your entertainment peso. Tourists and Mexicans alike flood the streets in the evenings, often dressed to the hilt and set to have a good time. Bars and discos clog the streets, each attempting to outdo the others in flashiness and decibel output. Although the Alameda and other areas also have some places to dance, discos in more run-down parts of town can get seedy. Women venturing out alone should be aware that they will most likely be approached by men offering drinks, dances, and their firstborn.

Different areas of the city boast different entertainment specialties. As a general rule, the best *discotecas* are found along Insurgentes Sur, and a few spill over into the Zona Rosa. Rock clubs abound in the Zona Rosa and a few exist around the Alameda. *Mariachi* bands lurk in Garibaldi Plaza, while *merengue* and *salsa* clubs are centered near the *zócalo* and in San Ángel and Coyoacán. Jazz bands, some *salsa* and traditional Mexican music, and generally lighter fare appealing to an older crowd can also be found in the city's southern suburbs.

For safety, the Zona Rosa offers the best lighting and least lonely streets, which are a problem in other areas. Taxis run all night, as do *peseros* on the major routes (see Getting Around, above). Try to avoid going out at night alone; as always, the bigger the group the safer you'll be.

## ZONA ROSA

### Bars

The Zona Rosa is a bar-hopper's dream come true. While taverns in this area are generally upscale and expensive, high price tags often mean live performers and tasty *botanas* (appetizers). Zona Rosa bars cater to all ages and tastes, from teenybopper to elderly intellectual. Many feature live music or beamed-in video entertainment. Women will probably feel safest in this area, but men still aggressively try to pick up anything with two X chromosomes. Catch a ride home in a *pesero* running all night along Insurgentes Sur (1-1.50 pesos).

**Harry's Bar and Grill,** Liverpool 155 (tel. 208-62-98), enter half a block north of Liverpool on Amberes. An international thirtysomething crowd carouses and chats amidst the dull din of a piped-in soccer match. Walls are cluttered with beer bottles and menus from bars and *cantinas* all over the Republic. Beers a hefty 12-14 pesos. Mini *botanas* 17-30 pesos. Open Mon.-Sat. 1pm-midnight.

**Bar Osiris,** Niza 22 (tel. 525-66-84). Suffers from mid-week attendance problems, but on weekends, it turns into a hard-rock party pit. Live bands perform after 8pm. Cover Fri.-Sat. 15 pesos. 6 beers 50 pesos. Open Wed.-Sun. 7pm-3am.

**Yarda's Bar,** Niza 39 (tel. 514-57-22). The packed dance floor shakes rhythmically with the pumping bass and techno tunes. The 30-peso pitchers of beer just can't compete with the 16-peso mixed drinks, says this young, ultra-suave crowd. Cover Fri.-Sat. 30 pesos. Open Mon.-Sat. 4pm-3am.

**Xcess,** Niza 39 (tel. 525-5317). A more mellow techno beat and fog machine compete with 6-peso ¼-*yardas* of beer (about ¼ liter) for the young dance crowd's attention. A huge picture of Elvis stares down upon all visitors. Open Thurs. (no cover) 2pm-2:30am, Fri.-Sat. (cover 30 pesos) 2pm-3am.

**El Chato,** Londres 117 (tel. 533-28-54), recognizable by the stained glass doorway. No glitz, no booming beat, but the somewhat older crowd likes it that way. A great place to wind down and to imbibe quality beer out of steins (12 pesos). Frequented by famous Mexican actors, politicians, and businessfolk. Occasionally blessed with visiting *trovas* from the Yucatán, during which a 30-peso cover charge take effect. Don't miss the informal jazz-piano bar with Sinatra sound-alikes an arm's reach away. Open Mon.-Sat. 1pm-1am.

### Discos

The Zona Rosa has some of the Republic's flashiest discos and highest cover charges—on weekend nights, the Zona can seem like the epicenter of the entire universe. Club-hopping, however, is becoming more difficult, as many discos are moving over to the high cover charge and open bar system. Long lines are sure signs that a disco has become the joint *du jour*. Inside, expect anything from a sweaty, throbbing mass of humanity to a slightly more reserved jacket-and-tie crowd enjoying the U.S. pop/rock fare. Sidewalk recruiters will likely try to lure in groups, especially those with high female to male ratios; hold out and you just might be offered a deal. If you can't find something to your liking here, head east to Insurgentes Sur, and then south along the thoroughfare—you'll run across the whole gamut of clubs.

**Rock Stock Bar & Disco,** Reforma 260 (tel. 533-09-06), at Niza. Even though Elvis has left the building, this chic-est of discos is usually packed with beautiful young Mexicans. Non-famous single men will have difficulty getting in. Follow the street signs through the rotating darkroom-style doors and upstairs into a huge open attic room in which railings, scaffolding, and metal cages are doused in fluorescent paint. Free barrels of chips and popcorn. Lively action, with everything from rave to underground rhythms. Thurs. cover 90 pesos for men, free for women.

Fri-Sat. cover 100 pesos for men, 70 pesos for women. Cover includes an open bar for most drinks. Open Thurs. 8pm-1am, Fri.-Sat. 8am-3am.

**Celebration,** Florencia 56 (tel. 208-29-33). Rigged with speakers heard 'round the world. Modern dance rock accompanies a stylish set and varied theme nights— you just might wind up boogeying next to masked horror aficionados. Scattered tables provide an oasis from the active dance action. Admission includes *barra nacional* (open bar, national brands). Cover 80 pesos. Open daily 7pm-3am.

**Papa's Disco,** Londres 142 (tel. 207-77-02). For the true dancing machine. Come prepared to shed a few pounds while experiencing a Latin grind mixed in with hard rock, pop, and techno. Wed.-Thurs. and Sun. cover 60 pesos for men, free for women. Fri.-Sat. cover 80 pesos for men, 40 pesos for women after 10pm. Cover includes *barra nacional.*

**Melódica,** Florencia 58 (tel. 523-22-42), just south of Londres and next to Celebration. This multi-club metamorphoses from a karaoke bar in the early evening to a happening pop-and-rock *discoteca* later at night. Mon.-Thurs. cover 80 pesos, Fri.-Sat. 100 pesos. Includes *barra nacional.* Open Mon.-Sat. 7pm-2:30am.

## CENTRO

Many of the bars here are popular among the desk-job jet-set, and some have as long and distinguished a history as the buildings that lord over them. Explore, but bear in mind that by midnight the Centro's streets are completely deserted and potentially dangerous. While the following bars spill over into the Alameda area, they are distinguished by their clientele and atmosphere.

**El Bar Mata,** Filomena Mata at 5 de Mayo (tel. 518-02-37). Live bands on Wed. and Sun. nights (cover 30 pesos) pack in a youthful crowd ready to party. Equals nearly everything the Zona Rosa has to offer mid-week, although on non-band nights (no cover) the clientele noticeably thins out. Open daily 6pm-2am.

**La Opera,** 5 de Mayo 10 (tel. 518-02-37), just west of Filomeno Mata. A restaurant by day, the place fills up at night with chatting couples downing cocktails. Baroque ceiling, mirrored walls, a grandfather clock, and dark wood booths. While relatively low-key today, showdowns, secret government conferences, even alliances were made and lost within these walls. A significant tourist minority tones down the formality. Drinks 12-19 pesos. Open daily 1pm-midnight.

**Bar de los Azulejos,** Casa de los Azulejos on Madero 14 (tel. 518-66-76), 2nd floor. Small bar tucked away in a corner of Sanborn's. Spiral staircase, leather chairs, and dimmed lights lend a touch of class appropriate for the historic building. A great place to relax in style and lose those troublesome, hard-earned pesos. Food available. Mixed drinks 12-18 pesos. 50% off domestic wines and liquors Mon.-Thurs. 4-6pm and Fri.-Sun. 6-8pm. Open daily 7am-11pm.

**Bar León,** Brasil 5 (tel. 510-30-93), just west of the Templo Mayor and cathedral. Appealing to a slightly older crowd, León offers nightly performances by *merengue* or *salsa* bands. Dark atmosphere invokes the Mexico of yesteryear. In business for 45 years. Bacardi rum 17 pesos, beer 12 pesos. Open Wed.-Sat. 4pm-1am.

## ALAMEDA CENTRAL

While bars and discos near the Alameda can't compare in luster to those in the Zona Rosa, prices are refreshingly low. Unfortunately, surrounding neighborhoods may be dangerous, especially late at night. Taxis are somewhat sparse in this area.

Especially popular is the **Hostería del Bohemico,** Hidalgo 107 (tel. 512-83-28), just west of Reforma. Leave the Hidalgo Metro stop from the Av. Hidalgo/Calle de Héroes exit and turn left. This romantic café is saturated with music, singing, and poetry in the evenings. Seating is on the outdoor terraces of both levels and all four sides of a lush, two-tiered courtyard with a burbling central fountain. The slice-of-a-tree tables and chairs are lit by old-fashioned lanterns, making it the perfect spot for intimate conversations. Guitars strum in the background. No cover, but coffees, cakes, and ice creams run high at 14 pesos each (open daily 5-11pm).

> ### C'mon! Big Bucks!
> If you're into spectacle but running low on pesos, head for the live drawing of the **Loteria Nacional** at the National Lottery Building, the art-deco structure at Juárez and Reforma. Every Monday, Wednesday, and Friday, crowds gather at 8pm to see if they've gotten rich quick. Uniformed boys draw the winning numbers from an immense golden ball and then shout them out robot-like, a hushed crowd hanging on their every syllable. Meanwhile, lottery officials circulate throughout the crowd, distributing free lottery paraphenalia. If you're looking for a cheap gift, snag a free set of Loteria Nacional matches and keychains.

## GARIBALDI PLAZA

Garibaldi Plaza hosts some of Mexico City's gaudiest and seediest nightlife. On weekend nights, roving *mariachis* compete for pesos with *ranchera* groups, who will play your favorite tune for 20-50 pesos. Tourists, locals, prostitutes, musicians, vendors, and the entire rainbow of human fruit flavors mingle here, many reeling from the plastic cup of liquor they just downed. Big nightclubs, each with their own *mariachi*, do their best to lure the crowds. Though they advertise no cover, per-drink prices are staggeringly high. Beware of pickpockets and purse-snatchers; *do* leave home without it—your credit card, wallet, and purse, that is.

Possibly one of the most peculiar attractions of the plaza is **Pulquería Familiar,** Honduras 4, on the northwest corner of the plaza. Supposedly the only *pulque* (fermented cactus juice) bar where women are admitted—accompanied, of course, by a male friend. Taste the precolonial alternative to beer. Have a glass of *blanco* (the pure stuff, 1.50 pesos) to get a feel for it; then move onto the fruity flavorings to actually enjoy the experience. Flavored liters of *pulque* run 8 pesos—mango comes closest to duplicating a nice tropical mixed drink (open daily 4pm-2am).

The plaza is at the intersection of Lázaro Cárdenas and República de Honduras, north of Reforma. Take Metro Line 2 to Bellas Artes and walk three blocks north along Cárdenas; Garibaldi is the plaza/construction site on your right. The Garibaldi stop on Metro Line 8 takes you three blocks north of the plaza. Exit to your left from the stop and walk south. The best time to visit Garibaldi is from 8pm-2am on weekends, but it's also the least safe then. Prostitutes turn tricks here, and the neighboring streets and *cantinas* can be dangerous. Women should take particular caution.

## COYOACÁN AND SAN ÁNGEL

While generally very safe sections of town, these two southern suburbs fall just outside many of Mexico City's public transportation axes. The Metro serves both until midnight, after which a taxi may be the best option.

**Arcano,** División de Norte 2713 (tel. 689-82-73), near the San Andrés park in Coyoacán. A live jazz/rock combo brightens the dark interior. The cover depends on the group. No cover Mon.-Wed. Open daily 8:30pm-1am.

**La Cueva de Amparo Montes,** Avenida de la Paz 32 (tel. 550-89-86), in San Ángel. Serenades, *salsa,* and the music of old Mexico make for a romantic alternative to the club scene. Fri.-Sat. cover 58 pesos. Music from 10pm. Open daily 1pm-2am.

## GAY BARS AND DISCOS

Mexico City offers the full range of social and cultural activities for gays and lesbians. Pick up a copy of *Ser Gay,* a free pamphlet available at Butterfly (see below) that details gay entertainment and art events in the city and provides a complete listing of all the gay bars in town.

**Butterfly,** Izazaga 9, near Metro Salto del Agua, ½ block east of Lázaro Cárdenas, just south of the cathedral. The biggest, brashest gay night spot in town. The dance floor is a crowded tangle of humanity. Video screens and a superb lighting system. Male revue on weekend nights. Tues.-Thurs. no cover, Fri.-Sat. cover 30 pesos with 2 drinks. Gay events throughout the city are advertised from here. Open Tues.-Sun. 7pm-2am.

**El Taller,** Florencia 37-A (tel. 533-49-84), in the Zona Rosa. Watch carefully or you'll miss the entrance to this underground bar. Well-known hangout for blue-collar gay men. Wed. and Sun. attract a twentyish crowd; private barroom attracts an older crowd. Male revue Wed. at midnight. Sun.-Tues. and Thurs. cover 20 pesos includes 1 drink. Wed. and Fri.-Sun. 35 pesos. Open Tues.-Sun. 9pm-3am.

**Botas Bar and Disco,** Niza 45 (tel. 514-46-08), in the Zona Rosa. Mirrors, a disco ball, blacklight bulbs, and a large-screen TV make for sensory overload. The gay crowd is mixed in with the tourists—all chilling at the tables or cutting the groove on the high-tech dance floor. Drinks 25-35 pesos. Tues.-Thurs. no cover, Fri.-Sat. cover 30 pesos. Open Tues.-Sun. 8pm-2am.

**Famoso 42,** Cuba 42 (tel. 355-75-59), between Allende and República de Chile in the *centro*. Couples cuddle in the dark corners or slow-dance to mellow musical fare: Mexican *merengue*, but mostly American top-40 ballads. Pauses in the music bring strippers, videos, and calls for drinks. Open Tues.-Sun. 4pm-2am.

# ■■■ SPORTS

Whether consumed by bullfighting, soccer, jai alai, or horse racing, Mexican fans share an almost religious devotion to *deportes*. If sweaty discos and cavernous museums have you craving a change of pace, follow the crowds to an athletic event and prepare yourself for a rowdy good time.

**Plaza México,** Insurgentes Sur (tel. 563-39-59). Accessible by the Metro station San Antonio (Line 7). Mexico's principal bullring. Bullfights begin Sun. at 4pm. Professionals fight only Dec.-April; *novilladas* (novices) replace *matadores* in off-season. The stadium seats 50,000 fans. Tickets are 15-80 pesos, depending on proximity to the ring and whether they fall on the shady or sunny side. If you're going cheap, try to bring sunglasses, a hat, and a pair of binoculars.

**Aztec Stadium,** SA-Tlalpan 3465 (tel. 677-71-98). Take shuttle train or *pesero* directly from the Tasqueña Metro station (Line 2). How big is it? Really big. In August 1994, 112,000 Mexicans—the biggest crowd in NFL history—turned out for a pre-season game between the Oilers and Cowboys. The Azteca is the greatest of the many stadiums where professional soccer is played. Read the sports pages of any newspaper for information on games. The season runs Oct.-July.

**Frontón México** (tel. 543-32-40), Pl. de la República, 3 blocks south of the Revolución Metro station (Line 2), facing the north side of the monument. Watch and bet on jai alai, the game played (much like racquetball) with a little ball and curious curved wicker *cestas* which the *Guiness Book of World Records* describes as the world's fastest sport. Officially dressy—men wear coats and ties, women dresses or skirts—but a decent shirt and jeans is the unspoken standard for admission. Games take place Tues.-Thurs. and Sat. starting at 9pm, Sun. at 7pm. Box office opens at 6:30pm. Admission 20 pesos. Betting (optional) starts at 1 peso.

**Hipódromo de las Américas,** Av. Ávila Camacho. Take a *pesero* labeled "Hipódromo" west along Reforma, or bus #17 from Metro Tacuba—the horsetrack is on the outskirts of the city. Races Thurs. and Sat.-Sun. at 2:15pm. Admission free unless you sit in the upper level, where purchase of food is obligatory.

---

### And In This Corner...

In a Republic where elections are all too often rigged, perhaps it's no surprise that **Lucha Libre** (fake, fixed wrestling) is so popular. Watch (usually) masked men of immense proportions pin each other to mats throughout the city. For information on the wheres and the whens, consult the sports section of *Tiempo Libre*. Expect to pay 12-24 pesos for the privilege of screaming and swearing at the wrestlers along with hundreds of screaming and swearing Mexicans.

# NEAR MEXICO CITY

## ■■■ TEOTIHUACÁN

For about 1,000 years, a consummately organized, theocratic society thrived in the Valley of Mexico; then it disappeared as mysteriously as it had arisen. The cultural and commercial center of this society was Teotihuacán, founded in 200 BCE. An important holy city, Teotihuacán drew hundreds of pilgrims and became something of a market town in order to accommodate their needs. Its influence on architecture and art was so great that many of the styles that developed here can be found in the legacies of civilizations as far south as Guatemala.

Scholars speculate that the city eventually collapsed under its own weight, that it grew so unwieldy that it could no longer produce enough food to keep its inhabitants well-fed. At its heyday between 150 and 450 CE, Teotihuacán covered nearly 42 square kilometers and scarcely accommodated a population of nearly 200,000. Archaeologists believe that the entire Calle de los Muertos was covered by huts and other residential structures. To make matters worse, importing food was complicated by the fact that residents of the city never discovered the wheel.

By 850 CE, not a single individual was left in the enormous urban complex. When the Aztecs founded Tenochtitlán in 1325, Teotihuacán, 50km northeast of their capital, lay in ruins. The Aztecs adopted the area as ceremonial grounds and believed its huge structures had been built by giants who inhabited the world during the era of the first sun. Believing that those buried in this hallowed place had become gods, the Aztecs called the area Teotihuacán, meaning "Place of the Gods."

The ruined city's latest incarnation is as the most-visited archaeological site in the Republic. The archaeological zone, more commonly referred to as **Las Pirámides,** covers a vast area. The ceremonial center, a 13-square-kilometer expanse, was built along a 2km stretch now called **Calle de los Muertos** (Road of the Dead) for the countless human skeletons that were discovered alongside it. The road leads from the Pyramid of the Moon to the Temple of Quetzalcóatl. Since the Teotihuacanos planned their community around the four cardinal points, Calle de los Muertos runs in what is almost a perfectly straight north-south line. The main structure, the **Pyramid of the Sun,** is on the east side and is squared with the point on the horizon where the sun sets at the summer solstice. On the north end of Calle de los Muertos are the Plaza and Pyramid of the Moon. The Palace and Temple of Quetzalcóatl stand on the east side of the southern end.

The best way to explore the ruins is from south to north. Start your visit on the west side of the southern end of the Calle de los Muertos, where a small **museum** does what it can to tell the story of the enigmatic civilization that inhabited the city. Displays compare the size of the ancient city with various present-day cities, illustrate the architecture and technology of the pyramids, describe the social, religious, and economic organization of the society, and exhibit *indígena* art. Although all the pieces you see are replicas (the originals are at the Museo Nacional de Antropología in Mexico City), the museum serves as a good introduction to the site.

Directly in front of you as you exit the museum is the expansive **Ciudadela,** where priests and government officials once lived. At the center of the Ciudadela is the **Temple of Quetzalcóatl,** once a giant walled-in stadium sheltering a group of ancient temples. Its four flanking platforms served as grounds for priestly ceremonies and dances. The central plaza houses an altar upon which the centennial sacrifice of the "New Fire" was celebrated. Although the temple has lately suffered tremendous erosion from the gods of rain and wind, on the east side of the pyramid you can still see the fierce heads of Tláloc, the rain god, and the serpent Quetzalcóatl, and and traces of the red paint that originally decorated them.

Continuing north along the Calle de los Muertos, you will cross what was once the San Juan river. On the west side of the street are the remains of two temples, known as the **Edificios Superpuestos,** that were built in two phases, 200-400 CE and 400-750 CE, atop older, partially demolished temples.

Farther to the north and east is the **Pyramid of the Sun,** the most massive single structure in the ceremonial area. Second in size only to the pyramid at Cholula, its base measures 222m by 225m—dimensions comparable to those of Cheops in Egypt. The pyramid rises 63m, but the grand temple that once crowned its summit is missing. The miniature temple that now stands atop the pyramid once served Tonacatecutli, the god of the sun. During the summer solstice, the sun falls vertically over the center of the pyramid, thereby bringing the temple that once existed on top in direct contact with its object of worship. The grueling climb to the top of the pyramid (don't worry, the platforms of the multitiered pyramid make convenient rest stops) pays off with a view of the entire site and surrounding valley.

Between the Pyramid of the Sun and the Pyramid of the Moon on the west side of the street is the **Palace of Quetzalpapalotl** (the *quetzal* butterfly). This columned structure was the residence of elites who staked out the area next to the ceremonial space and far from the residential complexes of the common folk; bird motifs and geometric patterns adorn the columns. The inner patio is one of the most beautiful sights of the ancient city; the colored frescoes and bird glyphs have survived years of decay and retain much of their original, intricate detail. Behind the first palace is the **Palacio de los Jaguars.** Although this palace is entirely restored, complete with fluorescent lights and plastic handrails, some of the original frescoes remain, with red, green, yellow, and white symbols that represent birds, corn, and water.

At the northern end of the Calle de los Muertos is the stunning **Pyramid of the Moon.** Although it appears to be as tall as the Pyramid of the Sun, it is in fact much shorter, but built on higher ground. Two somewhat different stages of construction are noticeable in the structure, and the tall steps of the lower section makes the climb more difficult than at the Pyramid of the Sun. A sculpture of **Chalchiutlicue,** a water goddess, was found here during excavations. The view from the summit down the Calle de los Muertos hints at the magnitude of Teotihuacán.

If you still have the energy, there are two other areas, signless and unmarked, to visit off the Calle de los Muertos on the outskirts of the excavated site. On the northeast side of the Pyramid of the Sun near entrance #4 is the **Tepantitla Palace,** which has some of the best-preserved frescoes on the site. You can still make out priests with elaborate headdresses and representations of Tláloc. The lower part of the mural displays the Teotihuacano ideal of paradise. On the southeast border of the site are **Atetelco, Tlamimilolpa, Zacuala,** and **Tetitla;** while each was once a palace, these days each of the structures can seem more like a crumbling maze. Keep your eyes peeled for vestiges of eagle and jaguar frescoes.

Be sure to bring plenty of water, a hat, and sunglasses; vendors sell water if you run out. Written guides sell for 20-30 pesos. Expect to spend about 15-20min. at the museum and another three to four hours exploring the ruins. (Site open daily 8am-5pm. Admission 16 pesos, free parking. To contact the Teotihuacán offices, dial 601-88 or 600-52; from Mexico City add the prefix 91-595.)

**Getting There:** Direct bus service from Mexico City to the pyramids is available from **Autobuses Teotihuacán** (every 15 min., 5am-6pm, 1hr., 9 pesos) located in the Terminal de Autobuses del Norte at *Sala* 8 (tel. 567-14-94). The same bus line runs from Tepexpan should you come from Texcoco or Chiconcuac. The last bus back from the pyramids to Mexico City leaves the main entrance at 6pm. A few miles before reaching Teotihuacán, the bus passes just to the right of the town of Acolmán, founded shortly after the Conquest by Franciscans. The majestic lines of the ex-monastery of Acolmán rise to the sky, breaking the monotony of the corn fields. Even at a distance, the architectural solemnity of this early religious settlement is evident. If you want to stop at the ex-monastery on your way back to Mexico City, take the Indios Verdes bus from the main entrance and get off at Acolmán.

# ■■■ TEPOTZOTLÁN

On the highway from Mexico City to Tula and Querétaro, the town of Tepotzotlán makes an easy daytrip from Mexico City. For those itching to escape the smog and bustle of the city, Tepotzotlán offers a glimpse of small-town life, and its church and monastery house fine examples of religious art. Unfortunately, its proximity to the city has made Tepotzotlán popular with tourists, and prices are high.

In the 16th century, Jesuits established a convent in Tepotzotlán where *indígenas* could study language, art, theology, and mathematics. Martín Maldonado, an *indígena* convert, donated the land to the missionaries in 1582. Construction of the buildings continued until the end of the following century, and the huge bell in the tower was added in 1762. To the rear of the Churrigueresque **Iglesia de San Francisco Javier** is the **Capilla de la Virgen de Loreto.** Behind it, the incredibly ornate **Camarín de la Virgen** (altar room) is fitted with a mirror so that visitors can see the decorations on the dome that crowns it.

After the expulsion of the Jesuits in 1767, the church and buildings became a reform school for priests. Early in this century, they were returned to the Jesuits, and in 1964, the whole complex became the **Museo del Virreinato** (tel. 207-91-37). Although the actual collection is somewhat sparse, the exhibit contains many treasures from the colonial period. Jesuit imagery predominates in the monastery's halls—St. Ignatius stares out from every other altar, and St. Francis Xavier is only slightly less ubiquitous. The popular "Chant" CD put out by the Benedictine Monks of Santo Domingo echoes throughout the halls, fitting the mood perfectly.

The **Iglesia de San Francisco Xavier** is a Churrigueresque masterpiece. Look out for *El Crucifix,* a 17th-century sculpture of Christ on the cross carved from a single piece of wood. Be sure not to miss the concealed entrance to the upper floor near the exit. The hall contains paintings of priests and nuns, a map of Mexico City from 1793, and a balcony with a great view of the surrounding area. The monastery's orchard is criss-crossed by cobblestone paths (open Tues.-Sun. 11am-5:45pm; admission 14 pesos; free Sun.).

The plaza outside the church is packed with immaculate eateries alongside a few hotels. Tepotzotlán's best lodgings are in the **Hotel Posada San José,** Plaza Virreynal 13 (tel. 876-08-35), nearly hidden right beside the Restaurant-Bar Pepe. The walls are bare brick, but the floors are carpeted and the bathrooms are tiled (singles 50 pesos; doubles 70 pesos). For cheap eats, head to **Restaurante Los Pericos,** Plaza Virreynal 7A (tel. 876-23-72), on the far side of the central part of the plaza. Dining under the shaded balcony is perfect for observing the plaza (open daily 8am-10pm).

**Getting There:** To get to Tepotzotlán, take the Metro to Cuatro Caminos (Line 2), then the yellow or blue bus from *salida* H or M. Buses run from 6am-10:30pm, leaving approximately every 20min. (4 pesos). To get back, catch a bus on Juárez across the street from the Hotel Posada San José to any of a number of Metro stations.

# Baja California

Peeled away from the mainland geological ages ago by earthquakes, Baja California is a 40,000-square-mile peninsula cradled by the warm, tranquil Sea of Cortés on the east and the cold, raging Pacific Ocean on the west. Baja claims one of the most spectacular and diverse landscapes in the world: barren desert mountains jut at breathtaking angles high into Baja's traditionally cloudless sky, whose color is contested only by the idyllic blue-green waters in the sea below. The paradisical beaches of the Bahía de Concepción are watched over by many of the thousands of species of cacti that thrive on Baja's otherwise barren hillsides.

Baja is 21km across at its narrowest and 193km at its widest, and its two principal mountain ranges, which partition the two coasts, reach heights of 10,000 feet. Until relatively recently, Baja was an unknown frontier of sorts; the only way to reach its rugged desert terrain was by plane or boat. With the completion of the Transpeninsular Highway in 1973, and the addition of both better toll roads in the north and ferry service, Baja has become a popular vacation spot among Californians, Arizonans, Mexicans, and others. Vacationers range in type from hardy campers setting out to tame the wild deserts of central Baja to the ubiquitous wealthy Americans who prefer a day on the beach, an evening when they can drown their inhibitions in many a *cerveza* and *margarita,* and a night of posh resort life, all without the inconvenience of changing their dead presidents into Mexican pesos.

Baja was said to be first inhabited by wandering Indian tribes, who left their mark in the form of cave paintings, most prominently in the Sierra de San Francisco of Baja Sur. In 1535, Spanish *conquistador* Hernán Cortés crossed the sea that today bears his name and established a colony in what is now the Bahía de la Paz. Though Cortés's colony was abandoned two years later, fleeting European settlements continued from 1538 to 1685: first by Sebastián Vizcaíno, explorers in search of pearls, and later the Jesuits, most prominently Padre Eusebio Kino in 1685. Baja's east coast was permanently settled in 1697 by Padre Juan María Salvatierra, who landed in Loreto with only six soldiers. There, he founded a mission that led to the Jesuit control of Baja for the following 70 years. Twenty-three missions were eventually built, but the Jesuits, with burgeoning wealth and power, were expelled by Spaniards in 1768. The Mexican-American war in 1846-48 finalized the international line, and prohibition in the U.S. brought shady business to such border towns as Tijuana and Mexicali. Nowadays, Californians from Burbank to Berkeley form the solid stream of tourists flowing into Baja to surf, fish, and drink to their hearts' content. The lower prices and lower drinking age, as well as the warm climate, fine beaches, and productive fisheries, are more accessible than ever.

Large resort hotels and condominium complexes are sprouting to house the human torrents, but they have a ways to go before filling Baja California. The heavily-Americanized Los Cabos on the southern tip are beautiful, but have close to as little integrity as Tijuana, the wasteland at the northern extreme. But much of Baja's middle section—from glorious Mulegé and Loreto to the oasis town of San Ignacio and thousands of undisturbed beaches along both coasts—is still pristine. The central mountains and desert beaches, down to the beautiful port city of La Paz, beckon a visit to this still-mysterious peninsula.

## ■■■ GETTING AROUND

### BY LAND

The completion of the Transpeninsular Highway has made it quicker to travel the peninsula by **car,** but driving through Baja is still far from easy. The road was not designed for high-speed driving; often you'll be safely cruising along at 60mph and suddenly career into a hidden, poorly banked, rutted curve that can only be taken at 30mph. Still, a car (especially if it's 4WD) is indisputably the best way to get around, since it opens up an entire world of hiking and camping opportunities—the only way to get close to the most beautiful and secluded areas of Baja.

The Ángeles Verdes (Green Angels) pass along Rte. 1 twice per day (see Once There, Transportation: By Car on page 36). Remember that extra gas (unleaded) may be in short supply along this highway, so don't pass a PEMEX station without filling your tank. All of Baja is in the Zona Libre (Free Zone), so strict vehicle permits are not required. If you will be driving in Baja for more than 72 hours, you only need to get a free permit at the border by showing the vehicle's title and proof of registration. The **AAA Guide to Baja** is absolutely essential if you're traveling by car. Pick one up (US$4, free for AAA members) at any AAA office in Southern California. It includes important auto information as well as valuable, detailed descriptions of off-road jaunts at just about any point along any highway.

All major towns in Baja are served by **bus.** The grueling 25-hour bus trip from Tijuana to La Paz costs 237 pesos; from La Paz you may zip directly to the mainland by **ferry** for as little as 61 pesos. If you plan to navigate the peninsula by bus, be forewarned that almost all *camiones* between Ensenada and La Paz are *de paso*. This means you have to leave at inconvenient times, fight to procure a ticket and then probably stand the whole way. A much better idea is to buy a reserved seat in Tijuana, Ensenada, La Paz, or Los Cabos, and traverse the peninsula in one shot while seated. Unfortunately, you'll miss the fantastic Mulegé-Loreto beaches.

Anyway you cut it, Baja's beaches and other points of interest off the main highway are often inaccessible via public transportation. Buses don't stop at coastal spots between Tijuana and San Quintín. Near Mulegé, Loreto, La Paz, and Los Cabos (capes) on Baja's southern tip, travelers tied to the bus system can make a short walk from the main road to some of the beaches. Some swear by hitching, as Baja has but one well-traveled main drag. Some tourists may not stop for thumbers, but many oblige if caught at a pit stop—PEMEX stations are thick with rides. Mexicans are much more amenable to thumbers, and usually provide an explanation if they don't pick you up. Remember, hitching is unpredictable and potentially hazardous; use common sense and don't hesitate to turn down a ride if something seems wrong. *Let's Go* does not recommend hitchhiking.

## BY SEA

**Ferry** service was instituted in the mid-1960s as a means of supplying Baja with food and supplies, not as a way for tourists to get from here to there—passenger vehicles may take up only the ferry space left over by the top-priority commercial vehicles. For those who plan to take their car aboard a ferry, it's a good idea to make reservations a month in advance; consult a travel agent or contact the ferry office directly (See La Paz, Practical Information on page 128 for details).

There are three different ferry routes: Santa Rosalía to Guaymas (8hrs.), La Paz to Topolobampo/Los Mochis (9hrs.), and La Paz to Mazatlán (17hrs.). The La Paz to Topolobampo/Los Mochis route provides direct access to the train from Los Mochis through the Barrancas del Cobre (Copper Canyon) Ferry tickets are generally expensive, even for *turista*-class berths, which cram two travelers into a cabin outfitted with a sink; bathrooms and showers are down the hall. It's extremely difficult to find tickets for *turista* and *cabina* class, and snagging an *especial* berth (a real hotel room) is as likely as stumbling upon a snowball in the central Baja desert; there are only two such suites on each ferry. This leaves the bottom-of-the-line *salón* ticket, which entitles you to a bus-style seat in a large, smelly room with few communal baths. For further ferry information contact the State Tourist Department (tel. 2-11-99 or 2-79-75; fax 2-77-22).

The cafeteria on the ferry isn't very expensive, but you'll probably want to bring food with you on the trip. If, as is likely, you find yourself traveling *salón*-class at night, ditch your seat early on and stake out a spot on the floor, or outside on the deck under the stairs—simply spread out your sleeping bag and snooze. A small storage room is available to store your belongings, but there's no guarantee that

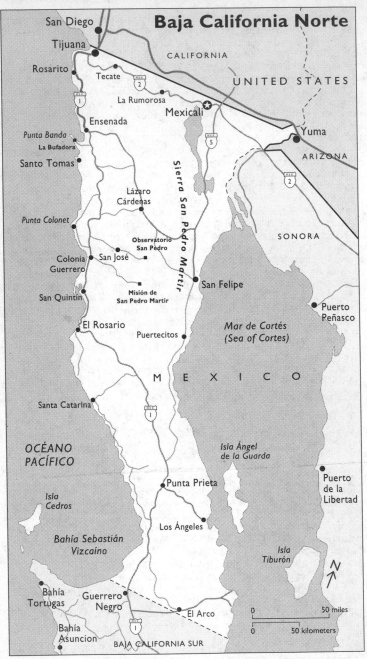

# Baja California Norte

San Diego

Tijuana

Rosarito

Tecate

La Rumorosa

CALIFORNIA

UNITED STATES

HEX 2

Mexicali

Ensenada

Punta Banda

La Bufadora

Santo Tomas

HEX 1

HEX 5

Yuma

ARIZONA

Lázaro
Cárdenas

Punta Colonet

Observatorio
San Pedro

Colonia
Guerrero

San José

SONORA

HEX 2

Sierra San Pedro Martir

San Quintín

Misión de
San Pedro Martir

San Felipe

El Rosario

Puertecitos

Mar de Cortés
(Sea of Cortes)

Puerto
Peñasco

M E X I C O

Santa Catarina

HEX 1

Isla Ángel
de la Guarda

OCÉANO
PACÍFICO

Punta Prieta

Puerto
de la
Libertad

Isla
Cedros

Los Ángeles

Bahía Sebastián
Vizcaíno

Isla
Tiburón

N

Bahía
Tortugas

Guerrero
Negro

El Arco

0          50 miles

0          50 kilometers

Bahía
Asuncion

HEX 1

BAJA CALIFORNIA SUR

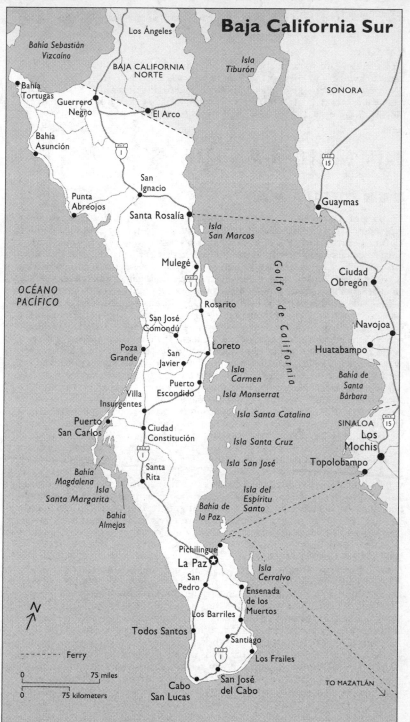

# Baja California Sur

your stuff is secure; to be safe, ask to retrieve your bags about an hour before arrival. A doctor or nurse is always on board in the (rare) event that someone gets seasick.

## BY AIR

Air travel can save you time, but it's not cheap. A flight from La Paz to Los Mochis takes 20 minutes (300 pesos); the flight between Tijuana and La Paz takes 1½ hours (912 pesos). **Aeroméxico** (tel. 83-27-00, ext. 1236), **Mexicana** (tel. 84-21-00), and **Aerocalifornia** (tel. 84-21-00) all have regular daily service from Tijuana to Los Mochis, Guadalajara, La Paz, Los Cabos, and Mexico City.

# BAJA CALIFORNIA NORTE

## ■■■ TIJUANA

Tijuana is Mexico in its rawest, most bleakly industrial incarnation. The most notorious specimen of the peculiar subculture that has grown up along the border, Tijuana is exactly how most of its thirty million yearly *gringo* visitors would have it. The city comes complete with English-speaking, patronizing club promoters; Mexican artisans selling fluorescent *sombreros* and day-glo souvenirs; and attractions covering every decadent way of blowing money, from a glitzy jai alai palace to dark, dingy strip joints, and Las Vegas-style hotels to wet, throbbing dance clubs.

Tijuana is good at being bad—it's been U.S. citizens' number one cheap party spot ever since Prohibition brought a "drought" to the 1920s. First settled by the Cochimie, Tijuana made it onto the map in 1829, when Don Santiago Argüello received the title to Tía Juana (Aunt Jane's) ranch. The ranch became part of the border in 1848, after Mexico lost its northern half to the U.S. in the Mexican-American War. Following WWII, Tijuana grew into an industrial workhorse; over the last decade, the promise of a factory job has attracted over one million people, including whole towns from Southern Mexico and refugees from Mexico City's slums. Men and women from all over the Republic come to Tijuana to study at the top-notch Ibero-American University, or to buy discounted foreign goods. Today's Tijuana is the fourth-largest city in Mexico, stretching out over a huge land area and boasting the fastest growth rate (13.6%) of the world's major cities.

Tijuana is inextricably linked to the U.S. *Gringo* greenbacks are exchanged for shots of tequila poured down tourists' throats and accompanied by shrill whistles, and American corporations bear some responsibility for the stinking pools of factory waste that fill the backyards of Tijuana's two million residents. It's hard to say whether it's the city's skanky charm, its cheap booze, or its sprawling, unapologetic hedonism that attracts tourists like flies. But it's not hard to say why Tijuana is perhaps the only city for which telling someone you're going there will elicit knowing chuckles on all seven continents.

### ORIENTATION

From San Diego to Tijuana, take the red **Mexicoach** bus (tel. 81-84-54 or 800-628-3745) from its terminal at the border (every half-hour, US$1). It will pass Plaza Pueblo Amigo on the Mexican side and eventually drop you off beside the Frontón Palacio on Revolución between Calles 7 and 8. An easier way might be to grab a trolley to San Ysidro at Kettner and Broadway in downtown San Diego (US$1.75), and to walk across the border. Transfers from airport buses are also available.

Driving across the border may seem appealing at first, but the hassles of obtaining Mexican insurance, parking, and the mobs of cars clogging the auto port of entry make this a bad idea for a daytrip. If you get into an accident and you don't have insurance, your car may be confiscated. It's a much better idea to leave your car in a lot on the U.S. side and join the throngs of people walking across the border for the

TIJUANA

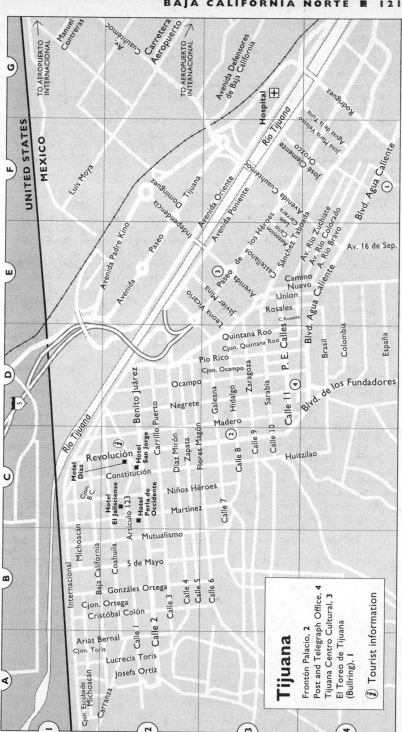

TO AEROPUERTO INTERNACIONAL

Manuel Contreras

Av. Cuauhtémoc

Carretera Aeropuerto

TO AEROPUERTO INTERNACIONAL

Avenida Defensores de Baja California

Hospital

Río Tijuana

José Clemente Orozco

Rodríguez

José María Velasco

Aguas de la Tuna

UNITED STATES

MEXICO

Luis Moya

Tijuana

Domínguez

Avenida Padre Kino

Independencia

Paseo

Avenida

Avenida Oriente

Avenida Poniente

Avenida Cuauhtémoc

Castellanos

de los Héroes

Cjon. Antonio Luis

Carrera

Sánchez Taboada

Av. Río Zuchiate

Av. Río Colorado

A. Río Bravo

Av. 16 de Sep.

Paseo de los Héroes

Leona Vicario

Javier Mina

③

Camino Nuevo

Union

Rosales

C. Rosales

Blvd. Agua Caliente

Blvd. Agua Caliente

①

Quintana Roo

Cjon. Quintana Roo

Pio Rico

Cjon. Ocampo

Ocampo

Negrete

Benito Juárez

Carrillo Puerto

Díaz Mirón

Zapata

Flores Magón

Galeana

Hidalgo

Zaragoza

Sarabia

Madero

Calle 9

Calle 10

Calle 8

P. E. Calles

Brasil

Colombia

España

Blvd. de los Fundadores

Calle 11

④

Huitzilao

Río Tijuana

②

Revolución

Hotel San Jorge

Motel Díaz

Cjon. B.C.

Constitución

Hotel El Jalisciense

Hotel Perla de Occidente

Artículo 123

Niños Héroes

Martínez

Calle 7

Internacional

Michoacán

Coahuila

Baja California

Mutualismo

5 de Mayo

Gonzáles Ortega

Cjon. Ortega

Cristóbal Colón

Calle 3

Calle 4

Calle 5

Calle 6

Arias Bernal

Cjon. Toris

Lucrecia Toris

Josefa Ortíz

Calle 1

Calle 2

Cjon. Escobedo

Michoacán

Carranza

**Tijuana**

Frontón Palacio, 2

Post and Telegraph Office, 4

Tijuana Centro Cultural, 3

El Toreo de Tijuana (Bullring), 1

ⓘ Tourist information

day. Parking rates start at US$3 per day and increase as you move closer to Mexico. Long customs lines when returning can be hellish on busy days. Bring proper ID to re-enter the U.S. A passport will ensure the speediest passage; while a driver's license or other photo ID is also acceptable, it will slow things down. Leave fruits, vegetables, and firearms behind (see "Leaving Mexico" on page 9).

If you arrive at the central **bus station,** avoid the cab drivers' high rates (50 pesos to downtown) and head for the public bus (every 5 min., 5am-10:30pm, ½hr., 2.75 pesos). When you exit the terminal, just turn to your left, walk to the end of the building, and hop a bus marked "Centro Línea." It will let you off on **Calle 3** and **Constitución.** Other *avenidas* run parallel to Constitución, notably **Niños Héroes** and **Martínez** to the west and **Revolución** (the main tourist drag), **Madero,** **Negrete,** and **Ocampo** to the east. *Calles* run east-west; *avenidas* run north-south.

## PRACTICAL INFORMATION

**Tourist Office:** Revolución at Calle 1 (tel. 88-05-55). English-speaking staff offers maps and advice. Open Mon.-Sat. 9am-7pm, Sun. 10am-5pm. A booth on Revolución between Calles 3 and 4 has maps and may be less crowded. **State Attorney for the Protection of the Tourist:** Same address as tourist office. Saul Caño Domínguez Francisco and staff take seriously any problems tourists may encounter—don't hesitate to call. Answering machine operates after hours.

**Customs Office:** (tel. 83-13-90), at the border. Open Mon.-Fri. 8am-3pm.

**Police:** Constitución at Calle 8 (tel. 38-51-60). There's usually a bilingual officer at the station.

**Post Office:** Negrete at Calle 11 (tel. 84-79-50). *Lista de Correos.* Open Mon.-Fri. 8am-7pm, Sat.-Sun. 9am-1pm. **Postal Code:** 22000.

**Telephones:** Tijuana's streets are paved with **LADATELs.** There is a reasonably priced *caseta* at Motel Díaz (see below), and at Hotel San Jorge, Calle 1 at Constitución (tel. 88-37-54), which sends and receives **faxes** (8 pesos per page). Open daily 7:30am-9:30pm. **Telephone Code:** 66.

**Telegrams:** (tel. 84-79-02; fax 84-77-50), to the right of the post office, in the same building. Open Mon.-Fri. 8am-7pm, Sat.-Sun. 8am-1pm.

**Consulates: U.S.,** Tapachula Sur 96 (tel. 86-23-95), in Col. Hipódromo, adjacent to the Agua Caliente racetrack southeast of town. In an emergency, call 619-585-2000 in the U.S. After hours, leave a message on the answering machine and they'll respond shortly. Open Mon.-Fri. 8am-4:30pm. **Canada,** German Gedovius 5 (tel. 84-04-61), in the Zona del Río. Open Mon.-Fri. 9am-1pm.

**Currency Exchange:** Banks along Constitución exchange currency at the same rate. **Bánamex,** Constitución at Calle 4 (tel. 88-00-21, -22, or 85-82-06). Open for exchange Mon.-Fri. 9am-5pm. *Casas de cambio* all over town offer better rates, but do not exchange traveler's checks.

**Bus Station:** (tel. 21-29-83 or -84). To reach the bus station from downtown, board the blue-and-white buses marked "Buena Vista" or "Camionera" on Niños Héroes between Calles 3 and 4 (2.75 pesos), or jump in a brown-and-white communal cab on Madero between Calles 2 and 3 (3 pesos). The cheapest carrier is **Transportes Norte de Sonora** (tel. 21-29-48), which serves Ensenada (7am, 1, and 5pm, 1½hrs., 21 pesos), Guadalajara (9 per day, 6:30am-2am, 36hrs., 293 pesos), Guaymas (every hr., 15hrs., 150 pesos), Hermosillo (every hr., 12hrs., 130 pesos), Los Mochis (every hr., 25hrs., 206 pesos), and Mazatlán (every hr., 26hrs., 239 pesos). **Autotransportes de Baja California** (tel. 21-29-82 to -87, ext. 2408), runs to locations in Baja, including La Paz (8am, noon, 6, and 9pm, 24hrs., 237 pesos), Loreto (8am, noon, 6, and 9pm, 18hrs., 181 pesos), Mexicali (every hr., 3hrs., 39 pesos), San Felipe (5 per day, 5am-4pm, 5hrs., 66 pesos; try to go through Ensenada, not Mexicali), and Santa Rosalía (8am, noon, 6, and 9pm, 15hrs., 143 pesos). **Greyhound** (tel. 21-29-82, ext. 2618) runs to Los Angeles (6:10, 7:15, and 8:15pm, 3hrs., US$18) and connects there to other locations. **Communal cabs** are all over town; some go to Rosarito (½hr., 4 pesos).

**Car Rental: Dollar,** Blvd. Sánchez Taboada 10521 (tel. 81-84-84), in front of the VW dealership. Starting at 242 pesos per day, including insurance and 200km free mileage. Open Mon.-Fri. 9am-6pm, Sat. 9am-2pm.

**Car Insurance:** If you'll be driving in Mexico, spend US$5 per day in San Ysidro to get insurance. There are several drive-through insurance vendors just before the border at Sycamore and Primero who distribute a free booklet with maps and travel tips (see "By Land" on page 116).

**Supermarket: Calimax,** Calle 2 at Constitución (tel. 88-04-54). Open 24 hrs.

**Library:** In Parque Teniente Guerrero. Open Mon.-Fri. 8am-8pm, Sat. 8am-1pm.

**Red Cross:** In an emergency dial 132. Some English spoken. Open 24 hrs.

**Pharmacy: Farmacia Botica "Sherr,"** Constitución 700 (tel. 85-18-20 or 83-39-38), at Calle 3. Some English spoken. Open 24 hrs. **Discount Pharmacy,** Av. Revolución 615 (tel. 88-31-31), between Calles 2 and 3, and at Revolución 1151 (tel. 88-38-38), between Calles 5 and 6. English spoken.

**Hospital:** Centenario 10851 (tel. 84-09-22), in the Zona del Río. Some English spoken. Open 24 hrs.

**Emergency:** Dial 134.

## ACCOMMODATIONS

Tijuana's budget hotels cluster on Calle 1 between Revolución and Mutualismo. The area teems with humanity during the day and is relatively safe. Come nighfall, however, the neighborhood becomes something of a red-light district, especially on Calle 1 between Revolución and Constitución. Avoid walking here at night if possible, and when returning to your hotel, head down Calles 2 or 3.

**Hotel El Jalisciense,** Calle 1 #1715 (tel. 85-34-91), between Niños Héroes and Martínez. Clean, smallish rooms house high, resilient beds and private baths without shower curtains. *Agua purificada* for post-workout refreshment. Check-out 1pm. A good deal: singles and doubles 60 pesos, 10 pesos each additional person.

**Motel Díaz,** Revolución 650 at Calle 1 (tel. 85-71-48). Large, spotless rooms with comfortable beds and nice bathrooms surround a parking lot. Rooms on the ground floor across the lot get plenty o' light; rooms upstairs have no windows. All include not one but (count 'em) *two* night tables, a phone for incoming calls only, and bathroom fans. Check-out 1pm. Singles 90 pesos. Doubles 120 pesos.

**Hotel San Jorge,** Constitución 506 (tel. 85-85-40), between Calles 1 and 2. A large, mirrored lobby leads up to bunker-sized rooms with hanger-filled closets. Clean private baths; the soft beds tend to cave in. Phone available for local calls. Check-out noon. Singles 66 pesos. Doubles 77 pesos. 11 pesos each additional person.

**Hotel Perla de Occidente,** Mutualismo 758 (tel. 85-13-58), between Calles 1 and 2. The healthy hike from the center of the action makes this a haven from noise. Large, soft beds and roomy bathrooms; life is sweet here. Stand-up fans available upon request. Check-out 1pm. Singles 50 pesos. Doubles 80 pesos.

## FOOD

Cheap *típico* restaurants line Constitución and the streets leading from glitzy Revolución to Constitución. Even cheaper are the mom-and-pop mini-restaurants—most are probably safe if the cooks, usually in full view, have clean hands. Avoid the ubiquitous taco stands. *Gringo* fast-food chains (think KFC) crowd Revolución, usually with slightly higher prices than their American counterparts. Tourist-oriented restaurants also line Revolución, and promoters outside try to lure in the masses. Remember to *always* pay in pesos, even if the menu quotes prices in dollars. Restaurants use exchange rates of 75%, or even 50%, of the going pesos-per-dollar rate.

**Los Panchos Taco Shop,** Revolución at Calle 3 (tel. 85-72-77). Orange plastic booths are packed with hungry locals eating cheap Mexican faves. *Tortillas* freshly rolled on the premises. Breakfast also served. New York steak taco US$1, bean *burritos* US$2.10. Get a 10% discount on the entire menu with a Mexicoach flyer coupon. Open Mon.-Fri. 8am-midnight, Sat. 8am-3am, Sun. 8am-2am.

**El Pipirin Antojitos,** Constitución 630 (tel. 88-16-02), between Calles 2 and 3. Load up your tacos with a counterful of condiments. Seating under the orange arches. *Flautas gigantes* 8 pesos, *super quesadilla* with meat and cheese 14 pesos. Open daily 8am-10pm.

**Hotel Nelson Restaurant,** Revolución at Calle 1, under the Hotel Nelson. Good, cheap food served in a clean, fan-cooled coffee-shop atmosphere at a convenient location. Cheap breakfast options include the "special breakfast" of 2 eggs, hot cakes, and ham for 10 pesos; 3 *enchiladas* are 10 pesos. Open daily 7am-11pm.

**Tía Juana Tilly's,** Revolución at Calle 7 (tel. 85-60-24), in the shadow of the jai alai palace. Still vaguely legendary; black-and-white photos tell the story of the nearly 50-year-old bar's earlier days. Live music and dance floor. Mexican plate (taco, *burrito,* and *enchilada*) US$4. Open Sun.-Thurs. 11am-11pm, Fri.-Sat. 11am-5am.

## SIGHTS

Fun in Tijuana revolves around clubs and money and their concomitant vices—shopping, drinking, and gambling. This said, tourist officials have begun to promote events not connected with fermented beverages. They seem to be succeeding; modern Tijuana has a wealth of amusements outside the conventional bar scene. For inexpensive diversion, do a bit of people-watching while strolling down **Revolución;** you'll see plenty of surprising and revolting sights, like tourists having their pictures taken with donkeys painted as zebras and wearing gaudy *sombreros.* When you get tired, relax in the beautiful and shady **Parque Teniente Guerrero,** Calle 3 and 5 de Mayo. It's one of the more pleasant parts of Tijuana and only a few blocks from Revolución. The **cathedral,** with its massive chandelier, is nearby at Niños Héroes and Calle 2. The **Morelos State Park,** Blvd. de los Insurgentes 26000 (tel. 25-24-70), features an exotic bird exhibit and picnic area (open Tues.-Sun. 9am-5pm; admission 3 pesos, 1 peso for kids). To get there, board the green-and-white bus on Calle 5 and Constitución.

The family-owned **L.A. Cetto Winery,** Cañon Johnson 8151 (tel. 85-30-31), just off Constitución at Calle 10, squeezes its specialty from grapes grown in the Valle de Guadalupe, northeast of Ensenada. Tours of the facilities are both entertaining and informative. Just don't try to remove a bottle from the storeroom (as one American woman recently did, causing a wine avalanche that broke and spilled thirty cases of wine bottles). Tours begin every 20 minutes, Tues.-Sun. 8:30am-6:30pm (US$1, with wine-tasting US$2, with wine tasting and souvenir goblet US$3).

Walk off your wine buzz with a visit to one of the new museums in Tijuana. The **Museo de Cera** (tel. 88-24-78), on Calle 1 between Revolución and Madero, is home to a motley crew of wax figures, including such odd bedfellows as Miguel Hidalgo, Dracula, Mikhail Gorbachev (complete with birthmark), Benito Juárez, and Tom Cruise (open Mon. and Wed.-Fri. 10am-7pm, Sat. 10am-8pm; admission US$1, under 6 free). The nearby **Mexitlan,** Calle 2 and Ocampo (tel. 38-41-01), showcases a vast field of over 200 intricate miniatures depicting famous historical, religious, and cultural monuments. Absorb Mayan architecture, Mexico City's Paseo de la Reforma, and Teotihuacán without having to consult a single bus schedule. Mexican folk art is also sold (open Wed.-Fri. 10am-6pm, Sat.-Sun. 9am-9pm; admission US$3.25).

## SPORTS

**Jai alai** is played every night at 8pm in the majestic **Frontón Palacio,** Revolución at Calle 7 (tel. 85-16-12). Two to four players take to the three-sided court at once, using arm-baskets to catch and throw a Brazilian ball of rubber and yarn encased in goatskin. The ball travels at speeds reaching 180mph; jai-alai is reputedly the world's fastest game. After each point, the winning one- or two-player team stays on the court while the losing team rotates out in king-of-the-hill style. The first team to score seven points wins; after the first rotation through the entire 8-team lineup, rallies are worth two points, not one. If you can, try to catch a doubles match—the points are longer and require more finesse. Players are treated like horses, with betting and odds. All employees are bilingual, and the gambling is carried out in greenbacks. (Seating US$3-15, but free-admission coupons are often distributed outside. 13 games, alternating singles and doubles, every night but Wed., 8pm-1:30am.)

Tijuana has two bullrings. **El Toreo de Tijuana** (tel. 86-12-19), downtown to the east off Agua Caliente and Cuauhtémoc, hosts *corridas* (bullfights) on chosen Sundays at 4:30pm from early May to July. A ticket allows you to watch six bullfights. More modern than its cousin, **Plaza Monumental** (tel. 80-18-08), northwest of the city near Las Playas de Tijuana (follow Calle 2 west), employs famous *matadores,* and hosts fights from August to mid-September. Tickets to both rings are sold at the gate and sometimes at the tourist booth on Revolución, between Calles 3 and 4 (tel. 85-22-10). Admission to the bloody spectacle ranges from US$8-40, depending on where you sit. The Plaza Monumental can be reached via the blue-and-white buses that wait on Calle 3 between Constitución and Niños Héroes.

## ENTERTAINMENT

If bullfighting turns your stomach, head for the **Tijuana Centro Cultural,** on Paseo de los Héroes at Mina (tel. 84-11-11, ext. 301; open daily 8am-9pm). The cultural center includes the **Space Theater,** an auditorium with a giant 180° screen that shows American OmniMax movies dubbed in Spanish. (Showtimes Mon.-Fri. every hr. from 3-9pm, and weekends every hr. from 11am-9pm. Adults 14 pesos, children 7 pesos. Center open daily 11am-8pm. Free.) A performance center (**Sala de Espectáculos**) and open-air theater (**Caracol al Aire Libre**) host visiting cultural attractions, including the **Ballet Folklórico.** The **Sala de Video** screens free documentaries, and the **Ciclo de Cine Extranjero** shows foreign films Wed.-Fri. at 6 and 8pm, weekends at 4, 6, and 8pm (8 pesos).

All of this is just swell, but if you've come to party, brace yourself for a frenetic good time. Strolling down Revolución after dusk, you'll be bombarded by thumping music and abrasive club promoters hawking two-for-one margaritas. All Tijuana clubs check IDs (18-plus), with varying criteria for what's acceptable. Many places also routinely body-search patrons for firearms.

**People's Sports N' Rock Member's Club,** Revolución and Calle 2 (tel. 85-45-72). Teeming masses of half-naked teenagers and collegiates writhe on the striped dance floor, surrounded by a more mellow crowd enjoying the margaritas (US$3). Neon bikes, golf clubs, and roller skates hang menacingly from the ceilings, spinning in the cool breeze emanating from the terrace. Lively even on weeknights. Cover Sat. US$2, other days free. Open Sun.-Thurs. 9am-5am, Fri.-Sat. 9am-6am.

**Iguanas-Ranas,** Revolución and Calle 3 (tel. 88-38-85). A younger crowd drinks and raises hell on the dance floor and surrounding tables amidst the pervasive clown motif. For a break, head to the tables on the outdoor terrace lined with international flags. Beer US$2, margaritas two for US$4. The liveliest place to go weeknights; packed on weekends. Open daily 10am-4pm.

**Caves,** Revolución and Calle 5 (tel. 88-06-09). Flintstonian entrance leads to a dark but airy bar and disco with orange decor, stalactites, and black lights. The cave-like dance floor lies below everything else. Managers with tequilas in hand target potential customers . No cover. Beer US$1.25 weekdays, US$2 weeknights. Margaritas 2 for US$3.50 every day. Open Sun.-Thurs. 11am-2am, Fri.-Sat. 11am-6am.

**Tilly's 5th Avenue,** Revolución and Calle 5 (tel. 85-90-15). The tiny wooden dance floor in the center of this upscale, balloon-filled restaurant/bar resembles a boxing ring. Side tables are illuminated by lovely stained-glass lamps. Beer US$1, margaritas 2 for US$3. Wed. night is "Students' Night"—all drinks are US$1. Open Mon. and Wed.-Thurs. 10:30am-2am, Fri.-Sun. 10:30am-5am. Closed Tues.

# ■■■ ROSARITO

Rosarito has long been a playground for the rich and famous. Originally part of one of the enormous *haciendas* that used to spread across Mexico's northern half, Rosarito was given to the powerful Machado family in 1827 by the future governor of Baja California. The estate—swallowing up 407,000 acres—was a virtual fiefdom. Greenbacks flooded the area in the 1920s, when Los Angeles developers bought the land to build a hotel and country club; by the 1930s, the resort had become popular among Hollywood big-wigs fleeing from the Prohibition-dried U.S.

ROSARITO

Modern Rosarito is a string of hotels, restaurants, shops, and beaches lining the toll-free Rte. 1 about 27km south of Tijuana. A favorite destination for tourists and semi-permanent U.S. expatriates, Rosarito is a virtual *gringo* colony—English is ubiquitous and prices are quoted in dollars. The town has expanded at breakneck speed to accommodate the steady stream of tourists seeking sand and surf, but the delicate ecosystem of the region has suffered; garbage and Corona bottles litter Rosarito's once-lonely beaches. On weekends, the sands overflow with people, volleyball games, and horses—finding a place for your towel may be a struggle.

**Orientation and Practical Information** Virtually everything in Rosarito is on the main street, **Boulevard Juárez,** which is a section of the highway. Street numbers are non-sequential; almost everything listed below is near the purple Ortega's Restaurant in Oceana Plaza.

To get to Rosarito from Tijuana, grab a yellow-and-white *taxi de ruta* (3-5 pesos per person) that leaves from Madero between Calles 5 and 6; they guarantee snug seating and make the trip in under 30 minutes. To return to Tijuana, the surest way is again a *taxi de ruta,* which can be flagged down along Juárez or taken from their starting point in front of the Rosarito Beach Hotel. Getting to Ensenada is more of an adventure, because you're at the mercy of buses passing by the Rosarito toll booth (*caseta de cobro*) on Rte. 1. To get to the toll booth, board the blue-and-white striped cabs marked "Primo Tapia" from Festival Plaza just north of the Rosarito Beach Hotel (3 pesos). Buses pass by frequently (about every ½hr., 15 pesos) but often with standing room only.

The **tourist office** (tel. 2-02-00), on Juárez at Acacias, has all the brochures you'll need and lawyers for the protection of tourists. Some English is cautiously spoken (open Mon.-Sat. 9am-7pm, Sun. 10am-5pm). The **police** (tel. 2-11-10) are located next to the tourist office. The **post office** (tel. 2-13-55) is on Acacias directly behind the tourist office (open Mon.-Fri. 8am-5pm, Sat. 9am-1pm). **Postal Code:** 72100. Make international calls from one of the **LADATELs** in town; one is in front of Hotel Brisas del Mar at Juárez and Acacias, another in front of Bánamex, and yet another in front of the Hotel Quinta del Mar, on north Juárez. **Telephone Code:** 661. **Bánamex** (tel. 2-15-56, -57, -58; 2-24-48 or -49), on Juárez at Ortiz, exchanges currency Mon.-Fri. 9am-5pm. On weekends, you'll have to go to a *casa de cambio,* which charges a commission. **Lavamática Moderna,** on Juárez at Acacias, is open Mon.-Sat. 8am-8pm, Sun. 8am-6pm (wash 6 pesos, dry 1.50 pesos). The well-stocked **Comercial Mexicana Supermarket,** at the north end of Juárez before Quinta del Mar (tel. 2-09-34), is open daily 8am-10pm. The **Red Cross** (tel. 132) is on Juárez and Ortiz just north of the tourist office and features a formidable ambulance fleet. **Farmacia Hidalgo** (tel. 2-05-57) is on Juárez at Acacias (open Mon.-Sat. 8am-10pm, Sun. 8am-9pm). The **IMSS Hospital** (tel. 2-10-21), is on Juárez and Acacias behind the post office (open 24 hrs.). In an **emergency,** dial 134.

**Accommodations** With one notable exception, budget hotels in Rosarito are either inconvenient or cramped. The exception is the outstanding **Hotel Palmas Quintero** (tel. 2-13-49), on Lázaro Cárdenas near the Hotel Quinta del Mar, three blocks inland from north Juárez and inward on the left. A friendly staff and dog welcome tourists to giant rooms with double beds and clean, private baths with hot water. Chill on the patio under the palm trees (singles US$13 or 25 pesos; doubles price TBA). **Rosarito Beach Rental Cabins** (tel. 2-09-68), on Lázaro Cárdenas two blocks toward the water, are so cheap that most cabins are already occupied by permanent residents. You get what you pay for—each bug-sized cabin contains bunk beds, a toilet, and a sink. Disney-castle spires make the cabins hard to miss. Management is around some days from 8am-2pm and 4-7pm. (Check-out 1pm. Key deposit US$5. Singles US$5, with shower US$10. Doubles US$8, with shower US$12.)

**Food** Food is one of Rosarito's strengths—fresh produce and seafood abound in the restaurants that line the sides of Juárez. For an economical seafood dinner, set a course for **Vince's Restaurant** (tel. 2-12-53), on Juárez next to Motel Villanueva. Enjoy a feast of soup, salad, rice, potatoes, and tortillas, with fish (your choice): *filete especial* (fillet of Halibut, 24 pesos); jumbo shrimp (40 pesos), and a veritable seafood extravaganza of fish, shrimp, octopus, and lobster (46 pesos) are but a few of your options. The casual atmosphere is enhanced by sturdy plastic plates and vacationers in swimwear. Another Vince's lives at Juárez across from the Quinta del Mar (open daily 7am-11pm). Fresh tacos are served at **Tacos Sonora,** on Juárez 306. Fish tacos or *quesadillas* 5 pesos (open daily 7am-until the last customer leaves). Sit down to a staggeringly cheap breakfast at **Ortega's Ocean Plaza,** Juárez 200 (tel. 2-00-22), in an offensively purple building. Prick your appetite with a cactus omelette (US$1.99), or catch the all-you-can-eat Mexican buffet Sat.-Sun. 8am-12:30pm (US$5.95; open Sun.-Thurs. 8am-10pm, Fri.-Sat. 8am-11pm; MC, Visa accepted).

**Entertainment**  People don't come to Rosarito to change the world; they come to dance and drink. Travelers live the dream at **Papas and Beer,** Calle de Coronales 400 (tel. 2-04-44), one block north of the Rosarito Beach Hotel and two blocks toward the sea. The open-air dance floor, bar, and two sand volleyball courts are packed with partyers on the weekends. Beer is eight pesos, mixed drinks 10-18 pesos. Cover charge is US$3-10 on Saturdays and holidays (open daily 11am-3am). Even the most gray-haired will be carded for the 18-year age requirement.

# ■■■ MEXICALI

The highly industrialized capital of Baja California Norte, Mexicali (pop. 1,000,000) nudges the state's borders with both the U.S. and the Mexican mainland. A rich and fertile valley cradles the city; nourished by soil deposits from the Colorado River and artificially irrigated by water from the nearby Morelos Dam, the valley is one of the most important agricultural regions in the Republic. Lured by the prospect of farming productive land, thousands of Chinese immigrants came to Mexicali around the turn of the century. By 1918, when xenophobic residents prohibited further immigration, there were 10,000 Chinese residents in Mexicali and only 700 Mexicans. The immigrants had to face formidable linguistic and cultural barriers; discrimination and even violence were not uncommon. In one gruesome incident, over 100 Chinese laborers were murdered in the mountains 170km south of town; to this day, the mountains bear the name "El Chinero" in memory of the event. Time diluted the locals' hatred and tensions have virtually disappeared—in today's Mexicali, Chinese food is wildly popular, and a Chinese accent-influenced dialect has emerged in the city center. Of late, several U.S. firms have relocated to Mexicali so as to take advantage of low labor costs; the 11 industrial plants which now ring the city have fueled a recent growth spurt. Sections of Mexicali, including the mall and surrounding plaza, wear the American façade so well that if not for the language, one could be in the States.

## ORIENTATION

Though far from the ordinary route between the U.S. and Mexico, Mexicali can still serve as a starting point for travelers heading south; trains run via Mazatlán to Guadalajara and Mexico City. The city lies on the California border 189km inland from Tijuana, with Calexico and the Imperial Valley immediately to the north. Because of its valley location, Mexicali experiences chilly winters and mega-hot summers.

Mexicali is perhaps one of the most difficult cities in Mexico to navigate. Run directly to the tourist office and pick up a deluxe **map,** or grab a basic one at the border. Mexicali is plagued with streets that zigzag haphazardly and street numbers slightly less patterned than the digits of $\pi$. The main boulevard leading away from the border is **López Mateos,** which cuts an irregular northeast-southwest path through the downtown area. Both north-south *calles* and east-west *avenidas* intersect Mateos, causing even more confusion. Cristóbal Colón, Madero, Reforma, Obregón, Lerdo, and Zaragoza (in that order, from the border) run east-west. From

MEXICALI

east to west, Altamirano, Morelos, México, and streets A-K run north-south, starting from where Mateos meets the border. Don't try to make sense of the border area (particularly the intersection of Morelos and Obregón) from a map; guesswork and a few well-directed questions might be your best bet.

To reach the border from the bus station, take the local bus marked "Centro" (every 10min., 5am-11pm, 1.50 pesos) from outside the bus terminal, just across the footbridge. Ride past the Vicente Guerrero monument and the enormous new mall to downtown; then walk down Mateos until the border crossing.

## PRACTICAL INFORMATION

**Tourist Office: El Comité de Turismo y Convenciones** (tel. 57-23-76; fax 52-58-77), a pink building at Mateos and Compresora facing the Vicente Guerrero monument and park, 3km from the border (open Mon.-Fri. 9am-5pm). Get a city map right across the border in the Comandancia building—see Telephones below. **Tourist cards** are available at the Federal Immigration office at the border.

**Police:** Calle Sur and Mateos (tel. 134, 54-21-32, or 52-91-98). They speak English. Open 24 hrs.

**Post Office:** Madero 491 (tel. 57-51-47), at Morelos. *Lista de Correos.* Open Mon.-Fri. 8am-3pm, Sat. 9am-1pm. **Postal Code:** 21000.

**Telephones: LATADELs** are all over the city; one is in the post office, another is on Madero between Alta and Azulea, and a swarm are outside the white "Comandancia de la Policía Fiscal Federal" building right across the border. If you need a *caseta,* there is one at the **Farmacia de Dios** (see below). Local calls 1 peso, long-distance within Mexico 2.80 pesos per min., calls to U.S. 5 pesos and up per min. **Telephone Code:** 65.

**Telegrams:** (tel. 52-54-92), in the same building as the post office. Open Mon.-Fri. 8am-4pm, Sat. 8am-1pm.

**Currency Exchange:** Exchange currency at any *casa de cambio* along Madero, or try **Bánamex** (tel. 54-28-00, 54-29-29, 54-22-48, or 54-26-39), at Altamirano and Lerdo, where traveler's checks are accepted. Open Mon.-Fri. 9am-5pm.

**Train Station:** (tel. 57-24-20), near the bus station, at Independencia and Mateos. To get there, turn off Mateos opposite Denny's onto Ferrocarrileros. Take the first right and it's on the right. Train service is typically slower than bus service (even *estrella* class), and *estrella* tickets are more expensive than bus tickets. Two trains leave daily—the *estrella* is air-conditioned, serves food and, theoretically, goes twice as fast as the grubby *burro.* The *estrella* leaves promptly at 10am daily and goes as far as Guadalajara, stopping at major cities; tickets are on sale only from 8-10am. The *estrella* is often booked far in advance. The *burro,* on the other hand, only sells tickets on the day of departure (5-9:40pm), so tickets are usually available. It departs at 9:50pm and tools along at 50km/hr. First and second class on the *burro* are different in only one respect: first-class tickets have assigned seats. *Estrella* class to Guadalajara takes 36 hours and costs 201 pesos; *burro* class takes 72 hours (care to spend three full days on a train?) and costs 112 pesos.

**Bus Station:** (tel. 57-24-10, 57-24-15, 57-24-22, or 57-24-55), near the intersection of Mateos and Independencia, about 4km south of the border. **Transportes Norte de Sonora** (tel. 57-24-10) sends buses to Guadalajara (every hr., 33hrs., 293 pesos), Guaymas (every hr., 11hrs., 116 pesos), Hermosillo (every hr., 9hrs., 97 pesos), Los Mochis (every hr., 17hrs., 172 pesos), Mazatlán (every hr., 24hrs., 239 pesos), Tepic (every hr., 30hrs., 269 pesos), and Tijuana (*de paso*, 3hrs., 34 pesos). **Caballero Azteca** and **Elite** (tel. 56-01-10) send buses to most of the above locations at higher prices, plus Chihuahua (10:25am and 3pm, 17hrs., 218 pesos), Juárez (3:30pm, 14-16hrs., 188 pesos), and Nogales (11:35pm, 9hrs., 105 pesos). **Autotransportes de Baja California** (tel. 57-24-20, ext. 2229) sends buses to Ensenada (5 per day, 8am-8pm, 14hrs., 56 pesos), La Paz (5:30pm, 27½hrs., 273 pesos), Puerto Peñasco (9am, 1:45pm, and 8pm, 5hrs., 48 pesos), San Felipe (5 per day, 8am-8pm, 2½hrs., 40 pesos), and a roller-coaster ride to Tijuana (every hr., 3½hrs., 39 pesos). **Transportes del Pacífico** (tel. 57-24-61) offers *de paso* service to Tijuana, and also goes to Obregón, Los Mochis, and most of the above locations for slightly higher fares than Norte de Sonora, but also offers second-class buses for around 15% less that take 2-6 hours longer. **Golden**

**State** (tel. 52-24-10 or 53-61-69) sends buses to Californian cities, including Los Angeles (8am, 2:30pm, and 10pm, 4½hrs., US$27), Palm Springs (8am, 2:30pm, and 10pm, US$22), and Pomona (8am, 2:30pm, and 10pm, US$27).

**Red Cross:** (tel. 132), at Quinte Durango, Colonia Pueblo Nuevo. Very little English is spoken. Open 24 hrs.

**Pharmacy: Farmacia de Dios,** at López Mateos and Morelos (tel. 54-15-18). With a name like this, how can you go wrong? Some English spoken. Features a telephone *caseta*. Open 24 hrs.

**Hospital: IMSS Centro de Salud** (tel. 53-56-16), Lerdo at Calle F, has an English-speaking staff. Otherwise, try the **Hospital Civil** (tel. 54-11-23 or 54-11-30).

## ACCOMMODATIONS

Budget hotels crowd the noisy bar strip on Altamirano between Reforma and Lerdo and line Morelos south of Mateos. Hotels on Madero close to Mateos will dig deeper into your wallet but are cleaner.

**Hotel México,** Av. Lerdo 476 (tel. 54-06-69), at Morelos. An excellent value. Newly remodeled, this hotel offers clean rooms situated around a central patio, each boasting A/C and a color TV. The office doubles as a grocery store. Singles 60 pesos. Double bed 100 pesos. King-sized and double bed 120 pesos.

**Hotel Imperial,** Madero 222 (tel. 53-63-33, 53-61-16, or 53-67-90), at Azulea. Rock-hard beds. Minty-fresh rooms are stocked with desks, squeaky fans, A/C, and color TVs. Private baths with narrow showers. Key deposit 5 pesos. Check-out noon. *Agua purificada*. Visa, MC accepted. Singles 85 pesos. Doubles 110 pesos.

## FOOD

With Mexicali's large Chinese-Mexican population, you can count on finding tasty chow mein—and more—around every corner.

**Restaurant Buendía,** Altamirano 263 (tel. 52-69-25). Despite sharing a name with the illustrious family of Gabriel García Márquez's epic, Buendía specializes in Chinese cuisine—but chefs are always happy to whip up some *antojitos*. Try one of the heaping Chinese plates that you simply won't finish: beef with broccoli, fried rice, egg roll, and fried chicken goes for 13 pesos. Three *burritos* are 18 pesos.

**Tortas El Chavo,** Reforma 414 at Altamirano, off Mateos, three blocks from the border. A fast-food joint with plastic booths; mirrored walls reflect the green-and-yellow "furniture." *Tortas,* any style, are seven pesos; *tacos de machaca* (tacos filled with strips of beef) cost 3.20 pesos. Open daily 8:30am-8pm.

**Café Yin Tun,** Morelos 379, has good A/C and Christmas colors all year long—red tablecloths, fake green plants. Chinese specials 10-15 pesos. The ubiquitous beef with broccoli and breaded shrimp 15 pesos each. Special plates with more exotic seafood offerings are 35 pesos. Open daily 9am-midnight. MC, Visa accepted.

## SIGHTS

Mexicali's **park, forest, lake,** and **zoo** (tel. 55-28-33) are located in the southwestern part of town, on Alvarado between San Marcos and Lázaro Cárdenas. Wink at birds in the aviary, pedal a paddleboat on the lake, or admire lions and tigers from the train that circles the park and nature reserve. The grounds contain carousels, bumper cars, a pool, and a science museum (open Mon.-Sat. 9am-5pm, Sun. 9am-6pm; admission 5 pesos). To reach the park area board a black and white *colectivo* marked "Calle 3" downtown. If you've got wheels, drive south on Azulea over the Río Nuevo. The road becomes Uxmal south of the river; turn left on Independencia, then right on Victoria. The city's **Parque Vicente Guerrero** (tel. 54-55-63), across from the mall and busier sections of the main street, has jungle gyms and picnic-spot and party-space rentals (open daily 9am-8pm).

## ENTERTAINMENT

Bullfights are regularly staged in the fall at the **Plaza de Toros Calafia** (tel. 57-01-81), on Calafia at Independencia in the *centro*. Wild and crazy rodeos rampage in the winter and spring at **Lienzo Charro del Cetys,** Cetys and Ordente. Check at the tourist office for schedules. Good, clean fun awaits at **Mundo Divertido,** an amusement park at Mateos 850 (tel. 52-56-75), across from Vincente Guerrero Park (open Mon.-Fri. noon-9pm, Sat.-Sun. 11am-10pm). To get to the park, board a blue-and-white bus marked "Centro Cívico" departing from Madero and Altamirano (every 10 min., 5am-11pm, 1.50 pesos). **Cinema Gamelos,** Juárez 21 (tel. 66-07-48), at Montejano in the **Centro Comercial Gigante** mall, screens American films (12 pesos).

# ■■■ SAN FELIPE

Although San Felipe may put on Mexican airs, it is a tourist-oriented beach town at heart. Christened by San Felipe de Jesús in 1721, San Felipe remained essentially isolated until the 19th century, when a U.S. firm began harvesting tons of seafood from the deserted shores of Bahía San Felipe. In the 1950s, northern snowbirds claimed the area as a regular hangout, bringing with them handfuls of greenbacks and a new industry—tourism—to the area. San Felipe offers a stellar selection of seafood and a beautiful stretch of beach teased by the warm, shallow waters of the Gulf. Although more than 200 *gringo* RV parks now line the coast of the greater San Felipe area, the town still attracts many Mexicans and has managed to maintain its charm.

**Orientation and Practical Information** San Felipe is 198km south of Mexicali at the end of sizzling-hot Rte. 5. The town is also accessible via a paved road from Ensenada—if coming from Tijuana, the Ensenada route makes for a more pleasant ride. A dirt-and-gravel road connects San Felipe to points south. *Los arcos* (a tall arched structure) is immediately recognizable when entering the village; Chetumal is the street continuing straight from the arches toward the sea. Hotels, restaurants, and banks cluster on **Mar de Cortés,** one block from the beach. **Malecón,** filled with seafood stands, is right on the beach. All cross-streets named "Mar" run parallel to the beach; from south to north, Manzanillo, Topolobampo, Ensenada, Chetumal, and Acapulco run perpendicular. To get downtown from the **bus station,** walk north on Mar Caribe to the Manzanillo; then turn right toward the water.

The **tourist office,** Mar de Cortés 300 (tel. 7-11-55), at Manzanillo, has English-speaking staffers (open Mon.-Fri. 8am-7pm, Sat. 9am-3pm, Sun. 10am-1pm). The **police** are on Mar Blanco Sur (tel. 7-13-50 and 7-10-21), just south of Chetumal. The **post office** (tel. 7-13-30) is on Mar Blanco between Ensenada and Chetumal, five blocks inland from Cortés (open Mon.-Fri. 8am-3pm, Sat. 9am-1pm). **Postal Code:** 21850. **Telegrams** (tel. 7-11-12) can be sent from the yellow office on Mar Bermejo between Puerto Peñasco and Zihuatanejo (open Mon.-Fri. 8am-1pm). **Farmacia San Angelín,** Chetumal at Mar de Cortés (tel. 7-10-43), has *casetas* for **long-distance calls** (calls US$1 plus credit card charges). **Faxes** 5 pesos per page to receive, 12 pesos per page to send (open daily 9am-9pm). **Telephone Code:** 657. **Bancomer,** Mar de Cortés Nte. at Acapulco (tel. and fax 7-10-51), near Rockodile Bar, exchanges currency from 9am-1:30pm and has a 24-hr. **ATM.**

The **bus terminal** (tel. 7-15-16) is on Mar Caribe, a 15-minute walk from the center of action. **Autotransportes de Baja California** runs buses to Ensenada (8am and 6pm, 3½hrs., 46 pesos), Mexicali (6am, noon, and 4pm, 2½hrs., 37 pesos), and "Plus" service to Mexicali (7:30am and 8pm, 2½hrs., 40 pesos) and Tijuana (7:30am and 8pm, 5hrs., 71 pesos). Ticket sales daily 6:30am-10:30pm. **Luggage storage** at the bus station costs 1.50 pesos. The **Red Cross,** at Mar Bermejo and Peñasco (tel. 7-15-44), has English-speaking staffers (open 24 hrs.). **Farmacia San Angelín** is on Mar de Cortés at Chetumal (tel. 7-10-43; open daily 9am-9pm). The **Centro de Salud** (tel. 7-15-21), on Chetumal near the fire and police station, has English-speaking staffers (open 24 hrs.). In an **emergency,** dial 134.

**Accommodations** There are two kinds of accommodations in San Felipe: those with walls and A/C, and those without. Travelers who prefer the former will end up paying *mucho dinero* for mediocre rooms. Another cheap option is to rent a room in a private residence; check with the tourist office for a list. Crammed between curio shops and administered from the liquor store next door, **Motel El Pescador,** on Mar de Cortés at Chetumal (tel. 7-11-83 or 7-10-44), offers rooms right on the beach with anemic A/C and private baths. Everything is negotiable. Check-out noon (singles 150 pesos; doubles 180 pesos). **Chapala Motel,** on Mar de Cortés and Ensenada (tel. 7-12-40), has clean baths, A/C, and TVs. Ask for a room with a kitchen, then chill your head in the fridge. Check-out 2pm (singles 220 pesos, 193 pesos during week; doubles 165 pesos; MC, Visa).

As any Californian with an RV can tell you, San Felipe is well-known for its trailer parks. The most famous is **Ruben's** (tel. 7-14-42), toward the end of Av. Golfo de California in Playa Norte. To reach Ruben's, turn left from Chetumal onto Mar de Cortés; it's a short drive up. Individual beachfront parking spaces are topped with two-story open-air bungalows. Each spot easily accommodates carloads of folks with sleeping bags; RVs can hook up to electricity, hot water, and sewer connections (office open daily 7am-8pm; US$20 per vehicle, up to three people, US$2 each extra person). Smack dab in the middle of town on Mar de Cortés, **Campo San Felipe** (tel. 7-10-12) lures campers with a fabulous beachfront location. A thatched roof shelters each fully-loaded trailer spot. (Trailer hookup US$11-16, depending on location. US$2 per extra person, children under 6 free. Hookups US$1 extra. Tent space US$10.) **Carmelita,** across from the Chapala Motel, is one of the private residences renting out rooms. Four rooms are available, housing single people or "married" couples only; they cost around US$20.

**Food** Mar de Cortés is crammed with restaurants advertising air-conditioned relief. Just one block over along the Malecón, *ostionerías* and fish *taquerías* serve up fresh seafood under shady thatched roofs for fewer clams. Shrimp tacos 4-5 pesos, full shrimp dinners 35-45 pesos. **Los Gemelos,** on Mar de Cortés at Acapulco (tel. 7-10-63), near Bancomer, and its identical neighbor with seating on the beach, **Restaurant El Club,** feature beef, chicken, and shrimp *enchiladas* (18 pesos) and Veracruz-style fish (27.50 pesos) on pristine white tablecloths below more than enough hanging plastic turtles. The *camarones al mojo de ajo* (45 pesos) is one of the world's most perfect meals. Ice-cold *agua purificada* available free. Placemats feature octopi playing tennis—really (open daily 7am-11pm).

**Sights and Entertainment** People come to San Felipe to swim in its warm, tranquil, and invitingly blue Gulf waters. The beach in town follows along the Malecón. It gets crowded on weekends. **Jet-skis** can be rented for around US$20 per hr. Try the beaches further south for scuba and snorkeling—they're clearer. A booth that rents jet-skis and beach buggies (US$25 per hr.) is located right next to Motel El Pescador. **Banana boats** wait along the beach in front of Bar Miramar, ready to take you for a 20-minute spin (10am-6pm, 10 pesos per person, min. 5 people).

Many local fishermen will gladly take vacationers on fishing excursions near **Isla San Felipe** and the recently planted artificial reefs; remember, fishing is generally poor when it's windy. Wooden, motor-powered boats launch at around 6 or 6:30am for a half-day (until 1pm) of fishing and seal-watching near the rocks of the Isla (about US$25 per person, US$20 with 4 or more). One company that organizes such trips is **Alex Sport Fishing** (tel. 7-10-52). **Enchanted Island Excursions** (tel. 7-14-31) offers longer boat tours to the islands, lasting up to three days or more.

The whole Bahía is generally clean, safe, and pretty; beaches outside of town are more isolated, but might require a long walk or a drive. Every beach is accompanied by a commercialized RV/trailer park, but, as always, beaches are free—you only need to pay if you're parking. **Playa Punta Bunda,** 3km south of town (follow Camino del Sur), **Playa del Sol, Playa Jalisco,** and **Playa de los Amigos** all come recommended by locals. Buses which run from the Central Camionera north to Mexicali will drop you off on the beach (5-10 pesos; see Practical Information: Bus Station, above), but it may be hard to catch a bus *back* to San Felipe.

ENSENADA

Take time to visit the **Shrine of the Virgin Guadalupe,** at the top of the *cerritos* (hills) near the lighthouse. After a scorching hike, you'll be rewarded with a spectacular view of San Felipe and the blue bay. Don't try to drive up unless you've got a 4WD vehicle—the loose sand won't be amused. Sixty-four kilometers south of San Felipe is the **Valle de los Gigantes National Park.** With cacti up to 15m tall, the park was the original home of the giant cactus which represented Mexico at the 1992 World's Fair in Seville, Spain.

Seasoned veterans nurse drinks at **Bar Miramar,** Mar de Cortés 315 (tel. 7-11-92). The oldest bar in San Felipe may look like a *cantina* from the 60s, but the patrons come for company, not glitz. Push a few cues over green felt on the pool tables out front. (Beer US$1.25, margaritas US$1.75. Happy hour Mon.-Thurs. 3-7pm. Open daily 10am-2am.) Younger folks usually head a few doors down to the high-profile, high-priced **Rockodile** (tel. 7-12-19), on the Malecón at Acapulco. Check out the volleyball court, pool table, and outdoor terrace. The decor looks like an attempt to combine Keith Haring with cave paintings. (Happy hour with US$1 beers and US$2 margaritas Sun.-Fri. 11am-6pm. Beer US$2, margaritas a pricey US$4. Open Sun.-Fri. 11am-2am, Sat. 11am-3am. Closed Mon.-Thurs. in winter.)

# ■■■ ENSENADA

The secret is out—beachless Ensenada is fast becoming a weekend hot spot. The masses of Californians that arrive every Friday evening have *gringo*-ized the town to an incredible degree; everyone speaks some English, and store clerks resort to calculators if you try to buy something with pesos. Still, Ensenada is less brash than its insatiable cousin to the north. Cooled by sea breezes, Ensenada is quite pleasant— particularly during the week, when fewer tourist-consumers populate the city—and the center of town is lively and even somewhat endearing.

The ride from Tijuana to Ensenada offers continuous views of the Pacific, and its last twenty minutes are breathtaking if you take the Ensenada *cuota* (toll road)—the buses do. There are three toll gates along the way, each charging US$1.61. Don't begrudge the money, though; your tolls pay for safe roads with guardrails, insurance, ambulance and towing service, Green Angel road assistance (tel. 6-46-85 in Ensenada; available daily 8am-8pm), and emergency phones every 2km. There are no streetlights, though, so it's best to drive in the daytime. Drive in the right lane only; the left is strictly for passing and the law is enforced. Along the toll road you'll enjoy views of the ocean, large sand dunes, stark cliffs, and broad mesas—if busing it, be sure to grab a seat on the right-hand side. Some great rest spots can be found along the road to absorb the view. Find a clearing, cautiously pull over, and park— you can hike down or walk along the lonely cliffs. The much less scenic *libre* (free road) is a poorly maintained two-lane highway that parallels the toll road to La Misión and then cuts inland for the remaining 40km to Ensenada.

**Orientation** Ensenada is 108km south of Tijuana on Rte 1. Buses from Tijuana arrive at the main terminal, at Calle 11 and Riveroll. Turn right as you come out of the station, walk 10 blocks, and you'll be at **Mateos** (also called **Primera**), the main tourist drag. **Juárez** (Calle 5) runs parallel to Mateos, while from north to south, Avenidas Ryerson, Moctezuma, Obregón, Ruíz, Gastelum, Miramar, Riveroll, Alvarado, Blancarte, and Castillo are perpendicular to it above the *arroyo,* a grassy trench crossed by small bridges; below the *arroyo,* Avenidas Espinoza, Floresta, Guadalupe, Hidalgo, Iturbide, and (later) Balboa also run perpendicular to Mateos. **Blvd. Costero** traces the shoreline, parallel to (and west of) Mateos. Streets are numbered, avenues are named; together they form a grid. *Calles* run northwest-southeast, while most *avenidas* run northeast-southwest (Juárez and Mateos are exceptions). After sundown, avoid the area near the shoreline and the regions bounded by Avenidas Miramar and Macheros, and Mateos and Cuarta. Always keep in mind while orienting yourself that the large residential Chapultepec Hills lie to the north, and the water to the west.

**Practical Information** The **tourist office,** Blvd. Costero 540 (tel. 8-24-11, 8-36-75, or 800-310-968; fax 8-85-88), at Gastelum, has maps and English-language papers (open Mon.-Fri. 9am-7pm, Sat.-Sun. 10am-3pm). The **Chamber of Commerce,** Mateos 693, 2nd floor (tel. 8-37-70, 8-23-22, or 4-09-96), at Macheros, is closer to the center of town and provides brochures and city maps. (Open Mon.-Fri. 8:30am-2pm and 4-6:30pm. The *caseta,* where maps are available, is open Sat.-Sun. 9am-5pm.) **Police** are at Calle 9 at Espinoza (tel. 6-24-21). The **post office,** on Mateos at Club Rotario 93 (tel. 6-10-88), one block past the *arroyo,* posts a *Lista de Correos* (open Mon.-Fri. 8am-7pm, Sat. 8am-2pm). **Postal Code:** 22830. **LADATEL** phones line Juárez and Mateos. **Telephone Code:** 617. **Telegrams** can be sent from Av. Floresta at Calle Tercera (tel. 6-40-18; open Mon.-Fri. 8am-6pm, Sat. 8am-2pm). **Banks** clump along Juárez at Av. Ruíz, but few will exchange traveler's checks. One that will is **Bancomer,** on Juárez at Av. Ruíz (tel. 8-11-08), though the wait is usually long (exchange checks Mon.-Fri. 9am-12:30pm; exchange currency Mon.-Fri. 9am-1:30pm). **ATMs** are along Juárez in the bank district, including one at **BanOro,** Juárez and Gastelum, that accepts Cirrus, Plus, MC, and Visa.

The main **bus terminal** (tel. 8-66-80) is serviced by **Transportes Norte de Sonora** (tel. 8-67-70), which runs from 7:30am-midnight (and sometimes later) to Guaymas (6 per day, 16hrs., 157 pesos), Los Mochis (6 per day, 20hrs., 237 pesos 1st class, 209 pesos 2nd class), Mexicali (8 per day, 5:30am-8pm, 4hrs., 55 pesos 1st class, 50 pesos 2nd class), and Tijuana (every ½hr., 1½hrs., 25 pesos 1st class, 20 pesos 2nd class). **Autotransportes de Baja California** (tel. 8-66-80) runs to Tijuana and Mexicali on the same schedule as TNS, and also to Guerrero Negro (6 per day, 10am-11pm, 10hrs., 94 pesos), La Paz (10am, 2, 8, and 11pm, 22hrs., 217 pesos), Loreto (10am, 2, 8, and 10pm, 16hrs., 160 pesos), San Felipe (8am and 6pm, 3½hrs., 46 pesos), and Santa Rosalía (6 per day, 10am-11pm, 13hrs., 123 pesos). **Transportes Aragón** (tel. 4-07-17), located on Riveroll between Octava and Novena, runs to Tijuana hourly from 6am-9pm (20 pesos one-way, 30 pesos round-trip); Aragón will drop you off in the center of Tijuana instead of on the outskirts of town. Students and senior citizens get a 50% discount. Local *urbano* buses (tel. 8-25-94) leave every 8-15 minutes from Juárez and Sexta, and on Segunda and Macheros (1.50-2 pesos).

**Viajes Las Dunas,** Costero 1001 at Alvarado (tel. 8-82-28), next to the Costa del Mar, has the best prices in town for car rental. A four-door automatic Corsica with 100 free miles runs about 270 pesos a day, including insurance (open daily 8am-2pm and 4-6pm). **Luggage storage** is available at the main bus terminal (3 pesos for the 1st 5hrs., 0.30 pesos each additional hr.). **Lavandería Lavadero** (tel. 8-27-37), on Obregón between Sexta and Séptima across from Parque Revolución, washes small loads (6 pesos), large loads (12 pesos), and dries everything in between (2 pesos for 8min.; open Mon.-Sat. 7:30am-7pm, Sun. 8am-1pm). **Supermarket Calimax,** Gastelum at Calle 4 (tel. 8-33-97), has better prices than the grocery stores on just about everything (open daily 7am-9:40pm). The **Red Cross** is on Blvd. de Jesús Clark at Flores (tel. 4-45-85; open 24 hrs.). **Farmacia del Sol** is at Cortés and Reforma (tel. 6-37-75), in the Limón shopping center. English spoken (open 24 hrs.). The **Hospital General** (tel. 6-78-00 or 6-44-44), on the Transpeninsular Highway at the 111km mark, is also open 24 hrs. In an **emergency,** dial 132 (Red Cross) or 134 (police).

**Accommodations** Budget hotels line Mateos between Espinoza and Riveroll and at Miramar. Most rooms are a 20-minute hike from the beaches and 10 minutes from the popular clubs. Although many owners quote prices in greenbacks, they also accept pesos. **Motel Pancho,** on Alvarado at Calle 2 (tel. 8-23-44), one block off Mateos, has big rooms, clean baths, and furry brown rugs. Although plagued with mosquitoes, it's close to bars. Bedstands are marked by those who spent a cheap night before you (check-out noon; singles and doubles 60 pesos). **Hotel Rosita** (tel. 8-16-25), on Gastelum between Calles 3 and 4, is also close to the bars. Rooms are dark and small, contain flies, and have no shower curtains. But the beds hold people, the bathrooms (even communal ones) are fairly clean, the showers work, and

ENSENADA

the toilets flush. (Singles for 1 or 2 people 25 pesos, 35 pesos with bath. Doubles for 2 or 3 people 40 pesos with or without bath. Each additional person 10 pesos. A 6-person room with no bath 60 pesos.) The beach between Tijuana and Ensenada is lined with RV parks. One close to Ensenada is **Ramona RV Park** (tel. 4-60-45), on km104 of the Transpeninsular Highway (US$9 for full hookup).

**Food** The cheapest restaurants in town line Juárez and Espinoza; eateries on Mateos and near the water jack up their prices. Fresh fruit stands abound, but the best bargains are at the supermarkets on Gastelum. As always, the *panaderías* have good breads at minuscule prices. **Asadero Chispa,** on Mateos at Guadalupe, has extremely tasty grilled tacos with meat and whole beans (4.50 pesos) and scrumptious *burritos* made with beans and beef strips on foot-wide *tortillas* (13 pesos). Seats are scarce at lunchtime (open daily 11am-11pm). **Cafetería Monique Colonial,** Calle 9 and Espinoza (tel. 6-40-41), is popular with locals. Diners sit in anxious anticipation of their breaded steak with salad and fries (22 pesos). No alcoholic drinks are served, and another boon to your health is provided by the home medical guide on the paper placemats (open Mon.-Sat. 6am-10pm, Sun. 6am-5pm). Chefs at **Las Parrillas** (tel. 6-17-28), Espinoza at Calle 6, grill up fresh meat cutlets on the flaming pit as customers make like Pavlov's dog. Squeeze onto a counter stool in the diner-like atmosphere and scarf *burritos* (17 pesos) and *super hamburgesas* with veggies, avocadoes, and chili (12.50 pesos; open daily 7:30am-11pm).

**Sights** Seeing Ensenada requires more than a quick cruise down Mateos. For a view of the entire city, climb the **Chapultepec Hills.** The steep road to the top begins at the foot of Calle 2; expect a 10-15 minute hike. Less taxing is a stroll down **Blvd. Costero,** where herds of curio shops make for hours of mindless shopping.

The mild, dry climate of Northern Baja's Pacific coast has made it Mexico's prime grape-growing area. **Bodegas de Santo Tomás,** Miramar 666 (tel. 8-25-09), though cursed with the number of the Beast, has produced wine since 1888 (thank God not 1666). Today, they distill over 500,000 cases of wine every year, including rosé and champagne. Tours (US$2) are conducted thrice daily, complete with complimentary wine tasting and an assortment of breads and cheeses.

The **Instituto Nacional de Antropología e Historia,** Ryerson 99 (tel. 8-25-31), at Virgilio Uribe, is the oldest building in town. Artifacts from all over Baja include a charming photograph of two elderly Cucapa men standing next to their shared young wife, whom they acquired during a robbery in a nearby town (open Tues.-Sun. 8am-3pm; free). A healthy 15-minute walk from Mateos is the **Museo de Ciencias,** Obregón 1463 (tel. 8-71-92; fax 8-63-35), at Catorce. Housed in an old wooden boat, the museum displays photographs of and information about the endangered species of Baja (open Mon.-Fri. 9am-5pm, Sat.-Sun. noon-5pm; admission 5 pesos).

Contemplate great men in the well-manicured **Plaza Civil,** on Costero between Riveroll and Alvarado. The three men immortalized in much-larger-than-life golden busts—Venustiano Carranza, Miguel Hidalgo, and Benito Juárez—all seem to be grimacing. The nearby gardens of the **Centro Cívico, Social, y Cultural de Ensenada** (tel. 6-43-10 or 6-42-33) are one block from Costero. High, flapping flags, each symbolizing a Latin American country, sprout from beds of flowering plants.

**Entertainment** Most of the popular hangouts along Mateos are members of the hybrid species known as the restaurant/bar/disco. Food and drink are served only until 8pm or so, when the hybrids metamorphose into full-fledged dance club monsters. On weekends, almost every place is packed with festive-feeling *gringos.*

Better known than Ensenada itself is **Hussong's Cantina** (tel. 8-32-10), on Ruíz between Mateos and Calle 2; now 102 years old, it's the prototypical Mexican watering hole. Gulp down beer (5-7 pesos) or a margarita (6 pesos) at the long, shiny bar (open daily 10am-1am). When you tire of the continuous stream of *mariachis,* cross the street to **Papas and Beer** (tel. 4-01-45), a high-tech music emporium popular with the young crowd who swig margaritas (16 pesos) and spend horse-choking wads of cash. Escape the congestion and decor by stepping onto the terrace, where hockey-rink-like plexiglass boards prevent carousers from cross-checking each other off the balcony to the street below. Thursday night is birthday night—it's everyone's birthday—and Friday is ladies' night; women get drunk for free, and men aren't let in until 10pm (cover US$5 after 8pm Thurs.-Sat.; open daily 10am-3am).

If you don't drink, don't like to party, join the gyrating mass of teens whirling and bopping to late-80s pop hits at **Roller Ensenada,** a roller rink on Mateos at Iturbide (tel. 6-11-59; open Mon.-Thurs. 2-10pm, Fri.-Sun. noon-10pm; admission 7 pesos per hr.). If you just want to zone out in front of a big screen, **Cinema Gemelos,** on Balboa and Mateos at the southern end of town (tel. 6-36-16 or 6-36-13), shows mostly subtitled U.S. features from 4-10pm (admission 10 pesos, 5 pesos for the 4pm show). Another branch is on Calle 11 at Reforma in the Centro Comercial.

# ■ NEAR ENSENADA

Ensenada is an excellent base from which to explore Baja's natural wonders. Unfortunately, to reach most of them, you'll need some wheels—preferably a 4WD or all-terrain vehicle. Cars can be rented in Ensenada (see Practical Information, above).

## BEACHES

Good sand to accompany your swim in the idyllic Bahía de Todos Santos can only be found outside of the city. To the north, **Playa San Miguel** presents an appealing option. To get there, drive north up Calle 10 until the toll gate; turn left at the sign marked "Playa San Miguel." Buses also run to this beach—catch a bus marked "San Miguel" departing from Gastelum and Costero. Buses back must be flagged down.

Somewhat less attractive beaches lie 8km south of Ensenada off the Transpeninsular Highway. The crowded **Playa Estero** is dominated by the Estero Beach Resort, which is so Americanized that finding a single Mexican anywhere on the beach may be an impossible task. Volleyball courts fill the beach's clean but hard and unforgiving sand. The **Estero Beach Museum** (tel. 6-62-35) displays Mexican folk art (open Wed.-Mon. 9am-6pm; free). To get to Estero, take a right at the "Estero Beach" sign on Rte. 1 heading south. Parking costs US$5 at the resort. Alternatively, Playa Estero can be reached by bus; catch one departing from the Plaza Cívica marked "Aeropuerto," "Zorrillo," "Maneadero," or "Chapultepec." **Playa El Faro** (tel. 7-46-30; fax 7-46-20) is similarly rife with volleyball courts and Americans, but has slightly better sand. It also offers the opportunity to camp on the beach. Tents line up along the sand; a group of four can camp, park their car, and use the bathrooms and showers for US$7 per night or US$1.50 per night for bathroom and shower privileges only. Full RV hookups are US$12 per night, and single rooms for two people with bath are US$30. El Faro has yet another bonus: a resident caged lion. Another nearby beach is **Playa Santa María.**

Heading onto the Punta Banda peninsula, you'll find lonelier beaches along the stretch known as **Baja Beach.** Horses are available for rent, and you can swim anywhere along the clean, soft-white sand, in front of a quiet scattering of Americans in semi-permanent RV parks. The rolling hills and marshes provide a pleasant backdrop for the scene. To get to Baja Beach, take a right onto the smaller peninsula which juts off the Punta Banda en route to La Bufadora. Look for a "Horses for Rent" and "Aguacaliente" sign. You can also take a bus to La Bufadora (see below) and ask the driver to let you off there, but don't count on a ride back. Hitching is also possible. Farther south you'll find passable beaches; try **San Quintín,** two hours south of town on the Transpeninsular Highway (Route 1) by car. Locals head toward San Quintín for three reasons: the cool climate, the lack of tourists, and the large clam population at **Molino Viejo** (6km south of the city of San Quintín). **Rosario,** another modest beach town, is 58km south of San Quintín on the highway.

GUERRERO NEGRO

## HIKING

The Ensenada area's most beautiful spots remain essentially undiscovered by most tourists. Breathtaking hikes around the mountains of the Punta Banda peninsula approaching La Bufadora can be completed on well-kept trails of a National Park quality. Take in spectacular views of cliffs, mountainside, and blue sea floating off into oblivion as you circle the peaks. Bring a picnic, as there are some good spots to stop, and bring a bathing suit—when you reach the bottom, you can relieve your sweat-doused body with a dip amidst the rocks in the chilly Pacific.

The best spot to enter the trails is **Cerro de la Punta,** on the road to La Bufadora near the end of the Punta Banda Peninsula. Turn right up a long driveway at the "Cerro de la Punta" sign (parking 10 pesos). You'll see a small clearing and a large house on the cliffs; here, you can hike up among the cacti to the top of the mountains for views of the surrounding area, or down beautiful trails on the oceanside.

Other stops earlier along the road to La Bufadora are equally scenic, and a few are adjacent to unique cave-like rock enclosures created when the mountain was blasted to build the road. The bus to La Bufadora (see below) will drop you off anywhere along this road, including Cerro de la Punta, but if you can't hitch you may be waiting quite a while for the bus back. **Punta Banda** itself is a pleasant little town with a grocery market, post office (open Mon.-Fri. 8am-3pm, Sat. 9am-1pm), and restaurant all around a small plaza just after the exit onto Baja Beach, which juts back towards the mainland. A good place to camp or park an RV in Punta Banda is **Villarino** (tel. 3-20-45 or 6-42-46; fax 3-20-44), adjacent to the plaza, which has modern shower and bathroom facilities and full hookups at US$5 per person per night.

Hiking options further outside of Ensenada include the **Parque Nacional Constitución de 1857** to the east; follow Rte. 3 to Ojos Negros and depart from there for the mountains. Be forewarned that you'll need an all-terrain vehicle or pick-up truck to make the trek. If you don't have such resources, tours are available from **Calibaja Tours** (tel. 8-16-41; fax 8-10-45) in Ensenada and other local agencies—ask at the Ensenada tourist office for details.

## LA BUFADORA

**La Bufadora,** the largest geyser on the Pacific coast, is 30km south of Ensenada. On a good day, the "Blowhole" shoots water 40m into the air out of a water-carved cave. Unfortunately, the droves of visitors, cheesy curio shops, and food vendors have made the area rather unpleasant. Yet despite the tourists and garbage everywhere, the geyser is interesting enough to make a trip. To get to La Bufadora, drive south on the Transpeninsular Highway (take a right onto the highway off López Mateos at the southern end of town), head straight past exits for the airport, military base, and Playa Estero, and take a right after about 20 minutes at the sign marked "La Bufadora." Continue on that road until its end, where the geyser will be heavily advertised (parking US$1 or 5 pesos).

# BAJA CALIFORNIA SUR

# ■■■ GUERRERO NEGRO

Twenty degrees cooler than the bleak Desierto de Vizcaíno to the southeast, Guerrero Negro (pop. 10,000), though dusty and painfully industrial, might earn a soft spot in the hearts of heat-weary northbound travelers—be prepared, though, for wind and lots of gray. In its physical makeup, Guerrero Negro resembles a beachtown without the beach; its sandy roads and salty breeze deceive travelers into thinking that ocean waters are nearby. Situated about halfway between Tijuana and La Paz and plagued with the constant rumble of Transpeninsular Highway traffic passing through town, Guerrero Negro is the place to spend a cool—even chilly—

night if you'd like to break up the killer 25-hour trans-Baja bus trip. If you're heading south, stock up on cold drinks; vast expanses of sweltering terrain lie ahead.

In Guerrero Negro, salt is God, king, and country. So saline is Guerrero Negro that even breathing deeply of the town's air can send the hypochondriac's blood pressure soaring. The town was founded 58 years ago when a North American company began extracting and exporting salt from the Laguna Ojo de Liebre. With a prevailing northeast wind, low levels of precipitation, and the availability of solar energy, the laguna was (and is) ideal for salt collection. The salt plant is now the world's largest; producing over six million tons of the stuff each year, the plant dominates the town's economy and attracts job-seekers from throughout the region.

**Orientation** Guerrero Negro sprawls along 3km of the Transpeninsular Highway (Carretera Transpeninsular). Its two main roads, the highway and **Avenida Baja California,** are home to basically all of the town's industrial and commercial centers; poor residential areas, filled with grim-looking shacks, lie one block off these roads to either side. The highway runs from the bus station at the south end to the riverbed and salt plant at the north end of town, where it turns. Av. Baja California continues into Guerrero Negro, jogging to the left at the park and church. Some of the town's oldest shops line Av. Baja California, along with antiquated communal houses erected for the first employees of the salt plant. Yellow minivans run up and down the Transpeninsular Highway every 15 minutes from 7am-10pm (3 pesos).

**Practical Information** The **police** (tel. 7-02-22) are in the Delegación Municipal on the left side of the highway, a few hundred feet before the salt plant. The **post office** (tel. 7-03-44) is off Av. Baja California, two blocks past the church (open Mon.-Fri. 8am-3pm). **Postal Code: 23940. Telephones** are in Farmacia San Martín (tel. 7-09-11 or 7-11-11), on the Transpeninsular Highway, 100m north of the clinic. Calls to the U.S. 10 pesos per min., within Mexico 4 pesos per min., local calls 2 pesos for 3min. (open Mon.-Sat. 8am-10pm, Sun. 9am-4pm). International collect calls or calling card calls are free at the wall phone in the lobby of Motel Brisa Salina, on the highway across from the Union 76 ball (the one farther from the bus station—there are two). **Telephone Code:** 115. Change money at **Bánamex** (tel. 7-05-55 to -57) on Av. Baja California, just in front of the plant (open Mon.-Fri. 8:30am-1pm). Travelers heading south should change currency here, as the 24-hr. Visa, MC, Cirrus, and Plus **ATM** is the last of its kind until you reach La Paz. **Supermarket CaliMex** (tel. 7-04-34) is on the highway at Adolfo Ruíz, 400m away from the same Union 76 ball (open daily 9am-8pm).

The **ABC Autotransportes de Baja California** terminal (tel. 7-06-11) is one of the first buildings from the highway on the access road. ABC sends buses north (6 per day, 6:30am-10pm) and south to La Paz and points in between (5 per day, 5am-11pm) and to Santa Rosalía and points in between (4 and 6:30am). Northbound buses head to Jesús María (45min., 10 pesos), Rosarito (2hrs., 14 pesos), Punta Prieta (4hrs., 23 pesos), Santa Inés (5hrs., 41 pesos), El Rosario (6hrs., 56 pesos), Lázaro Cárdenas (7hrs., 68 pesos), San Quintín (7hrs., 72 pesos), Col. Guerrero (7½hrs., 75 pesos), Santo Tomás (8hrs., 91 pesos), Maneadero (8½hrs., 91 pesos), Ensenada (10hrs., 93.50 pesos), and Tijuana (11hrs., 114 pesos). Southbound buses stop at Vizcaino (45min., 16 pesos), San Ignacio (2hrs., 26 pesos), Santa Rosalía (3hrs., 37 pesos), Mulegé (4hrs., 45 pesos), Loreto (6hrs., 67 pesos), Insurgentes (7hrs., 86 pesos), Ciudad Constitución (9hrs., 92 pesos), and La Paz (11hrs., 123 pesos).

The **Dr. Sergio Noyole Mirand Public Library,** in a white, octagonal building inside the park off Av. Baja California, contains Spanish books and displays an enormous salt crystal (open Mon.-Fri. 10am-1pm and 2-7pm, Sat. 10am-2pm). An **IMSS Hospital and Clinic** (tel. 7-04-33) is on the highway at Blvd. M. Zaragoza, ½ km north of the water tower.

**Accommodations** Five motor lodges line the access road. Rooms are expensive, and no one accepts credit cards. The farther you get from the bus station, the more prices tumble. The cheapest place in town, **Motel Gámez** (tel. 7-03-70), is on the Transpeninsular Highway between the IMSS Clinic and the salt plant. The motel fits its guests into small, newly painted yellow rooms, each with private baths (some lacking sinks) and its own peculiar defect. A dusty, cat–filled parking lot serves as a courtyard. Check-out 24 hrs. after checking in (singles 35 pesos; doubles 45 pesos). **Motel Las Dunas** (tel. 7-00-55 or -57) is on the highway below the water tank, a short walk north from the bus station, on the right side of the street. Immaculate rooms with large showers as worthy as those at more expensive spots. Lukewarm *agua purificada* is available free. The extremely courteous staff helps in every way possible. Check-out 1pm. Key deposit 10 pesos (singles 50 pesos; doubles 55 pesos; triples 60 pesos). No one sleeps better than the guests at **Motel Brisa Salina**, across from the Union 76 ball (the one farther from the bus station). The double mattresses are so thick and high that ladders would be helpful. Most rooms are furnished with an entire entertainment system: color TV and a radio. All sport wooden bureaus and chairs and surround a narrow, neatly trimmed, flowery courtyard. Free *agua purificada*. Check-out 1pm (singles 50 pesos; doubles 60 pesos, two beds 70 pesos; 5 pesos each additional person).

**Food** Many aspects of Guerrero Negro are difficult to swallow, and the city's food is no exception. If you're looking for food after 9pm, particularly during the low season, bless you. Some seafood is decent, though, and the town specialty is lobster caught in the *laguna*. **La Palapa** is on the highway across from the PEMEX station closer to the bus station. The dining room is decorated with model boats, shells, photographs of marine life, and plastic fish caught in nets. The big, blaring TV can distract you, and the clam cocktail (12 pesos) can tide you over as you await your octopus (20 pesos). Breakfast is served—french toast (12 pesos; open daily 8am-9pm). In the shadow of the water tower on the right side of the highway (coming from the bus station), **El Figón de Sal** (tel. 7-16-87) offers very reasonably priced food in a small, grocery store-like dining room. A *comida corrida* (15 pesos), *pollo en mole*, and *calamar ranchero* (squid in salsa) are all available. Locals rave about **Cocina Económica Lety**, next to the Union 76 ball (the one closer to the bus station)—you may want to take a look.

**Sights and Entertainment** Excitement comes to town between late December and early March with the thousands of gray whales who make the annual swim from the Bering Sea to reproduce in the waters offshore. During the rest of the year, more excitement might be found staring at a blank wall. If you time your visit correctly, you can commune with hundreds of whales in the **Parque Natural de las Ballenas Grises**, on the **Laguna Ojo de Liebre**, formerly a deep-water port facility of the salt company. In the early morning, whales swim right up to the docks; during the rest of the day, ascend a tall observation tower for a look. No public transportation is available to the park. To get there, head south on Rte. 1 toward Santa Rosalía for 8-15km. A sign points out the 30km dirt road to the *laguna*. Staffers at the park sometimes lead whale-watching tours in early January and February.

The **Bahía de los Angeles** is populated by dolphins, blue and gray whales, sea lions, and many species of birds. From January to March, **Servicios Turísticos Mario** (tel. 7-07-88), on the highway near the PEMEX closer to the bus station, offers tours to the Bahía (min. 10 people) and of indigenous cave paintings in the Sierra de San Francisco. Most cave painting excursions, however, leave from San Ignacio (see below). On a four-hour tour of the *laguna*, you'll visit the **Dunas de Solidad**, 10km of pearly white dunes whose configuration changes daily due to the movement of the tides. The dunes get their name from the first residents of the area, Don Miguel and Doña Fidela, a solitary Sinaloa couple who settled here after a three-month overland trek.

# ■■■ SAN IGNACIO

More than any other stop on the arid Baja Peninsula, San Ignacio (pop. 2,000), between Guerrero Negro and Santa Rosalía on the Transpeninsular Highway, seems like a tropical oasis. From a distance, the town appears to be a cruel illusion, a mirage of the mind—leafy date palms, flowering bushes, and broad swaths of green appear magically in the middle of the blistering desert. Happily, you are not dreaming. The area around San Ignacio is blessed with the most plentiful underground freshwater supply in all Baja California Sur. Indigenous peoples knew of the subterranean lakes and called the area "Cadeau-Caamanc," meaning "Creek of Reeds." In modern times, the underground water sources have been dammed up to form a murky lake used for swimming and irrigating local orchards.

Though hot during summer days, San Ignacio earns praise for more than just its terrain. Locals are extremely amiable, and the town is relatively undisturbed by *gringos* for most of the year. San Ignacio's intimate atmosphere, beautiful panoramic starscapes at night, and historic mission overlooking the *zócalo* are but a few of the reasons why the pleasure-seeking *flojos* (lazy people) who set eyes on the town never want to leave and end up settling down. San Ignacio is also a prime point of departure for cave painting tours.

**Orientation and Practical Information** A winding road canopied by swaying date palms leads from the Transpeninsular Highway to the *zócalo*. Remember, of course, that in tiny San Ignacio the arms and legs are remarkably close to the heart—within 10 minutes of pulling into town, you'll know San Ignacio better than your hometown. Life revolves around the *zócalo*, which is delineated by **Juan Bautista Luyando** and the mission on the north, **Morelos** to the south, **Juárez** on the east, and **Hidalgo** to the west. Ask any local for directions, and you'll get them.

There's no official tourist office in town, but to hear friendly, informative chatter about San Ignacio you can visit the elderly woman who owns the **caseta,** Hidalgo 24 (tel. 4-02-50), south of Bancomer. She speaks some English (open Mon.-Sat. 8am-1pm and 3-6pm). The **police** (tel. 4-03-77) are in the Delegación Municipal on Ocampo and Zaragoza (open daily 8am-3pm). The **post office** is in the gray stone building on Juárez next to the *zócalo. Lista de Correos* (open Mon.-Fri. 8am-3pm). **Postal Code:** 23930. A lone **public phone** stands in the north side of the *zócalo* (0.50 pesos for local calls). You can place calls and send **faxes** at a pricier *caseta,* as mentioned above (tel. 4-02-50; fax 4-02-90). Calls to U.S. 9 pesos per min., faxes 20 pesos per page (open Mon.-Fri. 8am-1pm and 3-6pm). **Telephone Code: 115. Telegrams** can be sent and received at **Telecomm** (tel. 4-01-55), on Juárez facing the *zócalo* (open Mon.-Fri. 8am-2pm). Exchange currency at **Bancomer** (tel. 4-01-20), on the southern side of the *zócalo.*

The **bus station** is 2km from San Ignacio on the Transpeninsular highway. *De paso* buses run to Tijuana, Ensenada, Guerrero Negro, San Quintín, Lázaro Cárdenas, and Rosario. The bus south stops by at around 6pm, though it's often late. **Nuevos Almacenos,** a good-sized **grocery store** with cool San Ignacio t-shirts, is on the corner of Juárez and Juan Bautista Luyando (tel. 4-01-22), facing the *zócalo* (open Mon.-Sat. 8am-noon and 2-7pm, Sun. 8am-noon). The **pharmacy, Boticas Ceseña** (tel. 4-00-76), is unmarked at Madero 24A, parallel to and east of Juárez and Hidalgo (open daily 8:30am-1pm and 3-7pm; dial 4-00-75 after hours). To reach the **Centro de Salud,** walk away from the highway down Hidalgo, which turns into Ocampo. Turn right on Independencia, a tiny dirt road; it's the large white building on the right-hand side (open daily 8am-3pm). If you have a medical **emergency** after hours, call Fischer Lucero (tel. 4-01-90). Don't expect much help from either the health center or the police—try them in an emergency only.

**Accommodations** San Ignacio has few accommodations, and those that exist aren't that cheap. The family living in **Restaurant Chalita,** Hidalgo 9 (tel. 4-00-82), rents bedrooms just oozing with local culture. The small, clean rooms have fans and black-and-white TVs. Check-out 1pm (singles 50 pesos). **Hotel Posada,** on Ocampo and Independencia (tel. 4-03-13), a three-minute walk down Cipres from Hidalgo, has standing fans and private baths with showers (singles and doubles 120 pesos; triples 140 pesos). **El Padrino RV Park** (tel. 4-00-89) is 500m from the *zócalo* on the road connecting San Ignacio to the highway. Full trailer hookup (US$10, without electricity US$7) comes with a complimentary margarita from the pleasant Flojo's Restaurant-Bar. Motorcycles cost US$3 to park. El Padrino also offers four clean and freshly-built budget rooms with private baths (singles and doubles US$12).

**Food** Most places to chow down are in the *zócalo*. As in other fishing towns along the Baja coasts, seafood dishes warrant preferential gastronomic attention. Eat outdoors under the wonderfully starry sky at **Restaurant-Bar Rene's,** just outside the *zócalo* off Hidalgo. Enjoy their specialty, the *calamar empanizado* (breaded squid, 20 pesos) with a beer (5 pesos). If you'd rather eat under a roof, head into their round thatched hut and stare out at the small adjoining pond (open daily 7am-10:30pm). **Restaurant Chalita,** Hidalgo 9 (tel. 4-00-82), is housed in an old-fashioned Mexican kitchen. Sit on random furniture, listen to the caged birds sing (do you now know why?), and find salvation in a warm plate of *pescado al mojo de ajo* (20 pesos), *enchiladas* (12 pesos), or *chiles rellenos* (15 pesos; open daily 7:30am-10pm). **Flojo's Restaurant-Bar** (tel. 4-00-89) is part of El Padrino RV Park (see above) and a five-minute walk from town. Even you will become *flojo* (slack) when you overstuff yourself on two chicken *burritos* with rice and beans (20 pesos) or breaded Italian meat (22.50 pesos). Lean back, watch the stars between the reeds of the enormous *palapa,* and listen to the crickets chirp while your food is cooked (open daily 7am-10:30pm).

**Sights** A colonial colossus towering over wild, leafy vegetation, the **Mission of San Ignacio,** on the northern side of the *zócalo,* was founded in 1728 by Jesuit missionary Juan Bautista. The construction of the mission proved a logistical nightmare; wood had to be hauled in from the Guadalupe mission in the Sierras, furniture was brought from Mulegé via a scorching four-day mule ride through the unpaved desert, and the paintings were carried by boat from the mainland. The mission is a beautiful achievement, well worth the difficulties—magnificent on the outside, cool inside, and heavenly at night, when illuminated by outdoor spotlights. Inside, look up to see a a flying gold angel seemingly suspended in the dome—he's holding a banner (a precursor to plane banners?) that reads "Gloria in Excelsis Deo." A particularly striking outside view of the mission poking above palms and huts in the evening can be seen from halfway between the *zócalo* and Hotel Posada, on the small path. The newly opened **Mission Museum** (tel. 4-02-22), on Loyando, 30m west of the mission, tells the story of the nearby cave paintings—some of which have recently been hypothesized to be up to 10,000 years old—and even has its own huge faux-cave painting (open Mon.-Sat. 8am-8pm).

The main tourist draw to San Ignacio are the real **painted caves,** 75km away in the Sierra de San Francisco. More than 500 paintings reside within a 12-square-kilometer area. Oscar Fischer of Hotel Posada and his son, Dagoberto, offer various tours to the caves (tel. 4-03-13 or 4-01-56). US$20 (during the tourist season) gets you a nine-hour trip to one cave and two petroglyphic zones. It leaves at around 8am and makes as many stops in between as requested. A two-day tour will take you to the more impressive **La Pintada** (and the minor) **El Ratón** caves. For US$60, you'll get transportation, a guide, and a mule. If you're planning to sleep comfortably during the trip, you'll need a tent and an additional mule (US$10) to carry it. Some adventurous travelers make the trip from cave to cave on foot (about 5 miles each way), saving all mule costs but leaving their bodies worn, to say the least. US$80 plus tent and mule costs gets you the grandest tour of all: a three-day, eight-cave extravaganza that will show you all the indigenous paintings you probably ever wanted to see and leave all but the most resilient travelers battle-worn. For the two- and three-day trip, it is recommended that you call at least two weeks in advance so

that the Fischers can arrange the excursion and clear it with the Mexican bureaucracy. The managers also run trips to the Laguna San Ignacio to spy on **gray whales.**
They leave earlier than 7am and cost US$45 per person. Note that prices for all tours
(caves and whales) assume groups of six or more. Six people are easy to assemble
during the tourist season (Oct.-May), but during the summer, depending on the size
of your party, you may end up paying more.

# ■■■ SANTA ROSALÍA

Not only is Santa Rosalía a convenient transportation hub for buses and ferries, it is
also heir to a rich and colorful history. Nobody knew that the area contained treasure until 1868, when José Villavincencio took a hard look at the crumbling blue-
green rock and discovered an enormously thick ribbon of copper winding through
the hills. A few small-scale, inefficient operations chiseled some of the ore out of the
hills, but most of the copper remained untouched until the French-owned, Roths-
child-financed El Boleo company bought out all competitors and embarked on a
mining venture of staggering proportions. Over 600km of tunnel was bored into the
hills, leaving the landscape pockmarked with dangerously unmarked and
unguarded mine entrances. One hundred men labored to build 40km of railroad
track between the mines and the village; even today, the ground is studded with
iron spikes and wedges. When the mining town was settled, the houses were built
in an orderly fashion according to rank, so that the wealthiest, highest-ranking officials would literally be highest up. Their old homes crown the two cliffs that sandwich central Santa Rosalía. Mountains of abandoned machinery and railroad cars
bristle with rust, returning their metals to the ground. Meanwhile, a multi-national
company is trying to sift the last fragments of copper out of the earth by hydromet-
allurgically reprocessing the five million tons of slag and tailings that litter the site.

**Orientation and Practical Information** If you're planning a visit to
Santa Rosalía, keep in mind that the town is unbearably hot and humid in the summer. Although Santa Rosalía borders the ocean, the Gulf breezes don't cool it off
nearly enough; even during summer nights, temperatures of 90°F and high humidity
will drench you with sweat. To get from the **ferry** to Obregón, Santa Rosalía's main
strip, turn right as you leave the ferry compound; Obregón is the second left.

The **post office** is on Constitución, between Calles 2 and Altamirano (open Mon.-
Fri. 8am-3pm). **Postal Code:** 23920. **Long distance calls** can be made from the bus
terminal. **Telephone Code:** 115. **Bánamex** (tel. 2-00-10 or 2-09-84), on Obregón,
changes traveler's checks and provides relief from the blistering heat with ice-cold
A/C. Find some excuse to go in and stay in (open Mon.-Fri. 8:30am-1pm). The **ABC
Autotransportes bus office** is on Constitución, six blocks inland from the highway;
from here, one bus heads south at 11am daily. All other buses depart from the **ABC
station** (tel. 2-01-50), across the street from the ferry office. Heading north, *local*
buses going as far as Guerrero Negro leave at 3pm and Tijuana at 5pm; *de paso*
buses going as far as Tijuana leave at 6pm, Mexicali at midnight, Guerrero Negro at
2am, and Tijuana at 4 and 5am. Going north, buses stop at San Ignacio (1hr., 13.50
pesos), Guerrero Negro (3½hrs., 38 pesos), Punta Prieta (7hrs., 50 pesos), El Rosario
(9hrs., 84 pesos), San Quintín (9½hrs., 89 pesos), Col. Guerrero (10hrs., 93 pesos),
Ensenada (13½hrs., 123 pesos), Tijuana (15hrs., 143.50 pesos), and Mexicali
(18½hrs., 179 pesos). Heading south, all buses go as far as La Paz (7 per day, 8:30am-
2am) and stop at Mulegé (1hr., 10 pesos), Loreto (3hrs., 28 pesos), Ej. Insurgentes
(4hrs., 45 pesos), Ciudad Constitución (4½hrs., 48 pesos), and La Paz (7hrs., 78
pesos). **Águila** also runs buses to Los Angeles, CA (6:30, 11:30am, and 5:30pm,
US$20 one-way, US$35 round-trip).

From Santa Rosalía, you can catch the **ferry** connecting Baja to Guaymas on the
mainland (7hrs., *salon* 61 pesos, *turista* 121 pesos). The boat leaves Santa Rosalía
only on Sun. and Wed. at 8am from the modern, blue-and-green **Sematur** office (tel.
2-00-13) on Rte. 1 (the Transpeninsular Highway) just south of town. Those with

cars must purchase their spot in advance as well as show a tourist card, registration, and proof of their Mexican insurance (cars up to 5m long 447 pesos; motorcycles 65 pesos; office open Mon.-Sat. 8am-noon). Departure days and times, prices, and office hours are in constant flux, so be sure to call the office or talk to a travel agent to confirm the schedule. To reach the docks, catch a bus from the **ABC Autotransportes** station, about 200m south of the ferry. Santa Rosalía's **public library** is right next to Hotel Olvera (open Mon.-Fri. 8am-8pm and Sun. 9am-1pm). The **Centro de Salud** (tel. 2-07-89) is at Juan Michel Costeau.

**Accommodations and Food** If you're going to stay in sweltering Santa Rosalía, consider popping the few extra pesos for A/C. The budget standout is **Hotel Olvera,** Calle Plaza 14 (tel. 2-00-57 or -67), about three blocks from the shore on Constitución. From the bus station, take a left and walk along the water towards town until you come to the old train engine in front of the town's two main streets—follow Constitución, the left one, and it's on your right, at the bridge. Enjoy spacious bathrooms, large double beds with patriotic American bedspreads, and free lukewarm *agua purificada.* Deal with the cool shower—that's okay in this town (singles 50 pesos, 60 pesos with A/C; doubles 65 pesos, 80 pesos with A/C).

If you're staying, that means you're eating, too. Sit outside under the fans at the cool **Terco's Pollito** (tel. 2-00-75), on Obregón, horizontally across from the Hotel Olvera. The *Combinación Mexicana* (*tamale, chimichanga, chile relleno, frijoles,* rice, and *tortillas*) goes for 25 pesos (open daily 7:30am-11pm). **El Boleo Bakery,** Obregón at Calle 4 (tel. 2-03-10), known for its architecture (see Sights), deserves a visit for its food as well. Dazzlingly cheap french bread (0.75 pesos), *pan dulce* (1 peso), and donuts (1.50 pesos) thrill customers (open Mon.-Sat. 9:30am-7:30pm).

**Sights** The wooden houses, general stores, and saloons along Santa Rosalía's streets recall the town's previous incarnation as a mining boom-town. Startling specimens of 19th-century French architecture include the long and many-windowed **Palacio Municipal,** the **Hotel Francés,** and **El Boleo Bakery.** Tasty, tender French bread (based on an old, secret recipe) is still available at bakeries around town. The most serendipitous of artifacts is the spectacular prefabricated white cast-iron **Iglesia Santa Bárbara,** at Obregón and Calle 1. Designed by Gustave Eiffel (of Tower fame) and installed in the 1890s, this church was originally destined for a mission in Africa, but the company that commissioned it forgot to pick up its order. French mining *concessionaires* spotted the iron church at the 1889 Exhibition Universale de Paris and decided Santa Rosalía couldn't do without it. Observers either love it or hate it; its outside panels look like they fell off an industrial washing machine. Those travelers looking for fun in the sun and abundant water sports would do better to make tracks for the heavenly beaches just south of Mulegé.

# ■■■ MULEGÉ

Heaven on earth may just be the 48-kilometer arc of rocky outcrops, shimmering beaches, and bright blue sea known as the Bahía de la Concepción, which neighbors Mulegé. The coves and waters look more perfect than those inhabited by Neverland's mermaids; best of all, Concepción's beaches are not cartoons. Grown sport fishers and shell collectors weep at the variety and sheer size of the specimens caught here, and divers fall under the spell of Mulegé's underwater sights. What are *you* waiting for? Located 136km north of Loreto and 300km south of dreary Guerrero Negro on the Baja peninsula, Mulegé proper (pop. 4,400) is a pleasant, charming town in its own right, but it is simply a base—abandon it during the day for the marvelous beaches to the south.

**Orientation and Practical Information** Soon after bearing left off the Transpeninsular Highway, the road into Mulegé forks. To the left is **Moctezuma;** to the right is **Martínez.** Both are soon crossed perpendicularly by **Zaragoza;** take a right onto Zaragoza to get to the *zócalo,* which is one block from the crossing of Martínez and Zaragoza. **Madero** heads east from the *zócalo* (away from the highway) and, after following the Mulegé River for about 3km, hits the water at the town beach, **Playa de Mulegé. Caranea** runs parallel to Moctezuma, Martínez, and Madero, and meets Zaragoza at the top of the hill, north of Moctezuma.

The **Hotel Las Casitas,** Madero 50 (tel. 3-00-19), serves as an unofficial **tourist office,** with plenty of information on beaches, camping, and fishing. Ask for Javier to get to the real nitty-gritty. English-speaking **Kerry Otterstrom,** who goes by the bizarre nickname "El Vikingo," has written and published a 180-page book on Mulegé and can tell you all there is to know about the town. He is a bartender at El Candil Restaurant (see below) and can be found there between 4-6pm. The **police** are located at Martínez and Callejón Galván, the continuation of Madero on the west side of the *zócalo.* The **post office** (tel. 3-02-05), on Martínez across from the PEMEX station, posts a *Lista de Correos* (open Mon.-Fri. 8am-3pm). **Postal Code:** 23900. **Minisuper Padilla,** on Zaragoza at Martínez (tel. and fax 3-01-90), one block north of plaza, has two **phones** for international calls. (7 pesos per min. to the U.S. Credit cards and collect calls free. **Faxes** 10 pesos to send, 5 pesos to receive. Open Mon.-Sat. 8am-10pm, Sun. 8am-8pm.) An unreliable public phone is located in the plaza. **Telephone Code:** 685.

The **bus station** is simply a sheltered blue bench at the turnoff to Mulegé from Rte. 1. All buses are *de paso,* a phrase which might roughly be translated as "inevitably arrives late and full." Northbound buses stop by once a day at 4:30pm; southbound buses make two appearances, at 9:30 and 11:30am. Northbound buses go to Santa Rosalía (1hr., 10 pesos), San Ignacio (2hrs., 22 pesos), Rosarito (6hrs., 55 pesos), Punta Prieta (8hrs., 65 pesos), Santa Inés (9hrs., 77 pesos), El Rosario (10hrs., 92 pesos), San Quintín (10½hrs., 103 pesos), Lázaro Cárdenas (11hrs., 101 pesos), San Vicente (13hrs., 117 pesos), Ensenada (14½hrs., 135 pesos), Tijuana (16hrs., 155 pesos), Tecate (17hrs., 163 pesos), and Mexicali (19½hrs., 190 pesos). Southbound buses stop at Loreto (2hrs., 20 pesos), Insurgentes (3hrs., 37 pesos), Ciudad Constitución (3½hrs., 40 pesos), and La Paz (6hrs., 72 pesos).

**Lavamática Claudia** (tel. 3-00-57) is on Moctezuma beside Hotel Terrazas (wash 9 pesos, dry 2.50 pesos, soap 2 pesos; open Mon.-Sat. 8am-6pm). The **Red Cross** (tel. 3-02-58, 3-03-80, and 3-01-39 for after-hours help; CB channel 14) is located on Madero 200m east of the plaza. **Farmacia Moderna** (tel. 3-00-42) is on Madero in front of the plaza (open daily 8am-1pm and 4-10pm). **Centro de Salud B,** Madero 28 (tel. 3-02-98), also referred to as the ISSTE clinic or the Puesto Periférico, treats medical emergencies (open 8am-2:30pm; 24-hr. emergency care).

**Accommodations** Economical hotels crowd the center of town, but they're far from the beaches. While haggling can bring room prices down, those with sleeping bags often find the best deals on the shore. On hot nights, rooms at **Casa de Huéspedes Mañuelita** (tel. 3-01-75), on Moctezuma next to Los Equipales, around the corner from Zaragoza, relieve the traveler with soft beds, table fans, and private showers. All of the large, mostly-clean rooms look onto a cluttered courtyard populated by pets, thriving grapevines, and a baby or two. Campers who simply need to use the bathroom and shower pay 6 pesos (singles 30 pesos; doubles 40 pesos). **Hotel Terrazas,** on Zaragoza at Caranea (tel. 3-00-09), two blocks north of the plaza, is a pleasant establishment with every modern convenience except TVs. From the bus stop, bear left off the highway, take a right at Mulegé's initial fork, and take a left on Zaragoza. It's two blocks uphill on the right. An excellent restaurant/ bar is in the lobby (see below). Rooms have a homey feel despite their high-quality-hotel-room nature. *Agua purificada* available, but receptionists often aren't. Checkout noon (rooms with two beds 75 pesos, with A/C 90 pesos). **Casa de Huéspedes Canett** (tel. 3-02-72), on Madero east of the *zócalo,* offers beds you can sleep on and private showers that work—not much more—but the rooms aren't filthy and you can't go wrong for the price (singles 15 pesos; triples 30 pesos). **Orchard RV Park** and **María Ísabel RV Park,** both just south of town and accessible from the

MULEGÉ

Transpeninsular Highway, are near a fresh-water oasis lagoon, on Madero about 1km toward the beach. They're expensive as RV parks go (about US$12 per night).

**Food** For those tired of shopping for cans of soda, bread, and other on-the-road staples, a few unremarkable restaurants cluster near the bus station. **Hotel Terrazas Restaurant,** however, is not unremarkable—it offers superb, home-cooked meals at extremely reasonable prices. You may have to wait a while for your shrimp omelette (18 pesos), *huevos con chorizo* (12 pesos), or *camarones al mojo de ajo* (25 pesos), but you'll be glad you did. Who knows, you may even find salvation (open daily 8am-noon and 6-10pm). **El Candil Restaurant,** north of the plaza on Zaragoza near Martínez, serves an enormous Mexican combination platter with rice, beans, *chiles rellenos,* and tacos (22 pesos; open Mon.-Sat. 7am-10pm, often later). For outstanding seafood, try **La Almeja** (tel. 3-01-84), at the end of Morelos near the lighthouse, about 3km from the center of town. The floor is the beach, and should you find a bit of shell in your tasty and filling *sopa de siete mares* (seven seas soup, which includes just about every creature that ever swam in water—for 22 pesos), you can spit it into the Sea of Cortés. *Piña colada* made with fresh pineapple and coconut only 12 pesos. Be forewarned that seafood cocktails contain stomach-inciting raw tomatoes. Purified water and ice are available (open daily 8am-11pm).

At night, most *norteamericanos* in the area meet at the bar of **Hotel Las Casitas** on Madero for drinking and dancing with no cover. On Friday nights, a Mexican *fiesta* and buffet will cost you 30 pesos (reservations required). The last watering holes to close are El Candil and the bar at **Hotel Vieja Hacienda,** on the plaza.

**Sights and Sand** Pre-Colombian cave paintings are located at **La Trinidad** and the **Cuevas de San Borjita.** Trips to La Trinidad, offered by Kerry Otterstrom of El Candil Restaurant (stop by between 4-6pm), include hiking, a 200m swim in a narrow canyon, and over 700 cave paintings said to be up to 14,000 years old. The trip requires that you swim and be in decent shape, but allows all ages (US$35 per person). Another trip to the San Borjita caves offers better paintings, but there's no swimming and the hiking isn't as good (US$50 per person). Long trips run up to 7 days, at US$50 per person per day, including hotel, food, and drink. The guide speaks English, Spanish, German, and French. Other tours are available, and also through **Salvador Castro Tours** at Hotel Las Casitas (tel. 3-00-19).

In town, Mulegé's lovely **mission** sits on a hill to the west. Walk down Zaragoza away from the *zócalo,* go under the bridge, and turn right on the shaded lane. The mission is not a museum; mass is still held every Sunday. If you want a great view of the whole town, river, and palms, climb the steps on the hill just behind the mission. Behind the old Delagación Municipal on Madero next to the Centro de Salud, winding steps rise to the **Antique Jail/Museum.** Locals dubbed the jail, in use until 1975, "El Carcel Sin Puertos" (The Jail Without Doors) because it permitted inmates to work in town during the day in order to pay their keep; prisoners were prevented from fleeing by the vast deserts surrounding the town. The back portion of the building, with its ancient graffitti and despondently dark prison cells, held the actual jail. Ignore the pigeons flying in the rafters of the museum, and focus on the relics of the Cochimi Indians, garish missionary robes, and the tale of poor Simon Hernández, who was executed at age 12 for stealing a busted gun (open some mornings 8am-noon or so; hours erratic).

Two beaches lie only 3km from the center of town. **El Faro** is at the end of Madero, which becomes a dirt road long before you reach the beach. Alternatively, reach the **public beach** by following the Mulegé River to the Sea of Cortés, where it drains. Be warned, though—with well-trodden black sand and light waves, neither beach can hold a candle to the beaches 18km south. Watch out for jellyfish, especially in June and July. Diving and other equipment can be rented at **Mulegé Divers** (see below). For an isolated beach within walking distance (for some) from town, walk to the PEMEX station about 4km south on the highway, continue about 20m south, and a dirt road will lead off to the left to a lonely beach with sand dunes and desert hills overlooking somewhat rocky sand. It's not nearly as good as beaches farther south, but it's more peaceful and closer to Mulegé.

# ■■■ BAHÍA DE LA CONCEPCIÓN

There's nothing like a swim in the warm waters of the Mar de Cortés followed by a carefree bask in the soft sand and dinner with friendly *norteamericano* RVers up the road. Forget the beaches of the northern peninsula—the Bahía de la Concepción, beginning 16km south of Mulegé, is the most brilliant star in Baja's constellation. Bare, cactus-studded hills drop straight down to the white sand beaches and translucent waters of the *bahía*. Many nomadic travelers hitch (known in Americanized Spanish as *"pedir ride"*) from Mulegé to the beaches, catching one of the RVs or produce trucks barreling down the Transpeninsular Highway towards the bay. If you hitchhike, you will be most successful getting rides right across the island from the bus stop. Many locals passing by will signal by pointing their fingers, meaning they're just driving locally and wouldn't be able to take someone to the beach. Some may assume hitchhikers need rides all the way to Loreto; travelers avoid this confusion by holding up a sign that reads "Playa Santispac" along with that internationally-known flexed thumb. Hitching back from the beaches is even easier; many people leaving the beach are heading back to Mulegé. *Let's Go* does not recommend hitchhiking.

If you're planning a day at the beach and unwilling to hitch, try checking at the bus station for the time of the first *de paso* bus south (9:30 and 11:30am in August 1995). Wait to pay the fare until the bus arrives, and don't get on until the driver assures you that he plans to stop at one of the beaches. But don't count on a bus to take you back; bus service to the beaches is infrequent, and drivers may not stop along the busy highway. Beach-hoppers might also consider renting a car for the day, as access to and from the beaches further south is limited.

The beaches are fantastic after dark, but only come at night if you plan to stay—it's impossible to hitch back, no buses run, and even stepping onto the curvy highway is dangerous due to oncoming cars. A final note for all beaches: don't expect to find cold water or even remotely cold *anything*. Ice is rare, so unless you relish the idea of downing a hot Coke in the pounding sun, bring a cooler with some drinks.

**Playa Punta Arena,** 16km south of Mulegé, is far enough from the road that the roar of the waves drowns out the noise from muffler-less trucks. From the highway, travel 2km down a rocky dirt road. Bear right at all forks in the road. A dozen palm-frond *palapas* line the beach with sand-flush toilets in back (*cabañas* or parking 20 pesos). The waters near the shore are great for clam fishing, but swimming may be hazardous due to manta rays. The Paleolithic peoples who once inhabited the caves on the hillside south of the beach left behind millions of discarded shells. If you walk down the dirt road to Playa Punta Arena but take a left instead of a right at the second fork, you'll end up at **Playa San Pedro** and **Los Naranjos RV Park,** where payments for your space may be made with freshly caught fish.

The next idyllic beach down is **Playa Santispac,** connected to its neighbor by a dirt path that begins on the right side of Playa Punta Arena, winds though mountains for 1km, and deposits you on the left side of Santispac. Yachts and sailboats bob in the blue-and-green striped waters of the harbor/cove here, and the shores are filled with RVs at the **Las Palapas Trailer Park**—during the high season, Santispac is the liveliest beach on the bay. In the summer, however, the sands are nearly deserted. Tent-pitching is permitted; a man comes around once a day to collect the 20-peso camping or parking fee. Otherwise, pay up at Ana's Restaurant. Use of bathrooms and fresh-water showers costs 5 pesos. Santispac is directly on the highway, so those hitching will find it more convenient than Punta Arena. At **Ana's Restaurant,** guests enjoy fried fish (22 pesos) and shrimp omelettes (18 pesos) while marveling at the exotic shells on sale to the right of the counter. The adjacent bakery sells cakes and huge loaves of bread (6 pesos; open daily 7am-8pm). **Kayak Concepción Bay** (U.S. tel. (619) 275-4225; local fax 3-01-90), in front of Ana's, rents kayaks

(US$25-45), mask-snorkel-fin sets (US$5 per day), wet suits (US$6 per day), and VHF radios (US$8 per day), all with a 10% tax. Prices drop for longer rentals. Fully-equipped, multi-day tours are also available at US$39 per person plus tax, including food and drink. Tours require a minimum of four people and start at Playa Santispac at 8am (open daily 8am-sunset).

If you're swimming during the spring months, watch out for mating sting rays; throughout the summer, manta rays are a threat. In case of a sting, treat the affected area with hot, salty water. The **hot springs** on the south end of Playa Santispac pro-vide the perfect source. Check out these hot, bubbly waters even if you haven't been nipped by an underwater creature.

Neighboring Playas La Posada, Escondida, Los Cocos, and El Burro (encountered in that order traveling south) cling to the neighboring southern coast. The farther one ventures from Mulegé, the less populated the beaches become. **Playa La Posada,** which looks essentially like a minuscule village, is covered by permanent homes, but large *palapas* house temporary visitors (25 pesos per day, including access to bathrooms). Two distant rocky islands and an overgrown islet are popular destinations for jet-skiers. **Playa Escondida** ("Hidden Beach") is at the end of a 500m dirt path winding through the valley between two hills; look for a white sign with black letters at the southern end of Playa Concepción. True to its name, the short, facility-less Escondida is nicely hidden from all civilization. **Playa Los Cocos** is iden-tified by its white garbage cans adorned with palm trees. A dozen *cabañas* where you can spend the night free of charge line the shallow, duck-filled beach. A grove of marshy trees and shrubs separates the strip from the highway. At **Playa El Burro,** you can rent a *palapa* next to hordes of RVs (20 pesos per day). Next is **Playa El Coyote,** with *palapas,* and **Estrella del Mar,** an across-the-street restaurant which serves meat *enchiladas* (10 pesos) and fried chicken (18 pesos) from October to April (open daily 8am-8pm). Part of this beach has been privatized by RV settlers; the better sands and *palapas* are down on the southern end.

Fifteen kilometers farther down the road, at the exquisite (and even less popu-lated) **Playa Resquesón,** a beautiful spit of sand broadens into a wide beach. On the spit, you can lie in the sand sandwiched by water on both sides. Even further south, two more spots—**La Ramada** and **Santa Bárbara**—are currently undergoing devel-opment. Newly-built *palapas* have tainted these virgin beaches, and developers hope that these two, whose large size approaches that of Santispac, will soon attract the tourist masses. Another nearly deserted stretch of sand is the last beach before the highway climbs into the mountains separating Mulegé from Loreto. All of these beaches are marked from the main highway.

Divers rave about this area; it teems with underwater life, including gigantic sea turtles. **Mulegé Divers,** Madero 45 (tel. 3-00-59), down the street from Hotel Las Casitas, rents scuba equipment, conducts boat excursions, and sells an unparalleled collection of Mulegé T-shirts. If you already know how to scuba dive, try the five-hour trip that leaves at 8am (US$40, minimum 2 people). Otherwise, a scuba instruction course (US$60) helps you get your feet wet. Five-hour snorkeling excur-sions begin at 8am and cost US$25, including equipment (minimum 2 people). If you rent your snorkeling gear and go at it alone, you'll pay US$10. Go out to the islands (rather than staying near the beach) for the best snorkeling. Make reserva-tions at least one day in advance (open Mon.-Sat. 9am-1pm and 3-6pm).

# ■■■ LORETO

Founded by Jesuit missionaries in 1697, Loreto (pop. 10,000) was the first capital of the Californias and a link in a chain of missions along the west coast of Baja. The Loreto mission, however, was cursed by the same bad fortune that doomed Jesuit communities up and down the peninsula: in 1829, a freakish combination of hurri-canes and earthquakes wiped out the entire town. Recent construction has belat-edly restored the **Our Lady of Loreto Mission** to its former beauty. Years ago, the

Mexican government began to lay the foundations for a major resort, but funds were diverted to other projects.

Twice cheated by history, Loreto remains a simple town despite its three luxury hotels. The town features a long, tranquil *malecón* overlooking the distant fishing boats, with plenty of benches shaded by the Beverly Hills-esque rows of palm trees. Loreto's central square is peaceful and spotless, filled with friendly residents basking in the shadow of the nearby historic mission. Most visitors are middle-aged *norteamericanos* who come to fish in the waters off Loreto's coast. Because the town remains slow-paced, its pleasant streets are relatively safe even at night. Take a stroll and you'll be courted by two competing but equally beautiful vistas—the calm blue waters of the Sea of Cortés on one side, golden mountains on the other.

**Orientation and Practical Information** The principal street in Loreto is **Salvatierra** (named after the founding Jesuit missionary Juan María Salvatierra), which connects the Carretera Transpeninsular to the Gulf. **Hidalgo** forks off and goes in the same direction (a rough continuation) when Salvatierra becomes a pedestrian walkway. **Independencia** and **Francisco I. Madero** run perpendicular to Salvatierra; Independencia intersects it just as it forks into Hidalgo, and Madero does so afterward (closer to the water). Away from the gulf, **Allende, León,** and **Ayuntamiento** cross Salvatierra before Independencia. **Malecón,** which leads north to the beach and outlines the entire width of the city at the coast, runs perpendicular to Hidalgo where Hidalgo ends. **Juárez** runs parallel to, and north of Salvatierra and Hidalgo. The **zócalo** is at Hidalgo and Madero. To get to the center of town from the **bus station,** walk down Salvatierra in the direction of the distant cathedral (10min.) or indulge in a taxi (10 pesos).

The Palacio Municipal, on Madero between Salvatierra and Comercio facing the *zócalo,* houses the air-conditioned **tourist information center** (tel. 5-04-11). The extremely amiable staff will be happy to hand out maps and brochures or point you anywhere you have the urge to go. Enough English is spoken (open Mon.-Fri. 9am-2pm and 4-6pm). An informal information center is located on Salvatierra between Independencia and Ayuntamiento in a small jewelry shop (tel. 5-02-59). The **police** (tel. 5-00-35) are on Salvatierra just before Ayuntamiento (on call 24 hrs.).

The **post office** is on Salvatierra and Deportiva (tel. 5-06-47), near the bus station, behind the Red Cross (open Mon.-Fri. 8am-3pm). **Postal Code:** 23880. International **collect** and **credit card calls** (6 pesos) can be made on Salvatierra at Independencia across from the supermarket (tel. 5-06-97; open daily 8am-9pm). Long-distance and credit card calls can also be made at the *nevería* across from Supermarket El Pescador, 8.20 pesos per min. to the U.S. (see below; open Mon.-Sat. 8am-9pm, Sun. 9am-1pm and 4-8pm). **Telephone Code:** 113. The **telegram office** (tel. 5-03-87) is next to the post office and has identical hours. **Bancomer** (tel. 5-03-14 or -15), is on Madero across from the *zócalo* (open for exchange Mon.-Fri. 8:30am-noon).

The **bus terminal** (tel. 5-07-67) serviced by **Águila** is on Salvatierra near Allende just off the highway, about 2km from Madero. *De paso* buses run north as far as Santa Rosalía, with stops in between (5hrs.) at 2pm and 5pm, and as far as Guerrero Negro (6hrs.) at 11pm. Buses run south to La Paz, and points in between (5hrs., 50 pesos), at 8am (*local,* with movies), 2pm, 11pm, and midnight. Northbound *local* buses also go all the way to Tijuana (3pm, 18hrs., 181 pesos) and Mexicali (9pm, 21hrs., 223 pesos) and all points in between. A PEMEX **gas station** stares at the bus terminal across the street. **Alfredo's** (tel. 5-05-90) rents cars for US$50 per day including insurance, plus US25¢ per km.

Stock up for the day at **Supermarket El Pescador,** on Salvatierra and Independencia (tel. 5-00-60; open daily 7am-10pm). Watch clothes spin at **Lavandería El Remojón,** on Salvatierra and Independencia (tel. 5-02-59), across from the jewelry store/tourist office. Wash, soap, fabric softener, and dry costs 10 pesos per load, up to 4kg (open Mon.-Sat. 8am-8pm, Sun. 8am-2pm). **Biblioteca Municipal,** on Juárez and Madero (tel. 5-03-41), carries a collection of Spanish-language tomes, but has no A/C (open Mon.-Fri. 8am-8pm). The **Red Cross** is on Salvatierra and Juárez (tel. 5-11-

11; open daily 9am-1pm and 3-8:30pm). **Farmacia Misión,** Salvatierra 66 (tel. 5-03-41), is between Ayuntamiento and Independencia (open daily 8am-10pm). The **Centro de Salud** (tel. 5-00-39), on Salvatierra 1km from the bus terminal, is open 24 hrs. The **IMSS** can be reached at 5-62-70. **Emergency medical numbers** are 5-03-97, 5-09-06, and 5-00-62.

**Accommodations** Budget accommodations in Loreto seem to have perished with the missions. The most economical hotel in town is **Hotel San Martín** (tel. 5-04-42), two blocks north of the *zócalo,* on Juárez near the water, where the furniture appears to have been selected at random. Rooms have private baths, fans, and hot water, but the mattresses are rather wimpy. Parking available; traveler's checks accepted. Check-out 1pm (singles and doubles 50 pesos; triples 60 pesos; bargaining may work). Close to the bus station is **Motel Salvatierra,** on Salvatierra and Ocampo (tel. 5-00-21). Clean, cool, air-conditioned rooms are a bit small. Check-out noon (singles 60 pesos, 70 pesos with cable TV; doubles 80 pesos, 90 pesos with TV; Visa, MC accepted). **El Moro RV Park,** Robles 8 (tel. 3-05-42), though not on the water, allows you to hook up a trailer (US$10), crash in your car (US$8), or just camp out (US$4). Showers are a two-dollar luxury. If no one is there, you can park on the honor system—leave your payment under the door (office open 7am-8pm).

**Food** A number of pricey restaurant-bars have popped up around the docks, proving that supply meets demand. Decent meals are served in establishments up and down Salvatierra, and a number of restaurants cluster conveniently near the bus terminal. **Café Olé,** Madero 14 (tel. 5-04-96), south of the *zócalo,* offers tasty meals and good-sized side portions. Order at the counter, then check the bulletin board for information about events in town. Fresh fish fillet with fries and refried beans will set you back 22 pesos, a jumbo *burrito* 13 pesos, while a rich sundae will cost you another eight pesos (open Mon.-Sat. 7am-10pm, Sun. 7am-2pm). Meat-eating diners watch in salivatory awe as chicken after juicy chicken roasts to warm, brown blissful salvation in the open pit outside **Sinaloa Pollo,** on Salvatierra and Ocampo. A whole chicken costs 35 pesos. Perhaps not coincidentally, half a bird goes for half as much (open daily 9am-10pm). The popular **Restaurant-Bar La Palapa,** on Hidalgo between Madero and López Mateos, fills the bellies of hungry diners inside an enormous reed hut. Admire the horseshoe-shaped oak bar and shark skeletons. Mexican combination platters burst with *enchiladas, quesadillas,* rice, and beans (29 pesos). *Huachinango* (red snapper) 29 pesos; stuffed baked potato 16 pesos.

**Sights** With shaded benches along the water and the sidewalk, the *malecón* is a popular place for an evening stroll. The **Museo de las Misiones** (tel. 5-04-41), which recounts the complete history of the European conquest of Baja California in pictures, artifacts, and words, is located next to the reconstructed mission, one block west of the plaza. Here you can also receive information on other missions scattered throughout the peninsula (open Mon.-Fri. 9am-5pm; admission 10 pesos).

If you're angling for a fresh seafood meal, you can rent a fishing boat and a guide (US$100 for 7hrs.) or go at it alone with some fishing equipment (US$7 per day) from **Alfredo's** (see Practical Information, above). **Arturo's Sports Fishing Fleet** (tel. 5-04-90; fax 5-00-22), on Hidalgo half a block from the beach, offers five-hour snorkeling trips (US$60, minimum 3 people; equipment US$80 extra). Try approaching these companies or others for a trip to **Coronado Island,** where wide, sandy beaches and herds of sea lions await. **Carmen Island,** another popular destination, contains an eerie ghost town and abandoned salt mines. North of Loreto, the road passes the beautiful **Bahía de la Concepción**—with its incredible expanses of coves, blue-green water, and barren, cacti-dotted mountains jutting into the cloudless sky—on its way to Mulegé. South of Loreto, the road winds away from the coast into rugged mountains and the **Planicie Magdalena,** an intensively irrigated and cultivated plain. The striking white stripes on the first hillside beyond town are formed by millions of clams, conch, oyster, and scallop shells—refuse left by the region's

Paleolithic inhabitants. Some caves on the hillside, inhabited as recently as 300 years ago, contain shells and polished stone.

# ■■■ PUERTO SAN CARLOS

Puerto San Carlos (pop. 6,000), 45 minutes west of Constitución on Rte. 4, is one of the last untouched natural wonders of Baja California, a stunningly beautiful spot as yet unspoiled by tourism. Sheltered from Pacific winds by a fragmentary crescent of islands, San Carlos is perched on the edge of Bahía Magdalena on the west side of the Baja Peninsula. Each year, an estimated 18,000 gray whales migrate from the Bering Sea southward through the Pacific to Bahías Magdalena and Almejas. Whale mating season lasts from mid-January to mid-March, and during this period the love-struck creatures wow crowds of locals with aquatic acrobatics. In a peculiar maneuver called "spy hopping," a huge hormonal whale will pop its head out of the water, fix an enormous eye on whatever strikes its fancy, and remain transfixed for minutes on end, staring hypnotically like a submarine periscope. Surprisingly, few travelers have discovered Puerto San Carlos' natural attractions, and tourist-watching is as popular as whale-watching among the locals.

**Orientation and Practical Information** To get to San Carlos, take a transfer bus from Ciudad Constitución (every hr., 45min., 10 pesos). Most amenities for visitors lie on San Carlos's two main streets, **La Paz** and **Morelos,** which are perpendicular to each other. If you do get lost, a passerby can probably tell you where to find anyone or anything you're looking for. Semi-official **tourist information** is available at two equally subjective sources. The tourist office (tel. 6-02-53) is on La Paz, next to the IMSS Hospital. The pink information booth at the edge of town near the PEMEX station provides maps of the bay and islands in tentative English.

The **post office,** on La Paz near México, posts a *Lista de Correos* (open Mon.-Fri. 8am-3pm). **Postal Code:** 23740. The **police** are on La Paz and Acapulco across from the church. Phone friends back home for 7 pesos per minute at the unmarked **Papelería Chokes,** at Morelos and La Paz (tel. 6-00-62; open Mon.-Sat. 8am-1pm and 3-7pm). **Telephone Code:** 113. From the small white **bus terminal** on La Paz and Morelos, **Autotransportes Águila** rolls to Constitución (11am and 2pm, 45min., 10 pesos). Strangely, not only does tiny San Carlos have two sources of tourist information, it also has four medical resources. The **Red Cross** is in the same building as the police. **Farmacia Jazmin** is on La Paz and México (tel. 6-00-56) facing the church. The **IMSS Instituto Mexicano Hospital** (tel. 6-02-11) is also on La Paz. The **Centro de Salud** is on La Paz (yes, yes), in front of Hotel Alcatraz.

**Accommodations and Food** Finding rooms in San Carlos is easy; simply head for the area around Morelos and (yep, you guessed it) La Paz. From the bus station, turn right onto La Paz, then left onto Madero to reach **Motel Las Brisas** (tel. 6-01-52 or -59), on Madero between La Paz and Veracruz. Basic, clean rooms with large fans surround an empty cement courtyard. If you're here when the whales aren't, console yourself by studying the fading courtyard mural dedicated to these gentle giants (singles 50 pesos, with TV 60 pesos; doubles 70 pesos). **Hotel El Palmar,** Acapulco at Vallarta (tel. 6-00-35), allows you to watch your modern color TV while lounging amidst an endless variety of flowery bedspreads and curtains—a floral feast for the fatigued desert traveler. Mattresses are somewhat incapable of cushioning the hard bed-frames. Marginally hot water (singles 60 pesos; doubles 75 pesos). **Hotel Alcatraz** (tel. 6-00-17; fax for reservations 6-00-86), on La Paz at the edge of town across from the Centro de Salud, is an upscale alternative—sporting spotless, comfortable rooms full of amenities such as A/C, refrigerators, *agua purificada,* antique chairs and bureaus, nice color TVs, and some waterfront views. Other services offered by the friendly staff at the Alcatraz include laundry service (20 pesos), long-distance phone service, and a public bath and shower with towel, soap, and shampoo (18 pesos). Check-out 1pm (singles 85 pesos; doubles 140 pesos). A **trailer park** at Playa la Curva outside of town offers full hookups for US$5. Dining in San Carlos is homey—literally. A string of combination restaurant-living rooms along La Paz and Morelos allow you to meet locals, their kids, and pets while you enjoy marine delicacies. More likely than not, the fish on your plate was alive the last time you brushed you teeth. **El Patio Restaurant-Bar** (tel. 6-00-17; fax 6-00-86), in front of Hotel Alcatraz on La Paz, welcomes you into white plastic Corona chairs under open skies. Enjoy an oyster cocktail (30 pesos) or chicken with *mole* (20 pesos) while you watch palm trees sway (open daily 7am-10pm).

**Sights** The islands and bays surrounding Puerto San Carlos teem with life-forms. The tiny **Islote de Patos** (Duck Islet) in the middle of Bahía Magdalena is home to numerous species of birds, including pelicans and white-necks. The gangly creatures crowd every inch of the beach, standing idly like expectant guests at a failed cocktail party. The sheer number of birds (and their malodorous excrement) make landing here difficult; it's best just to cruise by. Feisty Pacific waves at **Cabo San Lázaro** and **Point Hughes,** both on the western tip of **Isla Magdalena,** will keep even veteran surfers busy. Reed huts scattered along the beach offer protection from the oppressive midday sun. Fifteen species of clams and starfish lurk beneath the waters of these immaculate beaches. Farther south, the island narrows to less than 50m in width, tapering off into perfectly white sand tufted with occasional bits of foliage, unusual flowers, and cacti. An enormous, undisturbed colony of sea lions (*lobos marinos*) lives near the island's southern tip. The cheapest way to explore the island is to make an ad-hoc deal with one of the fishermen departing from Playa La Curva in front of the PEMEX station. Unless you plan to camp out on the islands, make definite pick-up plans before you disembark.

# ■■■ LA PAZ

La Paz (pop. 175,000) is a gem among the cities of Baja California, a shining star in a peninsula once dubbed the "intellectual wasteland of Mexico." At once a major port city and home to ten tranquil beaches along the Sea of Cortés, this eclectic and beautiful capital of the young Baja Sur state is where real live Mexicans vacation, leaving the honky-tonk Cabos to Americans. Locals know that there are few sights in the Americas more exquisite than a sunset on the waters off the port of La Paz.

La Paz's earlier days were spent as a quiet fishing village accessible only by sea, but frequently abused by pirates for the iridescent white spheres concealed in the oysters in its sheltered waters. John Steinbeck's *The Pearl* depicted the town as a tiny, unworldly treasure chest glittering with semi-precious orbs.

The city is said to have been founded at least five times: by Cortés in 1535, Sebastián Vizcaíno in 1596, Admiral Isidro de Atondo y Antillón in 1683, the Jesuits Juan de Ugarte and Jaime Bravo in 1720, and finally by José Espinosa, who created the city that would last, in 1811. La Paz's hour of reckoning came in the 1940s, when La Paz's oysters sickened and died, wiping out the pearl industry. Within two decades, however, restless tourists and developers were scouring the country in search of prime real estate, and soon after the institution of the Baja ferries and the completion of the Transpeninsular Highway in the 1960s, La Paz was rediscovered.

## ORIENTATION

La Paz overlooks the **Bahía de la Paz** on Baja's east coast, 222km north of Cabo San Lucas and 1496km southeast of Tijuana, on the Transpeninsular Highway (Rte. 1). The ferry is by far the cheapest way to get from La Paz to the mainland, but for those with a car, procuring a ticket is nearly impossible; ferries carry mostly commercial trucks and the few slots for other vehicles sell out far in advance.

**Sematur Company,** 5 de Mayo and Prieto (tel. 5-46-66), operates the ferry from La Paz to Topolobampo and Mazatlán (open Mon.-Fri. 8am-1pm and 3-7pm, Sat.-Sun. 8am-3pm, though their hours are constantly changing). In order to secure a ticket to

the mainland, be sure to get there early. Acquiring a *salón* ticket should be no problem on the day of departure, but for other classes, call ahead to make reservations. A travel agency might be the most trouble-free way to make reservations—it costs the same and allows you to pick up the tickets at the agency instead of having to wait in the long lines at the ferry office. One such agency is **Operadora de Mar de Cortés,** in the CCC complex on Bravo and Ortega (tel. 5-22-77; fax 5-85-99), a 15-min. walk from the center, and **Cabo San Lucas,** at Hidalgo and Madero (tel. 3-37-17; fax 3-37-07). Tickets can be picked up from 4-6pm the day before departure. Otherwise, tickets may be bought on the day of departure (for more on ferries see Baja California, Getting Around: By Sea on page 117). While the ferry dock in Pichilingue is a hike (17km) from the center of town, you needn't fret—**Autotransportes Águila** buses run down Obregón hourly from 9am-4pm (except 10am) for five pesos. When you get off the ferry, hurry to catch the 9am bus to the *centro*, since another bus won't leave until 11am. A taxi from dock to downtown, or vice versa, will set you back a good 40 pesos. For a more economical route from city to dock, catch the bus at the downtown terminal on Obregón between Independencia and 5 de Mayo.

During holidays, ferry demand is great. In order to get a vehicle on the ferry you will need—at a minimum—proof of Mexican insurance (or a major credit card with the car owner's name on it), car registration, permission for the importation of a car into Mexico, and a tourist card—oh, and three photocopies of each. Travelers themselves will at least need a tourist card. To get a permit, bring all of the paperwork to **Banjercito** (tel. 2-11-16), at the ferry stop in Pichilingue. Alternatively, the **AAA** in the U.S. can also get your permit for you. Try to procure all these documents at the border when entering Mexico (for details on bringing your car farther into Mexico

LA PAZ

see Planning Your Trip, Documents and Formalities: Driver's License and Vehicle Permits on page 7). If not, **Servicios Migratorios,** on Obregón between Allende and Juárez (tel. 5-34-93), can set you up in La Paz (open Mon.-Fri. 8am-3pm and 5-9pm). All of the paperwork must be in place before you purchase the ticket; otherwise, Sematur will deny you a spot whether or not you hold reservations.

Activity centers around the area delineated by **Constitución, Ocampo, Serdán,** and the shore. **The municipal bus system** in La Paz serves the city sporadically. In general, city buses run daily from 6am to 10pm every half hour (1.50 pesos). Flag them down anywhere, or wait by the stop at Degollado, next to the market. Get to the center, if arriving on a bus, by convincing your bus driver to drop you in the center after stopping at the station, as many buses are going that way anyway.

## PRACTICAL INFORMATION

**Tourist Office:** Obregón at 16 de Septiembre (tel. 2-59-39), in a pavilion on the water. Excellent city maps and information about Baja Sur, especially Los Cabos. English-speaking staff. Open Mon.-Fri. 8am-8pm.

**Immigration Office: Servicios Migratorios,** Obregón 2140 (tel. 5-34-93; fax 2-04-29. You must stop here to obtain a tourist card if you entered Mexico via Baja and are mainland-bound. Open Mon.-Fri. 8am-3pm. After hours, head to their outpost in the airport outside of town (tel. 2-18-29). Open daily 8am-10pm.

**Police:** Colima at México (tel. 2-07-81). Open 24 hrs.

**Post Office:** Revolución at Constitución (tel. 2-03-88 or 5-23-58). Open Mon.-Fri. 8am-6pm, Sat. 9am-1pm. **Postal Code:** 23000.

**Telephones:** Sexy **LADATELs** pepper the downtown area and *zócalo.* Some older pay phones still remain as well. If you must use a *caseta,* try the **Librería Contempo,** at Arreola 25A (tel. 2-78-75) and Obregón. **Telephone Code:** 112.

**Telegrams:** (tel. 2-67-07; fax 5-08-09), upstairs from post office. Send or receive a **fax** to/from the U.S. for 15 pesos per page. Mon.-Fri. 8am-6pm, Sat. 8-11am.

**Currency Exchange: Bancomer** (tel. 5-42-48), on 16 de Septiembre, ½ block from the waterfront. Other banks scattered in small downtown area. All open for exchange Mon.-Fri. 8:30am-noon. The exception is **BITAL** (Banco Internacional), 5 de Mayo at Revolución (tel. 2-22-89), where you will be greeted by talking doors and an **ATM.** Open for exchange Mon.-Fri. 8am-6:30pm.

**American Express:** Esquerro 1670 (tel. and fax 2-83-00 or 5-52-72, or toll-free 91-800-00-1552), at the intersection with La Paz, one block from the coastline. Open Mon.-Sat. 8am-2pm and 4-6pm.

**Airport:** West of La Paz, accessible only by 35-peso taxis. Served by **Aeroméxico** (tel. 2-00-91 or 2-16-36), and **Aerocalifornia** (tel. 5-10-22 or -23). To Chihuahua, Culiacán, Los Mochis, Mazatlán, Mexico City (twice a day), Tijuana, and Tucson.

**Bus Station:** There are three. The **main station** is on Jalisco and Independencia, about 25 blocks southeast of downtown. Two municipal buses, "Central Camionera" and "Urbano," service the terminal (1.50 pesos); catch them near the public market at Degollado and Revolución. These buses come infrequently (every hr. 7am-8pm), and the hike to the station is long, so consider taking a taxi (10 pesos). **Águila** and **ABC** (tel. 2-42-70) provide service from that station to points north, including Loreto (7 per day, 9am-10pm, 5hrs., 50 pesos), Mulegé (7 per day, 9am-10pm, 7hrs., 70 pesos), Santa Rosalía (7 per day, 9am-10pm, 8hrs., 78 pesos), San Ignacio (5 per day, 10am-10pm, 9hrs.), Ensenada (10am, 4, 8, and 10pm, 19½hrs., 217 pesos), Tijuana (10am, 4, 8, and 10pm, 21hrs., 237 pesos), and finally, Mexicali (4pm, 24½hrs., 273 pesos). If you're heading south, the best way to do so (although buses also leave from the main *central*) is to leave from the new **Enlaces Terrestres station,** Degollado and Serdán (tel. 3-31-80). They run buses to Todos Santos (6 per day, 7am-8pm, 2hrs., 10 pesos), Cabo San Lucas (6 per day, 7am-8pm, 3hrs., 17 pesos), San José del Cabo (8 per day, 6am-5:30pm, 3½hrs., 22 pesos), and others. To get to nearby beaches and Pichilingue, the **Águila en Malecón station,** Independencia at Obregón (tel. 2-78-98), is your spot. Buses run to Playas Palmira, El Coramuel, El Carmancito, Tesoro, and Pichilingue (every hr., 8am-6pm except 10am, up to ½hr., 2-5 pesos) and to Playas Balandras and Tecolote on weekends only (every hr., 8am-6pm, 45min., 6 pesos). The last bus back to La Paz leaves from Tecolote at 6:45pm and from Pichilingue at 6:30pm on weekdays, 7pm on weekends.

**Ferries: Sematur,** 5 de Mayo and Prieto (tel. 5-46-66). To Mazatlán (Sun.-Fri. at 3pm, 17hrs., *salón* 91 pesos, *turista* 182 pesos, cars up to 5m long 635.70 pesos, motorcycles 82.20 pesos) and Topolobampo (Mon.-Sat. at 11am except for "cargo only" days—call for precise info—8hrs., *salón* 60.70 pesos, *turista* 121.20 pesos, cars up to 5m long 387.50 pesos, motorcycles 48.60 pesos). Open erratically Mon.-Fri. 8am-1pm and 3-7pm, Sat.-Sun. 8am-3pm. Offices at the dock open daily 8am-8pm. Boats for Mazatlán leave Sun.-Fri. at 3pm (no *turista* on Wed.), for Topolobampo at 8pm. Free local calls can be made from the dock facility.

**Laundromat: Lavandería Yoli,** 5 de Mayo at Rubio (tel. 2-10-01), across the street from the stadium. Wash 5 pesos, 10-min. dry 1 peso. Open Mon.-Sat. 7am-9pm, Sun. 8am-3pm.

**Library: Biblioteca de las Californias,** 5 de Mayo and Madero (tel. 5-37-67). Books about Baja. Open Mon.-Fri. 8am-8pm.

**Bookstores: Librería Ramirez** (tel. 2-18-81), on 5 de Mayo between Revolución and Madero. Spanish-language classics and books about Baja. Open daily 10am-9pm. **Librería Contempo,** Arreola 25A (tel. 2-78-75), at Obregón. Used books in English. Bring the book you've just finished or the junk you hate, and trade it in for something from their selection at half price. Open daily 10am-9:30pm.

**Red Cross:** Reforma 1091 (tel. 2-11-11), between Ísabel la Católica and Félix Ortega. Open 24 hrs.

**Pharmacy:** The huge **Farmacia Baja California,** Independencia at Madero (tel. 2-02-40), features that bread-and-butter combination: medicine and furniture. Open Mon.-Sat. 7am-11pm, Sun. 8am-10pm.

**Hospital: Salvatierra,** Bravo at Verdad (tel. 2-14-96 or -97).

**Emergency:** Dial 06.

## ACCOMMODATIONS

The cluttered artistic look seems to be making a resurgence in the budget hotels of La Paz; a student of Mexican folk art could skip the Museo Antropológico and tour the lobbies of these hotels instead. There's a **CREA** youth hostel (tel. 2-46-15) in Forjatero youth center near the Technical University, but its distance makes the hotels a safer, more convenient, and, given the taxi and bus system, perhaps even a cheaper option. Make reservations during peak mid-winter and summer months.

**Pensión California Casa de Huéspedes,** Degollado at Madero (tel. 2-28-96). Bungalow rooms have concrete floors and beds on concrete slabs, but you have to admire the plastic turtle sculpture, sea shells, and dysfunctional washing machine. Prices include private baths and use of the communal kitchen and TV. If you're lucky, you might get a room that has a huge tree trunk running through the bathroom shower, blossoming into full treehood above your roof. Bring your own blanket. Padlocks on the doors provide security. Check-out noon. Singles 38 pesos. Doubles 52 pesos.

**Hostería del Convento,** Madero 85 (tel. 2-35-08), almost at Degollado. Identical to the Pensión California around the corner. Rooms are arranged in an open-air maze lined with old maps of Baja and Mexico, but alas, no map of the hotel. Light blue rooms and ceiling fans offer some relief from the sticky heat. Prices include private baths and use of communal kitchen, TV, and laundry facilities. Padlocks. Singles 38 pesos. Doubles 52 pesos.

**Hotel Yeneka,** Madero 1520 (tel. 5-46-88), between 16 de Septiembre and Independencia. Potentially the most unique hotel in all of Baja. It doubles as a museum of eccentric items: a 1916 model-T Ford, a pet hawk, and a live monkey who lives in the trees. Each Tarzan-hut room has been remodeled in matching twig furniture and painted fully with rainbow colors and animals. Singles 75 pesos. Doubles 85 pesos. Negotiable. The restaurant offers good food at reasonable prices and has English-language books and *agua purificada* (open until 11pm). No to credit cards, yes to traveler's checks.

**Hotel Posada San Miguel,** B. Domínguez 151 (tel. 2-18-02), just off 16 de Septiembre. Fountained courtyards, tiled arches, and wrought-iron scroll-work on windows and railings. Cubical rooms with sinks and large, comfortable beds. Singles 40 pesos. Doubles 50 pesos. Triples 65 pesos.

**Hotel La Purísima,** 16 de Septiembre 408 (tel. 2-34-44), between Revolución and Serdan. While the name discourages frolicsome behavior between guests ("La Purísima" means Immaculate Conception), the small, white rooms are otherwise adequate, with A/C, oddly-placed color TVs, and *agua purificada*. Don't be put off by the jail-like corridor. Check-out 1pm. Singles 60 pesos. Doubles 70 pesos.

## FOOD

On the waterfront you'll find decor, menus, and prices geared toward peso-spewing tourists. Move inland a few blocks and the zeros begin to fall from the back of food prices. Seafood meals are generally fresh. The **public market,** at Degollado and Revolución, offers a selection of fruits, veggies, and fresh fish.

**Antojitos de Sinaloa,** 16 de Septiembre 220 (tel. 2-54-89), between Revolución and Serdán. Enjoy very cheap and very tasty Mexican faves in a small, friendly, fan-cooled room. Yummy beef soup with veggies 13 pesos, *chilaquiles con frijoles* 8 pesos, *bistek ranchero* 13 pesos. Open Mon.-Sat. 7am-10pm, Sun. 9am-6pm.

**Restaurante El Quinto Sol,** B. Domínguez at Independencia (tel. 2-16-92). One of the few vegetarian joints in Baja. Menu includes sausage *à la soybean,* as well as an assortment of juices. Doubles as a health food store—get your dried fruits and vitamins. The large El Quinto salad brings you veggie variety and sets you back 15 pesos. Yogurt smoothie with fruit 8 pesos, vegetarian steak 21 pesos, frozen yogurt 3.50 pesos. Open Mon.-Sat. 7am-9:30pm.

**Restaurant Palapa Adriana** (tel. 2-83-29), on the beach off Obregón at Constitución, offers patrons a stunningly beautiful and serene view of the water 5 short meters away. Seafood soup 25 pesos, *huachinango* (red snapper, fried or grilled) 35 pesos, *pollo mole* 18 pesos. *Pulpo al ajo* 30 pesos. Sea breeze *gratis.* Open daily 10am-10pm. Visa, MC accepted.

## SAND AND SIGHTS

Instead of stretching curving expanses of wave-washed sand, the beaches of La Paz snuggle into small coves sandwiched between cactus-studded hills and calm, transparent water. To be sure, this is prime windsurfing territory. But be careful—La Paz lifeguards make appearances on weekends only, and only on popular beaches.

The best beach near La Paz is **Playa Tecolote** (Owl Beach), 25km northeast of town. A quiet extension of the Sea of Cortés laps against this gorgeous stretch of gleaming white sand, backed up by tall, craggy mountains. Even though there are no bathrooms, Tecolote is terrific for **camping.** On Tecolote, jet skis, banana boats, and boats to the nearby **Isla Espíritu Santo** are available. You may not be able to reach Playa Tecolote without a car on weekdays; **Autotransportes Águila** buses (6 pesos from the mini-station) run weekends only, except during peak seasons— spring break, July, and August. Plenty of other beaches are easily accessible by taking the "Pichilingue" bus up the coast (station on Obregón and Independencia, 5 pesos). Be forewarned that neither of these buses run back to La Paz after 6:30 or 7pm (see Practical Information: Bus Stations, above). The "Pichilingue" bus goes as far as the ferry dock, at which point you need to walk 2km further on the paved road to **Playa de Pichilingue.** This beach is a favorite among the teen set, who dig its eatery and public bathrooms. Young'uns splash in the shallow waters and ride in the paddle boats (10 pesos per hr.). Along the same bus route lies **Playa El Coromuel** near La Concha Hotel, where visitors and locals congregate on weekends. All three beaches are a hefty hike or a short ride away. Closer to town, there's fine swimming in the placid waters near the tourist office, and plenty of restaurants and hotels are nearby in case the big bad sun wears you down. Bear in mind that the farther you venture from La Paz, the better and more secluded the beaches get.

The aquatic fun in La Paz doesn't stop at the shoreline. **Baja Diving and Service,** Obregón 1665 (tel. 2-18-26; fax 2-86-44), just north of B. Domínguez, organizes daily scuba and snorkeling trips to nearby reefs, wrecks, and islands, where you can mingle with hammer heads, manta rays, giant turtles, and other exotica (scuba trips US$77 per day, snorkeling US$40 per day, including equipment, lunch, and drinks). Equipment is also rented (snorkeling US$8, scuba about US$45). Trips leave at 7:45am and return between 3-5pm. **Viajes Palmira,** on Obregón between Rosales and Allende, in front of Hotel Los Arcos, also offers trips.

If you tire of the ocean and want to escape the blistering sun, take a break at the **Museo Antropológico,** 5 de Mayo and Altamirano (tel. 2-01-62), which displays local art, reproductions of pre-Hispanic cave paintings, and exhibits on Baja's indigenous peoples (open Mon.-Fri. 9am-6pm, Sat. 9am-2pm; free). To step forward in history—chronologically, if not spiritually—visit the **Museo de las Californias** in the Casa del Gobierno (tel. 5-37-67), on Madero and 5 de Mayo, facing the *zócalo* and next to the library. Somber, life-size paintings of earlier missionaries inspire fear (open Mon.-Fri. 8am-8pm).

# ■■■ TODOS SANTOS

Popular with a particular sort of traveler, Todos Santos is paradise for the frugal surfer/painter set. Eighty kilometers north of Cabo San Lucas and 80km southwest of La Paz, Todos Santos is one of the few towns on the southern Baja coast which oozes culture, is easily accessible by bus, offers some budget accommodations, and though on the water, is largely unmutilated by resort development.

Yet another in the string of towns founded by Jesuit missionaries in the 17th century, the mission of Todos Santos was erected in 1723. By the late 1800s, Todos Santos was enjoying a sweet adolescence. The town became a major producer of sugar cane, sprouting five *molinos,* or sugar processing plants, which shipped tons of sugar cane and candy to the mainland. When a crippling drought struck the region in the early 1950s, the sugar processing industry stopped generating the profits it once had; the large brick chimneys scattered throughout town are all that remains of the sugar boom. Todos Santos's newest incarnation is as a haven for artsy *gringos* drawn by the town's serenity and cultural sophistication—John Steinbeck used to hang his hat here, and the fine arts center was the first of its kind on the Baja Peninsula. More recently, such Hollywood luminaries as Jack Nicholson and Drew Barrymore have spent time in Todos Santos, and the Fred Dryer TV series "Land's End" is being filmed partly in town for a year.

Todos Santos's permanent *gringo* residents constitute a unique dichotomy: artsy expatriates mingle with alcoholic surfers or ex-surfers, many of whom are living out their post-glory days in anonymity. Despite the influx of drunks and disillusioned cocaine users, the town maintains its somewhat Americanized charm on the strength of gourmet shops, a culturally- and ecologically-concerned populace, and a small community of intellectuals. Though fairly expensive when compared with the rest of Mexico, the town is still cheaper than the Californian cities whence its expatriates came; to them it represents an excellent way to avoid American pop culture and teach their children Spanish through immersion. But rumor has it that a large resort hotel, complete with yacht basin and water park, will one day be built on the land near Playa Los Lobos. Surf in solitude while there's still time.

**Orientation** Todos Santos's two main streets, running parallel and east-west, are **Colegio Militar** and **Benito Juárez.** Juárez is just north of Militar; north of and parallel to Juárez run Centenario and Legaspi. South of Militar and parallel runs Rangel. From east to west, Ocampo, Obregón, Topete, Hidalgo, Márquez de León, Morelos, Zaragoza, and (three blocks further west, at the end of town) Degollado run north-south. Activity centers around the area between Legaspi, Militar, Morelos, and Topete; León crosses Militar and Juárez at the church and main plaza. You may be dropped off near Degollado and Juárez, as this is where the Transpeninsular Highway (from La Paz) turns to head toward Los Cabos.

**Practical Information** Todos Santos has no tourist office, but the American-owned **El Tecolote Libros**, on Juárez and Hidalgo, dispenses (on request) invaluable English-language maps (which include hand-drawn directions to nature spots outside town) as well as English-language newspapers and newsletters. Tecolote also stocks *The Tequila Cookbook* and guidebooks. Buy a book while you're there (12 pesos), or swap the one you're carrying (as long as it's not *Let's Go: Mexico '96*; open daily 9am-5pm). The **police** are in the Delegación Municipal complex on Legaspi between León and Hidalgo. The **post office** on Colegio Militar and León (tel. 5-03-30) posts a *Lista de Correos* (open Mon.-Fri. 8am-1pm and 3-5pm). **Postal Code:** 23300. Make long-distance calls from the **public phone** in front of the Delegación Municipal, or at the bus station *caseta* on the corner of Juárez and Zaragoza for 9.35 pesos per minute to the U.S. (open daily 8am-7pm). **Telephone Code:** 114. **Telegrams** (tel. and fax 5-03-60) cost 18 pesos per seven words at the Delegación Municipal on Centenario and Hidalgo. Already, this paragraph costs about US$68.50 (open Mon.-Fri. 8am-2pm). To exchange currency, head for **Bancomer,** on Juárez and Obregon (tel. 5-03-90; open Mon.-Fri. 8:30am-1pm).

The **bus station** is Pilar's taco stand, at the corner of Zaragoza and Colegio Militar (tel. 5-01-70). *De paso* buses run south to Cabo San Lucas (8 per day, 7am-7pm, 1½hrs., 15 pesos), San José del Cabo (8 per day, 7am-7pm, 2hrs., 18 pesos), and north to La Paz (8 per day, 8am-9pm, 1hr., 12 pesos). Meet your recommended daily nutritional allowances at **Mercado Guluarte** (tel. 5-00-06), on Morelos between Colegio Militar and Juárez (open Mon.-Sat. 7:30am-9pm, Sun. 7:30am-2pm). The friendly, American-run **Perico Azul,** Centenario and Topete, is both a farmer's market, with naturally-grown organic foods, and a boutique (open daily 9am-6pm). Other markets are on Degollado and Juárez. The **laundromat** (tel. 5-03-41) on Pedrajo, three blocks west of Degollado, charges 7.50 pesos to wash and six pesos to dry. Soap is two pesos. For 25 pesos per load, they'll wash it for you (open Mon.-Sat. 8am-4pm, Sun. 8am-2pm). **Farmacia Todos Santos** (tel. 5-00-30), on Juárez between Morelos and Zaragoza, is run out of a disheveled house but provides 24-hr. service. In case of an **emergency,** the number 5-01-22 will get you help.

**Accommodations** Two of the town's four main hotels are in the center of town; the others are a 15-minute jaunt away. Falling asleep in Todos Santos should not pose a problem—the town is oppressively silent—but swarms of tiny mosquitos can be annoying. The **Hotel Miramar,** on Pedrajo at Mutualismo (tel. 5-03-41), though a 15-minute walk from the center, offers an excellent value in an otherwise overpriced town. From the center, head to the west end of town and turn south onto Degollado. Walk a fair distance on Degollado, past PEMEX and a supermarket, until you see a sign for "Hotel Miramar." Take the following right, and it's four blocks down on your left. Clean, well-kept, centrally cooled rooms, large bathrooms with cool blue tiles, a pleasant courtyard and pool, and *agua purificada* will reward you at the end of your hike. Check-out noon (singles 50 pesos; doubles 75 pesos; traveler's checks accepted). **Departamentos Gabi,** at Juárez and Morelos (tel. 5-00-06), is run out of a grocery store around the corner (Mercado Guluarte, see above). The pool is well-suited to those who enjoy bathing in full view of the street, but the adjacent outdoor *palapa* is shady and has an ice-cold *agua purificada* dispenser. Rooms, which are clean and have color TVs, also might have their own private corridor leading to the bathroom (singles 60 pesos; doubles 70 pesos; triples 80 pesos). The brand-new **Misión de Pilar,** at Hidalgo and Colegio Militar (tel. 5-01-14), charges 90 pesos for modern, spotless rooms with nice private bathrooms. Hopefully, fans and window-screens have by now been installed.

Two RV parks are hidden along the coast, south of town. To reach the closer one, **San Pedrito Trailer Park,** turn right off the Transpeninsular Highway, 6.9km south of town. (You've missed the turnoff if you pass a beer store.) Pass through an arch that straddles the road, drive 3.1km, bear left at a fork in the road, and you're there. To get to **Los Ceritos Trailer Park,** turn right 10km south of town at a blue-and-white sign that reads "RV Park." Past a fence and the old highway to Los Cabos,

2.6km down the dirt road, you'll hit the park. A bar, pool, restaurant, TV, and awesome surfing beaches await.

**Food** Budget eats aren't hard to find in Todos Santos. Several *loncherías* line Colegio Militar near the bus station, offering triple tacos and the like for nine pesos. Locals swear by the **Taquería El Sinaloense,** run out of the back of a painted bus on Degollado near Colegio Militar. Enjoy excellent meat tacos (4 pesos) under a *palapa;* the Sinaloan meat is grilled on a huge grill out back. The American-run **Alice's Restaurant,** on Degollado near Juárez, has what might be the best burgers in Baja, and they're only 12-15 pesos with fries. Sit at the counter and order the huge, great-tasting mushroom and onion cheeseburgers with fries (15 pesos) off the fluorescent surfboard menu (in English), and wash it down with an irresistible Snapple (6 pesos; open daily 10am-8pm). Restaurant-bar **Las Fuentes,** at Colegio Militar and Degollado (tel. 5-02-57), one block left of the bus station, has pleasant fountains and good food: English-Spanish menu offers fried *huachinango* (red snapper) with rice and salad for 24 pesos and breakfast for about 18 pesos. If you haven't tried *mole* yet, here's your chance: chicken *enchiladas* with *mole* are good and inexpensive (22 pesos). Come for the food, stay for the clean public bathrooms. 10% tax added (open daily 7am-9pm). When the sun goes down, avoid the deafening sound of silence and visit **El Rinconsito Bar,** inside the red-clay roofed Hotel California. Watch TV, or just peer at your cold *cerveza* (open 11am-10pm).

**Sights** Todos Santos offers a wealth of diversions, most within a three-block radius of downtown. Chief among these is the **Casa de la Cultura,** a long brick building at Topete and Legaspi. Head two blocks down Legaspi away from the cathedral, then bear left on Legaspi; the Casa is on the left, halfway down the hill. Artifacts of Pericúe civilization, pastel paintings by prominent Baja artists, and three amazing murals depicting slavery, industrialization, and "mind and muscle," done in 1933 by third- and fourth-grade students, and an old library each occupy a room around an airy promenade. The central area is filled with a mélange of photos, sculptures, and religious figures from the colonial period (open daily 8am-8pm; free).

Todos Santos's new pride and joy (among art fans, at least) is the **Todos Santos Gallery,** on Legaspi and Topete, opened in 1995 by the prominent artist Michael Cope. The gallery has plenty of contemporary Mexican paintings by Cope and others, displayed in a tasteful way (open Mon. and Wed.-Sat. 9am-5pm).

Cutting-edge bronze and clay sculptures, off-the-wall wall clocks, and ornate mirrors are on parade at the **Santa Fe Art Gallery,** Centario 4 (tel. 5-03-40), between Hidalgo and Marquez de Leon (open Wed.-Mon. 9:30am-5pm). Don't be shy when you visit **Casa Franco Gallery,** Juárez at Morelos (tel. and fax 5-03-56), directly behind the Santa Fe gallery. The furniture comes from Puebla, the bowls and pipes from Guadalajara, Todos Santos, and Puebla (open daily 9am-5pm). The white-washed, colonial-style **Manuel Márquez de Leon Teatro,** facing the *zócalo* on Legaspi between Hidalgo and Márquez de Leon, hosts many cinematic and thespian endeavors. Ask around to find out about upcoming shows.

If you overdose on art, don't forget that Todos Santos is surrounded by some of the world's most unspoiled (and unexplored) beaches. **La Posa,** only 2km from town, is perfect for that romantic stroll or uplifting solitary walk. Unfortunately, vicious undercurrents and powerful waves make this beach unequivocally unsuited for swimming. To get there, go up Juárez and turn left on Topete. Follow the road as it winds across the valley and comes to a white building that says "Do not pass." If you pass that, you're on the beach. Most other beaches are accessible via the Transpeninsular Highway south of town. These sights are isolated, and therefore both attractive and hazardous. Bring a friend, and plan to return before nightfall. To head south, turn left onto Degollado as you walk away from the town center. Roughly six blocks later, the city limits end. To catch a spectacular aerial view of the sea, turn right 1.5km south on the highway at the first possible fork in the road. Follow the main dirt path east for 2.5km; the path will bear left past an old fish plant and up a hill, which falls precipitously to the seashore. Below you is **Punta Lobos,** the stomping ground of the local sea lion population and a beach popular with locals. To your right rises a lighthouse.

A beautiful lake atop a mountain, **Sierra de la Laguna,** is accessible only by car (it's a 90-minute drive). One kilometer down the highway past the Punta Lobos turn-off, turn left at the fenced-off cattle ranch. A 45-minute drive brings you to Rancho La Burera, which serves as the trailhead for the *laguna*. Be social and make friends in town. Invite them to show you the way.

To reach the appropriately named **Playa de las Palmas,** continue 4.6km down the highway, and turn right when you see the white buildings on the left. Travel another 2.6km and you'll be bowled over by palm trees; just past these is the beach. The serene and deserted beach here is well-suited for swimming.

---

### Baseball a la Mexicana

If you're feeling energetic at night, you might want to take in a baseball game at the local stadium, off Degollado to the south. Follow the light towers—any local will show you the way. Admission is only 5 pesos, though a cold Tecate's another 5 pesos. Root, root, root for the home team—Los Tiburones (the Sharks)—while analyzing the odder aspects of Mexican League professional baseball: you'll see an all-sand playing field, umpires in bright blue pants, baserunners without batting helmets, players trading gloves between batters, lots of submarine-ball pitchers, some players on the same team in different uniforms, and huge crowds dancing between innings to popular dance music. Oh, and if, by chance, you catch a ball, don't even think about keeping it as a souvenir—you will first be swarmed by tiny kids paid by commission for every ball (and crushed beer can) they recover, and eventually you'll even be bothered by the police! Games are at 7pm some weeknights and 1 or 2pm on weekends.

---

# ■■■ LOS CABOS

The towns of **Cabo San Lucas** and **San José del Cabo** comprise the southwestern part of the Los Cabos district (pop. 58,871), which includes much of the coastline of Baja California's southern end. Readily accessible via air and water, Los Cabos ("The Capes") is much more developed than the majority of the peninsula; despite the construction of the Transpeninsular Highway, it is still the northern and southern extremes of Baja California that attract tourists and city-dwellers. Visitors are drawn to the cape by the stretch of beach leading from San José del Cabo to Cabo San Lucas, where luxury hotels form a glittering strip between the desert and the ocean, and sunbathing, sightseeing, gift-buying, sport-fishing, jet-skiing *norteamericanos* congregate by the thousands.

The area has a long history of trade with Asia, beginning in the 16th century when Vizcaíno seized on Los Cabos as protective port for the "Nao de China," a vessel often molested by pirates on its trips between Manila and Acapulco. Eventually, Los Cabos grew into an important stop for ships making trans-Pacific runs. Because the region had a permanent fresh water supply, thirsty Asian travelers called Los Cabos "Sure Water Port." Locals now make their living almost entirely off of tourism.

# ■■■ CABO SAN LUCAS

Perched on the southern tip of Baja, Cabo San Lucas is an eminent 1990s representative of the heavily-Americanized resort industry of Mexico. Though small (pop. 3,000), the town has surpassed such classic resorts as Acapulco in popularity among honeymooners due to its peaceful waters and ultra-modern pleasure domes. A favorite vacation destination among families looking for an easy, pampered escape from stress, Cabo San Lucas is particularly accommodating to those who desire neither a peek into real Mexican culture nor a word of Spanish, and don't want to deal with that hassle of changing their dollars into pesos—or of even learning what a peso is.

Cabo San Lucas has yet to develop extensive facilities for budget travelers. Prices at most restaurants are high, even by U.S. standards. And timeshare-hawking, smooth-talking quasi-tourist officials roam Cabo's streets, looking for the day's prey—an American with a credit card who, with a free dinner and some convincing words, might just make that most infamous of impulse purchases: a US$15,000 piece of the pie in a glitzy ocean-view suite.

Despite its influx of dollar-rich, culture-poor tourists, Cabo San Lucas—the first of the two *cabos* on the *vía corta* bus route from La Paz—does have some appeal to the budget traveler, mostly due to its beaches and rock formations: **El Arco** is the famous arch rock that marks the very tip of the Californias. Until recently a peaceful fishing village, Cabo San Lucas's economic boom is fast becoming a sad lesson in the effects of unbridled growth. Dolphins and whales, once a common sight close to the coast, have all but disappeared from the area. City officials have now begun to enforce stricter pollution laws, but their efforts may be too little too late.

Budget travelers would do best to visit Cabo San Lucas only for the day or to camp on the beach and simply treat the town as a big supermarket; buy your sunscreen and make tracks for cheaper San José del Cabo.

**Orientation** **Lázaro Cárdenas** is the main street in Cabo San Lucas, and it runs roughly southeast-northwest, diagonally through the town's grid of streets. **Paseo del Marina** forks off Cárdenas where the resort zone begins, continues south, and winds around the marina. From west to east, north-south streets (all branching off Cárdenas) include Ocampo, Zaragoza, Morelos, Vicario, and Mendoza. Further west, Cabo San Lucas, Hidalgo, Matamoros, and Abasolo cross Cárdenas and continue south into the resort zone, eventually meeting Marina. From north to south, the following streets are perpendicular to those above: Obregón, Revolución, 20 de Noviembre, Libertad, 16 de Septiembre, Niños Héroes, Constitución, and 5 de Mayo, and south of Cárdenas, Madero, Zapata, and J. Domínguez run east-west in the resort area. Continuing south on Marina, one will pass the posh resorts, and eventually arrive at the beach, **Playa de Médano.**

Restaurants and bars—and a high density of English-speaking Mexicans—are concentrated on Cárdenas between Morelos and the mountains on the western edge of town. To get to the center of the action from the bus station, walk on Zaragoza for two blocks toward the water to Cárdenas. The grid-like pattern of the city makes it difficult to get lost. You might be dropped off at a remote bus station; from there, cross the street and walk across the sandy little park in front of the yellow complex; continue to the next street, and stand across the street from the bus stop to catch a local yellow bus to the center (every 15min., ½hr., 2 pesos).

**Practical Information** Maps are dispensed by time-share hawkers all over the center of town. The "Marina Fiesta" salespeople have the best of the lot. The long-distance **caseta** at Cárdenas and Hidalgo (tel. 3-00-25; fax 3-00-19) charges three pesos for **international collect calls** and 12.50 pesos per min. to the U.S. (open daily 8am-10pm), but a better choice is one of the many **LADATELs,** including one next to the above *caseta.* Another resides at Cárdenas and Ocampo. **Telephone Code: 114. Banca Serfín,** at Cárdenas and Zaragoza (tel. 3-99-90 or -91), exchanges cash and traveler's checks Mon.-Fri. 8:30am-11:30pm, and greets you with a friendly **ATM** that's fluent in English. **Bancomer,** across the street, will also change money from 8:30am to 1pm, as will the *casa de cambio* on Cárdenas at Zaragoza (tel. 3-19-50). Most hotels and restaurants will gladly exchange dollars at lower rates. The main **bus station,** served by **ABC Autotransportes** and **Águila,** is located at Zaragoza and 16 de Septiembre. The two most common destinations are San José del Cabo (every ½hr., 7:15am-10pm, ½hr., 5 pesos) and La Paz (9 per day, 6am-7:30pm, 3hrs., 25 pesos) via Todos Santos (1½hrs., 12 pesos). One bus per day leaving at 4:30pm heads all the way north, stopping at La Paz (3hrs., 25 pesos), Cd.

Constitución (6hrs., 55 pesos), Ej. Insurgentes (6½hrs., 58 pesos), Loreto (8½hrs., 75 pesos), Mulegé (10½hrs., 95 pesos), Santa Rosalía (11½hrs., 103 pesos), San Ignacio (12½hrs., 107 pesos), Vizcaíno (13½hrs., 136 pesos), Guerrero Negro (14½hrs., 148 pesos), Punta Prieta (16hrs., 170 pesos), El Rosario (18hrs., 199 pesos), San Quintín (19hrs., 210 pesos), Ensenada (23hrs., 236 pesos), and Tijuana (26½hrs., 257 pesos). Rent cars from **Avis Rent-a Car** (tel. 3-46-07), at Plaza Los Mariachis across from the Giggling Marlin. VW Bugs start at US$30 a day, including insurance and unlimited mileage (open Mon.-Sat. 8am-2pm and 4-6pm).

The large yellow local supermarket, **Supermercado Plaza,** at Zaragoza and Cárdenas (tel. 3-14-50), is open daily 7am-11pm. An **English-language bookstore,** at Marina and Cárdenas (tel. 3-31-71), in the Plaza Bonita Mall, has U.S. magazines, popular novels, and *USA Today* (open daily 9am-9pm). Next door to the supermarket is **Farmacia Aramburo** (tel. 3-14-89; open 7am-10pm). In case of an **emergency,** dial the **police** (tel. 3-00-57 or 3-12-10) or the **Red Cross** (tel. 3-30-00).

**Accommodations and Food** Multi-million-dollar resorts with every service imaginable dominate San Lucas's coast line; *ergo,* simple, cheap beds are seriously lacking. In any case, during the winter high season make reservations early and be prepared to shell out more *dinero* than you would during the slower summer months. The only legitimate budget accommodation remaining may be the **Hotel Casa Blanca,** on Revolución and Vicario (tel. 3-02-60). Though slightly less luxurious than its U.S. counterpart on 1600 Pennsylvania Ave., the hotel provides the basics: clean, simple, cement rooms with fans and functional private bathrooms. Check-out 1pm (singles 75 pesos; doubles 85 pesos). From Cárdenas, to get to the **CREA Youth Hostel (HI)** (tel. 3-01-48), walk ten minutes down Morelos to Av. de la Juventud, and then turn right and hike five minutes to the Instituto Sur Californiano building. The street is not-well lit; lone travelers would be wise to check in before twilight or stay in town. You may well have the entire place to yourself, ruining perhaps the best thing about hostels—the company. Excitement over the cheapest beds in town is certainly dampened by the inconvenient location and hot hike to the beach. Bring your own pillow. Check-out 2pm. (Dorm bunk with communal bath 30 pesos. Singles with private bath 40 pesos. Bunk doubles with bath 60 pesos. Camping 20 pesos.)

Like their fellow shops and hotels, restaurants in San Lucas have been forced into submission by *gringo* tastes. Restaurant-bars gang up on tourists along the water; the cheap spots line Morelos, a safe distance from the million-dollar yachts. King of *taquerías,* the **Asadero 3 Hermanos,** Morelos at 20 de Noviembre, serves up scrumptious, cheap, and safe tacos (4-4.50 pesos). Sit at the outdoor counter next to the locals and chow down; one taco might fill you up—two definitely will (open daily 7am-1am). Growling stomachs gravitate toward the enormous rotating spits of chicken at **El Pollo de Oro,** Cárdenas at Morelos (tel. 3-03-10). Half a chicken 17 pesos, quarter-bird 10 pesos. Simple calculations reveal that the half chicken is the better deal (open daily 6am-11pm). **Mariscos Mocambo,** Morelos at 20 de Noviembre (tel. 3-20-22), dishes up *puro* seafood; gulp down oysters *al mojo de ajo* (37 pesos) or Chinese sea snail soup for 22 pesos (open daily 11am-10pm).

**Sights and Entertainment** All major activity in Cabo San Lucas revolves around the pristine waters that surround the coast. One of the best beaches in the area, **Playa de Médano** stretches east along the bay around the corner from the marina. Escape the blazing sun in one of the beach's many restaurants or *palapas.* The waters of the Playa de Médano are alive with parasailers and motorboats full of lobster-red, beer-guzzling vacationers. For watersports fun, try **Cabo Aguade-portes,** in front of the Hotel Hacienda, or **JT Watersports** (tel. 6-68-96; open 9am-6pm). Explore underwater life with complete snorkeling gear (US$9 per day) or skim above the foamy waves on a catamaran (US$35 per ½hr.). Reservations can be made at Hotels Pueblo Bonito and Finisterra.

The famous **Arch Rock** ("El Arco") of Cabo San Lucas rises only a short boat ride from the marina. To get there, walk through the Plaza Las Glorias hotel or the big Mexican crafts market further down Paseo Marina to the docks. Eager, English-speaking boat captains will be happy to take you on a 45-minute glass-bottom boat ride to El Arco and back (US$6). On the way, you may be treated to an inordinate number of tasteless or corny jokes, and apart from the picturesque Arch (which is usually home to sea lions), you'll see Sly Stallone's summer dwelling in the distance—those budget travelers with weak stomachs can turn the other way. The boat also stops at **La Playa del Amor** (yes, that's Lovers' Beach) right near El Arco and allows you to get out and head back later on a different boat for no additional charge. This beach, perennially mobbed, is the only one with access to both the rough, deep blue Pacific and the light, tranquil Sea of Cortés. Swimming is good on the gulf side, but beware the Pacific's currents; two unlucky swimmers died recently after being dragged out to sea on this side, which is aptly named **La Playa del Divorcio** (Divorcees' Beach). Seclusion-seekers may find the Pacific beaches to their liking. To get to these beaches, hop on a yellow bus (1.50 pesos) or walk out on Marina and turn right across from the Mexican crafts market. Slip out to the beach between massive condo complexes right after you pass the Terra Sol Hotel.

**Snorkeling** is also popular on Lovers' Beach and around the rocks between the marina and the beach, where tropical fish abound. Bring your own gear or dish out those dollars for rented equipment from one of the many vendors that populate the marina area (see above). The best snorkeling beach is said to be **Playa Santa María,** between Cabo San Lucas and San José del Cabo.

The five-peso bus ride to San José del Cabo provides access to more beaches along the way. Choose your spot carefully in order to avoid the crowds. **El Chileno,** halfway between the two towns, offers phenomenal opportunities for swimming as well as snorkeling in one of the only live coral reefs in the world, but **Tulé** boasts nicer surf. Just ask around to find names and descriptions of other good sites, and ask the driver to leave you at the beach of your choice. Beaches closer to (and in) San José, past El Chileno, are generally unswimmable due to the surf.

At night, you too can join rich Americans in the nightly ritual of alcohol-induced gastrointestinal reversal. Typical Cabo San Lucas bar decor is in the same booze-can-punish-vein—off-the-wall signs like "Sorry, We're Open" and "Wrong Way—Do Not Exit" vie for space with assorted driver's licenses. Begin (or end) your single-minded quest for inebriation at **Squid Roe,** Cárdenas at Zaragoza (tel. 3-06-55 or 3-12-69). Draw on the brown-paper-bag tablecloths with fluorescent crayons while avoiding the temptation to inhale the sawdust that carpets the floor. Beer 10 pesos, national mixed drinks 12 pesos (dancing—on any and all surfaces—from 10pm-3am; open daily noon-3am). A louder, middle-aged crowd at the expensive **Giggling Marlin,** Marina at Matamoros (tel. 3-11-82), enjoys quaffing a full mug or a tall *yarda* while hanging upside-down like the day's big catch (happy hour(s) 2-7pm, during which beer and margaritas are half-price; open daily 8am-1am).

## The Timeshare Circuit

Timeshare vendors disguised as "tourist officials" roam the streets of Cabo San Lucas. If you want to take advantage of what they have to offer for free, you must be 25 years old (or tell them you're 25—they'll believe you) and possess a major credit card. If you have both, and a free afternoon, it's quite possible to go on the Arco boat ride for free and order anything you want at an expensive restaurant in exchange for an hour and a half of "listening," ears closed but eyes open, mouth pleasantly grinning, and head nodding to the English-speaking con man's pitch. He will try to convince you to dump US$15,000 into his hands in exchange for yearly time at an exclusive, American-oriented resort in Cabo. Don't admit until after dinner that you're not prepared to spend $15,000 (unless you want a struggle). Other lures include a free car rental for a day and a free day at a resort.

# ■■■ SAN JOSÉ DEL CABO

Although golf courses and luxury hotels now separate San José del Cabo from the beach, and a few small-town institutions are being pushed out of their traditional locations in the *centro* by tourist information centers and gift shops, San José del Cabo remains peacefully Mexican, a haven from the Resortville that dominates the rest of the cape. Although the occasional timeshare salesperson will scope out the streets of San José for prey, his goal will be to lure the customer back to San Lucas or to the glitzy resorts in between—central San José itself is largely immune. In fact, "Los Cabos," when said colloquially, often refers only to Cabo San Lucas and the surrounding beaches and resort, and does not include quieter San José. Unlike its neighbor, San José has retained some historical and cultural points of interest.

Two Spanish missionaries, Nicolás Tamaral and José Echeverría, founded San José del Cabo on April 8, 1730. The two men immediately set out to convert the indigenous Pericúe, and established a Spanish mission on the banks of the nearby freshwater lagoon. The missionaries soon realized, however, that their soul-saving efforts were doomed to failure. The Pericúe resisted, eventually murdering Father Tamaral. The physical structure of the mission was destroyed by flooding in 1793; six years later it was rebuilt, only to be decimated in 1822 by the warship "Independencia," commandeered by Chilean insurgents. The town's mission and interesting Palacio del Gobierno remain intact, situated among the mostly quiet streets of the *centro*.

**Orientation** The **Transpeninsular Highway** on the west and **Avenida Mijares** on the east, both running north-south, connect the town with San José's broad sweep of beautiful beach 2km away. From north to south, cross-streets, running east-west between the above two include Obregón, Zaragoza, Doblado, Castro, Coronado, Gonzáles, and much further south along the resort-laden beach, Paseo San José. Between the two main north-south streets, Green, Degollado, Guerrero, Morelos, and Hidalgo run parallel from west to east. The conspicuous cathedral and *zócalo* are on Zaragoza near Hidalgo. To get to town from the Águila/ABC Autotransportes station, walk up hilly González and turn right on the highway. Zaragoza is three blocks and a sweaty forehead away. Turn right and follow Zaragoza to the cathedral, a good 10 minutes away.

**Practical Information** The **tourist center** (tel. 2-04-46 or 2-29-60, ext. 150) is in the beige building next to the *zócalo* on Zaragoza and Mijares. An English-speaking staff dispenses maps designed to help tourists spend money—street names are replaced by the names of restaurants, bars, and hotels (open Mon.-Fri. 8am-3pm). For **police,** call 2-03-61. The **post office** is on Mijares and González (tel. 2-09-11), several blocks toward the beach on the right-hand side. *Lista de Correos* (open Mon.-Fri. 8am-6pm, Sat. 9am-1pm). **Postal Code:** 23400. **Free local calls** can be made from the booth outside the tourist office. The *caseta* beside the cathedral, Hidalgo 9 (tel. 2-04-53; fax 2-00-14), between Zaragoza and Obregon, is open daily 8am-9pm. Place an **international call** for 12.50 pesos per minute, or send a **fax** for 1 peso per page plus phone charges. **Telephone Code:** 114. Change money at **Banca Serfín,** Zaragoza at Green (tel. 2-23-03 or -06; open for exchange 8:30am-noon), and at **Bancomer,** on Zaragoza and Morelos (tel. 2-00-30 or -40; open for exchange 8:30am-noon). Bancomer often has the better rates. **ATMs** can be found in many banks, including **Banco Unión** (tel. 3-34-34), near the *zócalo.* You can also take advantage of that bank's wonderfully clean, air-conditioned bathroom. Ah.

San José del Cabo is such a whirring, buzzing metropolis that it needs two **bus stations. Águila** and **ABC Autotransportes** launch buses from the station on Mijares at González (tel. 2-11-00) to La Paz (10 per day, 6am-7pm, 3hrs., 25 pesos), Cabo San Lucas (15 per day, 6:45am-10pm, 25min., 5 pesos), and Todos Santos (5 per day until 4pm, 1¼hrs., 22 pesos). One bus per day leaves for Tijuana (4pm, 28hrs.). The **Frailes/Delfines terminal** is on Doblado and Privera (tel. 2-19-06), a five-minute walk from the *centro* and about 10 minutes from Mijares. Frailes operates yellow-and-blue school buses labeled "Union de Transporte Urbano." You can hop on anywhere along the Transpeninsular Highway between Cabo San Lucas and San José del Cabo (every ½hr. to Cabos San Lucas, 5:30am-7:10pm, 25min., 5 pesos). **Dollar Rent-A-Car** (tel. 2-01-00; at the airport 2-06-71), across from the supermarket (see below), will set you on the road for US$49 per day plus US$11 per day insurance; free mileage. You need a credit card and at least twenty-five candles on your last birthday cake. To corral a **taxi**, call 2-04-01 or 2-01-05.

The **library** is located at Mijares 5 and Zaragoza, across a walkway and behind the tourist office. If you can't read Spanish, you'll have to be content with looking at the pictures (open Mon.-Fri. 7am-9pm). Buy groceries at the **Supermercado Aramburo** on Zaragoza and Guerrero (tel. 2-01-88 or 2-00-48; open daily 8am-9pm). **Farmacia Profesor Aurora** is on Green at Dobaldo (tel. 2-26-11), across from the Jardín de Niños (open daily 8am-2pm and 4-11pm). The ever-ready **Red Cross** (tel. 2-03-16 or -61) is on Mijares next to the post office.

**Accommodations and Food** As prices rise with the approach of the megaresorts, rooms in the center of town look less and less appealing: imagine waking up US$16-40 poorer, then having to face a scorching 25-minute walk to the beach. Many random rooms are for rent for about 30 pesos a day; look for signs, especially on Obregón. Otherwise, you can enjoy multi-colored bedspreads and ancient paint jobs at **Hotel Ceci,** Zaragoza 22 (tel. 2-00-51), 1½ blocks up from Mijares. Spanking clean, cold rooms put guests in a positive mood, ready to appreciate the pastel curtains and matching lampshades (singles 55 pesos, 65 pesos with A/C; doubles 75 pesos with A/C). If you choose the **Hotel Diana,** Zaragoza 30 (tel. 2-04-90), ask for a room downstairs—they're the best of the bunch. Spotless rooms with A/C, modern TVs, and clean bathrooms go for 100 pesos. **Trailer Park Brisa del Mar,** just off the highway to San Lucas when it reaches the coast, provides beach campers, communal bathrooms, and a bar with TV (full hookup US$3 plus tax, US$5 for tent).

Budget restaurants in San José del Cabo are being pushed out by real estate offices and fancy tourist eateries, leaving few options between taco stands and filet mignon. A healthy suspicion of anglophone restaurants will save you money: if the menus are printed in flawless English, the food is probably more expensive than it ought to be. Good, moderately priced meals hide near the Frailes bus terminal and along Zaragoza between the cathedral and the banks. The best deal in town might be found at the **Mercado Municipal** restaurant building, near the ABC bus station. Seven restaurants reside in the airy pavilion with central tables. Try **Dalia,** on your right as you enter. Tasty, safe meat or fish main dishes vary daily at 15-17 pesos; the selection might include such items as *hígado encebollado* (liver with onions) or *pescado empanizado* or *frito* (fried fish). **Restaurante Vista al Mar,** on Castro and Doblado, offers homecooked meals and an authentic Mexican ambiance absent elsewhere in town. Locals sit on the airy covered porch and heartily devour economical foods prepared by the family, such as *enchiladas* (11 pesos) and *pollo frito* (16 pesos). The menu is short but traditionally Mexican (open daily 8am-4pm). The food at **Cafetería Rosy,** on Zaragoza and Green, will leave you as riveted as Rosie. Seafood dishes like *sopa de camarones* (shrimp soup, 17 pesos), *pescado en mantequilla* (fish in butter sauce, 20 pesos), and *pollo a la naranja* (chicken in orange sauce, 18 pesos) are tasty and hearty. Squint at the tiny TV while you chow down under the cool thatched roof (open daily Oct.-May 8am-10pm; June-Sept. 8am-6pm).

**Sights and Entertainment** The most popular beach in town (for surfing, if not swimming) is **Costa Azul,** on Palmilla Pt. 1km south of the Brisa del Mar trailer park. Getting here is difficult; try to convince the driver to let you off. A 15-min. walk down Mijares will lead you to good beaches much closer to town. The newest luxury hotels mar the sand at some spots, but there's plenty of natural, clean coastline in between the artificial structures. If you want to swim, try the **Playa Palmilla,** 3km toward Cabo San Lucas from Costa Azul. Hitchhiking is frequently done along that road (see Cabo San Lucas, Sights on page 160).

SAN JOSÉ DEL CABO

Don't be scared away from the **Killer Hook Surf Shop** (tel. 2-24-30), on Hidalgo between Doblado and Zaragoza; they don't bite, and they can provide t-shirts and lots of useful stuff (snorkel gear US$8, fishing pole US$10, surf board US$15, all for 24 hrs.). The shop also repairs surfboards and provides tips. Pick up and drop off equipment at the shop (open Mon.-Sat. 8am-8pm).

If you can find time between trips to the beach, stop by **Los Cabos Centro Cultural** on Mijares. Feast your eyes on sea fossils, reproductions of wall paintings, regional antiques, and an original Pericúe home. Guided tours are available (open daily 9am-5pm). At night, **Eclipse** on Mijares (tel. 2-16-94), one block down from Doblado, pumps out rock tunes (never a cover; happy hour Tues.-Wed. 7-9pm; open Tues.-Sun. 7pm-3am). The real nighttime action, however, is in Cabo San Lucas, a piggy-bank-shattering 90-peso taxi ride away.

# Northwest Mexico

## SONORA

### ■■■ NOGALES

Pushed up against the border and straddled by two steep hills bearing tin houses and block-long Corona signs, Nogales can seem like the archetypal border town—cheap curio shops, off-track betting, and cheesy bars dominate its landscape. However, the cultural syncretism and fast-paced bustle which animate life in other border towns are notably absent here; more or less unalloyed by *gringo* influences, Nogales is a precious commodity. Yet some traces of tourism do linger among the street vendors who import and mark up goods from all over Mexico. They expectantly wait for pocketbook-happy Americans to dip below the border for a day and purchase tiny rag dolls as proof of having set foot in a foreign land.

In large measure, Nogales has kept its cultural distance from the U.S. by design. After the 1848 Treaty of Guadalupe ended the Mexican-American War, across-the-border raids became a serious problem. While the U.S. had the resources and the will to deter raids with force, Mexico defended itself by encouraging development on its side of the border. Born out of war as something of an unarmed fortress, Nogales has retained its distinctively Mexican identity even as it has become a gateway to the U.S. for Sonoran wheat, corn, and fruit.

#### ORIENTATION AND PRACTICAL INFORMATION

If you plan to venture beyond Nogales, obtain a **tourist card** at the frontier. It's much simpler and cheaper to get the card here than farther south. When you cross the border—which, incidentally, has a huge Taco Bell billboard (they really did "make a run for the border")—through the new arched crossing complex, turn right into the first building you encounter; it's the immigration and tourist office. (See "Entering Mexico" on page 8.)

The **bus terminal** and **train station** are directly across from each other on Carretera Internacional, 4.5km from town. To reach the center of town from the bus station, avoid the exorbitant taxi fare (25 pesos) and board one of the white buses (1.20 pesos) marked "Parque Industrial" or "Villa Sonora." From the bus terminal, cross the street and walk north to the end of the block; buses stop across the street (and not before) and downtown Nogales is the last stop. Relatively small Nogales makes for easy navigating. From east to west, **Pesqueira, Juárez** (which becomes López Mateos several blocks south), **Morelos, Obregón** (the main tourist drag), **Ingenieros,** and **Hidalgo** run parallel to each other and perpendicular to the border. If you're crossing the border by foot, you'll be on Pesqueira; by car, you'll drive in on Juárez. **Internacional** runs parallel to the tall picket fence that marks the border. Proceeding south, away from the border, **Campillo, Ochoa, Pierson, Aguirre, Vázquez, Díaz,** and **González** all run parallel.

> **Tourist Office:** To the left of the border from the Mexican side, in the Edificio Puerta de México (tel. 2-06-66). The friendly, English-speaking staff is best at directing visitors to curio shops or bars, but will also hand out a crude map of the downtown area and various other brochures. Open daily 8am-3pm.
> **Police:** Gonzalez and F. Guerra (tel. 2-01-16 or 2-01-14). English-speakers on hand in the afternoon. Open 24 hrs. **Highway Patrol:** tel. 4-18-30.
> **Post Office:** Juárez 52 (tel. 2-12-47), at Campillo, posts a *Lista de Correos*. **Postal Code:** 84000 (central Nogales).

**Telephones:** Downtown Nogales has a high concentration of **LADATEL** phones. Look for them at Obregón and Campillo, Obregón and Flores Guerra, and at the border in front of the tourist office. **Puesta del Sol,** Campillo 115 (tel. 2-00-16, fax 2-17-14), at Obregón, has a *caseta* where you can make international calls, plus a fax service (5 pesos per page). Local calls 2 pesos for 3 min. Open daily 8am-12:30pm. The *caseta* in the bus terminal (tel. 3-50-81, fax 3-50-82) is overpriced. International calls and a fax service. Open 24 hrs. **Telephone Directory:** 04. **Telephone Code:** 631.

**Telegrams:** Campillo 68 (tel. 2-00-81 or 2-15-51), is next door to the post office. Open Mon.-Fri. 8am-6pm, Sat. 9am-noon.

**Currency Exchange:** Banks line Obregón near the border. **Bánamex** has two central locations: one at Obregón and Ochoa (tel. 2-34-34; fax 2-34-88) resembles the control tower of the Starship *Enterprise* (open Mon.-Fri. 9am-5pm); another at Obregón and Uchón (tel. 2-34-81; fax 2-38-20) could pass for the *Enterprise's* docking station (open Mon.-Fri. 9am-3pm). Both exchange dollars, traveler's checks, and feature two 24-hr. **ATM** machines near their entrances.

**Train Station:** Two trains depart daily for Mazatlán (126 pesos *estrella,* 53 pesos *burro),* Guadalajara (206 pesos *estrella),* and about a zillion other southern destinations; the *burro* (slow) leaves at 7am and the *estrella* (fast) leaves at 3:30pm, though times are subject to change. Tickets go on sale from 6-7am and from 8am-3:30pm. Reservations for the *estrella* can be made from 8am on (tel. 3-10-91).

**Bus Station: Tres Estrellas de Oro** (tel. 3-16-03) sends its crew to Chihuahua (12hrs.), Mexicali (10hrs.), Tecate (11hrs.), and Tijuana (12hrs.). **Autotransportes Caballero Azteca** (tel. 3-02-33) goes to Ciudad Juárez (9:30pm, 10hrs., 95 pesos). **Transportes Norte de Sonora** runs to Hermosillo (3½hrs., about 50 pesos), Los Mochis (11hrs., about 100 pesos), Mazatlán (16hrs., 150 pesos), Guadalajara (26hrs., 200 pesos), and Mexico City (32hrs., 270 pesos). **Transportes del Pacífico** (tel. 3-16-06) sends buses to Guaymas (6hrs., 50 pesos), and Tepic (22hrs., 173 pesos). Buses also leave for Querétaro (32hrs., 265 pesos), Puerto Vallarta (26hrs., 200 pesos), and Magdalena (1hr., 15 pesos). **Pitíc** (tel. 4-59-99) runs to Guadalajara, Hermosillo, Los Mochis, Mexico City, and Monterrey. **Greyhound** buses (tel. in Tuscon: 602-287-5628) leave for Tucson (every hr., 7am-7pm and 9pm, US$6.50) from their station ½ block from the U.S. side of the border.

**Luggage Storage:** Available 6am-10pm at the bus terminal, one peso per hr.

**Market: VH Supermarket,** Obregón 375 (tel. 2-41-24), between Ramos and Rodriguez. Open Mon.-Sat. 8am-8pm, Sun. 8am-10pm.

**Laundromat: Nuevas Lavanderas de Nogales,** Ingenieros 332, between Gonzáles and Díaz, partially obscured by a large white awning. Wash 4 pesos; dry 30¢ per min. Drying time 30min. Open Mon.-Sat. 7am-7pm, Sun. 7am-2pm.

**Red Cross:** (tel. 3-58-00), on F. Elías. Open 24 hrs.

**Pharmacy: Farmacia San Xavier,** Campillo 73 (tel. 2-55-03), between Juárez and Morelos. English-speaking staffers (open 24hrs.), as does **Farmacia San Andrés** (tel. 2-02-36), behind the tourist office. Open Mon.-Sat. 8am-8pm, Sun. 8am-6pm.

**Medical Assistance: Seguro Social,** Escobedo 756 (tel. 3-59-85), at Obregón and Roccoedo (take the "Parque Industrial" bus). English spoken. Open 24 hrs. Some English is spoken at the **Hospital Básico,** Dr. Francisco Arriola 1277 (tel. 3-07-94 or 3-08-59). Open 24 hrs.

## ACCOMMODATIONS AND FOOD

A string of budget hotels is situated one block behind the tourist office on Av. Juárez and Obregón. As in most of northern Mexico, rates are steep. The **Hotel San Carlos,** Juárez 22 (tel. 2-06-27, 2-13-46, or 2-14-09), features a beautiful oasis in the lobby: an ever-plenished, ice-cold purified spring water dispenser. Large, clean rooms have A/C, color TVs with U.S. cable, massage-showers, and phones. Ask for a renovated room. Check-out 1pm (singles 94.50 pesos; doubles 111 pesos, 121 pesos for two beds; Visa, MC accepted). **Hotel Olga,** Juárez 17 (tel. 2-35-60), across from the San Carlos, offers basic, fairly clean rooms. Outdoor bathrooms are bearable (singles 70 pesos, 80 with bath; doubles 80 pesos, 100 with bath).

There are a fair number of overpriced restaurants packed in the center of Nogales. **La Posada Restaurant,** Pierson 116 (tel. 2-04-39), off Obregón, jazzes up with painted tiles and curious objects. The town's petit-bourgeoisie enjoy fresh foods here. *Burritos de machaca* (dried beef) 5 pesos, steak *milanesa* 24 pesos, *chimichanga* 7.50 pesos. Open daily 7:45am-10pm.

### SIGHTS AND ENTERTAINMENT

Most of the curio and craft shops line Obregón. You *may* get good deals if you bargain and know something about quality. In fact, vendors *expect* shoppers to bargain prices down. Often, low prices can be had by pretending to walk away uninterested, but keep in mind that these salesmen barely make enough to feed their children. Before buying, ask turquoise vendors to put the rocks to "the lighter test." Plastic or synthetic material will quickly melt under a flame. Likewise, when buying silver look for a ".925" stamp on the piece; if it's not there, the goods are bad.

At night, little transpires in Nogales. The usual bands of *gringos* patronize the bars on Obregón on weekends. During the week, the only source of evening entertainment may be the Nogales **movie theater** (tel. 2-50-02), on Obregón between F. Guerra and Torres, which shows first- and second-run films daily, 3:30-9:30pm.

## ■■■ PUERTO PEÑASCO

The town with the English sobriquet—Rocky Point—is catering more to American resort-mongers and less to budget travelers with each passing day. However, the dusty port is still worth a trip; its beaches are somewhat tranquil, and its streets are clean and (for the most part) inviting. Once a launching pad for shrimp boats, Puerto Peñasco dried up when overfishing decimated the shrimp population of the Sea of Cortés. Economically widowed, the town now courts investors with a dowry of tax breaks and other incentives. Just 65 miles off the border and about three hours from Tucson, Puerto Peñasco, like northern Baja, attracts a fair share of weekenders. Thirty miles north on the road to Sonoita is the **El Pinacate** volcanic area.

**Orientation** Puerto Peñasco's main road, **Blvd. Juárez,** runs parallel to the train tracks. From the bus station, take a left past PEMEX and follow Juárez for about 2km. An orange walking bridge, **Calle Armada Nacional,** crosses Juárez where Calle 13 intersects it and heads right, to Playa Hermosa. A few blocks farther down Juárez, at the **Plaza del Camaronero, Calle Fremont** heads left. Juárez continues through the *centro* to a rocky outcrop. **Constitución** forks to the left off Juárez about 10 blocks past Fremont and runs parallel to the tracks. Continuing south on Juárez will lead past the **Dársena**—the port area—and eventually to **Malecón,** Peñasco's old section, on the western edge of town. Playa Hermosa lies to the northwest; Playa Miramar lies to the south. Town activity centers around two intersections: Fremont & Juárez and Constitución & Juárez. Numbered *calles* run east-west and start with 1 at the southernmost at Playa Miramar; boulevards run north-south.

**Practical Information** Puerto Peñasco's **tourist office** (tel. 3-41-29) is in the Jim Bur shopping center on Juárez, next to Bancomer (office open Mon.-Sat. 9am-mid-afternoon). **Police** wait at Fremont and Juárez (tel. 3-26-26) but speak little English (open 24 hrs.). The **post office** (tel. 3-24-50 or 3-24-30) is at Chiapas, two blocks east of Juárez on Fremont. *Lista de Correos* (open Mon.-Fri. 8am-7pm). **Postal Code:** 83550. The **telegram office** (tel. 3-27-82) is in the same building. **Fax** service (open Mon.-Fri. 8am-7pm, Sat. 9am-1pm). **LADATELs** are not easy to find; one is at Juárez and Fremont. Casetas are located at the Jim Bur Plaza, in Cheiky's Pizza Restaurant (tel. 3-36-27; local calls 2 pesos for 3min., calls to U.S. 7.50 pesos per min; open daily 8am-11pm) and next to Tortilandia, on Juárez between Cuauhtémoc and Morúa (tel. 3-57-74 or 3-57-75; local calls 1 peso, calls to U.S. 9 pesos per min; open Mon.-Sat. 8am-11pm, Sun. 9am-10pm). **Telephone Code:** 638. **Ban-**

**comer** (tel. 3-24-30), on Juárez and Estrella, next to the plaza, exchanges currency and traveler's checks (open Mon.-Fri. 8:30am-2pm).

The **train station** (tel. 3-26-10) is off Constitución, two blocks north of the intersection with Juárez, right behind the Hotel Paraíso del Desierto. *Estrella* trains leave at 1:40pm for Mexicali (3hrs., 27 pesos), Hermosillo (6hrs., 45 pesos), Guaymas (8hrs., 60 pesos), Los Mochis (11hrs., 95 pesos), and Mazatlán (18hrs., 141 pesos). *Burro* trains leave at 3am for Mexicali (4hrs., 15 pesos), Hermosillo (10hrs., 25 pesos), Guaymas (12hrs., 33 pesos), Los Mochis (15hrs., 53 pesos), and Mazatlán (21 hrs., 79 pesos). **Buses** depart from Juárez and Calle 24 (tel. 3-20-19). **Transportes Norte de Sonora** and **Autotransportes de Baja California** collectively go to Guaymas (9:30am, noon, and midnight, 9hrs., 93 pesos), Hermosillo (9:30am, noon, and midnight, 7hrs., 74 pesos), Mexicali (8:30am, 5pm, and 1am, 4½hrs., 48 pesos), and Tijuana (8:30am and 1am, 8hrs., 76 pesos).

**Supermercado del Pueblo** (tel. 3-23-48) is on Constitución and Juárez (open daily 8am-10pm). Also try **Supermarket Jim Bur** (tel. 3-25-61), at the Jim Bur Plaza on Juárez (open Mon.-Sat. 8am-9pm, Sun. 8am-4pm). At **Lavamática Peñasco** (tel. 3-22-63), on Constitución at Morúa across from Hotel Paraíso del Desierto, a wash or dry costs five pesos (open Mon.-Sat. 8am-7pm). The **Red Cross,** on Fremont at Chiapas (tel. 3-22-66), is open 24 hrs., but little English is spoken. **Farmacia Don Antonio,** Juárez 89 (tel. 3-50-18), will meet your need for drugs (open Mon.-Sat. 9am-9:30pm, Sun. 9am-3:30pm). **Hospital Municipal,** Morúa and Barrera (tel. 3-21-10), is one block east of Juárez; little English is spoken (open 24 hrs.).

**Accommodations and Food** As a rule of thumb, always ask for prices in pesos instead of in dollars, even if the seller is reluctant. They are significantly lower. Budget rooms in Puerto Peñasco are a rare commodity. Cheap accommodations are being torn down left and right to clear space for expensive resort hotels, condominiums, and time-shares. One of the last remaining quasi-budget hotels is the **Motel Playa Azul,** Calle 13 and Pino Suárez (tel. 3-39-51). It offers well-outfitted, clean rooms at negotiable prices. You'll be lavished with an ancient TV that receives only one channel, generous A/C, and yes, a private bathroom with hot water. Bargain with the manager (singles 100-150 pesos; doubles 120-200 pesos). Otherwise, **Playa Miramar RV Park** (tel. and fax 3-25-87; in the U.S. call 602-994-4475 for reservations), on (go figure) Playa Miramar, rents scenic spots year-round with cable TV, full hookup, and hot water. Washers, dryers, and showers are also available. (Check-out noon. Key deposit 30 pesos, 72 pesos per day for 1 or 2 people, 12 pesos per day each additional person, 432 pesos per week. Beachfront spaces slightly higher.)

As always, *taquerías* are the spot for budget grub; try Juárez between Constitución and Calle 24, near the bus station. Most beachside restaurants cater to *gringos,* with their (high) prices quoted in U.S. dollars; insist on pesos. For just 17 pesos, **Asadero Sinaloa,** Juárez and Calle 24 across from the bus station, rewards customers with five pieces of chicken. Chicken tacos (3.50 pesos) make for more dainty eating. Nice insect-free, indoor seating (open daily 10am-10pm). Set apart by its toothsome handmade tortillas, **Asadero Sonora,** on Constitución in front of the train station, serves up grilled steak tacos (2.75 pesos; open daily 9am-4am).

**Sights and Entertainment** Puerto Peñasco's clean beaches are blessed with shallow, clear, and warm waters, and are rarely crowded. Shallow tide pools cradle clams, small fish, and colorful shells. **Sandy Beach** and **Playa Hermosa** are the best choices for swimming; both have curio shops, restaurants, and hotels galore. The beaches around **Rocky Point** and **Playa Miramar,** at the southern end of town, are less crowded, rockier, and rougher. Playa Miramar also brims with RV parks and condominiums. For the intellectual beach bum, the **Intercultural Center for the Study of Deserts and Oceans** at the **Playa Las Conchas** offers tours of its wet lab and museum Tues. at 2pm and Sat. at 4pm (open Mon.-Sat. 10am-5pm).

To get to Playa Hermosa, turn left on Calle 13 when heading south on Juárez; the beach is straight ahead five or six blocks down. To reach Playa Miramar, head south on Juárez and turn left onto Campeche near the Benito Juárez monument. Continue uphill on the unpaved road for three blocks; Playa Miramar will be on your left. To reach Playa Las Conchas, head south on Juárez, turn left on Fremont near the Plaza del Camaronero, take a right onto Camino a las Conchas, and follow the rock-slab road for three or four kilometers. To reach Sandy Beach, head north on Encinas or Juárez until the intersection with Camino a Bahía Choya. Take a left and follow that until taking another left on the road labeled "To Sandy Beach."

## ■ NEAR PUERTO PEÑASCO: EL PINACATE

Forty-eight kilometers north of Puerto Peñasco on Rte. 8 to Sonora is the **El Pinacate** volcanic preserve, the largest biosphere in the world. Encompassing over four million acres, and including the upper reaches of the Sea of Cortés, the biosphere was created in June 1993 to limit volcanic rock excavation and protect endangered species. The area constitutes a unique natural environment: the Pinacate lava fields, pockmarked by over 600 craters, form 30,000-year-old islands in a vast sea of sand thought to be one of the earth's biologically richest warm deserts. From inside the park, the only thing visible for miles around are fields of igneous rock and the monochromatic moonscape punctuated by purple, white, and red wildflowers. The people of the Tohono O'odham nation have lived in this region for tens of thousands of years, crossing the desert on foot from Arizona to bathe in the waters they consider to be sacred and healing, and extracting fresh water from *saguaro* cacti.

**Pinacate Tours** and **Ajo Stage Lines** lead tours into the area; ask at the tourist office for details. A guide is recommended, as the region is vast, isolated, and climatically harsh. Four-wheel-drive, high-clearance vehicles with partially deflated tires are necessary if you're going to tough it out alone. Bring tons of water, a shovel, a spare tire, and firewood. Camping is permitted, but don't leave anything behind and don't remove any souvenirs. The best time to visit is between October and April.

## ■■■ HERMOSILLO

The capital of Sonora, Hermosillo (pop. 700,000) is an expansive metropolis and a center for commerce and education. Beautiful cathedrals, government palaces, modern restaurants, and stylish open-air malls stand side-by-side with garbage-ridden, insect-infested sidewalks and marketplaces, and a prominent red-light district. Looming large above all are Hermosillo's radio-tower-covered mountains.

If you get an early start and the buses run on time, you can breeze from Tucson to the beaches of Guaymas or Mazatlán in a single day, skipping the lonelier parts of Sonora entirely. But if you get stuck, Hermosillo isn't a bad place to pass the night.

### ORIENTATION

Hermosillo lies on Rte. 15, the main north-south highway connecting the western U.S. and central Mexico, 271km south of the border. **Buses** depart from the main terminal on Blvd. Encinas, 2km east of the city center. To get from the bus station to the center of town, cross the street and catch the bus (1.50 pesos) marked "Circuito Norte-Mendoza" or "Centro," which run every 10 minutes from 5am-10:30pm. Taxis will ask 20 pesos for a trip to *el centro;* pay no more than half this and don't jump in until you agree on a price. To get back to the bus station from town, wait for a bus at Elías Calles and Matamoros, across from Optica Morfin.

At the junction of **Blvds. Luis Encinas** (also known as Transversal) and **Rosales,** the Hermosillo Flash helps the mapless (and those planning to hitch out of town) to orient themselves. After crossing the canal, Rosales passes the Centro Ecológico and rolls on down to Guaymas. Most of the activity lies inside the square area bordered by Rosales on the west, **Juárez** on the east, **Serdán** on the south, and **Encinas** on the north. The *zócalo* is bounded by **Colosio, Sonora, Guerrero,** and **Garmendia.** From west to east, the principal north-south streets are Rosales, Pino Suárez, Yañez, García Morales, Garmendia, Guerrero, Matamoros, Juárez, and González. From north to south, the east-west streets are Encinas, Niños Héroes, Oaxaca, Sonora, Colosio, Dr. Noriega, Morelia, Monterrey, P. Elías Calles, and Serdán. Maps can be bought at one of the many local *papelerías* (14 pesos). If you get lost, remember that the antenna-capped mountain is always to the south.

## PRACTICAL INFORMATION

**Tourist Office: Centro de Gobierno de Sonora,** Blvd. Paseo Canal and Comonfort (tel. 17-29-64; fax 17-00-60), on the 3rd floor. Walk south on Rosales over the canal, turn right, then walk one block west. More of an administrative office. Little English spoken. Poor maps and little information. Open Mon.-Fri. 9am-3pm.

**Police:** Periférico Nte. and Noreste (tel. 18-55-64). Little English spoken. Open 24 hrs. **Transit Police:** 16-08-77.

**Post Office:** Serdán and Rosales (tel. 12-00-11). *Lista de Correos.* Open Mon.-Fri. 8am-7pm, Sat.-Sun. 8am-noon. **Postal Code:** 83000.

**Telegrams:** (tel. 12-03-56; fax 13-19-24), in the same building as the post office. Also offers telex and fax service. Open Mon.-Fri. 8am-7pm, Sat. 8am-12:30pm.

**Telephones:** Farmacia Margarita (tel. 13-17-73), Morelia and Guerrero, has *casetas* upstairs in the back for long distance calls. Open daily 8am-midnight. **LADA-TELs** in the *zócalo,* but lines are long. Others on Serdán and Guerrero, at Morelia 90 between Guerrero and Garmendia, and in front of the post office. *Casetas de larga distancia* can be found at nearly every pharmacy and (oddly) hair salon. Just look for the blue *"teléfono público"* signs along the sidewalk. **Telephone Code:** 62. **Directory Information:** 04.

**Currency Exchange:** Banks line Encinas and Serdán. **Bancomer,** Serdán and Yañez (tel. 17-36-81), accepts traveler's checks. Open 8am-2pm. **Bánamex,** Serdán and Matamoros, is closer to the center. Open Mon.-Fri. 8:30am-4:30pm. You'll see 24-hr. **ATMs** at these two banks and elsewhere.

**American Express: Hermex Travel,** Rosales at Monterrey (tel. 17-17-18). Open Mon.-Fri. 8:30am-1pm and 3-6:30pm, Sat. 9am-1pm.

**Airport:** 10km west of town on Transversal toward Bahía Kino (tel. 61-23-51). **Aeroméxico** (tel. 16-82-06 or 16-84-67) to Guadalajara (5am and 3:30pm, 2hrs., 1258 pesos), Mexico City (7:55am, 9am, and 3pm, 2½hrs., 809 pesos), Tijuana (11:30am and 12:15pm, 1hr., 715 pesos), and other destinations. **Mexicana** (tel. 61-03-99 or 61-04-08) to Mexicali (4:15pm, 1hr., 485 pesos), Mexico City (9am, 3:30pm, and 8:10pm, 2½-4hrs., 809 pesos), and more.

**Trains: Estación Pitíc** (tel. 15-35-77), north of the city on Rte. 15. Take the bus marked "Anapolas" to get to the train station. Northbound *estrella* (fast) to Nogales and Mexicali leaves at 7am, and the *burro* (slow) at 11am. Southbound *estrella* to Los Mochis and Guadalajara leaves at 9pm, and the *burro* at noon. Travelers should make reservations for the *estrella* in advance; otherwise, tickets go on sale one hr. before departure at the station. *Estrella* trains are generally a bit more expensive than buses and a little slower. *Burro* trains are half as expensive as *estrella* trains and twice as slow (about 24hrs. from Hermosillo to Mazatlán).

**Buses:** All service out of Hermosillo is *de paso;* during holidays and weekends you'll need to lace up your boxing gloves in order to win a seat. Buses to Tijuana and Mexico City fill up early, so buy tickets at least a day in advance. The cheapest carrier is **Transportes del Pacífico** (tel. 17-05-80). First- and second-class buses. Second-class is only slightly slower, equally comfortable, and about 12% cheaper. To Guadalajara (every hr., 22hrs., 269 pesos; second-class 24hrs., 232 pesos), Los Mochis (every hr., 7hrs., 87 pesos; second-class 7hrs., 75 pesos), Mazatlán (every hr., 13hrs., 175 pesos; second-class 14hrs., 151 pesos), Mexicali (every hr., 9hrs., 112 pesos; second-class 9hrs., 97 pesos), Mexico City (every hr., 30hrs., 385 pesos; second-class 32hrs., 332 pesos) Nogales (3 per day, 4hrs., 49 pesos; second-class 4hrs., 42 pesos), Tijuana (every hr., 12hrs., 151 pesos; second-class 12hrs., 130 pesos), Guaymas (every hr., 1½hrs.), and Tepic (every hr., 17hrs.). **Transportes Norte de Sonora** (tel. 13-40-50) to most of the above, plus Acapulco (10 per day, 35hrs., 419 pesos).

**Luggage Storage:** At the bus station. 1-2.50 pesos per hr. Open Mon.-Fri. 7am-7pm, Sat.-Sun. 8am-6pm.

**Supermarket: Ley Centro,** Juárez at Morelia (tel. 17-17-76). The size of two U.S. football fields, with public toilets and hundreds of young clerks decked out in blue hats. Takes U.S. dollars at a good exchange rate. Open daily 6:30am-10pm.

**Red Cross:** Tel. 14-07-69, at Encina and 14 de Abril. Open 24 hrs. (Barely) English-speaking staff on hand daily 9am-5pm.

**Pharmacy: Farmacia Margarita** Morelia at Guerrero (tel. 13-15-90). No English spoken. Open 24 hrs. Also try **Benavides,** Serdán 81 (tel. 17-26-47) at Guerrero and Abasolo. Film developing available. Open daily 8am-9pm.

**Hospital:** Transversal at Reyes (tel. 13-25-56). Open 24 hrs. English spoken.

**Emergency: 06. Ambulance:** SON-527.

## ACCOMMODATIONS

Hermosillo offers many budget hotels, but few establishments fall into that accommodating middle bracket. Air-conditioning is costly but indispensable, especially in the blistering summer heat. For those scraping the very bottom of the barrel, five *casas de huéspedes* line Sonora, two blocks west of the park; two more are on Guerrero near Sonora. Prices here are very inexpensive, but the area, which also includes nicer hotels like the Montecarlo, is the city's red light district. Lone female travelers should be especially careful and might consider avoiding the area entirely.

**Casa de Huéspedes del Viajero,** Sufragio Efectivo 90, between Pino Suárez and Yañez. Walk south on Rosales until you begin to pass the tall hill (Cerro de la Campana) to your left. Turn left onto Efectivo before reaching the canal. Unbelievably large rooms in an 84-year-old building. Adobe construction and fans keep the rooms cool. Aging outdoor bathroom. Lock your bags, as there's not always someone at the entrance. Check-out noon. All rooms 30 pesos.

**Hotel Washington, D.C.,** Dr. Noriega 68 Pte. (tel. 13-11-83), between Matamoros and Guerrero. Friendly management. Good-sized rooms with erratic hot water, A/C, and clean bathrooms. You're set for a good night's sleep with the solid security and comfortable beds, but you might be serenaded by street music. LADATEL in the lobby. Check-out 1pm. Singles 60 pesos. Doubles 75 pesos. Each additional person 5 pesos.

**Hotel Niza,** Elías Calles 66 (tel. 17-20-28), between Guerrero and Garmendia. A grandiose Art Deco hotel of the bloated past. The pink atrium is graced with murals and a gigantic globe. Rooms branching off this centerpiece have A/C, color TV, and comfy beds. Check-out 1pm. Singles 95 pesos. Doubles 135 pesos. Visa, MC accepted.

## FOOD

For a cheap and quick refuel, head for the counters that line the entrances to the public market at Matamoros, Guerrero, and Monterrey. Although busy and smelly, some small counter-cafés are sufficiently sanitary. Choose wisely: look out for flies and dirty pans and tabletops. Most offer tacos for a paltry sum, but *Let's Go* does not recommend eating any potentially contaminated vegetables—especially here! Stick with *enchiladas, burritos,* and the like, also wonderfully cheap at about 3 pesos. Alternatively, taco and *torta* places cluster around Serdán and Guerrero, serving *taquitos* and *quesadillas* for 4-5 pesos and *comida corrida* for around 12 pesos.

**Restaurant Jung,** Niños Héroes 75 (tel. 13-28-81), at Encinas. A new age, vegetarian restaurant in an industrial-wasteland section of town. The *comida corrida* comes with wheat rolls, soup, fruit juice, an entree, plus *frijoles con queso,* whole-grain rice, and dessert (25 pesos). The adjoining herbal medicine, Eastern philosophy, and pseudo-psychology store is worth a peek, if only for the *agua purificada* it sells. Open Mon.-Sat. 8am-8pm. Visa, MC accepted.

**Jugos Serdán,** Serdán 165 (tel. 13-21-90), between Pino Suárez and Yañez. *Tortas* with beef, avocado, lettuce, and tomato (8 pesos) and a variety of fresh fruit drinks: *aguas frescas* (fruit juices) and *licuados* (fruit with milk) with flavors such as mango and coconut (6 pesos). Open Mon.-Sat. 7am-8pm, Sun. 9am-2pm.

**Restaurant Chapala,** Guerrero between Sonora and Oaxaca. Mexican golden oldies blare from the juke box while the crowd of mostly middle-aged single Mexican men drowns their collective sorrow in a couple of 40s of Tecate. Open-air kitchen. Choose chicken, fish, or meat, and you'll be given a fried serving with french fries, *frijoles, tortillas,* and salsa (15 pesos). Aside from the tipsy men, you might as well be in your Mexican aunt's house—if you're Mexican and you have an aunt, that is. Open daily 7am-10pm.

## SIGHTS

**Cuartel Catorce** (tel. 13-13-79 for Sec. de Educación, ext. 23), on Guerrero and Colosio, is a rough structure with formidable walls of brown brick. Built in 1908, the structure was used for 80 years as a military installation; now it is home to the Secretary of Culture and Education of Hermosillo. The colonnaded inner courtyard is an oasis; the room in the back of the courtyard, now an office, was once home to the army's cavalry (open Mon.-Fri. 8am-3pm). The nearby **Museo Regional de Historia,** on Encinas and Rosales at the University of Sonora, contains artifacts and exhibits on pre-Hispanic and colonial history (open Mon.-Fri. 8am-8pm, Sat. 9am-1pm).

On the other side of Rosales rise the tall steeples of **La Catedral de la Asunción,** on Tehuantepec and Comonfort. The architecturally eclectic cathedral was built in the late 19th century to replace Hermosillo's colonial town chapel (tel. 12-05-01; office and gift shop open Mon.-Sat. 9am-1pm and 4-7pm). Fugitives from the blistering sun can find refuge near the cathedral in the refreshingly shady **Plaza Zaragoza,** where looming trees surround an open-air bandstand. Other shady parks dot the streets near the plaza, collectively making for one of the more peaceful areas of Hermosillo, and a welcome change from the dusty, filth-ridden streets of the *centro.* For the kids, a **playground,** complete with basketball courts, dwells on the corner of Pino Suárez and P. Elías Calles.

Across the street from the Plaza Zaragoza is the majestic, grey-and-white **Palacio del Gobierno.** The Palacio, from where the state of Sonora is governed, should not be confused with the pink-brick **Palacio Municipal** nearby, where local government functions are carried out. Both are worth investigating for their architecture. The Palacio del Gobierno contains four murals surrounding its beautiful, tree-laden inner courtyard, where statues immortalize the Sonoran patriots and senators Jesús García Morales and Ignacio Pesquená. Two of the murals, the 1984 Azteche abstract work on the lower level and the 1982 Estrada above the stairs, depict *indígenas* battling Spaniards; the mural hidden behind the stairs depicts *indígena* slavery, and the main upstairs mural recounts the ancient *indígena* legend of the five suns and the evolution of humanity.

# ■ NEAR HERMOSILLO

## CENTRO ECOLÓGICO DE SONORA

Hermosillo's **Centro Ecológico de Sonora** (tel. 50-12-25), 3km south of downtown off Vildosola, is more than just your token neighborhood zoo: it boasts an impressive array of animal life, a mini-aquarium (complete with outdoor sea lions), and hundreds of species of plants from Sonora and elsewhere. Founded in 1985, the Centro is also home to groundbreaking biological research on its home state.

Among the animal exhibits, the Mexican grey wolf, bearded camels, and energetic monkeys are standouts. The most spectacular feature of the Centro Ecológico, however, is its incredible collection of cacti. In addition to adorning every animal exhibit, many of the Centro's over 340 species of cacti are labeled and displayed just outside the main pavilion. Watch especially for the rare and beautiful *cina* and *biznaga,* from which fruit and candy are made; the *pitahaya,* which features an unusual red fruit; and the *maguey bacanova,* the fanned-out, spiked cactus, which is the source of all those *tequilas* you've been downing. Note also the *seri,* from which exquisite (and tremendously expensive) baskets are crafted.

The Centro is an excellent place for children; they delight in the three Disney (or Disney-esque) flicks shown every Sat. and Sun. in the air-conditioned movie theater (noon-6pm; free). Clowns in residence on weekends and fun sprinklers to run under also elicit shrieks of happiness from the kiddies. The enthusiastic, knowledgeable, and under-utilized staff is happy to answer any questions about the Centro and its flora and fauna. Cafeterias and *agua purificada* can be found throughout the park (open Wed.-Sun. 8am-6pm; admission 4 pesos for adults, 2 pesos for children).

**Getting There:** To get to the Centro Ecológico, catch the orange-and-green striped bus marked "Luis Orci" from the corner of Guerrero and Dr. Noriega (20min., 1.50 pesos).

# ■■■ BAHÍA KINO

A pair of beach towns on the beautiful Sea of Cortés (or Golfo de California) together comprise Bahía Kino, a 13-mile stretch of sand, blue water, sun—and little else. **Kino Viejo,** a dusty, run-down fishing village, lies 4km down the road from **Kino Nuevo,** an Americanized strip of posh, secluded homes and condos. Kino (as the towns are collectively known by locals) is an ideal destination for a daytrip to the beach from Hermosillo. The soothing breezes and vast expanses of sand make the hot, rickety ride from the city worthwhile.

**Orientation** Bahía Kino is located 120km west of Hermosillo. **Buses** in Hermosillo leave from the old **Transportes Norte de Sonora** station on Sonora between Revolución and Gonzáles, near the *zócalo* (10 per day, 5:40am-5:30pm, 2hrs., 15 pesos each way). It's best to get an early start on a daytrip to Kino—try to catch an early-morning bus from Hermosillo and sleep (if you can) during the ride. Remember that missing the 5:30pm bus back to Hermosillo means spending the night in Kino.

To get from one Kino to the other, catch the bus (every hr., 1.50 pesos) on Nuevo's main (and only) road, **Av. Mar de Cortés,** or on **Blvd. Kino** in Kino Viejo. You must flag down the bus—be prepared to wait for it to finally rumble in. Another option is walking: those who make the 2.5 mile jaunt are refreshed along the way by vendors hawking Gatorade and other cold drinks. It is also quite possible to hitchhike between the two towns, though *Let's Go* does not recommend it.

**Practical Information** The **police** are available at Kino and Cruz (open 24 hrs.). Next to the police is the **post office** (open Mon.-Fri. 8am-3pm). **Long-distance phones** are available at the clothing shop at Kino and Tampico. (Local calls 1 peso per min.; long-distance calls in Mexico 3.50 pesos per min.; calls to the U.S. 7.50 pesos per min. Open daily 9am-7pm.) **Public bathrooms** are on the beach in Kino Nuevo; in Kino Viejo, some downright pleasant potties are available at the **Centro de Salud,** at Tampico and Kino. Bring your own toilet paper. Near both the post office and the police is the **Red Cross,** at Kino and Manzanillo, which has no phone but can be contacted via the Hermosillo **emergency** number (dial 06).

**Accommodations and Food** Lodging options for budget travelers in Kino are limited to rentable spots in Kino Viejo in which to pitch your tent or park your RV. It's easy for the more adventurous traveler to camp for free under one of the many *palapas* (thatched umbrella structures) on the Kino Nuevo beach. Locals claim the area is fairly safe. **Islandia Marina,** Guaymas and Puerto Peñasco (tel. 2-00-81), just off Blvd. Kino and right on the beach, charges 50 pesos per day for a spot. It is run by two Arizona women who own a purified water plant—you'll never be short on that precious commodity. If you *must* stay in conventional accommodations (and miss the 5:30pm bus back to Hermosillo and its inexpensive hotels) you can rent a **cabin** from Islandia Marina (134 pesos) or stay in one of Kino Nuevo's pricey hotels. **Hotel Saro,** 5735 Mar de Cortés (tel. 2-00-07), is the cheapest at 165 pesos for a single with A/C and private bath.

A decent budget meal can be found in Kino Viejo. Try **Dorita,** Av. Eusebio Kino and Sabina Cruz (tel. 2-03-49), for relatively inexpensive *platillos mexicanos* (13 pesos), *carne asada* (15 pesos), and breakfasts (12-14 pesos). Fill up on purified water there—it's free (open daily 7am-9pm). For a ritzier dining experience, try the

**Marlin Restaurant and Bar,** Puerto Peñasco and Guaymas (tel. 2-01-11). Fish dishes (25-30 pesos), slabs o' meat (18-40 pesos), and wine (35 pesos a bottle) are stand-outs (open Tues.-Sat. 1-10pm; Visa, MC accepted). For those prices, though, you might as well try Kino Nuevo's restaurant, **La Palapa,** Mar de Cortés and Wellington (tel. 2-02-10). It boasts a round, air-conditioned dining room and several outdoor decks overlooking the sea. Fish fillets 25-30 pesos, *ceviche* 20 pesos, chicken 18 pesos (open daily 8am-10pm).

**Sand and Sights** The beaches of Kino are peacefully deserted early in the week, but as the weekend approaches, so do the masses. Americans with homes in Kino tend to populate the beaches only during the winter, making for some long, lonely stretches of sand during the summer months. All beaches in Kino (as in all Mexico) are public by law, so you can plop down right in front of anyone's RV spot or faux-villa, and they can't do a damn thing about it. In general, the beaches are better in Kino Nuevo; swim the warm, calm waters of the Gulf there if you can.

In Kino Nuevo, aqua equipment can be rented from **Diversiones Marinas** (pedal boats 30 pesos per ½hr., rowboats and canoes 15-40 pesos per hr., volleyball court 15 pesos per hr.). Ask at **Hotel La Posada,** on Av. Mar de Cortés towards Kino Viejo, just before Kino Nuevo's main strip begins, about which local is currently renting out scuba/snorkeling gear.

# ■■■ GUAYMAS

Looking out over the Sea of Cortés, Guaymas is the principal port in Sonora and the proud home of an active shrimping fleet and busy seafood-processing plants. The area was originally inhabited by the Guaymas and Yaqui tribes, whose lives were turned upside down when the mission of San José was established in 1701 near the present-day city. A Spanish settlement followed in 1769, and the invasion continues to this day, as waves of suntanned *norteamericanos* drop by to take a break from the resort life of nearby San Carlos.

Guaymas proper, though a modern, well-established city, is no resort town. Although its port area offers a pleasant view of the sea and nearby mountains and its charming cathedral and companion park serve as a haven for weary travelers, Guaymas suffers from an acute lack of convenient beaches. Nevertheless, it's the nicest place to rest on the trip south to the more alluring resorts at Mazatlán, San Blas, and Puerto Vallarta: its cool ocean breezes, cleanliness, and civility give it a decided advantage over Hermosillo.

## ORIENTATION

Guaymas is 407km south of Nogales on Rte. 15. Municipal buses (1.50 pesos) run up and down Guaymas's main strip, **Av. Serdán.** Buses marked "Miramar" (1.50 pesos) and "San Carlos" (1.80 pesos) reach beaches north of the city from various points along Serdán; both buses run frequently from 6am-8pm. Some travelers at the junction of Serdán and the highway also try thumbing as they wait for the bus. The center of the city lies around the crossings of Calles in the low 20s and Serdán, and buses arrive right in the thick of things at Calle 14, right off (surprise) Serdán. Women should not walk alone more than two blocks south of Serdán after dark. The waterfront begins around Calle 23 and Serdán; coming up to the water, you'll immediately feel the cool ocean breeze begin to do battle with the blistering sun.

Northbound vehicles, including buses, are often stopped by narcotics police. Avoid spending the rest of your vacation in a prison cell by having your identification ready. Let them search whatever they want; it's better not to assert the right to privacy when dealing with humorless armed *federales* dressed in blue.

## PRACTICAL INFORMATION

**Tourist Office:** Carretera Internacional at Blvd. Luis Encinas (tel. 1-16-45), at the edge of town. Take one of the buses marked "Miramar" or "Lomalinda," which may be flagged down anywhere along Serdán (1 peso). The English-speaking staff provides directions to San Carlos, but has no maps of Guaymas. Open Mon.-Fri. 9am-2pm and 4:30-6:30pm.

**Police:** (tel. 4-01-04), stationed on Calle 11 at Av. 9, near the Villa School. Some English spoken. Open 24 hrs.

**Post Office:** (tel. 2-07-57), on Av. 10 between Calle 19 and 20. Open Mon.-Fri. 8am-7pm, Sat. 8am-noon. **Postal Code:** 85400.

**Telephones: LADATELs** are scattered all along Serdán. Two quieter locations are on Calle 19 Nte. at Av. 17 Pte. and in front of the Hotel Rubi. **Santa Martha Pañalera,** Serdán 80 (tel. 4-03-54; fax 4-05-40), at Calle 19, has booths for long-distance collect calls (7 pesos per min. to the U.S., 4 pesos per min. within Mexico; Sun. and after 8pm, 5.50 pesos to U.S., 2.50 pesos within Mexico). Open Mon.-Sat. 8am-9:30pm, Sun. 8:30am-noon. The long-distance **Computel** *caseta* at the Tres Estrellas de Oro station (tel. and fax 2-95-18) charges various rates to the U.S. **Faxes** 3 pesos. Open daily 6am-10pm. **Telephone Code:** 622.

**Telegrams:** (tel. 2-02-92), next to the post office. Open Mon.-Fri. 8am-7:30pm, Sat. 8-11am.

**Currency Exchange:** Banks are located along Serdán. **Bánamex,** Serdán at Calle 20 (tel. 2-00-71), exchanges traveler's checks and greenbacks, and has two 24-hr. **ATMs** that accept Visa, MC, Cirrus, and Plus. Open Mon.-Fri. 8:30am-2:30pm.

**Airport:** To reach the airport, catch a bus marked "San José" or "Itson" along Serdán (1.50 pesos). **Aeroméxico,** Serdán at Calle 15 (tel. 2-01-23), has daily flights to La Paz (3:55pm, 50min., 1525 pesos), Mexico City (3:55pm, 4½hrs., 890 pesos), Tucson (12:25pm, 55min., US$120) and Phoenix (12:25pm). Flights depart daily; on Wed. and Sat., add ½hr. to the departure time.

**Train Station:** The old train station and current office (tel. 2-00-70 or 2-49-80) are located on Serdán at Calle 30. Office open Mon.-Fri. 8am-noon and 2-5pm for information or reservations. Trains actually arrive and depart from **Empalme** (tel. 3-10-65 or 3-06-16), 10km south on the International Highway. Buy tickets at the Empalme station one hour before the train arrives. From anywhere along Serdán take the municipal bus marked "Empalme" to the end of the route, then transfer to the bus marked "Estación." The faster *estrella* train leaves at 9:40pm; the slow *burro* leaves at 2:30pm. They run to Obregón (*estrella* 1½hrs., 12.80 pesos; *burro* 2hrs., 7.15 pesos), Navojoa (*estrella* 2½hrs., 20 pesos; *burro* 3hrs., 11.15 pesos), Sufragio (*estrella* 5hrs., 34.50 pesos; *burro* 6½hrs., 19.25 pesos), Guamuchil (*estrella* 6½hrs., 45.80 pesos; *burro* 8½hrs., 25.50 pesos), Culiacán (*estrella* 7½hrs., 60.10 pesos; *burro* 10hrs., 32.30 pesos), Mazatlán (*estrella* 12hrs., 81.50 pesos; *burro* 17hrs., 45.40 pesos), Acaponeta (*estrella* 13hrs., 97.60 pesos; *burro* 18½hrs., 54.40 pesos), Tepic (*estrella* 15hrs., 115.45 pesos; *burro* 21¼hrs., 64.35 pesos), and Guadalajara (*estrella* 21hrs., 144.90 pesos; *burro* 28hrs., 80.75 pesos).

**Bus Stations:** The town's three bus terminals are on opposite sides of the street at Calle 14 and Rodríguez. **Transportes Norte de Sonora** (tel. 2-12-71) goes to Acapulco (3pm, 50hrs., 396 pesos), Ciudad Juárez (3:30am and 2:30pm, 13hrs., 156 pesos), Culiacán (every hr., 9hrs., 89 pesos), Guadalajara (every hr., 23hrs., 212 pesos), Hermosillo (every hr., 1¾hrs., 14 pesos), Los Mochis (every hr., 6hrs., 56 pesos), Mazatlán (every hr., 12hrs., 131 pesos), Mexicali (every hr., 12hrs., 116 pesos), Mexico City (11 per day, 31hrs., 312 pesos), Nogales (every hr., 10hrs., 106 pesos), Obregón (every hr., 1¾hrs., 14 pesos), Puerto Peñasco (11:30am, 9hrs., 93 pesos), San Luis (15 per day, 6hrs., 48 pesos), Tepic (every hr., 18hrs., 174 pesos), and Tijuana (every hr., 15hrs., 150 pesos). **Transportes del Pacífico** (tel. 4-05-76 or 2-30-19) offers fares to most of the above destinations for about 10% more, while their second-class service runs 3-5% less. **Transportes del Norte, Chihuahuenses,** and **Futura** operate out of the same station as TNS, offering similar prices and times. **Transportes Corral Baldomero,** across the street, offers service to Hermosillo (every hr., 7am-10pm, 1¾hrs., 16 pesos), Navojoa (every hr., 7:45am-10:45pm, 4hrs., 30 pesos), Nogales (4 per day, 5½hrs., 51 pesos), and Obregón (every hr., 7:45am-10:45pm, 1¾hrs., 16 pesos).

**Ferry Terminal:** (tel. 2-23-24), on Serdán about 1km past Electricidad. The boat steams to Santa Rosalía Tues. and Fri. at 8am (arriving at 3pm); tickets may be

GUAYMAS

bought on the day of departure from 6-8am or on Mon., Wed., or Thurs. from 8am-2pm (*salón* 43 pesos, *turista* 86 pesos, *cabina* 129 pesos). See "Getting Around" on page 116. To get to the terminal, hop on an bus heading away from the Carretera Internacional and get off at the "Transbordador" sign, on your right.

**Luggage Storage:** Lockers are available at the **Tres Estrellas de Oro** bus terminal. 10 pesos first 8hrs., 4 pesos every extra hr. Open 24 hrs.

**Market: VH Supermarket** (tel. 4-49-19), on Serdán between Calles 19 and 20. You can't miss it. Open Mon.-Sat. 7am-9pm, Sun. 7am-8pm.

**Red Cross:** (tel. 4-08-76), at the northern limit of Guaymas, at the 1980km mark on the Carretera Internacional. No English spoken. Open 24 hrs.

**Pharmacy: Farmacia Sonora,** Serdán at Calle 15 (tel. 4-24-00). Some English spoken. Open 24 hrs. **Farmacia Benavides** (tel. 2-03-90), on Serdán between Calles 18 and 19. Film developing available. Some English spoken. Accepts MC, Visa. Open daily 8am-9:30pm.

**Hospital: Hospital Municipal** (tel. 4-21-38), on Calle 12 between Avs. 6 and 7. Some English spoken. Open 24 hrs.

## ACCOMMODATIONS

**Casa de Huéspedes Lupita,** Calle 15 #125 (tel. 2-84-09), two blocks south of Serdán across from the jail (*cárcel*). A mammoth "house" with 30 rooms and 12 communal baths, every last corner glowingly clean. Iron gates on the doors and fans in every room allow for much needed ventilation. Although it's hot during the summer, an ice-cold *agua purificada* dispenser awaits downstairs at the office. Check-out noon. Towel deposit 10 pesos. Singles 30 pesos, with bath 40 pesos. Doubles 40 pesos, with bath 50 pesos.

**Hotel Rubi,** Serdán at Calle 29 (tel. 4-01-69). Look for the "HO EL" sign. Friendly management shows guests to large rooms equipped with black-and-white cable TV and A/C. Convenient location for those who want to work, *à la Gump*, on a shrimping boat. *Agua purificada.* Check-out 1pm. Singles (with 2 beds) 65 pesos. Doubles 80 pesos. Triples 100 pesos. Quads 120 pesos.

**Hotel Impala,** Calle 21 #40 (tel. 4-09-22; fax 2-65-00), one block south of Serdán. The hotel reveals its antiquity through the black-and-white photos of Guaymas's past gracing the walls. Rooms are renovated to modern glory with matching polyester bedspreads and curtains, A/C, and TV. Check-out 1pm. Key deposit 5 pesos. Parking available. Singles 80 pesos. Doubles 105 pesos. Triples 125 pesos. Quads 150 pesos. Visa, MC accepted.

## FOOD

Seafood is *the* Guaymas specialty. Local favorites include frog legs, turtle steaks, and oysters in a garlic/chile sauce. Unfortunately, if you want to sample these local delicacies, you're going to have to pay a fair sum for them. For a seafood meal that won't bust your budget, try **Los Barcos,** Malecón and Malpica. The **Mercado Municipal,** on Calle 20, one block from Serdán, sells fresh produce as well as clothes, flowers, toys, and carved goods. Hot dog and taco vendors line Serdán.

**S. E. Pizza Buffet,** Serdán at Calle 20 (tel. 2-24-46). Delight in an all-you-can-eat buffet of pizza, spaghetti, and salad (if you-can-eat-all that!). Buffet 14 pesos. Open daily 11am-11pm.

**Las 1000 Tortas,** Serdán 188, between Calles 17 and 18. The *torta* is king at this family-run joint (7-9 pesos each). Three types of delicious *comida corrida* (18 pesos) are prepared daily and served from noon-4pm. Energetic customers sit upright in orthopedic wooden chairs, while tired neighbors slouch in brown vinyl booths; everyone munches on *enchiladas* and *gorditas* (15 pesos). Tasty *burritos de machaca con frijoles* (15 pesos). Open daily 7am-8pm.

**Pan Rico** (tel. 4-11-24), Serdán between Calles 19 and 20, the bakery next door to the VH Supermarket. Probably the cheapest filler-upper in town. Pastries and mini-loaves of bread can be had for pocket change. Open Mon.-Sat. 8am-9pm, Sun. 8am-7pm.

## SIGHTS AND ENTERTAINMENT

Guaymas's **beaches** are to the north in **San Carlos** and **Miramar.** Yachts hover off the shore in San Carlos, and the beaches accessible to the budget crowd are dull and pebbly. In San Carlos, the beach gets better past the end of the bus route near Club Med and Howard Johnson's. The nicer (but smaller) beaches in Miramar are back along the bus route in front of the fancy villas. Camping is not advisable here, but if you must, opt for San Carlos over Miramar.

Take a stroll in the **Plaza de los Tres Presidentes,** on Calle 23 at Serdán, in front of the **Palacio Municipal,** a classic Colonial-style structure built in 1899; note the requisite flag flying atop. The blue bay waters, the towering (yet austere, by Catholic standards) green-and-white **Catedral de San Fernando,** and three bronze statues of (rather obscure) Mexican presidents complete the scene. The ideal place for a quiet walk, however, is the small park directly in front of the cathedral; benches and many a shade-providing tree make for a prime nap area. **Inmobilaria Cinematográfica** or **Cine de Guaymas,** Av. 11 at Calle 20 (tel. 2-14-00), two blocks off Serdán, shows mostly U.S. films with Spanish subtitles daily from 3:40-11pm (admission 12 pesos). For the best view in town—of Guaymas, the mountains, the port, and the bay—seek out the shady bench just off Serdán towards the water, between Calles 25 and 26. Feel the soothing sea breeze and smile. Sniffle. (Kleenex, please.)

# CHIHUAHUA

## ■■■ EL PASO, TEXAS

With its arid climate and disparate architectural landscape, modern El Paso (pop. 600,000) seems like a combination of an oversized strip mall and a Mexican mission town. At once a collegiate and military mecca, a symbol both of American westward expansion and its conversion to suburbia, and a city caught between two states, two countries, and two languages, El Paso suffers from a bona fide identity crisis.

The largest of the U.S. border towns, El Paso grew up in the 17th century, a stopover on an important east-west wagon route that trailed the Río Grande though "the pass" (*el paso*) between the Rockies and the Sierra Madres. As Spain extended its reach into the New World, El Paso became a center for missionary activity; some missions left over from the period of Spanish colonization can still be seen today. More recently, the city has been dominated by Fort Bliss, the largest air defense base in the West, and the Biggs Army Airfield.

The city's San Jacinto Square, buzzing with pedestrians, is a pleasant place to while away the time. After dark, El Paso is a lonely city: most activity leaves the relatively tame center of town and heads to the UTEP (University of Texas at El Paso) area or south of the border—to El Paso's raucous sister city, Juárez.

## ORIENTATION

Before leaving the airport, stop at the visitors center for maps and information, at the bottom of the escalators descending from arrival gates. To get to the city from the airport, take Sun Metro bus #33 (Mon.-Fri. every ½hr., 6:28am-9:28pm; Sat. every ½hr.-45min., 7:58am-9:28pm; Sun. every hr., 8:07am-7:07pm. 40min. to downtown. Adults 85¢, children 6-13 and students 40¢, seniors 20¢; exact change only). The stop is located on a traffic island outside the air terminal building, across from the Delta ticket window. Get off when the bus arrives at San Jacinto Plaza and you'll find yourself right in the thick of it, near most hotels and restaurants.

When the bus stops running late at night, budget travelers usually prefer the green, air-conditioned vans of the **K.C. Express Shuttle Service** to more expensive cabs. (Shuttle service US$6 and up. Open Sun.-Thurs. 4am-midnight, Fri. and Sat. 4am-3pm.) Alternative approaches to the city include I-10 (west/east) and U.S. 54

(north/south). El Paso is divided into east and west by **Santa Fe** and into north and south by **San Antonio.** Tourists should be wary of the streets between San Antonio and the border late at night.

## CROSSING THE BORDER

To reach the border from El Paso, take the north-south bus (every 10min., 30min., 25¢) to the **Santa Fe Bridge,** its last stop before turning around. Do not confuse the inexpensive bus with the costly trolley. Two pedestrian and motor roads cross the Río Grande: **El Paso,** an overcrowded one-way street, and **Santa Fe,** a parallel road lined with Western-wear stores, clothing shops, and decent restaurants. Entry to Mexico is 25¢ and the return trip costs 30¢.

If entering Mexico by foot, walk to the right side of the Santa Fe Bridge and pay the quarter to cross. Daytrippers, including foreign travelers with a multi-entry visa, should be prepared to flash their documents of citizenship in order to pass in and out of Mexico. You might even get your bag searched by a guard if you're one of those people who always breaks off the short end of the wishbone, but normally you won't even have to show ID. After stepping off the bridge, head left to the near back corner of the large grey building on your left—to the lonely, air-conditioned Juárez tourist office, where friendly, English-speaking employees will provide you with maps and information.

To enter the United States, cross over the Santa Fe Bridge by the large *"Feliz Viaje"* sign. Be ready to deal with U.S. border guards and show a valid visa or proof of citizenship. You may be searched or asked to answer a few questions proving that you are who you say you are. (See "Leaving Mexico" on page 9.) Once in El Paso, wait at the stop on the right-hand sidewalk just across from the bridge for the north-south bus, which runs until 9pm to San Jacinto Plaza.

## PRACTICAL INFORMATION

**Tourist Office:** 1 Civic Center Plaza (tel. 544-0062), a small round building next to the Chamber of Commerce at the intersection of Santa Fe St. and San Francisco St. Easily identifiable by the thin, water-filled moat that surrounds it. Well-stocked with brochures; sells **El Paso-Juárez Trolley Co.** tickets for day-long tours across the border leaving on the hour from the Convention Center. (Tickets US$10 adults, US$8 children 6-13, free for those 5 and under. Trolleys run 10am-5pm, April-Oct.; 9am-4pm, Nov.-March. Call 544-0062 for reservations, 544-0061 for recorded information.) Talk to Scott Rackley for everything you ever wanted to know about El Paso but were afraid to ask.

**Post Office:** 219 E. Mills (tel. 775-7563). Open Mon.-Fri. 9am-5pm, Sat. 8am-noon. **ZIP code:** 79910.

**Area Codes:** El Paso: 915. To direct dial Ciudad Juárez, dial 011-52-16, followed by the local number.

**Mexican Consulate:** 910 E. San Antonio St. (tel. 533-4082), on the corner of San Antonio St. and Virginia St. Dispenses **tourist cards.** Open Mon.-Fri. 9am-4:30pm.

**Currency Exchange: Valuta,** 307 E. Paisano (tel. 544-1152). Conveniently near the border. Open 24 hrs. **Traveler's Checks: Bank of the West,** 500 N. Mesa St. (tel. 532-1000), on the corner of Main St. and Mesa St. Open Mon.-Thurs. 9am-4pm, Fri. 9am-5pm.

**AmEx Office:** 3100 N. Mesa St. (tel. 532-8900). Open Mon.-Fri. 8am-5pm.

**Airport: El Paso International Airport,** northeast of the city center. Take a #33 bus from San Jacinto Square or any other central location. Daily departures to locations in Mexico, the U.S., and other countries on a host of carriers, most with connections at Dallas/Ft. Worth.

**Train Station: Amtrak,** 700 San Francisco St. (tel. 545-2247). Open Mon., Wed., and Sat. 11am-6:30pm, Tues., Thurs., and Sun. 9am-5pm.

**Bus Station: Greyhound,** 201 San Antonio (tel. 532-2365 or 1-800-231-2222), across from the Civic Center between Santa Fe St. and Chihuahua St. Daily service to and from New York (US$99), Los Angeles (US$35), Dallas, Phoenix, and other U.S. cities. **Storage lockers** US$2 for up to 6 hrs., US$4 for 6-24 hrs. Open 24 hrs.

**Public Transportation: Sun Metro** (tel. 533-3333) departs from San Jacinto Plaza, located at the corner of Main St. and Oregon St. Adults 85¢ per trip, students and children 40¢, seniors 20¢.

**Car Rental: Hertz** (772-4255), **Budget** (778-5287), **Dollar** (778-5445), **Thrifty** (778-9236), **Avis** (779-2700), **Alamo** (774-9855), and more, all at the airport.

**Hospital: Providence Memorial Hospital** (tel. 577-6011). Open 24 hrs. For immunizations, visit **El Paso City County Health District**, 222 S. Campbell St. (tel. 543-3560). When approaching the Mexican border, turn left on Paisano St. and walk three blocks. Immunizations (by appointment and on Wed. only) are not required to enter Mexico, but are recommended. Open Mon.-Fri. 8am-5pm.

## ACCOMMODATIONS

If you have a choice, stay in El Paso rather than Juárez, where there are fewer appealing accommodations. El Paso's budget hotels all cluster around the center of town, near Main St. Its posh hotel district is near the corner of San Francisco and El Paso, though you'd be better off choosing budget lodging near San Jacinto Square.

**Gateway Hotel,** 104 S. Stanton St. (tel. 532-2611; fax 533-8100), at the corner of S. Stanton and San Antonio. An excellent choice in El Paso—a stone's throw from San Jacinto Square and a favorite stop for middle-class Mexicans; speak Spanish to get respect and a room. Extremely clean and spacious rooms, amply furnished with large beds and closets. Strong running water. Thoroughly cleaned bathrooms, some with bathtubs. A/C upstairs. A diner downstairs will take the edge off your budget-travel-induced hunger. Reservations accepted up to five days in advance, except during festivals and holidays. Check-out 4pm. Parking US$1.50 for 24 hrs. Singles US$21, with TV US$28. Doubles US$27, with TV US$31. Double with king-size bed US$32, with TV US$33.

**Gardner Hotel/Hostel (HI-AYH),** 311 E. Franklin (tel. 532-3661). From the airport, take bus #33 to San Jacinto Park, walk one block north to Franklin, turn right, and head east 1½ blocks. The Gardner is two blocks up Mesa St. from San Jacinto Park. This 75-year-old establishment features clean rooms in the heart of downtown. Inexpensive singles and dorm rooms are rather small. Reception open 24 hrs. Locker rental 75¢, 50¢ for 4 or more days. Management is extremely vigilant of security concerns. **Hotel:** All hotel rooms include a color TV with cable (including HBO) and a phone. Check-out 1pm. Singles with a small bed and no bath, US$22.50. Larger singles with better furnishings, US$27.50, with bath US$35. Top doubles US$40. **Hostel:** Small, 4-person dorm rooms and shared bathrooms. Beautiful, spacious kitchen, common room, and an array of couches for lounging and socializing in the basement. Check-out 10am. Bed in 4-person dorm room US$12.50, non-members pay US$3 more. Linen $2 extra.

## FOOD

El Paso is a hybrid species with North American and Mexican ancestors. Well known *gringo* chains coexist with small mom-and-pop restaurants. Residents of the city claim to have the best Mexican food anywhere, and *cocina mexicana* does indeed dominate the culinary scene; *burritos* are the undisputed local specialty. Attention vegetarians: bean *burritos* and *chiles rellenos* are tasty meatless options, but beware of animal lard.

**Luby's Restaurant,** Texas and Campbell (tel. 533-5042). A local favorite, hence the friendly, bustling atmosphere and inexpensive fare. Choose from a variety of salads (79-99¢) and red meats, chicken, or fish. Pick up food along a cafeteria-style line and chow down in a well lit, spacious dining area. For breakfast, try the waffle with fresh fruit (US$1.49) or other offerings (US$1-2). Lunch and dinner US$2.85-4.35. Open Mon.-Sat. 7:30-10am (for breakfast) and 10:30am-6pm.

**Ben's Restaurant/Rinconcito Café,** 605 S. Mesa (tel. 544-2236), serves outrageously cheap—and tasty—*burritos* (US$1-1.50). Otherwise, try out the *comida corrida,* which includes a generous sampling of Mexican specialties (US$3.25). Prices include tax. Free delivery downtown. Open Mon.-Sat. 8am-5pm.

**Big Bun,** 500 N. Stanton (tel. 533-3926). Serves inexpensive tacos, *burritos,* and hefty burgers (99¢) with salsa on the side. Refills at the soda machine 45¢. *Burritos* US$.99-1.99, deli sandwiches US$1.69-2.94. Open Mon.-Sat. 7am-7pm.

**The Tap Bar and Restaurant,** 408 E. San Antonio St. (tel. 546-9049), near Stanton. Not dirt cheap, but reasonably priced for the U.S. Serves breakfast, including excellent *huevos rancheros* (US$3), as well as lunch and dinner—the Mexican Plate #1 (tacos, *chiles rellenos, enchilada,* rice, beans, and nachos for US$4.50) surpasses its generic title in taste. Other entrees US$1.50-$6.50. At night, use the radiance from the neon-lit mini dance floor to guide yourself to a table. Live *mariachis* every Sat. night (10:30-11:30pm) and sports on a big-screen TV. Popular with Gardner Hostel-dwellers, and one of the only places open after 7pm, outlasting even McDonald's. Full bar with endless varieties of beer. Open daily 7am-2am.

## SIGHTS AND ENTERTAINMENT

The majority of visitors to El Paso are either stopping off on the long drive through the desert or heading south to Ciudad Juárez and beyond. Nevertheless, downtown El Paso has more to offer than just a cross-border trip. For a whirlwind tour of the city and its southern neighbor, hop aboard the Border Jumper Trolleys that depart every hour from El Paso (see Practical Information: Tourist Office above).

Historic **San Jacinto Plaza** swarms daily with men and women of all ages. Street musicians play music that evokes El Paso's roots, namely *conquistadores* and cavalry. South of the square, on **El Paso Street,** hundreds of locals hurry along the thoroughfare and dash into stores in search of new bargains. Here, a pair of Wranglers can be had for as little as US$10. To take in a complete picture of the Río Grande Valley, head northeast of downtown to Rim Rd. (which becomes Scenic Drive) to **Murchinson Park,** at the base of the mountains; the park offers a commanding view of El Paso, Juárez, and the Sierra Madres.

For nightlife, try the **Cadillac Bar,** 1170 Sunmount (tel. 779-5881, open daily 6pm-2am). The gay hotspot is downtown at **The Old Plantation,** 219 S. Ochoa (tel. 533-6055), a dance club/bar (open Thurs.-Sun. 8pm-2am). For a wilder time, there is Juárez, with rowdiness, no minimum drinking age, and ubiquitous nightlife.

Strategic timing can make your visit to El Paso more entertaining. The town hosts the **Southwestern Livestock Show & Rodeo** (tel. 532-1401) in February and the **World's Finals Rodeo** (tel. 545-1188) in November. Fear not: El Paso's celebrations transcend its country-western roots. Another festival is the **Sun Bowl Parade** (tel. 533-4916) at **UTEP,** which also offers historical campus tours (tel. 747-5000).

During the spring and summer, the **El Paso Diablos** (tel. 755-2000), pride of the fabled Texas League, play the best minor-league baseball around. Game times at

---

### The Plymouth Conspiracy

Take that turkey right out of the oven: contrary to popular belief—if El Paso has any say in it—those straight-laced Plymouth pilgrims did not celebrate the first Thanksgiving on the North American continent. Residents of El Paso wistfully recount the story of Don Juan de Oñate, a Spanish noble who, in January 1598, led a caravan of colonists from Santa Barbara, Mexico (near the city of Chihuahua) north to the United States. For over four months, the procession slowly plodded along through the desert, subsisting on roots, berries, and water from cacti. Finally, on April 20, 1598 (nearly a quarter-century before the Mayflower even set sail), the colonists arrived at the Río Grande. There, they rested in the soothing environs of the river, and on April 30, Don Juan requested that his people don their finest duds for a feast to celebrate their safe arrival. Shortly thereafter, they continued to what is presently Santa Fe, New Mexico.

---

Cohen Stadium are as follows: April-May: Mon.-Thurs. 6:30pm, Fri.-Sat. 7pm, Sun. 6:30pm. June-Aug.: Mon.-Sat. 7pm, Sun. 6:30pm. Call to confirm. To reach the stadium (9700 Gateway North), take Sun Metro bus #41 or #42 from San Jacinto Plaza as far north as it goes and walk the rest of the way. Ask the driver for directions.

# ■■■ CIUDAD JUÁREZ

Although Ciudad Juárez (founded in 1581 by Spanish explorers) is separated from El Paso only by the narrow Río Grande, one truly steps into another dimension upon entering Mexico. Visitors are immediately bombarded by commotion on all sides and treated to a feast of bright paint and neon. Near the border, the city is hectic, rude, loud, and cheap; the further one proceeds towards the ritzy ProNaf area, the calmer, pricier, and more Americanized the establishments—and people—become. Merry bands of carousing *gringos* have infiltrated the entire border area. Although fleeing in the face of the American advance, Mexican culture can be found in the city's cathedral square and Parque Chamizal, a pleasant respite from the industrial production centers and poor residential areas that dot most of the cityscape.

## ORIENTATION

Most of Old Juárez (the area immediately adjoining the Santa Fe and Stanton bridges) can be covered on foot. Street numbers start in the 600s near the two border bridges and descend to zero at 16 de Septiembre, where Av. Juárez ends. Both Lerdo and Francisco Villa run parallel to Juárez. The ProNaf center can be reached by hopping the public bus "Ruta 8-A" (1.20 pesos) on Malecón between the Departamento de Población and Secretaria de Turismo across the street from the bus shelter. Most city buses leave from the intersection of Insurgentes and Francisco Villa or thereabouts; always ask the driver where the bus is headed and inform him of your destination. Taxis are always available in any part of downtown, but fees are steep; negotiate a price before getting in. During the daytime, Juárez is relatively safe for the alert traveler. However, as darkness increases, so does the ratio of drunk to sober people wandering the streets. Women should not walk alone or in dark places; everyone should avoid the area more than two blocks west of Juárez's main street, Juárez.

## PRACTICAL INFORMATION

**Tourist Office: Coordinación de Turismo,** Malecón and Francisco Villa (tel. 14-06-07), in the gray Unidad Administrativa Municipal building to the right of the Santa Fe bridge, looking at it from the Juárez side. You must first cross a pedestrian bridge. Few truly helpful brochures, but it has an amiable English-speaking staff. Open Mon.-Fri. 8am-6pm, Sat.-Sun. 9am-1pm.

**Police:** Oro and 16 de Septiembre (tel. 15-15-51). **Transit Police:** Tel. 12-31-97 or 14-17-04.

**Post Office:** Lerdo at Ignacio Peña. Open Mon.-Fri. 8am-5pm, Sat.-Sun. 9am-1pm. **Postal Code:** 32000.

**Telephone: Secrefax,** Av. Juárez (tel. 15-15-10 or 15-20-49; fax 15-16-11), a few feet from the Santa Fe bridge, partially obscured under a white awning. Offers long-distance service within Mexico (5.50 pesos per min.) and to the U.S. (9 pesos per min.). Calls to El Paso 4 pesos per min. Will send, receive, and hold **faxes** (call in advance), and ship UPS (60 pesos). Open 24 hrs. **LADATEL** phones are scattered throughout the city. Look for them on Juárez near 16 de Septiembre. **Telephone Code:** 16. **Telephone Directory:** 04.

**U.S. Consulate:** López Mateos Nte. 924 (tel. 13-40-48 or 13-40-50). From Juárez St., turn left on Malecón and right on López Mateos. Settle in for the long haul—it's quite a walk. In an emergency, call the El Paso tourist office: (915) 544-0062.

**Currency Exchange:** In Juárez, banks congregate near the bus station, on Juárez St., and on 16 de Septiembre. Most display their rates outside and are open Mon.-Fri. 9am-1:30pm. One of the biggest is **Comisiones San Luis,** on the corner of 16 de Septiembre and Juárez (tel. 14-20-33). Traveler's checks accepted. Open Mon.-Thurs. 9am-9pm, Fri.-Sat. 9am-9:15pm, Sun. 9am-6:15pm. Another place

CIUDAD JUÁREZ

that takes traveler's checks is **Chequerama,** (tel. 12-35-99) at Unión and Juárez. Open Mon.-Sat. 10am-7pm.

**Abraham González Airport:** (tel. 19-07-34, -35, or -14 for administration) about 17km out on Rte. 45 (Carretera Panorámica). Catch the crowded school bus marked "Ruta 4" and get off at the San Lorenzo Church. Then get the Ruta "Aeropuerto" (1.20 pesos each). Primary carrier is **Aeroméxico** (tel. 16-66-21), with flights to Chihuahua, Mexico City, and Monterrey.

**Train Station:** Ave. Eje Vial Juan Gabriel at Insurgentes (tel. 12-18-44). Walk down Lerdo until it ends and take Juan Gabriel. Service to Chihuahua and Mexico City.

**Bus Station: Central Camionera,** Blvd. Oscar Flores 4010 (tel. 10-72-97 or 10-74-04), north of the ProNaf center and next to the Río Grande mall. It's too far to hike from the border: take **Chihuahuenses** bus from the El Paso terminal to Juárez (US$5) or cram into the "Ruta 1A" at Av. Insurgentes and Francisco Villa (1.20 pesos). Station open 24 hrs. Services include so-so eateries and an overpriced *caseta.* **Chihuahuenses** (tel. 29-22-01 or 29-22-06), **Ominbus de México** (tel. 10-74-04), **Estrella Blanca,** and others offer service to Chihuahua (every ½hr., 5hrs., 68 pesos), Guadalajara (8:30am and 9pm, 24hrs., 290 pesos), Mazatlán (12:30pm, 24hrs., 271 pesos), Mexico City (7 per day, 26hrs., 340 pesos), and more. **Greyhound** serves the U.S., including Dallas (US$59), El Paso (every hr., 50min., US$5), Los Angeles (US$35), San Antonio (US$79), and others.

**Supermarket: Del Real Mexicatessen,** V. Guerrero and López Mateos, in ProNaf. Take a checkered bus (#8) on V. Guerrero and Av. 16 de Sept. (5 min. ride). Inside of Pueblito Mexicano. Open 9am-10pm.

**Laundromat: Lavasolas,** Tlaxcala and 5 de Mayo (tel. 12-54-61). Twelve other locations in town. Washers 7.30 pesos (large), 6.30 pesos (small); dryers 7 pesos. Open Mon.-Sat. 8am-8pm.

**Pharmacy: El Félix Super Farmacia,** 16 de Septiembre and Noche Triste (tel. 12-08-24), across from the cathedral. Turn right from Juárez. Open 8am-10pm.

**Red Cross:** In the ProNaf Center, next to the OK Corral (tel. 16-58-06). Open daily 9am-7pm.

**Hospital: Hospital Latinoamericano:** 250 N. Lopez Mateos (tel. 16-14-67, 16-14-15, or 16-15-65). English spoken. Open 24 hrs.

**Emergency:** Tel. 06.

## ACCOMMODATIONS

In Juárez, a typical cheap hotel meets only minimal standards and charges some of the highest "budget" rates in Mexico. Inexpensive lodging can be found along the main strip, Avenida Juárez; pricier places are located in ProNaf, around López Matelos and Avenida de las Américas.

**Hotel del Río,** 488 Juárez (tel. 12-37-76), is well worth the climb upstairs. Large, simple, and clean rooms, comfortably thick beds, A/C, and color TVs await. Beware of rimless showers; don't leave your soap on the floor. Room service and parking available. Check-out 1pm. Singles, doubles, or tightly-squeezed triples US$20. AmEx, MC accepted.

**Santa Fe,** Lerdo Nte. 673 at Tlaxcala (tel. 14-02-70, 14-03-82, or 14-09-41; fax 12-56-27). A/C cools well-kept rooms while large color TVs entertain residents. Baby cribs available. Singles 135 pesos. Doubles, some with balcony, 153 pesos. MC, Visa, AmEx accepted.

## FOOD

Eateries vary from clean, air-conditioned restaurants catering to tourists to roadside shacks with picnic tables and TVs blasting *telenovelas* in Spanish. The quest for food that will not cause a bacteriological mutiny in *gringo* bellies is long; the prudent will beat a path to Av. Juárez and Lerdo or to the ProNaf center. Weak-stomached travelers should avoid shacks. In general, *mariscos* (shellfish) are overpriced and less than fresh in Juárez.

**Cafetería El Coyote Inválido,** Juárez 615 at Colón (tel. 14-27-27). A bustling, clean, American-diner atmosphere. Come for the A/C alone. Hamburgers 14.50 pesos, *burritos* 9.50 pesos, and an array of Mexican plates (14-20 pesos).

**Hotel Santa Fe Restaurant,** (tel. 14-02-70). Roll from here to there on the wheeled chairs. Then roll back. But don't expect too many dining companions to share the fun. Sample the *enchiladas de pollo* or club sandwiches (15 pesos) and wash 'em down with a beer (8 pesos). Open 24 hrs. Visa, MC accepted.

**Restaurant/Bar Villa Española,** Juárez 614 (tel. 12-02-38). Dark and spacious, but lively at night. *Chilaquiles* 9 pesos, *enchiladas* 10.80 pesos. Three cheers for *agua purificada.* Open daily noon-2am. AmEx accepted.

## SIGHTS AND ENTERTAINMENT

In *el centro* stands the **Aduana Fronteriza** (tel. 12-47-07), where Juárez and 16 de Septiembre cross. Built in 1889 as a trading outpost and later used for customs, it is now home to the **Museo Histórico de la Ex-Aduana,** which exhibits the region's history during the Mexican Revolution. Peeking inside the antique wagons is not frowned upon (museum open Tues.-Sun. 10am-5pm; free). The ProNaf center contains the **Museo de Arte e Historia,** (tel. 16-74-14), which exhibits Mexican art of the past and present (open Tues.-Sun. 11am-6pm; admission .75 pesos, students free). Also at the ProNaf center, the **Centro Artesanal** sells handmade goods at maximum prices; haggle here. The "Ruta 8" bus will take you from *el centro* to ProNaf for 1.20 pesos; a taxi charges 30 times as much.

The deforested **Parque Chamizal,** near the Córdova Bridge, is a good place to escape the noise of the city, if not the heat, and enjoy a picnic with the Stubbs/Goldsteins. The **Museo Arqueológico,** Av. Pellicer in Parque Chamizal (tel. 11-10-48 or 13-69-83), houses plastic facsimiles of pre-Conquest sculptures as well as trilobite fossils, rocks, and bones (open Tues.-Sun. 9am-5pm). **The Guadalupe Mission,** on 16 de Septiembre and Mariscal (tel. 15-55-02), features antique paintings and altars.

The *toro* and the *matador* battle in traditional bullfights on occasional evenings during the summer at the **Plaza Monumental de Toros,** Paseo Triunfo de la República and López Mateos (tel. 13-16-56 or 13-11-82). General admission seating begin at 25 pesos, 40 pesos in the shade. Children 12 and under free. Call for dates and times. The **Lienzo de Charro,** on Av. Charro off República (tel. 27-05-55), also conducts bullfights and a *charreada* (rodeo) on Sunday afternoons during the summer. At the western edge of town, the **Juárez Racetrack** (Galgodromo, tel. 25-55-59 or 25-78-54) rises from Vicente Guerrero. Dogs run Wed.- Sun. at 7:30pm. Sunday matinees during the summer at 2:30pm. Horse racing can be seen only on closed circuit TV.

Juárez has so many bars that counting them can make you dizzy even before you carouse. Many establishments are unsavory, and even some of the savory ones can become dangerous; stick to the glutted strip along Av. Juárez or in the ProNaf area. On weekends, North Americans swarm to Juárez to join their Mexican friends in a 48-hr. quest for fun, fights, fiestas, and inexpensive dental work. **Mr. Fog Bar,** Juárez Nte. 140 (tel. 14-29-48), is quite popular. A cartoon crocodile adorns the mirrored walls of this dark and reddish drinking establishment. Dance floor in back. Beer 7 pesos, liquor 6 pesos (open daily 11am-1am).

# ■■■ NUEVO CASAS GRANDES

A 3½-hour ride through the expansive Chihuahuan Desert separates Juárez from its southern neighbor, Nuevo Casas Grandes. Try to snag a window seat; it makes the sweaty journey south a peaceful experience. Once properly positioned, a panorama of sparse shrubs, distant but awe-inspiring Sierra Madres, and the occasional *vaquero* steering his herd of cows will rush by.

The ruins of Paquimé (pah-kee-MEH) in **Casas Grandes** are the remains of what was once the most important city in pre-Conquest northern Mexico. Nuevo Casas Grandes may remind you of cities in the American West; here, pioneers of the fashion frontier sport cowboy hats and enormous brass belt buckles. The absence of tourists, particularly those from north of the border, lends this slow-paced, quiet town an authenticity rare in Northern Mexico.

**Orientation** Nuevo Casas Grandes lies southwest of Ciudad Juárez and northwest of Chihuahua. The only way to get there is by road. The **Estrella Blanca** station is on Obregón and 16 de Septiembre.

The town's streets are laid out in an easy-to-navigate grid, with the center of town situated where the parallel streets Jesús Urueta, Minerva, 5 de Mayo, 16 de Septiembre, 2 de Abril, and Domínguez intersect with Juárez, Constitución, and Obregón. From the bus terminal, turn left onto 16 de Septiembre and walk one block to reach **Constitución,** the town's wide main street, with railroad tracks running between its two halves. Be careful—especially after sundown—when venturing out beyond the 9-square-block area delineated by Juárez, Madero, Urueta, and 16 de Septiembre. Taxis loiter on 16 de Septiembre and Constitución, and on Minerva and Obregón.

**Practical Information** Everything listed below lies within the 9-block downtown area. The **tourist office** is at Juárez Nte. 605, on your left as you enter the lobby of Motel Piñón. It offers a few brochures and conversation in Spanish (open erratically, 9am-1pm and 4-6pm). The **police** await at Blanco and Madero, on the outskirts of town. The **post office** at 16 de Septiembre and Madero (tel. 4-20-16), one block from Obregón, posts a *Lista de Correos* (open Mon.-Fri. 8am-6pm, Sat. 8am-1pm). **Postal Code:** 31700. **LADATELs** cluster around the central square. **Telephone Code:** 169. Change money at **Casa de Cambio California,** Constitución 207 (tel. 4-32-32; open Mon.-Fri. 9am-2pm and 3:30-7pm, Sat. 9am-2pm and 3:30-6pm). **Bancomer,** 16 de Septiembre at Constitución (tel. 4-03-90) has a 24-hr. **ATM** that takes Visa. **Ferrocarriles Nacionales de México** (tel. 4-08-69 or 4-55-15) operates a second-class **train** to La Junta (Mon., Wed., and Fri. at 10am, 12hrs., 17 pesos).

Buses leave from the station on Obregón and 16 de Septiembre. **Estrella Blanca** and **Caballero Azteca** (tel. 4-07-80) run to Chihuahua (11 per day, 6:30am-3:30am, with a *local* at 8am, 5hrs., 52 pesos), Cuauhtémoc (5 per day, 7:30am-6:15pm, 6½hrs., 61 pesos), and Juárez (12 per day, 6:30am-2am, 3½hrs., 42 pesos). **Chihuahuenses** (tel. 4-14-75) runs all the way to Hermosillo (6:30pm and midnight, 105 pesos first class, 94 pesos second class), Monterrey (5 and 6am, 199 pesos), Nogales (5 per day, 5:30am-1:30am, 77 pesos first class, 70 pesos second class), Obregón (2pm, 150 pesos first class, 134 pesos second class), San Luis Potosí (9am, 236 pesos), Tijuana (3am, 2, 4, and 11pm, 199 pesos first class, 179 pesos second class), Torreón (2:30am, 137 pesos first class, 123 pesos second class), and Zacatecas (2:30am, 206 pesos first class, 180 pesos second class). Next door, **Omnibus de México** (tel. 4-05-02) sends buses to Chihuahua (*vía corta* 7 per day, 5am-10:30pm, 5hrs., 53 pesos; *vía larga* 7 per day, 4:30am-8pm, 8hrs., 79 pesos) and Juárez (10 per day, 6am-3am, 3½hrs., 44 pesos).

Stock up at **Hiperama,** Juárez at Minerva (tel. 9-21-04; open daily 9am-9pm). **Lavasolas Paquimé,** 50m from Juárez and Urueta will wash or dry for 3 pesos (open Mon.-Sat. 8am-8pm, Sun. 8am-2pm). **Farmacia Benavides,** Obregón at 5 de Mayo (tel. 4-55-55), is open daily 8am-10pm. The **Red Cross and Hospital** is on Carranza at Constitución (tel. 4-20-20; open 24 hrs.). In an **emergency,** dial 06.

**Accommodations** Stock up on water before you hit town because none of these hotels offer *agua purificada,* only *agua potable.* Accommodations with modern conveniences cluster on Constitución and Juárez between 5 de Mayo and Jesus Urueta. Check-out time for all of the following listings is 2pm, except Hotel Juárez (1pm). **Motel Piñón,** Juárez Nte. 605 at 5 de Mayo (tel. 4-06-55; fax 4-17-05), sits next to the Dodge/Chrysler dealership. Guests sit cozily among the wooden carvings in Chimenea's Ladies' Bar, discussing the pottery pieces from Paquimé that they had seen in the motel's personal museum, and reliving the sensation of diving into the blue waters of the outdoor pool. Clean, carpeted rooms with colorful bathrooms with strong hot water also offer cable TV (singles 105 pesos; doubles 115 pesos; ask for the discount; MC, Visa accepted). At the **Hotel Juárez,** Obregón 110, a block from the bus station (tel. 4-02-33), you can talk and talk and talk to the friendly, English-speaking owner, Mario; show him your book and he'll mark down a point for *Let's Go* on his *Let's Go* vs. *Berkeley* scorecard. Mostly-clean rooms are small and not incredibly well ventilated, but have ample lighting, a bed, and a passable shower (singles 37 pesos, 47 pesos with two people; doubles 57 pesos; 10% discount if you ask for it).

**Food** Dining out with the locals (and the local flies) is cheap, since tourists are few and far between. The low tourist count, however, means that nightlife is soporific, and the few bars in town do not welcome women. **Restaurante Constantino,** Juárez at Minerva (tel. 4-10-05), is convenient to every big hotel. Bilingual menu, but speak Spanish to avoid pointing. *Enchiladas de pollo* are served with fresh bread, chips, and salsa (22 pesos). *Comida corrida* is the best deal at 17.50 pesos. Large windows have a view of the plaza (open 7am-midnight). The clean and icily air-conditioned **Dinno's Pizza,** Minerva and Constitución (tel. 4-02-40), may be just what the homesick traveler desires, but with a twist (jalapeño pizzas run 22, 27, and 33 pesos for small, medium, and large; other unusual flavors include cherry, pineapple, and coconut). Look for the small cream-colored public phone across from the front desk (open daily 8am-11:30pm; Visa, MC accepted). Sit down in the simple, timeworn **Café de La Esquina,** 5 de Mayo at Obregón (tel 4-39-59), and enjoy the larger-than-life soccer trophies and photos. Popular with an older crowd looking for a spot to play a serious game of dominoes undisturbed. *Bistec à la mexicana* (Mexican-style beefsteak) is yours for 22 pesos, *huevos al gusto* for 12 pesos. You might want to bring along a portable cooling device (open daily 24 hrs.).

# ■ CASAS GRANDES (PAQUIMÉ)

Eight kilometers southwest of Nuevo Casas Grandes, the pre-Conquest city of Paquimé lay hidden underground for 600 years. Its architecture suggests that **Casas Grandes** (so named upon excavation) grew out of two different cultures: its many-storied *pueblos* resemble those in the southwestern U.S., but other structures show the influence of central and southern Mexico. Between 1000 and 1200 CE, Paquimé was the most important agricultural and trading center in northern Mexico. The inhabitants kept parrots and turkeys in adobe pens and built indoor aqueducts and hidden cisterns to supply the *pueblos* in times of siege. They earned their livelihoods by farming and by trading sea shells brought from the Pacific coast. Unquestionably the biggest achievement of Paquimé was its complex system of irrigation, drainage, and underground water pipes. First exhumed in the early 1970s, Paquimé is now an archaeological zone administered by the Mexican government. Unfortunately, once it had been exposed for archaeologists and tourists, its high mud walls began to crumble. Visitors should avoid eroding the thin walls.

There are three principal maze-like mounds of ruins in Paquimé, which form a striking scene with the dusty mountains and ice-blue sky as the backdrop. It's easy to tell the parts that have been restored (the darker, more solid walls) from the original (cracked-looking) walls, which are located primarily in the mound to the far right. Among the ruins lie a partially excavated **market** as well as a **ball court.** The short and narrow T-shaped doors allowed inhabitants to defend themselves by pummeling unwanted visitors as they lowered their heads to enter. Look also for the **House of the Macaws, House of Skulls,** and the **Cross Monument,** which points to the four cardinal directions.

The **museum** (tel. 2-40-37) adjacent to the site is a terrific architectural achievement. Designed to blend in with the ruins and have a low impact on the environment, the museum displays artifacts that have been found at Casas Grandes, with an emphasis on the many pieces of polychrome pottery. Southwestern U.S. history and natural history are foci of the "Sala de las Culturas," which features a large-scale

CHIHUAHUA

model of Mesa Verde. A cafeteria, central patio with fountains, A/V room, gift shop, and a path directly out to the ruins round out the circular stone, handicapped-accessible structure (open roughly 9am-5pm).

On summer afternoons, the dry and shadeless ruins can become a blazing inferno, as temperatures near or exceed 100°F. Be sure to bring sun protection, a broad-brimmed hat (cheap *sombreros* are available in town), and, most importantly, a gigantic bottle of water to quench your thirst. When traveling from Chihuahua or Juárez, pick up information on the dig ahead of time, because none exists at the site. Some information may be obtained at the tourist center and pottery store at the opposite end of the square, or at the Motel Piñon back in Nuevo Casas Grandes. As always, be wary: wandering the area alone is not a wise idea.

**Getting There:** To reach Paquimé, take the light yellow **municipal bus** at the corner of Constitución and 16 de Septiembre to the central park in Casas Grandes (hourly, 1.30 pesos). Get off 8 to 10 minutes later by the main plaza; cross the street to the plaza, and continue straight down a dirt road for ten minutes. You will pass through a series of small brick shacks, two large dips in the land, and perhaps three or four wandering dogs. (Ignore their salivating unless you have a piece of ham.) Follow the path as it turns right, then turn left at the next intersection. You have now arrived at the largest (but hardly the most interesting) group of ruins open to the public in Northern Mexico (open daily 10am-5pm; admission 10 pesos; free Sun.).

Almost any **taxi** driver will take you to the site and walk around with you for about 60 pesos per hour. In Casas Grandes (pop. 20,000), **Pueblo Viejo,** a store at the Independencia and Juárez, sells tourist information, postcards (1-3 pesos), and authentic Indian pottery.

# ■■■ CHIHUAHUA

The capital the Republic's largest state, Chihuahua (pop. 800,000) is the vibrant, historically-rich mecca of Northern Mexico. Founded in 1709, it did not take long for Chihuahua to quickly mature into a major trading and administrative center. The city supported mining operations in the resource-laden western range and cattle enterprises in the surrounding valleys. Today, the lumber industry of the Sierra Madre yields most of the city's income.

Exposed to the sandstorms of Mexico's vast northern desert, Chihuahua may seem little more than a far-flung outpost of the civilization to the south. This seclusion convinced Pancho Villa to establish the headquarters of his revolutionary División del Norte here. During the conflict, his band of cowboys, bandits, and vagabonds staged attacks against the Porfiriato, streaming down from Chihuahua and assaulting social inequities. The man is a legendary figure to most Chihuahuenses, and Quinta Luz, Villa's sprawling colonial home, shines as the city's major attraction. Wealthy Americans and Europeans also established themselves here in the late 19th century, and the European villas that dot much of the city are their legacy.

The peoples who converge on Chihuahua and the surrounding area are as diverse as the land itself. Mennonites came here in flocks in the 1920s, attracted by the bountiful pastures. Today they maintain their seclusion in the nearby town of Cuauhtémoc and in other agricultural communities nearby. Equally secluded but quite different, the *indígena* Tarahumara people live isolated in the nearby Sierra Madres. They arrive at the city market in the early morning to sell handmade crafts.

Chihuahua can become an amiable, almost charming on a still and sunny day, but beware—the winds that whip across the surrounding desert do not stop for mere budget-traveling mortals. When the gales slice through town—summoning dirt, garbage, and rain—the city becomes a river of sorrow.

## ORIENTATION

¡Ay! Chihuahua sprawls in every direction, reaching onto the surrounding mountains. Skewered by Rte. 45 (the Pan American Hwy.), it serves as an important transportation hub for northern Mexico. Trains arrive at the **Estación Central de los**

**FFNN,** just north of downtown. Trains heading off to Los Mochis and Creel via the Barrancas del Cobre leave from a station south of the city center off Ocampo, two blocks from 20 de Noviembre. To shorten the 20-minute walk to *el centro,* hop one of the public buses (1.20 pesos) that run up and down Ocampo to Libertad; alternatively, snag a cab (about 15 pesos), but set the price before you step in.

Upon entering Chihuahua, you have two options. Either get off early before reaching the central bus station, or stay put until you reach the **Central Camionera** on Blvd. Juan Pablo. In either case, you will have to board a municipal bus (1.20 pesos) for the cathedral. When it comes into view, get off and walk to the left from Av. Juárez to reach **Libertad,** which is a pedestrian-only shopping arcade between **Independencia** and **Guerrero.** Two other main streets, **Victoria** and **Juárez,** run parallel to Libertad, and **Av. Ocampo** crosses Juarez one block past the cathedral. Get off the bus at **Av. Carranza** and walk two blocks to the left to the tourist office in the Palacio del Gobierno. Running parallel to Juárez on the other side of Victoria are Doblado, Niños Heróes, Carrillo, and Progreso. From Av. Independencia, parallel streets (*calles*) have even numbers starting with Calle 2a that increase as you head south, and odd numbers to the north. *Avenidas* running north-south are named. Budget hotels and restaurants cluster on the streets behind the cathedral.

Chihuahua is a relatively clean-cut, sanitary city—you'll be reminded that you're in the state capital. The sidewalks are well-paved, shanty mini-restaurants harboring *turista* are few and far between, and there is a relatively high density of men and women in suits. At night, the cathedral is well-lit, casting an almost spiritual glow onto the plaza it faces. The same cannot be said of the surrounding environs. With the exception of Av. Victoria, which perpetually celebrates victory with the flashing lights of bars and discos, the streets are poorly illuminated. Although the crime rate is not high, women especially should avoid walking alone after dark.

## PRACTICAL INFORMATION

**Tourist Office:** (tel. 10-10-77 or 29-33-00, ext. 4515 or 106; fax 16-00-32), in the lower left corner of the central courtyard of the Palacio del Gobierno on Aldama across from the Plaza de Hidalgo. Attentive, wonderfully helpful, English-speaking staff will take the time to answer all your questions. Indispensable maps and brochures in English. Open Mon.-Fri. 9am-7pm, Sat. 9am-1pm.

**Police:** (tel. 81-19-00), Av. Homero across from the Ford plant at the exit to Juárez.

**Post Office:** (tel. 10-00-18 and 10-35-95). In the large stone Palacio Federal on Libertad, between Vicente Guerrero and Carranza, one block from the arcade. Open Mon.-Fri. 8am-7pm, Sat. 9am-1pm. *Lista de Correos.* **Postal Code:** 31000.

**Telephones:** In the more expensive hotels and scattered among the various parks and plazas. Long distance service available in the plaza in front of the cathedral. Silver **LADATELs** gleam in the sun all over the *zócalo.* **Telephone Code:** 14.

**Telegrams:** Opposite the post office in the Palacio Federal (tel. 10-47-83). Turn left upon entering the building. For **telex,** call 34-98-78. Open Mon.-Fri. 9am-7pm, Sat. 9am-noon.

**Currency Exchange: BanPaís** (tel. 16-16-59), on Victoria on the first block away from the front of the cathedral. Traveler's checks changed free. Open Mon.-Fri. 9am-1pm. For 24-hr. dollar exchange, go across the street to **Hotel San Francisco** (tel. 16-75-50). **ATMs** are located near the lobbies of all the tall banks downtown near the *zócalo.*

**American Express:** Vicente Guerrero 1207 (tel. 15-58-58), past Allende, where Guerrero curves to become Paseo Bolívar. Inside a travel agency. Open Mon.-Fri. 9am-6pm, Sat. 9am-noon.

**Airport:** (tel. 20-97-39), on Blvd. Juan Pablo II, 14km from town. Served by **Aeroméxico,** Victoria 106 (tel. 15-63-03; open 9am-6pm), **Transportes Aéreos Ejecutivos,** Coronado 421 (tel. 16-28-28; open daily 9am-7pm), **Servicio Aéreo López** (tel. 15-83-32 or -33; open daily 8:30am-1:30pm and 3-7pm), **Aerovías de México,** Victoria 116 (tel. 16-35-31 or -47; open 9am-7pm), **Taesa,** Ortiz Mena 3403 (tel. 11-68-68), **Line Star Airlines,** on Prolongación Av. de las Américas (tel. 26-04-09 or -07; open daily 9am-10pm), and **AeroLitoral,** Victoria 106 (tel. 15-63-03 or 16-11-71; open daily 9am-6pm). To Monterrey, Ciudad Juárez, Mexico

City, and El Paso. Ground transportation to town available from a booth to your right as you exit the baggage area. From downtown, board buses marked "Aeropuerto" on Ocampo and Victoria.

**Train Station: FFCC Chihuahua al Pacífico** (tel. 15-77-56; fax 10-90-59), the southern station near Quinta Luz. Walk south on Ocampo and turn right at 20 de Noviembre. Walk to Calle 24 and take a left (the street sign for Calle 24 is not visible but it is at the end of the enormous prison). After two more blocks you will see the black 754 FNM Region Norte display train, which stands in front of the station. *Primera* trains leave at 7am for Creel (4½hrs., 64.15 pesos) and Los Mochis (14hrs., 141.55 pesos). *Segunda* trains leave at 8am for Creel (18 pesos) and Los Mochis (39 pesos). Tickets purchased on the train are 25% more expensive. Children 5-11 travel at half-price. Tickets sold Sun.-Fri. 6am-2pm. Only cash accepted. Two stopovers are permitted at an extra cost of 15%. **FFCC Nacionales de México,** the northern station on Av. Tecnológico, has service to and from the north and the south.

**Bus Station:** Local buses stop on Ocampo between Juárez and Victoria (0.90 pesos). To reach the main station, (tel. 29-02-42), board the white-and-red "Central Camionero" on Ocampo and Victoria for the 20min. ride. When you reach the station, cross the large thoroughfare. The sprawling station will be directly ahead. **Omnibus de México** (tel. 20-15-80) sends its luxurious fleet to Aguascalientes (5 per day, 2:30pm-3:30am, 14hrs., 177 pesos), Casas Grandes (7:30, 11am, 2:30, and 3pm, 5hrs., 53 pesos), Durango (11:30am, 6, and 8:30pm, 9hrs., 110 pesos), Guadalajara (3am, 3, 7, and 9pm, 17hrs., 224 pesos), Juárez (every hr., 4hrs., 68 pesos), Matamoros (2:40am, 18hrs., 206 pesos), Mexico City (*local* 5 per day, 9:43am-midnight, direct 4:30 and 9pm, 22 and 18hrs., 272 pesos), Monterrey (6:30, 9:30pm, and 2:40am, 12hrs., 147 pesos), Querétaro (5 per day, 9:43am-midnight, 18hrs., 232 pesos), Saltillo (6:30, 9:30pm, and 2:40am, 10hrs., 133 pesos), San Luis Potosí (6 per day, 4:50am-9pm, 188 pesos), and Zacatecas (7 per day, 9:40am-4:30am, 12hrs., 155 pesos). **Autotransportes Rápidos Delicias** (tel. 20-07-51) runs to Delicias (every ½hr., 6:20am-6pm, 1¼hrs., 14 pesos) and other nearby towns. **Transportes Caballero Azteca** (tel. 29-02-42) sends buses at 8, 9am, 6:30, and 10pm to Tijuana (22hrs., 231 pesos) with stops in Tecate (21hrs., 220 pesos), Mexicali (18hrs., 195 pesos), and San Luis Río Colorado (18hrs., 185 pesos). Buses also run to Cd. Obregón (10pm, 20hrs., 207 pesos), Hermosillo (7:30 and 10pm, 14hrs., 146 pesos), Nogales (8am, 12hrs., 121 pesos), Monterrey (10am, 3, and 9:30pm, 12hrs., 142 pesos), Torreón (8, 10am, 3, and 9:30pm, 6hrs., 78 pesos), and Zacatecas (9am and 2pm, 12hrs., 155 pesos). **Greyhound** (tel. 29-02-43; open 7am-7pm) runs connections from El Paso to cities across the U.S. **Transportes Chihuahuenses** (tel. 29-02-42) sends buses daily to Guadalajara (1:55am, 1:24, 3, and 6pm, 18hrs., 222 pesos), Juárez (every hr. until 9pm, 5hrs., 69 pesos), Mazatlán (10:15am and 5:45pm, 18hrs., 202 pesos), Morelia (8:15pm, 20hrs., 248 pesos), Puerto Vallarta (4:30am, 27hrs., 302 pesos), Torreón (8 per day, 11:30am-midnight, 6hrs., 82 pesos), and Zacatecas (11 per day, 1:24pm-midnight, 12hrs., 155 pesos). **Turismos Rápidos Cuauhtémoc-Anahuac** (tel. 10-44-33) has service to Cuauhtémoc (every hr., 5-7am and 8pm-midnight, and every ½hr., 7am-8pm, 1½hrs., 17 pesos). **Estrella Blanca** has a slightly older, more breakdown-prone fleet that chugs to nearly all of the above cities for lower prices, but requires more travel time.

**Supermarket: El Fénix,** Libertad 505 (tel. 10-26-21), in the pedestrian shopping arcade. Open daily 9am-9pm.

**Laundromat: Lavafácil,** Universidad 3500 (tel. 13-82-85), in the Centro Comercial Soriana Mall. From the cathedral, turn left on Carranza, which later becomes Universidad. Brace for a 40-minute walk.

**Red Cross:** Calle 24 and Revolución (tel. 11-22-11). Open 24 hrs.

**24-hr. Pharmacy: Farmacia Mendoza,** Calle Aldama 1901 at Calle 19 (tel. 16-44-14). Walk down Aldama away from the cathedral past Plaza de Hidalgo. Little English spoken.

**Hospital: Hospital General,** Revolución and Colón (tel. 15-60-84 or 15-77-08), in Colonia Centro. **Clínica del Centro,** Ojinaga 816 (tel. 16-58-18 or -85).

**Emergency:** Dial 06.

## ACCOMMODATIONS

Hotels in Chihuahua are like the city itself—charm shines through the grit. Economical hotels lie between Victoria and Juárez in the area behind the cathedral.

**Hotel del Pacífico,** Aldama 1911 at Calle 21a (tel. 10-59-13, only works intermittently), a few blocks from the Palacio del Gobierno. A great bargain: although the lobby is dark and rooms have a yellowish glow, all are clean and have A/C, large bathrooms, rugs, and decent foam mattresses with cement bases. Parking available, as are a cafeteria and *agua purificada*. Check-out 2pm. Singles 50 pesos. Doubles 60 pesos. Triples 70 pesos. MC, Visa accepted.

**Hotel Apolo,** Juárez at Carranza (tel. 16-11-00 or -01; fax 16-11-02), in the center. A step up in price—and amenities. In the dark but majestic lobby you'll be greeted by sculptures, chandeliers, and paintings of the arrival of Apollo—even on the ceiling! All the clean, bright, and cool rooms are outfitted with A/C, nice tiled bathrooms, rugs, phones, and cheery colors. 3rd- and 4th-floor rooms have color TV (no extra charge). Cafeteria, bar, and parking. Check-out 2pm. Singles 85 pesos. Doubles 100 pesos. Ask for the discount. MC, Visa accepted.

**Hotel San Juan,** Victoria 823 (tel. 10-00-35 and -36), one block down Victoria from the cathedral, on your right. Ravenous, he could wait no longer. After hastily dropping his bags on the weathered wooden floor of his room, and stopping in the clean, tiled bathroom, Don Juan took a cursory glance at the oversized closet, made a call on the ancient phone, and rushed out through the courtyard, heading for the cheesy bar from which he could hear the strains of live *mariachi* music. Central A/C and color TV. Check-out 2pm. Singles 36 pesos. Doubles 46 pesos.

**Hotel Roma,** 1015 Calle Libertad (tel. 10-23-63). Walk a few short blocks down Libertad from the cathedral; it's on your right, across from the Centro Médico Quirúrgico. Basic but spacious, somewhat clean, and quiet rooms. Beds might cave in if you don't watch out. Decent tiled baths will calm you. Ask for a room with A/C. Singles 36 pesos. Doubles 46 pesos. Add 10 pesos for color TV.

## FOOD

Eateries in Chihuahua are not geared toward tourists. Some of the best meals can be found in small *cantinas*, where bands serenade drunken (and often rowdy) men.

**Rosticería Los Pollos** (tel. 10-59-77), Aldama near Allende. Cafeteria-style dining at its best and brightest. Plastic booths, mirrored walls, A/C, and a pleasant, friendly atmosphere spice up your meal of excellent ¼ *pollo en mole* with rice and *tortillas* (a jaw-dropping 5.75 pesos) and, to finish it off, sweet *arroz con leche* (3.50 pesos). Try the *caldo* with rice and *tortillas* (2.80 pesos). Open 9am-8pm.

**Dino's Pizza,** Manuel Doblado 301 (tel. 16-57-07), across from the Santa Regina. An American crowd enjoys the pictures of Venice, clean bathrooms, and a strategically-placed emergency exit in this family-run joint. Dino never treated ol' stumpy Barney Rubble this well. Quaint decor and a delectable salami pizza (4 different sizes: 20, 25, 30, and 36 pesos). The special (pizza, spaghetti, and salad) goes for 14.90 pesos. Open 8:30am-midnight. AmEx, MC, Visa.

**Mi Café,** Victoria at Calle 10 (tel. 10-12-38), across from Hotel San Juan. Put on your sunglasses to enter this bright, 50s-style diner with melon-colored vinyl booths, and an orange-and-white checkered ceiling. A 24-peso order of chicken comes with bread, soup, rice, potatoes, and dessert—a huge meal. *Comida corrida* 19 pesos. Open daily 7am-11:30pm. MC, Visa accepted.

**El Delfín del Norte,** Juárez 301 at Calle 3a (tel. 16-98-99). For that ritzy touch: a seafood haven. Funky shell lamps illuminate fillet of fish *a la veracruzana* (19.50 pesos) or *a la italiana*, in oyster sauce (22 pesos). Stare at the fish tank when you get bored. Open daily noon-midnight.

**Restaurant-Bar Degá** (tel. 16-77-70), at Hotel San Francisco, near the *zócalo*. Offers a rare (if pricey) chance at a vegetarian meal. The *plato vegetariano* (27 pesos) includes vegetarian soup, a soy steak, avocado, and white rice; the *ceviche vegetariano* (16 pesos) has mushrooms and olive oil. Fresh carrot, papaya, or grapefruit juice 7 pesos. Beware of the overpriced drinks. Open 11am-1am.

## SIGHTS AND ENTERTAINMENT

The stately and regal **Palacio del Gobierno** stands in the center of Chihuahua on Aldama. It dates to the 19th century, and a beautiful series of murals inside done by Aarón Piña Mora—as well as a monument to the revered Miguel Hidalgo, who was decapitated in the city—tell the story of Chihuahua. Start from the left and work your way around the mural. Look for a nude Emiliano Zapata. The giant **cathedral** is constructed in a rich 18th-century Baroque style.

The area southwest of the *zócalo* offers an excellent leafy retreat from downtown. At **Quinta Luz,** also called **Museo de la Revolución** (Pancho Villa's house; tel. 16-29-58), visitors can relive the turbulence of the revolution by looking through an extensive collection of documents and photographs, paintings of Señor Villa, the bullet-ridden Dodge in which he was assassinated, his household furnishings, and his vast collection of rifles and machine guns (still enough to outfit a small army). To reach Quinta Luz, hike 1.5km south on Ocampo. On the left you will pass a statue of Simón Bolívar, the lively Parque Lerdo, and a monument dedicated to Manuel Ojinaga. A few more blocks down Ocampo brings you to an intersection with a stone church. This is 20 de Noviembre; turn left and go two blocks to Calle 10 and Méndez, then turn right. Villa's house is two blocks down on the right (open daily 9am-1pm and 3-7pm; admission 3 pesos).

On the way to the Villa household is another, equally worthy, museum: the **Quinta Gameros Centro Cultural Universitario,** also called the **Museo Regional de Chihuahua.** This amazing architectural feat on the corner of Calle 4 and Paseo Bolívar is one of the most stunning mansions in Mexico, and best of all, the aristocrat who had it built (mining engineer Don Manuel Gameros of Chihuahua) never lived in it; the Revolution drove him to El Paso, Texas, where he died in 1920, 10 years after the mansion's completion. The house was seized by revolutionaries and at one point served as Pancho Villa's barracks. Some astounding art nouveau furniture and room ensembles now wow observers; look for the 10-foot-high toilet and the beautiful mahogany dining room woodwork. Upstairs, local painters exhibit their works (open Tues.-Sun. 10am-2pm and 4-7pm; admission 7 pesos, 3.50 pesos for children; an informational booklet costs 4 pesos).

Back in *el centro,* the basement of the cathedral hides the **Museo de Arte Sagro,** Libertad and Calle 2 (tel. 10-38-77). Pastoral religious paintings from the 18th century mingle with photos and portraits from the Pope's most recent visit to Chihuahua. Artists on exhibit include Miguel Cabrera, José de Puez, and Juan Rodriguez Torres (open Mon.-Fri. 10am-2pm and 4-6pm; admission 4 pesos, 1 peso for children). For those craving more secular pleasures, the recently-opened **Museo de Arte Contemporáneo** at Carranza and Aldama (tel. 29-33-00, ext. 3700), across from the Palacio del Gobierno has a formidable collection of modern art. Geometrical Sebastián sculptures and a Diego Rivera sketch of a two-headed man/beast are among the highlights. Rodolfo Morales's striking *Reunión de Mujeres,* an Altamirano sculpture, photos of Frida Kahlo and Rivera, and some powerful Quenteros woodcuts are also in the museum (open Tues.-Sun. 10am-8pm; admission 5 pesos, students or teachers 3 pesos; free Wed.).

Occasional bullfights rage in the **Plaza de Toros,** Cuauhtémoc and Canal. The **Lienzo Charro** on Av. Américas west of town, hosts weekend rodeos. Inquire at the tourist office for dates, times and prices. If bullfighting isn't up your alley, maybe bowling will be: **Juventus Bowl** boasts one of the more modern bowling facilities in the world (inquire at the tourist office for directions).

On Juárez between Guerrero and Carranza, a golden eagle bearing the inscription "Libertad" points to the door of the **prison cell** (tel. 15-15-26, ext. 394), where Padre Miguel Hidalgo, leader of an early bid for Mexican independence, was held for two months prior to his 1811 execution. Mexican history buffs, prepare to swoon: the small room displays some of Hidalgo's belongings and letters from early participants in the uprising (open Tues.-Fri. 10am-2pm and 4-7pm; admission 1 peso). Another eagle points to the **Templo de San Francisco** on Libertad and Calle 17, which contains Hidalgo's decapitated body.

At night, you might catch a flick at **Cinepolis,** Vallarta at Zaragoza, a 15-minute ride away—hop on a white-and-purple bus labeled "Cerro de la Cruz" in front of the Héroes de la Revolución building in the *centro* (every 8min. until 9:30pm, 1.20 pesos). Cinepolis owns 14 screens and charges 15 pesos (half-price Wednesdays), showing movies from 3-9:40pm. If the buses have stopped running, you'll have to take a 15-peso cab back. Closer to town is **Cinema Revolución,** Doblado 700.

# ■■■ CUAUHTÉMOC MENNONITE COLONY

Plagued by both drugs and drunkards, the city of Cuauhtémoc is a hot, flat metropolis of 300,000 at the center of a large agricultural area. What delivers Cuauhtémoc into the realm of worthwhile travel destinations is its startling population of Mennonites (40,000-60,000) centered in the Mennonite grounds just outside the city. Among the masses of Mexican businessmen, street vendors, and families around Cuauhtémoc's *zócalo,* a blond-haired, blue-eyed Caucasian in overalls or a long black dress will occasionally amble by—hardly a typical sight in Northwest Mexico.

The Mennonites are a pacifist religious group founded by Menno Simons, who formed a Calvinist sect in the 16th century in Zaxonia, a region of lower Germany. Mennonites eventually began to inhabit parts of the Netherlands and Switzerland as well, but the group was expelled from the above countries, and later from Prussia and Bohemia (Poland) for two main reasons: their refusal to serve in the military and their steadfast determination to privately educate their children. This path of exile led them to the Ukraine and Russia, and after being booted by the Czar (who then rescinded the expulsion too late), many fled to Canada in the early twentieth century. Sects ended up in the United States (the Pennsylvania Dutch is one of many groups), and eventually a large group settled in northern Mexico in 1922, whereby the Cuauhtémoc colony was founded.

The hard-working, almost compulsively clean group of Mennonites that now inhabits the agricultural fields just outside Cuauhtémoc's center is now known for the Chihuahua cheese sold worldwide that they produce, supposedly made from the same recipe as Wisconsin cheese. Each small community of Mennonites, called a *campo,* has a number and is laid out in an orderly manner, with a main street, several farms, a creamery, a church, and a school. Most Mennonites speak Low German, an archaic 17th-century dialect that even those fluent in High (modern) German would not understand, but some High German is starting to permeate the colony. Many of the Mennonite adults speak a good deal of Spanish (they need it for trade), but there are still many, mostly children, that do not.

Some hard-core Mennonites now object to the "wayward" concessions the Cuauhtémoc group has made to modern technology. They are traditionally known for refusing all electricity and motor-powered vehicles, but today's Cuauhtémoc Mennonites drive around in pickups instead of horses and buggies, listen to radios (and watch TVs, in secret), and use computerized machinery in producing their cheese. But traditional dress is still standard: wide-brimmed, white hats and a long, flowered dresses for women, tall hats and overalls for men. Varying degrees of liberality exist within the group—some even live within the city of Cuauhtémoc, dressing like Mexicans but attending church in the fields on Sundays, and intermarriage (and thus conversion of Catholics to the Mennonite faith) is not unheard of.

**Orientation and Practical Information** Cuauhtémoc is located approximately halfway between Creel and Chihuahua, a two- to three-hour bus ride from each. The city is 70km west of Chihuahua on a 4-lane highway, and a stop on the Chihuahua-Pacífico Railroad. The highway into Cuauhtémoc from Chihuahua continues past the city and into the **Mennonite area,** where the *campos* are organized by number: on the left, numbers start at one and go up; on the right they start in the mid 20's and count down, and after a certain point, deeper into Mennonite lands, the field numbers switch to the 100s. The center of Cuauhtémoc is at the beginning of the parallel numbered streets: Melgar (Calle 1), Calle 2a, and Calle 3a. The cross-streets Morelos and Allende delineate the *zócalo* with Melgar and 2a.

The **police** can be reached at 2-45-99. The **post office** is on 4a and Guerrero (tel. 2-03-14; open Mon.-Fri. 8am-6pm, Sun. 9am-1pm). **LADATEL phones** surround the *zócalo* and dot the downtown area. A public **long-distance** coin phone is at **Nutrivida,** Allende and 7a (tel. 2-33-36; open Mon.-Thurs. 8am-8pm, Sat. 8am-6pm, Sun. 9am-3pm). **Telephone Code: 158. Banks** cluster near the *zócalo*. **Banca Serfín,** Melgar at Allende (tel. 2-63-33) has an **ATM** (bank open 9am-1:30pm), but the ATM at nearby **Bancomer** may be more compatible. The **Estrella Blanca bus station,** Allende at Calle 9a (tel. 2-10-18) runs buses daily to Basaseachi (8, 10:30am, and 4:30pm, 5hrs., 38 pesos), Casas Grandes (7:30pm, 5hrs., 61 pesos), Chihuahua (every ½hr., 1½hrs., 15 pesos), Creel (6 per day, 7:30am-7:40pm, 3½hrs., 33 pesos), Guerrero (every hr., 1½hrs, 14 pesos), Hermosillo (8am, 12hrs., 152 pesos), Juárez via Casas Grandes (9:30am, noon, and 2:45pm, 9hrs., 99 pesos), Juárez via Chihuahua (10am, 6hrs., 80 pesos), and Obregón (10:30am, 12 hrs., 124 pesos). The **Centro Comercial** is a big-time **supermarket,** complete with clothes and trinkets, across from the *zócalo* (open Mon.-Fri. 9am-8:15pm, Sat.-Sun. 8:30am-8:30pm). In the city, **Farmacia Cuauhtémoc** (tel. 2-08-77) is open Mon.-Sat. 9am-9pm, Sun. 10am-2pm. **Farmacia Rocío** is in the Mennonite area, on the right before Campo 3-B near the caged ostriches. A 24-hr. **hospital** (tel. 2-44-61) is next door. In an **emergency,** dial 06.

**Accommodations** The best place to stay in Cuauhtémoc, hands down, is the **Motel Gasthaus,** the only Mennonite hotel (in all of Mexico, probably), smack in the middle of the Mennonite area on km 13, on the left after *Campo* 3-B if coming from the city. The establishment sparkles with an otherworldly cleanliness; you'll see your reflection in the spotless floors and immaculate white walls. The beds are comfortable and the bathrooms absolutely irreproachable. This may be the cleanest hotel in the Republic—keep it that way by adhering to the "No Spitting" sign on your cabinet. (Singles 50 pesos. Doubles 60 pesos. Rooms with private bath and TV 75 pesos. Huge suites with refrigerators, sinks, and stoves with full-sized ovens: doubles 100 pesos, quads 150 pesos.) The friendly owner will take you on a tour (see below) and/or bring you to/from the city of Cuauhtémoc (30 pesos for 4 people).

If you must stay in the city of Cuauhtémoc, there are a few options, none very attractive. The **Hotel Gran Visión,** on Allende between 7a and 9a, offers tidy, small-ish rooms with A/C, TV, and phones. Check-out 2pm (singles 60 pesos; doubles 70 pesos; MC, Visa accepted). More costly but worth it is the **Hotel Unión,** Allende at 5a (tel. 2-11-14 to -17). Here you'll find cavernous and clean rooms with modern lighting, chairs and tables galore, and comfortable beds and bathrooms. A/C, cable TV, and phones are included, of course. English is spoken—try bargaining. Check-out 2pm (singles 80 pesos; doubles 100-110 pesos; MC, Visa accepted).

**Food** If you're here to sample Mennonite culture, you might as well try their food—and get out of the dirty city and into the ultra-clean kitchen of a Mennonite restaurant. Most have sinks with hand soap *outside* the bathroom because they're used so much. A few restaurants line the main highway through the *campos*—try the **Travelers Restaurant** (tel. 2-64-70), between *Campo* 3-B and *Campo* 19. Traditional Mennonite foods are very rich and very tasty: the *impanadas de requesón* (*wren atje*—dough filled with Mennonite cottage cheese, pierogi-like, and covered with cream sauce, 15.50 pesos) and *fideos con crema* (*kilje*—noodles with ham or sausage, also drowned in cream sauce, 14 pesos) are not exceptions. Eat here more than twice, however, and your cholesterol count may hit quadruple digits (open daily 9am-9pm). In the city, **El Den,** Allende at 2a (tel. 2-38-43) has cafeteria-style service that includes *comida corrida* (17.50 pesos) and a hamburger with french fries (11 pesos; open daily 7am-10:30pm).

**Sights and Entertainment** There are a handful of ways to explore the Mennonite lands of Cuauhtémoc. **Public buses** head into the area (down the main highway) once per hour (15min., 3 pesos), letting passengers off anywhere along the way. Perhaps a better idea is to head directly to the **Motel Gasthaus**—the owner will pick up 4 people up from the city for roughly 30 pesos—and start your tour from there. He will also take a few people around in his car or pickup for about 50 pesos per person for the entire day, less for shorter excursions. Tours typically include a look inside an authentic Mennonite home, a tour of a cheese factory and a machinery plant, and a meal (at your expense) at a Mennonite restaurant, though the actual sights covered on a tour are up to you. The above tour is offered as well by the father-and-son team **Cumbres Friesen,** both of whom are Mennonites (David is the father, John is the son). They charge US$15 per person for a half-day tour.

If you want to check out the Mennonite colony on your own, you'll need a car to get from place to place. Take a left at the 2-B/22 sign if you want to get a good look at a Mennonite cheese factory in action. Follow the road heading down into the village for awhile. You'll pass a school and church (open only on Sundays) on your left, and take a right into the **Quesería América,** one of the 20-25 cheese factories in the 80 or so Mennonite villages in the area. Keep your eyes open for the old-fashioned timecards and the four vats in which cheese is processed: the first one you see is actually the last stage in the process, in which a cottage-cheese-like mixture is pressed, salted, and allowed to sit for 12hrs. Cool off in the refrigeration rooms, where milk-cartoning machines and cheese waiting to be shipped are kept. You'll encounter some stares and friendly offers to buy cheese or sweets in the lobby. The workers tend to be very shy, and some don't speak Spanish (never mind English!).

To see a genuine **Mennonite household,** take a left at the "Hotel La Estancia" sign at Campo 6A. Follow that road about 2km, and take a right down another road a little ways. You'll see a white house with a blue stripe around the bottom; it's surrounded by a white picket fence and tall trees, and it's home to the **familia Guenther.** The friendly, Spanish-speaking family will show you their huge but stark kitchen with its jam-filled pantry, their living room, and their special guest room with a valuable wooden chair. Big families are the norm among the Mennonites, and the Guenthers are no exception: Mrs. Guenther's 12 children all live within a few km radius. There's something in it for her in showing you her house, by the way: she'll offer for sale her traditional Mennonite knitted crafts. Outside, scope out the horizon for the **radio tower,** via which Mennonites communicated before they succumbed to that modern luxury, telephones. Before, they all had walkie-talkies. 10-4 *familia* Guenther.

# ■■■ CREEL

High amid the peaks of the Sierra Madres and lodged among pine forests, log cabins, and rolling hills and valleys, the small village of Creel (pop. 5,000, altitude 7,669 ft.) welcomes travelers with natural beauty, human warmth, and refreshing, mountain-pine air. The village in many ways resembles a frontier town of the late 1800s: smoke billows from the chimneys of the humble but picturesque huts to counter the chilly climate; the train rumbles through the middle of town at least twice a day; and horses, pigs, and cows are as common to Creel's streets as the rugged, cowboy-hat-wearing villagers to whom they sometimes belong. As you make your way up to Creel from the south, the sweltering Chihuahuan desert gives way to a land of spectacular gorges, looming peaks, and cool nights.

Creel is perhaps most popular as a base from which to explore the stunning Copper Canyon. Although tourism to the town has increased of late, government plans for expansion have not yet damaged the unique ambience of the town nor substantially altered the lives of the Tarahumara Indians, 50,000 of whom live in the Sierra Tarahumara mountains surrounding the town. Of Mexico's many *indígena* groups, the Tarahumara have best warded off modern Mexican culture, living in isolated caves and wooden houses and resisting all efforts to settle them in villages. They are a people remarkably well-adapted to their rugged environment—they fashion plows from the limbs of oak trees and are skilled in the preparation of 200 species of edible plants. The Tarahumara are famous for their non-stop long-distance sacred foot-races, which last up to 72 hours. Tarahumara pine-needle baskets, blankets, figurines, and violins are sold throughout town.

While many come to Creel to sell their crafts or to pick up supplies, the Tarahumara greatly value their seclusion and tend to shy away from contact with tourists. If you pass Tarahumara cave dwellings, look at the caves from the road, but don't take their obvious accessibility as an invitation to approach more closely or to walk in and have a look-see. Also, refrain from photographing the Tarahumara.

Home to a great many groups other than the Tarahumara, the countryside around Creel is a mixture of races and cultures. *Mestizos* (people of mixed Spanish and *indígena* ancestry) live in villages and ranches throughout the area. The Pima inhabit the areas northwest of Creel, while the Northern Tepehuan live south of the town. To the west live the Guarojio; farther west are the Yaqui and Mayo groups. All of these indigenous groups are linguistically related to the Tarahumara.

## ORIENTATION AND PRACTICAL INFORMATION

The **train station** is located just northwest of the *zócalo,* and the **bus station** is right across the tracks and further north. To reach the *zócalo,* walk one block along the tracks in the direction of Los Mochis and turn left. The main street, **Mateos,** runs parallel to the trains on the opposite side of the *zócalo.* Street numbers go up to the right and down to the left as you turn onto Mateos from the tracks. **Chapultepec,** further north, runs parallel to Mateos and up to the tracks.

**Tarahumara Information: Artesanías Misión** (tel. 6-01-50), on the north side of the *zócalo.* Although not an official tourist office, it is the best source of information on Creel and the surrounding area. Sells books about the Tarahumara and its language (Rarámuri), crafts, and a map of the region (9 pesos for the fold-up version; 18 pesos for a topographical map). A small selection of English and Spanish guidebooks is available. The mission supports the Tarahumara's cultural development, and the local hospital receives store profits. English-speaking staff. Open Mon.-Sat. 9:30am-1pm and 3-6pm, Sun. 9:30am-1pm. Traveler's checks accepted.

**Police:** (tel. 6-00-81), in the Presidencia Seccional, on the south side of the *zócalo.*

**Post Office:** (tel. 6-02-58), in the Presidencia Seccional on south side of the *zócalo. Lista de Correos.* Open Mon.-Fri. 9am-4pm. **Postal Code:** 33200.

**Telephones:** Long-distance service available at the *caseta de larga distancia* in the **Papelería de Todo,** Mateos 30 (tel. 6-01-22 or 6-02-22; fax 6-02-12). Collect calls three pesos. **Fax** available (3 pesos per page). Open daily 9am-8pm. **Telephone Code:** 145. No LADATELS in town, but black coin-operated long-distance phones are around. One is in **All-Rich (Todo Rico) Restaurant,** Lopez Mateos 37, at Chapultepec (tel. 6-02-05).

**Telegrams:** In the same building as the post office. Open Mon.-Fri. 9am-4pm.

**Currency Exchange: Banca Serfin** (tel. 6-02-50), next door to the Misión. Dollars exchanged 10am-1pm. 5.85% commission for changing traveler's checks. Open Mon.-Fri. 9am-1:30pm.

**Train Station:** Av. Tarahumara 57 (tel. 6-00-15), right in town on the tracks—you can't miss it. Trains leave daily for Chihuahua at 3:40pm (*primera,* 75 pesos) and 5:15pm (*segunda,* 20 pesos), and for Los Mochis at 12:26pm (*primera,* 78 pesos) and 2:10pm (*segunda,* 22 pesos). Ride out to the Divisadero Station at Barrancas del Cobre on the Los Mochis-bound train (*primera,* 24 pesos, *segunda,* 6 pesos). Tickets go on sale at 11:30am for the *primera* to Los Mochis and a half-hour before departure time for other trains. Some trains might be "full," in which case you should scramble on quickly and aggressively when the train arrives and purchase a ticket on board. Never count on a train leaving on schedule or even leaving at all. Some travel agents sell tickets ahead of time (see page 202 for more tips on dealing with trains). The station is open Mon.-Fri. 10am-4pm, Sat. 10am-2pm.

**Bus Station: Estrella Blanca** (tel. 6-00-73), a small white-and-green building across the tracks from the *zócalo.* To Chihuahua (7 per day, 7am-5:30pm, 5hrs.,

49 pesos) via Bolonya (45min., 5 pesos), San Juanto (1½hrs, 11 pesos), La Junta (2hrs., 23 pesos), and Cuauhtémoc (3hrs., 33 pesos). From the Restaurant Herradero at Mateos 39, **canyon buses** (tel. 6-02-79 or -30) leave for Batopilas (Tues., Thurs., and Sat. 7:15am, 8hrs., 40 pesos; return-trip leaves Batopilas at 4am). Vans also run to Batopilas (see page 199).

**Bicycle Rental: Expediciones Umarike,** López Mateos 9, next to Casa de Huéspedes Margarita (see below). Very friendly English-speaking staff will set you up with a bike (whole day 65 pesos, ½ day 40 pesos, 12 pesos per hour; helmet and gloves 15 pesos). Guide services and bicycle excursions with van support are available. Buy a good road and trail map of the area for 10 pesos.

**Market: Albarrotes Pérez,** on Mateos next to Cabañas Bertis. Open daily 8am-9pm. Fruit, vegetables, and a large selection of water is available.

**Laundromat: Lavandería Veno,** Francisco Villa 112 (tel. 6-01-39). Across the tracks from the police, near the bus station. 10 pesos per load for wash and dry. Open 9am-8pm; bring your load by 6pm if you want same-day service.

**Pharmacy: Farmacia Rodríguez,** Mateos 43 (tel. 6-00-52). Open Mon.-Sat. 9am-2pm and 3-8:30pm, Sun. 10am-1pm.

**Medical Services: Clínica Santa Teresita** (tel. 6-01-05), on Calle Parroquia at the end of the street, two blocks from Mateos. Little English spoken. Open Mon.-Fri. 10am-1pm and 3-5pm, Sat. 10am-1pm. Open for emergencies 24 hrs.; keep ringing the bell until someone comes.

## ACCOMMODATIONS AND CAMPING

As Creel has flourished, the number of hotels has multiplied and competition for tourists' pesos has become intense. The backpacking set, however, still inhabits most of Creel's rooms. Prices are often somewhat negotiable during low season, and budget rooms are not hard to find despite the increasing popularity of the region.

**Margarita's Casa de Huéspedes,** Mateos 11 (tel. 6-00-45), across from the *zócalo*. One of the liveliest places to stay in all of Mexico. You'll have no trouble finding it—a young emissary meets every train and bus to lead you to the house, where you mingle with Margarita's family, friends, and guests. Make it clear that you want to go to the *casa,* not the hotel. All rooms are freshly renovated, with floor tiles, pine furniture, and heating. To top it off, all prices include two home-cooked complete meals (breakfast 7am-9am, dinner 6-8pm, vegetarians accommodated). Margarita is not only good to tourists: between the 15 children she employs to meet potential guests and the 6 cooks on her payroll, Margarita provides jobs to a great many Creel residents. The staff speaks English. Tours offered (see below). Reservations accepted. Check-out noon. Fine rooms with two single beds and a private bath 60 pesos for one person, 80 pesos for two. Shared dormitories go for 20-40 pesos per head (prices are negotiable).

**Cabañas Bertis,** López Mateos 31 (tel. 6-00-86). Log-cabin feel with paneled walls, thick wool blankets, and fireplace or wood stove in each abode (wood supplied free). Small private bath and dining table included. Tours offered (see below). Singles 50 pesos. Doubles 100 pesos. Triples 150 pesos.

**Pensión Creel,** Mateos 61 (tel. 6-00-71; fax 6-02-00). Walk down Mateos away from the *zócalo*. The Pensión has some expensive and some budget rooms. Budget rooms, in the *hacienda,* further from downtown near the trails and woods, offer bunk or double beds in newly renovated cabins. The *hacienda* boasts shared bathrooms, a fully-equipped kitchen, and a large common room featuring a roaring fireplace and magazine shelf. A complimentary bus service transports you to the *hacienda,* though it is within walking distance. Prices range from US$5 if you have your own sleeping bag to $10 with breakfast. Mention *Let's Go* to Federico for the $10 discount rate. French and English spoken.

**Hotel Korachi** (tel. 6-02-07), across the tracks from the train station. A wanna-be hunting lodge. Wood and gas heaters in the bathroom. Clean bedrooms with dark, wood-paneled walls. Singles 40 pesos. Doubles 70 pesos. Strange but clean *cabañas* with animal skins on the walls sit under shady trees and include private bath and wood supply. Singles 70 pesos. Doubles 90 pesos.

For those who prefer to immerse themselves in nature, the campground and lodges around Lake Arareko are the way to go. The campground (10 pesos per night per head) is on the northwestern shore, on a hill overlooking the lake. The site sports 31 barbecue- and fire-pits, 12 latrines, hot showers, and picnic areas. **The Segorachi Cabin** fits 16, contains a living room, kitchen, fireplace, and grill, and guests are pampered with a laundry service and a complimentary boat for use on the lake. **The Batosarachi Lodge,** on the southeast corner of this vast body of water, houses up to 50 in the three Tarahumara-style cabins (each has bunk beds, a common room, heaters, and hot water). At both the Segorachi Cabin and the Batosarachi Lodge, guests can cook their own meals or let themselves be served.

## FOOD

Creel has yet to spawn gourmet restaurants that cater to jet-set tourists. There are, however, several inexpensive restaurants in town with friendly atmospheres and good, home-cooked fare. Picnicking spots abound on the quiet hillsides outside town—relish an even cheaper picnic lunch of fruit and bread there.

**Restaurant El Tungar** (tel. 6-01-30), at the tracks next to the railroad station, gives you a chance to sit at a counter with the locals and eat extremely cheap and yummy food in a warm, homey environment. Taste the tongue (5 pesos), the chili with meat and beans (3 pesos), or the *chile relleno* (5 pesos, 8 pesos with beans). No alcohol served. Open 7am-7pm.

**La Cabaña,** Mateos 36 (tel. 6-00-68), a few paces south of the *zócalo* on your left. You can almost hear the birds chirping and the sap dripping as you recline in one of the pinewood stalls. Take in the stuffed game, the landscape drawings, and a 25-peso platter of seafood. Big *burritos* 4 pesos. Open daily 8am-10pm.

**Jorge's,** Francisco Villa at Cristo Rey, south of the bus station. If thinking about the 80s leaves you hollow, don't fret; this is one place where you'll never have to ask "Where's the beef?" The burgers (12 pesos) and *enchiladas* (13 pesos) arrive bulging with sizzling meat. The owner also prides himself on bringing fresh seafood to Creel, of all places. Open 8am-11pm.

**All-Rich (Todo Rico) Restaurant,** López Mateos 37 (tel. 6-02-05), at Chapultepec. A large variety of meat, chicken, and seafood is served up in a bright, clean, and friendly atmosphere. Go American with two hamburgers with french fries (10 pesos), or go gourmet with filet mignon (32 pesos). Breakfasts 7.50-12 pesos. Make an international call between bites on their coin phone—the owner provides change. Open daily 7am-11pm.

**Restaurante Veronica,** Mateos 34. A simple joint, newly renovated with tile floors and popular with locals. Enjoy *carne asada* con papas (roasted meat with potatoes) for 17.50 pesos, or the *comida corrida* with a drink (12 pesos). Open daily in the winter 8am-11pm, in the summer 7am-11pm.

## SIGHTS AND ENTERTAINMENT

Almost all of Creel's sights lie outside the city and in surrounding areas, including the Sierra Tarahumara and the Barrancas del Cobre (Copper Canyon). For information on these destinations, see below. In Creel proper, you can visit the **Casa de las Artesanías del Estado de Chihuahua,** Avenida Ferrocaril 178 (tel. 6-00-80), in the old railroad station. There, local and Tarahumara arts, crafts, and a random assortment of historical relics are on display. But what steals the show is the mummy in the back room, which some Tarahumara claim as a relative and upon which local schoolchildren periodically sprinkle flowers (open Tues.-Sat. 9am-1pm and 3-7pm).

At night, a local *cantina* with a touch of class is **Laylo's Lounge and Bar,** inside **El Caballo Bayo** restaurant and hotel, López Mateos 25 (tel. 6-01-36). Its large concentration of men is classic *cantina,* but the shiny wood paneling and nice decor outdo most watering-holes. A pitch-black entryway lies between you and the inside—you must knock on the door and pass the cursory field-sobriety test (which consists of keeping your balance in the dark) before entering (open daily 2pm-1am). Many local hotels, including the **Motel Parador** and the **Hotel Margarita's** keep their guests entertained with night-time diversions at the bar, including *mariachis*. Parador rocks with live music and many all-too-willing dance partners—it is the job of the *animador* to get the women up and dancing with the male patrons. While most establishments in Creel close before 9pm, a few are open later, and the town usually has a few tourists roaming the streets or strumming guitars until near midnight. On Saturday nights, the **Casino de Creel** in front of the plaza offers outdoor and indoor dances, to which both locals and tourists are welcome (men 15 pesos, women 10 pesos; festivities run from 8pm-1am).

Creel's real draw, of course, is the canyon and surrounding countryside, and you'll need either a car, a tour guide, or a brave heart to get there. Read on.

# ■■■ LAS BARRANCAS DEL COBRE (COPPER CANYON)

The **Barrancas del Cobre,** four times the size of Arizona's Grand Canyon, is one of the most spectacular sights in all of Mexico. It actually comprises five canyons in an area more generally known as the **Sierra Tarahumara,** home of the Tarahumara Indians. The Barrancas del Cobre hibernate under drifts of snow during the winter months and explode with color during the rainy season (July-Sept.), when the canyon's plants are in full bloom. Any time of year, the Copper Canyon is one of Mexico's greatest natural wonders. The Barrancas are criss-crossed by the tracks of the **Chihuahua-Pacífico Railroad;** trains careen along canyon walls at death-defying angles, plunge into tunnels (there are 96 of them), and briefly skim the rim of the *barranca*. The railroad stretches from Chihuahua to Los Mochis; along the way it crosses the Continental Divide three times and soars to a height of 8000 feet. Passengers peering from train windows can glimpse a breathtaking series of landscapes—cactus-covered plateaus, mountains overgrown with cedars, unusual rock formations, snow-covered summits, blue skies, and canyon floors teeming with tropical vegetation.

The transterritorial railroad was the brainchild of Albert K. Owen, the founder of a utopian farmers' and workers' colony near Los Mochis, who saw the train as a link to western Mexico. Owen failed to see his project come to fruition, however, and it languished until a governor of Chihuahua, Enrique Creel, organized the construction of the first 125 miles of track. In 1900, a Kansas City businessman took over Owen's project, envisioning a single railroad stretching from western Missouri in the U.S. to Sinaloa. He tacked another hundred miles of track onto the route before his coffers ran dry 12 years later. Construction continued sporadically during the 1930s, but the Sierra Madres remained inaccessible by rail. Finally, technological achievements precipitated by World War II made it possible to bore some of the highest and longest tunnels in the world. The entire route was inaugurated in 1961, a utopist's pipe dream brought to life by the engines of war.

Two types of trains make the daily journey between Los Mochis and Chihuahua. The *primera* is for tourists: clean, air-conditioned, equipped with bathrooms, and blessed with large, comfortable seats, *primera* trains run close to schedule. The *segunda* trains screech along the same tracks, carrying livestock as well as passengers.

From the Los Mochis station, the *primera* departs at 6am, the *segunda* at 7am. From Chihuahua, the *primera* leaves at 7am, the *segunda* at 8am. A *primera* ticket from Los Mochis to Chihuahua costs 153 pesos, the *segunda* 40 pesos. The Chihuahua to Creel leg takes six hours by *primera*, while the Creel to Los Mochis track is a nine-hour journey. The *segunda* makes twice as many stops, adding about four hours to any *primera* travel time. The *primera* from Chihuahua arrives in Creel at 12:26 pm (75 pesos), and the *primera* from Los Mochis at 3:14pm (78 pesos).

The serious mountain scenery lies between Creel and Río Fuerte, so if you take the *segunda*, you'll zoom by some great views in the dark. For more expansive natural spectacles and less mountain wall out your window, grab seating on the left side of the train heading towards Los Mochis, and the right side if you're on the way to Chihuahua. Bring food for the trip or you will be forced to rely on either the *enchilada* saleschildren who run through the train during stops in small towns, or the *burrito* salespeople at Divisadero. Even worse, you may find yourself at the mercy of the bland, expensive train entrees. Between Creel and Chihuahua, the most noteworthy stop is Cuauhtémoc (see page 191).

At the **Divisadero station,** the jagged mountain edges overlap to create a maze of gorges and rocks at the rim of the Barrancas del Cobre. Eight hours out of Los Mochis on the *primera,* the train stops here for 15 minutes of sightseeing. Everyone on board scrambles out, sprints to the brink, gapes, and sprints back. On the *segunda,* it's less formal. Ask the conductor when the train is going to leave, and be back early. Resist the urge to buy anything from the Tarahumara, strategically positioned between the train and the canyon—better examples of their craft are available in Creel at lower prices.

Perhaps the most amazing thing about the expansive and magnificent Barrancas is what a well-kept secret they are. Few foreigners, even those familiar with Mexico, have ever heard of the Copper Canyon, and fewer still could place it. This bodes well for your visit: unlike the Grand Canyon, you certainly won't have to elbow your way through a crowd to look over the edge—on the contrary, you'll feel like the only person in this land hidden deep within the Sierra Madres.

## THE ROAD SOUTH TO BATOPILAS

Leaving Creel and heading south, a road winds its way through the most scenic parts of the Copper Canyon. Buses rumble past numerous nail-biting hairpin turns, balancing most of the way in one lane on the edges of steep cliffs that will make your heart pound both from excitement at the view and nervousness as you put your life in the hands of a stranger at the wheel. The road has been called North America's most spectacular by many, but, unpaved most of the way, it is also one of the continent's most treacherous. The first 25-km section of the road just south of Creel is happily two-lane, paved, and quite hikeable and hitchable.

On the right side heading south, still-inhabited **Tarahumara caves** are within view of the road. On tours, it's possible to go in and visit the homes for a small donation. Beds and other furniture, woodstoves with chimneys, and kerosene lamps adorn the insides of many of the dismal, stone-walled caves. You may feel somewhat awkward walking into a native family's home, but many Tarahumara must sacrifice their privacy for precious pesos.

Four kilometers down the road from Creel (and a left on a dirt road) lies the humble **San Ignacio Mission,** constructed in 1744 and still in use today—services are conducted in Rarámuri, the native language of the Tarahumara, Sundays at 11am. The mission can easily be combined in a day trip with the **Valle de los Hongos** (Valley of the Mushroom Rocks). The government now charges 10 pesos for each of the two sites, more to take photos. To reach the valley and mission by foot, walk down Mateos past the Motel Parador. When the road forks, take the smaller branch to the left, beside the cemetery. A kilometer or so out of town you will pass through the gates of the Tarahumara's *ejidos* (communal lands), containing the caves in which they live. After the cultivated fields, the valley is to the right and the mission at the bottom of the hill. On the way you will pass through small dells and plains surrounded by rocky cliffs, pines, and oak trees characteristic of the Tarahumara highlands. The stone mission is dedicated to Saint Ignatius Loyola, the community's patron saint. The Valley of Mushroom Rocks (also called the Valley of the Frogs or Ducks) contains immense, oddly shaped stones formed by the San Ignacio River.

Unguided travelers may also reach **Laguna Arareko,** an enormous lake 3km long and 8 acres in area. Just bear right when the road forks past Mateos and follow the path 7km southeast. The water here is cold and contains dangerous weeds below the surface, so swimming is discouraged. Two other options reasonably close to the lake are **Recohuata Hot Springs**—which requires a tour guide who will take you for a 1½-hour ride and then send you on a 600m hike down into the canyon (around 45 pesos)—and the **Valle de las Monjas** (Valley of the Nuns), nine kilometers away and a daytrip on horseback.

Twenty-two kilometers from Creel down the road to Batopilas is the town of **Cusárare,** which features its very own Jesuit mission constructed in the 18th century, the **Misión de Cusárare.** Check out its interior, done by the Tarahumara; you'll see crude wood floors and indigenous designs. There are no pews—people sit on the floor when it's used on Sundays. A boarding house for children and a small Tarahumara craft museum are nearby, but the most popular attraction in the town's vicinity is the **Cusárare Falls,** a nice but uphill 4km hike through a pine forest. Consider hiring a young guide for a few pesos so that you'll know which path to take to get the impressive falls.

Another 20km beyond Cusárare on the road to Batopilas, **Basíhuare** is an old overnight stop that once housed silver carriers headed for Batopilas. Excellent views of the canyon can be had here. 20km past Basíhuare is the crossing of the highest point of the **Río Urique.** Later, the road starts weaving around the narrowing canyon, offering spectacular vistas as you climb the **Cerro de 7 Pisos** ("Seven-floor Hill"), the nickname for the seven distinct layers that lead up along the rocky inner walls of the canyon on the most frightening stretch of this incredible one-lane path. The seven steps can best be seen from **La Bufa,** 60 km from Basíhuare and past the fork, a scenic lookout that has the most magnificent view of all. If you have good vision, you can make out the tiny thread that is the Río Urique far, far below and the yellow wooden bridge that runs across it. If you're driving, pull off onto the shoulder, and try not to look down. Get out, and gape. Then gape some more.

If you'd gone left at the fork instead of right, you would've come to **Norogachi,** a Tarahumara mission center at the river with a hospital, mission school and beautiful (but touristy) *Semana Santa* services, and **Guachochi,** a rocky, frontier-like village with both colonial and Tarahumara influences.

But the right fork, however, will take you to the more interesting town of **Batopilas.** On the way you'll pass the bridge across the Urique. There, you can get out and walk down into the bushes, a beautiful spot from which you can see a waterfall down below. Keep your eyes peeled for **Tescalama trees,** which have yellow flowers and grow out of the sides of sheer rock. The last quarter of the ride to Batopilas also has plenty of **piedra cobriza** (copper rock), which gives the canyon its copper tint.

**Getting There: Margarita's** and **Cabañas Bertis** both offer trips that cover Cusárare (mission and falls), Lake Arareko, a Tarahumara cave, and the **Elephant Rock.** It's a four-hour trip and runs about 45 pesos per person for at least 4 people; Bertis also runs a trip to San Ignacio Mission, Lake Arareko, Valley of the Mushrooms, and the Elephant Rock that's only two hours and costs 35 pesos per person. Tours that go as far as La Bufa and then back run 90-95 pesos from Margarita's, or 90 pesos per person (min. 6) from Cabañas Bertis. It's a 10-hr. round trip. On any trip—guided or not—remember to bring plenty of water and food, adequate footwear, and a sun hat. While Margarita's tours are among the cheapest, many other outfits in Creel offer group tours for those averse to roughing it. In all cases, the basic package involves walking, though for a few more pesos you can arrange to navigate on bikes, horses, or even donkeys. Pensión Creel, Hotel Nuevo, Chihuahua Tours (tel. 6-02-24, on Mateos and Flores), and Sartidora del Pacífico (across from the Cabañas Bertis) all run similar tours to popular sites. **Motel Parador,** Mateos 44 (tel. 6-00-75; fax 6-00-85), offers tours including a bag lunch that are somewhat more expensive.

## BATOPILAS AND SATEVO

**Batopilas** is a tiny town nestled in the depths of the canyon along the Río Urique, a rough 35km from La Bufa and a thrilling but scary 140km (6hrs. by van, 8hrs. by bus) from Creel. Batopilas was a silver-mining boom town discovered by Pedro de la Cruz in 1708. Its rich silver supply lasted until the late 1800s, which is why such a secluded place was the second city in all Mexico to receive electricity. Today, that electricity comes only between the hours of 6-9am and 8pm-midnight, a symbol of what little remains of Batopilas's glory days.

Everything in Batopilas centers around the old, stone plaza, which has a basket-ball court and a few benches. There you'll find the **post office** (**Postal Code:** 33400) and a long-distance **phone** that costs about 9 pesos per min. (open Mon.-Sat. 9am-3pm, Sun. 9am-1pm). A **library** and the municipal building with **police** are also at the plaza. The best place in town to stay is the **Hotel Mary,** Juárez 15, next to the church near the plaza. Large, basic, adobe rooms with ceiling fans are naturally cool and rustically charming. Check-out noon (30 pesos per person). The nearby **Hotel Batopilas** is also recommended by travelers to the region. The Hotel Mary's restau-rant, **Quinto Patio,** is the only restaurant in town that's reliably open. *Enchiladas* (12 pesos), *bistek* (17 pesos), and pork chops (17 pesos) are on the menu, but you're limited to whatever happens to be in the fridge at the time. The food isn't anything to write home about, but it's edible. Recommended by locals but errati-cally open is the **Puente Colgante** (Swinging Bridge) **Restaurant,** next to the swing-ing bridge (appropriately), down a short path on the far end of the plaza.

The magnificent **haciendas** in ruin along the river are poignant reminders of the excesses of the owners in the silver-mining days of Batopilas. The brown, castle-like **Hacienda Shepard** belonged to an American, and its ruins now stand in contrast with the green of the surrounding trees and canyon. Look for the *tescalama* tree growing sideways off the brown wall of the hacienda. Hikes from Batopilas leave daily. They go to mines, including the **Porfirio Díaz** mine in town and the more interesting **Peñasquito,** an hour hike up a steep hill; to the **Cerro Colorado,** a sec-tion of the old Camino Real to Chihuahua during the mining boom, a 12-hour hike; and to the lost mission of **Satevo** (see below). The best source of information about departing tours is the **Riverside Lodge,** in town diagonally across from the plaza on the bench side (not the basketball-court side). The "lodge" is a grand sight in itself, a veritable museum more than worthy of a look around. A restored *hacienda,* the lodge is now a very fancy package-tour inn—check out the incredible piano room, which looks like a room in a Newport mansion with paintings and portraits galore, a vintage piano, and an old 1911 treasure underneath a trapdoor on the floor. The historical photos on the walls may be the most interesting exhibits—included is an 1899 shot of Pancho Villa at age 22 (before he hung out in Batopilas with Sr. Shep-ard), a photo of gold bars stacked to the ceiling, and another of the day when the river ran as high as the hotel wall.

The most fascinating excursion from Batopilas is that to **Satevo,** a minuscule town with a spooky and beautiful mission. It's a 40-minute drive—you'll need 4WD or, better, pixie dust—or a two-hour walk. In the middle of the fertile valley and straddled by the towering canyon, out of nowhere, rises a lonesome, round mission shrouded in mystery. Why was it built here, of all places? When was it built (the 15th or 16th century are the best guesses, but no one knows)? And finally, how did the Tarahumara, barely able to find shelter for themselves, gather up the energy, spirit, and desire to build such a thing? In any case, it's a sight to behold, especially at sunset, when the rays carom off the red bricks of the roundhouse-like construc-tion, combining with the clouds and valley to create a heavenly scene. In order to look inside the mission you'll have to tip the poor family living next door, which has the key. The inside the mission is even eerier, with ancient tombs below and dark-ness above.

**Getting There:** Trips to Batopilas and back can be on the pricey side: Margarita's charges a house-mortgaging 1500 pesos for a round-trip for up to eight, but a private driver can be hired for less: **Sergio Rascón** of Cabañas Bertis will take up to a van-load for 800 pesos, and he's a particularly reliable and cautious driver—a necessity for such a trip.

## BASASEACHIC FALLS NATIONAL PARK

The Basaseachi Falls are one of the world's prominent waterfalls; with water falling 806 feet, the cascade is a truly spectacular sight. It is the highest waterfall in Mexico and the fourth highest in North America, and few waterfalls are blessed with such gorgeous surroundings. Named "Basaseachi," a Tarahumaran word meaning "place of the cascade" or "place of the coyotes," the word was Mexicanized with the added "c" at the end when it was made a national park preservation area, the only such area in the northern Sierra Madres. This is the spot you'll find on the posters, the sight most associated with the region, and a not-to-be-missed excursion from Creel and the Chihuahua-Pacífico Railroad.

Once at the village (from where you see the falls from above), the hike down to the base of the falls is a picturesque and fascinating 3-hour round trip trek, but a mere 30-minute hike down leads to the "window"—the best view of the falls, that from the side. The rest of the climb down is steep and difficult for many, so you might instead choose to turn around at the "window."

**Getting There:** Trips to the village of Basaseachi run 120 pesos per person (min. 6), which is a 127-km trip on unpaved roads or 210 less scenic kilometers on paved roads. Margarita's runs the trip for only 90 pesos per person. On the way you'll get a good glimpse of the Río Urique and its part of the expansive canyon.

---

### The Tarahumara Handshake

The Tarahumara Indians are a quiet bunch, and they generally won't complain if you take pictures or peer deep into their cave dwellings. But try to put yourself in their place; they might be offended or feel awkward and simply be too polite or intimidated to speak up. One interesting aspect of Tarahumara is the way they shake hands: it is a limp shake, with none of the fist-pumping action of the Western shake. If you do get a chance to shake a Tarahumaran's hand, keep this in mind; you can tell how Westernized the Tarahumaran is from how firm his or her shake is. Their clothing is also a good indication: traditional dress consists of a *tagora*, a cloth wrapped twice around the waist, sandals (*akaka*), and a *napatza*, a loose cotton shirt.

---

## SOUTH OF CREEL TO URIQUE

Creel to Urique is a 154km trip. Along the way, partly along the Chihuahua-Pacífico railroad, are Divisadero, Bahuichivo, and Cerocahui. **Divisadero** is a train stop 51km south of Creel on the Chihuahua-Pacíficio railroad. It can also be reached by road from Creel (Margarita's charges 60 to 70 pesos per person for an excursion). Aside from owning an amazing vista of a wide expanse of canyon—perhaps the fullest view of the Barrancas anywhere—Divisadero is also home to "La Piedra Volada," a large, precariously balanced stone, and a crazily expensive hotel and restaurant. It is technically possible (though quite difficult) to try a full-day hike between Cusárare and Divisadero, but an experienced guide is a must. A far more manageable and popular hike from Divisadero (that might force you to stay at the pricey hotel, as camping is not recommended) is down into the canyon—you can go as far as you want. A four-hour, 4km round-trip hike goes to the Tarahumara village **Bacajipare,** while the 27km descent to the bottom of the canyon from Divisadero takes eight hours each way. Guides for hire hang around the hotel, and they'll take you down to the Río Urique, to Bacajipare, or elsewhere.

**Bahuichivo,** in a clearing in the forest, is another stop on the railroad, 97km south of Creel. Another frontier-like town, it has a couple of restaurants and hotels, but it's usually used as a departure point for locations deeper in the canyon or Cerocahui and Urique, further south. **Cerocahui** is 17km southeast of Bahuichivo. From Bahuichivo, grab a white "Transportes Cañon Urique" van, which also goes to Urique, right at the Bahuichivo train station. The main attraction of this beautiful mountain village (pop. 600, elevation 5,000ft.) is the **Jesuit Mission,** founded in 1681 by the noted priest Juan María de Salvatierra and reconstructed in 1948. Gold and silver mines (**Sangre de Cristo**), the **Gallego Mountain** (38 stomach-wrenching km away), the **Misión Churo,** and well-known waterfalls including the **Yeparavo waterfall** (4km south), are among the possible excursions from Cerocahui.

The **Barranca de Urique,** the canyon in which the village of **Urique** sits, is the deepest of all of the Barrancas. Urique sits upon the river of the same name, and affords spectacular views of the canyon. Basic restaurants and hotels are available.

# SINALOA

## ■■■ LOS MOCHIS

Los Mochis is accustomed to playing host to strange bedfellows. In pre-Hispanic times, the city was inhabited by a diverse group of indigenous peoples which included Mayans, Ahomes, Zuaques, and Tehuecos. In 1872, the city was settled by a group of Americans led by Albert Owen, a socialist, and Benjamin Johnston, a businessman. While Owen set out to forge a socialist utopia—the fishing village of **Topolobampo** is his legacy—Johnston busied himself in founding the Sinaloa Sugar Co., whose smashing success propelled Los Mochis into the 20th century.

The nucleus of an extremely fertile region of crops, Los Mochis (often just called merely "Mochis") is an important stop on a cross-country voyage, linked to the Baja peninsula (by a ferry departing from Topolobampo) and the Barrancas del Cobre (by rail). The community has recently awakened to the revenue-generating potential of tourism: the local secretary of tourism recently initiated a program of instruction for the area's hotel and restaurant employees. With a little luck, such efforts may succeed in paving Los Mochis's coppery cliffs with a red carpet of hospitality. But much more than hospitality is needed to make this city more than an obligatory stopover. Although Los Mochis is a bustling agricultural and industrial city, it suffers from crowded, dirty streets, smoggy air, and little in the way of entertainment or of cultural interest.

**Orientation** The city is laid out in a simple grid. Activity centers around **Obregón** and **Hidalgo** and the perpendicular **Zaragoza, Prieta,** and **Leyva.** Past Obregón, Castro, Ordoñez, and later, 16 de Septiembre and 5 de Mayo run parallel; on the other side, past Hidalgo run Independencia, Juárez, Morelos, Madero, Bravo, Carranza, and Serdán. Perpendicularly, Flores runs after Leyva while Allende, Degollado, and Constitución run after Zaragoza on the other side.

**Practical Information** The ferry to La Paz leaves from Topolobampo at 9am every day except Sunday (*salón*-class tickets between Topolobampo and La Paz, 61 pesos; 387.50 pesos to bring a car onto the ferry; 49 pesos to bring a motorcycle). Check times and buy tickets at the **Sematur** office on Rendón 519 (tel. 2-01-41; fax 2-00-35; open Mon.-Fri. 8am-1pm and 3-7pm, Sun. 9am-1pm; hours erratic). Tickets must be purchased one day in advance (before 11am) at the Sematur office or on the day of departure on the ferry at Topolobampo. To get to the office, walk nine blocks from Juárez on Flores, and then turn left on Rendón.

In the mornings, a **bus** runs to Topolobampo every 20 minutes starting at 6am (4 pesos); the bus leaves from a small side street between Hidalgo and Obregón near the Hotel Santa Anita. The bus can also be flagged down on Cuauhtémoc between Prieta and Zaragoza, but it's advisable to take the bus from the station and to get there more than ½hr. early, as it's often crowded.

The **Chihuahua al Pacífico** train (tel. 2-08-47) runs back and forth from Los Mochis to Chihuahua, passing through the Copper Canyon and offering amazing views of the canyon at the Divisadero station, south of Creel, where fifteen minutes are allowed for tourists to get off, gape, and get back in. Unfortunately, the train is horribly unreliable; frequent problems, including derailments and avalanches make your plans to leave Los Mochis about as secure as a savings and loan investment (and the Fed can't bail you out of this one). The first class train passes through at 6am (75 pesos to Creel; 143 pesos to Chihuahua). If it does come, be in the station by 4:30am or earlier to get in the snail-paced ticket line. Hopefully, you'll have gotten to the front by the time the train leaves. If it looks like it's about to leave and you're still in line, ditch the line, box out a few angry train officials, bowl over anyone else in your path, and jump onto the train; what can the conductors do but sell you a ticket if you're already on? The train arrives in Creel around 4pm. A second-class train, even less reliable than the first, supposedly leaves at 7am and arrives in Creel after dark, depriving you of the spectacular canyon views. A better alternative to waiting in the ticket line is buying your ticket beforehand from a travel agency—one such option is **Paotam,** Rendón 517 (tel. 2-23-83). Another is **Viajes Conelva,** Leyva 357 Nte. (tel. 8-51-90; open until 7pm). No extra charge is added, and you'll have much more peace of mind come sunrise. The train-bound become the captives of cagy taxi drivers, who all report to a price-fixer worthy of Don Corleone (may his first child be a masculine one). Fares to downtown begin at 25 pesos. This desperate situation tempts otherwise scrupulous travelers to bluff their way onto the free bus to and from the Hotel Santa Anita. It's easy to get the public bus from the station back to town during the daylight hours (every 15min., 2.50 pesos)—just walk away from the station down the road about 100m—but a taxi is the only option in the wee hours.

If you miss the train and must get to Chihuahua or Creel, bless you. The most appealing option (which is sort of like saying the coolest spot in hell) is to grab a bus to Hermosillo from the Los Mochis bus station (8hrs.) and then catch the overnight Hermosillo-Chihuahua bus (1 per day, 8pm, 13½hrs., 165 pesos). From Chihuahua, buses run regularly to Creel (5hrs., 45 pesos).

Set office hours are the butt of town jokes. The **tourist office,** on Cuauhtémoc and Allende (tel. and fax 2-66-40), is on the left upon entering the Unidad Administración del Gobierno del Estado de Sinaloa. Walk down Calle Leyva two blocks past Blvd. Castro; turn left on Cuauhtémoc and walk for three more blocks. The office is on the far right corner (open daily 9am-1pm and 4pm-6pm). Another tourist information source is the **Cámara Nacional de Comercio, Servicios, y Tursimo,** on Prieto and Cuauhtémoc (tel. 2-04-77 or 2-08-97; fax 2-31-73), on the second floor. Ask for Lic. Francisco López Miranda for friendly help. The **Tourist Security** number is 91-800-90-392. **Police** life revolves around Degollado at Cuauhtémoc in the Presidencia Municipal (tel. 2-00-33). The **post office** lies at Ordoñez 226 (tel. 2-08-23), two blocks off Castro, between Prieta and Zaragoza (open Mon.-Fri. 8am-7pm). **Postal Code:** 81200. Cheap but noisy collect and calling card calls can be placed on **LADATEL** phones scattered throughout downtown. **Telephone Code:** 686. The lines at **Bancomer,** Leyva at Juárez (tel. 8-08-49 or 5-78-08), may be 30 minutes long. Consult clerks for authorization to change traveler's checks (open Mon.-Fri. 9am-2pm).

**Tres Estrellas de Oro** (tel. 2-17-97), **Norte de Sonora** (tel. 2-04-11), and **Elite** (tel. 8-49-67) operate out of the modern terminal at the corner of Juárez and Degollado. **Transportes Norte de Sonora** is usually the cheapest carrier, and sends buses to Mazatlán, Cuauhtémoc, Mexico City, and Tijuana. **Transportes del Pacífico** (tel. 2-03-47), on Morelos between Leyva and Zaragoza, is also relatively cheap. *De paso* buses run south to Mazatlán and north through Guaymas, Hermosillo, and Mexicali to Tijuana. Unfortunately, these buses are often chock-full by the time they reach Los Mochis. Seats are easier to obtain on the slower *de local* buses to Guadalajara, Tijuana, and Mazatlán, all of which run two or three times per day. All other buses are *de paso,* so be on your toes. Buses to El Fuerte and other nearby destinations leave from Zaragoza, between Ordoñez and Cuauhtémoc. For **taxis,** call 2-02-83.

The **Norte de Sinaloa** station (tel. 8-03-31) sends a large fleet of rickety green buses every 20 minutes to Guasave (1hr., 8 pesos), Guamuchil (2hrs., 13 pesos), Culiacán (3½hrs., 25 pesos), and Ahome (½hr., 3.50 pesos).

For fresh fish, fruit, and vegetables, check out the **market** on Obregón between Leyva and Zaragoza; on weekends it bustles with activity. Los Mochis's hippest threads get washed at **Lavamatic,** Allende 218 just before Juárez, for seven pesos per 3.5kg, then dried for eight more (open Mon.-Sat. 7am-7pm, Sun. 7am-1pm). The **Red Cross,** at Tenochtitlán and Prieto (tel. 5-08-08 or 2-61-17), one block off Castro, has 24-hr. ambulance service. **Farmacia Karla,** Obregón at Degollado (tel. 8-18-14 or -15), is open 24 hrs. Hit the **Hospital Fátima,** Blvd. Jiquilpán Pte. 639 (tel. 2-12-33) to check out the local medical scene. The **Centro de Salud** can be reached at 2-09-13. The **emergency** number is 06.

**Accommodations**   Budget hotels of variable quality are sprinkled throughout the downtown area demarcated by Castro, Juárez, Leyva, and Constitución. Mention that you're a tourist when negotiating a price at a hotel—Los Mochis's crusade to enhance tourism includes offering tourists lower prices at hotels. Arachnaphobes beware: crawling spiders are as ubiquitous as street noise. **Hotel Montecarlo,** Flores 322 Sur (tel. 2-18-18), a blue building at the corner of Independencia, is growing old gracefully. Large, very clean, rooms surround a quiet, palatial indoor courtyard. Central A/C, fans, and cable TV make your life happy. Take a room downstairs if you can—they're much cooler (singles 75 pesos, with two people 92 pesos; doubles 110 pesos). **Hotel Catalina** (tel. 2-17-72), is on Obregón near Degollado, across the street from the bus terminal. It'll impress you with large, clean, expensive-looking rooms with phones and a modern, high-tech lobby. Features include A/C, cable color TV with U.S. channels, and room service. Check-out 2pm (singles 90 pesos; doubles 130 pesos; 15 pesos per extra person). At **Hotel Hidalgo,** Hidalgo 260 Pte. (tel. 2-34-56), between Prieta and Zaragoza, ceiling fans and chilly colors (deep blue furniture and baby blue walls) cool the rooms. If there's a soccer game on the tube, the lobby becomes a local hang-out. All rooms are basic, mostly clean, have A/C, and offer thin mattresses and aging bathrooms (singles 60 pesos; doubles 80 pesos; extra people 10 pesos).

**Food**   The crowning virtue of this farming region is the **public market** between Prieto and Leyva along Castro, where prices are low and quality is high. The *taquerías* and *loncherías* in the market dish out cheap, home-brewed enigmas, many of which pack quite a wallop. Except for the *cantinas* (which women should avoid) and the corner *taquerías,* just about everything in town shuts down at 9pm; alcohol evaporates at 11pm. Put your ear to a conch and imagine you're near **El Farallón,** at Obregón and Flores (tel. 2-14-28 or 2-12-73). The first restaurant in the city to serve shellfish, also famous for its sea turtles before they were outlawed. Ornate fishing nets and stately wooden fish decorate the walls. Spectacularly good seafood is served here: flounder or sea bass (33 pesos), red snapper (39 pesos), and frog legs (30 pesos) flop onto your plate in huge portions. Cool, air-conditioned air mimics an ocean breeze (open 8am-10pm; AmEx, MC, Visa accepted). At **El Taquito** (tel. 2-81-19), on Leyva between Hidalgo and Independencia, pitch-black windows shade out the offending sun. Cold A/C will dry your sweaty skin and prevent the vinyl booths from sticking to the undersides of your thighs. Waiters in red jackets serve up hamburgers and fries (15 pesos) and Taquito-style shrimp (filled with cheese and wrapped in bacon) for 35 pesos (open 24 hrs.; MC, Visa accepted).

**Sights and Entertainment**   Los Mochis boasts a few modest amusements, but if you're stuck here for a day, head to Topolobampo. One of Los Mochis's founders, the sugar baron Benjamin Johnston, assembled the extraordinary collection of trees and plants standing in **Sinaloa Park,** on Prolongación and Castro. Hundreds of species inhabit this outdoor forest-museum, where *indígena* performers strut their stuff every Sunday beginning at 11am. Bark-watchers should check out the stump at the entrance to the park; careful observers have found a harem of wild animals and the insignia of the state of Sinaloa gouged into its roughened surface. The **Museo Regional del Valle del Fuerte,** Pte. Municipal at Castro (tel. 2-46-92), was once the home of another early settler and now houses his guns and detailed personal diary. Photographs documenting the growth and development of Northern Mexico are also on display (open Tues.-Sun. 9am-1pm and 3-7:30pm; admission

5 pesos). Across the street is the **Plaza Solidaridad,** which hosts performing groups every Sunday at 6pm. For a schedule of upcoming festivals and musical events at the Plaza Solidaridad and the nearby **Plazuela 27 de Septiembre,** consult the **Secretaria de Cultura y Acción Social** (tel. 5-04-05, ext. 38 or 39), in front of the tourist office. Adjoining the Plaza Solidaridad is the **Santuario del Sagrado Corazón de Jesús,** Los Mochis's oldest church. The **Cinema 70** is on Blvd. de la Plaza.

---

### Time Out: Topolobampo

Topolobampo is a decent place to spend the day, especially if you're stuck in life-less Los Mochis and willing to dish out the cash for an excursion—just about the only worthwhile activity there. When Albert Owen set out to forge his socialist utopia, he certainly didn't envision today's Topolobampo, a small fishing village helped along by the tourists who swim with many dolphins the port's warm waters and check out the wildlife in the bay. From the bus station, hang a left and follow the street to the shore, where boats and taxis run trips to the outlying attractions. For 70 pesos, a boat will usher you to **Playa El Maviri,** a fairly well-developed beach. Perhaps more interesting is **El Farallón,** a distant island where sea lions and pelicans run (er, swim and fly) free, and a hill juts out to the waters. While there are no beaches on island, snorkeling and swimming are still possi-ble. A full-day boat trip runs a wallet-shrinking 500 pesos round-trip for 5-6 peo-ple. Other destinations include the **Cerro de los Patos,** an area rife with ducks, the **Copus,** a large beach with fine sand, and the **Isla Verde,** a shallow lagoon.

---

# ■■■ MAZATLÁN

Mazatlán (pop. 314,000) means "place of the deer" in Nahuatl. A less appropriate name can hardly be imagined, since there is nothing even remotely pastoral or rumi-nant about this city. The only wildlife present—genus *Gringusmaximus,* species *norteamericanus*—roams the beaches in large herds.

Mazatlán is truly a city divided. The old city is traditionally Mexican, with a *zócalo,* busy streets, and bustling markets that lend it a genuine charm. Nearby on the shore is the **Olas Altas** (Tall Waves) neighborhood, with a peaceful beach, pleasant streets, and grand old hotels that evoke Mazatlán's glory days. Eight kilometers or so up the Avenida del Mar, however, lies another city entirely—the **Zona Dorada** (Golden Zone), home to high-rise hotels, dollar-dishing Americans, and patroniz-ingly friendly tourism agents. While Olas Altas is pleasant and the old city has its redeeming qualities, the Zona Dorada might depress some—with its Disney-castle clubs, pleasure palaces, time-share condos, overpriced gift shops, clubs, and offen-sive sights such as eight-year-olds selling cigarettes—but the honeymooners, Califor-nians, and families that come to swim and surf waters and pristine beaches of the Zona Dorada would argue otherwise.

Despite its eventful past, Mazatlán now offers little of historical or cultural interest to the traveler. The city's greatest assets are gifts of nature—glorious sunsets, a glit-tering ocean, and wide beaches. The Zona Dorada, spread along a highway, matches its Floridian prototypes gift shop for gift shop but boasts lower prices and nicer beaches. But it is Old Mazatlán and its shore that the *mariachis* evoke when they sing the classic bittersweet song of lost youth in Mazatlán.

## ORIENTATION

You can enter or leave Mazatlán by car, train, ship, or plane, but the bus is still the most economical way to get in and out of the city. The **bus station** is three blocks behind the Sands Hotel and about 2km north of Old Mazatlán. The area around the bus station, with several reasonably priced hotels and restaurants, along with a good beach and the vital "Sábalo" bus line only three blocks away, makes a convenient home base. You can catch the downtown-bound "Insurgentes" bus at the stand one block off the beach across from the chicken barbecuer.

On the far eastern edge of Mazatlán, the **Ferrocarriles del Pacífico** train station opens an hour before departures and closes soon after arrivals. Head for the better part of town: the yellow "Insurgentes" bus or the green, beat-up "Cerritos-Juárez" will take you to and from downtown. **Sematur** (tel. 81-70-20 or -21) operates passenger ferries every day but Saturday and Thursdays to and from Baja California's La Paz. The Sematur office and dock are on the southern end of Carnaval, which runs south from Ángel Flores. Meeting the ferry requires a hot 20-minute walk from *el centro;* the blue "Playa Sur" school bus (1.40 pesos) makes the trip, and for 8 pesos so will a taxi. Sematur accepts reservations up to a month in advance during the high season (Dec., July, and Aug.); make reservations at least two weeks ahead of your scheduled departure date. In any case, tickets are sold only on the day of departure, so be sure to reach the office at least two hours early to procure a spot, as capacity is limited to 40 people (open daily 8am-3pm).

The Mazatlán **airport** is 30km south of the city. The "Central Camionera" bus brings arrivals to their hotels, but no bus returns to the airport; resign yourself to a 72-peso (72 pesos?!) cab ride.

Built on a rocky spur jutting southwest into the Pacific, Old Mazatlán's downtown area surrounds and spills north of the *zócalo.* The main street running east-west is **Ángel Flores,** the southern boundary of the *zócalo.* Further south, the **malecón** follows the shore line. It starts as **Olas Altas** on the south end near Old Mazatlán, and it runs to the Zona Dorada 8km north, serving is the Zona Dorada's one main street; there it is called **Avenida del Mar.** In between the two areas, to the south of the fisherman's statue and north of Olas Altas, it is called **Paseo Clausen;** and to the far north, past Valentino's in the Zona Dorada, it's **Sábalo. El Cid Resort** is king of glitz in the Zona—it's a world unto itself.

Mazatlán's efficient **bus system** makes getting around the city a breeze. At some point, all municipal buses pass the public market on Juárez, three blocks north of the *zócalo;* if you get lost, you'll eventually return to familiar territory. The most useful bus line is the "Sábalo-Centro"; serviced by smaller, white, air-conditioned express buses, this line runs from the downtown market to Olas Altas and to Playa Sábalo in the Zona Dorada. The "Cerritos-Juárez" bus continues up to Playa Bruja at Puerta Carritos. The "Insurgentes" route services the bus and train stations, and "Playa Sur" goes to the ferry dock, lighthouse, and Olas Altas. Fare is 1.20-1.40 pesos; buses run every 15 minutes from 5am-11pm, and all fares rise by 10 centavos after 8pm. Feel free to wave down a bus at any point on its route—no official stops exist. For late-night disco hopping, you'll have to take a cab or a *pulmonía,* an open vehicle which resembles a golf cart that putters along at 60mph blasting raucous music. Always set the price before you commit yourself to a ride; standard fare between Old Mazatlán and the Golden Zone is 10 pesos. If you want to save the fare, it'll take you over an hour to walk the long path between the two sections, after which you may truly call yourself a man (or woman).

## PRACTICAL INFORMATION

**Tourist Office:** Olas Altas 1300 (tel. 85-12-20 or -21; fax 85-12-27). Walk down Ángel Flores past the *zócalo* until you reach the beach, and turn left—the office is in the big, beige Bank of Mexico complex, large and air-conditioned weekdays, with Mazatlán maps. Mucho English spoken. Open Mon.-Fri. 8:30am-2pm and 5-7:30pm, Sat. 9am-1pm.

**Police:** (tel. 84-44-99), on Rafael Quelna in Colonia Juárez. **Tourist Police** pass their days at Gabriel Ruíz and Santa Mónica (tel. 14-84-44). **Tourist Assistance:** 91-800-90-392.

**Post Office:** Juárez at Ángel Flores (tel. 81-21-21), across from the *zócalo. Lista de Correos.* Open Mon.-Fri. 8am-7pm. **Postal Code:** 82000.

**Telephones:** *Caseta* at Serdán 1512 (tel. 85-39-11; fax 85-01-08). International collect calls 8 pesos per min. Open 24 hrs. Public touch-tone phones are scattered throughout downtown and hotel lobbies. Small black pay phones accept old 100-peso coins or new centavo coins. Beige plastic phones take Mexican bank cards

MAZATLÁN

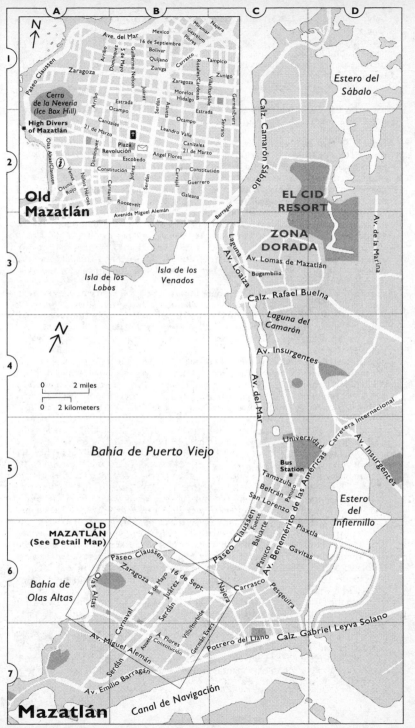

**Old Mazatlán**

N

Paseo Claussen
Zaragoza
Ave. del Mar
Cerro de la Nevería (Ice Box Hill)
High Divers of Mazatlán
Olas Altas/Claussen
Osuna
Venus
Rojo
Niños Héroes
Carnaval
Roosevelt
Avenida Miguel Alemán

Arribo
Domínguez
5 de Mayo
Guillermo Nelson
Juárez
Estrada
Ocampo
Canizales
21 de Marzo
Domínguez
Escobedo
Constitución
Serdán
Serdán
Azueta
Serdán

México
16 de Septiembre
Bolívar
Quijano
Zúniga
Zaragoza
Morelos
Hidalgo
Ocampo
Leandro Valle
Plaza Revolución
Angel Flores
Carnaval

Miramar
Gastelum
Flores
Najera
Carrasco
Rosales/Cárdenas
Villa/Iturbide
Tampico
Zúnigo
Estrada
Ocampo
Canizales
21 de Marzo
Constitución
Guerrero
Galeana
Carvajal
Germán Evers
Serrano
Barragán

Calz. Camarón Sábalo
Estero del Sábalo
EL CID RESORT
ZONA DORADA
Av. Lomas de Mazatlán
Bugambilia
Av. Loaiza
Calz. Rafael Buelna
Laguna del Camarón
Av. Insurgentes
Av. del Mar
Av. de la Marina

Isla de los Lobos
Isla de los Venados

N

0     2 miles
0     2 kilometers

Bahía de Puerto Viejo

Universidad
Carretera Internacional
Av. Insurgentes
Bus Station
Tamazula
Pánuco
Beltrán
San Lorenzo
Paseo Claussen
Fuerte
Baluarte
Pánuco
Av. Benemérito de las Américas
Piaxtla
Gavitas
Estero del Infiernillo

OLD MAZATLÁN (See Detail Map)

Bahía de Olas Altas

Paseo Claussen
Zaragoza
Olas Altas
Carnaval
5 de Mayo
Serdán
Juárez
16 de Sept.
A. Flores
Constitución
Villa/Iturbide
Germán Evers
Najera
Carrasco
Pesqueira
Av. Miguel Alemán
Serdán
Av. Emilio Barragán
Potrero del Llano
Calz. Gabriel Leyva Solano

Canal de Navegación

**Mazatlán**

only. Stainless-steel **LADATELs** are the best for international calls. **Telephone Code:** 64.

**Telegrams:** (tel. 81-22-20), in the same building as the post office. Open Mon.-Fri. 8am-7:30pm, Sat. 8-11am.

**Consulates: Canada,** Loaiza at Bugamblia (tel. 13-73-20), in Hotel Playa Mazatlán.

**Currency Exchange:** Banks throughout town exchange Mon.-Fri. 8:30-11am, and many have **ATMs.** *Casas de Cambio* are open all day in the north section of downtown.

**American Express:** (tel. 13-04-66; fax 14-13-62), in the Balboa Plaza Centro Comercial on Camarón Sábalo just before Balboa Towers. Open Mon.-Fri. 9am-6pm, Sat. 9am-1pm.

**Airport: Rafael Buelna International Airport,** 18km south of the city. **Aeroméxico,** Sábalo 310-A (tel. 14-11-11 or 91-800-36-202). To Mexico City (976 pesos), Los Mochis (549 pesos), Ciudad Juárez (876 pesos), Guadalajara (507 pesos), Hermosillo (1026 pesos), Monterrey (915 pesos), and Tijuana (986 pesos). **Mexicana,** on B. Domínguez and Av. del Mar (tel. and fax 82-77-22). To Denver (4 per day, US$316), Puerto Vallarta (7 per day, 477 pesos), Los Cabos (350 pesos), and Mexico City (821 pesos). **Delta** (tel. 82-41-55 or 82-13-49; fax 82-13-56). To Seattle and Fairbanks. **Alaska Airlines** (tel. 95-800-426-0333; fax 85-27-30). To San Francisco (7 per day, US$348) and Los Angeles (7 per day, US$274). **Aero-California,** El Cid Resort (tel. 13-20-42 or -18). To La Paz (7 per day, 411 pesos), Tijuana (7 per day, 976 pesos), Mexico City (818 pesos), and Guadalajara (491 pesos). All plane times and fares change frequently; be sure to call for the most up-to-date information.

**Train Station:** (tel. 84-67-10), in Colonia Esperanza on the eastern edge of town. One train leaves each day for Culiacán (*primera* 26 pesos, 3hrs., *segunda* 9 pesos), Obregón (*primera* 76 pesos, 10hrs., *segunda* 25 pesos), Hermosillo (*primera* 107 pesos, 16hrs., *segunda* 36 pesos), Nogales (*primera* 123 pesos, 18hrs., *segunda* 46 pesos), and Guadalajara (*primera* 70 pesos, 13½hrs., *segunda* 23 pesos).

**Bus Station: Transportes del Pacífico** (tel. 81-51-56) runs north to Los Mochis (21 per day, 6hrs., 75 pesos) via Culiacán (3hrs., 42 pesos), Guamuchil (5hrs., 59 pesos), and Guasave (5½hrs., 66 pesos). To Santa Ana (16 per day, 16hrs., 176 pesos) via Navojoa (9hrs., 102 pesos), Cd. Obregón (10hrs., 113 pesos), Guaymas (11hrs., 131 pesos), and Hermosillo (12hrs., 151 pesos). To Tijuana (15 per day, 26hrs., 240 pesos) via Nogales (18hrs., 184 pesos), Caborca (19hrs., 190 pesos), and Mexicali (24hrs., 240 pesos). South to Tepic (17 per day, 4hrs., 42 pesos) via Rosario (1hr., 10 pesos), Escuinapa (1½hrs., 13 pesos), and Acaponeta (2hrs., 22 pesos). To Mexico City (16 per day, 17hrs., 182 pesos), via Guadalajara (7hrs., 81 pesos), and Querétaro (15hrs., 145 pesos). **Elite** and **Transpacífico** (tel. 81-38-00) are slightly cheaper for some fares but runs less frequently, to Guadalajara (11am, 7:30, and 10pm, 7hrs., 81 pesos), Mexico City (10am, 17hrs., 159 pesos), Nogales (3:30pm, 18hrs., 184 pesos), and Tijuana (11am, 2, and 6:30pm, 26hrs., 255 pesos) and all points in between, including Culiacán (40 pesos), Guaymas (121 pesos) and Mexicali (229 pesos). 10 buses per day leave for Los Mochis (5am-3pm), and three more leave for Culiacán (6:30am-5pm). **Chihuahuenses** (tel. 81-53-81), along with **Transportes del Norte** and **Estrella Blanca** at the same number, run to Durango (7 per day, 8am-3am, 7hrs., 56 pesos), Guadalajara (8hrs., 94 pesos), Mexico City (6 per day, 11am-9pm, 18hrs., 211 pesos), Monterrey (10am, 18hrs., 177 pesos), Nogales (1pm, 20hrs., 224 pesos), and Tijuana (1:30 and 2:45pm, 26hrs., 258 pesos). In short, you can probably get a bus anywhere to the north or south within an hour of arriving at the bus station (if it's not sold out). The nicest buses are owned by Chihuahuenses, Elite, and del Norte; Estrella Blanca and del Pacífico are a step down.

**Ferry: Sematur** (tel. 81-70-20 or -21), port and office located at the end of Carnaval, south of *el centro*. To La Paz (3pm, 17hrs., *salón* 91 pesos and *turista* 181 pesos). Children aged 2-11 travel half-price. See Baja California: Getting Around, By Sea on page 117 for an explanation of the classes of ferries. You would do well to purchase tickets in advance at a local travel agency.

**Car Rental: Hertz,** Sábalo 314 (tel. 13-60-60, airport office 85-05-48; fax 13-49-55). Must be 21 years old.

**Laundromat: Lavafácil** (tel. 81-36-90), across from the bus station in the same pink building as the Hotel Fiesta. Wash 3.50 pesos, 10-min. dry 3.50 pesos. If they do it for you, it's 20 pesos per load. Open Mon.-Sat. 8am-4pm.

**Red Cross:** Zaragoza and Corona (tel. 85-14-51).

**Pharmacy: Farmacia Union,** Domínguez and Constitución 28 Sur (tel. 81-32-31), one block from Plazuela Machado. Open Mon.-Sat. 8am-9pm, Sun. 8am-3pm.

**Hospital: Clínica Siglo 21,** Domínguez 2301 (tel. 85-54-18), at Morelos, near Zaragoza park.

**Emergency:** tel. 06.

## ACCOMMODATIONS AND CAMPING

In the good ole' days, budget hotel rooms in Mazatlán cost about as much as those in other Mexican cities. Of late, many have jacked up their prices to resort levels. Nonetheless, high-quality cheap rooms do exist; simply avoid the Golden Zone, where rates are exorbitant even at the shabbiest joints. Budget hotels concentrate around three areas: in Old Mazatlán along the three avenues east of the main square (Juárez, Serdán, and Azueta); around the bus station; and on the pleasant waterfront area along Olas Altas, west of the center of Old Mazatlán. Large groups can even find cheap beds on Sábalo, near the beaches. Look and ye shall find.

The busiest seasons in Mazatlán are Christmas and the month following *Semana Santa.* At these times of year, check in early. At other times, prices are negotiable, especially for extended stays. Summer nights in Mazatlán are typically hot and humid; always inspect your room's ventilation system before paying. Also, traffic noise can become oppressive in Mazatlán, so avoid taking a room on the street.

RVers note: there's a trailer park, **La Pesta** (tel. 83-53-10), on Av. Rafael Buelna.

### Olas Altas

Back in the 1950s, long before wily developers began constructing multi-million-dollar pleasure pits along the north shore, the focal point of Mazatlán's fledgling resort scene was Olas Altas, a winding one-kilometer road hugging the shore southwest of town. Regal hot spots, built in the colonial style, still grace the old strip, but the majority of Mazatlán's tourists now bypass their aging displays, choosing instead the flashy young hotels from the north. Olas Altas is now a welcome oasis from the grime and noise of downtown or the frosted hair of the Golden Zone.

**Hotel Belmar,** Olas Altas 166 (tel. 85-11-11). Reminiscent of a resort of yesteryear, the opulent and assertive Belmar boasts hazy marble floors, dark wood paneling, and arches lined with colorful tiles. Monstrous, spotless, and nicely air-conditioned rooms with monstrous bathrooms. Match other guests ping for pong at the table tennis table. A swimming pool, deck, rocking chairs, and barber shop complete the picture. Oh, and there's parking available. Check-out 1pm. Singles with A/C and TV 60 pesos, with ocean view (no A/C) 70 pesos. Doubles with A/C and TV 70 pesos, with ocean view (no A/C) 80 pesos. AmEx, MC, Visa accepted.

**Hotel La Siesta,** Olas Altas Sur 11 (tel. 81-26-40 or 81-23-34, toll-free 91-800-69-770; fax 13-74-76). A jungly central courtyard spills over into the rooms. Slackers afflicted with trendy *ennui* can toy with the A/C, TV (10 extra pesos per night), or phone, or just lounge on the balcony overlooking the sea. Check-out 1pm. Singles 70 pesos. Doubles 85 pesos. Ask for a room with a view. AmEx, MC, Visa.

### Old Mazatlán

This is the noisier part of town and the hotels here are farther from the beach. In Mazatlán, that means you can't spit in the ocean from your window, so rooms here are on the cheap side. This area, especially the cathedral square, is well-trafficked after sundown—mainly by old men watching passers-by—and therefore somewhat safer than other parts of town. But if the discos are your scene, cabs will cost more from here than from the hotels west of the bus station.

MAZATLÁN

**Hotel del Río,** Juárez 144 or 2410, at Alejandro Quijano (tel. 82-46-54) is a few blocks from the shore. Offers nice 'n clean rooms and bathrooms. Stretch out on a pink wooden bed while a fan revolves rhythmically above your head. Look into my eyes. You're feeling sleepy. Singles 30 pesos. Doubles 50 pesos.

**Hotel San Fernando,** 21 de Marzo 126 (tel. 82-59-80), between Azueta and Serdán. Look forward to the tall ceilings and soft beds. Flamingoed bedspreads provide a touch of kitsch. Unfortunately, some walls are rotting, and the A/C leaks out holes in the windows, but still keeps the room cool. A good deal. Check-out noon. Singles 40 pesos. Doubles 50 pesos.

### Near the Bus Station

Hotels in this area are close to sandy beaches and the ritzy Golden Zone, and some rooms boast ocean views. Be warned: prices here are steep.

**Hotel Club Playa Mar,** Av. de Mar 139 (tel. 82-08-33), on the *malecón*. Sip piña coladas while lounging in the large swimming pool and admiring the tropical decor of the alcove which surrounds you. All classy and clean rooms offer A/C, modern TV, a private bath, and a bar-like area, with fridge and *agua purificada*. Parking available. Check-out 1pm. Singles and doubles 90 or 100 pesos, depending on TV type and bed size. Credit cards accepted.

**Hotel Emperador** (tel. 82-67-24), on Río Panuco across from the bus terminal. Four-story (not 4-star) hotel offers clean bathrooms and firm beds on concrete slabs. Basic and small but scrubbed and tiled rooms with A/C 60 pesos for 1-2 persons; without the luxuries 40 pesos for 1-2 persons; add 10 pesos for each additional person. MC, Visa accepted.

**Hotel Cabínas,** Av. del Mar 123 (tel. 81-57-52), also on the *malecón*. Run-down rooms adorned with paintings of clowns and Mexican dancers. Apartment suites for up to 6 guests with kitchen and ocean view rented on weekly basis (130 pesos per night). This joint is very popular with Mexicans—reservations are recommended. Otherwise, singles 50 pesos, doubles 60 pesos.

## FOOD

Mazatlán's restaurants serve up everything from standard *comida corrida* to charbroiled T-bone steak, a *gringo* favorite. Of course, most menus are glutted with "Mexican classics"—spicy guacamole, crisp nachos dripping with cheese, and *jalapeños*. Many eateries here are relatively cheap, although, like everything else, food prices escalate as you get sucked north toward the Golden Zone. Enjoy your meal with *Pacífico* beer, the pride of Mazatlán.

### Olas Altas

**Restaurant Fonda Santa Clara,** Olas Altas 66 (tel. 81-64-51), near Hotel Belmar. Sit outside on the low wooden chairs. Sip the local *Cerveza Pacífico*. Slip into a zen-like trance while listening to the rhythmically crashing waves. The seafood soup (19 pesos) is a meal in itself, but if that isn't enough, there's always *camarones mexicanos* (mexican shrimp, 24 pesos). On Sundays, you can sample the house specialty, *paella* (Spanish yellow rice with seafood, chicken, *chorizo*, and vegetables) for 25 pesos. Open daily 7am-11pm. MC, Visa accepted.

### Old Mazatlán

The busy **public market,** between Juárez and Serdán, three blocks north of the *zócalo,* serves the cheapest meals in the area. If you need a headless pig, this is the place. But quality meals such as jumbo shrimp, *antojito* platters, and steak can be had for staggeringly cheap prices—almost always under 10 pesos. *Comida corrida* runs a bargain-basement 5 pesos. Snacking opportunities exist outside in the *loncherías* and taco stands.

**Café Pacífico,** Constitución 501 (tel. 81-39-72), across from the Plazuela Machado. This famous pub is a relic, with all the charm of grand Old Mazatlán: good food

MAZATLÁN

and drink, a dark, artsy atmosphere, chummy service, and damn good music. A large-screen TV with ESPN distracts you, and cold A/C and a pool table add to the fun. Food is light and snacky—try the crab *al natural* (20 pesos) or the platter of assorted cheeses (18 pesos). Eat at the café (or outside on the Plazuela sidewalk seats), then see it on the front of Sinaloa promotional literature. Open daily 10am-midnight. AmEx, MC, Visa accepted.

**La Casa de Ana,** Constitución 515 (tel. 85-28-39), next to Café Pacífico. A mere 15 pesos buys you an enormous vegetarian lunch, including soup, salad, vegetable main course, beans, dessert, and *agua fresca*. They've washed the lettuce in *agua purificada* and disinfected it. Open Mon.-Sat. 8am-10pm, Sun. 8am-6pm.

**Santa Fe Restaurant,** 5 de Mayo at 21 de Marzo (tel. 85-13-45). Where the elite meet in Old Mazatlán. Demure waiters, decked out in green-and-white threads, weave quietly between ritzy tables. If you feel like letting out a long, happy groan, enter the air-conditioned room and order the charcoal-grilled chicken (28 pesos) or Santa Fe fish fillet (38 pesos). Try the Sunday brunch all-you-can-eat buffet, with breakfast and meat dishes, served from 7:30am-noon (25 pesos). Open 7am-10pm. Pay with a credit card, get a mint in return.

## North to the Golden Zone

As you move north, prices soar and *norteamericano* culinary influence becomes more pronounced. Look no further if you crave Caesar salads and *gringo* company.

**El Mambo Lonchería,** Espinoza Ferrusquilla 204 (tel. 85-04-73), across from the bus station. Mexican pottery, hanging seashells, eclectic art, a macaw, and a parrot that speaks more Spanish than some of the guests. Tasty, large, and cheap meals. Beware of the howling buses passing by. Shrimp (in several different styles) 18 pesos. *Huevos rancheros* 8 pesos. Open daily 7am-7pm, Sun. 7am-3pm.

**Restaurant Roca Mar,** Av. del Mar at Isla de Los Lobos (tel. 81-60-08), in the Zona Dorada. Like most of its neighbors along the beach, this place offers a full bar and a traffic-obscured view of the crashing waves. Prices tainted by tourism. Shrimp cocktail 19 pesos. Grilled fish 29 pesos. Open daily 10am-1am.

## SAND AND SIGHTS

Mazatlán's greatest asset is its 16km of beach. Just north of Old Mazatlán and along Av. del Mar sprawls **Playa Norte.** The *playa* is a decent stretch of sand if you don't mind small waves and the stares of local *machos* who play soccer here. Solo women should consider doing their swimming farther north. As you hone in on the Golden Zone, the beach gets cleaner, the waves larger, and Playa Norte eases into **Playa Las Gaviotas.** Just past Punta Sábalo, in the lee of the islands, basks **Playa Sábalo,** whose great waves and manicured golden sand are enjoyed to the point of abuse by crowds of *norteamericanos*. Most area beaches are patrolled by lifeguards, who use a color-coded flag system to inform bathers of local conditions. Air-conditioned "Sábalo-Centro" buses pass by all of these beaches.

As Playa Sábalo recedes to the north, crowds thin rapidly and you can frolic on the glorious beaches all by yourself. Take the yellow "Sábalo bus" to the last stop and walk left for the beach; you'll be at nearly deserted **Playa Bruja,** with tons of beautiful sand and four- to six-foot waves all to yourself. Swim at your own risk: there are no lifeguards. Camping is permitted, but be cautious after dark and camp in groups whenever possible. Solo women should avoid Playa Bruja, as assaults have been reported.

**Yate Fiesta harbor cruises** (no alcohol, lots of music) depart daily at 11am for a three-hour tour of Mazatlán by sea. Tickets (30 pesos, 25 pesos for children 5-10 years old) are sold at the yacht office (tel. 85-22-37 or -38; fax 85-04-15). To get there, take the "Playa Sur" bus to the end of the first dock, near the lighthouse.

For a 360° view of Mazatlán, the sea, and the surrounding hills, climb to the top of **El Faro,** the second-tallest lighthouse in the world. Once off the Playa Sur bus, hike up the twisting dirt road to the lighthouse. The walk (about ½hr.) is almost unbear-

MAZATLÁN

able in the summer; avoid the heat by ascending in the early morning or late evening.

The **Acuario Mazatlán,** Av. de los Deportes 111 (tel. 81-78-15 or -16), keeps piranhas and other feisty fish (249 breeds in all) in a slew of cloudy tanks. The aquarium, the largest in Latin America, also hosts performing sea lions and birds, and sports displays on fishing. The pet pigeons in the aviary are less interesting than the hooded orioles, bar-vented wren, and social flycatchers in the surrounding trees. The Acuario is one block back from the beach and north of the Sands Hotel; the turn-off is marked by a shimmering blue sign (open daily 9:30am-6:30pm; admission 18 pesos, 8 pesos for children aged 3-13).

Mazatlán's **tower divers** don't quite match the exploits of the cliff divers in Acapulco, but their acrobatic plunges are nevertheless extraordinarily dangerous. Performances take place daily from 10-11am and 4:30-5:30pm or whenever people are around to watch, weather and tides permitting, 50m from the **Monumento Mujer Mazutleca.** The best viewing angles are just south of the towers; on days when the water is too rough for diving, climb the tower to watch the waves break below. Walk to the waterfront on Zaragoza and head south to get to the towers. Be forewarned that the divers will not perform unless they can pull in a sufficient number of "tips" beforehand.

William Blake saw the universe in a grain of sand and eternity in an hour. You too may get bored at the beach. In this case, don't abandon Mazatlán—just hop on one of the boats to the **Isla de la Piedra,** where locals go to escape the crowds. Boats leave from the wharf on Av. del Puerto at Gutiérrez Najera. Buses to the wharf depart from near the public market (1.40 pesos). To walk there, take 21 de Marzo from the cathedral past Serdan to the water, then turn left on Av. del Puerta (3 pesos round-trip). **Islas Venados** (Deer Island) is a relatively deserted scrap of land with fine diving; catamaran boats leave for the island from the Agua Sports Center in the **El Cid Resort** (tel. 13-33-33, ext. 341) in the Golden Zone (10am, noon, and 2pm, 40 pesos). Waterpark mania has hit Mazatlán with the new **Mazagua** (tel. 88-00-41), located north of the Golden Zone near Puerta Cerritos. Go bonkers in the wave pool or shoot down slippery slides (open daily 10am-6pm; 35 pesos, children 3 and under free). To get there, take a "Cerritos Juárez" bus.

## ENTERTAINMENT

Hordes of *norteamericano* high schoolers ditch the prom and hit Mazatlán yearly for the opportunity to try to look ten years older, twist, and shout (and drink). Supply rises to meet demand, and more than a dozen discos and bars clamor for *gringo* greenbacks. Inside, only the occasional Mexican rock tune will remind you you're in a foreign country. If you address bartenders or bouncers in Spanish, they'll smile, pat you on the head, and answer in near-perfect English, never forgetting to address you as *amigo.* Ask them about their "business hours" and they'll stifle a laugh: these clubs keep the music pumping as long as the pesos stream from your pockets.

**Bora-Bora** (tel. 86-49-49), on Paseo del Mar at the southern end of the Golden Zone, next to the beach. Jammed with touring teenagers clad in neon (or nothing at all) and dancing on the bars. Those so inclined may dance in cages. Clubbers in search of more wholesome activities can head for the volleyball court and swimming pool. Fri.-Sun. cover 30 pesos. Drinks 8-12 pesos. Open daily 8pm-4am.

**Valentino's** (tel. 8-14-66), in the same building as Bora-Bora, caters to a more upscale and older crowd. Dancing and drinks, of course, are what packs 'em in. Open daily 8am-4am.

**Pepe Toro,** Av. de las Garzas 18 (tel. 14-41-66). Caters to gay men. The dance floor starts hopping after 11pm. Open daily 7am-2am.

**El Toro Bravo,** Av. del Mar 550 (tel. 85-05-95). Watch would-be cowpokes drink their bladders full, attempt to ride the bucking saddle, then slink off to the toilet, where the pokes will puke. A twentysomething crowd. Cover 10 pesos, 30 pesos when a live band takes the stage. Open daily 9pm-4am.

# Northeast Mexico

With an assortment of border towns, former colonial settlements, and the congested urban center of Monterrey, Northeast Mexico encompasses a land of remarkable contrasts. But long before there were slap-happy gringo revelers to cross the Río Grande or any semblance of industrial development, Spanish colonists scattered themselves here in the late 16th century, fighting floods, disease, and natives in their determined attempts to expand their empire.

In more recent times, the destiny of the *noreste* has been shaped by its unique position between Texas and the rest of Mexico; first lodged amidst the 19th-century Mexican-American conflicts, the region is now heir to the cultural legacy of two distinct lifestyles. And as NAFTA further erodes the border between the U.S. and Mexico, the cities of the Northeast must rise to the challenge of promoting both tourism and investment. Saltillo provides a colonial oasis for frazzled urbanites; Monterrey, the giant industrial complex, draws conventions and commerce; Tampico begrudgingly offers a salty port city experience; and Reynosa and Matamoros, the quintessential border towns, continue to struggle fiscally yet are always eager to please *gringo* tourists. The Northeast offers Mexico in a microcosm—extreme poverty, decaying and new-found grandeur, and a proud heritage.

## ■■■ BROWNSVILLE, TEXAS

Brownsville (pop. 110,000) has the feel of an old country-western movie, complete with arid streets, men sporting cowboy hats and polished leather boots, and a hot climate that makes a high-noon showdown completely understandable. But beyond this 100% *gringo* façade lies a pervasive Mexican influence—you can hear it in the bicultural lilt that colors most conversations. As the site of the first battle of the Mexican-American war, and now as a vital junction in the wake of the North American Free Trade Agreement (NAFTA), Brownsville has been shaped throughout its history by its contact with neighbors south of the border.

### ORIENTATION

The strikingly monochromatic streets of downtown Brownsville form a grid alongside a large bend in the Río Grande near the **International Bridge.** Route 4 from the northeast (International Blvd.) and Route 415 from the northwest (Elizabeth St.) converge at the tip of this bend. Running north-south, U.S. 83 and 77 cut through the middle of the city. Boca Chica Blvd. (U.S. 281 and 48) swoops from the Midwest to Brownsville. South Padre International Airport is at the eastern extreme of the city. Having paid attention in seventh-grade history class will now prove beneficial, as the streets north of Elizabeth St. (Brownsville's active commercial thoroughfare) are named for American presidents, starting with Washington and tapering off just before the Great Depression. Cross-streets are numbered beginning at Palm Blvd. and run east-west from this point.

Local buses, which travel long routes to all areas of Brownsville, run from 6am-7pm and cost 75¢; all buses leave on the hour or the half-hour from City Hall, which is on E. Washington St. between E. 11th and E. 12th. Look for the schedule by the window at the east end of the building or call 548-6050 for route and schedule information—be prepared to practice that Spanish.

### PRACTICAL INFORMATION

**Chamber of Commerce:** 1600 E. Elizabeth (tel. 542-4341). Loads of practical advice, plus the invaluable *Guide to Brownsville.* Smattering of brochures. Open Mon.-Fri. 8am-5pm.

**Brownsville Convention and Visitors Bureau:** 802 Farm Rd. (tel. (800) 626-2639 or 546-3721), at Central Blvd., adjacent to the Sunrise Mall and near Motel 6. Friendly and knowledgeable staff will load you down with incredible quantities of maps and brochures. From City Hall, take the "Jefferson Central" or "Los Ebanos" bus. Get off near the highway across from the pyramid-shaped tan building. Open Mon.-Sat. 8am-5pm, Sun. 9am-4pm.

**Police:** 600 E. Jackson (tel. 548-7000), 24 hrs. **Post Office:** Elizabeth St. and E. 10th. Open Mon.-Fri. 7am-9pm.

**Telephone Area Code:** 210

**Telegrams: Western Union,** 2814 International Blvd. (tel. 542-8695). Send or receive telegrams, messages, and money orders. Open daily 7:30am-8pm.

**Currency Exchange: Express Money Exchange,** 801 International Blvd. (tel. 548-0303), exchanges traveler's checks. Open daily 10am-6pm. *Casas de cambio* litter International Blvd., all offering nearly identical rates.

**Airports: Brownsville and South Padre International Airport,** at 700 S. Minnesota (tel. 542-4373). Taxis to downtown US$9. Currently offers five flights a day to and from Houston (departing Brownsville at 6am, 11:55am, 1:50pm, 4:45pm, and 7:05pm; departing Houston at 11:15am, 1:15pm, 4:25pm, 6:50pm, and 9:20pm). Less convenient is **Valley International Airport** (tel. 430-8600), in Harlingen, Texas, 25mi. (42km) northwest of Brownsville. From Brownsville, a taxi to the airport runs US$40-45. The bus charges US$24 for the lonesome cowpoke plus $12 a head for company. Some get free rides from the airport to Brownsville on one of the vans to the expensive hotels. Both airports are served by **Continental** (tel. (800) 231-0856).

**Bus Stations: Greyhound,** 1134 E. Charles St. (tel. 546-7171). Luggage locker US$1 per day. To McAllen (8 per day, 2hrs., US$10), Laredo (2 per day, 6hrs., US$17), Houston (5 per day, 9hrs., US$19), Dallas (6 per day, 12hrs., US$49), and San Antonio (7 per day, 7hrs., US$31). Schedule changes frequently; call ahead. Reservations can be made 1 day in advance. **Valley Transit Company,** 1305 E. Adams (tel. 546-2264), at 13th St. Lockers available for 75¢ per day. To Laredo (7:15am and 3:15pm, 6hrs., US$17), McAllen (every hr., 1:15pm-5:15pm, also 7:15pm and midnight, 2hrs., US$9), and Del Río (8 per day, US$51).

**Market: H.E.B. Store #1,** 924 E. Elizabeth (tel. 542-4191), across the street from the post office. Open Mon.-Sat. 7am-9pm.

**Laundromat: Holiday Laundry** (tel. 542-9002), Elizabeth and West 6th. About ½ mi. (1km) NW of the Int'l Bridge. Self-service wash US$1 per load, 50¢ per dry.

**Pharmacy: Maldonado's,** 1201 E. Adams (tel. 541-8122). Open Mon.-Fri. 9:30am-6pm, Sat. 9:30am-2pm.

**Emergency:** 911.

## ACCOMMODATIONS

Lacking the amenities of most American motels, lodging in Brownsville gently jostles the southbound traveler into the reality that is Matamoros hotel life. Brownsville prices, however, are certainly more American than Mexican. Expect to pay US$25-40 for a single in the downtown area; most national chains await several blocks east for slightly more. Although infinitely more convenient, the downtown area is more dangerous at night than the distant area along the North Expressway.

**Cameron Motor Hotel,** 912 E. Washington (tel. 542-3551). Take refuge from the interminable heat and relax in the inviting lobby/lounge. Upstairs are functionally furnished rooms with bath, TV, A/C, and telephones—enough equipment to drown out the noise from the couple next door. Singles US$32. Doubles US$45.

**Motel 6,** 2255 North Expressway (tel. 546-4699, fax 546-8982), off U.S. 77 and 802. The enticing advantages of a national chain (cable TV, free shampoo) might be worth the jaunt miles away from the heart and soul of Brownsville. US$29, US$6 second person, US$3 each additional person.

## FOOD

Catering primarily to local residents, Brownsville restaurants serve up the ever-popular Tex-Mex cuisine. Capitalist Darwinism thrives here; each armed with a unique *salsa* and their own ruthless posse of devoted patrons, cafés struggle to survive.

**Lucio's Café,** 1041 E. Washington (tel. 542-0907). Possibly the most popular eatery in Brownsville, the air at Lucio's is filled with conversation and the sounds of Mexican hits from the jukebox. House specialties include the *caldo de res* (beef soup, US$2.75) and *menudo* (beef tripe soup, US$3.75). While it specializes in Mexican food, Lucio's offers a full menu for all tastes. Ice-cold A/C. Open 24 hrs.

**Rutledge's Restaurant,** 1126 E. Washington, located in a narrow (read: 4ft.) alleyway between two buildings. Next to Zepeda hardware. Locals claim everyone has eaten at this burger-lover's mecca. With a wide selection under US$2, the history of this establishment is secondary to its unique atmosphere and great food.

**Texas Café,** in Market Square, adjoining City Hall (tel. 542-5772). The somber murals of Brownsville circa 1890 are appropriate for this café, a local institution for nearly 80 years. Perfect for a quick bite before you hop on the bus. *Enchiladas, menudo,* and simple grill food all under US$3.50. Open 24 hrs.

## SIGHTS

While visitors to Brownsville often see only a run-down border town, Brownsville is home to one of the top zoos in the nation for rare and endangered species, as well as several museums honoring the city's prominent role in American history. The **Gladys Porter Zoo,** 500 Ringgold St. (tel. 546-7187), off E. 6th St., offers a 31-acre tropical sanctuary where most animals live in open quarters surrounded only by waterways. The collection includes lowland gorillas, Sumatran orangutans, and white rhinos. Admission US$5.75 for adults, US$2.75 for children. Open daily 9am-8pm, though tickets are sold only until 5:30pm.

Housed in the old Southern Pacific Railroad Depot, the **Historic Brownsville Museum,** 641 E. Madison (tel. 548-1313), emphasizes the military legacy of the region (open Mon.-Sat. 10am-4:30pm, Sun. 2-5pm; admission US$2, US$.50 for children under 16). For a quick dose of Brownsville history, visit the **Stillman House Museum,** 1305 E. Washington St. (tel. 542-3929), where Concepción "Kino" Camarillo, the museum's caretaker for 46 years, will greet you at the home of Brownsville's founder. Renovations have restored this brick Greek Revival structure to its 1850s splendor (open Mon.-Fri. 10am-noon and 2-5pm, Sun. 3-5pm).

# TAMAULIPAS

# ■■■ MATAMOROS

The brightly-painted letters "H Matamoros" are barely discernible on many a pink storefront in this city (pop. 350,000). Like the formerly vivid façades, now faded by sun and rain, the significance of the letter "H" has been obscured by the passage of time. It refers to the title given to Matamoros—"Unconquerable and Heroic City"—after its residents quelled a separatist attack following the end of the Mexican-American War. In the years before the war, Matamoros had become an international commerce center, a legacy preserved today by the overzealous souvenir-shop owners who prey upon incautious foreign travelers. Contemporary fiscal realities are sorely visible just blocks from the *centro*—citizens are clutching at hope for the economic windfall promised by NAFTA.

## ORIENTATION

Matamoros lies 38km west of the Gulf Coast on the Río Bravo. Route 2, which follows the course of the river northwest to Reynosa (100km) and Nuevo Laredo

(350km), also passes through the center of Matamoros. Local buses (1.50 pesos) run from the airport to the city center every hour from 5:30am to 8:30pm, dropping off passengers at the corner of Abasolo and Calle 12, 6 blocks northwest of the plaza. Taxis charge 40 pesos for the journey into town—be prepared to haggle and agree on a price before entering the vehicle. Until 7pm, downtown-bound buses depart regularly from the train station for 1 peso.

If walking (beware of overwhelming heat) or traveling by car from Brownsville, you must cross the **International Bridge,** located at the northernmost part of Matamoros. Upon arrival in Mexico, you will pass the customs and tourist offices. To reach the center of town from the border area, take one of the *colectivos* labeled "centro" (1 peso). Most await passengers past the customs office and to the right, against the white wall. Taxi drivers will try to charge exorbitant rates to the market area, but the persistent should be able to whittle them down to 5-10 pesos.

In the center of town, streets form a grid pattern: numbered *calles* run north-south, named *calles* run east-west. The pedestrian mall, where vendors hawk their wares, lies between Calles 6 and 7 on Abasolo. The main plaza lies two blocks east, down Gonzalez. The International Bridge and its immediate area lie in a crook of the Río Grande; while the *Zona Rosa* is located 2 blocks north of Hidalgo near Calle 6. Calle Obregón twists from the bridge towards the crossing with Calles 5 and higher, which lead to the market. West of Calle 7 it becomes Calle Hidalgo. South of Hidalgo, the east-west streets are (from north to south) Iturbide, Herrera, Bustamante, Bravo, Matamoros, Abasolo, Gonzalez, Morelos, Guerrero, and Independencia. If you're returning to the border, catch a *pesero* (.80 pesos) marked "Puente.".

---

### Afta' NAFTA

On January 1, 1994, the North American Free Trade Agreement (NAFTA) took effect with the full support of President Bill Clinton of the United States, Prime Minister Brian Mulroney of Canada, and President Carlos Salinas de Gortari of Mexico. The treaty eliminated the tariffs, quotas, and subsidies that had protected Mexican industry and agriculture since the 1940s. Because of NAFTA, smaller Mexican-owned businesses are slowly being driven out of business by *maquiladoras,* U.S.-owned assembly and automotive-sector factories. On the other hand, freer trade means cheaper consumer goods for financially strapped Mexicans—a blessing in a nation plagued by constant inflation. Increased competition may eventually reap profits for cities in Northeast Mexico, but development is now exacting high human and environmental costs.

---

## CROSSING THE BORDER

The Mexican government publishes a series of pamphlets (available at the immigration office at the border or at most tourist centers) that detail the rules and regulations for entering the country. Although enforcement is decidedly lax, it's best to avoid problems at the border by preparing yourself in case of a (rare) inspection.

The two best options for crossing the border are by foot or in a private car whose entire documentation is with you. See "Driver's License and Vehicle Permits" on page 7. Due to prohibitive increases in insurance rates, few buses and taxis have crossed the border since 1989.

A 100m-long bridge joins Matamoros and Brownsville. Pedestrians pay 25¢ or .80 pesos to leave either country. Crossing by foot is as easy as dropping in a quarter and pushing through a turnstile. Autos pay US$1 or 32 pesos, but be sure you've checked your insurance before you cross—most U.S. insurance is null and void in Mexico. To get a three- or six-month permit at the border, you must show a driver's license, proof of citizenship, documentation showing ownership of the car, and license plate identification and registration. If you don't own the car yourself, bring a letter or rental contract to prove it's not stolen. The fee for the permit is determined on the spot according to the value of the car (you may unexpectedly find that you are driving a treasure chest), and can be paid in cash or with any major credit card. If you're going to Matamoros just for the day, park on the U.S. side and walk.

U.S. citizens need to obtain a **tourist card (FMT)** for travel beyond Matamoros. An FMT can be obtained at the immigration office to the right directly after the International Bridge or in the Matamoros bus station. Regulations state that a passport or birth certificate with ID are necessary to secure an FMT. If the officer marks only 30 days on your card, ask for more now—you don't want to have lots of explaining to do later at a highway checkpoint.

## PRACTICAL INFORMATION

Mexico does not observe U.S. Daylight Savings Time and thus, runs one hour behind Brownsville from April to October.

**Tourist Offices: Delegación Turismo.** Get your Matamoros maps in Brownsville at the Brownsville Chamber of Commerce, only two blocks from the border. Enterprising local cab drivers have established the shack-like **Informacíon Turismo** across from the Gran Hotel Residencial, where Obregón turns into Hidalgo; maps and other essentials are rarely available. Next door is the **Módulo,** which has a few brochures and pricey guides. No set hours—just pray that it's open.

**Police:** (tel. 2-03-22 or 6-07-00). Some English spoken. Open 24 hrs.

**U.S. Consulate:** 232 Calle 1 (tel. 6-72-70 or 6-72-72), at Azaleas. Open Mon.-Fri. 8am-10am and 1-4pm.

**Post Office:** In the bus station. Open Mon.-Fri. 8am-2:30pm. **Postal Code:** 87361.

**Telephones: LADATELs** are scattered along Abasolo between Calle 7 and 8 and in Plaza Hidalgo. Between González y Morelos and on Calle 5 is **Computel,** with long distance service and fax. Open Mon.-Sat. 8am-10pm. **Telephone Code:** 891.

**Telegrams:** Next to the post office in the bus station. Open Mon.-Fri. 9am-1pm.

**Currency Exchange:** Banks line Calle 6 and the Plaza Hidalgo. Open for exchange 9am-1:30pm. **ATMs** make advances on Visa at **Bancomer** (tel. 13-90-00) at Matamoros and Calle 6. **Red Banorte,** on the corner of Calle 6 and Morelos, offers a 24-hr. Cirrus **ATM.**

**Airport: Servando Canales Aeropuerto,** on Rte. 101, the highway to Ciudad Victoria, 5km south of town. **Aeroméxico,** Obregón 21 (tel. 13-07-02), offers service to (6pm, 1½hrs., 555 pesos) and from (3pm, 1½hrs., 555 pesos) Mexico City. Open Mon.-Sat. 10am-5pm.

**Train Station: Ferrocarriles Nacionales de México** (tel. 6-67-06), on Hidalgo between Calles 9 and 10. Slow daily service to Reynosa (13.5 pesos) and Monterrey (15.5 pesos) beginning at 9:20am. Buy a ticket ahead of time and arrive early for boarding. Crowds of vendors hop on at every stop to sell everything from tacos to ten-pound slabs of freshly butchered raw meat.

**Bus Station: Central de Autobuses,** Canales at Aguiles, off Calle 1. Any *pesera* (minibus) marked "Central" will pass the station; ask the driver to stop. Luggage lockers available in the 24-hr. restaurant for 6 pesos per day or 3 pesos for 2 hours. **Omnibus de México** (tel. 13-76-93), to Monterrey (12 per day, 4½hrs., 17 pesos), and Saltillo (12 per day, 71 pesos). **ADO** (tel. 12-01-81), to Veracruz with numerous stops in between (2 per day, 214.5 pesos), Tampico (2 per day, 8hrs., 82 pesos), and Tuxpan (1 per day, 121 pesos). **Noreste** (tel. 13-27-68) offers the cheapest and most frequent buses to Monterrey (16 per day, 4hrs., 55 pesos). Also offers frequent service to Reynosa (14 per day, 2hrs., 15 pesos). **Autobuses del Norte** (tel. 12-27-77), to Monterrey (7 per day, 4½hrs., 55 pesos), Saltillo (6 per day, 71 pesos), San Luis Potosí (3 per day, 113 pesos), and Mexico City (1 per day, *ejecutivo* 251 pesos; *primera*, 4 per day, 193 pesos).

**Market: Gigante,** directly across from the bus station, with a big red "G." Supermarket, general store, pharmacy, and cafeteria. Open daily 8am-10pm.

**Laundromat:** Iturbide 748 #202 (tel. 13-76-93). One block south of Hidalgo by Calle 7. Self-service wash and dry 4 pesos each. Open daily 7am-10pm.

**Red Cross:** Caballero at García (tel. 2-00-44). English spoken. Open 24 hrs. For emergency medical aid also try the **clínica** along Canales, 3 blocks from the Central de Autobuses toward the center of the city along Calles 4 and 5. Open 24 hrs.

MATAMOROS

**Pharmacy: Farmacia Aristos del Golfo,** on Calle 1 between Gonzalez and Morelos. Joined to the hospital. Cordial pharmacists speak limited English. Open 24 hrs. Many pharmacies in market area are open during the day.

## ACCOMMODATIONS

The stop, shop, and go attitude of many visitors to Matamoros is painfully apparent in the underdeveloped hotel trade. Although prices are entirely reasonable, expect the basics—and little more. The market area, where most of the budget accommodations are located, swarms with pedestrians until nightfall, after which one should take common-sense safety precautions.

**Hotel Majestic,** Abasolo 89 (tel. 3-36-80), between Calles 8 and 9 on the pedestrian mall. Not quite majestic, but solidly domestic. The brightly colored rooms conjure up vivid childhood memories of coloring eggs at Easter time. Despite the noise from the lobby and street, the soft beds and moderately clean atmosphere allow for a good night's rest. Singles 35 pesos. Doubles 45 pesos.

**Hotel Colonial,** Matamoros 601 (tel. 16-64-18), at Matamoros and Calle 6, across from Bancomer. The white exterior disguises unkempt, large rooms with that Matamoros *je ne sais quoi*. Between ceiling fans and checkerboard floors, however, there is enough comfort for a nice stay. Singles 32 pesos. Doubles 45 pesos.

**Hotel México,** Abasolo 87 (tel. 2-08-56), a few stores down from the Majestic. Yellow walls and refreshingly bare rooms emphasize the importance of the basics—running water and soft mattresses. Beware the street-side rooms. Singles 30 pesos. Doubles 60 pesos.

## FOOD

Caught between the two extremes of *gringo*-friendly restaurants and more local eateries, a safe bet in Matamoros is to follow the crowds at meal time. Several great smaller cafés are hidden between Calle 6 and Calle 9.

**Café y Restaurant Frontera,** Calle 6 between N. Bravo and Matamoros (tel. 3-24-40). Locals stop by to stare at the optical-illusion floor while digging into Mexican specialties for 7-10 pesos. Breakfast a bit less, larger meat and seafood entrees a bit more. Look for the heart-shaped sign. Open daily 7am-10pm.

**Cafetería Las Vigas,** Calle 8, between Morelos y Gonzalez 104 (tel. 13-99-05). Other than the huge omelettes (10 pesos) and most dinner fare—you name it, and you can have it for under 14 pesos—the music alone is enough to lower even the highest of stress levels. Breakfast specials 8-10 pesos.

**Cafetería 1916,** 191 Calle 6 (tel. 3-07-27), between Matamoros and Abasolo. Try *sincronizadas 1916* (flour tortilla with ham, chicken, and avocado) for 9.50 pesos or stay on the American thoroughfare of fried chicken (14 pesos). Dessert has been called "better than sex." You make the call. Open daily 10am-10pm.

## SIGHTS AND ENTERTAINMENT

Brash vendors pounce upon any sign of interest, so look both wary and weary. The old market, or **Pasaje Juárez,** has entrances on both Matamoros and Bravo between Calles 8 and 9. Bright *piñatas* and rows of glittering jewelry brighten the dim interior of **Mercado Juárez,** the new market, on Abasolo between Calles 9 and 10. Like its older cousin, the market overflows with souvenirs. The vendors in Pasaje Juárez are more eager to please and can be talked into a decent deal. Avoid succumbing to temptation, though—markets farther south offer higher quality and lower prices.

For a refreshing break from souvenir hunting, join the herds of *gringos* and sink into the ventilated, out-of-this-dirty-hot-world-if-only-for-a-few-short-hours atmosphere of **Las Dos Repúblicas** on Calle 9, between Matamoros and Abasolo (tel. 6-68-94; open daily 8am-8pm). This plush joint is geared toward pampering *gringos,* so don't be startled when the keyboardist starts hammering away at inexcusable renditions of "New York, New York." 18-oz. frozen Margaritas US$6; *piña de la casa* arrives in a real pineapple. You keep the pineapple, they keep US$7.

# ■■■ REYNOSA

Despite its growth from a 1749 Spanish colony to its present size of over 600,000, a small-town atmosphere and quiet charm have never left Reynosa. The surroundings recall memories of old Zorro movies—a celebration of Spanish and Mexican culture tempered only slightly by economic hardship. Unlike Matamoros, Reynosa downplays many of its sorely impoverished regions to create quite an appealing tourist trade from nearby McAllen, Texas. With industry and natural gas plants relegated to the outskirts of town, the *centro* is reserved for more urbane activities.

## ORIENTATION

Reynosa is 150km from Monterrey and 645km from Mexico City; it can be reached from McAllen, Texas by taking 23rd St. eight miles south into Hidalgo and then over the International Bridge. From Mexico, Route 2 from Matamoros and Route 40 from Monterrey both lead straight into town. The **Central de Autobuses** is located on Colón and Rubio at the southeast corner of town; the **train station** is at the southern tip of town on Hidalgo. *Peseros* run in nearly all directions for about .80 pesos; taxis will attempt to overcharge the unwary (and weary) traveler.

   **Hidalgo** is the chief north-south thoroughfare. Perpendicular to it from west to east are Allende, Zaragoza, Morelos, Matamoros, Guerrero, Méndez, and Colón. **Morelos** is the main east-west street, and perpendicular to it are Victoria, Díaz, Hidalgo, Juárez, Chapa, Canales, Mina, and Rubio.

## PRACTICAL INFORMATION

**Chamber of Commerce: Cámara de Comercio de Reynosa,** on Chapa and Allende. Open Mon.-Fri. 9am-4:30pm. The **Casa de la Cultura de Reynosa** next door is also extremely helpful to lost travelers.

**Police:** tel. 22-00-88 or 22-07-90.

**Post Office:** On the corner of Díaz and Colón by the train station. Open Mon.-Fri. 8am-8pm, Sat. 9am-1pm.

**Telephones:** Scattered throughout the plaza and Hidalgo marketplace; most are **LADATELs,** which make international calls. The east edge of the plaza (on Hidalgo) has a public fax office. Open 8am-10pm.

**Currency Exchange:** *Casas de cambio* are scattered all along Hidalgo and the plaza area, but most will not accept traveler's checks; the **Centro de Cambios "Reynosa"** Matamoros 505 (tel. 22-90-60), will. **Erika Viajes,** Ávila Camacho 1325, a decent trek from the plaza, provides most **American Express** services, including traveler's checks. **Bancomer Zaragoza,** on the west end of the plaza, offers 24- hr. Cirrus, Red, and Visa **ATMs.**

**Train Station:** Follow Hidalgo south from the main plaza for 6 blocks. Service to Matamoros (2:45pm, 2½hrs., 5.50 pesos) and Monterrey (11:40am, 4½hrs., 15 pesos). Transfer in Monterrey for further destinations.

**Bus Station:** On Colón at the southwest corner of town. Offers service to most major cities in Mexico and a few others further south. **Del Norte** offers *ejecutivo* and *primera clase* service to Monterrey (4 per day, 3hrs., 50 and 40 pesos), Mexico City (3 per day, 15hrs., 252 and 194 pesos), and Guadalajara (2 per day, 18hrs., 241 and 185 pesos). **Oriente** serves San Luis Potosí (6 per day, 96 pesos) and Tampico (7 per day, 6hrs., 91 and 82 pesos). **Omnibús de México** offers service to Monterrey (11 per day, 4hrs., 41 pesos), Saltillo (9 per day, 6hrs., 52 pesos), and Matamoros (14 per day, 2hrs., 17 pesos). **Noreste** serves San Luis Potosí (2 per day, 90.50 pesos) and Monterrey (15 per day, 4hrs., 41 pesos).

**Market: Gigante,** across from the bus station on Colón. Open daily 8am-10pm.

**Laundromat: Peña Villarreal Antonio,** Victoria Pte. 220 (tel. 22-42-34). Open Mon.-Sat. 8am-9pm.

**Red Cross:** tel. 22-13-14, on Boulevard Morelos, just south of town off Chapa.

**Pharmacy: Farmacias López** (tel. 22-14-16, fax 22-60-28) on Porfirio Díaz and Guerrero. Open Mon.-Sat. 7am-11pm. **Hospital: Hospital San Vicente** (tel. 22-50-93), on Zaragoza three blocks west of the plaza.

**Emergency:** tel. 06.

TAMPICO

## ACCOMMODATIONS

The many hotels around the plaza and *Zona Rosa* are pricey. Look for the best deals on south Díaz and Hidalgo streets near the train station.

**Hotel Avenida,** Zaragoza 885 Ote. (tel. 22-05-92). The central patio with the vivid chirping of birds is traditionally Mexican, but carpeted floors make this bargain very reminiscent of a U.S. chain. With its proximity to the main plaza and an A/C-TV combo, you just can't beat their prices. Singles 80 pesos. Doubles 95 pesos.

**Hotel Rey,** Díaz 556 Nte. (tel. 22-26-32), near the train station. The small, brightly colored rooms are amply furnished. Even the blue bathrooms are relatively clean and have hot water. Note, however, that A/C overshadows all in this steamy town, making the nearby roar of trains seem very insignificant. Singles 70 pesos. Doubles 80 pesos.

## FOOD

**Café Paris,** Hidalgo 815 (tel. 22-55-35). Elaborately woven seat cushions and oh-so-chic mirrored walls in this packed restaurant set the stage for a dining experience valued by locals as well as tourists. Breakfast tortillas and *enchiladas* 8-10 pesos, most meats 17-20 pesos. Don't miss the bar, where drinks run 6 pesos each. Open daily 7am-10pm.

**Café Sánchez** (tel. 22-16-65) on Hidalgo off the southwest corner of the plaza. Despite the classy paintings by Diego Rivera and the picture of Alameda Park, it is the food that really makes Café Sánchez shine. With a pastry/dessert cart and free sliced carrots and peppers dipped in vinegar as a precursor to great Mexican dishes (12-16 pesos), how can you go wrong? Open daily 7am-10pm.

**Café Veracruz,** Hidalgo 510 (tel. 22-12-68). Hidden behind brash vendors in the Hidalgo marketplace, Café Veracruz offers a wide selection of seafood platters. Three different types of fish and a soda go for 9 pesos. The dark atmosphere and blue neon lights give the feeling that you're getting away with something—i.e., the cocktail and seafood platter for 16.75 pesos. Open daily 10am-10pm.

## SIGHTS AND ENTERTAINMENT

There's nothing like the main plaza at nightfall, where couples, young and old, tend to congregate. The **Hidalgo marketplace** may not offer any substantial deals, but it is a great spot for people-watching. Also near the plaza is the **Casa de la Cultura de Reynosa,** which houses changing art exhibits and music recitals. For a sampling of Reynosa's history, visit the **Museo Histórico de Reynosa,** Ortega at Allende, which exhibits furniture, archaeological pieces, and photographs of the region.

The bars and clubs scattered about the *Zona Rosa* tend to be a very popular hang-outs for Mexican and American youths. Locals recommend **Pepe's, Concha,** and **Refrides,** but warn that most other clubs have had serious barroom brawl problems. For the truly adventurous, a **Patinadero** (roller-skating rink) is on Allende and Chapa (tel. 28-15-42). Open Mon.-Fri. 12:30-9pm, Sat.-Sun. 10am-10pm.

# ■■■ TAMPICO

While many travelers see Tampico (pop. 270,000) as little more than a pit stop in the race south, the city has had a remarkable history. Founded in the 16th century on the ruins of an Aztec village, Tampico was destroyed by pirates in 1623. Exactly 200 years later, Santa Ana ordered the city re-settled, citing its strategic location and excellent natural harbor. By the turn of the century, Tampico had become one of the two or three most important oil ports in the world.

If you've seen Humphrey Bogart in *The Treasure of the Sierra Madre,* you might think of contemporary Tampico as the dirty, unfriendly oil town that every *gringo* is itching to skip. Amenities have cropped up to make a brief stay tolerable for those heading south. The Plaza de Armas, with its vibrant greenery and live concerts in the early evening, provides refuge from the refuse-ridden streets. For an alternative escape, a nearby beach, **Playa Miramar,** is accessible by either the "Playa" or "Escollera" bus (1.50 pesos from López de Lara and Madero).

**Orientation and Practical Information** To get to the city center from the bus stop, take a yellow taxi (15-20 pesos), minibus (1.50 pesos), or *colectivo* (1.50 pesos, 3 pesos with luggage). The town is centered around the **Plaza de Armas** and the **Plaza de la Libertad,** which is currently walled off for construction work. To the north of the Plaza de Armas is **Calle Carranza,** to the east is **Olmos,** and to the south is **Díaz Mirón.**

The **tourist office,** Olmos Sur 101 (tel. 12-00-07), is on the second floor of the orange-and-white building east of the Plaza de Armas; enter just to the right of the ice cream stand, go up the stairs, and walk past the unemployment office (supposedly open Mon.-Fri. 9am-2pm and 3-7pm, but tourist officials tend to come late—or not at all—and leave early). The **police** (tel. 12-11-57 or 12-14-37) are located on Tamaulipas at Sor Juana de la Cruz. Call the **highway patrol** at 28-05-42. The **post office,** Madero 309 Ote. (tel. 12-19-27), is at the intersection with Juárez on Pl. de la Libertad (open for *Lista de Correos* and stamps Mon.-Fri. 8am-7pm, Sat. 9am-1pm). **Postal Code:** 89000. No LADATELs, but collect calls can be placed from **pay phones** in the plaza. **Telephone Code:** 12. The **U.S. Consulate,** Ejército Mexicano 503, Suite 203 (tel. 13-22-17), is in the northern *colonia* Guadalupe (open Mon.-Fri. 10am-1pm). Exchange currency at **Central de Divisa,** Hidalgo 215 Sur (tel. 12-90-00; open Mon.-Fri. 9am-6pm, Sat. 9am-1:30pm). Otherwise, try one of the many banks near the Plaza de Armas (most open Mon.-Fri. 9am-1:30pm). **Bánamex,** on Madero between Aduana and López de Lara, has a 24-hr. Cirrus/MC **ATM.**

**Trains** leave daily from the station in the small park at the corner of Héroes de Nacozari and Aduana (tel. 12-03-34), three blocks south of Pl. de Armas. Trains head to Monterrey (7:45am, 31.45 pesos) and San Luis Potosí (8am, 26.65 pesos). Connections offer service to Cuauhtémoc (3.30 pesos), Ciudad Victoria (14.10 pesos), San Juan (27.85 pesos), Ciudad Valles (8.40 pesos), and Ebano (3.30 pesos). The **bus station,** on Zapotal north of the city, has adjoining first- and second-class terminals. Facing the station from the road, first class is to the right and second class to the left. **Omnibus de Oriente** (tel. 13-45-47) serves Guadalajara (3 per day, 136 pesos), Querétaro (3 per day, 101 pesos), Reynosa (6 per day, 10hrs., 91 pesos), and San Luis (3 per day, 7hrs., 69 pesos). **ADO** (tel. 13-41-88) serves Jalapa (2 per day, 99.50 pesos), Matamoros (3 per day, 8hrs., 82 pesos), Puebla (3 per day, 96 pesos), Tuxpan (14 per day, 3hrs., 41 pesos), and Veracruz (13 per day, 118.50 pesos). **Futura** (tel. 13-46-55) serves Ciudad Victoria (7 per day, 37 pesos), Saltillo (9pm, 6hrs., 102 pesos), and Torreón (2 per day, 150 pesos).

The **Sixpack,** Díaz Mirón 405 Ote., three blocks east of the southeast corner of the Plaza de Armas (tel. 12-24-15), is a **market** which sells more than just beer (open daily 9am-10pm). If you need a pharmacy, try **Benavides** (tel. 19-25-25), Carranza 102 Pte., on the corner of Olmos at the northeast edge of the Plaza de Armas (open Mon.-Sat. 8am-11pm, Sun. 8am-10pm). The **Red Cross** (tel. 12-13-33 or 12-19-46) offers 24-hour ambulance service. English-speaking doctors can be found at the **Hospital General de Tampico,** Ejército Nacional 1403 (tel. 15-22-20 or 13-20-35), near the bus station. In an **emergency,** dial 06.

**Accommodations and Food** Quality budget hotels are rare in Tampico, but for those willing to pay an extra 20-30 pesos, many of the larger hotels provide excellent rooms. In the downtown area, there is **Hotel Capri,** Juárez 202 Nte. (tel. 12-26-80), between Calles Altamirano and Obregón. Clean, no-frills rooms are pleasantly livable, except for the missing toilet seat and noise from the street below (singles and doubles 40 pesos). An equally simple option near the bus station is **Hotel Allende,** Allende 122 (tel. 13-82-57). Exit the bus station to the right, take the first right, and walk uphill half a block (singles and doubles 42 pesos).

Seafood is the standard fare in Tampico; *cafetería de mariscos* is unavoidable. **Café Mundo,** López de Lara y Díaz Mirón (tel. 14-18-31), three blocks east of the

MONTERREY

Plaza de Armas, teems with regular customers. The menu is varied; most entrees come with beans, fresh bread, and coffee (15-17 pesos). *Torta de milanesa con queso amarillo* with french fries goes for 8 pesos; *orejita con papas rancheras* only 11 pesos (open 24 hrs.). Fans whiz away at **Cafetería Emir,** Olmos Sur 107 (tel. 12-51-39), where the red-and-white decor is accented by paintings of ships. Catch up on the latest *telenovela* while downing *tamales de pollo* (3.65 pesos each) or *enchiladas* (16.70 pesos; open daily 6am-midnight).

# NUEVO LEÓN

## ■■■ MONTERREY

Photocopying services operating from wooden shacks. Modest vendors occupying the steps of international banks. An architecturally avant–garde edifice rising beside an aging historic site. Elderly peasants begging at the gates of a fledgling public transit system. Towering modern buildings that try to measure up against the indomitable heights of the Sierra Madres. This is Monterrey—focused and formidable, smoggy and vibrant, a juxtaposition of wealthy entrepreneurs living just minutes away from members of a horribly impoverished underclass.

Since its modest beginnings in the late 16th century, Monterrey has known all too well that to slow down is to perish; this theme is ever-present in the energized, active lives of the 3.75 million *regiomontanos* who inhabit this important industrial base. Whether peddling watches along a commercial thoroughfare or striding, suit-clad, toward a new office in the *Zona Rosa,* citizens of Mexico's third-largest city are keenly aware of the importance of progress.

### ORIENTATION

As the largest city in northern Mexico, Monterrey serves as an important transportation hub. All **buses** in and out of the city pass through Monterrey's huge **Central de Autobuses** at Colón and Villagrán. To reach the city center from the bus station, simply take any bus going south on Pino Suárez, the thoroughfare to the left (east) as you exit the station. No. 18 stops at Pino Suárez and Colón and will let you off at the southern end of the central Gran Plaza. All local buses run from 6am-midnight. Easier still, walk two blocks east to the gray subway station at Cuauhtémoc and Colón. Take the **metro** (Line 2, 1.50 pesos) and get off at Padre Mier or Zaragoza.

The **train station** is at Calzada Victoria, six blocks west of the bus station. To get to the **bus station,** walk straight ahead on Victoria for two blocks, turn right on Bernardo Reyes, and then left on Colón. The bus and train stations are in the northern end of the city, 3km north of the *centro.*

Downtown, **Avenida Constitución** runs east-west along the Río Catarina, a 10km-long dry riverbed that has been converted into a series of athletic fields. The extensive grounds are a good place to kill a sleepy Sunday afternoon. From west to east, the largest streets running north-south across Constitución are Gonzalitos, Pino Suárez, Cuauhtémoc, Benito Juárez, Zaragoza and Zuazua. From north to south, streets running east-west and parallel to Constitución are Washington, 5 de Mayo, 15 de Mayo, Matamoros, Padre Mier, Hidalgo, and Ocampo. Around Morelos sprawls the *Zona Rosa,* bounded by Padre Mier to the north, Zaragoza to the east, Ocampo to the south, and Juárez to the west.

**Local buses** (1 peso) run with convenient regularity. Av. Benito Juárez is a good place to catch most buses. A bus stop is located on nearly every block; except for Constitución and Juárez, buses usually head in only one direction on any given street. Nearly all east-west streets and most north-south streets *west* of Juárez alternate in their directions. To get from the budget hotel area to the city center, Ruta #1 Central and Ruta #17 Pío X both run the lengths of Pino Suárez and Cuauhtémoc. To

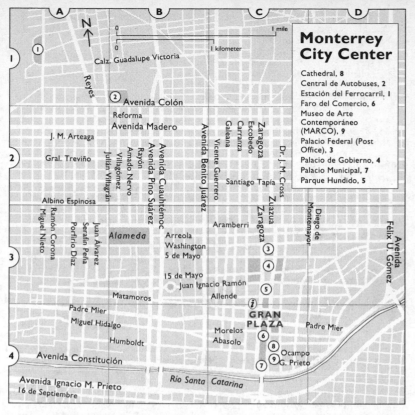

**Monterrey City Center**

Cathedral, 8
Central de Autobuses, 2
Estación del Ferrocarril, 1
Faro del Comercio, 6
Museo de Arte Contemporáneo (MARCO), 9
Palacio Federal (Post Office), 3
Palacio de Gobierno, 4
Palacio Municipal, 7
Parque Hundido, 5

get from the bus station to the Gran Plaza, Ruta #42 sails down Juárez and lets you off near the Palacio Municipal. Ruta #18 will also take you there. To get to points along Padre Mier, Hidalgo, or the Gran Plaza, be on the lookout for the Ruta #15 Macroplaza-Purísima bus. To reach points on the perimeter of the downtown area, Ruta# 69 circles the city and can be caught on Colón near the bus station. For more detailed route information, ask locals.

Although currently under-utilized by the bus-dependent locals, Monterrey's ever-expanding **subway** system provides cheap first-class service to the *Zona Rosa* as well as many east-west points along Av. Colón and north up Av. Simón Bolívar.

## PRACTICAL INFORMATION

**Tourist Office: Oficina de Turismo,** Zaragoza at Matamoros (tel. 345-08-70 or 345-09-02), also toll free from the U.S. (800) 235-2438 and in Mexico (91-800-83-222). Walk east down Matamoros; it's on the left just before the underpass. From the Gran Plaza, stairs lead down by the Congreso del Estado. Follow the blue "INFOTUR" signs for info and maps. English spoken. Open Tues.-Sun. 10am-5pm, but occasionally open on Mon.

**Police:** Arista and Washington, 3rd floor, for missing persons (tel. 340-77-77). To report theft or loss, contact police at the corner of Carranza and Roberto Martínez (tel. 345-11-11 or 345-30-46). Little to no English spoken.**Consulates: U.S.,** Constitución Pte. 411 (tel. 345-21-20), downtown. **U.K.,** Priv. Tamazunchale 104 (tel. 378-25-65). Both are open Mon.-Fri. 8am-5pm.

**Post Office:** Zaragoza at Washington (tel. 342-40-03), inside the Palacio Federal. Open for stamps Mon.-Fri. 8am-7pm, Sat. 9am-1pm; for registered mail Mon.-Fri. 8am-5pm. **Postal Code:** 64000.

**Telephones:** Most **LADATELs** are clustered in the *Zona Rosa;* long distance and fax service in the office on 5 de Mayo between Carranza and Galeana. No charge for collect calls. Open daily 9am-8pm. Most hotels also offer international services to guests for nominal fees. **Telephone Code:** 8.

**Currency Exchange:** Banks dot Madero near the budget hotels and flood the *Zona Rosa,* lining Padre Mier in particular, but many refuse to cash traveler's checks. Most open Mon.-Fri. 9am-1:30pm. **Casa de Cambio Trebol,** Padre Mier Pte. (tel. 342-21-40), across from the Banco Internacional, changes traveler's checks. Open Mon.-Fri. 9am-6pm, Sat. 9am-1pm. Traveler's checks 9am-2pm only, but they may run out of pesos.

**American Express:** Padre Mier Pte. 1424 (tel. 343-09-10), about 1.5km west of the *centro.* Take the #4 bus on Padre Mier from the *Zona Rosa.* Your best bet for changing AmEx checks. Open Mon.-Fri. 9am-1pm and 3-6pm, Sat. 9am-1pm.

**Airport:** Taxis charge 50 pesos for the 4km trip to the center, *colectivos* 40 pesos. Haggling for a lower price is occasionally possible. **Aeroméxico,** Cuauhtémoc 812 Sur at Padre Mier (tel. 343-55-60), to Guadalajara (8 per day, 489 pesos), Hermosillo (2 per day, 724 pesos), Mexico City (16 per day, 1½hrs., 496 pesos), and Villahermosa (2 per day, 956 pesos). **Mexicana,** Hidalgo 922 Pte. (tel. 340-55-11), to Mexico City (6 per day, 506 pesos). **Aerolitoral** (tel. 386-22-10), to Villahermosa (2 per day, 708 pesos). **American Airlines,** Zaragoza 1300 Sur (tel. 340-30-31). **Continental,** Insurgentes 2500 (tel. 33-26-82). All offices open Mon.-Fri. 9am-7pm, Sat. 9am-1pm. Make reservations at least 2-3 days in advance, more for weekend travel. Airfares subject to rapid change.

**Train Station: Región Noreste,** Calzada Victoria (tel. 375-46-04). Sometimes cheaper, but always slower than buses. To Matamoros (10 pesos), Mexico City (128 pesos), and Tampico (48 pesos).

**Bus Station:** Colón at Villagrán to Amado Nervo. The black hole at the center of a bus route universe. **Transportes del Norte,** (tel. 375-42-81) to Aguascalientes (5 per day, 9hrs., 102 pesos), Chihuahua (3 per day, 11hrs., 153 pesos), Guadalajara (5 per day, 10hrs., 145 pesos), Matamoros (5 per day, 4½hrs., 55pesos), Mazatlán (5 per day, 18hrs., 152 pesos), Mexico City (7 per day, 12hrs., 173 pesos), Querétaro (5 per day, 8hrs., 131 pesos), Reynosa (9 per day, 3hrs., 41 pesos), San Luis Potosí (11 per day, 6hrs., 82 pesos), Tampico (2 per day, 7hrs., 93 pesos), Zacatecas (8 per day, 5½hrs., 79 pesos), and an hourly service which runs 24 hrs. a day to Nuevo Laredo (47 pesos) and Torreón (5½hrs., 62 pesos). **Transportes Frontera,** (tel. 375-09-87) to Matehuala (14 per day, 4½hrs., 50 pesos), Mexico City (6 per day, 12hrs., 148 pesos), San Luis Potosí (14 per day, 6 hrs., 82 pesos), and Tampico (2 per day, 7hrs., 82 pesos). **Estrella Blanca,** (tel. 318-37-47) to Aguascalientes (6 per day, 102 pesos), Chihuahua (11 per day, 11hrs., 153 pesos), Guadalajara (6 per day, 10hrs., 145 pesos), Matehuala (15 per day, 4½hrs., 50 pesos), Mexico City (7 per day, 12 hrs., 173 pesos), San Luis Potosí (15 per day, 6½hrs., 82 pesos), and Tijuana (8pm, 419 pesos). **Rojo de Los Altos,** (tel. 374-72-73) next to Frontera, to Saltillo (every 15min., 24 hrs. a day, 13 pesos). **Futura** and **Turistar** have fewer, more luxurious buses (20-50 pesos more than above prices). The bus station has a 24-hr. pharmacy and an emergency medical unit.

**Market: Gigante,** on Colón, across from the bus station. Adjoining pharmacy. Open Mon. and Wed.-Sat. 9am-10pm, Tues. 9am-9pm. **Mercado del Norte,** also known as La Pulga. This endless maze of vendor stalls covers Reforma, the street just south of Colón. Entrance on Colón, two blocks east of the bus station. Everything from cologne to car tires is available. Haggle. Open from morning to dusk.

**Medical Emergencies and Assistance: Red Cross,** at Alfonso Reyes and Henry (tel. 342-12-12 or 375-12-12), 24 hrs. **Cruz Verde,** at Ciudad Madero and Ciudad Victorio (tel. 371-50-50 or 371-52-59). English spoken. Open 24 hrs.

**24-hr. Pharmacy:** In the bus station or **Benavides,** at Pino Suárez and 15 de Mayo. **Emergency:** Dial 06.

## ACCOMMODATIONS

Hotels conveniently located near the *Zona Rosa* inflate their rates to exploit tourists. Budget accommodations, catering more to local businessmen, are sprinkled throughout the underdeveloped area near the bus stations. Many rooms are full by early afternoon. Expect to find a moderately quiet fan-equipped room (with few or no bugs) for around 70 pesos. If you are staying in this area alone, take precautions when walking at night, since the streets become deserted around 10pm.

**Hotel Amado Nervo, S.A.,** Amado Nervo 1110 Nte. (tel. 375-46-32). Large, well-furnished rooms with full-length mirrors, toilet seats, and hot, giant-sized showers. Lounge areas offer ample relaxing space. Singles 63 pesos. Doubles 89 pesos.

**Hotel Nuevo León,** Amado Nervo 1007 (tel. 374-19-00). Despite the ever-present traffic below, the rooms come with plenty of space, soft beds, warm water and an attentive, helpful staff. Hallway phone available for use by patrons. Singles 65 pesos. Doubles 80 pesos.

**Hotel Conde,** Reforma Pte. 419 (tel. 375-71-59 and 372-18-79), a gray building concealed by the labyrinthine *Mercado del Norte*. From the bus station, take the Colón walkway. Walk one block south onto Reforma and four blocks east—Conde is on the left. Inviting, quiet rooms with rotary phones and color TVs are marred only slightly by the insect population. Singles 70 pesos. Doubles 92 pesos.

## FOOD

Barbecued meats, especially *cabrito* (goat kid), are a specialty of northern Mexico. Charcoal-broiled specimens in restaurant windows lure hungry passers-by. Popular dishes include *agujas* (collar bone), *frijoles a la charra* (beans cooked with pork skin, coriander, tomato, peppers, and onions), *machacado con huevos* (scrambled eggs mixed with dried, shredded beef), hot tamales, and for dessert, *piloncillo con nuez* (hardened brown sugar candy with nuts) or *glorias* (candy balls of goat's milk and nuts). Downtown Monterrey is littered with fast-food joints, while the bus station area is filled with cheap, but sometimes unsanitary restaurants.

**La Puntada,** Hidalgo 123 Ote. (tel. 340-69-85), east off Juárez in the *Zona Rosa*. Remarkably fast-and-friendly service is their hallmark. Designed for the Monterrey business person on lunch break, the service is fast, the atmosphere relaxing, and the conversation stimulating. Devour the ultra-fresh tacos, tortillas, and *hamburguesas* in an ultra-suave environment. *Chuletas de puerco* 14 pesos, tacos 10-11 pesos. Open daily 7am-10pm.

**Las Monjitas** (The Little Nuns), Escobedo 903 (tel. 344-67-13). In a devout country like Mexico, a restaurant in a dark, abbey-like building with servers dressed as nuns is entirely at home. While the prices of divinely inspired dishes of *carne asada* hover around 20 pesos, many lighter offerings are half as expensive. Amen. *Enchiladas* and *quesadillas* run about 12 pesos; most varieties of *flautas* 13 pesos. Open daily 8am-11pm.

**Restaurante Vegetariano Superbom,** Padre Mier 300 Ote., 2nd floor (tel. 345-26-63). Elevator music and earthy tones create an ambiance appropriate for the elite, but the prices are very pedestrian. Try the *comida corrida* (2 cheeses, rice, salad, and a fruit drink) for 14 pesos, or the breakfast buffet (20 pesos).

**El Cabrito,** Padre Mier 276B Pte. (tel. 345-12-30), off Cuauhtémoc. Quite possibly the place for a splurge: some of the best cuisine of the Northeast is available here—all prepared in an open kitchen with goat carcasses proudly hanging in the window. *Cabecitas* (head stew) is only 12 pesos, but *cabrito* (goat kid) and some of their finer carnivorous cuts run into the 30-peso range. Open daily 8am-10pm.

## SIGHTS AND ENTERTAINMENT

Monterrey's huge and loud **Gran Plaza** rubs visitors the wrong way. Revered architectural relics jostle with looming concrete structures, suggesting a kind of style-less collage. Yet by placing such prominent symbols of modernity side-by-side with historical sites, city planners demonstrate a commitment to honor the memory of the past even as Monterrey strides intrepidly into the future.

MONTERREY

The Gran Plaza is bounded by Washington on the north, Constitución on the south, Zaragoza on the west, and Zuazua on the east. At its northern extreme, just south of Washington, stands the **Palacio Federal,** which serves as the post office and is nearly hidden from sight by a ring of trees and an unkempt courtyard. Immediately to the south is the state capital building, the **Palacio de Gobierno,** a magnificent colonial structure graced by a columned front and a beautiful central courtyard. Outside sprawls the **Esplanada de los Héroes,** a plaza decorated with the statues of four famous Mexicans (Miguel Hidalgo stands at the northwest corner, Benito Juárez at the northeast, Morelos at the southwest, and Escobedo at the southeast). Soothing fountains mark the southern end of the plaza. South of the Esplanada is **Parque Hundido** (Sunken Park), a cool and verdant garden gateway for the city's young couples (isolated walkways on both sides aren't usually traversed by the solitary individual). A wall of water overlooks the park, and a monument to youth ironically faces away from the green depths, tactfully averting its eyes from the mature goings-on. Rising on both sides of the Parque Hundido and providing a harsh contrast to the park's natural overgrowth are three modern buildings: the colossal **Congreso de Estado** in which politicians cut deals, the **Palacio de Justicia,** where the blindfolded goddess carefully weighs both sides of local cases, and the **Teatro de la Ciudad** which offers experimental theater most nights of the week.

Further along the Gran Plaza sits **Fuente de La Vida** (Fountain of Life) which douses an immense statue of Neptune surrounded by cavorting nymphs and naiads. Under the potent Monterrey sun, the figures shine with a blinding brilliance. The most striking construction, however, is the bright orange **Faro del Comercio** (Lighthouse of Business) with its laser beacon atop that circles the skies at night. Built on the 100th anniversary of the Chamber of Commerce, all 30 meters of the lighthouse serve a purely symbolic purpose, a testament to the economic ambitions of Monterrey's leaders. Just across Zuazua from the Faro de Comercio is the resplendent, pale yellow **Catedral de Monterrey.** Forming the southern tip of the Gran Plaza is the **Palacio Municipal** and surrounding gardens. To the east lies the stylistically innovative **Museo de Arte Contemporáneo (MARCO)** (tel. 342-48-20), where changing exhibitions display the works of prominent Mexican painters, photographers, and other purveyors of art forms. An immense bronze dove guards the entrance. (Open Tues. and Thurs.-Sat. 11am-7pm, Wed. and Sun. 11am-9pm. Admission 10 pesos. Students with ID 5 pesos. Free Wed.)

The **Obispado,** former palace of the bishop of Monterrey, is now a state museum. The museum displays murals, paintings, and old weapons from the colonial era, but the decayed exterior and the view of the city from the site are more of a draw than the museum's collection (open Tues.-Sat. 10am-6pm, Sun. 10am-5pm; admission 10 pesos). Take bus #4 from Washington. Ask the driver to point out the stop.

The Cuauhtémoc Company, for over a century the major producer of beer in Monterrey, has converted one of its old factories into the **Jardines Cuauhtémoc,** one block south of the General Anaya subway stop on Line 2. The gardens are densely covered with trees and dotted with benches and tables. Sit in the shade, enjoy a complimentary *cerveza,* and think about Valenzuela's decayed screwball after visiting the three museums and the **Hall of Fame** (a collection of photographs and documents commemorating Mexico's baseball heroes) in the old factory.

The **Museo Deportivo,** part of the Hall of Fame, celebrates *charriadas* (rodeos), boxing, soccer, and bullfighting. Perhaps not surprisingly, the complex also contains a museum devoted to beer; located just to the north of the gate that leads into the gardens, the **Museo de la Cervecería** (tel. 375-22-00) foams over with beer culture artifacts, including beer mugs from various countries. An appointment must be made to see the brewery or the Museo de la Cervecería; check at other museums for information. The complex, with its red brick buildings and wild ivy, is reminiscent of K-House. The **Museo de Monterrey** adds just a dash of culture to the gardens with its tribute to leading Mexican artists and displays of modern artistic works.

Also worth a visit are the **Grutas de García,** 45km northwest of the city and accessible by car or bus. Once there, take the cable car railway in order to avoid the steep 700m uphill climb. Ticket for use of the cable car is included in the price of admission (open daily 9:30am-5:30pm, 20 pesos for adults, 12 pesos for children). The Grutas are a system of natural chambers; the dozens of sedimentary layers in their walls reveal that 50 or 60 million years ago the caves lay on the ocean floor. Take a **Transportes Monterrey-Saltillo** bus from the terminal; buses go to the Grutas de García only on Sundays and then only after 9am. The most convenient way to see the Grutas is on one of the organized OSETUR tours that leave from Ocampo and Escobedo behind Hotel Ancira every Thursday and Saturday, beginning at 1:30pm. (Ends 5:30pm back in Monterrey, 25 pesos per person. Make reservations by calling 47-15-33 or 47-16-14.)

# COAHUILA

## ■■■ SALTILLO

After a gorgeous trek through the mountains, Saltillo (pop. 700,000) materializes as the soothing colonial town of yesteryear. Unlike its booming neighbor, Saltillo retains the relaxing small-town feel that Monterrey has forsaken in its quest for economic prosperity. Few structures rise more than a few stories high, and some buses slow down and actually stop for pedestrians crossing the street. Saltillo's quiet charm and dry climate make it a refuge of sorts for harried *regiomontanos* and a pleasant destination for those en route to Mexico City or other tourist havens.

The capital city of Coahuila, Saltillo prides itself on its citizens and history. Two giants of Mexican history were born here—Venustiano Carranza, a revolutionary general dubbed the "father of the Mexican Constitution," and Francisco Madero, the first man to seize power from Díaz in 1911. The first inhabitants of the mountainous region surrounding the modern-day city were 400 Tlaxcalteca families, craftsmakers and weavers by trade. Brightly colored *sarapes* (woolen shawls) are still a symbol of the city's traditional lifestyle and distinctive culture, and Saltillo's streets burst with artistry and cultural pride from July 18 to August 3 during **Feria de Saltillo.**

### ORIENTATION

Nestled in a valley between the jagged Sierra Madre mountains, Saltillo lies 87km southwest of Monterrey, along the desolate Highway 40. Frequent buses plod to and from Monterrey, Guadalajara, San Luis Potosí, and Mexico City.

The **Central de Autobuses** is located about 3km southwest of the city center on Blvd. Echeverría Sur. Transport to and from the city center is cheap and easy. After you exit the bus terminal, cross the pedestrian overpass and catch minibus #10 from the small street perpendicular to the boulevard, on the side of Restaurant Jaslo. Make sure to ask if it's heading toward the *centro*. All buses cost .80 pesos and run daily 6:30am-11pm. Catch a return bus (#9) at the corner of **Aldama** and **Hidalgo,** a block down the street from the cathedral, in front of the entrance to the Mueblería Moderna furniture store. The train station is much closer to the city center (about 1km) but still a hike if you are laden with luggage.

Adequate, inexpensive lodging is available near the bus station, but most budget restaurants and sights of interest are located in the center of Saltillo, in or around the two main plazas. The center's streets form a slightly distorted grid not quite aligned with the four cardinal directions. The quiet **Plaza de Armas** contains the cathedral and is bordered by **Juárez** to the south and **Hidalgo** to the east. To the west **Plaza Acuña** is bordered by the narrow **Padre Flores; Allende** forms its eastern boundary. The oddly placed **Acuña** runs parallel to Padre Flores, one block west.

## PRACTICAL INFORMATION

**Tourist Office:** Acuña and Blvd. Francisco Coss (tel. 12-40-50), about 1.5km north of the center, in the old red railway station building. Accessible by the #1B minibus from the city center and train station. Relatively unhelpful and short on brochures, maps, and practical advice. Open daily 9am-5pm.

**Tourist Hotline:** tel. 91-800-90-392. For questions, problems, or emergencies.

**Police:** Treviño and Echeverría Ote. (tel. 15-55-61 and 15-51-62).

**Post Office:** Victoria 453 (tel. 12-20-90), after Urdiñola. Open for stamps and *Lista de Correos* Mon.-Fri. 9am-5pm, Sat. 9am-1pm. Other branches in the bus station and near the tourist office. Both open Mon.-Fri. 8am-3pm. **Postal Code:** 25000.

**Telephones: LADATELs** are few and far between. Collect and direct dial calls can be made from pay phones in the post office. Long distance calls paid for directly can be made from Café Victoria, Padre Flores 221. **Fax** available. Open daily 7am-10pm. Long distance lines in the bus station as well. **Telephone Code:** 84.

**Telegrams: Telecomm,** next door to the post office on Victoria. Open Mon.-Fri. 9am-5pm, Sat. 9am-noon. Office in bus station open Mon.-Fri. 9am-3pm.

**Currency Exchange:** *Casas de cambio* offer the best rates. Closest to the city center is **Casa de Cambio Coin,** Acuña 167 (tel. 14-12-96), across the street from Hotel San Jorge, which changes traveler's checks at decent rates. (Open Mon.-Fri. 9am-1:30pm and 3:30-6pm, Sat. 9am-1pm.) The banks which line Victoria, west of the Plaza de Armas behind the Palacio de Gobierno, will exchange dollars. Most are open 9am-1:30pm. **Bánamex,** at Allende and Ocampo, behind the Palacio de Gobierno, has a 24-hr. **ATM** that takes AmEx, MC, Visa, Cirrus, Plus, and more.

**Airport: Aeropuerto Plan de Guadalupe,** 20min. northeast of the city center off Hwy. 40. The **Saltillo Ramos Arizpe** bus from the bus station or along Acuña in the center can let you off nearby (until 10:30pm, 1 peso). A taxi from the *centro* will charge upwards of 20 pesos for the trip. **Tacsa** offers service to Piedras Negras (2 per day, 400 pesos) and Torreón (2 per day, 323 pesos). **Mexicana** offers an evening flight to Mexico City (7:45pm, 325 pesos). Tickets can be purchased at the travel agency in the Hotel San Jorge (tel. 14-95-84). Make reservations a day or two in advance.

**Trains:** E. Carranza, past the Alameda (tel. 14-95-84). Daily to Mexico City (10pm, 12hrs., 145 pesos first class, 102 pesos second class), and Piedras Negras (8:15am, 12-14hrs., 32 pesos).

**Bus Station: Central de Autobuses,** Echeverría Sur and Garza, accessible by minibus #9. **Transportes del Norte** (tel. 17-09-02), to Durango (5 per day, 8hrs., 99 pesos), Guadalajara (5 per day, 10hrs., 130 pesos), Mexico City (5 per day, 10hrs., 156 pesos), San Luis Potosí (4 per day, 5hrs., 77 pesos), Tampico (7pm and 10pm, 6hrs., 107 pesos), and Zacatecas (4 per day, 5hrs., 65 pesos). **Omnibus de México** (tel. 17-03-15) to Aguascalientes (8 per day, 6hrs., 87 pesos), Matamoros (6 per day, 7hrs., 71 pesos), Mexico City (2 per day, 10hrs., 157 pesos), and Reynosa (6 per day, 5hrs., 54 pesos). **Transportes Frontera** (tel. 17-03-16) to Guadalajara (6 per day, 10hrs., 131 pesos), Torreón (every 15min., 3½hrs., 35 pesos), and Zacatecas (hourly, 9:30am-8:30pm, also 12:30am and 1am, 5hrs., 56 pesos). **Autobuses El Águila** (tel. 17-01-83) to Celaya (2 per day, 11hrs., 114 pesos), Hermosillo (8:15pm, 25hrs., 296 pesos), Piedra Negras (5 per day, 77 pesos), and Uruapan (6:45pm, 13hrs., 184 pesos).

**Ángeles Verdes (Green Angels):** (tel. 12-40-50). A staff of English-speaking mechanics provide car repair assistance.

**Market: De Las Fuentes,** Treviño 328 (tel. 12-85-54), between Allende and Acuña, across Blvd. Echeverría Sur. Open Mon.-Fri. 9am-8pm, Sat. 9am-9pm, Sun. 9am-3pm. **Soriana,** at Blvd. Francisco Coss (tel. 12-30-13). Open Mon.-Sat. 9am-8pm, Sun. 9am-3pm. Both are small grocery stores.

**Laundry: Laundrymatic,** Mutualismo Pte. 310 at Allende, at the end of the gravel road just south of the tourist office. Self- and full-service wash and dry. Open Mon.-Sat. 9am-1pm and 3:30-7:30pm.

**Pharmacy:** In the bus station. Open 24 hrs.

**Red Cross:** Cárdenas and Rayón (tel. 14-33-33), northeast of the city center. Open 24 hrs. No English spoken.

**Hospital: Hospital Universitario,** Madero 1291 (tel. 12-30-00). Open 24 hrs. No English spoken.
**Emergency:** 06.

## ACCOMMODATIONS

Boulevard Luis Echeverría, which runs along the bus station, teems with places to rest your head. Although most of the hotels clustered in this area offer liveable and inexpensive rooms, downtown establishments boast more convenience and comfort for similar prices. Tourists tend to flock to the *centro,* while the Echeverría clientele consists largely of Mexican businessmen.

**Hotel Saade,** Aldama Pte. 397 (tel. 12-91-20 or 12-91-21), 1 block west of Pl. Acuña. Earth tones dominate the clean, well-furnished, and quiet rooms in this modern hotel. Solid location places you in the heart of it all. *Agua purificada* and hot water to chill or char. Singles 65 pesos. Doubles 75 pesos. TV 10 pesos extra.

**Hotel Premier,** at the corner of Allende and Múzquiz (tel. 12-10-50). Bright, spacious rooms and an attractive lobby with murals depicting the town's history are the perfect recipe for a pleasant stay. Rooms come with color TV and bottled water. Singles 80 pesos. Doubles 90 pesos.

**Hotel Urdiñola,** Victoria 207 (tel. 14-09-40), behind the Palacio de Gobierno. A marvelous central staircase stands before a charming courtyard, but its grandeur is reflected in the prices. Rooms are well-furnished with a matching set of mahogany furniture. This *gringo* retreat is equipped with *agua purificada,* TVs, and phones. Singles 92 pesos. Doubles 104 pesos.

**Hotel Central,** Echeverría 231 Ote. (tel. 17-00-04). Shiny yellow hallways open onto clean but somewhat drab rooms. The monotonous brown lacquer on the walls is enough to put you to sleep. Singles 40 pesos. Doubles 60 pesos.

**Hotel Saltillo,** Echeverría 249 Ote. (tel. 17-22-00). Immaculate white rooms come with phones, TVs, and hefty price tags. Disco, hair salon, and 24-hr. seafood restaurant. Singles 90 pesos. Doubles 100 pesos.

## FOOD

Like the residents of every other Northern Mexican city, *saltillense* claim that their *cabrito* and *carne asada* outstrip the other town's dishes. Perhaps because of its gastronomic chauvinism, Saltillo has stood its ground against fast-food chains and *cafeterías* that plague Monterrey. Be sure to sample *pan de pulque* (bread made with cactus juice), a Saltillo specialty. Restaurants on Allende and Carranza cater more to the tourist masses, while the cafés on smaller streets remain a local refuge.

**El Guaripas Taco-Grill,** Allende Nte. 746 (tel. 12-69-49), 6 blocks down Allende from Plaza Acuña. A gallery of Western pop culture. Mexican and U.S. favorites served up under the watchful eye of Einstein, Elvis, and Ronald Reagan. Shockingly pink tablecloths. Eight-course buffet Mon.-Sat. noon-4pm, 15 pesos. All you can drink 25 pesos. Open Mon.-Wed. 10am-6pm, Thurs.-Sun. noon-midnight.

**Restaurant Principal,** Allende Nte. 702 (tel. 15-00-15), just up the street from El Guaripas. A haven for the lover of *cabrito; cabrito en salsa de tomate* is 25 pesos. The large central space and open second floor balcony provide an invigorating, after-the-hunt feel while you down *cabecito* (19 pesos). Open daily 8am-9pm.

**Café and Restaurant Arcasa,** Victoria 215 (tel. 12-64-24). Beyond the inviting doors lies a hybrid between the family-run café and the sophisticated restaurant. Lunch 5-7.50 pesos. Mexican staples 9-12 pesos. Open daily 7am-midnight.

## SIGHTS

You won't tire from running from sight to sight in Saltillo; the city's few worthy points make for sedate yet satisfying enjoyment. Saltillo offers more beautiful and better-preserved architecture than other northern cities, and there are plenty of spots to lounge and enjoy the festive atmosphere. The **Plaza de Armas,** Saltillo's main plaza, breaks from the mold that shaped the crowded and noisy *zócalos* of larger Mexican cities. This paved plaza contains neither trees nor benches, though four statuesque torch-bearing females guard a central fountain. On the east side of the plaza stands the Churrigueresque **cathedral,** built over a 55-year period in the latter half of the 18th century. The cathedral's intricately wrought gray stone façade and equally elaborate interior retain a remarkable degree of detail to this day.

On the south side of the plaza is the **Cavie Museum,** which houses exhibits of regional literature and art, which change every two to three months (open Tues.-Sun. 9am-7pm; free). Knock on the door of the adjoining IEBA (Instituto Estatal de Bellas Artes) if the museum is closed during normal hours. The **Palacio de Gobierno** stands on the west side of the plaza and houses several murals depicting scenes from Mexican history (open Mon.-Sat. 10am-6pm, Sun. 11am-6pm; free).

Budding ornithologists might investigate the newly-opened **Museo de las Aves** (tel. 14-01-67), home to members of most species of birds native to the Americas, including several that are rare or nearly extinct. You, too, can learn about bird migration patters, songs, and the mechanics of flight. Take either Allende or Hidalgo uphill from the Plaza de Armas; the museum is housed in the large, canary yellow building in front of the parking lot. (Open Mon.-Fri. 10am-6pm, Sat. 2-6pm, Sun. 11am-6pm. Admission 5 pesos adults, 2 pesos children. Free Wed.)

**Plaza Acuña,** two blocks northwest of the Plaza de Armas, bustles with activity. Vendors spill out of the **Mercado Juárez,** in the northwest corner of the plaza, while xylophonists hammer away and guitar players and accordionists rove through the crowds. Almost romantic in a hyperactive sort of way, the plaza is a great place to people-watch or browse through the stalls that offer souvenir items, including hats, rugs, ukuleles, and colorful *sarapes* (open daily 8:30am-8pm).

Once you've had enough of the plaza scene, try relaxing (or napping) in the **Alameda,** just west of the city center (follow Victoria west from Plaza de Armas), or the **San Francisco Park and Church,** south of Plaza de Armas at Juárez and Cepeda. The refreshingly green Alameda is filled with winding paths; during the cooler hours of the day, these paths are navigated by herds of joggers.

Perched on a hill overlooking the city, **Plaza México** (or **El Mirador**), offers an astonishing panoramic view of the whole area and the unconquerable mountains around. Take Miguel Hidalgo uphill for a kilometer, turn left on General Cepeda and follow it for another 20-50m, turning onto the winding Gustavo Espinoza and up to the small plaza with benches and old street lamps. Just west of El Mirador stands the **Iglesia del Ojo de Agua,** a sparkling white church set up off the ground. Within the church is the spring which gave Saltillo its name. When Spaniards first saw the water spurt out of the ground here, they called the spot *saltillo,* or "little jump." It's considered good luck to drink the water here.

# ■ Central Mexico

## ZACATECAS

### ■■■ ZACATECAS

A charming city is the last thing a traveler expects to find in the prickly desert of Central Mexico—yet out of nowhere rises Zacatecas. The arid surroundings augment the colonial beauty of this town, perched between, on, and over mineral-laden hills. The lifeblood of Zacatecas once flowed through veins of silver. A silver trinket, given to early Spanish colonists by an indigenous Cascane in the mid-1500s, triggered the mining bonanza that was the city's *raison d'etre.* In the 200 years after the Conquest, the hills surrounding Zacatecas were stripped of over US$1 billion worth of silver and other precious metals. Among mining towns, Zacatecas was unusually fortunate: the arts flourished under the patronage of affluent silver barons, and the rows of grand colonial mansions downtown testify to an era of lavish consumption. In the early 19th century, one devout mine owner even paved a walkway from his home to the cathedral with solid silver bars.

The tumultuous history of modern Mexico has left its thumbprint on Zacatecas; in 1914 Francisco "Pancho" Villa's revolutionary forces triumphed here over Carranza's troops. As revolution atrophied into institution and the mines ran dry, Zacatecas emerged as a hub of sophistication rife with architectural, artistic, and natural treasures. A delightful dearth of tourism helps maintain their authenticity.

### ORIENTATION AND PRACTICAL INFORMATION

At the junction of several major highways, Zacatecas is easily accessible from many cities, including Guadalajara (318km south), Aguascalientes (129km south), and Chihuahua (832km north). All buses arrive and depart from the **central bus terminal** on the outskirts of town. City buses (0.80 pesos) and taxis (8 pesos to the *centro*) wait outside. Some *taxistas* will ask foreigners for double the going rate; if you think you're getting ripped off, bargain or take the bus. To get to *el centro,* take Ruta 7.

Unlike most Mexican cities, Zacatecas has no identifiable center of town. Instead, activity revolves around two streets, **Juárez** and **Hidalgo** (the latter is renamed González Ortega southwest of Juárez). As both streets are quite steep, walking around will firm you up and trim you down. Use the Juárez-Hidalgo intersection, which falls one block northwest of **Plaza Independencia,** as your point of orientation. Many of the city's colonial monuments are on or near Hidalgo. Zacatecas can get chilly, so sweaters and jackets come in handy.

**Tourist Office: Infotur,** Hidalgo 608 (tel. 4-05-52), at Callejón del Santero across from the cathedral. Young staff is helpful with specific queries. Useful map. No English spoken. Open Mon.-Fri. 9am-7pm, Sat. 9am-noon. **TIPS,** a Spanish-language weekly which lists cultural events, movie schedules, museum exhibits, and tourist services, is on sale at various newsstands; inquire at the tourist office.

**Police:** Héroes de Chapultepec 1000 (tel. 2-05-07). No English spoken.

**Post Office:** Allende 111 (tel. 2-01-96), off Hidalgo. Posts a *Lista de Correos.* Open Mon.-Fri. 8am-7pm, Sat. 9am-1pm. **Postal code:** 98000.

**Telephones:** Callejón de Cuevas 111 (tel. 2-88-06), up the alley from the corner of Café Zas, above the bookstore on the left. International collect calls 6 pesos. Open Mon.-Fri. 8:30am-9pm, Sat. 10am-2pm and 4-8pm. **LADATELs** are well-placed throughout the city. **Telephone Code:** 492.

**Telegrams:** Hidalgo at Juárez (tel. 2-00-60). Open Mon.-Fri. 8am-6pm, Sat. 9am-noon.

**Guided Tours: Cantera Tours,** López Velarde 602-6 (tel. 2-91-21, tel. and fax 2-90-65), at Camino La Bufa. Guided 3-hr. tour of the city 55 pesos, 5-hr. tour 75 pesos. 50% off for children under 15. Includes transportation and admission to museums. No English tours. Office open Mon.-Sat. 9am-2pm and 4-7pm.

**Currency Exchange: Bánamex,** Hidalgo 132 (tel. 2-59-20). Open Mon.-Fri. 9am-3pm. Will exchange until closing. **Bancomer,** Hidalgo 302 at Allende (tel 2-11-15). Open for exchange Mon.-Fri. 9am-2pm. The *casa de cambio* at Av. Torreón 107-B (tel. 2-32-08), on the northwest extension of Juárez, has rates just a few *centavos* below the banks'. Open Mon.-Fri. 9am-6pm, Sat. 9am-1pm.

**Airport:** (tel. 498/5-08-63 or 5-81-99). Accessible by *combis* from the Mexicana office (3pm, 20min., 20-25 pesos), or call the *combi* office (tel. 2-59-46). Only two airlines service the airport. **Mexicana,** Hidalgo 406 (tel. 2-32-48), has service to Los Angeles (Thurs.-Sat. and Mon., US$211.65), Mexico City (4:50pm daily, 401 pesos), Tijuana (10:15am daily, 828 pesos), and others. Open Mon.-Fri. 9am-7:30pm. **Taesa,** Hidalgo 306 (tel. 2-00-50 or 2-02-12), serves Chicago (Thurs. and Sat., US$189 plus tax), Oakland (this is their *especial;* Fri.-Sat., US$170), Mexico City (2-3 per day, 312-405 pesos), and a large selection of other cities throughout the Republic. Open Mon.-Fri. 9am-7pm, Sat. 10am-6pm.

**Train Station: Estación de Ferrocarriles** (tel. 2-12-04), on González Ortega southeast of *el centro.* Within walking distance of downtown. Ruta 8 and other buses pass the station. Trains south often arrive/leave 2-3 hours late. Trains north are usually not more than an hour late. The train to Mexico City (first class 8pm, 13hrs., 76 pesos; second class 5am, 13hrs., 44 pesos) goes via Querétaro (10hrs.) and other points in between. The train to Ciudad Juárez (first class 9:35am, 19hrs., 136 pesos; second class 11:40pm, 19hrs., 80 pesos) goes via Torreón (7hrs.) and other cities. Night tickets are sold 7-9pm; buy first-class tickets to Juárez 8am-departure; purchase on-board for second class to Mexico City.

**Bus Station: Central de Autobuses,** Lomas de la Isabélica at Tránsito Pesado (tel. 2-06-84). To get there from the *centro,* take the "Camionera Central" or Ruta 8 bus from the east end of Juárez. **Estrella Blanca** (tel. 2-06-84) has the most extensive service from Zacatecas, serving Aguascalientes (every ½hr., 6am-9pm, 2½hrs., 19 pesos), Mexico City (10 per day, 8:30am-3:30am, 8hrs., 102 pesos) and San Luis Potosí (9 per day, 10:15am-1am, 2½hrs., 28 pesos), among others. **Transportes Chihuahuenses** (tel. 2-00-42) goes to Ciudad Juárez (9 per day, 6:15am-12:15am, 18hrs., 224 pesos) and Guadalajara (5 per day, 2am-1:30pm, 5hrs., 66 pesos). **Omnibus de México** (tel. 2-54-95) sends travelers to León (7 per day, 4pm-6:40am, 4½hrs., 44 pesos) and Mexico City via San Luis Potosí (9 per day, 7am-1am, 8hrs., 118 pesos).

**Car Rental: Budget,** Mateos 104 (tel. 2-94-58). Deals start at 149.70 pesos per day plus 1 peso per km and 52 pesos for insurance. Renters must be 25 years of age and carry a valid credit card and driver's license.

**Laundromat: Rosa Blanca,** López Mateos 129 (tel. 2-97-80), ½ block downhill past the Hotel Colón. 3kg for 25 pesos. Same-day service. Open Mon.-Fri. 8am-7pm, Sat. 8am-5pm.

**Red Cross:** Calzada de la Cruz Roja 100 (tel. 2-30-05), off Héroes de Chapultepec. English spoken. Open 24 hrs.

**Pharmacy: La Perla de Zacatecas,** Hidalgo 131 (tel. 2-14-09). No English spoken. Open daily 9am-11pm.

**Hospital: Hospital General,** García Salinas 707 (tel. 3-30-04). Open 24 hrs.

**Emergency:** Dial 06.

## ACCOMMODATIONS

For no discernible reason, the less expensive hotels in Zacatecas tend to be dingier than budget hotels elsewhere in Mexico, and middle-range accommodations are hard to come by. Unless you're willing to fork over 70 pesos for a single, the hostels, though a bit far from the *centro,* are the most clean and least depressing option.

**CREA Youth Hostel (HI),** Lago La Encantada (tel. 2-02-23, ext. 10), southwest of the city. You'll never find it on foot; fortunately, orange-red "Ruta 8" buses (0.80 pesos) run from the Plaza Independencia and from the bus station. Ask drivers for the "Albergues CREA" or get off at the sign for La Encantada. The rooms are behind the dirt soccer fields and basketball courts. Also equipped with a swimming pool, and courts for volleyball and racquetball, the hostel is surrounded by rose bushes and kids. Small, sterile quads. Single-sex floors. Clean communal bathroom. 11 pesos per person; 25% discount with HI membership. Breakfast 9 pesos. Lunch and dinner 11 pesos each. Open daily 7am-11pm.

**CREA Youth Hostel II (HI)** (tel. 2-93-77), Av. de los Deportes, on the west side of the soccer stadium. Pretty far out of town. Ruta 11 and 13 buses pass by the hostel; when you see the dirt soccer fields on the left, get off and walk to your right, through the gate to the yellow building. Ruta 3 passes to the hostel's right; get off at the red arches and it's on your left. Curtainless showers in the larger rooms. Rooms fit 4-28 people. Hot water and cleanliness abound. Soccer fields, basketball courts, and weight room. 11 pesos per person. 25% discount with HI card. Breakfast 9.25 pesos. Lunch and dinner 11.25 pesos each. Open daily 7am-11pm.

**Hotel El Parque,** González Ortega 302 (tel. 2-04-79), near the aqueduct. A tad out of the way, but in a nice area with pleasant parks. Rooms are sort of dark, though the TVs brighten things up. Thin walls; the neighbors quiet down by about 11pm. Bedrooms and bathrooms are fairly clean. Singles 48 pesos. Doubles 58 pesos.

**Conda de Villareal,** Plazuela de Zamora 303 (tel. 2-12-00). Take Juárez to its southeastern end and it's a few blocks to your right, on the left-hand side. Central location may be its only virtue. Dim rooms have peeling paint, and bathrooms don't have much showering space. Hot water 24 hrs. Singles 30 pesos. Doubles 35 pesos, with two beds 40 pesos.

## FOOD

The sophistication of Zacatecas seeps out of its museums and mansions and into its restaurants—the city boasts a large assemblage of pocket-sized gourmet cafés. Coffee aside, however, budget meals in Zacatecas often fail to impress. Cheap generally means lesser quality, and expensive means, well, expensive. Not to be missed are the candies on sale near the Alameda (on Juárez or Torreón). One peso buys a sizable chunk of sugary-sweet *dulce con leche, camote,* or *cocada.*

**Café Acrópolis** (tel. 2-12-84), on Hidalgo near the cathedral. The brown vinyl booths are filled with middle-aged men and women and the odd bunch of teenagers gossiping over coffee. The consistent stream of 80s tunes is stellar. Breakfast 18-20 pesos. *Quesadilla* on pita bread 21 pesos. Open daily 8am-10pm.

**La Terraza** (tel. 2-32-70), in the *centro comercial* next to the cathedral. Although the menu is limited and the food is average, the pleasant atmosphere and outdoor tables overlooking the city create an ideal place for coffee and a snack. Burgers 5.50 pesos. Ice cream 5 pesos. *Licuados* 4.50 pesos. Open daily 10am-9:30pm.

**El Dragón de Oro** (tel. 4-09-90), González Ortega and Rayona, a few blocks up Ortega from Hotel El Parque. The Chiw Wong family cooks up huge portions of savory Chinese food, keeping the customers happy. Entrees can feed two travelers and their horses. Pastas 15-22 pesos. Seafood 30-35 pesos. Chop suey 25 pesos. Open daily 1-10pm and 11pm-midnight.

## SIGHTS

The 18th-century **cathedral,** on Hidalgo four blocks northeast of Juárez, combines three architectural styles. The northern façade is Churrigueresque, the southern façade is European Baroque, and the western façade, a richly carved celebration of the Eucharist, is among the country's most lavish examples of Mexican Baroque (open daily 7am-1pm and 6-9pm). Next to the cathedral, the **Palacio de Gobierno** is notable for the mural which surrounds its interior stairwell. Executed in 1970 by artist Antonio Pintor Rodríguez, the work traces the history of Zacatecas from the pre-Conquest era until the present. Much of the mural devotes itself to the mugs of Zacatecas's historical players (open Mon.-Fri. 8am-8pm).

Across Hidalgo and up the steep Callejón de Veyna is the **Templo de Santo Domingo.** Built by the Jesuits in 1746, the church contains eight impressive Baroque altars of gilded wood and an elaborate 18th-century German pipe organ (open daily 7am-1pm and 3:30-9pm; quiet, respectful visitors are welcome during services). Next door, in a building whose past incarnations include a monastery and a jail, is the **Museo de Pedro Coronel** (tel. 2-80-21). Containing the tomb, sculptures, and paintings of the Zacatecan artist Pedro Coronel, the museum houses one of the best modern art collections in Latin America. Works by Picasso, Braque, Chagall, and Miró jostle for space. Mesoamerican and African masks, as well as Japanese, Chinese, and Tibetan pieces break the Eurocentric spell (open Fri.-Wed. 7am-1pm and 3:30-9pm, Sun. 10am-5pm; admission 10 pesos).

The dramatic **Ex-Convento de San Francisco**, a worthy attraction in itself, houses the **Museo Rafael Coronel** (tel. 2-81-16) inside its spacious halls. To reach the museum from the cathedral, follow Hidalgo. At the first fork, bear left; at the second, bear right. The museum's reputation rests on its fabulous collection of masks from around the world. (Open Mon.-Tues. and Thurs.-Sat. 10am-2pm and 4-7pm, Sun. 10am-5pm. Admission 10 pesos. Free for kids 10 and under. Students, teachers, and those 60 and over pay half-price. Ex-convent open same hours. Free.)

Southeast of downtown, 39 rose-colored stone arches mark the end of Zacatecas's famous colonial aqueduct, **El Cubo.** Beside the aqueduct, the verdant **Parque Estrada** borders the former governor's mansion, now the **Museo de Francisco Goitia** (tel. 2-02-11; open Tues.-Sat. 10am-2pm and 5-8pm, Sun. 10am-5pm).

The **Cerro de la Bufa,** named for its resemblance to a Spanish wineskin, peers down from the city's highest crag. Adjacent to the Cerro is the **Museo de la Toma de Zacatecas** (tel. 2-80-66). Erected to commemorate Pancho Villa's decisive victory over federal troops in the summer of 1914, the museum lays claim to a fascinating array of revolutionary memorabilia, including photographs, cannon, and small arms (open Tues.-Sun. 10am-5pm; admission 5 pesos; half-price for students, seniors, and teachers; kids 10 and under free). The museum is flanked on one side by the early 18th-century **Capilla del Patrocinio,** whose gracefully sculpted façade and cloistered courtyards are carved from deep-red stone. Also near the museum are shops selling arts, crafts, and loads of geodes for rock jocks. A short but steep assault on the peak of the hill leads to the ornate Moorish **Mausoleo de los Hombres Ilustres de Zacatecas,** worth the hike if only for the view of the city it affords. An even better vista is available at the **Meteorological Observatory** behind the museum.

Unfortunately, public buses run to La Bufa only on Sun. and religious holidays (Ruta 9), and taxis suck up 15 pesos. The most appealing way to make the trip is by **teleférico** (suspended cable car), which runs between the peak of El Grillo and La Bufa every 10 minutes. The Swiss-made cars carry passengers on an eight-minute journey high above Zacatecas. Follow García Rojas northwest to its end to the cable car stop (open daily 10am-6pm, given good weather; 5 pesos each way).

The **Mina de Edén** (tel. 2-30-02) was one of the region's most productive silver mines until about 30 years ago, when continual flooding made mineral extraction increasingly futile. You may enter the mine from either the top or the side. The top entrance is 100m to the right as you leave the *teleférico.* From there, walk into the mountain, take the elevator down, and begin the tour. Otherwise, follow Juárez northwest along the **Alameda,** an oblong park lined by some of Zacatecas's grandest colonial mansions. Continue along Torreón until it ends, and then turn right. From there, a mini-locomotive whisks tourists into the mountain. A chilling guided tour (in Spanish) of the cool subterranean tunnels ensues. Tour groups cross rope bridges and follow the beam of a flashlight to learn something of the haunting myths of the mine (mine open daily 11am-6:30pm; admission 12 pesos).

Trips to La Bufa and Mina de Edén can be easily combined. At the end of the mine tour, go back the way you came or take the elevator up to El Grillo, where you can catch the *teleférico* to La Bufa; or do the reverse, beginning with the *teleférico,* then taking the elevator down to the mine. Either way, the entire trip takes 2-3 hours.

## ENTERTAINMENT

Much of Zacatecas's nightlife gets going on Thursday or Friday nights, when the university students slam the books shut and head to the bars and discos. Not surprisingly, the tourists' first choice is always **El Malacate** (tel. 2-30-02). The opportunity to boogie 50m above a pool of water 220m deep while enclosed by 320 meters of rock above and 600m to the side is a rare opportunity. Inside the club's walls of solid rock, tastefully decorated with helmets and shovels, partiers quaff expensive drinks and dance to the latest U.S. top-40 hits (cover 30 pesos; open Thurs.-Sat. 9pm-2:30am). At the same time, revelers can be found at a similar altitude, jamming to rock music just next to the *teleférico* station at **El Elefante Blanco** (tel. 2-71-04). The club offers a stunning view of Zacatecas at night, in addition to pool tables, foosball, and a happenin' dance floor (open Fri.-Sat. 9pm-2am). Things at **Nivel Siete** (tel. 2-41-19), on Tacuba, barely and rarely get out of control, but during the week it may be the only joint in town which serves up beer (5-8 pesos) past 10pm (open Mon.-Thurs. noon-1am, Fri.-Sat. noon-2am).

During daylight hours, the **Video Club de la Biblioteca Mauricio Magdaleno,** Jardín Independencia 1 (tel. 2-59-29), is the place to be. Free movies from just about every country and in just about every genre (including cartoons!) are shown twice a day at 11:30am and 5:30pm, Monday through Saturday. Look for the movie schedule in TIPS or inquire at the library. Also check out **Cinemas Zacatecas,** Constituyentes 300 (tel. 2-54-04), for the latest in Mexican and American films.

## ■ NEAR ZACATECAS: GUADALUPE

The **Museo de Virreinal,** also called the **Museo Regional de Guadalupe** (tel. 3-20-89), is 7km east of Zacatecas on the highway to Mexico City in the small and splendid village of Guadalupe. Highlights include the first series on the Virgin of Guadalupe, done by the 18th-century painter Miguel Cabrera, and a 1621 Gutenberg volume on mining (open Tues.-Sun. 10am-4:30pm; admission 13 pesos; free Sun. and for students and teachers with ID, children 13 and under, and those over 60). The collection of antique vehicles housed next door in the **Anexo al Convento de Guadalupe** (tel. 3-20-89) is worth a peek (open Tues.-Sun. 10am-4:30pm; free).

**Getting There:** Ruta 13 buses to Guadalupe (0.80 pesos) leave every 15 minutes from the Centro Comercial car-park at the corner of Salazar and López Mateos.

# AGUASCALIENTES

## ■■■ AGUASCALIENTES

Aguascalientes ("hot waters") presents the average visitor with just enough diversions to deserve a stopover. The pride and joy of the city is the eagerly anticipated **Feria de San Marcos,** three weeks of festivities from the second half of April until the first week of May. But aside from its yearly extravaganza, Aguas offers only a small range of attractions that commemorate its relatively undistinguished history. Residents, however, are proud of their past, and their government tries valiantly to promote the city; the streets of Aguas, dotted with modern buildings, Blockbuster Videos, and liquor stores are absolutely immaculate, and not a single cigarette butt defaces the honored Jardín de San Marcos. Aguas has erected museums for each of its 15 minutes of fame, including former public bathrooms recently declared a national monument, and perhaps more notably, the museum of political cartoons by the anti-Díaz satirist and Aguas native José Guadalupe Posada.

**Orientation** Aguascalientes is 168km west of San Luis Potosí, 128km south of Zacatecas, and 252km northeast of Guadalajara. Av. Circunvalación encircles the city, while Av. López Mateos cuts through town east-west. The **bus station** is a few blocks west on Av. Convención from the north-south Av. José María Chávez. All city buses are green and white; "Centro" buses (0.70 pesos) run from outside the bus station to the Mercado Morelos, two blocks north (on Morelos) from the Plaza de la

AGUASCALIENTES

Patria. To return to the station, "Central Camionera" buses traverse the length of Rivero y Gutiérrez (parallel to and one block north of Madero). The drivers of Aguas are one of the city's miracles—due to a recent (and strictly enforced) city ordinance, *everyone* here wears a seatbelt. Those strapped-in *taxistas* charge about seven pesos from the bus terminal to the center of town. From the Plaza de la Patria, most sights are either on **Montoro** (the street that runs east from the southeast corner of the plaza) or on **Carranza,** which begins to the west of the plaza, behind the *basílica.* When you plan your day in Aguas, keep in mind that the city absolutely *dies* during *siesta* (2-5pm), even for Mexico.

**Practical Information** The **tourist office** (tel. 15-11-55 or 16-03-47) is on the first floor of the Palacio de Gobierno, the first door to the right of the main entrance. Workers are helpful and have a so-so map. Some English spoken (open Mon.-Fri. 8am-3pm and 5-7pm, Sat. 9am-1pm). The **police** are on López Mateos at Héroes de Nacozari (tel. 14-20-50 or 14-30-43). English ain't spoke. The **post office,** Hospitalidad 108 (tel. 15-21-18), one block east of the plaza on Madero, then left on Morelos and right on Hospitalidad, posts a *Lista de Correos* (open Mon.-Fri. 8am-7pm, Sat. 9am-1pm). **Postal Code:** 20000. **LADATELs** are along the Plaza de la Patria. **Tabaquería Plaza,** Colón 102 (tel. 17-31-78 or 17-20-45), charges 9.50 pesos per min. to the U.S., and around 17 pesos to Europe. No collect calls (open daily 8:30am-9:30pm). **Telephone Code:** 49. For **telegrams,** there is **Telecomm,** Galeana at Nieto (tel. 16-14-27 or 16-12-52), located behind the Basílica, half a block to your left (open Mon.-Fri. 8am-6pm, Sat. 9am-1pm). **Bancomer,** 5 de Mayo 112 (tel. 17-19-00), a block from the Plaza de la Patria, has shorter lines and a slightly better buy rate than the competition (open for exchange Mon.-Fri. 8:30am-2pm). **Casa de Cambio Cedinsa,** Hospitalidad 104B (tel. 18-27-84), next to the post office, has better hours than its nearby competitors (open Mon.-Fri. 9am-6:30pm, Sat. 9am-1pm).

The **train station** (tel. 15-22-55) is on the Alameda two blocks east of Héroes de Nacozari. Keep in mind that southbound trains often leave 5-7hrs. late. Trains head north to Ciudad Juárez (first class 6:50am, 24hrs., 150 pesos; second class 9pm, 24hrs.) and south to Mexico City (first class 10:30pm, 12hrs., 63 pesos; second class 7:20am, 12hrs.). The **bus station** on Av. Circunvalación is served by **Omnibus de México, Estrella Blanca, Flecha Amarilla, Rojo de los Altos,** and a slew of smaller companies. **Estrella Blanca** (tel. 78-20-54) has decent fares and frequent service to every destination imaginable, including Guadalajara (every hr., 6am-noon, 2-8pm, and 11pm, 2¾hrs., 48 pesos), Mexico City (every hr., 8am-4pm, every ½hr., 10pm-2:30am, 6½hrs., 102 pesos), Monterrey (every hr., 9am-midnight, 8hrs., 102 pesos), and San Luis Potosí (every hr., 6am-11pm, 2¾hrs., 36 pesos). **Flecha Amarilla** runs to Guanajuato (12:30 and 10:30pm, 3½hrs., 28 pesos). **Rojo de los Altos** (tel. 78-20-54) sends the most buses to Zacatecas (every ½hr., 6am-8:30pm, 2½hrs., 19 pesos). **Luggage Storage** is available at the bus station (1.50 pesos per hrs.). **Benavides Farmacias,** Moctezuma 101 (tel. 18-19-54), across from Bánamex, is open daily 8am-10pm. English spoken. **Hospital Hidalgo,** Galeana 465 (tel. 17-19-30 or 17-29-83), is open 24 hrs. No English spoken. In an **emergency,** dial 06.

**Accommodations** Aguascalientes has plenty of hotels, both near the bus station and in the *centro.* Even if you're just passing through, consider the latter option thoroughly; it's an infinitely nicer part of town. Unfortunately, no matter where you stay, budget accommodations in Aguas lack character and modernity. During the Feria de San Marcos (mid-April-early May), prior reservations are a must.

The youth hostel, **Inajud,** on Av. de la Convención Oriente and Jaime Nuño (tel. 70-08-63), just a few km from the bus station, is a solid budget option. It's equipped with 24 beds for women, 38 for men, a track, baseball field, and volleyball and basketball courts. Communal bathrooms are modern and clean and the showers supposedly have hot water during open hours, it being Aguascalientes and all (shower early to be sure). Rooms come with lockers and locks. Make reservations a week in advance. The 11pm curfew is strict. (11 pesos per person. 20-peso bedding deposit.

Breakfast 9 pesos. Lunch and dinner 11.25 pesos. 10% discount with HI or AYH membership, 25% with Plan Joven. Open daily 7am-11pm.) The **Hotel Continental** awaits at Brasil 610 (tel. 78-28-29), at Guatemala, bordering the left side of the bus station as you exit. Translation A: convenient for the one-night-stay traveler. Translation B: a noisy, dirty, and depressing part of town. The rooms themselves also present a trade-off; in the cleaner, more modern part of the hotel, single travelers sleep under flowery spreads on individual beds, while all the double beds are in older, worn rooms. All rooms come with fans. The bathrooms, though aging, gush hot water (singles 40 pesos; doubles 50 pesos, with two beds 60 pesos).

There are a few affordable options closer to the *centro*. The most worthwhile is the somewhat pricey **Hotel Senioral,** Colón 104 (tel. 15-16-30), located right on the Plaza de la Patria. Comes with all the amenities: TV, phone, desk, fan, carpet, and purified water. Too bad the basics are lacking, what with thin walls, ancient furniture, small bathrooms, and cramped bedrooms. But hey, it's clean (singles 60 pesos; doubles 80 pesos). Across from the cathedral is **Hotel Rosales,** Guadalupe Victoria 104 (tel. 15-21-65). Behind the rose stone façade and the bright bus-terminal seats lurks a spooky courtyard and a tiny plastic man holding a lantern. The rooms probably housed guests in the same years that the city's public bathrooms provided relief (see Sights), but the management keeps them clean. Some have TVs, none have toilet seats (singles 55 pesos; doubles 65 pesos, with 2 beds 75 pesos).

**Food** "Average" just about describes the food of Aguascalientes. The city presents a *panadería* here, a taco stand there, and a nice cafetería every once in a while. The spacious wooden interior of **Mitla,** Madero 220 (tel. 16-36-79), a block north of Montoro near the plaza, could fit twice as many tables as it does. Luckily, the management likes to keeps things comfy. Sandwiches 10-15 pesos; *enchiladas* 14 pesos. The *menú del día* costs between 15-17 pesos (open daily 7:30am-11:30pm). At **El Greco,** Madero 434 (tel. 15-27-75), the wood decor, brick arches, and, of course, portraits of the restaurant's namesake attempt to produce a Spanish setting. But the joint's real strength is its food, as evidenced by its popularity with locals. Pancakes 8 pesos, *enchiladas de mole* 10 pesos. The *menú del día* runs 14 pesos (open daily 8am-midnight). Desperate vegetarians should check out the **Restaurant Vegetariano,** López Velarde 210. From the plaza, take Juárez one block north, go right two blocks, and make a left onto López Velarde, the extension of Hidalgo. In the small pharmacy/restaurant, 18 pesos buys you a buffet with *tostadas* and a jug of *agua fresca* (open Mon.-Sat. 1:30-5pm).

**Sights and Entertainment** The **Feria de San Marcos** (mid-April-early May) constitutes the soul of Aguascalientes. The sporting and cultural events play diverse roles in the residents' lives; for some, excitement stems from the cockfights, bullfights, and other sporting events, but for farmers whose livestock means their own livelihood, milking contests are the most highly anticipated event of the year. Many of the Feria's events occur in the **Jardín de San Marcos,** a 10-15-minute walk on Carranza from the **Plaza de la Patria.** The area around the Jardín was originally an Indian *pueblo,* but around the year 1600, *indígena* labor erected the **Templo Evangelista San Marcos** at the site. The church is most notable for housing José de Alsívar's *La Adoración de los Reyes Católicos.* In 1838, the city's aristocrats, having expanded their settlement from the area of today's plaza, claimed the Jardín (then surrounded by fields) as their own, and in 1842, the modernization process began. Today the Jardín is an immaculate park with leafy vegetation, sliced by red brick walkways and bordered at its four corners by the original *fuentes.*

Another focal point of the city's cultural and historical activities is the **Instituto Cultural de Aguascalientes,** popularly known as the **Casa de la Cultura,** Carranza 101 (tel. 15-00-97). Kiosks in the courtyard just drip with listings for arts events.

Those interested in Mexican politics and art should visit the **Museo de Guadalupe Posada** (tel. 15-45-56), on León next to the Templo del Encino, four blocks south of López Mateos. Posada, an engraver and cartoonist, is Mexico's most famous printmaker. His images of Porfirian excess helped turn public opinion against Díaz at the end of the dictator's reign. The museum holds 220 of the artist's original works, almost all skeletal figures caricaturing Díaz. *La Calavera Catrina* is world-renowned, depicting a society lady-*calavera* wearing an outlandish hat; her figure appears later in Diego Rivera's *Sueños de Una Tarde Dominical en la Alameda,* now on display in Mexico City. The museum also includes 100 works by Posada's mentor, Manuel Manilla, and an exhibit of contemporary art from around the world (open Tues.-Sun. 10am-6pm; admission 3 pesos, students and children 1.50 pesos).

The **Centro Cultural Los Arquitos,** on the Alameda at Héroes de Nacozari (tel. 17-00-96), is Aguascalientes's newest museum, and stands on ground that was declared a national monument in 1993 by ex-President Carlos Salinas de Gortari. The Arquitos served as public bathrooms from 1821 until 1973, but these johns were no average port-o-potties: during the 19th century, the bathrooms were the central water distributor for the city. In 1973, with the construction of Boulevard Convención (the road to encircle the city), the aqueduct which supplied the bathrooms was broken. The building was abandoned until Salinas's decree, and since then, it has undergone a magnificent restoration process. On November 11, 1994, the city opened a center which includes a gallery with rotating exhibits, a cafeteria (open Mon.-Fri. 9am-1pm and 3-8pm, Sat. 9am-1pm and 3-6pm, Sun. 9am-2pm), a bookshop, a video room that shows children's movies Fridays at 5pm, and a small museum (open daily 10am-2pm and 4-8pm).

The soft grays and rose-colored bricks of the **Basílica de la Asunción de las Aguascalientes** (open daily 6am-9pm) make it the most remarkable of the structures on the Plaza de la Patria. Its façade is Solomonic Baroque; look out for the sculptures of church patrons San Gregorio, San Jerónimo, and San Agustín. The cathedral's interior is graced with high ceilings, gold trimmings, and ornate icons, as well as paintings by José de Alcíbar, Andrés López, and Miguel Cabrera.

During the week, low-key good times can be had at the **Casa Verde,** Montoro 107 (tel. 15-33-32), where pool is 10.20 pesos per hour, dominoes 4.80 pesos per hour (open daily 10:30am-11pm). On weekends, shake your caboose with the locals at **Disco El Cabús,** Blvd. Zacatecas at Campestre (tel.73-04-32 or -38), in the Hotel Las Trojes (cover about 35 pesos; open Thurs.-Sat. 9pm-2am). Check out the laser light at **Excalibur,** Ayuntamiento 117-201, where each mixed drink will cost about ten pesos (cover roughly 30 pesos; open Thurs.-Sat. 9pm-2am). Both spots are 18+, and men must wear pants at El Cabús.

# SAN LUIS POTOSÍ

## ■■■ SAN LUIS POTOSÍ

Though founded in 1583 as a Franciscan mission, this town forgot its religious calling when somebody discovered silver in the mountains around town. In 1592, the town of royal fortune was given a royal name—San Luis, after King Louis IX of France. As the earth coughed up more and more shiny metal, miners optimistically tacked on yet another title—"Potosí," the name of a prosperous Bolivian mining town. Mining soon vaulted San Luis Potosí to the center of Mexico's export-based economy. Precious silver bought political clout, and the city eventually became the power-center of northern Mexico, including present-day Texas and Louisiana.

While San Luis Potosí may have lost its political pull, the city has grown comfortably over the past 400 hundred years. Today, sprawling San Luis is home to 800,000 people, its colonial charm still very much intact. Bands, magicians, and women blowing soap bubbles gather in the town plazas at dusk to entertain the assembled crowds of young and old. In a graceful bargain with modernity, automobile traffic along the cobblestone streets has been shunted away from the central plaza, creating a truly peaceful preserve of land in the middle of a vibrant and breathing city.

## ORIENTATION

San Luis Potosí is at the center of a triangle formed by Mexico's three largest cities—Monterrey, Guadalajara, and Mexico City. Five main highways (Rtes. 57, 85, 70, 49, and 80) snake their way into the city. To get downtown from the bus station, catch an "Alameda" or "Centro" bus (1 peso) and hop off at **Parque Alameda,** the first big stretch of green after the railway tracks. **Taxis** to *el centro* cost 10 pesos.

San Luis's main drag is **Avenida Carranza,** which runs east-west and passes the north side of the **Plaza de Armas,** the city's historic center. East of the plaza, Carranza is called **Los Bravos. Madero** runs parallel to Carranza/Los Bravos and one block south, touching the Plaza de Armas's south side. East of the plaza, Madero goes by **Othón.** The **Plaza del Carmen** is two blocks east of the plaza on Madero/Othón. Another block farther east lies the Alameda, where the bus from the station drops off visitors. The train station is on Othón opposite the Alameda. Zaragoza forms the east side of the Pl. de Armas; north of the plaza it goes by Hidalgo. On the west side of the plaza is the **Calle Cinco de Mayo,** known as **Allende** farther north. **Aldama** is one block west of 5 de Mayo.

## PRACTICAL INFORMATION

**Tourist Office:** Carranza 325 (tel. 12-30-68), to the right of the Hotel Panorama. Fish-stocked fountain imparts a touch of class. Friendly staff, great maps, lots o' info. Open Mon.-Fri. 9am-8pm, Sat. 9am-1pm and 4-8pm. **Tourist center,** first floor of the Palacio Municipal, on the northeast corner of the Plaza de Armas.

**Police:** (tel. 12-28-04 or 12-54-76), in the Palacio Municipal.

**Post Office:** Morelos 235 (tel. 2-27-40), between Salazar and Insurgentes, 1 block east and 4 blocks north of the Plaza de Armas. *Lista de Correos* posted Mon.-Fri. 9am-2pm. Open Mon.-Fri. 9am-5pm, Sat. 9am-1pm. **Postal Code:** 78000.

**Telephones:** No LADATELs are available, but a few of the old coin-operated payphones on Calle Hidalgo allow international collect calls. Also try **Computel,** Carranza 360, opposite the Hotel Panorama. International collect calls 5 pesos for 5 min. Open Mon.-Sat. 7:30am-9pm. **Telephone Code:** 48.

**Telegrams:** Escobedo 200 (tel. 12-33-18), at the south end of the Plaza del Carmen up the stairs to your right. Open Mon.-Fri. 9am-5pm, Sat. 9am-1pm.

**U.S. Consulate:** Mariel 103 (tel. 12-15-28), via the "Morales" bus. Open Mon.-Fri. 8:30am-1:30pm, but sometimes available in the afternoons. The police and the tourist office have consulate employees' home numbers in case of emergency.

**Currency Exchange: Casa de Cambio,** Morelos 400 (tel. 12-66-06), has better rates than the banks. Open Mon.-Fri. 9am-2pm and 4:30-8pm. Many banks around the Pl. de Armas open Mon.-Fri. 9am-1:30pm, including **Bánamex,** at Allende and Obregón, which has a 24-hr. Cirrus/MC **ATM.**

**American Express: Grandes Viajes,** Carranza 1077 (tel. 17-60-04).

**Airport:** (tel. 2-00-95). Served by **Mexicana,** Himno Nacional 145 (tel. 17-89-20). Flights to Mexico City, Monterrey, and Chicago. Office open Mon.-Fri. 9am-6pm.

**Trains:** From the station on Othón near the north side of the *Alameda.* Daily departures to Mexico City (10:22pm, 6hrs., 92 pesos), Monterrey (3:35pm, 8hrs., 69 pesos), and Aguascalientes (1pm, 6hrs., 24 pesos).

**Buses: Central de Autobuses** (tel. 12-74-11), two blocks south of the chaotic convergence of highways that wrap around the Glorieta Benito Juárez, 4km east of the city center along Av. Universidad. Endless bus companies; from here you can easily get anywhere in the northern half of the republic. **Primera Plus** (tel. 18-30-16) runs to Mexico City (9 per day, 5hrs., 62 pesos) and Querétaro (7 per day, 254 pesos). **Flecha Amarilla** (tel. 18-29-23), provides second-class service to Gogorrón (every 15min., 5am-9:40pm, 1¼hrs., 8 pesos), Guanajuato (8 per day, 4hrs., 35 pesos), Mexico City (9 per day, 5hrs., 67 pesos), and Morelia (12 per day, 58 pesos). **Estrella Blanca** (tel. 18-30-49) goes to Monterrey (every hr., 7hrs., 86 pesos), Saltillo (every hr., 5hrs., 67 pesos), and Zacatecas (7 per day, 3hrs., 28 pesos). **Transportes Tamaulipas** and **Noreste** (tel. 18-29-15) jointly trek to

Matehuala (6 per day, 2½hrs., 32 pesos), Monterrey (8 per day, 7hrs., 82 pesos), and Reynosa via Linares or Monterrey (3 per day, 90.50 pesos). They also offer connections in the U.S. with Greyhound. **Del Norte** offers service to Acapulco (2 per day, 167 pesos), Cuernavaca (every hr., 88 pesos), Mexico City (every hr., 78 pesos), and Saltillo (3 per day, 78 pesos).

**Car Rental: Arrendadora Automotriz Potosina,** Obregón 670 (tel. 14-26-00).
**Auto Repairs: Ángeles Verdes Auxilio Turístico,** Reforma 206 (tel. 12-60-63).
**Laundromat: Lavandería La Burbuja,** Nicolás Zapata 535. 15 pesos for 4kg. 2-hr. service. Open Mon.-Sat. 9am-7pm.
**Red Cross:** Juárez at Díaz Gutiérrez (tel. 15-33-22 or 15-36-35).
**24-hr. Pharmacy: Botica Mexicana,** Othón 180 (tel. 12-38-80), by the cathedral.
**Hospital:** Carranza 2395 (tel. 13-03-43 or 13-43-95), several km west of *el centro*.
**Emergency:** 06.

## ACCOMMODATIONS

Few good accommodations can be found near the bus station; for those who don't mind staying in this noisy part of town, a viable option is the youth hostel. Hotels closer to *el centro* typically boast commodious *cuartos* for reasonable prices.

**Villa Juvenil San Luis Potosí CREA Youth Hostel (HI)** (tel. 55-73-60), near the Glorieta Benito Juárez, two blocks to the left along the main street (Diagonal Sur) as you exit the bus station. Smallish, 4-person rooms are clean but somewhat run-down. Access to sports complex with basketball courts, soccer fields, swimming pool, and track. Curfew 11pm. 14 pesos per person, 10% discount with HI or AYH card, 25% discount with CREA card. Blankets, sheets, pillow, towel, and lockers. Breakfast 9 pesos, lunch and dinner 13 pesos each. Make reservations.
**Hotel de Gante,** 5 de Mayo 140 (tel. 12-14-93), half a block south of the Pl. de Armas's southwest corner. Spacious rooms have well-equipped bathrooms and a marvelous view of the plaza. The lounges on each floor provide space to hang out and chug the free bottled water. Singles 75 pesos. Doubles 85 pesos.
**Hotel Plaza,** Jardín Hidalgo 22 (tel. 12-46-31), on the south side of the Pl. de Armas. The rooms show visible signs of wear, but are quiet and have soft beds and efficient fans. What more can you ask for? A central courtyard illuminates hall-ways and TV-equipped lounges. Singles 45 pesos. Doubles 55 pesos.

## FOOD

Caught in the confluence of many gastronomic currents, San Luis Potosí has developed a unique cuisine. Both *tacos potosinos* and *enchiladas potosinas* are stuffed with cheese and vegetables, then fried. *Nopalitos* are tender pieces of cactus (spines removed) cooked in a salty sauce of garlic, onion, and tomato while *taquitos dorados* are thin slices of chicken or beef rolled in corn tortillas and deep-fried. *Chongos coronados* (curdled milk in sweet maple water) is a popular dessert. Many touristy restaurants lie on Carranza or one block north on Arista. While prices are jacked up along this strip, so is originality and the chance for a nice atmosphere.

**La Corriente,** Carranza 700 (tel. 12-93-04). A glass ceiling and sparkling fountain make for a very romantic atmosphere, tempered only slightly by the bull's head mounted on the wall. The house special, *chamorro pibil* (pig leg cooked in a banana leaf) accompanies the *comida corrida* (18 pesos) and a variety of other *antojitos mexicanos* (most 15 pesos). Open daily 8am-midnight.
**Restaurante Posada del Virrey-Cafetería,** Jardín Hidalgo 3 (tel. 12-70-55), on the north side of the Plaza de Armas. This popular plaza restaurant is housed in a building that was once home to Mexico's only female viceroy. 7 kinds of beer in huge, frosty mugs 6 pesos each. Avoid toasting the patriarchy. Breakfast 15-20 pesos. Spanish chicken 17 pesos. Open daily 8am-11pm.
**Yu Ne Nisa,** Arista 360 (tel. 14-36-31). Beyond the shelves of vitamins a celebration of vegetarianism awaits. The bright eating area is decorated with plants and matching green chairs. Veggie burgers available for only 12 pesos, and that *quesadilla* you've been craving is a rock-bottom 8 pesos. Open Mon.-Sat. 9am-7pm.

## SIGHTS

Dubbed the "City of Plazas" by hype-meisters, San Luis Potosí has three main town squares. The most central of these is the **Plaza de Armas** (also known as **Jardín Hidalgo**), replete with trees and relaxing *potosinos*. At the beginning of the 17th century, residents cheered bullfights in the dusty plaza from the balconies of the surrounding buildings. Since 1848, a red sandstone gazebo bearing the names of famous Mexican musicians has graced the plaza; on Thursday and Sunday evenings, it hosts a local band that attracts a romantically-inclined older crowd.

The west side of the Plaza de Armas is marked by the Neoclassical façade of the **Palacio del Gobierno.** Constructed in 1798 and briefly occupied by the exiled national government in 1863, the structure was renovated in 1950 and continues to serve as San Luis Potosí's administrative seat. On the second floor, in the **Sala Juárez,** is a diorama of the dramatic meeting between Juárez and Princess Salm-Salm, the wife of one of Maximilian's advisors. Legend has it that the princess begged Juárez for Maximilian's life on the eve of his execution. Plastic figures of the unmoved Juárez and the beautiful princess Salm-Salm are positioned in front of the table where Juárez signed Maximilian's sentence. As you enter the palace, go upstairs and turn left at the top of the staircase—the Sala Juárez is the first room on your left. Ask the guard to unlock the door (open Mon.-Fri. 9am-2:30pm).

Opposite the Palacio de Gobierno stands the **cathedral,** with two bell towers that toll a different melody every 15 minutes. Both magnificent and ominous, the cathedral was completed in 1710, but in 1855, when San Luis became a diocese, the building was "upgraded." Miners are said to have donated gold and silver to beautify the interior, and marble statues of the apostles (small copies of those at the Basilica of San Juan de Letrán in Rome) were placed in the niches between the Solomonic columns of the Baroque façade. Paintings can be admired in the sacristy (cathedral open daily 8am-7pm; tourists should avoid visiting on Sundays or during mass).

The **Palacio Municipal,** on the northeast corner of the plaza, was rebuilt after local citizens torched the original structure to protest Carlos III's expulsion of the Jesuits from Spanish America. A traditional red-stone courtyard leads to a painted stairwell and simple mosaic steps in pseudo-Pompeiian style. Sala Cabildo on the second floor features ceilings elaborately painted by Italian artist Erulo Eroli. One block west of the southwest corner of the Pl. de Armas is the **Antigua Caja Real** (Old Royal Treasury/ Monetary Repository), the city's only existing secular baroque building. The small sculpture which accents the corner of the façade is La Purísima.

East of the Plaza de Armas on Othón is the modest **Casa Othón,** home of the illustrious *poeta potosino* Manuel José Othón (1858-1906). The yellow walls of this museum contain manuscripts, memorabilia, and a furniture collection from the Othón household. Check out the bathtub (open Tues.-Fri. 10am-2pm and 4-6pm, Sat.-Sun. 10am-2pm; 1 peso recommended donation).

Nicolás Fernando de Torres, a rich *sevillano* of the early 18th century, made his fortune in San Luis Potosí. After his death, his estate was used to found a church and a convent of the ascetic Carmelite order. The complex encompassed a large area, but today only the **Iglesia de Carmen** remains on the northeast corner of the plaza of the same name. Many *potosinos* claim that the church is the most beautiful religious building in the city; it features hanging chandeliers, golden altars, and a huge mural of the crucifixion. Affixed to its façade are statues of San Eliseo, San Elías, and, at the very top, the Madonna (open daily 7:30am-1:30pm and 4-9pm; again, avoid visiting during religious ceremonies).

The pink sandstone **Museo Nacional de la Máscara,** Villerías 2 (tel. 12-30-25), in the Palacio Federal, half a block south of the Pl. del Carmen along Villerías, displays hundreds of masks from every Mexican region. Be sure to see the ceremonial masks used in colonial and pre-Hispanic times in pagan religious celebrations (open Tues.-Fri. 10am-2pm and 4-6pm, Sat.-Sun. 10am-2pm; free).

Two blocks south and one block west of the Plaza de Armas's southwest corner is the **Plaza de San Francisco.** The plaza is distinguished by its bronze fountain, quaint cobblestone streets, and red sandstone buildings. Elderly *potosinos* often congregate here, grasping grandkids and tossing crumbs to the pigeons. Soon after the city's founding, construction began on the **Iglesia de San Francisco,** on the west side of the plaza. Less ornate than its nearby counterparts, the orange stucco façade boasts a Sevillian clock (1785) and statues of St. Francis. Inside, the doorway to the Salón de Profundis depicts St. Frailón washing the sacred cuts of St. Francis. Each morning, Franciscans chanted the *De Profundís* in the salon, which is dominated by a magnificent Churrigueresque fountain (open daily 8am-7pm). The **Plaza de Aranzazu** (or western Pl. de San Francisco) is the simple space at the end of cobbled Universidad; classes of schoolchildren often take their afternoon recess here.

The **Museo Regional Potosino,** Galeana 450 (tel. 12-51-85), along the street on San Francisco's southern side, occupies the grounds of the former Franciscan convent. The government seized the land in 1950 and converted part of it into a museum. On the museum's second floor is the marvelous **Capilla a la Virgen de Aranzazu.** A shepherd found the altar's image of the Virgin in a prickly thicket, hence the name (*aranzazu* means "from within the thorns"). The *ex-votos* along the walls are a tradition among Mexico's faithful; each depicts a miracle that a parishioner has experienced. They are often painted anonymously and hung in the church near an image of the Virgin. A huge 18th-century hymnal stands to the right of the altar and next to the bishop's sedan chair. The first floor exhibits artifacts from all of Mexico, including an exhibition of prehispanic artifacts (open Tues.-Sat. 10am-1pm and 3pm-6pm; free). Three blocks east along Manuel Othón from the Plaza de Armas is the expansive **Alameda Juan Sarabía.** During the day you can admire its trees, benches, statues, and artificial ponds; avoid the Alameda at night.

The **Parque Tangamanga** has it all: three lakes for paddle-boating and fishing, a baseball field, electric cars, a jogging path, and grounds for driving and biking. The open-air **Teatro de la Ciudad** hosts frequent cultural and artistic events. To get to the park, catch a "Perimetral" bus (.80 pesos) on Constitución across from the Alameda. Get off at the Monumento a la Revolución and walk south for three blocks (open Tues.-Sun. 9am-6pm; free).

### ENTERTAINMENT AND SEASONAL EVENTS

Chic *potosinos* insist that **Arusha,** Muñoz 195 (tel. 17-42-30), is the best club in town. To understand the kitschy grandeur of the club's decor—which consists of a gigantic elephant head (fake), some stuffed animals (real), and a light system to create that jungle mood—you need to know that Arusha is a city in Tanzania. Now, party on. (Cover 25 pesos, drinks 7 pesos. No shorts, sandals, or sneakers—after all, this is Africa. Open Thurs.-Sat. 9pm-3am.) **Oasis,** on the highway to Mexico City, is an intimate joint with a loyal following (cover 25 pesos; open Thurs.-Sat. 8pm-2am). Taxis after dark to either club run about 10 pesos. A little closer to the *centro* is **Puff!,** Carranza 1145 (tel. 13-65-53). Appealing to the young collegiate crowd, this hip disco has no cover (open daily, and starts filling up at about 10pm).

The last two weeks of August mark the **Fiesta Nacional Potosina.** Concerts, bullfights, fireworks, and a parade guarantee that a swell time will be had by all.

# ■■■ MATEHUALA

The indigenous founders of Matehuala must have anticipated the trickle of backpackers who traverse this central Mexican crossroads: the town's name derives from a Huachichil phrase meaning "don't come." Unfortunate nomenclature aside, the city's 75,000 residents welcome visitors to their haphazardly laid-out streets.

Founded in 1590 as a mining colony meant to take advantage of the mineral deposits in the nearby mountains, today Matehuala promotes itself through its proximity to the remnants of this mining legacy at Real de Catorce. While its list of attractions may be sparse, Matehuala promises a relaxing stay; unlike many other Mexican cities, the city has slid into the modern age with grace. The motor scooters zipping past video stores cannot detract from Matehuala's parks and tranquil atmosphere.

## ORIENTATION

Matehuala is 261km from Saltillo and 191km from San Luis Potosí, and is located on Rte. 57, which runs though the eastern half of the city. The city is inaccessible by train. The **Central de Autobuses** is located on Calle 5 de Mayo, just south of the city and near the large, red **Arco de Bienvenida.** Cinco de Mayo runs north-south through the center of town. From the station, a *pesera* labeled "Centro" will take you to the downtown area for 0.80 pesos—get off when you first come to Hidalgo street across from the Promacen building. Taxis charge 8 pesos for the trip.

Even for its residents, the streets of Matehuala are terribly confusing. Some run for only a few blocks; others split into two forks or suddenly change names. A map is both invaluable and hard to come by. Try to procure one at the tourist office on Highway 57, or better yet, at the Monterrey or San Luis Potosí tourist offices. **Miguel Hidalgo** runs north-south through most of the city; **Benito Juárez** runs parallel to it, one block west. Most points of interest lie somewhere on or between these streets.

## PRACTICAL INFORMATION

**Chamber of Commerce: Cámara Nacional de Comercio de Matehuala,** Morelos 427. The only central tourist resource. Low on maps and pamphlets but high on knowledge. Open Mon.-Fri. 8am-1:30pm and 4-7:30pm, Sat. 8am-1pm.

**Tourist Office:** Next to Padregal Motel on Highway 57, north of the city (tel. 2-12-81 for Padregal Motel). Helpful but small-scale. Open Mon.-Fri. 10am-4pm.

**Police:** tel. 2-06-47.

**Post Office:** Leandro Valle and Negrete (tel. 2-00-73). Open Mon.-Fri. 8am-3pm, Sat. 9am-1pm. *Lista de Correos* Mon.-Fri. 8am-1pm. Postal Code: 78700.

**Telephones:** No **LADATEL**s available. Long distance service at **Domi's,** Morelos 701 off the Plaza de Armas. *Caseta de larga distancia* at Niño Artillero 111, west off Hidalgo behind the gas station. Open 9am-9pm.

**Telegrams: Telecomm,** Madero 119A (tel. 2-00-08). Open Mon.-Fri. 9am-7pm.

**Currency Exchange: Casa de Cambio San Luis Divisa,** at Colón and Hidalgo, just north of Hotel Matehuala (tel. 2-31-46). They also cash traveler's checks. Open 9am-8pm. **Banca Serfín,** at Reyes and Hidalgo (tel. 2-12-82), has a 24-hr. Cirrus/MC **ATM.**

**Bus Station: Central de Autobuses,** on 5 de Mayo south of the downtown area. Offers service to most major cities in northern Mexico and to a few others farther away. Consolidated service of **Transportes del Norte, Frontera, Estrella Blanca** (tel. 2-01-50), and **El Águila** (tel. 2-28-60) to Mexico City (4 per day, 8hrs., 113 pesos first class and 96 pesos second class), Monterrey (3 per day, 4-5hrs., 50 pesos), Nuevo Laredo (every hr., 3pm-6am, 9-10hrs., 108 pesos), Querétaro (2 per day, 6hrs., 70 pesos), Saltillo (3 per day, 3hrs., 45 pesos), and San Luis Potosí (every hr., 2½hrs., 32 pesos). **Noreste** (tel. 2-09-97) serves Monterrey (7 per day, 4hrs., 50 pesos) and Reynosa (3 per day, 6hrs., 68 pesos). **Tamaulipas** (tel. 2-27-71) to McAllen (3 per day, 6½hrs., 74 pesos), Monterrey via Saltillo (17 per day, 50 pesos), Real de Catorce (5 per day, 9 pesos), Reynosa via Linares (2 per day, 7hrs., 68 pesos), and San Luis Potosí (6 per day, 32 pesos).

**Market: Chalita,** Hidalgo between Constitución and Madero. Open Mon.-Fri. 9am-2pm and 3:30-8:30pm, Sat. 10am-2pm. An outdoor market selling crafts and souvenirs is located in front of the Templo de la Imaculada Concepción. Open 9am-6pm, sort of).

**Laundromat: Lavandería Acuario,** Betancourt and Madero (tel. 2-70-88). Self-service wash or dry 3kg for 8 pesos, 20 pesos for full-service. Open daily 8:30am-2pm and 4-8pm.

**Pharmacy: Farmacia Rex,** Madero and Morelos (tel. 2-02-49). Open 8am-10pm.

**Red Cross:** Ignacio and Ramirez and Betancourt (tel. 2-07-26).

**Emergency:** 06. Dial it.

## ACCOMMODATIONS

**Hotel Blanca Estela,** Morelos 426 (tel. 2-23-00), next to the video store. Reservations are recommended at this 11-room hotel. Fans cool small, clean, colorful rooms with TVs. Great hallway lounge space. Singles 65 pesos. Doubles 75 pesos.

**Hotel Matehuala,** Bustamante 134 (tel. 2-06-80), just north of the Plaza de Armas. High-ceilinged and well-furnished rooms look onto a big central space easily able to accommodate a pick-up game of *fútbol*. Singles 50 pesos. Doubles 60 pesos.

**Hotel María Esther,** Madero 111 (tel. 2-07-14). Dainty blue-and-white exterior encloses rooms with an outdoor balcony, a slightly beat-up couch, and a painting to take you away from it all. Singles 52 pesos. Doubles 65 pesos.

## FOOD

**Restaurant Fontella,** Morelos 612 (tel. 2-02-93), just south of Hotel Matehuala. Modern lamps illuminate a tranquil, flora-filled dining area, while the murals of the city evoke a sense of yesteryear. Try the *comida corrida* (15 pesos) or some of the breakfast options (under 13 pesos). Open daily 7:30am-2am.

**La Cava,** Callejón del Arte 1 (tel. 2-28-88), just east of Hotel Matehuala. The bright pink tablecloths and outdoor dining area provide a pleasant escape from the merciless sun. Traditional Mexican fare and a healthy assortment of sandwiches for under 15 pesos. Open daily 7:30am-10:30pm.

**Restaurant y Mariscos Santa Fe,** Morelos 709 (tel. 2-07-53), on the east side of the Plaza de Armas. The TV seems to have most patrons captivated. Endless options include *pollo empanizado* (14 pesos), *bistek ranchero* (13 pesos), and most seafood options for under 18 pesos. Open daily 7am-midnight.

## SIGHTS

Standing solemnly at the center of Matehuala between Calles Juárez and Hidalgo is the as-yet-incomplete **Templo de la Imaculada Concepción,** a copy of Saint Joseph's cathedral in Lyon, France. Construction began in 1905, but poor funding forced has slowed progress on the project. (Sigh. Maybe someday.) The large clock and seemingly impenetrable gray exterior of this Gothic-style edifice belie a beautiful interior flooded with light. Another cathedral, the **Templo del Santo Niño,** stands four blocks west on Constitución and is currently closed for renovations.

Just in front of the main cathedral is the **Plaza Juárez,** now permanently occupied by vendor stalls and small, makeshift cafés. Stretching out onto adjoining streets, the bazaar is collectively known as **Mercado Arista.** Leather and ceramic goods as well as the usual slew of cheap plastic toys and trinkets figure prominently here.

Two large parks stand at the northeast and southeast corners of the downtown area. Approximately three blocks east of Hidalgo between Bocanegra and Altamirano is the soothing and peaceful **Parque Vicente Guerrero** (also called the Parque del Pueblo). Vicente Guerrero's counterpart is the more lively **Parque Álvaro Obregón,** just south of Insurgentes. With basketball courts and benches aplenty, Álvaro Obregón draws entire families in the early evening hours.

# ■■■ REAL DE CATORCE

Only a stretch of pavement separates the stone-paved streets of Real de Catorce from the modernized Matehuala, but the two towns seem light-years away. Once a thriving mining town with 30,000 inhabitants, Real de Catorce now looms mysteriously on the side of a mountain, a veritable ghost town.

Real de Catorce sprung up with a glittery flash in 1772, when veins of silver and gold were uncovered in a remote part of the Sierra Madre. The etymology of the town's name, which literally means "Royal of Fourteen," is a matter of considerable debate: while *real* refers to a Spanish coin worth one-quarter of the *peseta*, the significance of *catorce* remains murky. Some hypothesize that there were 14 travelers in the group that first discovered silver in the region; dissenters assert that it took 14 days for the indigenous Huicholes to arrive at the mountain.

Despite the ghost-town hype surrounding "La Ciudad Increíble" (The Incredible City), several hundred people, including a colony of hippies, still call Real de Catorce home. Men and women still traverse the city's clumsily-constructed streets, pulling their horses and donkeys behind them, thinking of the glory that once was.

**Orientation and Practical Information** Today, tourists from all over Mexico travel to Real de Catorce to investigate this dusty anachronism of a town. Self-appointed tour guides, offering information and peyote—not necessarily in that order, or for free—abound in the back streets of the city. **Autobuses Tamaulipas** (tel. 2-08-40) offers trips from Matehuala leaving every 2 hours, 6am-6pm (round-trip18 pesos). Taking the last bus means spending the night at Real de Catorce. Buses leave from a station at Guerrero and Méndez, near el centro. Finding the station is quite tricky; ask a local to point you in the right direction. The 1½ hour trip is guaranteed to whiten the knuckles of the timid traveler: the bus rambles along a cobblestone road and a winding path chiseled into the mountainside. Real de Catorce lies at the end of a tunnel exactly 2300 meters long and one vehicle wide.

In the town itself, most services (i.e. the civil registry, police station, and municipal government) run out of the **Residencia Municipal,** just by the Plaza Principal. The **post office,** on Calle Constitución, is open Mon.-Fri. 9am-1pm and 3-6pm. The single **telephone** (tel. 2-37-33) will put you in touch with the hotels.

**Accommodations and Food** Real de Catorce has a conspicuous lack of decent budget accommodations and an unusual abundance of Italian restaurants. **Hotel Real,** Morelos 20, has colorful, spic-and-span rooms with that clean, pine-fresh scent. The central courtyard has a direct view of nearby mountaintops. (Singles 100 pesos. Doubles 115 pesos.) Italian dishes (15-20 pesos) are the forte of the hotel's restaurant. **Hotel Providencia,** Lanzagorta 29, is cheaper, but the bathrooms are shoddy and the walls dirty. (Singles 50 pesos. Doubles 100 pesos.) Although somewhat more expensive, the best option may be **Quinta La Puesta Del Sol,** a variation of a bed and breakfast across from the Capilla de Guadalupe. (Rooms with TV and bathroom run 100 pesos. Doubles 150 pesos.) The **Eucalipto Restaurant** on Calle Lerdo offers decently priced Italian food.

**Sights** Calle Lanzagorta runs past most major sights. The **Templo de la Purísma Concepción** is down the road on the right; ascend the white walkway to reach the entrance. Inside, the floor seems to be composed of rectangular blocks of wood; the blocks are actually doors to subterranean tombs, each of which contains several bodies. The cathedral houses a lifelike image of St. Francis, whose miracles have created a devoted following; on October 4, the saint's feast day (as well as that of the lesser known, though equally revered Saint Fabian Giraldo), the town attracts a flock of pious visitors hoping to pray at the cathedral. A side room has its walls filled with thousands of letters as testament to Saint Francis' ability to work miracles.

Across from the cathedral along Lanzagorta is the **Museo Parroquial** (open Thurs.-Sun., 10am-4pm), which exhibits relics from the town's past. Uphill on the right, after the cathedral (a steep climb) is the **Plaza Principal,** where today only a crumbling fountain remains. Next to the plaza is the **Casa de Moneda,** formerly a mint, whose third floor houses a photography exhibit of Real de Catorce. Enter the museum by the plaza (open daily 10am-4pm; free).

Turning right immediately after the Jardín, continue two blocks uphill, then head one painfully uphill block to the left. There the terraced steps of the **Palenque de Gallos** (cock-fight ring) echo the layout of a classical Athenian theater. (You will have to ask someone in the Casa de Moneda to unlock it for you.) The cliff known as **El Voladero** offers wonderfully breathtaking views of the surrounding mountains and valleys. To reach it, walk straight ahead on Calle Constitución up the hill. Further up Calle Zaragoza lies the Plaza de Toros, an unimpressive amalgamation of stone that was used for only six years as a bullfighting ring before its closure in 1868. Across the street is the stark white **Capilla de Guadalupe** (also called the Panteón), which overlooks a cemetery tightly paved with the graves of local saints.

# ■ Western Mexico

## NAYARIT

Nayarit entered the world's consciousness via Carlos Castañeda's book *Journey to Ixtlán*, which was inspired by the hallucinogens of a small town halfway between Tepic and Guadalajara. A state with diverse terrain, Nayarit is marked by volcanic highlands, lakes and rivers, and numerous beaches, many of which still remain undeveloped. A Pacific breeze keeps Nayarit's desert climate at relatively mild temperatures; this climate has in turn helped Nayarit become the Republic's greatest exporter of fruit, and reputedly of the lion's share of the nation's marijuana crop.

The Cora and Huichol peoples constitute the basis of the Nayarit culture. Bright color dominates their costumes and crafts, particularly in the famous Huichol *Ojos de Dios* (Eyes of God), crosses decorated with colored yarn culminating in brilliant squares at the tip. Folk music of Nayarit is ancient in origin and deeply religious.

### ■■■ TEPIC

The Nayarit capital and an important crossroads for the entire region, Tepic is a hard-working city (pop. 500,000) that fits its name well: it comes from the Nahuatl words *tetl* (rock) and *pic* (hard). Aside from a few historical sites and La Loma Park, the average visitor finds little of interest here. Travelers who visit Tepic usually just pass through on Rte. 15 or 200 or use the city as a base for exploring nearby towns.

**Orientation and Practical Information** As you leave the bus station, *el centro* is down the highway (Insurgentes) to the left; cross the street and catch one of the banana slug-yellow buses (6am-9pm, 1 peso) at the *parada*. **Avenida México,** running north-south six blocks west of the bus station, is downtown Tepic's main drag. Addresses on Av. México change from Norte to Sur about four blocks north of **Insurgentes,** the largest east-west street. The yellow minivan *combis* (6am-8pm, 1 peso; 8pm-midnight, 2 pesos) run back and forth along Av. México and Insurgentes. At its northern terminus, the many-fountained **Plaza Principal** (officially the **Centro Histórico**) is incessantly active, dominated on one end by the cathedral and on the other by the **Palacio Municipal.** Most tourist services lie on or near Av. México.

The **regional tourist office,** Avenida de la Cultura 74 (tel. 4-80-71 to -73; fax 4-80-74), is in the *colonia* Ciudad del Valle, just south of town and west of Av. México. Well-stocked with maps and brochures. A sprinkling of English spoken (open Mon.-Fri. 9am-8pm). The **police station** (tel. 2-01-63) is at Avenidas Mina and Oaxaca, but it's too far to walk and no buses go there. Cabs cost 8 pesos. The bus station holds a **post office** (tel. 2-45-03; open Mon.-Fri. 8am-2pm and Sat. 7-11am) and a **telegram office** (tel. 3-23-27; open Mon.-Fri. 8am-1:30pm). For telegrams, there is also **Telecomm,** Av. México Nte. 50 (tel. 2-17-11; open Mon.-Fri. 8am-7pm, Sat. 8am-noon). There are two **Computel** booths in the bus station; the one to the left as you enter is open 24 hrs. No collect calls. Credit card-only **TelMex** phones are in the bus station and along Av. México. **Telephone Code:** 321. Bundles of **banks** and *casas de cambio* clutter México Nte.; most banks are open Mon.-Fri. 9am-1pm, while *casas de cambio* are commonly open Mon.-Sat. 9am-2pm and 4-7pm. **Bánamex** and **Bancomer,** on Av. México Nte. a few blocks south of the plaza, have **ATMs.**

The **train station,** on Allende at Juárez (tel. 3-48-61 or 3-48-35), has a daily train to Guadalajara (noon, 5hrs., 17 pesos). To get there, hop on a "Ferrocarril" bus at the bus station or downtown at the corner of México Sur and Hidalgo. Tepic has a downtown **bus station,** located three blocks north of the plaza on Victoria, which serves local destinations, as well as the larger, long-distance station. Warning: not even locals have mastered the infinite municipal routes, so read the painted windows and ask the drivers questions. **Norte de Sonora** (tel. 3-23-15) runs the most out of both stations, with out-of-town service to Culiacán (every hr., 8hrs., 85 pesos) and dozens more. **Transportes del Pacífico** (tel. 3-23-13) goes constantly to Ixtlán (14 pesos) and Tequila (28 pesos), among others. **Elite** (tel. 3-13-28 or 3-23-26) rides in style to Guadalajara (9 per day, 5:30am-10:30pm, 4-4½hrs., 50 pesos), Mazatlán (every 2 hrs., 5hrs., 49 pesos), Mexico City (7 and 8:30pm, 12hrs., 160 pesos), and Nogales (8 per day, 12:10am-9pm, 24hrs., 273 pesos). **TriStar** (tel. 3-23-26) has extensive service, including Mexicali (every hr., 30hrs., 312 pesos) and Tijuana (every hr., 32hrs., 312 pesos). **Omnibus de México** serves Guadalajara (every hr., 10pm-2pm, 3½hrs., 50 pesos) and Mexico City (5 per day, 10am-11pm, 11hrs., 160 pesos). **Luggage storage** runs two pesos per article per hour, 12 pesos for 24 hrs.

One (but not the only) good **pharmacy** in Tepic is **Distribuidores de Medicina y Perfumería de Nayarit,** Av. México Nte. 376 (tel. 6-40-61). No English spoken (open daily 8am-10pm). The **Centro de Salud** (tel. 3-41-27) is on Paseo de la Loma. To make the 20-minute walk to the hospital from the bus station, take a left as you leave the building and another left at the intersection with Avenida México. After three blocks, take the right-hand fork at the rotary; two blocks later the hospital is on your left (open 24 hrs.). Cabs to the hospital cost eight pesos from the *centro*.

**Accommodations and Food**   If Tepic throws a few good experiences your way and you decide to stay a night or two, head for the **Hotel Nayar,** Martínez 430 (tel. 3-23-22), left on your way out of the bus station and another left on the first street; continue for a block, turn right, and go up half a block. The rooms are large but sparsely furnished. Lucky guests get a token *objet d'art*. Bathrooms are roomy enough and clean, but no shower curtains (singles 40 pesos; doubles 40 pesos, two beds 55 pesos). An alternative to Nayar is its next-door-neighbor, the **Hotel Tepic,** Martínez 438 (tel. 3-13-77), beside the bus station. The rooms are tiny and basic. Singles come with a desk, mirror, closet, and bed with a concrete frame—avoid plopping down after a long bus ride. The private bathrooms are so small you could relieve yourself, take a shower, and brush your teeth at the same time (singles 32 pesos; doubles 40 pesos, two beds 47 pesos). For both hotels, light sleepers beware: the noxious and noisy Central de Autobuses starts grinding at around 6am. The area just north of the Plaza Principal and west of Av. México hosts a slew of hotels. Try the **Hotel Sarita,** Bravo 112 Pte. (tel. 2-13-33), 3½ blocks west of Av. México. Very simple red-and-white tiled rooms come furnished with hot water, towels, fans, and some with TVs (singles 50 pesos; doubles 55 pesos, two beds 65 pesos).

Tepic is well-endowed with agricultural goodies. Mangos and *guanábanas* (soursops) make their way to the stalls at Mercado Juan Escutia, on Mérida and Zaragoza, four blocks south and three blocks east of the Museo Regional (see below). For a more formal meal, head for **Altamirano,** México Sur 109 (tel. 2-13-77), where peach stucco walls and bright green seats host slews of businessfolk taking advantage of a scrumptious plate of *enchiladas con pollo y crema* (15 pesos; open daily 7am-10pm). **Restaurant Vegetariano Quetzalcóatl,** León Nte. 224 at Lerdo, four blocks directly west of Plaza Principal, provides a *cenaduría* atmosphere without the meat. Stuff yourself on the Sat. buffet (18 pesos) or sample the *comida corrida* (16 pesos). Vegetable soup 5 pesos (open Mon.-Sat. 8am-8:30pm). For the health-conscious, another option is a stroll through La Loma Park to **Girasol,** Paseo de la Loma 201 (tel. 3-42-93). To reach the restaurant, walk up Insurgentes by the park until you get to Restaurant El Jardín; cross the street, cross the bridge, and hike right on through the park on the paved road. Across the street at the road's end, Girasol serves 90s-style vegetarian food. Soy burger 6 pesos (open daily 8:30am-10pm).

**Sights**   In front of the Plaza Principal is the **Catedral de la Purísima Concepción de María,** a church marked by twin 40m-tall towers. Legend says the church was erected in the 16th century to protect the cross that miraculously appeared on that

NEAR TEPIC

spot in 1540. South of the Plaza Principal at México Nte. 91 is the **Museo Regional de Nayarit** (tel. 2-19-00). The museum houses a small collection of Toltec and Aztec bones, pottery, and artifacts (open Mon.-Fri. 9am-7pm and Sat. 9am-3pm). Also south of the plaza, at México and Abasolo, is the **state capitol,** a gracefully domed structure dating from the 1870s. At Av. México's southern end, turn west (uphill) on Insurgentes and you'll come to **La Loma,** a huge and enchanting park. If you're lucky, the miniature train that circles the park will be in service.

## ■ NEAR TEPIC: MEXCALTITÁN

Home to under 500 people, Mexcaltitán is situated on an oval island with a perimeter of only 1000m. On June 28 and 29, when the streets are still streets, Mexcaltitán hosts La Fiesta de San Pedro y San Pablo, when the town blesses the waters on which its prosperity is built. When the water is low and the festival has passed, there isn't much to do in Mexcaltitán but see the **Museo del Origen,** on the *zócalo,* which traces the island's history. Aztec artifacts and the histories of the inhabitants' ancestors all find cases here (open Tues.-Sun. 9am-1pm and 3-6pm; free).

The island has managed to spawn a few restaurants, all of which play the only culinary game in town—shrimp. *Camarón al diablo, camarón al mojo de ajo, coctel de camarón;* Gump-like, the list goes on forever. Try **Alberca** (ext. 134), on Hidalgo, all the way to your right as you step off the *lancha,* for some of the island's best in a restaurant built on the water. Shrimp meals are about 25 pesos (open daily 8am-7pm). If you miss the last boat, there is an as-of-yet nameless **hotel** on the island at Venecia 5 (ext. 128). To reach it, walk straight across the island from the *lancha* dock. The rooms are clean yet entirely plain, except for the loud blue tiles screaming for attention from below. Enormous shower space. (One bed 50 pesos, two beds 60 pesos, three beds 90 pesos. Four beds and A/C 120 pesos.) On Mexcaltitán, all **telephones** work on an extension system. The sole number is (323) 2-01-98.

To reach Mexcaltitán, travel first to **Santiago Ixcuintla,** a village notable for its blue-domed cathedral. Buses run frequently from Tepic to Santiago (12 per day, 6:30am-6:30pm, 1-1½hrs., 11 pesos). From the bus station in Santiago, follow Calle Bravo Sur, cross the bridge, and walk for about five blocks; a left on any block will lead to the market and Ocampo Pte., which is the pick-up and drop-off point for *combis* and taxis. *Combis* (25min., 7 pesos) bound for La Batanga leave in conjunction with *lancha* times, about a half-hour before each leaves. Alternatively, take one of the buses that leaves from the local terminal, about 50m to your right as you exit the main station. From La Batanga, a boat takes passengers to and from the island (2 pesos). Boats leave from La Batanga at 9:45am, noon, 3, and 4:45pm; they return at 10am, 12:45, 3:45, and (warning!) the last boat leaves at 5:30pm. Always check with *combi* drivers and boat owners to confirm times.

Back in Santiago, change money at **Bánamex** (tel. 5-00-54), 20 de Noviembre at Hidalgo (open Mon.-Fri. 8:30am-1pm). **Transportes Norte de Sonora** (tel. 5-04-17) sends buses mainly to Tepic (every ½ hr., 5am-7pm, 11 pesos), but also to Mazatlán (6 per day, 6am-4pm, 4hrs., 35 pesos), San Blas (8:30, 9:30am, and 12:30pm, 2hrs., 11 pesos), and Puerto Vallarta (8:30am, 5hrs., 37 pesos). Should the last bus leave without you, the **Hotel Casino** (tel. 5-08-50), Ocampo and Rayón across from the *combi* lot, has wall-to-wall-carpeting, TVs, A/C, and hot water for big spenders, but for half the price, you still get hot water (singles 35 or 70 pesos; doubles 55 or 80 pesos). The trip to Santiago may be worth it if only to taste the goodies at **Panificadora El Gran Sabór,** Hidalgo 13, two blocks from the *zócalo.* Delicious pastries can go for less than a peso, and make a great snack (open Mon.-Sat. 5am-8pm).

## ■■■ SAN BLAS

San Blas has the feel of a creaky old sea salt, wounded long ago during a glorious adventure, who now insists that his scars should remain uncovered. The entire town could use a paint job, and the city's fort, destroyed during the wars of Independence, has been nothing more than a pile of rubble for over a hundred years. The dark waves off of San Blas make the water look like a worn swatch of blue corduroy. Awesome and abundant beaches, over 300 species of birds (just listen as you exit the bus station), and nearby nature preserves attract *norteamericano* expatriates, birdwatchers, and tourists en route to Puerto Vallarta. Only the swarming *jejene* gnats protect San Blas from enterprising developers with visions of Vallarta in their heads. As San Blas is also a haven for surfers, the *zócalo* is a cool-dude sort of place; skate-rats, surfers, and video game junkies swagger about into the wee hours.

**Orientation and Practical Information** San Blas is 69km northeast of Tepic by Rtes. 15 and 54. Buses run hourly to and from Tepic (2hrs., 11 pesos) and from Las Varas, south of San Blas. The **bus station** is just behind the *zócalo,* across from the cathedral. **Calle Juárez,** San Blas's main drag, runs parallel to the bus station on the opposite (south) side of the *zócalo.* **Batallón** runs perpendicular to Juárez from the *zócalo*'s center and leads to the closest beach, **Playa Borrego.**

The **tourist office,** Juárez 28 (tel. 5-00-01), is across from Restaurant McDonald (see below); head west past Batallón. The office has recently been converted into a shop for Huichol art, run by the **Comunidad Cultural Huichol.** It's rarely open during the low season, but desperate travelers may seek help at Michoacán 26, next to Casa María. The English-speaking staff distributes maps (open daily during high season 9am-9pm). The **police** (tel. 5-00-28) are on Sinaloa opposite the bus station; it's the last door in the Palacio Municipal as you walk away from the *zócalo* (open 24 hrs.). Rates could be better at the **Bánamex** on Juárez, east of the *zócalo* (open Mon.-Fri. 8:30-10:30am). Then again, rates are even worse at the *casa de cambio,* Mercado 32 (tel. 5-02-68), with another entrance on Juárez across from the bank (open daily 8am-2pm and 4-6pm). San Blas's **post office** (tel. 5-02-45) is at Sonora and Echeverría, one block north and one block east of the northeast corner of the *zócalo* (open Mon.-Fri. 8am-1pm and 3-6pm, Sat. 9am-1pm). **Postal Code:** 63740. The **telegram** office is at Sonora 56 (tel. 5-01-15; open Mon.-Fri. 8am-2pm). A *caseta de larga distancia,* Juárez 3 (tel. 5-06-10 or -11; fax 5-06-65) places collect calls, 5 pesos for 5 min. (open daily 8am-10pm). **Telephone Code:** 321.

**Transportes Norte de Sonora** runs **buses** from San Blas's station to Guadalajara (8:30am, 6hrs., 48 pesos), Tepic (12 per day, 6:30am-7pm, 1½hrs., 11 pesos), Santiago Ixcuintla (8:45am, 1, 3, and 6pm, 1½hrs., 10 pesos), and more. **Farmacia Económica** is at Batallón 49 (tel. and fax 5-01-11). English spoken (open daily 8am-2pm and 4-9pm). The **Centro de Salud** (tel. 5-02-32) is on Batallón and Campeche, five blocks south of the *zócalo.* No English spoken (open 24 hrs.). **Clínica IMSS,** Batallón 10 (tel. 5-02-27), is two blocks towards the *zócalo* from the Centro de Salud (open for consultation 8am-5pm; afterwards, enter on Canalizo).

**Accommodations and Food** Finding a place to sleep in San Blas isn't too difficult during the off-season, but autumn storms bring mile-long waves and bed-seeking surfers. In September and October you'll need to make reservations. The blood-sucking mosquitoes near the water make camping a no-no and rooms inland the best choice. **El Bucanero,** Juárez 75 (tel. 5-01-01), is reminiscent of a creaky pirate ship. The most popular place in town, El Bucanero is outfitted with large, dim rooms with high ceilings, clean bathrooms, a swimming pool, and a huge fading crocodile in the lobby. Hot water and fans make things comfy. (Low season singles 77 pesos, doubles 99 pesos. High season singles can cost 98 pesos, doubles 130 pesos. Prices vary.) The sign outside **Casa María,** Batallón 108 (tel. 5-06-32), says *"mi casa, tu casa,"* and the friendly folks mean what they say. Simple, white concrete rooms are set around a grassy, if slightly overgrown courtyard. The amenities just keep coming: parking, purified water, postal service, and a communal kitchen with refrigerator and dishwashing basin. Two of the rooms lack private baths, but the communal one is clean (singles 40 pesos, 50 pesos with bath; doubles with bath 50 pesos). Larger parties should scout out **Bungalows Portolá,** Paredes 118 (tel. 5-03-86), three blocks from the *zócalo* towards the market on Batallón, then a left and a right. Each space is well-kept and has beds for four, with a clean bathroom and dining room/kitchen. Colorful decor and amenities galore, starting with purified water and ending with the car and bike rental the proud owner runs from his office. Prices stay the same during high and low season (two people 120 pesos; three people 138 pesos). A **trailer park** with all the standard services, plus a guard, is **Los Cocos** (tel. 5-00-55), on Batallón just before the Playa Borrego (two people 45 pesos).

San Blas doesn't teem with restaurants, but those that exist are reasonably priced. While there's no Mayor McCheese at **Restaurant McDonald,** Juarez 36 (tel. 5-04-32), opposite the tourist office, the joint is just as popular with locals and travelers as the real Mickey D's. The little flowering plants give the place an odd, shimmering feel—imagine painting a black and white movie light blue. Try the chicken special (17 pesos) or a *plato de fruta* (7 pesos; open daily 7am-10pm). **La Familia,** Batallón 60 (tel. 5-02-58), is a family joint, right down to the tablecloths, TV, and conversation-starting wall-mounted shark's teeth. Chicken costs 18 pesos, *quesadillas* are 12 pesos (open daily 7:30am-10pm; due to economic pressures, they may not open until noon during the low season). For a slightly fancier, but comfortable atmosphere, head to the mask-happy **La Hacienda,** Juárez 41 (tel. 5-07-72). Delicious chicken *fajitas* for 22 pesos; mahi mahi 17 pesos (open Wed.-Mon. 2-10pm).

**Sand and Sights**  At the southern end of Batallón, **Playa Borrego** is easily accessible from town; unfortunately, it's egg-white bland. Borrego's sand is gray and its mosquitoes ravenous. Quiet, pretty, and swimmer-friendly, **Playa del Rey** lies off the coast of Borrego, and is accessible by *lancha* (about 3.50 pesos) from Borrego.

San Blas's initial attraction is the smooth water, packed sand, and long waves of **Playa Las Islitas.** During the stormy months of Sep. and Oct., the beach's waves are said to stretch for a good kilometer, and some surfers actually go the distance from Matanchen Bay to Las Islitas on a single wave. To reach Las Islitas, take the bus that leaves from near the market behind the church on the *zócalo* (9 per day, 7:30am-5pm, 15min., 9 pesos) or a taxi for 20 pesos. Walking is tough and takes a while. Don't settle for the first few stretches of sand that greet you—prettier coves and seclusion await farther along the shore.

While the winding jungle boat ride to **La Tovara** springs can be expensive, seeing a live crocodile just might make all the pesos worthwhile. Locals hype La Tovara—not the beaches—as San Blas's can't-miss attraction. Guides navigate the shallow, swampy waters en route to La Tovara, pointing out rare and interesting birds and the stilted huts left over from the set of the film *Cabeza de Vaca*. (Don't believe anyone who tells you the huts were left behind by an ancient and mystical people.) Just as it becomes necessary to duck the logs under which the boat passes, the path clears to reveal hordes of turtles and huge fish. It's best to journey to La Tovara early in the morning, when the water is still calm and the birds are as yet undisturbed by the *lanchas*. Trips can be arranged through the tourist office or with the boat owners themselves at the small docking area at Juarez's eastern end. Boats typically leave after 7am and return around 4pm; expect to pay 100-120 pesos per group or boat, depending on the tour. The excursion takes three hours, less if the meal at the restaurant (not included in the price) is skipped.

San Blas's town center stood on a hill overlooking the bays until a fierce battle during the wars for Independence left the old center ruined. The short hike to the top of the hill, called **La Contaduría,** affords a beautiful view of the city and coast. The splintering stone fortress that protected the city impresses from above, while an 18th-century church stands further downhill. To reach the ruins, head east on Juárez as if leaving town. Just before the bridge and the sign that says "Cape Victoria 7," turn right onto the dirt road behind the houses and restaurants; veer right off that road onto a stone path that winds uphill and leads to the top of La Contaduría.

After hours in San Blas, there's not much to do except down a few at the local watering hole. **Mike's CantaBar,** above Restaurant McDonald, rarely gets wild or crazy, but it's an interesting place to pass the evening. Mike no longer performs vintage rock, but he sings live salsa in what looks like an antique airport lounge (no cover; open daily 7pm-2am, live music Fri.-Sun.).

---

### The Huichol Indians of Nayarit and Jalisco

The Huichol Indians of Nayarit and Jalisco are believed to be the oldest native group in Mexico, and 2,000-year-old petroglyphs attributed to them have been discovered along Mexico's west-central coastal area. Originally, each Huichol piece was done by hand, depicting a unique mythological scene. Gold and jade were used to produce intricate designs on bowls and animal figurines. Spanish traders exchanged glass beads for the gold the Huichol used, and today the materials of choice are colored beads imported from (naturally) Czechoslovakia. The Huichol are also known for yarn paintings, a craft more common in cities, where the material is readily available. But the many Huichol who still live in rural mountain regions are easily taken advantage of by agencies that purchase their work for a paltry sum and sell it for fifty times the price the artisan was paid. Furthermore, Huichol artists are often coerced into reproducing identical designs and figures, a practice in conflict with traditional Huichol beliefs. The **Comunidad Cultural Huichol** of San Blas, a three-year-old non-profit organization, works to give Huichol artists a forum to express their art without exploitation.

---

# JALISCO

## ■■■ GUADALAJARA

To fully appreciate Guadalajara (pop. 5 million), you sometimes need to squint—both the city's history and its sophisticated charms have been obscured of late by industrial development and the construction of endless rows of flat, unspectacular one-story houses.

Founded by the most brutal of the *conquistadores,* Nuño de Guzman, Guadalajara was from its inception a city where Spanish values were dominant—de Guzman killed so many *indígenas* that few pre-Conquest traditions survived. When pro-Independence convulsions disrupted life in 19th-century Mexico City, Guadalajara, then something of a frontier town, attracted Spanish colonists who wanted to be both far from the capital and in a comfortably Spanish environment. Calling themselves *tapatíos,* the new arrivals helped to forge a distinctive culture. Over the years, the icons of this culture—tequila, *mariachi,* and the hat dance—have become important symbols for the entire Republic.

Today, Guadalajara is the second largest city in the Republic and a great place to spend a few days. The city boasts pocket parks galore, a bounty of fine museums, four large plazas, and stately colonial architecture. Markets in and out of the city provide no shortage of vintage *jalisciense* crafts, and local artists, thespians, dancers (including the renowned Ballet Folklórico), and street performers continue to celebrate Guadalajara's fine arts tradition. Meanwhile, the university, the second oldest in Mexico, keeps Guadalajara young and shades its urban bustle with a measure of highbrow intellectual sophistication.

### ORIENTATION

Buses run every hour from Guadalajara's **airport** to the *antigua* **bus station** in the south of town (5 pesos). From there, any "Centro" bus will take you into the center of town. *Combis* into town wait outside the terminal exits and leave hourly (5:45am-9:45pm, 5 pesos). A **taxi** to or from the airport costs up to 50 pesos, depending on the time of day. A new law mandates that taxis use fixed rates and a meter, on a 5 peso per 3km scale. Drivers follow that law like a mantra, and there's this bridge in Brooklyn...Actually, most *taxistas* ignore the law because they feel lawmakers didn't give them a fair shake. Try to get them to use the meter, but at least pin down the price before entering.

The **intra-city bus system** runs far, wide, and frequently. Though somewhat rough around the edges (usually crowded, always noisy, and sometimes uncomfortable), minibuses (1 peso), regular buses (1.30 pesos), and the big blue **TUR** buses (3.50 pesos) are an excellent way to get just about anywhere in the city. Buses #60 and 62 run the length of Calzada Independencia, from the train station to the Parque Mirador. The electrically wired "Par Vial" bus goes down Independencia, turns onto Vallarta, and travels west, turning just short of López Mateos. Coming back eastward it cruises Hidalgo, three blocks north of Juárez. Bus #258 from San Felipe, three blocks north of Hidalgo, runs from near the **Plaza Tapatía** down López Mateos to the **Plaza del Sol,** nightclub central. Bus #24A runs the length of López Mateos, from Zapopan to beyond the Plaza del Sol, in both directions. TUR bus #707A circles from the *centro* on Juárez west to López Mateos, down to Mariano Otero at the Plaza del Sol, up to Niños Héroes, and north on 16 de Septiembre and Corona to the start of the route. Buses run from 6:30am-10:30 or 11pm.

A new bus station, the well-organized and clean **Nueva Central Camionera,** has arisen in the town of **Tlaquepaque,** southeast of Guadalajara on the highway to Mexico City. Each of the station's seven terminals has been outfitted with **LADA-TELs** and a hotel information booth. The hotel booths work on a promotional basis with a select group of Guadalajara hotels, where you may receive discounts. The well-informed staffers can give you directions to almost any destination, but don't trust their quotes for hotels they don't promote. Buses and taxis (10-27 pesos; the earlier in the day, the cheaper) all head downtown from directly in front of any terminal. Prices are fixed for taxis running from the station, so buying a ticket at the taxi kiosk may prevent a potential rip-off.

Finding your way around outside the *centro* can be difficult, as streets change names at the borders between Guadalajara's four sectors. The city's **shopping district** centers around the intersection of Juárez and Alcalde/16 de Septiembre. The **Plaza Tapatía** is an oblong area that contains the **cathedral,** the **Teatro Degollado,** many churches and museums, and countless stores. The area west of Tapatía, with many of the most expensive hotels and restaurants, modern buildings, as well as the university and the U.S. consulate, is the most prosperous part of town.

The poorer *colonias* (suburbs) can be dangerous at any time of day. Check with the tourist office before blazing new trails. Throughout Guadalajara, it is wise to stick to lit streets after dark and to take taxis after 11pm. Solo women travelers should avoid Av. Independencia after this hour as well, as the street has a magnetic field that attracts raucous, drunken men. The area east of Independencia is generally considered a more unsafe part of town. A massive sewage explosion in 1992 has also brought a resurgence of cholera to the city; while many say that it's no longer a problem, vaccinations against the infection are recommended.

Guadalajara recently opened the first part of its **subway** system, and the one completed line (of four) runs efficiently (every 5-10min., 6am-10pm, 1.50 pesos). Line 1 runs from the northern boundary of the city, Anillo Periférico Norte, more or less along Federalismo to Anillo Periférico Sur. There is a stop at Federalismo and Juárez. Line 2 has not been completed, but it runs from Juárez and Av. Alcalde/16 de Septiembre to Av. Patria in the east.

## PRACTICAL INFORMATION

**Tourist Offices: State Office,** Morelos 102 (tel. 658-22-22 or 658-00-49, ext. 114), in the Pl. de la Liberación, next to the Pl. Tapatía. Lots of helpful information, maps, *Guadalajara Weekly* (the free tourist paper), and *Very Oír,* which lists cultural events for the month. Complete listing of hotels, restaurants, and emergency hotlines. English spoken. Ask about tours. Open Mon.-Fri. 9am-8pm, Sat.-Sun. and holidays 9am-1pm. An **Oficina de Relaciones Públicas** is in the Palacio de Gobierno off Corona. Limited information, but it has some good pamphlets on downtown Guadalajara. Open Mon.-Fri. 9am-3pm and 4-8pm, Sat. 9am-1pm.

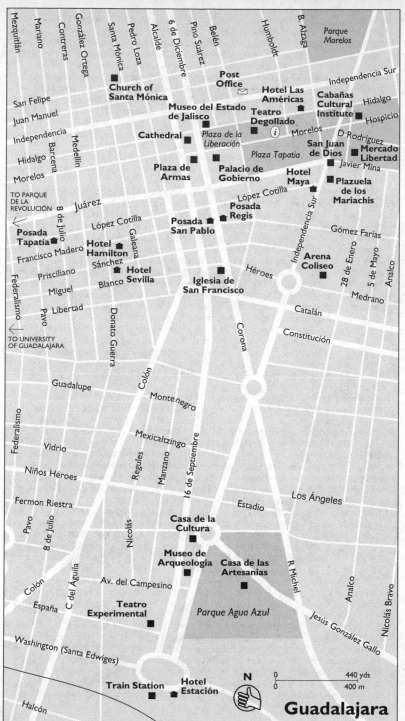

Guadalajara

**Police:** Independencia Nte. 840 (tel. 617-60-60 or 618-02-60). On call 24 hrs.

**Post Office:** (tel. 614-92-20 or 614-40-99), on Carranza, between Juan Manuel and Calle de Independencia (*not* Independencia Sur), one block north of the Teatro Degollado. Open Mon.-Fri. 8am-9pm, Sat. 9am-1pm. City mailboxes rumored to be unreliable. **Postal Code:** 44100, 44101 for surrounding area.

**Telephones: LADATELs** are all over the *centro*. **Mayahuel,** Paseo Degollado 55 (tel. 614-66-13 or -55), just towards the Cabañas Institute from the tourist office, offers long-distance service to the U.S. at 7 pesos per min., to Europe 9 pesos per min. No collect calls. Open Mon.-Fri. 9:30am-7:30pm, Sat. 10am-2pm. Blue phones take peso coins. **Telephone Code:** 3.

**Telegrams: Palacio Federal,** Alcalde and Juan Álvarez (tel. 614-26-64), and at the airport. Open Mon.-Fri. 9am-6pm, Sat. 9am-noon.

**Tours: Panoramex,** Federalismo 944 (tel. 810-51-09 or 810-50-05). Trips to Ajijic, Chapala, Tlaquepaque, Tonalá, and others. Budgets of all sizes accommodated. English tours available. City tour plus Tlaquepaque (daily 9:30am and 2:30pm, 5hrs., 65 pesos); Chapala and Ajijic (Tues., Thurs., and Sat.-Sun. 9:30am, 6½hrs., 90 pesos). Open Mon.-Fri. 9am-7pm, Sat. 9am-2pm.

**Consulates: U.S.,** Progreso 175 (tel. 825-27-00 or 825-29-98; fax 826-65-49). Open Mon.-Fri. 8am-noon. **Great Britain and Northern Ireland,** Quevedo 601 (tel. 615-90-93), between Eulogio Parra and Manuel Acuña. Open Mon.-Fri. 10am-2pm. **Canada** (tel. 625-34-34, ext. 3005 or 616-56-42; fax 615-86-65), at Fiesta Americana Hotel, Local 30 on the Minerva traffic circle (catch a "Par Vial" bus). Open Mon.-Fri. 9:30am-1:30pm. **Australia,** López Cotilla 2030 (tel. 615-74-18). Open Mon.-Fri. 8am-1:30pm and 3-6pm. For others, try the **Oficina de la Asociación Consular** (tel. 616-06-29), or the state tourist office, which has complete listings.

**Currency Exchange:** At banks and *casas de cambio,* rates are exceptionally high for cash and traveler's checks. **Bancomer,** Corona 140 (tel. 669-47-55 or 00000-63), at López Cotilla. Open for exchange Mon.-Fri. 8:30am-1pm. **Bánamex,** Juárez at Corona (tel. 679-32-52), is open for exchange Mon.-Fri. 9am-2pm. The block of López Cotilla between Colón and Maestranza is a *mercado* with only one product: money—making for good exchange rates. A particularly good rate on U.S. dollars is at **Cambios I. Gonzáles Machuca,** López Cotilla 218 (tel. 613-12-96 or 613-36-36). Open Mon.-Sat. 9am-7pm.

**American Express:** Vallarta 2440 (tel. 615-89-10), at Plaza los Arcos. Take the "Par Vial" bus and look for the office on your right after about 15 blocks. Financial services and travel agency. Open Mon.-Fri. 9am-2pm and 4-5pm, Sat. 9am-noon.

**Airport: Aeropuerto Internacional Miguel Hidalgo** (tel. 688-57-66, 688-53-82, or -76), 17km south of town on the road to Chapala. *Combis* run hourly (5:45am-9:45pm) from town to the airport, leaving from the Mexicana office (Díaz de Leon 951, via minibus #625 along Avenida Juárez). Don't pay more than 50 pesos for a cab. Served by **Aeroméxico** (tel. 614-50-00 or 688-57-67), **Mexicana** (tel. 613-50-97 or 688-51-00), **American** (tel. 616-40-90 or 688-56-46), and **Delta** (tel. 630-35-30, 688-56-53, or 688-55-25).

**Train Station:** (tel. 650-08-26 or 650-10-82), at the foot of Independencia Sur, just before the tunnel, south of the *centro.* To get to the station from the intersection of Independencia and Juárez, take a taxi (5 pesos) or bus #60 or #62. You can also walk to Independencia, only a block from the station, and take bus #45 north to the intersection with Juárez. Prices vary widely depending on train and class of ticket. To Mexico City (9pm, 11½hrs., 33.55-177.70 pesos), Tepic (first class 9:30am, 4hrs., 29.45 pesos), Mexicali (first class 9:30am, 37hrs., 231 pesos) and points in between. Second class leaves at noon. Advance ticket sales to points north Mon.-Fri. 9am-1pm, to Mexico City 9am-8pm daily. Same-day sales 7:30am-time of departure. Open daily 5am-10pm.

**Bus Station: Nuevo Camionera Central,** in Tlaquepaque. To reach the station from downtown, catch a bus on Av. Revolución, or on Av. 16 de Septiembre across from the cathedral. Both the red-and-white bus #275 (or 275A) and a blue TUR bus marked "Nueva Central" will take you there. In a taxi, be sure to specify the *new* bus station, since some drivers may zip you to the old station and then make you pay extra to go to Tlaquepaque. 30-odd carriers insure easy access to the northern half of the Republic. **Terminal 1: Servicios Coordinados** (tel. 600-

06-54 or 600-02-70) sends buses to Guanajuato (5:30pm, 5hrs., 52 pesos) and Mexico City (9 per day, 8hrs., 121 pesos). **Terminal 2: Autobuses del Occidente** (tel. 600-00-55) to Colima (2¾hrs., 43 pesos). **Terminal 3: Transportes del Pacífico** (tel. 600-08-54) to Mexico City (7 per day, 5am-1pm, 8hrs., 121 pesos) and Puerto Vallarta (11 per day, 4:30am-midnight, 6hrs., 78 pesos). **Terminal 4: Autocamiones del Pacífico** (tel. 600-04-50) to Nogales and 12 points in between (4 per day, 3:30am-11:30pm, 28hrs., 274 pesos), Puerto Vallarta (6 per day, 5:30am-11:30pm, 6hrs., 67 pesos), and Tijuana (9 per day, 12:30am-10pm, 36hrs., 292 pesos). **Terminal 5: Línea Azul** (tel. 600-02-31) to San Luis Potosí (first class 11 per day, 9:30am-midnight, 5hrs., 66 pesos; second class 23 per day, 6hrs., 57 pesos). **Terminal 6: Omnibus de México** (tel. 600-02-91, 600-07-18, or 600-04-69) to Ciudad Juárez (4 per day, 11am-11pm, 22-24hrs., 291 pesos) and Zacatecas (16 per day, 6:30am-midnight, 5hrs., 67 pesos). **Terminal 7: Estrella Blanca** (tel. 679-04-54, -55, -66, or -34) is the parent company of numerous smaller lines, including **Rojo de los Altos** and **Transportes del Norte.**

**Car Rental:** Most places are on Niños Héroes or at the airport. **Budget,** Niños Héroes 934 (tel. 613-86-34, 613-02-86, or 613-00-27). **Dollar,** Av. Federalismo Sur 540-A (tel. 826-79-59 or 825-50-80; at the airport 688-56-89; fax 826-42-21). Renters need a driver's license, major credit card, and 21 years under their belt. Prices start at 85 pesos per day plus 0.75 pesos per km.

**Laundromat: Kwikwash,** López Cotilla 1234 (tel. 626-51-85). Wash and dry 4kg for 25 pesos. Same-day service. Open Mon.-Sat. 8:30am-8pm, Sun. 9am-3pm.

**English Bookstores: Sandi Bookstore,** Tepeyac 718 (tel. 621-08-63), almost at the corner of Av. de las Rosas in Colonia Chapalita. Take bus #50 from Garibaldi or the green "Plus" bus from Juárez. Extensive selection of new books and North American newspapers. Open Mon.-Fri. 9:30am-2:30pm and 3:30-7pm, Sat. 9:30am-2pm. The **Hyatt** carries day-old copies of the *New York Times;* the **Sanborn's** department store at Juárez and Corona carries a wide range of magazines.

**Cultural Information: Departamento de Bellas Artes,** Jesus García 720 (tel. 614-16-14). Seasonal calendar of events. Open Mon.-Fri. 9am-3pm.

**Red Cross:** Accqui and Juan Manuel (tel. 613-15-50, 614-56-00, or 614-27-07), near the Plaza Morelos. English spoken.

**Pharmacies: Farmacia de Descuento,** Pedro Moreno 518 (tel. 614-29-50). No English spoken. Open Mon.-Sat. 8am-10pm, Sun. 8am-9pm. **Farmacia Guadalajara,** Javier Mina 221 (tel. 617-85-55). Minimal English spoken. Open 24 hrs.

**Hospitals: Green Cross Hospital** (tel. 614-52-52 or 643-71-90). English spoken. **Hospital del Carmen,** Tarascos 3435 (tel. 813-12-24).

## ACCOMMODATIONS

Guadalajara is full of cheap places to stay. Many hotels offer discounts for extended stays. *Posadas* are an excellent option—they're small, family-run establishments that provide large, well-furnished rooms, better security, and for a few extra pesos, frequently include meals. The drawbacks are less privacy and curfews. Check at the tourist office for a list. Guadalajara also has an excellent hostel (see below). Outside of the hostel and the *posadas,* reservations are only necessary in February and October, when thousands flock to Guadalajara for its cultural festivals.

### Near Plaza Tapatía

With room prices more or less consistent (and prices often based as much on haggling ability as quality), bedding down in the *centro* isn't a bad idea. It's probably safer, though noisier, than other options, and convenience is a definite plus.

**Posada San Pablo,** Madero 218 (tel. 613-33-12). One of the best deals in town. A plant- and canary-covered courtyard give way to large clean rooms with ceilings over 4.5m high. Some rooms have balconies and TVs. The angel of a manager keeps travelers coming from every corner of the world, and she has their postcards to prove it. Clean bathrooms and hot water. Singles 50 pesos. Doubles 60 pesos, with 2 beds 70 pesos. Add 20 pesos per person for a complete (and clean) breakfast and lunch meal plan. Prices are flexible.

**Posada Tapatía,** López Cotilla 619 (tel. 614-91-46). An abandoned *posada* until it was resurrected in August 94. The new owners are doing a good restoration job, allowing the place to retain its old charm. Clean, well-kept rooms with high ceilings, large mirrors and a dresser. Singles 45 pesos. Doubles 60 pesos.

**CODE Youth Hostel,** Av. Prolongación Alcalde 1360 (tel. 624-65-15). Take bus #52 or 54 from the Jardín de San Francisco or anywhere on Alcalde or the northern part of 16 de Septiembre. The CREA is just past the traffic circle. The clean, single-sex rooms hold 20 metal bunks each. Rooms come with bedding, pillows, and lockers, but you need to bring your own lock. Water is hot and the management friendly. Curfew 11:30pm. 15 pesos per person, and a 25% discount with HI membership. Reception open Mon.-Fri. 8am-9pm, Sat.-Sun. 9am-3pm and 5-9pm.

**Hotel Las Américas,** Hidalgo 76 (tel. 613-96-22). Comfortable, but the off-white color scheme is a bit bland. Wall-to-wall carpets, curtains, and gleaming lobby and hallways. Water is a perk here: in the shower, it's hot; in the pitchers they leave for you, it's purified. For 10 pesos your black-and-white TV magically becomes color and you get a fan. Terrific location, but traffic noise can be problematic. Singles 60 pesos. Doubles 65 pesos, with 2 beds 80 pesos.

**Hotel Sevilla,** Sánchez 413 (tel. 614-91-72). Rooms have TVs, dark rugs, and curtains, and retro characteristics: cherry-red phones, bright purple bedspreads, sky-blue bathrooms, and oh-so-tasteful landscape photos. Clean and spacious enough. Restaurant downstairs. Singles 50 pesos. Doubles 70 pesos, with 2 beds 80 pesos.

**Posada Regis,** Corona 171 (tel. 613-30-26). Large, clean rooms with high ceilings and huge chandeliers. Every day, a movie is screened in the dark courtyard. Deals for multi-night stays during low season. Singles 92 pesos. Doubles 115 pesos. Student singles (much smaller) 35 pesos. Student doubles 60 pesos.

**Hotel Hamilton,** Madero 381 (tel. 614-67-26). Sonar would help here—dark side-street location, dark rooms, dark maroon bedspreads, and metal doors painted black. Pink bathrooms are cramped. Big brown flowery curtains. Singles 40 pesos. Doubles 50 pesos. Triples 55 pesos. Add 15 pesos for TV.

**Hotel Maya,** López Cotilla 39 (tel. 614-46-54). Walls, showers, and bedspreads are all basic, all a dizzying sky blue—the rooms feel like large, underwater cells. At least they're clean. Singles 55 pesos. Doubles 70 pesos.

## East on Javier Mina

Javier Mina and the dark side streets off of it can become dangerous at night. If the cheaper options above don't work out (or if you just want to be closer to Plaza de los Mariachis) these hotels are basic, modern, and clean options.

**Hotel Ana Ísabel,** Javier Mina 164 (tel. 617-79-20 or 617-48-59). Like a cruise ship (not that budget travelers would know) with its narrow hall, small rooms, tiny TVs, and minuscule sinks. Clean. Hot water. Singles 50 pesos. Doubles 65 pesos.

**Hotel Azteca,** Javier Mina 311 (tel. 617-74-65 or -66). An elevator whips you upward from the snazzy lobby. Plenty of furniture, fans, and linoleum-esque floors. Pistachio-green bathrooms want to be loved. Comfy, but could be roomier for the money. Singles 50 pesos. Doubles 66 pesos, with 2 beds 80 pesos.

## West to University

The university campus, located eight long blocks west of Pl. Tapatía, is considerably more peaceful than the rest of the *centro*. Because most university-related action ends by nightfall, you gain nothing but tranquility by staying in this area. A pleasant option is **Hotel La Paz,** La Paz 1091 (tel. 614-29-10), near Donato Guerra on bus route 51 or 321. Clean, basic rooms come equipped with desks, floral bedspreads, TVs, and phones. But peace has its price—it's in the boonies (singles 50 pesos; doubles 55 pesos, with two beds 75 pesos; triples 90 pesos; TV 15 pesos extra).

## South to Train Station

Before opting to bed down in this industrialized part of town, remember that there's nothing to do around here but sleep, and better hotels await in Guadalajara's lively *centro*. If you must, **Hotel Estación,** Independencia Sur 1297 (tel. 619-00-51), is—

unfortunately—just to the right as you leave the station. The gray-and-peach rooms have seen years of use, but the staff does its best to maintain them. The rooms and bathrooms appear untainted (singles 40 pesos; doubles 50 pesos, with 2 beds 80 pesos; TV 10 pesos extra). Six long blocks from the station is **Hotel Flamingos,** Independencia Sur 725 (tel. 619-99-21). Catch the #60 or #62 bus and get off at Los Ángeles if you have bags. It's the cheapest hotel you'll find, which means small, noisy, and dark rooms, with beds the size of pillows and bathrooms without toilet seats. On the up side: the place is clean and there's a cafeteria in lobby (singles 34.50 pesos; doubles 45.85 pesos; triples 50.60 pesos; ask about discounts longer stays).

## FOOD

Guadalajara has tons of budget eateries as well as upscale French, Italian, and Japanese restaurants for those with money to burn. *Birria* makes an appearance on many a storefront menu. Hearty but not heart-smart, *birria* is a local specialty made by stewing meat, typically pork, in tomato broth thickened with cornmeal and spiced with garlic, onions, and chiles.

### Near Plaza Tapatía

Well-priced snacks are easy to find here, and that doesn't refer to the Dunkin' Donuts or Mickey D's just around the corner from your hotel. Ice cream is everywhere; sidewalk stalls are common (just be careful), and *panaderías* stuff the area southwest of Plaza Tapatía, primarily the blocks enclosed by Pavo, Sánchez, Galeana, and Juárez.

**Hidalgo 112,** at...Hidalgo 112 (tel. 614-54-47). No sign out front, so look for the faded red awning. A glorified juice bar with pine tables and traditional blue glass. Read the paper and chat with locals after the lunchtime rush. Fantastically cheap. Large fruit yogurt with granola served in a huge martini glass (6.50 pesos), as well as juices (2-2.50 pesos) and sandwiches (from 3 pesos). Soy burgers (4 pesos). *Quesadillas* 1 peso each. Open Mon.-Sat. 7am-10pm, Sun. 7am-5pm.

**Restaurante La Alemana,** Blanco at 16 de Septiembre (tel. 613-11-48). Sort of a diner, with live German music nightly, great cheap food, and free-flowing beers from the huge wooden bar. A favorite of Mr. Maximilian Diehn, lover of *Lederhosen, bratwurst,* and all things *deutsch.* Family joint by day, buddy joint by night. Huge plate of *enchiladas con pollo* 8 pesos. Open daily 9am-11.30pm.

**El Farol,** Moreno 466 (tel. 613-03-49), second floor. *Comida típica* at low prices. Prized tables overlook bustling Moreno. Friendly owner makes a mean *chile relleno.* Complementary *buñuelos,* a *tortilla* dessert dripping with sugary syrup. Entrees 10-16 pesos. *Enchiladas* 10 pesos. Open daily 9am-midnight.

**Restaurant Acuarius,** Sánchez 416 (tel. 613-62-77), across from Hotel Sevilla. New Age Mex-style. Break out your peasant shirt and brandish your cosmic consciousness. Wonderful management. Freshly squeezed O.J. 5 pesos. Soy burgers 9 pesos. Vegetarian *comida corriente* 22.50 pesos. Open Mon.-Sat. 9:30am-6pm.

**La Chata,** Corona 126 (tel. 613-05-88). Checked tablecloths, wooden chairs, traditional music, and a great downtown location. Open kitchen makes everything hot. Entrees around 20 pesos. *Huevos* 10 pesos. Open daily 8am-midnight.

### East to Javier Mina

Restaurants near Javier Mina will fill your stomach, but not with anything that tastes particularly thrilling going down. The exception is **Restaurant del Pacífico,** Plaza de los Mariachis 31 (tel. 617-82-28), where the *carne asada* (14 pesos) is perfect. Many a beer is drunk here; brews are 4.50-6 pesos (open daily 9:30am-late). **Restaurant Flamboyen,** Independencia Sur 164 (tel. 613-97-59) is in the Hotel de los Reyes. Not flamboyant, and certainly not meant for a king, but the bar stocks all sorts of wacky drinks. Sandwiches 12-16 pesos. Beer 6 pesos (open Mon.-Wed. 7am-midnight, Thurs.-Sat. 7am-2am, Sun. 7am-10pm).

GUADALAJARA

## West from Chapultepec to López Mateos

Most places below cluster near the intersection of Vallarta and Chapultepec, on the "Par Vial" bus route. Hopping a #321 bus from outside of the Fiesta Americana also does the trick and stops closer to restaurants on Chapultepec. It's worth the trip— the extra pesos you drop here buy superior food and even a measure of elegance.

**Los Itacates Fonda,** Chapultepec Nte. 110 (tel. 825-11-06). Fancy *típico* restaurant with a sizeable selection of Mexican delicacies. Full of middle- and upper-class Mexican families. Ceramic plates and locally produced crafts adorn the stucco walls. Great breakfast buffet 18 pesos. Four *enchiladas de mole* 15 pesos, *huevos a la mexicana* 10 pesos. Open Mon.-Sat 8am-11pm, Sun. 8am-7pm.

**Restaurant Samurai,** Vidrio 1929 (tel. 826-35-54), the small street a block north of the Niños Héroes monument on Chapultepec. Japanese food served up in a room in a family's house. Very cozy, very quiet, very tasty. *Comida corrida* (Japanese style) of rice, soup, and main course 12 pesos. *Tonkatsu* 25 pesos. Complete meals 18-30 pesos. Sushi on weekends (20 pesos). Open daily noon-10pm.

**Recco,** Libertad 1973 (tel. 125-07-24), just off Chapultepec. The waiters look mighty suave in those white dinner jackets; patrons in T-shirts or shorts will feel under-dressed. Popular for business lunches. A rejuvenating appetizer plate of *fettucine alfredo* (to find Martinez-esque salvation in—¡viva 95!) 14 pesos. Broiled sea bass 46 pesos. Menu in Spanish and English. Attentive Italian owner speaks English almost fluently. Open daily 1:30-11:30pm.

**Café Don Luis,** Chapultepec 215 (tel. 625-65-99), at Libertad. Coffees and desserts. A great place to revive your sleepy bones after a *siesta;* Angel's Kiss (Kahlúa, coffee, and eggnog) is love at first sip (8.50). Open daily 10am-2pm and 5-10pm.

**Las Margaritas,** López Cotilla 1477 (tel. 616-89-06), just west of Chapultepec. Inventive (and expensive) vegetarian food. Yellow-and-green Middle Eastern motif and tasty hippie tunes. *Casserole Las Margaritas* (rice, veggies, mushrooms, tuna, and cheese) 20 pesos. Sandwiches 15-20 pesos. *Comida corrida* 18-20 pesos. Open Mon.-Sat. 9am-9pm, Sun. 10am-6pm.

**Bananas Cafe,** Chapultepec Sur 330 (tel. 615-41-91). Not a fruit in sight. Instead, very loud music and video screens, with bunches of giggly students singing along to Guns-n-Roses tunes. Long haired waiters dressed in black put Bananas on the hipster map. Mostly snack food and drinks. Sandwiches 7-15 pesos. Beer and drinks 6-12 pesos. Open Mon.-Sat. 8:30am-midnight, Sun. 4:30pm-midnight.

**La Hacienda de Jazo,** Justo Sierra 2022 (tel. 616-82-80), just off Chapultepec Nte. In a courtyard so quiet you'll forget you're in a city. Lionel Richie and friends are piped in. Lively and sophisticated lunch bunch. Meat and fish entrees 22-37 pesos. Say you beer, say me 7 pesos. Open Mon.-Fri. noon-10pm, Sat. noon-7pm.

### Peel it, Slice it, Suck it, Dice it

Mangos may be the banana republics' most delicious offerings, but the fruit's sumptuous flavor is often passed over by foreigners who can't figure out how to eat the damn thing. There are two types of mangos: the red or green *paraíso,* the larger of the two, and the yellow *manila,* a smaller and less stringy fruit.

You can tell a lot about people from how they eat their mango. Some seem to find an acute enjoyment from sucking the fruit, turning it into almost an erotic art, while more prim folks can't stand the messiness involved. The easiest way to eat a mango is to pluck an end with your fingernail, peel it like a banana, and suck away. But for hygiene's sake, consider a fancier option: cut along both sides of the seed, leaving you with two pieces and a seed with some fruit around the edges. Next, peel the skin around the seed and chomp away. Then take your two bowl-shaped pieces and cut down into the fruit, creating a grid in the pulp. Turn the skin inside-out and scrape your pieces onto a plate. Diced mango! Alternatively, cut the fruit into strips, shove them into your mouth, and use your teeth to scrape off the pulp. Mangos are sometimes sold on a stick, and one can eat the fruit like ice cream by turning and sucking—be sure to lean over as you eat. And the one vital rule of mango-eating: never, ever wear a white shirt.

## SIGHTS

The rich history and culture of Guadalajara may no longer be plainly evident on its streets, but the city's distinguished legacy is not hard to spot in its monuments. Statues commemorating everyone from the *niños héroes* to (who else?) Benito Juárez are ubiquitous. All of Guadalajara's plazas are always clean and crowded, and often jolted by massive power surges when visited by party-hardy *mariachis*. And of course, Guadalajara has some mean museums—they're the best introduction to Mexican culture and history outside of Mexico City.

### Downtown

Downtown Guadalajara's four plazas punctuate the city's sidewalks and concrete with greenery and space. Horse-drawn carriages wait at the corners of some plazas, offering hour-long tours for about 50 pesos. (If you're desperate for some equine companionship, look for them on the Independencia side of the Mercado Libertad.) The spacious **Plaza de la Liberación,** with its large, bubbling fountain, is surrounded by the cathedral, Museo Regional, Palacio de Gobierno, and Teatro Degollado. A modern sculpture depicts Hidalgo breaking the chains of slavery in commemoration of his 1810 decree, signed in Guadalajara, to abolish the trade.

The **Palacio de Gobierno,** built in 1774 and on the plaza's south side, is a Churrigueresque building graced by a mural by José Clemente Orozco; the sight of Miguel Hidalgo's feverish eyes looking down from the wall strikes fear in the heart of many an unsuspecting visitor. A second Orozco mural covers the ceiling in the echoing **Sala de Congreso.** The mural depicts enslaved *indígenas* and the heroism of Hidalgo and Juárez (both open Mon.-Sat. 9am-9pm).

The imposing **cathedral** faces the Teatro Degollado across Plaza de la Liberación. Begun in 1558 and completed 60 years later, the cathedral is a mélange of architectural styles. After an 1848 earthquake destroyed its original towers, ambitious architects replaced them with much taller ones. Fernando VII of Spain donated the cathedral's 11 richly ornamented altars in appreciation of Guadalajara's help during the Napoleonic Wars. One of the remaining original altars is dedicated to Our Lady of the Roses; it is this altar, and not the flamboyant flowers, that gave Guadalajara its nickname, "City of Roses." Californians, including SMR and LRK, might disagree.

Inside the sacristy is the *Assumption of the Virgin,* a painting by the showy 17th-century painter Bertolemé Murillo. The towers, known as the *cornucopias,* can be climbed with the permission of the cathedral's administrators, who hole up in the side of the building facing the Teatro Degollado. There are entrances on this side, or just walk through the church to the back. The 60m jaunt to the top of the towers affords the best view in town. You may be able to take pictures of the church and sacristy, but be respectful (church open Mon.-Sat. 8am-7pm; tourists unwelcome on Sun.). On the cathedral's west side is the arboreal **Plaza de los Laureles;** to the north, the **Plaza de los Mártires** commemorates *tapatíos* who have died in various wars.

A building constructed in 1696 on the north side of the Plaza de la Liberación houses the **Museo Regional de Guadalajara** (tel. 614-99-57, 614-52-64, or -57). The museum chronicles the history of western Mexico, beginning with the Big Bang. The first floor covers the country's pre-Hispanic development and includes meteorites, mammoth bones, metalwork, jewels, and some Aztec art lamenting the Spanish Conquest. Collections of colonial art, modern paintings, and an exhibit on the history of the Revolution occupy the second floor (open Tues.-Sun. 9am-3:45pm; admission 13 pesos, 6.50 pesos for students, and free for everyone on Sun.; movies, plays, and lectures in the museum auditorium).

Attend the Ballet Folklórico at 10am on Sunday mornings to get a good look at the **Teatro Degollado,** a neoclassical structure on the Plaza de la Liberación's east end. The theater's interior features gold-and-red balconies, a sculpted allegory of the seven muses, and Gerardo Suárez's depiction of Dante's *Divine Comedy* on the ceiling. You can visit anytime, provided there is no performance scheduled. Tickets (tel. 614-47-73) are available at the theater box office (see Entertainment, below).

GUADALAJARA

The **Plazuela de los Mariachis** is on the south side of San Juan de Dios, the church with the blue neon cross at Independencia and Javier Mina. Immediately after sitting down, roving musicians will pounce—using every trick in their musical bag, the *mariachis* will try to separate you from your pesos. Prices for songs are completely variable; a good *mariachi* who likes you or a bad one without much choice may perform a song for only 15 pesos, post-haggling. But too much haggling may turn a good *mariachi* into a bad one, so keep the performance in mind.

From the **Plaza Tapatía,** constructed in 1982, you can spy the dome of the 190-year-old **Hospicio Cabañas** at the corner of Hospicio and Cabañas, three blocks east of Independencia. It was here that Hidalgo signed his proclamation against slavery in 1811; the building has since served as an orphanage and an art school. For its main chapel, Orozco spent 1938-39 painting a nightmarish rendition of the Four Riders of the Apocalypse; some regard the work as Orozco's best. *Espejos* (mirrors) are available free for those who don't want to strain their necks; alternatively, lie down on one of the many benches set up for reclined viewing. The *hospicio* also houses a collection of Orozco drawings and lithographs recently moved from his home (open Tues.-Sat. 10:15am-6pm; admission 8 pesos, 4 pesos with student ID, 2 pesos for children 13 and under, 10 pesos for camera rights—no flash).

The **Mercado Libertad,** at Javier Mina and Independencia, is promoted as the largest covered market in the Americas. It probably isn't, but there are still oodles of sandals, leather goods, *sarapes,* jewelry, and a few odd guitars filling tier after tier of booths. And be careful where you glance, or you may end up bargaining yourself into a "deal" you never wanted in the first place (open daily roughly 9am-8pm, but some merchants do not open on Sun.). A more authentic market is **El Baratillo** on Javier Mina, approximately 15 blocks east of Mercado Libertad. El Baratillo lasts all day Sunday and sometimes stretches for 30 or 40 blocks. Everything imaginable is peddled here, from hot *tamales* to houses. From Mercado Libertad, walk two blocks to Gigantes and catch bus #37 or 38 heading east.

### South

Almost everything is for sale inside the **Casa de las Artesanías de Jalisco** (tel. 619-46-64 or 619-51-79), on González Gallo, the street which bisects Parque Agua Azul. Pottery, jewelry, clocks, hammocks, china, blankets, *equipales,* chessboards, shirts, and purses, are all high-quality and have all been carted over from Tlaquepaque and Tonalá (see "Near Guadalajara" on page 262). Prices are higher here than in the villages (open Mon.-Fri. 10am-7pm, Sat. 10am-4pm, Sun. 10am-2pm).

### West

Guadalajara's **Zona Rosa,** the upper-class shopping district, centers on Chapultepec, west of the university. Cultural activity in the city's wealthier areas focuses on the **Plaza del Arte,** one block south on Chapultepec from its intersection with Niños Héroes. National artists bare their souls on a rotating basis in the plaza's **Galería de Arte Moderno** (tel. 630-27-22; open Tues.-Fri. 6am-8pm, Sat. 10am-5pm). The **Teatro Jaime Torres Bodet,** also in the Plaza del Arte, has book expositions, concerts, and other performances. Stand-up comedy and performance art periodically enliven the premises with laughter and pretension, respectively (open Mon.-Fri. 10am-8pm, with extended hours for some exhibitions).

### ENTERTAINMENT AND SEASONAL EVENTS

Although there is no lack of things to do at night in Guadalajara, the streets usually become deserted after dark and are often dangerous. Listings of cultural events appear in the magazine *Very Oír* (ask for it at the tourist office), in *The Guadalajara Weekly,* and on the kiosks and bulletin boards of places like Hospicio Cabañas. There's almost always something going on.

The **Ballet Folklórico** has toured the world, entertaining audiences with amazingly precise rhythmic dance, authenticated with the traditional garb of each representative region and polished with amusing stage antics. There are two troupes in

Guadalajara, one affiliated with the University of Guadalajara and the other with the state of Jalisco. The former, reputedly better, performs in the Teatro Degollado on Sunday at 10am. Tickets (15-60 pesos) are sold the day before the show at the Teatro Degollado ticket office (tel. 658-38-12; open daily 10am-1pm and 4-7pm). Spend the extra pesos for a seat in front and arrive a half-hour before the show because seats are not reserved within sections, and performances nearly always sell out. The **Ballet Folklórico de Cabañas,** the state troupe, performs Wednesdays at 8:30pm in the theater of the Hospicio Cabañas (tickets 25 pesos).

University facilities, scattered throughout the city, have created a market for high culture on a low budget. The **Departamento de Bellas Artes** coordinates activities at a large number of stages, auditoriums, and movie screens throughout the city. The best source of information on cultural events is the blackboard in their lobby at García 720 (see Sights, above), which lists each day's attractions. The **Instituto Cultural Cabañas** presents live music on an open-air stage in the Hospicio Cabañas at least once a week. Drop by the Hospicio Cabañas ticket counter (see Sights, above), or look for flyers with the Cabañas insignia (a building with pillars) for schedules.

For Luis Buñuel retrospectives and other vintage screenings, head to the cinema at Bellas Artes. The **Cine Cinematógrafo,** at Vallarta 1102 (tel. 25-05-14), just west of the university, is a repertory film house that changes its show weekly (tickets 3 pesos). For more mature company and some live *música romántica,* try the **Copenhagen,** Américas 930A (tel. 817-26-89), at López Mateos near the statue of Columbus (cover 15 pesos; open daily 1pm-1am, music toots Mon.-Sat. 10pm-1am). Alternatively, try **La Hosta,** at México and Rubén Darío (open daily 1pm-1am).

Clubbing hits hardest on the Plaza del Sol, near the southern end of López Mateos. While many of the clubs are *privado* (meaning many of their patrons pay membership fees), they are often open to the public.

**Osiris** (tel. 622-42-70), at Jardines de los Arcos on Lázaro Cárdenas. Receives rave reviews from locals. When it's private, you can get in by convincing the bouncers of your foreign origin (it shouldn't be hard). Cover 20 pesos.

**Ciros,** Mariano Otero 2409 (tel. 631-62-32), by the Plaza del Sol. Two clubs in one: its left half is a slightly upscale *privado* club, while the right half is a louder, brighter video bar. Cover for left half 20 pesos; for video bar men 50 pesos, women 10 pesos, with an open bar. Open Wed.-Sun. 9pm-3am. The club side closes during parts of low season.

**Pasaje,** Mariano Otero 1989 (tel. 121-13-63), a few doors down from Ciros. The ultimate in glam; thick smoke clouds a packed dance floor, while the majority down a drink and soak up the flashing lights and big screen TVs. Come prepared: preferably with a date in expensive clothing. The bouncers have loads of fun making people wait. Open Wed.-Sun. 4-8:30pm with no alcohol and a 5-peso cover for the under-18s; 9pm-3am 30-peso cover for adults.

**Gay clubs** support more nightlife here than in any other city outside of the capital. The upscale Zona Rosa along Chapultepec is a favorite gathering place. The best-known gay disco is **Unicornio,** López Mateos. Other hangouts include **S.O.S.,** La Paz 1413 at Escoza (closed Sun.), which has incredibly vibrant drag shows, and **Monica's,** Álvaro Obregón 1713, which is popular with a younger crowd (open Wed.-Sun. 11pm-4am). The **Jesse James,** Ramos Millán 955, is a honky tonk complete with country-western music. A mixed gay and straight crowd frequents **Chivas López Cotilla** and **Degollado.**

Thursday and Sunday evenings, finding a bench in the Plaza de Armas, across from the Palacio de Gobierno, is an impossible task—the Jalisco State Band draws crowds of locals enjoying free performances of gusto-packed music. The music doesn't get going until about 7pm, but seat-seekers should arrive before 6:15pm. Powerful speakers bring the show to other plazas, including the Plaza de los Mártires. The **Plaza de los Fundadores,** behind the Teatro Degollado, serves as a stage every afternoon for the clown-mimes who are popular among locals. Watch and give tips, but unless you like being the butt of jokes, keep out of the mime's eye.

In February, Guadalajara hosts a few weeks of cultural events to kick off the Lenten season. The **Fiestas de Octubre,** a month-long festival of cultural and sporting events, take place in October, as part of the processions of Our Lady of Zapopan (see Near Guadalajara, below). Marked by parades, dancing, bullfights, fireworks, tons of food, and displays representing each state in the Republic, the highly anticipated *fiestas* are great fun.

## SPORTS

**Bullfights** take place almost every Sunday from October to April in the **Plaza de Toros,** at Nuevo Progreso on the northern end of Independencia (take bus #60 or #62 north). During bullfight season the ticket and information office is at Moreno 887A (tel. 626-90-90 or 625-19-74), but the Plaza de Toros is open year-round (tel. 637-99-82 or 651-85-06). More popular, colorful, and distinctly Mexican are the *charreadas* (rodeos), held in the **Aceves Galindo Liendo** rodeo ring, near the east side (south end of Calzada Independencia) of Parque Agua Azul.

Even for a Mexican city, *fútbol* is huge here. The *Chivas,* the local professional team, are perennial contenders for the national championship—conversations turn nasty, brutish, and short at the mention of the *Pumas,* the team's Mexico City rival. Matches are held from September through May in **Jalisco Stadium,** at the University of Guadalajara and in **Estadio 3 de Marzo,** at the Universidad Autónoma. The ticket office for the former is in front of the Plaza de Toros (tel. 637-05-63 or 637-02-99) and at Colomos Pte. 2339 (tel. 641-50-51) for the latter.

# ■ NEAR GUADALAJARA

## TLAQUEPAQUE

The "village" of Tlaquepaque, as it exists in the minds of tourists, is little more than the strip along Independencia, where upscale shops set in old colonial mansions sell silver, handicrafts, leather, ceramics, plastic toys, and junk. Some even sell tickets to rock concerts. Though completely geared towards tourists, Tlaquepaque offers the best quality and prices for *artesanías* in the Guadalajara area. Just off its main square lies the *mercado,* where cheaper goods of lesser quality can be found.

The **Museo Regional de las Cerámicas y los Artes Populares de Jalisco,** Independencia 237 (tel. 635-54-04), has an interesting collection of antique regional crafts, as well as newer pieces for sale (open Tues.-Sat. 10am-4pm, Sun. 10am-1pm; free). Another fun, if touristy, spot is **La Rosa de Cristal,** Independencia 232 (tel. and fax 639-71-80), where artisans blow glass by hand, then sell their inflated works at inflated prices (glass-blowing Mon.-Fri. 10:30am-1:30pm, Sat. 10:30am-noon; shop open Mon.-Sat. 10am-7pm, Sun. 10am-2pm).

There are only two hotels in the town. **Posada en el Parián,** Independencia 74 (tel. 635-21-89), has clean rooms outfitted with a small wooden dresser, chair, and chest, but the adobe color scheme darkens the quarters; bathrooms are aging. Rooms go for 50 pesos for one *cama matrimonial,* 60 pesos for two individual beds, and 75 pesos for two larger beds. Reserve in advance or arrive early. The **Hotel Tlaquepaque,** Juárez 36 (tel. 635-00-87), features very turquoise rooms of the could-be-cleaner variety (singles 40 pesos; doubles 60 pesos). The central block of restaurants along Independencia boasts a number of relatively identical establishments, all expensive, and all with outdoor tables. Of these restaurants, **Paco's,** Progreso 1517, stands out for its people-watching potential. *Mole poblano* 23 pesos. *Quesadillas* 15 pesos (open daily 10:30am-2am). *Mariachi* groups hang out in front of all the restaurants—they'll perform at your table for a hefty 35-40 pesos.

**Getting There:** Reach the town by the #275 (or 275A) bus route or via the Tlaquepaque-marked TUR bus; for the main markets, get off at Independencia, marked by a Pollo-Chicken joint to the left; if the driver turns left off Niños Héroes, you've gone too far. To get back to downtown Guadalajara, hop back on a #275 or

TUR bus at the corner of Niños and Independencia. The Nueva Central is ten minutes away in the opposite direction on either of the above buses.

## ZAPOPAN

Northwest of Guadalajara, the town of Zapopan is famous for the **Basílica de la Virgen de Zapopan,** a giant edifice erected in the 16th century to commemorate a peasant's vision of the virgin. The walls of the church are hung with many decades' worth of *ex-votos,* small paintings on sheet metal recognizing the Virgin's aid in curing diseases. The image of the Virgin herself was made by natives from corn stalks in the 16th century. Pope John Paul II visited the shrine in 1979, and a statue of the pontiff holding hands with a beaming *campesino* boy now stands in the courtyard in front of the church. Every October 12 since the mid-18th century, the figure of Our Lady of Zapopan has made her way from Guadalajara's cathedral to Zapopan. While the procession only lasts a few hours, the statue is frequently exchanged from church to church throughout Guadalajara in the months before the procession. Each move occasions serious partying. For tourists, the **Casa de Artesanías de los Huichol,** a museum and crafts market for Huichol handwork, remains Zapopan's focal point. Clothing, *ojos de dios* (eyes of God, crossed rods decorated with yarn designs), and *makrames* (colorful designs of yarn on wood) sold here are on the cheap side (open Mon.-Fri. 9am-1pm and 4-7pm, Sat. 10am-1pm; free).

**Getting There:** To reach Zapopan, catch the #275A bus northbound on Av. 16 de Septiembre (25min., 1.50 pesos); hop off at the big church.

## TONALÁ

A less accessible, mercifully less touristed version of Tlaquepaque, **Tonalá** is most fun on Thursday or Sunday—on these market days, Tonalá springs awake from its near-perpetual *siesta.* Tonalá specializes in inexpensive, conservatively decorated ceramics. Good quality, low-priced silver also abounds, and costs considerably less than in downtown Guadalajara. While Tlaquepaque offers a greater variety of handicrafts, Tonalá retains a more authentic feel—some women weave multi-colored rugs and sew dolls, while patient ceramics merchants paint personalized messages onto their products. In Tonalá, the soft sell rules; merchants will take the time to talk with you, and you won't feel obligated to purchase anything.

**Getting There:** Buses #103 and 104, which run through downtown Guadalajara along Moreno, or TUR bus #706, which runs along 16 de Septiembre (3.50 pesos), are the best way to reach Tonalá; the trip takes about 30 minutes.

## LAGO DE CHAPALA

Forty kilometers south of Guadalajara, **Lago de Chapala** is Mexico's second largest lake. Tucked along the serene northern shore of the lake, the small villages of **Chapala** and **Ajijic** are a peaceable mix of Mexican tourists, tons of *norteamericano* retirees, local artists, and residents. While living in Ajijic in the 1940s, D.H. Lawrence wrote *The Plumed Serpent.* Although industrial waste has made swimming in the lake unsafe, the mountains which haunt the lake's opposite shore keep the whole area beautiful. English-speakers will feel at home in Chapala and Ajijic: there are so many expatriates here that half of the signs are in English.

### Chapala

In Chapala, the bus station's main entrance lies on the town's main north-south strip, **Madero.** The lake is Chapala's southern and eastern boundary. **Hidalgo** (known as Morelos east of Madero) runs west to Ajijic from two blocks north of the lake. The *mercado de artesanías* is on the waterfront four blocks east of Madero's terminus, on Ramón Corona.

Reach Chapala's **tourist office,** Aquiles Serdán 26 (tel. 5-31-41), by going west on Hidalgo from the Restaurant Superior, then hanging a left about 200m later at the yellow Italian restaurant; it's on the right-hand side (open Mon.-Fri. 9am-7pm, Sat. 9am-1pm). A **Computel** is in the plaza on Madero (fax 5-49-53), and charges four pesos per five minutes on collect calls to the U.S. **Telephone Code:** 376. Currency exchange is possible at **Bancomer,** Madero 212 (tel. 5-45-15 or 5-45-78; open for exchange Mon.-Fri. 9am-1pm). An **ATM** is also available. Or try **Bánamex,** Madero 222 (tel. 5-22-71 to -73; open for exchange Mon.-Fri. 9am-2:30pm).

If you plan on spending the night in Chapala, the **Hotel Nido,** Madero 202 (tel. 5-21-16), which once played host to dictator Díaz's weekend soirées, is the place to go. The airy hotel has clean, simple rooms with floral stencils, hot water, a pretty courtyard, and a pool. (Singles 75 pesos. Doubles 95 pesos. Add 20 pesos for TV. Restaurant open Mon.-Fri. 8am-9pm. Breakfasts 8-14 pesos, shrimp cocktail 18 pesos.) At **Casa de Huéspedes Las Palmitas,** Juarez 531 (tel. 5-30-70), parallel to Madero behind the plaza, a sunny lobby with checkered floors and parakeets leads to large, basic rooms with good beds and hot water. The hotel has been in the family for two generations (singles 35 pesos; doubles 40 pesos, two beds 60 pesos). For eats, head to Madero, where restaurants churn out tasty fish dishes. Expatriates are practically cemented to the sidewalk tables outside of **Restaurant Superior,** Madero 415 (tel. 5-21-80). If you don't mind their company, good food goes for excellent prices. Three *burritos* 10 pesos, *pollo con mole* 18 pesos, hamburgers 8 pesos (open Wed.-Mon. 8am-10pm, Tues. 8am-5pm). More *típico* food is served at **Chabela's Fonda** (tel. 5-43-80), at the far-right corner of the plaza's restaurants as you face them from Madero. Sunday brunches swarm with locals taking advantage of the 12- to 16-peso *menú del día* (open daily 8am-7pm). Near the entrance to the *mercado* (where prices are higher than they are in Guadalajara), local youths try to sell **horseback rides** to tourists for about 15 pesos an hour. Unless you'd like a tour of the not-so-interesting (nor prolific) sights of Chapala at a slower-than-crawling pace, you'd do well to pass up their offers.

**Getting There:** You can get to Chapala from the *antigua* bus station (every ½ hr., 6am-9pm, 45min., 10 pesos). Get off at Chapala's **bus station,** the final stop, located on the north side of town. Buses back to Guadalajara leave from the station on the same schedule as they come in.

## Ajijic

Just down the road from Chapala is the prettier village of Ajijic. The number of expatriates in town keeps the quality of facilities and the number of extended-stay apartments high. Across from the *zócalo,* **Suites Plaza Ajijic,** Cólon 33 (tel. 6-03-83), rents sunny, super-clean apartments with bedrooms, bathrooms, kitchens, and dining tables, not to mention closets and clean, comfortable furniture (singles and doubles 90 pesos, 450 pesos per week). At **Las Casitas,** Carretera Chapala Pte. 20 (tel. 6-11-45), the rooms are dark and the *centro* is a bit of a walk away; on the other hand, what would a budget accommodation be if all were perfect? Prices are excellent for a good living space; one- to two-person bungalows go for 80 pesos with all the amenities, including kitchens. The couch folds out and cots are available for a third and fourth person (90 and 100 pesos, respectively). Next door, the **Posada Las Calandrías,** Carretera Chapala Pte. 8 (tel. 6-10-52), has larger, clean and furnished apartments, a gleaming pool, an assortment of English-language books in the reception area, and a great view of the lake from the second-story balcony—but the prices are higher (doubles 115 pesos; quads 184 pesos).

For a great lunch, try **Danny's,** Carretera Chapala Ote. 2A, located just off the highway half a block from the road to the *zócalo.* Breakfasts are for homesick *gringos,* with the Grand Slam (eggs, pancakes, bacon, and sausage) going for 14.50 pesos, while lunch becomes local with Mexican combos from 13.50-22 pesos (open Mon.-Sat. 8am-5pm, Sun. 8am-1pm). Feeling fancy? Try the lunch buffet at **Hotel Nueva Posada,** Donato Guerra 9 (tel. 6-14-44), where the sumptuous Italianate interior and sculpted gardens leading down to the lake are especially popular with retirees. Daily specials go for 21 pesos. (open daily 8am-11pm).

**Getting There:** *Camiones* leave Chapala for Ajijic from Madero at Manzanillo, one block north of the plaza (every 15min., 6:15am-8:30pm, 15min., 2 pesos). They first weave through the village of San Antonio, then go on to Ajijic. Get off at **Colón,**

the north-south strip, or when the street you're on changes from **Constitución** to **Ocampo.** The *zócalo* is one block inland. To get back to Guadalajara, buses can be caught along the highway outside Ajijic (4 run 6-8:30am, then hourly until 6:30pm, 45min., 11 pesos). Alternatively, catch one of the *camiones* along Constitución back to Chapala.

# ■■■ PUERTO VALLARTA

In 1956, tabloid headlines were touting Puerto Vallarta as an unspoiled paradise. Richard Burton and Elizabeth Taylor's torrid affair while Burton was on location shooting *Night of the Iguana* helped paint Puerto Vallarta as the world headquarters of sensuality. Back then, neither highway nor telephone wire linked the town to the outside world; then Taylor bought a house, and the radical facelift began. Thirty-five years and millions of dollars later, Puerto Vallarta is a world-class resort with stunningly groomed beaches, luxurious hotels, and gorgeous mansions.

While Puerto Vallarta revolves around tourism, tourist-mania can take a variety of forms. In the south end of town, where the best swimming beach lies and where the more reasonably-priced hotels are located, there is a certain, if somewhat artificial, charm—the buildings are white-stuccoed, the roofs are red-tiled, and the streets are cobbled. On the north side of the river, larger nightclubs and more expensive clothing stores find a home, while still further north international resorts line the highway. Around and near Puerto Vallarta, the mansions and property that are the fodder of glossy brochures sparkle in their own sensual luxuriance.

## ORIENTATION

Running roughly east-west, **Río Cuale** bisects Puerto Vallarta before hitting the ocean. The southern half of town contains virtually all the cheap hotels, best beaches, budget restaurants, and dance clubs. The glitzy northern area could be mistaken for a U.S. beach resort; it houses nearly all of the city's tourist services.

The main streets in the southern half are **Insurgentes** and **Vallarta,** which run north-south two blocks apart, and **Francisco Madero** and **Lázaro Cárdenas,** which run east-west one block apart. The central bus and *combi* stop is on Insurgentes between Madero and Lázaro Cárdenas. Rte. 200 from Manzanillo runs into town south of the river, becoming Insurgentes. Insurgentes and Vallarta run north from Lázaro Cárdenas to the two bridges that link the south and north sections.

The main streets in the north are **Morelos,** the continuation of Vallarta, and **Juárez,** one block east. Four blocks north of the Vallarta bridge is the **Plaza Mayor,** whose cathedral serves as a landmark. The ritzy waterfront between Pl. Mayor and 31 de Octubre, called the **Malecón,** contains overpriced restaurants, clubs, and cheesy T-shirt shops. North of the Malecón, Morelos becomes **Perú** and runs through a working-class neighborhood before joining the coastal highway. North along the highway lie the **airport** and **marina.**

Taxis charge about 15 pesos to travel between the **Playa de los Muertos** and the entrance to the highway. **Municipal buses** and **combis** which operate daily from 6am-10:30pm, cost 1.30 pesos. Northbound buses and *combis* originate at the southern end of Insurgentes, run across the Insurgentes Bridge, head west on Libertad for a few blocks, north on Juárez, and onto the highway. In the opposite direction, buses enter the city on Av. México, which becomes Díaz Ordaz and then runs into Morelos, crossing the Vallarta Bridge before heading back. Any municipal buses operating south of the Sheraton or labeled "Centro," and all *combis* pass the Plaza. Buses and *combis* labeled "Hoteles" will pass the hotel strip. For the most part, buses stop only at the clearly marked *parada* signs and at the covered benches.

From the airport, there is a bus stop on the same side of the highway, 30m to your right as you leave the airport area (5am-11pm, 1.30 pesos). Specifically-marked airport taxis run out of the airport, although one can ride in on a city taxi.

## PRACTICAL INFORMATION

**Tourist Office:** (tel. 2-02-42), in the Presidencia Municipal, on the north side of the Pl. Mayor; enter on Juárez. Loaded with maps and other information. English spoken. Open Mon.-Fri. 9am-9pm, Sat. 9am-1pm.

**Police:** (tel. 3-25-00), at Iturbide and Morelos. On call 24 hrs.

**Post Office:** Mina 188 (tel. 2-18-88 or 2-37-02), just off Juárez, two blocks north of the Pl. Mayor. *Lista de Correos.* Open Mon.-Fri. 8am-7:30pm, Sat 9am-1pm. **Postal Code:** 48300, but the last two digits vary even within Puerto Vallarta.

**Telephones: LADATELs** can be found at Lázaro Cárdenas and Constitución. A more expensive option is **Computel,** Madero 296 (tel. 3-18-50), but they do not allow collect calls. Open daily 7:30am-9:30pm. **Telephone Code:** 322.

**Consulates: U.S.,** Miramar at Libertad (tel. 2-00-69), just north of Río Cuale. Open Mon.-Fri. 9am-1pm. **Canada,** Hidalgo 226 (tel. 2-53-98; fax 2-35-17). Open Mon.-Fri. 9am-1pm.

**Currency Exchange: Bánamex** (tel. 2-08-30), on the Pl. Mayor, changes money Mon.-Fri. 9am-2pm. *Casas de cambio* are everywhere, especially near the Malecón. Their rates are lower than the banks; better deals are generally found away from the beach. Hours are typically Mon.-Sat. 9am-2pm and 4-8pm.

**American Express:** Morelos 660 (tel. 3-29-55 or 3-29-26), at Abasolo. English is spoken. Open Mon.-Fri. 9am-2:30pm and 4-6pm, Sat. 9am-1pm.

**Airport:** 8km north of town via the highway. Buses labeled "Ixtapa" or "Juntas" pass the airport; catch them on Lázaro Cárdenas or Insurgentes. **Aeroméxico** (tel. 4-27-77 at Plaza Genovesa; tel. 1-18-97 or 1-10-55 at the airport), **Mexicana** (tel. 4-89-00 at Centro Comercial Villa Vallarta; tel. 1-12-66 at the airport), and other airlines have frequent flights to Guadalajara (314-395 pesos one-way), Mexico City (465 pesos one-way), and Los Angeles (US$295 one-way).

**Bus Station:** Each bus line operates out of its own office-depot on the south side of the city. **Elite,** Basilio Badillo 11 (tel. 3-11-17), at Insurgentes, serves Ciudad Juárez and 21 points in between (5pm, 36hrs., 340 pesos), Guadalajara (every hr., 7am-4pm, 8 more 10:30pm-1:30am, 6hrs., 78 pesos), and Mexico City (4 per day, 5-11pm, 14hrs., 193 pesos). **Primera Plus** and **ETN** both operate from Lázaro Cárdenas 258. **Primera Plus** (tel. 3-16-16) serves Colima (1pm, 6½hrs., 77 pesos), Guadalajara (7 per day, noon-1am, 5½hrs., 80 pesos), Manzanillo (first class 8am and 1pm, 5hrs., 57 pesos; second class 5 per day, 7am-10:30pm, 6hrs., 44.50 pesos), and Melaque (first class 8am and 1pm, 3½hrs., 44 pesos; second class 3 per day, 7am-2pm, 5hrs., 34.50 pesos). **ETN** (tel. 3-29-99 or 3-06-46) serves Guadalajara (6 per day, 9am-12:30am, 5hrs., 105 pesos), Mexico City-North (6:30pm, 12hrs., 255 pesos), and Querétaro (Sat. at 8:30pm, 11hrs., 200 pesos). **Transportes Cihuatlán,** Madero and Constitución (tel. 2-34-36), sends the most south to Manzanillo (5 per day, 5am-4pm, 5hrs., 43.50 pesos), and Barra de Navidad (4:30 and 11:30pm, 4¼hrs., 44.50 pesos). **Transportes del Pacífico,** Insurgentes 282 (tel. 2-10-15), to Guadalajara (first class 11 per day, 7am-1pm, 6hrs., 76 pesos; second class 7 per day, 6am-11pm, 6½hrs., 68 pesos), Mexico City (first class 6pm, 14hrs., 190 pesos), Morelia (first class 10pm, 12hrs., 135 pesos), and Tepic (every ½hr., 4:15am-10:15pm, 3½hrs., 26 pesos). **Transportes Norte de Sonora,** Carranza 322 (tel. 2-66-66), sends buses to San Blas (noon and 3:30pm, 3-3½hrs., 28 pesos) and Tepic (7 per day, 5:30am-7pm, 3-3½hrs., 26 pesos).

**Car Rental:** Almost all car rentals have offices on Calle Francisco Medina Ascencio, the hotel strip. **Dollar,** Francisco Medina 1736 (tel. 2-42-56). **Budget,** Medina 1004 (tel. 3-11-20, 2-29-80, or 1-18-88; fax 1-12-10). **Avis,** Medina 1004 (tel. 2-29-80; fax 1-12-10). **National,** Medina 1680 (tel. 2-05-15 or 2-27-42; fax 3-03-75), and at the Airport Sheraton.

**Market: Super Mercado Gutiérrez Rico,** at Constitución and Serdán (tel. 2-13-67), provides a huge array of supermarket-type foodstuffs. Open daily 6:30am-10pm.

**Laundromat: Lavandería Automática Blanquita,** Madero 407A (tel. 3-25-47). 12 pesos for 1-3kg. Same-day service. Open daily 8am-9pm. Many laundromats line Madero. Look for the best deals away from the beach.

**Red Cross:** (tel. 2-49-73 or 2-15-33) Open 24 hrs.

**Pharmacy: Farmacia CMQ,** Basilio Badillo 365 (tel. 2-13-30 or 2-29-41), half a block inland from Insurgentes, plus 4 other locations. All open 24 hrs.

**Hospital: CMQ Hospital,** Basilio Badillo 365 (tel. 3-00-11 or 3-19-19). English spoken. Open 24 hrs. **Hospital Medasist** (tel. 3-04-44) has a bilingual staff and 24-hr. emergency service.

## ACCOMMODATIONS AND CAMPING

Puerto Vallarta's sleeping options queue up in ascending socioeconomic order, from the beach south of town (free) to the Sheraton (laughably expensive) in the north. The best budget hotels are south of Río Cuale, on or near Madero. Make sure the fan works before whipping out your wallet. June is the least expensive month of the year, December the most expensive.

Officially, Puerto Vallarta frowns on shiftless beach bums, but most travelers who choose to camp encounter no problems. Even many of the stray dogs are friendly. Some beachfront clubs have night guards who may keep an eye on those who request their permission before bedding down. Many people dig into the sand behind the Hotel Los Arcos or the Castle Pelícanos, which is government property, or into the open space between the J. Newcombe tennis courts and the Sheraton.

**Hotel Belmar,** Insurgentes 161 (tel. 2-05-72), right in the middle of the south side. The most for your money. Whoever picked the colors was in a giddy mood—the walls and floor are bright, with bedspreads to match. All of the well-lit rooms have either street-side or interior balconies that look up and down the hotel's entrails. Small bathroom doors make you feel as if you're entering a telephone booth, but the facilities are well-scrubbed and come with shower curtains. Some rooms have TV. Singles 65 pesos. Doubles 80 pesos. Triples 100 pesos.

**Hotel Azteca,** Madero 473 (tel. 2-27-50). Clean and simple rooms are almost lovable. The brick exterior and giant leafy jungle plants set it apart in this sky-rise-dominated town. Restaurant and long-distance phone for patrons. Fans and hot water. Singles 30 pesos. Doubles 40 pesos. Triples 50 pesos. 1-3 person room with kitchen 60 pesos. Prices rise in winter.

**Hotel Yasmin,** Basilio Badillo 168 (tel. 2-00-87), one block from the beach. A refreshing courtyard with tables and chairs gives way to very clean, airy rooms with fans, floral stencils, desks, psychedelic bedspreads, and spotless bathrooms. But it's location, location, location that makes the difference; the waves are as close as they'll get for these prices. Singles 75 pesos. Doubles 85 pesos.

**Hotel Villa del Mar,** Madero 440 (tel. 2-07-85), two blocks east of Insurgentes. A nautical motif gives new meaning to the word tacky. All rooms are clean and furnished. Spic-and-span bathrooms have shower curtains. Quiet. Singles 40 or 45 pesos. Doubles 50 or 55 pesos. Prices rise in winter and during *Semana Santa.* Visa, MC accepted.

**Hotel Hortencia,** Madero 336 (tel. 2-24-84). A lobby with modern furniture, TV, and tiled floors opens into a sunny forest of a patio. Big rooms with white walls, ceiling fans, wood furniture, and desks. Curtained showers and baths sufficient, but the years of use are beginning to show. Singles 40 pesos. Doubles 45 pesos.

## FOOD

Puerto Vallarta's Malecón specializes in tourist traps with *norteamericano* cuisine, but elsewhere on the north side exist some excellent, decently-priced restaurants. Near the beach on the south side, *gringos* can find many upscale restaurants built with them in mind, especially on the blocks enclosed by Basilio Badillo to the south, Olas Altas (the beachfront), Lázaro Cárdenas, and Constitución. Cheaper down-home eateries are plentiful around Madero near Insurgentes, and in the **market** on the north side, where Insurgentes crosses Río Cuale (open Mon.-Sat. 8am-8pm). Taco and *quesadilla* stands prosper south of the river, near the cheap hotels.

### South

**Cafe de Olla,** Basilio Badillo 168 (tel. 3-16-26), next to Hotel Yasmin. Good Mexican and U.S. fare served up by friendly, attentive folk. Great-smelling grilled food and iced tea lure both Mexican and *norteamericano* vacationers. Beautiful burgers 20 pesos. Chicken, beef, cheese, or mushroom turnovers 35 pesos. Open Wed.-Mon. noon-11pm.

**La Fonda China Poblana,** Insurgentes 222 (tel. 2-40-49). A ground floor adorned with photos of people getting down in the restaurant gives way to an airy second floor devoid of decor but outfitted with a balcony. *Chile relleno* 15.70 pesos, *enchiladas suizas* 17.80 pesos. Open 24 hrs.

## North

**Fonda El Patio,** Calle Francia 139, off the highway, directly in front of Centro Comercial Villa Vallarta. Literally, a patio. Delightful yellow tablecloths, abundant flora and fauna, and open air. Run by an ex-hotel chef and his family, this place knows how to keep things delicious *and* clean. Watch them make the most scrumptious *tortillas* you've ever tasted (they could make a meal by themselves) on the outdoor *comal.* Menu changes daily, but all meals come with *agua fresca,* soup, rice and beans *de olla*—not refried! Chicken in *mole* is only 15 pesos. Fillet of breaded fish goes for 17 pesos. Popular with locals. Open Mon.-Sat. 1-6pm.

**Mi Casa Buffet,** at Iturbide and Miramar, up four very steep blocks on Iturbide. An all-you-can-eat buffet; watch a pound of flesh attach itself to each of your hips. The menu, which changes daily, might feature vegetable or rice soup, *pollo en mole,* barbecued pork, or beef stew. Bread and *tortillas* are a given. Feels so much like Mexico, you'll forget you're in Puerto Vallarta. Buffet 10 pesos. *Agua fresca* 2 pesos. Open Mon.-Sat. 2-9pm.

**La Lechuga,** Hidalgo 224 (tel. 3-13-74), just south of the church and above the Canadian consulate. A vegetarian restaurant with a self-proclaimed *ambiente bohemio*—you'd think you're in Greenwich Village. Bright colors dominate, especially in the painting of the parrots in the sunset; escape the barrage by choosing a table on the balcony. *Comida corrida (agua fresca,* soup or salad, and an entree) 14 pesos. Open Mon.-Sat. 12:30-5:30pm. From Wed.-Mon. 6pm-midnight, it becomes the ritzier, more expensive **Abadía Basso.**

**El Pollo Vagabundo,** México 1295 (tel. 2-43-99), a few blocks south of the Sheraton next to Hotel Buenaventura. As down to earth as a millipede, it fits its industrial neighborhood well. Food is excellent—the name may stem from the fact that there's not much chicken on the menu. Breakfast special 15 pesos. *Chilaquiles* 9-14 pesos. BBQ ½-chicken 30 pesos. Open daily 8am-10:30pm.

**Restaurant Buffet,** Iturbide 270 (tel. 2-30-73), a few blocks inland from Plaza Mayor. 100% vegetarian cuisine, with a strong Indian influence—check out the photos. Small, white-walled, and simple, with your choice of dishes on the right. Buffet 20 pesos. Open Mon.-Sat. noon-8pm.

**El Barzón,** Av. Francisco Medina 2715 (tel. 4-45-00), km 4.5 on the road to the airport, near Playa de Oro in the Hotel Zone. All the trappings of a beach-front restaurant—red-tiled roof and flaming open-air grill—but located on the highway. Mexican music plays and not a word of English spoken. A haul if you're staying farther south, but the heavenly *tortillas* are worth crawling for. Specialty is group deals, with all kinds of meat, cheese, guacamole, and beer (4 people 109 pesos, 6 people 159 pesos). BBQ chicken 18 pesos. Open daily 11am-7pm.

## SAND AND SIGHTS

To really enjoy Puerto Vallarta, one must cultivate a taste for its 40km of coastline. Some of the least crowded and most gorgeous beaches stretch along the coast south of town on the road to **Mismaloya** (see Near Puerto Vallarta below). The best beach within the Puerto Vallarta city limits is **Playa de los Muertos** (Beach of the Dead), a popular strip in front of the south side's best hotels—despite its name. It begins at its southern end with a rocky cliff dotted with small white homes, and runs north to a small dock which separates it from the **Playa de Olas Altas** (Big Waves Beach). To get there, walk all the way west on Lázaro Cárdenas and then south along Playa de Olas Altas, or take the street of the same name and turn right on Rodríguez.

While water sports generate a lot of activity during the morning hours, things slow to a trickle by mid-afternoon. **Parasailing** (US$30 a shot) is particularly popular; parachutes are scattered on the Playa de Olas Altas, and their owners will descend upon you like vultures if you look even remotely interested. **Señor Scuba,** Rodríguez 121 (tel. 8-00-37), two blocks south of Hotel Los Arcos, rents scuba equipment (US$5 per piece, US$10 for a tank, plus a credit card deposit), and offers diving lessons and trips. Waverunners (US$35 pesos per ½hr.), sea kayaks (US$10 per hr.), and fishing trips (US$20-30 per hr.) are available as well, but snorkeling and scuba expeditions (US$15-65 to Los Arcos, depending on equipment) can be a bit cheaper. Your best bet is to rent a mask and fins for US$5 each, plus deposit (open Mon.-Sat. 10am-6pm). Another Señor Scuba is at Mismaloya Beach (tel. 8-06-60, ext. 3081; open daily 10am-5pm). On the northern beach, near Sheraton, the currency of choice is also the U.S. dollar—in bulk. Parasailing is even more popular here.

Municipal efforts to render the **Río Cuale** a cosmopolitan waterway meet with limited success for about 400m inland and fail completely thereafter. Anyone alone should be careful when walking this stretch of the river and should avoid doing so altogether after dark. **Isla Río Cuale,** between the two bridges, supports small stores selling simple baubles, bangles, and *botanas.* The **Museo del Cuale,** at the seaward end of the island, is mainly an archeological exposition of Mesoamerican culture. The museum is made necessary by the Law of Conservation of Brain Cells—since the rest of Puerto Vallarta kills 'em, another place has to stimulate them (open Tues.-Sun. 10am-3pm and 4-6pm; free).

The river can also be reached from the north via Zaragoza, which merits a walk. Stairs lead up the mini-mountain beginning behind the Church of Guadalupe, breaking out amid bougainvillea and hibiscus into the wealthy **Zaragoza** neighborhood, known locally as **Gringo Gulch.** The prominent bridge spanning the apex of the street connects Elizabeth Taylor's humble *pied-à-terre* with Richard Burton's.

## ENTERTAINMENT

After dark, Puerto Vallarta offers something for everyone, whether it's a cocktail in the moonlight or the chance to thrash across a crowded dance floor. Most of the upscale action is along Díaz Ordaz on the northern waterfront, where clubs and restaurants cater to suntanned professionals holding pricey rum drinks and bopping to U.S. top-40 tunes. On the Malecón, one can have a serious conversation about the latest melodramatic twist in *90210* or *Melrose Place* with any of the hundreds of American teeny-boppers who congregate there. Discos cater to those who can spring a 20- to 30-peso cover charge in high season and pay ten pesos for a cold one. For cheap fun, nothing beats the **pool hall,** Madero 279 (tel. 2-24-57). Pool is ten pesos per hr. and dominoes 3 pesos per hr., but the middle-aged men don't look too highly upon (and sometimes look too long at) female visitors (open daily 9am-2am).

Puerto Vallarta is home to a thriving, if small, gay scene, and gay men are generally accepted here. Lesbians, however—as in most of Mexico—meet with a less open-minded reception. Two clubs in Vallarta are frequented primarily by gay men: **Los Balcones** and the **Zótano.** For those clubs with covers, save a small fortune by obtaining free passes (which may not be honored during peak tourist season) from the condo-hawkers who lurk around the Malecón. Most discos aren't worth visiting until 11pm or midnight; the time is well-spent tossing back drinks in cheap bars.

**Carlos O'Brian's Bar & Grill & Clothesline** (tel. 2-14-44), Díaz Ordaz at Pipila. The only things hanging out to dry are intoxicated high school students who've forgotten the names of their hotels. Teens bounce between here, **Zoo,** and **Kahalua,** a few blocks south on the waterfront. It's the biggest party in town—block-long lines wrap around the building all night. Inside, "Tequila" starts playing, the American DJ starts yapping, and the contest is on—who can have the most fun? Open daily noon-2am.

**Zótano,** Morelos 101 (tel. 3-06-77), on the Plaza Río next to the Vallarta Bridge. This basement rocks! Wall-to-wall dancing, perhaps because there's no room at the bar. Almost exclusively gay men. Open daily 9pm-4am.

**Los Balcones** (a.k.a Los Espejos), Juárez 182 (tel. 2-46-71), at Libertad. International crowd practices looking lazy-languid on the balconies overlooking Juárez and Libertad. When the house music plays, the floor itself seems to dance, buckling and slithering to the beat beneath patrons' feet. Mostly gay couples and a few lesbian couples hang out here. Starts hopping at 11:30pm. Open daily 9pm-4am.

**Christine** (tel. 4-02-02), next to Hotel Krystal in the hotel zone. Those who can afford the 40-peso cover and don't mind a quick frisk at the door can witness the laser shows and gushes of cold smoke from the ceilings. The staggered seating, floor lights, and seven large screens give it a 21st-century feel. *Norteamericano* disco, house, and pop. Men: the dress code says you must wear long pants. And keep those shirts tucked in! Call ahead for discount info. Open daily 10pm-late.

**Cuiza,** on Isla Río Cuale, at the foot of the Vallarta Bridge. Find a table on the shady patio, order a margarita, and listen to the jazz. Entertainment gets no mellower than this. Promotes itself as a "twilight" spot. Frequented by Mexican professionals and lots of *nuevo-wavo gringo* couples. Live music Wed. and Fri.-Sun. 8-11pm. Open daily 6pm-1am.

**Ándale,** Olas Altas 425 (tel. 2-10-54). Video bar and restaurant caters to a teeming crowd of *norteamericanos* and Mexicans of all ages who down shots to collective shouts of ¡*ándale!* Watch mom and pop get plastered as the kids look on in disbelief. Open daily 8:30pm-3:30am.

# ■ NEAR PUERTO VALLARTA

Puerto Vallarta's best beaches start a few kilometers south of town. The first few you come across are monopolized by resorts and condos, and though they're nicer and quieter than the ones back in town, access to them is usually only through the hotels. Farther down the coast lies **Los Arcos,** a group of pretty rock islands hollowed out in places by pounding waves. Similar rocks litter much of Mexico's Pacific coast, but the powerful waves of Bahía de Banderas render these formations more impressive than most. The coastline here lacks sand, but it still serves as a platform from which to start the 150m swim to the islands. Bring a mask or goggles or risk missing the tropical fish that flit through the underwater reefscape. Flippers avail against the heavy currents, and be careful where you step—the coral is sharp enough to draw blood. Use caution and swim with a friend. To get to Los Arcos, take the bus to Mismaloya and ask the driver to stop at Hotel de los Arcos.

The beautiful crescent beach of **Mismaloya** lies just around the bend to the south. Best known as the setting of *Night of the Iguana* and Arnold Schwarzenegger's *cinéma vérité* classic, *Predator,* Mismaloya has recently been encircled by large hotels and is only slightly less crowded than the beaches in town. The area still harbors remnants of both movie sets.

The road veers away from the coast just beyond the **Boca de Tomatlán.** This narrow cove contains only a small beach but offers a breather from the touristy hubbub of the northern coastline. A couple of small restaurants cater to *gringos*.

The last place to check out on the southern road is **Chico's Paradise,** 5km inland from the Boca de Tomatlán. Take in a gorgeous view of the **Tomatlán Falls** while having a drink at Chico's huge and airy *palapas.* You'll have to take a **taxi** (25 pesos from Mismaloya) or a long-distance Transportes Cihuatlán bus (see "Practical Information" on page 266; 4-5 pesos) to get there unless you have your own vehicle.

Farther south along the coast lie the beaches of **Las Ánimas, Quimixto,** and **Yelapa,** all of which are accessible only from the ocean. Las Ánimas and Quimixto are twins—long stretches of unoccupied sand backed by small villages and a few *palapas* offering seafood to tourists. Quimixto also offers a small waterfall to those who tire of the beach. The trip can be made in an hour by foot from the beach, or in a half-hour by rented mule. Scuba trips (organized by Señor Scuba and others) also make their way from downtown Puerto Vallarta and Mismaloya to these beaches.

**Yelapa,** destination of the popular boat ride is, in a way, a bit of a fake. Yelapa is supposed to be a secluded peasant fishing village, but its seemingly simple *palapa* huts were designed by a *norteamericano* architect whose definition of rustic included interior plumbing and hot water. Many of these *palapas* are occupied for only part of the year, and short- and long-term rentals can be arranged easily for widely varying and sometimes surprisingly low prices. The beach fills with hawkers and parasailers during the day, but the town, a 15-minute walk from the beach, remains *tranquilo*—with waterfalls and nude bathing upstream and poetry readings downstream, nobody's ready to leave. Don't miss the secluded swimming hole at the top of the stream that runs through town; follow the path uphill along the stream, and just before the restaurant, duck under the water pipes to the right of the trail and head up the track. About 15m before it rejoins the stream bed, an inconspicuous trail leads off to the left to a deep pool which overlooks the bay.

The cheapest way to get to the boats-only beaches is via the **Autobús Acuático** water shuttle. It leaves twice a day (10:30 and 11am) from the Muelle de los Muertos and stops at Mismaloya, Las Ánimas, and Yelapa. It's cheaper to take the #2 bus or an **Autotransportes del Pacífico Camioneta** from the municipal bus station near Muelle de los Muertos to Mismaloya or La Boca and catch the water shuttle from there. It cruises by there about 20 minutes after it leaves Los Muertos. Passage from Mismaloya to Yelapa costs 15 pesos. Boats return at noon and 4pm, but don't miss the last one or you'll be stranded.

If you prefer something more organized, **cruises** to points south of Vallarta leave the marina every day from 9am on, and return around 4pm. The cheapest cruises to Yelapa are 80 pesos, but most are more of a splurge. Tops is 130 pesos, including food and drink. Information about the dazzling variety of tours can be found in the tourist office, at any large hotel, or in the marina. Tickets and cruise information can be obtained from **La Jungla Travel Agency** (tel. 2-47-99). If you are over 25 (in some cases 23), gainfully employed, and have a major credit card, you can save money from La Jungla on all of the above activities, or on a 24-hour jeep rental (US$80).

Lots of new developments, condos, and resort facilities offer freebies to potential buyers; the most common deal is an invitation to eat a free breakfast or lunch at the resort, spend a few hours enjoying its facilities, and then buy tickets (usually at half-price) to any or all of a list of popular tours and cruises. The catch is that you have to listen to their ultra-high-pressure sales pitch which can verge on coercion. Don't under any circumstances relinquish your credit card number. Remember, you are under no obligation to do anything whatsoever.

# ■■■ BAHÍA DE NAVIDAD

Along with Guadalajara and Puerto Vallarta, Bahía de Navidad forms one vertex of Jalisco's "Tourist Triangle." Power is not shared equally within the triarchy, however: with the exception of December and the *Semana Santa,* few tourists are spotted on the placid shores of Bahía de Navidad. The *bahía,* a sheltered cove of talcum sand and shimmering water, is home to the towns of **Melaque** and **Barra de Navidad.** Only a few kilometers apart, the two towns are in the midst of steady growing pains. Barra retains the charm and authenticity of a small Mexican town—so small, in fact, that it has neither bank nor *panadería*—but tourism is still the lifeblood of this hamlet. Restaurants, hotels, and clubs are sprouting with great frequency, while the fishing industry occupies less space on Barra's new agenda. The Xanadu-esque hotel at the end of the bay may be a symbol for future development, but in the meantime, Barra remains a small, relatively quiet *pueblito.*

Melaque is somewhat larger and slightly less touristed than its sister, and caters less to outsiders and more to the needs of its own citizens; perhaps its less spectacular waves pre-determined its role in this partnership. Despite these differences, come the *temporada alta* (high season), the two towns are indistinguishable, as an incredible influx of tourists, especially Canadians, dominates the bay. Bahía de Navidad has become the winter home of many foreigners who annually visit their expatriate comrades. Both towns' beaches are spectacular, their crimson sunsets framed between the two spits of the cove.

Melaque and Barra de Navidad are 55km northwest of Manzanillo on Rte. 200, or 240km southwest of Guadalajara on Rte. 54. The towns themselves lie a few kilometers apart: two if by sea, five if by highway. Northbound buses hit Barra first and southbound ones do the reverse.

**Municipal buses** or **combis** (both 1 peso) connect the two towns every 15 minutes or so (7:30am-10pm), but it's better to take one of the larger buses heading to Manzanillo that leave on the hour from both towns' bus stations. These cost the same as municipals or *combis,* but are faster and more comfortable. Of course, the 30- to 40-minute walk along the beach between the towns is the true hard-core budget option; don't go alone and take a cab after dark (15-18 pesos), as some women have been harassed along this stretch.

# ■■■ MELAQUE

**Orientation and Practical Information** Melaque's **bus station** (tel. 5-50-03) is on **Carranza Gómez Farías,** the parallel-to-the-beach main drag. From the bus station, turn left on Gómez Farías and walk two blocks to reach **López Mateos.** Another left turn takes you to the plaza, a few blocks inland. López Mateos and **Hidalgo,** one block beyond it and parallel to it, are the main cross streets towards the ocean.

The **police** (tel. 5-50-80), on López Mateos, north of the plaza, are available 24 hrs. The **post office,** José Clemente Orozco 13 (tel. 5-52-30), is two blocks left of the plaza as you face the beach and 1½ blocks towards the beach on Orozco, in the green building on your left. *Lista de Correos* (open Mon.-Fri. 8am-3pm, Sat. 8am-noon). **Postal Code:** 48980. For access to **telephones,** visit the *caseta de larga distancia* at Corona 60. From the plaza, take Hidalgo towards the beach and make a left opposite the market. Public telephones (good for long-distance) are by the bus station. **Telephone Code:** 335. Despite its size, Melaque has no bank (neither does Barra de Navidad). A **casa de cambio** (tel. 5-53-43) across from the bus station changes dollars at a poor rate, but there's no commission and, well, it's the only option (open Mon.-Sat. 9am-2pm and 4-7pm, Sun. 9am-2pm).

**Buses** leave from the bus station (see above). The only carrier is **Autocamiones Cihuatlán,** which rides to Guadalajara (first class 7 per day, 5hrs., 61 pesos; second class 15 per day, 6½hrs., 47.50 pesos), Manzanillo (first class 5 per day, 1¼hrs., 12.50 pesos; second class every hr., 1¾hrs., 9.50 pesos), and Puerto Vallarta (first class 9:15am and 1:30pm, 3½hrs., 43.50 pesos; second class 12 per day, 5hrs., 34 pesos), among others.

You can tidy those whities at the **Lavandería Industrial Hotelera** at Gómez Farías 26, next to the bus station, for six pesos per kg (same-day service; open Mon.-Sat. 8am-4pm). The **Red Cross** (tel. 5-23-00) is 15km away in Cihuatlán, accessible by buses which leave every 15min. from the plaza (3-4 pesos), or by taxi (38 pesos). **Super Farmacia Plaza,** López Mateos 48 (tel. 5-51-67), is south of the plaza (open Mon.-Sat. 8am-2pm and 4-9pm, Sun. 8am-2pm and 6:30-9pm). The **hospital** (often called **Centro de Salud**), on Cordiano Guzmán, between Corona and G. Farías, is open 24 hrs. for emergencies (for consultations Mon.-Sat. 9am-2pm and 5-9pm).

**Accommodations and Camping** Melaque is larger than Barra de Navidad and has more hotels; most budget accommodations are inland, near the *centro.* A bargain occasionally lurks among the beachside bungalows. All rates rise during the high season, when Melaque's supply and demand curves stretch themselves to accommodate a heavy influx of foreign tourists. Check with expatriates to locate good deals. **Bungalows Villamar,** Hidalgo 1 (tel. 5-50-05), just off the beach. Large, well-scrubbed beachside bungalows have two bedrooms, each with two double beds, lots of dark wooden furniture, and a sizeable all-purpose room with a fully equipped kitchen. Decks look out onto well-kept flowery grounds and spectacular views of the ocean. English spoken. (One person 55 pesos, 2 people 85 pesos, 3 people 125 pesos, 4 people 150 pesos. Up to 8 people per bungalow. Call in advance to reserve during high season.) **Hotel Hidalgo,** Hidalgo 7 (tel. 5-50-45), half-way between the plaza and the beach, is a friendly, family affair. Small, clean rooms with chests of drawers and spotless but microscopic bathrooms surround the court-yard, living room, and kitchen (which also serves as the family's laundry room). Ask the management to turn on the fan, since there are no switches in the room (singles 35 pesos; doubles 50 pesos). **Hotel San Nicolás,** Gómez Farías 54 (tel. 5-00-66), half a block west of López, has aging but clean rooms with pretty bedspreads, fans, chairs, closets, and chests. Narrow but entirely adequate bathrooms. A few rooms have bay views and small balconies above the street (singles 40 pesos, 80 pesos in winter; doubles 50 pesos, 100 pesos in winter). **Playa Trailer Park,** near the beach at Gómez Farías and López Mateos (tel. 5-50-65), contains 45 lots with electricity, water, and sewer hook-ups. Bathrooms (1 peso) and showers (6 pesos) are accessible to the public. A two-person trailer spot or camping site costs 45 pesos. Security is provided 24 hrs. Reservations are recommended.

Many people park trailers or pitch tents at the far western end of Melaque, between the sandy beach and rock formations. The site is flat but strewn with litter, rocks, vehicles, and tents. If you need room for only one tent, a far better spot lies along the shore, just before the rocky beach. Otherwise, hunt for more creative sites between the two towns. A small, land-locked lagoon separates the beach and jungle; people pitch tents on the oceanside or crash among the crabs between Melaque and the lagoon. Campers should respect the rights of local landowners: at least one landowner has posted a "no camping" sign.

**Food** During the summer, restaurants ship in shrimp from the north, but come high season, local fishing boats catch everything that is served on the waterfront. Lobster is trapped here illegally; aid the persecuted crustacean's cause by ordering oysters. More authentic (and less expensive) Mexican places can be found near the central plaza. Cheaper still are the sidewalk food stands that materialize after the sun sets and the nameless, dirt-floored eateries in the *mercado* and near the bus station.

**La Flor Morena,** Juárez 21, receives locals and expatriates alike who flock here to chow down on great, filling Mexican food at unbelievably low prices. Feast on vegetarian dishes, *tostadas* (2-4 pesos), or scrumptious tacos (2 pesos each; open Tues.-Sun. 6-11pm). **Los Pelícanos** lies near the end of the row of *palapas* on the beach, 200m beyond the huge pink Hotel Casa Grande. The proprietor, New Yorker Philomena "Phil" García, considers herself the fairy godmother of the road-weary *gringo* and is a fixture of the local expatriate scene. Unfortunately, Philomena recently underwent major surgery and her restaurant is for sale; then again, a buyer may not come along for another five years. In the meantime, enjoy breakfast (around 10 pesos), lunch, or dinner with her wise and weathered husband, Trinidad García (open daily 8am-11pm, off-season daily 9am-7pm).

**Sights and Entertainment** The beach gets more crowded and the waves get smaller toward the western end of Melaque's sandy strip. Restaurants and aqua-activities also increase in density to the west. **Jet-ski rentals** run 120 pesos per ½hr., and are available Mon.-Thurs. at the far west end of the beach at Restaurant Moyo (tel. 7-11-04). On weekends, jet-skis can be rented on the beach and at the Hotel Casa Grande. You can see the whole beach from the water by hopping aboard one of the banana boats zipping by (15 pesos per person for a 10-min. ride).

Although few people actually come to Melaque for the nightlife, few refuse when it's thrust upon them. **Disco Tango,** where Gómez Farías runs into Vallarta, monop-olizes the action and is the after-hours oasis of Melaque's under-30 (but over-18, mind you) tourist crowd (open daily 10pm-3am, roughly). Alternatively, head over to Barra, where tourists and natives alike get down on weekends. For something a bit more mellow and smoky, you can always twirl cues with the middle-aged men at **Billiard San Patricio,** Melaque's pool hall, on Orozco and Juárez, about 3 blocks from the plaza (pool and *carambola* 6 pesos per hr., dominoes 2.50 pesos per hr.; open daily 10am-11pm).

# ■■■ BARRA DE NAVIDAD

**Orientation and Practical Information** Barra de Navidad's bus stop is at Veracruz 226, on the corner of Nayarit. Veracruz runs roughly parallel to **Legazpi,** the main street that hugs the beach. Turn left on Veracruz from the bus station to get to *el centro.* The **tourist office,** Veracruz 174 (tel. 5-53-99), serves all of Jalisco. English is spoken in the mornings (open daily 9am-8pm). **Police** wait 'round-the-clock at Veracruz 179 (tel. 5-53-99). No English spoken. The **post office,** Guanajuato 100, is 1½ blocks inland from the plaza on the right-hand side. *Lista de Correos* (open Mon.-Fri. 8am-3pm, Sat. 9am-1pm). **Postal Code:** 48987. **Telephones** are available at the *caseta* next to Hotel Pacífico on Legazpi. Public phones are on Veracruz next to the police station. **Telephone Code:** 335. The **telegram office** (tel. 5-52-62) is at Veracruz 96, on the corner by the plaza (open Mon.-Fri. 9am-4pm). Barra has no bank, but a **casa de cambio,** Veracruz 212 (tel. 5-61-77), exchanges dollars at a poor rate (open Mon.-Sat. 9am-2pm and 4-7pm, Sun. 9am-2pm).

**Buses** depart from **Primera Plus,** Veracruz 228 (tel. 5-52-65) to Guadalajara (first class 5 per day, 5hrs., 62 pesos; second class 13 per day, 6½hrs., 48.50 pesos) and Puerto Vallarta (first class 9am and 1pm, 3½hrs., 44.50 pesos). You can purchase tickets for **ETN,** Veracruz 204, which has connections in Manzanillo. **Lavandería Jardín,** Jalisco 71, just left on Veracruz before Morelos (at the lagoon) will wash and dry 3kg for 15 pesos (open Mon.-Fri. 9am-2pm and 4-5pm, Sat. 9am-2pm). Near the center of town lies **Farmacia Marcela,** Veracruz 172 (tel. 5-54-31), a family store where the wife speaks some English (open daily 9am-2pm and 4-10:30pm). For medical attention, the **Centro de Salud,** on Puerto Navidad, is down Veracruz and out of town. Make a right just after the signs for El Márquez, just before Veracruz becomes a highway. The Centro is the second building on the right, the one with the red-and-white gate. No English is spoken. Emergency service 24 hrs.

**Accommodations and Camping** Budget accommodations in Barra are available only to the keen-eyed (or *Let's Go-*armed) traveler. Most hotels are on or near the water and cater to the well-heeled tourist. However, persistent and frugal groups can find bargains in doubles, triples, and quads at the nicer hotels. Of course, all prices are subject to hikes during the *temporada alta.* Reasonable accommodations are sometimes available in private residences—ask around and look for signs in restaurants. The best spot to camp or park your trailer is the extreme south end of town, on the sandbar near the breakwater. Campers can use a toilet and a shower in one of the nearby sand-floored eateries; look for the hand-lettered signs that read "Sanitario/Regadera." **Posada Pacífico,** Mazatlán 160 (tel. 5-03-59), features comfortable white rooms, a pleasant courtyard, flashy shower curtains, and killer fans. The friendly *dueña* lets guests park in the driveway if there's room. (Singles 50 pesos, 60 pesos in winter. Doubles 60 pesos, 80 pesos in winter. The four newly-constructed bungalows go for 80 pesos, 150 pesos in winter.) **Casa de Huéspedes Caribe,** Sonora 15 (tel. 5-52-37), between Legazpi and Veracruz near Hotel Pacífico, has a family feel. Despite renovations and the devaluation of the peso, the dirt-cheap prices have not risen in over a year. Recently installed wooden doors lead to rooms with cute beds, spotless red floors, clean private bathrooms, and fans (25 pesos per person, winter rates skyrocket; discounts for stays longer than a week). **Bungalows Karelia,** on Legazpi, on the beach next to the Hotel Bogavante, are a good deal for three or more people. Airy but worn suites house a refrigerator, table, chairs, stove, fan, and kitchen utensils (suites for 2 people 120 pesos, for 3 people 140 pesos, for 4 people 160 pesos; prices rise during high season).

**Food** For delicious, inexpensive Mexican food in a pleasant atmosphere—checkered tablecloths enclosed by soft pink walls—try **Restaurant Paty** (tel. 7-07-43), on the north corner of Veracruz and Jalisco. Grilled *pollo* is 12 pesos. Small *pozole* goes for 6 pesos, large for 8 (open daily 7am-11:30pm). **Restaurante Marcela,** Guanajuato 61 (tel. 7-07-52), a block inland from the plaza, is a local favorite. As you enter, a traditional painting of the Last Supper is to your left, a television to your right; big wooden chairs in the back, white plastic seats in the front; traditional tablecloths adorn the tables, and each is topped with a vase of plastic flowers; here, old Mexico meets the tourist industry, but there's no question as to which category the *sabrosa* food belongs. *Enchiladas* 4 pesos. *Huevos a la mexicana* served with beans and rice 7 pesos (open daily 7am-11pm). The beachside tables at **Restaurant Pacífico,** Legazpi 206 (tel. 5-59-10), offer great sunset viewing and a stirring vista. The breakfast special is a bargain at 9 pesos (open daily 8am-10pm).

**Sights and Entertainment**   **Mariner,** Legazpi 154, across the street from the church, rents surfboards, body boards, and skindiving equipment (each 5 pesos per hr. plus deposit of passport or credit card; open daily 9am-9pm).

The short trip across the lagoon to the village of **Colimilla** is pleasant; the steep price for small groups is not. For 30 pesos round-trip, a *lancha* will deposit up to eight passengers at the far end of the lagoon or amid Colimilla's palms, pigs, cows, and open-air restaurants. A 1km stroll from here is the deserted **Playa de los Cocos,** which has larger breakers than those in Barra. If you don't want to swim back, remember to set a time to be picked up. In a *lancha,* the full trip runs 160 pesos. Up to eight people can tour the lagoon behind Barra for 50 pesos. For 80 pesos per hour, up to four people can zoom off in the same *lancha* full of equipment for tuna or marlin fishing. Operators have formed a cooperative, so prices are fixed. Their office and docks lie at the very end of Veracruz (open daily 7am-7pm).

Bibliophiles and those in search of brain food should not miss **Beer Bob's Book Exchange,** Mazatlán 61, a few blocks to the right as you face the Posada Pacífico. Expatriate Bob runs one of the few stores of its kind—purely a book *exchange,* no cash involved. In the back room sits Bob and company, watching TV, playing cards, or engaging in "some serious beer drinking." This is Barra's expatriate core, a welcome spot for travelers to stop by and pick up a good read.

At **El Gaeón/Aladino's,** on Legazpi, the all-age clientele throbs as one; everyone out past midnight parties here (cover 10 pesos; beer 4 pesos, mixed drinks 8 pesos). Things get pretty hot amid the potted plants next door at **Casablanca** (tel. 5-05-40), especially on Fridays, when live shows pull out all the stops, and on Saturdays, when Mexicans 18+ and *gringos* boogie together (cover Fri.-Sat. 10 pesos; open Tues.-Sun. 8pm-2am). Those who prefer singing to dancing may want to mellow out at the **Bar Roof Garden Café/ Rocky's Sports Bar,** down Jalisco, a local hangout just beyond Restaurant Paty. There, somebody will sing "New York, New York" all night if you won't. (Beer 4-5 pesos. Happy hour 6-9pm. Downstairs open daily 11am-9pm, upstairs 6pm-3am.) A number of two-for-one happy hours along Legazpi make the giddy trip towards inebriation that much cheaper.

---

### El Cristo del Ciclón

A source of sinful pride for Barra is the Iglesia de San Antonio, on the corner of Jalisco and Veracruz, four blocks south of the bus station. The church is a modern structure famous for its miraculous icon, *El Cristo del Ciclón* (Christ of the Hurricane). Its arms, instead of extending to form the traditional crucifix, are bent and, though still attached to the body, droop earthward as if in a shrug. Local lore has it that when Hurricane Lilly furiously struck the bay at dawn on September 10, 1971, a young girl burst into the church begging the icon for help, causing Christ's arms to detach from the crucifix in order to hold the hurricane back and save the town from destruction (church open daily 7am-9pm; masses Mon.-Sat. 7:30am and 7:30pm, Sun. 8am, noon, 7:30, and 8:30pm).

# COLIMA

## ■■■ MANZANILLO

Residents of Colima state point proudly to Manzanillo, the home of the state's finest beaches and the brightest hope for its economic future. The workhorse port of Mexico's Pacific coast, Manzanillo attracts ships from as far away as Russia. A navy repair station faces the city's main plaza, and *el centro* is a dynamic, sweaty, work-a-day place unappealing to the purely beachgoing tourist. Those officials and investors who seek to transform Manzanillo into the next Cancún are up against conventional wisdom, which holds that a working port can never become a truly world-class resort.

Most tourists avoid central Manzanillo altogether and stay north or west of town at the glossy resorts on the city's two bays of golden-brown sand. Thanks to a fortuitous combination of currents and latitude, Manzanillo is cooler in the summer than either Puerto Vallarta or Acapulco. Its reasonably priced hotels all lie in the midst of the loud and brazen port action—a disadvantage for some visitors to this beach-happy region, but a blessing for those seeking a change of environment. Downtown Manzanillo's hustle and bustle can be exciting, with stylish youngsters cruising the *zócalo* by night and sailors from around the globe roaming the streets in search of t-shirt souvenirs by day. The courts near the *zócalo* are always occupied by spectators watching games of *fútbol* and basketball. A 20-minute bus trip separates the active *centro* from the beaches.

Those seeking only sand and surf would do better to repair to some secluded village, such as Cuyutlán or Barra de Navidad, where there is no metropolis between the hotels and the Pacific. Even the smaller towns outside of the Manzanillo city limits tend to be grimier than most Mexican beach towns. But for those budget travelers excited by the prospect of beautiful beaches *and* a real city, Manzanillo will certainly deliver.

### ORIENTATION

Manzanillo lies 96km west of Colima and 355km south of Guadalajara. The **Jardín Obregón,** Manzanillo's plaza (also called the *zócalo),* is the most useful orientation point in town. The plaza faces north onto the harbor, but boxcars often obstruct the glorious view of PEMEX tankers. Sigh. **Morelos** runs along the north (waterfront) edge of the plaza, **Juárez** along the south. **Avenida México,** Manzanillo's main street, runs south from the plaza. Most hotels and services are nearby. The local bus labeled "Centro" runs from the station to the corner of 21 de Marzo and Hidalgo (0.50 pesos). From the corner, a right turn onto Allende and another one onto México will lead you to the *zócalo.* A taxi (tel. 3-23-20) from the bus station to the center of town costs five pesos.

Two blocks east of México and one block south of Juárez stands an elevated patch of rocky terrain that serves as a residential district. If you find yourself hopelessly stranded on one side and wish to cross, you may weave your way through—the climb is not terribly taxing, and it affords you a panoramic view of the city.

### PRACTICAL INFORMATION

**Tourist Office:** Blvd. Costera Miguel de Madrid 4960 (tel. 3-22-64 or 3-22-77), 2 blocks past Fiesta Mexicana. Catch a Miramar bus (1.20 pesos), and tell the driver where you're headed. Staffed by young 'uns who try to be helpful—just hope one of their boyfriends doesn't call. Little English spoken. Open Mon.-Fri. 9am-7pm, Sat. 9am-1pm.

**Police:** On Avenida Teniente Azveta in the Edificio Federal (tel. 2-20-10).

**Post Office:** Juárez and 5 de Mayo (tel. 2-00-22). *Lista de Correos.* Open Mon.-Fri. 8am-7pm, Sat. 9am-1pm. **Postal Code:** 28201.

**Telegrams: Telecomm** (tel. 2-30-30), in the Palacio Municipal, to the left of the stairs as you enter. Open Mon.-Fri. 8am-10pm, Sat. 9am-1pm.

**Telephones: Computel,** México 302 (tel. 2-47-52) and on Morelos ½ block east of the *zócalo* (tel. 2-02-05). International collect calls 5 pesos for 5 min. Open daily 7am-10pm.

**Currency Exchange: Banco Internacional,** México and 10 de Mayo (tel. 2-21-50 or 2-08-09), has slightly better rates and is open for exchange longer than its competitors. Open Mon.-Fri. 8am-7pm, Sat. 9am-2:30pm. **ATMs** at **Banamex** across from the Banco Internacional.

**Airport:** (tel. 4-15-55), in Playa de Oro, on the highway between Barra de Navidad and Manzanillo. Taxis to the airport 78 pesos. *Colectivos* (32 pesos) take passengers to the airport 2hrs. before take-off and leave from Manzanillo's *centro;* call the airport to make arrangements. **Aeroméxico,** Carrillo Puerto 107 (tel. 2-17-11), one block west of México and three blocks south of the *zócalo.* Open Mon.-Fri. 9am-2pm and 4-7pm, Sat. 9am-2pm.

**Train Station:** On Niños Héroes near Morelos (tel. 2-00-40), east of the plaza. To Guadalajara (11:10pm, 7½hrs., 21.25 pesos), and some 30 stops en route. Office open daily 8am-10pm.

**Bus Station:** On Hidalgo, at the outskirts of town between Laguna Cuyutlán and the ocean. Taxis to the *centro* 5 pesos. **Sociedad Cooperativa de Transportes** (tel. 2-04-35) has buses to Armería *(ordinario:* every 15min., 5:15am-10:15pm, 1¾hrs., 4 pesos; *primera clase:* every ½hr., 5am-10pm, 1¼hrs., 4 pesos), Colima *(ordinario:* every 20min., 4am-10:15pm, 2hrs., 10 pesos; *primera clase:* every ½hr., 5am-10:15pm, 1½hrs., 10 pesos), and Tecomán (every 20min., 5am-10:15pm, 1½hrs., 10 pesos). **Tres Estrellas de Oro** (tel. 2-01-35) rides in style to Mexico City (7:30pm and 9pm, 12hrs., 149 pesos), Lázaro Cárdenas, Zihuatanejo, Acapulco, Tijuana, and Mazatlán. **Autobuses del Occidente** (tel. 2-01-23) also serves Mexico City (6 per day, 12hrs., 124 pesos). **Autocamiones Cihuatlán** (tel. 2-05-15) serves Guadalajara and points in between *(primera plus:* 6 per day, 6hrs., 73 pesos; *segunda clase:* 13 per day, 8hrs., 57 pesos) and Puerto Vallarta *(primera plus:* 8am and noon, 5hrs., 56 pesos; *segunda clase:* 11 per day, 7hrs., 29 pesos). **Autotransportes del Sur de Jalisco** (tel. 2-10-03) serves Colima (every 15min., 5am-9:45pm, 2hrs., 7 pesos).

**Laundromat: Lavi-Matic,** Hidalgo 1 (tel. 2-08-44), all the way down México until it intersects a major street; it's on the southeast corner of the small plaza. Same-day service (if you bring your load early enough). 5 pesos per kg, 3kg minimum. Open daily 8am-7pm.

**Red Cross:** (tel. 6-56-51),Calle Avenida Parotas in Valle de las Garzas. Open 24 hrs.

**Pharmacy: Farmacia Manzanillo,** Juárez 10 (tel. 2-01-85 or 3-24-11), on the south side of the *zócalo.* English spoken. Open daily 8am-11pm. **Farmacia Continental,** at Playa Miramar (tel. 3-02-86), across from Juanitos, at km 14 on the Miramar Hwy. Dr. Joseph Cadet speaks English. Open Mon.-Sat. 10am-2pm and 5-9pm.

**Hospital:** tel. 2-00-29. Open 24 hrs.

## ACCOMMODATIONS

Aside from a few t-shirt and souvenir shops, downtown Manzanillo does not seem to go out of its way to cater to tourists. Hotels in the center of town are more worthwhile than those near the bus station, which is in a relatively dangerous neighborhood. Many hotels boast hot water, and *agua purificada* can often be found in the lobby. **Camping** on Playa Miramar is feasible during Semana Santa and in December, when bathroom facilities are available and security is heightened.

**Hotel Flamingo,** Madero 72 (tel. 2-10-37), 1 block south of the *zócalo.* No flamingos here, but still the best bet for your money. Clean, basic rooms were probably decorated by Charlie's Angels; check out the pea-green furniture. The place could use more ventilation, and the fans don't really help. Bathrooms are clean. Singles 50 pesos. Doubles 70 pesos. Reservations recommended.

**Hotel Emperador,** Dávalos 69 (tel. 2-23-74), 1 block west of the plaza's southwest corner. Above a restaurant whose aromas make the mouth water; these aromas, sweet bedspreads, and clean bathrooms may be the hotel's only virtues. Entirely adequate but barren rooms, some without windows, are a claustrophobe's nightmare. Single bed 30 pesos. Double bed 45 pesos, two single beds 50 pesos.

**Hotel Miramar,** Juárez 122 (tel. 2-10-08). Groovy-cool staircases lead up to large, worn rooms that appear to have been untouched since the birth of rock-and-roll. You could fit a small roller rink onto any of the vast, checkered balconies. Could use a paint job and some general maintenance, though rooms are spacious and are supplied with a desk, closet, and large bathroom. Those who are lucky enough to land the neon pink and white striped bedspread should write to 1 Story St., Cambridge, MA 02138. Singles 40 pesos. Doubles 60 pesos. Triples 75 pesos.

**Casa de Huéspedes Petrita,** Allende 20 (tel. 2-01-87), 4 blocks down México. Cell-like rooms feature odd window screens and a clunky (though functional) communal bathroom. Try to snag the triple with the squeaky-clean bathroom. Singles 25 pesos. Doubles 30 pesos. Triples 50 pesos, with bathroom 60 pesos.

## FOOD

Manzanillo is sprinkled with a few good restaurants, but because tourists mostly put up closer to the beach, the market is strictly local and the food downtown is adorned with few culinary frills.

**Restaurant Emperador,** Dávalos 69 (tel. 2-23-74), below the hotel of the same name. The blank walls and fluorescent lights aren't nearly as pleasing to the eye as the food is to the palate. Specialty *comida corrida:* a gargantuan dinner of vegetable soup, fillet-of-fish, and steamed vegetables, including rice, tortillas, and a glass of *agua fresca* for a mere 11 pesos. Open daily 8am-10:30pm.

**Los Naranjos,** México 366. Look hard: the sign outside is hard to spot. If there's a table available here at lunchtime, consider yourself lucky—this joint is popular with locals. Breakfast doesn't attract quite so big a crowd. Entree with a mountain of tortillas, rice, and beans, with a very generous serving of juice; 14 pesos.

**Restaurante Chantilly** (tel. 2-01-94), on the plaza at Juárez and Moreno. Serves Mexican staples in a diner-like setting to crowds of newspaper-reading professionals. Though the food is nothing to write home about, the view of the *zócalo* makes it a good spot for people-watching. Waffles 9 pesos. Shrimp cocktail 30 pesos. Three chicken *enchiladas* 12 pesos. Open Sun.-Fri. 7am-10pm.

## SIGHTS

Of the two nearby beaches, **Bahía Manzanillo** and **Bahía Santiago,** the former has more expensive hotels and cleaner golden sand. Unfortunately, its beach slopes steeply, creating a strong and sometimes dangerous undertow. The beaches at Bahía Santiago, though twice as far from *el centro* and bordered by a noisy highway, are safer for swimming and are more popular with sun worshippers.

The closest good beach on Bahía Manzanillo, **Playa Las Brisas,** has a few secluded spots, but parts of the beach are crowded with luxurious hotels and bungalows. To get to Las Brisas from downtown Manzanillo, take a taxi (16-18 pesos) or the "Las Brisas" bus (2 pesos). Catch the bus on México or on the highway going toward the airport and Barra de Navidad. Alternatively, catch the "Miramar" bus and ask the driver to let you off at the *crucero* (crossroads). From the crossroads, turn left to populated shores or stake out a private piece of beach right at the junction.

The "Miramar" bus continues west of Peninsula Santiago, gear-grinding toward other excellent beaches on Bahía Santiago. Because this part of the bay is not used for shipping, the water is cleaner than at Las Brisas. The "Miramar" buses (2.60 pesos to the Bahía) leave every 15 minutes from the train station, three blocks east of the plaza on Niños Héroes. The best place to get off is where everyone else does—at **Miramar Beach,** where a footbridge crosses the highway. This is the most crowded section of the beach, but it boasts top-notch beachfront restaurants from which you can rent body boards and surfboards (5-10 pesos per hr.). Crowds disappear 20m east or west of the beach club that owns this stretch of sand. The waves are adequate for body boarding or body surfing, but you'd have about as much luck with your surfboard here as you would in a swimming pool.

Even calmer waters await at **Playa la Boquita,** which is recommended for children. Also oozing tranquility is **Playa Audiencia,** a small but magnificent cove with calm waters, light brown sand, a few small boats, and a gorgeous rocky vista. To reach the *playa,* take a Las Hadas bus (3 pesos) from either Niños Héroes or from anywhere on Miramar Highway to the Sierra Radison. Then, dodge the crabs along the path to the beach. The bus ride back to town offers a spectacular view of the peninsula.

## ■ NEAR MANZANILLO

### PARAÍSO

**Paraíso** may soon be destroyed by the gods for its hubris, but while it exists it outclasses its unsightly sister city, nearby **Armería.** A well-paved road connects the two towns, cutting through 7km of banana and coconut plantations before it dead-ends into the black sands that surround Paraíso's few hotels and thatched, beachfront restaurants. A shoreline strewn with an endless row of lawn chairs and umbrellas backs the emerald green surf. Paraíso is popular among Mexicans as a destination for daytrips and weekend vacations; during the high season and on Sundays, the beachfront has a true family atmosphere, and the town's single dirt road is often crammed with buses and cars blaring music for the entertainment of all. But on a lazy summer weekday, the beach is almost deserted, and a few lucky swimmers have the waters all to themselves.

Just before the main road becomes the beach, you'll see Paraíso's only other street, **Avenida de la Juventud** (extravagantly called **Calle Adán y Eva** by locals) which runs along the back of the beachfront restaurants. The first building on the beach and to your left is **Hotel Equipales,** where you'll find funky green walls enclosing clean rooms and cramped bathrooms. To reach the hotel by phone, call the town's *caseta* (tel. 4-60-24 or 4-60-26; singles 25 pesos, doubles 50 pesos). Farther to the left lies **Hotel Paraíso** (tel. 8-10-09). For those staying on the beachfront, expect big, well-maintained rooms, spotless showers, and a pool crammed with kids. A new section across the street boasts slightly nicer rooms, but not nice enough to justify the added distance from the shore—and the higher prices. (Singles and doubles 90 pesos, in the new section 125 pesos.) At the opposite end of the strip sits **Posada Valencia,** where the beds are waist-high, the rooms are clean, and the bathroom tiles are scrubbed spotless. Alas, the plain cement floors put a damper on it all. Hot water is available mornings and evenings. Direct phone calls to the *caseta.* (Singles 50 pesos, Doubles 80 pesos.)

Alternatives to spending the night in a hotel abound. For campers, Paraíso's extensive beach makes a soft pillow, and the Hotel Paraíso offers showers (5 pesos) and free bathrooms to anyone who should care to use them. Hotel Equiplaes also offers bathroom (1 peso) and shower (3 pesos) use. Some *enramada* owners may let you hang your hammock under their thatched roofs. In high season (especially Dec. and April), rooms may be available in private Paraíso houses; ask around.

**Restaurants** run the slim gamut from rustic *enramadas* to cement-floored *comedores.* Predictably, locally caught seafood dominates menus, which barely differ from place to place in both offerings and prices. **Restaurant Paraíso,** in the Hotel Paraíso (see above), is as popular as the hotel pool. Uniformed waiters provide snazzy service. Tasty shrimp dishes cost 28 pesos (open daily 8am-6pm). The restaurants at Hotel Equipales and Posada Valencia (see above) also offer a pleasant atmosphere and reasonable prices. Make long-distance calls across the street from the bus stop in the *tienda rural* (tel. 4-60-24 or 4-60-26). Fee for use of the phone is derived from a simple formula: "give me whatever you think is appropriate." No, that's not a joke (open Mon.-Sat. 9am-9pm, Sun. 9am-6pm). And remember to bring plenty of cash on your trip to Paraíso, because there's no credit in Paradise.

NEAR MANZANILLO

**Getting There:** Buses to Paraíso leave from the corner outside Restaurant Camino Real in Armería (every 45min., 6am-7:30pm, 2 pesos). The stop is three blocks from where most buses arrive, on the corner of Netzahualcóyotl (the main street) and 5 de Mayo. Buses return from Paraíso to Armería from the same place they stopped (where the remains of the paved road meet Adán y Eva).

## CUYUTLÁN

If you're a budding Thoreauvian hungry for solitude and silence, then **Cuyutlán** (pop. 1650) should be on your agenda. In the off-season, shut-up buildings and empty streets give the place a ghost-town feel and the huge golden head of Benito Juárez is often the only face visible amidst the palm trees of Cuyutlán's green and white *zócalo*. On weekdays during the summer months, the beach is as deserted as the *zócalo*, its dark sand pounded by wild waves while nary a soul watches. Summer weekends are slightly busier, but it is only during the high tourist season (Dec.-May), that lifeguards and a well-planned *malecón* make Cuyutlán's beaches especially attractive.

Cuyutlán's most unusual distinction is the renowned **green wave,** a phenomenon that occurs regularly in April or May. Quirky currents and phosphorescent marine life combine to produce 10m swells that glow an unearthly green. The town itself reaches high tide during the **Festival of the Virgin de Guadalupe** (the first twelve days of December), when twice a day, at 6am and 6pm, men, women, and children clad in *traje de indios* process 3 miles to the town's blue church. The celebrations peak on the twelfth day, when *mariachis* accompany the procession and the marchers sing *las mañanitas* in tribute to the Virgin.

The road from Armería, 15km to the northeast, becomes **Yavaros,** running east-west, parallel to the coastline, as it enters town. It intersects **Hidalgo,** which runs north-south, along the east side of the town square; a left at this intersection takes you to the beach. Buses coming from Armería (every ½hr., 6am-7:30pm, 2.50 pesos) make a right at the intersection onto Hidalgo and head away from the beach before stopping at the *parada* (bus stop) which serves as a bus station on Hidalgo. **Veracruz,** Cuyutlán's other mighty boulevard, is parallel to Yavaros, one block off the beach and three blocks from Yavaros.

Most of Cuyutlán's municipal services are within one block of the *zócalo*. The owners of the Hotel Morelos will **change money** if they have the cash. Bring an adequate supply of *pesos* just in case. The only **telephone** is at Hidalgo 47 (tel. 4-18-10), one block inland from the *zócalo*. Call there to reach any of Cuyutlán's establishments. Again, pay what's appropriate. (Open 24 hrs. **Telephone code:** 332.) **Farmacia del Carmen** is at Hidalgo 117 (open Mon.-Fri. 4-8pm, Sat.-Sun. 9am-2pm and 4-8pm). For those who fall sick, a **Centro de Salud** is one block west of the *zócalo* on Yavaros at Madero. (Consultation Mon. 4-6pm, Tues.-Fri. 9am-2pm and 4-6pm, Sat. 9am-noon.) The **police** reside at Hidalgo 143 (tel. 4–18-10, ext. 113), one block south of the *zócalo*.

Waves, both green and blue, lap at the doorsteps of most nearby budget hotels. The **Hotel Morelos,** Hidalgo 185 at Veracruz, offers incredibly plush, spacious rooms with fans and hot water, and what seems like all the flowers in Cuyutlán. (30 pesos per person, mid-June-Oct. 25 pesos per person; with kitchen 35 pesos per person.) In the **Hotel Fénix,** Hidalgo 201 at Veracruz, the rooms may be taller than they are wide, but there's a fan in each one, and the bathrooms are tidy enough to use. What's more, the family atmosphere is sure to leave travelers feeling warm and fuzzy inside (35 pesos per person). The **Hotel San Rafael,** Veracruz 46, is the oldest hotel in Cuyutlán. Wooden-shuttered windows look out on seaside patios and a swimming pool. Plain white rooms have a closet and small tables, and the clean bathrooms have hot water. (Singles 50 pesos. Doubles 100 pesos.) Across from the hotel is **La Discoteque Mania,** a disco and video bar that's usually open in the winter and during *Semana Santa*.

Camping sites and outdoor cabañas are available at **Cabañitas del Ejido Cuyutlán,** a short walk from Posada del Sol. The sites include an open-air *cabaña* with a table, electricity, security, and access to showers and toilets (8 pesos for 24 hrs.). Unofficial camping sites lie 200m from Cuyutlán's hotels, in a private patch of black sand. Some travelers string up a hammock in one of the *palapas* near the hotels—most of them are vacant in summer. For two pesos, campers and daytrippers can use the toilets and showers at Hotel Morelos.

Almost all the food in Cuyutlán is served up in the hotel restaurants. Seafood is the obvious specialty, but other Mexican staples are definitely available. Almost all the restaurants are on Yavaros.

**Getting There:** Buses leave from the *parada* for Armería every half-hour from 6:30am to 8pm (3 pesos; see Paraíso: Getting There). There is no public transportation between Paraíso and Cuyutlán.

# ■■■ COLIMA

The capital of Colima state is hardly a tiny village (pop. 10,000), but it manages to maintain a certain small-town benevolence and informality—its streets and parks are delightfully clean and its civic-minded inhabitants, many of whom work for the state government, are remarkably friendly. Studded with little museums and theaters, under-touristed Colima provides relief from the well-trodden coastal route and is a great place to shake the sand from your shoes. Founded in 1523, Colima is rich in tradition and culture, and retains the picturesque, sophisticated air of an aging antique. Alas, progress is catching up with the city: afternoon serenades in the *zócalo* battle with cruising cars blaring techno music and the slews of storekeepers hawking hip clothing. When the cathedral doors are propped open to keep the pious masses cool, the organ's somber strains are drowned out by the pulsating beat of the pop music being played in the plaza.

## ORIENTATION

A string of plazas runs east to west across downtown Colima. The arcaded **Plaza Principal,** flanked by the cathedral and the Palacio de Gobierno on the east side, is the business center of town and houses its lone gazebo. On the other side of the cathedral and *palacio* is the smaller, quieter **Jardín Quintero,** marked by the large fountain in its center. Three blocks farther east on **Madero** (which runs along the north side of the plaza) is the large, lush **Jardín Núñez,** the other significant reference point in town. Many tourist services are on **Hidalgo,** which parallels Madero one block to the south. The main **bus station** is 2km out of town, but mini-buses zip by incessantly. All intra-city buses charge 1.20 pesos.

## PRACTICAL INFORMATION

**Tourist Office:** Portal Hidalgo 20 (tel. 2-43-60 or 2-83-60), on the west side of Pl. Principal, across the *zócalo* from the Palacio de Gobierno. Extremely helpful staff. Info on the city and the state of Colima. Open Mon.-Fri. 8:30am-3pm and 6-9pm, Sat. 9am-1pm.

**Police:** Juárez at 20 de Noviembre (tel. 2-18-01).

**Post Office:** Madero 247 (tel. 2-00-53) at Revolución, on the northeast corner of the Jardín Núñez. *Lista de Correos.* Open Mon.-Fri. 8am-7pm, Sat. 8am-noon. **Postal Code:** 28000.

**Telephones: Computel,** Morelos 234 (tel. 4-59-05), on the south side of Jardín Núñez. International collect calls 6 pesos for 10min. Open daily 7am-10pm. Blue international phones are just about everywhere. **Telephone Code:** 331.

**Telegrams:** Madero 243 (tel. 4-59-96), 1 door from the post office. Open Mon.-Fri. 6am-6pm, Sat. 9am-noon.

**Currency Exchange: Banamex,** Hidalgo 90 (tel. 2-01-03), 1 block east of Pl. Principal. No commission and a good rate, but Acapulco might freeze over as you wait in line. Money exchange in the basement. **ATM.** Open Mon.-Fri. 9am-1:30pm. **Majapara Casa de Cambio** (tel. 4-89-98, fax 4-89-66), on the corner of Morelos and Juárez at Jardín Núñez. Slightly better rates. Open Mon.-Fri. 9am-2pm and 4:30-6:30pm, Sat. 9am-2pm.

COLIMA

**Train Station:** At the southern edge of town (tel. 2-92-50). Taxi fare from the *centro* 4.50 pesos, from suburban bus station 4 pesos. Second-class service to Guadalajara (1:30pm, 6hrs., 16 pesos) and Manzanillo (3pm, 2hrs., 6 pesos). Offices open daily 9am-3pm.

**Bus Stations:** The well-mopped and airport-like **Central de Autobuses** is 2km out of town and accessible via numerous buses (1.20 pesos), or taxi (5 pesos). **La Linea** (tel. 4-81-79) operates the most buses to Guadalajara (*Linea Plus:* 11 per day, 3hrs., 50 pesos; *Ordinario:* 8 per day, 3hrs., 43 pesos). **Autotransportes del Sur de Jalisco** (tel. 2-03-16) runs second-class buses to Guadalajara via Pihaumo (every hr., 5am-6pm and three evening departures, 3hrs., 37 pesos) and to Manzanillo (27 per day, 2hrs., 7 pesos). **ETN** (tel. 2-58-99 or 4-10-60) has first-class service to the Guadalajara airport (3pm and 9:30pm, about 3hrs., 80 pesos). **Tres Estrellas de Oro** (tel. 2-84-48) has first-class service to Mexico City (8pm, 9:30pm, and 11pm, 20hrs., 143 pesos), and connects in Tecomán to Acapulco, Zihuatanejo, Lázaro Cárdenas, Tijuana, and Mazatlán. **Omnibús de México** (tel. 4-71-90), your best bet to the east, goes to Aguascalientes (2pm, 7pm, and 10pm, 6hrs., 71 pesos) and Mexico City (7:45pm, 8:30pm, and 10pm, 20hrs., 136 pesos). **Primera Plus** (tel. 4-80-67) runs first-class buses to Manzanillo (10 per day, 1½hrs., 20 pesos). **Sociedad Cooperativa Colima** operates from the suburban bus station and is accessible via numerous bus routes or a taxi (5 pesos) from *el centro*. To Armería (every 30min., 4:30am-10pm, 5 pesos), Tecomán (every 5min., 4:30am-10pm, 4.50 pesos), and Manzanillo (direct or via Tecomán, every 30min., 4:30am-10pm, 10 pesos). Suburban buses go to Comala (see: Near Colima), Zapotitlan, Cofradía, and San Antonio.

**Luggage Storage:** Available at the central bus station.

**Laundromat: LavaTec,** Rey Coliman 4. Same-day service. Wash or dry about 5 pesos. Open Mon.-Sat. 8:30am-8:30pm.

**Red Cross:** Aldama at Obregón (tel. 2-14-51 or 2-22-42). Open 24 hrs.

**Pharmacy: Farmacia Colima,** Madero 1 (tel. 2-00-31 or 2-55-37), at the northeast corner of the Pl. Principal. Open Mon.-Sat. 8:30am-9pm, Sun. 9am-2pm.

**Hospitals: Hospital Civil,** San Fernando at Ignacio Zandoval (tel. 2-02-27 or 2-09-11). **Centro de Salud,** Juárez at 20 de Noviembre (tel. 2-00-64 or 2-32-38). Dr. Armando López speaks English. Open Mon.-Fri. 7am-2:30pm.

**Emergency:** dial 06.

## ACCOMMODATIONS

Colima certainly isn't teeming with budget accommodations, but a smattering of inexpensive hotels line Jardín Núñez and outlying streets. Higher-quality (and higher-priced) hotels cluster near the university. Because Colima does not anticipate the same *gringo* crowds as its beachside cousins, expect most fellow lodgers to be natives. Purified water is often not available.

**Hotel La Merced,** Hidalgo 188 or Juárez 82 (tel. 2-69-69). The entrance is on the west side of Jardín Nuñez—wind through the walkway and parking lot to reach the reception desk. A colorful motel-esque establishment with an outdoorsy feel. Rooms sport a desk, bureau, chest, and ceiling fan. Private baths with showers that boast hot water. Singles with a double bed 60 pesos. Doubles with both a single and double bed 75 pesos. Triples 90 pesos. Quads 105 pesos.

**Casa de Huéspedes,** Morelos 265 (tel. 2-34-67), just off the southeast corner of Jardín Núñez. A stairwell populated by billions of plants leads up to dusty rooms with cramped bathrooms. Bring your own toilet paper. The aged woman who runs the hotel and her adult children are exceptionally friendly. Singles 30 pesos, Doubles 50 pesos.

**Hotel San Lorenzo,** Calle Cuauhtémoc 149 (tel. 2-20-00). From Pl. Principal go west 2 blocks to Calle Cuauhtémoc and walk left 3 blocks. Very clean rooms with private bathrooms, hot water, two towels, and June Cleaver curtains. Don't expect many friendly *charlas* with the management. Singles 45 pesos. Doubles 55 pesos. Triples 65 pesos.

COLIMA

## FOOD

Most restaurants in Colima serve up the traditional *pozole blanco* (hominy), but others tread the cutting edge, affecting a modern air. Huge *equipales* (Colima's traditional bamboo chairs) scoop hungry Euro-types into cafés serving wine and cheese, but *típicos* are few and far between. A few pleasant establishments cluster around the Plaza Principal, but a jaunt down any of the plaza's sidestreets will lead to more authentic, less expensive eateries.

**Samadhi,** Medina 125 (tel. 3-24-98), 2½ blocks north of Jardín Núñez. Walk down Juárez (the western border of the Jardín); Samadhi is next to the church. The name could not be more appropriate for the meditative atmosphere, referring to the point one reaches at maximum concentration. Enter the leafy courtyard enclosed by soft yellow, orange, and pink walls; then savor some delicious vegetarian food. Breakfast Samadhi (orange or carrot juice, a fruit plate with yogurt, cereal, granola, and honey) goes for 14.50 pesos. Nachos 9 pesos. Three *enchiladas rojas* 13.50 pesos. Open Fri.-Wed. 8am-10pm, Thurs. 8am-5pm.

**Cenaduría Morelos,** Morelos 299 (tel. 2-93-32) at Domínguez, 1 block off the southeast corner of Jardín Nuñez. One of Colima's many *cenadurías* (eateries), Morelos is as *sabroso* as they get. The waitresses are pleasant until you question their restaurant's cleanliness—at that point, pride takes over as they explain their establishment's history as a lesson in hygiene. The moral? Enjoy the lettuce and diced turnip that comes with the *pozole, tostadas, sopes,* sweet *enchiladas,* or *taquitos.* All entrees 8 pesos. Open Tues.-Sun. 5-11pm.

**Los Naranjos,** Barreda 34 (tel. 2-00-29), almost a block north of Madero, just behind the Plaza Principal. *Periódico*-perusing middle-age men sip coffee between mellow lilac and beige walls. *Carne asada* "Los Naranjos" 28 pesos, *antojitos* 8-10 pesos. Open daily 8am-11pm.

**Los Portales,** Portal Morelos 25 (tel. 2-85-20), on the south side of the Pl. Principal. Eat your meal outdoors by the plaza in a funky *equipale*—people-watching doesn't get any better than this. Entrees 10-16 pesos, *antojitos* 4-7 pesos. Open daily 8am-10pm.

## SIGHTS

In Colima's well-maintained **Plaza Principal,** the gazebo and decorative fountains of the **Jardín Libertad** lure bureaucrats on their lunch hour to the garden's white benches. The double arcade around the plaza encompasses the **Museo Regional de Historia de Colima,** the Hotel Ceballos, and a handful of stores and sandwich shops. The commercial establishments continue along the pedestrian malls, which radiate from the plaza's corners.

On the east side of the plaza, much of the state government is housed in the **Palacio de Gobierno.** An inviting beige and white building with a breezy courtyard, the *palacio* also contains a four-wall mural, completed in 1954 by Jorge Chávez Carrillo in honor of the bicentennial of Hidalgo's birth. The intricate mural, covering the walls of the staircase closest to the Plaza Principal, moves counterclockwise through Mexico's tumultuous history. It begins with a powerful depiction of the Spanish conquest and ends at the Mexican Revolution with Pancho Villa's infamous heroism.

Adjoining Colima's municipal complex is the renovated colonial **Santa Iglesia Cathedral,** a pawn in the battle between humanity and nature—or, depending on your perspective, between Catholicism and the ghost of indigenous religions. The Spanish first built a church on this spot in 1527, but an earthquake destroyed the original wood and palm structure; fire consumed its replacement. Undeterred, the Spanish built another church. The cathedral's Neoclassical interior sparkles with gilt paint, chandeliers, and polished marble. In the pulpit designed by Othón Bustos rests a statue of San Felipe de Jesús, the city's patron saint. Avoid visiting during services (Mon.-Sat. 7:30, 11:30am, and 7:30pm, Sun. 7, 8, 11am, noon, 6, 7, and 8pm).

A block south of the tourist office, on the west side of Plaza Principal, stands **Teatro Hidalgo,** completed in 1883. Unmarred by the passage of time, the theater's four tiers of side-seating barely touch the high ceiling, and its swooping red curtains lend the stage a 19th-century ambiance. Occasional performances enliven the majestic interior beyond those large wooden doors; inquire at the tourist office.

Colima's **Museo de Las Culturas de Occidente** (tel. 2-31-55), on Calle Calzada Galván, is an excellent museum devoted to local pre-Hispanic art. It's newly improved after an extensive remodeling project. Rarely seen outside the state, the Colima ceramic figurines on display here are among the most playful and captivating artifacts in Mexico. To get to the museum, take the bus towards University of Colima from Av. Rey Coliman and get off at Casa de la Cultura, the university's arts center. (Open Tues.-Sun. 7am-9pm.) The museum's café, **Dalí,** is a sight in its own right. Prints by you-know-who drip from the walls under dim, smoky Euro-light. While the food isn't exactly in the budget range, it's almost worth it to drink *cervezas* with the college crowd between pale blue walls. Every night between 9 and 10pm, Sensitive Mexican Man (not Scott) stands on the café's small platform wailing love songs, a guitar cradled in his arms. *Muy romántico.* (Open daily 8:30am-12:30pm, 4-11:30pm.)

Colima's newest museum, the **Museo de Historia,** Portal Morelos 1 (tel. 2-92-28), is at 16 de Septiembre and Reforma on the south side of the Pl. Principal, next to the bookstore. The museum houses a small collection of pre-Hispanic ceramics (open Tues.-Sat. 9am-6pm, Sun. 5-8pm.; free). Next door the university runs a gallery featuring an eclectic art collection. (Open Tues.-Sat. 9am-2pm and 5-8pm, Sun. 5-8pm. Free.) Also sponsored by the institution is Colima's **Museo Universitario de Culturas Populares** (tel. 2-68-69), at Manuel Gallardo and 27 de Septiembre, which boasts a collection of traditional dresses and masks, figurines recovered from nearby tombs, and descriptions of the pre-Aztec western coast; provided you dig archaeology and read Spanish, these descriptions serve as a useful complement to the pieces. A gift shop sells handmade reproductions of local ceramics (museum open Mon.-Sat. 9am-2pm and 4-7pm). Getting there is an easy 15-minute walk north on 27 de Septiembre from the Plaza Principal. Alternatively, catch the #17 bus on Filomena Medina next to the pharmacy between Zaragoza and Guerrero and take it to the corner of Medina and Gallardo. The museum is half a block to your left.

# ■ NEAR COLIMA

## VOLCANOES

In Nahuatl, Colima means "place where the old god is dominant." The old god is **El Volcán de Fuego** (3820m). Recorded eruptions date back to the pre-Conquest era, and on June 24, 1994, lava was visible from the capital as El Fuego once again erupted, asserting its status as an active volcano. But before you cross Colima off your list of places to visit, know that the tourist office assures that the volcano is not a threat to the city. (Of course, Guadalajara wasn't supposed to get hit by an earthquake, and…) Near the top of El Fuego, which still emits small amounts of smoke and lava, is the **Joya Cabin,** which lacks all amenities except a roof. Because of the frequency of volcanic activity, the park is only open sporadically; if you're planning a trip to the top, call the **police** ahead of time (tel. 2-18-01). **El Nevado de Colima** (4240m), stands taller than its neighbor but is dormant and not much fun at parties. Still, travelers sometimes make the climb. As always, think safety. The ascent should not be attempted by solo travelers, or by those with little hiking experience.

**Getting There:** Guadalajara-bound *locales* (from the new bus station) pass through the town of **Atenquique,** 57km away. From here a 27km-long unimproved dirt road runs to the summit of El Fuego. The trip is only recommended for four-wheel-drive vehicles, though logging trucks based at the factory in Atenquique make trips up the road to spots near the summit. Buses from **Guzmán** (83km away) limp up to Joya, whence you can make your epic assault on the summit.

## LAGUNA CARRIZALILLO AND LAGUNA LA MARÍA

If you don't mind insects, frogs, and huge lizards, and you just have to get away from it all, think about going to **Laguna Carrizalillo,** 27km north of Colima. Daytrippers come here to bask in peace. Two pesos buys access to the lagoon area for a day, but due to administrative problems, *cabañas* are currently not available at Carrizalillo.

Larger, closer to the volcanoes, and more visited is **Laguna La María,** whose calm, green waters surrounded by a dense wall of plant life attract flocks of ornithologists in search of tiny yellow Singing Wilsons. If birds aren't your thing, try fishing either from the shore or from a rented *lancha* (about 20 pesos per hour). Two pesos buys access to the lagoon for a day. The proprietor of the *cabañas* will rent fishing poles. (Four-person *cabañas* 125 pesos, 150 pesos for six people.)

**Getting There:** Buses (about 4 pesos) marked "Cofradía" or "Zapotitlán" supposedly chug up and down the mountain road to La María every hour from 7am to 4pm. Ask the driver for the return time before boarding, and confirm it once again when you reach La María. The voyage up to the lagoon can take anywhere from 40 to 90 minutes, but those who survive the painfully bumpy ride are rewarded with a magnificent view of the mountains just before the bus reaches the tiny crossroads that leads to the lagoon. To get to the entrance from here, follow the wooden sign that says La María (a 15-minute hike). The bus back leaves from the same crossroads on the opposite side of the street. To make accommodations reservations at La María, ask at the Colima **tourist office** (tel. 2-43-60).

## COMALA

South of the lagoons and just 9km north of Colima is the picturesque town of **Comala,** known as "El Pueblo Blanco de América" (The White Town of America). Originally, all the façades in town were white, with red-tiled roofs, huge porches, and windows filled with flowers. Today, Comala's small-town feel persists in the *zócalo,* which is surrounded by cobblestone streets and dotted with white benches, fountains, and orange trees. The south side of the *zócalo* is lined by a row of lively restaurants in which mariachis and trumpeters perform and waiters supply patrons with a steady stream of free *botanas* (Mexican appetizers) to whet the appetite for *cervezas* and *ponche* (mezcal with tropical fruit juices), one of the region's vertigo-inducing traditional drinks.

To the east of the *zócalo* lies the **Iglesia San Miguel del Espíritu Santo,** whose unfinished bare-bricked rear endows it with additional character. Watch your head as you enter, for perched above is a sinister flock of pigeons. Once inside, you are met not by ornate stained-glass windows, but a sky blue ceiling. The nave of the church is occupied by still more birds, chirping a deafening cacophony. On the other side of the *zócalo* are the city offices, where a four-wall mural commemorates Comala's 130 years as a city and celebrates the "richness of its soil." Unfortunately, the birds who have control of the church have also settled across the way, and have graciously added their own artistic expression to the mural. One door over is the office of Comala's municipal president, Arnoldo Ceballos Fierros, who can be contacted for further information (tel. 5-50-10 or 5-50-20). **Salón Comala Bucaramanga,** Progreso 15 (tel. 5-55-11), in the center of it all, is popular among locals. A load of shrimp goes for 35 pesos (open 8:30am-6pm).

Comala's main claim to fame is its colony of *indígena* artisans who craft wooden furniture, leather goods, clocks, and bamboo baskets in accord with the dictates of pre-Hispanic traditions. A small *tianguis (indígena* market) stands just outside Comala's *centro.* It's past the strip of restaurants by about 200m. It's a 15 to 20-minute walk from the *zócalo* (open Mon.-Fri. 8am-3pm, Sat. 9am-2pm).

**Getting There:** Buses to Comala leave from Colima's suburban bus station (every 15min., 6am-10:30pm, 1.20 pesos).

# ▧ El Bajío

A vast, bowl-shaped plateau of fertile soil, rolling farms, and verdant hillsides sits slightly below central Mexico's volcanic range. Since the 16th century, the Bajío's silver-rich underground has brought the region prosperity and steered the course of its history. The area's richest mines were discovered by local aristocrats by 1550, but it was not until 1750, when the silver trade was rerouted through Mexico City, that the Bajío's cities ascended to the ranks of the wealthiest and most influential cities in Mexico. As the city of Guanajuato began to supply most of the country's minting silver, it became the commercial and banking center of this thriving region, trading manufactured goods for crops from the nearby agricultural towns of Salamanca, Irapuato, León, San Miguel, and Celaya. A flourishing economy eventually brought the Bajío both a measure of sophistication and a population of U.S. expatriates, drawn to the region's vibrant social life and distinguished history.

# GUANAJUATO

## ■■■ GUANAJUATO

Guanajuato is simply beautiful. During the ride into the city, the highway winds through lush mountains split at the base by winding streams, passing rows of *nopales* (prickly-pear cacti) that blend surreally into the landscape. The hills continue into a city where the legacy of colonial days lives on in apolitical forms; serpentine slate streets overflow with monuments to the ostentation of Guanajuato's silver barons. The contours of the city's history—the peaks of economic success and the pits of horrific repression—are as treacherous as the city's streets. In 1558, massive veins of silver were discovered in the area. Over the next 200 years, the city became one of Mexico's wealthiest, supplying much of the world's silver.

Guanajuato is also the birthplace of Diego Rivera, the muralist whose earliest works are infused with impressions of the city. During the **Festival Internacional Cervantino,** held in October in honor of the author of *Don Quijote,* Guanajuato sponsors performances of drama, classical music, and ballet in an atmosphere of Dionysian debauchery. Though the town's boom days are over, tourists continue to visit from around the world, while Guanajuato's university students and musicians drive an animated and youthful social life that glitters as brightly as silver.

### ORIENTATION

Guanajuato is 56km southwest of Dolores Hidalgo and 44km north of Irapuato. The shortest way from Mexico City is via Celaya on Rte. 45. Buses run to Guanajuato from both León and Irapuato. Guanajuato's **bus station** is 3km west of town; from there, catch the "El Centro" bus (1.40 pesos) or take a taxi (10 pesos).

Guanajuato has been adding streets for the last 30 years or so in an attempt to make the city accessible to cars. Whether the government has succeeded is debatable, but no one denies that what was once a difficult city to navigate is now next to impossible. Many streets are not open to traffic, and few follow a linear path. At the center of the city, from northwest to southeast, are the **Plaza de la Paz,** the *basílica,* and the Jardín Unión. **Avenida Juárez** zig-zags west to the market, then changes names as it turns uphill to Plaza de la Paz for a short time, passing the tourist office and the bus station; to the east of the plaza, the schizophrenic street calls itself **Avenida Sopeña.** Roughly following the path of Juárez/Sopeña, the **Subterránea** is an underground avenue built beneath the former bed of the river, which now flows in an adjacent concrete channel. When you become lost (and you will), remember

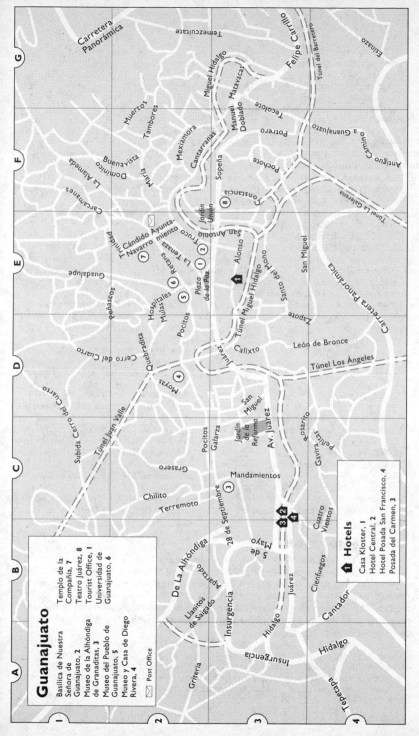

**Guanajuato**

Basílica de Nuestra
Señora de
Guanajuato, **2**
Museo de la Alhóndiga
de Granaditas, **3**
Museo del Pueblo de
Guanajuato, **5**
Museo y Casa de Diego
Rivera, **4**

Templo de la
Compañía, **7**
Teatro Juárez, **8**
Tourist Office, **1**
Universidad de
Guanajuato, **6**

◹ Post Office

**⬆ Hotels**

Casa Kloster, **1**
Hotel Central, **2**
Hotel Posada San Francisco, **4**
Posada del Carmen, **3**

that the tunnel is always downhill from you. Buses (6am-10:30pm, 1.40 pesos) cross the city above and underground. Taxis within the city cost five to eight pesos.

## PRACTICAL INFORMATION

**Tourist Office: Subsecretaria de Turismo,** Plaza de la Paz 14 (tel. 2-15-74; fax 2-42-51), on your right as you pass the *basílica* going uphill. While their map is sadly reminiscent of a placemat made by a 3rd grader and the brochures are simple, asking questions proves very informative. English spoken. Open Mon.-Fri. 8:30am-7:30pm, Sat.-Sun. 10am-2pm.

**Police:** Alhóndiga 8 (tel. 2-02-66 or 2-27-17), one block from Juárez. On call 24 hrs.

**Post Office:** (tel. 2-03-85), on Ayuntamiento, down the street from the Universidad de Guanajuato. Follow Truco, the street bordering the right side of the *basílica* as you face it from Plaza de la Paz, for one block and turn left. Open for stamps and *Lista de Correos* Mon.-Fri. 8am-8pm, Sat. 9am-1pm. **Postal Code:** 36000.

**Telephones: Lonchería y Caseta de Larga Distancia Pípila,** Constancia 9 (tel. 2-00-75), behind the Templo de San Diego. Open Mon.-Sat. 9:30am-9:30pm, Sun. 11am-2:30pm. **Telephone Code:** 473.

**Telegrams:** Sopeña 1 (tel. 2-04-29), east of Teatro Juárez. Open Mon.-Fri. 8am-6pm, Sat. 9am-1pm.

**Currency Exchange:** Banks line Juárez and the Plaza de la Paz. **Banco Mexicano,** Sopeña 18 (tel. 2-15-59), one block east of the Teatro Juárez, has a decent exchange rate but won't exchange traveler's checks. Open for exchange Mon.-Fri. 9am-1:30pm. **Centro Cambiario Mavaq,** Plaza de la Compañía 12-A (tel. 2-94-99), directly in front of the Templo de la Compañía's main entrance, has a good rate. Open daily 9am-5pm.

**Bus Station: Central de Autobuses,** west of the *centro.* **Flecha Amarilla** (tel. 3-13-33), to Aguascalientes (5 per day, 5:40am-6:10pm, 3½hrs., 28 pesos), Dolores Hidalgo (every 20min., 5:30am-10:30pm, 1½hrs., 9 pesos), Mexico City (4 per day, 5:30am-1:20pm, 5½hrs., 59 pesos), Morelia (7 per day, midnight-3:10pm, 4hrs., 27 pesos), Querétaro (6 per day, 6:40am-4:40pm, 3hrs., 23.50 pesos), San Luis Potosí (3 per day, 7:50-11:30am, 3hrs., 35 pesos), and San Miguel de Allende (6 per day, 6:45am-2:30pm, 2hrs., 14.50 pesos). **Estrella Blanca** (tel. 3-13-44), offers first-class service to Guadalajara (4 per day, 8am-10:30pm, 5hrs., 55 pesos) and Monterrey (7 per day, 2-9:30pm, 10hrs., 128 pesos). **Primera Plus** (tel. 3-13-33), goes to Puerto Vallarta (9:45pm, 9hrs., 130 pesos). **Omnibus de México** (tel. 3-13-56), serves Zacatecas (9pm, 5hrs., 54 pesos).

**Laundromat: Lavandería Automática,** Manuel Doblado 28 (tel. 2-67-18). Wash and dry 3kg for 22 pesos. Same-day service. Open Mon.-Sat. 9am-2pm and 4-8pm.

**Red Cross:** (tel. 2-04-87), on Juárez west of the market. English spoken by some volunteers. 24-hr. emergency service.

**Pharmacy: Farmacia La Perla de Guanajuato,** Juárez 146 (tel. 2-11-75). Makes deliveries. No English spoken. Open daily 9am-9pm.

**Hospital:** (tel. 3-15-73 or -77), behind the bus station. Dr. Adolfo Sánchez Leva speaks English. Open for consultation Mon.-Fri. noon-2pm and 5-8pm.

**Emergency:** 06.

## ACCOMMODATIONS

Guanajuato is chock full of accommodations within the range of the budget traveler. The quiet, pretty neighborhood around the *basílica* is home to some inexpensive hotels, often occupied by young people of all nationalities; Guanajuato frequently plays two-day getaway for students at language institutes in San Miguel de Allende or Mexico City. Those visiting Guanajuato on weekends or during the Festival Cervantino in October should make hotel reservations in advance. During the festival, many prices double.

**Casa Kloster,** Alonso 32 (tel. 2-00-88). Leaving the *basílica,* head to your right on Juárez and make an immediate left at the first open alley. Take the first left (that's Alonso), and it's on your right. Well-kept rooms come with yellow-and-black tiled floors; some get bright *quetzal*-patterned bedspreads. Spotless communal bathrooms are modern, save the "no toilet paper in the toilet" rule. Rooms surround an open courtyard filled with flowers, plants, and birds. Ebullient guests. 35 pesos per person. Reservations are recommended.

**Hotel Central,** Juárez 111 (tel. 2-00-80), across the street from the Posada San Francisco, one block from the market. Formerly included the right side of the courtyard as well, until joint owners parted ways and split the building into two separate establishments. Competition has been good for the place; rooms are spotless, equipped with beds with pink spreads that sink in the middle, a desk, and a mirror. If you're shy, all showers come with curtains or sliding glass doors. Hot water 24 hrs. Singles 45 pesos. Doubles 55 pesos. Add 10 pesos for TV.

**Posada Del Carmen,** Juárez 111-A (tel. 2-93-30). Adjacent to Hotel Central, with virtually identical rooms. Not all bathrooms come with shower curtains. Singles 45 pesos. Doubles 50 pesos.

**Hotel Posada San Francisco,** Juárez 178 (tel. 2-24-67), at Gavira, the big pink hotel next to the market. Very clean, very carpeted bedrooms with shiny bathrooms. All rooms come with TV, or watch in the 2nd-floor lounge, with a suit of armor to keep you company (he won't talk, hog the remote, or steal your nachos). Classier than the cost. Singles 70 pesos. Doubles 100 pesos.

## FOOD

Guanajuato's restaurants make their money off the *comida corrida,* generally referred to as *la comida* or *el menú.* The meal begins at around 12:30pm and runs until early evening, depending on the restaurant. At the peak hour (around 2:30pm), restaurants are crowded with students, local workers on their lunch breaks, and tourists. A *comida* generally includes soup, salad, tea or *agua fresca,* a *plato fuerte,* and sometimes a dessert. Inexpensive restaurants cluster around Guanajuato's plazas and near the *basílica;* prices rise near the Jardín Unión, as the *gringos*-per-square-inch ratio rises. The Mercado Hidalgo has many fruit and taco stands.

**Truco No. 7,** at (hey!) Truco 7 (tel. 2-83-74), the first left beyond the basílica. Decent prices, good food, and great company: The Doors, The Beatles, and just about everyone in town. Tremendously popular with both local and U.S. students. High ceilings, fine pottery, and a funky *equipale* on which to enjoy a Mexican or American meal. *Carne asada* 15 pesos, *comida corrida* 13 pesos, and *huevos* 4-8 pesos. Cappuccino 4 pesos. Open daily 8am-11:30pm.

**Cafetería y Restaurante Pinguis** (tel. 2-14-14), on the Jardín Unión. Look for the red awning across from Posada Santa Fe. Excellent central location and low prices make it a great breakfast place. A bulletin board advertises local cultural events, while the adjacent wall shows the management's appreciation for Diego Rivera and Frida Kahlo. Clientele is a bizarre cocktail of students, *señores* sipping coffee over the newspaper, and whoever wanders in off the Jardín. *Menú del día* 13 pesos. Eggs 4-6 pesos. Juices 2.50-3 pesos. Open daily 8am-10pm.

**Rincón de San Fernando,** Plaza de San Fernando 43, on the southeast corner, off Juárez before it curves into Plaza de la Paz. The food is tasty and prepared with care. Yellow walls are still adorned with the paintings of the site's original Arabic café. *Comida corrida* 12 pesos. Tacos and *flautas* 4-8 pesos. Ketchup fanatics may want to give the *coctel de aguacate* a whirl (5 pesos). Open daily 8am-6pm.

**Restaurant Vegetariano,** Calixto 20 (tel. 2-20-62), visible from Juárez, up the small hill just beyond the turn for Plaza de la Paz. Red-checkered tablecloths, teapots at every table, and orange-and-white shelves stocked with oats give the place a country-home feel. Very reasonable. *Menú del día* 13 pesos. Breakfast 10 pesos. *Licuados* 3-4 pesos. Open Mon.-Sat. 8am-about 7pm.

## SIGHTS

The **Museo y Casa de Diego Rivera,** Pocitos 47 (tel. 2-11-97), chronicles the life of Guanajuato's most famous native son. Arranged chronologically, the works reveal the influence of Parisian friends like Picasso and Modigliani who encouraged Rivera's move from landscapes to Cubist sketches and elongated nudes. By 1920, however, the bright colors and simple tones of Rivera's Mayan-influenced style asserted

GUANAJUATO

themselves. Don't miss the outstanding watercolor illustrations for the *Popol Vuh* (the sacred book of the Maya) which imitate Mayan iconography. Note also Rivera's sketch for a section of the mural commissioned in 1933 by New York's Rockefeller Center—the mural was destroyed after a portrait of Lenin was discovered in it. This sketch, which portrays a woman enslaved by a machine with the head of Adolf Hitler, was not incorporated into the final composition. The museum also includes a photo-mural reproduction of Rivera's *Sueños de Una Tarde Dominicial en la Alameda*, a brightly colored piece composed of 75 representations (open Tues.-Sat. 10am-1:30pm and 4-6:30pm, Sun. 10am-2:30pm; admission 5 pesos; students and teachers 2.50 pesos; free for those over 70 or under 13).

The **Museo de la Alhóndiga de Granaditas** (tel. 2-11-12), on Calarza at the west end of Pocitos, is fairly conventional. Constructed as a granary between 1797 and 1809, this building witnessed some of the most crucial and bloody battles of the fight for Mexican independence. Today, the Alhóndiga is an ethnographic, archaeological, and historical museum. A chamber on the first floor charts the course of Mexican nationhood. Other exhibits display the work of *indígena* artisans of the Bajío region—check out the masks, firecrackers, engraved machetes, tapestries, and candy horse skeletons designed for consumption on *El Día de los Muertos* (Day of the Dead). Another gallery shows Romualdo García's photographs of Mexicans on the eve of the 1910 Revolution. While the hall, which contains huge busts of the heroes of 1910, is nothing short of stunning, the museum's finest exhibit traces the social history of Guanajuato from the Conquest through the Revolution.

For many who visit, the museum's most impressive possessions are the three murals gracing the building's stairwells. The works are often mistaken for that of José Clemente Orozco, Diego Rivera, or David Alfaro Siqueiros; the actual painter, José Chávez Morado, was a contemporary of all three. *Abolición de Esclavitud* (1955), the earliest of the three murals, follows Mexico's history from the Conquest, when Indians were oppressed slaves, to the Revolution, by which time native groups had regained some measure of power. (Open Tues.-Sat. 10am-2pm and 4-6pm, Sun. 10am-2:30pm. Doors close ½hr. before closing time. Admission 13 pesos. Free Sun. and for students, seniors, and those 13 and under. Photo permit 1 peso.)

The **Museo del Pueblo de Guanajuato,** Pocitos 7 (tel. 2-29-90), next to the university, was inaugurated in 1979. It features rotating exhibits on the first and third levels, from nude photography that would make the NEA squirm to samples of El Bajío's finest pottery. The second floor features a permanent exhibit of 18th- and 19th- century Mexican painting (open Tues.-Sat. 10am-1:30pm and 4-6:30pm, Sun. 10am-3pm; admission 5 pesos, children 10 and under free).

The newest museum in Guanajuato is the **Museo Iconográfico del Quijote,** Manuel Doblado 1 (tel. 2-67-21), east of the Jardín Unión. Housed in a gorgeous colonial mansion, its 10 big galleries contain over 600 works of art inspired by Cervantes's anti-hero Don Quijote, including paintings, sculptures, stained-glass windows, candlesticks, and clocks. Artists like Dalí, Picasso, Daumier, and Pedro Coronel have all interpreted Quijote; so have scores of lesser-knowns, as you'll soon see (open Tues.-Sat. 10am-6:30pm, Sun. 10am-2:30pm; free).

The **Jardín Unión,** in the heart of the city and one block east of the *basílica*, is the town's social center. This triangular plaza boasts enough shops, cafés, and guitar-strumming locals to appease the wild beast of tourism. Looking down on the Jardín from the nearby hill is the **Monumento a Pípila,** which commemorates the miner who torched the Alhóndiga's front door. The angry, titanic Pípila looks most impressive at night, when he is illuminated by spotlights. While the view of Pípila from below is striking, the monument itself affords a magnificent panoramic vista of the city. To reach the statue, follow Sopeña to the east and take the steep Callejón del Calvario to your right across the street from Lavandería El Centro (a 10-min. climb), or hop a bus marked "Pípila" from Plaza de la Paz.

The **Teatro Juárez** (tel. 2-01-83) faces one corner of Jardín Unión. After designing the theater to suit his tastes, Porfirio Díaz inaugurated the building in 1903 for a Verdi opera. The theater has an unabashedly gaudy Romanesque façade (try 12 columns, 12 lampposts, eight statues, and two bronze lions). The auditorium betrays its Moorish design: half-circles, arabesques, and endlessly weaving frescoed flowers in green, red, yellow, and brown make the interior seem like a gigantic Turkish carpet. In addition to housing government offices, the Teatro Juárez still hosts plays and the main events of the Festival Cervantino (open Tues.-Sun. 9am-1:45pm and 5-7:45pm; admission 4 pesos, camera permit 2 pesos).

Another self-aggrandizing Porfirian edifice is the **Palacio Legislativo de la Paz,** the state capital, across from the Posada de la Condesa near the *basílica.* Christened by Díaz in 1900, the building is an adaptation of the Greek Parthenon. Italian marble, wall and floor mosaics, and a decorative zinc ceiling ornament the interior (open for viewing Mon.-Fri. 10am-5pm; free).

Perhaps the most beautiful of Guanajuato's many natural attractions is the **Ex-Hacienda de San Gabriel de Barrera** (tel. 2-06-19). Seventeen glorious gardens, each laid out in a different style, cover about three acres. Cobbled paths, well-groomed flora, and whistling birds make the gardens a stroller's dream. The *ex-hacienda* itself, a 16th-century structure, abuts the gardens; its rooms contain furniture, silverware, and paintings from the era in which it was built. To get there, take a bus from Juárez for the "Central de Autobuses" (1.40 pesos) and tell the driver you're headed to San Gabriel de Barrera (open daily 9am-7pm; free).

In the **Basílica de Nuestra Señora de Guanajuato,** looming over the Pl. de la Paz, dozens of candelabra illuminate the lush Doric interior, including its fine ornamental frescoes and paintings of the Madonna by Miguel Cabrera. The wooden image of the city's protector, Nuestra Señora de Guanajuato, rests on a pure silver base and is believed to be the oldest piece of Christian art in Mexico (open daily 7am-8pm).

Next to the university and one block north of the basilica is the more interesting Jesuit **Templo de la Compañía.** Finished in 1765, the temple was shut down just two years later when the Jesuits were expelled from Spanish America. The exterior is one of the most striking in the region and still has four of the original five Churrigueresque façades. In the back of the church, in the ex-sacristy, is an art exhibit containing some of the church's original collection. At the end of the exhibit is a spooky *relicario,* a wood shelf enveloped in gold leaf, holding a collection of human bones (church open daily 7:30am-9pm; exhibit open daily 10:30am-2pm and 4:30-5:30pm; a five-peso donation is requested to support the restoration process).

The most famous alley in the city, the **Callejón del Beso** (Alley of the Kiss), is located off Alonso just before it hits Plaza de la Paz. Local lore has it that two lovers who lived on opposite sides of the alley were kept apart by their families but could

---

### Mmmm...Mummies

Museums in Guanajuato explore the historical, the artistic, the monumental, and the macabre. A museum of the latter variety is the **Museo de las Momias** (tel. 2-06-39), next to the city cemetery. The minerals and salty water of Guanajuato's soil naturally mummified the 108 corpses now on display in the museum. A guide points out the purplish, inflated body of a drowning victim; a woman buried alive, frozen in her attempt to scratch her way out of the coffin; two fashionable Frenchmen; a man who died by hanging, and another who was stabbed. Some buried babies still wear the colorful attire of saints to ensure divine intercession on their ride to heaven. The museum's oldest mummy has been around for 130 years, while its youngest has been on display for 10. The mummies are the most popular sight in Guanajuato, drawing a larger crowd than the less ghastly museums downtown. At the exit, vendors hawk morose candy figurines of the most memorable mummies, some wearing little sombreros, others wrapped in cellophane scavenged from ketchup bottles. The museum is west of town; to get there, catch a "Momias" bus (1.40 pesos) in front of the Cine or Mercado (open daily 9am-6pm; admission 5 pesos; students and children 5-10 years old 3 pesos; adults over 60 and children under 5 free).

GUANAJUATO

still kiss each other from their balconies. At some points the alley is an amazing 68cm wide—no wonder the city government has felt a need to make its streets more automobile-friendly.

**Mercado Hidalgo,** one block east of the tourist office, went up in 1910 with a monumental Neoclassical arch as an entrance. Inside, both the seafood *coctelerías* and the vendors who sell musical instruments are trustworthy. While Guanajuato's famed ceramic mugs have declined in quality, woolen items are still cheap and the wide variety of *sombreros* will satisfy even the most discerning of heads (most vendors vend daily 9am-9pm).

About 20km from Guanajuato, on top of a mountain 2850m above sea level, is the **Monumento a Cristo Rey,** completed in 1956. The mountain, called the **Cerro del Cubilete,** is considered the geographical center of Mexico. The dark bronze statue of Jesus which lords over it is 16m tall and weighs more than 80 tons. Although the statue is striking, you may spend more time observing the surrounding landscape; kilometers of blue hills are visible from the summit. Take the "Cristo Rey" bus from the bus station (1hr., around 5 pesos).

## ENTERTAINMENT AND SEASONAL EVENTS

Each year, for two or three weeks in late October, Guanajuato stages the **Festival Internacional Cervantino.** The city invites repertory groups from all over the world to make merry with the *estudiantinas,* the strolling student minstrels of the Universidad de Guanajuato. Institutionalized in 1973, the festival got its start in 1954 as a production of the university's theater. The festivities take place mostly at local theaters, but Guanajuato's many museums and churches are also transformed into stages for the events. Dramatic productions are always sold out, so reserve early.

From June 22 to 26, Guanajuato celebrates the **Feria de San Juan** at the Presa de la Olla with cultural events, fireworks, and sports. Shorter celebrations occur on **Día de la Cueva** (July 31), when residents walk to a cave's entrance to honor San Ignacio de Loyola, first patron saint of Guanajuato and founder of the Compañía de Jesús. After the worshippers hold mass, they party. December religious celebrations include the famous *posadas,* which re-create Mary and Joseph's search for budget accommodations in Bethlehem without their trusty *Let's Go: Israel and Egypt.*

The rest of the year, theater, dance, and music are performed; check the tourist office for information, or consult posters around town. On Thursday and Sunday nights in the Jardín Unión, the state band performs three melodies of deceased *guanajuatense,* beginning at around 7pm. Student groups present films almost every day of the week. Call the **Teatro Principal** (tel. 2-15-26), the **Teatro Cervantes** (tel. 2-11-69), or the **Teatro Juárez** (tel. 2-01-83) for specifics (tickets about 10 pesos).

The core of Guanajuato's nightlife rests in the bar/café scene. Discos do exist, but they come to life only on weekends. The bars and cafés in the immediate vicinity of the Jardín Unión are friendly and comfortable, even for single women. If things slow down on the Jardín, it's because they're picking up at the **Guanajuato Grill,** Alonso 20. Neon lights, posters of sports heroes and half-naked men and women, a nightly DJ with bass-booming speakers, and a *zócalo*-style gazebo in the center of the bar for those who wish to be seen has the grill bursting at the seams with thirsty students when school's in. The bouncers can be selective, and generally discriminate against men. Beer 7 pesos (no cover; open Tues.-Sat. 8pm-2am). For the opposite type of crowd—older and more mellow—there's **Damas de las Camelias,** Sopeña 32. Decorated by Juan Ibañez, a student of the Spanish director Luis Buñuel, the bar's walls display cave-style paintings and pictures backed by tin foil (open Fri.-Sat. 6pm-6am, Sun.-Thurs. 6pm-late). Just when you thought a bar couldn't get any mellower, **Chez Santos,** Juan Valle 19, shows up at the door. Located off Juárez just before turning up into Plaza de la Paz, the bar is set in a former horse stable—its high stone walls and large wooden beams across the ceiling make you want to whinny. The dark, romantic lighting calls for candlelight; unfortunately, there is none, so it's a bit hard to see. On the club scene, the most offbeat one in town is **El Rincón del Beso,** Alonso 21-A (tel. 2-59-12), east of Casa Kloster. Nightly sing-alongs and riotous poetry interpretations attract large crowds. Things get moving at around 11pm. Beer 9 pesos, drinks 17 pesos (no cover; open daily 6:30pm-3am).

# ■■■ DOLORES HIDALGO

Mexico's official "Cradle of Independence" has never eclipsed its label. The small town of Dolores Hidalgo has little more to offer than a thriving ceramics industry, a few museums, a church, and its amazing story: the mild-mannered Don Miguel Hidalgo y Costilla, an iconoclastic Dolores priest, was plotting to sever Mexico's relations with the Spanish crown when he discovered that the government of New Spain had learned of his plans. He took decisive action. On Sunday, September 16, 1810, the people of Dolores were awakened at 5am by the tolling of the parish church bell—the *Grito de Dolores.* Hearing the bell, residents tumbled out of bed and gathered at the church; Hidalgo delivered a ringing speech to his parishioners proclaiming Mexico's independence from Spain. Then, calling his flock to arms, Hidalgo rallied an army to march on the capitol. In doing so, the priest signed his own death warrant and paved the way for an independent Mexico.

Today's Dolores Hidalgo is trying desperately to build a tourist industry on its rich history and pottery, but for travelers, the town rarely serves as more than a daytrip from San Miguel or Guanajuato. Perhaps because its tale is so ingrained in the Mexican consciousness, visitors to Dolores are primarily nationals; North Americans and Europeans still elicit serious stares from locals.

## ORIENTATION AND PRACTICAL INFORMATION

Dolores Hidalgo sits in the middle of the state of Guanajuato, 50km northeast of the state capital and 42km away from San Miguel de Allende. To get downtown from the bus station at Hidalgo and Chiapas, walk straight out the door, take a left (you're on Hidalgo), and go three blocks. This brings you to the **Jardín,** the tourist office, **Plaza Principal,** and the **Parroquia.** The **Río Dolores** runs east-west through the city; streets are arranged in a grid parallel and perpendicular to the river. A map is useful since streets have different names on opposite sides of the plaza. There is a well-labeled map in the plaza, or you can buy a good one at the tourist office for ten pesos. The budget option: copy down the street names from the plaza's map—the town is small, and the points of interest all lie within three blocks of the center.

**Tourist Office: Delegación de Turismo** (tel. and fax 2-11-64), on the Plaza Principal in the arcade to the left of the Parroquia. Enthusiastic and helpful staff supplies free English brochures and a city map which provides street names for only the north and east sides of the Plaza Principal. They also sell more comprehensive guides to Dolores for 10 pesos and to Guanajuato State for 15 pesos. Open Mon.-Fri. 9am-4pm and sometimes 5-7pm, Sat.-Sun. 10am-3pm.

**Police:** (tel. 2-00-21), in the Cárcel Municipal on San Luis Potosí, one block north of the Plaza Principal. Some English spoken. Available 24 hrs.

**Post Office:** Puebla 22 (tel. 2-08-07). From the Plaza Principal, go south on Jalisco one block and take a left on Puebla. *Lista de Correos.* Open Mon.-Fri. 9am-4pm, Sat. 9am-noon. **Postal Code:** 37800.

**Telephones: Restaurante Plaza** (tel. 2-01-52), on the south side of the plaza. International collect calls 5 pesos per 10min. Open Mon.-Sat. 9am-2pm and 4-8pm. No LADATELs, but a few pay phones in the plaza. **Telephone Code:** 418.

**Telegrams:** Puebla 22 (tel. 2-04-63), in the post office. Open Mon.-Fri. 8am-6pm, Sat. 8am-noon.

**Currency Exchange: Casa de Cambio Cordisa,** Jalisco 11 (tel. 2-13-35), at the corner with Puebla, has similar rates and better hours than the bank on the Plaza Principal. Open daily 8am-7pm.

**Bus Station:** Hidalgo at Chiapas. **Flecha Amarilla** (tel. 2-06-39) runs to Guanajuato (every 20min., 5am-9:10am, 1½hrs., 9 pesos), Mexico City via San Miguel de Allende and Querétaro (every 40min., 5am-7pm, 11:30pm, and 1:30am, 5hrs., 49

**DOLORES HIDALGO**

pesos), San Luis Potosí (11 per day, 5:30am-8pm, 3hrs., 24 pesos), and San Miguel de Allende (every 20min., 5:20am-9:50pm, 40min., 6.50 pesos).

**Public Toilets:** To the left of the Parroquia in the narrow arcade around the corner from the tourist office (0.50 pesos).

**Pharmacy: Farmacia Dolores,** Plaza Principal 21 (tel. 2-09-48). Little English spoken. Open daily 9am-9pm.

**Hospital: Hospital Ignacio Allende,** Hidalgo 12 (tel. 2-00-13). English spoken. Open 24 hrs.

**Emergency:** 06.

## ACCOMMODATIONS

Given the low demand for overnight lodging, rooms in Dolores Hidalgo are scarce. Most budget hotels here ask for a fair share of your precious pesos, but reciprocate with amenities and quality service. Expect prices to rise and rooms to fill up from roughly September 8-17, when Dolores is overrun by Independence Day celebrants.

**Posada Hidalgo,** Hidalgo 15 (tel. 2-04-77), half a block south of the Jardín. Just the basics, but some basics! Comfortable beds, stone tile, hot water, and a generally spotless living space. Miguel would be proud. Could use a bit more light, though. Singles 60 pesos, with TV 65 pesos. Doubles 70 pesos, with TV 80 pesos.

**Hotel Posada Cocomacán,** Plaza Principal 5 (tel. 2-00-18), at Querétaro and Guanajuato, on the Jardín. Wood furniture, tiled walls, and romantic lighting in rooms off a sunny courtyard. Clean bathrooms. Singles 70 pesos. Doubles 85 pesos.

**Posada Dolores,** Yucatán 8 (tel. 2-06-42), a block west of the Plaza Principal. The clean, stark, pastel rooms are full of international travelers. Communal bathrooms are decent, but not all of the private or communal toilets have seats. Singles 25 pesos, with bath 30 pesos. Doubles 30 pesos, with bath 50 pesos.

**Hotel Caudillo,** Querétaro 8 (tel. 2-01-98), across the street from the Parroquia. Clean rooms with rugs, dressers, 70s bedspreads, 24-hr. *agua caliente*, black-and-white TVs, and that musty something that defines motels. Bathrooms are adorned with a mélange of locally made tiles—as if you hadn't seen enough ceramics already. Friendly and attentive management. Singles 70 pesos. Doubles 85 pesos.

## FOOD

In Mexico, there's no escaping the *chicharrón* (pork rind), and in Dolores Hidalgo the popular snack has become...an ice cream flavor! The Jardín is flanked by vendors pushing long carts loaded with rows of metal casks. Wrapped in towels to keep out the Mexican heat, the containers contain a crazy variety of ice cream flavors— *elote* (corn meal), *cerveza* (beer), *aguacate* (avocado), and tequila. Hand a vendor five pesos and he'll cram a mammoth portion into a cone or a plastic cup. However tempting though the combination of your favorite snack with your favorite drink may be, Mexican ice cream is known to harbor more than a few nasty amoebas, so verify the product's hygienic integrity before placing that spoon in your mouth.

Nothing can compare to making a meal out of ice cream, but the restaurants in Hidalgo try to provide satisfying alternatives. Around the Jardín most restaurants are reasonably priced, and those that aren't betray themselves by their touristy clientele.

**Eduardo's Pizza,** Veracruz 5 (tel. 2-21-24), in the Plaza Veracruz, one block east and one block south of the Jardín. Really good pizza and really groovy decor— empty boxes of Honey Smacks, vinyl records, and cigarette cartons dance on a grid of strings just short of the ceiling. Wonderfully friendly management. Personal pizzas start at 12 pesos. Medium vegetarian (normally enough for two) 29 pesos. Beer starts at 3 pesos. Open daily noon-10pm, or until the last client leaves.

**Restaurant La Esperanza** (tel. 2-03-60), in the Mercado Hidalgo. From the Plaza Principal, walk west on Michoacán half a block, then turn right into the market and walk 50m; if you get to Yucatán (the street, of course) you've gone to far. Not fancy, just good cheap food—a classic *mercado* restaurant, save the spacious dining area. *Comida corrida*, with soft drink, 15 pesos. Open daily 6am-5:30pm.

**Restaurant El Delfín,** Veracruz 2 (tel. 2-22-99), at Guerrero. Serves up seafood, hence the red-and-white checkered tablecloths. Vines on the wall add a nice touch. *Huachinango* (red snapper) around 22 pesos. Shrimp 35 pesos. Seafood soup 15 pesos. Beer 2.50 pesos. Open daily 9am-7pm.

## SIGHTS AND ENTERTAINMENT

Most of Dolores's sights lie within four blocks of the bus station. The beautiful **Parroquia de Nuestra Señora de los Dolores,** where the *Grito de Dolores* was sounded, still stands in the Plaza Principal, though the original bell now graces Mexico City's Palacio de Gobierno. Constructed between 1712 and 1778, the church, with its intricate façade and towers of pink stone, is the most awe-inspiring structure in town. Mexican presidents return here on the anniversary of Hidalgo's proclamation and repeat his words verbatim (open daily 5:30am-noon and 4-9:30pm).

The **Museo Casa Hidalgo,** at Morelos and Hidalgo, one block from the Plaza Principal, is the niftiest stop in town. The museum was Hidalgo's home from 1804 until 1810, and many of the rooms remain as they were in 1810. Many of Hidalgo's belongings are on display. Documents and works of art relating to the independence movement fill rooms off a central courtyard. This includes a fabulous Metepec **Tree of Life,** with Hidalgo at its center. The Metepec are famous for this type of art; the tree is done with brightly painted pottery, and figures of the Independence movement decorate the branches on this particular piece. Watch your head—the doorways were made for 18th-century Mexicans (open Tues.-Sat. 10am-6pm, Sun. and holidays 10am-5pm; admission 14 pesos; free Sun. and for kids under 13, adults over 60, and teachers and students with ID).

The **Museo de la Independencia,** Zacatecas 6, lies less than one block northwest of the Parroquia. To your right as you enter is a display honoring Dolores Hidalgo's favorite musical son, José Alfredo Jiménez (1926-1973). The display includes one gold and two platinum records; some of his *sarapes;* awards given to him in Los Angeles, Hollywood, Phoenix, San Antonio, and Chicago; a photograph of an elaborate altar built for him in the wonderful country of Colombia; and his Dolores Hidalgo birth certificate. The museum's melodramatic murals, statues, and dioramas focus on life under Spanish rule, Independence, and the life and works of the town's other idol, Miguel Hidalgo (open Fri.-Wed. 9am-5pm; admission 3 pesos, free for students, children under 12, and adults over 60).

The pottery industry here is almost as big as the Independence industry, and ceramic shops abound in Dolores Hidalgo. Don't spend your time searching for the most authentic pieces, because pottery in Dolores is a dynamic art; different artists have different specialties, and the style changes with the times.

# ■■■ SAN MIGUEL DE ALLENDE

Accompanied by a group of *indígena* converts, Franciscan friar Juan de San Miguel founded San Miguel el Viejo in 1542. The village's first years were difficult ones. In the heart of Chichimec territory, the *pueblo* was repeatedly attacked, and its residents were very nearly decimated. Things changed, however, in 1555, when silver was discovered in Zacatecas—the viceroy of New Spain made it a priority to blaze a path between his office in Mexico City and the ore. As it fell on a straight line between these two points, San Miguel received official protection. No longer a target for Chichimec attacks, the settlement swelled into a city, and by the end of the 16th century, it had been re-christened San Miguel el Grande.

San Miguel's moment in the spotlight came on September 16, 1810, when Hidalgo led his rebel army into the city. Convinced by Ignacio Allende of the righteousness of Hidalgo's pro-independence mission, San Miguel became a staunch opponent of Spanish rule—before pushing on to the capital, the army spent three days in the city recruiting new soldiers. In 1826, the infant republic recognized Allende's role in the drive for independence by adding his name to San Miguel's.

Today's San Miguel has become a serious attraction among foreign students, and the city carries a reputation as the home of many a *norteamericano* expatriate. The icon of all this *gringo*-ization is Neal Cassady, the prototype of Kerouac's hero in *On the Road*, who collapsed in San Miguel while walking near the railroad tracks and died soon afterwards. Of course, not all the expatriates who call San Miguel home aspire to Cassady's philosophy towards life: of late, retired suburbanites have started flocking to town. Fortunately, San Miguel's expat community sees the city as far more than a Florida-like vacationland; in fact, many Americans come here with the desire to assimilate inconspicuously. Bilingual children are already entering adulthood, the product of two cultures, and few have trouble participating in both—witness the American and Mexican fathers and sons who take part in Sunday afternoon basketball games at Parque Juárez or the young blonde child discussing a Disney flick in fluent Spanish with his Mexican counterpart. It's no wonder that the expatriate invasion has caused so few tensions—most natives are well-disposed to *gringos* and are eager to practice their English or help them with Spanish.

Renowned for its artisanry and academics, San Miguel has another resource that prospective visitors often overlook—a mild climate. The town is almost never oppressively hot, thanks to its 2000m elevation. Unlike other colonial towns of similar elevations, San Miguel is also a very green city, with plenty of trees, flowers, and hills to appreciate in the comfortable outdoors. Beware the ides of June and July, however. Cold afternoon drizzle or drenching day-long downpours can turn the cobblestoned streets into gushing streams..

### Just Call Me Blondie

*"¡Miren, miren, el huerito!"* shout the schoolgirls. *"Pss, pss, ¡huera!"* hiss the men. *"¡Que huero!"* gasps the twentysomething woman. Nothing more than average comments in the day of a fair-haired person in Mexico. *Huero, -a* means blonde, and few Mexicans will hesitate to show their amazement and excitement upon seeing anyone with a full head of naturally yellow hair and a heartbeat. And it's no wonder: television, magazines, and politics are all dominated by light-skinned, and more often than not, fair-haired people. This, despite the dark complexions and Indian heritage of an overwhelming percentage of Mexico's population. Remember, though, that often a fair-skinned, black-haired Mexican receives the label *huero* from his companions. So while being the object of endless catcalls is frustrating, *"huero"* in a casual sense is often an affectionate term.

## ORIENTATION

San Miguel lies midway between Guanajuato and Querétaro, 428km northwest of Mexico City. To get from the **bus station** to the center (known as the **Jardín de Allende** or **Plaza de Allende**), take a bus (1.40 pesos) or a taxi (8 pesos). The **train station** lies another kilometer west of the bus station on the same road.

Most attractions are within walking distance of the Jardín, and the streets form a near-grid. Streets south of the Jardín that run east-west change their names every few blocks. A good source of current information on the town is the weekly U.S. expatriate newspaper *Atención,* available at the public library (see Practical Information), supermarkets, bookshops, and newsstands.

## PRACTICAL INFORMATION

**Tourist Office: Delegación Regional de Turismo** (tel. 2-17-47), on the Pl. de Allende next to the Parroquia and Restaurante La Terraza. Knowledgeable and helpful staff speaks English and distributes tiny but handy maps. Open Mon.-Fri. 10am-3pm and 5-7:30pm, Sat. 10am-5pm, but expect it to open about ½hr. late.

**Police:** (tel. 2-00-22), in the Presidencia Municipal. On call 24 hrs.

**Post Office:** Appropriately at Correos 16 (tel. 2-00-89), one block east of the Jardín. *Lista de Correos.* Open for registered mail Mon.-Fri. 8am-6pm and Sat. 9am-1pm, for all other services Mon.-Fri. 8am-7pm, Sat. 9am-1pm. **Postal Code:** 37700.

**Telephones: El Toro,** Macías 58-A (tel. 2-11-00), across from the Hotel Sauto. International collect calls 4.50 pesos. Open Mon.-Sat. 8am-8pm, Sun. 8am-2pm. **La Esquinita,** Correos at Recreo (tel. 2-36-21 or 2-39-39), charges 3 pesos per 10min. on international collect calls. Open daily 10am-2:30pm and 5-10pm. The only **LADATEL** in town is inside the post office and is coin-operated. **Telephone Code:** 415.

**Telegrams:** Correo 16-B (tel. 2-32-15; fax 2-00-81), adjacent to the post office. Open Mon.-Fri. 9am-1pm and 3-6pm, Sat. 9am-noon.

**U.S. Consular Representative:** Macías 72 (tel. 2-23-57), opposite Bellas Artes. Open Wed. 9am-1pm and 4-7pm, Mon.-Tues. and Thurs. 4-7pm, or by appointment. In case of emergency dial 2-00-68 or 2-09-80. For other countries, contact the **Delegación Regional,** Calle Balza 18 (tel. 2-25-42 or 2-13-83).

**Currency Exchange:** Better rates and shorter lines are more likely to be found at a *casa de cambio* than at one of the large banks. **Deal,** Correo 15 (tel. 2-29-32), has a good rate, good hours, and a few branches around town. Open Mon.-Fri. 9am-6pm, Sat. 9am-2pm. **Bánamex,** on the west side of the Jardín, has a 24-hr. **ATM.**

**American Express:** Hidalgo 1 (tel. 2-18-56). Full financial and travel services. Holds cardholders' mail and cashes traveler's checks. English spoken. Open Mon.-Fri. 9am-2pm and 4-6:30pm, Sat. 9am-2pm.

**Train Station: Ferrocarriles Nacionales de México** (tel. 2-00-07), 2km west of town. To Mexico City (1:09pm, 6hrs., 35 pesos) and Nuevo Laredo (2:35pm, 17hrs., 101.05 pesos) via San Luis Potosí.

**Bus Station:** (tel. 2-22-06), on Calzada de la Estación, 1km west of the center. From the *centro,* take a "Central Estación" bus. **Herradura de Plata** ("Silver Horseshoe," tel. 2-07-25) has a nifty replica of its namesake on its price board, plus service to Mexico City (*plus* 3 per day, 6am-12:30pm, 3½hrs., 53 pesos; second class every ½hr., 5am-7:40pm, 4hrs., 43 pesos). **Flecha Amarilla** (tel. 2-00-84) to Aguascalientes (12:20 and 2:20pm, 4hrs., 42 pesos), Dolores Hidalgo (every 20min., 6am-8pm, 45min., 6.50 pesos), Guanajuato (9 per day, 6:45am-5pm, 1½hrs., 14.50 pesos), Querétaro (every 40min., 5:20am-8pm, 1¾hrs., 11 pesos), and San Luis Potosí (6 per day, 7:30am-6:40pm, 4hrs., 29.50 pesos). Other lines sell tickets for buses they run out of Querétaro and Celaya.

**Car Rental: Gama Rent-a-Car,** Hidalgo 3, Interior 1 (tel. 2-08-15). Prices start at 115 pesos per day and 0.70 pesos extra per km plus 15% IVA tax. Special weekly rates. Drivers must be 25 years of age with a license and a major credit card, plus one other form of ID. Open Mon.-Fri. 9am-2pm and 4-7pm, Sat. 9am-2pm.

**Car Repair: Pablo Arteaga Silva,** San Antonio Abad 1 (tel. 2-13-20), at the very northwest edge of the *centro.* Open Mon.-Fri. 9am-3pm and 4-8pm, Sat. 9am-2pm.

**Laundromat: Lavamágico,** Pila Seca 5 (tel. 2-08-99). Will pick up (8am-noon) a dirty 4kg load and return it cleaned for 16 pesos. Open Mon.-Sat. 8am-8pm.

**English Bookstore: El Colibrí,** Sollano 30 (tel. 2-07-51). Superb (but expensive) selection of paperback fiction. Open Mon.-Sat. 10am-2pm and 4-7pm.

**Public Library: Biblioteca Pública,** Insurgentes 25 (tel. 2-02-93), next to La Española. An important feature of expatriate social life. Free language exchange (see Entertainment). They get rid of old paperbacks by selling them for 1-3 pesos each. Open Mon.-Fri. 10am-2pm and 4-7pm, Sat. 10am-1:30pm.

**Red Cross:** (tel. 2-16-16), km1 on the Carretera Celaya. 24-hr. emergency service.

**Pharmacy: Farmacia Allende,** San Francisco 3 (tel. 2-00-74), half a block from the Jardín. No English spoken. Open daily 9am-9pm.

**Hospital: Hospital de la Fe,** Libramiento a Dolores 43 (tel. 2-17-71, 2-22-33, or 2-67-98), near the bus station. Brand spankin' new. Open for consultation Mon.-Fri. 9am-2pm and 5-8pm, Sat. 9am-2pm. Emergency service 24 hrs. English spoken.

**Emergency:** Dial 20-911.

## ACCOMMODATIONS

Despite the large number of students who visit the town, San Miguel has few budget accommodations. Instead, many hotels provide continental breakfast and/or TV or offer a stellar location on the Plaza Principal to justify their costliness. For short stays during the busy summer months (especially July), you may want to make a reservation several days in advance. If you're planning an extended stay, check for notices of rooms for rent on the bulletin board at the Instituto Allende, Ancha de San Antonio 20, southwest of the Jardín, and in popular *norteamericano* cafés and hotels.

**The San Miguel International Hostel,** Organos 34 (tel. 2-06-74). You'll come for a day and stay for a month. A communal effort: Michael the manager hires help on a work-for-food basis, guests are expected to perform morning chores, and everybody knows your name—feel free to join the courtyard conversations. Well-stocked with English books, a bathtub, a sitting room, and a piano. Free kitchen use (including free pasta and spices), optional afternoon Spanish lessons (1hr., 10 pesos), and a washing machine (5 pesos per load, including soap). Clean single-sex dorm rooms for 4-10 people. 30 pesos per person, 25 with HI or ISIC membership, continental breakfast included. Also, two private single rooms and one private double (50 pesos, 60 pesos with bath). Reservations not accepted.

**Casa de Huéspedes,** Mesones 27 (tel. 2-13-78). Serene, flower-filled courtyard complete with lounge chairs and back issues of the *New Yorker*. Immaculate rooms (with throw rugs and adobe-colored tiles), some with kitchens, and a wonderfully friendly staff. Singles 50 pesos. Doubles 80 pesos. Month-long stays are common: singles 1200 pesos, doubles 1500 pesos. Reserve well in advance.

**Hotel Posada de Allende,** Cuna de Allende 10 (tel. 2-06-98), around the corner from the Parroquia. Pretty much a *posada típica;* aging and small (just four rooms), but the rooms are clean and spacious, with high ceilings and a pool-green color scheme. Rooms off of a small courtyard, one wall of which is the Parroquia. Terrific location. Singles 60 pesos. Doubles 85 peso, with two beds 95 pesos.

## FOOD

The sweet aroma of international cuisine wafts through the cobbled streets of San Miguel, and fine restaurants grace almost every corner. Unfortunately, their prices are as *norteamericano* as their clientele. But a few places around town, including some *gringo* favorites, do serve large portions at bargain prices. The walkway on the east side of the Jardín is crowded with taco stalls serving locals and foreigners, and more of the same hides in and around the *mercado* on Colegio. *Elotes* and *tortas* can be found in the tiny square on Insurgentes between Macías and Hidalgo. Fresh fruit and vegetables come to town on Tuesday with the market.

**La Gruta,** Cuadrante 5 (tel. 2-41-19), just down the street from Posada Allende. A cozy place a few feet below street level. All types come here for some tasty Italian cooking. *Pasta oriente* (with chicken and veggies) 19 pesos. Small pizza with two toppings (a light meal for two) 25 pesos. Open Wed.-Mon. 1-11pm.

**Olé-Olé Café,** Loreto 66 (tel. 2-08-96), up past the *mercado*. A fake bull, walls stuffed to the limit with bull-fighting posters, and the bright pink-and-red decor make this in no way a *típico* joint, but the food and prices are right on. Specialties are *fajitas* (chicken 20 pesos, beef 25 pesos) and garlic-style mushrooms (25 pesos). Open daily 1-8pm.

**Las Palomas,** Mesones 60. A taco stand you can trust. Afternoons, the counter seats are occupied by local teens snacking, flirting, and gossiping. Tacos 1.70 pesos. *Gorditas* 2.50-3.50 pesos. Open daily 9am-9pm.

## SIGHTS

The best way to experience San Miguel is on your own two feet. Starting at 9am on Tuesdays and Fridays, groups assemble in front of the church in the Jardín for 90-minute tours of the city (around 30 pesos, but the money goes to charity, so cough it up). The public library gives guided **home and garden tours** of the city in English on Sundays at noon (60 pesos; be there at 11:30am or so). San Miguel boasts some beautiful orchid-filled courtyards, but some say the tours are something of a real estate pitch. While you're walking, 64 hectares await at the **Jardín Botánico,** on the outskirts of town. The garden commands some excellent vistas, and includes a small lake and extensive cactus life (open sunrise to sunset; admission 5 pesos, free for children under 10). Inquiries should be directed to the Cante organization, Mesones 71 (tel. 2-29-90; fax 2-40-15). Alternatively, just wander in the vicinity of the Jardín.

Almost every street has an interesting shop or café, and without exerting yourself much, you'll come across some magnificent churches and artisans' shops.

**La Parroquia,** next to the Jardín, is one of the most distinctive churches in central Mexico. Its façade and tower were designed by the *indígena* mason Zeferino Gutiérrez, who is said to have learned the Gothic style from postcards of French cathedrals. Inside, medieval-style banners and glittering chandeliers hang from above, where a few murals grace the walls' highest points. At the front is a tremendous four-piece, gold-leaf altar (open daily 5:30am-8am and 9am-9pm).

The **Museo Histórico de San Miguel de Allende,** on the corner of Canal and Cuna de Allende, just west of La Parroquia, resides in Allende's former home; his status is evident from this magnificent, partly Baroque mansion. The eclectic museum combines tributes to Allende with seemingly unrelated exhibits on astronomy and paleobiology and enough charts to put you to sleep (open Tues.-Sun. 10am-4pm; free).

At the corner of Canal and Macías, two blocks west of the Jardín, stands the enormous **Iglesia de la Concepción.** Graced by the representation of the Immaculate Conception which crowns its two-story dome, the church was finished in 1891. Pairs of Corinthian columns adorn the church's lower level and its interior features polychrome sculptures of St. Joseph and the Immaculate Conception (open daily 7am-7pm; avoid mass Mon.-Fri. 7:30am and 7pm, Sun. 9:30am, 11:30am, and 7pm).

Founded in 1712, the **Templo del Oratorio de San Felipe Neri** lies at the corner of Insurgentes and Loreto, two blocks east of the library. Rebuilt many times, the church is an amalgamation of styles—its interior is mainly Neoclassical while its engraved Baroque façade shows *indígena* influences (open daily 6:30am-12:30pm and 6:30-8:30pm). On the west side of the church, the towers and the dome belong to the **Santa Casa de Loreto,** a reproduction of the building of the same name in Italy (enter on the right side of the altar in San Felipe Neri). The floors and the lower wall friezes are covered with glazed tiles from China, Spain, and faraway Puebla (open Mon.-Fri. 4:30-7:30pm, Sat.-Sun. 7:30am-6:30pm).

One block east of the Jardín at Juárez and San Francisco, the **Iglesia de San Francisco** includes a dark red Neoclassical tower attributed to the architect Tresguerras. Finished in 1799, the church's Churrigueresque façade honors many saints. Several small paintings in the interior are so enveloped in darkness that you'd have to be a bat to appreciate them (open Tues. 7am-1:30pm and 5:30-8:45pm, Thurs. 10:30am-8:45pm). To the left as you face San Francisco is the **Iglesia del Tercer Orden,** one of the oldest and most decayed churches in San Miguel. Constructed by the Franciscan order between 1606 and 1638, the main façade contains an image of St. Francis and symbols of the order (open daily 7am-1:30pm and 5:30-8:45pm).

Reverberating with the calls of tropical birds, the **Parque Juárez,** three blocks south of the Jardín on Aldama and then Carranza, is the greenest park in San Miguel. Die-hard cagers can often join a pick-up basketball game involving both *gringos* and locals. Some of the most elegant houses in San Miguel surround the park.

## ENTERTAINMENT AND SEASONAL EVENTS

The Bellas Artes and Instituto Allende have bulletin boards crammed with information on upcoming jazz, classical guitar, and folk concerts, as well as theatrical productions and lectures by both locals and *gringos.* The **Biblioteca Pública** (see Practical Information) sells the magazine *Atención* (3 pesos), details of events.

What, did you think all these students came here to learn? Most nights it seems everyone in town is at **Mama Mía,** Umarán 8 (tel. 2-20-63), probably because the place is so damn big. If you somehow miss all the herds of people, it's just west of the Jardín's southwest corner. To the right as you enter is the official Mama Mía Bar, with a dance floor, live *salsa* or rock (sorry, no ABBA), and a bouncy younger crowd movin' to the beat (cover 10 pesos; open daily 10pm-3am). On the left is the LOUD video bar (open daily 7pm-late), and directly in front of the entrance is a run-of-the-mill bar (open daily 9am-late). **Coco,** Macías 85 (tel. 2-26-43), is a bit more tranquil. Live music of all types every night with no cover—but no dance floor either, so you're forced to sit, eat, listen, and love it. Large pizzas 60 pesos. *Huevos al gusto* 10 pesos. Beer 6 pesos during the day, 7 pesos at night (open 8am-about 2:30am, kitchen closes at 10pm). The party doesn't start at **El Ring,** Hidalgo 25 (tel. 2-19-98), until around 2:30am, when indefatigable elite members of San Miguel's club-hopping brigade begin to trickle in from other spots. The place rocks with the latest dance hits from the U.S. and Latin America. For males, no shorts or sandals (cover Sat. 30 pesos, Sun. 15-pesos including 2 drinks; open Wed.-Mon. 11pm-4am).

San Miguel is reputed to have more *fiestas* than any other town in Mexico. Beyond national and religious holidays, San Miguel celebrates the birthday of Ignacio Allende on January 21, the Fiesta de la Candelaria on February 2 (marking the start of spring and the birthday of El Padre de Miguel), and the festival of San Miguel's guardian saint from September 14 to October 3. On September 29, mass is held, and the following Saturday a celebration begins with the singing of *Las Mañanitas* at 4am. On that day, bulls run free through the center of the city in imitation of the *encierro* in Pamplona, Spain; seek cover behind a concrete barrier. The International Chamber Music Festival is held August 1-15 at Belles Artes

# QUERÉTARO

## ■■■ QUERÉTARO

Positioned between Mexico City and Guadalajara on the busiest stretch of highway in the Republic, Querétaro has been fêted by fate. It was here that Emperor Maximilian, abandoned by Louis Napoleon and captured by Juárez's troops, ascended Cerro de las Campanas (Hill of the Bells), pressed a gold coin into each assembled soldier's hand, and uttered his famous last words: "Mexicans, I am going to die for a just cause: the liberty and the independence of Mexico. May my blood be the last shed for the happiness of my new country!" The year was 1867. Between 1910 and 1920, Mexico was wracked by violence—in a single decade, war snatched away one in eight Mexicans and left Carranza's forces running the nation. Perhaps hoping to inaugurate the peaceful era Maximilian had prematurely proclaimed, Carranza chose to draft the new constitution, a durable document which still governs the Republic, in Querétaro.

While Mexico gave up much here—the Treaty of Guadalupe Hidalgo, which compelled the Republic to cede its northern territories to the U.S., was signed in Querétaro—the city proudly brandishes the marks of its history. Indeed, much of what is attractive about modern Querétaro is hardly modern at all; the city is notable for its colonial architecture, 18th-century aqueduct, centuries-old brick streets and *callejones,* and numerous fountains and squares. Unfortunately, the city's charms are obscured by poverty, pollution, and uncomfortably crowded streets and buses.

### ORIENTATION

Querétaro is on Routes 120 and 57. Its streets form a grid, and nearly all important sites are within walking distance of the balloon-filled **Jardín Zenea.** 16 de Septiembre, Madero, Corregidora, and Juárez bound the Jardín on the north, south, east, and west, respectively. The **bus station,** whose modernity puts most international airports to shame, is on the very south side of town. To reach downtown, walk out of the station towards the highway, where you can catch buses labeled "Centro" (1.40 pesos). The **train station** is a good distance from the Jardín, about two blocks beyond the end of Corregidora in the northernmost part of the city.

## PRACTICAL INFORMATION

**Tourist Office: State Tourist Office,** Pasteur Nte. 4 (tel. 12-14-12, 12-09-07, or 12-12-87). From the Jardín, take 5 de Mayo, and it's just to your left at the end of the Plaza de Armas. Friendly English-speaking staff so knowledgeable they could do without the Internet program at their fingertips. Hands out helpful maps and lists of local cultural events. City tours in English or Spanish begin daily 10:30am (2hrs., 10 pesos). Open for tourist information daily 9am-9pm. Administrative offices open Mon.-Fri. 9am-3pm and 6-9pm.

**Police:** Constituyentes Pte. 20 (tel. 12-15-07). Always on call.

**Post Office:** Arteaga Pte. 7 (tel. 12-01-12), two blocks south of the Jardín Zenea, between Juárez and Allende. *Lista de Correos.* Open Mon.-Fri. 8am-5pm, Sat. 9am-1pm. **Postal Code:** 76000.

**Telephones:** A *caseta* is at 5 de Mayo 33 (tel. 12-09-76 or 12-11-67). Collect calls to the U.S. 15 pesos, to Europe 17 pesos, but the cost covers calls as long as 1½hrs. Open 24 hrs. Open Mon.-Sat. 9:30am-2pm and 4:30-9pm. Blue international **LADATELs** are everywhere, but most are coin operated. **Telephone Code:** 42.

**Telegrams:** Allende Nte. 4 (tel. 12-01-63), one block west of the Jardín. Open Mon.-Fri. 8am-6pm, Sat. 9am-noon.

**Currency Exchange: Bancomer,** Juárez 15 (tel. 12-06-77). Open Mon.-Fri. 8:30am-3pm, for exchange 9:30am-1:30pm. A good alternative is **Cambios La Posada,** Allende Nte. 2, next to the telegram office. Open Mon.-Sat. 9am-6pm.

**Train Station:** (tel. 14-46-77), on Cuauhtémoc north of Av. Universidad. To get to the station from the Jardín, walk to Av. Universidad (about five long blocks), go left two blocks to Cuauhtémoc, and go right the three or so blocks to the tracks (about 20-25 minutes). Otherwise, cabs will run around 7 pesos. Trains leave for Ciudad Juárez (12:45 and 11:30pm, 103.40 pesos), Guadalajara (12:40am), Mexico City (3 per day, 6am-4pm, 14.75 pesos), and Nuevo Laredo (12:55pm).

**Bus Station:** To get to the stunningly modern station, "Ruta 25" passes on Zaragoza, "Ruta 8" on Constituyentes, and "Ruta 72" on Universidad—all are labeled "Central." As you enter, the right half (Accesos 1 and 2) provides first-class service, and the left half (Accesos 3 and 4) provides second-class service. In Accesos 1 and 2, **Primera Plus** (tel. 11-40-01) serves Aguascalientes (7 per day, 6am-11:15pm, 4½hrs., 63 pesos), Guadalajara (5 per day, 12:15am-10pm, 5½hrs., 70 pesos), Mexico City (every 20min., 4:30am-9pm, 2¾hrs., 42 pesos), and Morelia (6 per day, 4:10am-5:30pm, 3hrs., 33.50 pesos). **Omnibús de México** (tel. 29-00-29) serves Acapulco (midnight, 8hrs., 149 pesos). In Accesos 3 and 4, **Estrella Blanca** (tel. 29-02-02) has buses every hour (6:15am-6:15pm) to Pachuca (5hrs., 33 pesos) and San Juan del Río (1hr., 7 pesos). **Oriente** (tel. 29-02-58) serves Monterrey (4:30pm, 10hrs., 114 pesos) and Nuevo Laredo (4:30pm, 13hrs., 156 pesos). **Flecha Amarilla** (tel. 11-40-01) runs to Dolores Hidalgo (every 40min., 1¾hrs., 15.50 pesos), Guadalajara (every ½hr., 12:30am-4:20pm, and slightly less often until 10:40pm, 6-7hrs., 64 pesos), Irapuato (every hr., 6:20am-8:10pm, 1½-2hrs., 17 pesos), Manzanillo (3 per day, 1:30am-7:20pm, 12hrs., 101 pesos), Mexico City (every 10min., 6am-9pm, 2¾hrs., 34 pesos), Morelia (every 30min., 3½-4hrs., 26.50 pesos), and San Luis Potosí (every hr., 6:15am-9:15pm, 3½hrs., 132 pesos). **Herradura de Plata** (tel. 29-02-45) sends buses to San Felipe (every 20min., 6am-10:40pm, 3hrs., 22.50 pesos), San Juan del Río (every 20min., 5am-8pm, 45min., 7 pesos), and San Miguel de Allende (every 20min., 6am-10:40pm, 1hr., 11 pesos).

**Laundromat: Lavandería Automática La Cascada,** Comercial Mexicana, local 18 (tel. 16-56-96). 3kg for 25 pesos. Same-day service available. Open Mon.-Fri. 9am-8pm, Sat. 9am-2pm.

**Red Cross:** At Balaustradas and Circuito Estadio (tel. 29-06-65 or 29-05-45).

**Pharmacy: Farmacia Guadalupe,** Madero 32 (tel. 14-10-15). No English spoken. Open daily 8am-10pm.

**Hospitals: Hospital Seguro Social,** Zaragoza at 5 de Febrero (tel. 16-17-57). **Hospital General,** 5 de Febrero 101 (tel. 16-00-39 or 16-20-36).

**LOCATEL:** (tel. 14-33-11 or 14-28-89). Will find lost people.

## ACCOMMODATIONS

Despite a small-scale tourist industry, good and inexpensive accommodations are not difficult to find in Querétaro's *centro*. If impersonal hotels aren't your thing, there are some cheap but rickety *posadas* downtown—look for them on the south side of the Jardín.

**CREA Youth Hostel,** (tel. 23-11-20), on Av. Ejército Republicano. Just four blocks east of the Jardín or on bus route 14 (0.80 pesos)—ask for CREA. Archetypally basic. Single-sex dorms and 4-8 bunks per room. Bedrooms and bathrooms are clean, and there's a playing field and athletic complex just outside the reception. 11 pesos per person (25% discount with HI or Plan Joven). 20-peso bedding deposit. Breakfast 9 pesos, lunch and dinner 11.25 pesos. Check-out 2pm. Open daily 5am-11pm, but call if you're locked out.

**Hotel Hidalgo,** Madero Pte. 11 (tel. 12-00-81), one block west of the Jardín. Pleasant colonial architecture and central location. All rooms are clean, cute, and soaked with the smell of air freshener. Rooms with terraces are the breeziest and most spacious of the lot. Attracts families, international travelers, and some escapees from cult-like *gringo* expatriate communities. English-speaking management. Singles 50 pesos. Doubles 60 pesos. The attached restaurant is very inexpensive. *Menú del día* 13.50 pesos.

**Hotel del Márquez,** Juárez Nte. 104 (tel. 12-04-14 or 12-05-54), three long blocks north of the Jardín. Huge rooms sport carpets, bedspreads, TVs, and telephones. Illuminated by something like track-lighting, beautiful tiled bathrooms are equipped with 24-hr. hot water. Singles 55 pesos. Doubles 70 pesos.

## FOOD

In Querétaro, finding the meal that suits you is simple. Inexpensive restaurants face the Jardín Zenea, pricier *loncherías* and outdoor cafés rim the nearby Plaza Corregidora, and taco, *torta*, and other fast-food stands line 5 de Mayo. Wherever you go, expect to find a diverse local crowd of businesspeople and youngsters. But you'd better hurry: many restaurants stop serving their *menú del día* at 5 or 6pm.

**Restaurante de la Rosa,** on Juárez at Peralta (tel. 24-37-22), across from the Teatro de la República. Basic, tasty Mexican food served by the swellest, sweetest women in town. They'll eagerly encourage you to "practice your Spanish" while you chow down. Breakfast specials (8-10 pesos), *menú del día* (until 5 or 6pm) 14 pesos, *pollo a la mexicana* 16 pesos. Open Mon.-Sat. 9am-10pm.

**Restaurante Manolo's,** Madero 6 (tel. 14-05-40), on the south side of the Jardín. Tranquil and relaxed with white-and-yellow walls and wooden chairs. The white-tiled kitchen is open to show the cooks at work. Try the *paella. Menú del día* 16.90 or 21.90 pesos. *Huevos al gusto* 11.50 pesos. Open daily 8am-9pm.

**Ibis Natura Vegetana,** Juárez Nte. 272 (tel. 14-22-12), half a block north of the Jardín Obregón. A long, narrow restaurant in a health-food store set up soda-fountain style, complete with a wooden counter, reflecting stainless-steel ceiling, and pretty good food. Yogurt 4.20 pesos. Soyburger 7.30 pesos. Hearty *menú del día* 17.25 pesos. Open daily 8am-9:30pm.

## SIGHTS

While Querétaro doesn't hurt for tourist attractions, the most intriguing spot in town is the **Convento de la Santa Cruz** (tel. 12-02-35), south of the Jardín. Follow Corregidora to Independencia and turn left; after walking a few blocks, you'll reach the convent; it occupies a plaza dedicated to the founders of the city. Nearly everything inside Santa Cruz is original—the clay pipes and water-catching system date from the city's aqueduct days. Devoted Maximilian-fan-clubbers will want to make a pilgrimage to the room in which Emperor Maximilian spent his last minutes, which has been left exactly as it was on the day of his execution. In one courtyard, trees grow thorns in the form of crucifixes; according to legend, the thorns began growing into crosses after one of the original friars stuck his cane in the ground near the trees. It is said that these are the only trees of their kind in the world; attempts to plant seedlings in other locations have supposedly failed. The tree is of the *mimosas* family, and is known simply as the *Árbol de la Cruz* (Tree of the Cross). (Open with 15-25min. guided tours Mon.-Sat. 9am-2pm and 4-6pm, Sun. 9am-4:30pm. Some donation expected. A few English-speaking guides available.)

Northeast of the Alameda, along Calzada de los Arcos, at the end of Independencia, the **Acueducto** rises above the city. Stretching for 1280m and reaching heights of 23m, the aqueduct dominates the valley in which it lies. Now an emblem of the city, the aqueduct, with its 74 arches of pink quarry stone, was constructed between 1726 and 1738 as a gift to a perpetually parched community from the Marqués del Villas del Águila. Up 5 de Mayo to the east of the Jardín is the **Plaza de la Independencia** or **Plaza de Armas,** a monument to the aforementioned *marqués.* Stone dogs hang around his statue, drooling respectfully into a fountain.

The plaza is bordered by old square-rimmed trees and beautiful colonial buildings, including the **Casa de la Corregidora,** home of Doña Josefa Ortíz de Domínguez, heroine of the Independence movement. The *casa* is now the seat of the state's government, so only the courtyard may be viewed (open Mon.-Fri. 9am-3pm and 6-9pm, Sat. 8am-9:30pm). Built from 1675 to 1680, the colorful **Templo de la Congregación,** one block north of the Casa de la Corregidora at Pasteur and 16 de Septiembre, has two white towers and a central dome. The church's frescoes and stained glass are splendid, and the pipe organ is one of the most elaborate in Mexico. The image of *La Guadalupana* is by Miguel Cabrera (open daily 7am-9pm; avoid mass Mon.-Fri. at 8, 10am, and 8pm, and much more often Sat. and Sun.).

The newly-remodeled **Teatro de la República** stands at Ángela Peralta and Juárez (tel. 12-02-58). Many historic events have transpired here: in 1867, the final decision on Emperor Maximilian's fate; in 1917, the drafting of the constitution; and in 1929, the formation of the Partido Nacional de la Revolución (PNR), the precursor of today's ruling Partido Revolucionario Institucional (PRI). Inside, viewers can see the **Sala de Constituyentes,** where the constitution was drafted (both open Tues.-Sun. 10am-2pm and 5-8pm).

The **Museo Regional** is located in the **Ex-Convento de San Francisco,** at Corregidora and Madero (tel. 12-20-31; fax 12-20-36), to the east of the Jardín Zenea. Exhibits include various artifacts culled from the dustbin of history, such as the table upon which the 1848 Treaty of Guadalupe Hidalgo was signed with the U.S. While exhibits of contemporary art and craftwork greet you at the entrance, the entire upstairs area is devoted to colonial-era religious paintings and artifacts relating to Querétaro's military and political history (open Tues.-Sun. 10:30am-4:30pm; admission 14 pesos, free Sun. and for students and teachers with ID, seniors, and kids under 13).

Overshadowing the Museo Regional is the newer **Museo de Arte de Querétaro,** Allende 14 (tel. 12-23-57), across the Jardín at Pino Suárez. The original edifice, an 18th-century Augustinian monastery, was rebuilt in 1889. An exhibit on local architecture supplements the bounty of Baroque paintings. European canvases, 19th- and 20th-century Mexican art, and the work of the 20th-century *queretareano* Abelarto Ávila round out the formidable collection (open Tues.-Sun. 11am-7pm; admission 5 pesos, free Tues. and for students with ID, seniors, and children under 12).

The **Cerro de las Campanas** (Hill of the Bells), named for the peculiar sound its rocks make when they collide, is where Emperor Maximilian first established his military headquarters then later surrendered his sword to General Escobedo in 1867. To reach the monument, walk a few blocks north of the Jardín Zenea on Corregidora and turn left onto General Escobedo. Proceed on Escobedo until the street ends at Tecnológico, then take a right, and you will come to the monument. The walk should take a half-hour. To the left of the Cerro de las Campanas and up a low hill, Maximilian's family built a small chapel over the ground where the emperor and two of his generals were shot. Three small white memorials inside designate the places where each took his last breath. Up the stairs to the left of the chapel stands a large stone sculpture of Benito Juárez, the man responsible for Maximilian's execution (open daily 7am-6pm; free).

For lazing around, nothing beats the shady trees of the **Alameda Hidalgo.** Across from the bus station, the Alameda, which was built in 1790, includes a duck pond, green lawns, a skating rink good enough for star skater Paul Frey, two soda fountains, and (wouldn't you know it) a monument honoring Hidalgo.

## ENTERTAINMENT AND SEASONAL EVENTS

Local entertainment, like most everything else in Querétaro, revolves around the Jardín Zenea. Open-air brass band concerts are given in the gazebo Sunday evenings from 6-8pm, and myriad jugglers, *mariachis,* and magicians perform there less regularly. Balloons in bunches big enough to fly you to Chicago are sold around the *jardín,* enlivening the already festive plaza. *Mariachi* goes strong in the Jardín de los Platitos, where Juárez meets Av. Universidad north of the *zócalo.* Things start to heat up at about 11pm on Fridays and Saturdays.

Call the **Academia de Bellas Artes** (tel. 12-05-70), Juárez Sur at Independencia, to find out what the students of the Universidad Autónoma de Querétaro have in store for the public. If you're lucky, you might catch a ballet recital, piano concert, theatrical event, or even a folk dance presentation.

More fun than monster trucks, **Querétaro 2000** (tel. 20-68-10 or -13), on Boulevard Bernardo Quintana, is a huge swath of parks and facilities, including a pool, football field, basketball court, gym, cafeteria, restaurant, amusement park, library, a Hall of Fame, an open theater, and an area for camping (open daily 7am-9pm).

Querétaro's student body spends its pesos at a number of discos. The most upscale spot in town is **Discoteca Misiones** (tel. 18-00-22 or 18-02-62), at km229 on the highway to Mexico City in the five-star Hotel Ex-Hacienda Jurica. More convenient to *el centro* is **Tiffani's,** at Zaragoza Pte. 67. The local twentysomething crowd does its thing at **JBJ,** Blvd. Bernardo Quintana 109 (tel. 13-72-13 or 13-01-48). Next to the disco is the JBJ Bar, which has karaoke and pool tables. Also happening is the disco **Van Gogh,** at Prolongación Pasteur Sur 285 (tel. 12-65-75). Many establishments open their doors only on weekends.

The annual **Feria de Querétaro** takes place during the second week of December. The **Feria de Santa Ana,** complete with bulls running through mobbed streets, takes place July 26. Be aware that bull-running can be dangerous to spectators; bulls sometimes run out of control and have been known to injure passers-by. Try to observe the bulls from the safety of a balcony.

# MICHOACÁN DE OCAMPO

Because many of the region's indigenous Purépeche subsisted by the rod and the net, the Aztecs dubbed the lands surrounding Lake Pátzcuaro "Michoacán," or "country of fishermen." The distinctive language the Purépeche spoke and the terraced agricultural plots they built have convinced scholars that they were not originally indigenous to Lake Pátzcuaro but in fact migrated to the area from what is today Peru. Unlike other societies, the Purépeche successfully defended themselves against the aggressively expansionist Aztecs. Purépeche hegemony lasted from around 800 CE, when they first settled Michoacán, until the Spanish arrived in 1522.

Since the colonial period, Michoacán has become an agricultural juggernaut, parlaying mild weather, abundant rains, and red, fertile soil into huge corn harvests. Of late, the forest-covered mountain ranges which surround Michoacán have begun to attract hunters and wildlife enthusiasts, and tourists looking for pretty beaches and inexpensive handicrafts have started to make their way to the state.

## ■■■ MORELIA

Morelia, founded in 1541, drifts in and out of the 20th century like a busy, dizzy honeybee caught between equally scrumptious hunks of *pan dulce.* Vendors hawk

GUANAJUATO          QUERÉTARO

Briseñas   Vista
              Hermosa
*Lago de Chapala*
San José   Sahuayo   Ixtlán   Zinápara
de García            Zamora
Jiquilpan
                              Cuitzeo
         15   Carapan   *Lago de*
                          *Cuitzeo*   51   Maravatío
         37         Quiroga   Morelia      Zinapécuaro
Paracho   *Lago de*   Tzintzuntzán        51   Ciudad
Ciudad            *Pátzcuaro*                      Hidalgo
Guzmán   JALISCO   Peribán   Zirahúen      Tiripetío   Zitácuaro
              Uruapan         14
COLIMA                  Sta. Clara   Pátzcuaro   Villa
                        del Cobre              Madero
         Buenavista
                    120
                  Nueva
Telpacatepec       Italia   La Huacana   Tiquicheo   MÉXICO

Coahuayara   Coalcomán               Churumuco

*Punta*                      *Presa de*
*San Telmo*                  *Infiernillo*                PUEBLA
                  Arteaga   37   Infiernillo   Ciudad Altamirano
Chocola
       200   Las Peñas   Lázaro Cárdenas
                  Playa Azul                GUERRERO
*OCÉANO PACÍFICO*
                                        N
                  0        40 miles    ↑
**Michoacán de Ocampo**   0        40 kilometers

extension cords and Chicago Bulls caps in the crowded *centro;* nearby stand incongruous relics of Morelia's colonial magnificence—rose-colored stone arcades and grand, white-washed houses, their windows big as doors. The capital of Michoacán, Morelia (pop. 500,000) is swollen with bureaucrats, students, and poor *indígenas.* The city sometimes feels like an over-sized flea market glutted with *norteamericano* mass-culture, but its sophisticated air and bustling, eminently habitable feel charm visitors without drawing crowds of tourists.

## ORIENTATION

Situated 287km west of Mexico City on Rte. 15, Morelia is the largest city on the route heading northwest from the D.F. to Guadalajara, another 312km up from Morelia. The streets in Morelia form a large grid, and navigating the city is relatively uncomplicated. Most sights are well within walking distance of the *zócalo* and the adjacent **cathedral;** both are on **Avenida Madero,** Morelia's main thoroughfare. North-south street names change at Madero, while east-west street names change every other block; Madero never forsakes its name. Where there are two street names on a corner, the newest-looking placard is usually correct.

The "Ruta Verde" *combi* (1.30 pesos) runs between the **train station** to **Plaza Carrillo,** six blocks south and two blocks west of the *zócalo*. To get there from the train station, cross the street and wait at the *parada* (stop). Getting downtown from the **bus station** requires a ten-minute walk. Go left (east) as you leave the building, take the first right onto Valentín Gómez Farías, walk three blocks, and then make a left on Av. Madero—the *zócalo* is three blocks ahead. Alternatively, take a taxi from

MORELIA

the station for five pesos. In general, if you need a cab, head for the bus station, where they cluster in large numbers 24 hours a day.

## PRACTICAL INFORMATION

**Tourist Offices: State Tourist Office,** Nigromante 79 (tel. 17-23-71), at Madero Pte. in the Palacio Clavijero, two blocks west of the *zócalo*. From the bus station, walk three blocks south on Valentín Gómez Farías to Av. Madera Pte. and turn left—the office is on the far corner. A friendly, young staff distributes maps. Ask for the monthly list of local cultural activities. Free walking tours of the city (occasionally in English) leave from here Sat.-Sun. at 11am. English spoken daily 9am-3pm. Open daily 9am-8pm.

**Police:** (tel. 12-00-73 and 12-22-22), on 20 de Noviembre, one block northwest of the Fuente de las Tarascas at the end of the aqueduct. On call 24 hrs.

**Post Office:** Av. Madero Ote. 369 (tel. 12-05-17), five blocks east of the cathedral. Posts a *Lista de Correos*. Open Mon.-Fri. 8am-7pm. **Postal Code:** 58000.

**Telephones:** 24-hr. long-distance service in the bus station, but no collect calls. The **Computel,** Eduardo Ruiz 553 (tel. 13-96-47), across the street from the bus station, makes international collect calls for 5 pesos per 5min. Open daily 7am-9pm. *Casas de larga distancia* dot the city center (usually around 8 pesos per min. to the U.S). A **fax** service is on Madero opposite the *zócalo*. **LADATELs** exist but are hard to find; the post office has some that are coin-operated. Credit card-operated LADATELs are at Pino Suárez and Serdán, one block east of the *zócalo* and one block north of Madero. **Telephone Code:** 43.

**Telegrams:** Av. Madero Ote. 371 (tel. 12-06-81), next to the post office. Open Mon.-Fri. 8am-6pm, Sat. 9am-noon.

**Currency Exchange:** Banks are concentrated on Av. Madero east of the cathedral. **Bancomer,** Madero 21 (tel. 12-29-90), changes at an excellent rate 9am-12:30pm. A **casa de cambio** near the *zócalo* at Ocampo 178 and Zaragoza (tel. 2-84-48), gives a good rate. Open Mon.-Fri. 9am-6pm, Sat. 9am-1pm.

**Airport: Aeropuerto Francisco J. Múgica** (tel. 13-67-80), on the Carretera Morelia-Cinapécuaro at km27. **Aeroméxico** (tel. 13-01-40), **Mexicana** (tel. 13-80-05), **Taesa** (tel. 12-00-72), and **Aeromar** (tel. 13-68-86). Destinations include Mexico City and Guadalajara.

**Train Station:** (tel. 16-16-97), on Av. del Periodismo. To Lázaro Cárdenas (5:20am, 11hrs.), Mexico City (10:30am and 10:40pm, 10½hrs.), and Uruapan (first and second class 5:30am, 3½hrs.).

**Bus Station:** Ruíz at V. Gómez Farías (tel. 13-55-89). **Herradura de Plata** (tel. 12-29-88) to Mexico City (28 per day, 4¼hrs., 72 pesos) and Toluca (9 per day, 5:30am-5:30pm, 3½hrs., 44 pesos; second class 16 per day, 4am-12:30am, 3½hrs., 35.50 pesos). **Flecha Amarilla** (tel. 13-55-89) to Guadalajara (8 per day, 5am-7:30pm, 6hrs., 48 pesos), Guanajuato (7 per day, 6:10am-5:50pm, 4hrs., 27 pesos), Querétaro (24 per day, 4hrs., 26.50 pesos), and San Luis Potosí (15 per day, 4am-8:30pm, 7hrs., 58 pesos). **Ruta Paraíso/Galeana** (tel. 12-55-05) goes to Pátzcuaro (every10 min., 5am-8pm, 1hr., 10 pesos) and Uruapan (every 20min., 5am-8pm, 2¼hrs., 20 pesos).

**Public Transportation:** Buses and *combis* (both 1.30 pesos) serve the city from 6am-10pm, but during rush hour they inevitably overflow with passengers and move slowly through the gridlocked streets. *Rutas* 1, 2, and 4 traverse Av. Madero regularly in both directions, and are useful for getting to and from the Parque Cuauhtémoc and the aqueduct.

**Laundromat: Lavandería Automática Ivon,** Plaza Servicentro, local 30 (tel. 14-31-58), by the Plaza las Américas. 3kg for 18 pesos. Same-day service. Open Mon.-Fri. 9am-8:30pm, Sat. 9am-7:30pm.

**Red Cross:** Ventura 27 (tel. 14-51-51 or 14-50-25), at the end of Banuet, next to the Parque Cuauhtémoc. Staff speaks some English. Open 24 hrs.

**Pharmacy: Farmacia Fénix,** Allende 69 (tel. 12-84-92), behind the *zócalo*. Open Mon.-Sat. 9am-9pm, Sun. 9am-8:30pm.

**Hospital: Hospital General Dr. Miguel Silva,** at Isidro Huarte and F. de Mogil (tel. 12-22-16). No English spoken. Open 24 hrs.

**Emergency:** Dial 06.

## ACCOMMODATIONS

Morelia carries a multitude of budget hotels south of Av. Madero and just west of the cathedral, many of which play host to foreign tourists of all sorts, students, and Mexican travelers. The only very difficult time to find a room is during *Semana Santa*, but there is also slight influx of summer school students during the July and August sessions. For some reason, cable TV is common among Morelia's budget establishments, which are typically clean and equipped with hot and purified water.

**CREA Youth Hostel (HI),** Chiapas 180 (tel. 13-31-77), at Oaxaca. Take a taxi for 6 pesos or walk west on Madero Pte. and turn left on Cuautla. Continue south on Cuautla for seven blocks, then turn right on Oaxaca and continue three blocks to Chiapas. The Ruta Amarilla *combi* runs to Oaxaca. Very happening for a Mexican youth hostel. Plenty of sports facilities, but only available for use with a permit from the sports office. Beds 11 pesos. Breakfast 9 pesos, lunch and dinner 11.25 pesos. Open daily 7am-11pm.

**Hotel Colonial,** 20 de Noviembre 15 (tel. 12-18-97). Cozy courtyard graced by stone arches and pillars. Glows a deep yellow. High ceilings, large windows, and a friendly staff. All rooms with bath and TV. Very popular with all types of travelers; reserve ahead. Singles 45 pesos. Doubles 55 pesos, with two beds 70 pesos.

**Hotel El Carmen,** Ruíz 63 (tel. 12-17-25), three blocks north of Madero between Juárez and Morelos. Melon-colored lobby and fresh-smelling, small rooms. Tiled walls, firm mattresses, and color TVs with cable. Bedrooms and bathrooms are clean, but the latter have no shower curtains. The neighborhood gets a little feisty after about 10pm. Singles 50 pesos. Doubles 60 pesos, with two beds 90 pesos.

**Hotel Mintzicuri,** Vasco de Quiroga 227 (tel. 12-06-64), across from the Posada Don Vasco (below). Cozy, wood-paneled rooms with especially clean rugs for a budget joint. A map of Michoacán to the left as you enter, and a mural of General Morelos to your right. Rooms come with phones and cable TV. Singles 55.20 pesos. Doubles 69 pesos.

**Posada de Villa,** Padre Lloreda 176 (tel. 12-72-90), three blocks south of the Museo de las Artesanías. Huge rooms with soft beds. The bathrooms are a bit trodden but extremely clean, scrubbed down by the sweet Mama Bear of a manager. Hot water and powerful water pressure. Free parking. Rooms for long-term rent, with kitchen, stove, dining table, and wardrobe, are available (900 pesos per month). Regular singles 40 pesos. Doubles 50 pesos, with two beds 60 pesos.

## FOOD

Finding good, cheap food is a breeze in Morelia—almost every thoroughfare has at least one family-run restaurant that opens onto the street and dishes out inexpensive *comida corrida* (usually around 7 pesos). Restaurants on the *zócalo* tend to be more pricey, but they're a great place for breakfast.

**La Fuente,** Madero Ote. 493B (tel. 12-64-11), one block east of the post office. A fun and colorful vegetarian restaurant with a stage for mid-afternoon guitar strummings (daily 2:30-4:30pm). Groups of healthy teens take advantage of the slightly pricey but 100% natural food. Even the ice is purified. Whopping *energéticas* (fruit salads with yogurt and granola) 13-18 pesos. *Licuados* (shakes) 6-8 pesos. *Menú del día* 17 pesos. Most entrees 21.95 pesos. Open daily 1-7:30pm.

**Restaurant-Bar La Huacana,** Aldama 116 (tel. 12-53-12), at Obeso. The gargantuan oil painting of the town of Huacana's plaza behind the stage makes a nice backdrop for the large cafeteria-like dining area. Stone walls provide great acoustics for the *mariachis* who play Mon.-Fri. 3-5pm. *Comida corrida* 15 pesos. Most *enchiladas* 15 pesos. Breakfasts 8-10 pesos. Open daily 8am-10pm.

**Hindú Vegetariano Govina,** Morelos Sur 39 (tel. 13-38-86). Don't expect any reposeful poses of Shiva, the goddess Aditi, or battles scenes between the Pandavas and the Kauravas—just good vegetarian food. Located in a former hotel restaurant, and the stained glass and wall designs have stayed behind. *Comida corrida* 13-15 pesos. Soy burgers 4 pesos. Open Mon.-Sat. 9am-5:30pm.

## SIGHTS

In 1986, for its 100th birthday, the **Museo Michoacano,** Allende 305 (tel. 12-04-07), one block west of the *zócalo* at Abasolo, got a great big facelift. The museum was spiffed up, and exhibits were divided into five categories: ecology, archaeology, the colonial period, the struggle for freedom, and independent Mexico. The most notable object on display is a huge, anonymous painting completed in 1738, *La Procesión del Traslado de las Monjas de una Universidad a su Convento Nuevo* ("The Procession of the Nuns from the University to Their New Convent"). Comments penned by Diego Rivera call the well-observed painting ground-breaking and note that it was produced in an era when religious themes dominated Mexican art. As if to underscore Rivera's point, a number of ecclesiastical paintings hang nearby, including works by Miguel Cabrera and a trio of indigenous 19th-century artists—Manuel Ocaraza, Félix Parra, and Jesús Torres. Near the stairway, a mural by Alfredo Zalce portrays those who have shaped Mexico's history and skewers those who blindly admire U.S. mass culture (open Tues.-Sat. 9am-7pm, Sun. 9am-2pm; admission 14 pesos, free Sun. and for those under 13 and over 60).

Overlooking the *zócalo,* the massive **cathedral** had been 65 years in the making when it was completed in 1745. Out of dry corn cobs and orchid nectar, *indígenas* sculpted *Señor de la Sacristía,* the oldest treasure of the church, and in the 16th century, Felipe II of Spain donated a gold crown to top off the masterpiece. In the 19th century, a bishop tipped the careful balance that had existed between Neoclassical and Baroque elements by removing the elaborate Baroque filigree from the altarpieces and frescoes and renovating the church's interior in the sober Doric Neoclassical style (open daily 9am-8:30pm).

The former residence of José María Morelos, the parish priest who led the Independence movement after Hidalgo's death, is now the **Museo de Morelos,** Morelos 323 (tel. 13-26-51), one block east and two blocks south of the cathedral. The museum displays Morelos' religious vestments, military ornaments, and uniform, as well as other mementos of the surge for independence (open Mon.-Sat. 9am-7pm, Sun. 9am-6pm; admission 10 pesos, free Sun. and for those under 13 or over 60). More of a civic building than a museum, the **Casa Natal de Morelos** (Birthplace of Morelos; tel. 12-27-93) stands at Corregidora 113, at García Obeso, one block south of the cathedral. Glass cases preserve Morelos' war-time cartography, communiqués, and letters. Also notable are murals by Alfredo Zalce and a shady courtyard watched over by the martyr's bust (open Mon.-Sat. 9am-7pm; free).

The peach-colored **Casa de Cultura,** Morelos Nte. 485 (tel. 12-41-51), 3½ blocks north of Madero, is a gathering place for artists, musicians, and backpackers. The *casa* houses a bookstore, art galleries, a theater, and a lovely café. Dance, voice, theater, guitar, piano, and sculpture classes are offered, and concerts, book presentations, art festivals, and literature workshops are given. The on-premises **Museo de la Máscara** exhibits a small collection of masks from all over the Republic (open Mon.-Fri. 10am-2pm and 4-8pm, Sat.-Sun. and holidays 10am-6pm; free).

The **Casa de las Artesanías,** Humbolt at Juan de San Miguel (tel. 12-12-48), is a huge craft museum and retail store. Crafts are organized by the town of their origin; on display are colorful macramé *huipiles,* straw airplanes, geometrically decorated pottery, carved wood furniture, and guitars. The *museo* is impressive, but better prices await in Pátzcuaro (open Mon.-Sat. 10am-8pm, Sun. 10am-6pm; free).

The city's **aqueduct,** built in 1788, sides a pleasant pedestrian avenue perfect for evening strolls in the western part of the city. Nearby, the well-lit **Plaza de Morelos** is marked by an equestrian monument to Morelos commissioned during the Porfiriato and inaugurated by the very revolutionary forces that would topple him.

Drag the kids off to the zoo in the **Parque Benito Juárez** (tel. 24-13-12). To reach the park, take the "Guenda" *combi* from the corner of Allende and Galeano or a St. Maria bus heading south on Nigromante (open daily 10am-5pm; admission 3.50 pesos, children under 10, 0.50 pesos).

## ENTERTAINMENT

Listings of events can be found at the Casa de Cultura (see Sights, above) and at the tourist office. The **Casa Natal de Morelos** (see Sights, above) shows artsy films the last Tues.-Thurs. of every month at noon and 7pm (admission 1 peso). Conferences, music talks, and other events take place here on Fridays at 7pm (free). **Cinema Victoria,** Madero Pte. 944-C (tel. 12-43-10), two blocks west of the Hotel San Jorge, features Hollywood's latest interspersed with slice-and-dice hyper-violent flicks (admission 5 pesos). For older *norteamericano* movies, check out **Sala Eréndira** (tel. 12-12-87) on Santiago Tapia behind the Palacio Clavijero.

See plays at 8pm on Wednesday night in the **ISSTE Morelos Theater,** on Av. Madero in the western part of the city. The theater's university and amateur groups perform picaresque plays, pantomime, and—hold on to your black garters!—a Spanish version of *The Rocky Horror Picture Show.* If you find heavenly bodies more fascinating than the scantily-clad ones of *Rocky Horror,* head for the **Planetario** (tel. 14-24-65), in the Centro de Convenciones. (Shows Fri.-Sat. 7pm, Sun. 6:30pm. Arrive ½hr. early. Must be 7 or older. Admission 6 pesos.) To get there, take the Ruta Rojo #3 *combi* on Av. Allende/Valladolid.

**La Casona del Teatro,** Aquiles Serdán 35, one block north of Madero, hosts comedies (in Spanish) Fri.-Sat. at 8:30pm and Sun. at 7:30pm (15 pesos). The coffee shop/theater is popular with students and bohemian types who play chess and drink coffee (3.50 pesos) until showtime. Snacks and sandwiches are also available (2-7 pesos; open daily 11am-11pm). A similar hangout is the bookstore-café **La Librería,** Calzada Fray Antonio de San Miguel 324 (tel. 12-02-87), which sometimes has films and music. Live jazz gets going Wed.-Sat. at 6pm at the **Cantera Jardín,** Aldama 343 (tel. 12-75-78; cover around 20 pesos).

While the **Bomba Y Jungle Bar,** Justo Mendoza 60 (tel. 12-09-17), is usually pretty fun, the joint jumps most energetically on Wednesdays, when women pay 10 pesos and men pay 60 pesos to take advantage of the *barra libre* (open bar). University students flock to **XO Klub,** Av. Campestre 100 (tel. 15-55-14), and **Siglo 18,** Blvd. García León and Turismo (tel. 24-07-47), discos where the only requirement is that you buy 20 pesos worth of drinks (both open Thurs.-Sun. 9pm-2am). Down the street, local teens and a teeny handful of *gringo* students celebrate birthdays with buckets of budget Coronas at **Carlos 'n Charlie's,** Av. Carmelinas 3340 (tel. 24-37-39), near the Hotel Calinada (open daily 1pm-2am). Also popular but a smidgen more sedate is **Canta Bar,** Lázaro Cárdenas 2225 (tel. 15-53-54). Domestic drinks cost about five pesos (cover about 10 pesos; open Thurs.-Sun. 9pm-2am). Up the same alley, **Bola Suriana,** on Bartolomeo de las Casas, a few blocks east of the Museo de Artesanías, anchors the local Latin music scene. Also very popular among the younger crowd are **Freeday,** Av. Campestre 374 (tel. 15-66-61), and **La Antigua,** Av. Camelias (tel. 15-90-47).

# ■■■ PÁTZCUARO

Michoacán de Ocampo's earthy jewel, Pátzcuaro (pop. 40,000) is slowly becoming a travelers' favorite. And no wonder: there is something marvelously pure about Pátzcuaro, something entirely uninterrupted about the relationship here between people, their land, and their history.

Cool and rainy in the summer months, Pátzcuaro is surrounded by land that bends and lilts, rolling up and over hills and stretching itself to the shores of Lake Pátzcuaro. It was this land that had been ruled by the Purépeche; it was here that the Spaniards sent Bishop Vasco de Quiroga to replace Nuño de Guzmán, who had ruled the region with an iron fist. Inspired by the humanitarian ideals of Thomas Moore, Bishop Quiroga defended the Purépeche from landowners and mining magnates. In order to encourage economic development, Quiroga taught the residents of each Purépeche village around the lake a different craft. Soon the communities were trading with one another, and the area became fairly prosperous. In today's

Pátzcuaro, the legacy of Quiroga's efforts is on display for all to see; the stores which line the town's cobblestone streets are stuffed with stacks of locally produced woolen sweaters, meticulously carved wooden toys, and decorative masks.

Tourists typically come to Pátzcuaro to buy high-quality crafts or to use the town as a base for visiting the smaller towns which surround Lake Pátzcuaro.

## ORIENTATION

Rte. 14 leads into Pátzcuaro from Morelia (70km) and Mexico City, first crossing Quiroga and Tzintzuntzán to the north and nearby Tzurumútaro to the east, and then continuing on to Uruapan, 67km to the southwest.

The quickest way to reach *el centro* from the **bus station** is by *combi* (1.50 pesos) or city bus (1.20 pesos). Make sure the vehicle you're using is in fact going to the center—drivers may neglect to change signs when they change routes.

Pátzcuaro encompasses two distinct areas: while the downtown is perched on a hill, 5km north lies a residential part of town that fronts the lake. Downtown centers around Pátzcuaro's two main squares. **Plaza Bocanegra,** the smaller of the two, is all bustle and thick crowds. One block south on **Dr. Benito Mendoza** (which borders both plazas' west sides) is the larger **Plaza Quiroga.** Quiroga is elegant and quiet, and features a central fountain and well-shaded, rosebush-lined paths. Streets more or less form a grid, changing names at each plaza. Keep in mind that addresses on the plazas are not given with the street name, but rather the name of the *portal* (arcade). For example, at Plaza Quiroga, Benito Mendoza becomes **Portal Hidalgo.**

To reach the **lake** from downtown, jump on a public bus labeled "Lago," "San Pedro," or "Sta. Ana"; these buses pass by the east side of Plaza Bocanegra, Portal Regules, and Portal Juárez nearly every five minutes (1.20 pesos). *Lanchas* (boats) depart for the island of Janitzio and other points around the lake (14 pesos).

The summers here can be mighty wet, so bring along some raingear.

## PRACTICAL INFORMATION

**Tourist Office: Delegación Regional de Turismo,** Ibarra 2, Int. 4 (tel. 2-12-14), at Benito Mendoza, just past the northwest corner of Plaza Quiroga. It's in the medical building; the office is the 3rd door on the right in the courtyard. Helpful staff and a good map, but no English spoken. Open Mon.-Sat. 9am-3pm and 4-7pm, Sun. 9am-3pm. Also, a smaller information booth is on the Plaza Bocanegra next to the library. No English spoken. Open daily 10am-1pm (roughly).

**Police:** Ibarra 9 (tel. 2-00-04).

**Post Office:** Obregón 13 (tel. 2-01-28), half a block north of Plaza Bocanegra. *Lista de Correos.* Open Mon.-Fri. 8am-7pm, Sat. 9am-1pm. **Postal Code:** 61600.

**Telephones: Hotel San Agustín,** Portal Juárez 27 (tel. 2-05-38), on Plaza Bocanegra. International collect calls 5 pesos. Open daily 8:30am-10:30pm. **Telephone Code:** 434.

**Telegrams:** Títere 15-A (tel. 2-18-00 or 2-12-25; fax 2-00-10), one block east and one block north of the library. Open Mon.-Fri. 8am-6pm, Sat. 9am-noon.

**Currency Exchange:** Almost all banks exchange until noon only. **Banca Serfín,** Portal Morelos 54, on the north side of Plaza Quiroga, has good rates. **Sociedad Cambiaría Pátzcuaro,** Benito Mendoza 7 (tel. 2-02-40), will also change dollars. Open daily 9am-2:30pm and 4:30-6:30pm.

**Train Station:** (tel. 2-08-03), at the bottom of Av. de las Américas near the lakefront. Daily service to Mexico City (first class 9:30pm, 47 pesos; second class 8:40am and 9:30pm, 26 pesos; both 12hrs.) and Uruapan (first class 7am, 7 pesos; second class 7am and 6:45pm, 4 pesos; both 2hrs.).

**Bus Station:** Off Circunvalación, south of town. **Herradura de Plata** (tel. 2-10-45), runs to Mexico City (first class 7 per day, 9:15am-12:15am, 5¾hrs., 80 pesos; second class 8 per day, 7:35am-midnight, 7hrs., 60 pesos), and on the same schedule to San Juan del Río (second class 5hrs., 36.50 pesos) and Toluca (first class 4hrs., 80 pesos). **Flecha Amarilla** (tel. 2-09-60) goes to Guadalajara (11:30pm, 6hrs., 50 pesos) and San Luis Potosí (first class 10am, 6hrs., 78 pesos; second class 7pm, 8hrs., 66 pesos). **Galeana** (tel. 2-08-08) serves the following destinations from 5:40am-9pm: Morelia (every 15min., 1hr., 10 pesos), Santa Clara del Cobre (every 40min., 25min., 3 pesos), and Uruapan (every 15 min., 1¼hrs., 10 pesos).

**Luggage Storage:** Available at the bus station until midnight. Two pesos per hr.

**Laundromat: Lavandería Automática,** Terán 14 (tel. 2-39-39), two blocks west of Plaza Quiroga. 3kg for 14 pesos, wash and dry. Takes 3-5hrs. Open Mon.-Sat. 9am-2pm and 4-8pm.

**Public Library:** On the Plaza Bocanegra in the Ex-Templo de San Agustín (see Sights). Contains a small selection of books in English. Open Mon.-Fri. 9am-7pm.

**Pharmacy: Principal,** Benito Mendoza 1 (tel. 2-06-96). Open daily 9am-10pm.

**Hospital:** Romero 10 (tel. 2-02-85). English spoken Mon.-Fri. 9am-1pm and 4-6pm. Open 24 hrs.

**Emergency: Cuerpo de Rescate,** Lib. Ignacio Zaragoza (tel. 2-21-65). English-speakers can be contacted. 24-hr. service.

## ACCOMMODATIONS

Pátzcuaro is home to just enough hotels to accommodate its small tourist industry. The few that do exist are ideal for the budget traveler—adequately kept and well-priced. Expect to lodge with large numbers of Mexican, European, and some American travelers.

**Posada de la Salud,** Serrato 9 (tel. 2-00-58), three blocks east of either plaza, half a block past the *basílica* on its right. Beautiful courtyard, gorgeous carved furniture from Cuanajo, cloud-soft mattresses, and clean bathrooms. A cold, damp must tends to linger in the rooms during the rainy season. Hot water 24 hrs. Singles 45 pesos. Doubles 80 pesos.

**Hotel Valmen,** Lloreda 34 (tel. 2-11-61), one block east of Plaza Bocanegra. A great deal if you don't mind a mushy bed. Aztec tile and squawking birds fill the court-yards. Well-lit rooms, some with balconies, though the plumbing is a bit erratic. Excellent double-locks on doors. Popular with international travelers. Lock-out 10pm. 35 pesos per person.

**Posada de la Rosa,** Portal Juárez 30 (tel. 2-08-11), on the west side of Plaza Bocanegra. Red tiles and lots of sunlight. Simple, musty rooms with a lone, breath-taking lightbulb hanging from the ceiling. Rooms with a view onto the plaza are the nicest. The communal bathroom is a little rickety but fairly clean. Singles and doubles 30 pesos, with bath 40 pesos.

## FOOD

Fish from the nearby lakes can be found in restaurants throughout the city. *Pescado blanco* is far and away the most plentiful and popular dish. *Charales* (smelts), served in the restaurants along Pátzcuaro's lakefront and on Janitzio, are fried, sardine-like fish which are eaten whole and by the fistful. Their popularity is proving an environmental nightmare (they are consistently overfished), so try to resist. *Caldos de pescado* (fish broths) bubble in large clay vats outside open-air restaurants, particularly on Janitzio. These spicy soups, loaded with fish and sometimes shrimp, crab, and squid, are a meal in themselves.

Most of the restaurants by the docks close at 7pm. More formal restaurants with tablecloths and locally crafted furniture ring Plaza Quiroga. Less formal and less expensive restaurants tend to be closer to Plaza Bocanegra and the market.

**El Buho,** Tejerías 8 (tel. 2-14-39), two blocks east of Pl. Bocanegra. Pottery, wood chairs, little flowers on each table, and splashes of Chaplin and Marilyn Monroe on the walls. A down-to-earth sort of place. The food (basic Mexican and American) is fresh and carefully prepared and makes its way into the mouths of young backpackers without burning holes in their pockets. Also popular among local youth. *Burritos* 10 pesos. Small pizza 25 pesos. Open daily 8am-10pm during the summer months, December, and *Semana Santa.* Otherwise open daily 5-10pm.

**Restaurant y Cafetería La Casona,** Quiroga 65 (tel. 2-11-79), on the north side of Plaza Quiroga. White walls, wooden beams, and black metal chandeliers give the

place a classy, minimalist look. Older working men eat their four-course *comidas* here. Complete breakfasts 10-18 pesos, fish 16-45 pesos. Open daily 8am-9pm.
**Restaurant El Patio,** Plaza Quiroga 19 (tel. 2-04-84), on the south side of the plaza. Pricey, but the food is good and the ambience pleasant. The sophisticated decor blends still-lifes, empty wine bottles, and pillars of rough stone. Fresh 'n tasty beef and fish lure tourists, families, and middle-aged folks. Breakfasts 12-22 pesos. Fish 26-36 pesos. *Filete ranchero* 30 pesos. Open daily 8am-10pm.

## SIGHTS

Pátzcuaro's unique handcrafts—hairy Tócuaro masks, elegant Zirahuén dinnerware, and thick wool textiles—are sold in the Plaza Bocanegra's **market** and in the small shops along the passage next to Biblioteca Gertrudis Bocanegra. Bargaining is easier in the market or when you buy more than one item, but don't expect much of a discount on the arrestingly handsome wool articles—thick sweaters, brilliantly colored *saltillos* and *ruanas* (stylized ponchos), rainbow-colored *sarapes,* and dark shawls—Pátzcuaro's specialty. Regardless of how much you plead and beg, retailers stick to their prices, wavering 10-15 pesos at most. Still, these items are far from expensive. Most vendors are open 8am-8pm daily.

When Vasco de Quiroga came to Pátzcuaro, he initiated not only social change but bold architectural projects as well. Quiroga conceived the **Basílica de Nuestra Señora de la Salud,** at Lerín and Serrato, as a colossal structure with five naves arranged like the fingers of an extended hand. Each finger was to represent one of Michoacán's cultures and races, with the hand's palm as the central altar representing the Catholic religion.

Today the basilica features a grandiose Romanesque altar. Intricate parallel stripes of frescoed arabesques cross the high, concave ceiling of the church, forming impressive vaults. An enormous glass booth with gilded Corinthian columns and a dome protects the statue of the *Virgen de la Salud;* when Vasco de Quiroga asked a Tarascan artisans to design an image of the Virgin in 1546, they complied by shaping her out of *tatzingue* paste made from corn cobs and orchid honey, a typical 16-century statue-making technique. Native groups had used this method to create idols of their own gods before the Conquest and continued the practice to mold the images of the Virgin and saints. The resulting statue is durable and incredibly light, weighing only 4-5 kilograms (open daily 8am-8pm).

Down the street from the basilica, on Lerín near Navarette, is the **Casa de Artesanías.** Originally a convent for Dominican nuns, this complex now contains craft shops, a small gallery of modern Mexican art, and a mural depicting Vasco de Quiroga's accomplishments. The *casa* sells cotton textiles and superb musical instruments (guitars, flutes, and *güiros*) at decent prices (guitars 80-500 pesos). For woolens, the market is still your best bet (open daily, loosely from 10am-2pm and 4-7pm, though individual shops often forgo *siesta* for tourist pesos).

The **Museo Regional de Artes Populares** (tel. 2-10-29), one block south of the basilica at the corner of Lerín and Alcanterillas, displays pottery, copperware, and textiles produced in the region. Particularly appealing are the *maque* and *laca* ceramics collections (open Tues.-Sat. 9am-8pm, Sun. 9am-3pm; admission 7 pesos; free for children under 13 and on Sun.).

Statues of Pátzcuaro's two most honored citizens stand vigil over the town's principal plazas. The ceremonious, banner-bearing Vasco de Quiroga inhabits **Plaza Quiroga,** a vast and well-forested space which seems more like a humble city zoo than a *zócalo.* The massive, bare-breasted Gertrudis Bocanegra looks out from the center of **Plaza Gertrudis Bocanegra.** A martyr for Mexican independence, Bocanegra was executed by a Spanish squadron in the Plaza Quiroga in October of 1817. Locals claim that bullet holes still mark the ash tree to which she was tied.

**Biblioteca Gertrudis Bocanegra,** on the plaza of the same name, occupies the former site of an Augustine convent. The library's multicolored mural, *La Historia de Michoacán,* by Juan O' Gorman, illustrates the history of the Purépeche civilization from pre-Conquest times to the Revolution of 1910 (open Mon.-Fri. 9am-7pm).

When the next-door **Teatro Caltzontzín,** once part of the Augustinian convent, became a theater in 1936, an as-yet-unfulfilled prophecy was uttered: one Holy Thursday, the theater will crumble as punishment for the sin of projecting movies in a sacred place. If you dare, Mexican and U.S. movies are there for the watching. Check the posted schedule for times and flicks (admission 5 pesos).

Three kilometers east of the city, at the end of Av. Benigno Serrato, is **El Humilladero** (Place of Humiliation), where the cowardly king Tangaxhuán II surrendered his crown and his daughters to Cristóbal de Olid and his Spanish troops. Two peculiar features distinguish this chapel: on its altar stands a rare monolithic cross, undoubtedly older than the date inscribed on its base (1553); and on the chapel's façade are images of gods which represent the sun and the moon. To reach it, take a *combi* marked "Panteón" or "El Cristo" (1.50 pesos).

## ENTERTAINMENT AND SEASONAL EVENTS

Aside from mellowing out in restaurants, there isn't much to do in Pátzcuaro at night. For a worthy diversion, though, try the off-beat **El Viejo Gaucho,** Iturbe 10 (tel. 2-03-68), a bar and restaurant where Mexican and Cuban folk music, dramatic readings, and an open mike provide nightly entertainment. Yellow lightbulbs illuminate the setting and Frida Kahlo posters adorn the walls—all in all, El Viejo is an odd-bird for Michoacán. Burgers (12-15 pesos), thick-crusted pizzas (20-35 pesos), and delicious *empanadas* (5 pesos each) entertain the tastebuds (cover 10 pesos per person; open Tues.-Sun. 5pm-2am). **El Rincón Video Café,** on Quiroga just east of the Plaza Quiroga's northeast corner, attracts younger locals looking for a hangout or in the mood for some tunes (open Tues.-Sun. 5-11pm).

Pátzcuaro hosts several fiestas during the year. Soon after Christmas celebrations are done with, Pátzcuaro is electrified by a pair of **pastorelas,** celebrated on January 6 to commemorate the Adoration of the Magi, and on January 17 to honor St. Anthony of Abad. On both occasions, citizens dress their domestic animals in bizarre costumes, ribbons, and floral crowns.

A few months later, Pátzcuaro's *Semana Santa* attracts devotees from all over the Republic. The city's order of celebration differs slightly from the rest of Michoacán. On Thursday, all the churches in town are visited to accompany the Nazareth, and on the night of Good Friday, the **Procesión de Imágenes de Cristo** is held, during which images of a crucified Christ are carried around town. The faithful flock from all over the state on Saturday for Pátzcuaro's **Procesión del Silencio,** celebrated everywhere else the day before. On this day, a crowd marches around town mourning Jesus's death in silence. Pátzcuaro and the surrounding regions party down on Sunday—with a religious flavor, of course. Along with *Semana Santa*, the most important celebration of the year is **Noche de Muertos** (Nov. 1-2), which holds special importance for the Tarascans. Candle-clad fishing boats row out to Janitzio on the first night, heralding the start of a two-night vigil in the graveyard. The first night commemorates lost children; the second remembers deceased adults.

# ■ NEAR PÁTZCUARO

## AROUND LAGO DE PÁTZCUARO

The tiny island of **Janitzio,** inhabited exclusively by Tarascan *indígenas* who speak the Purépeche dialect, subsists on its tourist trade. The town's steep main street is lined with stores selling woolen goods, hand-carved wooden chess sets, masks, and assorted knick-knacks. Between the shops—the bulk of which are quite pricey—are numerous restaurants all offering *pescado blanco* and *charale*. A low hill towers over the island; atop it is a statue of Morelos so big it can be seen clearly from Pátzcuaro. Inside the statue, a mural traces the principal events in both Morelos's life and the struggle for independence that he led. From the mural, stairs lead to the cuff of Morelos's sleeve, where openings in the statue permit a spectacular view of the lake (open daily 10am-6pm; admission 1 peso).

**Getting There:** To get to the island, first hop on a **bus** labeled "Lago" at the corner of Portal Regules and Portal Juárez at Plaza Bocanegra. The bus (0.60 pesos) rambles to the docks, where you'll buy a **ferry** ticket (round-trip 14 pesos). Ferries leave when they fill up (about every 5min. on weekends, every 20min. during the week, 9am-5pm; the ferries leave with more frequency 10am-4pm) and reach the island in about 30 minutes. Be sure you know when the last boat leaves the island for Pátzcuaro, as Janitzio does not accommodate the stranded.

From the ferry, the serene towns of Jarácuaro, Nayízaro, Puácuaro, and Ihuatzio are visible along the verdant lake shore. Before docking, the ferry is surrounded by local fishermen who paddle out in canoes and briefly demonstrate the use of their butterfly-shaped nets in the hopes of earning a small contribution. To reach the other towns around the lake, take a second-class **Flecha Amarilla** bus.

## TZINTZUNTZÁN

Tzintzuntzán (Place of the Hummingbirds) was the last great city of the Tarascan empire. Before his death in the middle of the 15th century, the Purépeche lord Tariácori divided his empire among his three sons. When the empire was reunited some years later, Tzintzuntzán was chosen as its capital. Its former glory relegated to history, Tzintzuntzán's claims to fame are the delicate, multi-colored ceramics displayed on tables along Calle Principal.

The **Yácatas,** a peculiar pre-Conquest temple, sits on a hill just outside the city on the road to Pátzcuaro. To reach the entrance, walk up the street in front of the market and convent. It's a bit of a hike—follow the road all the way around the hill until you reach the small museum/ticket booth. The bases of the structures—all that remain today—are standard rectangular pyramids. The missing parts of the *yácatas,* however, are what made them unique; each was originally crowned with an unusual elliptical pyramid constructed of shingles and volcanic rock. The pyramids are situated along the long edge of an artificial terrace 425m long and 250m wide. Each building represents a bird. The museum at the entrance includes some Mesoamerican pottery and a gift shop (site open daily 9am-6pm; admission 10 pesos, free Sun.). Also of interest is the 16th-century Franciscan **convent** closer to town. The olive shrubs that now smother the extensive, tree-filled atrium were originally planted by Vasco de Quiroga over 450 years ago (open daily 7am-6pm).

**Getting There:** Tzintzuntzán is perched on the northeastern edge of the Lago de Pátzcuaro, about 15km from Pátzcuaro on the road to Quiroga and Morelia. Second-class buses leave from the station in Pátzcuaro every 15 minutes (25min., 3 pesos). To get back to Pátzcuaro, hop on the appropriately labeled bus from outside the convent. Bring a sweater; Tzintzuntzán can be chilly and damp.

## SANTA CLARA DEL COBRE

Santa Clara del Cobre, 16km south of Pátzcuaro, has an extensive history as the crafter of copper mined in nearby towns. Nearly every store in town sells copper plates, pans, bowls, and bells. Prices here are only slightly better than elsewhere in Mexico, but Santa Clara is unbeatable for quality and variety. For a quick look at some highly imaginative pieces, step into the **Museo de Cobre,** close to the plaza. Santa Clara celebrates the **Feria de Cobre** in the first half of August. Like Quiroga, there is little to see in Santa Clara beyond *artesanías;* budget only a couple of hours for a trip here from Pátzcuaro.

**Getting There:** To reach Santa Clara from Pátzcuaro, take a Galeana bus (every 30 min., 7am-8pm, 20min., 4-5 pesos).

## ZIRAHUÉN

If you're into camping, Zirahuén makes for a fun trip from Pátzcuaro. Not as large as Lake Pátzcuaro, Zirahuén (Where Smoke Rose) has other merits. It is more open, unobstructed by marshes and islands, and if you find an area untouched by the lake's algae, it's clean enough for swimming. To **camp,** hike up one of the ridges that border the lake and set up in any one of the spots that overlook the water; the landowner—if there is one—may ask you to pay a few pesos. An excellent locale is the sizeable piece of lakefront on the west (left, as you face the lake) side of town. The strip, about 15m in width, is covered by grass cut short by grazing horses and is located in front of a few abandoned wooden shacks. From the center of town, follow any of the streets leading to the left until you reach the lakefront cut off by the hill bordering Zirahuén's west side. On weekends, the lakefront fills with locals in search of a *tranquilo* place to relax. Be warned: heavy afternoon rains during June and July can turn summer camping into a soggy experience.

Zirahuén offers much for the non-camper as well. At the end of the street bordering the town plaza lie a series of informal lakefront restaurants, where a stack of *tortillas,* a plate of rice, salad (beware), and fresh white fish will run you a mere 8 pesos. Next to the restaurants sits a *lancha* dock, where a ride around the lake costs 15 pesos in a collective boat, 120 pesos for a private ride (up to 5 people). For those not inclined towards camping, the only other lodging options are the beautiful but expensive lakefront *cabañas*.

**Getting There:** To reach the town, take the bus from the second-class station in Pátzcuaro (3 per day, 20min., 2 pesos) or catch one of the Zirahuén-bound cabs from Obregón and Industrial, past the post office, a block north of Plaza Bocanegra. The taxis leave much more frequently than the buses, but with a somewhat loose schedule (about every 20min., 6 pesos). To get back, cabs leave from the very end of the paved highway as it hits Zirahuén, on the town's south side (about 8 pesos).

# ■■■ URUAPAN

Surrounded by red soil, rolling hills, and rows upon rows of avocado trees, Uruapan (pronounced ur-WA-pan, pop. 200,000) sits amidst a checkerboard of ex-*encomienda* farmland. Farmers and their families come to Uruapan to sell what they have grown and to buy bags of fried plaintains, wristwatches, and other necessities of modern life. Uruapan is no mere market town, though: thick traffic, smoggy air, and a Kentucky Fried Chicken collectively symbolize the city's development into a commercial center. Tourists typically come to the city to explore the nearby waterfall, national park, and Paricutín Volcano.

**Orientation** About 175km west of Morelia and 320km southeast of Guadalajara, Uruapan makes a good stopover on the way to or from Playa Azul (260km to the south) and other Pacific coast resorts, or a side trip from Morelia or Pátzcuaro. Everything in town is within easy walking distance of the *zócalo,* known as **Jardín de los Mártires** on its west side and **Jardín Morelos** on its east end. The statue in the center faces south, looking down **Cupatitzio.** **Emiliano Carranza** runs into the southwest corner of the square from the west, and **Obregón** is its continuation on the eastern side of the plaza. Watch out with all the "Carranzas"—**Venustiano Carranza** runs into the *zócalo's* north side, and **Manuel Ocaranza** runs one block west of Cupatitzio into the plaza's south side. The east and south sides of the square are lined with various *portales* (arcades), and **Ocampo** runs along its western edge. To reach the center from the **bus station** on Benito Juárez in the northeast corner of town, hail a taxi (6 pesos) or hop aboard a bus labeled "El Centro" (1.40 pesos).

**Practical Information** The **tourist office,** Ocampo 64 (tel. 3-61-72), is on the basement level of the Hotel Plaza. Good map available, and some English spoken during weekdays (open Mon.-Sat. 9am-2pm and 4-7pm, Sun. 9am-2pm). The **police** are at Eucalyptos and Naranjo (tel. 4-06-20; open 24 hrs.). The **post office,** on Reforma 13 (tel. 3-56-30), is three blocks south of *zócalo* on Cupatitzio and left one block (open Mon.-Fri. 8am-7pm, Sat 9am-1pm). **Postal Code:** 60000. For **long-distance calls,** try the **High Life Perfumery,** 5 de Febrero 12A (tel. 3-62-11); international collect calls cost 10 pesos (open Mon.-Sat. 9am-2pm and 4-8:30pm, Sun. 10am-2pm). **LADATELs** are rare; look in front of the Comedor Vegetariano, next to the big TelMex office. **Telephone Code:** 452. To change money, try **Centro Cam-**

**biario,** Portal Matamoros 19 (tel. 4-79-17; open Mon.-Fri. 9am-2pm and 4-7pm, Sat. 9am-2pm). Higher exchange rates and an **ATM** await at **Banca Serfín,** Cupatitzio 17 (tel. 3-54-11; open for exchange Mon.-Fri. 9am-1:30pm).

The **train station** (tel. 4-09-81) is located on Lázaro Cárdenas in the eastern part of town, and is accessible by the "Zapata," "Zapata Revolución," or "Foviste" buses. Regular and first-class trains run to Mexico City (second class 6:30am, first and second class 7:10pm, 13hrs., 31 or 55 pesos) and Lázaro Cárdenas (10am, 6hrs., 18 or 31.50 pesos). The station office is open Mon. and Wed.-Sat. 8am-7pm, Sun. and Tues. 9am-12:30pm and 4-7pm. **Buses** leave from Benito Juárez, in the northeast corner of town. To reach the station from the *zócalo,* take either the "Central Camionera" or "Central" bus (1.40 pesos). **Galeana** (tel. 4-00-90) serves Morelia (every 20min., 4am-9pm, 2hrs., 20 pesos) and Pátzcuaro (every 20min., 4am-9pm, 1hr., 10 pesos). **Flecha Amarilla** (tel. 4-39-82) runs buses to Celaya (5 per day, 7:20am-10pm, 5hrs., 142 pesos), Manzanillo (10am, 8hrs., 71 pesos), Mexico City (3 per day, 7:20am-10pm, 9hrs., 73 pesos), Querétaro (4 per day, 9am-10pm, 6hrs., 48.50 pesos), San Luis Potosí (3 per day, 9am-4pm, 8hrs., 82 pesos), and Zamora (6 per day, 10:45pm-12:15pm, 2hrs., 17 pesos). **La Línea** (tel. 3-18-71) is a good bet for Guadalajara (14 per day, 5hrs., 41-55 pesos) and Toluca (9 per day, noon-1am, 5hrs., 60-67 pesos). **Primera Plus** (tel. 4-39-82) gives first-class service to Guadalajara (5 per day, 6:15am-7:15pm, 5hrs., 55 pesos), León (9am and 1:45pm, 6hrs., 62 pesos), Mexico City (north station 4 per day, 7am-10:30pm; west station 11pm, 7hrs., 94 pesos), Morelia (4 per day, 9am-1:45pm, 2hrs., 25 pesos), and Zamora (5 per day, 6:15am-7:15pm, 2hrs., 24 pesos).

A laundromat, **Autoservicio de Lavandería,** Emiliano Carranza 47 (tel. 3-26-69), at García, four blocks west of the *zócalo,* washes 3kg for 19 pesos (open Mon.-Sat. 9am-2pm and 4-8pm). **Farmacia Fénix,** Carranza 1 (tel. 4-16-40), is at Ocampo. No English spoken (open daily 8am-9pm). The **Red Cross,** Del Lago 1 (tel. 4-03-00), is a block down from the **Hospital Civil** on San Miguel (tel. 3-46-60 or -81), seven blocks west of the northern edge of the *zócalo* (both open 24 hrs.).

**Accommodations** The cheapest hotels in Uruapan are, unfortunately, the "cheapest" in every sense of the word—the norm for truly inexpensive spots is tattered bedspreads, horrendously filthy bathrooms, and a fraternity of jumbo *cucarachas* who host 24-hour parties you're constantly being invited to. Even worse, many of these inexpensive joints let rooms by the hour; unless you've packed your suede underwear, you'll want to pay a few more pesos to avoid these sleazy establishments, many of which ooze from the eastern edge of the *zócalo.*

Fortunately, cheap and sleazy is not the only option for Uruapan's budget travelers. For a good, clean night's sleep, try the **Hotel Los Tres Caballeros,** Constitución 50 (tel. 4-71-70). Go north up Portal Santo Degollado (the *zócalo's* eastern street) into the market for about two blocks; the hotel is on the right. The rooms and bathrooms here are small, but clean and loaded: mirrors, wooden furniture, pitchers of *agua purificada,* fresh towels, and posters of Mexico are par for the course (singles 40 pesos; doubles 50 pesos). If you need to recharge, it might be worth spending the extra pesos to spend the night at the **Hotel Regis,** Portal Carillo 12 (tel. 3-58-44 or 3-59-66), on the south side of the *zócalo.* The four-storied hotel is blessed with spotless rooms, each equipped with a TV, phone, fan, and desk. The interior courtyards are pleasant and the location excellent. Prices vary vastly depending on business and season (singles 70-126.50 pesos; doubles 80-161 pesos). **Hotel Villa de Flores,** Carranza 15 (tel. 4-28-00), a block and a half from the *zócalo,* features spotless bathrooms, massive, breezy rooms, and a beautiful flower-filled courtyard that attracts hummingbirds and lounging humans. The restaurant offers a 12-peso *comida corrida* (singles 75 pesos; doubles 95 pesos).

**Food** Tucked into an important agricultural region, Uruapan offers cheap and tasty food. Fresh fruit abounds, the market (half a block north of the *zócalo* on Constitución) is sizable, and around the *zócalo,* vendors sell delicious one-peso hotcakes for breakfast. Between Constitución and Pátzcuaro y Quiroga (walk half a block down Constitución to a door on the left and up the stairs) is an outdoor square where, for very little money you can get a great dinner, lunch, or snack. The restaurants in and around the *zócalo* offer fewer alternatives than the market and street stands. Hotel restaurants are the most common option for a sit-down meal, and cafés specializing in coffees and desserts unleash their aromas up and down Carranza. A delightful rarity in Uruapan is the simple **Comedor Vegetariano,** Aldama 14 at Morelos, a block south and a block east of the *zócalo.* The white-walled restaurant with plastic-covered tablecloths specializes in food, not appearances. A *menú del día* (15 pesos) is served Mon.-Sat. 1-4:30pm, and a buffet (20 pesos) Sun. 1-4:30pm. At all other times, delicious *tortas* (4 pesos) and juices (4 pesos) are offered (open daily 8am-8pm). While the look at the **Café Tradicional de Uruapan,** Carranza 5-B, is fancy coffeeshop, the tables here are often pulled together to accommodate groups of families, teens, and middle-aged men sipping their *café* so slowly that they might lose a race with a Mexican train. Specialties are breakfast, snacks, and coffee, but the management is currently attempting to remodel the place into more of a restaurant. *Huevos rancheros* 9 pesos, *tamales* 2.50 pesos, *capuchino* 6.50 pesos (open daily 8:30am-10pm). The restaurant at the Hotel Regis, **Los Faroles,** is also quite nice. Locals and guests swing by to watch the *Canal de las Estrellas* and leisurely munch on their food. Four *quesadillas* 15 pesos, eggs 10-11 pesos, pancakes 10 pesos. Massive *comida corrida* 20 pesos (open daily 7am-11pm).

**Sights and Entertainment**    If you haven't the time to catch the natural wonders surrounding Uruapan, the **Parque Nacional Barranca del Cupatitzio** at the western end of Independencia fringes the town with a bit of jungle. Endless, dense green bush is split by the Río Cupatitzio and concrete walkways for visitors, where locals hawk hand-made goods. Although the grounds are a bit littered, the park makes for an excellent afternoon walk or picnic (open daily 8am-6pm; admission 2 pesos for adults, 1 peso for children). Uruapan's other daytime attraction is the **Museo Regional de Arte Popular** (tel. 4-34-34) on the *zócalo,* which displays Michoacán crafts. The building once was the first hospital in the Americas; today it is home to a smattering of ceramic dining equipment and a small collection of masks (open Tues.-Sun. 9:30am-1:30pm and 3:30-6pm; free).

At night, Uruapan comes out to play. **Temetsi,** Independencia 15 (tel. 4-06-29), attracts crowds of all ages, depending on what's playing. You can count on jazz, rock, blues, *música romántica, mexicana,* or *latina* in the evenings from Friday to Sunday and sometimes on Thursday. The place is technically a café, but a wild enough crowd may find dance space between the tables (cover 5-25 pesos; open daily 9am-11pm). A bit outside of town on the road to Tzaráracua is **La Scala Disco,** Madrid 10 (tel. 4-26-09), in Colonia Huerta del Cupatitzio. Wednesday through Sunday local youths dance to U.S. top-40 mixed with Mexican dance music (cover 20 pesos; open 9pm-2am; the cab ride should cost 8 pesos). Nearer the *zócalo* and accessible by foot is **La Kashba,** Ocampo 64 (tel. 3-37-00), in the Hotel Plaza. It

---

### The Virgin of Guadalupe vs. The Prince of Darkness
### Round 1: Down by the River

At Uruapan's Parque Nacional Barranca del Cupatitzio, young boys will give you a tour of **La Rodilla del Diablo** ("The Devil's Knee") for a small fee. Legend has it that the river at one time dried up, leaving the surrounding lands stark and bare. One day, the friar Juan de San Miguel led a procession to the river's dry mouth, carrying an image of the Virgin. The friar halted the procession, sprinkled some holy water on the Virgin's image and on the rocks at the river's mouth. Suddenly, Satan appeared, saw the Virgin, and retreated into the rocks, resuming the flow of water. One rock still bears the mark of the hiding place of the Príncipe de la Tinieblas (Prince of Darkness).

attracts a post-collegiate crowd that dances and drinks to a different artist each night (cover 12-50 pesos; open Tues.-Sun. 8pm-4am).

# ■ NEAR URUAPAN

## PARICUTÍN VOLCANO

A visit to the beautiful, black, and still-active Paricutín Volcano makes a cool daytrip from Uruapan. In 1943, the volcano erupted. By the time it quit spewing lava eight years later, there was little dust left to settle—the land had been coated in a thick and hardening layer of porous lava. Along the way, entire towns had been consumed and a 700m, dark-side-of-the-moon sort of mountain had sprung up. In one area, the lava covered an entire village except for the church steeple, which now sticks out of a field of cold, black stone. You can rent horses and a guide to ascend the volcano (70 pesos). Before you do, however, reconcile yourself to some serious haggling and some serious saddle sores—wooden saddles are the rule here. Unless you're feeling manic, allow at least four or five hours for a guided trip or for a journey into the valley to see the steeple.

**Getting There: Paraíso** buses run to Paricutín and nearby Angahuán from the bus station (every ½hr., 5am-7:45pm, 40min., 5.50 pesos).

## TZARÁRACUA AND TZARARECUITA

The waterfalls at **Tzaráracua** (sah-RA-ra-kwa), 10km from Uruapan on the road to Playa Azul, cascade 20m into a series of small pools. The first waterfall, called Tzaráracua, is about 1km from the small parking lot—walk or ride a horse there. Possessed of an incredible single-mindedness of purpose, guides and their horses surround visitors upon arrival at the lot. Expect to pay 25 pesos for a round-trip to the first falls, 50 pesos to the second. Alternatively, hoof it to the waterfall on your own two feet—the path to the falls descends a flight of cobbled stairs and requires about 20 minutes of walking. The path is lined with tiny restaurants selling drinks and food, and culminates at the base of the falls. Look but don't swim—the water at the bottom is littered with trash and has a dangerous current. A worker will take you over the water in a suspended boxcar (2 pesos), and more horses await to take you on to Tzararecuita and back to the entrance (30 pesos) or just up the hill (10 pesos).

**Tzararecuita,** with two smaller pools free of pollution and perfect for swimming, is another 1.5km beyond the large pool. Skinny-dipping is popular in the chilly water, but watch out for peepers and keep a close watch on your clothes.

**Getting There:** Buses marked "Tzaráracua" supposedly leave from the south side of the *zócalo* every hour (2.50 pesos), but during the week the schedule is so imprecise that you could be there all day; Sundays are a bit more reliable. Taxis should run you 25 pesos. For solo travelers and those trying to make their remaining pesos go a long way, things are much simpler: catch a bus headed for Nueva Italia or Playa Azul from the Central and beg to be let off at Tzaráracua. No matter how you get to the falls, getting back to Uruapan can be quite difficult; while buses supposedly head back to the city every hour, in actuality they rarely come. The best bet is hiking up to the highway from the small lot and flagging down an Uruapan-bound bus. Be persistent; now is the time on Shprokets when we jump up and down and wave our arms, like a little birdie, *ja?*

## PARACHO

If guitars are on your shopping list, go to Paracho, 30km north of Uruapan. Carefully crafted six-strings pack just about every store. Fantastic bargains are available for all varieties of guitar. In the first week of August the town holds an internationally renowned **guitar festival.** Musicians and craftspeople partake in a musical orgy that includes classical concerts, fireworks, dancing, and guitar-strumming competitions.

**Getting There:** To get to Paracho, hop a **Paraíso** bus bound for Zamora or Paracho (every 15min., 4am-8:20pm, ½hr., 6 pesos) from the Central Camionera.

# HIDALGO

## ■■■ TULA

The signs on the road leading into Tula admonish visitors and residents to keep the town clean because of its historical significance. That significance, however, could be easily overlooked—the quiet *zócalo,* bustling market, and plentiful taco stands do little to distinguish Tula from other Mexican towns. Today, most visitors are drawn to the Toltec archaeological site just outside the city. Tula lies within easy daytrip range of Mexico City (80km along Rtes. 57 and 85) and Pachuca (75km).

**Orientation and Practical Information** Downtown Tula consists of a few commercial streets surrounding a central *zócalo.* To reach the *zócalo* from the **bus station,** turn right down Xicotencatl and then left at Ocampo. Follow the signs to the centro, turning left down Zaragoza and then right on Hidalgo. To get to Tula from Mexico City, take an AVM bus from the Central de Autobuses del Norte. The ticket window is at the far end of the terminal in *Sala* 8. Buses leave every half-hour throughout the day and run 16 pesos.

There is no **tourist office,** but the town is small and friendly enough that people on the street will probably be willing and able to answer any question. The **police** are on 5 de Mayo 408 (tel. 2-01-85). The **post office** is hidden on Av. Ferrocarril. From the top of Av. 5 de Mayo, head downhill Av. Vicente Guerrero, along the train tracks, and continue straight ahead (open Mon.-Sat. 9am-3pm). **Postal Code:** 42800. Make calls at **Teléfonos de Mexico,** Av. 5 de Mayo 3 (tel. 2-00-41), near Mina (open Mon.-Sat. 8am-10pm, Sun. 8am-3pm). There is also a *caseta* at the bus station (open daily 8am-9pm). **Telephone Code:** 773. The small gray **telegram** office (tel. 2-00-37) is behind the market and the white Loconsa building, in a construction zone. From Zaragoza, head right downhill on 5 de Mayo and left at Av. Colegio Militar (open Mon.-Fri. 9am-9pm, Sat. 9am-noon). Change money at **Bánamex,** Leandro Valle 102 (tel. 2-39-03), down Juárez from the *zócalo,* which also has an **ATM** (open Mon.-Fri. 9am-5pm).

Buses run out of the **Autotransportes Valle de Mezquital (AVM)** terminal (tel. 2-02-25 or -64), on Xicotencatl. 1st-class buses run to Celaya (9 per day, 3½hrs., 38 pesos), Irapuato (8 per day, 5hrs., 48 pesos), León (6 per day, 6hrs., 59 pesos), Mexico City (every ½hr., 6am-8pm, 2hrs., 16 pesos), Pachuca (every ½hr., 4:30am-7:30pm, 2hrs., 15 pesos), and Querétaro (9 per day, 2hrs., 32 pesos). For a cab, call **Taxi Sitio Tula** (tel. 2-00-39).

If struck by the need to wash your clothes, **Lavandería E La,** 5 de Mayo at Mina, will clean your duds for 7 pesos per kg (open Mon.-Fri. 8am-8pm, Sat. 8am-6pm). The **IMSS Clínica Hospital,** Ocampo at Xicotencatl (tel. 2-10-46), in the large brown building, is open for emergencies around the clock. The **pharmacy** is in the same building (open Mon.-Fri. 8am-7:30pm, Sat. 8am-9pm).

**Accommodations and Food** Because Tula is a small town and most people come through just to see the ruins, the budget room is a rare animal. A few cheap and clean hotels do exist. The best deal in town is the **Auto Hotel Cuéllar,** 5 de Mayo 23 (tel. 2-04-42). A proudly-flown Mexican flag flaps atop this ultra-pink joint. A smattering of wooden furniture and occasional patches of homey carpeting hug the rosy walls and tiled floors. Bathrooms feature showers with sliding glass doors (singles 55 pesos; doubles 65 pesos, with TV 85 pesos). A second option offering scarcely better conditions is **Hotel Cathedral,** Zaragoza 106 (tel. 2-08-13), right off the plaza. The creamy interior is pleasant, and large globular bulbs illuminate worn brown carpeting. The bathrooms are trial-size, and you don't get quite enough pop for your peso (singles 60 pesos; doubles 75 pesos).

If a good hotel is a rare animal in Tula, moderately formal restaurants are on the verge of extinction here. You'll probably be dining solo at **Restaurant Casa**

**Blanca,** Zaragoza 3 (tel. 2-22-74), at Hidalgo, which sports peach-colored walls hung with weavings. The color-splashed tables hold a five-course *comida corrida* (17.50 pesos) and a hamburger platter with fries and *refresco* (14 pesos). More typical is the **Restaurant El Ranchito** (tel. 2-02-03), on Zaragoza half a block before Hidalgo. Old women swat flies in the TV-equipped rear area, while cooks up the front dish out a 15-peso *comida corrida* with *postre* and *refresco* (open daily 6am-midnight).

**The Ruins** The current archaeological site is but a fraction of an expansive national park dedicated to preserving the plants and animals of the semi-desert area. From Tula's central plaza, **taxis** will take you to the site for seven to eight pesos. The town-to-ruins walk is long but manageable. From the plaza, turn left on Zaragoza (the first street toward the bus station). When you reach Ocampo, a sign points to the "Parque Nacional Tula"; turn right, and head towards the highway. One street before the main highway, turn left on the road marked by the stone statue. The park lies about 1km up, off the road to the left. Taxis aren't available at the site itself for the return, but *peseros* pass frequently on the highway (1.40 pesos).

Once the Toltecs' greatest city, ancient Tula was constructed at the foot of a hill in a region of brooding volcanic mountains. In the final years of Teotihuacán (around 700-750 CE), a band of Chichimecs and Toltecs, led by Mixcoatl-Camaxtli, wandered through the Valley of Mexico before conquering the Otomí area between present-day Tula and Jilotepec. It is believed that Mixcoatl-Camaxtli then led his people to what is now the state of Morelos, where he had a son before losing his throne. This son, Ce Acatl Topitzin, eventually recovered his father's throne and moved the capital to the foot of the mountain called Xicuco, where he founded Tula.

Ce Acatl Topitzin (a.k.a Quetzalcóatl) is the most venerated king in *indígena* history and mythology. After many years at Tula, he abandoned the city in 884 CE and led many of his followers to the Gulf coast because of strife with neighbors who did not agree with his peaceful ways and who rejected the god for whom he was named. In the years following Quetzalcóatl's departure, several kings expanded Tula into the center of the mighty Toltec empire. Hundreds of years later, the Aztec Emperor Moctezuma brought about his own downfall when he welcomed the recently-arrived Cortés because he believe the *conquistador* was the same light-skinned Quetzalcóatl who had fled to the east so many years before.

The Toltecs, whose name means "builders" in Nahuatl, relied on irrigation for their agricultural success and modeled their architecture after the style of Teotihuacán. During the 200-year-long Toltec heyday, the kingdom abandoned its once pacific stance for the violence and viciousness for which it is now notorious. When crop failures and droughts weakened the Toltec capital in 1165 CE, the Chichimecs lashed out at the Toltecs and destroyed Tula. The ruins of the city are architecturally mediocre, partly because the Toltecs experienced internal instability—at one point Quetzalcóatl urged the Toltecs to evacuate the city, prompting some residents to bury their belongings and move to the region called Tlapallan. Tula was eventually absorbed by the Aztec empire, and to this day, Aztec ceramics and pottery can be found scattered among the ruins.

From the entrance area, a dirt path zigzags through two sets of vendor stalls before arriving at the main plaza. The first structure you see to your right (north) as you reach the main plaza is **Ballcourt #1,** just north of the large Edificio de los Atlantes. This court, nearly 200 ft. long, once held a depiction of a ball player in ritual dress, which is now located in the archaeological sponge that is the Museo Nacional de Antropología in Mexico City.

To the left (south) is the monumental **Edificio de los Atlantes,** also called the **Edificio de Tlahuizcalpantecuhtli** (try to say that in one breath!), likely the ceremonial worship building. Along its northern side and currently covered by a tin roof is the **Coatepantli,** which depicts jaguars and serpents in procession, as well as a deity in headdress and heart-devouring eagles. Reliefs of serpents feasting on live humans adorn the adjacent wall. Standing atop the pyramid are the Atlantes, figures of carved warriors; close inspection of the Atlantes (each a whopping 9.6m tall) reveals traces of red pigment, the only remnants of the many colors the statues once wore. Each statue is actually composed of several sections of stone, carefully designed to resemble the battle garb of the ancient *guerreros*. In their left hand each carries an *atlatl* (dart thrower), while the right hand holds a sheaf of arrows. A butterfly-shaped breastplate covers each figure's front, and a wide, knotted belt protects the lower regions of their anatomy. Strapped to their backs is a huge solar disk.

Immediately west of the Edifico de los Atlantes is the **Palacio Quemado,** or burnt palace; it is thought to have been an administrative center in ancient Tula—or perhaps the city market. A *chac-mool,* or messenger to the gods, was originally found in the central patio; now the black figure with a gaping mouth reclines near the steps to the Edifico de los Atlantes, under the awning. Like many other indigenous cultures that built their largest buildings on the eastern boundary of the plaza to witness the sunrise, and inspire awe and maintain socio-political control (i.e. Tenochtitlán, Teotihuacán, etc.), Tula's **Templo Principal** once towered over the others. On the east side of the expansive green plaza, this building may have served as living quarters for the high priests or rulers of the city. Not fully excavated and overgrown with weeds, it's not possible to climb the Templo Principal from the front, but you can scramble up a steep rocky path in its southeast corner. On the west side of the plaza sulks a second ballcourt. The level side closest to the plaza served as an altar where pre-game rites were likely held. Adjoining the ballcourt on the interior of the plaza is **El Tzompantli,** a small platform built by the Aztecs. Tzompantli means "place of skulls" and was used to display the victims of sacrifice.

The only other excavated structure of interest in the area is **El Corral,** 1.5km north of the main plaza. El Corral's distinctive, rounded shape leads archaeologists to believe that it was dedicated to the god of the wind. A dirt path from the northern border of the main plaza leads north to the wind god's shrine. The **Museo Jorge R. Acosta,** at the entrance to the ruins, concerns itself with Toltec religion, crafts, recreation, and socioeconomic hierarchy. Inside is a copy of the *chac-mool,* as well as a history of the different groups that occupied the site and some of their remains.

The only written guide available is a small book (20 pesos). The museum complex also includes a cafeteria, bathrooms, and an information desk where you can request a free guided tour and brochures (site open daily 9:30am-4:30pm; admission 14 pesos, free Sun. and holidays; museum free with admission).

# Veracruz

## NORTHERN VERACRUZ

### ■■■ JALAPA (XALAPA)

Upon arrival in Jalapa, the lucky traveler realizes that she has stumbled upon a rare gem. Perched high upon a mountain slope, Jalapa (or sometimes Xalapa, pop. 288,000) surprises visitors with its decaying colonial beauty, its lush surroundings, and its subculture of talented artists. As well-informed visitors know, Jalapa is home to a world-class museum, the University of Veracruz, and an emerald necklace of magnificent parks and gardens.

The capital of the state of Veracruz since 1885, Jalapa was first settled by Nahuatl speakers who dubbed the area "spring in the sand." After the Spanish conquest, Jalapa's annual fairs earned the city the economic importance it continues to enjoy today. Downtown Jalapa is the busy, giddy center from which the rest of the city ripples outward, merging gracefully with the raw beauty of the Veracruz landscape. Steep cobblestone streets provide a magnificent view of the lush peaks surrounding Jalapa at every turn, while the bustling avenues give constant evidence of a city fairly bursting at the seams with artistic energy. Taken together, Jalapa's sophistication and beauty make it a favorite destination for foreigners and Mexicans alike.

#### ORIENTATION

Jalapa lies 104km northwest of Veracruz along Route 140 and 302km east of Mexico City. Trains and first- and second-class buses typically stop in Jalapa, though buses run more frequently to more destinations. The **train station** is at the extreme northeast edge of the city, a 40-minute walk or 6-peso taxi ride from *el centro*.

The first-class ADO and the second-class AU **bus terminals** are both housed in a state-of-the-art building at 20 de Noviembre 571, east of the city center. The station offers long-distance phones, telegraph service, a pharmacy, shopping, food, and drink. Taxis to the *zócalo* run 6 pesos. To catch a bus to the *zócalo* (1.20 pesos), first exit the station complex by descending the long, terraced steps to street level; from there, buses marked "Centro" or "Terminal" head downtown.

Jalapa, like many other hilly towns, can be quite confusing. Its main east-west street is Enríquez; Enríquez defines the north side of **Parque Juárez,** which more or less functions as the *zócalo*. East of the park, Enríquez splits into a north branch, Xalapeños Ilustres, and a south branch, Zamora. Zaragoza runs roughly parallel to Enríquez/Zamora, one block south. West of the Parque Juárez, Enríquez becomes Av. Camacho and gradually turns toward the northwest. Clavijero and Revolución, on the west and east sides of the park, head north and uphill from Enríquez.

#### PRACTICAL INFORMATION

**Tourist Office:** A kiosk in the bus station, to the far left as you enter the terminal after leaving the bus area, is the best source of information. Friendly staff has brochures and the answers to most of your questions. Open daily 8am-10pm.

**State Tourist Office,** Camacho 191 (tel. 18-72-02), a 30-minute walk west from the *zócalo*. Any yellow minibus heading west on Enríquez will get you there (1.20 pesos). The office will be on your left. Less helpful than the above tourist office. Map available. Brochures for other parts of the state and country. No English spoken. Open Mon.-Fri. 9am-9pm, Sat. 9am-1pm.

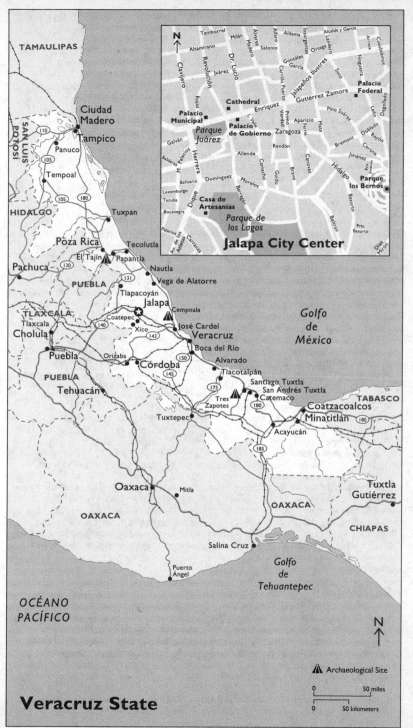

TAMAULIPAS

Ciudad
Madero
Tampico
Panuco

SAN LUIS
POTOSÍ
110
105
Tempoal
105
180

HIDALGO

Tuxpan

Poza Rica
El Tajín
130
Pachuca
Papantla
Tecolutla

131
Nautla
PUEBLA
Tlapacoyán
Vega de Alatorre
Jalapa
Cempoala
Coatepec
140
TLAXCALA
Xico
José Cardel
Tlaxcala
143
Veracruz
Cholula
Boca del Río
Orizaba
150
Puebla
Córdoba
Alvarado
PUEBLA
145
Tlacotalpán
Tehuacán
175
Santiago Tuxtla
San Andrés Tuxtla
Tres
Catemaco
Zapotes
180
Tuxtepec
Coatzacoalcos
TABASCO
Acayucán
Minatitlán
180
185
TABASCO

Golfo
de
México

Oaxaca
Mitla
Tuxtla
Gutiérrez
OAXACA
OAXACA
CHIAPAS
Salina Cruz

Puerto
Ángel
Golfo
de
Tehuantepec

OCÉANO
PACÍFICO

N

▲▲ Archaeological Site

0          50 miles
0       50 kilometers

Veracruz State

**Jalapa City Center**

N

Tamborrel
Milán
Alcalde y García
Altamirano
Álvarez
Aldama
Arrese
Clavijero
Madero
Insurgentes
Cuauhtémoc
Revolución
Ortega
Nogueira
Dr. Lucio
Gonzáles
Soto
Juárez
García
Opiloga
Carrillo Puerto
Jalapeños Ilustres
Palacio
Cathedral
Gutiérrez Zamora
Federal
Palacio
Enríquez
Leño
Municipal
Primo
Verdad
Palacio
Aparicio
Doblado
Parque
de Gobierno
Zaragoza
Ferriz
Rayón
Juárez
Mata
Corona
Galván
Rendón
Bremont
Jiménez
Allende
Camacho
Canovas
Hidalgo
Balderas
Dominguez
Morelos
Guido
Bravo
Parque
Herrera
Belisario
Barragán
Basurto
los Berros
Luxemburgo
Casa de
Tacuba
Artesanías
Priv.
Bocanegra
Parque de
Basurto
los Lagos
Palacios
Díaz
Mirón

**Police:** Officially at the Cuartel San José, at the corner of Arteaga and Aldama (tel. 18-18-10), but the hordes of heavily armed cops that hang out across the street from the cathedral at the Palacio de Gobierno can help in an emergency.

**Post Office:** In the Palacio Federal, at Zamora and Diego Leño (tel. 17-20-21). Open Mon.-Fri. 8am-8pm, Sat. 9am-1pm. Open for *Lista de Correos* Mon.-Sat. 8am-1pm. **Postal Code:** 91001.

**Telephones: LADATEL** phones are outside the Palacio de Gobierno on Enríquez and outside the post office. Booths in small office on Calle Guerro 9, off the southwest corner of the Parque Juárez. Open daily 9am-10pm. **Telephone Code:** 28.

**Telegrams: Telecomm,** Zamora 70, around the corner from the post office. **Fax** service also available. Open Mon.-Fri. 8am-6pm, Sat. 9am-1pm. Telegram service also available at the bus station.

**Currency Exchange: Banco Internacional,** on Enríquez, one block west of Restaurant Terraza Jardín. Open Mon.-Fri. 9am-1:30pm. **Bánamex,** at the corner where Enríquez splits into Zamora and Xalapeños Ilustres, has an **ATM** that accepts Plus, Cirrus, MC, and Visa. **Casa de Cambio Jalapa,** Zamora 36 (tel. 18-18-45). Open Mon.-Fri. 9am-1:30pm and 4-6pm.

**American Express:** Carrillo 24 (tel. 17-41-14; fax 12-06-01), three blocks east of the *zócalo* off Enríquez. Helpful staff will change money or traveler's checks, but only when the office has the cash. They will also hold mail for card members. Open Mon.-Fri. 9am-8pm. Cashier open Mon.-Fri. 9am-2pm and 4-7pm. AmEx shares the office with **Viajes Xalapa,** a full-service travel agent. Hours and phone number same as AmEx.

**Buses:** From **CAXA** (Central de Autobuses de Xalapa), first-class **ADO** buses run to Campeche (8:15pm, 15hrs., 179 pesos), Catemaco (8am, 4½hrs., 47 pesos), Coatepec (3:40 and 6pm, ½hr., 2 pesos), Mérida (8:15pm, 18hrs., 210 pesos), Mexico City (every hr., 4:30am-midnight, 5hrs., 57.50 pesos), Papantla (13 per day, 7am-11:15pm, 4hrs., 44.50 pesos), Puebla (11 per day, 6am-11:55pm, 3hrs., 33 pesos), San Andrés Tuxtla (12 per day, 8am-midnight, 4hrs., 45 pesos), Santiago Tuxtla (2:30 and 5:30pm, 3½hrs., 43 pesos), Tuxtepec (6am and 3:30pm, 5½hrs., 45 pesos), and Veracruz (every 20min., 5:30am-11pm, 2hrs., 19.50 pesos). **Autobuses Unidos (AU)** goes direct to Mexico City (every hr., 8:50am-11:50pm, 5hrs., 50.50 pesos), Puebla (every hr., 2:25am-8:15pm, 3hrs., 28 pesos), Tlaxcala (1:40am and 10:05am, 3hrs., 28.50 pesos), and *ordinario* to Veracruz (every 15-30 min., 4:30am-9:30pm, 15.50 pesos).

**Market:** Revolución at Altamirano, two blocks north of the Parque Juárez. Open daily 8am-sunset. **Chedraui** is a supermarket in the Plaza Crystal mall, on the corner of Independencia and Lázaro Cárdenas. Open daily 8am-9pm.

**Laundromat: Lavandería Los Lagos,** Dique 25 (tel. 17-93-38), right around the corner from Casa de Artesanías. 3.5kg washed and dried for 13 pesos. Open Mon.-Sat. 9am-2pm and 4-7pm.

**Library: Biblioteca de la Ciudad,** Juárez 2. Open Mon.-Fri. 8am-10pm, Sat. 8am-9pm, Sun. 8am-8pm.

**Red Cross:** Clavijero 13 (tel. 17-81-58 or 17-34-31), a block north of Parque Juárez. 24-hr. ambulance service. English-speaking staff available Tues. and Sat. night.

**Pharmacies: Farmacia del Dr. Rancón,** on the corner of Saraga and Revolución (tel. 8-09-35). Open 24 hrs. Many other pharmacies nearby on Revolución and on Enríquez by Terraza Jardín.

**Emergency:** Dial 06.

## ACCOMMODATIONS

And the Lord God, seeing the plight of the weary budget traveler, was moved to take pity upon her, and said, "Let there be Jalapa." He filled it with comfortable, economical, and convenient accommodations, and grouped them mostly on Revolución, close to the *zócalo,* the market, and the parks. (Warning: this utopian Garden has mosquitoes.) All rooms in the hotels listed have private baths with showers.

**Hotel Limón,** Revolución 8 (tel. 7-22-07), half a block up Revolución from Enríquez; go up past the left side of cathedral. The Platonic form of the urban budget hotel, the lovely Limón, established in 1894, is no lemon. Medium-sized, spotlessly clean rooms surround a patio with *mudéjar*-tile walls. Color TV and piping hot water 'round the clock. Safe-deposit boxes. Try to get a room at the far end of the hotel; rooms facing Revolución pick up every last noise from the street below. Reservations accepted. Singles 30 pesos. Doubles 35 pesos, with 2 beds 42 pesos. A few larger rooms, up to 5 beds (75 pesos, 5 people max.).

**Hotel Citlalli,** Clavijero 43 (tel. 18-34-58). Two blocks up the hill from Enríquez, west of Restaurant Terraza Jardín. This hotel has all the amenities (TV, phone, *agua purificada,* huge sparkling bathrooms), even if it's a bit short on character. Clean white stucco rooms with wood accents, bordering on the sterile. Quiet street. Singles 45 pesos. Doubles 60 pesos. Triples 75 pesos.

**Hotel Continental,** Zamora 4 (tel. 17-35-30). Large rooms in this former mansion retain an air of musty elegance gone-by. All open onto a dark, yet attractive garden patio; the restaurant on the first floor serves a 7-peso *comida corrida* (open Mon.-Sat. 1-6pm). Singles 34 pesos. Doubles 40 pesos, with 2 beds 45 pesos.

**Hotel Plaza,** Enríquez 4 (tel. 17-33-10), just east of Palacio de Gobierno. Two floors of faded but spacious rooms. Most second-floor rooms wrap around an open-air patio and have elegant varnished wooden doors original to this early 20th-century structure. Singles 35 pesos. Doubles 40 pesos, with 2 beds 45 pesos. Up to 6 people (with 4 beds) 75 pesos.

## FOOD

Filled with high-quality cafés and cheap eateries, Jalapa is a true culinary paradise. Particularly cheap cuisine can be found in the market and at the many stands around it. Look out for *mole xiqueño,* a type of *mole* unique to the region. The market at La Rotonda, six blocks north of Enríquez on Revolución, is the place for cheap, filling *tortas.* Vegetarian restaurants are on Murillo Vidal, south of the post office.

**La Sopa,** Callejón del Diamante 3-A (tel. 17-80-69). Two blocks east of the *zócalo,* in the crowded alley off Enríquez. Hip hangout under a vaulted ceiling. Decor by local artists. When it's crowded, join an occupied table and make a friend. *Comida corrida* 9 pesos. *Antojitos* at night. Open daily 1-6pm and 7:30-11pm.

**Café de la Parroquia,** Zaragoza 18 (tel. 17-44-36), near the south side of the Palacio de Gobierno. Like its famous cousin in the Port of Veracruz, La Parroquia's 61 tables fill with folks looking for fine fare. Many a heated political discussion takes place over their excellent *café lechero.* Sandwiches start at 5 pesos, omelettes at 9. Open daily 7:30am-10:30pm. Also on Camacho west of Parque Juárez, on the way to the Teatro del Estado (tel 17-71-57). Open Mon.-Sat. 8am-midnight.

**Restaurant Terraza Jardín** (tel. 18-97-13), on Enríquez, across the street from the Parque Juárez. Outdoor tables swim with conversation and chess games. Inside is merely a large, plain room with more tables. Breakfast of corn flakes, toast, juice, and coffee 9 pesos. Club sandwich 12 pesos. Open Mon.-Sat. 8am-11pm.

## SIGHTS

The inscription above the entrance to the galleries of Jalapa's **Museo de Antropología** admonishes the Mexican visitor to pause, for "this is the root of your history, your crib and your altar." Below, a massive Olmec head stares grimly out across three millennia. Displayed in spectacular marble galleries and outdoor gardens, the museum's other Olmec heads are perhaps the most impressive of the 3,000 items on display. The heads commemorate leaders of the little-understood Olmecs, who ruled the Gulf Coast of Mexico around 1000 BCE, but were unknown to archaeologists until the 1930s, when the remains of their civilization were found in a Veracruzan rain forest. The main gallery contains artifacts of the Olmecs, Totonacs, and Huastecs. A group of Totonac figurines and masks subvert the austerity of the Olmec heads with their merry smiles, while nearby the Huastec deity Tlazoltéotl, associated with procreation, stands sculpted in soft, minimalist relief.

To walk to the museum, walk east on Enríquez/Camacho past the tourist office. Turn left on Av. Xalapa and walk on for several blocks; the museum is on the left. The walk takes approximately 45 minutes—you might want to catch one of the yellow buses on Enríquez marked "Tesorería" (1.20 pesos). Taxis are about 6 pesos.

Explanatory signs are in Spanish (open daily 9am-5pm; gift shop and cafeteria; admission 10 pesos, students and teachers 6 pesos; wheelchair accessible, though it's necessary to have an attendant help with the small steps at the entrance).

Some of Jalapa's most popular sights are its public parks and gardens, the hallmarks of a rich and livable city. The **Parque Ecológico Macuitepetl** is primarily a preserve for the flora and fauna indigenous to the Jalapa area, but also serves as one of the city's principal recreational areas. A brick path meanders past smooching lovers to the summit of an extinct volcano 186 meters above the city. A spiral tower near the summit offers a commanding view of the city and mountains. To get there, take a "Mercado-Corona" *colectivo* from Revolución and Altamirano to the park's entrance (1.20 pesos), or hail a taxi (6 pesos). South of Parque Juárez on Dique lies the **Paseo de los Lagos,** where a bicycle path traces the perimeter of several urban lakes. On sunny afternoons, the park is dotted with children, chirping birds, panting joggers, and still more amorous young couples. Like any urban park, though, it can be dangerous at night. At the west end of the park, near Dique, the **Casa de Artesanías** (tel. 17-08-04), a non-profit state-run handicrafts store, features work by Veracruzan artisans. Fine pieces, including meticulously embroidered shirts, are cheaper here than in private shops (open Mon.-Fri. 8am-8pm, Sat.-Sun.10am-1pm).

Through the east entrance of the **Palacio de Gobierno,** off Enríquez on the side opposite Parque Juárez, lies a marble courtyard with a staircase marching upward into the bureaucratic chambers above. The banister is guarded by bronze *conquistadores,* their swords beaten into lampposts instead of plowshares. The mural on the wall, by Mario Orozco Rivera, depicts a family overcoming ignorance and injustice. Note the gory figure on the left—no smooching here. Nearby, the terraces of **Parque Juárez,** built in 1892, share their view of the city and mountains with a small café. Carefully cut hedges line the walkways and enclose beds of flowers. In order to enjoy the view from the terrace, you may have to dodge the droves of young lovers who congregate here in the evenings like nighthawks circling a street light. Blame it on the sun, the mountains, the university, whatever—if the sight of so much liplocking makes you feel lonely, go smooch the luscious lips on an Olmec head.

## ENTERTAINMENT

Jalapa is bursting with cultural opportunities. Ask at the State Tourist office or the bus station kiosk, or pick up a copy of a local newspaper for information about concerts, dance, and theater. The **Agora de la Ciudad** cultural center, located at the bottom of the stairs in the Parque Juárez (tel. 18-57-30), has a screening room, gallery space, and loads of information and schedules about local events. The **Teatro del Estado** (tel. 17-31-10), a 10-minute walk east of Parque Juárez on Enríquez/ Camacho, at the corner of Ignacio de la Llave, holds enticing performances—the **Orquesta Sinfónica de Jalapa** and the **Ballet Folklórico de la Universidad Veracruzana** appear regularly. A city with more than 6,000 students, Jalapa is also one of the major destinations in Mexico for aspiring artists. **La Unidad de Artes,** Belisario Domínguez 25, posts announcements of exhibitions, plays, and recitals by students.

On weeknights, life is lived in the cafés along Enríquez and Zaragoza. The newly opened **Tierra Luna,** Diego Leño 28 (tel. 12-13-01), brews a great *capuchino* (4.50 pesos) and has frequent live music for its young clientele's listening pleasure (open Tues.-Thurs. 8am-10pm, Fri.-Sat. 8am-11pm, Sun. 10am-6pm). Jalapa is also rife with movie theaters, including **Cine Jalapa,** Camacho 8, which shows first-run movies from abroad. As the weekend approaches, however, people migrate from café tables to bars and dance floors around the city. The best deal in town is **La Sopa,** an artists' hangout offering live music Wed.-Sat. nights (no cover). Also located near the *centro* are **B42** (tel. 12-08-93) on Camacho just west of Parque Juárez—follow the lines of people. A popular disco, it plays music for all tastes for just a 15-peso cover.

**7a Estación,** 20 de Noviembre 57 (tel. 17-31-55), located just below the bus station, is a disco favored by locals and tourists alike. From 8-10pm get in free; afterwards the cover is 15 pesos (open Mon.-Sat.). Local students say the best place to hang out is the **Plaza Crystal** on Av. Lázaro Cárdenas, a mall featuring several bars, including **Next,** which offers pool, darts, table hockey, and disco. **Fandango** and **Escape,** across the street from Plaza Crystal on Garibaldi, are particularly favored by the younger crowd. To get to the Plaza Crystal, take a bus marked "Sumidero" or "Circunvalación" from the bus stop on Zaragoza, located down the stairs on the left side of the Parque Juárez. Be prepared to take a cab back, however; the buses will probably stop running before you do.

# ■ NEAR JALAPA

## COATEPEC

A colonial town located just 8km from Jalapa, **Coatepec** makes for both an easy escape from the hustle and bustle of downtown Jalapa and a rest stop on the way to Xico. Renowned for an odd combination of orchids, coffee, and ice cream, Coatepec's *zócalo* is ringed with cafés and *heladerías* (ice cream stores) serving up dozens of exotic flavors. Walk along Cuauhtémoc, off of Aldama, if you want to pack up some of that famous coffee and take it home—the street is overflowing with small shops eager to sell it to you. As for the orchids, at **Inverandero María Cristina,** Miguel Rebolledo 4 (tel 16-03-79), by the *zócalo,* you can watch the flowers grow and even buy one of your very own (70 pesos).

**Getting There:** To get to Coatepec, take a bus marked "Terminal" from the eastern stop on Enríquez in front of the 3 Hermanos shoe store (1.20 pesos). Get off at the Excelsior Terminal, a roundabout lined with buses about 10 minutes away from the city center. From there, catch a bus marked "Coatepec." The trip takes about 20 minutes and will let you off at the Excelsior station next to Coatepec's *zócalo.*

## XICO AND CASCADA DE TEXOLO

**Xico,** located 19km from Jalapa, is a rustic foothill town even further removed from the frantic pace of Jalapa's jam-packed streets; here, there are almost as many mules on the road as there are automobiles. Xico is known for its cuisine (*mole xiqueño* can be found on many menus throughout Jalapa) and its nine-day festival dedicated to the town's patron saint, Mary Magdalene, which begins on July 22. During the festival, Xico adorns itself for events including bullfights and a running of the bulls.

The **Cascada de Texolo** (Texolo Falls), located 3km from Xico, is perhaps the town's main attraction and its strongest asset. Immortalized in the film *Romancing the Stone,* the dramatic waterfall crashes in a gorge alive with vivid greenery, the songs of passing birds, and the constant drum of water as it spills into the river below. There is a restaurant and viewing area across from the falls; a bridge leads to the other side of the gorge, where several paths yield stunning views of other waterfalls and the area's lush vegetation.

**Getting There:** To get to Xico from Jalapa, take a bus marked "Terminal" from the stop on Enríquez to the Excelsior Terminal about 10 minutes away (1.20 pesos). From there, take a "Xico" bus (45min., 2.50 pesos). From Coatepec, take a bus marked "Xico" from the bus stop at the corner of Juárez and Cuauhtémoc. (From the Excelsior stop, cross the *zócalo* and continue one more block. Turn left on Av. Juárez.) The ride costs 1.20 pesos and lasts 20 minutes.

To get to the falls, start from the blue sign that says "Entrada de la Ciudad" at the entrance to Xico and walk up the hill, going left of the restaurant located at the fork in the road. At the top of the hill, turn left and continue walking along this road as it descends from the town into a coffee plantation. Quite a ways into the journey, you will come to another fork in the road; bear right and continue until the falls' restaurant comes into view. To get back to Xico, you can either hoof it all the way up or ask the restaurant owner to drive you for 12 pesos—that's *his* taxi parked outside. Buses for Jalapa depart from both Xico's *zócalo* and the city's entrance (2.50 pesos).

# ■■■ TUXPAN (TUXPAM)

As the sun rises over the Río Tuxpan, boats of fishermen set out for the day. Much like their Olmec, Huastec, and Totonac predecessors almost 500 years ago, boys standing on the shore fling their nets into the water, draw them back, and fling them out again. The scent of freshly caught *mariscos* pervades Tuxpan's markets, and occasional breezes carry the salty smell of sea far inland. Fruit vendors traverse the streets near the riverfront, selling bananas and mangos by the bag. Framed by smokestacks bellowing clouds of gray waste, Tuxpan's active *centro* can sometimes seem overwhelming. But relief is at hand: Playa Azul is just 12km away. On weekends, the beach overflows with families splashing about and digging in the sand.

**Orientation** Tuxpan is 347km northeast of Veracruz and 328km northwest of Mexico City via Rte. 130. Rte. 180 connects Tuxpan and Papantla and continues north to Tampico. The city spreads along the northern bank of Río Tuxpan; activity is concentrated on two park-like plazas, **Parque Rodríguez Cano** and **Parque Reforma.** The streets do not follow the cardinal directions, but remember that the bridge lies on the eastern edge of town. Streets perpendicular to the bridge and parallel to the water run roughly east-west. Parque Rodríguez Cano is on the waterfront, just south of the busiest part of town; it is bordered by the white cathedral to the west and, on its north side, the yellow **Presidencia Municipal.** The larger **Parque Reforma** is between Juárez and Madero, four blocks west up Juárez and one block inland from Rodríguez Cano. **Humboldt,** lined with shops and restaurants, forms its eastern boundary. From the **ADO bus station,** head left 50m to the water, and then right (west) along Reyes Heroles for three blocks; you will be at Parque Rodríguez Cano. Walk one block north back to Juárez, then left (west) three blocks and *viola!* Parque Reforma is on your right. To get to the beach, take the "Playa" bus east from the riverfront road from the bench along the boardwalk by the ferry station, just across from Parque Cano (every 10min., 6am-8:30pm, 2.50 pesos).

**Practical Information** The **tourist office** (tel. 4-03-22 or 4-01-77) is in the Palacio Municipal, Juárez 20, in Parque Rodríguez Cano. Enter on the Juárez side—it's a small, unmarked office across from Hotel Florida offering no maps but some brochures and friendly practical information (ostensibly open Mon.-Sat. 8am-3pm and 4-7pm). The **police** can be found at Galeana 38 (tel. 4-02-52 or 4-37-23), next door to the Red Cross (open 24 hrs.). To reach the **post office,** Clavijero 28 (tel. 4-00-88), walk north under the bridge past the vendors. Continue straight ahead, crossing the wide Cuauhtémoc; Clavijero is the small street running northwest (open Mon.-Fri. 8am-6pm, Sat. 8am-1pm). **Postal Code:** 92800. No LADATELs exist, but many stores in the *centro* offer **long distance telephone service,** including **Papelería La Violeta,** Morelos 21 (tel. 4-38-00; open Mon.-Sat. 9am-2pm and 4-8pm, Sun. 9am-2pm). Pay phones that allow long-distance collect calls are located across from Banco Internacional on Juárez, west of Parque Reforma. A credit card phone in the telegram office takes MC, Visa, and AmEx. **Telecomm,** Ortega 20 (tel. 4-45-43), just beyond the "Pollo Feliz" sign on the left-hand side of the street, provides **telegram** and **fax** service (open Mon.-Fri. 9am-8pm, Sat. 9am-1pm; for money orders Mon.-Fri. 9am-5pm, Sat. 9am-noon). **Telephone Code:** 783. **Bancomer** (tel. 4-12-58) is on Juárez at Zapata (open Mon.-Fri. 9am-1:30pm). For a 24-hour **ATM** that accepts virtually any card, try **Bánamex** (tel. 4-08-40) just southwest of Parque Reforma. There are no *casas de cambio* in Tuxpan.

In Tuxpan, each **bus** line has its own station. **ADO,** Rodríguez 1 (tel. 4-01-02), three blocks east of Parque Cano down Reyes Heroles, has first-class service to Jalapa (7 per day, 6hrs., 57.50 pesos), Mexico City (10 per day, 6hrs., 57 pesos), Papantla (5 per day, 2hrs., 12.50 pesos), Poza Rica (25 per day, 1½hrs., 9 pesos), Tampico (every hr., 3hrs., 41 pesos), and Veracruz (8 per day, 6hrs., 76.50 pesos). **Estrella Blanca,** Cuauhtémoc 18 (tel. 4-20-40), two blocks past the bridge, a left on Constitución, and then three blocks west. Offers second-class service to Guadalajara

(5 per day, 20hrs., 134 pesos), Mexico City (9 per day, 8hrs., 57 pesos), Monterrey (7 per day, 125 pesos), Tampico (every hr., 5hrs., 38 pesos), and nearly all points in between. Buses tend to run off schedule; call or stop by to confirm departure times. **Omnibus de México,** Vicente Guerrero 30 (tel. 4-11-45), at the bridge, has first-class service to Mexico City (7 per day, 6hrs., 57 pesos), Querétaro (6pm, 8hrs., 83 pesos), and Tampico (9:15am and 5:15pm, 3hrs., 41pesos).

**Mercado Rodríguez Cano,** west of and diagonally across from the ADO station, sells fruits, fish, clothing, and souvenirs (open roughly 9am-6pm). **Farmacia Popular,** Independencia 4 (tel. 4-03-11), is on the riverfront side of the market (open 24 hrs.). The **Red Cross,** Galeana 40 (tel. 4-01-58), is eight blocks west of *el centro* along the river, next to the police station (24-hr. emergency ambulance service). **Hospital Emilio Alcar,** Obregón 13 (tel. 4-01-99), is one block west of the bridge, then a block and a half inland and up the inclined driveway on the right. No English spoken (open 24 hrs.). In an **emergency,** dial 06.

## Accommodations
Budget accommodations in Tuxpan are concentrated near the two central parks, ensuring a reasonable measure of safety into the evening hours. **Hotel Parroquia,** Escuela Militar 4 (tel. 4-16-30), to the left of the cathedral on Parque Rodríguez Cano. Rooms with spacious bathrooms and windows open onto balconies overlooking the park and river—all at one of the cheapest places in town. Full-length mirror and fan provide those little extras (singles 46 pesos; doubles 57.50 pesos). **Hotel El Huasteco,** Morelos 41 (tel. 4-18-59), is half a block east from the northeast corner of Parque Reforma. While the small, windowless rooms are not easy on the claustrophobic, impeccable cleanliness and functioning A/C more than compensate (singles 52 pesos; doubles 68 pesos). **Hotel del Parque,** Humboldt 11 (tel. 4-08-12), on the east side of Parque Reforma, puts you right in the thick of things if you can deal with a little noise—the hotel is right above a gym/Tae Kwon Do studio. Tiled floors lead to drab rooms. Some have a gorgeous view of the plaza, some have seatless toilets, some have both (singles and doubles 50 pesos).

## Food
As the battle has already been lost, it's hardly worth heading for the hills: soulless hotel cafeterias have colonized Tuxpan. Most of the cafeterias serve *antojitos mexicanos* and seafood; the drab culinary landscape is brightened only by a few pizza joints. Decorated with a sea motif, **Barra de Mariscos del Puerto** (tel. 4-46-01), at Juárez and Humboldt across from the southeast corner of Parque Reforma, offers *parrillada de mariscos,* a veritable seafood menagerie that for 30 pesos can feed two (open daily 8am-midnight). In a dramatic departure from Tuxpan's culinary heritage, **Pizzas Cat's,** Juárez 44 (tel. 4-73-86), offers some interesting variations on traditional Italian dishes to its under-25 clientele. Popular items include *spagueti* (5 pesos) and the *pizza española* (17 pesos; open daily 7am-10pm). Crowded during the day, the open-air **Cafetería El Mante,** Juárez 8 (tel. 4-57-36), one block west of Rodríguez, boasts a clientele nearly as large as O.J.'s defense team. Enjoy *enfrijoladas con bistek* (15 pesos) or the many regional *antojitos* (5-12 pesos) while soaking in the warm glow from bright orange tablecloths—or from the steamy love scenes in the ever-present *telenovelas.*

## Sights and Entertainment
*Tuxpeños* are justly proud of their river's relaxed beauty and scenic shores. Palm trees and benches line the boardwalk, which parallels the water and offers views of the men and women hauling in the day's catch. Goods are sold up and down the river; under the bridge, piles of pineapples, bananas, shrimp, and fish can be had for a bare minimum at the huge open-air market which flows from the indoor market on Calle Rodríguez. Located on the waterfront, the reposeful **Parque Rodríguez Cano** comes alive every Monday at 5:30pm for the **Ceremonia Cívica,** when government officials make speeches and schoolchildren march in an orderly procession. On the west side of the Parque Reforma is the **Museo Regional de Antropología e Historia.** Located inside the Casa de la Cultura, the museum showcases Huastec and Totonac carvings, figurines, and

other archaeological remnants. Most of the introductory information is in Spanish (open Tues.-Sun. 10am-2pm and 4-6pm; free).

Twelve kilometers from the city center, Tuxpan's **beach** can be crowded and slightly dirty, especially in the high season, but the wide expanse of fine sand continues far enough for you to stake a private claim somewhere down the line. Buses (2.50 pesos) marked "Playa" leave Tuxpan for the beach every 15 minutes from 6am-10pm; the last bus returns to Tuxpan at 8:30pm.

Though there are a number of **bars** in Tuxpan's *centro,* the best nightlife in town can be found a few blocks down the river after the crowds in the Parque Reforma thin out. **Mantarraya,** Reyes Heroles at Guerrero (tel. 4-22-04) keeps the young crowd hopping to American pop and techno hits (cover 20 pesos, including 2 drinks). Just past Allende on Reyes Heroles, facing the river, **La Puesta del Sol** (tel. 4-73-66) serves food, beer, and mixed drinks to quiet customers enjoying the live music, both tropical and *salsa.* A block away is the classy **Charlôt** (tel. 4-40-28), which serves appetizers and drinks both indoors and out (open Tues.-Sun. noon-midnight). Turn right on Pérez to find the glowing neon entrance of **La Bamba** (tel. 4-62-09), a high-tech bar featuring large-screen music video entertainment and serving cocktails and beers by the bucket to a professional crowd.

---

### ¡Viva la Revolución!

Get in touch with the power-hungry dictator in you at the **Casa de la Amistad México-Cuba.** You might expect a glowing tribute to Mexico-Cuba relations; brace yourself. The museum is an unmediated and unqualified exaltation of the life of Fidel Castro, from his stay in Tuxpan to his rise to power in Cuba. Containing a map of Fidel's journey aboard the *Granma* to Cuba in 1953, an old warehouse serves as the first "gallery." Photographs of a macho, young, beardless Fidel line the walls. Nearby is the *pièce de résistance,* a colorful mural depicting a valiant Fidel leading his fellow boatsmen to victory under the watchful gaze of good guys Benito Juárez, José Martí, and Simón Bolívar. Atop the stairs is a room containing photographs of crowds in Havana and Fidel at the U.N. The final room on the caretaker's tour is propaganda central—pictures of doctors and farmers symbolizing Cuba's social progress, as well as a proud look back through the guestbook and the diverse crop of visitors expressing support for the Cuban Revolution. To get to the museum, take a blue ferry (.70 pesos) across the river. Walk right (west) along the sidewalk and continue straight up the dirt road, past the overgrowth to the paved sidewalk, and turn left and enter to the side of the two small white building with the boat out front (open daily 9am-2pm and 3-7pm; free, but donations are requested, of course).

---

# ■■■ PAPANTLA

Crawling up the green foothills of the Sierra Madre Oriental, Papantla (pop. 125,000) looks out onto the magnificent plains of Northern Veracruz. The town's hilly topography and *indígena* vibrance preserve an as-yet-unspoiled look into the pre-colonial past of Mexico. Papantla is one of the few remaining bastions of Totonac culture, a living testament to a civilization that once dominated the northern half of what is now Veracruz. The Totonacs were conquered by the power-hungry Aztecs around 1450, but the vanquished soon took their revenge. With assistance from the Totonacs, Cortés crushed the Aztec Empire in the 16th century—but Totonacs fared little better under Spanish rule. The culture managed to persist here, however, and when Totonac rebels rose in 1836, Papantla was their stronghold. Today, ancient rituals persist in the flight of the *voladores,* a thrilling acrobatic ceremony once laden with religious meaning, now performed for the benefit of delighted tourists and enshrined in a huge statue overlooking the city. The noisy *zócalo* is crowded with locals, while *indígenas* continue to don traditional dress: men wear wide white bloomers, women lacy white skirts and embroidered blouses with shawls.

The city also makes a terrific base for exploring **El Tajín,** the ruins of the Totonac capital and one of the most impressive archaeological sites in the Republic. The ruins are 12km south of the city (see page 333).

**Orientation** Papantla lies 250km northwest of Veracruz and 21km southeast of Poza Rica along Rte. 180. Downtown hustle and bustle centers around **Parque Téllez,** the white-tiled plaza. The cathedral rises on its southern side while **Enríquez** borders on the north. Sloping downhill to the north are **Juárez** (on the east side) and **20 de Noviembre** (on the west side), both perpendicular to Enríquez. To get from the ADO station to *el centro,* turn left onto Juárez out of the station and veer left at the fork. Taxis (4 pesos to the *centro*) pass frequently along Juárez. If you arrive at the second-class bus station, turn left outside the station and ascend 20 de Noviembre three blocks to the northwest corner of the plaza.

**Practical Information** Elusive tourist officials keep their distance from the **tourist office** (tel. 2-01-23), on the second floor of the **Palacio Municipal,** on the west side of the plaza (supposedly open Mon.-Fri. 10am-4pm and 6-8pm). More helpful with practical information is the **Chamber of Commerce,** Ramón Castaneda 100 (tel. 2-00-25). Follow Lázaro Muño (the narrow street running east from the plaza) four blocks downhill and turn right (uphill) for 1½ blocks (open Mon.-Fri. 10am-2pm and 4-8pm, Sat. noon-8pm). **Police** (tel. 2-00-75 or 2-01-50) are in the Palacio Municipal (open 24 hrs.). The **post office,** Azueta 198, second floor (tel. 2-00-73), posts a *Lista de Correos* (open Mon.-Fri. 9am-1pm and 4-7pm, Sat. 9am-noon; for registered mail Mon.-Fri. 9am-1pm and 3-5pm). **Postal Code:** 93400. The pharmacy on the eastern side of the plaza has **LADATEL** service; collect calls 7 pesos (open daily 9am-10pm). **Hotel Tajín,** Nuñez y Domínguez 104 (tel. 2-10-62), charges 15 pesos for collect calls (open 24 hrs.). **Telephone Code:** 784. The **telegram office** is located at Enríquez 404 (tel. 2-05-84), about five blocks east of the *zócalo* (open for telegrams Mon.-Fri. 9am-8pm, Sat. 9am-noon; for **money orders** Mon.-Fri. 9am-1pm and 3-5pm, Sat. 9am-noon). **Bánamex** (tel. 2-00-01), Enríquez 102, exchanges currency and has a 24-hr. **ATM** for MC, Visa, Cirrus, and Plus (open Mon.-Fri. 9am-1:30pm).

Papantla has two **bus stations.** The first-class **ADO** station, Juárez 207 (tel. 2-02-18) serves Jalapa (8 per day, 4hrs., 44.50 pesos), Mexico City (5 per day in the evening, 6hrs., 51 pesos), Tuxpan (3 per day, 2hrs., 12 pesos), and Veracruz (5 per day, 4hrs., 46.50 pesos). The second-class terminal, commonly called **Transportes Papantla,** 20 de Noviembre 200, offers frequent service to Poza Rica (every 10-15min., 6am-11:30pm, 35min., 4 pesos). Pay after boarding.

**Poza Rica** (21km northwest of Papantla) is a nearby transportation hub. Their **ADO** station (tel. 2-04-29 or 2-00-85) runs buses to Jalapa (16 per day, 4hrs., 48.50 pesos), Mexico City (22 per day, 5½hrs., 47 pesos), Papantla (18 per day, 30min., 4 pesos), Tuxpan (33 per day, 1½hrs., 9 pesos), Veracruz (15 daily, 4½hrs., 49.50 pesos), and Villahermosa (9 per day, 12hrs., 148 pesos).

The **Red Cross** (tel. 2-01-26) is on Pino Suárez, at Juárez (open 24 hrs.). **Farmacia Aparicio,** Enríquez 101-E (tel. 2-02-68), is on the northern border of the plaza (open daily 7am-10pm). **Clínica IMSS** (tel. 2-01-94), 20 de Noviembre at Lázaro Cárdenas, provides emergency medical assistance. From the ADO station, take a right and walk two blocks to Cárdenas (no sign except "Clínica IMSS"), then turn left; IMSS is half a block up on your right (open 24 hrs.).

**Accommodations** Few accommodations are available in tiny Papantla. **Hotel Tajín,** Nuñez y Domínguez 104 (tel. 2-01-21), half a block to the left as you face the cathedral, displays in its lobby a carved stone wall from El Tajín. Perched on a hill above the city, balconies and lounge areas afford panoramic views. Amenities include bottled water, black-and-white TVs, and phones. Laundry service available (singles 69 pesos, 93 pesos with A/C; doubles 93 pesos, 120 pesos with A/C). The dark rooms and crusty bathrooms of **Hotel Pulido,** Enríquez 205 (tel. 2-00-36), are enlivened (sort of) by fans, flowery sheets, and amusing curtains. The hotel's court-yard/parking lot is a noisy social center late into the night; ask for a second-floor room away from the cars revvin' their engines until the wee hours (singles 40 pesos; doubles 60 pesos). Large glass windows and a curious combination of bold colors lends an Brady-esque feel to **Hotel Totanacapán,** 20 de Noviembre at Olivo (tel. 2-12-24 or 2-12-18), four blocks down from the plaza. Hallway murals are quite pleas-ant, but the ever-vigilant Carol Brady would have replaced some of the furniture by now (singles 70 pesos, 90 pesos with A/C; doubles 90 pesos, 110 with A/C).

**Food** Papantla's few restaurants serve regional delicacies to tourists looking for the real thing. Most eateries, in celebration of Papantla's traditional role as a live-stock center, stick to beef and pork offerings with just a smattering of seafood. **Res-taurant Tajín,** Jesús Nuñez y Domínguez 104, half a block east of the cathedral, serves up a homey atmosphere complete with flowers and numerous pictures of El Tajín. Breakfast specials 8-12 pesos, *comida corrida* 12 pesos (open daily 7am-10pm). Large murals of early colonial settlers and a view of the plaza enliven **Sor-rento,** Enríquez 105 (tel. 2-00-67), a popular tourist hangout for breakfast. Meal spe-cials include *camarones fritos* (14 pesos) and steak *enchiladas* (12 pesos; open daily 7am-10pm). Nearby is the **Restaurant Enrique,** Enríquez 103 (tel. 2-16-45), just across from the main entrance to the cathedral, which serves fairly expensive and fairly fancy seafood. *Casuela de mariscos* is a tasty and tempting dish prepared in a clay western pot (25 pesos; open daily 10am-6pm).

**Sights and Entertainment** Papantla's biggest attractions are the relics of its Totonac heritage. South of the plaza is the **Catedral Señora de la Asunción,** remarkable not so much for its interior, which houses four large murals of Christ's life and death, but for the stone mural carved into its northern wall, measuring 50m long and 5m high. Called **Homenaje a la Cultura Totonaca,** the mural was created by Teodoro Cano to honor local Totonac heroes and folklore figures. Its focus is the plumed serpent Quetzalcóatl, whose image runs along the full length of the carving. At the far left of the mural is a representation of the Dios del Trueno (god of thun-der), who announces the coming of the rains. From left to right, the mural follows a rough chronological outline, moving from the mythical first family of the Totonacs to the discovery of corn, which represented an end to the group's nomadic lifestyle and established Totonac agricultural civilization. The mural moves on to depict the Pyramid of the Niches, the focal point of El Tajín, flanked by faces with characteris-tic round cheeks, smallish noses, and smiles. Next, the ballplayers from the courts of El Tajín vie for the right to ritualistic death and deification. Six faces belonging to fig-ures important in the history of Papantla are carved near the god's open jaw. These six individuals are Serafín Olarte, a Totonac leader; Simón Tiburcio, a Mexican colo-nel; Vicente Herrera Hernández, a Mexican general; Jorge de Castro Cancio, a pro-fessor; Gildardo Muñoz, a poet; and Celestino Patiño Pérez, a linguist.

The cathedral's spacious courtyard commands a view of the *zócalo.* Called the **Plaza de los Voladores,** the courtyard is the site of the ceremony in which *vola-dores* acrobatically entreat the rain god Tlaloc to water the year's crops. In early June, during the 10-day **Festival of Corpus Christi,** the *voladores* perform as often as thrice a day. During the festival, Papantla comes alive with artistic expositions, fireworks, traditional dances, and cockfights.

Papantla's latest effort to enshrine its *voladores* is the **Monumento al Volador,** a gigantic flute-wielding *indígena* statue erected in 1988 atop a hill and visible from all over town. To get to the monument, where you can read explanatory plaques and see Papantla in its entirety, walk up Reforma along the right side of the cathe-dral and up the narrow alleyway, following the road as it curves left; then make a sharp left before the road starts to slope down and walk uphill.

A time-worn mural decorates the inside of the *zócalo*'s centerpiece, a domed kiosk. Painted by Arturo Cano in the 1960s, the mural represents the Totonac conception of creation. The four cardinal points are personified as warriors, each representing different natural calamities that have befallen Mesoamericans. The *zócalo* is furnished with a set of benches inlaid with mosaics and framing small paintings of the Totonacs rendered in a style typical of northern Veracruz.

The town's two markets are situated next to the central plaza. **Mercado Juárez,** at Reforma and 16 de Septiembre, off the southwest corner of the *zócalo,* specializes in poultry and veggies but is neither particularly colorful nor low-priced. **Mercado Hidalgo,** on 20 de Noviembre, off the *zócalo*'s northwest corner on a small triangular block, vends more arts and crafts items than can be found at Juárez; look for regional foods as well as traditional handmade clothing. You'll find both men's garb (striking white sailor shirts and baggy white pants) and women's clothing (white or light-colored dresses, intricately embroidered near the shoulders and neck).

# ■■■ EL TAJÍN

The impressive ruins of El Tajín only hint at the thriving Totonac civilization that once spread across modern-day northern Veracruz. Named for the Totonac god of thunder, El Tajín served as the political and religious center of the Totonac people. Marked similarities between buildings at this site and those at Teotihuacán reflect the influence of Aztec and Mayan practice. A modern concrete building welcomes visitors to the ruins, as do hordes of eager vendors. Just by the entrance stands a large pole, the apparatus of the *voladores.* June through August, the *voladores* perform almost hourly; the rest of the year, they descend through the air only on weekends. The daring acrobats—who typically request a ten-peso donation when they are through—generally perform after a large group has finished touring the ruins. A **museum** near the entrance to the ruins displays pottery and carvings discovered at El Tajín, but most of the plaques lack explanatory information.

From the museum building, a straight gravel path leads to the ruins themselves. Off to the right and under a shady half-canopy of trees stand several introductory plaques. Other plaques, written in Spanish, English, French, German, and Totonac are scattered throughout the site, although many are vague, even unreadable. The best sources of information are the blue uniformed "rangers" stationed throughout El Tajín. Native Totonacs themselves, the rangers may offer to give you an *ad hoc* tour of a certain area and will eagerly answer any questions you pose, although their English proficiency is limited.

The **Plaza del Arroyo,** the central rectangular plaza formed by four tiered pyramids, lies just to the left of the gravel road. Each pyramid is pointed toward the northeast at a 20° angle, in a feat of architectural planning maintained in all the early buildings at this site. The heart of El Tajín is just past the pyramids. Two identical, low-lying, slanted constructions to the left of the observation area form a central ballcourt in which the famous one-on-one game called **pok-ta-pok** was played. While the game vaguely resembled soccer, feet weren't allowed to make contact with the ball. Every 52 years, a contest was held between the most valiant ballplayers; the winner won the honor of offering his heart for sacrifice. Another I-shaped court can be seen north of the eastern pyramid.

Across from the plaza is an elevated central altar surrounded by dark, black stone temples; two of these temples can be climbed. Just left of the altar is a split-level temple that displays a statue of Tajín, the god of thunder. This area was known as the **Central Zone,** and is unique because the styles and functions of the buildings here vary considerably. To the northwest stands **El Pirámide de los Nichos,** a fascinating structure with seven levels and a total of 365 niches corresponding to the days of the year. Each niche was once painted in red and blue. The Totonacs marked time in 52-year epochs, during which a single flame was kept continuously burning. At the end of each epoch, the carefully nurtured flame was used to ritually torch many of the settlement's buildings. Each new epoch of rebuilding and regeneration was inaugurated by the lighting of a new flame. Today, ritual ceremonies are held annually at the pyramid, at the vernal equinox. Farmers place seeds in the niches and later retrieve them for planting.

Farther north and atop a hill is **Tajín Chico,** accessible either by a series of large stepping stones or an easy-to-ascend staircase off to the west. Whereas Tajín was a public religious and social center, archaeologists hypothesize that Tajín Chico was where the ruling class and political elite actually lived. Newly uncovered in the Tajín Chico area is **Building I,** where several colored paintings, representing different gods from the Tajín pantheon, are visible. While some buildings here are in good condition, most have yet to be excavated and are off-limits to the public. As a result, park officials don't mind if visitors scamper up the higher buildings to get a view of the site and surrounding hills. A good deal north of Tajín Chico is a partially unearthed palace for the god Tajín; its façade displays a Mayan-influenced arch of great interest to scholars retracing patterns of cross-cultural interaction in Mesoamerica. One of the buildings just to the northwest, which may soon be open to visitors, is the **Complex of the Columns,** where an account was found of some-one called 13-Rabbit, likely a religious leader. East of Tajín Chico, down the hill and around the curve in the gravel road, is the **Great Xicalcoliuhqui,** a tremendous recreational area still being unearthed.

The entrance to El Tajín site is beside the "Archaeological Zone" billboard and 300m down the access road off Rte. 180. (Site open daily 9am-5pm. Admission 16 pesos, Sun. and holidays free. Mexican students get in free; flash your student ID if you have one.) Bring lots of water; the sun here can be merciless. Brochures about El Tajín are distributed at the Tuxpan and Papantla tourist offices.

**Getting There:** El Tajín is accessible via *pesera* from the bus stop in Papantla on Calle 16 de Septiembre, one block east of the cathedral's southeast corner. Buses run on the half-hour (roughly) and cost 2.50 pesos. The bus will first pass through El Chote and then stop at the entrance to El Tajín. To return to Papantla, walk down the access road to the main highway. Cross the road to the bus stop to catch a *pesera* running back to Papantla (2.50 pesos). Service is also available from the **Transportes Papantla** second-class terminal in Papantla; from here it's necessary to go through El Chote and switch buses before arriving at the site.

---

### Los Voladores of Papantla

Papantla's *voladores* are renowned for their graceful acrobatics. The performance begins with five elaborately costumed men climbing a stationary pole to a platform about 20m above the ground. Having consumed courage-enhancing fluids, four of the hardy five start to "fly"—hanging by their feet from ropes wound around the pole, spinning through the air and slowly descending to earth. Meanwhile, the fifth man plays a flute and dances on the pole's pin-head. Originally, each of the four fliers corresponded to one of the four cardinal directions; positions assumed during descent were related to requests for specific weather conditions. Lately, however, the performance has lost its meteorological significance and has been subjugated to commercial exigencies like so many other expressions of *indígena* religion. Instead of performing once every 52 years, the *voladores* now fly as often as tourists can afford to feed them pesos.

---

# ■■■ VERACRUZ

The oldest port city in the Americas swelters in colonial decay and modern resurrection. Cortés landed here on Good Friday, 1519, christened the city "La Rica Villa de la Vera Cruz," and marched on to conquer the Aztec empire. Since then, Veracruz has been a place where Mexico has rubbed up against the rest of the world. The city prospered as the only port in New Spain officially permitted to trade with the mother country. It supported the liberals of the fledgling Republic who sought to open Mexico to European trade and influence. It was here that Juárez proclaimed

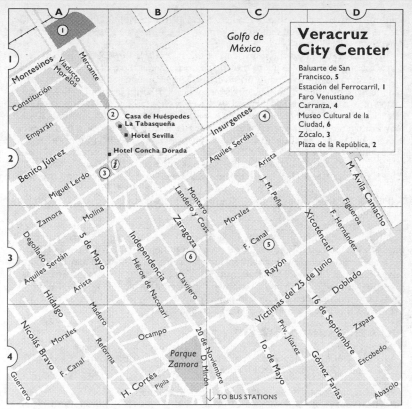

the laws of the Reforma, and here that he staged the reconquest of Mexico from the Hapsburg Emperor Maximilian. Twice the city was occupied by American troops, first in 1847 during the Mexican-American War, and again in 1916, when Woodrow Wilson feared German arms were on their way to Mexico's conservative president.

Today Veracruz's streets continue to fill with sailors—as well as tourists—from around the world. Modern Veracruz (pop. 327,500) sprawls along Mexico's Gulf coast, merging gracefully with **Boca del Río** (pop. 143,800), the prosperous home of the area's best beach and most chic discos. A hot, humid urban sprawl that drips with sweat into the night, the twin cities are buffeted by strong winds called *nortes,* a display of nature's force which some people find disagreeable and others spectacular. What impresses visitors even more, however, is something distinctively *veracruzana*—the nearly untranslatable qualities of *sabor,* rich and alluring flavor, and *ambiente,* unique and enchanting atmosphere.

## ORIENTATION

Veracruz lies on the southwestern shore of the Gulf of Mexico. Tampico is 421km to the north via Route 180; Jalapa, the state capital, sits 140km inland via Route 140; Puebla and Mexico City are due west on Route 150, 304km and 421km respectively; Oaxaca is 421km to the south.

Veracruz's **Central de Autobuses** houses both the first- and second-class bus stations. First-class ADO lies directly on Díaz Mirón, the city's major crosstown street. Second-class AU opens onto La Fragua, one block to the east. Both stations are located 14 blocks south of **Parque Zamora,** where Díaz Mirón feeds into Independencia, the main downtown drag. The *zócalo* lies on Independencia, seven blocks

**VERACRUZ**

south of Parque Zamora. Buses labeled "Díaz Mirón" travel along Díaz Mirón to Parque Zamora and points farther downtown (1.40 pesos). Taxis will take you downtown for 6.50 pesos.

The **train station** is at the north end of the Plaza de la República, a square just northeast of the *zócalo*. To get to the *zócalo*, turn right at the exit and walk toward the opposite end of the Plaza in front of you. The Plaza ends at Lerdo; take a right and follow it into the *zócalo*. The city's **airport** is 8km south of town on Route 150.

Downtown Veracruz is laid out grid-style with streets either parallel or perpendicular to the coast. **Díaz Mirón** runs north-south and converges with **Avenida 20 de Noviembre** south of downtown at the **Parque Zamora.** Here, the two streets become **Independencia,** the main downtown drag. Independencia forms the western boundary of the *zócalo*, also called the Plaza de Armas or Plaza de la Constitución. The northern boundary, **Lerdo,** runs east and becomes the southern limit of the **Plaza de la República,** home of the train station and post office, and drop-off point for many municipal bus routes. **Insurgentes,** one block south of the *zócalo* behind the cathedral, runs east into **Camacho;** the two streets serve as Veracruz's waterfront promenade.

The *centro* is generally safe, but visitors should be wary nevertheless. Dress plainly and be careful in giving the name of one's hotel to recent acquaintances—thieves will chum up to tourists in the *zócalo* and then rob them at their hotel. Do not walk far from the downtown-Díaz Mirón area after dark. Women may find themselves the object of more male attention in Veracruz than in smaller towns; this unwanted attention will typically come in the form of invitations to discos and city tours from random men. A firm and polite refusal will be grudgingly accepted during the day, but at night it may well be taken as a challenge to overcome.

## PRACTICAL INFORMATION

**Tourist Office:** (tel. 32-19-99), in the Palacio Municipal on the east side of the *zócalo*. Helpful staff speaks some English. Maps and brochures. Open daily 9am-9pm. **Seguridad Para el Turista** (tel. 91-800-90-392) offers medical and legal services for tourists.

**Police:** (tel. 38-06-64 or 38-06-93), in the Palacio Municipal.

**Post Office:** Pl. de la República 213 (tel. 32-20-38), several blocks north of the *zócalo*. Facing the Palacio Municipal, walk east on Lerdo for two blocks to Aduana, then turn left and walk two blocks to Pl. de la República. Open for stamps and *Lista de Correos* Mon.-Fri. 8am-8pm, Sat. 9am-1pm. **Postal Code:** 91700.

**Telephones: LADATEL** phones on the northeast and southwest corners of the *zócalo*. Booths in El Portal, on the corner of Callejón Miranda and Molina, just southeast of the *zócalo* (tel. 32-22-60). Collect calls 11.50 pesos. Local calls 2 pesos. Open daily 9am-midnight. **Telephone Code:** 29.

**Telegrams:** (tel. 32-25-08) on the Pl. de la República next to the post office. Open Mon.-Fri. 9am-5pm, Sat. 9am-noon. **Fax** and **money orders** also available.

**U.S. Consulate:** Víctimas del 25 de Junio 388 (tel. 31-01-42). On the corner with Gómez Farías, several blocks south of the *zócalo*. Open Mon.-Fri. 9am-1:30pm. The addresses and phone numbers of several other consulates in Veracruz are readily available at the tourist office.

**Currency Exchange: Bancomer,** Independencia at Juárez (tel. 31-00-95), one block north of the *zócalo*. Open Mon.-Fri. 9am-noon. **Bánamex,** on Independencia on the opposite corner (tel. 32-32-00), is open for exchange Mon.-Fri. 9am-1:30pm, and also has an **ATM** that accepts Cirrus and Plus cards. For "friendlier" rates, try **La Amistad Casa de Cambio,** Juárez 112 (tel. 31-24-52), near the banks. Open Mon.-Fri. 9am-6pm. Big hotels will change cash, but it is virtually impossible to change traveler's checks on weekends.

**American Express:** Camacho 222 (tel. 31-45-77), across from Villa del Mar beach. Catch the "Villa del Mar" bus from the corner of Serdán and Zaragoza; the office is on the right. They won't cash traveler's checks, but will hold client mail. Open Mon.-Fri. 9am-1pm and 4-6pm, Sat. 9am-noon.

**Airport:** (tel. 34-00-08), on the highway to Mexico City, 8km south of downtown Veracruz. Both **Aeroméxico** and **Mexicana** are represented by **Viajes Carmi,**

Independencia 837 (tel. 31-27-23), north of the *zócalo*. Open Mon.-Fri. 9am-1:30pm and 3:30-7:30pm, Sat. 9am-1pm. **Aeroméxico** has a separate office at Simón Bolívar 723 (tel. 35-01-42). **Mexicana** also has its own office at the corner of 5 de Mayo and Serdán, northeast of the *zócalo* (tel. 32-22-42). Open Mon.-Fri. 9am-1:30pm and 3:45-7:30pm, Sat. 9:30am-1:15pm. Office at the airport (tel. 38-00-08). Open daily 6am-11pm.

**Train Station: Ferrocarriles Nacionales de México** (tel. 32-33-38), at the north end of the Pl. de la República. First class to Mexico City (10pm, 12hrs., 50 pesos), or second class (7:20, 8:20, and 10am, 28 pesos). Ticket booth open Mon.-Sat. 6-9am, 10-11am and 4-9:30pm. Sun. 6-10am and 7-9:30pm.

**Bus Station:** First-class **ADO** buses leave from Díaz Mirón 1698 (tel. 37-56-77), about 20 blocks south of the *zócalo*. Service to Cancún (10:35pm, 233 pesos), Catemaco (7 per day, 7am-5:15pm, 3hrs., 28 pesos), Jalapa (every 20 min., 6am-11:30pm, 2hrs., 19.50 pesos), Mexico City (every hr., 84 pesos), and Oaxaca (every 15-30 min., 7:15am-8:15pm, 94.50 pesos). Second-class **AU** buses leave from the station on the block behind the ADO station (tel. 37-23-76). Direct service to Córdoba (4:30, 5:30, and 6:30pm, 22.50 pesos), Jalapa (every hr., 2hrs., 16.50 pesos), Mexico City (every hr., 7hrs., 66.50 pesos), and Orizaba (4:30, 5:30, and 6:30pm, 26 pesos), *ordinario* to Puebla (every hr., 51.50 pesos) and Salina Cruz (8:25 and 10:15pm, 74 pesos). **Cristóbal Colón** has first-class service to Oaxaca (11:30pm, 88 pesos) and Tuxtla Gutierrez (6 and 7pm, 109 pesos). **Autotransportes Los Tuxtlas** has second-class service to Catemaco (every 10 min., 3hrs., 22 pesos), San Andrés Tuxtla (every 10 min., 2¾hrs., 21 pesos), and Santiago Tuxtla (every 10 min., 2½hrs., 19 pesos).

**Taxis: Taxis Por Teléfono de Veracruz** (tel. 34-62-99) will send you a taxi at a higher price than if you flag one down yourself. Veracruz is divided into zones, with set fares for taxi travel between them. Fares outside zones are negotiable.

**Car Rentals: Fuster,** Blvd. Ávila Camacho 1291 (tel. 32-81-47; fax 32-81-48). Small VW for 90 pesos per day, plus .70 pesos per km under 100km. Open daily 8am-8pm. **Fast Auto,** Lerdo 245 (tel. 31-83-29), just west of the *zócalo*. VW for 155.77 pesos, including insurance and 100km. Open Mon.-Sat. 6am-7pm, Sun. 9am-1pm.

**Cultural Center: Instituto Veracruzana de la Cultura,** in a purple building on the corner of Canaland Zaragoza. Houses visiting artistic exhibitions of all kinds. Bulletin board with announcements of city-wide events. Open Mon.-Fri. 9am-9pm, Sat. 9am-7pm, Sun. 10am-noon. Free.

**Supermarket: Chedraui,** Díaz Mirón 440 (tel. 31-42-75), four blocks south of Parque Zamora on the way to the ADO station. Open 8am-9pm.

**Laundromat: Lavandería Automática Mar y Sol,** Madero 572, near the intersection with Serdán. 3kg washed and dried for 14 pesos for same-day service, 10 pesos for next-day pick-up. Open Mon.-Fri. 9am-2pm and 4-8pm, Sat. 9am-5pm.

**Red Cross:** (tel. 37-55-00), on Díaz Mirón between Orizaba and Pérez Abascal, one block south of the Central de Autobuses. No English spoken. 24-hr. emergency service and ambulance on call.

**Pharmacy: Farmacia El Mercado,** Independencia 1197 (tel. 32-08-83). Open daily 7am-2am.

**Hospital: Hospital del IMSS,** Díaz Mirón 61 (tel 22-19-20) or the **Hospital Regional,** 20 de Noviembre 284 (tel 32-36-90).

**Emergency:** Dial 06.

## ACCOMMODATIONS

Veracruz has three peak seasons: *Carnaval* (the week before Ash Wednesday), *Semana Santa* (the week before Easter), and summer vacation (July and August). The city is full of hotels, but many fill up well in advance during the first two peak periods, and some change their rates during some or all of them. At other times, reservations are necessary but prices are relatively affordable. Rooms with ceiling fans or large windows are commonplace and not so pricey, but you'll have to scrape out the insides of your wallet to get a room with air conditioning.

## Downtown Area

These hotels are either on the *zócalo* or around the corner to the northeast, on Morelos. Some inexpensive hotels on the *zócalo* may be patronized by couples without baggage. The area is full of revelers all night every night, and is therefore fun, loud, and relatively safe.

**Hotel Concha Dorada,** Lerdo 77 (tel. 31-29-96), right above the east end of *zócalo* bars. Spotless. Recently remodeled, with a TV and a telephone in every room. Intemperate revelers can dive from the window of a plaster-and-pastel bedroom right onto a *marimba* in the *zócalo* below. Singles 69 pesos with fan, 80 with A/C. Doubles 75 pesos with fan, 92 with A/C.

**Hotel Sevilla,** Morelos 359 (tel. 32-42-46), at the intersection with Lerdo. Corner double rooms are a bargain in the off-season, receiving refreshing cross-breezes (and cross-*marimba*). Large rooms have a color TV and ceiling fan, but few have toilet seats. In some rooms, the paint is divorcing itself from the walls. A/C 15 pesos extra. Singles 50 pesos, 95 pesos during *Carnaval* and *Semana Santa*. Doubles 75 pesos, 115 pesos during holidays.

**Casa de Huéspedes La Tabasqueña,** Morelos 325 (tel. 32-05-60), 100m north of Lerdo on Plaza de la República. Here, introverts can escape the explosive *zócalo* into their own personal caves. Small, graying stucco rooms are have ceiling fans, though some lack windows. Free shampoo samples will leave your hair shiny and full of body. Singles 35 pesos. Doubles 60 pesos. Prices may rise during holidays.

## Diaz Mirón and Bus Station

The hotels near the *zócalo* enjoy a much better location for downtown sight-seeing and carousing, but these establishments will do if those are full or if you have to catch a red-eye bus. Hotels close to the bus station tend to be very noisy, for obvious reasons. At night, it's probably best to take a cab back to this area.

**Hotel Acapulco,** Uribe 1327 (tel. 31-87-27), halfway between the bus station and the *zócalo*. Friendly family offers spotless, comfortable rooms. Beds sport cedar headrests handmade by the owner. Very clean bathrooms. Ceiling fans in all rooms. Happily free of noisy bus traffic. Singles 46 pesos (69 pesos peak season). Doubles 58 pesos (86.50 pesos peak season).

**Hotel Central,** Díaz Mirón 1612 (tel. 32-22-22), next to the ADO station. A modern-looking joint straight out of *Metropolis,* complete with a marble lobby. Ask for a room with a balcony from which to watch buses zip by. TV, phone, and large bathrooms. Luggage storage. Singles 80 pesos, 100 pesos with A/C. Doubles 90 pesos, 120 pesos with A/C.

**Hotel Rosa Mar,** La Fragua 1100 (tel. 37-07-47), behind the ADO station and across the street from the AU station. Clean, but could use more regular maintenance. Little black-and-white TVs in the rooms entertain those waiting for an early-morning bus. Singles 45 pesos. Doubles 55 pesos. 15 pesos extra for A/C, 5 pesos extra for color TV.

## FOOD

It's that coastal thing—all the menus in Veracruz are stuffed with seafood. Shrimp, octopus, red snapper, and a host of other sea beasts are hauled in daily from the Gulf. The cheapest way to enjoy these delicacies is to head for the **fish market** on Landero y Coss between Arista and Zaragoza. But don't let the proximity to the water fool you; most of what's served has been in the freezer for weeks. Watch out for *ceviche* (raw seafood marinated in acidic juices): it's delicious, but if prepared improperly, it can make you very, very sick. Never eat it in the market—bad shrimp *ceviche* could kill you.

**Gran Café de la Parroquia,** Gómez Farías 34, at the corner of Paseo del Malecón (tel. 32-18-55). A Veracruzan tradition since 1810, the Gran Café has served every Mexican President, plus a whole host of other luminaries, including Colombian author Gabriel García Márquez. You'd think it served the whole Republic from the crowds that flock to it every night, and it's no wonder: the food's great and the *ambiente* impeccable. Watch the masses collectively effervesce as you enjoy the light breakfast Porfirio Díaz used to eat here: papaya (4 pesos), sweet bread (3 pesos), and their delicious *café lechero* (4.50 pesos). Open daily 6am-1am.

**Restaurant El Pescador** (tel. 32-52-52), on Zaragoza between Morelos and Arista. Ahoy, matey! Hanging models of sailing vessels and a menu chock-full of seafood remind you that you're in a port town. Most dishes 15-28 pesos; a two-person seafood extravaganza goes for 98 pesos.

**Alaska** (tel. 31-78-73), in the Parque Zamora. You can't miss the huge sign. This is where many locals go to retreat from the tourist battalions closer to the *zócalo*. If you've been craving the *nieves* you see all over town, this is the place to be—all of the frozen treats your health-conscious heart could possibly desire are made with *agua purificada*. Simple fare at low prices; the view of the beautiful park is free. *Antojitos* 6-9 pesos. Open daily.

**El Tiburón,** Landero y Coss 167 (tel. 31-47-40), at Serdán. As a boy, the owner of this overwhelmingly blue home-cooking restaurant, El Tiburón González, was afraid of sharks. He kept all his limbs, though, and now he's one of the best salsa dancers in Veracruz. *Comida corrida* 9 pesos. *Sopa de mariscos* with crab, shrimp, squid, and fish in a paprika broth, 26 pesos. Breakfast 3-18 pesos.

**Kabuki,** Rayón 500 (tel. 32-70-05). Walk up Independencia until you hit Parque Zamora, and turn left on Rayón; the restaurant is on the right side of the street. A trickling waterfall and a small wooden bridge at the entrance bring a little piece of Japan to Veracruz. Unfortunately, so do the prices. You might have to hawk your Honda hatchback for one of the more expensive dishes, but most fall within the realm of affordability. Sushi 19-28 pesos, noodle dishes 9-30 pesos. MC, Visa accepted. Open daily 1pm-midnight.

## SIGHTS AND SAND

In the evening, the hymns of the cathedral spilling out into the *zócalo* yield to the seductive rhythms of *marimba*. Crowds gather on benches and outside bars to drink in music that doesn't relent until daybreak. On Tuesday, Thursday, and Saturday nights around 8pm, *veracruzanos* young and old gather for the slowly swaying *danzón,* an old Veracruz tradition. The band strikes up a tune, and couples—men in white wearing straw hats, women clutching their sandalwood fans—file out onto the makeshift dance floor where they sway to the nightly rhythms.

### Museums and Monuments

For one take on the city's history, visit the **Museo Histórico de la Revolución Carranza** by a small park near the waterfront, on Insurgentes between Hernández and Xicoténcatl. The museum, also called Museo Constitucionalista, is upstairs and to the left in a yellow colonial lighthouse which also houses offices of the Mexican Navy. The lighthouse, its twin on Morelos dedicated to Benito Juárez, the *Aduana Maritima* (Maritime Customs) on the Plaza de la República, and the post and telegraph offices, are all architectural legacies of the Porfiriato. The museum is really a monument to Venustiano Carranza, the president who restored unified constitutional rule to Mexico, thus ending the civil wars following the Revolution. Inside, a sharp sailor will point out Carranza's flags and spittoons. One room is a small shrine of photographic idolatry: Carranza with a crippled boy, with various bigwigs, riding in a car, reading the paper, etc. A drawing of Carranza's skeleton shows where the bullets hit when he was assassinated on May 21, 1920. In one corner, a glass case holds some of Carranza's personal effects, among them a gold pocket watch and chain, ornamented by a silver coin imprinted with the face of Simón Bolívar. The sailor at the museum's front desk can provide you with a written guide explaining (in English) many of the exhibits (open Tues.-Sat. 9am-5pm).

For a deeper glimpse into the past, visit the **Museo Cultural de la Ciudad,** Zaragoza 397 (tel. 31-84-10). Paintings, models, dioramas, and Spanish explanations tell the history of the city from pre-Hispanic times to the present. The museum's most interesting attraction is a relic from its days as an orphanage. In the back stairwell, a stained-glass window depicts Talinmasca, an orphan whose transgressions, legend has it, brought thunder, lighting, and the fierce autumn winds called *nortes* to the area (open Mon.-Sat. 9am-4pm; admission 3 pesos).

Down the street to the right (Canal), between Farías and 16 de Septiembre, lies the **Baluarte de San Francisco.** This 17th-century bulwark protected inhabitants from swashbuckling pirates like Frances Drake; it is all that remains of the old city wall. The museum inside the fort displays a beautiful collection of pre-Hispanic gold ornaments. The roof of the fort affords a great view of the city (open Tues.-Sat. 10am-4:30pm; admission 13 pesos; Sun. and holidays free).

The major colonial fortification in the city, and Veracruz's most important historic site, is the **Castillo de San Juan de Ulúa** (tel. 38-51-51), on the northeastern edge of the harbor. To reach the fort, take the bus of the same name (.80 pesos) from the east side of the Pl. de la República, in front of the Aduana building. The point where the first Spaniards landed at Veracruz, it is named "San Juan" because it was on the first day of San Juan that the ships arrived, and "Ulúa" for the greetings that the indigenous inhabitants offered the sailors as they disembarked. Begun in 1582, it was part of the system of fortifications built around the Spanish Caribbean to protect the Spanish trade fleet and treasure from privateers. The fort's defenses are incomprehensible without a mini-guidebook (the tourist office can tell you where to buy one) or the services of a guide (15 pesos in Spanish, 30 in English, for 1-5 people). Its drawbridge was dubbed the Bridge of Sighs when the building became a brutally inhumane prison. Going around clockwise you pass its three cells—Heaven, Purgatory, and Hell, all of which flooded regularly. On the walls in Purgatory are the wooden pegs used by Inquisitors to tie prisoners to the walls. The perpetual darkness of Hell, surrounded by walls nine meters thick, caused prisoners to lose their sense of time and their sanity. To maintain yours, cross the bridge back to the fort and head for the side facing the city, where you can enjoy the view while feeding crumbled crackers to the harbor's hungry angelfish (open Tues.-Sat. 9am-4pm; admission 14 pesos, children 5 pesos; free Sun.).

### Beaches and Beyond

The beaches in Veracruz are not world-class, but they are a refreshing break from the central Mexican heat. The harbor is a case study in the toxic impact of big oil in big cities. Locals still swim in the water, but considering the health risk, the short trip south to **Playa Villa del Mar** is a better idea. There, the beach is fairly clean and reasonably uncrowded. Restaurants, juice-bars, and some expensive hotels line **Blvd. Camacho** across the street from the beach. Playa Villa del Mar is a fairly pleasant hour-long walk from the *zócalo* along the waterfront; it is also accessible via one of the frequent buses from the corner of Serdán and Zaragoza (1.50 pesos) marked "Villa del Mar" or "Boca del Río." If you share El Tiburón Gonzalez's shark-phobia, fear not: the only sharks you'll see are in the **Acuario de Veracruz** (tel. 32-79-84), on the north end of the beach. The salt-water tank is enclosed by an enormous concave window arching over visitors' heads, allowing sharks to swim straight at them before veering directly over their hair-raised scalps (open daily 10am-7:30pm; admission 15 pesos, children 5 pesos).

The best beach in the Veracruz area is **Mocambo,** in the neighboring city of Boca del Río, a 25-minute bus ride away. Take a "Boca del Río" *colectivo* from Zaragoza and Serdán (1.20 pesos) and ask to be dropped off at Playa Mocambo. A sign saying "Playa" will point you down a short driveway on the opposite side of the road. At the bottom, veer left to head for the beach, or go straight into the **Balneario Mocambo** (tel. 21-02-88), a clean, Olympic-sized public pool surrounded by *cabañas* and palm trees and equipped with changing rooms and a pool-side bar-restaurant (open daily 9am-5pm; admission 12 pesos, children 6 pesos). The bus back to Veracruz will pick you up at the top of the drive.

Dedicated followers of fashion might want to check out **Guayaberas Finas,** Zaragoza 233 (tel. 31-84-27). *Guayaberas* are traditional, dressy, short-sleeved shirts with thin pleats running down the front. The shirts are designed for hot weather in the Caribbean, and are visible everywhere in Veracruz on the backs of *marimba* players and the older men in town. Guayaberas Finas is one of the most famous brands; their best *guayabera* is made of a Japanese poly-linen blend, following a Cuban design (240 pesos; open Mon.-Sat. 9:30am-2pm and 4:30-8pm). Inexpensive *guayaberas* start at 50 pesos and can be found all over the city.

## ENTERTAINMENT AND SEASONAL EVENTS

The city's best and liveliest entertainment is free every night in the *zócalo*. Crowds start to gather around 7pm for incredible puppet shows, parades, karate demonstrations, and just about everything else that attracts passers-by (and their pesos).

Going downtown to visit the discos is like reading *Playboy* for the articles, but here goes. **Discotheque La Capilla,** Independencia 1064, in the Hotel Prendes between Lerdo and Juárez, teems with tourists hopping to top-40 hits (cover and minimum vary; open Thurs.-Sat. 10pm-3:30am). The same folks operate **Borsalino's,** Landero y Coss 146 (tel. 31-48-81), a bar which magically transforms itself into a disco Thurs.-Sat. from 9pm-3am. South of the city center are two clubs that cater to gays: **El Cid,** Américo Vespucio 178, opposite the Estadio Pirata Fuente, and the more raucous **Hip-Pop-Potamus,** just off Camacho in Colonia Costa Verde.

Boca del Río is developing a much hipper dance scene; some locals say the atmosphere there is beginning to rival that of the *zócalo*. Cover charges are high, however (as much as 45 pesos), and you'll have to shell out 12 pesos more for a cab ride from downtown, since the buses stop running at around 11pm, just as the clubs are opening. Ask for **Blue Ocean** on Blvd. Camacho (tel. 37-63-25) and nearby **Club Ocean,** Ruíz Cortines 8 (tel. 37-63-27).

**Bars** are ubiquitous in Veracruz. A row of practically indistinguishable bars along the north side of the *zócalo* is haunted by *marimba* players and Chiclets-pushers; you might also try one of the various indoor bars located on and near Landero y Coss, east of the *zócalo*. They're cheaper, but may be tuneless. The stakes—and the testosterone levels—are high at **Billares Maupome,** at the intersection of Landero y Coss and Serdán, where they charge 8 pesos per hour to shoot pool (open 9am-midnight, sometimes later).

If two hours of air-conditioning appeals to you, you might want to catch a movie—who cares what's showing? For English-language films, check out **Plaza Cinema,** Arista 708. At Díaz Mirón 941, between Iturbide and Mina, is **Cinema Gemelos Veracruz** (tel. 32-59-70). Admission for all cinemas is 10 pesos.

Veracruz's **Carnaval**—a nationally renowned, week-long festival of parades, concerts, and costumes—takes place in late February or early March (during the week before Ash Wednesday). Its reputation is amazing; partisans claim that only Rio's Carnival and New Orleans's Mardi Gras swing harder. For information, contact the tourist office. Make reservations early.

# ■ NEAR VERACRUZ

## CEMPOALA RUINS AND JOSÉ CARDEL

One of the most impressive archaeological sites in the state of Veracruz, the ruins at **Cempoala** (or sometimes Zempoala) lie 40km north of Veracruz, off Route 180. Buses from Veracruz run to nearby **José Cardel,** making the ruins an easy excursion.

Cempoala was one of the largest southern Totonac cities, part of a federation that covered much of Veracruz in pre-Hispanic times. In 1469, the Aztecs subdued Cempoala and forced them to join their federation. Cortés arrived in 1519, attracted to the glitter of the seashells in the stucco used to build the structures (thinking, of course, that it was gold). The Totonacs and their chief, Chicomacatl (famous, primarily, for having been enormously fat), welcomed the Spaniards and lent Cortés soldiers for his campaign against Montezuma at Tenochtitlán in 1521. It was at Cempoala that Cortés defeated (and imprisoned) Panfilo de Narváez, who had been sent by Diego de Velázquez, the governor of Cuba, to teach the cocky *conquistador* some respect for his higher-ups.

The ruins sit on a field surrounded by lush vegetation and distant hills. A museum, to your left as you enter, displays a small collection of pottery and figurines unearthed here, and sells a much-needed English mini-guide to the ruins (3 pesos). Once a city of 30,000 people, Cempoala was ruled from the large structure at the north end of the site, which is known as the **Main Temple** but was actually the palace. Just south and to the right of the Main Temple is a more mysterious structure known as **Las Chimeneas.** The top of Las Chimeneas affords a view of Cempoala's ruined walls and the structures they once enclosed, all originally covered by a layer of stucco that no longer glitters like gold, but is still visible around the base of many buildings. Off to the west, facing Las Chimeneas at the edge of the site, is the base of the **Great Pyramid** (on the left). Nearby, flanked by mountains, stands the **Temple of the Wind God** (on the right). Ringing the area are a variety of other structures dedicated to different gods, including the **Temple of the Sun,** which can be recognized by the circular stone mound in front where the Totonacs used to place the hearts of people sacrificed as religious offerings. In the **Temple of Death,** the structure closest to the entrance, archaeologists found a tomb containing a representation of a goddess as well as the bridles of Cortés's horses.

Next to the white building (soon to be a museum) left of the entrance, guides will point out stonewares that date back to as early as 1027 CE. Here on display is a representation of a god reflecting the planet Venus, a stone used for corn grinding, and the circular goal used in the sacred game of *pelota.* If a player succeeded in getting the ball through the small goal, he received the honor of being sacrificed to the gods. Lucky guy (open daily 9am-6pm; admission 10 pesos, free Sun.).

**José Cardel** would be nothing special, except that it's strategically positioned at the intersection of the coastal highway and the road from Jalapa. Should you need to stay in José Cardel, however, the town has plenty of amenities. Most services cluster around the *zócalo.* The **police** station (2-03-52) is in the Palacio Municipal, on the north side of the *zócalo.* **Bancomer,** on the south side of the *zócalo,* is open for exchange Mon.-Fri. 9am-2pm. The **Red Cross** (tel. 2-02-26; 24-hr. ambulance service) is four blocks west of the *zócalo* on Emiliano Zapata, the street leading into town from Route 180. On the southeast corner of the *zócalo,* **Farmacia Santiago** (2-04-31) is open 24 hrs. Small **restaurants,** *refresco* stands, and a movie theater round out the *zócalo.* The **Hotel Plaza,** Independencia 25 (tel. 2-02-88), sits across from the ADO bus station and offers huge Barbie-esque pastel rooms, each with A/C and color TV (singles 70 pesos; doubles 90 pesos). The hotel's restaurant is open daily 7am-11pm. For a clean and cheap no-frills room, head for **Hotel Garelli** (tel. 2-05-69), on Flores Magón and Benito Juárez (singles 25 pesos; doubles 50 pesos).

**Getting There:** To reach Cempoala from Veracruz, you must first take a bus to José Cardel, a trip of 45 minutes. From its station on Díaz Mirón, ADO runs first-class buses to José Cardel (4 per day, 6 pesos). Much more convenient is Autotransportes Teziutecos, whose second-class station is located on La Fragua (every 10 minutes, 5am-9:15pm, 3 pesos). In José Cardel, ADO buses stop on Independencia, two blocks south of the southwest corner of the *zócalo.* The second-class bus station stands on the south side of the *zócalo.*

To reach Cempoala from José Cardel, get a *colectivo* (1.20 pesos) from the second-class bus station; they leave every half-hour. Ask the driver to let you out at *las ruinas.* The trip takes about 10 minutes. In Cempoala, you'll be dropped at the intersection of Av. Prof. José Ruiz and Av. Fco. del Paso y Troncoso Norte. Walk 100m on Fco. del Paso y Troncoso Norte, where a ticket booth marks the entrance to the site. If driving from Veracruz, follow Rte. 180 past the city of José Cardel until you come to the Cempoala city turn-off. Proceed until an obscured sign for the ruins appears on the right (about 1km before town; the sign says "Zona Arqueológica").

To get back to José Cardel, stand across the street from where you were dropped off; the miraculous hybrid of Mexican transport, the taxi-*colectivo,* leaves every 15 minutes from this spot, packed full with five or six passengers at 2 pesos each. A regular taxi costs about 20 pesos. Buses run all afternoon and into the evening.

# SOUTHERN VERACRUZ

Southern Veracruz retains a relaxed and intimate feel largely because the verdant volcanic hills of La Sierra de los Tuxtlas remain virtually untouristed. Most local residents make their living from tobacco farming or small-scale cattle ranching. **Catemaco** monopolizes the area's fun-in-the-sun business because of its proximity to fine lake-side beaches and Gulf Coast sands. Nearby **San Andrés Tuxtla,** the region's largest city, offers a healthy range of hotels, restaurants, and swanky Mexican cigars. In **Santiago Tuxtla,** life is even slower than in Catemaco. With only two hotels and a small museum, the fastest moves in town are made at the recreation center's foosball tables.

Local color is supplied by the over-hyped but still vital *curandero* culture. *Curanderos* (medicine men), called *brujos* (witches) by locals, practice a mixture of conjuring, devil-invocation, and natural healing. Their rituals combine elements of European, African, and pre-Hispanic traditions; some incantations are recited in Nahuatl and the *diablo* they invoke is probably a spiritual descendant of the Tuxteco god Huichilobos. Locals may visit *curanderos* to heal a snake bite, or to discover if a spouse is being unfaithful; some *curanderos* head to Catemaco, where they hawk their services to *gringos* in search of spooky thrills.

# ■■■ CATEMACO

While the rest of the Sierra de los Tuxtlas languishes off the beaten track, the world (or at least much of Mexico) beats a path to Catemaco's door during the holidays. The city drinks at the edge of a large lake bordered by rocky beaches and peppered with idyllic islands. The natural beauty of the Tuxtlas range's green, river crisscrossed slopes, makes Catemaco a tremendously popular destination with Mexican tourists during *Semana Santa,* Christmas, and summer vacation. Catemaco is also a favorite hangout for a sizeable number of foreign tourists, a sort of fresh-water Margaritaville for members of the international beard-and-sandal brigade. On the first Friday in March, Catemaco hosts an annual gathering of shaman, medicine men, and witches from all over Mexico. As a result, traditional *curandero* culture has become grist for the tourist mill here, and several *palapa*-roofed Corona bars have slapped the term *"brujo"* onto their names. For disbelievers, swimming and scenic lake-isles, bars, and dance clubs offer more than enough entertainment.

**Orientation and Practical Information** Catemaco lies along Rte. 180 and is a frequent stop for both first- and second-class buses. Buses frequently run from Catemaco to major cities like Mexico City, Veracruz, and Jalapa, as well as to San Andrés Tuxtla and Santiago Tuxtla. Streets in Catemaco are poorly marked, but the basilica on the *zócalo* is usually visible. **Carranza** runs along the west side of the *zócalo,* while **Aldama** runs parallel on the east side. The waterfront is only a block downhill from Aldama at the *zócalo.* South of the *zócalo,* Aldama becomes **Madero** and runs parallel to the lake. Carranza curves westward and meets Rte. 180 at the southwestern corner of the town. The entire town can be covered on foot in 10 minutes, and all services huddle around the *zócalo.* The **ADO** and **AU** station sits on Aldama north of the *zócalo,* one block behind the basilica. **Autotransportes Los Tuxtlas** stops two blocks south of the *zócalo* on Cuauhtémoc, which runs parallel to and one block north of Aldama.

**Las Brisas Hotel,** Carranza 3 (tel. 3-00-57), provides **tourist information.** Señor Agustín Moreno is the official "State Tourist Coordinator" for Catemaco and the coastal areas. He speaks no English but will gladly show you a map of the region and will sell you an informative brochure in Spanish for five pesos. He's there 8am-1pm daily, wearing a *guayabera* and a smile. The **police** are in the Palacio Municipal (tel. 3-00-55), on the *zócalo* (open 24 hrs.). The **post office** is on Mantilla, between the lake and Hotel Los Arcos (open Mon.-Fri. 9am-4pm, Sat. 9am-1pm; often open all afternoon, contrary to official hours). **Postal Code:** 95870. The **telephone** *casetas* in town do not allow international collect calls, but the larger hotels may let you call collect for a hefty fee. Best bet: call from elsewhere. **Telephone Code:** 294. The **telegraph office** (tel. 3-00-52) is on Carranza, a short distance southwest of the *zócalo* (open Mon.-Fri. 9am-3pm). Them dollars ain't no good in this town: there are no banks that can exchange money. Head to the **Bánamex** in San Andrés. If push comes to shove, **Hotel Los Arcos,** on the lake at Madero 7 (tel. 3-00-03, fax 3-02-50) will exchange dollars at extremely unfavorable rates. Those pesky negative externalities of money-exchange monopolies...

First-class **ADO buses** (tel 3-08-42) leave for Córdoba (9:30pm, 5hrs., 52 pesos), Jalapa (7am, 5hrs., 47 pesos), Mexico City (9:30 and 10pm, 9hrs., 109.50 pesos), Puebla (10pm, 6hrs., 87 pesos), Veracruz (5 per day, 6am-6:15pm, 2½hrs., 28 pesos), and Villahermosa (12:20pm, 5hrs., 53 pesos). **AU** (tel. 3-07-77) goes to Jalapa (9:15pm, 5hrs., 38.50 pesos), Mexico City (8:05pm, 9hrs., 95 pesos), Puebla (9:15pm, 7hrs., 74 pesos), San Andrés (8:05 and 9:15pm, 20min., 2 pesos), and Veracruz (9:15 pm, 2½hrs., 23 pesos). **Autotransportes Los Tuxtlas** goes to San Andrés (every 10 min., 20min., 2 pesos) and Santiago (every 10 min., 40min., 4 pesos). **Farmacia Nuestra Señora del Carmen,** at the corner of Carranza and Boettinger (tel. 3-00-91), attached to the Hotel Acuario, is open daily 7am-9pm. The **Centro de Salud,** on Carranza (tel. 3-02-47), is in a white building with a blue roof three blocks south of the *zócalo,* on the left. Some English spoken. Medical services are available 24 hrs. In an **emergency,** dial 06.

**Accommodations** There are plenty of hotels in Catemaco, but don't expect to find room if you arrive unexpectedly during Christmas (or *Semana Santa*). Even if you make reservations far in advance, you'll have to cough up plenty of cash, gold, and myrrh, as rates during holidays rise to celestial levels. On the other hand, you'll practically have the town to yourself on a weekday during the off-season. Most hotels are concentrated around the *zócalo* and the waterfront. Dozens of young Mexicans and tie-dyed foreigners gather on the beaches with guitars and sleeping bags. It is not safe to camp on the beaches, however, since crime has recently been a problem in the area (see "Near Catemaco: The Gulf Coast" on page 345 for other camping possibilities). The **Hotel Julita,** Playa 10 (tel. 3-00-08), on the waterfront one block downhill from the *zócalo,* is a very good deal, boasting an unbeatable location and large rooms with springy beds. Wake up to the squawking of lake birds; then catch breakfast at the restaurant downstairs (singles 30 pesos; doubles 60 pesos; peak season singles 40 pesos; doubles 60 pesos). **Hotel Acuario,** at the southwest corner of the *zócalo* at Boettinger and Carranza (tel. 3-04-18), provides large, relatively clean rooms with 70s curtains, some with balconies. The lobby has a sitting area and TV (singles 25 pesos; doubles 40 pesos, with 2 beds 60 pesos).

**Food** When choosing a waterfront restaurant, pay attention only to the establishment's view of the lake, since food tastes pretty much the same everywhere. *Mojarra* and *topote* will hop right from the lake onto your plate, but make sure to have them fried, since parts of the lake are polluted. *Mojarra* is prepared in a variety of ways, while the bite-sized *topote* is fried up whole and heaped with *tamales*. Shrimp, much of it from surrounding rivers, is also a local specialty. **Restaurant La Casona del Recuerdo,** Aldama 6 (tel. 3-05-76), just off the *zócalo,* is a haven from the busy waterfront. The terrace in back overlooks a peaceful wooded garden. *Mojarra* goes for 14 pesos, shrimp 19.50 pesos (open daily 8am-8pm). On the waterfront, across from the Hotel Julita, **7 Brujas** (tel. 3-01-57) serves the standard seafood dishes, plus a great view of the waterfront from the 2nd floor of their nifty circular building. Take your very own *bruja* doll home (5 pesos; open daily 8am-10pm). Diagonally across from Hotel Julita, **Restaurant La Ola** serves hotcakes for five pesos and fries up a mean *mojarra* (open Mon.-Sat. 8am-9pm, Sun. 8am-10pm).

**Sights and Entertainment** The rocky beaches of **Laguna Catemaco** inspire no hyperbole, but a dip in the lake can be a refreshing break from the hot Veracruz sun. The water immediately in front of town is not safe for swimming. A hiking path runs along the edge of the lake—walk down from the *zócalo* to the waterfront and turn left. The trail, bordered by trees knotted with character, will guide you the 1.5km to **Playa Expagoya** and then another 0.5km down the road to the more secluded and sandy **Playa Hermosa,** the first swimmable beach on the trail. The path is not safe at night, as there's the potential for crime.

The lake is nearly circular, about 15km across, and several small islands dot its smooth surface. The waterfront is lined with long, flat-bottomed, brightly-colored boats equipped with chairs and canopies. Referred to in Catemaco as *lanchas,* these vessels lie ready to take you on an hour-long trip to the best-known island of the lot, **Isla de Changos.** A tribe of semi-wild, red-cheeked *changos* (mandrills, a kind of baboon) was brought from Thailand for a scientific experiment by the University of Veracruz in 1979, who wanted to see if the animals could survive in their new environment. Lo and behold, 17 years later the *changos* are alive and well and posing for snapshots. Knowing that the *lanchistas* bring coconuts and tortillas, the bravest *changos* climb right into the boat to pose for camera shots and collect their reward. En route to the island, you'll pass close to a cave-shrine that stands on the spot where a woman had a vision of the Virgin Mary over a century ago. The *lanchas* leave from the docking area below the *zócalo.* Launch prices are pre-set and clearly posted. A standard tour of the lake, including the Isla de Changos and the shrine of the Virgin, costs 120 pesos for one to six passengers and 25 pesos for each additional passenger. To see only the Isla de Changos will cost 70 pesos for one to six passengers. Negotiate with the *lanchistas* for longer trips, including an exploration of the rivers that feed the lake or a trip to the tropical forests of the national park on the lake's western shores.

Catemaco's **bars** and **discos** are the best in the area, serving just as many residents of the Tuxtlas as those of Catemaco itself. **Chanequa's,** in the Hotel Playa Azul (tel. 3-00-42 or 3-00-01), some distance outside of Catemaco, is said to be the hottest. It is possible to walk there, but somewhat difficult and, at night, dangerous. A launch will take you to the hotel for 20 pesos. The **7 Brujas** (tel. 3-01-57), two doors down from the restaurant of the same name, is a small, well-advertised bar that serves many non-Catemacans (beers 2 5 pesos, cocktails 8 pesos; open daily 8am-10pm). For **discos,** locals recommend **Jahac 45,** four blocks south on the waterfront from the Hotel Julita and one block to the right, which converts from a video bar to a disco on Friday and Saturday nights at 9pm. Not to be outdone in the numerical theme, there's **Luna 90,** a disco above Restaurant La Luna (cover 5 pesos; open Sat.-Sun. after 9pm). Coming back from the discos, it's best to take a cab or walk in groups, since Catemaco is not safe after dark.

# ■ NEAR CATEMACO: THE GULF COAST

The Gulf Coast whispers seductively to those who believe that waves crash more crisply in the absence of Corona bars and souvenir shops. The coast's beaches are not spectacular, but they are secluded—cattle roam the spaces between fishing villages with no telephone lines and only the most basic services. The state of Veracruz wants to pave the road to the coast and to develop the region for tourism. When this will happen is anyone's guess, but the sage traveler will visit the area before it does.

Getting to the Gulf Coast near Catemaco is an adventure. Public transportation to the area is limited to **Transportes Rurales's** small Nissan pickup trucks, affectionately dubbed *piratas* by locals. A four-door vehicle with wooden benches built into its caged-in bed, a *pirata* can carry the entire population of a small town. Men are expected to yield indoor seats to children and the elderly. The pickups depart from the intersection of two unmarked streets on the eastern edge of town. To get there, follow the lakefront to the restaurant Casa Azul, then take a left. After about three blocks, the street will end and you'll see the pickups gathered on the cross-street to the right. They leave for **Sontecomapán** every 20 minutes and for points farther out every hour, 6am-6pm daily. The road is paved as far as Sontecomapán, but after that it's dirt, mud, and stones all the way.

Sontecomapán is a small town beside an eponymous saltwater lake that empties into the Gulf of Mexico. *Lanchas* are available for excursions on the lake. Sontecomapán is accessible by pickup truck (4 pesos). Farther down the road lies the village of **La Barra,** a small fishing community where Laguna Sontecomapán empties into the Gulf of Mexico. To get there, ride a pickup 8km beyond Sontecomapán until the road forks. Your *pirata* will normally follow the left fork; you can either negotiate with the driver to take the right fork instead, or you can hop off, take a right, and hike the 5-6km to La Barra yourself. Once there, locals will show you a modicum of hospitality if you introduce yourself politely; chances are, a friendly *viajero* will be allowed to set up camp near someone's home.

The *pirata* route comes closer to the coast near **Playa Jicacal** and **Playa Escondida.** The pickups take about 40 minutes to travel from Catemaco to the intersection of two dirt roads, where signs clearly indicate the ways to both beaches. A hilly, 2km walk through a lush and remote rural area leads to Playa Jicacal, a long, slightly stony beach where the only footprints lead to a few modest fisherman's shacks and—inevitably—a *refresco* stand and snack bar. The beach is said to be safe for camping, and hammock-hanging sites may be available. Safety goes hand and hand with good manners, and campers who wish to crash on the beach would do well to ingratiate themselves with the *jicacaleños*.

On the left, facing the water, a bluff thick with tropical vegetation rises 250m above sea level. A road leads up to the **Hotel Playa Escondida,** whose terrace restaurant offers a commanding view of the green Sierra de los Tuxtlas as it fades into the Gulf of Mexico along the extended crescent of Jicacal. The hotel may stretch your budget (singles 80 pesos, doubles 90 pesos), but it's the perfect hideaway for those fleeing the law or chasing true love. During peak season, make reservations by calling their number in San Andrés (tel. 91-294-2-16-14). The only access to Playa Escondida is down a long staircase high above the small rocky beach and the bluffs that enclose it. The staircase and its spectacular view belong to the hotel and are open only to guests. Swimming is possible at both beaches, but a strong undertow sometimes makes taking a plunge dangerous even for the natatorial expert.

At the end of the *pirata* route is the tiny village of **Montepío,** 40km (a 2–hour ride) from Catemaco. The town consists of a handful of buildings, including a little light blue church whose façade is barely big enough to accommodate the door. There are some very modest restaurants, a **pharmacy** (open daily 10am-2pm), and a **health clinic** (open 24 hrs.) scattered around the church and along the road. Montepío is less spectacular than Playa Escondida, but it does offer a long, narrow beach framed by a tall bluff and volcanic rocks on one end and the green hills of the Sierra on the other. Locals rent horses for 15 pesos per hour. Pick-up trucks, which pass every hour between 6am and 6pm, take travelers to a nearby **biological research station,** where young scientists may tell you about the flora and fauna of the area and show you the snakes and monkeys they're studying. The new **Hotel Posada San José** (tel. 91-294-2-10-10, in San Andrés) stands on the banks of the small river leading to the beach. The *posada* is pretty clean and features a restaurant serving a 15-peso *comida corrida*. The beach is said to be safe for camping. Day-trippers are beginning to discover Montepío, so if you want the town to yourself, plan on spending the night.

Alternatively, you can take a *pirata* headed for **Coyame,** 12km from Catemaco, where you can watch the cool waters that are bottled to make the soft drink of the same name bubble up from underground springs. You can stop off at **Nanciyaga,** 7km from Catemaco *en route* to Coyame, an area which prides itself on being the northernmost tropical rainforest on earth and the cradle of the Olmec civilization. Here, there are guided tours through the forest, rowboats and kayaks, mud baths, as well as the inevitable restaurant and, of course, shaman. The people at **Parque Ecológico Educativo Nanciyaga** (tel. 3-01-99; fax 3-06-66) can arrange other activities ranging from cabin stays to ritual steam baths. You can also take a *lancha* here from Catemaco; you'll have to haggle for the price.

# ■■■ SAN ANDRÉS TUXTLA

Lodged between the lush lakeside resorts of Catemaco and the Olmec artifacts of Santiago, San Andrés Tuxtla (usually just San Andrés) is the relatively untouristed anchor that keeps the Sierra de los Tuxtlas peacefully down-to-earth. A quiet, content little town, San Andrés serves mainly as a center for the tobacco and cattle industries of the surrounding countryside, and offers a cache of budget hotels, an entertaining *zócalo,* remarkably friendly people, and some nearby natural attractions. The spring is the hottest time of year, but unlike other parts of the Gulf Coast, San Andrés always cools off at night. During the summer, thunderstorms can punctuate the afternoon and evening, but are quickly forgotten.

**Orientation and Practical Information** Located midway between Catemaco and Santiago Tuxtla on Route 180, San Andrés is built on and around a volcanic range that hugs the Gulf Coast. The downtown area lies in the slightly raised center of a valley. Branching off Rte. 180, **Juárez,** the city's main street, descends a steep hill, crosses a small stream, and gradually ascends to the cathedral, at the north corner of the *zócalo.* As Rte. 180 swings around north of the city, it becomes **Blvd. 5 de Febrero.** The **bus station** housing AU, ADO, and Cuenca lies at the edge of town, at the intersection of Rte. 180 and Juárez, which leads to *el centro.* When leaving the station, turn left and walk downhill toward the *zócalo.* The walk takes about 10 minutes; a taxi will charge 3 pesos to most points downtown.

The tourist office is in the **Palacio Municipal,** on the corner of Juárez and Madero right in front of the cathedral (open Mon.-Fri. 9am-1pm and 4-6pm, but you may have trouble finding someone there). The friendly folks at **Turística Sanandrescana,** Zamora 299 (tel. 2-33-55; fax 2-32-44), are happy to answer questions. Zamora intersects Piño Suárez at the **Fénix** super-store. From the Palacio Municipal, take a left and go straight until you see the orange "Fénix" sign down the street on your left (open Mon.-Fri. 9am-2pm and 4-8pm, Sat. 9am-2pm). The **police** are located on Pasaje Rascón, on the side of the Palacio Municipal opposite that of the tourist office (tel. 2-02-35; open 24 hrs.). The **State Police** are on Zamora, three blocks north of Pino Suárez, on the right. The **post office** is at La Fragua and 20 de Noviembre (tel. 2-01-89), one block from the *zócalo,* behind the cathedral (open Mon.-Fri. 8am-8pm, Sat. 9am-1pm). **Postal Code:** 95700. **Pipisoles,** Madero 6B, has 3 *casetas de larga distancia,* and charges 5 pesos for collect calls (open Mon.-Fri. 8am-10pm, Sun. 9am-1pm). There are no **LADATEL** phones in San Andrés. The **telegram office** is on Constitución 93 (tel. 2-08-20; open Mon.-Fri. 8am-6pm, Sat. 9am-noon). Exchange your money at **Bánamex** (tel. 2-03-50), on the south side of the *zócalo* (open for exchange Mon.-Fri. 9am-1:30pm). They also have an **ATM** that accepts Plus, Cirrus, MC, and Visa cards.

Buses run frequently to all nearby destinations as well as to more distant points such as Oaxaca, Tampico, Mexico City, Jalapa, and Veracruz. On the highway down the hill from the station, **Autotransportes Los Tuxtlas** (usually called "Las Rojas" by the locals, owing to the color scheme of their vehicles) runs buses from 6am-6pm to Catemaco (4 pesos) every 10 minutes and to Santiago Tuxtla (2 pesos) slightly less often. **ADO** (tel. 2-08-71) goes to Jalapa (6 per day, 10:20am-2:10pm, 5hrs., 45 pesos), Mexico City (15 per day, 1:30am-10:40pm, 8hrs., 109.50 pesos), Puebla (9:30 and 10:40pm, 6hrs., 85 pesos), Veracruz (every 30-50 min., 12:20am-10:30pm, 2½hrs., 26 pesos), and Villahermosa (10 per day, 7am-10:30pm, 5hrs., 55 pesos). **AU** (tel. 2-09-84) goes to Jalapa (9:50pm, 5hrs., 36.50 pesos), Mexico City (8:40pm, 9hrs., 93.50 pesos), Puebla (9:50pm, 6hrs., 72.50 pesos), and Veracruz (9:50pm, 2½hrs., 21 pesos). **Cuenca** goes to Tuxtepec (4:50am and 1pm, 3hrs., 25.50 pesos).

SAN ANDRÉS TUXTLA

**Lavandería Tintorería Roxy,** at Agosto 776 (tel. 2-12-94), will wash and dry 3kg of your dirtiest duds for 11 pesos (open Mon.-Sat. 8am-8pm). **Farmacia El Fénix** is at Juárez 2 (tel. 2-27-27), across from the cathedral (open Mon.-Sat. 8am-10pm). The **Red Cross** is at Boca Negra 25 (tel. 2-05-00), north of the *zócalo* (open 24 hrs.). Ask for *servicio de ambulancia* to go directly to the hospital at the edge of town.

**Accommodations and Food** San Andrés remains almost tourist-free; budget accommodations are abundant and unfailingly available. Three of the best hotels are within spitting distance of each other, just north of the cathedral. To get to them from the cathedral, follow the street on the left of the church as you face it, then take a left. Take the first left onto Pino Suárez and you're there. The **Hotel Colonial,** Pino Suárez 7 (tel. 2-05-52) offers airy, pleasant, spacious rooms with slightly less pleasant bathrooms. The furnished sitting area looking over the rooftops of San Andrés makes up for what the showers lack (singles 25 pesos; doubles 35 pesos, with two beds 40 pesos). Across the street, the darker rooms of the **Hotel Figueroa** at Pino Suárez 2 (tel. 2-02-57) are similarly outfitted with fans, but lack toilet seats. Rooms on the central courtyard look across to the home of the friendly family that runs the place, while others line the arcaded balcony. A little dog named Cookie completes the picture (singles 23 pesos; doubles 40 pesos, with two beds 46 pesos).

Several sidewalk cafés on the *zócalo* serve breakfast and large coffees, and afford a pleasant view of simple small-town life. A number of good lunch spots line Madero, while the cheapest sidewalk stands proliferate in and around the market, which is downhill from the cathedral about two blocks off 16 de Septiembre. Under the *palapa* roof of **Restaurant La Caperucita,** Juárez 108 (tel. 2-05-11), downhill from the cathedral, *frijoles* and filet mignon cohabit in harmony. The friendly owners' specialty is a large and filling fried *misantleca* (a big fried disk-o-dough stuffed with meat, 12 pesos). They also serve delicious tacos, fruit shakes, and *refrescos* at mind-bogglingly low prices (open daily 7am-midnight). In the evening, people of all ages gather at **Restaurant del Parque,** Madero 5 (tel. 2-01-98), in the Hotel del Parque on the *zócalo*. This is where the wealthy politicos make deals over coffee. The service is excellent and the chicken soup delicious (6 pesos; open daily 8am-11:30pm). The friendly folks at **El Pequeño Archie,** on Pino Suárez just downhill from the hotels, heap tortillas atop their delicious meals. A *comida corrida* goes for 9 pesos. The location across the street from the movies makes it an excellent choice for pre-theater dining (open daily 8:30am-11pm).

**Sights and Entertainment** The sheer number of video rental stores in San Andrés just about says it all: this is not exactly a town that parties till dawn. Unless you brought your travel VCR along, you might be hard up to find nighttime entertainment. Most of the action centers on the *zócalo,* where folks in San Andrés gather to meet, gossip, see, and be seen. On Sunday nights, families bring their children and the square becomes a little kiddie carnival, with balloons and small electric cars for hire. **Cinemas San Andrés,** on Pino Suárez across from El Pequeño Archie, brings English-language movies to the big screen for 7 pesos. For anything more high-paced than people- and/or film-watching, you'll have to catch the bus to **Catemaco,** where most of the Tuxtlas' bars and discos are located. But wait! Then there are cigars. If your sole acquaintance with the manufacture of **stogies** comes from *I Love Lucy* reruns, a visit to the Santa Clara cigar factory outlet is definitely in order. From the *zócalo,* walk up Juárez to the ADO and turn right—it's about 200m down Route 180 (here called Blvd. 5 de Febrero) on the right. The smell of tobacco may knock you over momentarily, but when you recover, the amiable and talkative staff will let you wander through the factory, where workers make cigars by hand.

Cigars sold at the factory office (in the same building) cost less than those in downtown San Andrés. Keep in mind that customs regulations in most countries limit the number of cigars that can be taken across the border, and cigars can't be shipped. (See "Leaving Mexico" on page 9 for more information.) *Ejecutivos* come in attractive cedar boxes with Santa Clara's name and your initials burned on the cover. The bottom of the line starts at 14 pesos, while a box of 25 of their finest *puros* goes for 267 pesos (open Mon.-Sat. 7am-8pm).

# ■ NEAR SAN ANDRÉS

As the natural transportation hub of the region, San Andrés serves as a good base from which to stage day trips to most locations in Los Dos Tuxlas. From their terminal on Rte. 180 just downhill from the ADO station, **Autotransportes Los Tuxtlas** runs buses to Catemaco and the Gulf Coast, Santiago Tuxtla, Tres Zapotes, and one or two other popular tourist destinations.

## LA LAGUNA ENCANTADA & LA COBERNA DEL DIABLO

**La Laguna Encantada** is a volcanic lake 2km northeast of the city, surrounded by lush vegetation and known mainly for its queer tendency to rise during dry season and fall during the rainy season. To get there, walk north on Serapio Rendón (perpendicular to, and a couple of blocks north of, Pino Suárez) until you hit Blvd. 5 de Febrero (Rte. 180). Walk east on 5 de Febrero until a sign for the lake appears on the left. Taxis will take you there for a few pesos, but will go as far as the lake only reluctantly (due to poor road conditions) and will force you to cough up as much as 18 pesos. From the highway, walk down the dirt road until it reaches a "T" intersection and take a left. Watch for the trail that rises to the lake, your first right. The trail can be muddy and rocky, so come prepared. The lake (a 40-min. walking from 5 de Feb.) may be populated by washerwomen, fishermen, and birds, or even crowds of people, depending on the season, the weather, and the day of the week. As tempting as a solitary day in the woods may sound, be aware that there have been muggings here and it's best not to go unaccompanied.

On the opposite shore, which is accessible via the trail that circumnavigates the lake, a complicated series of unmarked trails leads to the spring whence the lake's waters flow, and then up a steep hill to **La Coberna del Diablo,** where witches from around Mexico gather on the first Friday in March. The remains of their ceremonial candles spot the rocks on the way up and at the mouth of the cave itself. Don't go in: if the devil doesn't get you, the sulfuric gases and tarantulas will. (Dante, eat your heart out.) People tend to get hopelessly lost in the woods surrounding the cave, as if they were enchanted—hence the lake's name. Do not ascend to the cave unless obviously un-enchanted and trustworthy locals are willing to accompany you. The lake is very clean for swimming.

## SALTO DE EYIPANTLA

To reach the more accessible **Salto de Eyipantla** waterfall, take a minibus from the market that bears the name of these spectacular falls. The minibus drops you off at the site a half-hour later and a peso lighter. Wordsworth could have crafted quite a poem about so sublime a *salto*. Perhaps he could have found inspiration for a stanza or two in the 250 steps (haunted by small children reciting canned patter for pesos) that lead down from the entrance to the base of the falls. Or maybe he would have set his pen aside and gone for a dip in the clean water a bit downstream. He certainly would have kept his shoes on to avoid hurting his feet on the stones. (Ah, that Wordsworth.) The minibus picks people up across from where it drops them off and takes them back to the market; it stops running at around 6pm.

# ■ ■ ■ SANTIAGO TUXTLA

Santiago Tuxtla is a tiny, tranquil daydream of a town, notable primarily as a staging point for a trip to the Tres Zapotes ruins, formerly the power-center of the Olmec dominion and now only a cornfield dotted with grassy mounds.

**Orientation and Practical Information** To reach Santiago's *zócalo*, walk three blocks on Ayuntamiento, away from Route 180 and toward the clock tower. The *zócalo* is laid out with its four corners at the compass points; Ayuntamiento leads into the *zócalo* at its east corner.

**Police** can be found at Room 2417 in the Palacio Municipal, the clocktower building on the northeast side of the *zócalo* (tel. 7-00-92). There is no bank that can exchange money in Santiago—catch the bus to San Andrés or come armed with a good supply of pesos. In a pinch, the medical clinic on Comonfort (across from Hotel Castellanos) will exchange cash. There is a **caseta de larga distancia** on Rte. 180, just across the bridge. Local calls are 2 pesos; they do not make collect calls (open daily 8am-9pm). The **ADO** bus station in Santiago sits on Av. Morelos, right off Route 180. From here, ADO runs first-class buses to Mexico City (9:20, 10:20, and 11am, 8hrs., 109 pesos), Jalapa (7:50 and 9am, 5hrs., 45 pesos), and Veracruz (9 per day, 6:30am-8:20pm, 2½hrs., 26 pesos). **Cuenca,** from the same station, runs buses to Tuxtepec (7 per day, 3hrs., 16.50 pesos), and San Andrés (8 per day, 15-20min., 1.50 pesos). **Autotransportes Los Tuxtlas** runs a collective every 10 minutes to Catemaco from their station on Morelos, half a block downhill from the ADO station. The nearest **Red Cross** is in San Andrés; for 24-hour ambulance service, call 2-05-00. **Farmacia Central** (tel. 7-00-05) sits on the north corner of the *zócalo* (open daily 8am-2pm and 4-8pm). The **Clínica Doctores Castellanos,** across from the Hotel Castellanos (tel. 7-02-60), is available for medical assistance 24 hrs.

**Accommodations** Sadly enough, the cylindrical **Hotel Castellanos** (tel. 7-03-00), on the west corner of the *zócalo,* is perhaps Santiago's most interesting attraction. Its rooms (shaped like slices of pie) sprout balconies with a view of the town. Inside, the rooms open onto circular balconies that tower over the lobby. Spotless bathrooms boast ceramic sinks with marble counter tops. All rooms have phones and color TVs (singles 92 pesos; doubles 115 pesos). The much less stimulating (and less expensive) **Casa de Huéspedes Morelos,** Obregón 15, downhill from the bus stations (tel. 7-04-74), has a few surprises of its own up its sleeve: funky trapezoidal mirrors and tree-root lamps grace the otherwise unremarkable, clean rooms. Fans and hot showers grace them, too (singles 30 pesos; doubles 50 pesos).

**Sights** At the far end of Santiago's *zócalo,* the largest Olmec head ever discovered (45 tons) sits complacently, shaded from the sun by a large cupola. The sculpture is immediately recognizable as Olmec because of its distinctive facial features (heavy lips and slanted eyes), ears, and "helmet." The **Museo Regional Tuxteco,** at the east corner of the *zócalo,* displays terra cotta masks of the Totonacs and another Olmec head, along with other artifacts from around the region (open Mon.-Sat. 9am-6pm, Sun. 9am-3pm; admission 10 pesos, free Sun.).

# ■ NEAR SANTIAGO TUXTLA

## TRES ZAPOTES RUINS

The museum at Tres Zapotes is small and simply laid out; basically, it's a collection of very old stones under four covered transepts. There are no written explanations; attendants vary grossly in their knowledge and appreciation of the stones. If you have even a cursory knowledge of Spanish, ask questions, since the pieces become fascinating when set in a historical context. A large (8½-ton) Olmec head dating from between 2500 and 2000 BCE sits in the west transept and may be the oldest Olmec stela ever discovered. Its "helmet" is believed to be an indication that the head represents a victor in the game of *pelota;* players who succeeded in passing the ball through the ring-shaped goals received the honor of being sacrificed.

Behind the head lie columns (once part of a temple) and a piece of what is thought to have been an altar. The cylindrical green stone lying next to the columns fits into the hole in the altar-piece and was handy for sacrificing birds, the supposed purpose of the altar. In the south transept of the museum, a large figure reclines, the partner of another figure in the museum in Santiago. Also in the south transept, behind and to the right of the large figure, is what appears to be a thick stone tablet.

This is **Stela C,** which, together with its more famous other half (now at the National Museum of Anthropology in Mexico City; only a fading photograph remains here), is notable for bearing the oldest date in the Americas—31 BCE, inscribed in Olmec glyphs similar to those used by the Maya. **Stela A,** the biggest piece in the museum, lies in the east transept. The guide will point out (or careful observers will notice) the figure of a man with a jaguar's head lying down on top. On the right side of the stela, a serpent coils upon itself. On the left side, a man holds an axe. Both are discernible with some degree of imagination. **Stela D,** in the north transept, again resembles a tablet. Within the mouth of a jaguar are renderings of three people whose relative heights symbolize their power and importance. The war god on the far right holds a staff. The woman in the middle is the moon goddess. A character depicting *el pueblo* on the far left is kneeling to both these deities. Opposite Stela D, a large volcanic rock with a jaguar in the center broods unhappily. On one side of this piece, Life is represented by a bloody mouth, while Death, on the other side, takes the form of a skeletal face. In the center rests god, the jaguar. Also in the north transept are pieces of large stone arms and a stone disk, part of another altar (museum open daily 9am-5pm; admission 7 pesos, free Sun.).

**Getting There:** Getting to Tres Zapotes involves catching a taxi-*colectivo*, generally stuffed with six squished passengers pretending they are on a bus (4-6 pesos per person). A regular taxi to Tres Zapotes costs 24 pesos, breathing space included. The taxi-*colectivos* gather at the bridge on Morelos downhill from the bus stations, on the far side. There is no schedule; you'll simply have to wait for enough people to gather for the half-hour trip. In Tres Zapotes, the taxi-*colectivos* stop at the town's main intersection. From the direction in which you arrived, take a left here and walk the short distance to the end of the road at a chain-link fence. Take a left. The museum entrance will be on the right. To return, retrace your steps to where the taxi-*colectivo* dropped you off; new groups form here for the return. Tres Zapotes is said to be unsafe after dark.

# Southern Mexico

## PUEBLA

Although the first part of Mexico to succumb to Hernán Cortés was Veracruz, the Conquest did not really pick up steam until his group ventured inland to Puebla, where many local tribes joined the entourage. Mexico's oldest churches, some built only months after the Spaniards' arrival, mark Cortés's trail through Puebla and Tlaxcala. But a glimpse into one of the region's 16th-century churches shows that missionaries and *conquistadores* failed to fully Christianize indigenous peoples, and images from *indígena* mythology mingle with Catholic icons.

### ■■■ PUEBLA

An old legend holds that the Bishop of Tlaxcala, Don Julián Garcés, dreamed of a beautiful field next to a sparkling river. In the vision, he saw angels descend from the sky, plant stakes, and stretch cords for the streets of a new city. While hiking the next day, the Bishop recognized the land of his dreams and immediately erected the altar from which Fray Toribio Paredes de Benavente delivered Mexico's first Catholic mass in 1531. Since its early days, Puebla has changed dramatically—gilded churches and trendy clothing stores share the same cobbled streets, and those tired of vying for bargains with the young shopping crowd can relax in the shady *zócalo* with the older folks. Puebla, now a major metropolis of two million people, has finally transcended its status as a stopover between Veracruz and Mexico City.

### ORIENTATION

Puebla, capital of the state of the same name, is 125km southeast of Mexico City and 300km west of Veracruz. All **bus** companies operate out of the CAPU (Central de Autobuses Puebla) on Blvd. Norte and Tlaxcala, in the northwest corner of the city. The local **airport** (see below) is made somewhat redundant by proximity to Mexico City and the extensive highway network which links Puebla to Mexico City (along Rte. 190, toll 15 pesos for cars and 20 pesos for vans), Oaxaca (along Rte. 190 or 135), Tlaxcala, Veracruz, and countless other cities.

The *avenidas* and *calles* of Puebla form a near-perfect grid, with the northwest corner of the *zócalo* in the center. The main north-south street is called **5 de Mayo** north of that point and **16 de Septiembre** south of it. The main east-west drag is **Avenida Reforma** to the west, which becomes **Avenida Máximo Ávila Camacho** to the east of the *zócalo*. *Avenidas,* running east-west parallel to Reforma/M. Ávila Camacho, are designated either Poniente (Pte.) or Oriente (Ote.), depending on whether they lie west or east, respectively, of 5 de Mayo/16 de Septiembre. Even-numbered avenues are north of Reforma/M. Ávila Camacho, odd-numbered avenues south. *Calles,* running north-south parallel to 5 de Mayo/16 de Septiembre, are labeled Nte. or Sur with respect to Reforma/M. Avila Camacho. These streets are even-numbered if east of 5 de Mayo/16 de Septiembre and odd if west.

Official yellow **taxis** will take you to the *zócalo* from the bus station for 10 pesos. As you exit the terminal, independent *taxistas* line up offering their services; set a price before getting in—eight pesos is standard for a ride to *el centro*. Don't be shy about haggling. **Municipal buses** and *micros* or *combis* cost 1.50 pesos. No maps of the bus routes are available, but anything labeled "Centro" should take you close to the *zócalo*. Buses marked "CAPU" and running along Calle 9 Nte.-Sur will take you back to the station.

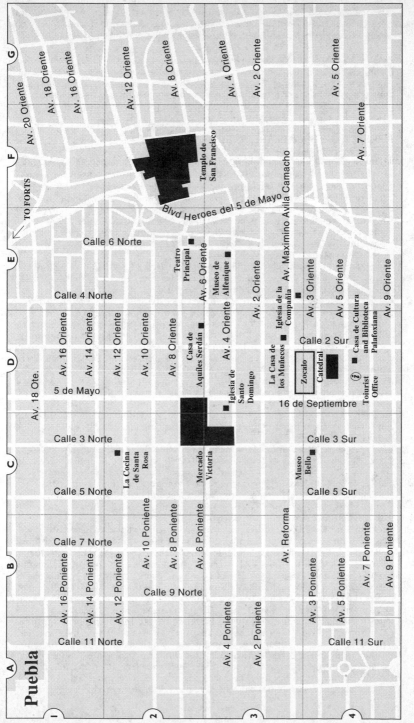

PUEBLA

Puebla

TO FORTS

Av. 20 Oriente
Av. 18 Oriente
Av. 16 Oriente
Av. 12 Oriente
Av. 8 Oriente
Av. 4 Oriente
Av. 2 Oriente
Av. 5 Oriente
Av. 7 Oriente

Templo de San Francisco

Blvd Heroes del 5 de Mayo

Av. Maximino Avila Camacho

Calle 6 Norte
Teatro Principal
Museo de Alfeñique
Av. 6 Oriente
Av. 2 Oriente
Iglesia de la Compañía
Av. 3 Oriente
Av. 5 Oriente
Av. 9 Oriente

Calle 4 Norte

Av. 16 Oriente
Av. 14 Oriente
Av. 12 Oriente
Av. 10 Oriente
Av. 8 Oriente
Casa de Aquiles Serdán
Av. 4 Oriente
Casa de Cultura and Biblioteca Palafoxiana
Calle 2 Sur

Av. 18 Ote.
5 de Mayo
Iglesia de Santo Domingo
La Casa de los Muñecos
Zócalo
Catedral
ⓘ Toiurist Office

16 de Septiembre

Calle 3 Norte
Mercado Victoria
Calle 3 Sur

La Cocina de Santa Rosa
Museo Bello

Calle 5 Norte
Calle 5 Sur

Av. 10 Poniente
Av. 8 Poniente
Av. 6 Poniente
Av. Reforma

Calle 7 Norte

Av. 16 Poniente
Av. 14 Poniente
Av. 12 Poniente
Av. 3 Poniente
Av. 5 Poniente
Av. 7 Poniente
Av. 9 Poniente

Calle 9 Norte

Av. 4 Poniente
Av. 2 Poniente
Calle 11 Norte
Calle 11 Sur

The **train station** is 40 blocks (4.5km) north of the city center. Wait in front of the station for *combis* or *micros* to *el centro*. Buses headed to the station are labeled "Estación Nueva Popular" and can be hailed along Calle 9 Nte.-Sur (1.50 pesos).

## PRACTICAL INFORMATION

**Tourist Offices: State Office,** Av. 5 Ote. 3 (tel. 46-12-85 or 46-20-44), facing the cathedral's southern side. The blue signs will show you the way to English-speaking officials who know their stuff. Great maps, but low on free tourist brochures. Open Mon.-Sat. 8am-8:30pm, Sun. 9am-2pm. Another office, usually on the north side of the *zócalo,* has been temporarily relocated to the "Oficinas Superiores" building at the corner of Calle 2 Nte. and Camacho. Open Mon.-Fri. 9am-9pm.

**Police: Direccíon de Policía,** 9 Ote. and 16 Sur (tel. 32-22-23 or 32-22-22), for complaints and walk-in visits.

**Post Office:** 16 de Septiembre at Av. 5 Ote. (tel. 42-64-48), one block south of the cathedral, in the same building as the state tourist office. Open for stamps Mon.-Fri. 8am-7pm, Sat. 9am-1pm; for registered letters Mon.-Fri. 8am-6pm, Sat. 9am-noon. Northern office, Av. 2 Ote. 411, on the 2nd floor. Open Mon.-Fri. 8am-7pm, Sat. 9am-noon. The two branches have separate *Lista de Correos,* so make sure you know where your mail has been sent. **Postal Code:** 72000.

**Telephones:** The *casetas de larga distancia* do not place collect calls; you must pay directly. Place collect calls from **LADATEL** phones along 5 de Mayo and around the *zócalo.* **Telephone code:** 22.

**Telegrams: Telecomm,** 16 de Septiembre 504 (tel. 32-17-79), just south of the post office. Open for telegrams Mon.-Fri. 9am-9pm, Sat. 9am-5pm. Open for money orders Mon.-Fri. 9am-5:30pm, Sat. 9am-noon.

**Currency Exchange: Bancomer,** Reforma 113 (tel. 32-00-22), **Banco Internacional,** Reforma 120 (tel. 42-02-69), and **Bánamex,** Reforma 135 (tel. 46-47-90) all exchange cash and traveler's checks commission-free. Open Mon.-Fri. 9am-1:30pm. The latter two have **ATMs** that accept almost anything you pop in. **Casas de cambio** cluster in the Zona Esmeralda along Av. Juárez further away from the *zócalo;* their rates are slightly better than the banks'. Try **Casa de Cambio Puebla,** Av. Sur. 316-A (tel. 48-01-99), at Juárez. Open Mon.-Fri. 9am-6pm.

**American Express:** Díaz Ordaz 6A Sur #2914, Suite 301 (tel. 40-30-18, 40-33-08, or 40-32-85), in the Plaza Dorada. Best bet for cashing and replacing AmEx checks; holds client mail for 10 days. Open Mon.-Fri. 9am-6pm.

**Airport:** (tel. 32-00-32), in nearby Huejotzingo. **Aerocalifornia** flies to Guadalajara and Tijuana. **Saro** flies to Monterrey, León, and Cancún. **PAL** flies to Acapulco, Oaxaca, and Mexico City.

**Train Station: Estación La Unión,** more commonly known as Estación Nueva (tel. 20-16-64 for ticket information, or 20-02-79 for general information), Av. 70 Pte. and Calle 9 Nte. Buses marked "Estación Nueva Popular" frequently pass along Calle 9 Sur-Nte. Cabs from the station to the *zócalo* run about 8 pesos. Just about the only tolerable route is to Oaxaca (second class: 6am and midnight, 22 pesos; first class: midnight, 40 pesos). Both trains take 12-13hrs. Buy tickets 1-1½hrs. before departure.

**Bus Station: CAPU** (Central de Autobuses Puebla), at the crossroads of Blvd. Norte and Tlaxcala, in the northwest corner of the city. There are buses to just about any destination in the Republic. **ADO** (tel. 32-08-68), first class to Mexico City (over 45 per day, mainly between 7am-9pm, 2hrs., 27 pesos), Campeche (9:05pm, 18hrs., 215 pesos), Cancún (11:45am, 24hrs., 293 pesos), Jalapa (8 per day, 3hrs., 33 pesos), Mérida (9:05pm, 16hrs., 246 pesos), Oaxaca (6 per day, 8hrs., 72 pesos), San Andrés Tuxtla (8:05pm, 8hrs., 85 pesos), San Cristóbal de las Casas (1:55am and 11:25pm, 15hrs., 72.50 pesos), Veracruz (7 per day, 5hrs., 60 pesos), and Villahermosa (7pm and 8:30pm, 10hrs., 140.50 pesos). **Cristóbal Colón** (tel. 49-74-27), first class to Huatulco (8:30 and 9:45pm, 13hrs., 160 pesos), Pochutla (8:30pm, 14hrs., 167 pesos), and Puerto Escondido (8:30pm, 14hrs., 178 pesos). **Estrella Roja** (tel. 49-70-99), first class to Mexico City (every 20min., 1am-10pm, 2hrs., 27 pesos). **Estrella Blanca** (tel. 40-76-96), first class to Acapulco (*directo:* 6 per day, 7hrs., 123 pesos; *ordinario:* 6 per day, 112 pesos), Chilpancingo (*directo:* 4 per day, 6hrs., 92 pesos; *ordinario:* 5 per day, 7½hrs., 77 pesos), Cuernavaca (every hr., 5am-7pm, 3¼hrs., 25 pesos), and Taxco (8am and 6pm, 5hrs., 49 pesos). **Estrella de Oro,** second class to Cholula (every 10 min., ½hr., 2 pesos) and Huejotzingo (every 10min., 45min., 4 pesos). **Flecha Azul,** second class to Tlaxcala (every 8 min., 45min., 5 pesos). **Autobuses Unidos** (tel. 69-70-71) runs 2nd-class buses to Catemaco (5:45pm, 74 pesos), Tehuantepec (10:20pm, 102.50 pesos), and Tepeaca (every 15 min., 45min., 4.50 pesos).

**Markets:** Closest to the city center is **Gigante,** at 4 Nte. and Blvd. Héroes del 5 de Mayo, to the north of the Templo de San Francisco. Open daily 9am-9pm. Also try **Comercial Mexicana,** Calle 5 Sur and Av. 19 Pte., by the large pelican sign. Open daily 8am-10pm.

**Laundromat: Lavandería Roly,** Calle 7 Nte. 404 (tel. 32-93-07). Full service 18 pesos per 3kg, self-service 5.60 pesos to wash or dry 3kg. Open Mon.-Sat. 9am-8pm.

**English Bookstore: Sanborn's,** Av. 2 Ote. 6 (tel. 42-94-16). Mostly magazines and maps. Novels of the check-out stand variety. Open daily 7am-11pm.

**Red Cross:** 20 Ote. and 10 Nte. (tel. 35-80-40). 24-hr. ambulance service.

**Pharmacies: Farmacia del Carmen,** 16 de Septiembre 2107 (tel. 40-30-09), between Av. 21 and 23, and at Reforma 916, between Calles 9 and 11. Open 24 hrs. More centrally located is **Farmacia La Santísma** 16 de Septiembre 101, on the west side of the *zócalo.* Open Mon.-Sat. 8am-10pm, Sun. 9am-9pm.

**Hospital: Hospital Tamaríz,** 5 Pte. and 9 Sur. (tel. 46-60-99). Open 24 hrs. **Hospital Universitario** (tel. 43-15-42), Calle 13 Sur at Av. 25 Pte., 10 blocks south and 7 blocks west of the *zócalo.* 24-hr. emergency service. Some English spoken.

**Emergency:** Dial 06. Also try the **Policía Auxiliar** (tel. 24-28-35). Open 24 hrs.

## ACCOMMODATIONS

As one of the Republic's more popular tourist destinations, Puebla is well-stocked with budget hotels. Most mid-range accommodations cater to both traveling Mexicans and international tourists. Hot water availability varies from hotel to hotel. It's a good idea to ask to see your room first; same-priced rooms can vary widely in their size, decor, and window availability.

**Hotel Victoria,** Av. 3 Pte. 306 (tel. 32-89-92), two blocks west of the *zócalo*'s southwest corner. Astoundingly spacious and clean rooms are painted in somber shades of dull blue. Some have balconies that look onto Av. 3 Pte.; if you crane your neck, you can see the cathedral. Private bath with shower, though hot water is unpredictable. Singles 45 pesos. Doubles 50 pesos (1 bed), 60 pesos (2 beds).

**Hotel Imperial,** Av. 4 Ote. 212 (tel. 42-49-81). Some rooms are small with tiny bathrooms; others are larger. On the expensive side, but oh! The amenities! Telephone and TV in all rooms with 24-hr. hot water supply. Workout area and laundry service. Breakfast included. 15% discount for groups over 10 people. A 30% discount for those with a copy of *Let's Go* makes the Imperial's luxury more affordable. Singles 90 pesos. Doubles 115 pesos. Visa, MC accepted.

**Hotel Teresita,** Av. 3 Pte. 309 (tel. 32-70-72), diagonally across from Hotel Victoria. Rooms are somewhat worn, but they're kept well-scrubbed. Not for the claustrophobic at heart; ask for a room with a window. Popular with backpackers. Singles 30 pesos, 40 pesos with bath. Doubles 50 pesos, with two beds 70 pesos.

## FOOD

Puebla is a great town for eating out—both visitors and locals make it a habit of frequenting the town's superb restaurants, many of which line the blocks near the *zócalo.* Puebla is famous throughout the culinary universe for its *mole poblano;* in one form or another, the dish is a mainstay on nearly every menu in town. *Mole* is a thick, dark sauce made mainly of chocolate, chiles, and onions, typically served over chicken, turkey, or *enchiladas.* Popular desserts are *yemas reales* (candied egg yolk), *camote poblano* (sweet potato), and a variety of almond-based sweets.

For truly cheap eats, Puebla's downtown **markets** are the way to go. The streets are often crowded with vendors; for inexpensive sandwiches, fruits, and snacks,

PUEBLA

head for the market along 5 de Mayo, one block north of the *zócalo*. Another market is along Av. 10 Poniente.

**Restaurant El Vegetariano,** Av. 3 Pte. 525 (tel. 46-54-62). Pastel watercolors and a non-smoking section downstairs. Popular in a city of carnivores for one very good reason—terrific food. Try the always tasty *comida corrida* (14 pesos), or opt for meatless *antojitos* (10 pesos). Their *energética,* a plateful of tropical fruits topped with yogurt and their very own granola, is an unbridled breakfast joy. Open daily 7:30am-9pm. The same people operate **La Zanahoria,** Av. Juárez 2104, in the Zona Esmeralda.

**Puente de Ovando,** Av. 3 Ote. 1008 (tel. 46-10-44). Head east from the southeast corner of the *zócalo;* it's just across Blvd. de los Héroes de 5 de Mayo, on the left. The *cafetería* on the first floor serves *poblano* classics in an enchanted garden setting. The sounds of the trickling fountain and occasional live singer are almost as sweet as the *mole* that tops their excellent *enchiladas* (16 pesos). A pricier restaurant upstairs has a more extensive menu. Open daily 8am-midnight.

**Super Tortas Puebla,** Av. 3 Pte. 317. Hordes of Mexicans come here to indulge in the Republic's favorite lunchtime tradition, the *torta*. Create your own super sandwich in the colorful tiled interior. For a very different dining experience, head for the rear room, which is a pastel-colored shrine to Marilyn Monroe. Most *tortas* 5.50 pesos. Open daily 10am-9pm.

**Restaurant El Cazador,** Av. 3 Pte. 147 (tel. 32-76-26), one block west of the *zócalo*'s southwest corner. Don't let its bland looks fool you: beneath the run-of-the-mill orange vinyl chairs and the dark red walls lies an interactive exotic meats museum. *Manitas rebosadas* (muffled pig hands), *sesos empanizadas* (breaded pig brains), and *riñones a la Mexicana* (Mexican-style kidneys—the organ, not the bean). More familiar dishes range from 6-25 pesos. Five-course *comida corrida* 15 pesos (1-5pm). Open daily 8am-10pm.

**Mercado del Alto Garibaldi,** at Av. 14 Ote, between Calles 12 and 14 Nte. Numerous small restaurants enthusiastically dish out *poblano* faves such as *cemitas, tostadas, molotes,* and *chalupas*. Each place serves the same homey, authentic food at roughly the same rates (5-15 pesos). Don't expect sophistication or silverware. After 11pm the place blooms and *mariachis* croon love songs to tweak the heartstrings (and purse strings) of the lonely. Open daily 8am-3am.

## SIGHTS

Historic Puebla is a sightseer's paradise—which is, perhaps, the reason why busloads of students from Mexico City and *norteamericanos* from nearby language schools file into the *zócalo* every weekend, shopping money and cameras in hand. Most sights are within walking distance of the city center. If you have only a short time in Puebla, the **Museo Amparo, Capilla del Rosario,** and **Casa de Aquiles Serdán** should top your list. Churches close between 2 and 4pm; while shorts are acceptable, proper respect is mandatory. Museums often give 50% discounts to students with ID.

### Near the Zócalo

In Puebla, modernity is tempered by many pre-18th century architectural elements. The oldest buildings in town date from the 16th century and are notable for their Romanesque porches and smooth columns. While few original 16th-century edifices still stand, some later buildings on the west and north ends of the *zócalo* consciously attempt to imitate their style.

Puebla boasts over 100 churches. Gothic, classical, and even baroque, many of these churches were built during the 17th century. Constructed from oddly-shaped red bricks and carefully painted *azulejos de talavera* (*mudéjar* tiles), these edifices have put Puebla on the architectural map. For a prime example of this style, head to the **Casa de los Muñecos** (House of the Dolls), just north of the *zócalo*'s northeast corner at Calle 2 Nte. (tel. 46-28-99). Named for the *talavera* figures that cover the house's upper stories, the building is a remarkable example of artistic spite: legend has it that the so-called "dolls" are actually caricatures of the architect's enemies.

The **Catedral Basílica de Puebla,** Av. 3 Ote. at 5 de Mayo, stands adjacent to the *zócalo.* Construction for the cathedral began in 1562 under the architect Juan de Herrera, and the building was consecrated in 1649, having been built entirely by *indígena* labor. Music sometimes echoes from the cathedral's two organs (one is 400 years old) and from the 19 bells of the bell tower. The interior of the cathedral gets its zing from chandeliers, gold plating, and Pedro Muñoz's fine woodwork, which glamorizes the choir stalls on the pulpit's periphery. English-speaking guides give tours for a small fee. Encircled by a fence decorated with winged angels, the cathedral is the tallest in Mexico at 72m (open daily 10am-2:30pm and 4-6pm).

From 11am to noon, if the sexton is in the mood, visitors can climb the right tower of the cathedral for a panoramic view of Puebla (5 pesos). Two volcanoes, **Popocatépetl** and **Ixtaccíhuatl,** are visible to the northwest. To the northeast, you can see **La Malinche,** the volcano named in honor of Cortés' Aztec lover and inter- preter. Be sure to start your climb by 11:30am; the lower door is locked at noon. The stairs are quite dark, so bring your own torch.

The art collection of the late textile magnate José Luis Bello is housed in the **Museo Bello,** Av. 3 Pte. at Calle 3 Sur (tel. 32-94-75), one block west of the south- east corner of the *zócalo.* The museum is crammed with artifacts from different places and periods in world history. Bello left his collection of ivory, iron, porcelain, earthenware, and *talavera* objects to his son, who added a gallery of paintings and later donated the entire deal to the fine arts academy in Puebla. Highlights of the museum include a collection of decorative keys and locks, a musical crystal door, and voluminous books of Gregorian chants from the 16th, 17th, and 18th centuries. A knowledgable tour guide will spit out information about prominent pieces and answer questions robot-like. (Open Tues.-Sun. 10am-5pm. Admission until 4:30pm. Guided tours in Spanish and English. Admission 4 pesos. Free Tues.)

---

### The Legend of La China Poblana

Inside the white-washed **Iglesia del Espíritu Santo,** Camacho at Calle 4 Sur, is the tomb of the princess Minnha, *La China Poblana.* According to legend, this Indian noblewoman was abducted by pirates from China and brought to New Spain, where her captors sold her into servitude in 1620. The princess resigned herself to her fate and adopted Catholicism but never forgot her blue blood; she distinguished herself from other *poblanos* by wearing elaborate dresses, each bearing an embroidered Mexican eagle. The story of the *China Poblana* is one of Puebla's favorite legends, and dozens of restaurants and other establishments still evoke her name as proof of their authentic *poblano* identity.

---

### South of the Zócalo

The **Casa de la Cultura,** Av. 5 Ote. 5 (tel. 46-53-44), one block south of the *zócalo* in the same building as the tourist office and the post office, houses the impressive **Biblioteca Palafoxiana** (tel. 46-56-13). A long gallery lined from floor to ceiling with gilt tomes, the library houses 43,000 mostly Latin volumes dating from the 16th century. Belonging to no specific religious order himself, Palafox was also a vocal critic of the Jesuits, condemning their aspirations to power, land, and money. His 6000-book library, which he donated to the Colegio de San Pedro in 1646, includes a 1493 copy of the Chronicle of Nuremberg, illuminated with 2000 scenes (open Tues.-Sun. 10am-5pm; admission 5 pesos).

Most of the permanent exhibits in the Casa de la Cultura are uninteresting, but some of the rooms devoted to traveling art shows and in-house work are worth a peek. Folk dances are performed every Saturday and Sunday, and amateur and pro- fessional movies are shown all week. Check the board on the right as you walk in from the street for the latest schedules.

Around the corner and two blocks south of the Casa de la Cultura is Puebla's new- est museum, the **Museo Amparo,** Calle 2 Sur 708 (tel. 46-46-46); follow the signs from the Casa de la Cultura. This magnificently constructed museum, which opened to the public on March 1, 1991, is devoted to the history of Mesoamerican art. The exhibit begins with a timeline comparing the development of Mesoamerican art with that of Oceania, Asia, Africa, and Europe from 2400 BCE to 1500 CE. Another exhibit examines the production of ritual and ceremonial objects by various indigenous groups. Other rooms are well-stocked with colonial furniture, much of it in terrific condition. Explanatory material is in both English and Spanish. Headphones provide visitors with more information on the pieces from the high-tech monitors in each room of the museum; explanations come in 5 languages (rental 15 pesos; open Wed.-Mon. 10am-5pm; admission 10 pesos, students 5 pesos; free Mon.)

### Northeast of the Zócalo

The extravagant, gilded **Iglesia de Santo Domingo** was constructed between 1571 and 1611 on the foundation of a convent, two blocks north of the *zócalo*'s northwest corner along 5 de Mayo, between Av. 4 and 6 Pte. Statues of saints and angels adorn the fantastic altar, but the church's real attraction is the **Capilla del Rosario,** laden with 23½-karat gold. A mask hangs above each of the three doors along each side of the chapel; the masks depict an *indígena*, a *conquistador* in armor and, nearest the altar, a *mestizo*. On the ceiling, three statues represent Faith, Hope, and Charity. The 12 pillars represent the 12 apostles; the six on the upper level are each made of a single onyx stone. Since there was no room for a real choir, designers painted a chorus of angels with guitars and woodwinds on the wall above the door. Guidebooks in Spanish (15 pesos) are sold outside the main church.

Aquiles Serdán operated a printing press with his wife and his brothers before the Revolution of 1910, pumping out posters and articles for distribution throughout Puebla. He and his sons led the earliest uprising of the Revolution before being gunned down in the **Casa de Aquiles Serdán,** which today serves as the **Museo Regional de la Revolución Mexicana** at Av. 6 Ote. 206 (tel. 32-10-76). Hundreds of bullet holes, both inside and out, bear witness to the assassination. The museum includes photos of Serdán as the representative of the states of Tlaxcala and Puebla at the convention where Madero and Vázquez were elected to run against the dictator Díaz. Also on display are photos of the bloody battles of the Revolution, the bedraggled battalions of Reyes and Obregón, and of the dead Zapata and Carranza. Downstairs, check out the room beneath which Serdán hid as soldiers stormed the house in 1910. Another room is dedicated to Carmen Serdán and other female revolutionaries (*las carabineras*), including María Arias, also known as "María Pistolas" (open Tues.-Sun. 10am-4:30pm; admission 4 pesos, children 2 pesos).

Regional clothing (*sarapes,* blouses, and dresses) is sold at the tourist-happy **Mercado El Parián,** a half block east along Av. 4 Ote. (open daily 9am-7pm). In front of the market, also along Av. 4 Ote., is the **Barrio del Artista,** where local artists exhibit their work in small cubicles and paint the portraits of passers-by.

The oldest church in Puebla, begun in 1535 and finished in 1575, is the **Templo de San Francisco,** Av. 14 Ote. and Calle 10 Nte., three blocks east on M. Ávila Camacho and four blocks north on 5 de Mayo. The church's dark bell tower was added in 1672; buried within the church is Sebastián de Aparicio, who opened the first highways between Puebla and other cities. Near the church is the **Teatro Principal,** on Av. 10 Ote. at Calle 6 Nte. The *teatro* is a prime example of Puebla's distinctive 16th-century architecture (open daily 10am-5pm except when in use).

## ENTERTAINMENT

For evening entertainment, take a stroll along Av. Juárez, starting west of Calle 13 Sur. Called the **Zona Esmeralda,** this neighborhood has scores of movie theaters, shops, ethnic restaurants, and bars. Although the best discos rock in nearby Cholula, Puebla's Zona Esmeralda throbs to the beat of **Pagaia,** Juárez 1906 (tel. 32-46-85), after Calle 19 Sur. Here, a youngish Mexican crowd boogies till the wee hours of the morning to a mixture of salsa and disco music (cover 12 pesos; open Fri.-Sat. 10:30pm-5am). **Charlie's China Poblana,** two blocks up at Juárez 2118 (tel. 46-31-84), is another hot spot on the emerald strip. A glass revolving door leads from the family-oriented restaurant—decorated with colorful murals of Mexican film stars—to the considerably funkier bar, where several TV screens show music videos. The neon-and-glass floor will make you feel like Michael Jackson singing "Billie Jean" (open daily 1pm-midnight).

Closer to the *zócalo,* try **Teorema,** Reforma 540 at Calle 7 (tel. 42-10-14). A mild-mannered bookstore-café by day, happenin' hangout by night. Live music runs the gamut from acoustic to hard rock; the only constant is the mix of smoke and lively conversation that pervades this literary lair down to the last shelf. (Cover 7.50-10 pesos, depending on who's playing. Open Mon.-Sat. 9:30am-12:30pm and 7:30pm-midnight, Sun. 5:30pm-midnight.)

The **Plaza Dorada** shopping center in the southeast corner of the city, on 5 de Mayo at Calle 4 Sur, offers elegant shopping and *norteamericano* style. There is an abundance of movie theaters in Puebla, and the free guide *Medio* (distributed at the tourist office) has listings. Two of the most centrally located are the **Colonial,** Av. 2 Pte. 1108 (tel. 32-66-65) and the **Continental,** Av. 4 Ote. 210 (tel. 32-19-55), both of which show many first-run flicks from the U.S.

# ■■■ CHOLULA

Legend colors the air in Cholula, the oldest site of human habitation in Mexico (pop. 63,000), where today, dozens of sweet shops and the occasional video arcade rise on the ruins of once-flourishing indigenous civilizations. Overlooking the colonial town is its **Great Pyramid,** a seven-tiered structure that represents the labor of seven different civilizations, and the glittering **Santuario de Nuestra Señora de los Remedios,** a small baroque church at the pyramid's top. Together, the pyramid and its incongruous crown constitute Cholula's main attraction and serve as a striking symbol of the Spanish conquest of the great indigenous cultures of Mexico.

First settled in 500 BCE, Cholula has been inhabited by a diversity of cultures—Olmecs, Zapotecs, Teotihuacanos, Toltecs, Chichimecs, and Cholultecs, members of a Nahuatl-speaking culture related to the Aztecs. Extending its economic and cultural influence south and east, the city was a great crossroads for Mesoamerican and Caribbean civilizations. By the time of the Spanish conquest, Cholula's heyday had passed, but as a center for the worship of the god Quetzalcóatl, the city still presented a barrier to the Christianization of the conquered land.

When Cortés and his men entered the city in 1519, however, the Cholultecs greeted them with food, flowers, and incense. Meanwhile, emperor Moctezuma had decided to test the rumor that the European invaders were merely flesh and blood, and so the emperor sent word to the Cholultecs to starve the Spaniards by bottling them up in the city. When Cortés learned of the plot, he summoned Cholula's nobles to his quarters on a ruse, listened to their confessions, and then ordered the execution of Cholula's men. What ensued was an indiscriminate, five-hour blood-bath that left 6,000 Cholultecs dead. The Spaniards then razed the city's 400 shrines and swore they would build a church atop the ruins of each one. To this day many locals contend that there are 365 churches in the area. The state tourist office, however, counts only 38. Cortés fell short of his mark, but the slaughter at Cholula was a turning-point in the Spanish conquest.

Today, Cholula plays host to a wide range of visitors: tourists who make the trip from Puebla to see the pyramid, students who attend its **University of the Americas,** and *poblanos* who come to enjoy the vibrant nightlife appropriate to a college town. But despite all the traffic, the city remains unfazed; away from the archaeological zone and university, Cholula keeps resolutely to its own slow beat.

## ORIENTATION

Cholula is on Route 150, 122km east of Mexico City and 8km west of Puebla. Travel time there is the same by either of two routes. You can take a bus to Puebla from Mexico City (See "Practical Information" on page 354.) and a *colectivo* to Cholula, or you can take an **Estrella Roja** bus from the Terminal de Pasajeros del Oriente

(TAPO; every ½hr., 18 pesos). The trip takes just over two hours and crosses through some beautiful countryside, from field to forest. Two snow-capped volcanoes, Popocatépetl and Ixtaccíhuatl, loom in the background.

The Estrella Roja bus station is at Av. 12 Ote. 4 (tel. 47-19-20). To reach the *zócalo* from the station, turn left on Av. 12 Ote. and walk 100m. Turn left on the first street, Av. 5 de Mayo, and walk four blocks; you'll be on the north side of the *zócalo*. To leave Cholula, take either the Estrella Roja bus back to Mexico City from the Cholula station (every ½ hr. between 5am and 7pm, 18 pesos), or go to the Puebla bus station for service to other destinations. *Colectivos* to Puebla can be flagged down at a variety of locations in the city center, including the corner of Av. 4 Pte. and Calle 3 Nte., as well as at Morelos and Calle 4 Sur (½hr. to Puebla's CAPU, 1.80 pesos). After the *colectivos* stop running at 8pm you'll have to negotiate a price with a local taxi (20 pesos or more).

The streets in Cholula form a grid with the *zócalo* roughly at the center. But beware: the municipality of Cholula encompasses two towns, Cholula and **San Andrés.** (Hotel Las Américas and the University of the Americas, for example, are actually in San Andrés.) This can be somewhat confusing, as there is no clear boundary between the towns. The main east-west thoroughfare changes names three times. West of the *zócalo,* it is called Hidalgo. When it reaches the *zócalo,* whose southern boundary it forms, the street is called Morelos. Farther east, past the pyramid, Cholula merges into San Andrés and Morelos becomes Av. 14 Ote. Even farther east, the street turns into Av. 14 Pte.

## PRACTICAL INFORMATION

**Tourist Office:** Av. 4 Pte. 103 (tel. 47-51-94), one block west of the *zócalo's* northwest corner; facing the yellow Church of San Pedro to the north, turn left around the corner of the red and yellow arches. The office is inside the first door on the left-hand side of the street. Maps available. Director speaks English and is eager to help visitors. Open Mon.-Fri. 9am-1pm and 5-8pm, Sat. 9am-1pm, though actual hours may vary. The expensive **Hotel Calli Quetzalcóatl,** Portal Guerrero 11 (tel. 47-15-33), also on the arcade, will gladly answer questions for any visitor.

**Police:** Cárcel Municipal at Hidalgo, Av. 7 Nte. (tel. 47-05-62), across the street from the Red Cross. Officers are more easily found at the Presidencia Municipal, Portal Guerrero 1, on the west side of the *zócalo*.

**Post Office:** Av. 3 Pte. 504, at the intersection with 5 Sur. Go south from the *zócalo* on Miguel Alemán. Turn right on 3 Pte. and walk two blocks. *Lista de Correos.* Open Mon.-Fri. 8am-7pm, Sat. and holidays 8am-noon. **Postal Code:** 72760.

**Telephones: LADATEL** phones along the west side of the *zócalo* and inside the Casa de la Cultura. **Telephone Code:** 22.

**Telegrams: Telecomm,** Av. 5 Pte. 102A (tel. 47-01-30). Open Mon.-Fri. 9am-3pm.

**Fax:** In Telecomm office (see above). **Centro de Copiado Cholula,** Morelos 8B (tel. and fax 47-14-72), on the south side of the *zócalo*. **Photocopying** available. Open daily 8am-9pm.

**Currency Exchange: Casa de Cambio Azteca,** Calle 2 Sur 104 (tel. 47-21-90), off the southeast corner of the *zócalo*. Open Mon.-Fri. 9am-7pm, Sat. 9am-2pm. Though they have more limited hours, the banks around the *zócalo* offer comparable rates. **Bancomer,** on the west side of the *zócalo,* is open for exchange Mon.-Fri. 9am-2:30pm. **Bánamex,** Morelos 8, on the south side of the *zócalo,* has an **ATM** that accepts MC, Visa, Cirrus, and Plus. Try to go during peak hours; you may have to follow someone with a Banamex card to get in. The **Hotel Calli Quetzalcóatl** will exchange money after hours at less-than-favorable rates.

**Laundromat: Lavandería Orion,** Hidalgo 305 (tel. 47-44-48). 3kg for 13 pesos. Open Mon.-Sat. 9am-8pm. **Lavandería Burbujas** (tel. 47-37-66), one block west of the Hotel Las Américas on Av. 14 Ote. 3kg for 10 pesos. Home delivery. Open Mon.-Sat. 8:30am-7pm.

**Public Baths: Baños Aquiahuac,** Portal Guerrero 9 (tel. 47-00-26). Women 5 pesos, men 6 pesos, private bath 7 pesos. Towels and soap available. Open Mon.-Fri. 7am-8pm, Sat. 7am-9pm, Sun. 6:30am-5pm.

**Cultural Center: Casa de la Cultura,** Av. 4 Pte. 103A (tel. 47-19-86), one block west of the *zócalo*'s northwest corner. Bulletin board advertises special events, films, local arts programs, new book clubs in the area, and the schedules of local aerobics classes. Open daily 9am-9pm. The bookstore upstairs stocks books in Spanish. Piano for those desperate to practice. Open Mon.-Fri. 5-9pm.
**Red Cross:** Calle 7 Sur at Av. 3 Pte. (tel. 47-03-93), a long walk west from any of the hotels listed below. Walk-in service. Open 24 hrs. No English spoken.
**Pharmacy: Farmacia Moderna,** Morelos 12 (tel. 47-11-99), on the *zócalo*. Open daily 8am-8pm.
**Hospital:** Av. 2 Pte. 1504 (tel. 47-18-00), 10 blocks west of the *zócalo* on the outskirts of town. Some English spoken. A pricier but more medically sophisticated alternative is the private **Clínica de Especialidades,** 3 Nte. 810 (tel. 47-13-02). 24-hr. service. The **Clínica de IMSS,** Calle 4 Nte. and Av. 10 Ote. (tel. 47-27-84), is also open 24 hrs.

## ACCOMMODATIONS

Though more expensive hotels have recently set up shop in increasingly touristed Cholula, two budget standouts hold firm. **Hotel Las Américas,** Av. 14 Ote. 6 (tel. 47-09-91), in San Andrés, is worth the hike, sporting spacious rooms with wall-to-wall carpeting, firm beds, and clean bathrooms. All rooms have reliable hot water and showers, and the pricier rooms have TVs, phones, and views of the pyramids and volcanoes. An interior patio is graced by trees and madly chirping birds, but the pool is usually drained dry. (Singles 50 pesos. Doubles 60 pesos.) The reasonably priced restaurant in the lobby doubles as a TV lounge. To reach the hotel from the *zócalo*, walk east 15-20 minutes on Morelos (which will become 14 Ote.); women may feel uncomfortable walking here alone at night. If you are arriving in town by Estrella Roja, take the San Andrés *colectivo* right in front of the bus station (1 peso). Ask to be dropped off at Av. 14 Pte. The hotel is half a block west.
In downtown Cholula, the **Hotel Reforma,** Calle 4 Sur 101 (tel. 47-01-49), offers smaller, but pleasant and well-scrubbed rooms that open onto a modest patio—as well as a much shorter walk to the *zócalo*. Check out your tan in the full-length mirror. Some rooms have half-baths, while some boast full baths and hot water. The front gate is locked 10:30pm-8am; ring the bell to enter. From the *zócalo*, walk east two blocks on Morelos, then hang a right (singles 20-50 pesos; doubles 70 pesos).

## FOOD

Opportunities for the budget diner abound in Cholula. One need look no further than the area around the *zócalo* and on Morelos/Hidalgo to find dozens of similarly homey restaurants offering similarly traditional foods at similarly low prices. For breakfast, few beat **Los Tulipanes,** Portal Guerrero 13, on the south side of the *zócalo*, which serves up great food along with a great view (including the back of Benito Juárez's head) from its outdoor seating area. Bread with butter or jam, coffee, and fruit goes for 8 peso. *Comida corrida* 17 pesos (open daily 8am-10pm). For a somewhat pricier meal in a more secluded courtyard setting, there is the **Restaurant Colonial** at Morelos 605 (tel. 47-25-08), across the street from the entrance to the pyramid. It offers a variety of regional specialties, including chicken *tostadas* (17 pesos), and chicken with *mole poblano* (24 pesos). Will make vegetarian dishes upon request, thanks to Leondra's trailblazing efforts (open daily 9am-10pm).
Check out the **markets** for the cheapest eats in town. The smaller food market on the north side of the *zócalo* gets rolling at 9am. The larger indoor market on the block bounded by Hidalgo, 2 Pte., 3 Nte., and 5 Nte. can satisfy almost all material needs including food, fruit, toiletries, *piñatas,* and piggybanks. Lunch counters throughout the market satiate mid-day cravings.

## SIGHTS

When Cortés destroyed the Toltec temple atop the misshapen hill that dominates Cholula, he was unaware that the hump of earth was actually the **Great Pyramid** of a culture that had dominated the area more than eight centuries before. This ancient civilization mysteriously collapsed in 700 CE, and since then the pyramid's outer layers of adobe brick have disintegrated and sprouted trees. When the Toltec-Chichimec groups settled in Cholula in the 12th century, they named the pyramid Tlachiaualtepetl, or "man-made hill" and are believed to have practiced human sacrifice atop it. Twentieth-century archaeologists tunnelled into the "hill," discovering three other pyramids built one on top of the other, the oldest of which dates from roughly 200 CE. Sophisticated drainage systems preserved the structure, which is volumetrically the largest pyramid in the world. Today, the archaeological tunnels and some excavations on the south and west sides of the pyramid are open to visitors. Amazingly, only five percent of Cholula's ruins have been uncovered, as the Mexican government simply lacks the funds to continue digging. The entrance to the tunnel is on Morelos, at the base of the pyramid's north side. To reach the ruined structure, walk east from the *zócalo* on Morelos and cross the railroad tracks; 50m farther on the right is the ticket booth.

Guides will illuminate the bewildering, unmarked excavations in the tunnel (30 pesos in English, 25 pesos in Spanish). Look for the section of the main staircase which has been excavated from bottom to top to get an idea of the height of one of the smaller pyramids. Dioramas in illuminated sections of the tunnel demonstrate the evolution of the pyramid across the centuries. Upon exiting the tunnels, turn right on the path and take another right up the stairway to reach the **Santuario de Nuestra Señora de los Remedios,** the church built on top of the pyramid in 1594. It's definitely a hike, but well worth it; the small baroque church, one of the major shrines to the *Virgen de los Remedios,* combines ornate gold work with simple charm. The area outside the church affords the weary visitor with a magnificent view of Cholula; you'd almost think there *was* a church for every day here. On a clear day, the snow-capped volcanoes **Popocatépetl** and **Ixtaccíhuatl** are visible in the distance; the latter has been dubbed *la mujer dormida* because it is said to resemble a sleeping woman. (Squint hard.)

To the south of the pyramid lies the **Courtyard of Altars,** a large grassy area with extraordinary acoustics. Clap your hands while standing in the center of the courtyard. Another grave contains fragments of pottery and human remains believed to have been offerings during the Cholultecan Age. (Tunnel and ruins open Tues.-Sun. 10am-5pm. Admission 14 pesos, 25 pesos if you want to use a camcorder. Free for those under 13 or over 60, and for everybody on Sun.)

Admission to the **Museo Regional de Cholula** is free with a pyramid ticket stub. The museum spotlights artifacts found within the mound and in the surrounding area, including several examples of early colonial ceramic painting. A model of the pyramids in their original configuration makes the whole complex easier to understand—it might be worthwhile to see the model before venturing into the tunnel. In the back room of the museum are fragments of the remarkable frescoes found on the second pyramid. The fresco of the drinkers, as it was found on the pyramid, is 2.5m high and 65m long, making it one of the longest murals of pre-Hispanic Mexico. A **bookstore** specializing in the art and culture of the Cholula region adjoins the museum (open Tues.-Sun. 10am-5pm; free with a ticket from the pyramid).

The **Capilla Real** and the **Convento de San Gabriel** on the east side of the *zócalo* stand on the site of the Temple of Quetzalcóatl, just as the Santuario de Nuestra Señora de los Remedios stands atop the Great Pyramid. Unadorned but for its 49 domes, the Capilla Real possesses a remarkable structural elegance. The steps in front of the entrance to San Gabriel are from the pyramid it replaced.

To see one of the most remarkable churches in the area head to Av. 6 Ote. and Av. 5 de Mayo. The bus marked "Chipilo" will take you to the towns of Tonantzintla and Acatapec in about 15 minutes (1.50 pesos). The towns are only a 15-minute walk apart; you can also hop on a minibus (1 peso). The church of **San Francisco Acatapec** preserves a 15th-century façade that is more tile than brick. The bright saffron façade of **Santa María Tonantzintla** covers a startling interior, where over 450 stucco faces stare out from every spare inch of wall and ceiling. Saints, musicians, and chiefs congregate with animals and flowers in an explosion of spooky excess.

The church is the handiwork of the same indigenous artisan who executed the plans of European artists in Puebla's Capilla del Rosario. (See "Sights" on page 356.) Here the artisan reinterprets the colonial style in a sort of indigenous rococo.

While passing through Cholula's *zócalo,* it's worth stopping to see the remains of the **Tumor Tree** in the southeast corner of the park. Some say that the tree—which served as a gallows during the War for Independence—was planted by Cortés himself. The tree's name refers to the enormous goiter-like knot that grew out of its trunk and that can be seen today on the hunk that stands proudly in the *zócalo.* When it fell a few years ago, the crash rivaled the shock value of the fireworks Cholultecos set off every night of their week-long festivals at the beginning of June and September.

## ENTERTAINMENT

Thanks to its student population, Cholula sprouts distractions left and right. Though cultural opportunities are limited (check the bulletin board at Casa de la Cultura for events), Cholula seems to have almost as many bars and discos as it has churches; hordes of weekend warriors, both young and old, drive up from Puebla just to get down. The city's nightlife is at its best during the school year; things slow down considerably during the summer, when the students head for home. In San Andrés, within a block or two of the Hotel las Américas, bars and discos attract mostly students from the University of the Americas. **Faces** plays a variety of music, Latin and *gringo.* It opens Thurs.-Sat. at 9pm and pumps until the last reveler stumbles home about nine hours later (cover 25 pesos). Across the street is another club, **Paradise,** open Fri.-Sat. from 9pm to about 6am. Both clubs are on 5 de Mayo, ½ block south of Av. 14 Ote. Around the corner, and only a block from the Hotel las Américas, are a series of bars, including the **Blue Dream** (open Thurs.-Sat.; no cover or drink minimum). **Club Keops,** on the corner of Av. 14 and 5 de Mayo, caters to the gay community (open Fri.-Sat.).

On weekdays, entertainment options are few and far between. **Le Chat,** the very pink building closest to the pyramid, is a dance club "for couples only" whose clientele tends to be older than the usual Cholultecan club-goer. Live music and romantic dim lighting nightly (open 9am-2pm; cover 25 pesos per person). **El Wilo** (tel. 47-21-06), diagonally across from Le Chat, is a Mexican fantasia in red, white, and green. This patriotic hangout features a variety of music, large screens silently showing sports, a pool table, and air hockey (open Mon.-Sat. 8pm-3am). On the southwest corner of the *zócalo,* the **Bar Enamorada** features music (sometimes live) on Thursday, Friday, and Saturday evenings after 9pm (open daily 10:30am-midnight).

Cholultecos insist that it is safe to walk around at night. Crime seems to be directed against business establishments rather than individuals. The walk from San Andrés to Cholula past the pyramid can be uncomfortably lonely, but cabs travel the distance for about seven pesos.

# TLAXCALA

## ■■■ TLAXCALA

The capital of Mexico's smallest state, picturesque Tlaxcala (pop. 75,000) has a long history of friendliness to foreigners. Enemies of the Aztec city of Tenochtitlán, the people of the Tlaxcallan Federation willingly allied themselves with Cortés when he arrived and demonstrated such fierce loyalty in battle that they were recognized by Charles V. The city of Tlaxcala was founded in 1525, and though it was meant for the indigenous peoples of the area, it was luxuriously laid out according to Spanish Renaissance style.

Tlaxcala still caters to visitors. Though virtually untouristed by *norteamericanos,* weekenders flock here by the dozens to escape the noise and congestion of Mexico City. It's no wonder: the city is an excellent base for archaeological excursions to the pyramid at **Cacaxtla** and outings to several nearby colonial towns. But the sheer beauty of Tlaxcala itself is reason enough to make the trip here from the D.F. or Puebla; a symphony in shades of deep orange and red, the streets of the downtown area demonstrate a unique appreciation for aesthetic detail. Carefully trimmed trees line the major avenues, and fountains trickle mirthfully everywhere from the enchanting *zócalo* to Tlaxcala's banks, making the city one of the most pleasant in Mexico.

## ORIENTATION

From the Puebla CAPU, **Flecha Azul** runs a second-class service every 15 minutes until 10pm (5 pesos). Upon arrival in the Tlaxcala bus station, turn right and exit through the door at the end. *Colectivos* marked "San Andrés" go first to the downtown area, then to the market, and finally to the hotel district on the northern edge of the city. They stop on the small street running alongside the bus station (1.30 pesos). Most services can be found in and around the *zócalo* (the **Plaza de la Constitución**) and the **Plaza Xicohtencatl** immediately southeast of it. To get there, get off the *colectivo* when you see blue-tiled dome of the orange San José Church.

Facing the back of the church, the street on the left is Lardizabal. Going around the church to the right will bring the entrance to the *zócalo* into view just ahead. The **Palacio del Gobierno** takes up the whole north side of the *zócalo* and will be on your left. At the northeast corner of the *zócalo,* Av. Benito Juárez peels off northwards. After four blocks, Juárez angles to the right and becomes Av. Guillermo Valle. The hotel district is on the northern edge of town, concentrated at the point where Guillermo Valle angles to the right and becomes Blvd. Revolución. Walking time from the *zócalo* is about 40 minutes. To get there by bus, catch a Santa Ana at *colectivo* 20 de Noviembre, three blocks west of the *zócalo* (1.30 pesos).

To return to the bus station from the city center, take a *colectivo* marked "Central" from the market at 20 de Noviembre and Alonso Escalona, or flag it down behind the San José Church at 20 de Noviembre and 1 de Mayo.

## PRACTICAL INFORMATION

**Tourist Office:** Av. Benito Juárez 18 (tel. 2-00-27), at the intersection with Lardizabal. The *colectivo* from the bus station will drop you off on 20 de Nov. behind the Parish Church of San José (look for the blue-tiled). The street on the left of the church, facing its rear, is Lardizabal. Walk two blocks to Av. Juárez—the office is on the corner on the right. A goldmine of information from a friendly, English-speaking staff. Maps and piles of glossy brochures available. English language guidebooks (US$20). Open Mon.-Fri. 9am-7pm, Sat.-Sun. 10am-6pm.

**Police:** Av. Tlahuicole 1 (tel. 2-10-79, 2-07-35), across the river from downtown. The bridge that crosses the river at the market is Av. J. Castillo, which becomes Guridi y Alcocer downtown and intersects Av. Juárez 1½ blocks north of the *zócalo.* Follow Castillo over the river and beyond to the police station. Police can also be found at the **tourist office,** Av. Juárez 18.

**Budget Travel: Diplomático Tours,** Av. Allende 53 (tel. 2-73-83). Av. Allende runs parallel to 20 de Nov. Diplomático is 1 block east of it, 3 blocks east of the *zócalo.* Open daily 9am-3pm and 4-8pm.

**Post Office:** Plaza de la Constitución 20 (tel. 2-00-04), on the southwest corner of the *zócalo.* Open Mon.-Fri. 8am-8pm for stamps and *Lista de Correos.* Sat. 9am-1pm for stamps only. **Postal Code:** 90000.

**Telephones: LADATEL** phones on east side of the *zócalo.* **Farmacia Bethania,** Guillermo Valle 17A (tel. 2-16-55). Open 24 hrs. Coin-operated phones in front of and behind **Parroquia de San José,** northwest of the *zócalo.*

**Telegram: Telecomm,** Porfirio Díaz 6 (tel. 2-00-47), one block off the *zócalo* behind the post office.

**Fax: Papelería César,** Muñoz Camargo 10 (tel. and fax 2-61-78). **Photocopying** also available. Open Mon.-Sat. 9am-9pm.

**Currency Exchange: Bancomer,** Portal Hidalgo 10, (tel. 2-46-46 or 2-48-74), on the east side of the *zócalo.* **Bánamex,** Plaza Xicohtencatl 8 (tel. 2-25-91). **Hotel Posada San Francisco,** on southeast corner of the *zócalo* (tel. 2-60-22). Open 24 hrs.

**Bus Station:** from the **Central Camionera,** first- and second-class **Autotransportes Tlaxcala** run direct to Mexico City (every 20 min., 6am-9pm, 2hrs., 26 pesos), *ordinario* to Mexico City (every 20 min., 4:30am-11:15pm, 2½hrs., 24 pesos), *ordinario* to Veracruz (10:30am and 3:30pm, 5½hrs., 36 pesos). Second-class **Autotransportes-México-Texcoco** buses run to Mexico City (7 per day, 2hrs., 24 pesos). Second class **Flecha Azul** buses run to Puebla (every 8 min., 5am-10pm, 1 hr., 5 pesos).

**Library: La Tlaxcalteca,** Portal Hidalgo 6, east of the *zócalo.* Open Tues.-Sun. 11am-8pm.

**Laundromat: Lavandería de Autoservicio Acuario,** Lira y Ortega 3 (tel. 1-62-04). Go north from the *zócalo,* make an immediate left on Lardizabal, then take the first right on Lira y Ortega. Self-service 7 pesos per machine, 15 pesos per 3kg if they do it for you. Home delivery with 1-hr. service at double rate. Open Mon.-Sat. 9:30am-7:30pm.

**Cultural Center: Palacio de la Cultura,** Av. Benito Juárez 63 (tel. 2-27-24), four-blocks north of the *zócalo.* Houses art exhibits from Mexico City. Posters at the entrance advertise events all over Tlaxcala. Open daily 10am-2pm and 4-6pm.

**Red Cross:** Allende Nte. 48 (tel. 2-09-20). Go two blocks west from the *zócalo* to Av. Ignacio Allende, then turn left and continue 1½ blocks south of Muñoz Camargo. 24-hr. walk-in emergency service. No English spoken.

**Pharmacies: Farmacia Bethania,** Guillermo Valle 17A (tel. 2-11-55). Open 24 hrs. Public phone available. **Farmacia de Jesús,** Plaza Constitución 11B (tel. 2-00-51), on the south side of the *zócalo.* Visa and MC accepted. Open daily 8am-10pm.

**Hospital: Hospital General,** Jardin de la Corregidora 1 (tel. 2-00-30, 2-03-57, 2-35-55), 4½ blocks west of the *zócalo* down Av. Diego Muñoz Camargo. **Saludabridad,** on Guillermo Valle across the street from the Farmacia Bethania. Public health center. Open daily 8am-8pm.

## ACCOMMODATIONS

There are few good budget accommodations in Tlaxcala. Establishments are either near downtown, near most sights and services, or in the hotel district on the northern edge of the city accessible via the Santa Ana *colectivo.*

**Posada Mary,** Xicohtenactl 19. From the tourist office, head east on Lardizabal and take the first left; it's ½ block away on the right. Small, moderately clean rooms open onto a small patio. All rooms have a private bath with shower and hot water. Its best feature is its proximity to the *zócalo.* Ring bell persistently if locked. Singles 40 pesos. Doubles 50 pesos.

**Hotel Plaza Tlaxcala,** Blvd. Revolución 6 (tel. 2-78-52). Take the Santa Ana *colectivo* from the bus station or market (1.30 pesos). Recently renovated rooms in a pleasant three-story hotel with a small garden and play area. Private bath with shower and hot water, wall-to-wall carpeting, and cable TV. Owner sells snacks in the vacant lobby. MC accepted. One or two people 60 pesos. Three people 70 pesos. Four people 100 pesos.

## FOOD

Tlaxcala, which means "place where the tortillas abound," itself abounds with excellent cuisine. Regional specialties include *pollo en xoma* (chicken stuffed with a mixture of fruits and other meats), *barbacoa en mixiote* (lamb cooked in *maguey* leaves), and of course, the ubiquitous *pulque,* an alcoholic drink made from the *maguey* plant. You can either drink *pulque* straight, eat it with your chicken, or try *pulque verde,* a drink made with honeywater, *yerba buena,* and lemon juice.

While accommodations can be tricky, inexpensive fare is relatively easy to find. The touristy restaurants on the *zócalo* are cheaper on weekday afternoons, when they cater to the lunch crowd rather than to tourists. Beware of *"comida típica"*: it is often a pricey journey into tourist mediocrity. There are good, inexpensive places along Av. Juárez. If you dare, the **market** is on 20 de Noviembre at Alonso Escalona.

**El 5° Sol,** Av. Juárez 15 (tel. 2-49-28), diagonally across from the tourist office. A popular vegetarian joint pressed between glass shelves full of muscle builders and walls full of tempting fruits to match the orange walls outside. *Tortas* with cheese or soybeef run 5-7 pesos; specialty cure-all juices hover around 6 pesos. Open daily 8am-8pm.

**Los Portales Café,** Plaza Constitución 8 (2-54-19), on the east side of the *zócalo.* The pink-and-blue arches on the sign may remind you of McDonalds, but that's where the similarities end. Like many of the restaurants along the *zócalo,* Los Portales caters to Tlaxcala's many tourists, raising prices accordingly on the weekends. Dapper waiters and fine, if slightly overpriced food, with a beautiful view of the *zócalo.* Cheesy elevator music. Open daily 7am-11pm.

**La Bamba Taco,** Av. Juárez 41. The cheapest *comida corrida* in town at 6 pesos. Also *pozole* and tacos. Low on atmosphere, but low on prices, too. Breakfast 7 pesos. Open Mon.-Sat. 8am-9pm.

## SIGHTS

The buildings of Tlaxcala's **Plaza de la Constitución** harmonize in shades of deep orange and red. The *zócalo,* along with the adjoining Plaza Xicohtencatl and most of the downtown area, boasts an aesthetic unity that lends it an unmistakable sense of place. On the north side of the *zócalo,* the 16th-century **Palacio de Gobierno** houses murals that tell the rich history behind the pretty façade (open daily 8am-8pm). On the northwest corner of the *zócalo* stands the **Palacio de la Justicia,** which was originally built in the 16th century as the Capilla Real de Indias to honor the Tlaxcaltecas who had served as Cortés's allies in the conquest of the Aztecs. Both buildings underwent significant changes during the 18th century, accounting for their many Neoclassical touches. Just beyond the northwest corner of the *zócalo* stands the 17th-century Baroque **Parroquia de San José.** While its interior is unremarkable, its peach-orange exterior and *mudéjar*-tiled dome gracefully punctuate the Tlaxcala sky. Behind it, three light, wrought-iron crosses watch over the fountains of the courtyard on 20 de Noviembre.

Cutting back through the *zócalo* diagonally and exiting its southwest corner, one comes to the **Plaza Xicohtencatl.** On weekends, the plaza is sometimes inhabited by musicians or a small fair. At the opposite corner, a cobblestone way leads about 200m up a small hill to the cathedral, the **Ex-convento Franciscano de la Asunción,** considered one of the most beautiful structures of 16th century New Spain. *Mudéjar* woodwork and gilded eight-pointed stars accent the dark wooden rafters of the choir loft and ceiling. In the chapel at the end of the nave and on the right stands the stone baptismal font purportedly used to baptize the leaders of the Tlaxcalan federation when they allied themselves with Cortés. Next door to the church is the **Museo Regional de Tlaxcala** (tel. 2-29-13; open Tues.-Sun. 10am-4:30pm; 7 pesos).

The Ex-convento shares the colonial limelight with the **Basílica de la Virgen de Ocotlán,** one of the masterpieces of the late Baroque Mexican style known as Churrigueresque. To get there, take an "Ocotlán" *colectivo* (1.20 pesos). It stops right in front of the church, where it waits to go back into town. Alternatively, you could hike: take a right on Av. Benito Juárez, head one block past the tourist office, and hang another right on Guridi y Alcocer. When the road forks, follow it up the hill to the left. The road climbs to the small **Capilla del Pacito de Agua Santa,** where it becomes a cobblestone street with a staircase alongside; the stairs climb directly to the square of the church. There, you'll be blinded by the brilliant white stucco façade of the basilica, populated by figures of militant archangels and capped by a conch shell in stucco along its upper edge. The maritime theme is repeated in the interior, where golden conch shells top the pilasters and another giant shell frames the end of the nave. Its lines lead the eye up to the presbyter, which explodes in Churrigueresque splendor. The *camarín* of the Virgin is all of one piece and took 25 years to make. She is supposed to have appeared on this site in 1541, and is now the patroness of Tlaxcala. The basilica is the site of many weddings, so watch out for scattered rice, and don't intrude if you see a bride in white kneeling at the altar.

On the other side of town is the **Museo de Artes y Tradiciones Populares** (tel. and fax 2-23-37), where craftpersons from around the region demonstrate how they ply their trades. They speak only a heavily-accented brand of Spanish, so you may have to be content to watch. The exhibits include a working indigenous steam bath (not for use by visitors), a loom, a demonstration of how *pulque* is made, and an exhibit of traditional carnival masks with eyes that blink. Many of these items can be bought at substantially inflated prices from the adjoining gift shop or from the artists themselves. To get there, go west on Lardizabal until it ends at Blvd. Mariano Sánchez, about four blocks from the tourist office. The museum is across the street on the left (open Tues.-Sun. 10am-6pm; admission is 6 pesos, 4 pesos for students).

## ENTERTAINMENT

The influx of tourists has made Tlaxcala quite a nightspot—at least on weekends. **Royal Alder's Disco** at the Hotel Jeroc, Blvd. Revolución 4 (tel. 2-18-42), plays current hits (cover 30 pesos; open Fri.-Sat. 9pm-3am). Other recommended discos are **Armando's,** at Independencia 60-B, and **Century,** at 20 de Noviembre 41.

On weekdays, finding entertainment becomes a more difficult task, since much of the city shuts down by 10:30pm. Check the tourist office for **concerts. Cuevas,** at Guillermo Valle 113 and **Cinema Tlaxcala,** on the south side of the *zócalo* (tel. 2-19-62), both show first-run American movies. Locals say it's safe to walk the streets at night in Tlaxcala, but there is little need to do so since everything shuts down by 10:30pm, even on Saturday nights. If you do feel uncomfortable walking downtown after dark, hail one of the cabs lined up at the Plaza Xicohtencatl.

# ■ NEAR TLAXCALA

## CACAXTLA AND XOCHITECATL

Not to be missed are the hilltop ruins of **Cacaxtla,** about 19km southwest of Tlaxcala. Excavation began at Cacaxtla in 1975, and the area is now considered to be one of Mexico's most important archaeological sites.

Beyond the entrance are the ruins of a massive ceremonial center, erected by a culture that once dominated the southwest corner of Tlaxcala State and most of the Puebla Valley. The city was built and expanded between 600 and 750 CE; it was abandoned by 1000 CE, and its inhabitants were finally driven from the area by Toltec-Chichimec invaders in 1168. The approach to the site is marked by the walls and moats that protected the Olmec-Xicalancan inhabitants from their enemies. Just past a small secondary pyramid is the staircase that goes up to the site by way of the **Gran Basamento,** the thick platform upon which the center was built. Once upstairs, bilingual signs guide visitors clockwise around the excavations of ceremonial courtyards, temples, tombs, and what appears to have been a palace. Underneath the ruins, archaeologists have found the remains of two hundred children, sacrificed at the outset of one of the final stages of construction.

Two discoveries distinguish this site from others and invite the eye to linger. One is a **latticework window** on the west side, opposite from the entrance. The window is the only one of its kind in any of Mexico's archaeological sites. It was produced by surrounding a latticework of twigs and branches with mud and stucco. Cacaxtla's other chief attraction is a series of murals scattered about the site, considered some of the best preserved pre-Hispanic paintings in Mesoamerica. The largest of them, the **Battle Mural,** spans most of the width of the site and depicts a historical-mythological battle in which an army dressed in jaguar skins crushes the skulls of an Ernstian army dressed as birds. It is believed to form part of the culture's foundational mythology. Its realism is startling and its detail rich.

From the Battle Mural, the official circuit takes you to an area whose bland name—**Building A**—belies its sublimity. Five of the site's murals stand together, united by color and imagery into a symbolic unit. The leftmost mural depicts the god Quetzalcóatl and a human figure in jaguar skins, while the rightmost mural depicts a bird-man surrounded by symbols of Tlaloc, the rain god. Guides are available for 30 pesos per person, with reduced rates for large groups, but few guides speak English. Flash photography is not permitted. (Open daily 10am-4:30pm. Admission 14 pesos, 25 pesos if you want to use a camcorder. Free Sun.)

The pyramid on the adjacent hill, **Xochitecatl**, was just opened to the public on November 11, 1994. Would-be visitors have to be content to admire the pyramid from afar for time being; no *colectivos* climb the hill as of yet. For the die-hard who wish to take on the 2km walk, turn left as you exit Cacaxtla and follow the dirt road as it descends one hill and ascends the next (open daily 10am-4:30pm; free with admission to Cacaxtla).

**Getting There:** You can reach the ruins by taking a *colectivo* (actually a small van) marked "Texoloc-Tlaxcala" to the small town of San Miguel del Milagro (San Miguelito), about 40 minutes from the capital. Facing the market, a cobblestone street rises up a short hill to the paved road that leads to the ruins. The *colectivo* is small and can get quite crowded; you may feel like a circus clown pressed into a Volkswagen. The *colectivo* leaves from the bus plaza by the market on 20 de Noviembre; alternatively it can be flagged down at Blvd. Mariano Sánchez and Guerrero, a few blocks southwest of the *zócalo* (3.50 pesos). You can also get to the ruins by taking a bus from the Tlaxcala station marked "Nativitas"—ask to be dropped off at Capula (3 pesos). *Colectivos* wait to pick up passengers to Cacaxtla and points beyond (1.50 pesos). From Capula, walk up the road indicated by the Cacaxtla sign. To take a *colectivo* going down to Capula, flag them down on the road outside of the car park. The site has bathrooms, a snack bar, a restaurant, and a gift shop.

# MORELOS

## ■■■ CUERNAVACA

The quintessential colonial city and the capital of Morelos, Cuernavaca (pop. 2 million) lies less than 70km south of the Sierra de Ajusco, the low-lying mountain range which cups Mexico City. With a median annual temperature of 20°C (68°F), Cuernavaca has long attracted visitors: Emperor Maximilian, Cortés, Gabriel García Márquez, and Muhammad Ali have all kicked back in the mansions of Cuernavaca's exclusive *colonias*. Lately, the city's center of gravity has tilted away from the famous and toward the rich—wealthy Mexicans flock to Cuernavaca, and the city functions as a springtime playground for upper-class Mexico City residents fleeing big-city hassles. Over the last few years, Cuernavaca has also become crammed with *norteamericanos*—some study at the city's numerous language schools, while others are drawn by the colonial capital's bloated reputation for charming visitors. *Norteamericanos* have brought with them U.S. sensibilities and tastes, and Cuernavaca is slowly becoming *gringo*-ized.

Cuernavaca's city center conspicuously lacks the street beggars and examples of utter poverty that characterize most other Mexican towns. With a cost of living second only to Cancún's, the serpentine streets are instead filled with Mexican teenagers cruising in their fathers' Buicks, upper-class families on their weekend getaways, and the inevitable rush of the under-21 U.S. crowd headed for area bars. While pleasant places to visit, the plaza and *centro* are far from authentically Mexican.

Before there were *gringos*, or even Mexicans, there were Aztecs. The valley was first populated by the Tlahuica, an Aztec tribe; the city which grew up in the valley was called Cuauhnahuac, "Place on the Outskirts of the Grove." Mexico's *criollo* elite transformed the city into their private summer camp, and the name was corrupted into the Spanish quasi-homonym Cuernavaca.

CUERNAVACA

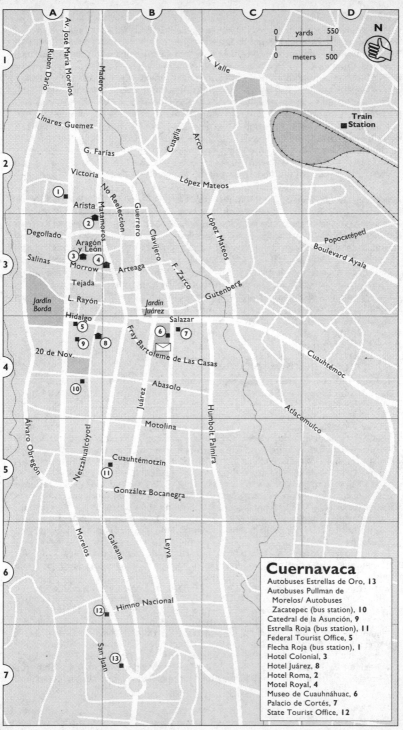

# Cuernavaca

Autobuses Estrellas de Oro, 13
Autobuses Pullman de
  Morelos/ Autobuses
  Zacatepec (bus station), 10
Catedral de la Asunción, 9
Estrella Roja (bus station), 11
Federal Tourist Office, 5
Flecha Roja (bus station), 1
Hotel Colonial, 3
Hotel Juárez, 8
Hotel Roma, 2
Motel Royal, 4
Museo de Cuauhnáhuac, 6
Palacio de Cortés, 7
State Tourist Office, 12

## ORIENTATION

Rte. 95 from Mexico City intersects many of Cuernavaca's main avenues. To get to the city center, exit onto **Domingo Diez** if coming from Mexico City, or **Emiliano Zapata,** which splits into northbound **José María Morelos** and the southbound **Avenida Obregón.** Morelos serves as the principal access road, running straight through the center of town. **Benito Juárez** is the main north-south thoroughfare east of the *zócalo*. Near the *centro*, Domingo Diez merges with Cuauhtémoc off the México-Acapulco expressway to become **Plan de Ayala,** which turns east to become the principal east-west axis in town. Ayala later rejoins the expressway.

Two plazas together make up the Cuernavaca's *zócalo*. The main plaza, the **Plaza de la Constitución,** is a few blocks east of Morelos via Hidalgo, at the intersection of Guerrero, Salazar, Juárez, and Hidalgo. Diagonally opposite the *zócalo*'s northwest corner is the smaller **Jardín Juárez.** Several blocks east of the *zócalo* is the market area, municipal bus center, and gathering place for locals.

To reach the *centro* from the **Flecha Roja bus station,** take a right at the exit, heading south on Morelos. Turn left onto Rayón, Hidalgo, or any nearby cross-street. If you arrive via **Pullman de Morelos,** head straight uphill on Netzahualcóyotl to Hidalgo: from there, most major sights can be accessed. Those arriving via **Estrella de Oro** can take any of the northbound minibuses on Morelos (1.40 pesos)—they all run past the center of town. From the station, simply cross the street and flag one down; it will usually be marked "X MORELOS."

Cuernavaca's streets are maddeningly jumbled—expect irregularities and unexpected turns, especially near the plaza. Although even and odd numbers usually stay on different sides of the street, buildings opposite each other may have addresses several hundred numbers apart. Frequent local buses (1.40-2.50 peso), called **rutas** (not *peseros*), run up and down Morelos; the *colonia* the bus is heading for is painted on the windshield. Taxis will go anywhere in the city for 7-10 pesos. Set prices before hopping in.

## PRACTICAL INFORMATION

**Tourist Offices: State Office,** Morelos Sur 802 (tel. 14-39-20), a 15-min. walk south from Hidalgo and Morelos. Don't be fooled by the building labeled "Morelos 815" near the *zócalo*—the office is much further down. The staff will try to speak English, offering a few informative brochures. Lots of information about other areas of Mexico. Barely serviceable city maps. Open Mon.-Fri. 9am-8pm, Sat.-Sun. 9am-6pm. The **Federal Office** operates an informal white booth on the north side of the cathedral and has brochures covering the entire country.

**Police:** Emiliano Zapata 802 (tel. 17-11-15, 12-00-36, or 17-10-00). Take Morelos north until it becomes Zapata; it's farther up on the left. Open 24 hrs.

**Post Office:** Plaza de la Constitución 3 (tel. 12-43-79), on the southwest corner of the *zócalo*. Open Mon.-Fri. 8am-7pm, Sat. 9am-1pm. **Postal Code:** 62000.

**Telephones:** LADATELs are easy to find around the *zócalo*, along Morelos Sur, and in the bus stations. For a good old-fashioned *caseta*, there's **Telcom,** Salazar 8, on the eastern edge of the *zócalo*. Open Mon.-Fri. 8am-8pm, Sat. 9am-5pm. **Telephone Code:** 73.

**Telegrams: Telecomm** (tel. 18-05-67), to the right of the post office. Open for telegrams Mon.-Fri. 9am-8pm, Sat. 9am-1pm. For money orders Mon.-Fri. 9am-5pm, Sat. 9am-noon. Public **fax** service.

**Currency Exchange: Bánamex** (tel. 12-57-20), at Matamoros and Arteaga, one block north of Jardín Juárez. **ATMs** for MC, Visa, Cirrus, and Plus. Currency exchange 9am-1:30pm. **Casa de Cambio Gesta,** Morrow 9 (tel. 14-01-95 or 18-37-50), at Comonfort. Exchanges many international currencies. Open Mon.-Fri. 9am-2pm and 4-6pm. Nearby is the **Casa de Cambio Divisas de Cuernavaca,** Morrow 12A (tel. 12-85-68 or 18-35-62), which also has offices at Guerrero 208 and in the Plaza Los Arcos in the northern part of town. Open Mon.-Fri. 9am-5pm.

**American Express:** (tel. 14-22-66), in the Las Plazas Shopping mall on the northern side of the *zócalo*. Holds mail, provides many travel services (tickets, hotel reservations, car rentals), and will exchange when pesos are available. Open Mon.-Fri. 9am-2pm and 4-6pm, Sat. 10am-2pm.

**Train Station:** Leandro Valle 33 (tel. 12-80-44). Service to Iguala and Puebla.

**Bus Stations:** First- and second-class buses arrive at small terminals scattered about town. **Flecha Roja,** Morelos 503, four blocks north of Jardín Borda. 1st-class service to Acapulco (8 per day, 5hrs., 85 pesos), Grutas de Cacahuamilpa (every 40min., 6am-6pm, 1hr., 9 pesos), Mexico City (nearly every ½hr., 5:30am-9pm, 1¼hrs., 19 pesos), Taxco (12 per day, 1½hrs., 14-17 pesos), and northern cities including San Luis Potosí (90 pesos), Matehuala (121 pesos), Saltillo (161 pesos), and Monterrey (176 pesos). The **Tres Estrellas del Centro** desk in the same building offers local service to Chalma (6 per day, 1¼hrs., 12 pesos) and Toluca (every 30min., 6am-9pm, 12 pesos). The station has 24-hr. **luggage storage** (5 pesos for the first 5hrs., 1 peso per hr. after) and long-distance phones (open daily 7am-9:30pm). **México-Zacatepec (LASER)/Pullman de Morelos,** Netzahualcóyotl 106 (tel. 14-36-50), at Abasolo, two blocks south of the *zócalo.* To Aguascalientes (10pm, 7½hrs., 121 pesos), Zacatepec (every hr., 9am-6pm, 6.50 pesos), and small cities throughout Morelos. **Estrella de Oro** (tel. 12-30-55), on Morelos Sur at Las Palmas Circle, 10 blocks south of the intersection of Reforma and Hidalgo. First-class service to Acapulco (8 per day, 3½hrs., 58 pesos), Ixtapa/Zihuatanejo (2 per day, 8hrs., 103 pesos), Mexico City (5 per day, 1¼hrs., 17 pesos), and Taxco (3 per day, 1½hrs., 15 pesos). **Estrella Roja,** Galeana 401 at Cuahtemotzin, seven blocks south of the *zócalo,* has 1st-class service to Cuautla (every 30min., 6:15am-10pm, 1hr., 9 pesos) and Puebla (every hr., 5am-7pm, 3hrs., 25 pesos). 2nd-class **Estrella Roja** and **Ometochtli,** on López Mateos at the south end of the Mercado. Buses load in the parking lot across the highway that runs perpendicular to Degollado. Buses to Tepotzlán (45min., 5 pesos).

**Academic Programs for Foreign Students:** A number of centers provide summer- and term-time instruction in Spanish. Weekly tuition includes 6hrs. per day of language instruction and may also include both group excursions to sites and placement in local homes. **Cuauhnahuac,** Morelos Sur 1414, Col. Chipitlán (tel. 12-36-73). US$220 (US$180 off-season) per week; no lodging. Highly recommended. Open Mon.-Fri. 8am-3pm. **Spanish Language Institute,** Bajada de la Pradera 208 (tel. 17-52-94), in Colonia Pradera. Very popular with small groups and for historical excursions (US$150 per week). Open Mon.-Fri. 8am-3pm. **Experiencia,** Leyva 1130, Col. Las Palmas (mailing address Apartado Postal C-96; tel. 16-65-79). Offers reliable bilingual programs. **The Mexican Immersion Center,** Piñanona 26 (tel. 15-79-53), in Colonia Jacarandas is highly regarded by students and run by a very friendly woman (US$155 per week). **Cemanahuac,** San Juan 4 (tel. 12-64-19), Colonia Las Palmas.

**Markets: Superama** (tel. 12-81-20), at Morelos, just behind Helados Holanda north of the cathedral. Open Mon.-Sat. 7:30am-9pm, Sun. 8am-8pm. Alternatively, an excellent fruit and vegetable market is located in the triangle formed by Blvd. Alfonso López Mateos, accessible by heading east on Degollado, up the pedestrian bridge, and past the vendor stands.

**Laundromat: Nueva Tintorería Francesa,** Juárez 2 (tel. 12-91-71), next to the Palacio de Cortés. Loads washed, dried, and folded for 12 pesos per kg. Open Mon.-Fri. 9am-7pm, Sat. 9am-2pm.

**Red Cross:** Ixtaccíhuatl at Río Panuco (tel. 15-05-51 or 15-35-55).

**Pharmacy: Farmacia Blanco,** Morelos 710 (tel. 18-23-93), just north of the Flecha Roja bus station. Farther south, **Farmacia de Nazareth,** Morelos 104 (tel. 14-37-24 or 12-48-67).

**Medical Assistance: Centro Quirúrgico,** Juárez 507-B (tel. 14-23-38). A pricey doctor for every ailment. Free help at **IMSS** (tel. 15-50-00).

**Hospital: Hospital Civil,** Morelos 197 (tel. 14-17-44 or 18-83-17), directly across the street from the cathedral. 24-hr. emergency treatment free, except for the cost of supplies. Long lines at all hours.

**Emergency:** 06.

## ACCOMMODATIONS

Cuernavaca has become a chic upper-class getaway, so rooms are chronically over-priced. The cloud has a silver lining, though—even the barest of hotels are often outfitted with a swimming pool or lush courtyard. Cheap lodgings line Matamoros for several blocks north of the *zócalo*. Although there are some extremely inexpensive *casas de huéspedes* along Aragón y León, you'd do best to pass them up—many of the guests have customers of their own, a fact that becomes apparent at night.

For an extended stay, it's possible to lodge with a local family through one of the city's Spanish-language schools. Students choose from a list of families willing to provide room, board, and language practice. **Cuauhnahuac** is especially willing to lend their family list to backpacking visitors who wish to spend time with *cuernavaquence*. Sharing a room with a student costs US$16 per day for room and board; for a private single, you pay US$30. Contact José Camacho at Cuauhnahuac. Also try the bilingual language school, **Experiencia,** Leyva 1130 (tel. 12-65-79), in Colonia Las Palmas (see Practical Information: Academic Programs, above).

**Hotel Colonial,** Aragón y León 104 (tel. 18-64-14), uphill and west of Matamoros, in the middle of the block. This pretty orange colonial home has found new life as a small hotel. A relaxing central courtyard and hospitable staff. Green-and-brown rooms enlivened by tiled floors and spotless bathrooms. Singles 60 pesos. Doubles 70 pesos, with two beds 80 pesos. TV 15 pesos extra.

**Motel Royal,** Matamoros 19 (tel. 18-64-80), two blocks north of Jardín Juárez. The walls and the lounge furniture are saturated with pink paint. Rooms are slightly run down with mattresses from the sixties, but cleanliness prevails and the greenery outside keeps things cool. Singles 70 pesos. Doubles 80 pesos. TV 15 pesos extra. Credit cards accepted.

**Hotel Juárez,** Netzahualcóyotl 117 (tel. 14-02-19), half a block south of Hidalgo. Rooms are somewhat bare, but the sleepy atmosphere, wooden furniture, and cool pool beckon to the weary traveler. Some rooms are bright and airy, but others offer only slits for windows. Singles 65 pesos. Doubles 85 pesos.

**Hotel Roma,** Matamoros 405 (tel. 18-87-78), three blocks north of the Jardín Juárez. Don't sleep late—hot water only from 6-9am and 8-10pm. Worn rooms have peeling paint and dark bathrooms. Quiet, though. Make reservations for weekend stays. Singles 45 pesos. Doubles 58 pesos.

## FOOD

Stuffed full with tourists, Cuernavaca has more than its share of budget eateries, so tasty, cheap food is never far away. For your main meal, take advantage of one of the excellent restaurants around the plaza; head up the side streets (try Aragón y León) or the larger thoroughfares Galeana and Juárez for lighter, less expensive fare. In the market, a *comida corrida* costs about 12 pesos *con refresco*. Beware of dirty dishes and old, unclean frying oil.

Along Guerrero, north of the plaza, street vendors sell mangos, *piñas* (pineapples), and *elotes* (corn on the cob), along with pocket combs, sunglasses, and digital watches. The health drinks sold at the Eiffel Kiosk in the Jardín Juárez include everything from the standard fruit and milk *licuados* to a spinach concoction not even Popeye could love. Drinks are cheap (4-12 pesos), delicious, and hygienic.

**Marco Polo Pizzería,** Hidalgo 26 (tel. 12-34-84), on the 2nd floor. Named for the ultimate traveler (though he somehow managed without *Let's Go: The Silk Route*), this pizzeria offers a view of the cathedral and surrounding mountains from the balcony. Candles add atmosphere to complement the deliciously filling puffy pizzas (starting at 14 pesos). Open daily 1-10:30pm.

**Restaurant Los Arcos,** Jardín de Los Héroes 4 (tel. 12-44-86), on the south side of the *zócalo*. Flanked by lush plants and a bubbling fountain, nice, mosaic-inlaid outdoor tables are ideal spots from which to watch the day slip-slide away. Musicians of all abilities serenade the clientele. *Comida corrida* 17 pesos. Carry-out sandwiches (*para llevar*) 5 pesos. Open daily 7:30am-midnight.

**Gin Gen,** Rayón 106 (tel. 18-60-46), 2½ blocks west of the Jardín Borda. A Mexican breed of the ever-popular Chinese restaurant. Chinese fans and figurines clutter the walls. Try the steak fried rice (19 pesos) or chicken lo mein (26 pesos). Dine-in or carry-out. Open daily 1-10pm.

**Fonda FIJI,** Benito Juárez 500 (tel. 18-96-96). Popular with the local office lunch crowd, this slightly upscale version of the *típico* family-run streetside eatery offers a solid 12-peso daily menu. Filling *antojitos* 12-15 pesos. Open daily 8am-6pm.

**Helados Virginia Cuernavaca,** Hidalgo 22 (tel. 12-97-42), just east of Marco Polo Pizzeria. Ordinary appearance. Out of the ordinary ice-cream flavors, including *arroz* (rice), *elote* (corn on the cob), and *jícama* for 4 pesos. Open daily 8am-9pm. Another branch farther south at Juárez 300.

## SIGHTS

Cuernavaca's popularity has little to do with scintillating sights. The **Plaza de la Constitución,** the larger of the two plazas which comprise the *zócalo,* extends east from the Palacio de Gobierno and is home to the machine that is the Morelos state bureaucracy. The heart and soul of the city, the tree-shaded plaza glows with fiery red *flamboyanes* (royal poinciana) and is speckled with cafés and wrought-iron benches. Food vendors and *mariachis* engage in a Darwinian struggle for pesos.

A bulbous kiosk designed by Gustave Eiffel and commissioned by Cuernavaca's Viennese community stands in the **Jardín Juárez,** at the northwest corner of the Pl. de la Constitución, north of the Palacio de Gobierno. Throughout the day, the garden is filled with mobile orange shoeshine booths, vendors hawking helium balloons, mobs of *cuernavaquence,* and large U.S. tour groups. Thursdays and Sundays at 6pm, a local band commandeers the kiosk and belts out polkas, classical music, and *rancheras* (Mexican country music). The kiosk houses a fruit drink stand, and a long list describes the health benefits of each ingredient.

At the southeastern corner of the Pl. de la Constitución, east of Benito Juárez, the **Palacio de Cortés** stand as a stately reminder of the city's grim history—Cortés set Cuernavaca on fire in 1521, then built this two-story fortress from the remains of local buildings, situating the fortress atop a sacred pyramid. Completed in 1524 (when Cortés left to destroy Honduras), the building functioned as a prison in the 18th century and as the Palacio de Gobierno during the dictatorship of Porfirio Díaz.

A grant from the former British ambassador to Mexico (none other than Charles Lindbergh's father-in-law) transformed the Palacio de Cortés into the **Museo Cuauhnahuac.** On the first floor of the museum, archaeological and anthropological exhibits deal with pre-Hispanic cultures. Timelines highlight the histories of the Toltec, Olmec, Mayan, and Aztec peoples; illustrated parchments document the Xochilimilca, Chalcha, Telcaneca, and Tlahuica cultures. Perhaps one of the most interesting displays is the collection of indigenous drawings and depictions of the Spanish arrival, in which valiant eagle and tiger warriors in full regalia battle the invaders. Second-floor exhibits on the Conquest and Mexican history include the first public clock ever to toll in Mesoamerica and some original clothing and furnishings from the palace. Examples of an Asian influence abound in early furniture and decorations, as Spain had invaded the Philippines in 1565 and maintained a steady trade with the islands throughout Mexico's colonial period. A collection of rare photographs chronicles the Revolution of 1910 and ethnographic displays mark the march of "progress" in Tlahuican daily life.

One of Diego Rivera's greatest works is on the western balcony of the second floor of the palace. Painted during the building's stint as the Palacio de Gobierno, the mural was commissioned by then-U.S. ambassador to Mexico Dwight D. Morrow as a gift to the people of Cuernavaca. Rivera's mural depicts Mexico's history from the Conquest until the Revolution of 1910, proceeding chronologically from right to left. A statue of Morelos towers over the museum's south patio (museum open Tues.-Sun. 10am-5pm; admission 14 pesos; free Sun. and for students with ID).

Black soot has darkened the tall walls and towers of the **Catedral de la Asunción,** three blocks down Hidalgo from the *zócalo,* at Morelos. Construction on the three temples of the cathedral began in 1525, making this one of the earliest churches in the Americas. The florid reliefs adorning the cathedral are good examples of the wildly ornamented, post-Baroque Churrigueresque style. Removal of the aisle altars 20 years ago revealed some fabulous Japanese frescoes depicting the persecution and martyrdom of Christian missionaries in Sokori, Japan. Historians speculate that these frescoes were painted in the early 17th century by a converted Japanese artist who had settled in Cuernavaca. The simple altar is highly unusual—seven baskets holding candles hang within a faceless box. The cross over a skull and bones on the north entrance to the main temple is an emblem of the Franciscan order (open daily 7am-7pm).

Site of glamorous soirées during the French occupation of Mexico, the **Jardín Borda** (tel. 12-00-86) is today a Sunday gathering spot for young couples and families on picnics. The stone entrance is on Morelos, across from the cathedral. In 1783, the priest Manuel de la Borda built a garden of magnificent pools and fountains next to the ostentatious residence of his relative, José de la Borda. The Jardín Borda's grandeur quickly gained fame, and in 1864, Emperor Maximilian and his wife Carlota established a summer residence there. Maximilian's dignitaries glided in delicate boats on the giant pool in the park's northern end, which is portrayed in a painting hanging in the city's museum. Today it takes a vivid imagination to recognize the park's faded splendor amid the sometimes non-functional fountains and cracked sidewalks. However, the modern additions to the garden—an art collection near the entrance, a small theater where weekly cultural events are held, and a museum inside Maximilian's old summer home—are welcome replacements for its past elitism. Unlike the fountains and sidewalks, the mango trees, tropical ferns, ornamental plants, and giant palm trees have flourished through the years. Patchwork rowboats are available for rent (5 pesos per ½hr.)—you too can emulate the emperor's cronies (open Tues.-Sun. 10am-5:30pm; admission 5 pesos, free Wed.).

The **Pyramid of Teopanzolco** squats on a glistening green lawn at the center of a public park, near the southern end of Teopanzolco, southeast of the market on Guerrero. As is frequently the case in Mexico, the pyramid actually consists of two pyramids, one within the other. The first stairway leads to a ledge, at the bottom of which a second stairway, belonging to the second pyramid, begins. Like other pre-Hispanic peoples, the Tlahuica increased the size of their monuments by encasing outdated ones in new construction. A chilling partial staircase suggests that the new pyramid was unfinished when Cortés arrived. To get to the site from the marketplace or along Morelos, hop on local bus #10 and ask the driver to let you off at the *pirámide*. If you're in the mood to break in those walking shoes, head north along Morelos (the cathedral will be on your left), turn right on Pericón, and go right on Río Balsas to Teopanzolco (open Tues.-Sun. 10am-5pm; admission 10 pesos).

## ENTERTAINMENT AND SEASONAL EVENTS

Cuernavaca's popularity as a vacation spot fuels a fairly glitzy nightlife, and the city's *norteamericano* expatriates, now over 20,000 strong, lend a north-of-the-border feel to many festivities. Bars in Cuernavaca are modern and highly commercialized, and several have live nightly entertainment. Around the *zócalo*, many of the clubs cater to tourists; some have no cover charge but expect patrons to buy drinks.

Discos are typically open from 8pm to 4am on Friday and Saturday. To deter the fistfights and *broncas* (brawls) that used to plague Cuernavaca's clubs, some now admit only male-female couples and require reservations; most, however, do not enforce these business-diminishing rules. The most popular discos in town are not on the *zócalo* but down neighboring side streets. Many lie just out of walking distance (especially at night) and are best reached by *rutas* or a taxi after 11pm. Students from local language schools get free passes and avoid cover charges.

**Barba Azul,** Prado 10 (tel. 13-19-76), appeals to the early 20s, hard-hitting-techno crowd, and draws both tourists and locals. Drinks 12-15 pesos (cover 40 pesos; open Fri.-Sat. 10am-5am). **Samanna,** Doming Diez 1522 (tel. 13-47-27), is where the late twenty- and thirtysomething crowd packs it in to flaunt their dancing prowess, shaking their collective booty to a live *salsa* and tropical mix (Fri.-Sat. cover 30 pesos; open Wed.-Sat. 8pm-4pm). **Kaova,** Av. Morelos Sur 302 (tel. 18-43-81), offers a rock/dance hybrid to a largely collegiate crowd (Fri.-Sat. cover 30 pesos after 10pm; open Wed.-Sat. 9pm-3:30am). **Ta'izz,** Chapultepec 50 (tel. 15-40-60), bops to U.S. top-40 favorites. Fog machines and light shows seduce the younger crowd (cover 40 pesos; open 9pm-4am). **Shadée,** at the end of Gutenberg, east of the *zócalo,* is a smaller disco oriented toward a gay crowd that jumps with youthful sweat and tentative accents nurtured at nearby language schools. Drinks 15 pesos (cover Thurs.-Sat. 35 pesos; open Mon.-Sat. 9pm-4am). Free entertainment is generally available in the main plazas at 6pm on weekends, when *mariachis* practice for their evening gigs.

Cuernavaca's movie houses charge eight to ten pesos per flick. Downtown, **Cinema Las Plazas** (tel. 14-07-93), across from the Jardín Juárez, screens imports and high-quality Mexican films. The colonial **Cine Alameda,** Matamoros 1 (tel. 12-10-50), one block north of the *zócalo,* shows popular titles on its ultra-wide screen. **Teatro Morelos,** on Morelos, about a block and a half north of Jardín Borda, shows excellent Mexican films (10 pesos, with student ID 5 pesos). For more audio-visual stimulation, feast your eyes and ears at **Las Palmas Video** (tel. 18-82-86), about 1.5km down Juárez and at the foot of the hill. Lounge on comfortable couches while watching the latest videos beamed from the U.S. by satellite.

**Harry's Grill,** Gutenberg 93 (tel. 14-19-17), beside the Las Plazas mall north of the *zócalo,* throbs with U.S. top-40 dance hits, old telephone booths, airplane propellers, and *norteamericano* license plates. The well-heeled crowd must get a kick out of Harry's slogan: "A Sunny Place for Shady People." The pick-up scene here is no less than frantic, and the folks are lively, loud, and fun to watch. Hors d'oeuvres are free, but drinks are fairly expensive: beers cost ten pesos (open daily 1pm-2am).

On Sat. and Sun., the **market** in the Jardín Juárez specializes in silver jewelry; don't be afraid to bargain. The **Feria de la Primavera** (Festival of Spring) brings with it parades and costumes for 10 days a year at the vernal equinox (March 21-22).

# ■ NEAR CUERNAVACA

## XOCHICALCO

Ceremonial center, fortress, and trading post rolled into one, Xochicalco is the most impressive archaeological site in the state of Morelos. Built in the 7th century during the Toltec Classic period, Xochicalco suffered periodic invasions by the Olmecs, Maya, Zapotecs, and Mixtecs. Archaeologists speculate that the site may even be the mythical city of **Tamoanchan,** the place where wise men came to begin the cult of the new god Quetzalcóatl, as well as to synchronize civil and religious calendars. By the time of the Conquest, the city had become a tributary of Tenochtitlán, the capital of the Aztec empire.

Although its Nahuatl name means "Place of the Flowers," the hilltops where Xochicalco stands are arid in the summer. Lizards and roadrunners dart away as you pass through the rocky terrain, and more oxen than tourists make the trek to the ruins. Even during the rainy season, when dew seeds the hills with green grass, an eerie loneliness pervades the site.

A rocky path leads from the parking lot to the ruins. The tourist center offers small but invaluable brochures and maps for 3 pesos. The ruins are best explored in a generally circular manner, starting at the elevated plaza up to the left of the first patch of greenery.

On the right side of the first plain, the **Pirámide de las Estelas** (Structure A) and the **Great Pyramid** (Structure E) just south of it nearly dwarf the three smaller structures on the left. The Great Pyramid forms the northern boundary of the **Plaza Central,** which can be reached by continuing straight (south) and taking the small slope down to the left. This area was most likely a trading center for the local and regional populations—many ancient area roads have been found to converge here. Twin pyramids on the east and the west sides of the plaza, labeled **Structure C** and **Struc-**

ture **D,** were used in the worship of the sun, one oriented towards the sunrise, the other toward the sunset. At the center of the Plaza is a carved obelisk that bears two hieroglyphs related to the god Quetzalcóatl. The obelisk's shadow plotted the trajectory of the sun between the pyramids.

The southwest corner of this plaza offers a great overhead view of the **Eastern Ballcourt** below. To reach it, walk down the stone steps between Structures C and D. Nearly as far as the eye can see, straight ahead and off to the left, are unexcavated remnants of this sprawling city. Continue down the narrow rocky path directly to the right for the ballcourt. A statue found here bears a remarkable likeness to another found in Copán, Honduras, an indication of Xochicalco's possible trading range. Continuing west is the **Palacio,** a building with many of its rooms still intact. Because of its proximity to other ceremonial areas, the palace may have been the living quarters of a group of high priests. Further ahead is the small **Building A** and a large hill which holds the unexcavated **La Malinche,** another group of living quarters and a ceremonial area. From atop this hill, a row of 21 altars connecting the ballcourt to La Malinche are visible. While only small pedestals remain, at one time these altars were used to mark the 260 days of the ceremonial calendar.

After heading back up the hill to the central plaza, make way to the base of the **Great Pyramid (Structure E).** Atop this pyramid rest the remains of an even more ancient structure. Follow the path down to the left (west) and over to the stairway/ porticos section. This area was used to limit access to the main part of the city, in case of invasions or revolution. The design simply did not work well enough; Xochicalco did eventually fall to a revolution.

Past the portico and up two sets of impressive stairways rebuilt in 1994 is the **Plaza Ceremonial,** which served as the main ceremonial center of the city. As you enter, the top of the Pirámide de las Estelas is accessible and holds a small temple inside, enclosing a huge pit in the center that was the burial site for high priests and a place for ritual offerings. In the center of the plaza is the renowned **Pyramid of the Plumed Serpet (Quetzalcóatl).** Sloppily reconstructed in 1910, it bears carved reliefs of Quetzalcóatl, the great feathered serpent who was a god-hero to the Toltecs. Xochicalco's commercial partnership with southern cultures is reflected in the embrace Quetzalcóatl bestows upon a priest in an elaborate Mayan headdress.

On the rear (west) end of the plaza is the tremendous **Montículo 2,** the highest area of the site, and supposedly where the rulers of Xochicalco lived. The eastern side was intended for daily activities, while the west end was exclusively ceremonial. Exit the Plaza Ceremonial on the north side and head west down the slope to the **Hall of the Polichrome Altar,** where a colored altar rests beneath an authentic reconstruction of the roofing used by the Toltecs. Further down is a cistern used for water storage, a sauna used for pre-game initiation rites, and **Teotlachtli,** the northern ballcourt. Here, two massive rings of rock are attached in the middle, unlike most ballcourts in Mesoamerica, which have only one ring. Teams competed for the privilege of being sacrificed atop the Pyramid of Quetzalcóatl; the players' strong hearts were believed to feed the sun. Nearby, the foundations remain of the **Calmecac,** the palace in which Toltec and Aztec priests underwent training and initiation.

Continue west along the weed-ridden path, around the back of the base of Montículo 2 until you reach a large stone amalgamation. A small opening in the corner (with steps leading up) allows access to the stuccoed interior of the underground observatory where ancient astronomers followed the cosmos. On summer solstices, Aztec sages and stargazers peered through a shaft in the ceiling to trace the path of the sun; by so doing, they hoped to verify and adjust the Aztec calendar. The observatory is open from 11am-2pm. A guide gives periodic presentations as soon as a good-sized group has assembled (site open Tues.-Sun. 9am-5pm; admission 14 pesos; free Sun. and for students with ID).

**Getting There: Flecha Roja** runs buses (5 pesos) directly to Xochicalco. Alternatively, snag a bus to Miacatlán (5 pesos) from the **Autos Pullman** station, at Abasolo and Netzahualcóyotl, one block south of the cathedral in Cuernavaca. Ask the driver to drop you off at the Crucero de Xochicalco. **Taxis** wait at the *crucero,* and for seven pesos will take you to the site. Otherwise, the uphill walk to the site (4km) will take about an hour. Taxis usually sit at the site entrance, but it may be a good idea to ask your taxi driver to pick you up at a specified time. Buses rarely stop at the *crucero* on their way back to Cuernavaca; instead, hail a nearby taxi and ask to go to the *caseta* (2 pesos), a nearby bus stop. Buses go back every 30 minutes or so.

## TEPOZTLÁN

In northern Morelos, the quiet *pueblo* of Tepoztlán occupies one of the state's most scenic and utterly impenetrable sites—towering cliffs form a natural fortress that allows entrance only from the south. Proceeding along Rte. 95-D toward Tepoztlán, keep your eyes peeled for **Popocatépetl** and **Ixtaccíhuatl,** two massive volcanoes which surge from the ground. The cobbled *indígena* village is a bastion of pre-colonial life; ancient customs still hold sway, and Nahuatl is the predominant language. On Sundays, the *zócalo* comes alive with vibrant market activity. During the rest of the week, however, the town is groggy, leaving for visitors only the summer sun and the elderly residents arguing over crops and politics. Wobbling on a peak 360m above the village are the archaeological sites for which the town is famous. The thin air may leave you breathless and thirsty, so prepare accordingly.

The valley of Tepoztlán is charged with ages of myth, legend, and magic. It is thought that the god-hero of the Toltecs, Quetzalcóatl, was born here about 1200 years ago. Even today, rumor has it that cellular phones and compasses are unable to work in the area. Celebrations still take place every September 8, when the *pulque* flows and the dance floor fills in honor of Tepoztecatl. *Los chinelos*—colorfully attired folk dancers—may invite you to join their traditional dance, *el salto.*

Travelers also come to visit the **Pyramid of Tepozteco,** perched on the northern ridge of the cliffs that rise above one end of town, about 3km above the valley. Some say the pyramid was a Tlahuica observatory and defense post for the valley, while others swear it served as an Aztec sacrificial temple. The 10m-tall structure has a porch inscribed with barely discernible Tlahuica glyphs. To reach the pyramid, follow Av. 5 de Mayo north out of town (passing the *zócalo* on your right) until you reach its end. The hour-long climb is steep and strenuous, but is made bearable by the cooling shade of trees. If you intend to climb, be sure you are equipped with appropriate footwear, water, and spirit; many halfhearted attempts at climbing end in disappointment (open Tues.-Sun. 9am-4:30pm, but irregularly; admission 10 pesos; free Sun. and for students and teachers with ID).

The **Museo de Arte Prehispánico,** at the rear of Capilla Asunción (accessible only from the back street), holds a collection donated to the city by the poet Carlos Pellicer. The impressive display includes pottery pieces and clay figures of Olmec, Zapotec, Mayan, Totonac, and Aztec origin, as well as many objects from Teotihuacán. There are also photographs of the Republic's key archaeological sites (open Tues.-Fri. 10am-2pm and 4-6pm, Sat.-Sun. 10am-6pm; admission 3 pesos, 1.50 pesos for students and teachers with ID).

Because of its natural beauty, vernal climate, and proximity to Mexico City, the area around Tepoztlán attracts an ever-growing population of wealthy *norteamericanos.* Unfortunately, these foreigners have started to drag the entire town upscale, and Tepoztlán completely lacks moderately priced accommodations. **La Cabaña,** 5 de Mayo 54, across from the Pullman de Morelos station, rents bare but clean rooms, all with communal baths and *agua purificada.* Knock on the black gate to get inside (singles 25 pesos; doubles 50 pesos). The market offers many cheap eateries.

**Getting There:** Visit Tepoztlán from either Cuernavaca or Mexico City. **Ometochtli** buses to Tepoztlán leave from the Cuernavaca market (5 pesos). In Tepoztlán, they arrive and depart from in front of the *zócalo* or a depot outside town. If you arrive at the Ometochtli depot, follow the main road; it will curve to become Av. 5 de Mayo. Pullman de Morelos in Mexico City operates buses every half-hour from Taxqueña for 15 pesos. In Tepoztlán, buses arrive and depart from the *zócalo,* close to the market.

## MALINALCO

Although located in the state of México, the Aztec ruins of Malinalco are most easily reached from Cuernavaca. On the bus ride to the ruins, *campesinos,* loaded down with the straw baskets and woolens they plan to sell in Mexico City, chew tobacco, spit on the steel floor, and chat about crops and harvests in Spanish and Nahuatl.

Most important buildings in Malinalco are situated around the *zócalo* and bear their identification (i.e. *farmacia, cantina, hotel*) in the same multi-colored inscriptions. Inside the *zócalo,* vendors display everything from sandals to fried fish. In front of the plaza, the town's massive church, the **Parroquia del Salvador Divino,** inspires awe. Built in the 16th century by Augustinian monks, the church boasts frescoes that depict the stations of the cross, and a spine-chilling room in which at least a dozen Christ figures suffer all sorts of torments. The outside, however, masks its former glory with dark, decaying, soot-covered walls (open daily 9am-6pm; free).

Though Malinalco has no tourist office, the **Casa de Cultura de Malinalco,** on one corner of the *zócalo,* can help you find the ruins and just about anything else you might need (open Mon.-Sat. 9am-2pm and 4-7pm, Sun. 10am-1pm).

To get to the ruins from the *zócalo,* follow the blue pyramid signs along Guerrero and go straight. Take a left on Milgar, a right at the next blue arrow, and another right at the blue sign that appears to lead visitors into someone's driveway.

Malinalco was the sacred ground for the rituals that officially transformed an Aztec youth into a *caballero tigre* or *caballero águila* (tiger or eagle warrior). Because of the importance of these rituals and the ground they were performed on, Malinalco was terraced and completely fortified from the outside. On the open circular stone platform—the first structure on the right as you enter—prisoners were bound to a pole with only arms left free and made to wrestle the recently initiated warriors. If the over-matched prisoner won consecutive bouts with two *águila* and two *tigre* warriors, he was matched against a left-hander. If the prisoner defeated the lefty, he was granted freedom. Defeat, on the other hand, had macabre consequences—the small rectangular basin in front of the entryway to the pyramid was used to hold the prisoner's blood after his ritual sacrifice. Behind the pyramid, the bodies of the sacrificed were burned to ashes on the oval bed of rock.

The **Temple of Initiation** for eagle and tiger warriors is a massive monolithic structure. All of its statues, rooms, and façades were carved from one giant slab of stone. Two stone jaguars guard the Temple's steep steps. To the right of the entrance to the inner chamber, the broken figure of an eagle warrior sits on the head of the feathered serpent Quetzalcóatl. The frame of the chamber entrance is fashioned into the fanged, open-mouthed head of a serpent. Inside the circular chamber, three supine eagles and a jaguar are carved on the floor. In the hole behind the first eagle, the beating hearts of the sacrificed awaited the initiates who would devour them.

To the right of the Temple of Initiation stand the remains of *temascál,* an ancient predecessor to the sauna. Behind the *temascál,* you can still make out the small cells

---

### Popocatépetl and Ixtaccíhuatl

Overlooking Morelos and Puebla are two snow-capped volcanoes, **Popocatépetl** (5452m) and **Ixtaccíhuatl** (5282m), respectively the second- and third-largest peaks in the country. These magnificent mountains, which are open to both experienced climbers and less audacious backpackers, are themselves shrouded in indigenous mythology. Legend has it that the warrior Popocatépetl ("Smoking Mountain" in Nahuatl) loved Ixtaccíhuatl ("Sleeping Woman"), the emperor's daughter. Once, when he went off to battle, Ixtaccíhuatl heard erroneously that he had been killed; she subsequently died of lovesickness and grief. When Popo (as he was known to friends) learned of his lover's death, he built the two great mountains. On the northern one he placed her body, and on the southern one he stood vigil with a torch. Locals pay their respects to the supine, death-pale Ixtaccíhuatl on the mountain's snowy summit.

in which the elderly *sacerdotes* most likely used to live. Walking to the end of the platform and looking down, you'll see the ruins of the prisoners' cells situated about 15m below the whole complex. The remaining wall-bases suggest very narrow and painful punishment chambers (open Tues.-Sun. 10am-4:30pm; admission 14 pesos, free Sun. and for students with ID).

**Getting There:** Getting to Malinalco requires a transfer in the small village of Chalma. **Tres Estrellas del Centro,** in the Flecha Roja station in Cuernavaca, sends six buses daily to Chalma (1¾hrs., 12 pesos). From Chalma, you'll have to hail a taxi to Malinalco (20min., 15 pesos, 3 pesos if shared).

# ■■■ CUAUTLA

Known until 1869 as Ciudad Morelos, in recognition of José María Morelos and his contributions to the War for Independence, Cuautla is truly the powder keg of Mexican history. The town was Emiliano Zapata's stronghold during the Mexican Revolution, and both heroes are immortalized in two of the town's three main plazas. Today, Cuautla survives primarily on the memories of its proud past, and only in small part from the tourism brought by historical relics and the many *balnearios* (hot water springs) that dot the area.

**Orientation** Cuautla is located in the central part of eastern Morelos, about 42km east of Cuernavaca on the Cuernavaca-Cuautla highway or Rte. 138. A new toll road now provides fast service to Mexico City, but Cuernavaca remains the best port of entry. The town's layout is reminiscent of Italy's boot-like structure, but nearly everything of interest except the far-flung spas lies within a six-block radius of the *centro.* The center consists of three large plazas running in a straight line, each two blocks from the next. The southernmost plaza with the Zapata statue is the **Jardín Revolución del Sur.** Two blocks north is the *zócalo,* or **Plaza del Santo Domingo,** and two blocks farther is the **Plaza de San Diego** and the **Alameda.** The main drag connecting the plazas is **Galeana.** Note that it changes names nearly ten times; it is known as Guerrero near the Jardín del Sur, and as Obregón, 19 de Febrero, Hidalgo, and Independencia farther north.

To get to the *zócalo* from the Estrella Roja station, exit to the left on Vázquez and make a right onto 2 de Mayo. Continue for two blocks, and you'll run right into the southeast corner of the *zócalo.* From the Cristóbal Colón station, take a right on 2 de Mayo and walk three blocks before running into the plaza. *Rutas* (minibuses) heading to nearby cities and the *balnearios* usually gather in the Jardín del Sur and just northeast of the Alameda area. The main routes are along Obregón and Reforma.

**Practical Information** For tourist information, a small **tourist desk** is located on the ground floor of the Convento de San Diego across from the Alameda in the northernmost plaza. Short on legible maps, but the extremely helpful staff speaks some English. For **tourist help,** dial 91-800-90-392. The **police** (tel. 3-10-50 or 2-00-26) await at the Palacio Municipal on the *zócalo.* The **post office,** Ramírez Ferrera 4 (tel. 2-01-10), is open Mon.-Sat. 8am-7pm. **Postal Code: 62740. LADATELs** dot the *zócalo* area, and **casetas** are located in most pharmacies and along Guerrero on the east side of the *zócalo.* **Telephone Code:** 735. The **Cambio de Divisas Alameda,** Plaza Fuerte de Galeana 84 (tel. 2-53-53), just north of the Alameda, probably offers one of the best rates among the few *casas de cambio* in Cuautla. **Bánamex,** Galeana 33 (tel. 2-01-06), by the *cine,* has an **ATM.**

Cuautla has two main **bus stations,** both of which are best reached from Cuernavaca (via Estrella Roja) or Mexico City's Taxqueña station. The large **Cristóbal Colón** station, on 2 de Mayo at Reforma, serves Amecameca (every 20min., 9am-6pm, 6 pesos), Mexico City (every 15min., 6:30am-9pm, 1½hrs., 19 pesos), Oaxaca (2:30 and 8:30pm, 8hrs., 60.50 pesos), and Tlalmanalco (every 20min., 9am-6pm, 7 pesos). **Estrella Roja,** on Costeño at Vázquez, serves Cuernavaca (every 15min., 5am-8pm, 1½hrs., 9 pesos), Mexico City (every 20min., 5am-6pm, 2hrs., 18.50

CUAUTLA

pesos) via Oaxtepec (ask to be let off, 20min., 5 pesos). **Farmacia Afil,** 2 de Mayo 13 (tel. 2-76-31), is just east of the *zócalo.* Medical consultations also available (open daily 9am-9pm). The **Red Cross** is at Calleja de Retirada 53 (tel. 2-21-95) and offers 24-hour service. A nearby **hospital** is the **Sanitorio Aguilar Sánchez,** Constituyentes 180 (tel. 2-09-00), where little English is spoken. In an **emergency,** dial 06.

**Accommodations and Food** Just outside the sphere of the American tourist crowd, Cuautla's hotels offer clean, well-kept rooms for low prices to a largely Mexican clientele. Some places fill up and charge more on weekends, so try to book reservations during the week. **Hotel España,** 2 de Mayo 22 (tel. 2-21-86), is just east of the *zócalo.* The beautiful ivy-covered courtyard centers around somewhat small but well-furnished rooms. Bathrooms sparkle, but hold off on those afternoon showers—there's only hot water from 6-10am and 6pm-midnight (singles 50 pesos; doubles 60 pesos). At the **Hotel Jardines de Cuautla,** 2 de Mayo 94 (tel. 2-00-88), you'll find a relaxing yellow courtyard but no lush gardens as the name suggests. Two classes of rooms—remodeled and unfortunate. Both offer clean bathrooms, somewhat soft beds, and a quiet night's sleep (singles 50 and 80 pesos; doubles 80 and 120 pesos). **Hotel Colón,** Guerrero 48 (tel. 2-29-90), on the southwest corner of the *zócalo,* is right in the middle of the action. The place is slightly run-down and can be noisy, but unique, extra-large, family-sized rooms are the perfect option for groups of four to six. The blue-green color scheme brings a little piece of the ocean to this landlocked town (singles 40 pesos; doubles 60 pesos; quads 80-100 pesos).

Small eateries dot Galeana and the three plazas, but most are remarkably alike, with similar clientele and menus. **Tony & Tony's Pizzas,** on the southwest corner of the *zócalo,* can whip up some mean pasta dishes. Try the *napolitano spaghetti* for 13 pesos. **Emy's,** across from the Colón bus station, packs in the lunchtime crowd for its daily menu with all five Mexican food groups: appetizer, meat, cheese, soft drink, and dessert.

**Sights and Entertainment** Vestiges of Cuautla's revolutionary history are scattered throughout the *centro.* The **Jardín Revolución del Sur,** the farthest south of the three plazas on Galeana, holds both Emiliano Zapata's body and numerous monuments to his memory. A small and easy-to-miss bronze relief sits in the plaza's southwest corner. Commanding center stage, however, is a massive statue of Zapata on his legendary horse, with a hand on the shoulder of a peasant who looks up at him with admiration and gratitude. Zapata, from the nearby town of Anenecuilco, established Cuautla as his headquarters during the struggle for land reform. Here was proclaimed the Plan de Ayala, Zapata's program for the return of land from the landholders to the rightful hands of the peasants whose families, according to ancient documents, had originally owned it. The gilded plaster statue, while tacky and inelegant, serves its purpose. Under the statue's base rest the remains of Zapata, who was betrayed and killed by Venustiano Carranza's agents.

Two blocks north is the **Plaza del Santo Domingo,** which serves as the town's *zócalo.* The **Iglesia de Santo Domingo,** on the east side of the plaza, was built in 1652 and served as a stronghold during the War for Independence. The southwest corner nearly hides the **Casa de Morelos,** an inconspicuous red building where General Morelos once stayed when organizing the struggle for freedom in the south. The museum inside is poorly kept but does hold several interesting revolutionary relics (open Tues.-Sun. 10am-3pm).

Further north is the **Plaza del San Diego,** named for the nearby **Iglesia** and **Convento de San Diego.** Whereas the Plaza del Sur commemorates the Mexican Revolution, here, the War for Independence and José María Morelos are the objects of veneration. The convent on the west side doubles as a museum, holding many flags and weapons from both wars (open Tues.-Sun. 9am-5pm; free). Inside is also the **Casa de la Cultura,** which hosts a weekly speaking series and provides limited tourist information. The small statue of Morelos outside, in front of the movie theater, honors the 1812 battle in the Alameda, just northeast of the plaza.

After catching all the history in town, head for a nearby *balneario* (spa) to soak in the sun and the supposedly beneficial effects of the springs. The best springs lie several miles out of town, but several within the city limits are easier on the budget. **Agua Hedionda** (tel. 2-00-44) boasts five sulfur pools and a natural water temperature of 90 degrees. As the name suggests, the sulfur here is strong—it may be a good idea to show up with a stuffy nose. Rumor has it that these waters can heal ulcers (open Fri.-Wed. 7am-6pm). **El Almeal** (tel. 2-17-51), on Virginia Hernández, is more of a pool than a spring. However, it does offer campgrounds and sports facilities galore for the cash-strapped traveler. *Rutas* run from the *centro* to each of the spas; catch one at the marketplace or along the Plaza de la Revolución del Sur.

The **Centro Vacacional Oaxtepec** (tel. 6-01-01) puts the *balnearios* within Cuautla to shame. Inside are over 20 giant pools with water slides and palm trees, a lake for boating and fishing, and courts for nearly every sport. Connecting it all is a free shuttle service and a sky-tram (*teleférico*). Under a huge geodesic dome-complex are the sulfur springs that give Oaxtepec its name. Restaurants and equipment rental facilities abound (resort open daily 8am-6pm; admission adults 18 pesos, children under 12 and seniors 9 pesos). To get there, catch a Oaxtepec *ruta* from the marketplace or Plaza del Sur (2.50 pesos) in Cuautla. *Rutas* returning to Cuautla pass by the main road in front of the resort. Cross the street to flag one down.

For the party animal, **The Sha,** Plaza Fuerte de Galeana 84 (tel. 2-91-87), is the closest thing that Cuautla has to a night spot. A young crowd shakes and sways to a hard-hitting rock and dance mix (open Wed.-Sat. 8pm-3am).

## ■ NEAR CUAUTLA

### POPOCATÉPETL AND IXTACCÍHUATL

Veiled in Aztec mythology, the snow-capped **Popocatépetl** ("Smoking Mountain") and **Ixtaccíhuatl** ("Sleeping Woman") overlook the state of Morelos and nearby Puebla. Both peaks can be climbed to a small degree on well-marked tourist trails, after which tourist organizations offer group trips to the very tops of the peaks. To get to Popocatépetl, take a bus to Amecameca (every 15min., 1½hrs., 6 pesos) from Cuautla's Cristóbal Colón bus station. In Amecameca, minibus drivers will charge you a hefty sum for the trip to Tlamacas, a small village at the base of the mountain—note that the minibuses from Amecameca generally do not operate on weekends. From here, another *pesero* runs to the beginning of the trail. The small **Tlamacas Lodge** provides dorm-style housing and somewhat pricey meals in its cafeteria. The lodge organizes assaults on the mountains and rents equipment at about 100 pesos per person. Before beginning your climb, register at the **Club Socorro Alpino** (Alpine Assistance Club) and inform them of your expected return date.

To reach Ixtaccíhuatl, take a bus to Tlalmanalco (every 20min., 2hrs., 7 pesos) from Cuautla's Colón bus station. From here, a *pesero* runs to San Rafael, which rests at the base of Ixtaccíhuatl. Alternatively, join one of the trips that leaves from the Tlamacas Lodge. Realize that both mountains can be very dangerous and that it is unwise to climb alone or without proper equipment. Travelers have lost their lives due to inclement weather, so inquire about the current conditions before making plans, and always bring both warm clothes and raingear.

# GUERRERO

## ■■■ TAXCO

Since silver was discovered here in 1534, Taxco (pop. 150,000) has spun itself into a chaotic web. Pedestrians squeeze past each other in narrow alleys. Cobblestone *callejones* (alleys) pick their way up, over, and around rolling green hills. And tour-

TAXCO

ists buzz through it all, drawn like bees to the sweet honey of countless jewelry shops. Beneath all the swarming confusion and old-fashioned beauty are the veins of silver which have shaped Taxco's history.

After absorbing the land which includes present-day Taxco in 1440, the Aztec Empire ceded control over the area to the Spaniards, who changed the city's name to Taxco, a corruption of *tlachco,* the Nahuatl ball game. The discovery of silver attracted everyone from fortune seekers to merchants to miners—amid the inhospitable mountains of central Mexico, Taxco had suddenly become a boom town.

The dust had settled by the 18th century, and population growth had slowed. In 1928, however, a road was paved between Acapulco and the previously isolated Taxco. Soon after, Taxco was declared a national monument; the government decreed that all new buildings would be built in the colonial style and that all new streets would have to be cobbled. However, little more than lip service was paid to the city's past until 1932, when Professor William Spratling, "Don Guillermo" to locals, gave up teaching and opened a silver workshop in Taxco. He taught the silversmith's craft to locals, and his jewelry quickly gained international repute. Spratling's legacy is evident—today more than 300 silver shops operate in the area, attracting a staggering number of North American and European tourists.

## ORIENTATION

Taxco is at the northern end of Guerrero state, 185km southwest of Mexico City. **Avenida J. F. Kennedy,** the principal artery, circles the town. To get to *el centro* from any spot in the city, look for the highly visible **Catedral de Santa Prisca** atop the hill and work your way up to it on any one of the many small alleys.

Taxco's most interesting sights and shops cluster around the cathedral and adjacent *zócalo* (also called the **Plaza Borda**). *Combis* run along three main routes: from **Los Arcos** (the north entrance to town where Av. Kennedy begins) down Av. Kennedy to the south end of town; from Los Arcos up **La Garita,** through the center and out **Cuauhtémoc-San Nicolás-San Miguel;** and along the **Panorámica,** another avenue bordering Taxco on the west. *Combis* (1 peso) run from 7am to 8pm everywhere in town; white taxis charge three to eight pesos. But in small Taxco, reliable feet remain the best mode of transportation. To get to the *zócalo* from the **Flecha Roja bus station,** look for the church steeple and head uphill, ascending through the narrow market area. Its maze-like nature may be confusing at first, but as soon as you reach the top of the first incline, start climbing and go up to the next level as soon as you can. From **Estrella de Oro,** turn right on Kennedy and head down to Flecha Roja (be sure the numbers are decreasing).

Once at the *zócalo,* finding your way around may be confusing. If you are standing with your back to the cathedral, Cuauhtémoc runs diagonally off to the left and leads to the Plazuela de San Juan. Sloping downhill on the right is a passageway that lands at Plaza Bernal and the adjoining streets Alarcón and Juárez.

## PRACTICAL INFORMATION

**Tourist Office:** Kennedy 1 (tel. 2-07-98). From the *zócalo,* go down Juárez to Garita, or take the "Garita" *combi.* Information is surprisingly minimal; no regular hours. Generally open daily 9am-7pm. A better source of information may be the **tourist booth** (tel. 2-06-48) at the **Estrella de Oro** bus station, where free promotional maps and advice are dispensed liberally. Open daily 8am-11pm.

**Police:** Kennedy 71-B (tel. 2-06-66), at the **Carcel Municipal.** From the *zócalo,* head downhill to Kennedy and hang a left. Open 24 hrs.

**Post Office:** Kennedy 124 (tel. 2-05-01). A hike; turn right when you come down from the hill and just keep on goin'. Open Mon.-Fri. 8am-7pm, Sat. 9am-1pm. **Postal Code:** 40200.

**Telephones:** Long distance service in **Farmacia de Cristo,** Hidalgo 18 (tel. 2-11-19), down the road from Pl. San Juan. Collect calls about 10 pesos. Open 8am-10pm. Phonecard-operated **LADATELs** can be found around town. Many mini-supermarkets sell phonecards. **Telephone Code:** 762.

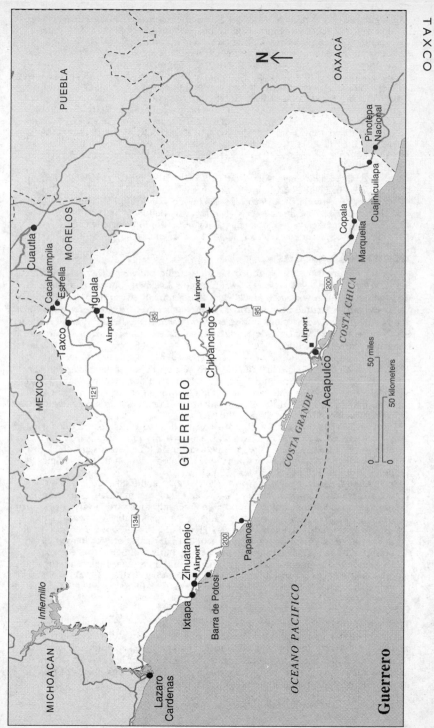

TAXCO

PUEBLA

OAXACA

N

Pinotepa
Nacional

Cuajinicuilapa

Copala

Marquelia

COSTA CHICA

Cuautla

MORELOS

Cacahuampila

Estrella

Iguala

200

Taxco

Airport

Airport

Chilpancingo

95

95

Airport

MEXICO

121

Acapulco

COSTA GRANDE

GUERRERO

50 miles

50 kilometers

0

0

134

Zihuatanejo

Airport

200

Papanoa

Ixtapa

Barra de Potosi

MICHOACAN

Infiernillo

OCEANO PACIFICO

Lazaro
Cardenas

**Guerrero**

**Telegrams:** Alarcón 2 (tel. 2-48-85), near the *zócalo,* at Plaza Bernal. Open Mon.-Fri. 8am-3pm, for money orders Mon.-Fri. 9am-3pm.

**Currency Exchange: Banca Confia** (tel. 2-45-10), on the *zócalo.* Open Mon.-Fri. 9am-1:30pm. **Bancomer,** at Cuauhtémoc and Pl. de San Juan. **ATM** for Visa cash advances. Open for exchange Mon.-Fri. 9am-1:30pm. **Bánamex,** Juárez 17 (tel. 2-44-55), has an **ATM** accepting MC, Visa, Cirrus, and Plus. Banks will change traveler's checks, and most silver dealers accept dollars.

**Bus Stations: Estrella de Oro,** Kennedy 126 (tel. 2-06-48), at the southern end of town. From the *zócalo,* head downhill and hang a right on Kennedy. To Acapulco (4 per day, 5hrs., 55 pesos), Chilpancingo (4 per day, 2hrs., 25 pesos), Cuernavaca (9am and 4pm, 1½hrs., 15 pesos), and Mexico City (5 per day, 2hrs., 29-34 pesos). **Flecha Roja,** Kennedy 104 (tel. 2-01-31), straight downhill from the cathedral. To Cuernavaca (7 per day, 1½hrs., 17 pesos) and Mexico City (every 1-2hrs., 5am-8pm, 29 pesos).

**Laundromat: Lavandería Automática La Cascada,** service available through Bora Bora Pizza (see Food, below). Inquire within.

**Pharmacy: Farmacia de Cristo** (see Telephones). Other pharmacies line Cuauhtémoc. Different pharmacies stay on duty every night; at the IMSS hospital you can get an emergency dose of medicine if you need it immediately.

**Hospital: IMSS,** Kennedy 114 (tel. 2-03-36). 24-hr. emergency/ambulance service.

## ACCOMMODATIONS

Maybe they figure true silver shoppers shouldn't mind plunking down large quantities of it for lodgings—who knows?—but Taxco's so-called "budget" accommodations aren't so budget-oriented at all. They're not terribly overpriced, just swanky and conveniently located near the *zócalo*—and big believers in paying for what you get. Make advance reservations during *Semana Santa,* Día de San Miguel (end of Sept.), or the Feria Nacional de la Plata, a two-week celebration of silver (late November-early December).

**Hotel Los Castillos,** Alarcón 3 (tel. 2-13-96), just northeast of the *zócalo* off Plaza Borda. A lovely hotel: carefully carved doors, brick floors, embroidered orange sheets, bottled water, and exquisitely tiled bathrooms. A few rooms have bathtubs. Expensive shop of the Castillo silversmith family downstairs. Singles 85 pesos. Doubles 110 pesos. Triples 140 pesos.

**Hotel Los Arcos,** Alarcón 7 (tel. 2-18-36), just next to Hotel Los Castillos. First-floor rooms are luxurious duplexes with beds upstairs and a sitting area and bath downstairs. Clean, white-washed rooms with smallish bathrooms and thick towels. Top-floor terrace offers an enchanting late-night view of the city. Singles 85 pesos. Doubles 115 pesos. Triples 135 pesos.

**Hotel Casa Grande,** Pl. de San Juan 7 (tel. 2-01-23), on the small plaza down Cuauhtémoc from the *zócalo.* Don't miss the 2nd-floor reception area (actually, it's only a table). Rooms center around a cool central courtyard. Somewhat worn beauty, but a good deal nonetheless. Singles 55 pesos. Doubles 70 pesos.

**Casa de Huéspedes Arellano,** Pajaritos 23 (tel. 2-02-15). From the *zócalo,* walk down the street to the right of the cathedral. Take the stairs almost immediately on the right and descend into the market. The hotel will be on the left, about 3 levels down. The building is home to a family and their pets. Terrace on the 2nd floor is a great place for getting some sun and chatting with backpackers. Singles 40 pesos, with bath 50 pesos. Doubles 50 pesos, with bath 60 pesos.

## FOOD

The narrow cobblestone streets of Taxco lack the push-cart vendors and sidewalk cafés that are so common in other Mexican cities. *Taquerías* and *torterías* are virtually extinct around Plaza Borda, but as you descend into the swarming market areas, their numbers increase. Cold breakfasts are the specialty of the *neverías*—plentiful in town alleys—which sell coffee, *licuados,* pastries, delicious pieces of *pan de queso* (custard-like Mexican cheesecake), and other goodies.

**El Rincón del Abuelo,** Callejón del Nogal 1 at Cuauhtémoc. Can you spot grandpa in the corner, next to the 1950s *Readers Digests?* He's feasting on veggie rice and cheese (12 pesos) and washing it down with a deluxe *agua de piña* (7 pesos). Mmmm. Go, grandpa. You've got good taste. Open daily 8am-11pm.

**Bora Bora Pizza,** Delicias 4 (tel. 2-17-21), on the unmarked street that slopes up to the right from Cuauhtémoc, just off the *zócalo.* Fishing nets and basket lamps dangle from the ceiling. Dimly lit with low tables and stools. Pizzas start at 15 pesos, spaghetti at 13 pesos. Open daily 5pm-midnight.

**Restaurant Meléndez,** Cuauhtémoc 6 (tel. 2-00-06), inside the relatively inexpensive Hotel Meléndez. Once a sunlit hotel lobby, now a tranquil dining area and quasi-shrine. Delicious 5-course *comida corrida* 20 pesos, full breakfast 18 pesos. Open daily 7:30-11am and 1-4pm and 7:30-9:30pm.

**La Concha Nostra,** Pl. de San Juan 7, in the Hotel Casa Grande. Lovely views of the city at night from their balconies, plus lots of MTV and a pool table upstairs. Popular with the city's many language students. Pizza. Open daily 8am-late.

## SIGHTS

On sale in hundreds of silver shops throughout town, Taxco's most famous sights sparkle and swagger and fluctuate in value. For an example of original silver craft, stop at **Los Castillos** (see Accommodations). Like many Taxco families with traditions in silverwork, the Castillo family keeps its workshop (right on top of their store) open for tourists to visit. Skills are passed down through the generations—the work of the youngest Castillo, Alejandra, figures prominently (open Mon.-Fri. 9am-7pm, Sat. 9am-6pm, Sun. 10am-3pm, but the workshop is often closed).

If you're dipping so deep into your wallet that you can feel your knees, head for **El Mercado de Artesanías,** off Veracruz just behind Santa Prisca, for browsing, bargaining, people-watching, and snacking. Sure, merchants here sell silver, but they also peddle pomegranates and painted ashtrays. The market is open daily from 10am to 6pm but is most crowded during *siesta,* when confused *gringos* hit Taxco's version of a mall instead of sleeping.

A major attraction is the *zócalo's* **Catedral de Santa Prisca,** with its beautiful baroque façade of pink stone. Intense white light illuminates the 40m towers until 9pm. On foggy nights, the towering nave and blue-tiled dome are lit up as well. Don José de la Borda hired two Spanish architects, Diego Durán and Juan Caballero, to design and build the church for Borda's son Manuel, a priest. Begun in 1751, the church took only seven years to complete. Among the designs and figures on the façade, the outstanding features are the Churrigueresque *interestípite*—decorative inverted columns with a Corinthian flourish at the bottom. Inside the church, a canvas by renowned 18th-century Mexican artist Miguel Cabrera depicts the martyrdom of Santa Prisca, who was tortured and killed by Roman guards in the first century for defending Christians (open daily 6am-8pm). For a small *propina* (tip), you can climb the 113 steps of the left tower of the cathedral for a spectacular view (inquire inside; climbing permitted after 2pm only).

The **Casa Humboldt,** Alarcón 6 (tel. 2-55-01), down the street past the Hotel Los Arcos, is one of the oldest colonial homes in town. With its unusual bas-reliefs in Moorish *mudéjar* style, the *casa* served as the temporary home of South American explorer Alexander von Humboldt, whose bust still overlooks the interior. The beautifully restored house contains artifacts discovered in the basement of the Santa Prisca cathedral (open Thurs.-Sat. 10am-5pm, Sun. 9am-3pm; admission 10 pesos, students and teachers with ID 5 pesos). The **Museo de Arqueología Guillermo Spratling,** Delgado 1 (tel. 2-16-60), down the street to the right of Santa Prisca, displays pre-Conquest art, mostly from cultures along Mexico's west coast. William Spratling, the *norteamericano* who taught locals the art of silver-smithing, donated his ceramics and figurines to the museum (open Tues.-Sat. 10am-5pm, Sun. 9am-3pm; admission 10 pesos, students and teachers free with ID).

The **Convento de San Bernandino,** in the Plaza del Convento, was built in 1592 as a Franciscan monastery. A fire destroyed the building two centuries later, and in 1823 it was reconstructed in Neoclassical style. The struggle for independence officially ended when the Plan of Iguala was signed within the walls of this ex-convent in 1821. Now a school convenes under its roof (open daily 10am-5pm; free).

## On the Silver Trail

Though unscrupulous sellers and cheating craftspeople occasionally pass off *alpaca* (fool's silver) or *plateados* (silver-plated metals) as the real McCoy, buying silver in Taxco is usually a safe bet. Larger pieces, such as necklaces and bracelets, are consistently striking. Many proprietors speak English and accept U.S. currency, but stick with Spanish and talk pesos while bargaining, or risk being charged tourist prices. In general, the farther one walks from the Pl. Borda, the cheaper the sterling products become. Bargain at stores with silver workshops by faking out the clerk and heading straight for the artisan. Most shops have two prices: *menudeo* (retail) and *mayoreo* (wholesale), the latter for those profit-oriented people who load their bags with silver in Taxco to resell at lofty prices back home. Remember that only the official ".925" stamp on the object's side guarantees that your shiny new charm is indeed silver; inspect merchandise carefully before purchasing anything.

## ENTERTAINMENT AND SEASONAL EVENTS

After silver shops close, most of Taxco gathers at the **Plaza Borda** in front of the illuminated façade of Santa Prisca. Most Mexican discos are open during the week, but Taxco's discos don't even bother to open their doors until the weekend. For those still up for dancing after a day of hiking up and down Taxco's relentless hills, there are only two real choices. In the **Disco Escaparartes,** Plaza Borda 2, the great music has plenty of locals dancing and drinking (open Thurs.-Sun. 9pm-3am). At video-bar **Güiri-Güiri,** Cuauhtémoc 2, video games and folk art complement the modern, wood-paneled bar, and a large video monitor shows MTV clips and occasionally U.S. football. The outdoor terrace affords a mind-blowing view of Santa Prisca, the *ex-convento,* and much of eastern Taxco (occasional live music 9pm-midnight; two-drink min.; open Fri.-Sun. 7:30pm-1:30am). Boards around the plaza announce the day's movies at Taxco's three theaters.

Taxco's crowded streets somehow accommodate a tsunami of tourists during its two major festivals. The **Feria Nacional de la Plata,** a national contest of silverworkers designed to encourage silver artisanship, runs in the first week of December. **Semana Santa** festivities are even more popular in Taxco. On Good Friday, hooded *penitentes* carry logs made out of cactus trunks on their shoulders or subject themselves to flagellation in order to expiate their sins and those of the town.

## ■ NEAR TAXCO: GRUTAS DE CACAHUAMILPA

While the above-ground scenery around Taxco has an awe-inspiring rugged grandeur, it is the beauty of an extensive network of caves that compels tourists to forget about silver shopping and venture forth from the city limits.

According to legend, the Grutas de Cacahuamilpa were once a hideaway for runaway *indígenas*—a Tetipac chief is said to have regained his lost throne by having his daughter emerge from the caves disguised as a deity and pronounce the return of the former chief to power. Twenty huge *salones* (halls) consume the visitor with their stalactites, stalagmites, and rock formations in curious shapes, sizes, and colors. The columns and ceilings—some as high as 85m—are the work of the subterranean stream that developed into the Río San Jerónimo. Explorers hoping to traverse the caves have not always had great success—the make-shift grave of an English spelunker is the highlight of any tour of the *grutas.*

Tours leave on the hour from the **visitor's center** and afford little opportunity for traipsing about on your own. After dishing out a bit of history, the guide directs the crowd's attention to rock formations which, he claims, bear remarkable likenesses to familiar people and things. The crowd oohs and ahhs as the guide points out stoned images of Santa Claus, Dante, and—what else—the Virgin of Guadalupe. Some of the guides employed by the caves speak English, but only for a good-sized group of *gringos.* Beware of the slick pavement; shoes with good traction are helpful (caves open daily 10am-5pm; admission 15 pesos, children 10 pesos).

**Getting There:** Buses run to the Grutas de Cacahuamilpa from Taxco's **Flecha Roja** bus station (every ½ hr., 8am-5pm, 45min., 5 pesos), and the last one returns to Taxco at 6pm. The bus will drop you at the crossroads, where you also catch the return bus. Take a right down the street; the cave entrance lies just after the curve. Catching a bus back may prove difficult. You may be forced (especially during the afternoon *siesta*) to consider other forms of transportation, including some uncomfortably crowded *colectivos* that stop at the site. Cacahuamilpa is 30km north of Taxco, 36km south of Ixtapán, and 69km southwest of Cuernavaca.

# ■■■ CHILPANCINGO

Home to the Universidad de Guerrero, Chilpancingo is a consummate college town: students rush through its streets with backpacks and books in hand, supporting the city's thriving cheap entertainment and food industries, and the *zócalo* feels something like a campus quad with its modern architecture and abstract sculptures.

The capital of the state of Guerrero, Chilpancingo is tucked midway between Acapulco and Taxco beneath green-laced mountains. Its relative lack of tourist attractions means that few foreigners stop by, making it an ideal place to take a rest from the sea-to-silver route, observe student culture, watch a couple of political demonstrations, and then return to the *gringo* trail.

**Orientation and Practical Information** Chilpancingo is located 130km north of Acapulco and 270km south of Mexico City. Streets run in straight lines, forming easy-to-follow blocks, and their names are clearly marked.

To get to the *zócalo* from the **Estrella de Oro** bus station, take a left on Juárez from the station's front entrance and continue several blocks until Juárez rams right into the square. From the **Estrella Blanca** station, take a right on 21 de Marzo and continue one block until you hit Juárez, make a right and keep on going—you'll pass the Estrella de Oro station a few blocks down. From either station, you can also catch a *combi* heading in the right direction—just ask to be left off at the *zócalo.*

Limited **tourist information** is available from the **Sendatur** office (tel. 2-05-37) in the Estrella Blanca bus station. The **police** (tel. 2-20-62) are at Guerrero, six blocks up from the Red Cross. Officers can also be found in the *zócalo.* The **post office** is located at Hidalgo 9 (tel. 2-22-75), 1½ blocks up from the *zócalo.* It posts a *Lista de Correos* (open Mon.-Fri. 8am-7pm, Sat. 9am-1pm). **Postal Code:** 39000. **LADATELs** line the *zócalo.* **Telephone Code:** 747. For currency exchange, head to **Bancomer** (tel. 2-25-75), in the *zócalo,* which is open for exchange 9am-1:30pm. **Bánamex,** next door to Bancomer, also exchanges traveler's checks and cash from 9am-1:30pm. It also has an **ATM** that accepts Cirrus, Plus, MC, and Visa.

**Estrella de Oro,** Juárez 53 (tel. 2-21-30), leaves for Acapulco (first class 4pm, 2hrs., 33 pesos), *ordinario* to Acapulco (every hr., 2½hrs., 24 pesos), Cuernavaca (6 per day, 2½hrs., 38-57 pesos), Mexico City *de local* (7 per day, 3½hrs., 74 pesos), Mexico City *de paso* (7 per day, 4½hrs., 60 pesos), and Taxco (3 per day, 6:20-11am, 2½hrs., 34 pesos). **Estrella Blanca** (tel. 2-06-34), at 21 de Marzo, a few blocks down from Estrella de Oro, sends buses direct to Acapulco (every ½hr., 5:40am-9:15pm, 2hrs., 22 pesos), Cuernavaca (6 per day, 2½hrs., 34 pesos), Mexico City (11 per day, 4hrs., 48 pesos), and Taxco (3 per day, 2½hrs., 32 pesos).

If you get a boo-boo, go to the **Farmacia Nueva Alameda,** Catalán at Zapata (tel. 2-70-13). Open 24 hrs. If you get a really bad boo-boo, consult the **Red Cross,** Apresa at Juárez (tel. 2-65-14). Some English spoken. Ambulance service 24 hrs. To do something about the person causing all the boo-boos contact the police (see above) in an **emergency.**

**Accommodations and Food** Chilpancingo, not being most travelers' number-one destination, doesn't offer many hotel options—but what few there are happen to be happily inexpensive. **Hotel María Isabel,** Madero 1 (tel. 2-48-80), at the corner of Abasolo near the *zócalo,* is the shining star of Chilpancingo's accommodations pool, featuring large rooms with lovely tile floors and user-friendly bathrooms. Some have brand new color TVs; rooms without TVs are slightly less spectacular but worthwhile nonetheless. Ceiling fans and hot water (singles 50 pesos, with TV 80 pesos; doubles 65 pesos, with TV 85 pesos). Much less expensive (and less appealing) is the **Hotel Chilpancingo,** Alemán 8 (tel. 2-24-46), whose spartan cement rooms might test your budget-traveling happy-go-lucky patience. Unfortunate bathrooms (singles 30 pesos; doubles 50 pesos).

Good food isn't hard to find in this town. The streets, especially around the *zócalo,* are crawling with student-packed taco joints that offer authentic food at low, low prices. For something a little more upscale, try **Bib's Restaurant,** on the second floor of Trujano 2 (tel. 1-11-66). It's not exactly sophisticated, but green tablecloths, large planters, and great views of the *zócalo* from the window-side tables give it a slight edge. Standard Mexican fare in the 10-20-peso range (open Mon.-Sat. 8am-8pm). **Restaurant Cuauhtémoc,** 1½ blocks down from the *zócalo* at Alemán 14 (tel. 2-32-23), is a popular restaurant that tends to get crowded at *comida* time; maybe it's the *mariachis* who stop in on occasion, or perhaps it's the *telenovelas* on TV that draw people in such large numbers. *Comida corrida* 12 pesos (open Mon.-Sat. 8am-11pm). A sidewalk café with plenty of outdoor seating, **La Parroquia,** Bravo 2 (tel. 2-29-28), in the corner of the *zócalo,* tends to attract a professional crowd. Standard fare, plus burgers (10 pesos) and filet mignon (25 pesos; open daily 7:30am-10:30pm).

**Sights and Entertainment** Chilpancingo's main attraction is the **Museo Regional de Guerrero,** in an old government building on the *zócalo* which now serves as the Instituto Guerrerense de la Cultura. Though the beautiful and historic building may be more interesting than the museum itself, it's still worthwhile to peek into the courtyard and take a look at the murals depicting the history of Guerrero. Some ancient items unearthed nearby are also sporadically positioned around the courtyard (open Tues.-Sat. 11am-6pm; free).

Lovers of all things *folklórico* may want to take a look at **La Casa de las Artesanías,** a short ride from the *zócalo* via the "Jacarandas" *combi.* Their name says it all: *artesanías* of all shapes, sizes, and prices can be found in the house. So, shop (open Mon.-Fri. 9am-9pm).

If the sights are on the paltry side, never fear: you're in a college town. What Chilpancingo lacks in museums, it makes up for in bars. A good place to start your search for other forms of not-so-intelligent nightlife is the **Casino del Estudiante,** Guerrero at Madero, just off the *zócalo.* Basically, it's a student hangout that houses bulletin boards with local events listings to complement some very popular pingpong tables. Otherwise, just hit the *zócalo* and keep walking until something catches your eye; chances are it'll be filled with college students engaging in some raucous R&R. **Ton's Que** (tel. 2-12-32), on the *zócalo,* is one of many such establishments, as well as **Rodash Video-bar** (tel. 2-48-80), in the Hotel María Isabel, which doubles as a sports bar come *fútbol* season (open daily 5:30pm-1am).

# ■■■ ZIHUATANEJO AND IXTAPA

It's no wonder that Zihuatanejo is so popular with tourists: its beautiful beaches and tranquil environment offer a relatively unmatched serenity. But before Zihuatanejo started slapping prices on everything and printing menus in broken English, it was little more than a pier on which to unload the day's catch. Centuries before it became a sun-soaked tourist trap, Zihuatanejo's pre-Conquest matriarchal society lent the town its original name—Cihuatlán, from the Nahuatl words *cihuatl* (woman) and *tlan* (place). When the Spanish arrived, they malaproped the name as Zihuatanejo and developed the harbor into a trading center of measurable importance. In the 19th century, however, ports like Manzanillo and Acapulco assumed Zihuatanejo's lucrative trade with Asia and the city reverted to a fishing village.

The recent remodeling and development of the area around the scenic Playa del Palmar, including the creation of the tourist complex at Ixtapa, began in 1978. Masterminding the operation was the Bank of Public Works and Services, contracted by the Mexican government to provide tourists with "a picturesque town on the shore of a small, peaceful bay." Even though Ixtapa's artificial façade reveals the cold hand of urban planning, the government development scheme seems to have worked: witness the planeloads of tourists from around the world that arrive daily to bathe in the sun and in the Pacific. Given the resort's awesome beaches, the developers could hardly have gone wrong.

Although designed by the same people, the beach resorts of Zihuatanejo and Ixtapa have very little in common. Ixtapa is nothing but a line of skyscraping hotels, burst full-grown from the collective mind of its developers, along an extremely attractive beach. Ixtapa has a few tourist-oriented stores located near the hotels, but excluding the tourist authorities, it has no public services, no downtown, no residential district, and no cheap anything. Nor does it have the pollution, overcrowding, or thriving slums that plague its neighboring resort Acapulco—at least not yet. Zihuatanejo, the area's commercial center and the only base for budget travelers, fills these voids. All of the area's ritzy hotel complexes operate outside of town, where tourists hole up in their air-conditioned suites, venturing out mainly to bake on the beach or catch dinner in town. On the waterfront, maître-d's of the innumerable seafood restaurants compete aggressively, flaunting their menus for passing tourists to see, while the calm waters prod along fishing boats and refresh the occasional swimmer. Downtown, cheap hotels, open-air restaurants, and boutiques jostle for elbow-room; taxis constantly zoom by, offering every last *gringo* their services. In fact, downtown Zihuatanejo looks like a small town in which everyone simultaneously decided to open a souvenir shop/hotel/pharmacy/restaurant. Luckily, the easy-going proprietors lend the town a relaxed atmosphere. This combination of frenetic activity and cheerful informality makes the area one of the Pacific coast's premier vacation spots.

## ORIENTATION

Zihuatanejo and Ixtapa rise from the Pacific coast, 115km southeast of Playa Azul and Lázaro Cárdenas and 268km northwest of Acapulco. **Estrella Blanca** and **Estrella de Oro** buses stop in Zihuatanejo, providing the most frequent service to the two towns. The Estrella Blanca station lies just outside the *centro,* and can be reached by a *micro* (minibus) (every 5min., 9am-6pm, 5min., 1 peso). To reach Estrella de Oro from the **Playa Municipal,** take Juan N. Álvarez until it becomes Paseo de la Boquita. Stay on Boquita as it veers left and becomes Paseo del Palmar at the Plaza Kioto. Estrella de Oro is on the left at the next corner. **Taxis** from Estrella de Oro to the center of town (or back) cost 6 pesos, while those from the Estrella Blanca station cost 7 pesos. A better way of getting from Estrella Blanca to the center of town is to catch one of the buses heading left as you leave the station (1 peso). The resort crowd flies into Zihuatanejo's international **airport,** 16km south of the city on the highway to Acapulco. **Mexicana** and **Aeroméxico** are the only carriers that provide service to this area. Taxis to and from Zihuatanejo cost about 30 pesos.

Downtown Zihuatanejo forms a rectangle of about 25 square blocks bounded by the major streets **Morelos** (formerly Paseo Zihuatanejo) to the north, **Juárez** (formerly Paseo del Cocotal) to the east, **Paseo del Pescador** (a.k.a. the waterfront) to the south, and **5 de Mayo** to the west.

Ixtapa consists of a single access road, **Blvd. Ixtapa,** which parades past a phalanx of huge luxury hotels to the west and overpriced stores to the east. It terminates abruptly after the last resort. A smaller road off the boulevard continues to the northwest beaches. Buses shuttling between the two cities leave from the intersection of Juárez and Morelos in Zihuatanejo across from the yellow Elektra electronics store, and from various bus stops on the boulevard in Ixtapa (about every 15min., 6am-7pm, 15-25min., 1 peso from any stop). Cab fare between the two towns runs about 15-20 pesos.

If an address listed below is not on Blvd. Ixtapa, it is in Zihuatanejo.

## PRACTICAL INFORMATION

**Tourist Office: City Office** (tel. 4-20-82, ext. 121, or 4-20-01, ext. 120), in a booth on Juan N. Álvarez to the left of the small town square and the basketball court as you face the beach. Maps and basic information. Some English spoken. Open Mon.-Sat. 9am-3pm and 6pm-8pm. **State Office,** in a *caseta* on Blvd. Ixtapa in front of Hotel Presidente (tel. 3-19-67 or 3-19-68), has piles of maps and pamphlets. Some English spoken. Open Mon.-Fri. 9am-2pm and 4pm-7pm.

**Tourist Police:** In Ixtapa (tel. 4-20-40, 4-23-66, 4-53-60, or 4-53-55).

**Police:** In the Palacio Municipal (tel. 4-20-40, 4-23-66, 4-53-60, or 4-71-71 for *el director*), in Zihuatanejo.

**Post Office:** (tel. 4-21-92), off Paseo del Palmar. Walking north from Estrella de Oro, it's down the side street to the right. If you see the end of Las Palmas on your left, you've gone too far. It's on the east side of the big white building at the end of the street. *Lista de Correos.* Open Mon.-Fri. 8am-6pm. **Postal code:** 40880.

**Telephones:** At **Money Exchange,** on Galeana between Ascencio and Bravo. Collect calls 5 pesos. Open daily 8am-9pm. **Teléfonos Públicos,** Juárez, across from Banco Mexico. Collect calls 5 pesos. Open daily 8am-9pm. **Telephone code:** 753.

**Telegrams: Edificio Telecomm** (tel. 4-21-63), just one door over from the post office. Open Mon.-Fri. 9am-1pm and 3-5pm, Sat. 9am-noon.

**Currency Exchange: Banco Mexicano,** Los Mangos and Juarez (tel. 4-51-60). Open Mon.-Fri. 9am-1:30pm. Changes U.S. dollars 9:30am-12:30pm, Canadian dollars 9:30-11:30am. **Money Exchange,** on Galeana (tel. 4-35-22 or 4-36-22). From the Playa Municipal, walk one block north on Cuauhtémoc and take a right on Bravo. Take the first left onto Galeana and follow the signs. It's the humble wooden building on the left. Rates on the dollar around. 50 pesos less than the banks, but no commission. Open daily 8am-9pm.

**Airport:** (tel. 4-20-70), on the coast to the south. **Aeroméxico,** Álvarez 34 (tel. 4-20-18). Open Mon.-Sat. 9am-6:30pm. **Mexicana, Guerrero,** and **Bravo,** next to Farmacia Coyuca (tel. 3-22-10, 4-22-08, or 4-27-09). Open Mon.-Sat. 9am-6:45pm, Sun. 9am-2pm and 3-5:45pm.

**Bus Stations: Estrella de Oro,** Paseo Palmar 54 (tel. 4-21-75). Departures between 8am-11pm. To Acapulco (4 per day, 4hrs., 37 pesos), Cuernavaca (4 per day, 7-10hrs., 103 pesos), Mexico City (7 per day, 9hrs., 103 pesos), plus many other destinations. **Estrella Blanca** (tel. 4-34-77), outside of town. To Acapulco (15 per day, 7am-9:30pm, 4hrs., 43pesos), Huatulco (7:45pm and 9:30pm, 15hrs., 139 pesos), and Puerto Escondido (7:45pm and 9:30pm, 11hrs., 117 pesos).

**Laundromat: Super Clean,** Catalina Gonzales 11 (tel. 4-23-47), east of Cuauhtémoc. 18 pesos/3kg (min.). Free pick-up and delivery. Open Mon.-Sat. 8am-8pm.

**Red Cross:** (tel. 4-20-09), on the right side of Av. de las Huertas as you leave town. 24-hr. emergency and ambulance service.

**Pharmacy: Farmacia "Coyuca,"** Guerrero and Bravo (tel. and fax 4-53-90). You can't miss the huge blue sign. Will deliver. Open daily 8am-11pm. A 24-hr. branch with the same name at Fuente del Sol, at the traffic circle heading toward Ixtapa.

**Medical Services: Centro de Salud,** Paseo de la Boquita at Paseo del Palmar (tel. 4-20-88). Open for consultations Mon.-Sat. 8am-3pm. The tourist office recommends the private **Sanatorio de la Salud de Especialidades,** Antonio Nayas 11 at Cuauhtémoc (tel. 4-47-76 or 4-34-37). Open 24 hrs.

## ACCOMMODATIONS AND CAMPING

Zihuatanejo supports a youth hostel on the outskirts of town and a slew of reasonably priced hotels downtown. Farther inland from the downtown area, hotels become dirtier and less expensive. Accommodations tend to cluster along Bravo, the western end of Álvarez, and Morelos. Somewhat more upscale and better maintained establishments line the streets between Bravo and the waterfront. Most lodge a diverse mix of Mexican and foreign visitors. During the winter months, some prices are subject to slight increases. As with many of Mexico's hotels, stays longer than a week can earn discounts.

The tourist office frantically discourages unofficial camping, possibly because they believe *gringos* can't do without the amenities of a five-star hotel, but more likely because they hate to see tourist dollars slip away. Those who choose not to heed their warnings frequent the point beyond and to the northwest of Playa Las Gatas on the Bahía de Zihuatanejo. Empty sand awaits northwest along Ixtapa's Playa Palmar away from the hotels, or on Isla Ixtapa for those who accidentally miss the last boat back. Despite the heavy presence of police officers, it's probably not a wise idea to camp alone, and groups of any size run the safety risks common to all touristed beaches at night.

**Casa Elvira** (tel. 4-20-61), on Paseo del Pescador, two blocks west of the basketball courts. A striking menagerie including birds, plants, and ducks. Small but adequate singles come with *agua purificada* and a fan; larger doubles include a couch. Friendly manager. Communal porch with 3 chairs, 20 plants, and a whole lot of character. Right on the beach. Singles 30 pesos. Doubles 50 pesos.

**Hotel Casa Aurora,** Bravo 27 (tel. 4-30-46), between Guerrero and Galeana. Magnificent upstairs rooms with floral bedspreads, A/C, hot water, and desks await two lucky travelers. Everyone else misses out on the funky sheets and hot water. The furnished, sunny patio makes rooms on the second level ideal. All rooms include either A/C or a fan and are 30 pesos per person.

**Casa Bravo,** Bravo 11 (tel. 4-25-48), west of Juárez. Big, cozy rooms with TVs, towels, soap, toilet paper, and a jug of *agua purificada*. Private bathrooms of the feel-free-to-shower-barefoot variety. No hot water. Balconies in some rooms overlook the street. Singles 50 pesos. Doubles 70 pesos. Triples 100 pesos.

**Hotel Villa del Ángel,** Cuauhtémoc 5 (tel. 4-25-29), 1 block north of the beach, on the east side of the street just north of Álvarez—don't be misled by the office on the ground floor. Fear not the dark, concrete stairwell—bright, melon-colored rooms with striped bedspreads and a ceiling fan await. Balcony buffs might consider splurging for the large and well-furnished terraces. Singles 40 pesos. Doubles 70 pesos, with balcony 80 pesos. 10 pesos off with a student ID.

**Villa Deportiva Juvenil,** on Morelos (tel. 4-46-62). From Juárez and Morelos, hike west for about 15 min. Ignore the signs urging you to the center and hang a left at the sewage plant. (Those aren't *mariscos* you smell.) It's the next building on the right. The distance from the *centro* is the only drawback. Well-maintained single-sex rooms with 4-8 bunks cooled by a single fan. Sheets, blanket, and pillow supplied (20 peso deposit). Clean bathrooms with hot water. Check-out 9:30am. 15-day max. stay. Restaurant serves breakfast (10.50 pesos), lunch, and dinner (both 13.50 pesos). Basketball court lit at night (open 7am-11pm). 15 pesos per person. HI membership gets you a 10% discount, with Plan Joven 25%. Reservations for groups of 10 or more recommended at least 20-30 days in advance.

**Casa Tulipanes,** Calle Pedro Ascencio 3 (tel. 4-36-61, fax 4-26-69), just to the left as you face Hotel Zihuatanejo. It's the mysteriously unmarked white building with sky-blue trim. Easy on the wallet but—unless you're a concrete connoisseur— hard on the eyes. Boasts 23 good-sized rooms cooled by fans. Free use of the pool at Hotel Zihuatanejo. Singles and doubles 40 pesos. Triples 55 pesos.

## FOOD

Most hotels in Ixtapa include meals in the price of a room, so the resort has failed to spawn the swanky restaurants so common in Acapulco and Puerto Vallarta. In Zihuatanejo, however, you should have little trouble finding a budget meal. Vendors lining the streets of Juárez sell *pollos rostizados* (roasted chickens) for about 20 pesos; one bird is a meal for two. In general, restaurants farther inland are cheaper, less polished, and more likely to offer something besides seafood. While restaurants along the shore are maintained with Ixtapa's timid tourists in mind, the streets just inland from the water are dotted with small restaurants with lots of character.

**Los Braseros,** Ejido 21 (tel. 4-48-58). Culinary delights you would expect to find only in Ixtapa, but for a fraction of the cost. House specialties are the *platos combinados,* consisting of a massive plate of stir-fried meat, vegetables, or both, with hot tortillas on the side (about 20 pesos). Sample some *ballena* (whale), advertised as "A Tradition!" Other entrees on the eccentric menu include the *beso* (kiss) and the *gringa.* The nimble chef prepares all food on a big grill in front of the restaurant, while 10 functioning fans keep the interior cool. The "TutiFruti" (crepes topped with fruit salad and yogurt) is a yummy way to end your meal; however, at 19 pesos it will denude your wallet somewhat. Open daily 4pm-1am.

**Pollos Locos,** Bravo 15 (tel. 4-40-44), next to the Casa Bravo. Prototypical beachside chicken joint comes complete with high tin roof and roaring open barbecue—the only thing missing is the beach. Once the fire cranks up, the inviting smell of chicken barbecued over wooden coals (16 pesos) wafts around the block. All meals come with onions, rice, and hot delicious homemade flour tortillas. To be safe, don't touch the salad (amoeba alert!). *Quesadillas* 8 pesos. Open daily 1-11pm.

**Tamales y Atoles "Any,"** Ejido and Guerrero (tel. 4-73-73 or 4-73-03), in front of Comermex. Cool and relaxed atmosphere. Traditional Guerreño fare. House specialties include the *"Consomé Any,"* a chicken consommé served with carrots, avocado, potato, rice, and garbanzo beans; tortillas are included (20 pesos). Eight different kinds of *tamales* (4 pesos). Open daily 8am-midnight.

## SAND AND SIGHTS

Neither Zihuatanejo's self-conscious charm nor Ixtapa's resort façades could ever eclipse the area's natural beauty. In Zihuatanejo, four stretches of sand line the water. They are, clockwise from the municipal pier, Playa Principal, Playa La Madera, Playa La Ropa, and Playa Las Gatas. Ixtapa overlooks the unbroken stretch of Playa del Palmar on the Bahía del Palmar, but the prettiest beaches lie beyond Laguna de Ixtapa: Playa Quieta, Playa Linda, and at the bay's west edge, Isla Ixtapa.

### Zihuatanejo

Downtown Zihuatanejo's beach, **Playa Principal,** is the least interesting of the area's sands, but its waters float the boats of local men, women, and children who are sometimes willing to take visitors for a spin in their crafts. On one side, its short and narrow sands are bordered by the seafood restaurants and basketball courts of Paseo del Pescador; unobstructed ocean water hugs the other. The largest catch of the day, typically on the display on the pier, may give timid swimmers a start. Overpriced deep-sea fishing trips leave from the Municipal Pier daily and cater to the serious fishing enthusiast. **Playa La Madera,** named after the wood once exported from its shores, is slightly more attractive than its downtown cousin. To reach it, walk 15 minutes east on one of the trails along the shoreline (some scrambling over rocks is involved), or walk east along the canal on Paseo de la Boquita, cross the canal at the bridge, and follow the signs to Playa La Madera. Here the shoreline is longer, though the beach is cut off by a few small restaurants at the base of a hill.

Zihuatanejo's two best beaches are **Playa La Ropa** and **Playa Las Gatas,** neither of which can be reached by walking along the bay's shores. La Ropa ("clothing") takes its name from the silks and other garments that washed ashore following the shipwreck of a trading vessel from Asia. Protected from the rough Pacific by the shape of the bay, La Ropa's crescent of sumptuous white sand attracts tourists from the hotels on the surrounding cliffs but is still relatively uncrowded during the week. On weekends, many locals stake a claim along the shimmering shore.

Taxis to La Ropa run 8-10 pesos. The walk takes 30 to 40 minutes and can be uncomfortably hot, even at night. If you must strain yourself, follow Paseo de la Boquita along the canal, cross over, and head toward the airport, as if going to La Madera. Bypass the Madera access road and follow the signs to La Ropa. The shortest route to the beach requires an immediate right turn into the drive of Playa Club La Ropa after passing the small park scattered with benches and flower pots. Hotel Catalina Sotavento's access road also leads to La Ropa. Make your way through the multi-tiered experience of the hotel complex and down the stairs to the bay. The imposing gate at the foot of the stairs (which has a large gap underneath) is often locked at night.

**Playa Las Gatas** was named for the sharks that once inhabited the waters close to shore. Long before the Spanish conquistadors settled the area, Tarascan King Caltzonzín built an artificial breakwater to create a safe swimming space for himself and his daughters; the sharks had to search elsewhere for sustenance. Since then, a natural reef that supports an abundance of marine life has grown over the original stone barricade.

In spite of its name, Las Gatas is one of the area's most crowded beaches. Ready to tame the swarm, a barrage of restaurateurs attempt to anchor tourists to wicker chairs and away from the water by brandishing their *cocos locos* (potent combinations of lime juice, natural syrup, tequila, gin, vodka, and rum mixed in coconut shells—sobriety anyone?). Las Gatas's white sands, coral reefs, and calm waters make for excellent snorkeling. Crowds notwithstanding, it is well worth the trip.

To get to Playa Las Gatas, walk along the shoreline from Playa La Ropa. In several spots you will have to use your hands, but the hike isn't terribly difficult. Follow the dirt road as far as Restaurant-Bar Capricho del Rey (look for the pink flags); from there, strike out across the rocks. Ten minutes later you'll be lounging on a beach chair at Las Gatas, *refresco* in hand. A road also leads to Playa Las Gatas; the strenuous walk takes well over half an hour. A less tiring and more popular way to reach Las Gatas is to pile into one of the *colectivo* boats from Zihuatanejo's municipal pier (every 15min., 9am-5pm, round-trip about 15 pesos). Buy tickets at the base of the pier at the western end of Paseo del Pescador; the boats leave from halfway down the pier. Save your ticket stub for the trip back.

A variety of snorkeling and scuba excursions, around US$25, are available beachside at Carlo Scuba and Oliviero's Scuba in Ixtapa, Antonio at Playa las Gatas, and at the Zihuatanejo Scuba Center.

## Ixtapa

While most of Zihuatanejo's crescent beaches are protected from the waves, three-footers pound Ixtapa's endless stretches of sand. Ixtapa would be beach heaven, except that the prices are as vicious as *las gatas*—a snack will cost you an arm and a leg and leave you feeling gnawed. All of Ixtapa's hotels are four- or five-star, and all of its restaurants, beachfront and otherwise, cater to the same free-spending clientele. But persevere. Buy some food and drink in cheaper Zihuatanejo and take the bus to paradise. Stride into a glittering hotel lobby as if you owned the place. In a swimsuit—having shed backpack, grimy jeans, and your copy of *Let's Go*—you just might blend in.

Ixtapa's **Playa del Palmar** weighs in as the resort's longest beach and one of the most beautiful stretches of sand in the world. Parts of its waters are a bit rough or dirty for swimming, though. Red flags indicate dangerous undertows, purple and blue signal contamination, yellow flags mean caution, while green flags mark calm seas good for swimming. Black flags imply the obvious: don't even think of swimming. Many of Palmar's waters in front of the hotels are red flag areas. To the southeast, however, lounges invite loiterers while parasailers make circuits during daylight hours until gas and demand run out (around 60 pesos). To the northwest, past existing hotels and the foundations for new condominium projects, lie perfectly sloping sands kissed by deep blue waves custom-designed for body surfing. To get to Playa del Palmar, take the bus from Zihuatanejo, get off in front of any hotel, and walk through the lobby. To reach the northwestern end of Palmar, drive down Blvd. Ixtapa until it dead-ends by Laguna de Ixtapa, or walk (15min.) along the beach or road.

To the northwest of Ixtapa are **Club Med, Playa Quieta,** and **Playa Linda,** less crowded and more stylish than the beaches at Ixtapa or Zihuatanejo. To drive here from Ixtapa, follow the boulevard northwest beyond most of the hotels and turn right at the sign for Playa Linda. If you're driving from Zihuatanejo, the access road from Route 200 is more convenient; go past the exit for Ixtapa in the direction of Puerto Vallarta and take the next left, marked Playa Linda. The road skirts Laguna de Ixtapa and hits the beach farther northwest. A taxi to Playa Linda or Playa Quieta costs about 15 pesos from Ixtapa, or 40 pesos from Zihuatanejo. Crystal clear water and bodysurfing waves await at **Playa Cuatas,** across the street from the tennis courts at Club Med on Playa Linda. Bring a lunch; there are no services here.

Some claim that of all the area's beaches, the most picturesque are those on **Isla Ixtapa,** about 2km offshore from Playa Quieta. Although the view is nice, the beach itself doesn't measure up to Playa del Palmar. Activity picks up in a few shoreside restaurants by day, but the island's 10 acres remain uninhabited at night. Boats to Isla Ixtapa leave from the municipal pier in Zihuatanejo between 9 and 10am and start their return journeys between 4 and 4:30pm (round-trip 35 pesos). While a bit pricey, the service runs on the clock the customer sets. A more economical way to get there is to take a bus or taxi to Playa Quieta, and then take a boat from there (around 15 pesos). Three stretches of beach ring the island. The two with northeastern exposure sustain crowds, small restaurants (no bargains), and snorkel gear booths (2.70 pesos for 1 set, 4.20 pesos for 2). The third is prohibitively rough and therefore generally deserted. Several dealers on the island rent scuba equipment. Prices are higher than at Las Gatas, and snorkeling conditions are worse because of the choppy water.

## ENTERTAINMENT

In the end, a beach is a beach is a beach. The real differences between the sleepy fishing village of the past and the glamorous resort town of the present are only apparent when you start looking for fun away from the water. This is tough in Zihuatanejo; a good deal of time there is spent boating, fishing, and chatting with boat owners. For wholesome entertainment, take the wife and kids to **Fantasía,** Vicente Guerrero 13 (tel. 3-16-24), just south of Ejido. Air hockey tables, foosball, and an array of video games tease away your pesos. Even the toddlers will be entertained with coin-activated rides seemingly transplanted from the storefronts of American supermarkets.

By contrast, Ixtapa provides the area with its rowdiest nighttime entertainment. **Señor Frog's** (tel. 3-06-92) blares American pop music across the boulevard. There's no cover, so ordering right (like *pasta al burro* for 25 pesos or *aros de cebolla—* onion rings—for 10 pesos) buys you extended hours of B-52s tunes at a table or by the bar. (Restaurant open daily 6pm-midnight. Bar open 6pm-whenever you run out of money.) **Christine,** Blvd. Ixtapa 429 (tel. 3-03-33), in the Hotel Krystal, prides itself on being "the most beautiful disco in the world," with its tiered seats and hanging vines. Mexican tourists and *gringos* alike swing their hips to the nightly light show at 11:30pm. (Open daily 10pm-6am. Cover 40 pesos. Call ahead to ask about discounts sometimes offered Mon.-Wed.)

# ■■■ COSTA GRANDE

The Guerrero coast north of Acapulco is often called the Costa Grande to distinguish it from its smaller counterpart (Costa Chica) to the south. Trade with Asia centuries ago left some of the area's inhabitants with Polynesian features. Of specific interest are Barra de Potosí, 20km southeast of Zihuatanejo, and Papanoa, another 60km farther along Route 200.

## BARRA DE POTOSÍ

For the *gringo* whose head is spinning from ruins, cathedrals, and souvenirs, there is no better tonic than a spell at **Playa Barra de Potosí.** Life here could not get more *tranquila*. Words spoken at the playa roll lazily off the tongue and waft effortlessly out to sea. *Camionetas* putter along the single sandy road, bouncing the inhabitants back and forth to their secluded homes. Now and then, someone stirs for a bit of fishing. The owners of the 12 or so open-air *enramadas* (informal "restaurants" with thatched roofs), just past the strip that constitutes "town," are proud of Playa Potosí's laid-back friendliness—and its fabulously cheap prices. In keeping with the casual spirit of the place, no restaurant seems to have a menu; they'll whip up whatever you want and then pull a price out of the air only after you remind them about your *cuenta* (don't be afraid to live large—baby lobsters often go for about 10 pesos). Friendly beyond belief are the folks at **Enramada Bacanora** (the third *enramada* on the beach as you enter the *enramada* area); by the time you finish your breakfast conversation with Chico and Ester, it may be time to order lunch.

Visitors to Barra de Potosí are expected to sleep in the hammocks that adorn each *enramada*. (Flex your travel-savvy and sleep on the diagonal, so as to support your back.) The owners don't care if you sack out in their hammocks forever—as long as you buy a meal from them every now and then. *Baños*, too, are free of charge. The owners will let you leave your pack in the *enramadas* for as long as you like. The *enramadas* farthest from the lagoon, toward the crossroads, tend to be the most magical in Barra de Potosí—the friendliest, safest places for all these gracious amenities. The mosquitoes are also free, so bring plenty of repellent.

Those still unskilled in the art of hammock-snoozing can give their backs a break at the wonderful (and wonderfully pink) **Hotel Barra de Potosí** (tel. 4-82-90, 4-82-91, or 4-34-45), an unfinished resort hotel that has nevertheless opened its doors for business. The completed portion of the hotel is gorgeous, while the half-constructed, abandoned remains of the hotel's top two floors save it from spoiling Potosí's charm. The top rooms which include a view of the beach, TV, cooler, washing machine, dining room, and kitchen, go for 250 pesos; from there, prices can drop to 100 pesos as amenities are whittled away. Visa, AmEx, and MC are accepted. Look for the signs—the hotel is just behind the empty white tourist booth. North of the hotel, nothing exists aside from a few private homes—save yourself the inevitable trek back to the access road.

If you simply *must* exert yourself while in Barra de Potosí (something the locals may not understand or appreciate), your only option is to hike the dirt road to the lighthouse on top of **Cerro Guamiule** (2000m), the nearby peak that guards the southern entrance to the bay. After a half-hour walk, you will be rewarded with a view of the bay and its 20km of beaches.

From Playa Potosí, the southernmost beach on the bay, walk north along the shore to the aptly named **Playa Blanca** (3km). You will pass **Playa Coacoyul** (8km), **Playa Riscaliyo** (19km), and pebbly **Playa Manzanillo** (24km) before reaching another lighthouse (26km), which overlooks the northern edge of the bay. All beaches are free of tourists in the summer months, but fill up with a few hundred Mexican visitors during Christmas.

**Getting There:** To reach Playa Potosí, get off a second-class bus at Los Achotes, which is little more than a *crucero* (crossroads) between Zihuatanejo and Petatlán. From Zihuatanejo, the microbus leaves the bus station behind the market, just east of Juárez (every 10min., 9am-6pm, ½hr., 2 pesos). Either warn the driver of your unfamiliarity with the area before boarding, or look for the highway signs that say Zarco 2 and Laguna de Potosí 10; the sign for Los Achotes is just a few meters ahead but easy to miss. From the *crucero,* hop on one of the fairly frequent *camionetas* (flatbed pick-up trucks) that travel the dirt road to the playa (every ½hr. during the day, ½hr., about 3 pesos). Pretend you're just naturally alert and avoid the low crossbar when boarding; then grab a seat on the right side where the roof blocks the sun's glare. Many hitch a ride with one of the residents; *Let's Go* does not recommend hitching. The last *camioneta* returns to the *crucero* at 5pm. Do not walk the 6km—it's farther, hotter, and bleaker than it seems. To return, take a *camioneta* back to the *crucero* and wait for the Zihuatanejo-Petatlán microbus. From the *cruc-*

*ero,* with your back to the beach, Zihuatanejo is to the left and Petatlán to the right. Traveling time to Barra de Potosí is approximately 1-1½ hours.

# ■■■ ACAPULCO

Once upon a time, Acapulco was the stunningly beautiful playground of the equally glamorous packs of the rich and famous. Hollywood legends once celebrated their silver-screen successes by dancing the Mexican nights away in its chic clubs, politicians spent their honeymoons hopping between its attractive shores, and scores of passengers on "The Love Boat" found televised love always exciting and new on the path from the Aloha Deck to the docks at Acapulco Bay. But time passes and fairy tales fade: Acapulco's glamour went out just about the time that Gopher hung up his cruise-ship whites and got himself elected to the U.S. Congress.

Today, Acapulco is two things—a slim, glitzy fingernail of a resort with beaches to one side and downtown to the other, and a slum that reaches up into the hills behind the resorts. This second, grimmer Acapulco was born when the heavily monied stopped vacationing on Acapulco's shore and hotel jobs could no longer keep pace with the waves of immigration drawn seaward from the interior by the prospect of plentiful pesos. But now more than ever, everyone in Acapulco is driven by money—either the need to spend it or the need to earn it. Vendors crowd the streets and cling to slow-moving or indecisive visitors; restaurant owners wave travelers inside with their menus. Peddlers of everything from Chiclets to "free information" run at tourists like eager bulls. Most of Acapulco's visitors tend to be older *norteamericanos,* Europeans, and Mexicans who think fondly of Acapulco as "the city that never sleeps." Indeed, perhaps the best time to visit the city is at night, when darkness shrouds the grime and allows the glitter of the street lamps to evoke Acapulco's fairy tale past.

## ORIENTATION

The fading grandfather of Mexico's Pacific resorts, Acapulco sits 400km south of Mexico City and 239km southeast of Zihuatanejo/Ixtapa. The crescent-shaped city opens to the south around Acapulco Bay. Route 200 feeds into **Avenida Costera Miguel Alemán** (sometimes labeled Av. Presidente Alemán, but always referred to simply as **La Costera**). This thoroughfare traces the contour of the bay and connects Acapulco's three main districts: the **Peninsula de las Playas**, the older city center, and the relatively new strip of luxury hotels that extends from **Parque Papagayo** to the naval base. Landmarks along the Costera make easy reference points for locating the city's major sights, most of which lie on or near this divided highway. (This is especially useful because street numbers in Acapulco are rarely posted, and when visible, tend not to follow any logical numerical sequence.) The Peninsula de las Playas forms the southwestern curve of the crescent and shields the bay from Pacific breakers. The Costera begins on the southern (seaward) side of the peninsula at Playa Caleta, and continues past the **zócalo,** the strip, and finally to the naval base.

The city's **Estrella de Oro bus station** is on Av. Cuauhtémoc, just northeast of Parque Papagayo. To get from the station to the *zócalo,* take any bus heading southwest (1.40 pesos). To make the walk to the *zócalo* (45min.), follow Cuauhtémoc southwest until it becomes Escudero, which ends at Av. Costera Miguel Alemán. Turn right; the *zócalo* is two blocks ahead. The city's second bus station is **Estrella Blanca** at Av. Ejido 47. Instead of walking, take a bus marked *"zócalo"* (1.40 pesos) or hire a taxi (8 pesos).

**Buses** blaring musical horns cruise the length of the Costera, Av. Cuauhtémoc, and other major streets from 5:30am to midnight. The old blue-and-white school buses charge 1.40 pesos; the fare is slightly higher on the modern, air-conditioned "Paseo Acapulco" and "Acatur" buses (2 pesos). Buses marked "Cine Río-La Base" connect the *zócalo* with the naval base via both Cuauhtémoc and the Costera; those marked "Hornos" or "CICI" stick to the Costera. Because bus numbers mean about

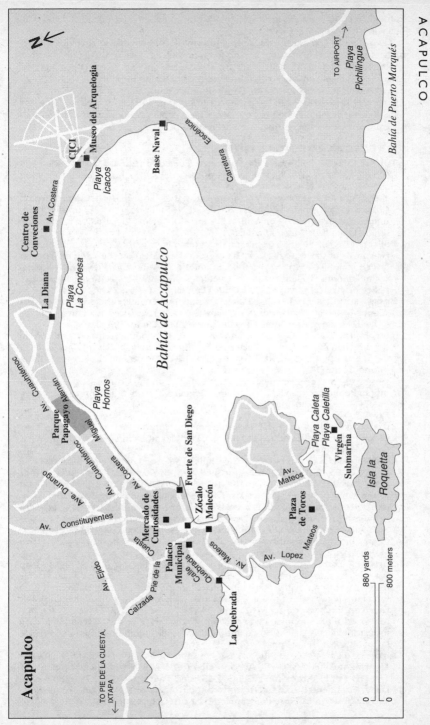

ACAPULCO

as much as street numbers in Acapulco, it's best to read the destinations painted on bus windshields, or ask the driver.

**Taxis,** usually VW Bugs, swarm up and down every street. Fees are ridiculously high and rising. A ride from the *zócalo* to either bus terminal or Playa Caleta costs 8 pesos, to Pie de la Cuesta 30 pesos, to Puerto Marqués or the airport 50 pesos. Always bargain and always set the price before you climb in.

A cheaper option is the door-to-door **collective company;** call 66-90-58 or 86-49-33 one day in advance with flight information. Some English is spoken. They will pick you up 90 minutes before your scheduled departure for domestic flights and 120 minutes before international departures (18 pesos).

## PRACTICAL INFORMATION

**Tourist Offices: Secretaria de Fomento Turístico (SEFOTUR),** Costera 187 (tel. 86-91-64 or -67). Some English spoken. Maps, brochures and information about Acapulco, Ixtapa, Zihuatanejo, and nearby towns. Open Mon.-Fri. 9am-2pm and 4-7pm. In an emergency, contact the state's **Tourist Assistance Bureau,** Costera 4455 (tel. 84-44-16 or 84-70-50, ext. 165), in front of CICI in the Centro Internacional Acapulco Convention Center. More of an office than an information booth. Open daily 9am-midnight.

**Police:** (tel. 85-06-50 or 85-08-62), on the ground floor of the Cocos Condominium, two-thirds of the way to Playa Caleta from the *zócalo* on the Costera. **Tourist police** (tel. 85-04-90) are the folks in and around the *zócalo* wearing virginal white uniforms. To find lost people, vehicles, and valuables, or to quickly contact police or medical services, dial **LOCATEL** (tel. 81-11-00), 24 hrs.

**Post Office:** Costera 215 (tel. 82-20-83), a pink building near the *zócalo*. Open for stamps Mon.-Sat. 8am-8pm, Sun. 9am-1pm; for registered mail and *Lista de Correos* Mon.-Fri. 8am-7pm, Sat. 9am-3pm. **Postal Code:** 39300.

**Telephones: Caseta Carranza,** Carranza 9. Walk two blocks from the *zócalo* in the direction of the strip, and make a left onto Ignacio de la Llave. Collect calls to the U.S. 15 pesos. Open daily 8am-10pm. **LADATELs** line the Costera. **Telephone Code:** 74.

**Telegrams:** In the Palacio Federal (tel. 82-26-21), on the Costera next to the post office. Public **fax** 83-84-82. Open for telegrams Mon.-Sat. 9am-8pm; for money orders Mon.-Fri. 9am-5pm, Sat. 9am-noon.

**Travel Agency: M and M Tours,** Costera 26-A L-2 (tel. 84-89-60; fax 84-83-25), a few blocks west of the Hard Rock Café, on the opposite side of the street. Tours of the city and its environs, as well as daytrips and excursions to Mexico City. Open daily 8am-10pm.

**Consulates: U.S.,** Costera 187, in the Club del Sol Hotel mezzanine. Mr. Bon Urbaneck (tel. 85-12-00 or 85-66-07; for messages, 85-66-00 ext. 273), keeps office hours Mon.-Fri. 10am-2pm. **Canada** (tel. 85-66-21), in the Club del Sol Hotel, next to the U.S. Consulate. Contact Ms. Diana McLean. Open daily 10am-2pm. **U.K.** (tel. 84-16-50) in the Hotel Las Brisas, Carretera Escénica. Derek Gore, who is also responsible for Australians and New Zealanders, holds office hours Mon.-Fri. 9am-2pm and 4-7pm. For other consulates, call or stop by the **Casa Consular** in the Centro Internacional Acapulco (tel. 81-25-33 or 84-70-50, ext. 116 or 117). Open Mon.-Fri. 9am-2pm and 4-7pm.

**Currency Exchange:** Banks lining the Costera near the *zócalo* and on the strip have decent rates. All open Mon.-Fri. 9am-1:30pm. On the strip, you won't be able to open your eyes without spotting a *casa de cambio*—usually open until 8pm with rates comparable to banks. **Bánamex,** next to the post office, has an **ATM.**

**American Express:** Costera 1628 (tel. 69-11-22 to -24; fax 69-11-88), on the bottom floor of the shopping center. Will exchange traveler's checks and hold mail for cardholders. Efficient, air-conditioned office also functions as a travel agency. Open Mon.-Sat. 10am-7pm.

**Airport:** (tel. 84-03-03), on Rte. 200, 26km south of the city. **Delta** (tel. 84-07-16), **Continental** (tel. 66-90-63), **Aeroméxico** (tel. 85-16-00), **Mexicana** (tel. 84-12-15 or 84-14-21), **American** (tel. 66-92-48), and **Taesa** (tel. 85-21-74 or 86-56-00). Delta, Continental, and American have their offices at the airport, Aeroméxico and Mexicana in La Torre de Acapulco (just east of bus stop #18).

**Bus Stations: Estrella de Oro** (tel. 85-87-05), on Cuauhtémoc, about 10min. east of the northeast corner of Parque Papagayo. From the Costera, turn down the block opposite the Ritz—Cuauhtémoc runs perpendicular a few blocks up. To: Chilpancingo (every ½hr. from 5:15am, 2hrs., 29 pesos), Cuernavaca (5 per day, 70 pesos), Guadalajara (3:01 and 5:01pm, 210 pesos), Mazatlán (6:03am and 9:48pm, 224 pesos), Mexico City (over 22 per day, 5hrs., 89 pesos), Monterrey (10:01pm, 262 pesos), Morelia (5 per day, 127 pesos), Puebla (3 per day, 110 pesos), Querétaro (1:35 and 9pm, 146 pesos), Taxco (3 per day, 4hrs., 55 pesos), Tijuana (9:48pm, 448 pesos), and Zihuatanejo (every ½hr., 4hrs., 37 pesos). **Estrella Blanca,** Av. Ejido 47 (tel. 82-10-71). To Cuernavaca (2:15am and 9:35pm, 92 pesos), Mexico City (every hr., 5hrs., 111 pesos), Puebla (9:05pm, 137 pesos), and Querétaro (3 per day, 156 pesos).

**Laundromat: Ghost Cleaners,** José María Iglesias 9 (tel. 82-70-22), one block west of the *zócalo.* 4kg for 25 pesos. Same-day service. Open Mon.-Fri. 8am-2pm and 4-8pm, Sat. 8:30am-2pm.

**Red Cross:** (tel. 85-41-00), on Ruíz Cortínez, along Madero north of the *zócalo* into the hills. Take a bus labeled "Hospital Y." 24-hr. emergency service, but no English spoken. 10-peso service fee. 24-hr. doctor available through the **Sociedad de Asistencia Médica Turística** (tel. 85-58-00 or 85-59-59). English spoken.

**Pharmacy: Faber Farmacia,** Azueta 6, next to the mini-super of the same name. Open 24 hrs. **ISSTE Farmacias,** Quebrada 1 (tel. 82-34-77), directly behind the cathedral on the *zócalo.* The storefront faces Independencia. Open daily 8am-8pm.

**Hospital: Hospital General del IMSS,** Ruíz Cortínez 128 (tel. 85-17-30 or 85-08-62), north of the *zócalo* along Madero. Take any bus marked "Hospital Y." Medical appointments can be made here with English-speaking private physicians. 24-hr. emergency service.

## ACCOMMODATIONS

After it gets dark, sacking out on the beaches of Acapulco Bay is a dumb idea. Tourists report that their bags have been stolen from their sides in broad daylight as they closed their eyes on the beach. The same unsavory character who looked hungrily at your wallet when you bought that greasy *quesadilla* in the *zócalo* is ten times as shady when it's dark—twenty when your eyes are closed.

Fortunately, budget accommodations are more plentiful and easier to find in Acapulco than anywhere else on Mexico's Pacific coast. Many taxi drivers at the bus stations will offer to take you to their personal favorite; these middlemen charge no fee (but do hang around for a tip) and generally plug fairly economical places. Be sure to clarify the agreement before you step in the car. If you have time, though, it's a snap to locate Acapulco's budget neighborhoods and make your own comparisons. Acapulco is a haggler's dream: be certain to inquire about discounts before paying for a room. Don't be afraid to turn your back and walk away from unrelenting managers—there are plenty of options elsewhere. However, haggling is impossible (and reservations a must) during *Semana Santa,* when rooms are nearly double the off-season prices.

Most of the best deals in the city look out on Calle La Quebrada, which runs from the church behind the *zócalo* to the top of the La Quebrada cliffs. Other cheap hotels squeeze onto Teniente José Azueta and other cross streets between Quebrada and the Costera. To reach Quebrada from the *zócalo,* walk up the alley to the left of the cathedral and take the first left. To get to Teniente José Azueta, make a right onto the Costera (facing the bay) and another right at the second street corner.

**Casa de Huéspedes La Mamá Hélène,** Juárez 12 (tel. 82-23-96; fax 83-86-97), 1½ blocks west of the *zócalo.* Large, fan-cooled rooms with small details—dried flowers, vanities with slightly scratched mirrors—that lend the place a sort of warm *je ne sais quai.* Water is on the chilly side. A favorite of the European backpacking crowd. Owner Hélène, a transplanted Frenchwoman, speaks English, makes a mean cup of coffee, and is happy to offer tourist information or lend out her English-language books. Go, Hélène. Singles 50 pesos. Doubles 80 pesos.

**Hotel Angelita,** Quebrada 37 (tel. 83-57-34). Wicker furniture with pink cushions in the lobby. Rooms are bright and airy (if slightly tacky), with fans and clean, private bathrooms. Watch cable TV with the proprietors in the lobby. Singles 35 pesos. Doubles 60 pesos.

**Hotel Asturias,** Quebrada 45 (tel. 83-65-48). Look for the pink-and-black sign next to Angelita. If you tire of bouncing *centavos* off the springy mattresses, turn your attention to the pool, the small collection of English-language novels, and cable TV in the lobby. Private bathrooms with hot water. The kind management will guard the packs of wayfaring travelers, guests or not, free of charge. Singles 40 pesos, 50 pesos high season. Doubles 70 pesos, 80 pesos high season.

**La Torre Eiffel,** Inalámbrica 110 (tel. 82-16-83). The "tower" is the four-story pink-and-white building across from El Mirador, a long hike all the way up Quebrada. Worth the climb if you're not hell-bent on hitting the beach. Big, sunny rooms, some with marble decor in the bathrooms. Fabulous views of La Quebrada and the hills from large breezy patios with shocking pink furniture. Industrial-strength fans and a nice pool. Hot water mornings and evenings. Singles 30-40 pesos. Doubles 80 pesos.

**Casa de Huéspedes Anita,** Teniente José Azueta 12 (tel. 82-50-46), about two blocks inland from the Costera. Slightly crumbling bathrooms with hot water 24 hrs. Some very, very pink decor that closes on you like the fist of a baby. Some rooms have terraces that overlook the street. 30 pesos per person, 60 pesos high season. Up to five people per room.

## FOOD

Acapulco's restaurants don't aspire to traditional culinary authenticity (unless you count the McMexican burger), but they're a godsend for Americans homesick for Yankee cuisine, fast-food style. Denny's, Pizza Hut—and yes, even McDonald's—have invaded the Costera. Unfortunately, these restaurants sell their gringo food at prices gringos are used to—you won't see many locals here.

As usual, *típico* spots serve the cheapest meals; look to the hundreds of *fondas* (food stands) throughout the city as well as in the market, which spans several square blocks and is located inland from the Costera between Mendoza and de León. Another source of inexpensive fare (and a break from the Acapulco heat) are the supermarkets that line the Costera between the strip and the *zócalo*, notably Gigante, near Hornos, and Comercial Mexicana, just inland from La Diana. Prices are lower here than at the supermarkets further along the strip.

Only slightly more expensive than the *fondas*—and generally much better—are the restaurants between Costera and Quebrada, south and west of the *zócalo*. In Acapulco, seafood reigns supreme. *Tacos* or *quesadillas* stuffed with *cazón* (baby shark hash) are inexpensive, traditional, and satisfying. Another budget option are *picaditas,* Mexican "pizzas" made with fried corn dough and layered with beans, cheese, and just about anything else you want to toss on top.

### Near the Zócalo

Prices begin to climb as you inch north and west from the *zócalo* toward the strip.

**100% Natural,** Costera 248 (tel. 85-13-72, ext. 100), a 20-25 min. walk from the *zócalo,* near Hornos. Other branches line the Costera. Forget your gastrointestinal woes, folks—it's all *purificada.* Eat veggie sandwiches, salads, and *quesadillas* to your heart's content, and wash it down with a cool tropical shake or (gasp!) water. Veggie sandwiches 13 pesos. *Enchiladas* 16 pesos. Tropical shakes 7 or 10 pesos. Open daily 8am-midnight.

**The Fat Farm/La Granja del Pingui,** Juárez 10, at Iglesias. It's two restaurants in one! A smooth cultural crossroads between the U.S. and Mexico, paved with burgers (10 pesos), apple pie (8 pesos), and *piñatas.* English-language menu features mashed potatoes and meatloaf; Spanish-language menu offers tacos and *tamales.* Peruse English-language novels while watching MTV. Open daily 9am-10pm.

**Pizza's Real,** Independencia 7 (tel. 83-72-29), one block down the street behind the *zócalo*. A neighborhood joint that serves up pizza topped with just about anything. The walls are lined with 70s photos of pizza surrounded by beer and condiments. Savor the cheesy atmosphere while chowing down on the thin-and-crispy pizzas. Delivery available. Pizza 12-38 pesos. Open daily noon-1am.

**Mariscos Nacho's,** Azueta and Juárez (tel. 82-28-91), one block from the Costera. An open-air seafood place. The red and white tablecloths, tiled floor, and potted plants give it an air that many other restaurants are missing. Seafood with rice (17 pesos). Delicious *camarones al mojo de ajo* (shrimp in garlic sauce, 30 pesos). *Quesadillas de cazón* 7 pesos. Open daily 9:30am-9:30pm.

**Tepoznieves,** in the corner of the *zócalo* near the Costera. Branches throughout the city. *Nieves* in every flavor imaginable, from rose petal to *mezcal* to—yikes!—corn on the cob. The scrumptious frozen treats also come in more traditional flavors, such as strawberry and rum raisin. Can't decide? Try them all; they're very, very generous with the tasting spoons. Small *nieve* 4 pesos, medium 6 pesos. Open daily 10am-10:30pm.

## Playa Caleta

There are plenty of restaurants in the beach area, but most are low in quality and devoid of ambiance. Caleta's cheapest cuisine can be found within the *fondas* across the street from Playa Caletilla, where dozens of families set up stalls and sell the same food at the same prices. If you do want to sit by the sea, however, **Restaurant El Costeño,** at the boat launch on Playa Caletilla, off the Costera, is one of about 15 look-alike, taste-alike establishments on Caletilla. Like its neighbors, it tends to be a bit expensive, with a fish fillet going for about 20 pesos and *arroz con mariscos* for under 25 pesos (open daily noon-10pm). For a cheaper meal that involves more than seafood, try **Restaurant/Bar Mar Azul,** Gran Vía Trópica 1, above the fountain with the baby-blue railing (*tortas, huevos,* and *cervezas* all under 10 pesos; open daily 7am-11pm).

## On the Main Strip

The many Chi-Chi restaurants between Playa Condesa and La Base cater mainly to tourists who apparently don't fret about cost. One more moderately priced establishment is **Los Tres Amigos,** Costera 115, at Playa Condesa, where mariachi and *veracruzana* music drown out the dull roar of the waves nightly. The outdoor grill will serve up *brochetas* (shish kebab) for 30 pesos or *picadas* for 18 pesos, but the music can be heard just as well from the bar (open daily 6pm-whenever you feel like leaving). **Jovito's,** across from the Fiesta Americana at Playa Condesa, also provides moderately priced *tacos de mariscos* for budgeteers who stray from the *zócalo*. Lounge at tables that look like little huts. Shrimp *tostadas* and seafood *flautas* 15 pesos (open daily noon-2am).

## SAND AND SIGHTS

### Península de las Playas

World-renowned representatives of Acapulco, the cliff-divers at **La Quebrada** never fail to impress. These buff young men judge the speed of the incoming waves as well as the distance between the opposing cliffs on the south side of the peninsula before diving from 25-35m heights into the shallow waters of the inlet below.

The **Unión de Clavadistas La Quebrada** (Divers' Union) adheres to a rigid daily agenda—dives occur at 12:45, 7:30, 8:30, 9:30, and 10:30pm. The last two dives of the day are undertaken by torchlight. You can watch from the terrace bar of the **Restaurant La Perla** in Plaza Las Glorias, and the terrace of Don Carlos, in the same building; both provide an equally good view of the death-defying acts with a "complimentary" drink starting at 20 pesos. You can preserve your proletarian credentials (and also a fair amount of pesos) by joining the masses on the platform across from the point where the dives originate (5 pesos, under 10 free). Alternatively, if you pay your pesos and gawk from one of the two higher platforms conveniently located near the divers' dressing room, you might be able to meet the dashing heroes. The cliffs are at the southwestern end of La Quebrada, a 15-minute walk up the hill from the *zócalo*.

Signs all over Acapulco's beaches request that you not pollute the sea, but it may be a bit too late. Those who like to live dangerously can swim relatively free of tourists at **Playas Caleta** and **Caletilla.** Many buses marked "Caleta" run down Costera and Cuauhtémoc and head for these beaches. At the westernmost tip of Acapulco Bay, on the seaward side of the peninsula, they lie adjacent to each other and are known as the "morning beaches" because of their eastern exposure. Their waters are calm and good for swimming, and attract many a local beach-goer. Between them, a short causeway links the mainland to what otherwise would be a tiny island.

All sorts of equipment are available for rent on Playa Caleta; canoes, paddle boats, and flatboats are available on the beach's eastern side. On its western side, just before Playa Caletilla, is a stand that rents sailboats and bronco motor boats. In addition, inner tubes are available all over the beach.

Perhaps the most remarkable attraction at Playa Caleta is the aquarium at the far end of the boat launch, aptly called **Mágico Mundo Marino.** Not only are there sea lions, alligators, and other denizens of the deep blue yonder, but the 20-peso entrance fee (15 pesos for children 3-12) allows you to spend the whole day lounging by the pool or partaking of the two giant waterslides. Due to its cleanliness and unique location, the view from the aquarium's pool and rocks probably tops that of any beach in Acapulco (open daily 9am-7pm).

The **Plaza de Toros Caletilla,** Acapulco's main bull ring, sits beyond the abandoned yellow jai-alai auditoriums 200m west of the Caletilla beach area. *Corridas de toros* begin in December and go through Easter week, when the best-known *matadores* appear. Buy tickets at the Centro Kennedy box office at the Costera and Álvaro Saavedra (tel. 85-85-40) or at the ring box office starting at 4:30pm on the day of the fight. Bullfights erupt on Sundays at 5pm.

## City Center

Hanging out in the *zócalo,* **Plaza Álvarez,** is a far better way to learn about the life of Acapulco's inhabitants than cruising around all day in a bus. Huge trees cast shadows over stone benches, old men sit at their shoeshine stalls, and couples bask for hours in sidewalk cafés. Occasionally, a roving band of *mariachis* wakes the shade-dwellers. The plaza is bounded on one side by the Costera and on the other by the **Catedral de Nuestra Señora de Soledad,** whose blue-tiled dome is visible from higher points around the bay. Masses are Sundays at 7am, 8:30am, 10am, 11:30am, 1pm, 6pm, 7pm, and 8pm, and daily at 7am, 8am, 7pm, and 8pm.

The city's **Palacio Municipal** crowns a hill just inland from the *zócalo.* Go to the top of the white flight of stairs to the right of the cathedral, take a right through the tunnel, and the *palacio's* entrance is around the corner to your left and up another flight of stairs. This circular structure encloses a courtyard, and from its patio most of the old city is visible. Before it became Acapulco's city hall, the building served as a jail; the Mexican painter Sofia Bassi Zolorio did time here. Indicted for murdering her husband, hers became a *cause célèbre* until prominent Mexicans—claiming that her art represented an important contribution to society—secured a pardon for her. During the time of her confinement in the late 1960s, Bassi Zolorio covered a number of the prison's walls with paintings. The *palacio's* small auditorium bears one of the most striking of these works, a surrealistic self-portrait involving a rendition of the artist's imagined trial and execution. The best-known mural in the building is Roberto Cueva del Río's *Patria Es Primera,* which covers all four walls of the north stairway. Other works are scattered around the former prison, including a representation of Mexico's presidents hatching from eggs and a chronicle of Acapulco's transformation from small-time fishing village to big-time resort (palace open Mon.-Fri. 9am-9pm; no shorts or swimsuits).

The **Fuerte de San Diego** was built in 1615 to ward off pirates, among them Sir Francis Drake, who hung around the bay looting ships arriving from Asia. In 1776, an earthquake leveled all of Acapulco, destroying the fort that stood on the Costera, a five-minute walk east of the *zócalo*. The fort was later restored to its original pentagonal shape, and during the Revolution it proved secure enough to hold back Morelos's rebel forces for a full four months. While its strategic importance has vanished, the fort remains a working military compound. Civilian visitors can visit the fort and its attached museum. After hours it becomes a make-out spot for young *acapulqueño* couples who come to pay sensual homage to its glorious history (museum open Tues.-Sun. 10:30am-4:40pm; admission 14 pesos, students, teachers, children, and senior citizens free and for all on Sun.).

## Parque Papagayo

The green grass and cool shade of Parque Papagayo offer relief from too many days of hot sand and bright sun. Sandwiched between **Playas Hornos** and **Hornitos** (the "afternoon" beaches), the park, like the beaches it borders, caters largely to a Mexican crowd. Its many diversions include roller skating, boating (on an artificial lake), and go-cart racing. The park also encloses a small but well-equipped amusement park, a *plaza de toros* (but no bullfights), and a concrete toboggan run, whose starting gate at the top of a little hill is accessible by what is likely the only ski lift in Mexico. You can also reach the summit by cable car or a winding road. Of interest, too, is the park's **aviary;** crested cranes, peacocks, buzzcocks, emus, guinea fowl, flamingos, and toucans inhabit the netted sanctuary. For schedules of rodeos and other park activities, call the park office (tel. 85-24-90; open Mon.-Fri. 9am-8pm, Sat. 9am-noon). For further information, contact the PR department (tel. 85-27-56).

## East of La Diana

Gatekeeper of the luxury hotel fantasy land, a statue of Diana the huntress stands oddly on a traffic island in the middle of the Costera. From her post to the city's easternmost reaches, Acapulco is a conglomeration of resorts, each providing room and board, a swath of sand, built-in entertainment, and door-to-door package tours. You could spend your vacation in this part of Acapulco and forget you were in Mexico were it not for the **Instituto Guerrerense de la Cultura,** Costera 4834 (tel. 84-38-14). Part of a state-wide program, the institute was created to develop city spirit and promote regional arts and culture. Paintings by local artists are for sale in the gallery (open daily 9am-2pm and 5-8pm). The **archaeological museum** housed in the Instituto has a small collection of pre-Hispanic artifacts (open daily 9am-2pm and 5-8pm; free).

The **Acapulco Cultural and Convention Center** hosts a Mexican *fiesta,* a cultural show that features the **Mexico Traditional Ballet.** While the show is largely a money-making "cultural experience" for tourists, it affords travelers who are willing to pay the price a fascinating encounter with a rope performer as well as an opportunity to glimpse the regional dances of Veracruz, Oaxaca, Jalisco, Puebla, Chiapas, and Guerrero. The budget-breaking shows happen Mondays, Wednesdays, and Fridays at 8:15pm (dinner at 7:30pm), and cost 80 pesos (cover), 100 pesos (cover and drinks), or 150 pesos (cover, drinks, and dinner). Those itching for extravagance should call 84-70-50, ext.448 for reservations.

The **CICI waterpark** is a state-owned tourist attraction. For 30 pesos (children 2-10, 25 pesos), artificial waves will toss and hurl you headlong down the long, winding water slides. Trained dolphins perform at 12:30, 2:30, and 5pm (open daily 10am-6pm). To reach the park, head east on Costera until you see the walls painted with bright blue waves and the larger-than-life dolphins, or simply get off the bus labeled "CICI" at the stop labeled "CICI" (duh). The bus marked "Base" passes the blue wave walls as well; just yell to be let off.

## Puerto Marqués

Lacking the pre-packaged polish of the strip only a few kilometers away, the beach town of **Puerto Marqués** encompasses an unremarkable ribbon of sand lined wall-to-wall with restaurants so close to the water that the bay's waves tease diners' feet. Puerto Marqués would be simply one more seaside village were it not for the magnificent view on the approach from Acapulco. The **bus** ride to this bay (where thieving Sir Francis Drake stalked thieving, bullion-laden Spanish galleons) is the real attraction, thanks to a magnificent vista from the top of the hill before descending into town. Get on the bus labeled "Puerto Marqués" at the beginning of the run to ensure yourself a waterside seat (45min., 1.40 pesos). In Acapulco, buses to Puerto Marqués pass by the post office on the opposite side of the street about every half hour, 5:30am-9pm. It might be easier to catch the bus across the street from La Diana, where it's guaranteed to stop. As the bus rambles along, the Bahía de Puerto Marqués and the pounding surf of Playa Revolcadero come into full view.

The serenity of the tiny bay makes it an ideal spot for either waterskiing or learning to sail. Rates depend on the season; amiable sailboat owners are generally more than happy to help out the novice *gringo* sailor free of charge. Scuba and snorkeling equipment can also be rented at the beach. A popular afternoon's anchorage for sailboats is **Playa Pichilingue,** a small, often deserted patch of sand on the Bahía de Puerto Marqués that is inaccessible by land.

Restaurants along the water can be expensive; walk one block inland for the more reasonably priced fare.

## ENTERTAINMENT

Dinner is traditionally served late in Acapulco, and many visitors spend a lot of time and money on the final meal of the day, filling their tanks in preparation for Acapulco's legendary night life. Those up for some day's-end booty-shaking head for the chic **discos,** either on the strip or in the Zona Rosa. Remember that loud music is no guarantee of a good-sized crowd; try to peer inside before paying the cover charge. Be warned that many of Acapulco's larger, glitzier discos like **Fantasy** (tel. 84-67-27), at Carretera Escénica Las Brisas, and nearby **Extravaganza** (tel. 84-71-54), where the cover averages 80 pesos, require reservations on Friday and Saturday nights—without them, no amount of pleading and name-dropping will get you inside. If you intend to be sexually active with strangers during your stay, keep in mind that Acapulco is one of the cities with the most reported AIDS cases in Mexico; condoms are an absolute must here.

**Baby O** (tel. 84-74-74), at the intersection of the Costera and Nelson, five minutes from La Base, cranks out modern pop and rock all night long. Baby is the farthest out along the Costera and attracts a younger crowd than the high-tech Fantasy and Extravaganza. In its huge, cave-like interior, videos and the latest dance tunes rock the willing. Wednesday is ladies' night (cover 70 pesos; open Tues.-Sun.10:30pm-5am). Also try **Atrium,** Costera 30 (tel. 84-19-01), for drinks (open bar) and fake palm trees (cover varies by gender, about 120 pesos; open daily 10pm-4am). These and other discos at the east end of town—such as **Magic,** at the Costera and Yucatán (tel. 84-88-16), one block toward the *zócalo* from Boccaccio's (cover 50 pesos, open daily from 10:30pm)—are notorious for picking and choosing their crowd. Bouncers first admit single women, then male-female couples, and finally, if room permits, single men. If you find this practice offensive, prohibitive, or just too darn reminiscent of the late 70s, you may wish to frequent discos farther west.

Acapulco is an exceptionally popular destination for gays and lesbians. **Gallery,** De Los Deportes 11 (tel. 84-34-97), one block inland from the Calinda Quality Inn, is popular for its famous female impersonators, which attract a mixed crowd to both the 11pm and 1am shows (cover 50 pesos; dancing begins daily at 10pm). The **Open House Bar,** Plaza Condesa M. Alemán at Piedra Picuda Puerta 4 (tel. 84-72-85), is another popular option (no cover; open nightly 8pm-4am).

## ■ NEAR ACAPULCO: PIE DE LA CUESTA

Pie de la Cuesta is truly magnificent. Life is peaceful here; the sun lingers beautifully over the Pacific horizon just before dropping out of view. A single-lane highway runs through Acapulco's hills to Pie de la Cuesta, ending in the narrow road that separates the Pacific from the placid waters of Laguna de Coyura, and the hustle of Acapulco from the serenity of a small beach community.

Those seeking a place to wash Acapulco's sand from their feet don't do it at Pie de la Cuesta; the overpowering surf here sometimes precludes aquatic activity. It's fun to admire the valiant natives dodging violent waves, but many take pleasure in the lagoon instead, the site of the area's best waterskiing. Several ski clubs line the lagoon (ski rental about 120 pesos per hr.). Rest and relaxation is all too often interrupted, unfortunately, by aggressive *lancha* agents. Their tours of the lagoon inevitably include the area where the exploding helicopter scene from *Rambo* was filmed. Rates average 8 pesos per person in a *colectivo* boat. The *lancha* agents notwithstanding, the serenity of Pie de la Cuesta is worth at least a daytrip. The air is cleaner here, the water bluer, the surf stronger, the beach less crowded, and the scenery even more stunning than in Acapulco.

Pie de la Cuesta extends along one main road, beginning at the Oasis snack shop (also the bus stop) and ending at the naval base. Travelers on a budget have at least three options for spending a night (or a month) here. **Villa Nirvana** (tel. 60-16-31), on the ocean side of the road about 100m from the Oasis (look for the blue gate), is a utopian fantasy hotel complete with a swimming pool. Rooms are spacious, as are the bathrooms. Each room is graced by a huge porch with cushioned chairs and a hammock (singles 100 pesos; doubles 150 pesos; breakfast 10 pesos and up). **Hotel Puesta del Sol** (tel. 60-04-12), just past Villa Nirvana, off a side street on the ocean side of the road (watch for the sign on the lagoon side), has a restaurant, pool, and tennis court—the place is virtually a luxury resort. All rooms have refrigerators and 40 boast ocean views. Those that don't run about 10 pesos less (rooms for 1-4 people 100 pesos; *cabañas* for up to 5, with kitchen, 200 pesos; breakfast starting at 10 pesos). You can camp or find trailer hook-ups at the **Acapulco Trailer Park** (tel. 60-00-10); their office is in the "mini-super" just before Quinta Dora near the base. The trailer park has 60 sites, with spots on either the lagoon or the ocean side, and 15 clean bathrooms (sites for 1 car and up to 2 people 30 pesos).

Medical assistance is available at **Farmacia del Doctor,** a few buildings down from El Zanate near the eastern end of the lagoon. To speak with Dr. Luis A. Rios, go to the pharmacy when it's open (Mon.-Sat. 8am-2pm and 4-8pm), or knock loudly. English is spoken. There is also a phone at the pharmacy from which local calls can be made for 3 pesos. The **Red Cross** can be reached by calling 85-09-43, and the **police,** situated at the easternmost point of the bay, are at 85-06-50.

**Getting There:** Buses to and from Pie de la Cuesta leave from Escudero in Acapulco daily 5:30am-9:00pm and stop on Costera across the street from the post office near the *zócalo*. The ride takes anywhere from 25 minutes to an hour, depending on traffic and costs 1.40 pesos.

# OAXACA

## ■■■ TUXTEPEC

After years of neglect by Oaxaca's highland capital, Tuxtepec is now booming—and the signs of growth are everywhere, from the massive Corona brewery on the city's edge to the dozens of new storefronts that lie in its shadow. In the past two decades, the city's population has skyrocketed from 20,000 to about 110,000; boom and beauty rarely go hand in hand, and Tuxtepec poses no exception to the rule. Consequently, busy and hard-working Tuxtepec is a far cry from the sleepy colonial towns that lure tourists to the state. But even if concrete and Corona factories aren't high on your agenda, Tuxtepec is still a decent place to pass a night en route from the Gulf to Oaxaca, and makes a good base for exploring the surrounding countryside.

**Orientation** Tuxtepec is on the northern frontier of Oaxaca state, 222km from the state capital and 165km south of the city of Veracruz. The Papaloapán River forms a U-shaped bend here, with the opening of the "U" facing west. The *zócalo,* **Parque Juárez,** is in the southeast part of the city, near the river's northward bend. City services are concentrated along the streets that stretch westward from the *zócalo* toward another square near the end of downtown, **Parque Hidalgo.** The principal street, **Avenida Independencia,** two blocks south of the *zócalo,* marks the southern boundary of the downtown area. Parallel to it are, from south to north, Avs. 20 de Noviembre, 5 de Mayo, Libertad, and Carranza. North-south streets form a grid with these in the downtown area. Note that there is a Calle Juárez three blocks west of the *zócalo,* and a Blvd. Juárez a few blocks west of Parque Hidalgo.

The **ADO** station is in the northwest part of the downtown area, on Ortiz and Primero de Mayo. To get downtown, take a right on Ortiz as you exit the station; the wide street on the second block to the right is Camacho. *Colectivos (urbanos)* going to the right head downtown (1 peso). From the **AU** station, take a right onto Matamoros and walk 3½ blocks to Independencia. *Colectivos* going left head for the vicinity of the *zócalo.* From the other stations, take a left and then the first right. Independencia will be three blocks down. *Colectivos* are not plentiful in Tuxtepec, so it may be best to take a cab to the *zócalo* or to a hotel (5 pesos). The second-class stations are no more than 15 minutes from the *zócalo* (follow the flow of traffic on 5 de Mayo). The ADO station is about 25 minutes from the *zócalo.* Go down Camacho to the traffic circle and, from the opposite side of the circle, go down Matamoros one block. Then take a left on Libertad and walk seven blocks to the *zócalo.*

**Practical Information** Tuxtepec has no tourist office, but the **chamber of commerce,** Av. Libertad 290 (tel. 5-08-86), on the northwest corner of the *zócalo,* can provide limited information, or at least a guide to Tuxtepec in Spanish (open Mon.-Fri. 9am-2pm and 5-7pm, Sat. 9am-1pm). The only full-service **travel agent** in town is **Sotelo Viajes,** Morelos 118 (tel. 5-26-65), near the intersection with 5 de Mayo, six blocks west of the *zócalo.* The **police** (tel. 5-31-66) await in the Palacio Municipal on the south side of the *zócalo.*

The **post office** is on Independencia, two blocks south of the *zócalo* (open Mon.-Fri. 8am-7pm, Sat. 9am-1pm). **Postal code:** 68300. **Telegrams** and **faxes** can be sent from the **Telecomm** office, Av. Carranza 875 (tel. 5-05-01), four blocks north of Independencia between Aldama and Morelos (open Mon.-Fri. 9am-1pm and 3-7pm, Sat. 9am-noon). There are **long-distance telephone** *casetas* at Calle Juárez 17, just off Independencia (open Mon.-Sat. 8am-9:30pm, Sun. 8am-3pm). **Telephone Code:** 287. **Bánamex,** Independencia 36 (tel. 5-23-28), just southwest of the *zócalo,* accepts both cash and traveler's checks and has a Cirrus/Plus **ATM** (open Mon.-Fri. 9am-2pm). **Bancomer,** Independencia 437 (tel. 5-08-63), is farther west down the same street (open Mon.-Fri. 9:30am-noon).

Tuxtepec is home to four **bus stations.** From its station on Ortiz and Primero de Mayo, **ADO** (tel. 5-04-73) runs first-class buses to Acayucán (7 and 9am, 3hrs., 27 pesos), Córdoba (9am and 1pm, 4hrs., 27.50 pesos), Jalapa (5am, 5hrs., 45 pesos), Mexico City (7 per day, 7am-midnight, 8hrs., 90 pesos), Oaxaca (7:30am, 10:30pm, and midnight, 6hrs., 36 pesos), Puebla (5 per day, 7am-11pm, 6hrs., 65.50 pesos), Tuxtla Gutierrez (1am, 9hrs., 104 pesos), and Veracruz (7 per day, 5:30am-6:30pm, 3hrs., 28.50 pesos). **AU** (tel. 5-04-73), on Matamoros, sends buses to Jalapa (3 per day, 5hrs. 40 pesos), Mexico City (10 per day, 5am-11:40pm, 8hrs., 79 pesos), Puebla (6 per day, 7:35am-10pm, 6hrs., 57.50 pesos), Tehuantepec (1am, 6 hrs., 41.50 pesos), and Veracruz (5 per day, 3hrs., 24.50 pesos). From the same station on Matamoros, **Cuenca** (tel. 5-02-37) leaves for Oaxaca (6 per day, 10am-midnight, 6 hrs., 30 pesos) and San Andrés (6am and 5:30pm, 4 hrs., 25.50 pesos). Cuenca also has a station at Libertad 1475 (tel. 5-11-27). Buses depart from the **Autobuses de Trópico** station, Libertad 1215B (tel. 5-28-95), between Ocampo and Degollado. The only place in Tuxtepec to **rent cars** is **Mayabell,** Mutualismo 264 (tel. 5-34-29), between Carranza and 18 de Marzo.

**Oaxaca State**     OCÉANO PACÍFICO

The **markets** are on Independencia between Calle Juárez and Arteaga, near the *zócalo,* and on 5 de Mayo and Matamoros, near the second-class bus stations. There is a **supermarket, Superperchín,** on Independencia 314 (tel. 5-04-35), near the *zócalo* (open Mon.-Sat. 8am-9pm, Sun. 8am-3pm). The folks at **Lavandería Super-Clean,** Av. 5 de Mayo 1309, between Ocampo and Degollado, will do your dirtiest laundry with same-day service. **Farmacia Albatros,** 20 de Noviembre 996 (tel. 5-25-82), at the intersection with Aldama, is open 24 hrs. The **Red Cross,** Madero 110 (tel. 5-00-57), one block west of Blvd. Benito Juárez, is open 24 hrs. for emergency assistance. In case of **emergency,** call the **Policía Preventiva** (tel. 5-15-45) anytime.

**Accommodations** Tuxtepec has several inexpensive hotels, one of them on Independencia, the other three clustered together on Hidalgo, 1½ blocks north of the *zócalo.* The best location is occupied by **Posada Guadalupana,** Independencia 808 (tel. 5-11-95), between Matamoros and Aldama, about halfway between the two squares and three blocks south of the second-class bus stations. The rocking chairs around the *posada's* patio provide an escape from the bustle of Independencia. Older rooms are clean but lack hot water and are beginning to show their age; newer rooms are spacious but plain with equally clean bathrooms (old singles 25 pesos, new singles 35 pesos, with TV 45 pesos; old doubles 32 pesos, new doubles 45 pesos, with TV 55 pesos). **Hotel La Misión,** Hidalgo 409 (tel. 5-23-81), one block west and 1½ blocks north of the *zócalo,* offers a breezy sitting room, TV in the lobby, and freshly cut flowers on the cedar reception desk. Matching lacquered cedar doors open into spacious rooms. The clean bathrooms come with free shampoo (singles 35 pesos; doubles 40 pesos).

**Food** Tuxtepec is a solidly working- and middle-class city, so there are lots of affordable restaurants along Independencia and the blocks just north of it, and a string of lunch counters off the southwest corner of the *zócalo*. For super-cheap eats, head to the **markets** on Independencia and Calle Juárez, and on 5 de Mayo and Matamoros. In case you're wandering around in a catatonic state and have forgotten you're near a Corona brewery, the ubiquitous plastic Corona chairs and tables will remind you. A good, inexpensive breakfast (juice, coffee, eggs, and *frijoles* for 7 pesos) and a solid *comida corrida* (9-10 pesos) can be had at **Cocina Económica La Flor de Café,** Independencia 35, near the *zócalo*. Juice is fresh-squeezed and delicious (4 pesos; open Mon.-Sat. 10am-2pm and 4-9pm, Sun. 10am-2pm). At **Los Caporales,** on the second floor of Independencia 560 (tel. 95-44-05), between Aldama and Matamoros, silk flowers and faux marble tabletops provide a refreshing break from the pervasive Corona theme. *Comida corrida* (12 pesos) served before cable TV. And never, ever underestimate the power of A/C (open daily 8am-10pm).

**Sights and Entertainment** When it comes to tourist attractions, Tuxtepec comes up pretty empty-handed. The city serves travelers mainly as a base for daytrips to the surrounding area. When you return to Tuxtepec at night, dusty and tired, you can keep yourself amused at the **Centro Recreativo "Alf,"** 20 de Noviembre 1364 (tel. 5-40-09), near Parque Hidalgo. At the center you can shoot pool with the locals (3 pesos per ½hr.), rattle the foosball table, or catch some table hockey. The center serves snacks, pizza, and *refrescos;* the premises are alcohol-free (open daily 11am-midnight). If you feel like sitting still and zoning out, head next door to **Cinema Plus,** 20 de Noviembre 1364, which screens movies in English for 7 pesos. **Cinema Tuxtepec,** Blvd. Camacho 945 (tel. 5-01-76), on the way to the ADO station from the city center, offers Mexican skin flicks on Thursdays and Fridays and English-language movies the rest of the week (8 pesos).

In the evening, locals gather in the squares and on the few terraces along Independencia that offer views of the river. At the east end of town, Independencia fades into a quiet parkway that wraps around a bend in the river. The opposite shore is lush and only sparsely developed—if you squint, it looks sort of picturesque. If you would rather find crowds than escape them, you might head to one of the two discos in town. **Fetiche** (tel. 5-23-39) is at Av. 2 and Calle 3, west of the ADO station, while **Chichos** is on Blvd. Juárez (cover charge is 15-20 pesos; open Thurs.-Sat. 9pm-3am and Sun. 6-11pm). **Bars** line Independencia, but don't rely on them to lubricate your walk home from the discos—they all close around 11pm. Tuxtepec is generally safe, but crime is on the rise, and care should be taken at night.

## ■ NEAR TUXTEPEC

The area around Tuxtepec is renowned for its scenic beauty; unfortunately, most of it is not easily accessible by bus. The sites along the road to Oaxaca are perhaps the easiest to reach; they are served by an AU bus en route to **Valle Nacional,** a small tobacco-growing town 58km from Tuxtepec, where Porfirio Díaz once built a work camp for his political enemies. On the way there, the bus passes through **Chiltepec,** a town famous among gastronomes for its renditions of regional cuisine, and crosses a small suspension bridge on its way to **Jacatepec.** Other destinations are accessible by *colectivo* from the Mercado Flores Magón, on 20 de Noviembre between Riva Palacio and Blvd. Juárez, two blocks west of Parque Hidalgo. Another bus passes through **San Lucas Ojitlán** and **Jalapa de Díaz,** 42km and 70km from Tuxtepec, respectively. Ojitlán is notable for its *artesanías,* while Jalapa is known for its brightly-colored *huipiles.* Consult the Tuxtepec Chamber of Commerce for information on other destinations. Many of the towns around Tuxtepec are accessible by taxi, but rates are as steep as the mountain roads. Expect to pay 90 pesos round-trip to Chiltepec and 160 pesos round-trip to Valle Nacional.

# ■■■ OAXACA DE JUÁREZ

Perched on a giant plateau that gracefully interrupts the Sierra Madre del Sur's descent into the Oaxaca Valley, the city of Oaxaca (pop. 214,000) is a rare beauty. Nicknamed "City of Jade" after Hernán Cortés began to build his beloved (but unfinished) estate here in 1535, Oaxaca's deep green stone buildings have since aged to a dignified yellow. Throughout the streets, this style has been lovingly preserved and imitated, giving Oaxaca the feel of a city that lives and breathes its own remarkable history. Especially in the early morning, the city is strikingly beautiful; at first light, the city's high, green, gracefully aging silhouettes are spectacular.

A relatively affluent and cosmopolitan city, Oaxaca has recently become a major destination for tourists of all ages and nationalities who are lured by its prestigious museums, outstanding archaeological sites, and its sheer attractiveness. Even so, it manages to maintain a friendly, small-town atmosphere; the *zócalo,* lined with sprawling jacaranda trees and outdoor cafés, is one of the most amiable in the Republic. Expect to see all of Mexico in evidence here: merchants, *indígenas,* and professionals jostling elbows, *norteamericanos* jabbering away at the city's fine language schools, and restless students, some tearing around on expensive motorcycles, others agitating for labor reform. But neither tourism nor politics can do anything to diminish Oaxaca's cultural richness—nor its colonial charm. From dawn to dusk, when the streetlights play up and down the stone faces of its magnificent churches, Oaxaca is a wonder to behold.

## ORIENTATION

Oaxaca de Juárez rests in the Oaxaca Valley, between the towering Sierra Madre del Sur and the Puebla-Oaxaca range, 523km southeast of Mexico City, 435km south of Veracruz, and 526km west of Tuxtla Gutiérrez. Principal access to Oaxaca from the north and east is via Route 190.

While most of Oaxaca's streets form a grid, orienting yourself can be difficult; many streets change names as they swing by the *zócalo.* The large English-language maps posted around the *zócalo,* at the bus stations, and in the lobbies of fancy hotels clearly mark all sights. The *zócalo,* on Hidalgo (one of the few streets that does not change names), consists of two squares. The main square lies between Hidalgo and Trujano/Guerrero, and the **Plaza Alameda de León** just to the northwest is sandwiched by Hidalgo and Independencia.

Oaxaca's downtown is circumscribed by a busy peripheral expressway, called the **Periférico** in the south but known by other names as it loops north. **Avenida Hidalgo** divides *el centro* into two principal areas: the budget district lies south of Hidalgo, while expensive hotels and restaurants cluster around the *zócalo* north of and on Hidalgo. Most of Oaxaca's sights are snuggled between lavish private residences in the neighborhood north of Hidalgo. **Avenida Macedonio Alcalá** splits downtown into east and west sections, serving for a few blocks north of the *zócalo* as a pedestrian walkway, the **Andador Turístico.** South of the *zócalo,* Alcalá becomes Bustamante. Oaxaca's other principal streets are **Independencia,** parallel to Hidalgo, and **García Vigil/Cabrera,** one block west of Alacalá, which forms the western boundary of the *zócalo.* Twelve blocks north of the *zócalo,* **Calzada Niños Héroes de Chapultepec** (the Pan-American Highway) runs east-west.

To reach the *zócalo* from the **first-class bus station** (home to **ADO, Cristóbal Colon, UNO,** and others), cross the street and catch a bus marked "Centro," heading west on Chapultepec (1.20 pesos). The bus runs south on Juárez. If you get off at Hidalgo, the *zócalo* will be three blocks to the east. To make the 20-minute walk from the station, head west on Chapultepec for six blocks to Alcalá and turn left. Walk twelve blocks to the main plaza.

From the **AU station,** take the *colectivo* marked "Centro," which will eventually head down Independencia. Ask to be let off at García Vigil, which will put you at the north end of the Plaza Alameda. The main square is one block south. If you care to make the 2km walk from the station (not recommended after dark), take a left com-

OAXACA DE JUÁREZ

ing out the door and walk to the stoplight. Take a right onto Madero and follow it to the **train station.** A 25-minute walk stretches ahead of you: turn right as if coming out of the station, walk five long blocks, then turn left (east) onto Independencia, which will lead you to the *zócalo*. Alternatively, you could take a *colectivo* marked "Centro" or "Independencia" from the train station, get off at García Vigil, and walk one block south to the *zócalo*.

From the **second-class bus station**, head left across the large road (the Periférico). On the other side, pick up Trujano (perpendicular to the Perférico) and follow it east for eight long blocks until you hit the *zócalo*. **Taxis** charge 10 pesos from any of these stations. It's a good idea for travelers to take taxis when crossing town late at night. Be aware, that cabbies charge extra from 11pm and 5am.

## PRACTICAL INFORMATION

**Tourist Offices:** El Secretario de Desarollo Turistico maintains three offices in the city; one is at Independencia 607 (tel. 6-38-10 or 6-09-84), at Garcia Vigil on the Pl. Alameda de León. Open daily 9am-3pm and 6-8pm. The office at 5 de Mayo 200 (tel. 6-48-28) contains the **Agencia del Ministerio Público,** which will act as a liaison to consulates in case of accident or robbery. Open daily 9am-3pm and 6-8pm. The third office is at Alcalá 100, and is open daily 9am-8pm. All three locations employ at least one English-speaking staffer. Good maps distributed.

**Police:** Aldama 108 (tel. 6-36-18 or 6-26-26), south of the *zócalo* between Miguel Cabrera and Bustamente. Some English spoken. Open 24 hrs.

**Post Office:** (tel. 6-26-61), in the Pl. Alameda de León. *Lista de Correos.* Open Mon.-Fri. 8am-8pm, Sat. 9am-1pm. Open for *Lista de Correos* Mon.-Fri. 8am-2pm. **Postal Code:** 68000.

**Telephones: LADATEL** phones are in the *zócalo,* at La Iglesia de Santo Domingo, and at the ADO station. *Casetas* available at **Computel,** Hidalgo 204 (tel. 4-80-84). Collect calls 5 pesos per min. 50% off at night and on Sun. Open daily 7am-10pm. **Telephone Code:** 29.

**Telegrams:** Independencia at 20 de Noviembre (tel. 6-49-02), around the corner from the post office. Open for telegrams Mon.-Fri. 8am-6pm, Sat. 9am-noon. Open for money orders Mon.-Fri. 9am-6pm, Sat. 9am-noon.

**Consulates:** In an emergency, go first to the Agencia del Ministerio Público (above), whose staff will get consular assistance. **U.S.,** Alcalá 201 #204 (tel. 4-30-54). Hidden under an arched doorway. Open Mon.-Fri. 9am-2pm. In an emergency call tel. 4-14-04. **Canada,** Dr. Liceaga 119 #8 (tel. 3-37-77; fax 5-21-47), open Mon.-Fri. 9am-2pm. **Germany** and **Great Britain,** Hidalgo 817 #5 (tel. 3-08-65), open Mon.-Fri. 9am-2pm.

**Currency Exchange:** Thundering herds of banks encircle the *zócalo;* hours for currency exchange vary. **Bánamex,** Hidalgo 821 (tel. 6-59-00), one block east of the *zócalo,* has a Cirrus/Plus **ATM.** Open for exchange Mon.-Fri. 9am-noon. **Bancomer,** García Vigil 120 (tel. 6-33-33), two blocks north of the *zócalo* at Morelos is open for exchange Mon.-Fri. 9am-noon. Also try the many *casas de cambio;* their rates are less favorable, but their hours are longer.

**American Express:** Valdivieso 2 (tel. 4-62-45 or 6-27-00), off the northeast corner of the *zócalo*. Money wired (10min. from the U.S.). Mail held for holders of AmEx traveler's checks or cards. Currency exchanged at slightly unfavorable rates. Services available Mon.-Fri. 9am-2pm and 4-6pm, Sat. 9am-1pm. It also houses a travel agency that sells plane tickets and first-class bus tickets to Mexico City and Puebla. English spoken. Office open Mon.-Fri. 9am-8pm, Sat. 9am-6pm.

**Airport: Aeropuerto Juárez,** on Rte. 175, 8km south of the city. Taxis to the airport cost 30 pesos. Transportation to the airport can be arranged through **Transportes Aeropuerto,** Pl. Alameda de León (tel. 4-43-50). With advance notice, they'll pick you up at your hotel (*colectivo* 10 pesos, *especial* 39 pesos). Office open Mon.-Sat. 9am-2pm and 5-8pm (for Sun. service reserve on Sat.). **Mexicana,** Independencia at Fiallo (tel. 6-34-14, airport tel. 6-57-97). Five daily flights to Mexico City (50min., 577 pesos). **Aeroméxico,** Hidalgo 513 (tel. 6-37-65, airport tel. 1-50-44). 1 daily flight to Mexico City (50min., 517 pesos), Tuxtla Gutierrez (45min., 464 pesos), Villahermosa (2½hrs., 565 pesos). **AeroCaribe,** at the Mex-

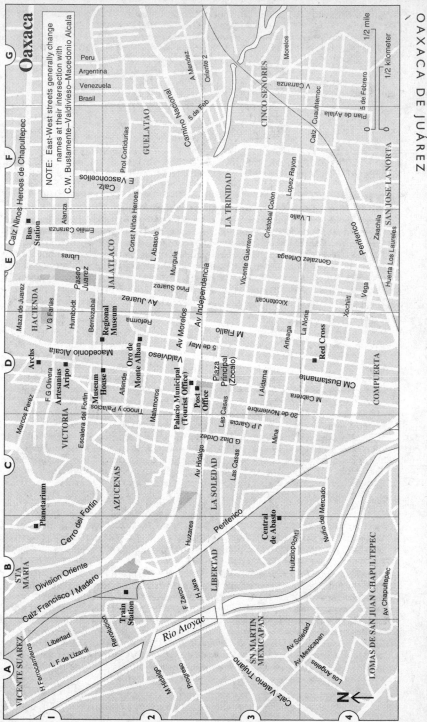

OAXACA DE JUÁREZ

# Oaxaca

NOTE: East-West streets generally change names at their intersection with C.W. Bustamante–Valdivieso–Macedonio Alcala

Peru
Argentina
Venezuela
Brasil

0    1/2 mile
0    1/2 kilometer

**G**

Morelos
V Carranza
CINCO SEÑORES
Calz. Cuauhtémoc
Plan de Ayala
5 de Febrero
Huerta Los Laureles   SAN JOSE LA NORTA
Zaachila
Periférico
Vega
Xochitl

**F**

A Mendez
Oriente 2
5 de Feb
Camino Nacional
Prol Cordurias
GUELATAO
Calz E Vasconcellos
LA TRINIDAD
Lopez Rayon
Cristobal Colon
L Valle
Gonzalez Ortega
Arteaga
La Noria
Red Cross

**E**

Calz Niños Heroes de Chapultepec
Bus Station
Alianza
Emilio Caranza
Libres
JALALACO
Const Niños Heroes
L Abasolo
Murguia
Pino Suarez
Vicente Guerrero
Xicotencatl
COMPUERTA

**D**

Maza de Juarez
HACIENDA
V G Farias
Humboldt
Berriozabal
Reforma
Av Juarez
Av Morelos
Av Independencia
5 de May
M Fiallo
Artesanias
Macedonio Alcala
Regional Museum
Paseo Juarez
Oro de Monte Alban
Valdivieso
I Aldama
M Cabrera
CM Bustamante

**C**

Marcos Perez
Archs
F G Olivera
Aripo
VICTORIA
Escalera del Fortin
AZUCENAS
Tinoco y Palacios
Allende
Matamoros
Palacio Municipal (Tourist Office)
Post Office
Plaza Principal (Zocalo)
Las Casas
J P Garcia
G Diaz Ordaz
20 de Noviembre
Mina
LA SOLEDAD
Av Hidalgo
Huzares
Periférico
Nuño del Mercado
Central de Abasto
Huitzilopochtli
Pochtli

**B**

Planetarium
Cerro del Fortin
Division Oriente
Calz Francisco I Madero
Train Station
F Zarco
H Jara
LIBERTAD
Rio Atoyac
SN MARTIN MEXICAPAN
Los Angeles
Av Soledad
Av Mexicapan

**A**

STA MARIA
VICENTE SUAREZ
H Ferrocarileros
Libertad
L F de Lizardi
Revolucion
M Hidalgo
Progreso
Calz Valerio Trujano
LOMAS DE SAN JUAN CHAPULTEPEC
Av Chapultepec

Museum House

**N**

**1**  **2**  **3**  **4**

icana offices (tel. 6-02-29) to Cancún (1 per day, 4¾hrs., 1,012 pesos) and Mérida (1 per day, 3hrs., 997 pesos). **Airport Information:** tel. 1-50-36.

**Train Station: Ferrocarriles Nacionales de México** (tel. 6-22-53 or 6-26-26). In a stone building set back from the road on the western end of Madero. Second class to Puebla (7:35am, 27.20 pesos; tickets sold daily 6-11am) and Mexico City (7pm, 26.10 pesos; tickets sold daily 3:30-6pm). Lines are absolutely tremendous; arrive very early, and get reservations one week ahead.

**Bus Stations:** Only partial listings are given; it is possible to go almost anywhere in the Republic at any time of day or night. **First-class station,** Niños Héroes de Chapultepec 1036, 12 blocks north and 4 blocks east of the *zócalo*. From this station, **ADO** (tel. 5-17-03) runs to Mexico City (24 per day, 6am-11:45pm, 9hrs., 91 pesos), Puebla (6 per day, 7hrs., 66 pesos), Veracruz (8:30am and 8:15pm, 9hrs., 94.50 pesos), Tuxtepec (2 and 11:30pm, 4hrs., 36 pesos), and Villahermosa (7pm, 12hrs., 121 pesos). From the same station, **Cristóbal Colón** (tel. 5-12-14) goes to Mexico City (11 per day, 6:30am-midnight, 91 pesos), Puebla (4 per day, 2:25-11:15pm, 7hrs., 66 pesos), Puerto Escondido (9:30am and 10:30pm, 9hrs., 84 pesos), Pochutla (9:30am and 10:30pm, 8hrs., 73 pesos), San Cristóbal (7:30 and 10:15pm, 12hrs., 94 pesos), Santa Cruz Huatulco (9:30am and 10:30pm, 7½hrs., 66 pesos), Tehuantepec (9 per day, 5hrs., 40 pesos), and Tuxtla Gutierrez (7:30 and 10:15pm, 11hrs., 85 pesos). Also from the first-class station, **Autobuses Cuenca del Paloapan** (tel. 5-09-03) runs buses to Guelatao (every hr., 8 pesos), Tuxtepec (6 per day, 5hrs., 30 pesos), and Veracruz (midnight, 9hrs., 52 pesos). To reach Mexico City in true style take the **UNO** bus; it's the next best thing to a corporate jet (4 per day, 9hrs., 125 pesos). UNO also goes to Puebla (6:30pm, 7hrs., 92 pesos). **Autobuses Sur** runs to Matamoros (5 per day, 7:30am-7pm, 46 pesos) and Mexico City (5 per day, 7:30am-7pm, 9hrs., 73 pesos). The **AU** station, Prolongación de Madero 1104 (tel. 2-63-55), is northwest of the *zócalo* and can be reached by the *colectivo* marked "Monumento," from the Periférico across from the 2nd-class terminal. AU runs second-class buses to Mexico City (12 per day, 9hrs.). AU tickets can also be purchased at their office on Díaz Ordaz 516 (tel. 4-24-68; open Mon.-Fri. 8am-8pm, Sat. 8am-2:30pm). The **second-class station** is just past the Central de Abastos (big market), across the Periférico from the western end of Trujano. From this station, **Estrella del Valle** (tel. 4-57-00 or 6-54-29) runs buses to Puerto Escondido (direct service 8:30am and 10:30pm, 9hrs., 52 pesos; *ordinario* every 2hrs., 9hrs., 40 pesos), and Santa Cruz Huatulco (10pm, 7½hrs., 49 pesos). The station is full of small regional bus lines, many without signs or ticket windows. Frequent service to every small town near Oaxaca; each town is served by only 1 line, usually for under 3 pesos. Ask the staff of each line. The **Hotel Mesón del Ángel bus stop,** Mina 518, between Mier y Terán and Díaz Ordaz, serves as a 3rd bus station. From here, **Autotransportes Turísticos** (tel. 6-53-27 or 4-31-61) runs buses to Monte Albán (5 per day during off season, every ½hr. during peak season, 30min., roundtrip 10 pesos).

**Car Rental: Hertz Rent-a-Car,** La Bastida 115 (tel. 6-24-34), off the **Andador Turístico** at the north side of the small park. Must be over 21, with a driver's license and credit card. Small VWs 111 pesos per day, plus 52 pesos for insurance and 0.86 pesos per km under 200 km. Open daily 8am-2pm and 4-7pm. **Budget,** 5 de Mayo 315 (tel. 6-44-45), around the corner from Hertz. Must be over 21, with license and credit card. Small VWs 216 pesos, including insurance and mileage (no limit). Open daily 8am-1pm and 4pm-7pm.

**Markets: Central de Abastos,** at the west end of Trujano or Las Casas, across from the 2nd-class bus terminal. Beware of pickpockets. **Benito Juárez produce market,** between 20 de Noviembre and Aldama, and Cabrera and Las Casas.

**Laundromat: Super Lavandería Hidalgo,** J.P. García 200 (tel. 4-11-81), at Hidalgo, one block west of *zócalo*. 3.5kg washed and dried for 20 pesos. Open Mon.-Sat. 8am-8pm.

**Bookstore: Librería Universitaria,** Guerrero 104 (tel. 6-42-43), off the southeast corner of the *zócalo*. Small selection of used paperbacks in English (about 10 pesos), and a number of English-language books about Mexico. Open Mon.-Sat. 9:30am-2pm and 4-8pm.

**Libraries: Biblioteca Pública,** Alcalá 200. A beautiful specimen. Open Mon.-Fri. 9am-8:30pm. **Biblioteca Circulante,** Alcalá 305. Open Mon.-Fri. 10am-1pm and 4-7pm, Sat. 10am-1pm. The **Instituto de Artes Gráficas** (see "Sights" on page 415) also has a library with many English-language art books.
**Cultural Center: Instituto Oaxaqueño de las Culturas,** Calz. Madero at Av. Técnica (tel. 6-67-14), near the AU station. Hosts plays, dance performances, and concerts. Check the monthly "Guía Cultura," available at tourist offices, libraries, and museums, for current information.
**Red Cross:** Armenta y López 700 (tel. 6-44-55 or 6-48-09), between Pardo and Burgoa. Ambulance service. English spoken. Open 24 hrs.
**Pharmacies: Farmacia Zarate,** Hidalgo 411 (tel. 6-42-80), 2½ blocks west of the *zócalo;* a 2nd store around the corner at J.P. García 100 (tel. 6-07-20); a 3rd at Hidalgo and Mier y Terán (tel. 6-79-22). Will bring medicine to your hotel during working hours. All open daily 7am-midnight. **Farmacia Héroes de Chapultepec** (tel. 3-35-24), half a block east of 1st-class bus station. Open 24 hrs.
**Hospitals: Hospital Civil,** Porfirio Díaz 400 (tel. 5-31-81), 1.5km out of town, offers free medical service. Private hospitals include **Instituto Mexicano de Seguro Social (IMSS),** Chapultepec 621 (tel. 5-20-33), and **Hospital Vasconcelos,** Morelos 500 (tel. 6-36-52), at Padre Ángel. Also try **ISST** (tel. 5-31-44).

## ACCOMMODATIONS AND CAMPING

As Oaxaca attracts more *norteamericanos,* some old budget standbys have upgraded their rooms in an attempt to attract more upscale tourists. But bargains still await the penny-pinching soul, especially in the busy blocks south of the *zócalo,* which are within easy walking distance of the second-class bus station and all major sights and services. Reservations are a must on *fiesta* weekends, especially during the Guelaguetza in July.

Outside the downtown area are a number of trailer parks. The **Trailer Park Oaxaca,** Violetas 900 (tel. 5-27-96), is near the *Zona Militar* in the northeast part of town. To get there, take the "Colonia Reforma" bus from the stop on García just north of Hidalgo. The **Trailer Park San Francisco,** Madero 705, in the northwest part of town, is accessible on the "Santa Rosa" bus from the same García stop.

### Near the First-Class Bus Station

**Casa Arnel,** Aldama 404 (tel. 5-28-56), in the Colonia Jalatlaco, a 20-min. walk from the *zócalo.* Take a right coming out of the bus station, walk two blocks, and turn right on Aldama; it's seven blocks down, across from a stone colonial church. From the *zócalo,* walk north on the *andador turístico,* make a right on Constitución before the Iglesia de Santo Domingo and follow it for 6 blocks, turning left on Calz. de la República. A couple of blocks will bring the church into view; turn right and continue until you see the yellow and red "Casa Arnel" sign. Spotless, homey rooms open onto a quiet jungle-like courtyard, complete with parrots and laundry facilities. Large English-language library and tourist information. An international backpacking crowd chats over breakfast in the morning, and coffee and *refrescos* at night. Singles 30 pesos, 60 pesos with bath. Doubles 60 pesos, 80 with bath. Discounts for extended stays.

### North of the Zócalo

The northern part of town is more prosperous, residential, tranquil, and attracts more tourists than the southern. Hotels here offer some of the best deals in town.

**Hotel Reforma,** Reforma 102 (tel. 6-71-44), four blocks east of the *zócalo.* Rustic, hand-carved wood furniture lets you pretend you're on a *hacienda;* the view from the rooftop table allows you to take in the city. Spotless bathrooms and plenty of sitting areas in the wide hallways. Singles 50 pesos. Doubles 60 pesos.
**Las Bugambilias,** Reforma 402 (tel. 6-11-65). The friendly Cabrera family rents six rooms upstairs in their spacious home, complete with double beds and flawlessly clean bathrooms you could bathe a whole family in. Home-cooked breakfast and home-style camaraderie included. 66 pesos per person, up to two people. In front

of the house is the cozy (and often full) **La Olla Café,** which serves *tortas* (7 pesos) and coffee in *talavera* mugs, as well as a 15-peso *comida corrida.* Beautiful *mudejár* tile and darkwood interior. Open Mon.-Sat. 8am-9pm.

**Hotel Pombo,** Morelos 601 (tel. 6-26-73), between Vigil and Díaz, one block north of the *zócalo.* Fascinating bathrooms: some are shaped like trapezoids, most smell like fireplaces, and all boast water warmed by wood-burning heaters. Rooms without bath are slightly bigger than soap dishes. Dark, musty interior, but an excellent location. Singles 30 pesos, 40 pesos with bath. Doubles 35 pesos, 50 pesos with bath.

### South of the Zócalo

South of the *zócalo* you'll find a legion of budget hotels; often four or five share the same block, particularly along Díaz Ordaz. Because of their proximity to the market and second class bus terminal, many of these hotels front noisy, dirty streets; if that's not your thing, ask for a room in back. Special caution should be exercised when walking in this area at night.

**Youth Hostel El Pasador,** Fiallo 305 (tel. 6-12-87), two blocks south of the *zócalo.* Formerly a painting school—be sure to add something of your own to the studio wall of the artist/owner. Hip hangout with a stereo and TV in the dining room. Common kitchen. Bedding provided. Clean bathrooms. No curfew or min./max. stay. Quiet time 11pm. Closed noon-2pm for cleaning, but only when full. Safety deposit box available (5 pesos). 25 pesos per person. Key deposit 10 pesos.

**Hotel Chayo,** 20 de Noviembre 508 (tel. 6-41-12), one block south of Aldama. Concrete furniture that would make the Flintstones proud. Clean bathrooms sport pristine white tile. Recently remodeled. Singles 53 pesos. Doubles 60 pesos.

**Hotel Pasaje,** Mina 302 (tel. 6-42-13), three blocks south of the *zócalo.* Well-scrubbed rooms open onto a plant-filled courtyard. Dim lighting and artsy posters attempt to deflect attention from the unfortunate color scheme. Singles 40 pesos. Doubles 70 pesos.

**Hotel Lupita,** Díaz Ordaz 314 (tel. 6-57-33), three blocks west and one block south of the *zócalo's* southwest corner. Not to be confused with the more expensive Hotel Fortín, with which it shares a patio. Fair-sized rooms with grubby bathrooms. Walls so pink you'll feel like you're sleeping in Pepto Bismol. Singles 30 pesos, 45 pesos with bath. Doubles 40 pesos, 50 pesos with bath.

### FOOD

With food to please every palate, Oaxaca is a city to grow fat in. Even in heavily touristed areas, fresh, well-prepared meals at good prices await the jaded traveler. Like many regions in Mexico, Oaxaca has its own take on *mole,* a delicious sauce made of myriad ingredients from chiles to chocolate. Many restaurants also serve up *tlayudas,* large, crisp tortillas topped with just about anything you can think of. *Botanas oaxaqueñas* also make an appearance on menus throughout the city; they are plates full of regional goodies including chile, *quesillo* (boiled string cheese), *chorizo* (sausage), and *guacamole.* When sampling goodies on the streets, exercise caution. Most pastry vendors cover their snacks with glass or plastic, but some don't, and huge flies tend to descend upon unattended delicacies. And be careful of the *nieves,* frozen treats that taste like sorbet—they're delicious, but make sure to ask where the water came from before you dig in.

The **markets** (see "Practical Information" on page 410) offer delicious chocolate breads, *chapulines* (dried crickets), and spiced *jícama* (a beet-shaped fruit), as well as the usual inexpensive fare. The cafés in the *zócalo* offer great views at fairly high prices, but if you order something less expensive (breakfast, coffee, or drinks), you'll get to sit and watch Oaxaca for hours on end.

**Flor de Loto,** Morelos 509 (tel. 4-39-44), west of García Vigil. So good that words cannot describe it. Vegetarian and regional specialties in a hip atmosphere. Specializes in crêpes, peculiar and delicious. Excellent *comida corrida* only 16 pesos. Open Mon.-Sat. 8:30am-10pm, Sun. 8:30am-9pm.

**Restaurant Quickly,** Alcalá 100 (tel. 4-7-76), on the *andador turístico* just north of the *zócalo*. Hunker down to big portions with local *artesanías*. Handmade tablecloths create a warm atmosphere. *Comida corrida* 12 pesos (and they have a vegetarian *comida*, too!). Open Mon.-Fri. 8am-10:30pm, Sat.-Sun. 2-10:30pm.

**La Soledad,** Mina 212 (tel. 6-38-07), three blocks south and two blocks west of the *zócalo*. A chocaholic's fantasy: it serves seven deliciously decadent types of hot chocolate with heaping baskets of fresh bread, and—for the die-hard cocoa fiend—even offers chocolate *tamales* (3 pesos). *Tlayudas* and *botanas*, too (20 pesos for a two-person plate). Buy some chocolate to go from the store in front— it's hard to resist. Open Mon.-Sat. 7am-8pm, Sun. 7am-4pm.

**Café Alex,** Díaz Ordaz 218 (tel. 4-07-15). A fancier version of the good storefront places south of the *zócalo*. An extensive menu that runs the gamut of Mexican cuisine, with English explanations for the uninitiated. Garden seating available. Breakfasts 4-12 pesos. *Moles* 17 pesos. *Comida corrida* 12 pesos. Open Mon.-Sat. 7am-9pm, Sun. 7am-noon.

**El Biche Pobre '2',** Calzada de la República 600, 1 block west of Casa Arnel on Hidalgo (not the main downtown Hidalgo). Popular with local families. Pretty wood-paneled ceilings. The *botana surtida*, a 2-course collection of *oaxaqueña* specialties, is one of the best deals in town (20 pesos). Open daily 1-6pm.

**La Tropical,** Mina 106 (tel. 6-67-52). A juice bar serving exotic concoctions to complement the orange-and-green decor. A great place to watch Oaxaca pass by while sipping at a banana or strawberry *licuado* (4 pesos). *Tortas* start at 3.50 pesos. Call for home delivery. Open daily 8am-8pm.

## SIGHTS

Oaxaca's **zócalo,** composed of two plazas, is always congested with people. Early in the morning, vendors set up stalls filled with expensive, exotic pastries, women sell fruit from baskets, and toy dealers hawk huge multi-colored balloons. Every evening between 7 and 9pm, live concerts given by local rock groups, *marimba* performers, and the state brass band send music reverberating throughout the square. Often the activity in front of the Palacio de Gobierno is of a political nature. By 10pm, however, foreigners dominate the *zócalo*.

Throughout Oaxaca's streets, vendors sell knitted cotton blankets, *sarapes*, jade bookends, *oaxaqueño* guitars, wooden letter openers, masks, and straw baskets. Make clear from the beginning whether you intend to buy or not; entrepreneurs become indignant if they think you're just stalling to fetch a better price, and many resent foreign tourists for seeking cut-rates on *artesanías*. Start your haggling for *sarapes* and musical instruments at half the asking price. Eavesdropping on the final price other tourists pay is typically useless; most tourists shell out more than twice the bargain rate. On Saturdays, be sure to visit the *tianguis* set up in Oaxaca's biggest market, the **Central de Abastos** (across the Periférico from the western end of Mina), where virtually every resident of Oaxaca state is either buying or selling food, art, or crafts. Bring someone with a good sense of direction and beware of pickpockets—these quick-fingered thieves are clever.

The **Catedral de Oaxaca** and the **Palacio de Gobierno** (not to be confused with the Palacio Municipal, which contains the tourist office) sit on opposite sides of the *zócalo*. Originally constructed in 1535, the cathedral was damaged and finally destroyed by a series of earthquakes. In the 18th century it was rebuilt with *oaxaqueño* green-brown stone and ornamented in filigree. The ornate bishop's seat, in the central altar, provides a structural focus (open daily 7am-8pm).

Inside the **Palacio de Gobierno,** on the south side of the *zócalo*, a mural by Arturo García Bustos presents an informative collage of *oaxaqueño* history. The center panel is dominated by Benito Juárez, his wife Margarita Masa, and one of his oft-repeated phrases, *"El respeto al derecho ajeno es la paz."* ("Respect for the rights of others is peace.") Also appearing in this panel are two other Juárez-era reformers. On the wall to the right as you ascend the staircase is a portrait of Sor Juana Inés de la Cruz, the poet, nun, theologian, and astronomer. Considered Mexico's first feminist, she impersonated a man for several years in order to attend the

OAXACA DE JUÁREZ

university in Mexico City, and penned a diatribe against misogynists called *Hombres Necios* (Foolish Men). Sor Juana eventually made her way onto the front of 1-peso bills (Palacio de Gobierno open 24 hrs.).

Walking north from the *zócalo* on Alcalá (the *andador turístico*), you will arrive at the **Museo de Arte Contemporáneo de Oaxaca,** Alcalá 202 (tel. 4-71-10). The museum's colonial building is known as the Casa de Cortés, although historians insist that it is not in fact Cortés's Oaxaca estate. The beautifully constructed museum contains rotating exhibits by contemporary artists like Rufino Tamayo and Juan Rulfo, and features a foreign film series on weekend nights (open Wed.-Mon. 10:30am-8pm; donations solicited).

There are churches, it seems, on every street in downtown Oaxaca, and most merit at least a brief visit. The **Iglesia de Santo Domingo,** farther up Alcalá from the Museo de Arte Contemporáneo and six blocks north of the *zócalo,* deserves a special trip. The church is the tallest building in Oaxaca, and its Baroque interior has some of the most stunning internal decoration of any church in the Republic. Waves of gilded stucco dance elegant arabesques around arches, across ceiling vaults, and above altars and chapels. Construction on the church began in 1575, the structure was consecrated in 1611, and improvements and artistic work continued after that. Built 2m thick as protection against earthquakes, the walls served the convent well when it saw service as military barracks for both sides during the reform wars and the Revolution (open daily 7am-1pm and 4-8pm).

The ex-convent next door was converted in 1972 into the city's prestigious **Museo Regional de Oaxaca** (tel. 6-29-91). The frescoes, paintings, and stucco work have withstood a century of military abuse. The museum fastidiously organizes its archaeological and ethnographic exhibits into sections focusing on each of the state's *indígena* peoples. The superb exhibits cover every facet of *indígena* life, even the *teohanacatl* (hallucinogenic mushrooms) used by the Mixtecs. A must-see exhibit displays Mixtec jewelry found in Tomb 7 at nearby Monte Albán. Elaborately worked gold, silver, and copper artifacts, some set with jewels, reveal the sophistication of Mixtec metalworkers. Explanatory signs are in Spanish (open Tues.-Fri. 10am-6pm, Sat.-Sun. 10am-5pm; admission 14 pesos; free Sun. and holidays).

For a glimpse of the modern, stop in at the small **Instituto de Artes Gráficas,** Alcalá 507 (tel. 6-69-80), opposite the Santo Domingo church. Prints and graphic art from around the world are on display; exhibits change every three months. The museum also houses an amazing art library containing many English-language volumes (open Wed.-Mon. 10am-8pm; free).

Another renowned museum, the **Museo de Arte Prehispánico de México Rufino Tamayo,** Morelos 503 (tel. 6-47-50), at Díaz three blocks north of the *zócalo,* shows off the *oaxaqueño* artist's personal collection of pre-Conquest objects. The figurines, ceramics and masks that Tamayo collected were selected for their aesthetic value as well as for anthropological interest. Pieces are arranged in roughly chronological order rather than by culture (open Mon. and Wed.-Sat. 10am-2pm and 4-7pm, Sun. 10am-3pm; admission 10 pesos).

The **Teatro Macedonio Alcalá,** on 5 de Mayo at Independencia, two blocks east of the *zócalo,* is one of the most beautiful buildings in Oaxaca and an illuminating example of the art and architecture that flourished in Mexico under Porfirio Díaz. Díaz's regime had a serious case of *afrancesamiento,* the taste for French art and French intellectual formulas. Oaxaca, the birthplace of Díaz, remained a favorite of the dictator, and his support was instrumental in this theater's construction. On the ceiling, scantily clad Muses float above the giant candelabra (occasionally open for shows Mon.-Sat. at 8pm, Sun. at 6pm).

A minor but funky and absorbing attraction is the museum of religious art at the **Basilica of Our Lady of Solitude,** Independencia 107 (tel. 6-75-66), 4½ blocks west of the *zócalo.* It houses the astonishing array of objects sent from around Oaxaca and the world as gifts to the Virgin, who is said to have appeared here in 1620. The museum's packed cabinets overflow with everything from model ships to shell-and-pasta figurines to wedding bouquets (open Mon.-Sat. 9am-2pm and 4-7pm, Sun. 9am-2pm; admission 1 peso).

---

### Benito Who?

Five blocks north of the post office on Vigil is the **Casa de Benito Juárez,** García Vigil 609 (tel. 6-18-60), once home to Mexico's famous ex-president. The house hardly looks like the spot where a poor, 19th-century Zapotec *campesino* grew up. Here's the story: Benito's older sister left the Juárez home in Guelatao to come to Oaxaca as the domestic servant of the wealthy Masa family. The Masas were *paisanos* from Spain and good friends with the equally wealthy Salanueva family. The Salanuevas took interest in young Benito, adopted him and brought him to Oaxaca. His subsequent education and upbringing qualified him to marry the Masas's daughter, Margarita, and to embark on a career in law and reform-minded politics. The house—living room, bedrooms, kitchen, well and "bookbinding/weaving shop"—is a replica of 19th-century upper-middle-class *oaxaqueño* life (open Tues.-Sun. 9am-1pm; admission 5 pesos, free Sun.).

---

## ENTERTAINMENT AND SEASONAL EVENTS

Nightlife in Oaxaca is a bit livelier than in most towns south of Mexico City. Crime is on the rise, however, and care should be taken when venturing out at night.

**Discos** and **bars** are packed—and dripping with sweat—on Friday and Saturday nights. All clubs listed here charge a 30-peso cover, unless otherwise indicated. **Eclipse,** Porfirio Díaz 219 (tel. 6-42-36), at the corner of Matamoros, is popular and convenient. A young crowd boogies under plastic-and-pipe palm trees and groovy mood lighting (cover 30 pesos Fri. and Sat., 10 pesos on Sun.; open Thurs.-Sat. 10:30pm-3am, Sun. 6-11pm). The colonial patio at **Principal** shines in the glow of the bar's purple-and-green neon lights. Watch the dancing from the second floor of the patio, or gyrate on the dance floor with your eyes locked on the videos flashing above your head (cover 20 pesos; open Fri.-Sat. 9pm-3am). The only place in Oaxaca for live salsa is a local favorite, **Candela,** Allende 211 (tel. 6-79-33). A stylish crowd gathers under the moons and stars that hang from the ceiling (cover 15 pesos; open daily 10pm-1:30am). An older but funky crowd gathers for conversation, *sangría,* and occasional live music at **Hipótesis Café,** Morelos 511, a bar, café, and self-proclaimed bohemian hangout. When no one is playing, customers are invited to strum a tune on the café's communal guitars (open Mon.-Sat. 1pm-1am).

Oaxaca offers a fair number of cultural opportunities for a city its size. Every night there are films and talks, and some evenings there are dance performances, concerts, and theater. Many events are free; see the listings in the *Guía Cultural,* available at museums and tourist offices, or in the English-language *Oaxaca Times,* also available at the tourist office.

By far the biggest summertime festivity is **La Guelaguetza** or **Los Lunes del Cerro** (Mondays of the Hill), held on the third and fourth Mondays of July. The festival features costumed performers representing the different peoples of Oaxaca, each demonstrating fantastic regional dances in Oaxaca's largest amphitheater. Tickets are pricey—mid-section seats go for 150 pesos and front-section seats go for 200 pesos—but if you arrive 2-3 hours early, you can get a good seat in the back section, free of charge.

## ■ NEAR OAXACA

### ATZOMPA, ARRAZOLA, CUILAPÁN, AND ZAACHILA

A culture and lifestyle different from the sophistication of Oaxaca de Juárez emerges in these small towns, all of which lie near Rte. 131.

**Atzompa** is where that magnificent blend of clay and sprouts, the **Chia Pet,** was invented. The pottery which is the town's specialty can be had here at better prices than in Oaxaca. Atzompa's Casa de Artesanías is a publicly funded forum that brings together the work of the town's specialized artisans. Selection is good at the Casa, but bartering is easier with the artisans themselves. Ask to be dropped off near the Casa, and then knock on just about any door in town; nearly everyone who doesn't work in Oaxaca is a potter.

**Arrazola** is the hometown of Manuel Jiménez, one of Mexico's most famous artisans, and the original creator of the brightly colored wooden animals that now rank among Mexico's most sought-after handicrafts. His coyotes will cost you more than your entire trip. Fear not, though; everyone else in town is copying Jiménez's work and selling figurines from *refresco* stands at relatively low prices. What the copies lack in grace and originality they attempt to make up for in intricacy and elaborate painting.

**Cuilapán** is home to an isolated but lovely 17th-century Dominican monastery, once the home of one of the most powerful and wealthy religious orders in Mexico. The ruined monastery's crumbling stone arcades frame the fields of the surrounding valley and the sinews of the hills that embrace it (gates open daily 10am-6pm; admission to grounds free, 7 pesos to interior).

**Zaachila,** the last political capital of the Zapotecs after they abandoned Monte Albán, hosts a fascinating market each Thursday. Drop your pesos on preserved bananas, squealing pigs, and stoic turkeys. The middle of town is dominated by the fuchsia-pink and bright yellow cathedral. Behind the church, a street heads uphill to an archaeological site that has been only partially uncovered. (Perhaps what lies underground is more interesting than what can be seen.) Until 1962, locals prohibited excavations, on the grounds that their Zapotec heritage should not be dissected by outsiders. Few potential sites have since been explored, but two Mixtec tombs with well-preserved architecture and jewelry have been uncovered. The treasure of gold, turquoise, jade, and bone artifacts has been spirited away to museums in Oaxaca and Mexico City, but the tombs—the only decorated tombs in Oaxaca—are easily accessible. In the tomb on the right side as you enter, you can view stone reliefs depicting owls and the god of death.

**Getting There:** All four towns are accessible in the course of a day under ideal conditions, though your best bet is to start out in Arrazola or Atzompa and move from there to the other cities rather than starting in Cuilapán or Zaachila, where most buses are headed back to Oaxaca rather than other points in the countryside.

The towns can be easily reached by minibus or taxi-*colectivo* from Oaxaca. The bus to Zaachila and Cuilapán leaves from the second-class bus terminal every 15 minutes (1 peso). Buses to Atzompa and Zaachila pass along the southbound side of the Periférico outside the second-class terminal, but only zip by every half-hour. A taxi-*colectivo* is probably a better option; taxis leave from Mercedes, on the edge of the large market next to the second-class station, the Central de Abastos. Ask which of the red-and-white cabs is headed for your destination. Travel time from Oaxaca to Aztompa, Arrazola, or Zaachila is about 15 minutes; allow 10 minutes for the trip to Cuilapán. It's easy to hop from one town to the next; take either a bus or a taxi-*colectivo* to Aztompa, 8km off the main road, then take either form of transportation back to the main road (1 peso). From there, flag down a bus or taxi-*colectivo* headed for Arrazola or Cuilapán/Zaachila (6 pesos by taxi-colectivo). Repeat this procedure to get from Arrazola to Cuilapán/Zaachila.

## SAN BARTOLO COYOTEPEC AND POINTS SOUTH

**San Bartolo Coyotepec,** 12km south of Oaxaca on Rte. 175, is the source of the ink-black pottery that pops up everywhere in the city. Fine pieces are available here at fairly low prices. If you didn't pick up quite enough brightly colored animals in Arrazola, head to **San Martín Tilajete,** 21km south of Oaxaca and about 4km off the main road. Four kilometers farther south, **Santa Tomás Jalietza** specializes in weaving on back-strap looms. In **Ocotlán,** 33km out of the city, leather goods, wrap-type traditional clothing, and herbal remedies can be had for a song. Swashbuckle your way through Mexico with one of the swords produced here. Market day is Friday; most of the action is between 10am and 5pm.

**Getting There:** All of the above towns are accessible by bus or taxi-*colectivo.* Taxis leave from the south end of the Central de Abastos (2 pesos for San Bartolo, 3-6 pesos for others, excluding Ocotlán). A *colectivo* leaves for Ocotlán every 20 minutes between 7am and 8pm from the second-class terminal, passing through San Bartolo and near the other towns. The last bus leaves Ocotlán for Oaxaca at 8pm.

## GUELATAO

The *pueblito* of **Guelatao,** 57km north of Oaxaca, became a national monument on March 21, 1967 (the centenary of the victory of Mexican forces over the French occupation) when the government ordered the construction of a civic plaza, a museum, statues, and a mausoleum to honor Benito Juárez, Guelatao's native son. Guelatao now seems less a living town than a memorial park, adrift in the Cuenca del Papaluapan mountain range. Should you catch it between national holidays, political campaigns, and TV docu-drama filmings, you will find Guelatao empty and peaceful. The tiny **Museo Benito Juárez** delineates Juárez's life. The museum balcony commands a view of Guelatao's rugged landscape.

**Getting There:** To get from Oaxaca to Guelatao, take a Benito Juárez bus, the line farthest to the right as you enter the second-class terminal (tel. 6-57-76). Get an early start for this trip; the 2½ hour ride is rough (8 pesos). The crowded bus back to Oaxaca passes about every two hours.

# ■■■ OAXACA TO MITLA

The road from Oaxaca to Mitla, the Pan-American Highway (Rte. 190), cuts through a valley full of artisanal towns, *mezcal* distilleries, and archaeological sites.

Just 9km outside of Oaxaca de Juárez is **Santa María El Tule,** one of Mexico's great roadside attractions. The tree in the church courtyard, commonly known as the **Tule Tree,** is over 2000 years old and is believed to weigh 636,100 metric tons—it absolutely dwarfs the tiny church. With an astounding perimeter of 57.9m, it is believed to have the largest girth of any tree on earth. Ask the bus to driver to drop you off at El Tule; then ask for *"el árbol."*

The walls of the Iglesia de San Jerónimo Tlacochahuaya illustrate Zapotec decorative techniques as applied to Catholic motifs. At the end of the 16th century the Dominicans built this church and convent 21km east of Oaxaca in **Tlacochahuaya,** far (in those times) from worldly temptations (church open daily 7am-noon).

The **Dainzú** ruins, just off the road branching for **Macuilxochitl,** 22km east of Oaxaca, date from Monte Albán's final pre-Conquest epoch. At the base of the tallest pyramidal monument, a series of magnificently carved figures represent ballplayers in attitudes similar to the "dancers" at Monte Albán. Two humans and two jaguars, gods of the sport, supervise the contest. Up the hill from the pyramid, another game scene is hewn in the living rock (open daily 10am-6pm).

Roughly 20km from Oaxaca, a turn-off leads north to **Teotitlán del Valle,** a community closely resembling an ancient Zapotec city. The source of most of the beautiful woolen *sarapes* produced in Oaxaca, Teotitlán's 200 to 300 families earn their livelihood largely by spinning and weaving. Many allow tourists to visit their workshops, and a live demonstration impresses more than any museum ever could.

About 33km east of Oaxaca, a southerly turn-off leads to **Tlacolula,** an ancient village that hosts a lively market every Sunday morning. Busloads of tourists flood Tlacolula every week, but outsiders have yet to obscure the market's *indígena* roots. Look out for the *sarapes, tapetes* (rugs), baskets, oxen yoke, and pottery. The market is officially open until 6pm, but activity starts to wind down at around 2pm.

**Yagul,** 8km east of Tlacolula, was a Zapotec city later inhabited by the Mixtecs. Less impressive archaeologically than Mitla, rarely-visited Yagul is perhaps more striking aesthetically. The city is built into the skirts of a hill overlooking a spectacular mountain-ringed valley. Most of the more famous buildings and tombs are in the acropolis, the area closest to the parking lot about 2km north of the highway. The restored ballcourt, the largest of its kind in the Oaxaca valley, once hosted a little-understood ceremonial game. As you face the ballcourt, the **Court of the Triple Tomb** is on the left. Carved with an image that is probably a jaguar, the tomb is in three sections; stone faces cover the largest portion. Beyond the ballcourt, the **Council Hall** rises above a patio; behind the hall is the **Palace of the Six Patios,** believed to have been the home of the city's ruler. Heading back to the parking lot, take the trail that climbs uphill to the rocky outcropping to catch a spectacular view of the cactus-covered hills. Look for the small stone bridge; it's behind the tomb on your right as you climb the hill (open daily 8am-5:30pm; admission 7 pesos, free Sun.).

**Getting There:** All the destinations listed above are accessible via a Mitla-bound bus, which leaves the second-class station in Oaxaca every 15 minutes from 8am-8pm, seven days a week (2.50 pesos to Mitla). If you ask the driver ahead of time, you can get off almost anywhere. There are also frequent buses directly to many of these locations. Most people visit these sites on daytrips, but if you'd like to stay overnight, inquire at the Oaxaca tourist office for information about guest houses.

# ■■■ MITLA

Tucked away in a mostly Zapotec-speaking village, the archaeological site at Mitla, 46km due east of Oaxaca, is smaller and somewhat less popular with tourists than the immense Monte Albán. It's best to visit before 11am, when buses from Oaxaca first begin to arrive.

Mitla was built by the Zapotecs, whose high priest probably lived in Mitla and shared power with a sovereign based in Monte Albán or Zaachila. When the Spaniards arrived in the valley, Mitla was the only ceremonial center of the Mesoamerican Classical period still in use. Ironically, the Catholic archbishop of Oaxaca built his home to echo the horizontal lines of the Zapotec priest's residence in Mitla, thus paying architectural tribute to an ancient indigenous religion virtually exterminated by Catholicism. By the time of the Conquest, however, Mixtecs had appropriated Mitla from the more pacific Zapotecs, transforming the city into the largest and most important of the late Mixtec cities.

Walking about 2km from the bus stop and then through the village, you'll happen onto the doorstep of the Catholic church and the entrance to the official archaeological zone. The ticket booth is on the far side of the red-domed church. To the left of it, behind the church, is a group of three patios that comprise the **Group of the Church.** One of the patios has been almost completely buried by the Catholic church, and only a few of the original palace walls remain visible. The central patio is on the other side of the church; here and in the surrounding rooms you can still see pieces of Mixtec decorative paintings glowing red against the stone. The paintings are believed to tell the history of Mitla.

More impressive ruins are across the road in the fenced-in area that encloses the **Group of the Columns.** Explanatory signs throughout this area are in English. Beyond the entrance are two patios joined at one corner. The tombs of the pyramids form a cross, and for years Spaniards thought this proved that the Mixtecs somehow knew the story of Jesus. Engineers have since discovered that the shape of the tombs protected them from the huge earthquakes that shook the area at the time of their construction.

On the second patio in the Group of the Columns, two tombs in the temples to the east and north of the courtyard are open to visitors. In the east temple stand large stones covered in a characteristic mosaic pattern. The roof of the tomb in the north temple rests on a single huge column, still referred to as the **Column of Life** by *indígenas*. Some make a pilgrimage here each year to embrace the column; in exchange for the hug, the column tells them how much longer they will live (site open daily 8am-5pm; admission 10 pesos, free Sun.).

Beyond the Group of the Columns is a daily bazaar selling mostly *típico* clothing. Although prices are high, bargaining is expected, and the selection is extraordinarily large. On the central plaza back in town, the unexciting **Frissell Museum** contains thousands of figurines from Mitla and other Mixtec sites, all arranged around a court-yard. Some descriptions are in English (open daily 9am-5pm; admission 10 pesos).

Many visitors come to Mitla not to visit the ruins but to hike in the cactus-covered, stream-laced hills around it. If you must stay in Mitla, try the **Hotel Zapoteca,** 5 de Febrero 12 (tel. 8-00-26), on the way from the bus stop to the ruins. The stucco-walled rooms are big and the bathrooms are acceptably clean. Rooms upstairs are a bit nicer. An inexpensive restaurant is attached (singles 45 pesos; doubles 60 pesos).

**Getting There:** Buses to Mitla leave Oaxaca's second-class terminal every 15 min-utes, from 8am-8pm. The last bus leaves Mitla at 8pm (2.50 pesos either way).

# ■■■ MONTE ALBÁN

Monte Albán, one of the most important and spectacular pre-Hispanic ruins in Mex-ico, stands regally atop a green mountain 10km from Oaxaca de Juárez. The mono-lithic, geometrically precise stone structures of the ruins are cradled only by expansive blue skies.

Monte Albán flourished during the Classic Period (300-750 CE), when it shared the spotlight with Teotihuacán and Tikal as a major cultural/ceremonial center of Mesoamerica. While its original name is unknown, Monte Albán was the greatest of the Zapotec capitals—in its cosmopolitan heyday, the city's art and architecture drew on a mixture of Olmec and Mayan influences. Incredibly, the huge complex of tombs, pyramids, platforms, and temples was originally built without wheels or pack animals. The entire complex was but one of 260 Zapotec cities in the Oaxaca Valley. Eventually, the Mixtecs conquered and appropriated the Zapotec settlement. In the centuries that followed, many of the civilizations of the Oaxaca Valley left a piece of their heritage here. Today, descendants of the Zapotecs constitute the fourth-largest language group in Mexico.

Archaeologists have divided the history of the site into five periods. Objects from **Monte Albán I,** dating from about 500 BCE, generally show the influence of the old-est civilization in Mesoamerica, the Olmecs. By the end of Monte Albán I, the city was the largest and most important community in Southern Mesoamerica. During the period known as **Monte Albán II** (100 BCE-300 CE) the Zapotecs consolidated their empire and expanded their commercial trading routes. It was an era of wild cultural cross-fertilization: the Maya borrowed the calendar and writing system already in use at Monte Albán, while the Zapotecs borrowed from the Maya their steep staircased pyramids and *juego de pelota,* a ball game played on a special court. Flourishing simultaneously with Teotihuacán, Monte Albán reached its apogee dur-ing the period known as **Monte Albán III** (300-750 CE). Almost all of the extant buildings and tombs as well as several urns and murals of *colanijes* (richly adorned priests) come from this period. Burial arrangements of variable luxuriousness and size show the tripartite social division of the period: priests, clerks, and laborers lived apart, died apart, and were buried in very different tombs. For reasons that remain unknown, Monte Albán shriveled up and died around 750 CE. Construction ceased, and control of the Zapotec empire shifted from Monte Albán to other cities such as Zaachila, Eta, and later Mitla. In the midst of this disastrous period, known as **Monte Albán IV** (750-1000 CE), the Mixtec people invaded from the northwest and took over many of the Zapotec cities. During **Monte Albán V,** from 1000 CE to the arrival of the Spaniards, the city functioned as both a fortress and a sacred necropo-lis. The members of the Mixtec nobility were buried in the elaborate, treasure-filled tombs left by the Zapotecs; when the most noteworthy, **Tomb 7,** was discovered in 1932, the treasure found within more than quadrupled the number of previously identified gold Mixtec objects.

As you enter the **Central Plaza,** the most prominent building to the right is the **Northern Platform.** Bear left as you enter the site, and walk along the eastern boundary of the Central Plaza; the first structure on the left is the ball court. Origi-nally smothered in stucco, the steps of the court were not spectators' stands, but rather part of the playing area. After passing a series of related substructures, you'll reach two pyramids which dominate the center and southern end of this side of the plaza. The inclined walls were originally flat and covered with stucco like the ball court and frescoes.

**Building P,** the first of the two pyramids, fascinates archaeologists because of an inner stairway feeding into a tunnel to the central structures a few meters away. The tunnel apparently allowed priests to pass into the central temples unseen by the public. The second of the two pyramids, the **Palace,** was once a wealthy Zapotec's residence; it is graced by a patio-courtyard and a garden in which a cruciform grave was discovered.

Directly outside the palace are the four central monuments of the plaza. **Buildings G, H,** and **I** together constitute what was likely the principal altar of Monte Albán. Directly to the east, between the central Building H and Building P, is the small, sunken **Adoratorio,** where archaeologists dug up an intricate jade bat mask. This is Monte Albán's oldest structure, dating from Monte Albán II. A sacred icon and the most famous piece from this period, the mask contains 25 pieces of polished, forest-green jade with slivers of white conch shell forming the teeth and eyes of the bat. Unfortunately, the mask has long since flown to a new perch in the Museo Nacional de Antropología in Mexico City.

The fourth of the central structures, **Building J** is formed in the bizarre shape of an arrowhead on a platform and contains a labyrinth of tunnels and passageways. Unlike any other ancient edifice in Mexico, it is asymmetrical and built at an angle to the other structures around the plaza. Its broad, carved slabs suggest that the building is one of the oldest on the site. Many of the glyphs depict an upside-down head below a stylized hill; the glyphs are thought to represent a place and a name. Archaeologists speculate that this image indicates a conquest, the head representing the defeated tribe and the name identifying the region conquered.

Behind Building J stands the highest structure at Monte Albán: the **Southern Pyramid.** On both sides of the staircase on the plaza level are a number of stelae carved with rain gods and tigers. The stela on the pyramid's right side contains a precise date, but archaeologists lack the point of reference needed to coordinate this date with the modern calendar. The neighboring stela is believed to depict the king of Monte Albán. If you climb only one pyramid in Mexico, make it this one: the top affords a commanding view of the ruins, the valley, and the mountains beyond.

Along the western border of the Central Plaza are the foundations of **Building M,** followed by the **Platform of the Dancers** at the foot of Building L. The low platforms in front of Building M were apparently designed to make the plaza—which was built around inconveniently located rock formations—more symmetrical. In front of Building M and to the left as you face it are the haunting reliefs known as the **Dancers.** Among the most interesting examples of pre-Conquest sculpture, the reliefs date from the 5th century BCE, and are nearly identical to contemporary Olmec sculptures along the Gulf Coast. Many are accompanied by glyphs and number schemes which were part of an elaborate system of writing and calendar-keeping. Beyond the Platform of the Dancers, the **Northern Platform,** which is almost as large as the Central Plaza itself, dominates the entire site. Steps rise to meet a sunken patio. **Building B,** to the left as you face north on top of the steps, is believed to be a Mixtec-influenced addition to the site.

The path exiting the site passes the gift shop and cafeteria on the way to **Tomb 104.** Duck underground, look above the entrance, and gaze at the urn. It is covered with a motif which interweaves images of the maize god and rain god. Near the parking lot is the entrance to **Tomb 7,** where the spectacular cache of Mixtec ornaments mentioned above was found.

The **museum** at the site's entrance was recently remodeled; it offers a chronological survey of Monte Albán's history and displays sculpted stones from the site's earlier periods. Unfortunately, the truly spectacular artifacts from the site have been hauled off to museums in Oaxaca and Mexico City (site open daily 8am-5pm; admission 14 pesos, 25 if you want to use a camcorder, free Sun. and holidays).

**Getting There:** Buses to Monte Albán leave from the Hotel Mesón del Ángel, Mina 518, between Mier y Terán and Díaz Ordaz in Oaxaca. Monte Albán is only 10km from Oaxaca, but the ride through mountainous terrain takes 30 minutes. The normal procedure is to buy a round-trip ticket, with the return fixed three hours after arrival at the site (about the right amount of time for a full perusal); if you want to stay longer you can pay an extra four pesos to come back on one of the later buses. During high season, buses from the hotel leave daily every hour between 8:30am and 5:30pm; during low season, buses leave five times per day during the week and six times per day on Sunday (10 pesos round-trip). To avoid the tourist hordes, leave early. Travel agencies around the *zócalo* in Oaxaca arrange special excursions to the ruins, some with English-speaking guides. Expect to pay around US$30 per person.

# ■■■ OAXACA TO THE PACIFIC

By bus, nine arduous but beautiful hours separate Oaxaca from the beaches of the Pacific coast. With little more than weekly markets to interest tourists, the tiny villages on the way provide only minimal services.

Second-class **Estrella del Valle** buses running from Oaxaca to Pochutla (see Oaxaca, Practical Information: Bus Stations on page 412) also stop in **Ocotlán** (see Near Oaxaca on page 417) and **Miahuatlán,** two hours by bus from Oaxaca and located in a region renowned for its *mezcal*. Market day (Monday) brings textiles of all types, tall wood *pilones* (for pounding corn or other seeds into tortilla flour), and *huaraches* (sandals) made out of strips of salvaged car tires (steel-belted radials are best). **Buses** from Miahuatlán head north to Oaxaca and south to Pochutla roughly every half-hour from 6am-8pm.

If you're heading for the coast, chances are you'll touch down in **Pochutla**—while a few buses go directly to the coast, most transfer here. While known for its black coral jewelry, Pochutla is important mainly as a bus-hopping spot.

**Currency** can be exchanged in Pochutla at **Comermex,** Lázaro Cárdenas 57 (tel. 4-01-45), open Mon.-Fri. 9am-noon. From its station on Lázaro Cárdenas 84, 100m from the second-class station, **Cristóbal Colón** (tel. 4-02-74) runs first-class buses to Huatulco (10am and 3:30pm, 1hr., 8 pesos), Mexico City (4:30pm, 13hrs., 153 pesos), Oaxaca (10am and 4:30pm, 9hrs., 73 pesos), Puebla (4:30pm, 11hrs., 132 pesos), San Cristóbal (10am and 10:30pm, 11hrs., 93 pesos), Tehuantepec (10am and 3:30pm, 3½hrs., 34 pesos), Tuxtla Gutiérrez (10am and 10:30pm, 10hrs., 79 pesos). From the Lázaro Cárdenas station across the street, underneath the yellow "Hotel Posada San José" sign, **Estrella del Valle** (tel. 4-01-38) runs first-class buses to Mexico City (6:15am and 7:15pm, 13hrs., 120 pesos) and Oaxaca (9:30am and 11pm, 6hrs., 36-40 pesos). Second-class buses go to Puerto Ángel (every 20min., 1.50 pesos), Puerto Escondido (every hr., 1hr., 8 pesos), and Zipolite (every 20min., 2.50 pesos). From its station on Lázaro Cárdenas 94, just up the street from the "Elvis," **Gacela** and **Estrella Blanca** (tel. 4-03-08) run semi-direct to Acapulco (8 per day, 8hrs., 87 pesos), *ordinario* to Acapulco (every hr., 7:15am-2:30pm, 10hrs., 75 pesos), Huatulco (every hr., 8:30am-8:30pm, 1hr., 7 pesos), direct to Mexico City (5pm, 12hrs., 140 pesos), and direct to Puerto Escondido (6:15, 7:15, and 8:15pm, 1hr., 7 pesos). **Hotel Posada San José,** across from the bus stop and down a small road next to the Estrella del Valle station (tel. 4-01-53) offers surprisingly comfortable, fan-cooled rooms opening onto a courtyard with—joy of joys—a pool and palm trees. Pay extra for A/C (singles 36 pesos, with color TV 50 pesos; one-bed double 40 pesos, with TV 55 pesos; Visa, MC accepted).

# ■■■ TEHUANTEPEC

East of Oaxaca de Juárez, the North American continent narrows to a slender strip of land just 215km across, known as the Isthmus of Tehuantepec. Inhabitants of the region have resisted assimilation into the mainstream of Mexican-*mestizo* culture, preserving instead a unique Zapotec tradition most visible in Tehuantepec (pop. 60,000), the oldest of the isthmus's principal cities. Zapotecs captured the town from the Mixtecs prior to the Spanish conquest, only to surrender Tehuantepec to Cortés without a fight in exchange for special privileges. When Cortés failed to provide what he had promised, the people of Tehuantepec revolted; today, they're still bucking patriarchal authority. Tehuantepec is a matriarchal society; the birth of a daughter is cause for celebration, and men turn their wages over to their wives, who control family finances. The ebb and flow of rural life is punctuated by frequent *fiestas*, during which women often dance together, clothed in embroidered silk *huipiles* (blouses) and long, billowing *enaguas* (skirts). Decked out in vibrant traditional garb with balloons tucked into their hair, these women make Carmen Miranda look dowdy. Don't be surprised if a band of women, parading through the streets on a *fiesta* day in floppy straw hats, approaches you with a shot of *mezcal*. (Drink it if you can—it's rude to refuse.) But liberation is limited even in Tehuantepec: while women enjoy a uniquely privileged social and economic status, they still can't ask men to dance.

**Practical Information** For tourist information, visit the **Chamber of Commerce,** across the street from the Hotel Donaji (open Mon.-Fri. 9am-2pm and 4-7pm, hours unstable). For information about the town, visit the reception desk of Hotel Donaji. The **police** (tel. 5-00-01) are in the back of the Palacio Municipal, on the south side of the *zócalo*. The **post office** is on the north side of the *zócalo* (open Mon.-Fri. 8am-7pm, Sat. 8am-1:30pm). **Postal Code:** 70760. The **telegraph** office is next door to the post office (open for money orders Mon.-Fri. 9am-5pm, Sat. 9am-noon, for telegrams and **faxes** Mon.-Fri. 9am-8pm, Sat. 9am-noon). **Telephones** are available in Hotel Donaji from 7:30am-11pm. There are no LADATEL phones in town. U.S. dollars or traveler's checks can be exchanged at **Bancomer,** 5 de Mayo 3 (tel. 5-00-21), between the *zócalo* and Salina Cruz (open Mon.-Fri. 9am-noon).

**Buses** leave from a handful of stations, all a 20-minute walk from the *zócalo*. From its station on Av. Héroes and the highway, **Cristóbal Colón** (tel. 5-01-08) travels to the most destinations, including Huatulco (2am and 3pm, 4hrs., 26 pesos), Mexico City's TAPO (6:30, 7:30, and 9:15am, 12hrs., 120-158 pesos), Oaxaca (6 per day, 5hrs., 40 pesos), Pochutla (2am and 3pm, 5hrs., 35 pesos), Puebla (9:15pm, 10hrs., 134 pesos), Puerto Escondido (2am and 3pm, 6hrs., 45 pesos), San Cristóbal (12:30am and 1pm, 8hrs., 60 pesos), and Tuxtla Gutiérrez (12:30am and 1pm, 5hrs., 46 pesos). From the same station, **ADO** runs to Juchitán (5 per day, midnight-8:30pm, 5 pesos) and Tampico (10pm, 215 pesos).

The **public library** is in the **Casa de la Cultura,** down a short alley off Guerrero next to the Centro de Salud (open Mon.-Fri. 9am-1pm and 4-8pm, Sat. 9am-2pm). The **market** is on the west side of the *zócalo*. The **Red Cross** (tel. 5-02-15) is on the highway to Salina Cruz, past the bridge (ambulance service 24 hrs.). The **Farmacia del Rosario** (tel. 5-01-18) is on Romero two blocks south of the *zócalo* (open daily 7:30am-10pm). The **Centro de Salud** (tel. 5-01-80) is on Guerrero two blocks east of Juárez and northeast of the *zócalo* (open 24 hrs.).

**Accommodations and Food** Tehuantepec has a few small hotels and *casas de huéspedes,* all within a few blocks of the *zócalo* and all clean. **Casa de Huéspedes el Istmo,** on Hidalgo, 1½ blocks north of the post office, offers rooms that are spacious and reasonably clean, if heavy on the concrete. Communal bathrooms are tolerable and ceiling fans are pleasurable (singles 20 pesos; doubles 30 pesos, with bath 40 pesos). **Hotel Donaji,** Av. Juárez 10 (tel. 5-00-64), is south of the *zócalo*. Neat little rooms have full-length mirrors, fans, and clean bathrooms. A/C available for a hefty price (singles 50 pesos; doubles 70 pesos, with two beds 75 pesos). **Hotel Oasis,** Melchor Ocampo 8 (tel. 5-00-08), southwest of the *zócalo*, offers crumbly stucco rooms, decent bathrooms, and a breezy patio (singles 50 pesos; doubles 60 pesos, with 2 beds 75 pesos; A/C 25 pesos extra).

Tehuantepec doesn't have many cheap restaurants, but at night vendors set up tables for inexpensive sit-down dining. **Café Colonial,** Romero 66 (tel. 5-01-15), two blocks south of the *zócalo,* serves a *comida corrida* (16 pesos), pancakes (10 pesos), and meat dishes (18-24 pesos; open Mon.-Sat. 8am-10pm, Sun. 8am-6pm). **Restaurante y Mariscos Ángel** (tel. 5-02-12) is on 5 de Mayo between the market and the highway. *Quesadillas* infiltrate the sinister hegemony of seafood. Fish is 18-20 pesos, super *licuados* are 6 pesos (open daily 7am-midnight). To reach the ever-chic **Scarú,** Leona Vicario 4 (tel. 5-06-46), take Juárez south until it ends at a park. Make a left and walk 1½ blocks; it's ahead and to the left. A good example of 18th-century Tehuantepecano architecture, the building has a back patio with columns rising to meet colonial tile. It's a bit pricey, but the atmosphere is unparalleled, with live *marimba* music Thurs.-Sun. from 2-7pm.

**Sights and Entertainment** The oldest building in town is the old Dominican **monastery,** now the **Casa de la Cultura,** down a short alley off Guerrero, next to the Centro de Salud. The monastery was commissioned by Cocijo-pii, the last of the Zapotec kings, who converted to Christianity and quickly handed over the reins of the city when the Spanish arrived at his doorstep. Today, the 16th-century structure's colonial frescoes vie for attention with contemporary paintings (open Mon.-Fri. 9am-1pm and 4-8pm, Sat. 9am-2pm).

Tehuantepec's real attractions are its *fiestas.* Each of the town's 14 *barrios* (neighborhoods) hosts an annual celebration lasting 8-12 days, beginning on the eve of the feast day of the neighborhood's patron saint. The feast days are concentrated in the summer, so *fiestas* tend to bleed together into an undifferentiated season of revelry. The festivities begin on May 1, with the *barrio* of Santa Cruz Tagolaba's *fiesta,* and continue through the second Sunday in October, when the *barrio* of Jaliso begins its celebration—with a hiatus during most of July. Of all the festivals, the most colorful and spectacular are those of Sandonga, beginning on May 28, Santa María, from August 14-20; and Laborío, September 6-10. When it's *fiesta*-time, Tehuantepec sparkles with dances, parades, fireworks, and special masses. Daytime festivities are relatively safe, but after dark, things can get dicey; to protect yourself from inebriated bullies trying to provoke fights, attach yourself to a group of friendly locals. Brush up on your dance steps, and keep a good hangover cure up your sleeve. And remember: women run the show.

# ■■■ BAHÍAS DE HUATULCO

With its wide, palm-lined streets, shiny new electric lights, and sprawling resorts, Huatulco is a paradise for those who like their vacations packaged, planned, and posh. If everything looks new here, that's because it is: Mexican government officials settled on the area as a prime candidate for resort development in the 1980s, and began building from the bottom up. As a result, the entire city feels something like a seaside country club; even the *zócalo* smacks of freshly poured concrete and professional landscaping. The bulk of the visitors are moneyed Mexicans and *norteamericanos* drawn to Huatulco's reputation as—for better or for worse—"the new Cancún." Though backpackers may feel out of place amidst the shiny cars and bulging wallets coursing through Huatulco's streets, the city still merits a visit—precisely because those government officials knew what they were doing. Huatulco's bays are breathtakingly beautiful, filled with sapphire-blue waters and lined with lush vegetation. Because most remain undeveloped, visitors from nearby Puerto Ángel or Puerto Escondido should find much of Huatulco a pristine idyll, as of yet untouched by the hands of luxury hotel builders. But rest assured, the developers will come. The days of Huatulco's raw beauty are almost certainly numbered.

## ORIENTATION

Huatulco is located 750km from Mexico City via Routes 150, 190, and 175, and 950km from Acapulco on Route 200. The small downtown area, **La Crucecita,** contains most of the area's services and budget accommodations. Streets are unusually well-marked; the *zócalo* is bordered on the west by **Gardenia** and on the east by **Bugambilias.** The main street, **Carrizal,** lies one block east of Bugambilias and leads south to the most developed of Huatulco's bays.

Huatulco consists of nine bays in all: San Agustín, Chachacual, Cacaluta, Maguey, Órgano, Santa Cruz, Chahué, Tangolunda, and Conejos, from north to south. Of these, **Santa Cruz** is the most developed, with hotels and some tourist services clustered on its main road, **Blvd. Santa Cruz.** Home to mostly luxury hotels, **Tangolunda** is only slightly less developed than Santa Cruz; its main thoroughfare is **Blvd. Benito Juárez.** Feeding into the two roads is **Blvd. Chahué,** which runs from La Crucecita to the bay of the same name.

## PRACTICAL INFORMATION

**Tourist Office: Asociación de Hoteles y Moteles** (tel. 7-08-48), in Santa Cruz on Blvd. Santa Cruz and Monte Albán. Helpful staffers speak good English and have reams of information to hand out. Open Mon.-Fri. 9am-2pm and 4-6pm, Sat. 9am-1pm. **Espacio 2000,** Guamuchil 210 (tel. 7-00-27), ½ block from the *zócalo.* An information booth with loads of pamphlets and maps. Also puts out a helpful guide to Huatulco. Open Mon.-Fri. 9am-2pm and 4-8pm.

**Police:** Blvd. Chahué 100, in the pink government building. In case of emergency, call tourist officials, also in government building 24 hrs. (tel. 7-02-10); they can provide an English-speaking interpreter and other assistance.

**Post Office:** Blvd. Chahué 100 (tel. 7-05-51), in the pink government building. *Lista de Correos.* Open Mon.-Fri. 9am-1pm and 3-6pm, Sat. 9am-1pm. **Postal Code:** 70989.

**Telegrams: Telecomm,** next to the post office. Open Mon.-Fri. 8am-6pm, Sat. 9am-noon.

**Telephones: Telefónico,** Bugambilias at Flamboyan (tel. 7-03-14). 10.30 pesos per min. to U.S. Open Mon.-Sat. 7:30am-9:30pm, Sun. 8am-1pm and 4-9pm. There are **LADATEL** phones all along Carrizal, Blvd. Santa Cruz, and Blvd. Benito Juárez. **Telephone Code:** 958.

**Currency Exchange: Bancomer,** Blvd. Santa Cruz at Pochutla (tel. 7-00-03), will exchange cash and traveler's checks. Open Mon.-Fri. 9am-1:30pm. Next door, **Bánamex** (tel. 7-03-22), in addition to exchanging cash and traveler's checks, houses a 24-hr. **ATM.** Open Mon.-Fri. 9am-1:30pm. Large hotels also exchange money at slightly less favorable rates.

**Airport:** 19km from Santa Cruz. **Aeromar** (tel. 1-00-52) flies daily to Mexico City (55min., discount price 325 pesos), **AeroMorelos** (tel. 1-04-44) flies to Oaxaca (3 per day, 35min., 297 pesos), and **Mexicana** flies to Mexico City (3 per day, 55min., discount price 325 pesos). Mexicana also has an office in the Castillo Huatulco Hotel on Blvd. Santa Cruz (tel. 7-02-23). Open Tues.-Fri. 9am-6pm, Sat. and Mon. 9am-2pm and 3-6pm.

**Bus Stations: Estrella Blanca,** Gardenia 8 (tel. 7-01-03), at the corner of Palma Real, leaves for Acapulco (first class 5 per day, 5:30am-11:30am, 9hrs., 96 pesos), *ordinario* to Acapulco (8 per day, 9hrs., 82 pesos), direct to Mexico City (6:30pm, 12hrs., 186 pesos), Pochutla (every hr., 1hr., 7 pesos), Puerto Escondido (3 per day, 5:15-7:30pm, 2hrs., 17-20 pesos), and Salina Cruz (6 per day, 2½hrs., 23 pesos). **Cristóbal Colón** (tel. 7-02-61), down Gardenia at the corner of Ocotillo, runs to Córdoba (3:30pm, 10hrs., 121 pesos), Mexico City-Taxqueña (2:30 and 5:30pm, 12½hrs., 144 pesos), Oaxaca (5:30 and 11pm, 7hrs., 66 pesos), Puebla (5:30pm, 11hrs., 125 pesos), Puerto Escondido (4 per day, 2hrs., 19 pesos), San Cristóbal (11am and 11:30pm, 10hrs., 85 pesos), and Tuxtla Gutiérrez (11am and 11:30pm, 9hrs., 72 pesos). **Estrella del Valle** (tel. 7-01-93), on Jazmín between Carrizal and Sabali, runs an *ordinario* to Oaxaca (8:30am and 12:30pm, 8hrs., 37 pesos) and direct to Oaxaca (10:15pm, 8hrs., 37 pesos).

**Car Rental: National** (tel. 1-02-93), on Blvd. Juárez in front of the Sheraton in Tangolunda. Small VW 280 pesos per day, including mileage and insurance. Credit card and driver's license required. Make reservations at home to avoid paying steep rates. Open Mon.-Sat. 8:30am-2pm and 4:30-7pm, Sun. 9am-1pm.

**Market: 3 de Mayo,** on Guamuchil off of the *zócalo*. *Artesanías,* food, and small kitchens for snacks.

**Laundromat:** Carrizal at Flamboyan (tel. 7-05-85), across from Hotel Busanvi. 3kg for 19.50 pesos; self-service 4kg for 16.50 pesos. Open Mon.-Sat. 8am-9pm. Self-service after 4pm only.

**Red Cross:** Carrizal, across from Gran Hotel Huatulco (tel. 7-11-88). Open 24 hrs.

**Pharmacy: Farmacia del Centro,** Bugambilias at Flamboyan (tel. 7-02-32). Open Sun.-Fri. 8am-10pm, Sat. open 24 hrs. Pharmacies take turns staying open all night.

**Hospital: Hospital del IMSS** (tel. 7-01-24 or 7-03-83), on Blvd. Chahué past the government building. 24-hr. service. No English spoken.

**Emergency:** In case of emergency, call tourist officials at any hour, also in the government building (tel. 7-02-10); they can provide an English-speaking interpreter and other assistance.

## ACCOMMODATIONS AND CAMPING

Tourist officials frown upon camping as a way to escape Huatulco's high-priced hotel scene, but concede that camping is allowed on Chahué and Cacaluta. The other bays are off-limits partially because they lack security; if you don't mind taking the chance, camp at will. The main problem is actually getting there—many of the bays are accessible only by boat. Under no circumstances should you try to camp on Santa Cruz or Tangolunda; the hotel owners would be very unhappy.

If camping isn't your thing, brace yourself for a rocky ride through the world of Huatulco's budget accommodations. All affordable rooms are located downtown in La Crucecita, but even though they're somewhat removed from the ocean, they tend to be a bit overpriced.

**Hotel Posada San Agustín,** Carrizal 1102 (tel. 7-03-68), at the corner of Macuil. Tidy white stucco rooms have spotless bathrooms, ceiling fans, and small balconies with a view of either the street or bougainvillea. Cold water. Single or one-bed double 50 pesos, 60 pesos high season. Two-bed double 80 pesos, 90 pesos high season.

**Hotel Busanvi,** Carrizal 601 (tel. 7-00-56). Rooms vary quite a bit, from spacious two-bed doubles with equally spacious and clean bathrooms to a shoebox-sized single with a bathroom so small the sink's outside. Ask to see your room first. Color TV in some rooms, ceiling fans in all. Singles 50 pesos. Doubles 95 pesos.

**Hotel Benimar,** Bugambilias at Pochote (tel. 7-04-47). Small, overwhelmingly yellow rooms with weak ceiling fans and disproportionately large—if undermaintained—bathrooms. Try to bargain the prices down; it shouldn't be hard. Singles and doubles (2 beds) 80 pesos, 110 pesos high season.

## FOOD

Huatulco's cuisine tends to run the financial spectrum, from pricey French food to cheap *típico* kitchens. As a general rule, the closer the restaurant is to the *zócalo*, the more expensive it will be. Carrizal is lined with small kitchens that offer lots of food (and virtually no atmosphere) at low prices.

**Restaurant-Bar Gina,** Guarumbo 201 at Carrizal. Standard *típico* fare, served on standard plastic tables. Breakfast of eggs, rice, beans, *tortillas,* and (guilt-free) O.J. for 10 pesos. Open daily 7am-9pm.

**Oasis Café,** Bugambilias at Flamboyan (tel. 7-00-18), at the *zócalo*. A culinary cross-roads, all held under a green awning with a view of the city center. *Enchiladas* 12 pesos, T-bone steak 28 pesos, sushi 18-35 pesos—you decide! Open daily 7am-midnight; Japanese food served 2-11pm only.

**Restaurant-Bar La Tropicana,** Guanacastle at Gardenia (tel. 7-06-61), on the *zócalo*. The cheapest option on the *zócalo*, serving a hefty *comida corrida* for only 14 pesos. White tiles—and yes, plastic chairs—give it that down-home feel. Open 24 hrs.

PUERTO ÁNGEL

## SIGHTS AND ENTERTAINMENT

Spread across some 35km, Huatulco's nine bays pose a challenge to those determined for a change of scenery. Santa Cruz, Tangolunda, and Chahué can all be reached by any *colectivo* heading down Carrizal or Blvd. Chahué marked with the name of your desired destination (1.50 pesos). As for the rest, a little ingenuity can go a long way. A boat is probably the easiest method to reach them, but also the most expensive; it is possible, however, to take a taxi to Conejos, Maguey, and San Agustín. Shave some pesos off the San Agustín fare by first catching a bus to nearby Santa María Huatulco for 4 pesos, and taking a taxi from there.

Those looking for outdoor adventures in Huatulco will not be disappointed—but surprise, surprise: adventure comes at a price. **Deportes Acuáticos y Diversiones** (tel. 7-00-51, ext. 604), located in the Castillo Huatulco Hotel, offers a variety of "ecological excursions," from a full-day biking and hiking tour of the rainforest (250 pesos per person) to private boat trips to the bays (800 pesos for up to 6 people, sport fishing equipment included). It also offers bike rentals (20 pesos per hr., 50 pesos per day). A less expensive option is **Rent-a-Bike**, on Flamboyan at Bugambilias (tel. 7-06-69), which organizes low, medium, and high level bike tours to the bays for 45 pesos per person.

Huatulco's night scene is just getting off the ground, so to speak, leaving antsy travelers with few options. Most large hotels have their own bars, but the only full-fledged disco is **Magic Circus,** on Blvd. Santa Cruz (tel. 7-00-17; fax 7-00-37), a sort of multimedia extravaganza (cover 40 pesos except Wed.; open Wed.-Sat. 10pm-late; open bar Thurs.).

# ■■■ PUERTO ÁNGEL

With no bank or newsstand and only a fledgling post office, Puerto Ángel's turquoise shores are a natural haven for urban escapists. The town is popular with Mexican families, Europeans, and those who want to simmer at Zipolite without enduring its primitive facilities. Unlike its neighbor, Puerto Ángel has fairly advanced accommodations and tourist services. The modest port may no longer be a beachside Eden, but neither is it a built-up resort town. Hotels and restaurants intermingle with homes and businesses, and nightlife is almost non-existent. But the food is good, the cove beautiful, the crowd cosmopolitan, and the living tranquil.

## ORIENTATION

The southward bulge in Oaxaca's coastline culminates in Puerto Ángel, 240km south of Oaxaca de Juárez via Rte. 200. Puerto Escondido, 68km to the west on Rte. 200, is easily reached by **bus** from Pochutla (every hr., 6am-8pm, 1hr., 4 pesos). **Taxis** provide a link between Puerto Ángel and nearby towns for about 2 pesos *colectivo* or 10 pesos *especial*. If you must take a taxi, do what you can to get the *colectivo* rate and don't let drivers con you into paying baggage-carrying fees.

The road from Pochutla becomes Puerto Ángel's main drag at the edge of town; **Avenida Principal** descends a hill, then wraps around Playa Puerto Ángel, becoming **Blvd. Virgilio Uribe.** The thoroughfare then turns away from the beach to curve around the large hill which halves the town. Soon after leaving the first half of town, the road branches off to the left; this branch leads to private homes and sheer cliffs. The main road crosses a small creek (really a glorified puddle) and forks at a sign for Hotel Ángel del Mar; the upper, right-hand road rambles farther down the coast to Zipolite, and the lower, left-hand road heads for the Playa Panteón. The only significant side street in town climbs the hill directly across the street from the pier on Playa Puerto Ángel; it starts out as **Vasconcelos,** then curves to the left, becomes **Teniente Azuela,** and arrives back at Uribe in front of the naval station.

## PRACTICAL INFORMATION

Services in Puerto Ángel are less than minimal; most must be begged, borrowed, or imported from nearby Pochutla. There is no **police** station, but naval officers around the base stand in for the cops. The **post office**, on Uribe at the beginning of town, sells stamps and posts a *Lista de Correos* (open Mon.-Fri. 9am-4pm). **Postal Code: 70902. Telegrams** are in the **Telecomm** office next door to the post office (open Mon.-Fri. 9am-3pm). The **long distance-caseta,** Vasconcelos 3 (tel. 4-03-98), is opposite the pier (open Mon.-Sat. 7am-10pm, Sun. 2-10pm; collect calls 5 pesos, Mon.-Fri. 7-9am and 2-4pm). **Telephone Code: 958. Change money** in Pochutla at **Comermex,** Lázaro Cárdenas 57 (tel. 4-01-45), up the street from the bus stations (open Mon.-Fri. 9am-1pm). The same **colectivo** goes to Pochutla (every 20min., 7am-7pm, 1 peso), then doubles back and heads to Zipolite (1 peso) and Mazunte (2 pesos). Hop aboard anywhere along Uribe. **Farmacia Ángel** is up Vasconcelos on the right, opposite the Hotel Soraya (open Mon.-Sat. 7am-2pm and 4-9pm). The owner's husband is a doctor and is available 'round-the-clock in case of medical emergency. Everyone knows the doctor; any cab driver can take you directly to his home. Limited **medical services** are available at the **Centro de Salud,** at the top of Vasconcelos to the left on a dirt path (open Mon.-Sat. 8am-2pm and 4-8pm; for emergencies 24 hrs.). Some medical services are also available (in emergencies only) at the naval base. The nearest **hospital** (tel. 4-02-16) is between Puerto Ángel and Pochutla. The **Agency of Public Ministry,** next to the base, will contact police in an **emergency.**

## ACCOMMODATIONS

Puerto Ángel supports a slew of cheap, attractive hotels and *casas de huéspedes,* making the town a good base for daytrips to the sultry sands of Zipolite. Budget lodgings are strung along the hills on the inland side of the main road between the two beaches. Hammock spaces are inexpensive and fill up quickly. Only expensive hotels have hot water; some hotels have running water only at certain hours. Inexplicably, hotels in Puerto Ángel tend to contain books in various languages.

**Pensión Puesta del Sol,** past the naval base but before the fork that leads to Playa Panteón and Zipolite. There is a sign on the right pointing up a steep driveway. Comfortable, well-furnished rooms and sparkling bathrooms. Communal areas (including bathrooms, terraces, cafeteria, and TV room) are attractive and very well kept. Everything absolutely glows. Fans and mosquito screens. Breakfast served. Cold water available 24 hrs. Singles 35 pesos, without bath. Doubles 50 pesos, with bath 60-70 pesos.

**Casa de Huéspedes Gundi y Tomás,** on Iturbide just before the bridge and across from the naval base. Stone-and-brick terraces rambling uphill overlook the beach. Nets or screens render each room mosquito-proof. Communal bathrooms are very clean. Breakfast served. Spanish lessons, English-language books, tourist info, and backpacking company are all readily available. Singles 30-35 pesos. Doubles 50 pesos. Hammocks 10 pesos.

**Posada Rincón Sabroso,** on the high hill at the entrance to town. Look for the sign on the inland side of the road near the pier. Forget the beaches: just lie on the hammock in front of your room looking out over the cove. Every surface has been expertly scrubbed—the joint sparkles. Varnished tree branches hold the toilet paper. Laundry facilities. Running water 7-10am and 5-9pm. Singles 50 pesos, 60 pesos high season. Doubles 60 pesos, 70 pesos high season.

**Casa de Huéspedes Leal,** at the base of the hill next to the stairs rising to Guni y Tomás. Simple rooms jazzed up with some multi-colored paint. Communal baths. Guest book serves as testament to their international clientele; write a note in your native language before you leave. Singles 20 pesos. Doubles 35 pesos.

## FOOD

Food in Puerto Ángel is usually fresh and filling. Reasonable prices and excellent seafood make the beachfront *palapa* restaurants attractive to budget travelers.

**King Creole,** at the western end of Playa Panteón. For some of the best international cuisine in the Republic, try this friendly spot on the sand. Filet mignon with baked potato, fresh vegetables, and garlic bread about 40 pesos. Incredible desserts and vegetarian and creole specialties.

**Restaurant Villa Florencia** (a.k.a Lulu), in town on the landward side of Iturbide, east of the naval station. Yummy food. International books line the walls. Watch the traffic go by; when it does, stand up and dance around. Pasta galore, including tortellini (20 pesos). Pizzas 20-24 pesos. Restaurant and bar open daily 7am-11pm.

**Restaurant El Capy** (tel. 4-30-02), downstairs from the *casa de huéspedes* of the same name, on the dirt road between the 2 beaches, to the right as you descend to Panteón. The proprietor-fisherman catches everything El Capy serves. A hangout for international beach bums. Delicious sea fare: shrimp in garlic 20 pesos, breaded filet of fish 22 pesos. Open daily 7am-9pm.

### SIGHTS

Of Puerto Ángel's two beaches, the smaller **Playa Panteón,** on the far side of town, is the worthier. The water here is calm and warm, the coves great for exploring. To rent a boat at Playa Panteón, inquire at **Restaurant El Amigo del Mar, Restaurant Susy,** or any of the beachside restaurants. The hourly price will depend on your Spanish, the price of gasoline, and the time of year. You can also rent snorkeling equipment at Restaurant Susy (10 pesos per hr.). Scuba and snorkel equipment is available day and night from **Grupo Técnico Deportivo** in the Hotel La Cabaña (tel. 4-31-16); a daytime scuba dive trip costs US$25, while a night-time trip is US$50. The beach closer to the pier, **Playa Puerto Ángel,** has become somewhat polluted and dirty, but folks still take the plunge. **Elías Tarias,** the small, white-roofed restaurant on the side of the pier away from Playa Panteón, rents boats as well.

A few kilometers east of Puerto Ángel sprawls **Playa Estacahuites** (pronounced "a STACK o WHEATIES"), a nudist beach. In a small, secluded cove ideal for snorkeling, Estacahuites attracts enough visitors to its shore that thefts are common. To reach Playa Estacahuites from town, head east on Uribe as if you were going to Pochutla. Just outside of town you'll spot a huge Corona sign. Turn right at the sign and the beach will be at the end of the dirt path; it's well worth the 20-minute hike.

### ■■■ ZIPOLITE

The road to paradise is newly paved. Zipolite, once a remote hippie beach, can now be easily reached from Pochutla by the *colectivo* that travels from Puerto Ángel to Mazunte. The word *zipolite* means "place of the dead"—it refers to those who have lost their lives in the unforgiving surf. Of course, cynics would note that for every person who has lost their life in the waves, ten have lost their former lives to Zipolite's hypnotizing combination of wind, water, and marijuana.

Newcomers to Zipolite are teased for wearing watches, while oldtimers often can't tell you how long they've been here. The crowd is uniformly young and mostly from Mexico, Europe, and the U.S.; the presence of a few hard-core hippies gives the town a somewhat seedy edge. Come here to stroll naked down the long beach, check in with the international vagabond set, and generally partake of the friendly fringe atmosphere. Do it soon, though, because where paved roads go, hotels and souvenir shops soon follow.

**Orientation and Practical Information** Zipolite lies just 4km west of Puerto Ángel; see Puerto Ángel: Practical Information on page 429 for details on *colectivo* schedules. If you need information in Zipolite, ask someone who's naked—the ones without tan lines have been here the longest. There is a **pharmacy** and a small **general store** on the road near the east end of the beach. Zipolite has no potable water, and bottles of *agua purificada* cost twice as much here as they do in Puerto Ángel—stock up before you come. There is no telephone service.

**Accommodations and Food** Accommodations in Zipolite are casual to the max. The *palapas* along the beach offer food, drink, and hammocks. **San Cristóbal,** near the west end of the beach, offers particularly nice *cabañas* (25 pesos for 1-2 people). They also have clean bathrooms with cold-water showers. By far the grooviest place on the beach is **Shambhala,** on the slope at the west end, which offers small concrete rooms with beds, mosquito netting, and little else to hordes of eager international youth (singles 20 pesos; doubles 30 pesos; hammocks 5 pesos). Shambhala also boasts an attached mostly-vegetarian restaurant and Buddhist meditation center. Unlike many places on the beach, it is drug-free.

For fish and seafood, the *palapas* are ready and waiting. **La Choza,** near the west end of the beach, whips up a tasty *huachinango* (red snapper), which at 20 pesos is the most expensive dish on the beach. **El Hongo** has yummy spaghetti carbonara, **Lo Cósmico,** the last place on the west end before Shambala, yummy crabs.

**Sand and Sights** Zipolite offers a remarkably high concentration of people doing absolutely nothing. Waves break cataclysmically offshore, slamming the carefree souls who frolic naked in the surf. The waves come in from two directions (southeast and southwest) at 45-degree angles to the beach. This creates a series of channels that vacuum unsuspecting swimmers out to sea. Though ferocious, these channels are not very wide: if you find yourself being pulled away from shore, do not attempt to swim directly towards the beach; rather, swim parallel to the beach until you're clear of the seaward current. Zipolite is unfortunately plagued by theft, so keep an eye on everything or leave it locked up. A final warning: scorpions patronize Zipolite, so either give your cut-offs a good shake before jumping into them or blend in with the locals by going about your business in the buff.

If you *must* get out and do something, catch a *colectivo* to Mazunte, two towns past Zipolite. There you will find the recently opened **Museo de la Tortuga,** an aquarium which holds nine of the eleven turtle species in the world, and all six of the freshwater varieties. Don't begrudge the admission price; your pesos go toward conservation. Guides speak English and Spanish (open Tues.-Sat. 10am-4:30pm, Sun. 10am-12:30pm; admission 10 pesos, children and students with ID 5 pesos).

# ■■■ PUERTO ESCONDIDO

Puerto Escondido (pop. 20,000) is the heroine of a familiar tale. Less than two decades ago, it was a quiet *indígena* fishing village where visitors had to wheedle overnight lodging from local families. Today, the Pacific crashes beneath the boards of droves of stocky surfers who head for Playa Zicatela at the crack of dawn, as sun-worshippers from the world over look on. And though Puerto Escondido no longer seems like a remote outpost, this fabulous stretch of beach between two magnificent outcroppings of rock still plays host to amiable international company. Where only a handful of scantily clad *extranjeros* used to gleefully romp, hotels now outnumber hippies, drug use has dwindled, and nudity is history. Excellent food, exotic drink, and kitsch trinkets compete for pedestrians' pesos and lend the *paseo* an urban air. Rife with the conveniences and exciting nightspots Puerto Ángel lacks, Puerto Escondido establishes its own fast pace between peak tanning hours.

## ORIENTATION

Like any self-respecting seaside village, Puerto Escondido has its own airport. It is also connected to the rest of the world by land; Rte. 175 (paved) and Rte. 131 (mostly unpaved) wind treacherously through the Sierra Madres toward the coast, while an expertly paved coastal road, Rte. 200, twists through ramshackle fishing towns and coastal forests on its way to Acapulco.

Puerto Escondido is built on a hill. The **Carretera Costera** (Rte. 200) cuts across the hill, bisecting it into an uptown of well-marked, perpendicular residential streets and *la zona turística,* a downtown maze of paths leading to the beach. Rte. 131 from Oaxaca crosses Rte. 200, becomes **Pérez Gasga,** and twists downhill to form a pedestrian walkway behind the beach. Beyond the walkway, it meets Rte. 200 again 1km east of *el crucero,* just west of a bridge crossing Laguna Agua Dulce. (The intersection of Rte. 200 and Pérez Gasga is usually called *el crucero.*) The **airport** is 3km west on Rte. 200, a tough walk or short cab ride (8 pesos) to the *centro.* **Bus stations** cluster north of *el crucero,* just off Rte. 131, and are one of the few reasons for visitors to stray this far uphill from the beach. To get from the stations to the center of town, walk down Route 131 until you hit Rte. 200. Cross *el crucero* and wind your way down Pérez Gasga until you reach the pedestrian mall.

**Cabs** from *el crucero* transport the weary traveler downtown or to the *playas* for seven pesos. Taxis charge 8 pesos to go anywhere in town, no matter how short the distance. To leave town, hike the steep hill to *el crucero* or take a cab from either end of the pedestrian mall. Unless your surfboard is weighing you down or it's 105°F (both possible), the walk is easy. *Colectivos* and taxi-*colectivos* run along the Carretera Costera and in the uphill part of town.

## PRACTICAL INFORMATION

**Tourist Office:** An information booth at the beginning of the pedestrian walkway, next to the taxi stand. Maps available. English spoken. Highly irregular hours.

**Police:** (tel. 2-07-21), just downhill from the tourist office. Available 24 hrs.

**Post Office:** (tel. 2-09-59), Calle 7 Nte. at Oaxaca, 10 very long blocks north of Hidalgo on Rte. 131 and to the right in a blue building with an antenna. *Lista de Correos.* Open Mon.-Fri. 8am-7pm, Sat. 9am-1pm. It's a good 45min. uphill walk from the beach. Catch a microbus or a taxi-*colectivo* at *el crucero,* or buy stamps from one of the many vendors on Pérez Gasga. **Postal Code:** 71980.

**Telephones:** (tel. 2-04-87), on Pérez Gasga across from Farmacia Cortés. No collect calls. Open Mon.-Sat. 9am-10pm, Sun. 9am-1pm. Make collect calls from one of the pay phones on Pérez Gasga. **Telephone Code:** 958.

**Telegrams:** (tel. 2-09-57), next door to the post office. Open for telegrams and **fax** service Mon.-Fri. 9am-1pm and 3-7pm, Sat. 9am-noon. Open for **money orders** Mon.-Fri. 9am-1pm and 3-5pm, Sat. 9am-noon.

**Currency Exchange: Bánamex** (tel. 2-06-26), on Pérez Gasga, halfway between *el crucero* and the pedestrian mall. Open for exchange Mon.-Fri. 9am-1:30pm and has a 24-hr. **ATM** that accepts Plus, Cirrus, MC, and Visa. **Money Exchange** (tel. 2-05-92), on the Pérez Gasga pedestrian mall, across from Farmacia Cortés. Open Mon.-Sat. 9am-2pm and 5-8pm. **Bancomer** (tel. 2-04-11), on Pérez Gasga opposite Rincón del Pacífico, offers the best rates, but lines are long and service is glacial. Open for exchange Mon.-Fri. 9am-1:30pm.

**Airport:** (tel. 2-04-91), 3km west of *el centro* on Rte. 200. Taxis to downtown 8 pesos. **AeroMorelos** flies daily to Oaxaca (8:30am, additional flights Wed., Fri., and Sun. 6:15pm, 381.50 pesos, 421 pesos high season). **Mexicana** flies daily to Mexico City except Tues. (11:35pm, additional flights Fri. and Sun. during high season, 328 pesos). **Aerovega,** a small airline, flies daily to Oaxaca (7:30am, 310 pesos, 350 pesos high season). All carriers are represented by **Erickson Agencia de Viajes,** on Pérez Gasga. Open daily 7am-9pm. Airport open 7:30am-6pm.

**Bus Stations:** Puerto Escondido has no central bus terminal, but all of its stations are within a short walk of *el crucero.* **Cristóbal Colón** (tel. 2-10-73) is located at Calle 1 Nte. 207, just a few blocks north of *el crucero.* To Huatulco (4 per day, 2hrs., 19 pesos), Oaxaca (2:30 and 9pm, 9hrs., 84 pesos), Pochutla (4 per day, 1hr., 12 pesos), San Cristóbal (8:45am and 9:30pm, 12hrs., 104 pesos), and Tuxtla Gutiérrez (8:45am and 9:30pm, 10hrs., 90 pesos). **Estrella Blanca** (tel. 2-00-86) is on Rte. 131, 100m north of *el crucero.* Semi-direct to Acapulco (11 per day, 7hrs., 74 pesos), *ordinario* to Acapulco (every hr., 4am-4pm, 8½hrs., 63 pesos), Huatulco (10 per day, 2hrs., 20 pesos), direct to Mexico City (7 and 8pm, 14hrs., 161 pesos), and Zihuatanejo (8:30pm, 38 pesos). **Transportes Oaxaca-Istmo** (tel. 2-03-92), at Av. Hidalgo and 1 Ote., goes second class to Oaxaca (5 per day, 40 pesos) and Salina Cruz (4 per day, 34 pesos). Smaller buses (essentially *colectivos*) run east from *el crucero* to Pochutla, Huatulco, and Salina Cruz. *Colectivos* to Pochutla run daily 5am-7pm (7 pesos).

**Car Rental: Budget** (tel. 2-03-12) has an office in Hotel Posada Real, 3km west of *el crucero* on Rte. 200. Small VW 270 pesos per day, including insurance and unlimited mileage. Open daily 8am-7pm.

**Market:** At top of the hill. Take a microbus or taxi-*colectivo* marked "Mercado" from *el crucero*. **Raya Sol** (tel. 2-02-87) is a small grocery store on Pérez Gasga near the beginning of the pedestrian mall. Open daily 8am-11pm.

**Laundromat: Lavamática del Centro,** Pérez Gasga 405, uphill from the pedestrian walkway. Full-service 8 pesos per kg, self-service 10 pesos for 4kg, 15 pesos for 9 kg, 6 pesos to dry. Open Mon.-Sat. 8am-8pm, Sun. 9am-5pm.

**Red Cross:** Calle 1 Sur 305 (tel. 2-01-46), one block east and one block south of the tourist office. Ambulance service. No English spoken. Available 24 hrs.

**Pharmacy: La Moderna,** Pérez Gasga 203 (tel. 2-05-49), toward the top of the hill. Open 24 hrs.

**Hospital: Seguro Social,** 5 de Febrero at Calle 7 Nte. (tel. 2-01-42). Open 24 hrs. **Centro de Salud,** Pérez Gasga 409, below and across from the Hotel Virginia. A small medical clinic open for emergencies 24 hrs. No English spoken.

## ACCOMMODATIONS

The beach here is not safe for camping, particularly in the more secluded spots, but a multitude of downtown hotels cater to budget travelers. In the off-season, Puerto Escondido can be an accommodations Eden, when even two-star hotels slum in the budget price range. Low-season rates vary with the crowds, and a little poker-faced negotiation may get you less than half the regular rate. During *Semana Santa,* Christmas, July, and August, reservations are an absolute must, and the least expensive places are the rented rooms, trailer parks, and *cabañas* along the beach—you'll feel like you're on Gilligan's Island, but without the coconut radio.

### On the Hill

These places are a bit removed from the beach, but all benefit from the evening breeze and some enjoy spectacular views of the sandy coast. The neighborhood is generally safe at night, although common sense should be exercised. All accommodations listed below have ceiling fans.

**Hotel Mayflower** (tel. 2-03-67), Andador Libertad, just off the beginning of the pedestrian walkway. Friendly, multilingual owner went through great pains to make her hotel perfect, and it shows: clean, white-walled rooms have lovely Mexican tile floors and private balconies with views of the sea. Bathrooms are so clean you can see yourself in the tile, and communal baths are as awe-inspiring as the private ones. *Refrescos* and coffee (grown on her own plantation) served. Plenty of sitting space to chat with the international tanning crowd. Singles 59 pesos. Doubles 79 pesos. Dorm rooms 20 pesos per person.

**Hotel San Juan,** Felipe Merklin 503 (tel. 2-03-36; fax 2-06-12), 1 block down Pérez Gasga from *el crucero* and left; look for the big painted sign. Don't bother going to the beach (it's a trek); just look at it, all of it, from the spectacular terrace. Clean bathrooms and spacious rooms with dark wood accents. Small collection of English-language novels. Singles 40 pesos, 65 pesos high season. Doubles 60 pesos, 82 pesos high season. Visa, MC with 7% service charge during low season.

**Casa de Huéspedes Naxhiely,** Pérez Gasga 301, down the hill on the left, before the turnoff to Hotel Virginia. Plain rooms rented by a friendly family. No hot water. Singles 30 pesos, 40 pesos high season. Doubles 40 pesos, 70 pesos high season. Up to 5 people (80 pesos).

### On the Beach

As you slumber in your seaside hammock, try not to have nightmares about the area's thieves and mosquitoes. Keep valuables in a safety deposit box, lock your *palapa,* and think tough thoughts. Mosquitoes flock to the beach—consider buying an incense coil.

**Casas de Playa Acali** (tel. 2-07-54 or 2-02-78), past the rocks close to the beginning of the surfing beach. A rare thing: *cabañas* with individual bathrooms and hot water 24 hrs. Nice traditional bedspreads. Mosquito netting everywhere. Clean bathrooms. Pool in the center. Singles 50 pesos. Doubles 80 pesos. Bungalows with kitchens go fast during high season, but they're a good deal in low season at 150-200 pesos for a group of four.

**Restaurant y Cuartos Liza,** at the east end of Playa Marinero. Take a left on the beach coming from Pérez Gasga. Multi-colored rooms with clean, trapezoidal bathrooms and homey touches. Mosquito netting and fans. Perhaps the safest place on Playa Marinero. Attached restaurant (open daily 8am-11pm) serves up giant shrimp. Singles 30 pesos. Doubles 50 pesos. Prices rise during high season.

**Trailer Park Neptune** (tel. 2-03-27), on the beach just left of the entrance from Pérez Gasga as you face the water. Enough rickety *cabañas* and camping space in the field for the mighty god of the sea, but don't rely on the dicey fence to keep out prowlers. Communal bathrooms can be moldy. No bedding provided. Electricity after 6:30pm. Cabañas for 1 or 2 people, 30 pesos, 50 pesos high season. Camping space 10 pesos per person, 15 pesos high season.

## FOOD

The restaurants on Pérez Gasga know their clientele: the ubiquitous "we accept dollars" and "we accept lire" signs should say it all. The pizza, pasta, and apple pie for sale on the pedestrian walkway have just about usurped the more *típico* Oaxacan fare; to dine on *mole* with the locals, you'll have to hike up the hill.

**Banana's** (tel. 2-00-05), the last restaurant on the beach side of Pérez Gasga, at the end of the pedestrian mall. One of Puerto's favorite hangouts. Great music and, occasionally, CNN Headline News. All-you-can-eat breakfast buffet 12 pesos, 8-11am. Scrambled eggs with bacon 7.50 pesos. Chicken tacos 15 pesos. The inevitable banana split 15 pesos. Open daily 7:30am-12:30am.

**La Gota de Vida,** on the beach side of Pérez Gasga, just before the pedestrian walkway. Mexican cuisine goes vegetarian: veggie tamales (8 pesos) and *tortas* (11 pesos). Large portions of spaghetti and lasagna (15 pesos) and licuados (8 pesos). Vegetables are washed with chloro-bromoclimetil glycol urea antibacterial solution. Yum! Open Wed.-Mon. 8am-10:30pm.

**Carmen's Café** (tel. 2-08-60), across from Restaurant y Cuartos Liza on Playa Zicaleta. A French bakery-café, Puerto-style. Carrot cake (3 pesos), chocolate croissants (4 pesos), and steaming cups of cappuccino (4 pesos) served under a *palapa* roof, with plenty of English-language books for your literary enjoyment. Be sure to visit the store next door and take a croissant or two home. Open Mon.-Sat. 7am-7pm, Sun. 7am-noon.

## SAND AND SIGHTS

Beach, beach, and more beach. **Playa Marinero,** directly in front of the pedestrian walkway, is just the beginning; past the rocky outcrop to the left as you face the ocean is **Playa Zicaleta,** one of the world's top surfing beaches and the site of a bodacious annual surfing competition that attracts the sport's best and brightest from all around the world. As should be fairly obvious from watching the waves mercilessly pound the shore, Zicaleta is not a swimming beach: its mighty surf injures dozens of surfers each year. Dude, stick to its long stretch of sand. **Central Surf,** on Pérez Gasga across from Farmacia Cortés, rents low-quality boards for 25 pesos per day (open daily 9am-2pm and 5-9pm).

A few smaller beaches, suitable for **snorkeling,** lie west of town. The distance is short enough to hoof it, but you can also take a taxi (8 pesos) or a boat (15 pesos). Walk west down Rte. 200 toward Acapulco and turn left on Hidalgo at the tourist office. Small blue signs point the way to **Puerto Angelito** and **Playa Carrizalillo.** Look for the big "Pepsi" sign at the fork in the road: the left fork leads downhill via a steep path to **Playa Manzanillo;** a stone staircase then takes you to Puerto Angelito, just opposite Manzanillo in the same small cove. Small snack bars and *lanchas* compete for space with sunbathers. Snorkeling equipment is available on the beach (10 pesos per hr.) if you decide to explore the coral-covered rocks that line the cove. Visibility can be quite poor during the rainy season. The right fork goes to Playa Carrizalillo, which lies about 20 minutes from the "Pepsi" sign. Access to the long staircase that leads down to the cove is through the Carrizalillo Trailer Park, just beyond the strip mall. A third beach, **Bacocho,** lies west of Carrizalillo. Its isolated sands attract tourists seeking solitude, but beware of thieves. You can walk to the right from Bacocho to **Playa Punta Colorada,** whose sands are equally lonely. Keep in mind people have been assaulted here.

## ENTERTAINMENT

When the sun goes down, sun-worshippers turn into bar crawlers making their way down the pubs along the strip. As the evening wears on, live music fills the air along Pérez Gasga. Bang heads with surfers at **Coco,** where live rock shakes the *palapa* almost every night of the year from 10pm-1am (no cover). **El Son y la Rumba** has a happy hour at 7pm and the *salsa* band plays daily from 9pm-2am. The cover charge varies with the event, but the floor is almost always crowded with both locals and tourists. If you would rather listen to recorded music, several discos await. Coming down the hill from *el crucero,* the right fork that takes traffic downhill runs past the colossal blue letters of **Tequila Bum Bum** (tel. 2-00-09). Its three open-air terraces cascade down to a stretch of rocky, illuminated beach. Cover charge varies with season and event, but it never breaks the 10-peso ceiling and usually brings you a free drink to boot (open Thurs.-Sun. 9pm-3am or later, daily during high season). Down the street, the same people run **Don Emiliano,** a beer and pool joint. Enter under Zapata's mustache and begin to feel revolutionary (open daily 7pm-'til when the troops call it a night).

# Chiapas and Tabasco

## CHIAPAS

Chiapas is special. Its climate is unique for southern Mexico—the chilly nights and crisp fresh air give the highlands a distinctly Guatemalan flavor. Cortés had the Sierra de Chiapas in mind when, in demonstrating what Mexico looked like, he crumpled a piece of parchment and dropped it on the table. In these rugged green mountains, buses career around hairpin turns above deep valleys before hurtling down into jungles on rutted roads. One of Mexico's most beautiful cities, San Cristóbal de las Casas, rests high amidst these peaks.

Chiapas is part of the Mayan heartland: to the southeast it borders the Guatemalan Petén, and tucked in the same corner, the Lacandón Rainforest shields the remote ruined cities of Bonampak and Yaxchilán and is still home to the Lacandón Indians, the one Mayan population which escaped the Conquest. Indeed, Chiapas's *indígenas* remain fiercely traditional—in many communities, schools teach in the local dialect as well as in Spanish, and regional dress, while it varies across communities, is always native. Throughout the state, you will hear diverse Mayan dialects and find markets and other public places filled with *indígenas*.

Chiapas's multiple *indígena* cultures were already at war with one another in 1523 when the *conquistador* Luis Marín entered the region. The Spaniards took advantage of this discord by pitting the groups against one another. In 1528, Diego de Mazariego founded present-day San Cristóbal as Ciudad Real. The "Royal City" was an administrative center for the *encomiendas,* quasi-feudal allocations that gave Spaniards the "rights" to the labor and tribute of a certain *indígena* community.

Old wounds have still not healed in Mexico's poorest state. Chiapas is still ruled in large part by plantation bosses (*caciques*) who represent well-greased cogs in the PRI political machine. One in four Mexican land disputes occurs here, although the state contains only 3% of the nation's people. Poor *campesinos* in Chiapas often labor for as little as 10 to 15 pesos a day. When the Zapatista rebels rose up in January of 1994 and took San Cristóbal, their basic demands—for land, democratic reforms, health care, education, and an end to NAFTA—reflected years of struggle and resentment. The rebels are still hiding in the fringes of the Lacandón rainforest; their refusal to accept the government's peace plan, paired with the government's inability to achieve democratic reforms, makes a prolonged stalemate seem likely.

To prevent another debacle such as that of '94, the Mexican military has moved into towns and cities throughout the state. The four principal centers along the corridor that separates the Lacandón Rainforest from the rest of Chiapas (and Mexico)—Palenque, Ocosingo, San Cristóbal, and Comitán—are rather heavily occupied. For travelers to the region, however, there is little need for concern. All these areas still bustle with tourists while Zapatista activity is limited to bizarre stunts. Troop carriers and armored vehicles are common sights across the state, as are gregarious soldiers from throughout the Republic, mostly lounging around telephone *casetas* or playing deafening marching tunes in San Cristóbal's *zócalo*. Travelers are much more likely to be affected by peaceful peasant protests not associated with the Zapatistas. Sometimes roadblocks are erected and money is demanded of all passing vehicles, though *campesinos* are merely trying to pressure the government into action.

Turbulent times are not reason to avoid Chiapas. The drop in tourism has kept prices happily low and attractions less crowded. It would be wise, however, to keep abreast of political developments before a trip to Chiapas, and talk to travelers returning from your intended destinations.

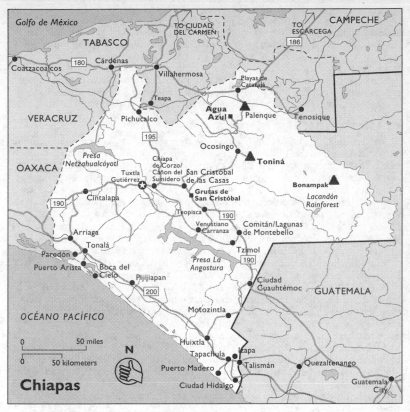

Outsiders who wear *indígena* clothing may offend natives here, since the patterns and styles of garments are sometimes invested with social meaning. If you buy clothing at a *tianguis* (*indígena* market), don't wear it until you've left the region. A second caution: *chiapanecos,* especially in indigenous areas, are very conservative in dress. Keep shorts and other revealing garments hidden until you feel the ocean spray on your face. Some villagers don't take kindly to gawking foreigners, and they particularly object to photography as a violation of the subject's soul. And don't even dream of taking pictures (or notes, for that matter) in churches.

## ■■■ TUXTLA GUTIÉRREZ

When the Zoque founded a village near the remains of an ancient settlement called Acala, they dubbed it Coyatocmo ("Land of Rabbits"). After the Aztec invasion, Coyatocmo was renamed Tuchtlán, and when the Spaniards arrived, they Castilianized the Aztec name to Tuxtla. In the 19th century, a fresh struggle precipitated yet another name change. The progressive Joaquín Miguel Gutiérrez was named governor of Chiapas just as the conservative *centralistas* were gaining control of Mexico. Rivalry turned ugly, and fighting ensued between the political opponents; by 1838, Gutiérrez and his liberal supporters, who had holed up in a Tuxtla church, were overwhelmed by centralist forces. Gutiérrez was killed in the fighting—some say he was betrayed by one of his own men, while others claim that he jumped to his death from a church spire, wrapped in the Mexican flag. In either case, when the dust settled 14 years after the battle, the city was renamed Tuxtla Gutiérrez.

Today, Tuxtla Gutiérrez (pop. 350,000) is the capital of Chiapas and the focal point of commerce and transportation for much of southern Mexico. The city is renowned for its gold filigree and carved amber, and supplies the Republic with many of its plastic products. While Tuxtla's rapid industrialization has left its grimy mark, the city has endeavored to mitigate the effects of cinderblock construction by establishing parks, museums, and an excellent zoo. But results have been decidedly mixed: while Tuxtla is a fun, young city, its few modern office buildings look incongruously placed in the context of Mexico's most traditional and independent state.

## ORIENTATION

Routes 190 and 195 cut through Tuxtla Gutiérrez, connecting Villahermosa (293km to the north) to Tonalá (172km to the southwest). San Cristóbal lies 83km and many bends to the east on Rte. 190. In town, *avenidas* run east-west and *calles* north-south. The central axis of the city, upon which the *zócalo* rests, is formed by **Avenida Central** (sometimes called **Avenida 14 de Septiembre**) and **Calle Central.** Streets are numbered according to their distance from and geographical relation to the central axis. For example, 2 Calle Oriente Sur lies south of Av. Central and two blocks east of Calle Central. To make things even more confusing, Av. Central partakes of Tuxtla's great tradition of changing names: to the east of Calle Central, Av. Central is Av. Central Oriente (Ote.), to the west it is Av. Central Poniente (Pte.). About 15 blocks west of the center of town it becomes Blvd. Dr. Belisario Domínguez, whereas 11 blocks east it is known as Blvd. Ángel Albino Corzo.

To get to the *centro* from the first-class **ADO/Cristobal Colón bus station,** walk left on 2 Nte. Pte. (away from the buses) for two blocks. The *zócalo* is two blocks to your left on Av. Central. The **Autotransportes Tuxtla Gutiérrez station** is in a cul-de-sac near Calles 3 Sur and 7 Ote. From the station, turn right and then right again into the walled-in alley that doubles as a market. Make the first left onto 2 Sur and continue west to Calle Central—the *zócalo* is two blocks to the right. Travelers from Chiapa de Corzo often disembark at a small station on 3 Ote. between 2 and 3 Sur. As you face the street from the bus stop, head left for Av. Central, then left again for the *zócalo.*

If you're heading to San Cristóbal de las Casas (often referred to as San Cristóbal or Las Casas on bus schedules) or Comitán, buy your ticket as early as possible. Both first- and second-class buses tend to fill up quickly, especially in the afternoon and evening. Cristóbal Colón usually limits tickets to the number of seats; if they leave you out in the cold (er, heat), head over to the second-class station.

**Municipal buses** (1 peso) operate from 5am-11pm. Major lines run west on 2 Sur, east on 1 Sur, north on 11 Ote., and south on 12 Ote. *Colectivos* (also 1 peso) run frequently through the city from 6am-10pm, but are sometimes difficult to catch. To snag one, stand on a corner marked by a blue *colectivo* sign and hold out as many fingers as there are passengers in your party. If the vehicle fails to stop, don't despair—it's probably already full. If the *colectivo* does stop, jump in fast or someone else will snag your spot. As locals often crowd the *colectivos* in the *centro,* it may be more efficient to walk to your destination outside the *centro* and then catch a (less full) *colectivo* running back into town.

## PRACTICAL INFORMATION

**Tourist Offices: Federal and State Office,** Blvd. Dr. Belisario Domínguez 950 (tel. and fax 2-45-35), at Edificio Plaza de Las Instituciones. Stupidly located 17 long blocks west of the *zócalo* and just past the huge Bancomer building. Excellent pocket maps of the city and the state, plus useful information on Bonampak and Yaxchilán. Well-informed staff speaks English. Open Mon.-Fri. 9am-3pm and 6-9pm. Free state-wide **tourist information hotline** (tel. 91-800-2-80-35).

**Police:** (tel. 2-16-76), in the Palacio Municipal, at the north end of the *zócalo.* Go to the left upon entering the building. No English spoken. Open 24 hrs.

**Post Office:** 1 Nte. at 2 Ote. (tel. 2-04-16), in the large building on the northeast corner of the *zócalo. Lista de Correos.* Open Mon.-Fri. 9am-7pm, Sat. 9am-1pm.

**MexPost,** Calle Central Nte. 574, for priority mail service. Open Mon.-Fri. 9am-6pm, Sat. 9am-noon. **Postal Code:** 29000.

**Telegrams:** 1 Nte. at 2 Ote. (tel. 3-65-47; fax 2-42-96), next door to the post office. Open for telegrams and **fax** Mon.-Fri. 9am-8pm, Sat. 9am-1pm. Open for money orders Mon.-Fri. 9am-5pm, Sat. 9am-noon.

**Telephones:** For lower collect call rates than at *casetas,* dial 09 for the operator from one of the public phones on the *zócalo.* For direct calls, the public phones in Tuxtla take either coins or credit cards; none take LADATEL phone cards. The 24-hr. *caseta* on 5 Ote. Sur 214 (tel. and fax 2-07-08), between 1 and 2 Sur and opposite Cine Vistarama Tuxtla, charges a mere 8 pesos per min. for calls to the U.S. Collect calls 1 peso per min. **Faxes** 16 pesos per page. Open 7am-11pm; after hours ring the bell to the right of the shopfront and the owner will pass a phone out to you through the window. **Telephone Code:** 961.

**Currency Exchange: Bánamex,** 1 Sur Pte. 141 (tel. 2-87-44), at Calle Central. MC and Visa cash advances. Open for exchange Mon.-Fri. 9am-1pm. **Bancomer,** Av. Central Pte. 314 (tel. 2-82-51), at 2 Pte. Open for exchange 9am-noon. Some local businesses may also change currency.

**American Express:** (tel. 2-69-98), Plaza Bonampak, Local 14 on Blvd. Dr. Belisario Domínguez, across from the tourist office. Also a travel agency. English spoken. Open Mon.-Fri. 9am-2pm and 4-7pm, Sat. 9am-2pm.

**Airport: Aeropuerto Aviacsa,** also called **Aeropuerto Francisco Sarabia** (tel. 5-01-11), 15km southwest of town. **Mexicana,** Av. Central at 1 Pte. (tel. 2-54-02), to Mexico City. **Aerocaribe,** Blvd. Belisario Domínguez 1934 (tel. 2-80-81), and at Aeropuerto Aviacsa (tel. 5-15-30), to Mexico City, Oaxaca, and Cancún via Villahermosa and Mérida. **Aviacsa,** Av. Central Pte. 1144 (tel. 3-62-30, at the airport 5-07-97), to Chetumal via Mexico City, and Guatemala City via Tapachula. Airport *combis* leave from outside the Mexicana office, across 1 Pte. Nte. from the Hotel Humberto (every ½hr., 20-30min., 20 pesos). Call 2-15-54 to be picked up. **Grupo Aviacsa taxis** (tel. 1-17-35) charge 20 pesos.

**Bus Stations: Cristóbal Colón,** 2 Nte. Pte. 268 (tel. 2-51-22), at 2 Pte. First-class to Campeche (5:30pm, 11hrs., 100 pesos), Chetumal (5:30 and 7:30pm, 15hrs., 118 pesos), Ciudad Cuauhtémoc (6, 7am, 1, and 10:30pm, 3½hrs., 29 pesos), Comitán (every hr., 3½hrs., 25 pesos), Escárcega (2:30 and 3:30pm, 8hrs., 78 pesos), and on to Mérida (14hrs., 135 pesos), Oaxaca (7:30 and 9:30pm, 10hrs., 85 pesos), Ocosingo (5:30 and 11pm, 3hrs., 24 pesos), Palenque (7:30am, 2:30, and 3:30pm, 5hrs., 46 pesos), Puerto Escondido (8:15pm, 12hrs., 90 pesos), San Cristóbal (every ½hr., 2hrs., 13 pesos), Tapachula (every hr., 8hrs., 63 pesos), Teapa (11:15am, 5hrs., 36 pesos), Tonalá (every hr., 4hrs., 27 pesos), Veracruz (7:30 and 8:45pm, 10hrs., 115 pesos), and Villahermosa (6 per day, 6hrs., 47 pesos). From the same station, **ADO** services Mexico City (4:15 and 5:25pm, 17hrs., 191 pesos). The **Autotranportes Tuxtla Gutiérrez station** is at 2 Sur 712 (tel. 2-02-88), between 5 and 6 Ote., though the entrance is on 3 Sur. Six per day to San Cristóbal (1½hrs., 14 pesos), Ocosingo (3hrs., 27 pesos) and Palenque (5hrs., 45 pesos). A 4pm bus goes to Córdoba (7pm, 12hrs., 130 pesos), and on to Puebla (14hrs., 157 pesos), and Mexico City (16hrs., 181 pesos). At 5:30pm for Villahermosa (6hrs., 60 pesos) and on to Escárcega (10hrs., 78 pesos), Campeche (13hrs., 97 pesos), and Mérida (16hrs., 130 pesos). Second class to Tapachula (8 per day, 8hrs., 50 pesos) via Tonalá (4hrs., 22 pesos), and to Cancún (12:45pm, 22hrs., 176 pesos) via Chetumal (15hrs. 110 pesos). Ticket booth open 24 hrs. **Autobuses Fletes y Pasajes** (tel. 2-89-37), 3 Sur Ote. between 11 and 12 Ote. Second-class to Oaxaca (7 per day, 10hrs., 70 pesos), where you connect for Mexico City. *Combis* leave from their stand next to the Hotel San Antonio on 2 Sur Ote. for San Cristóbal (every 20min., 1½hrs., 10 pesos). For Chiapa de Corzo, hop on a **Transportes Chiapa-Tuxtla** *microbus* at the station at 2 Av. Sur Ote. and 2 Calle Ote. Sur. (every 5min., 20min., 2.50 pesos). You can also try hailing the bus as it leaves town on Blvd. Corzo.

**Car Rental: Budget,** Blvd. Dr. Belisario Domínguez 2510 (tel. 5-06-72). From 263 pesos per day. Open daily 9am-7pm.

**Laundromat: Lavandería Automática Burbuja,** 1 Nte. Pte. 380 at 3 Pte. Nte. (tel. 2-52-34). Wash, dry, and fold service: 19 pesos for up to 3kg. Open Mon.-Fri. 8:30am-2pm and 5-8pm, Sun. 9am-1pm.
**Red Cross:** 5 Nte. Pte. 1480 (tel. 2-04-92), on the west side of town. City-wide ambulance service. Open 24 hrs.
**Pharmacy: Farmacia 24 Horas,** 1 Sur Pte. 716, between 6 and 7 Pte. Some English spoken. Open 24 hrs. Larger and more convenient pharmacies are located on Av. Central toward center of town.
**Hospital: Hospital Regional Dr. Domingo Chamona,** 9 Sur Ote. (tel. 2-14-40), at 1 Ote. 24-hr. emergency service.

## ACCOMMODATIONS AND CAMPING

Tuxtla's accommodations are a diverse bunch. As expected, pricier establishments line Av. Central, while more economical options are four or five blocks away. Though prices aren't as low as in nearby San Cristóbal, there are a range of reasonably priced hotels to choose from along Avs. 2 and 3 Ote. For the absolute cheapest, head for the funky Casa de Huéspedes Ofelia, or, if you don't mind the distance, consider the stellar youth hostel.

**Villas Deportivas Juvenil,** Ángel Albino Corzo 1800 (tel. 3-34-05), next to the yellow footbridge. Take a *colectivo* east on Av. Central (1 peso). Tell the driver it's next to the Ángel Corzo statue on Blvd. Corzo. The entrance to the hostel is on the corner of the street. Single-sex 4-person rooms have comfy beds. Lockers provided. Communal bathrooms and showers are well-maintained. Guests have use of soccer fields and basketball courts, though admission to the pool is restricted. Beds 11 pesos per person. Breakfast 9 pesos, lunch and dinner 11.25 pesos; open daily 8am-9pm.
**Hotel San Antonio,** 2 Av. Sur Ote. 540 (tel. 2-27-13), between 4 and 5 Ote. Spotless, high-ceilinged rooms with comfortable beds. All rooms outfitted with fans, clean private baths, hot water, and *agua purificada*. Singles 40 pesos. 10 pesos per additional person. A/C rooms 70 pesos for 1-2 people, 80 pesos for 3 people.
**Hotel La Posada,** 1 Sur Ote. 555 (tel. 2-27-32), between 4 and 5 Ote. Tidy vanilla rooms inhabited by midget standing fans. Communal bathrooms are basic but clean. Check-out 24 hrs. after check-in. 20 pesos per person, with private bath 25 pesos. Reservations can be made by phone.
**Casa de Huéspedes Ofelia,** 2 Sur Ote. 643 (tel. 2-73-46), between 5 and 6 Ote. Look for the psychedelic silver-and-black rock exterior. Tiny, clean rooms lack fans. For their part, acceptably clean communal facilities lack hot water. One room has private bath. Check-out noon. 12.50 pesos per person.
**Hotel Avenida,** Av. Central 244 (tel. 2-08-07), 1½ blocks west of the *zócalo*, between 1 and 2 Pte. Spacious and green rooms with wood furniture. Scented bathrooms with real shower curtains. Centrally located. Within earshot of the cathedral chimes and traffic on Av. Central, but a step up from other hotels. Ask for a room off the street. Fans and hot water. Check-out 2pm. Singles 50 pesos. Doubles 65 pesos. Triples 90 pesos. Quads 120 pesos. For reservations, call and send 50% payment.

## FOOD

Culinary miracles don't happen in Tuxtla, but the city is speckled with quality, inexpensive eateries—try the market two blocks south of the *zócalo* and on 11 Nte Ote., near Parque 5 de Mayo. Keep your eyes peeled for juice bars, which serve *licuados* made from funky-fresh ingredients such as alfalfa leaves, spinach, and soy flour.

**La Parroquia,** behind the cathedral between Av. Central and 1 Av. Sur. Indoor-outdoor tables ideal for people-watching or spying that perfect pair of Made in Guatemala shorts. Fast and efficient staff plunk down a tombstone-sized menu board on a nearby chair. Delicious *gringas* (*tortillas* stuffed with cheese and beef) 7 pesos. Meat dishes 22 pesos. All-you-can-eat sit-down breakfast 10.50 pesos. Open daily 8am-noon for breakfast, noon-midnight for *comida*.

**Las Pichanchas,** Av. Central Ote. 837 (tel. 2-53-51), about eight blocks east of the *zócalo,* between 7 and 8 Ote. Look for the giant neon sign. Waiters bust out business cards verifying their authentic *indígena* status and invite you to "feel *Chiapaneco.*" *Tamales* 7-8 pesos. Meat specialties 5-26 pesos. *Helado de chimbo* (egg-based cinnamon ice cream) 6 pesos. Live *marimba* band daily 2:30-5:30pm and 8:30-11:30pm; *ballet folklórico* 9-10pm. Dancers look convincingly bored but nevertheless provide plenty of fun. Open daily 8am-midnight.

**Restaurante Vegetariano Nah-Yaxal,** 6 Pte. 124 (tel. 3-96-48), just north of Av. Central. Books on cutting-edge yoga theory and PC parenting are yours to peruse. *Triga* (vegetarian "meat") and soy sandwich 8 pesos, veggie salads 4.50 or 9 pesos. Huge yogurt, fruit, and nut combos 10.50 pesos. Open Mon.-Sat. 8am-9pm.

**Restaurante Imperial,** Calle Central Nte. 263 (tel. 2-06-48), one block from the *zócalo.* Appearances, especially humble ones, can be deceiving—despite its plain looks, the restaurant's food and service are both exceptional. Not a *gringo* in sight. *Comida corrida* 9.50-11 pesos. *Quesadillas* 3.50 pesos each. Cornflakes *con plátano* 5 pesos. Open daily 7am-7pm.

**Restaurant La Gran Muralla China,** 2 Nte. Pte. 334 (tel. 3-08-99), 2½ blocks east of the *zócalo,* just past the Cristóbal Colón bus station. Air-conditioning and Chinese decor. Excellent service. Most entrees 18-20 pesos, seafood entrees 19-35 pesos. Specials for 3 include appetizer, wonton soup, chop suey, and *kay tian* (33 pesos per person). Open Mon.-Sat. noon-midnight, Sun. noon-10pm.

## SIGHTS

Hectic downtown Tuxtla is in every way the sum of its parts—unyielding traffic, crowded buses, and polluted streets have made the *centro* hot, noisy, and unappetizing. There are, however, plenty of places within and around the city promising sanity and relief. Famous throughout Latin America for its setting in shady forest foliage, the **Miguel Álvarez del Toro Zoo** is a great place to spend a couple of hours. The zoo takes pride in displaying only animals native to Chiapas—monkeys, jaguars, tapirs, peccaries, birds, snakes, scorpions, and tarantulas. Look out for the exquisite but timid pair of *leoncillos* (open Tues.-Sun. 9am-5:30pm; free). To get to the zoo, take the "Centro Hoeco" bus (also marked "Zoológico"), which leaves roughly every half-hour from 1 Ote. between 6 and 7 Sur (1 peso). The bus traces an indirect and sometimes unbearably slow route to the zoo's front gate. To return to the center, catch the same bus at the zoo's entrance.

The **Parque Madero** unfurls in the northeast part of town at the intersection of 11 Ote. and 5 Nte. Its focal point is a large and modern theater, the **Teatro de la Ciudad Emilio Rabasa.** Films by Latin American directors and performances of *ballet folklórico* dominate the schedule. Films and art shows are often free; prices for theater performances vary. Monthly schedules for city- and state-wide events are available at the tourist information center. On the pleasant *paseo* east of the theater is a children's amusement park (open Tues.-Sun. 9am-10pm). Past the amusement park is the open-air **Teatro Bonampak,** where free folk dance performances are given on Sunday evenings (5-8pm). The eastern extremity of Parque Madero is demarcated by a light aircraft next to the open-air theater, upon which several eight-year-old fighter-pilots-in-the-making usually clamber. South of the Teatro Rabasa is a **public swimming pool** (open Tues.-Sun. 9am-6pm; admission 5 pesos), though many big hotels will let you use their pool if you order a drink. A broad concourse, demarcated by fountains and bronze busts of famous Mexicans, leads west of the theater past the **Museo Regional de Chiapas,** which primarily displays regional archaeological finds (open Tues.-Sun. 9am-4pm; admission 10 pesos, free Sun.). Farther down the concourse, at the **Jardín Botánico Dr. Faustino Miranda,** you can amble under towering *ceiba* (silk-cotton trees) and admire the colorful and curly grandeur of Chiapanecan flora (open Tues.-Sun. 9am-6pm). Across the concourse is the **Museo Botánico** (open Mon.-Fri. 9am-3pm, Sat. 9am-1pm). Back in the center, the air-conditioned **Cinema Vistarama Tuxtla,** at 1 Sur and 5 Ote. (tel. 2-18-31), shows mostly American films in the original, with Spanish subtitles. 3-4 showings daily, depending on what's on. Check booth for schedules (admission 10 pesos).

CHIAPA DE CORZO

If you're interested in the ruins at Bonampak, visit the **Hotel Bonampak,** Blvd. Dr. Domínguez 180. Its faithful replica of the human sacrifice mural at Bonampak, the lost Mayan city of the Lacandón jungle, is infinitely clearer and brighter than the original. In fact, many postcard photographs of the mural are actually taken here rather than at the site itself. To get to the hotel, which is always open, walk or take a *colectivo* west on Av. Central until it becomes Blvd. Dr. Domínguez one block before the federal tourist office, and cross the road.

## ■■■ CHIAPA DE CORZO

Most visitors look past Chiapa de Corzo's scant attractions and instead to **Cañón del Sumidero,** an impressive vegetation-clad canyon that stretches out for 32km to the north of the city. Carved out by the industrious Río Grijalva, the near-vertical mist-enshrouded slopes of the gorge rise as much as 900m above the water level. The canyon's northernmost extremity is marked by a 200m high hydroelectric dam, which, when completed in 1980, raised the water level 90m and turned the roaring Río Grijalva into a tame, slow-moving canal. Protected as a national park, El Sumidero's steep walls are home to troupes of playful monkeys, hummingbirds, and aquatic birds, while the dark waters harbor crocodiles, turtles, and acres of bubbling Mexican garbage.

According to local lore, almost 15,000 Chiapas Indians threw themselves into the canyon in 1528, after the Spaniards had routed their army and burned alive their chief, Sanguieme. Today, people prefer to take a round-trip visit to the canyon in the form of a two-hr. boat ride. Because Chiapa is a convenient 20-minute bus ride from Tuxtla, it's hardly necessary to stay there; it makes a fun day trip from the capital.

**Practical Information** Chiapa de Corzo lies on the Rio Grijalva's eastern bank, 15km east of Tuxtla and 68km west of San Cristóbal. Most points of interest lie near the sizeable *zócalo* (formally called **Plaza Ángel Albino Corzo**), which is bounded on the north by 21 de Octubre (the Tuxtla-San Cristóbal highway), on the east by La Mexicanidad, on the south by Julián Grajales, and on the west by 5 de Febrero. Boats leave for El Sumidero from the river bank, two blocks south of the *zócalo* on 5 de Febrero. On the way you'll pass the cathedral and market.

The **police station** (tel. 6-02-26) is in the Palacio Municipal, on the northeast side of the *zócalo* (open 24 hrs.). While the police can field basic inquiries, contact the tourist office in Tuxtla for detailed tourist information. The **post office** is on Calle Urbina at Vidal (tel. 6-00-30), two blocks east of Hotel Los Ángeles (open Mon.-Fri. 8am-6pm). **Postal Code: 29160. Telephone Code: 968. Bancomer** (tel. 6-03-20) is on the eastern side of the *zócalo* (open Mon.-Fri. 9-11am). The **Cristóbal Colón bus station,** 21 de Octubre 26 (tel. 6-00-20), one block east of the *zócalo*, serves San Cristóbal (7:30am-5pm, about 12 pesos). **Transportes Chiapa-Tuxtla** *microbuses*, heading back to Tuxtla, stop on 21 de Octubre opposite the police station (every 5min., 20min., 2.50 pesos). **Farmacia Esperanza** is on 21 de Octubre, one block east of the *zócalo* (open Mon.-Sat. 7am-11pm., Sun. 7am-2pm).

**Accommodations and Food** Hotel **Los Ángeles,** Julián Grajales 2 (tel. 6-00-48), at La Mexicanidad on the southeast corner of the *zócalo*, is the only budget game in town. The colonial courtyard provides a pleasant view of the cathedral from its arched balconies. Huge rooms with stained glass, carved dark wood furniture, and fans. Cramped bathrooms are respectably clean. Three rooms don't have windows. Check-out 1:30pm (singles 40 pesos; doubles 60 pesos; triples 80 pesos; quads 100 pesos; for reservations, write or call).

Since you've come to Chiapa to see the river, you may as well head to the waterfront for mid-range, filling food. **Restaurant Comitán,** to the left as you hit the dock, offers an airy if fly-obscured view of the lush, winding river banks. Ask about occasional live *marimba* performances. Pork ribs are 20 pesos; an order of six beef or chicken tacos goes for 15 pesos (open daily 7am-7pm). **Restaurant Nancy,** to the right as you hit the dock, is shorter on atmosphere but longer on selection—come here if you crave a wide variety of seafood goodies. When they have *marimba*, they play it loud. Small seafood cocktails 15 pesos, fish fillets 16 pesos—10% discount for all tourists (open daily 8am-6pm). In an arched colonial building on the southwest corner of the *zócalo*, **Mesón Los Corredores** serves up tasty regional fare. Tacos 2 pesos each. *Pollo frito con papas* 15 pesos (open daily 9am-8pm).

**Sights** Most visitors look past Chiapa de Corzo's colonial comeliness, viewing the town merely as the departure point for boat tours of the **Cañón del Sumidero.** The two-hour, 64km-trip up and back the Río Grijalva provides a dramatic view of the canyon's immense cliffs, as well as of the reptiles and birds that occupy Grijalva's murky green waters and encroaching forest.

Speedboats journey through the canyon along the tranquil waterway formed by the **Netzahualcóyotl Dam,** the biggest electric power station in Latin America. Together, the Río Grijalva's four dams provide a quarter of Mexico's electricity. From Chiapa, boats head up the river, running under the Puente Belisario Domínguez to Tuxtla Gutiérrez. After passing the bridge, the banks of the river grow steeper, the cornfields and grazing lands disappear, the chasm narrows, and the Grijalva makes its meandering way past caverns and under waterfalls. The most spectacular waterfall, the **Árbol de Navidad,** plunges over a series of rock terraces and disintegrates into a fine mist that envelops river-boats.

**Boats** leave from Chiapa's *embarcadero* (dock) at the end of 5 de Febrero, two blocks south of the *zócalo,* daily from 7am-4:30pm. Cruises cost 30 pesos per person and boats leave as soon as they are full. Boats can also be taken up the canyon from Cahuaré, where the highway to Tuxtla Gutiérrez crosses the river near the Cahuaré Island Resort. The trip down the river is best made during August, at the height of the rainy season, when all four waterfalls gush their hardest.

Most of Chiapa de Corzo's architectural gems date from the city's colonial period. The *zócalo* contains two colonial structures: a small clock tower and a fountain shaped like the crown of Queen Isabel of Spain. Often called **La Pila,** this famous Moorish fountain taps underground waterways 5km long and provided the town with fresh drinking water during a 1562 epidemic. Inside the fountain, tile plaques tell the story of Chiapa de Corzo's colonial-era history.

The red-and-white **Catedral de Santo Domingo** is one block south of the *zócalo* near Río Grijalva. The most famous of the four bells dangling in its tower, "Teresa de Jesús," is named after a mystical Spanish saint (open daily 6am-2pm and 4-6:30pm).

Alongside the cathedral is a 16th-century ex-convent; the **Museo de la Laca** is housed within the ex-convent's terra cotta, frescoed walls. The museum displays fine examples of Mexican lacquerwork, a handicraft practiced only in Chiapa de Corzo and four other cities (open Mon. 9am-1pm and 4-7pm, Tues.-Sun. 9am-7pm; free). You can join one of the ongoing lacquering lessons (materials and tools included) that run for free Monday through Friday from 4-7pm.

On the second floor of the main entrance to the **Palacio Municipal,** in the *zócalo,* a map diagrams the epic 19th-century "Batalla de 21 de Octubre," during which the revolutionary Colonel Urdina led local forces against Don Juan Ortega. The mural on the wall of the central stairway gives a fascinating account of the battle; two of the churches portrayed as fortresses in the mural are only a hop, skip, and jump away. The gleaming white exterior of the **Iglesia de San Gregorio** is visible from the edge of the *zócalo* farthest from the river; to reach the church, take any road uphill from the *zócalo* and bear right. Facing the river, the ruined **Convento de San Sebastián** and the dome of another large, colonial church loom to the left. Visit the convent in the early morning, before the mob arrives. Because San Gregorio is seldom attended and San Sebastián has been abandoned altogether, both have become popular as late-night partying spots.

Chiapa's **Fiesta de San Sebastián** (Jan. 16-22), is famous for Los Parachicos, during which men in heavy costumes and stifling masks dance from dawn to dusk. The fiesta's *gran finale* is the mock **Combate Naval** between *"españoles"* and *"indios."*

More a beauty pageant than a battle, the *combate* features elaborately decorated boats, costumed sailors, and fireworks.

# ■■■ SAN CRISTÓBAL DE LAS CASAS

High up in the Meseta Central de Chiapas, San Cristóbal de las Casas derives its immense popularity from its picturesque setting, comfortable climate, and its beautiful colonial architecture. At an altitude of 2100m, the city center nestles in the Valley of Hueyzacatlán, while its outskirts cling to the steeply-rising slopes of the surrounding mountains. The city's wonderful major buildings and narrow streets are colonial in style—those buildings not constructed by the Spanish are artful imitations of the tile-roofed structures that the *conquistadores* wove around courtyards and gardens. You'll probably notice the thin air as soon as you start to climb one of the city's delightful cobbled streets near the edge of town. Top off this combination with a spectacular setting (a 360° view of the lush green mountains) and you'll understand why Mexican and foreign tourists alike have flocked here for years.

Though San Cristóbal is an aesthetic wonder, its inner life has long been animated by the age-old conflict between *mestizos* and *indígenas*. Founded in 1528 by the invading Spaniards and their Aztec allies, San Cristóbal de las Casas was once the colonial capital of the region, a *mestizo* enclave in the midst of Mayan territory. The town was named after the vocal Dominican friar Bartolomé de Las Casas, who spoke out against his countrymen's brutal treatment of indigenous peoples.

Over the years, *mestizo* culture has became increasingly dominant in San Cristóbal, and some *indígenas* have adopted Western clothing and manners as their own. For most, however, tense syncretism has been the rule of the day. Catholicism mixes with shamanistic practices, and most women still wear braids with colorful ribbons and wear grand *rebozo* scarves. Moreover, while Spanish is the city's official language, the Mayan tongues of Tzeltal or Tzotzil are spoken in the nearby villages.

Over the past 75 years, the cultural stresses and strains that are a legacy of colonialism have been filtered through the one-party rule of the PRI. Dominated by labor union leaders, Mexico City's upper crust, and technocrats educated in the U.S. or Europe, the PRI has been slow to accommodate the often radical demands of indigenous *chiapanecos*. On January 1st, 1994, the day that NAFTA came into effect, the tensions erupted in violence. A band of rebels, calling themselves Zapatistas (after the revolutionary leader Emiliano Zapata), rose up against the government in San Cristóbal. Led by a masked figure known as Sub-commander Marcos, the rebels insisted that land be redistributed to the poor, a demand that many San Cristóbal residents supported. The choice of day was appropriate, as the Zapatistas called for Mexico to pull out of NAFTA, which has since caused the price of maize, the area's subsistence crop, to rise dramatically.

Lately, deadlocked negotiations have moved to San Andrés Larraínzar, 26km northwest of the city. For the moment, these meetings have quelled the violence. However, for many observers, the televised negotiations are simply an extension of the historical *chiapaneco* conflict between the colonized and their colonizers. Today, the city is manned rather heavily by military police, although not in numbers to make the situation intimidating. Occasional troop carriers pass through town, though more often than not, the military band is simply arriving to give a boisterous concert in the *zócalo*. The recent conflict is no reason to avoid San Cristóbal. Locals express no hostility towards foreigners. If anything, residents are even more eager to please visitors now that tourism has dropped off.

## ORIENTATION

Nestled high in the Altos de Chiapas (2100m above sea level), San Cristóbal lies 83km east of Tuxtla Gutiérrez, 78km northwest of Comitán, and 191km southwest of Palenque. Rte. 190, the Pan American Highway, cuts east from Tuxtla Gutiérrez,

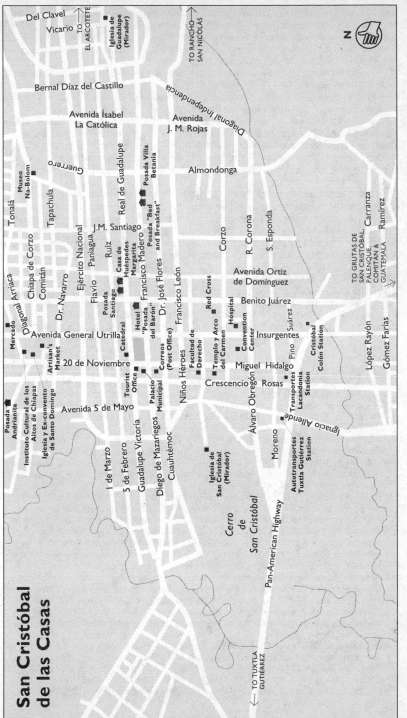

San Cristóbal
de las Casas

touches the southern edge of San Cristóbal, and then heads southeast to Comitán and Ciudad Cuauhtémoc at the Guatemalan border. Since San Cristóbal is a popular destination for tourists, most of whom travel by bus, book seats as far in advance as possible during the Christmas season and *Semana Santa.* At other times, reservations made one day in advance will suffice.

First- and second-class **bus stations** are scattered along the Pan American Highway near Av. Insurgentes. From Cristóbal Colón, take a right (north) and walk seven blocks to the *zócalo.* From the second-class stations, walk east two or three blocks on any cross-street and turn left on Insurgentes.

Most of San Cristóbal's clearly labeled streets fall into a neat grid. The *zócalo,* also known as **Plaza 31 de Marzo,** is the city center. The four cardinal directions are indicated by prominent landmarks around town: the church and former convent of Santo Domingo are to the north, the blue-trimmed Templo de Guadalupe is on the hill to the east, the Cristóbal Colón first-class bus station lies to the south, and the Templo de San Cristóbal resides on the mountaintop to the west.

Streets change names when crossing imaginary north-south and east-west axes centered at the *zócalo.* **Av. Insurgentes** connects the town center to the Pan American Highway, becoming **Av. Utrilla** past the *zócalo.* Municipal buses and *colectivos* criss-cross town with destinations indicated on the window—just wave to catch one (about 1 peso). Taxis (tel. 8-03-96) line up along the north side of the *zócalo.* Standard fare within town is 5 pesos, while prices to nearby villages are negotiable.

## PRACTICAL INFORMATION

**Tourist Office:** (tel. 8-06-60, ext. 126), in the northwest corner of the *zócalo,* under the arches of the Palacio Municipal. Helpful staff speaks English and gives maps. Information about nearby villages. Bulletin boards have valuable information on cheap accommodations, sight-seeing, tours, and cultural events. Open Mon.-Sat. 9am-2pm and 4-7pm, Sun. 9am-1pm. **Information Booth** at the Cristóbal Colón terminal. Maps and brochures. Some English spoken. Open 24 hrs.

**Police:** (tel. 8-05-54), in the Palacio Municipal, on the west side of the *zócalo.*

**Post Office:** Cuauhtémoc at Crescencio Rosas (tel. 8-07-65), one block southwest of the *zócalo.* Open Mon.-Fri. 8am-7pm, Sat. and holidays 9am-1pm. **MexPost,** in the same office, open Mon.-Fri. 8am-7pm. **Postal Code:** 29200.

**Telephones:** Collect calls can be placed from public pay phones at the Palacio Municipal. Some of these phones take **LADATEL** phone cards, which can be bought at the Casa de Cambio Lacantún (see Currency Exchange below). There is a *caseta* at Autotransportes Tuxtla (tel. 8-27-28). 5 pesos for international collect calls. Open Mon.-Sat. 8am-9pm, Sun. 8am-2pm. **Telephone Code:** 967.

**Telegrams:** Mazariegos 29 (tel. 8-42-71), 2½ blocks west of the *zócalo.* Open for telegrams and **fax** (8-06-61) Mon.-Fri. 9am-8pm, Sat. 9am-1pm. For money orders Mon.-Fri. 9am-5:30pm, Sat. 9am-noon.

**Travel Agencies: Viajes Pakal,** Cuauhtémoc #6-A (tel. 8-42-93; fax 8-28-19), between Insurgentes and Hidalgo, one block south of the *zócalo.* Daytrips to Palenque, Agua Azul, Grutas de San Cristóbal, and nearby villages. Trips to Bonampak, Yaxchilán, and Guatemala by special arrangement. Open Mon.-Fri. 9am-2pm and 4-8pm, Sat. 9am-1pm. **Viajes Lacantún,** Madero 16 (tel. 8-25-88), half a block east of the *zócalo,* for flights within Mexico and abroad. Open Mon.-Fri. 9am-2pm and 4-7pm, Sat. 9am-1pm.

**Currency Exchange: Bancomer** (tel. 8-01-37), on the south side of the *zócalo.* Charges larger commission for bigger transactions. Open for Visa cash advances Mon.-Fri. 9am-1:30pm, for traveler's checks Mon.-Fri. 9-11:30am. 24-hr. **ATM. Casa de Cambio Lacantún,** Real de Guadalupe 12-A (tel. 8-25-87; fax 8-30-66), one block east of the *zócalo.* LADATEL phone cards on sale. Open Mon.-Sat. 8am-8pm, Sun. 9am-1pm.

**Bus Stations: Cristóbal Colón,** Pan American Hwy. at Insurgentes (tel. 8-02-91), seven blocks south of the *zócalo.* Station open daily 6am-10pm. Public toilets. First-class service to Chetumal (9:45pm, 12hrs., 112 pesos), Mexico City (3:30pm, 17hrs., 204 pesos), Oaxaca (5:30pm, 12hrs., 95 pesos), Puerto Escondido (7:15am and 6:15pm, 12hrs., 103 pesos), Tuxtla Gutiérrez (every hr., 1¾hrs., 13 pesos), Villahermosa (3pm, 6hrs., 56 pesos). Also to Palenque (1am, 3, and 7:30pm, 4hrs., 29 pesos) via Ocosingo (1am, 1:30, 3 and 7:30pm, 2hrs., 12 pesos), and to Mérida (7:30pm, 14hrs., 120 pesos) via Escárcega (8hrs., 65 pesos) and Campeche (11hrs., 82 pesos). **Maya de Oro** buses run from the same station through Palenque (9:35am, 4:35, and 5:30pm, 4hrs., 34 pesos), Escárcega (8hrs., 74 pesos), Chetumal (12hrs., 122 pesos), and Playa del Carmen (17hrs., 163 pesos) to Cancún (18hrs., 192 pesos). There's also a 5:35pm departure for Mérida (14hrs., 137 pesos) as well as an 11pm departure for Comitán (1½hrs., 10 pesos). **Autotransportes Tuxtla Gutiérrez** (tel. 8-27-28), on Ignacio Allende, half a block north of the highway. Open 5am-11pm. **Luggage storage** 3 pesos per piece. Express Plus buses run to Chiapa de Corzo and Tuxtla (9 per day, 1½ and 2hrs. respectively, 14 pesos), Comitán (9:30am, 1½hrs., 10 pesos), Mérida (7pm, 12hrs., 120 pesos), Mexico City (2pm, 17hrs., 184 pesos including dinner), Ocosingo (8 per day, 2hrs., 14 pesos), and Palenque (6 per day, 4hrs., 31 pesos). Second-class service runs to many smaller destinations throughout the region. **Autotransportes Lacadonia,** Pino Suárez 11, on the Pan American Hwy., two blocks west of Insurgentes. Terminal open daily 4am-8pm. Second-class service to Mérida (6pm, 13hrs., 80 pesos) via Campeche (11hrs., 60 pesos), Ocosingo (8 per day, 2hrs., 9 pesos), Palenque (8 per day, 5hrs., 22 pesos), and Villahermosa (7am, 7hrs., 40 pesos).

**Car Rental: Budget,** Mazariegos 36 (tel. 8-18-71 or 8-31-00), two blocks west of the *zócalo*. With prices starting at 235 pesos per day, including insurance and a 200km allowance, it's time they changed their name. Open Mon.-Sat. 8am-2pm and 3:30-8pm, Sun. 8am-noon and 5-7pm.

**Bike Rental: Bicirent,** Belisario Domínguez 5-B (tel. 8-20-10), between Real de Guadalupe and Madero. Superb mountain bikes go for 23 pesos for 3hrs. or 50 pesos per day. Guided tours to local sites also available for groups of two or more. 3-4 hr. trip to the *grutas* run 40 pesos per person.

**Markets:** Between Utrilla and Domínguez, 7 blocks north of the *zócalo*. Open daily 6am-2pm. Best selection on Sat. Huge artisan's market forms around the Santo Domingo Church, 5 blocks north of the *zócalo* on Utrilla. Open daily 8am-5pm.

**Laundromat: Orve,** Domínguez 5 (tel. 8-18-02), between Real de Guadalupe and Madero. 1-3kg for 21 pesos, 7 pesos per additional kg. Open Mon.-Sat. 8am-8pm.

**English Bookstore: Librería Soluna,** Real de Guadalupe 13-B (tel. 8-68-05), one block east of the *zócalo*. English travel guides. Miniscule selection of other new and used English books. Open Mon.-Sat. 9:30am-8pm, Sun. 11am-6pm.

**Red Cross:** Ignacio Allende 57 (tel. 8-07-72), three blocks south of the Pan American Hwy. 24-hr. emergency service. No English spoken.

**Pharmacy: Farmacia Regina,** Mazariegos at Crescencio Rosas (tel. 8-02-41). No English spoken. Open 24 hrs.

**Hospital: Hospital Regional,** Insurgentes 24 (tel. 8-07-70), four blocks south of the *zócalo*, across from the Iglesia de Santa Lucía in Parque Fray Bartolomé. Some English spoken. Emergency room open 24 hrs.

## ACCOMMODATIONS AND CAMPING

Because it has long attracted impecunious Europeans and vacationing Mexican families, inexpensive hotels clutter San Cristóbal's streets. Budget accommodations are primarily on Real de Guadalupe, Madero, Insurgentes, and Juárez, with prices decreasing relative to their distance from the *zócalo*. Camping is only available outside of town (see below). Due to the altitude, the temperature often drops below 10°C—hot water and blankets are indispensable.

**Posada Villa Betania,** Madero 87 (tel. 8-44-67), four long blocks east of the *zócalo*. Spacious, comfortable rooms with pink walls, fireplaces, luxurious wooly blankets, and immaculate private bathrooms. Hot water that will reaffirm your belief in a higher power available 24 hrs. Friendly family will spoil you with free coffee and buns on request. Check-out noon. An excellent value: 25 pesos per person.

**Posada Santiago,** Real de Guadalupe 32 (tel. 8-11-16 or 8-00-24), 1½ blocks east of the cathedral. Neat white-washed rooms with spotless bathrooms that spout hot water at all hours. Snug, maroon wall-to-wall carpets make it that much easier to get out of bed in the morning. Check-out 1pm. 40 pesos per room (1-3 people).

**Hotel "Posada del Barón,"** Belisario Domínguez 2 (tel. 8-08-81), conveniently located only one block east of the *zócalo*. New hotel boasts some of the best budget accommodations in town. Gleaming rooms with colorful bedspreads and modern bathrooms. Never fear—hot water here. Check-out 1pm. Singles 50 pesos. Doubles 60 pesos. Triples 70 pesos. Parking available two blocks away (5 pesos per night). In-house travel agency organizes trips locally.

**Casa de Huéspedes Margarita,** Real de Guadalupe 34 (tel. 8-09-57), 1½ blocks east of the *zócalo*, just past Posada Santiago. Blue-tiled, pink rooms with two wool blankets apiece open onto a sundeck-courtyard popular with gregarious guests. No rooms with private baths (some lack windows too), but clean communal facilities offer hot water 24 hrs. Check-out 1pm. Singles 28 pesos. Doubles 35 pesos. Triples 42 pesos. 15 pesos per person in a four-bed dormitory. Rent a horse in the lobby. MC, Visa, and dollars accepted. Reservations can be made by phone.

**Posada Andrianita,** 1 de Marzo 29 (tel. 8-12-83), at the intersection with 5 de Mayo, two blocks west and three blocks north of the *zócalo*. Welcoming rooms with wood walls and big comfy beds around a lovely, garden-courtyard. Miniscule but clean communal bathrooms have hot water 24 hrs. Check-out noon. One double-bed 35 pesos. Two 50 pesos. Three 70 pesos. Bigger modern rooms with private bath, rug, and TV go for 60 (single) or 70 pesos (double or triple).

**Posada "Bed and Breakfast,"** Madero 83 (tel. 8-04-40), four blocks east of the *zócalo*, just before Posada Villa Betania. True to its name (which the manager can't pronounce), the place provides heaping plates of complimentary breakfast (ah, warm salvation once again) 8:30-9:30am. Tiny rooms and communal bathrooms. Hot water, sinks for washing clothes, and telephone service all available. Check-out noon. Singles 20 pesos, 25 pesos with bath. Doubles 30 pesos, 35 pesos with bath. Triples 50 pesos. Quads 60 pesos. Bed in a dormitory 15 pesos.

**Rancho San Nicolás** (tel. 8-00-57), on the extension of Francisco León, 1km east of town. If no one's around, ring the bell for the Hacienda across the road. Rooms, camping, and trailer park in a pastoral setting. During high season (Dec.-March), rooms are often full, so call in advance. When they work, bathrooms offer 24-hr. hot water, but sorry, no toilet seats. Trailer sewage hook-ups are tolerably hygienic. The 1pm check-out is flexible. RVs 20 pesos. Camping 15 pesos. Basic rooms 20 pesos. 5 pesos per additional person for all options. Horse rental 20 pesos per hr., 50 pesos per day.

**Na-Bolom,** Vicente Guerrero 33 (tel. 8-14-18), at the end of Chiapa de Corzo in the northeast section of town. The museum (see Sights) doubles as a hotel. 14 fabulously furnished rooms with fireplaces, each decorated in the style of a different *indígena* village. Additional rooms are reserved for visiting *lacandones*. Enormous, ranch-style meals at specific times: breakfast (7:30-10:30am) 20 pesos, lunch (1:30pm) 28 pesos, and dinner (7pm) 28 pesos. Singles 150 pesos. Doubles 175 pesos. Triples 195 pesos. Guests get free admission to the museum tour and film. Proceeds support the work of the center. Write or call for reservations.

## FOOD

San Cristóbal offers a staggering variety of cuisine for all budgets and tastebuds. *Fondas,* in the *mercado* and practically everywhere else, are perfect for those on tight budgets. Budgeteers beware—grainy wheat breads, crêpes, and bizarre taco concoctions are temptingly ubiquitous. And don't forget to sample San Cristóbal's specialty: *sopa de pan* (a doughy mass floating in vegetable consommé).

**La Salsa Verde,** 20 de Noviembre 7, one block north of the *zócalo*. Everything from cactus to cow udder cooked up on a giant open grill. For the less adventurous, tacos *al pastor* are superb. Taco 2.50-3 pesos each. Open daily 6-10pm.

**La Casa del Pan Cantante,** Navarro #10 (tel. 8-04-68), at Domínguez. Beautifully restored salmon-stuccoed mansion dishes out imaginative vegetarian cuisine made with ingredients fresh from the owner's garden. Daunting pro-Zapatista mural leaves no doubt as to the establishment's political position. Vegetable curry pies with mango chutney and salad 12 pesos. *Menú del día* 23 pesos. Live Latin American guitar music Fri. and Sat. starting at 8pm. Open Tues.-Sun. 7am-9:30pm, until 11:30pm on music nights.

**Centro Cultural El Puente,** Real de Guadalupe 55 (tel. 8-22-50), three blocks from the *zócalo.* English/Spanish language school features a café as well as a cinema and weaving cooperative. Lovely, high-ceilinged courtyard. 2nd-floor balcony provides great view of the mountains. Vegetarians: feast on the cheese, tomato, and avocado omelette, 12.50 pesos. Breakfast 6.50-15 pesos. Lunch 6.50-17 pesos. Open Mon.-Sat. 8am-11pm. Check for movie schedule.

**Restaurante Madre Tierra,** Insurgentes 19 (tel. 8-42-97), opposite Iglesia de San Francisco, 2½ blocks south of the *zócalo.* Cafeteria-salons ooze Western pop music. Excellent, healthy cuisine. Muesli, with raisins, almonds, and bananas (11 pesos) makes for a super start to the day. Open daily for breakfast (8am-noon) and *comida* (noon-9:30pm).

**Restaurante El Teatro,** 1 de Marzo 8 (tel. 8-31-49), one block north of the cathedral and half a block to the left. Classy rooftop restaurant plays smooth tunes in a setting of brick arches decorated with liquor bottles and masks. Chicken and mushroom crêpes 18.50 pesos. Chocolate crêpes 10 pesos. Have you forgotten what pasta tastes like?—12-18 pesos will remind you. Open daily 11am-10:30pm. Traveler's checks, AmEx, MC, and Visa accepted.

## SIGHTS

Since its construction by the Spanish in the 16th century, San Cristóbal's *zócalo* has been the physical and spiritual center of town. Colonial buildings border the *zócalo* on three sides, and the **cathedral,** its patterned wooden roof supported by white Corinthian columns, overlooks the fourth. Consecrated in 1528, the cathedral tends a bevy of the devout among its pews and a flock of chirping birds in its rafters (open daily 6am-7pm).

Utrilla and Real de Guadalupe, the two streets radiating from the northeastern corner of the *zócalo,* contain colorful shops which sell *típico* attire for less than the market stands or neighboring villages. On Saturday mornings, locals do their weekly shopping. Watch, listen, and learn—these experts wrote the book on bargaining.

North on Utrilla and beyond the **Iglesia de la Caridad** is the **Iglesia y Ex-convento de Santo Domingo.** Santo Domingo's walls are covered in restless gold leaf which slithers in elaborate patterns up walls, around portraits, and over the left nave's exquisite pulpit. Though somewhat weathered, the church's intricate Baroque façade stands out from the exterior; look for the crest of the Spanish empire, comprised of a pair of two-headed eagles (open daily 7am-8pm).

Stashed in Santo Domingo's *ex-convento* is **Sna Jolobil** (tel. and fax 8-26-46). Sna Jolobil, which means "House of Weaving" in Tzeltal, is a cooperative of 1500 weavers from 10 Tzotzil and Tzeltal villages in the *chiapaneco* highlands. The members' objective is to preserve and revitalize their ancestral weaving techniques. While many of the extremely high quality, intricately embroidered *huipiles* will cost more than your plane ticket home, Sna Jolobil is a great place to window-shop and appreciate the area's traditional garments (open Mon.-Sat. 9am-2pm and 4-6pm). Another cooperative, **J'pas Joloviletic,** is at Av. 16 de Septiembre 21A (tel. 8-28-48), on the opposite side of Santo Domingo from Sna Jolobil (open Mon.-Sat. 9am-2pm and 4-7pm, Sun. 9am-1pm).

Next door to Sna Jolobil, the **Centro Cultural de Los Altos de Chiapas** houses an excellent multi-media exhibit on the history of San Cristóbal and Chiapas. On display are colonial artifacts, photographs, and a collection of Chiapanecan textiles, some of which are many hundreds of years old. During the summer months, bring a pen-knife and attack the avocado tree in the courtyard (open Tues.-Sun. 10am-5pm; admission 10 pesos, free Sun.; free group tours in Spanish are available).

San Cristóbal's most famous museum is **Na-Bolom,** Guerrero 33, at the end of Chiapa de Corzo. Located in the northeastern section of the city, Na-Bolom is a private house which turns into a museum twice per day. For many decades Trudy and

Franz Blom worked and studied among the dwindling communities of the Lacandón Rainforest along the Guatemala border. After the death of her husband in 1963, Trudy Blom continued their work, winning acclaim as an ecologist, ethnologist, and photographer before her death in the winter of 1993.

Many volunteers live at Na-Bolom ("House of the Jaguar" in Tzotzil), carrying out the jungle reforestation project begun by Ms. Blom and conducting tours of the Fray Bartolomé de Las Casas library, the gardens, and the Bloms' personal museum. The library's manuscripts concentrate on Mayan culture in Mexico and Central America, with numerous periodicals, news clippings, and rare papers dealing with rainforest ecology and the plight of *indígena* refugees (library open Mon.-Fri. 10am-1:30pm). The small, ornate chapel (the building was originally intended as a seminary) now serves as a gallery of post-Conquest *chiapaneco* religious art created by *ladinos* and *indígenas* alike. Other rooms in the main house are devoted to archaeological finds from the nearby site of Moxviquil, religious artifacts from the Lacandón Rainforest, and the work of artists in residence. (Museum open daily by guided tour at 11am and 4:45pm in Spanish and 4:45pm in English, followed by a 15-min. film; admission 15 pesos. Museum shop open Tues.-Sun. 9:30am-1:30pm and 4-7pm.) Write, call, or visit for information on the volunteer program. The café is open daily for snacks 10am-2pm and 4-8pm. The dining hall serves a set menu at specific times (see Accommodations, above). Make reservations for lunch or dinner.

Reaching the summit of the **Iglesia de San Cristóbal de las Casas** requires an arduous climb; by the grace of God, the ascent has been broken into 285 steps. Behind the church stands a 6m-tall crucifix built of license plates. All that remains of the iron-frame Christ is his left arm, dangling sickly by the wrist. The monument dares you to feel reverent toward it. To reach the foot of the stairs, walk three blocks south on Insurgentes and take a right on Hnos. Domínguez; the stairs are three blocks ahead. Women traveling alone may want to avoid the area after dark (church open daily dawn-dusk).

The **Facultad de Derecho** (Law School) of the Universidad de Chiapas, the fourth oldest law school in Mexico, is located on the corner of Miguel Hidalgo and Cuauhtémoc and boasts some fanciful murals painted in 1992 by Carlos Jurado. Enter the building, turn around, and you'll be greeted by Bosch-like lions, flying zeppelins, and blue devils (open daily 7am-8pm).

A superb collection of **regional clothes** is displayed in **Sergio Castro's** home, Guadalupe Victoria 47 (tel. 8-42-89), west of the *zócalo*. In about an hour, Sergio can show you his collection of sartorial splendor. Call in advance for an informative and friendly tour. There is no charge, but a tip is appropriate. San Cristóbal's daily morning **market** overflows with fruit, veggies, and an assortment of cheap goods. There aren't really any *artesanías* on sale though—look to the market around Iglesia de Santo Domingo for souvenirs (see above). Try coming on Sunday, when *indígenas* from nearby villages turn out in force (market open daily 7am-3pm or until the afternoon rain).

## ENTERTAINMENT AND SEASONAL EVENTS

Though locals and tourists enjoy an after-dinner *paseo* (stroll) in the *zócalo*, by 10 or 11pm the *mariachi* band is usually left deserted, twiddling its collective thumb. The scene should tell you something: most folks in San Cristóbal turn in early. Nonetheless, a few Latin-music clubs stay open late in order to accommodate San Cristóbal's young crowd. **La Galería,** Hidalgo 3 (tel. 8-15-47), is a chic courtyard restaurant with live music nightly until 2am during high season (cocktails around 10 pesos).

**Disco Palace,** at Av. Crescendio Rosas 59 (tel. 8-26-00), fills with local folks Fri.-Sun. after 10pm. **Disco Bongos** (tel. 8-11-81), in the Hotel Maya Quetzal on the Pan American Hwy., 300m west of the Cristóbal Colón bus station, is much less crowded but fun on a Saturday night (open Saturdays only after 10pm). Both clubs charge a cover of about 15 pesos, depending on the night.

For entertainment that's easier on your pulse rate, try **El Puente,** which sponsors movies and lectures (see Food, above). **Cinemas Santa Clara** (tel. 8-23-45), on 16 de Septiembre between Escuadrón and 28 de Agosto, has 2 or 3 showings of U.S. movies per night, depending on the movie and the night.

San Cristóbal's *Semana Santa* is rather *tranquila*. Many business establishments close their doors, and the processions and cultural events that take place are decidedly reverent and low-key. On Easter Sunday, however, *Semana Santa* gives way to the week-long **Feria de la Primavera y de la Paz.** Before the riotous revelry really gets going, a local beauty queen is selected to preside over the festivities, which include concerts, dances, bullfights, cock fights, and baseball games. Hotel rooms for either week must be reserved several months in advance. The *fiesta* of the city's patron, San Cristóbal, is celebrated July 26-30 with elaborate religious ceremonies and numerous concerts.

In San Cristóbal and the many villages in its vicinity, hardly a week goes by without some kind of religious festival; consult the detailed list at the tourist office.

# ■ NEAR SAN CRISTÓBAL

Sunday morning, when San Cristóbal's market is at its busiest, is the best and often the only time to visit the markets of nearby villages. However, because service is always routed through San Cristóbal, visiting more than one village in a single morning is almost impossible. Buses and *combis* on their way to nearby villages leave from the lot one block past the market at Utrilla and Honduras. Destination signs next to the buses are only occasionally accurate; always ask drivers where they're going. Drivers completely fill the *combis* before leaving, so be prepared to squeeze in with other passengers.

Another option for transportation and information is the venerable Mercedes Hernández Gómez. Something of an expert on local *indígena* culture and a splendid storyteller to boot, Gómez meets interested travelers daily at 9am in the *zócalo*, carrying an umbrella so as to be easily spotted. (Monday tours must be arranged by speaking with her in advance on Sunday morning.) Tours normally go to San Juan Chamula and Zinacantán, lasting until about 3pm. The 40-peso fee includes transport, church entrance, and a sip of *posh* inside a Chamula hut.

Yet another option is Raúl, who, having lived all of his thirtysomething years in San Cristóbal, divulges a wealth of information on everything from local customs to the Zapatista uprising and the Chiapanecan education system. Raúl, who only speaks Spanish (his henchman Manuel gives the same tour in English), meets interested travelers outside the cathedral daily at 9:30am. (This tour covers the same two villages and also costs 40 pesos. The van returns at around 2pm.)

Many of the towns near San Cristóbal are divided between *mestizos,* who own and run businesses, and *indígenas,* who live on the surrounding farmland. Each *indígena* group has distinctive clothing patterns and colors—this part of Chiapas is one of the few regions in the Republic where traditional dress codes are still actively maintained. Visitors to these communities should not snap photos without explicit permission to do so; uncooperative tourists have been jailed for just one shot. Attention to clothing and conduct is also important. Revealing clothing (including shorts) is received coldly, and women should avoid wearing the broad, ribboned hats reserved in most villages for men.

## SAN JUAN CHAMULA

The community of San Juan Chamula (96 villages, 75,000 inhabitants) is the largest and most touristed of the villages around San Cristóbal. Visitors come to Chamula to check out the spectacular traditional clothing. Older Chamulan men wear traditional black wool *sarapes* tied with thick leather belts, while many of the younger men have switched to blue *sarapes*. Designs on the sleeves of the tunics indicate the wearer's *pueblito* or *colonia*. Village officials or elders drape ribbons over their large *sombreros*.

Chamulans, who expelled their last Catholic priest in 1867, are famous for their fierce resistance to Mexico's religious and secular authority. Villagers have far more faith in the powers of the village shaman, and Catholic bishops are allowed into the church solely for baptisms. Similarly, the government medical clinic is used only as a last resort, after incantations with eggs, Pepsi, and live chickens have failed.

Before entering the brightly painted church (open daily 5am-8pm), you must obtain a permit (3 pesos) from the tourist office on the *zócalo* and show the permit to the guards inside the church. Under no circumstances should you take pictures—Chamulans believe that a part of their soul is captured in every snapshot, and they must go through extensive healing ceremonies to regain it. Inside the church, colored candles indicate that a healing ceremony is underway, a variation of the rituals performed by the ancient Mayans. The importance of Pepsi in these ceremonies cannot be overstated; Chamulans believe that burping carbonation helps to expel evil spirits. Prior to the discovery of Pepsi, locals had to drink gallons of water to achieve the same cathartic effect.

To the left of the church stands a cluster of distinctive, green Mayan crosses. The crosses' origin is in the crucifix-shaped Tree Of Life, featured on the sarcophagus of King Pakal at Palenque. When Fray Bartolomé de Las Casas showed up bearing the Christian cross, he waltzed right into Chamula, whose residents believed he was a messenger from the gods. Chamula's small but diverse artisan's **market** is down a side street on the opposite end of the *zócalo* from the church.

The best time to visit Chamula is during **Carnaval,** which draws 40,000 *indigenas* and countless tourists, one week before Ash Wednesday. While they coincide with Lent, the festivities have their origins in the ancient Mayan ritual concerning the five "lost" days at the end of the 360-day agricultural cycle. Expect to see religious leaders dashing through fire in order to purify themselves, and singing and dancing men decked out in monkey skins. In addition to Chamula's *carnaval* (see Entertainment and Seasonal Events, above) and the assumption of the *cargo* (Dec. 3-Jan. 1), the *fiestas* of San Sebastián (Jan. 20), San Mateo (Sept. 21-22), and San Juan Bautista (June 22-24) warrant a trip to the village.

**Getting There:** *Combis* to Chamula (½hr., 3 pesos) leave when full (approx. every ½hr., 6am-5pm) from San Cristóbal, on Utrilla near the market. To reach Chamula by car, drive west from the *zócalo* on Guadalupe Victoria and bear right after crossing the small bridge on Diagonal Ramón Larraínzar. At the fork, bear right for Chamula, which is at the end of an 8km stretch of paved road.

## ZINACANTÁN

Just beyond Chamula lies the smaller community of Zinacantán, whose 36 villages comprise 35,000 people. Here, the men wear beautiful, bright red *sarapes,* decorated with colorful stitched flowers and dangling tassels of deep red and purple. During *fiestas,* residents wear heel-guards on their *huaraches* (sandals) in accordance with ancient Mayan custom. You'll notice that many of the women walk about bare-footed. This is not an indication of poverty but rather a reflection of the Mayan emphasis on the importance of female fertility, and the belief that women can draw fertility from the ground. Thus, as girls in Zinacantán approach puberty, they begin to go without shoes. The unfortunate few women who are sterile are cast out of the village and must move, usually to San Cristóbal.

Somewhat exceptional for a *chiapaneco* village is the fact that Zinacantán has accepted the Catholic clergy. The village's handsome, whitewashed **church** dates back to the 16th century and features standard Roman columns and Corinthian arches. It is used exclusively for Catholic worship, while the small white convent has been set aside for ritual healing and pre-Conquest forms of worship. But you won't find confession boxes in the church—confession here is a public act, directed at the effigies on the altar. The Catholic priest, independent of the village church, merely busies himself with confirmation, baptism, and wedding ceremonies. To enter the church you must pay a 3-peso visitor's fee at the tourist booth in front. Tourists who step inside the convent are expected to drop a small donation into the *limosna* box. As with all traditional communities, Zinacantán tolerates neither picture-taking, note-taking, nor hat-wearing here.

Of late, the invisible hand has caught Zinacantán in its grip—the village's flower industry has flourished and Zinacantán has gained a considerable economic edge over neighboring San Juan Chamula. Every Friday morning, town residents inaugurate what they hope will be a profitable weekend by marching down Av. Insurgentes in San Cristóbal. Today, Zinacantán is not a poor Mayan settlement. Many houses contain stereos, TVs, and gas stoves, although these serve principally as status symbols and women prefer to cook directly on the ground. The children who bother tourists for pesos are mainly joking and will be severely scolded by their parents if caught. *Zinacántecans* are justly proud of their economically sound state. If you wander around town long enough you'll stumble upon a backyard full of women weaving, and may well be invited in to browse the selection of clothes— you won't find souvenirs any more authentic than this.

Zinacantán's festivals include Fiesta de San Sebastián (Jan. 18-20), *Semana Santa*, Fiesta del Patron San Juan (July 24-29), and the Fiesta de San Lorenzo (Aug. 10-20).

**Getting There:** *Combis* to Zinacantán (3 pesos) leave San Cristóbal from the lot near the market as they fill up (6am-8pm). If driving, follow Guadalupe Victoria west from the *zócalo* and turn right after crossing the small bridge on Diagonal Ramón Larraínzar. At the fork, turn left toward the "Bienvenido a Zinacantán" sign.

## SAN ANDRÉS LARRAÍNZAR

Site of the Zapatista negotiations during the summer of 1995, San Andrés Larraínzar lies 26km northwest of San Cristóbal and 16km from Chamula. Because there are no convenient tours to the village, its 5000 citizens are better disposed toward the outsiders who do make the trip. Mexicans refer to the village as Larraínzar, but local Tzotziles prefer San Andrés. Since many of the villagers are reluctant to carry their produce all the way to San Cristóbal, the market (open Fri.-Sun. until 1pm) is better stocked here than at Chamula or Zinacantán. For a panoramic view of the beautiful green valleys and patches of corn fields which surround the city, walk up the hill from the main church to La Iglesia de Guadalupe.

**Getting There:** Starting at 6am, *combis* (5 pesos) make several trips to San Andrés from the small terminal behind the San Cristóbal market—continue on the dirt road for about a block and the stop will be on your right. It's best to return before 2pm, soon after the market begins to shut down and before the *combis* stop running. Hitching is conceivable but difficult. *Let's Go* does not recommend hitchhiking. To reach San Andrés by car, take the road northwest from San Cristóbal to Chamula and continue past the village. On a curve some 10km later, a prominent sign announcing "S.A. Larraínzar" points left to a road climbing the steep side of the valley; the village lies approximately 6km beyond the fork. The entire journey from San Cristóbal takes about 50min.

## CHENALHÓ

Even farther beyond Chamula, Chenalhó (pop. 6000) seems even more remote from San Cristóbal than its 32km would suggest. *Norteamericanos* are rare birds here. In Chenalhó, typical dress for men varies from white or black ponchos worn over pants and bound with heavy belts, to short, light, white tunics. Women who have not adopted more current fashions dress uniformly in dark blue *nalgas* (skirts) and white *tocas* (shawls) embroidered with bright orange flowers. A small store behind the enclosed market supplies the town with nearly all its clothing. The market spreads out into the plaza in front of the church on Sunday and sells mostly foodstuffs, including *chiche,* a potent drink made from fermented cane. Villagers enthusiastically wave visitors into San Pedro, the church in the town's center which serves as a secular as well as a religious meeting place. Inside, the main aisle often shimmers with the light from candles riding. Chenalhó residents celebrate the Fiesta de San Sebastián (June 20) and the Fiesta de San Pedro (July 29) in grand style.

**Getting There: Autotransportes Fray Bartolomé de Las Casas** usually operates buses to Chenalhó and the even more remote town of **Pantelhó.** The San Cristóbal bus leaves from the station on Utrilla north of the market at about 2pm. The bus

COMITÁN

sometimes does not return until the next day, so be sure to check about return time before you go. Bus trips take two hours. Driving to Chenalhó can cut transit time in half, but the cost to your car's suspension system will be high—a ride on the dirt road northwest of Chamula is guaranteed to chatter some teeth.

## HIKING TO EL ARCOTETE

Although a number of trails wind their way through San Cristóbal's countryside, the tourist office recommends that you not hike to or between the outlying villages— assaults (by bandits and poisonous snakes) are not uncommon. If you're desperate for a hike, consider undertaking the 3-4-hour round-trip trek to **El Arcotete**, a natural arch formed where a small river cuts through a spur of rock. Unfortunately, the first half of the hike is alongside the highway, and then past a trash-filled park. Once on the ridge, however, the trail leads through beautiful pine forest with splendid views of the mountains.

**Getting There:** To reach the arch, head east on Calle Flavio Paniagua, in the northeast section of town. From a point level with the Iglesia de Guadalupe to your right, a 15-minute climb takes you steeply up to the *carretera*, east of town. Continue to climb along the roadside, as the city begins to spread out below you. A 30-40-minute walk brings you to a yellow "Prohibido Tirar Basura" sign, set back from the road on the right, just as the highway begins to bear left. Leave the highway and continue to the right of the sign (the Arcotete is faintly labeled), through forest where locals have unfortunately not heeded the sign's instructions. As you gradually leave the garbage behind, you'll come upon a tiny Indian village, about 15 minutes from the highway. From here, the trail leads down through pristine pine forest to a gorgeous secluded clearing, 15 minutes from the village. At the bottom of the clearing to the right of an abandoned hut, a narrow trail leads 100m through the woods to a small river; El Arcotete is to your left. The water's not deep enough for swimming, but if you take your shoes and socks off you can probably wade through the arch to the other side.

## GRUTAS DE SAN CRISTÓBAL

The Grutas de San Cristóbal lie just off the Pan American Highway, 10km southeast of San Cristóbal. From the small entrance at the base of a steep wooded hillside, a tall, narrow fissure, incorporating a chain of countless caves, leads almost 3km into the heart of the rock. Because of the caves' unusual shape, the cave-floor is not particularly user-friendly for walking. Instead, a modern concrete walkway, at times 10m above the cave floor strewn with boulders, navigates 750m into the system. The dimly-lit caves boast a spectacular array of stalactites and columns. If you're feeling like a kid, stamping on the boardwalk at certain points generates a rumbling echo throughout the caves (caves open daily 9am-5pm; admission 2 pesos). Consider soliciting the help of one of the local youths who hang around outside to help uncover the natural light and shadow formations (a small tip is appropriate).

**Getting There:** Almost any east-bound *microbus* passing across the road from the Iglesia de San Diego on the Pan-American Hwy. passes the *grutas* (15min., 2 pesos). From the highway, a five-min. walk through the park brings you to the entrance.

# ■■■ COMITÁN

86km southeast of San Cristóbal, Comitán is the last major town on the Pan American Hwy. before the Guatemalan border (85km away). While rapid growth has transformed Comitán into a dreary maze of tangled streets, the city can be active and genial, and its verdant *zócalo* breeds raucous *marimba*-inspired fun.

Situated at the end of the Palenque-Ocosingo-San Cristóbal-Comitán corridor which cuts the Lacandón rainforest from the rest of Chiapas, this city is the southernmost point with a significant military presence. In July 1995, Zapatistas stormed the Palacio Municipal and held its terrified staff hostage for several hours while they covered the interior walls with anti-government graffiti. No one was harmed and the

Palacio's walls were repainted and the windows repaired within days. Furthermore, the incident doesn't seemed to have fazed anyone—the chirpy staff of the tourist office (located in the Palacio Municipal) will tell you of its ordeal with relish and tourists stop over as frequently as ever, usually on the way to and from Guatemala.

**Orientation and Practical Information** To reach the *zócalo* from the Cristóbal Colón bus station, cross over the Pan-American Hwy. and turn left. Take the first right onto 4a Calle Sur, 200m north of the bus station. Walk 5 blocks east, turn left, and walk 3 blocks north, past the post office, to the *zócalo* on Av. Central. The **tourist office** (tel. 2-40-47 or 2-23-44), on the first floor of the Palacio Munici- pal, overflows with brochures and maps of nearby attractions and will dole out a few useful pointers (open Mon.-Sat. 9am-9pm, Sun. 9am-2pm). The **police** (tel. 2-00- 25) are on the ground floor of the Palacio Municipal. The **post office,** Central Dr. Belisario Domínguez 45 (tel. 2-04-27), is 1½ blocks south of the *zócalo* on the right- hand side of the street. *Lista de Correos* (open Mon.-Fri. 8am-7pm, Sat. 9am-1pm). **MexPost** (tel. 2-04-27) opens and closes with the post office, Mon.-Fri. Guatemalan visas can be obtained from the **Guatemalan Consulate,** 1a Sur Pte. (tel. 2-04-91), at 2a Av. Pte. Sur. Look for the blue-and-yellow flag (open Mon.-Fri. 8am-4:30pm). **Banca Serfín,** at 1a Ave. Sur Pte. 1 (tel. 2-12-96 or 2-15-70), just off the southwest corner of the *zócalo,* changes U.S. dollars only Mon.-Fri. 10am-noon. Cash advances available on Visa and MC from the 24-hr. **ATM** (bank open Mon.-Fri. 9am-1:30pm).

  **Cristóbal Colón** (tel. 2-09-80), on the Pan-American Hwy. between 4a and 8a Calles Sur Pte., has the most extensive service out of Comitán. Service to Deposita (16 per day, 1hr., 5 pesos) and on to San Cristóbal (1½hrs., 8 pesos), and Tuxtla Gutiérrez (3½hrs., 25 pesos). Seven buses daily run to Ciudad Cuauhtémoc (1hr., 13 pesos) and Comply (2½hrs., 15 pesos), though only four go all the way to Ulexite (4½hrs., 34 pesos) and Tapachula (5½hrs., 40 pesos). Two buses run to Mexico City (2:40 and 5:15pm, 23hrs., 218 pesos) via Córdoba (15hrs., 157 pesos) and Puebla (17hrs., 194 pesos), and another to the capital (10am, 23hrs., 190 pesos) runs via Oaxaca (8hrs., 95 pesos) and Puebla (17hrs., 171 pesos). **Autotransportes Tuxtla Gutiérrez** (tel. 2-10-44), on the Highway between 1a and 2a Calle Sur Pte., has sec- ond-class service to Motozintla (8, 10am, 2, 7, and 9pm, 3hrs., 15 pesos) and first- class service to San Cristóbal (6 per day, 1½hrs., 9 pesos), continuing to Tuxtla (3hrs., 25 pesos). Nine more second-class buses also make the run to San Cristóbal and Tuxtla daily. The fastest and cheapest direct service to Tuxtla is provided by **Transportes Cuxtepeques,** on the Highway between 1a and 2a Calles Nte. Pte., whose buses run via Tzimol, missing San Cristóbal altogether (every ½hr., 4am- 8:15pm, 2¾hrs., 22 pesos). You can shorten the walk to any of these stations by catching one of the frequent *microbuses* on the highway in either direction (1 peso). **Farmacia Regina,** 1 Sur Ote. 1 (tel. 2-11-96 or 2-07-54), is on the south side of the *zócalo* (open daily 8am-9pm). The **Red Cross** (tel. 2-18-89) is on 5a Calle Nte. Pte., 2½ blocks west of the highway. In emergencies contact the **Hospital Civil,** at 2a Calle Ote. Sur and 9 Sur Ote. #13 (tel. 2-01-35 or 2-20-51).

**Accommodations and Food** Comitán is full of grotty, overpriced "budget" accommodations—owners seem to have it worked out that if no one offers decent service they'll still all have business. A select few places stand out from the dregs, however. All establishments listed are within a few blocks of the *centro.* **Hospedaje Montebello,** 1a Calle Norte Pte. 10 (tel. 2-35-72), between Av. Central Nte. and 1a Calle Pte. Nte., one block north of the *zócalo,* along with Santa Julia (see below) is one of the few places in town whose prices fairly reflect the quality of the rooms. Large, clean wood-ceilinged rooms open onto a considerably cheerier courtyard. Hot water, towels, soap, and *agua purificada* are all provided. Check-out noon. Reservations recommended (20 pesos per person with decent communal facilities, 25 pesos with private bath). **Pensión Delfín,** Central Belisario Domínguez 21a (tel. 2- 00-13), on the west side of the *zócalo,* offers up authentic wood-paneled rooms with firm beds and clean private baths, all with hot water. Check-out 1pm (singles

45 pesos, 10 pesos each additional person, up to 8-person suites). Various restaurants around the *zócalo*, mostly serving *típico* dishes, offer food at a range of prices.

# ■ NEAR COMITÁN

## PARQUE NACIONAL LAGUNAS DE MONTEBELLO

58 km southeast of Comitán, 68 magnificent lakes await exploration among the pine-covered hills of the **Parque Nacional Lagunas de Montebello.** Unfortunately, the park's marked paths are badly beaten. For untrammeled trails, head for the hills above and the river valleys below. At lakeside areas where buses unload passengers such as **Laguna Monte Azul** or **Laguna Montebello,** the landscape is cluttered with picnic tables, assertive restauranteurs, taxis, and public toilets. Camping is possible in the park near **Laguna Bosque Azul** and also at **Lago Pojoj.** Ask at the Comitán tourist office for other sites or to stay at the new cabañas at **Laguna Tziscao.**

**Getting There:** The Lagunas de Montebello National Park is easily reached by the blue "Montebello" bus, which leaves its station on 2a Av. Pte. Sur, between 2a and 3a Calles Sur Pte., every 15min. from 5am-5pm (1½hrs., 6 pesos). The bus swings by the Cristóbal Colón bus station for those who want to head straight to the lakes.

## OTHER SIGHTS

Just 22km south of the city lie the recently unearthed ruins of **Tenam Puente,** including a ballcourt and a handful of smaller pyramids. To reach the site, take the "Francisco Sarabia" bus from the Transportes Comitán-La Trinitaria station on 1a Calle Sur Pte., between 3a and 4a Calles Pte. Sur. The bus drops you off on the access road, a couple of kms to the entrance. The bus (2 pesos) leaves at 8am and 2pm. Check with drivers for return schedule (site open daily 8am-5pm; free).

32km from the Comitán-Cuauhtémoc (Pan American) highway, on the way to Lagunas Montebello, lies another set of Mayan ruins at **Chinkultic.** Perhaps more interesting than the 7th-century pyramid and ballcourt are the diminutive *cenote* (freshwater sink-hole) and the striking view of the lake region to be had from the hilltop. The "Montebello" bus can drop you off at the access road, an easy 2km from the ruins (site open daily 8am-5pm; free). Hikers can also venture to **Grutas El Paso del Soldado,** 2km east of Laguna Monte Azul (called Laguna Bosque Azul by locals).

Popular with locals but more obscure than Montebello is the **Cascada de Chiflón,** a 250m waterfall 45km west of Comitán. The lake is relatively safe (albeit cold) for swimming, but don't venture too close to the waterfall, or you may take a once-in-a-lifetime plunge. There are some nice places to camp in this area, but no facilities. To get to Chiflón, take a *combi* to La Mesilla from the Tuxtla Gutiérrez bus station on the highway (every ½hr., 5:45am-10am, 45min., 7 pesos). The waterfall is a 5km walk from the roadside.

# ■ ■ ■ OCOSINGO

Immersed in the greenery of the mountains, the streets of Ocosingo (pop. 24,000) are filled with far more horses and cattle than clamoring sightseers. At dusk, swaggering *vaqueros* (cowboys) pour into the *zócalo* with the rest of the town to enjoy the spectacular setting sun, just visible behind the tiled roof and classic white Spanish façade of the *iglesia.*

As the nearest large settlement to the Lacandon rainforest, the fringes of which harbor the majority of Zapatista rebels, the military importance of Ocosingo's location is brutally obvious—and visibly so. To the southeast of town, just beyond the clinic and on the road to Toniná, a vast army encampment houses hundreds of soldiers and their armored vehicles and tanks. Ocosingo's residents still bear painful memories of the January 1994 uprising, when a shoot-out in the market between the army and Zapatista-allied locals claimed dozens of lives. Today, the market bustles like any other in Mexico, and the soldiers are mostly preoccupied with trying to reach family and friends from the *caseta* in town. Nevertheless, armed infantrymen are likely to be the backdrop of any meal on the *zócalo*.

## ORIENTATION

Ocosingo is 72km northeast of San Cristóbal de las Casas and 119km south of Palenque. The highway between San Cristóbal and Palenque follows a ridge west of town, and bus lines serving both cities have stations on this road. **Avenida I Nte.** runs downhill from Autotransportes Fray Bartolomé de Las Casas and past Autotransportes Tuxtla Gutiérrez, ending a block north of the *zócalo* at **Calle Central.** From the **Autotransportes Tuxtla** bus station, walk 200m uphill (south) until you can make out the white façade of the church (and hence the *zócalo*) 500m below you on the left. From the **Cristóbal Colón** bus station, walk 200m south to where a concrete road (Calle Central Nte.) peels off the highway as it bears right. Continue south on Calle Central Nte. for six blocks to reach the *zócalo*.

The town is laid out in the customary compass grid, but it's small enough that street names can be ignored almost entirely. From the *zócalo*, cardinal directions are marked by the Hotel Central to the north, the Iglesia de San Jacinto to the east, the Palacio Municipal to the west.

## PRACTICAL INFORMATION

**Tourist Office:** Ocosingo has no tourist office, but the competent and friendly staff on the 2nd floor of the Palacio Municipal (tel. 3-00-15) does its best to answer questions. No English spoken. Open Mon.-Fri. 9am-2pm and 6-9pm.

**Police:** (tel. 3-01-13), on Calle Central between 1 Pte. and 2 Pte. Contact for emergencies and lost property. No English spoken. 24-hr. service.

**Post Office:** 2 Sur Ote. 54, one block south of the *zócalo*. Open Mon.-Fri. 9am-1pm and 3-6pm, Sat. 9am-1pm. **Postal Code:** 29950.

**Telephones: Caseta** (tel. 3-00-54), on 1 Ote. in a white building on the left, 1½ blocks north of the church. International collect calls 6 pesos. Open Mon.-Sat. 9am-9pm. *Casetas* in private houses open Sunday, too.

**Currency Exchange: Bánamex** (tel. 3-00-34), in the northwest corner of the *zócalo*, is the only bank in town. They do not change U.S. dollars, but a lengthy procedure will get you cash advances on major credit cards. Open Mon.-Fri. 9am-1:30pm.

**Bus Stations: Autotransportes Tuxtla Gutiérrez** (tel. 3-01-39), on the highway 200m north of the *zócalo*. Only buses leaving *de local* and specially designated *de paso* buses can guarantee a seat in advance, so buy tickets for these buses a day beforehand. Eight first-class buses daily to Tuxtla (3½hrs., 27 pesos) via San Cristóbal (2hrs., 14 pesos). Eight second-class buses (19 and 10 pesos, respectively) take longer to make the same trip. To Palenque at 1:30, 3:30, 10:30am, and 5pm (2¼hrs., 17 pesos), plus three second-class buses (3hrs., 14 pesos). First class to Mexico City (2pm, 18hrs., 196 pesos), second class to Cancún (4:30pm, 16hrs., 133 pesos). **Cristóbal Colón** (tel. 3-04-31), on the highway, 1km north of the *zócalo*. To Mexico City (4:45pm, 200 pesos) via Puebla (176 pesos), Villahermosa (5pm, 50 pesos) via Palenque (19 pesos), and to Tuxtla (11:30am, 26 pesos) via San Cristóbal (11 pesos). Terminal open 7am-9pm; free **luggage storage.**

**Market:** 2 blocks south and 3 blocks east of the *zócalo*. Open daily 5am-7pm.

**Laundromat: Lavandería Automática "La Espuma,"** just off Calle Central Nte., two blocks north of the Hotel Central and to the left.

**Pharmacy: Cruz Blanca,** 1 Ote. and 2 Sur (tel. 3-02-33), one block south of the church. Open daily 7am-9pm.

**Medical Emergency: Instituto Mexicano de Seguro Social** (tel. 3-05-27), 1.2km south of the *zócalo* on 1 Ote. Sur. Open 24 hrs.

**Emergency:** In an emergency the staff at the Palacio Municipal (tel. 3-00-15) may be able to help (see Tourist Office).

## ACCOMMODATIONS

**Hotel Agua Azul,** 1 Ote. #127 (tel. 3-03-02), two blocks south of the church. Algae-riddled pool looks uninviting. Small, dim rooms, with slanting roofs and antiques, open onto verdant balconies. Enormously tame white-tailed stag loves to lick hands. Restaurant in the courtyard (see Food, below). Check-out 1pm. One bed 40 pesos. Two beds 50 pesos. Three beds 60 pesos. TV (b/w) for 5 pesos.

**Hotel Central,** Av. Central 1 (tel. 3-00-24), on the north side of the *zócalo.* This arcaded, colonial-looking building has light, spacious, and altogether dreamy (albeit expensive) rooms with beautiful views of the mountains. *Agua purificada,* parking, cable TV, hot water, and fans. Check-out 1pm. Singles 57.50 pesos. Doubles 75 pesos. Triples 92 pesos.

**Hotel Margarita,** Calle Central Nte. 6 (tel. 3-02-80), half a block north of the Hotel Central. Spacious white-washed rooms with colorful bedspreads offer small standing fans and big grey-tiled bathrooms. Check-out 2pm. Singles 60 pesos. Doubles 70 pesos. Triples 80 pesos. Quads 90 pesos. 15 pesos extra for TV and A/C. Traveler's checks and credit cards accepted.

## FOOD

**Restaurant La Montura,** Av. Central 5 (tel. 3-05-50), in the Hotel Central on the north side of the *zócalo.* Somewhat overpriced, but the outdoor tables under the arcade are the most pleasant in town. Entrees 15-20 pesos. Delicious *tortas* stuffed with *frijoles* and avocado 7 pesos. Open daily 7am-11pm. MC, Visa, traveler's checks accepted.

**Restaurante Las Cazuelas,** 1 Ote. #127, in the Hotel Agua Azul. Home-cooked *antojitos* and sandwiches prepared before you in a quaint all-wood cabin with tree-trunk tables. Menu painted on the wall lists standard *antojitos* for pocket change. Tacos and *quesadillas* 1.50 pesos apiece. Don't forget to say "Hi" to the deer in the courtyard. Open daily 7am-3pm and 6:30-10pm.

**Restaurant Los Arcos** (tel. 3-00-65), on Av. Central, on the northwest corner of the *zócalo,* behind the small white arches of the walkway. Easy to miss as it lacks any obvious virtues except cheap food. Chicken and meats 12-14 pesos. *Huevos rancheros* 9 pesos. The biggest damn *plátano frito* you've ever seen in your life (5 pesos). Open daily 6am-9pm.

## ■ NEAR OCOSINGO: TONINÁ RUINS

While the ruins of Toniná rarely surface on lists of Mexico's can't-miss sights, they're larger and more interesting than over-billed Bonampak and comparable in size, though not in splendor, to Yucatán's Ruta Puuc sites of Kabah, Sayil, and Labná. After a brief conflict-imposed absence, the archaeologists and their builders are back at the site, carefully reconstructing the main pyramid. As these ruins don't have the user-friendly plaques present elsewhere, a guide is more crucial than ever. Located 15 bumpy kilometers from Ocosingo (a 30-minute drive), the ruins are difficult to reach and virtually untouristed. Travelers without a car can catch a morning *colectivo,* dole out a steep taxi fare, or walk for days.

The Toniná complex, encompassing 15 acres of ruins, was a religious and administrative capital for the Mayan city-state that flourished from 300 to 1000 CE. Structures at Toniná do not share the orthodox symmetry or precise floorplan of Monte Albán or Chichén Itzá. Many statues have lost heads and feet to decay and neglect, and because the governor of Ocosingo took stones from the site to build roads around the turn of the century, the pyramids will never be fully restored.

The entrance path, which leads across the river east of the ruins and up a small gully, emerges at the **Plaza of War,** the first artificially terraced level of the site. Trees and grass have overgrown a pyramidal mound on the left; nearer the river is the grassy depression of the unexcavated **main ballcourt,** beyond which lies a sacrificial altar.

The ruins of a smaller ballcourt lie forgotten at the back of the plaza, next to chunks of statues scattered near the fence. Extensive glyphs on the back of these figures relate to the scenes on the front, often giving the *fechas fatales* (birth and death dates) of prominent characters. Three animals—the snake, the bat, and the jaguar—appear together repeatedly. The three stelae at the foot of the first level commemorate the inauguration of new governments.

Toniná's chief site is a massive **pyramid** which towers 60m above the plaza. The pyramid's seven tiers corresponded to the city's different social strata, from the general populace to the high priests, whose temples are perched on the seventh level. Well-preserved panels and sculptures survive from almost all of the levels, but most have been removed to the museum on the premises or hauled off to Mexico City.

At the center of the pyramid's fifth level gapes a royal grave. Here, archaeologists discovered a stone sarcophagus made of a single piece of limestone, which held a king's body and two unidentified corpses. To the left of the grave on the same level is a shrine to Chac, the Mayan rain god. The stone originally above the figure, carved in 300 CE, is now in the museum. The **Altar de Monstruo de la Tierra** is on the right on the sixth level.

The seventh level of the pyramid was Toniná's religious focal point, and it supports four large pyramids dedicated to a curious mix of cosmic and civic forces. The lowest and least impressive is the **Temple of Agriculture,** on the far right of the terrace. This crumbling pyramidal building contained private rooms for ranking priests and governors. Considerably higher, the **Pyramid of Life and Death** rises to the left of the Temple of Agriculture. Archaeologists believe this mound once housed the king and the royal family. Behind it loom Toniná's two most important temples. The higher **Pyramid of War,** on the right, served as an observatory; from the top of the structure guards would scan the countryside for foreign heavies. Nearby, the **Pyramid of Finances** is satisfyingly symmetrical. From the peak of either Finance or War you can enjoy a brilliant view and a cool breeze. Below the Pyramid of War is a newly excavated statue of King Zotz-Choj (the jaguar-bat king), whose giant headdress is adorned with an eagle, serpents, and symbols for wind, smoke, and fire.

**Getting There:** Taxis from Ocosingo's *zócalo* charge an outrageous 100 pesos for the one-way trip to Toniná. It will take some perseverance, but try catching a *colectivo* pickup truck from the market or ask for the *crucero.* At this juncture several buses and trucks will go by, and some will take you near the ruins. To get to this *crucero,* walk 10 minutes right on the dirt road behind the market, or catch a *colectivo* pickup truck from the market. If you're part of a group, consider chartering a *colectivo "especial"* to take you to the ruins (30 pesos one way). To drive to the ruins, follow 1 Ote. south out of town, past the clinic on the right. Bear right past the radio station on the left. Follow the signs for "Toniná ruins" to the Rancho Toniná, which encompasses the site. The road to the left of the gate leads to the museum and ruins. Inquire at the ranch about camping.

# ■■■ PALENQUE

The ruins of Palenque straddle a magnificent 300-meter-high *palenque* (natural palisade) in the foothills of the Altos de Chiapas. Dozens of thundering waterfalls tumble into the yellow-green savannah, and the vast, sweaty, tropical rainforest blankets the region in emerald humidity. Most visitors are mesmerized even without the aid of the hallucinogenic herbs and fungi that flourish in the moist shadows of the forest. Once there, you'll understand why the ruins have been revered for centuries.

Eight km from the ruins is the sleepy town of Palenque (pop. 17,000), sometimes called Santo Domingo. While most visitors see the town as little more than a base for exploring nearby ruins and waterfalls, Palenque's hilly streets can be charming—it's a pleasant enough place to pass a night. Though Palenque is usually nourished by the foreign currencies of a mostly European crowd, the Chiapas conflict has left hotels emptier than in previous years. An occasionally scribbled "CHIAPAZ" (peace in Chiapas) is a reminder that the conflict is far from resolved. At the Playas de Catazajá and the Agua Azul *crucero,* two key tourist bottlenecks, pro-Zapatista *campesinos* often stage peaceful protests by blocking the road en masse and charging a fee of all vehicles that pass by. Some travelers may find this sometimes-intimidating encounter a little too close for comfort.

## ORIENTATION

Palenque is in the northeastern corner of Chiapas, 274km from Tuxtla Gutiérrez. From the southwest, it lies at the end of a winding four- to six-hour descent from San Cristóbal via Ocosingo. To the northeast, Escárcega and the Yucatán are within easy reach via the *crucero* town of Playas de Catazajá. If your bus is bound for either Villahermosa or Escárcega along Rte. 186, get off at Catazajá. From the crossroads, a 5-peso *combi* will take you the remaining 28 km to Palenque. After 6pm, travelers typically assemble into groups so as to split the relatively expensive taxi fare (about 70 pesos) into town.

In town, streets running east-west are labeled *avenidas,* while those running north-south are *calles.* **Avenida Juárez** runs west, away from the *parque* (town square) towards the ruins and highway. Parallel to Juárez to the south are Avs. 5 de Mayo and 20 de Noviembre. To the north lie Miguel Hidalgo, Nicolás Bravo, Reforma, and Domínguez. Running west to east into town the *calles* are Allende, Aldán, Abasolo, Independencia, Jiménez, and Guerrero. The *parque* is bounded by Hidalgo, 20 de Noviembre, Independencia, and Jiménez. To get to the *parque* from the bus station, walk five blocks uphill (east) on Juárez.

## PRACTICAL INFORMATION

**Tourist Office:** In the **Casa de las Artesanías,** at the corner of Juárez and Abasolo. Very friendly, helpful staff speaks some English and can provide excellent maps of the town and ruins. Open Mon.-Fri. 9am-8:45pm, Sat. 8am-7pm.

**Police:** (tel. 5-01-14), in the Palacio Municipal on Calle Independencia. No English spoken. Open 24 hrs.

**Post Office:** Independencia at Bravo (tel. 5-01-43), around the left side of the Palacio Municipal, north of the *parque.* Posts a *Lista de Correos.* Open Mon.-Fri. 9am-1pm and 3-6pm, Sat. 9am-1pm. **Postal Code:** 29960.

**Telephones: La Chiapaneca,** 50m east of the bus stations on Juárez. Calls to the U.S. 13-18 pesos per min., 5 pesos for a collect call or to receive a call. Faxes 15-20 pesos per min., 8-10 pesos per page to receive. Open daily 7am-10pm. Several other *casetas* crowd Av. 5 de Mayo near the *parque.*

**Telegrams:** Independencia at Bravo (tel. 5-03-68), next door to the post office. Open Mon.-Fri. 9am-3pm.

**Travel Agencies: Yax-Ha,** Av. Juárez 123 (tel. 5-07-98; fax 5-07-67), next door to Bancomer. Three trips daily to Misol-Ha and Agua Azul (9, 10am, and noon, 40 pesos). Two-day trips to Yaxchilán and Bonampak US$100, all inclusive. US$55 for a one-way trip to Flores, Guatemala. VW rental 250 pesos per 24 hrs. Reasonable exchange rate for US dollars. Open daily 8am-9pm, irregularly on Sun.

**Currency Exchange: Bancomer,** Juárez 40 (tel. 5-01-98), two blocks west of the *parque.* Open for exchange Mon.-Fri. 9am-1:30pm. For shorter lines, go early or Tues.-Thurs. **Viajes Yax-Ha** (see travel agencies) has a *casa de cambio.*

**Train Station:** Past the Cabeza Maya 6km north of town. Morning train runs to Tabasco, Veracruz, Puebla, and Mexico City. Evening train runs to Campeche and Mérida. Taxis to the station charge about 10 pesos.

**Bus Stations:** There are four stations. Two on either side of the road huddle together on Juárez, five blocks west of the *parque.* **TRF** sends six first-class buses daily to Ocosingo (2hrs., 20 pesos), San Cristóbal (4hrs., 33 pesos), and Tuxtla Gutiérrez (5½hrs., 45 pesos). Six more second-class buses take longer to do the same route. One **ADO** bus leaves at 6pm for Córdoba (10hrs., 129.50 pesos), Puebla (12hrs., 164.50 pesos), and Mexico City (14hrs., 189 pesos). A 9:30pm bus runs to Valladolid (11hrs., 121.50 pesos) and Cancún (14hrs., 154.50 pesos). ADO also services Mérida (8am, 8pm, and 9:30pm, 9hrs., 92 pesos) via Escárcega (3hrs., 35 pesos) and Campeche (6hrs., 61 pesos) as well as Villahermosa (8 per day, 2¼hrs., 24.50 pesos). Two buses (**Cristóbal Colón** at 9am and **Maya de Oro** at 4pm) come by *de paso* for Ocosingo (19 pesos), San Cristóbal (29 pesos) and Tuxtla (46 pesos). Maya de Oro also passes by in the other direction (9 and 9:45pm) for Chetumal (7hrs., 82 pesos), Playa del Carmen (11hrs., 143 pesos) and Cancún (12hrs., 158 pesos). **Autotransportes Tuxtla Gutiérrez** (tel. 5-10-12) provides swell first-class service to Tuxtla (8am, 12:30, 3, 6:30pm, and midnight,

45 pesos) via Ocosingo (17 pesos) and San Cristóbal (31 pesos). Six more second-class buses leave in between.

**Taxis:** (tel. 5-01-12). 20 pesos to the ruins.

**Laundromat: Lavandería "Ela,"** 5 de Mayo at Allende, opposite the Hotel Kashlan. 5 pesos per kg. Open Mon.-Sat. 8am-1pm and 4-7pm.

**Pharmacy: Farmacia Central,** Av. Juárez near Independencia. Will change dollars at slightly unfavorable rates but without the hour-long wait at nearby banks. Open daily 8am-2pm and 4-9pm.

**Medical Services: Centro de Salud y Hospital General** (tel. 5-00-25), at the western end of town, near the gas station. 24-hr. emergency service. No English spoken.

## ACCOMMODATIONS

Palenque's hotels are quite expensive. You can try to bargain, but rates are typically posted behind the reception desk, rendering them virtually immutable. Staying in one of the hotels *en route* to the ruins allows you to immerse yourself in the striking mountain landscape, but makes it more difficult to reach cheap restaurants or the market. Although these roadside hotels are expensive, hippie-haven **Mayabell Trailer Park and Camping** (tel. 5-05-97; fax 5-07-67) allows guests to pitch a tent, string up a hammock, or put down a sleeping bag under a *palapa* for about 10 pesos per person (plus 10 pesos for hammock rental). Electricity, water, and decent sewage facilities are available for trailers (10 pesos per car). The few rooms boast terracotta honey-comb tiles, plaid bedspreads, standing fans, and private bathrooms (singles 60 pesos, 10 pesos per additional person). There's also a swimming pool, and the trailer park is 1km from Montiepa Falls. An attached restaurant serves *antojitos* and snacks, all for up to 12 pesos. 3-hr. guided horseback tours of the jungle available (120 pesos). Mayabell is 6km from town and 2km from the ruins, and is accessible by *combi* (2-5 pesos).

All of the hotels listed below are in the town center, within easy walking distance of the *parque* and bus station. Camping outside of a campground might be unsafe.

**Posada Canek,** 20 de Noviembre 73 (tel. 5-11-13), between Independencia and Abasolo, half a block from the *parque*. Immensely popular modern hotel with large rooms, firm beds, and flowered sheets. Four rooms have gorgeous balcony views of the mountains. Singles are put up in a five-person dormitory with toilet but external shower. Two or more people get their own room with private bath. Check-out 10am. 20 pesos per person. Make reservations a few days in advance.

**Hotel Vaca Vieja,** 5 de Mayo 42 (tel. 5-03-77 or -88), three blocks east of the *parque,* in a quiet part of town. Spacious, spotless, modern rooms and bathrooms. Comfortable beds, dauntless ceiling fans, and balcony views of the mountains (upstairs only). Check-out 2pm. Singles 40 pesos. Doubles 60 pesos. Triples 70 pesos. Prices rise by 10 pesos during the high season. Credit cards accepted with a 6% surcharge, dollars at a less-than-enticing rate.

**Hotel Lacroix,** Hidalgo 10 (tel. 5-00-14), just off the *parque* and opposite the Iglesia de Santo Domingo. Popular with generations of archaeologists, Lacroix has been around since 1956 and is the oldest hotel in town. A wild mural complete with a giant skull and a dancing Mayan decorates the entrance and jungle-like veranda. Clean rooms with ceiling fans. Often full. Check-out noon. Singles 50 pesos. Doubles 60 pesos. Triples 70 pesos. Reservations can be made by phone.

**Hotel Santa Elena** (tel. 5-10-29), on Jorge de la Vega Domínguez, one block west and one block south of the bus stations, next to the Hospital General. Unique wood-paneled rooms equipped with fans and soapy-green bathrooms with hot water. Check-out 1pm. Singles 40 pesos. Doubles 45 pesos. Triples with 3 double beds 80 pesos. Telephone for reservations.

**Casa de Huéspedes Hotel "San Antonio,"** Independencia 42 (tel. 5-09-55), four blocks north of the post office. Uninspiring apple-green rooms with fans and hot water serve up off-the-beaten-path peace and quiet. Check-out noon. Singles 30 pesos. Doubles 40 pesos. Triples 55 pesos. Quads 75 pesos. Six people 85 pesos. Reservations recommended.

**PALENQUE**

## FOOD

Palenque's restaurants cater to tourists, and any place devoid of foreigners is consequently best avoided. Despite *gringo*-orientation, the prices aren't all that outrageous and the food is pretty good. For the cheapest produce, try the market on Velasco Suárez, four blocks west and four blocks north of the *parque*. If you plan to spend the day at the ruins, you might want to brown-bag it—the sole on-site eatery is a glorified snack bar.

**Restaurante Las Tinajas,** 20 de Noviembre 41, at Abasolo. High-backed chairs, indirect lighting, suave music, and perhaps the best-named dishes in town. Excellent vegetarian options—try the *tlacoyos* (beans and shredded cheese wrapped in fried tortillas, 12 pesos), *chimichangas* (chicken in place of the beans, 11 pesos), or a *licuado* (4.50 pesos). Credit cards accepted. Open daily 8am-11pm.

**Restaurant Maya,** Independencia at Hidalgo (tel. 5-00-42), right on the *parque*. Tasty, touristy fodder at reasonable prices. Breakfast combo of yummy granola, juice, toast, and coffee 14.50 pesos. Credit cards accepted. Open daily 7am-11pm.

**Restaurant Rocamar,** 5 de Mayo at Independencia, near the *parque*. Prices here are on the high side, but the menu is long and exciting. Squid, conch, octopus, and other sea beasts prepared in a variety of ways for 10-30 pesos. Open daily 8am-8pm.

**Restaurant Yunuen,** 5 de Mayo 42 (tel. 5-03-88), at Chiapas annexed to the Hotel Vaca Vieja, three blocks east of the *parque*. Small, friendly, and very inexpensive cafeteria. Breakfast specials 6-11 pesos. Feast on the *pollo a la palencana*—fried bananas, two cheese tacos, rice, beans, salad, and chicken for 19 pesos. Traveler's checks accepted. Open daily 7am-11pm.

## SIGHTS

During the Mayan Classic Period (300-900 CE), one of Palenque's ancient names meant "Place of the Sun's Daily Death"—the city was obviously of great import to the Maya. Though impressive, the ruins only hint at the former magnitude of the city, as less than 10% of the pyramids have been shorn of their dense jungle blanket.

Palenque owes much of its finery, including its unparalleled stucco bas-relief sculptures, to an early ruler, the club-footed god-man King Pakal (615-683 CE). According to inscriptions made at the time of his death, Pakal lived into his fifth *katan* (20-year period) and was then succeeded by his elderly son Chan-Bahlum. Chan-Bahlum celebrated his ascension by building a great pyramid-crypt (Temple of the Inscriptions) for his father. After Chan-Bahlum died, Palenque slipped into oblivion. When Cortés arrived in the 16th century, he marched right past withered Palenque without noting its existence.

Upon entering the site, you pass the tomb of Alberto Ruz, an archaeologist so devoted to restoring Palenque that he insisted on being buried there. To the right rises the steep **Temple of the Inscriptions.** Named for its magnificent tablets, the Temple was the burial place of King Pakal, and was the first substantial burial place discovered in the Americas. After his disappointing discovery of six unimpressive skeletons, Ruz bored into the interior of the crypt; he discovered the perfectly preserved, elaborately carved sarcophagus of the king. Scholars assert that the first bodies Ruz discovered were symbols of the absolute power Pakal had wielded since age 12 and were charged with bearing the king's elaborate personal effects through the underworld. Visitors can scramble down the slippery stone steps to view the royal crypt. The hollow duct, which allowed Pakal's spirit to exit the underworld and communicate with Palenque's priests, is visible on the right after the staircase.

Next to the Temple is a trapezoidal **palace** complex, consisting of four patios and a four-story tower. This immense complex is replete with religious tributes, such as the relief on the north side depicting the nine gods of the underworld. Other carvings laud the godlike priests and royal families that inhabited its many chambers. The palace's T-shaped air tunnels cooled the air and doubled as representations of Ik, the god of the breezes. Clamber down the staircase from the top of the platform to explore the extensive, dimly-lit network of underground passageways. Flat-nosed masks of the rain-god Chac, which glare accusingly off to the north end's stuccoed walls, reveal the influence of the Olmecs, and suggest a deep-seated societal fear of drought. An exclusively female steam bath and latrines have also been excavated.

A trail leads up the mountainside to the left of the Temple of Inscriptions. About 100m along this trail, on the right, is the **Temple of the Lion.** Descend the pitch-black stairwell inside the structure and you'll come upon the site of the ancient well where a few faint traces of paint are slowly surrendering to the green slime of the jungle. The trail continues up the hill for 7km before reaching the tiny *indígena* village of Naranjo. Guides can be found for this difficult hike through beautiful terrain.

The path between the palace and the Temple of Inscriptions fords the recently reconstructed aqueduct before leading up to the **Sun Plaza,** another landscaped platform comprised of the **Temple of the Sun,** the **Temple of the Cross,** the **Temple of the Foliated Cross,** and the smaller **Temple 14.** The Temple of the Cross was named for a stucco relief of a cross which was found inside and which inspired a flurry of hopeful religious theories among the *conquistadores.* To their dismay, this Maya group is the only one known to have worshipped the cross. For the Maya, the cross represented the tree of life, a snake as its horizontal branch, a bird perched atop it. The outer layer of stucco has worn away, but the inner sanctum protects a large sculpted tablet and reliefs on either side of the doors.

About to be swallowed again by the jealous jungle, the **Temple of the Foliated Cross** lies across the plaza from the Temple of the Sun. Despite the overgrown path, the inner sanctum here contains a surprisingly clear carved tablet. The tablet was carved with an unusual tree (or cross) whose branches are remarkably similar to some of those found in a temple at Angkor-Wat, Cambodia, but nowhere else.

To the south, through the wall of trees, several unreconstructed temples surround the uncleared **Plaza Maudslay.** From Temple 14 head downhill (north) and past the palace lie to the vestiges of a **ballcourt.** From the absence of stone rings, archaeologists suppose that wooden ones were used instead.

To the left of the ballcourt is the **Temple of Frederick, Count of Waldeck** who lived here for three years while studying the ruins in the 1830s. The four other temples which share the platform with the Temple of the Count comprise the **North Group.** Waterfall enthusiasts may catch a glimpse of the **Queen's Bath** (so named for its formerly exclusively female clientele), a small set of falls just through the trees from the North Group. A second set of falls, **Cascada Montiepa,** is hidden in the jungle, 600m down the road from the ruins. At the right-hand bend follow the path into the woods. Unfortunately, overgrown banks and shallow water make swimming impractical.

The archaeological site is open daily from 8am-4:45pm. The crypt is open from 8am-4pm. Visiting the ruins at night is prohibited and extremely unsafe. (Admission to the site 16 pesos. Free Sun. Small map available at gate for 2 pesos. Guided tours available.) *Combis* to the site run from 6am-6pm and cost 2 pesos; catch them off Juárez on Allende. Do not take popular shortcuts to the back entrance of the ruins from the campgrounds or the road—it is said that rapes and robberies have occurred on these trails, and the dense jungle leaves you isolated even if there are many other tourists nearby.

# ■ NEAR PALENQUE

## CASCADAS AGUA AZUL AND MISOL-HA

Both of these large *cascadas* (waterfalls) have overflowed with tourists of late, and for good reason. **Agua Azul,** 62km south of Palenque, is a breathtaking spectacle: the Río Yax jumps down 500 individual falls, then slips into rapids, whirlpools, and calm swimming areas in between. There is a tiny beach and swimming area 20min. upstream from the falls—if you swim, stay close to the bank and swim with a friend, as more than 100 people have met their watery end here.

Since the 4km walk from *el crucero* is tiresome, it's best to spend only a day at the falls, returning to Palenque in the afternoon. If need be, though, hammock or sleeping space is available at the campground here (hammock space 7 pesos, plus 3 pesos for rental; pitch a tent for 10 pesos per person). At Misol-Ha there are both camping spaces and *cabañas* available.

The falls at **Misol-Ha** are 24km from Palenque and only 2km from the highway crossing. There's a large cataract here, and the swimming area is clean and relatively safe. A small restaurant serves up a few good dishes at reasonable prices. **Buses** between Palenque and Ocosingo or San Cristóbal will stop at the crossroads for either Agua Azul or Misol-Ha (2 pesos from Palenque). Since few buses pass after 4pm, leave the falls in the early afternoon. Hitchhikers report that steady pick-up truck traffic makes catching a ride fairly easy (admission to each of the falls costs 2 pesos per person, 5 pesos per carload).

**Getting There:** The most painless way to visit Agua Azul and Misol-Ha is aboard a **Transportes Chambalu** *combi* (35 pesos round-trip). *Combis* leave daily from the Palenque station at Hidalgo and Allende at 10am and noon. After a 30-minute photo stop at Misol-Ha, the van continues to Agua Azul. Passengers are dropped off right by the falls for a three-hour swimming session. The whole trip takes about six hours.

# ■■■ TONALÁ

If, while in Chiapas, you're hit by a sudden and irresistible urge to lie on a beach—any beach—then head for Tonalá. While the beaches near Tonalá don't compare with Oaxaca's golden stretches of sand, **Puerto Arista,** and especially **Boca del Cielo,** are pleasant enough spots to spend a few hours. During *Semana Santa,* Christmas, and weekends in July and August, the beaches fill up with Chiapanecan families. At all other times, the sand is uninhabited, except for *zancudos blancos,* vicious biting insects that make sleeping in hammocks impossible.

With more funeral homes than pharmacies, Tonalá itself is a hot, inhospitable town. Furthermore, crossing Avenida Hidalgo, the main street (which doubles as the coastal highway), often entails risking your life. Tonalá is a suitable enough destination for lunch, but you'll soon want to move on to the beach or further afield.

**Orientation and Practical Information** Tonalá lies 223km northwest of Tapachula along Rte. 200 and 172km southwest of Tuxtla Gutiérrez on Rte. 190. All **bus stations** are on **Avenida Hidalgo,** Tonala's deadly main street. To get to the *zócalo* from the **Cristóbal Colón** bus station, take a left and head six blocks south. Both the **Autotransportes Tuxtla Gutiérrez** and **Fletes y Pasajes** bus stations are south of the *centro,* so you need to turn right and walk two blocks and four blocks north, respectively. As the coastal highway, Av. Hidalgo runs roughly north-south through town. To the east, Av. Rayón parallels Hidalgo, while to the west run Avenidas Matamoros, Juárez, and Allende. From north to south, Calles Madero, 16 de Septiembre, 5 de Febrero, Independencia, and 5 de Mayo run east-west, completing the grid that makes up the city center.

The **tourist office** is at Hidalgo and 5 de Mayo (tel. 3-27-87), two blocks south of the bus station and above the Autotransportes Tuxtla station. The helpful staff provides maps of town and answers questions about the area (open Mon.-Fri. 9am-3pm and 6-9pm, Sat. 10am-1pm). The **police** station (tel. 3-01-03) is two blocks north of Cristóbal Colón and to the right on Calle Libertad. The **post office,** Zambrano 27 (tel. 3-06-83), two blocks north and half a block east of the *zócalo,* posts a *Lista de Correos* (open Mon.-Fri. 8am-7pm, Sat. 9am-1pm). **Postal Code:** 30500. **Telephones** are in the Cafetería La Diligencia (tel. and fax 3-20-81), on Independencia off Hidalgo, south of the *zócalo.* 13 pesos per min. to call or **fax** the U.S. 5 pesos per page to receive a fax. International collect calls 5 pesos (open Mon.-Sat. 7:30am-9pm, Sun. 8am-2pm). **Telephone Code:** 996. **Bánamex,** Hidalgo 137 at 5 de Febrero (tel. 3-00-37 or 3-10-77), half a block south of the *zócalo,* is open Mon.-Fri. 9am-1:30pm.

First-class **buses** leave the **Cristóbal Colón** station incorporating **Maya de Oro** (tel. 3-05-40), six blocks north of the *zócalo,* for Chetumal (4pm, 21hrs., 154 pesos),

Mexico City (6 and 8:15pm, 13hrs., 177 pesos), Puebla (8:15pm, 11hrs., 152 pesos), Tuxtla Gutiérrez (every hr., 4½hrs., 27 pesos), Tapachula (every hr., 4hrs., 36 pesos), Veracruz (12:15am, 16hrs., 99 pesos), and Villahermosa (10:30am, 6:30, and 10:30pm, 9hrs., 91 pesos) with the 10:30 bus going on to Coatzacoalcos (63 pesos). **Autotransportes Tuxtla Gutiérrez** has first-class service to Mexico City (6pm, 13hrs., 165 pesos) via Puebla (11hrs., 145 pesos) and also to Tapachula (5:30am, 4hrs., 35 pesos). Second-class buses also run to Tapachula (8 per day, 4½hrs., 27 pesos) and Tuxtla (9 per day, 4hrs., 22 pesos; office open 5am-8pm). **Fletes y Pasajes** (tel. 3-25-94) on Hidalgo, 50m south of the bridge and 3½ blocks south of the *zócalo,* sends second-class buses to Mexico City (4, 5:45, 7, and 8:30pm, 13hrs., 127-140 pesos) via Córdoba (8hrs., 80-88 pesos), with the 7 and 8:15pm buses passing through Puebla (11hrs., 110-115 pesos). Also to Oaxaca (5 per day, 9hrs., 60 pesos) and Tapachula (6 per day, 4hrs., 30 pesos; office open daily 6am-10pm). **Taxis** (tel. 3-06-20) cruise up and down Hidalgo and hang out in the *zócalo* (25 pesos to Puerto Arista). If you're getting up early, the 24-hr. **radio-taxis** (tel. 3-10-44) opposite the Colón bus station will come and rouse you at your hotel at any hour.

The **market** is on Matamoros, several blocks southeast of the *zócalo.* Walk south on Hidalgo and right on 5 de Febrero or Independencia to Matamoros (open until 2:30pm, though stalls outside stay open until 6-7pm). The **Red Cross** (tel. 3-02-76) is on Av. Joaquín Miguel Gutiérrez (open 24 hrs.). **Clínica de Especialidades,** Hidalgo 127 (tel. 3-12-90), at Independencia south of the *zócalo,* is a pharmacy. One doctor speaks English (open daily 7am-2pm and 5-8pm; open 24 hrs. for emergency medical service). **Hospital General,** Av. 27 de Septiembre at Mina (tel. 3-06-87), is six blocks south of the *zócalo* and 3 blocks east before the gas station (open 24 hrs.). Call **Locatel** (tel. 3-06-04) at the Palacio Municipal to report a theft, missing person, items lost and found, or for general **emergencies** (open daily 9am-2pm and 6-8pm).

**Accommodations and Food**   Hotels in Tonalá are overpriced and under-cleaned. Singles at **Hotel Tonalá** (tel. 3-04-80), a few blocks south of the Cristóbal Colón station, aren't big enough to swing a cat in. Doubles are larger and come with TVs. Clean private bathrooms have cold water. Check-out 1pm (singles 55 pesos; doubles 95 pesos; triples 135 pesos). Cheaper accommodations come at a price at **Hotel Thomás** (tel. 13-00-80). Blue cell-like rooms are equipped with pre-historic ceiling fans, and the bathrooms are in dire need of a fix-up. Check-out 2pm (singles 35 pesos; doubles 40 pesos; triples 70 pesos).

The pink **Restaurante Nora,** Independencia 10 (tel. 3-02-43), is just east of Hidalgo and a block south of the *zócalo.* 3-course *comida corrida* 18 pesos. Meat dishes 11-23 pesos (open Mon.-Sat. 7:30am-10pm; traveler's checks and credit cards accepted). A little more upscale, **Restaurante Colonial** (tel. 3-02-39), in Hotel Galilea on the southwest corner of the *zócalo,* serves up giant portions of *antojitos,* eggs, and sandwiches. Tasty shrimp and mushroom *queso fundido* (12.50 pesos).

**Sand and Sights**   18km southwest of Tonalá, **Puerto Arista** offers 32km of gray sandy beach and the pounding waves of the Pacific. Be especially careful in the late afternoon, when the current tends to flow out to sea. Most beachside restaurants can provide hammocks for the night (about 10 pesos), although they may not even charge you if you enthusiastically patronize their establishment. Obviously, ask before setting up your own hammock or tent on someone else's property.

**Hotel Playa Escondida** is at the left end of the beach (singles about 30 pesos; doubles about 50 pesos; campers use facilities for 2 pesos). For calmer seas, head to the sheltered saltwater estuary of **Boca del Cielo,** 15km further down the coast. As the estuary is less than 100m wide, you can wade and then swim across to the beach-front restaurants and open ocean. To get there with your wallet and clothes in a less-than-soaked condition, hop in a *lancha* (15-20 pesos). There are no hotels in Boca del Cielo, so you'll want to base yourself in Puerto Arista or Tonalá. Every 20 minutes, *colectivos* run to both Puerto Arista (5 pesos) and Boca del Cielo (7 pesos) from their stand on 5 de Mayo, 1½ blocks west of Hidalgo.

# ■■■ TAPACHULA

Only a few kilometers from Tapachula, jaguars, pumas, *chakalakas* (turkey-like fowl), and packs of peccaries (akin to wild boars) roam the jungle in a fertile river basin which drains the southernmost part of the Republic, 4000m below the majestic volcano Tacaná. From the city center you wouldn't know it; the hot, dirty streets of Chiapas's second city (pop. 300,000) present a different world entirely. Only the *zócalo* provides welcome relief from Tapachula's assault on the senses. Topiary trees, their leafy crowns trimmed square and joined to one another, form a green canopy over the *zócalo's* two square blocks. During the rainy season, hundreds of mostly Guatemalan immigrants crowd under these trees, reading newspapers or socializing. Relaxing outdoor cafés provide sanctuary from the rampant *marimba* music that echoes through the city. For tourists, Tapachula is primarily a point of entry into Guatemala.

## ORIENTATION

Tapachula is 18km from Talismán at the Guatemalan border on Rte. 200 and 303km west of Guatemala City. Tonalá lies 220km to the northwest, along the Pacific coast. *Avenidas* run north-south, and *calles* run east-west. *Calles* north of Calle Central are odd-numbered, while those south of the central axis are even-numbered. Similarly, *avenidas* east of Av. Central are odd-numbered, while those west have even numbers. Tapachula's main plaza is located at 3 Calle Pte. between 6 and 8 Av. Nte., northwest of the center.

## PRACTICAL INFORMATION

**Tourist Office:** (tel. 5-54-09), in the Antiguo Palacio Municipal, just south of the Iglesia de San Agustín on the west side of the *zócalo*. Brochures, maps, and enthusiasm. Open Mon.-Fri. 9am-3pm and 6-9pm.

**Police:** (tel. 5-28-51), Palacio Municipal, at 8 Av. Nte. and 3 Calle Pte. Open 24 hrs.

**Post Office:** 1 Calle Ote. 32 (tel. 6-10-28), between 7 and 9 Av. Nte. Posts a *Lista de Correos*. Open Mon.-Fri. 8am-7pm, Sat. 9am-1pm. **MexPost** (tel. 2-04-27), in the same office, is open Mon.-Fri. 8am-7pm. **Postal Code:** 30700.

**Telephones:** Long-distance *casetas* are located on 17 Calle Ote., 1 block west of the Cristóbal Colón bus station, and also right across from the station (tel. 6-75-19). Collect calls 15 pesos. Open daily 7am-11pm. **LADATELs** at the Cristóbal Colón bus station or at the Cine Maya on 2 Av. Nte. at 1 Calle Pte.

**Consulate: Guatemala,** 2 Calle Ote. 33 (tel. 6-12-52), between 7 and 9 Av. Sur. U.S. and Canadian citizens need only a passport to acquire a visa. U.K. citizens don't need a visa for Guatemala. Go first to Copias "Motta" on Calle Central and 9 Av. Nte. to photocopy the first page of your passport and to obtain a visa application. Visas usually take less than ½hr., but arrive early in case of crowds. Visas free for Canadian and U.S. citizens. Open Mon.-Fri. 8am-4pm. Ring the bell after hours for emergencies.

**Currency Exchange: Bánamex,** Av. Central Nte. 9 (tel. 6-29-24). 24-hr. Cirrus and **Plus ATM** and cash advances on MC and Visa. Open Mon.-Fri. 9am-2pm. **Casa de Cambio,** 4 Av. Nte. and 3 Calle Pte. (tel. 6-51-22), changes U.S. dollars and traveler's checks at good rates. Open Mon.-Sat. 8am-7:30pm, Sun. 7am-1pm.

**Airport:** On the road to Puerto Madero, about 17km south of town. Served by **Aeroméxico,** 2 Av. Nte. 6 (tel. 6-20-50), **Aviacsa,** Av. Central and Calle 1 Pte. (tel. 6-31-47 or 6-14-39), and **Taesa,** 1 Calle Pte. 11 (tel. 6-37-32; fax 6-37-02).

**Train Station:** Av. Central Sur 150 (tel. 6-21-76), at the end of the *avenida* behind a miniature plaza and a small market. Slow, cheap, unreliable service to, among others, Veracruz, Huixtla, Tonalá, and Arriaga. Second-class only.

**Bus Stations: Cristóbal Colón,** 17 Calle Ote. at 3 Av. Nte. (tel. 6-28-81). Open 24 hrs. To Ciudad Cuauhtémoc (5 per day, 4½hrs., 27 pesos), and on to Comitán (6hrs., 40 pesos) and San Cristóbal (7½hrs., 54 pesos), Huixtla (every hr., 1hr., 7 pesos) and Tonalá (3hrs., 36 pesos), Tuxtla Gutiérrez (every hr., 6½hrs., 63 pesos), Mexico City (6 per day, 18hrs., 212 pesos) via Oaxaca (10½hrs., 106 pesos) and Puebla (15hrs., 188 pesos), and Villahermosa (7am and 6pm, 13hrs.,

133 pesos). Also Escárcega (7:30am, 12:30, 1, and 5pm, 17hrs., 146 pesos) via Palenque (13hrs., 112 pesos); the first two go on to Chetumal (21hrs., 190 pesos). All destinations east of San Cristóbal, including Mérida and Cancún, involve a change-over in Tuxtla. Take the 7:30am "Lujo" to Tuxtla to connect for Mérida (23hrs.) or Cancún (24hrs.). **Autotransportes Tuxtla Gutiérrez** (tel. 6-95-13), 11a Calle Ote., between 3a and 4a Av. Norte. Booth open 24 hrs. Also first-class service to Huixtla (8 per day, 1hr., 5 pesos), Tonalá (3½hrs., 28 pesos), and Tuxtla (7hrs., 50 pesos), and to Córdoba (3pm, 11hrs., 130 pesos), Puebla (14hrs., 170 pesos), and Mexico City (16hrs., 192 pesos). **Fletes y Pasajes,** 3a Av. Norte and 9a Calle Ote (tel. 6-76-03), has second-class service to Oaxaca (4, 7am, 1, and 6:30pm, 12hrs., 88 pesos), Tonalá (6 per day, 3½hrs., 28-31 pesos), and to Córdoba (3:30 and 5pm, 12hrs., 117-129 pesos), and on to Puebla (15hrs., 143-157 pesos) and Mexico City (16hrs., 160-176 pesos). From the station on 7a Calle Pte., between 2a Av. Nte. and Av. Central Nte., white **Paulino Navarro** (tel. 6-58-87) *microbuses* run to Puerto Madero (every 15min., 45min., 3 pesos).

**Border Crossing Transportation:** "Ahuacatlán" buses leave their station on 5a Calle Pte. and 12a Av. Nte. for Talismán (every 10min., 30min., 2.50 pesos). For those who don't want to spend any time in Tapachula, the bus swings by the Cristóbal Colón bus station, on 17a Calle Ote., on its way to the border. Cross the border on foot, and then catch a **Galgos** bus line to Guatemala City. If need be, take a taxi from the *zócalo* to Talismán (about 50 pesos).

**Red Cross:** 9 Av. Nte. at 1 Calle Ote. (tel. 6-19-49 or 6-35-06), across from the post office. 24-hr. ambulance service. No English spoken.

**Pharmacy: Farmacia 24 Horas,** 8 Av. Nte. 27 (tel. 6-24-80), at Calle 7 Pte. No English spoken. Delivery to anywhere within the city available 7am-11pm.

**Hospital:** (tel. 6-17-12), on the highway to the airport. Service 24 hrs.

## ACCOMMODATIONS

Due to the huge influx of Guatemalan refugees, budget accommodations are a dime a dozen in Tapachula, especially near the market. Unfortunately, many hotel rooms are as noisy and dirty as the rest of the city. The first two listings provide clean, pleasant accommodations at reasonable prices.

**Hotel 5 de Mayo,** Calle 5a Pte. #22 (tel. 6-39-43), just off Av. 12a Nte., 1½ blocks west of the *zócalo*. Reception area is upstairs past four bare concrete blocks, supposedly for supporting flower displays. A pleasant little hotel, completely refurbished in June 1995, has been repainted in an assortment of purple pastel colors. Small but spotless and new rooms with ceiling fans, bathrooms, and communal facilities. Check-out 1pm. Singles 25 pesos. Doubles 30 peso, with 2 beds 40 pesos. Triples 45 pesos. Rooms with private bathrooms cost 35, 40, 50, and 60 pesos, respectively, and a quad goes for 70 pesos.

**Hotel San Agustín,** 12a Av. Nte. #14 (tel. 6-14-53), between 1a and 3a Calles Pte., two blocks west of the *zócalo* on 3a Calle Pte. and ½ block south. Sprawling 55-room complex with a parking lot and chapel—although its main draw is the big, clean pool and sun deck. Gigantic but bare whitewashed two-room suites with rudimentary bathrooms and standing fans. Color TV and sodas for sale in the lobby. Check-out 1pm. One double bed 40 pesos. Two 60 pesos. Three 90 pesos. Four 120 pesos. Squeeze in as many as you like.

**Hotel Tabasco,** Av. Central Nte. 123 (tel. 6-51-33), just north of 17 Calle Ote., very conveniently located two blocks west of the Cristóbal Colón bus station. For budgeteers who need a cheap place for the night before an early-morning departure. Street noise free of charge; hot water unavailable at any price. *Agua purificada* in the hall. Drab, bare concrete singles are not worth 30 pesos. Doubles 50 pesos. Triples 70 pesos.

## FOOD

A moderately priced meal is not hard to come by in Tapachula, but don't expect a feast. The tiny Chinatown on 1a Calle Pte., one block southeast of the *zócalo*— don't blink or you'll miss it—promises relief (and you guessed it, warm salvation) from *frijoles* and *tortillas,* but portions are often small for the price. Cheaper Chinese (and other) food can be had at the **San Juan food market** on 17a Calle Pte., north of the *centro.* Take a 0.90-peso "Framboyanes" *combi* from 7a Calle Pte., between 10a and 12a Av. Nte. to get there (market open daily 5am-5pm). **Mercado Sebastián Escobar,** on 10 Av. Nte. between 5a and 3a Calles Pte., sells produce and baked goods.

**La Quinta Carmelita,** Calle Central Ote. 76 (tel. 5-40-07), about 1½km east of downtown, past the army barracks. Take any eastbound *colectivo* on Calle Central (1 peso). Thirst-quenching, authentic lemonade in a big glass goblet (5 pesos) looks just like frogspawn. *Queso fundido especial* (12 pesos) is decadent. *Comida corrida* 8.50-12 pesos. Open daily 7am-midnight.

**La Parrilla,** 8 Av. Nte. 20 (tel. 6-40-62), in the southwest corner of the *zócalo.* Perfect breakfast spot to read the paper or contemplate the huge birds painted on the walls. Breakfasts 7.50-16 pesos. Eggs 5-10 pesos. *Antojitos* 3-10 pesos. Grilled chicken 15 pesos. Open 7am-1am. Dollars and Quetzales accepted.

**El Charco de las Ranas,** 4 Av. Nte. 21, between 1a and 3a Calle Pte., next to the Hotel Fenix. Friendly open-air joint allows you to get away from *comida corrida.* Breakfast 12 pesos. *Tortas* 7 pesos. Open daily 7am-10pm.

## SIGHTS

Tapachula offers a few distractions for those who want to tarry on their way to or from Guatemala. The **Museo Regional del Socunusco** (tel. 6-41-73), in the Antiguo Palacio Municipal on the west side of the *zócalo,* houses a small collection of Olmec/Mayan ceramic and stone artifacts. Note the mural on the stairway depicting a child sacrifice. Upstairs, a jade-encrusted skull with gold beads for eyeballs grins gruesomely (open Tues.-Sun. 10am-5pm; admission 10 pesos; free Sun.).

Next door, the second-floor of the **Casa de la Cultura,** 8 Av. Nte. 24 (tel. 6-11-57), hosts occasional and temporary art exhibits (open Mon.-Fri. 9am-1pm and 4-8pm; free). There is an adequate-but-not-spectacular beach at **Puerto Madero,** 27km away, accessible from the second-class bus station Paulino Navarro on Calle 7 Ote. between Av. Central Nte. and Av. 2 Nte. (every 15min., 45min., 3 pesos).

# ■ CROSSING THE BORDER TO GUATEMALA

Those crossing the border on foot from Tapachula, Mexico to Talismán, Guatemala will be besieged by money changers and self-appointed "guides." Plan to cross the border early in the day to avoid bureaucratic delay, early and unofficial closings, and wasted time in Talismán. **Buses** from Tapachula (see Tapachula: Practical Information, above) drop off passengers at the entrance to the Mexican emigration office. Enter the building and present your **passport** and Mexican **tourist card** to officials behind the desk. Then follow the crowd across the bridge, which charges a toll of approximately 3 pesos. Proceed to a small building on the left to have your passport stamped by Guatemalan authorities; there is a charge of five quetzales.

The **money changers** on the Guatemalan side of the border generally give better rates for pesos than those on the Mexican side, but your best bet is to avoid small money changers and head for the **Banco de Quetzal,** on the Guatemalan side. **Buses** to Guatemala City leave about every two hours from 7am-2pm, and also at midnight and 4am. Don't travel at night, since this route has been recently plagued by assaults. Should you have to spend the night, the **Hotel José Ricardo,** just past the official buildings on the right, offers nice, clean rooms with bathrooms and hot water. They lock the front door, which is reassuring. The various eateries in Talismán can turn seedy when the drunks come out of the woodwork. Women traveling alone should be very careful.

The Tapachulan tourist office recommends that tourists do not cross the border at Ciudad Hidalgo, as the bridge there is long and deserted—travelers are particularly vulnerable to assault.

# TABASCO

Perched on the lush, flat Isthmus of Tehuantepec, Tabasco connects the Yucatán to the Gulf coast and the rest of the country. False etymologies flourish in Mexico, but *tabasco* may well descend, as is rumored, from the *indígena* word *tlapalco,* meaning "moist land." *Tabasqueños* proudly boast that their state is one of the wettest places on earth, second only to the Amazon Basin. Whether this claim is valid or not is a moot point—dotted by lakes and swamps, criss-crossed by rivers, and swathed in dense, humid jungle, Tabasco sees an awful lot of rainfall. In Tabasco, a traveler without rain gear is a very unhappy traveler indeed.

The Olmec culture flourished in the area now within Tabasco's boundaries. Because few Olmec artifacts exist, their civilization remains draped in mystery, but archaeologists do know that the Olmecs worshipped the jaguar as a divine creature. Manifest reminders of this obsession linger in many of the Olmecs' monumental and grotesque stone carvings, in which man and feline inseparably intertwine. The Olmecs' art, architecture, astronomy, and calendar were adopted and refined by the later Mayan and Toltec cultures. To attract tourists, Villahermosa recently underwent a cosmetic make-over, relocating most of the state's archaeological treasures to two museums in the city center—Parque-Museo La Venta and the Museo Regional de Antropología.

Tabasco's most important Mayan ruins, **Comalcalco,** lie an hour northwest of the capital, easily reached by bus or car. Some tourists stay in **Villahermosa** to visit the ruins of Palenque in Chiapas three hours away. Those bent on seeing Mexico's less accessible ruins can fly from Villahermosa or Tenosique into the **Lacandón Rainforest** to explore **Bonampak** and **Yaxchilán.**

# ■■■ VILLAHERMOSA

By 1596, the Spanish colonists were weary enough of defending the coast against British and Dutch pirates that they migrated inland up the Río Grijalva to found Villahermosa. The city was relatively poor and substantially isolated, an agricultural center of minor importance accessible only by the river. All that has changed, however, in the past 50 years. In the 1940s, railroad tracks were laid which connected Villahermosa to the rest of the Republic. The discovery of oil in the region in 1974 completed the transformation and gave the ailing city a shot in the arm.

Rail lines and petro-profits have turned Villahermosa (pop. 1.6 million) from boondock to boomtown, a dense urban forest of satellite antennae, luxury hotels, and apartment complexes. Swimming in oil revenue throughout the 80s, the state of Tabasco invested billions in improving its capital. New museums, monuments, bus stations, libraries, and parks sprang up across town. Development recently culminated in the completion of the ultra-modern Tabasco 2000 complex, which includes government buildings, a planetarium, and a sparkling shopping mall.

## ORIENTATION

Tabasco's state capital lies only 20km from the border with Chiapas. Escárcega, the major crossroads for Yucatán-bound travelers, is 298km (or 4hrs.) east of Villahermosa via Rte. 186. Coatzacoalcos, where the Mexican isthmus tapers to its narrowest, lies 169km to the west via Rte. 180, and Tuxtla Gutiérrez, Chiapas's capital, is 293km to the south.

First- and second-class **buses** depart from the eastern part of town. An international **airport** lies northwest of the city, 14km from the downtown area; taxis shuttle between the airport and *el centro* (40 pesos *especial,* 15 pesos *colectivo*).

Downtown Villahermosa lies between the Río Carrizal to the west and the Río Grijalva to the east, while the fingers of the **Laguna de las Ilusiones** tickle the northern half of the city. The *zócalo* and city center are to the south, on the west bank of the Grijalva. The spine of the downtown area is **27 de Febrero.** The straight-as-an-arrow **Paseo Tabasco** connects the Tabasco 2000 complex to *el centro,* intersecting 27 de Febrero in front of the cathedral. *Saetas* (public buses, 1 peso) and *combis* (1.10 pesos) run from 6am to 10:30pm.

To reach downtown from the **first-class ADO station,** walk two and a half blocks to the right on Mina to Méndez. From there, take a *combi* labeled "Tierra Colorada Centro-Juárez" and get off a few minutes later at **Parque Juárez.** Most hotels are south of the park on either Madero or its parallel cousin Constitución. Walking from the station to Parque Juárez takes 15 to 20 minutes; upon exiting the terminal, head straight ahead (east) across Mina and down Fuentes or Merino five blocks to Parque de la Paz. On the far side of the park, turn right (south) on Madero; Parque Juárez and the hotel zone are six blocks away.

To get downtown from the **second-class bus terminal,** cross Grijalva on the pedestrian bridge to the left of the station exit and jump on a bus labeled "Indeco Centro" (1 peso). Disembark at Parque Juárez on Madero; the hotels are to the south. To make the 25-minute walk from the station, cross the bridge and continue south on Mina for three blocks until you reach the ADO station (see above). Alternatively, take a taxi to avoid the bus hassle or the long walk from the station (5 pesos).

## PRACTICAL INFORMATION

**Tourist Offices: Instituto de Turismo,** Centro Administrativo de Gobierno, Tabasco 2000, Paseo Tabasco 1504 (tel. 16-36-33). Pass between the pillars of the first building on the right in the Tabasco 2000 complex. The tourist office is on the ground floor, halfway down on the right. Although primarily an administrative office, English-speaking staffers are happy to answer questions. Brochures and maps. Open Mon-Fri. 9am-3pm and 6-9pm, Sat. 9am-1pm. **Tourist Information Booths** at the airport and Museo La Venta. Usually open daily 7am-4:30pm.

**Police:** 16 de Septiembre at Periférico (tel. 13-21-10). No English. Open 24 hrs.

**Post Office:** Saenz 131 (tel. 12-10-40), at Lerdo, three blocks west of Madero and one block south of Zaragoza. Open Mon.-Fri. 8am-7pm, Sat. 9am-1pm. **Postal Code:** 86000.

**Telephones:** Long-distance calls are best made from pay phones on the street, since many *casetas* do not allow collect calls or don't exist at the locations indicated on the tourist office's map. **Café La Barra,** Lerdo 608 (tel. 12-20-06), up the stairs across from the main telegram office, will make collect calls for 3 pesos. Regular calls to the U.S. 9 pesos per min. Open Mon.-Sat. 7am-1pm and 3:30-8pm. **Telephone Code:** 93.

**Telegrams:** Lerdo 601 (tel. 12-11-90 or 12-24-94), at Saenz, around the corner from the post office. Open for telegrams and fax Mon.-Fri. 8am-7pm, Sat. 9am-1pm. Money order service closes 1hr. early.

**Currency Exchange: Bánamex,** Madero at Reforma (tel. 12-00-11). Good rates and super-efficient service. Take a ticket and wait to get served. Open for exchange Mon.-Fri. 9am-5pm. 24-hr. **ATM** for cash advances on MC and Visa. **Bancomer,** Juárez at Zaragoza (tel. 14-00-50), a few blocks west of Madero. Open Mon.-Fri. 9am-1:30pm.

**American Express:** Simon Salart 202 (tel. 91-800-5-00-44), at Fedencia. Some English spoken. Open Mon.-Fri. 9-11:30am and 4-6pm, Sat. 9am-1pm.

**Airport:** (tel. 12-11-64), on the Villahermosa-Macupana highway. **Aeroméxico,** Madero 718 (tel. 14-09-78). Also a travel agency. Open Mon.-Fri. 8am-7pm, Sat. 9am-1:30pm. **Mexicana,** Av. Los Ríos 105 (tel. 16-31-32), at Complejo Urbana in the Tabasco 2000 complex. Open Mon.-Fri. 9am-6:30pm, Sat. 9am-5:45pm. To Mexico City. **Aviacsa,** Av. Fco. J. Mina 1025 (tel. 14-57-70 or -80). To Mexico City, Mérida, and Cancún. **Aerocaribe,** Av. Los Ríos 105, in the Tabasco 2000 complex. To Cancún via Mérida, and to Oaxaca via Tuxtla.

**Bus Stations:** The first-class terminal is at Mina 297 at Merino, a couple of blocks east of Juárez. **ADO** (tel. 12-21-42 or 12-14-46) to Campeche (5 per day, 6hrs., 75 pesos), Cancún (8, 10, and 11:15pm, 11hrs., 152.50 pesos), Chetumal (8, 9, 10, and 11pm, 6hrs., 92.50 pesos), Escárcega (5 per day, 3hrs., 48.50 pesos), La Venta (5 per day, 2hrs., 20.50 pesos), Mérida (5 per day, 9hrs., 105.50 pesos), Mexico City (7 per day, 11hrs., 165 pesos), Oaxaca (6pm, 12hrs., 121 pesos), Palenque (8 per day, 3hrs., 24.50 pesos), and Veracruz (5 per day, 7hrs., 80.50 pesos). **Cristóbal Colón** (tel. 12-29-37) goes south to Teapa (5 per day, 1hr., 9 pesos), Tuxtla Gutiérrez (8 per day, 6hrs.), and Tapachula (6 and 9pm, 14hrs.) and west to Oaxaca (7:30 and 9:30pm, 12hrs., 121 pesos). **UNO** (tel. 14-58-18) has *servicio de lujo* tickets which must be bought 5 days in advance. **Luggage storage** 7am-11pm, 1 peso per piece per hr.

**Car Rental: Agrisa** (tel. 16-00-80) in the Holiday Inn annexed to the Tabasco 2000 shopping mall. The cheapest option is the VW sedan at 183 pesos per day and 90¢ per km. Open daily 8am-8pm.

**Market: Pino Suárez,** encompassed by Pino Suárez, Constitución, Hermanos Zozaya, and Grijalva, one block from the river, in the northeast corner of town. Open daily 6am-6pm.

**Supermarket: Bonanza,** Madero at Zaragoza (tel. 4-22-80). Open daily 7am-9pm.

**Laundromat: Lavandería Omni Klín,** Constitución 904. 5 pesos per kg. Same-day service if clothes brought in before 10am. Open Mon.-Sat. 8am-8pm.

**Red Cross:** (tel. 13-35-93 or 13-34-39), on General Sandino in Colonia 1 de Mayo. Take the "1 de Mayo" bus from Madero. 24-hr. ambulance service to any point in the city. No English spoken.

**Pharmacy: Farmacia Canto,** Madero 602 (tel. 12-20-99). MC, Visa accepted. Open daily 7am-11pm.

**Medical Services:** A good clinic is **Clínica 39,** Zaragoza 1202 (tel. 12-20-49), at Carmen Buen Día. English-speaking staff. Not free. Open daily 7am-8pm.

## ACCOMMODATIONS AND CAMPING

Unremarkable hotels in the *centro* provide basic rooms at mid-level prices. A budget bargain is therefore nowhere in sight. **Camping** and **trailer parking** are allowed in La Choca Park in Tabasco 2000 at no charge and with no facilities to speak of. Reservations for most establishments can be made by phone.

**Hotel Madero,** Madero 301 (tel. 12-05-16), near 27 de Febrero. An old Spanish building, which, though it could use some maintenance, manages to rise above the mediocrity. Private bathrooms with "hot water" that's closer to room temperature, but just fine for Villahermosa's heat. Manager stores packs and dispenses great maps. Check-out 1pm. Singles 40 pesos. Doubles 50 pesos. Triples 80 pesos.

**Hotel Tabascoob,** Constitución 514 (tel. 14-53-22). Pretty pink paint job and bright bed covers almost make up for the small size of the rooms. Fans but no hot water. Clean bathrooms. Check-out 1pm. Singles 50 pesos. Doubles 60 pesos. Triples 70 pesos. Deluxe rooms with A/C and TV are 15 pesos extra.

**Posada Hotel Brondo,** Pino Suárez 209 (tel. 12-59-61), near Sánchez Mármol. Some rooms are resplendent in cool pastel, others are tragically spartan. Fans and hot water. All doubles have private, clean bathrooms. Singles are served by communal facilities which are just a miracle. Check-out 1pm. Suites for up to four people come with kitchen and living room. Prices range from 44-104.50 pesos.

**Casa de Huéspedes Teresita,** Constitución 224 (tel. 12-34-53). 10 small, moderately maintained rooms off a jazzy upstairs lobby where the cheerful manager watches TV round the clock. Bathrooms have no hot water, but rooms have fans and some have balconies. Alligator hanging on the wall grins vacantly at passersby. Check-out noon. Singles and doubles 20 pesos. Triples 25 pesos. Add 5 pesos for private bath. Reservations must be paid in advance.

## FOOD

Despite booming development and a sincere desire to attract tourism, Villahermosa's restaurants are not suited to the gourmand-on-a-budget. You'll generally find yourself choosing between snack-joint *taquerías* and the cheaper restaurants, where price unfortunately reflects food quality. The main produce market operates off Pino Suárez near Zozaya, a few blocks from Puente Grijalva.

**Aquarius,** Av. Mina 309 (tel. 14-25-37), just east of Juárez and a short jaunt from the first-class bus station. Small, friendly health food/vegetarian place. The *comida* *del día* (1pm-about 7pm) is an excellent deal: salad, soup, main dish, dessert, and one free fruit drink all for 18.50 pesos. Breakfasts 10.90-17.90 pesos. Adjoining store sells squirrel food and other wholesome goodies. Open Mon.-Sat. 7:30am-10pm, Sun. 8am-9pm. Credit cards accepted. Other outlet at Av. Zaragoza 513 (tel. 12-05-75) has shorter hours.

**Restaurant Madan,** Madero 408 (tel. 2-16-50), diagonally across from Hotel Oriente. A/C, black-and-white photos of old Villahermosa, cheap food, and many elderly men smokily discussing politics. Not for the devout anti-cigarette crowd. Tacos 12.50 pesos. Three-course *menú del día* 19 pesos. Credit cards accepted. Open daily 7am-11:30pm.

**El Torito Valenzuela,** 27 de Febrero 202 at Madero (tel. 14-11-89), right next to the Hotel Madero. The cleanest and most popular of the downtown *taquerías*. Steaming, veggie-packed tacos for 2-3.50 pesos a pop. *Quesadillas* 9 pesos. *Comida corrida* 15 pesos. 3 eggs, many styles 9 pesos. Open daily 8am-midnight.

**Café Bar Impala,** Madero 421 (tel. 12-04-93). A well-preserved 1940s joint serving great *tamalitos de chipilín*, *panuchos* (cold tortillas with shredded meat and beans), and tacos (all 1.50 pesos apiece). Open daily 8am-8pm.

## SIGHTS

While exploring a ruins site at La Venta, Tabasco, in the early 1940s, U.S. archaeologist M.W. Sterling discovered six massive sculpted stone heads. Further studies indicated that La Venta was a principal ceremonial center of the Olmecs. In the late 1950s, many of the monumental pieces were moved to an archaeological park in northern Villahermosa, the **Parque-Museo La Venta.**

The Olmecs numbered only 250,000 at the height of their civilization (between 800 and 200 BCE), but their distinctive artistic style influenced groups from the Ríos Sinaloa and Panuco in northern Mexico to the Nicoya Peninsula in Costa Rica. The Olmecs worshipped the jaguar as a divine creator, and sculptors at La Venta produced numerous jade carvings in the animal's image. Some human faces were given a "jaguar mouth" to symbolize the intermingling of the divine and the mortal. The Olmecs' colossal sculptures range from 2 to 10m in height. Each of the spherical heads wears a war helmet, and the faces are characterized by thick eyelids, a wide nose, and prominent lips. Three of the giant heads, along with 30 other stone pieces, are now in the Parque-Museo La Venta.

Doubling as archaeological park and zoo, the site is enchanting. La Venta's Olmec sculptures take center-stage, displayed along a pathway which winds through a verdant jungle only minutes from the *Zona Remodelada*—only the traffic on Grijalva reminds you that you're actually in a sizeable city. Buzzing mosquitoes keep the unprepared tourist cruising along at a slightly-faster-than-these-bloody-insects-can-fly pace. Plaques along the way illuminate the faded Olmec art. While a few creatures, notably the crocodiles, put in cameo appearances along this pathway, most are located at the park's northern edge. Here, birds flit through the aviary, grand felines bask in the sun, and cheeky monkeys toy with those iguanas foolish enough to enter their pit. You can get a good look at the jaguars, which roam around their enclosure in the south of the park, halfway around the archaeological walk, near the giftshop.

To get to the *parque-museo*, take the "Tabasco 2000," "Circuito #1," or "Parque Linda Vista" **bus** (1.10 pesos) from Madero in the center to the intersection of Tabasco and Grijalva. Walk northeast on Grijalva for ten minutes until you reach the "La Venta" entrance (site open daily 9am-4:30pm; admission 10 pesos; 2-hr. tours in Spanish or English about 25-45 pesos for 1-35 people).

Return to Paseo Tabasco through the **Parque Tomás Garrido Canabal,** which lies on the Laguna de las Ilusiones and surrounds the Parque-Museo La Venta. Landscaped alcoves hide benches and fountains. Climb the 40m *mirador* for an excellent view of Villahermosa and look for the manatees that swim in the *laguna* below. The main entrance is at the corner of Tabasco and Grijalva (admission free).

Northwest on Paseo Tabasco, away from the city center and Río Grijalva, is **Tabasco 2000,** a long strip of sparkling new buildings that includes the city's cement block Palacio Municipal, a convention center, several fountains, a shopping mall, and a **planetarium** (tel. 16-36-41) with Omnimax shows dubbed in Spanish (shows Mon.-Fri. 5:30 and 6:30pm, Sat.-Sun. 6 and 7:30pm; admission 7 pesos). To reach Tabasco 2000, take the "Tabasco 2000" bus from the city center. Tell the driver where you want to get off, as the bus continues past Tabasco 2000.

The catalyst for the creation of the Parque-Museo La Venta was Carlos Pellicer Cámara, Tabasco's most famous poet. His name graces the **Museo Regional de Antropología Carlos Pellicer Cámara,** the main attraction at Villahermosa's new **Center for the Investigation of Olmec and Mayan Cultures** (CICOM). The museum describes archaeological sites near Villahermosa, including Palenque and Comalcalco. The first floor concentrates on the life, times, and arts of the Olmecs and the Maya, while the top floor includes representative pieces from all of Mexico's indigenous tribes. Guide books (in English or Spanish) are available at the ticket counter. From the *Zona Remodelada,* the museum is best reached by a 15-minute walk south along the Río Grijalva. The crowded #1 and "CICOM" buses pass frequently (open daily 9am-7:30pm; admission 5 pesos).

## ENTERTAINMENT

Villahermosa presents two basic nightlife options: the discos in the luxury hotels and the cultural activities sponsored by the Instituto de la Cultura.

The hottest mix of *salsa,* tropical music, and visual stimuli are found at **Video Bar Factory,** on Av. Méndez (open Tues.-Sat. 10pm-3am), **Tequila Rock,** on the part of Paseo Tabasco that extends into the Holiday Inn (open Wed.-Sun. 10pm-3am), and **Estudio 8** (tel. 14-44-66), in the Hotel Maya on Paseo Tabasco before Tabasco 2000 (open Thurs.-Sun. 9pm-2 or 3am). An older crowd packs into **Disco KU,** on Av. Sandino, and at the ambitiously named **Snob,** Juarez 106 in the Hyatt (both open Tues.-Sat. 10pm-3am). Taxi drivers are well-acquainted with disco hot spots and are the only efficient means of reaching them.

For mellower diversion, head for **Galería El Jaguar Despertado,** Saenz 117 (tel. 14-12-44), near Reforma in the *Zona Remodelada.* The café in the back sometimes features live classical music, but even if the tunes are absent, the fountain, the original Mexican art, and the gallery upstairs attract an interesting mix of intellectuals and thinkers (open Tues.-Sat. 3:30-10pm).

The **Instituto de Cultura Tabasco** (tel. 12-90-24), in the Edificio Portal del Agua on Magallanes, publishes a monthly calendar of musical, theatrical, and other cultural events; look for it in museums and major hotels.

# ■ NEAR VILLAHERMOSA

## COMALCALCO

Whereas La Venta documents Tabasco's Olmec past, Comalcalco demonstrates the Maya's dominance over the area in the later Classic period (200-700 CE). One of the northernmost Mayan settlements, Comalcalco has yielded evidence of contacts with other Yucatecan Mayan settlements, as well as with the Toltecs, Mexica, and Totonacs. The site's most distinctive feature is its architecture: unlike those of other Mayan cities, the pyramids and buildings of Comalcalco were constructed from packed earth and clay and later covered with stuccoed oven-fired bricks. Eroded but still imperial, the ruins contrast dramatically with the jungle behind them. Do not climb the temples—Uzi-toting guards are serious about the *"no subir"* signs.

With 10 levels, the hulking 25m-high **pyramid** to the left of the entrance to the site is Comalcalco's best-known landmark. The north face bears traces of the elaborate stucco carvings that once completely covered the structure's sides. Behind the pyramid stretches the north plaza, surrounded by a series of ruined minor temples and mounds. If you look closely at the dilapidated walls, you can see the insides of Comalcalco's brickwork and oyster-shell mortar.

From the plaza, a well-worn path leads up the side of the acropolis area and passes a group of three temples on the way. As with the main pyramid, vestiges of elaborate decorative carvings can be seen on each of these temples.

Farther up the acropolis, turn right to reach the **Tomb of the Nine Knights of the Night,** named after the nine bas-relief figures on the walls of the tomb. Visible from the acropolis, three sides of Comalcalco's **ballcourt** (to the left) remain unexcavated and covered with tropical vegetation. Several temples and administrative buildings, including one known as **The Palace,** stand in pieces atop the acropolis against a backdrop of tall, square brick columns and several roofless rooms (site open daily 10am-5pm; admission 10 pesos).

**Getting There:** The archaeological zone lies 34km northwest of Villahermosa, 2km from the town of Comalcalco. It can be reached by the bus that travels to Paraíso via Comalcalco. Get off at Comalcalco and walk back a block on Méndez to its major intersection with Rte. 187. From this corner catch a *combi* (about 2 pesos) and ask the driver to let you off at the access road to *las ruinas.* From here, the walk to the site is a pleasant 1km. You can also take a taxi (*especial*) directly to the site from the Comalcalco bus station (about 5 pesos).

## TABASCO COAST

In terms of natural beauty, the beaches of the Tabasco Coast pale in comparison to those of the Jalisco Coast or Quintana Roo. Generally speaking, however, Tabasco's beaches are clean and good for swimming, although oil drilling has not had a salutary effect on the coastal ecosystem.

Most of the small resort towns offer budget accommodations, and all are adept at preparing delicious seafood. Each about 70km from Villahermosa, the westernmost resorts on the coast, **El Paraíso** and **El Limón,** can be reached by bus. From Villahermosa and El Paraíso, buses run daily to the resort at **Puerto Ceiba,** where you can rent boats to explore its lagoon. From there, you can reach a number of small fishing villages that owe their livelihoods to oysters. Farther to the west and harder to reach, **Pico de Oro** and **Frontera** both bask on the sandy shore and provide possibilities similar to those at the closer El Paraíso and El Limón.

**Getting There:** To catch a bus after visiting the ruins, wait where the access road intersects Rte. 187 and flag down a blue bus or green-and-white *combi* marked "Paraíso" Many buses leave El Paraíso for Villahermosa. Check the return times at the corresponding Villahermosa bus stations. Buses leave from the *zócalo.*

## ■■■ TEAPA

An hour's drive south of Villahermosa along roads flanked by banana groves, Teapa (pop. 35,000) attracts visitors to its sulfuric spa and splendiferous caverns. Together, the sites make a full daytrip from Villahermosa. The town itself is slow-moving; its dilapidated, leafy *zócalo* and quiet streets make for peaceful strolling.

**Orientation and Practical Information** Getting to Teapa from Villahermosa via public transport is easy: catch a first-class **Cristóbal Colón** bus (5 per day, 1hr., 9 pesos), or a more frequent first-class **Transportes Villahermosa-Teapa** bus from the Central Camionera off Grijalva (every 30min., 6am-9pm, 9 pesos). The Transportes Villahermosa-Teapa bus lets you off at Teapa's main bus terminal on Méndez, from which local buses whisk you to either the spa or the caves. If you arrive by Cristóbal Colón, walk 200m to the left to the clock tower/arch on Méndez. The *zócalo* is a 10-min. walk to the left, the main bus terminal 10 min. to the right.

The **police** (tel. 2-01-10), in the Palacio Municipal on Méndez, are available around the clock. In Teapa, the **post office** is in a shack at Netzahualcóyotl 109 (tel. 2-02-54), the terminus of a dead-end street, two blocks from Méndez. From the church, head toward the bus stations on Anastasio Luque and take the first left. *Lista de Correos* (open Mon.-Fri. 9am-3pm). **Postal Code:** 06080. The long-distance **telephone** *casetas* do not accept collect calls. **Telephone Code:** 932. Dollars only can be changed at **Bancomer,** Av. Méndez 125 (tel. 2-00-36), one block before the church (open Mon.-Fri. 9am-12:30pm). The **Cristóbal Colón bus station** (tel. 2-03-52) is 200m up the road to the right from the clock tower/arch on Méndez. First-class buses run to Tuxtla Gutiérrez (5 per day, 5hrs., 36 pesos) via Pichucalco (30min., 4 pesos) and to Villahermosa (5pm, 1hr., 9 pesos). Second-class buses run to Villahermosa every hour (station open daily 7am-10pm). Ask kindly and you can leave **baggage** behind the counter. Villahermosa is much more easily reached by hopping into one of the red **taxis** in the center of town. They leave as soon as they have five people (approximately every 20min., 45min., 10 pesos). Notoriously unreliable **trains** connect Teapa to Mexico City (24hrs.) via Coatzalcoalcos (6hrs.), and Mérida (25hrs.). The **train station office** (tel. 2-00-03) is open Monday through Friday from 8am-4pm. To get there, take a taxi from the center. **Farmacia Espíritu Santo,** Calle Dr. Ramón Medina 106 (tel. 2-00-93), is open daily from 7am-10:30pm, but provides 24-hour service if you ring the bell in the upper-left-hand corner of the doorway. Pharmacies on Méndez have a wider selection of goods during the day.

**Accommodations and Food**  Teapa's accommodations are a scant bunch without a bargain in sight. Rooms at **Casa de Huéspedes Miye,** Méndez 211 (tel. 2-00-11), in the center of town, are the best budget deals available. Rockers in the lobby and fully curtained rooms are in good shape. Most rooms have shiny private baths, but communal baths are also clean. The owner swears there's hot water but the communal shower dribbles only cold. Check-out 1pm (singles 25 pesos, 30 pesos with bath; doubles 30 pesos, 40 pesos with bath; triples 40 pesos). More expensive is the **Hotel Quintero** (tel. 23-07-95), the blood-red modern building on the Calle E. Bastar side of the church and by far the most comfortable place around. Rooms have brick floors, fans, baths, hot water, and phones. Upstairs rooms have balconies. Check-out 1pm. Reservations recommended (singles 60 pesos, 75 pesos with A/C; doubles 70 pesos, 90 pesos with A/C; triples 80 pesos, 100 pesos with A/C; MC and Visa accepted). Across the park from the church on Av. Plaza de la Independencia, **Hotel Jardín** (tel. 2-00-27), is a third option. Most plainly furnished lime-green rooms have two double beds. Ceiling fans seem to work only at take-off speed—fasten seatbelts, please. Saggy ceilings complete the decor. No hot water. Check-out 2pm (all rooms 50 pesos, but haggle during the low season).

A visit to Teapa is not complete without a visit to **La Bella Sultana,** Av. Carlos Romanos 275, a long walk from the center, just before the bus terminal. From the *zócalo,* head past the clock tower/arch, the dry bridge and one eatery. Look for the airy corrugated iron roof opposite the PEMEX station 200m further down. Fantabulous budget dining doesn't get any better than this. Cheery, Christmasy tablecloths complement the excellent service. Tacos start at 2 pesos apiece (open daily 6am-1pm, and 4pm-12:15am). Easier on the feet but not the wallet is **Restaurante Cheje** in Hotel Quintero, an air-conditioned but pricey alternative. Pasta dishes 12-15 pesos. Breakfasts 12-20 pesos (open Mon.-Sat. 7am-10pm; bar open noon-10pm).

# ■ NEAR TEAPA

## LAS GRUTAS COCONÁ

Just a few kilometers from town, **Las Grutas Coconá** were discovered in the late 1800s by the Calzada brothers during a hunting trip. A path winds for 500m into the hillside, passing impressive caverns and underground lagoons along the way. A flashlight isn't necessary for the visit, but if you haven't brought your own, hiring an eight-year-old guide is one way of seeing the caves with a flashlight (a small tip is the norm). 150m into the cave system, shine your light into the roof of the tunnel on the bend. Sometimes you can catch the tiny bats during their *siesta.*

Further on you'll enter a breathtaking, acoustically-funky domed cavern replete with mighty stalactites. Beyond, a wooden walkway leads over a pool into a dripping cave. The final cave is draped in gloom and can only be explored with a flashlight. On the way back, look for a left-hand turnoff where a lone lightbulb has given life to a cluster of ferns. Here you can limbo beneath a 3-ft. ledge to reach a secluded emerald pool filled with blind fish.

**Getting There:** *Combis* for the *grutas* leave from Calle Bastar on the right hand side of the church every 20 minutes except during lunchtime (noon to 2pm). The *combis* are clearly marked "Grutas" and cost 1 peso. Taxis charge 10-15 pesos. To get back to town, catch the *combi* (open daily 9am-6pm; admission 3 pesos).

## EL AZUFRE SPA

**El Azufre Spa,** 5km west of Teapa on the way to Pichucalco, is a classic case of a fine resource gone to pot at the hands of Mexican (mis)management. The site sports three pools, a picnic area, *cabañas,* and a modest restaurant. The pungent, sulfuric tepid springs are unfortunately diminished by their dilapidated surroundings. The tiled, shallow swimming pools which collect the spring water are chipped and cracked, an inch of slimy, green ooze meets your every step, and the water is filled with gunk. If you can join the Mexican families in ignoring the conditions, you might enjoy the pleasant outdoor setting. Since the communal showers spout nothing but air, don't expect company on that smelly bus ride home. Should you become addicted to the waters, huge rustic *cabañas,* featuring three single beds and oodles of hammock hooks, can be rented for 100 pesos (admission 10 pesos).

**Getting There:** To reach El Azufre from Teapa, take the **Pichucalco** bus (every hr., 1.50 pesos from the bus terminal at Méndez and ask the driver to let you off at the short access road to the spa. A Pichucalco-bound taxi-*colectivo* will cost you 5 pesos. To return, walk back to the highway and flag down a returning vehicle.

# ■ Yucatán Peninsula

Too engrossed in hunting for slaves to watch where he was going, Hernández de Córdoba mistakenly ran aground here in 1517. When the freshly disembarked sailors asked the locals where they were, the Mayans, naturally not understanding Spanish, replied something to the effect of "We haven't a clue what you're talking about." Unfamiliar with the Mayan language, Córdoba only caught the last few syllables of their reply, *"Tectetán,"* and erroneously dubbed the region Yucatán before shoving off again. This encounter established a paradigm that would hold throughout Yucatán's history; misunderstood and continually molested by outsiders, it would never be fully conquered. Today the peninsula's culture remains essentially Mayan, but foreign influence fights on. Maya is still the first language of most of the inhabitants, *indígena* religions persist (often with a Catholic veneer), and fishing, farming, and hammock-making out-produce big industry and commerce. Burgeoning tourism, however, is threatening the traditional *yucateco* way of life. As international nomads discover the peninsula's fine beaches, beautiful colonial towns, and striking Mayan ruins, more workers are drawn by the dubious allure of the tourism industry. Many of those not working in the hotels or restaurants find themselves weaving hammocks for *viajeros* in Mérida, fishing lobster for visitors to Cancún, or acting as multi-lingual guides at archaeological sites.

The peninsula's geography consists mostly of flat limestone scrubland or rainforest dotted with an occasional *cenote* (freshwater sink-hole). Because of the highly porous limestone subsoil, there are no above-ground rivers in Yucatán. Poor soil and the lack of water make farming difficult, so maize remains the staple crop. The prominence of the rain god Chac at most Mayan ruins testifies to the eternal importance of the seasonal rains, which fall from May to late summer.

Since the Maya conquered the peninsula around 500 BCE, the Yucatán has known several masters. Many of the buildings in the Maya's illustrious city of Chichén Itzá are the creations of Toltecs and were built after the tribe took the peninsula in the 11th century. The Spaniards landed on the Caribbean coast but did not attempt to penetrate the region until they reached Campeche, which was taken and lost several times before being securely fortified during the mid-16th century. The Montejo family orchestrated the Spanish conquest in the Yucatán, establishing Mérida on the site of a Mayan village in 1542. More recently, other European influences have shaped Yucatán's cities—most notably in Mérida, where the Elysian Paseo Montejo reflects a French influence.

Colonialism brought more than just forts and stone cathedrals, however. Spanish settlers received vast land grants and convinced displaced *indígenas* to labor on their estates. Oppressed and humiliated, the *indígenas* rebelled against the white *ladino* overlords repeatedly in 1546, 1585, 1610, and 1624. After gaining independence from Spain, *ladinos* only stepped up their exploitation of Mayan peoples and lands. Thousands of Mayans were conscripted as debt laborers on the expanding *henequén* plantations. In 1847, Mayan discontent exploded in a bloody racial struggle, known as the Caste War, which enveloped the peninsula. At the height of the Mayan advance a year later, only the cities of Mérida and Campeche remained in *ladino* hands. A rebel Mayan community survived in eastern Yucatán as late as 1901, sovereign decades after Mexican troops had retaken most of the peninsula.

Yucatán's most recent culture shock resulted from the completion of Rte. 180, which links the peninsula with mainland Mexico. Desiring to maintain their historical isolation from the rest of the Mexican Republic, proud *yucatecos* originally resisted the federal highway plans. Despite new competition in shipping and transportation from the south and the ongoing invasion of sun- and ruins-seeking foreigners, Yucatán retains its distinctive character: *yucatecos* have held on to their native drawl and continue to brew the dark beers considered to be the nation's finest.

Mayan culture thrives in the peninsula's small towns, where the only evidence of Western influence arrives in the form of the weekly Coca-Cola truck. In the expanses between the touristed archaeological sites, *yucateco* women continue to carry bowls of corn flour on their heads and wear embroidered *huipil* dresses. The Yucatán's state borders form a "Y" down the center of the peninsula. The eponymous Yucatán state sits in the crest of the "Y," Quintana Roo sees the Caribbean sunrise on the eastern coast, and Campeche faces the Gulf Coast to the west. "The Yucatán" refers to the peninsula, not the state, whereas "Yucatán" without the article can refer to either entity.

# CAMPECHE

While its countryside is pocked with Mayan ruins and its coastline is over 200km long, Campeche pulls in fewer visitors than Yucatán to the north or Quintana Roo to the east. In large measure, tourists avoid the state because Campeche lacks a kind of swaggering grandeur—ruins, for example, are modest, relatively inaccessible, and rarely visited. All this could be set to change in the wake of recent developments, however. In tandem with the exciting new archaeological discoveries which are being made in the gigantic Calakmul Biosphere Reserve, the state has begun a recent push to promote itself as an ecotourism paradise. Off-the-beaten-track travelers can take in the jungle-clad ruins of Becán, Xpujil, Chicaná and the mysterious, unknown Calakmul, believed to rival Chichén Itzá and Tikal in size.

## ■■■ ESCÁRCEGA

The town of Escárcega is best known to travelers as a critical transit point at the intersection of the Yucatán's Rtes. 261 and 186. From the first-class **ADO station** the principal routes are north to Mérida (9 per day, 6hrs., 57.50 pesos), east to Chetumal (8 per day, 4hrs., 44.50 pesos), west to Villahermosa (8 per day, 4hrs., 48.50 pesos), and southwest to Palenque (2am, 1pm, and 10:30pm, 3hrs., 35 pesos). Other connections include Campeche (7 per day, 3hrs., 26.50 pesos), Cancún (1, 2, 8:30, and 11:30am, 10hrs., 104.50 pesos), Córdoba (2:30, 3, 5, and 9:30pm, 154 pesos), Mexico City (5 per day, 17hrs., 213 pesos), Puebla (9:30pm, 15hrs., 189 pesos), and Veracruz (5, 7:30, and 10:30pm, 9hrs., 129 pesos). The 10:30pm departure for Palenque is with **Cristóbal Colón,** which continues on to San Cristóbal (7hrs., 66 pesos) and Tuxtla Gutiérrez (8½hrs., 81 pesos). One km down Av. Hector Pérez Martínez, the second-class terminal runs buses to similar locations.

As buses leave around the clock for most destinations, it's unlikely you'll be stranded in Escárcega. If you're too exhausted to continue, however, head into town on Av. Martínez. One railway crossing and two traffic lights later, take a right for Escárcega's small *zócalo,* decorated with a garishly modern clock tower and neatly clipped trees. Escárcega is not the safest of places after dark, so take a taxi if it's late. The fading green **Hotel Las Tres Hermanas** (tel. 982/4-01-10), right on the *zócalo,* provides brightly painted, comfortable rooms along with plenty of street noise. Private bathrooms lack both hot water and toilet seats, and some even sprout fluffy moss. Best of all, however, the hotel is just three blocks from the second-class bus station (singles 30 pesos; doubles 50 pesos, with two beds 60 pesos; triples 70 pesos). To refuel before getting back on that bus, head for **Cocina Económica La Tabasqueña,** one block west of the post office on the *zócalo* and across the railroad tracks. Breakfast eggs run about 6 pesos (open daily 7am-8pm).

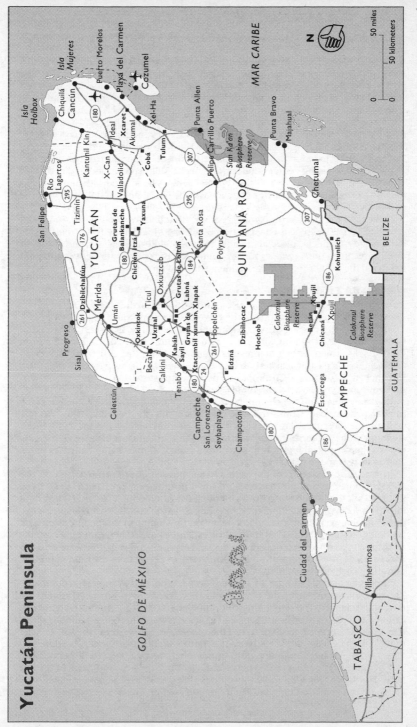

# Yucatán Peninsula

ESCÁRCEGA

MAR CARIBE

GOLFO DE MÉXICO

**YUCATÁN**

**QUINTANA ROO**

**CAMPECHE**

**TABASCO**

GUATEMALA

BELIZE

Isla Holbox

Isla Mujeres

Puerto Morelos

Playa del Carmen

Cozumel

Chiquilá

Cancún

Xcaret

Akumal

Xel-Ha

Punta Allen

Ideal

Tulum

Cobá

Felipe Carrillo Puerto

Sian Ka'an Biosphere Reserve

Punta Bravo

Majahual

Chetumal

San Felipe

Río Lagartos

Kantunil Kin

X-Can

Valladolid

Yaxuná

Santa Rosa

Tizimín

Grutas de Balankanche

Chichén Itzá

Oxkutzcab

Grutas de Loltún

Polyuc

Mérida

Umán

Oxkintok

Ticul

Uxmal

Kabáh

Sayil

Grutas de Labná

Xtacumbil xunaan

Xlapak

Hopelchén

Kohunlich

Xpujil

Becán

Chicaná

Progreso

Dzibilchaltún

Calkini

Tenabó

Edzná

Dzibilnocac

Hochob

Sisal

Celestún

Campeche

San Lorenzo

Seybaplaya

Champotón

Escárcega

Calakmul Biosphere Reserve

Ciudad del Carmen

Villahermosa

Progreso

Becal

50 miles

50 kilometers

180

295

176

180

261

24

180

261

184

307

295

186

307

186

180

# ■■■ CAMPECHE

Campeche was once a Mayan settlement called "Ah Kin Pech," or "Place of the Serpents and Ticks." Soon after Francisco Hernández de Córdoba's arrival on the Yucatán Peninsula, the city was renamed and its destiny redirected. By 1540 "Ah Kin Pech" had become "Campeche," and the construction of an important trading port was underway. Trade ships loaded with precious logwood dye dropped anchor in Campeche's port, frequently forced to seek shelter from vicious and persistent winds. The wounded ships attracted Dutch, English, and French buccaneers, and forced the Spanish to surround Campeche with stark bulwarks and a stone wall. By the time the fortification was complete, the city's economic import was waning. When the Bourbons rose to power in Spain in the 18th century, Ciudad del Carmen, a deep-water departure port in the Bahía de Campeche, soon surpassed Campeche as the regional trading center. Modern Campeche still plays second fiddle, though now the industry is tourism and the regional centers lie to the north and east. But the city has retained its character—sections of the old stone wall still stand, and the *baluartes* (bulwarks) and forts still guard (at least in spirit) the city center.

These days the city exerts as much energy attracting *extranjeros* as it once did repelling them. The recent construction of an airport and a highway from Mérida have made Campeche more accessible to tourists. Results are starting to show: three gargantuan hotels and a tourism complex have popped up between the old town and the waterfront, and the building still goes on.

## ORIENTATION

An easy 252km southwest of Mérida and 444km northeast of Villahermosa, Campeche is a popular stopover for travelers en route between the northern Yucatán and the rest of Mexico. The most direct link between Mérida and Campeche is Rte. 180 (2hrs. by car). From the south, take coastal Rte. 180 from Ciudad del Carmen, which merges at Champotón with Rte. 261 from Escárcega. Campeche is then easily reached via the new toll (*cuota*) highway, which runs from Haltunchen, just north of Champotón. Speed bumps (*topes*) make the curving scenic route via Seybaplaya excruciatingly slow.

All major routes into the city intersect the peripheral highway that encircles it. A smaller circular road, **Circuito Baluartes,** falls within the outer highway, circumscribing the old city. All main roads converge on the Circuito in the city center. **Avenida Gobernadores** comes in from the Mérida highway northeast of the city, crosses the peripheral highway, and passes the airport, train station, and bus terminals on its way to the Circuito.

To reach the *zócalo* from the first- and second-class **bus terminals,** catch the "Gobernadores" bus (1 peso) across the street from the station. There are no fixed stops, so ask the bus driver to drop you off at Baluarte de San Francisco. Turn right into the old city and walk four blocks on Calle 57 to the *zócalo*. If you'd rather make the 15-minute walk from the station, head left on Gobernadores and bear left as it becomes the large, divided Circuito Baluartes. Three blocks later, turn right on Calle 57 through the stone arch of Baluarte de San Francisco and walk four blocks to the *zócalo*. **Taxis** from the airport to the *zócalo* cost 25 pesos; from the train or bus stations they charge five pesos.

Campeche once fit into the 40 square blocks surrounded by the seven *baluartes*. The wall which completed the city's fortification was mostly dismantled around the turn of the century. The *centro*'s narrow, cobbled streets are identified by numbers. East-West streets have odd numbers, and increase from 51 to 65 in a southerly direction. Calle 8 runs north-south between the *zócalo* and the western city wall. Parallel to Calle 8, to the east, lie Calles 10 to 16. The *zócalo* lies near the sea, bordered by Calles 8, 10, 55, and 57. To the west, outside the city wall, Avs. 16 de Septiembre and Av. Ruíz Cortínez also run parallel to Calle 8 between the old city and the sea front. North of the *centro,* Calle 8 becomes Malecón Miguel Alemán, running past Iglesia de San Francisco uphill to Fuerte de San José El Alto. Av. Resurjimiento, the coast road south of the city, runs past the youth hostel and Fuerte San Miguel on its way to San Lorenzo and Seybaplaya.

A confusing network of **buses** links Campeche's more distant sectors to the edge of the old city. The fare on regular buses and minibuses ranges from 1-2 pesos. The market, where Gobernadores becomes Circuito Baluartes, serves as the hub for local routes. Buses sometimes stray from their routes and have no established stops, but it is possible to flag them down at almost any point on their route. Buses only come in as far as the Circuito, so you'll have to get around the city center on foot. They run from 6am-11pm.

## PRACTICAL INFORMATION

**Tourist Offices: Federal Tourist Office,** Calle 12 #153 (tel. 6-67-67; fax 6-60-68), between Calles 53 and 55, next to Iglesia del Jesús. Friendly staff doles out maps and brochures. Luís speaks some English. Open Mon.-Fri. 9am-3pm and 6-9pm.

**Police:** (tel. 6-36-06), on Calle 12 between Calles 57 and 59. Open 24 hrs.

**Post Office:** 16 de Septiembre at Calle 53 (tel. 6-21-34), in the Edificio Federal. Open for stamps, registered mail, and *Lista de Correos* Mon.-Fri. 8am-8pm, Sat. 8am-1pm. Express mail next door at **MexPost** (tel. 1-17-30). Open Mon.-Fri. 9am-6pm. **Postal Code:** 24000.

**Telephones: Computel,** Calle 8 #255 (tel. and fax 1-01-29), between Calles 57 and 59. Calls to the U.S. about 13 pesos per min. International collect calls 5 pesos per 5min. Open daily 7am-10pm.

**Telegrams:** (tel. 6-43-90), opposite MexPost in the Edificio Federal. Money orders, telegrams, and **fax.** Open Mon.-Fri. 8am-6pm, Sat. 9am-noon (money orders), 9am-1pm (fax and telegrams).

**Travel Agencies: Agencia de Viajes Jaina,** Av. Ruiz Cartinez #55 (tel. 6-22-23, ext. 352), in the Hotel Ramada. Edzná tours, leaving at 9am and returning at 2pm, around 75 pesos per person. Special Ruta Puuc tours Sat. 5am-10pm (price negotiable). Open Mon.-Fri. 9am-2pm and 5-8pm, Sat. 9am-1pm. **Prof. Augustín Zavala y Lozano,** at Calle 16 #348 (tel. 6-44-26), gives 3-hr. tours of Edzná (about 60 pesos). **Destino Maya,** Av. Miguel Alemán 162 (tel. 1-37-26; fax 1-09-34), above Cine Estelar, reached by climbing the narrow stairway at the opposite end of the building from the cinema. This tour operator will put together any manner of package from Edzná to Tikal, including food and accommodations. Better deals for groups. Open Mon.-Fri. 9am-3pm and 6-9pm, Sat. 9am-2pm.

**Currency Exchange: Bancomer,** Av. 16 de Septiembre 120 (tel. 6-66-22), between Calles 59 and 61. Open Mon.-Fri. 9am-1:30pm. Another branch (tel. 6-40-52) on Circuito Baluartes at Calle 55 at the market. Open Mon.-Fri. 9am-2pm. **ATM** gives cash advances on Visa.

**American Express:** (tel. 1-10-00), Calle 59 in Edificio Belmar, next to Ramada Inn. English spoken. Open Mon.-Fri. 9am-2pm and 5-8pm, Sat. 9am-1pm.

**Airport:** (tel. 6-31-09), on Porfirio, 10km from the city center. **Aeroméxico** (tel. 6-58-78 and 6-56-78), at the airport, serves Mexico City, Houston, and Acapulco.

**Train Station:** (tel. 6-51-48 or 6-39-99), 3km northeast of the city center on the way to Chiná. To Mérida, Mexico City, and anywhere along the way. 2nd class daily at 10:30pm, *mixto* Mon.-Sat. at 8am. Price calculated by distance traveled (.05 pesos per km). *Mixtos* include passengers, chickens, and all sorts of weird stuff. Tickets go on sale 1hr. before the train is supposed to arrive.

**Bus Stations: First-class terminal,** Av. Gobernadores 289, four blocks north of Circuito Baluartes at Baluarte San Pedro. **Baggage check** (3 pesos per day), waiting room, and restaurant. **Autotransportes de Oriente (ADO)** services Mérida (13 per day, 3hrs., 31 pesos) and Valladolid and Cancún (11:30pm, 4 and 6hrs., 60.50 and 103.50 pesos). Catch the **Cristóbal Colón** *de paso,* leaving at 8pm for Palenque (5½hrs., 61 pesos), Ocosingo (7½hrs., 80 pesos), and San Cristóbal (9½hrs., 104 pesos), Chetumal (noon, 5hrs., 70.50 pesos), Mexico City (2:30 and 7pm, 20hrs., 239.50 pesos), and Villahermosa (9:30am, 1:05, and 11pm, 6hrs., 75 pesos). **Camioneros de Campeche** buses leave from the **second-class terminal,** around the corner on Calle Chile. To Iturbide (5 per day, 15 pesos). Five buses daily take the long route to Mérida (26 pesos) via Bolonchén, Kabah, Santa Elena, Uxmal (18.50 pesos), and Muna (20 pesos). Five buses also go to Escárcega (every 2hrs., 3½hrs., 19.50 pesos). **Autobuses del Sur** sends buses to Chetumal (6:45am and 10pm, 6hrs., 53.50 pesos) and Villahermosa via Escarcéga (about every 2hrs., 3½hrs., 19.50 pesos).

**Taxis:** (tel. 6-52-30.) 3 stands: at the intersection of Calles 8 and 55, to left of the cathedral; at the intersection of Calle 55 and Circuito, near the market; and at the intersection of Gobernadores and Chile, near the bus terminal. Basic rate for intra-city travel 5 pesos; to the airport 30 pesos.

**Car Rental: Hertz** (tel. 6-88-48), in the lobby of the Hotel Baluartes at Ruíz Cortínez and Calle 59. Rentals start around 150 pesos per day, though rates vary with season. Check by the office for details.

**Market:** On Circuito Baluartes, at the eastern extremes of Calles 53 and 55. Unexceptional handicrafts and cheap food. Open daily sunrise-sunset, Sun. until 3pm.

**Supermarket: Super Diez** (tel. 6-79-76), in the Pl. Comercial A-Kin-Pech on 16 de Septiembre behind and across the street from the post office. Open daily 7am-9:30pm. **Super Maz**, on Av. Resurjimiento in the Plaza Universidad, near the hostel. Open daily 7am-10pm.

**Laundromat: Lavandería y Tintorería Campeche,** Calle 55 #22 (tel. 6-51-42), between Calles 12 and 14. 5 pesos per kg. Same-day service if dropped off in the morning. Open Mon.-Sat. 8am-4pm.

**Red Cross:** (tel. 5-24-17), on Av. Las Palmas at northwest corner of city wall. Free 24-hr. emergency service.

**Pharmacy: Farmacia Gobernadores,** next to the ADO station. Open 24 hrs.

**Medical Services: Seguro Social** (tel. 6-52-02), on López Mateos south of the city. **Hospital General,** Av. Central at Circuito Baluartes (tel. 6-09-20), four blocks south of the market.

## ACCOMMODATIONS AND CAMPING

In a city often overlooked by tourists, few budget accommodations have cropped up. Several middle-range establishments hover just out of the range of backpackers' pesos. Unfortunately, many of the cheaper places have sunk to unusually low levels of cleanliness and maintenance, leaving a void in the 50-peso price range. Nature lovers and those bent on camping might investigate La Casona de San Lorenzo (see below), located 15km outside of town.

### In the Old City

**Colonial Hotel,** Calle 14 #122 (tel. 6-22-22 or 6-26-30), between Calles 55 and 57, 2½ blocks from the *zócalo*. A Jurassic joint magnificently restored. Freshly painted rooms in pop art pink, blue and green with high, beamed ceilings. Water closets, pastel boudoir sets, internal phones, hot water, ceiling fans, and mono-grammed sheets. Quaint, cheerful courtyard with tables. Check-out 1pm. Singles 60.95 pesos. Doubles 69 pesos. Triples 86.25 pesos. 15 pesos for each additional person. Add 20 pesos for A/C. Prices may rise to 75 pesos (singles/doubles) and 95 pesos (triples) around Dec. 1995. Reservations must be paid in advance.

**Hospedaje Teresita,** Calle 53 #31 (tel. 6-45-34), between Calles 12 and 14 in a residential part of the old city, three blocks northeast of the *zócalo*. There's good reason why this is the cheapest place in the *centro*. Large, bare, concrete-walled rooms have wobbly fans. Lacks privacy. Foul-smelling communal bathrooms. Check-out 1pm. Rooms 30 pesos. Two rooms have OK private baths, 40 pesos.

### On The Coast Road

**Youth Hostel Villa Deportiva Juvenil Campeche** (tel. 6-18-02), on Agustín Melgar, several blocks east of the water and the coastal highway. From the *zócalo*, take the "Lerma" bus south along the coastal highway to the intersection with Melgar and walk the remaining few blocks. Reasonably comfy, single-sex 2-bunk rooms with lockers and spiffy bathrooms. Table tennis, and supposed access to the monstrous pool. Fans, but no hot water. Full in July, August, and December. Call to reserve. Curfew 11pm. Check-out 11am. Bunk rental (includes towel, blanket, and pillow) is 15 pesos per night plus 20-peso deposit. Breakfast (7-8:30am) 9 pesos, lunch (1:30-2:30pm) 11.25 pesos, and dinner (until 11pm) 11.25 pesos.

Another option along the coastal road is **La Casona de San Lorenzo,** on Carretera Campeche-Seybaplaya, about 15km from town. From May to Sept., this secluded, beachfront hacienda, currently undergoing renovations, has one particular draw for wildlife enthusiasts: the beach is a nesting ground for sea turtles. On any given evening during these months, a short stroll down the beach will literally bring you face-to-face with these serene creatures.

The hacienda's guest rooms feature brand new private bathrooms and tiled floors, but, as yet, remain completely bare of furniture. However, hammock hooks are everywhere. String one up indoors for 15 pesos (hammocks provided). For 10 pesos per person you can camp just outside or put up a hammock under the rickety roof. No camping on the beach from May to Sept. Meals provided at 10 pesos a pop (one free breakfast with this book). *Agua purificada* and coffee at all hours. Use of the kitchen, TV, and stereo. There are no services within walking distance. Snorkeling gear can be borrowed free of charge.

Stays must be arranged with the hacienda's proprietors—just go to one of their offices and let them know you want to stay. Contact either Luis Márquez at the main tourist office on Calle 12 (see Tourist Office) or Enrique at Destino Maya (see Travel Agencies). After hours, call Enrique (tel. and fax 6-69-57). The only way to reach San Lorenzo by public transportation (short of paying a steep taxi fare), is by the "Seyba-playa" bus, which leaves from behind the market approximately every 1½hrs. (2.50 pesos, last bus 7pm). Make sure to tell the driver to drop you off at "San Lorenzo" as it's not an official stop. A paved road leads from the highway to a guard hut 50m away. Let the guard know you're staying with Luis and Enrique at the hacienda. A seven-minute walk will take you past two right-hand turn-offs to a "Save the Turtles" sign. Take the third right here to the hacienda, just down the road on the left.

## FOOD

*Campechanos* will tell you that there are two culinary experiences required of every first-time visitor to the city: dinner at San Pancho (see below) and a sampling of *pan de cazón*, the region's favorite specialty (three or four stacked *tortillas*, filled with baby shark and refried beans, and covered with an onion, tomato, and chile sauce). Other local dishes include *pámpano en escabeche* (pompano broiled in olive oil and flavored with onion, garlic, chile, peppers, and a dash of orange juice) and *sincronizadas* (shredded turkey and refried beans, spiced up with onions and habanero chiles, and served on deep-fried *tortillas*). A reasonable range of budget eateries line the streets in the vicinity of the *zócalo*. The dirt-cheap places in the market may serve up just that: dirt, cheap—watch your health. Save for San Pancho, all the listings are within a few blocks of the *zócalo*. Plan your meal times to accom-modate the whims of proprietors, many of whom take long *siestas*.

**Cenaduría Portales** (tel. 1-14-91), better known as **San Pancho** for its proximity to Iglesia de San Francisco. Take either the "Las Palmas" or "Concordia" bus (1 peso) up Malecón Miguel Alemán to the church. Cross the plaza east of the church and head left to another smaller square. The restaurant huddles beneath the arches straight ahead. San Pancho's fine, cheap food is enhanced by the gleaming, terra-cotta clock tower of the old governor's building that occupies two sides of the plaza. Watch the *sincronizadas* (2.50 pesos) and sandwiches (6-7 pesos) being prepared before your eyes. Open daily 7pm-midnight. Visa, MC accepted. San Francisco is an area you don't want to hang around in too long after dark—after dinner, get straight back on the bus.

**Restaurant Del Parque,** Calle 57 #8 (tel. 6-02-40), at Calle 8 on the *zócalo*. Serves light, local fare: soups, sandwiches, desserts, giant-sized alcoholic and non-alco-holic drinks, and regional dishes—*pan de cazón* 15 pesos. MC, Visa accepted.

**Nutrivida,** between Calle 10 and 12. A small health food store stocked with teas, whole-wheat bread, and delicious homemade yogurt with fresh fruit. Courtyard provides ample room for munching soy burgers with or without wheat germ. Fresh-squeezed orange juice. Open Mon.-Sat. 8am-2:30pm and 5:30-9pm.

**Restaurant La Parroquia,** Calle 55 #9 (tel. 6-80-86), between Calles 10 and 12. Chatty locals and a wall-mounted TV compete for attention in this friendly cafeteria. Slings hearty portions of seafood and meats from 13 pesos. Tasty *filete de pescado* comes with *tortillas* (15 pesos). Open 24 hrs. Traveler's checks and credit cards accepted.

## SIGHTS AND SAND

Campeche's primary points of interest are related to its history as a fortified colonial outpost from the 16th to the 19th centuries, repeatedly under threat from marauding pirates. You can visit several of the pirate-repelling *baluartes* (bulwarks) simply by following the Circuito Baluartes around the old walled boundaries.

The area's most extensive exhibit, the **Museo Regional de Campeche,** Calle 59 #38 (tel. 6-91-11), between Calles 14 and 16, was being renovated but should reopen by Dec. 1995. It contains well-documented exhibits describing nearby ruins and displaying the jewelry, pottery, and funerary artifacts of the local Maya. The museum inhabits the 18th-century Casa del Teniente del Rey (House of the King's Lieutenant; formerly open Tues.-Sat. 8am-8pm, Sun. 8am-1pm; admission 13 pesos).

While the Museo Regional is undergoing renovation, some of its smaller items, most notably the wonderful jade masks, are on display in the **Fuerte de San Miguel,** a few km south of town near the youth hostel. Walk, or preferably drive, south along the coastal road, then turn left on Carretera Escénico just after Melgar. A short climb inland will take you to San Miguel. The top of the fort affords a pleasant view of the southern half of the city (open Tues.-Sun. 8am-2pm and 5-8pm, though parts of the exhibit close at 5pm; admission 1 peso, free Sun.).

San Miguel's counterpart north of the city **Fuerte de San José El Alto** is a few km from the *centro.* If you don't have a car, take the "Bellavista" or "San José El Alto" bus from the market or make the long walk—head north on Gobernadores, turn left on Cuauhtémoc, left on Calle 101, and right on Calle 7. The bus will drop you halfway up the hill; a five-minute walk takes you to the fort at the top. Built in 1792, San José was amazingly defensible when in use. The path leading to the portcullis winds deliberately so that battering rams could not be used on the gate. The fort's moat, which encircles the building, supposedly was rife with vicious spikes; the water was obscured with chalk so as to hide them from anyone thinking about jumping in. As San José is higher than San Miguel, the view is more spectacular; miles of green shoreline to the north give way to the urban waterfront of the city to the south. In the distance you can make out the lighthouse and Fuerte de San Miguel (open Tues.-Sun. 8am-8pm; admission 1 peso, free Sun.).

In the **Baluarte de la Soledad,** across from the *zócalo* off Calle 8 near Calle 57, the **Museo de Estelas Maya** houses a small collection of well-preserved Mayan stelae and reliefs taken from sites in Campeche state, including a phallus the size of a torpedo. Informative texts in Spanish and pictographs elaborate on sculpted figures' occupations. Visitors may also climb the walls of the fort, which is surrounded by a park. A showroom across from the museum occasionally features free exhibits (museum open Tues.-Sat. 8am-8pm, Sun. 8am-1pm; admission 3 pesos).

In the **Fuerte Santiago** at the northern corner of the city, the **Jardín Botánico Xmuch'haltún,** Calles 8 and 51 (tel. 6-68-29), makes an inviting stop. Over 250 species of plants thrive in an open-air courtyard shaded by trees and marked by walkways, benches, and fountains. It takes only 10 minutes to walk through the garden, soothe your mind, and refresh your soul (open Mon.-Fri. 8am-3pm and 6-8:30pm, Sat. 9am-1pm and 6-8pm, Sun. 9am-1pm; guided tours Mon.-Fri. from 5-6pm).

Campeche's **cathedral** rises above the *zócalo.* Don Francisco de Montejo first ordered the construction of the cathedral in 1540, but builders did not complete the massive structure until 1705. The cathedral's main attraction is its façade, which includes human figures and obscure carvings. Inside, you'll find the *Santo Entierro* (Holy Burial), a sculpture of Christ in a carved mahogany sarcophagus with silver trim (open daily 7am-noon and 5-8pm; free).

A little farther from the center of town, the **Iglesia de San Francisco,** on Av. Gustave Díaz (the extension of Malecón Alemán), built in 1518, claims to be the oldest church on the American mainland. Inside, yellow Corinthian arches project towards an ornate altar (open daily 8am-noon and 5-8pm). A few blocks south of *el centro,* the **Iglesia de San Román** houses El Cristo Negro. An object of great veneration among *campechanos,* it is supposedly one of only three black Christs in the republic (open daily 6am-noon and 4-8pm; free).

> ### Who Said a Beach is a Beach is a Beach?
>
> To say that Campeche's beaches are not its strong point is a gross understatement. Locals know to head south for sand and sunbathing. For those planning to stay at San Lorenzo, the water is good for swimming, though the beach is mostly stony. The closest, half-decent stretch of sand is to be found at **Playa Payucán.** Payucán offers good snorkeling opportunities for those with their own equipment—rentals are not available. Buses for **Seybaplaya,** 2km from the beach, leave from behind the market (4 pesos; see Accommodations: San Lorenzo). For those seriously looking for beachy bliss, head for the gorgeous sands of **Sabancuy,** a long 130 km to the south. And please, don't forget the sunscreen—or else.

## ENTERTAINMENT AND SEASONAL EVENTS

Campeche sponsors various free outdoor musical events, including the *ballet folklórico* in the *zócalo.* Every Friday night at 8pm, an impressive light and sound show at Puerta de Tierra on Calles 59 and 18 retells in Spanish the dramatically dialectical story of residents repulsing pirates. The performers' awful acting is as entertaining as the historical account. Weather-permitting, a *ballet folklórico* follows the conclusion of the show. A small museum houses a collection of amazingly well-preserved muskets, crossbows, and powder kegs from the 17th century. (Light and sound show, 13 pesos, 50% discount with student ID. Tour is given in the language common to most people present; translated text in three other languages is projected onto the wall throughout the show. Museum open daily 8am-2pm and 4-9pm. Admission free.) The wildly popular **Noche de Trova,** including music and performances by the *ballet folklórico,* is celebrated in the Parque de Guadalupe on Wednesdays at 8pm and in the *zócalo* on Thursdays at 8pm. For a complete schedule of events, ask for the *programa de actividades* at the tourist information center. St. Román is Campeche's patron, and two weeks of both religious and secular festivities, starting September 15, celebrate his feast.

**Atlantis** (tel. 6-22-33), at the Ramada Inn on Av. Ruiz Cortínez, lords over Campeche's nightlife. (Cover 25 pesos. Women free Sat. before midnight. Thurs. is singles night and free. Open Thurs.-Sat. 10pm-3am.) Near the university on López Mateos, **La Cueva de Las Ranas** attracts Campeche's aspiring rock stars and a hipster student crowd from 9pm-3am.

## ■ NEAR CAMPECHE: EDZNÁ

If you're already in Campeche, it's easy and worthwhile to visit the nearby ruins of **Edzná** (House of the Grimaces), where hieroglyphics date back to 652 CE. Despite its lack of elaborately sculpted detail, the **Edificio de Cinco Pisos** (Building of the Five Floors), which towers above the surrounding valley atop the **Gran Acropolis,** is supremely elegant. Sixty-five stairs, some adorned with hieroglyphics over 1300 years old, lead up to tiers of columns crowned by a magnificent five-room temple. During its Mayan heyday, the perch atop the monument afforded a view of the network of irrigation canals criss-crossing the valley close to the Río Champotón, 20km to the west. The canals were built without the use of wheels, metal tools, or domesticated animals. Nearby, among the many thistle bushes, are the remains of a ballcourt and several other temples of a central plaza which are presently being excavated by Guatemalan refugees and Mexican archaeologists. Also on display are some of the 19 stelae found at Edzná, one crafted as early as 672 CE, others made during the 10th-century evacuation of the ceremonial center.

Mosquitoes at Edzná can be so vicious that you may want to ask Luís at the tourist office what the current state of affairs is before you leave several pints of valuable blood in the jungle. A canteen of water and plenty of repellent are a must (site open daily 8am-5pm; admission 13 pesos, half-price with any student ID, free Sun.).

**Getting There:** Buses leave for Edzná from the market in Campeche (about every 1½hrs., beginning at 7am, 1½hrs., 3 pesos). Arrive early, because buses fill up quickly. Ask the driver to let you off at the ruins access road—although the sign says 2km, the site is about 500m away. Only one bus returns to Campeche so be sure to ask the driver when to be back at the highway entrance. During *Semana Santa*, July, and August, the city sponsors cheap guided tours to the ruins every morning at 9am from the Baluarte San Carlos. In the off-season, tours are supposed to run on Saturday and Sunday at 9am (ask for details at the tourist office).

# CAMPECHE TO MÉRIDA: THE MAYAN ROUTE

Often called **La Ruta Maya,** the long route between Campeche and Mérida (254km on Rte. 261) traverses the Puuc Hills, an area that was home to about 22,000 people during the Classic period of Mayan civilization (4th-10th centuries). Decimated by diseases introduced by the Spanish, the Maya slowly surrendered most of their cities and ceremonial centers to the jungle. Beginning in the 18th century, the Mayan population began a recovery. While today's Puuc Maya live in towns with paved roads and plumbing, women continue to wear traditional embroidered *huipiles* and Maya remains the dominant language.

Uxmal, Kabah, the Grutas de Xtacumbilxunaan, and Dzibilnocac can be reached by **public bus** (the first three from either Campeche or Mérida, the last from Campeche only). First-class buses take the short route. Be sure to board a bus that follows the long route (*vía larga*), and ask the driver to let you off close to the sites. The return trip can be tricky. Find out in advance when buses or *combis* will pass the site, and wave your arms wildly to flag down a ride.

To guarantee a return ride, rent a car or go on an organized tour. In Campeche, the state tourist office can refer you to guides who will take you on a private tour to any of these sites (see Campeche, Practical Information: Tourist Office on page 481). From Mérida, the cheapest way to see the sites is to take the special Autotransportes del Sur "Ruta Puuc" bus that leaves daily at 8am. The bus stops for two hours at Uxmal and about 40 minutes at Kabah, Sayil, Xlapak, and Labná and returns to Mérida at around 3:30pm. Even though it doesn't include admission to the ruins, the 31-peso bus fare is one serious bargain (see Mérida, Practical Information: Bus Stations on page 498). The state tourist office in Mérida has information on tours organized by travel agencies—most offer standard daytrips to Uxmal and Kabah and to Chichén Itzá (see Mérida, Practical Information: Travel Agencies on page 496). Agencies will also organize private tours to any site on the peninsula. The condition of the roads on this stretch is very good, even when it rains, but inclement weather often means that you will have the site to yourself.

Most sites harbor at least a small gift shop that sells *refrescos* and postcards, but hotels and restaurants are scarce. The sole exception is Uxmal. Those who cannot afford the sky-high rates there have two options: base yourself in Campeche or Mérida, or take advantage of the cheap accommodations and dining in **Ticul,** 28km away off Rte. 261.

Edzná is the closest ruin to Campeche (see page 485). Dzibilnocac and Hochob lie 88km south of the highway at Hopelchén, which itself is 41km east of Campeche. A few hundred yards north of the Campeche-Mérida state border, the Sayil-Oxkutzcab road veers east. Sayil (5km from the crossroads), Xlapak (10km), and Labná (14km) lie along the road before it terminates at the Grutas de Loltún

(30km). This road is paved, but the paths themselves are often quite muddy. Continuing north on the highway after the turnoff to Sayil, Kabah is 5km down the road; 23km past Kabah lies Uxmal.

# ■■■ DZIBILNOCAC

Dzibilnocac consists of a set of three excavated temples in various states of decay, surrounded by low pyramidal mounds. The first temple showcases a wall atop a once-symmetrical structure, while the middle temple features two corbel-arched cave-like rooms partially filled with rubble.

The third temple is Dzibilnocac's prize. A tall, narrow building with rounded corners, it has rooms on several stories and has retained part of its stucco façade. Climb to its highest level for a closer view of a gruesome mask of the rain god Chac. At the middle levels, observe simple reliefs executed without perspective or depth in the style of cave paintings. From the top of this temple, you can see larger pyramidal mounds bulging out from under the thick underbrush.

Though this site spreads over little more than one square km, several roads and paths allow you to explore neighboring farms and cornfields. Very often, smaller ruins or pyramids rise from the middle of an otherwise-cleared field. Temples in the area tend to decay faster than they would in nature's hands alone—local farmers dismantle the structures for inexpensive building materials. Make sure that your legs and ankles are completely covered with long pants and thick boots, as the area is rife with poisonous snakes.

**Getting There:** The Dzibilnocac ruins hide some 61km off Rte. 261, near the small town of **Iturbide.** To reach this village by car, exit Rte. 261 at Hopelchén and drive south toward Iturbide. You'll soon reach a prominent sign at a fork pointing the way (straight on, *not* to the right) to Iturbide. When you reach the village, bear right around the *zócalo,* passing Iturbide's yellow church, and continue out of town on a slightly worse, if less rocky, road. (During the rainy season, the road can be treacherous; strongly consider walking.) 50m into the forest, the right branch of the fork in the road ends at the ruins. If you don't have a car, take the **Camioneros de Campeche** bus from Campeche's second-class bus station to Iturbide (5 per day, 3hrs., 15 pesos). The last bus (if it comes at all) leaves Iturbide for Campeche at 3:30pm. Some of those who miss the bus hitch back to Hopelchén on Rte. 261, where buses run later into the afternoon (12 per day, 1½hrs., 9 pesos). Ruins open daily 8am-5pm; free.

**Dzibalchén,** between Iturbide and Hopelchén, has no hotels, but stranded travelers can spend the night there in a tent or on a hammock. Ask at the Palacio Municipal for bathroom facilities and hooks. Restaurants near the *zócalo* are open during daylight hours. Buses to Campeche leave Dzibalchén early each morning.

# ■■■ HOCHOB

Hochob is a perfect spot for experiencing the ruins in silence and solitude, and campers will be hard-pressed to find a destination so deserted and yet so accessible. Traveling to Hochob is ill-advised in the rainy season, when roads tend to wash out.

Hochob's three temples cluster around a central plaza which swells modestly from the flat rainforest. Deep-relief geometric patterns molded in stucco cover the well-preserved temple to the right of the entrance, the front of which once formed an enormous mask of Chac, the door representing his gaping mouth.

The top of the ruined pyramid immediately to the left of the temple provides a good view of both the site and the nearby rainforest. A crumbling façade at the far end of the plaza still bears traces of geometric motifs, behind which a spire-topped temple rests on a steeply sloping pyramid (ruins open daily 8am-5pm; free).

**Getting There:** The Hochob ruins lie closer to the town of Dzibalchén than do the ruins of Dzibilnocac, but they are more difficult to reach without a car. Take the road out of Dzibalchén for about 1km toward Campeche, then follow the sign pointing left to the town of **Chencoh,** 9km down a rough but passable dirt road. In town, make a left at the second intersection of roads lined with stone walls. After passing a small elevated concrete platform on the right and a barnyard full of pigs and turkeys, turn left again and follow the dirt track some 4km into the jungle. Pock-marked with potholes, this road becomes especially dangerous in heavy rain. Just after most visitors throw in the towel, the road forks. Bear left, and soon the outline of temples will appear against the sky. Park at the small *palapa* below Hochob's hill-top site, and continue up the road on foot.

There is no public transportation from Dzibalchén (or anywhere else) to Chen-coh, and vehicles pass even less frequently here than on the stretch of road to Itur-bide. Those who catch rides ask their driver to let them off at the access road to Chencoh, 1km before Dzibalchén.

# ■■■ GRUTAS DE XTACUMBILXUNAAN

Along the main highway, 31km past Hopelchén, a turn-off to the left leads to the Grutas de Xtacumbilxunaan (shta-kum-bill-shoe-NAN, Caves of the Sleeping Girl), which are perched 1km off the highway. A custodian leads a tour past deep *cenotes* (natural wells) that once supplied all of the water for Bolonchén (3km away), and points out barely discernible shapes on the cavern's walls and ceilings. Although these caves compare poorly to the grand caves at Loltún, even novice spelunkers will have a good time poking around (open Tues.-Sun. 9am-5pm; tours in Spanish given only during daylight hours; free, but guide expects a tip).

**Getting There:** The Grutas lie 1km down a well-marked access road that crosses Rte. 261 2km south of Bolonchén. Drivers of second-class buses typically drop pas-sengers at the access road.

# ■■■ TICUL

A bustling provincial town off the Campeche-Mérida highway, Ticul (pop. 40,000) is a convenient and inexpensive base from which to explore the nearby Ruta Puuc sites of Uxmal, Kabah, Sayil, Xlapak, and Labná, as well as the Grutas de Loltún. Stay-ing in Ticul is a welcome relief from Mérida—the town's busy residents simply don't have time to heckle tourists. For those with wheels, a number of *cenotes* and colonial buildings can be sought out in nearby towns—Teabo (30km southeast of Ticul), Mayapán (45km to the northeast), and Holcá (105km to the northeast) await exploration. Maní (15km east of Ticul) features a colonial monastery; Tekax (35km to the southeast) a hermitage; and Tipikal, an impressive colonial church.

**Orientation and Practical Information** Ticul's streets form a grid with the main drag, **Calle 23,** passing east-west through the center. Even-numbered streets run north-south. Most commercial activity transpires between the *zócalo* (Calle 24) and Calle 30, four blocks to the west.

**Police** headquarters (tel. 2-00-10 or -11) are on the northeast corner of the *zócalo* on Calle 23 (open 24 hrs.). Ticul's **post office** (tel. 2-00-40) is in the Palacio Munici-pal on the *zócalo* (open Mon.-Fri. 8am-2:30pm). **Postal Code:** 97860. The **tele-gram office,** Calle 21 #192-C (tel. 2-01-46), is in the blue-and-white building behind the post office (open Mon.-Fri. 9am-3pm). **Banco del Atlántico,** Calle 23 #195, off the *zócalo,* changes U.S. dollars and traveler's checks (open Mon.-Fri. 9am-2pm). Make cheap **calls** from the long-distance *caseta,* Calle 23 #210 (tel. 2-00-00), between Calles 26 and 28 (open 8:30am-10pm). Calls can also be made from the Hotel Sierra Sosa (see below; 8 pesos per min. to the U.S.). **Telephone Code:** 997.

**Combis** gather at Parque de la Madre, Calle 23 between Calles 28 and 30, collect-ing passengers for Oxkutzcab and Muna (3 pesos each). *Combis* for Santa Elena (3 pesos) leave from Calle 24 on the *zócalo*. From Muna, 6 **buses** run daily to Campeche (20 pesos) via Uxmal and Kabah. Hourly buses head north to Mérida (7 pesos). The town's pedal-powered **taxis** transport passengers (mostly *rebozo-bedecked señoras*) for a couple of pesos. **Farmacia San Jose,** Calle 23 #214-J (tel. 2-03-93), is between Calles 28 and 30 (open 8am-1pm and 4-10pm). Dr. Estela Sanabria can be reached at the same number for 24-hr. **medical assistance,** though no one in the pharmacy speaks English.

**Accommodations and Food** Ticul has several hotels and good restaurants. **Hotel San Miguel** (tel. 2-63-82), on Calle 28 opposite Parque de la Madre, offers a variety of small, clean, battleship-gray rooms with ceiling fans and basic tiled bathrooms. Check-out 1pm (singles 25 pesos; doubles 32 pesos, with two beds 38 pesos). **Hotel Sierra Sosa** (tel. 2-00-08; fax 2-02-82), on Calle 24, on the northwest corner of the *zócalo*, has rooms with saggy beds, ceiling fans, and TVs. Rooms with windows go hand-in-hand with considerable street noise. Comfort yourself with free coffee and *agua purificada*, but prepare to be "bugged" all night long. Check-out noon (singles 40 pesos; doubles 55 pesos; triples with TV 50 pesos).

A 15-minute walk from the *zócalo*, the blue-doored **Restaurant Margarita,** on Calle 34, dishes up incredibly cheap yet very good *antojitos* and sandwiches. The eatery amounts to three tables parked in a concrete hallway with napkins so coarse they feel like they've been recycled eight times. Dinner for a dollar: 4 yummy *panuchos*, doused in pepper and dripping grease, plus a soda, are only 5.50 pesos (open daily 7am-noon and 7-11pm). **Restaurant Los Delfines** (tel. 2-04-01), on Calle 27 between Calles 28 and 30, serves shrimp dishes, stuffed chiles, and jars of lemonade under a big *palapa* (open daily 11am-6pm). Ticul's **market** is just off Calle 23 between Calles 28 and 30 (open daily sunrise-sunset).

**Getting to the Ruins** Public transportation in Ticul is not geared to ruin-happy tourists. While Uxmal and Kabah are fairly accessible given a modicum of luck with *combi* transfers, the absence of traffic on the Sayil-Oxkutzcab road will leave the car-less traveler frustrated and stranded. In general, you shouldn't rely on direct service, but should reconcile yourself to changing buses. To reach the ruins around Uxmal, take a Mérida-bound bus from the Ticul bus station (tel. 2-01-62), on Calle 24 behind the main church to Muna (every ½hr., 3 pesos). *Combis* for Muna leave from Parque de la Madre, Calle 23 between Calles 28 and 30. From Muna, board a southbound bus or *combi* for Uxmal, Kabah, or other sites. Alternatively, you can reach the ruins by catching a *combi* in the *zócalo* to Santa Elena (30min., about 3 pesos). Change *combis* at Santa Elena for Uxmal (16km towards Mérida) or Kabah (south towards Campeche). *Combis* are most plentiful in the morning.

To reach the Grutas de Loltún, snag a *combi* to Oxkutzcab at Parque de la Madre; you'll be let off at the intersection of Calles 23 and 26 (15min., about 3 pesos). *Combis* leave for Loltún from the lot across from Oxkutzcab's market "20 de Noviembre." Tell the driver to let you off at the *grutas* (10min., about 3 pesos), as everyone else is probably headed for the agricultural cooperative 3km further down the road. Because the road is more crowded with *combis*, it's easier to reach the Grutas than Uxmal or Kabah. Hitchhikers will rarely find rides on any of these roads.

# ■■■ UXMAL

The largest site along the Ruta Puuc, Uxmal (oosh-MAL) is as wondrous as you've heard. The combination of proud pyramids, finely sculpted reliefs, and immense masks here is simply without peer. Though many of the stone sculptures originally unearthed at Uxmal have been lost to the twin greed of museums and thieves, the ancient city's fabulous architecture maintains today the grandeur that drew 25,000 people to the site at its height.

**Orientation and Practical Information** Uxmal is on Rte. 261, the longer highway route (*vía ruinas*) between the state capitals of Mérida (79km north) and Campeche (175km southwest). 23km to the southeast lies the next Ruta Puuc site, Kabah. 5km south of Kabah, the Sayil-Oxkutzcab road branches off Rte. 261 and heads east past Sayil, Xlapak and Labná, and the caves at Loltún.

**Autotransportes del Sur (ATS)** sends six buses a day from Mérida to Uxmal (1½hrs., 10.50 pesos). If you're willing to make a long day of it, several Ruta Puuc ruins can be explored in one day from Mérida (see Mérida, Practical Information: Travel Agencies and Car Rental on page 496). A frugal option is the ATS "Ruta Puuc" bus, which visits Uxmal, Kabah, Sayil, Xlapak, and Labná all in one day (31 pesos; see Mérida, Practical Information: Bus Stations on page 498). From Campeche you'll have to take the Camioneros de Campeche bus which takes the *vía larga* to Mérida (5 per day, 3hrs., 18.50 pesos). Ask the driver to stop at the access road to the *ruinas*. To return, grab a passing bus at the *crucero* just outside the entrance to the ruins. The last buses to Mérida and Campeche pass at 8pm and 7pm, respectively.

A modern **tourist center** containing a small museum, restaurant, gift shop, photographic supply shop, and bathrooms greets you at the entrance to the ruins. The **Kit Bolon Tun auditorium,** also in the tourist center, features documentaries on the Ruta Puuc and a 15-minute film of the events which take place at Uxmal in celebration of the biannual equinox (5 shows per day in Spanish and 3 in English; free).

**Accommodations and Food** Room prices being a function of location, Uxmal's accommodations are prohibitively expensive. Consider staying 30min. away in Ticul, where hotel rooms cost half as much. In Uxmal, the cheapest option from an expensive bunch is **Rancho Uxmal** (tel. 47-80-21), 4km north of the ruins on Rte. 261. From the highway near Uxmal, you can reach Rancho Uxmal by hopping aboard a passing bus or *combi* (about 2 pesos). Concrete-floored rooms feature two double-beds and toilet seat-less pretty pink bathrooms. The pool is usually in service during peak season (singles 100 pesos, 20 pesos per additional person). Four concrete platforms beneath *palapas* are available for tent-pitching or hammock-slinging (15 pesos per person, including the use of communal toilets and showers; hammock rental 10 pesos). The adjacent restaurant of the same name is also expensive, serving a variety of tasty local dishes for 20-40 pesos. Diners have access to the hotel pool and are entertained Thurs.-Sat. at 2pm by a group of Mayan folk dancers (restaurant open daily 7am-9:30pm; traveler's checks accepted).

**Sights** According to the **Chilam Balam,** a Mayan historical account written in phonetic Spanish, Ah Suytok Xiu and his warriors from the Valley of Mexico invaded Yucatán toward the end of the 10th century. Xiu and his successors dominated Uxmal until the city's strength was sapped by 12th-century civil warfare. Because their priests foretold the coming of white, bearded men, the Xiu did not resist when the conquistadors attacked Uxmal. The last Xiu ruler of the city was Ah Suytok Tutul Xiu, whose descendants still live in the Puuc region. When Tutul Xiu was baptized as an old man, his godfather was Francisco de Montejo, conqueror of the Yucatán.

The 40m-tall near-pyramid visible upon entering Uxmal is the **Temple of the Magician.** The pyramid was built by a dwarf-magician who, it is claimed, hatched from a witch's egg and grew to maturity in the space of a single year. The legend of the dwarf-magician's birth struck terror into the heart of the governing lord of Uxmal, who challenged him to a contest of building skills. The dwarf's pyramid, built overnight, easily outclassed the governor's Great Pyramid, still visible to the right of the Governor's Palace. Grasping at straws, the spiteful ruler complained that the base of the dwarf's pyramid was neither square nor rectangular but was actually elliptical. Having undermined the legitimacy of the dwarf-magician's triumph, the governor proposed that he and his adversary compete to see who could break a *cocoyol* (a small, hard-shelled fruit) on their heads. The dwarf-magician, in whose skull a turtle shell had been placed, easily cracked open the *cocoyol.* The governor crushed his unaltered skull trying to match the dwarf fruit for fruit.

The elegant south-facing arch leads to the **ballcourt.** Note the glyphs on the rings through which well-padded players tried to knock a hardened rubber ball. Emerging from the ballcourt, head right along a narrow path to the **Cemetery Group,** a small, leafy plaza bounded by a small pyramid to the north and a temple to the west. Stones that once formed platforms bear haunting reliefs of skulls and crossbones.

Returning to the ballcourt, head south to the well-restored **Great Pyramid,** built by the governor in his contest with the dwarf-magician. The architecture and crude latticework reveal the influences of northern Campeche. To the west, the pyramid looks down on the jagged face of the Palomar, behind which lie the jungle-shrouded remains of the **Chenes Temple.**

The **House of Turtles** and the **Palace of the Governor** top a man-made escarpment east of the Great Pyramid. The two-story House is on the northwest corner of the escarpment and is adorned along its upper frieze with a series of sculpted turtles. (Symbolizing rain, turtles were venerated by the Maya.) Over 100m long and built on three landscaped terraces, the palace is typical of Puuc style. The eastern frieze is covered by 20,000 decorations, which together form 103 masks of Chac.

From the Palace of the Governor, try to spot the overgrown, pyramidal **House of the Old Woman,** which lies to the east. About 400m south of the house is the **Temple of the Phalli.** Phallic sculptures hang from the cornices of this ruined building and spurt rain runoff from the roof. Experienced guides are available to give more detailed tours of the site. Expect to pay about 30 pesos per person as part of a group. However, it's much more fun to impress other tourists by pretending to read the plaques in Mayan (accompanied by a slow, wise nodding of the head).

### Bright Lights, Ruined City

Uxmal's nightlife consists of a light-and-sound show celebrating Mayan history and culture. The Spanish version (12 pesos) begins at 7pm and ends after the last of the Campeche-bound buses passes. If you know Spanish, join the hilarious Mexicans in their primal chanting of "Chaaaac, Chaaaac." The English version (18 pesos) begins at 9pm; some have hitched a ride back with other English-speaking spectators. (Site open daily 8am-5pm. Admission 23 pesos, free Sun. Parking 8am-5pm and ½hr. before each show, costs 4 pesos.) Guidebooks are available at the bookstore. Bring a raincoat—the chanting might actually work.

## ■■■ KABAH

Once the second largest city in the northern Yucatán, Kabah was built with the blood and sweat of many slaves. The most elaborate of Kabah's structures is the **Codz Pop Temple** ("rolled mat" in Mayan), which was named for the odd shape of the rain god Chac's nose. The temple's broad façade displays nearly 300 masks of Chac, each comprised of 30 carved pieces. The elaborate Chenes style of the temple is unique to the Codz Pop—its neighbors to the east, **El Palacio** (a 25m pyramid) and **Las Columnas,** were executed in plainer fashion. The site is thought to have served as a court where justices settled disputes with the aid of the gods.

Across the highway, a short dirt road leads in three directions. An unrestored group of temples lies to the right, the nearly camouflaged West Group is to the left, and a beautifully sculpted arch resides directly ahead. The arch marks the beginning of the ancient *sacbé* (paved, elevated road) which culminated in a twin arch at Uxmal. The perfect alignment of the archway with the north-south line is testimony to Mayan astronomical understanding (site open daily 8am-5pm; admission 10 pesos, free Sun. and holidays).

**Getting There:** Bisected by Rte. 261 on its way from Campeche to Mérida, Kabah lies 23km southeast of its Ruta Puuc cousin, Uxmal. The remaining Ruta Puuc ruins are accessible via the Sayil-Oxkutzcab road, which branches off Rte. 261 5km south of Kabah. Because of its location on the Campeche-Mérida highway (*vía ruinas*), Kabah can be easily reached by any second class bus running between the two capitals (see Campeche and Mérida, Bus Stations on page 481 and page 498, respectively). Buses will stop at Kabah only if a passenger notifies the driver beforehand or if the driver sees a person wildly gesticulating on the shoulder of the highway. To make things easy, hop on an ATS "Ruta Puuc" bus (see Mérida, Practical Information: Bus Stations on page 498). Since almost all the tourists who come to Kabah have cars, many hitchers find rides back to Uxmal or onto the Grutas de Loltún.

# ■■■ SAYIL

The **Palace of Sayil,** "Place of Red Ants," is an architectural standout among the region's ruins. Between its three terraced levels, the building's 50 rooms exhibit unparalleled ornamental diversity. Walls are carved with rows of slender columns; the second-story frieze depicts the descending serpent-god's body; and elegant second-floor chambers open onto pleasant porticos, each graced by bulging columns. Climb to the top for a gorgeous panoramic view of the rolling, verdant Puuc hills. Behind the palace sits a *chultún* (plastered catch basin) that ancients used to collect rainwater for use during the dry season.

The path continues past the palace to **El Mirador** (the lookout), a lofty temple with grandiose columns. Left of El Mirador, the path leads deeper into the jungle, where the extremely graphic **Estela del Falo** (Stela of the Phallus) will make even the most sexually liberated of visitors blush profusely. A few other temples are barely visible through the dense jungle undergrowth (site open daily 8am-5pm; admission 10 pesos, free Sun. and holidays).

**Getting There:** The only public transportation to Sayil is the Autotransportes del Sur "Ruta Puuc" bus (31 pesos), which leaves Mérida daily at 8am and also stops at several other ruins (see Mérida, Practical Information: Bus Stations on page 498). Buses do run, however, from Mérida to Kabah, 10km away on the main highway (see Kabah). Hitching from Kabah to Sayil is not unheard of. Many solicit lifts from enthusiastic four-wheeled travelers at other nearby sites.

# ■■■ XLAPAK

Nowhere is the fear of drought so apparent as in the ruined palace of Xlapak (shla-PAK), where the rain god Chac still reigns supreme. Aside from the remarkable crowd of hook-nosed faces peering out from the surface of the partially restored edifice, Xlapak is less interesting than other sights along La Ruta Puuc.

The masks of Chac at Xlapak and at other ruined sites face east—and so do most churches built in Mexico by the Spaniards. The churches were designed to face back across the Atlantic toward Spain, while the masks pointed east because death was thought to reside in that direction. The western and eastern sides of the buildings are built in contrasting styles, evidence of changing Mayan architectural tastes.

**Getting There:** There is no public transportation to Xlapak. Some people have solicited rides from nearby sites. Xlapak can be reached via the "Ruta Puuc" bus, which sweeps through five sites in the course of a day (see Mérida, Practical Information: Bus Stations on page 498). Biking from nearby towns is also an option. See Kabah for information on buses from Mérida to Kabah, 15km northeast of Xlapak (site open daily 8am-5pm; admission 7 pesos, free Sun.).

# ■■■ LABNÁ

Labná's buildings were constructed towards the end of the late-Classic period (600-900 CE), when the Puuc cities were connected by a *sacbé* (white road). Today, a short reconstructed section of the *sacbé* runs between Labná's two most impressive sights: the palace and the stone arch. When the Yucatán flooded, the raised *sacbé* allowed the Mayans to pass from one city to another. However, more common than floods were droughts. To weather parched conditions, the Maya constructed huge *chultunes* (catch basins), many of which are found at Labná. The *chultunes* collected both water (up to 8000 gallons in each) and the bodies of peasants who couldn't afford to be buried.

Labná's **palace** is on the northern side of the site, to your left as you enter. While the construction of this building occupied the Maya for several centuries, the edifice was never actually completed. Labná's palace is reminiscent of the one at Sayil insofar as both boast an exceptionally ornate second-floor façade. Nearby mosaics depict figures in palm huts, reminding present-day visitors that the stone palaces once housed only the privileged few.

Labná is famed for its picturesque **stone arch,** 3m wide and 6m high. Its western façade is intricately decorated in a trellis pattern, while the eastern side remains more bland. Previously thought to have been the entrance to another temple, archaeologists now believe that the arch served as a ceremonial point of entry for victorious warriors returning from the battlefield.

Beyond the arch, on the unrestored base of a pyramid, stands the **observatory,** also known as **El Mirador** (the lookout). Its notable façade rises over the box-like structure and bears sculptures attached by tenons or dowels. The terracing around the temple contained many *chultunes*. The top of the observatory affords a view of the entire site, and keep your eyes peeled for falcons' nests (site open daily 8am-5pm; admission 10 pesos, free Sun.).

**Getting There:** The final destination on the "Ruta Puuc" bus, Labná lies 42km east of Uxmal, and 4km beyond Xlapak (see Mérida, Practical Information: Bus Stations on page 498).

# ■■■ GRUTAS DE LOLTÚN

The Grutas de Loltún are 58km east of Uxmal on the Sayil-Oxkutzcab road. Below a dense jungle of mahogany and *ceiba*, 1.5km of enormous caverns wind through the rock. The ancient Maya first settled this area in order to take advantage of the Grutas' water and clay. Hundreds of years later, Mayan *campesinos* returned to the caves seeking refuge from the Caste War (1847-1848). Important caverns include the **Room of the 37 Inscriptions,** which includes many still-visible markings, and the **Na Cab** (House of the Bees), where you can see the *ka'ob* (grindstones) left by the Maya. Ancient inhabitants broke off the stalactite tips in the **Gallery of Fallen Rocks** to use as spears and arrows. In the **Gallery of the Five Chultunes,** a sculpted jaguar head drips water into cisterns while a huge warrior and eagle look on. The **Cathedral** is a palatial room that once hosted Mayan feasts and assemblies. The shadowy silhouette above the entrance is popularly believed to represent the Virgin of Guadalupe. Several caves contain partially hollow stalactites and columns—thump one with the heel of your hand and listen to the soft booming sound reverberate throughout the cave system. Archaeologists speculate that the Maya used these formations as a musical means of underground communication.

Entrance to Loltún is allowed only at 9:30, 11am, 12:30, 2, and 3pm, when a guide leads a tour through the caves. Guides speak Spanish and fluent gibberish with the odd mangled English word thrown in. Bear in mind the exorbitant rates charged by above-ground guides when leaving a tip for the free guide service (admission 17 pesos, 7 pesos Sun.). As you exit the caves (0.5km from the entrance), you'll stumble upon the conveniently located **Restaurant El Huinoc de Loltún,** which serves up a good range of local dishes for about 15-20 pesos. Having lunch with a rental-car-key-toting fellow traveler may well make your return trip a lot easier.

**Getting There:** To get to Loltún, catch a bus as far as Muna or Ticul, hop in a *combi* headed for Oxkutzcab, and then pray for deliverance for that last leg of the journey. A pick-up truck in Oxkutzcab's *zócalo* may be willing to make the trip, though it will cost you at least 20 pesos.

MÉRIDA

# YUCATÁN

The rich history of Yucatán draws thousands of visitors each year, who come to scramble up and down the majestic Mayan ruins and explore the state's old colonial towns. The glorious past is a palpable presence here, as 16th-century churches still stand proud, and snippets of spoken Mayan can be heard in restaurants and on street corners. While the beaches don't compare with those of the Caribbean coast, the peninsula's flat porous limestone often gives way to *cenotes* (freshwater sink holes) of all shapes and sizes, whose waters offer a refreshing dip for sun-soaked travelers. Several endless cave systems, many of which were used by the ancient Maya, await more adventurous types. Nature lovers might choose to head to one of the coastline's marshy national parks, which are home to hundreds of species of birds. But there's more to the state than most tourists have come to see: the tangled histories of *indígenas* and *ladinos,* embodied in the *mestizos* of mixed descent, are still a source of tension that simmers just below the surface.

## ■■■ MÉRIDA

Built atop the ruins of the Mayan capital of T'ho, modern Mérida is haunted by pre-Hispanic history—the stones of the city's fortress-like cathedral even bear traces of the Mayan temples from which they were stripped. The Maya called this site "place of the fifth point," to indicate that it was the center of the universe, the spot between the four points of north, south, east, and west. Today, Mérida (pop. 1.5 million) isn't the center of the universe, but it's certainly the center of Yucatán—it's the state's capital and key commercial center. Panama hats, made from the leaves of the *jipijapa* plant and the *guano* palm, come from Becal in the neighboring state of Campeche, hammocks arrive from the nearby *pueblito* of Tixcocób, and *henequén* is trucked to Mérida from all over Yucatán before being exported as hemp.

Of late, Mérida has become a magnet for immigrants from around the world. *Meridaños* of recent Lebanese and Syrian descent have made their presence felt in the city, and a small French community is responsible for the Paseo Montejo, Mérida's version of the Champs-Elysées. Mérida is also a big destination for jet-setting tourists who arrive by the plane-load and spend their days shopping and their nights whispering sweet nothings in music-filled parks. Perhaps the tourists are lured by Mérida's anomalous charm—while it is the largest city on the Yucatán Peninsula, it has yet to succumb to big-city indifference. Street cleaners struggle to maintain its reputation as "The White City," intimate conversations swirl about the *zócalo,* and every Sunday promenading families come out to enjoy *Mérida en domingo.*

### ORIENTATION

Rte. 180 rushes over from Cancún (322km) and Valladolid (168km) to the east, becoming **Calle 65,** which passes through the busiest part of town one block south of the *zócalo.* Those approaching on Rte. 180 from Campeche, 153km to the southwest, end up on **Avenida Itzáes** (also called **Avenida de la Paz**), which runs north-south, or on Calle 81, which feeds into the north-south Calle 70. Both intersect Calle 59, the best route to the center of town, running east to a point one block north of the *zócalo.* **Paseo Montejo** begins at Calle 47, running north as Rte. 261. The *zócalo* fills one city block, bordered by Calle 61 to the north, Calle 62 to the west, Calle 63 to the south, and Calle 60 to the east. To reach the *zócalo* from the **second-class bus terminal,** head east to Calle 62, walk three blocks, and turn left (north); the *zócalo* is three blocks ahead. Alternatively, take a taxi (10 pesos). From the **train station,** take a taxi (10 pesos), catch the "Seguro Social" bus, or walk six blocks west on Calle 55 and three blocks south on Calle 60. Mérida's international **airport** is 7km southwest of the city on Rte. 180 to Campeche. Bus #79, labeled "Airport," runs between the terminals and a midtown

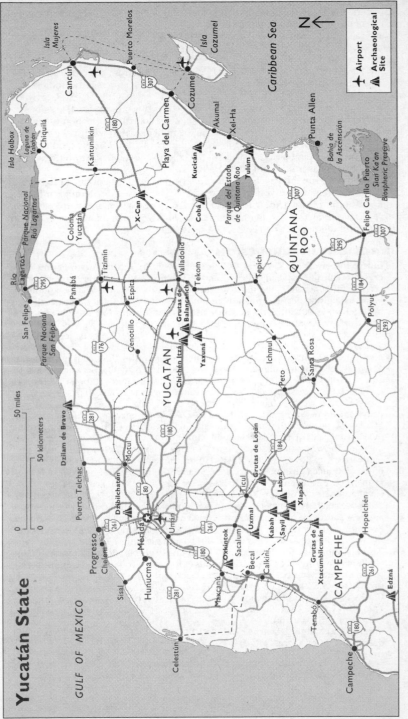

MÉRIDA

stop at the corner of Calles 67 and 60 (every 20min., 5am-9pm, ½hr., 80 pesos). A taxi from the airport costs about 25 pesos.

Mérida's consistently-gridded one-way streets have numbers instead of names. Using the streets which border the *zócalo* as rough directional axes, numbers greater than 60 usually lie west or south, smaller than 60 north or east. Addresses in Mérida are given using an "x" to separate the main street from the cross streets and "y" (meaning "and" in Spanish) to separate the two cross streets if the address falls in the middle of the block. Thus "54 #509 x 61 y 63" reads "Calle 54 #509, between Calles 61 and 63." Mérida's **municipal buses** (*camiones*) meander along idiosyncratic routes. Precise information is available at the tourist information office, but the city is small enough that a bus headed in the right direction will usually drop you off within a few blocks of your desired location. Locals and tourists tend to catch buses at their boarding points, usually in the center, a few blocks from the *zócalo*. City buses run daily from 5am-11pm (1.50 pesos).

**Taxis** do not roam the streets soliciting riders. You must call for one or have your hotel or restaurant call for you. There are stands along Paseo de Montejo, at the airport, and at the *zócalo*. Expect to pay at least 10-15 pesos for a trip within the *centro*. Taxi-*colectivos*, on the other hand, charge only 1.25 pesos for any destination in the city; dropoffs are on a first-come, first-serve basis.

## PRACTICAL INFORMATION

**Tourist Information: Central Office** (tel. 24-92-90), in the Teatro Peón Contreras, on Calle 60 between Calles 57 and 59. Helpful staff dispenses large numbers of colorful pamphlets, the most useful of which is *Yucatán Today*, a monthly guide listing practical information and local events. Additional offices at the airport (tel. 46-13-00) and at the second-class bus station, opposite the ADO information window. All offices open daily 8am-8pm.

**Police:** (tel. 25-25-55 or 25-73-98), on Av. Reforma (Calle 72) between Calles 39 and 41. Catch the "Reforma" bus. Some English spoken.

**Telephones:** It's impossible to place collect calls to the U.S. from most Mérida *casetas*. **Tel World,** Calle 60 #486-A (tel. and fax 24-76-00), between Calles 55 and 57. Calls to U.S. 12.73 pesos per min. Same rate for **faxes,** though a 5.50-peso service charge gets slapped on top. You can receive a fax for 4.20 pesos per page, plus the same service charge. A **photocopier** is available at 35¢ per page. Open daily 7am-10pm. You can always buy a **LADATEL** phone card (in denominations of 20 or 60 pesos) at the stand in the Palacio del Gobierno on the *zócalo*. Dialing 09 from any card-operated phone will connect you with a Mexican English-speaking operator who can connect you to a foreign operator. **Telephone Code:** 99.

**Telegrams:** (tel. 28-23-69; fax 24-26-19), in the same building as the main post office. Entrance is around the corner on Calle 56A. Forget about sending a **fax** (40 pesos); you can receive for 9.20 pesos per page. Open Mon. Fri. 8am-6pm.

**Travel Agencies: Yucatán Trails,** Calle 62 #482 (tel. 28-25-82, 24-hr. urgent tel. 25-75-94; fax 24-19-28), between Calles 57 and 59. Canadian owner Denis Lafoy is a genial source of information on Mérida and the Yucatán. Good, all-inclusive deals on daytrips to Ruta Puuc sites (transport, guide, lunch, and entrance fee included). Prices vary. Open Mon.-Fri. 8am-2pm and 4-7pm, Sat. 8am-1pm. **Travel Club,** Calle 59 #501 (tel. 25-75-94), on the second floor, just west of Calle 60. Super-low off-peak VW Beetle rentals (110 pesos, 160 pesos during peak season) include insurance and 300km free. Open daily 8am-8pm.

**Consulates: U.S.,** Paseo de Montejo 453 (tel. 25-50-11 or 25-55-54), at Av. Colón. Unless you have an emergency, try to go on Thurs. or Fri. Open Mon.-Fri. 7am-1pm. **U.K.,** Calle 58 #498 (tel. 28-61-52; fax 28-39-62 or 28-61-52), at Calle 53. Open Mon.-Fri. 9am-1pm.

**Currency Exchange: Bánamex** (tel. 24-10-11 or 24-11-32), in Casa de Montejo on the *zócalo*. 24-hr. Cirrus, MC, and Visa **ATM**. Open Mon.-Fri. 9am-5pm.

**American Express:** Paseo de Montejo 494, office #106 (tel. 28-42-22 or 28-43-73; fax 28-42-57), between Calles 43 and 45. English spoken. Open Mon.-Fri. 9am-2pm and 4-6pm, Sat. 9am-1pm. Money exchange desk closes 1hr. early.

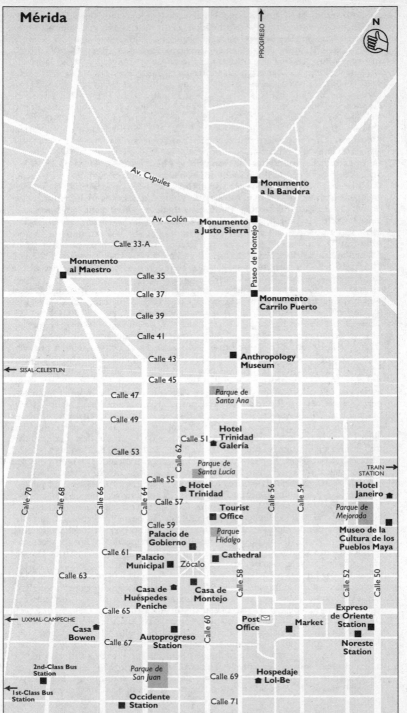

Mérida

N

PROGRESO

Av. Cupules

Monumento
a la Bandera

Av. Colón

Monumento
a Justo Sierra

Paseo de Montejo

Calle 33-A

Monumento
al Maestro

Calle 35

Calle 37

Monumento
Carrilo Puerto

Calle 39

Calle 41

SISAL-CELESTUN

Calle 43

Anthropology
Museum

Calle 45

Calle 47

Parque de
Santa Ana

Calle 49

Calle 51

Hotel
Trinidad
Galería

Calle 62

Calle 53

Parque de
Santa Lucía

TRAIN
STATION

Calle 55

Hotel
Trinidad

Hotel
Janeiro

Calle 70

Calle 68

Calle 66

Calle 64

Calle 57

Calle 56

Calle 54

Parque de
Mejorada

Tourist
Office

Calle 59

Palacio de
Gobierno

Parque
Hidalgo

Museo de la
Cultura de los
Pueblos Maya

Calle 61

Palacio
Municipal

Zócalo

Cathedral

Calle 63

Calle 58

Calle 52

Calle 50

Casa de
Huéspedes
Peniche

Casa de
Montejo

Calle 65

UXMAL-CAMPECHE

Casa
Bowen

Calle 60

Post
Office

Market

Expreso
de Oriente
Station

Calle 67

Autoprogreso
Station

Noreste
Station

2nd-Class Bus
Station

Parque de
San Juan

Hospedaje
Lol-Be

1st-Class Bus
Station

Occidente
Station

Calle 69

Calle 71

**Post Office:** (tel. 24-35-90), on Calle 65 between Calles 56 and 56A, 3 blocks southeast of the *zócalo* in the Palacio Federal. *Lista de Correos* and stamps. Open Mon.-Fri. 7am-7pm, for stamps only Sat. 9am-1pm. Branches at Calle 58 between Calles 49 and 51, at the airport, and at the main bus station. **Postal Code:** 79000.

**Airport:** On Rte. 180, 7km southwest of the city. Post office, telegrams, long distance telephone, and car rental. **Aeroméxico,** Paseo Montejo 460 (tel. 27-95-66 or 27-90-00), between Calles 35 and 37, and at the airport (tel. 46-14-00). **Mexicana,** Calle 58 #500 (tel. 24-67-54 or 23-12-92), and at the airport (tel. 46-13-32). **Aerocaribe,** Paseo Montejo 500-B (tel. 28-67-86), at Calle 47, and at the airport (tel. 28-67-90). **Aviateca** (tel. 46-12-96) Calle 58 between 45 and 43, between Calles 49 and 51, and at the airport (tel. 46-13-12). **Continental** (tel. 46-13-07), at the airport. The carriers listed above reach most cities in Mexico and the southern U.S., with limited destinations in Europe.

**Train Station: Ferrocarriles Nacionales de México** (tel. 23-59-44 or 23-58-55), on Calle 55 between Calles 46 and 48, northeast of the *zócalo*, go to Progreso, Campeche, Córdoba, Palenque, Valladolid, and Tizimín. Traveling by train is cheaper but much slower than by bus. Buy tickets an hour before departure or on board. Check at the information booth for schedules. Open daily 7am-10pm.

**Taxis: Palacio Municipal,** on the northwest corner of the *zócalo* (tel. 28-56-65). **Mercado Municipal,** at Calles 56 and 65 (tel. 23-11-35), in **Parque de la Maternidad** at Teatro Peón Contreras (tel. 28-53-22), and dozens of other *sitios* throughout the *centro*. Taxis are on call 24 hrs.; a ride within town will run you 10-15 pesos, to the airport 25 pesos. You're much better off making use of the *camiones* (municipal buses; see Orientation above).

**Bus Stations:** Most bus lines operate out of the main second class terminal, **Unión de Camioneros,** Calle 69 #544, between Calles 68 and 70, three blocks west and three blocks south of the *zócalo*. **Autotransportes del Oriente (ADO)** (tel. 23-22-87), sends buses to Cancún (every hr., 4:30am-midnight, 6hrs., 41 pesos), Chichén Itzá (every hr., 5am-8pm, 2hrs., 16 pesos), Chiquilá in time for the early ferry to Isla Holbox (12:30am, 6hrs., 40 pesos), Playa del Carmen (6 per day, 7hrs., 49.50 pesos), Tizimín (4pm, 3½hrs., 27 pesos), and Valladolid (every hr., 5am-midnight, 3hrs., 20.50 pesos). From the same terminal, **Autotransportes del Sur (ATS)** goes further afield to Campeche (every hr., 3hrs., 25 pesos), Escárcega (5 per day, 5½hrs., 44 pesos), Palenque (6 and 11:30pm, 14hrs., 101 pesos), San Cristóbal (6pm, 14hrs., 101 pesos), Uxmal (6 per day, 1½hrs., 10.50 pesos), and Villahermosa (5 per day, 9½hrs., 80.50 pesos). **Autotransportes Peninsulares** (tel. 24-90-55) sends a 6:30pm bus to Ticul (10 pesos) plus two cheap, slow buses to Chetumal (8hrs., 52.50 pesos). From the **first-class terminal** around the corner on Calle 70 between 69 and 71, **ATS** provides a special **Ruta Puuc bus** (8am, 31 pesos, admission to sites not included) which visits the archaeological sites of Uxmal, Kabah, Sayil, Xlapak, and Labná, returning around 3:30pm. **ADO** has first-class buses to Campeche (every ½hr., 2½hrs., 31 pesos), Cancún (6 per day, 4hrs., 58 pesos), Escárcega (6 per day, 5hrs., 57.50 pesos), Mexico City (10am, noon, 4, and 7:15pm, 22hrs., 240 pesos), Palenque (8am and 10pm, 8hrs., 92 pesos), Puebla (9:45pm, 20hrs., 246 pesos), Valladolid (7 per day, 2hrs., 29 pesos), Veracruz (2:45 and 9pm, 16hrs., 186 pesos), and Villahermosa (12 per day, 9hrs., 105.50 pesos). From the same terminal, **Caribe Express** and **Línea Dorada** send 4 buses each to Chetumal (6hrs., 66 pesos). Línea Dorada also provides first-class service to Ticul (6 per day, 1hr., 12.50 pesos). The **Cristóbal Colón bus** leaves at 5:30pm for Tuxtla Gutiérrez every day (15hrs., 135 pesos), passing through Campeche (2½hrs., 31 pesos), Escárcega (5hrs., 57.50 pesos), Palenque (8hrs., 92 pesos), Ocosingo (10hrs., 111 pesos), and San Cristóbal (12hrs., 123 pesos). The **Expreso de Oriente** station on Calle 50 between Calles 65 and 67, sends hourly buses at 15min. past the hour during the day to Cancún (6-6½hrs., 41 pesos), via Pisté/Chichén Itzá (2½hrs., 16 pesos), and Valladolid (3hrs., 20.50 pesos). Oriente also services Izamal (approximately every hr., 1¼hrs., 8 pesos). A smattering of smaller stations serve towns throughout the state. **Líneas Unidas del Sur de Yucatán** go to Mayapán (5:30am and 8pm, 1¼hrs., 12 pesos) from the **Autobuses del Noreste** station on the corner of Calles 50 and 67. Noreste services Río Lagartos (6:45am, 4:30, and 5:30pm, 3hrs.,

40.50 pesos) and Tizimín (8 per day, 2½hrs., 31 pesos). **Autobuses de Occidente,** on Calle 71 between Calles 64 and 66, go to Celestún (12 per day, 2hrs.). **Autoprogreso** buses shuttle between Mérida and Progreso (every 10min., 5am-10pm, 45min., 4.50 pesos), leaving from the station on Calle 62 between Calles 65 and 67. *Combis* leave the Parque de San Juan nearby for Dzibilchaltún (35min., 3.50 pesos) and Ticul (1½hrs., 10 pesos) every 20 min. or so.

**Car Rentals: México Rent-a-Car,** Calle 60 #495 or Calle 62 #483-A (tel. 27-49-16), both offices between Calles 57 and 59. VW Beetles, including insurance and unlimited *kilometraje,* go for 130 pesos a day (160 with credit card). Open Mon.-Sat. 8am-12:30pm and 6-8pm, Sun. 8am-12:30pm. Also see Travel Agencies above.

**Market:** More than four square blocks of covered stalls and street vendors, extending south of Calle 65 and east of Calle 58. All manner of food, clothing, toys, handicrafts, and junk for sale. Open dawn-dusk. **San Francisco de Asis** (tel. 24-33-08), on Calle 65 between Calles 50 and 52, across from the market in a huge gray building. Open daily 7am-9pm.

**Laundromat: La Fe,** Calle 61 #518 (tel. 24-45-31), between Calles 62 and 64, half a block from the *zócalo.* Have faith. Laundry service 13 pesos per 3kg (there is no self-service laundromat in Mérida). Open Mon.-Fri. 8am-7pm, Sat. 8am-4pm.

**English Bookstore: Dante** (tel. 24-95-22), in Teatro Peón Contreras, Calle 60 at 57. Post cards, guidebooks, maps, videotapes, and magazines in English, French, and Spanish. Open Mon.-Fri. 8am-9:30pm, Sat. 8am-2pm and 5-9pm, Sun. 10am-2pm and 4-8pm. Credit cards accepted.

**Red Cross:** Calle 68 #533 (tel. 24-77-74), between Calles 65 and 67. 24-hr. emergency and ambulance services (tel. 24-67-64). Some English spoken.

**Pharmacy: Farmacia Canto,** Calle 60 #513 (tel. 28-50-27), between Calles 63 and 65. Open 24 hrs.

**Hospital: Centro Médico de las Américas,** Calle 54 #365 (tel. 26-21-11 or 26-26-19), at Calle 33A. 24-hr. service, including ambulance. English spoken. Also **Clínica de Mérida** (tel. 25-41-00, 25-44-22, or 25-73-98), on Av. Itzáes between Calles 25 and 27. English spoken.

## ACCOMMODATIONS

You came to the Yucatán to see ruins? You'll see some all right—in Mérida's aging hotels. Ensconced behind old, sometimes nondescript façades, 200-year-old colonial mansions greet guests with leaky roofs and faulty plumbing. These fading dinosaurs are unique budget accommodations, though, and many enclose beautiful courtyards with sun-bleached frescoes, gurgling fountains, and towering palms.

**Hotel Trinidad Galería,** Calle 60 #456 (tel. 23-24-63; fax 24-23-19), at Calle 51. Sprawling complex of assorted rooms houses an art gallery and a pool out back. Containers brimming with guppies are everywhere. Friendly, helpful staff. Parking available. Check-out 1pm. Rooms start at 45 pesos for a single, 55 pesos for a double. For a bigger room you'll pay about 30 pesos more. The 1 room with A/C goes for 100 pesos. 20% surcharge if you pay by credit card.

**Casa Bowen,** Calle 66 #521-B (tel. 24-07-28 or 28-61-09), between Calles 65 and 67, halfway between the main bus station and the *zócalo.* A colonial mansion, carefully whitewashed on the inside with a leafy courtyard and second-floor balcony—mingle with assorted international guests in new wicker arm chairs. Large, elegant rooms and attractive bedspreads. Check-out 1pm. Double-bed singles 45 pesos. Doubles 50 pesos, with two beds 55 pesos. Rooms with kitchenette and fridge 65 pesos, with A/C 90 pesos. Squeeze in an extra person anywhere for 15 pesos. Dollars accepted at a rip-off rate.

**Hotel Trinidad,** Calle 62 #464 (tel. 23-20-33 or 21-30-29), between Calles 55 and 57. Furnishings of the past and paintings of the avant-garde future (many by the owner) are the highlights of this restored colonial mansion. Lobby moonlights as an art gallery and breakfast café. Guests have access to the pool at the nearby Hotel Trinidad Galería. Check-out 1pm. Ground floor singles 45 pesos. Doubles 50 pesos. Add 5 pesos for private bath. Modern rooms upstairs boast 15-ft. ceilings and breezy balconies. Singles 75 pesos. Doubles 80 pesos. 10 pesos per additional person. 12% surcharge if you pay by credit card.

**Hotel Janeiro,** Calle 57 #435 (tel. 23-36-02 or 23-83-73), between Calles 48 and 50, a hike from the bus station. This towering concrete block makes up in practical affordability for what it lacks in colonial charm. Sky-blue rooms done in neat, dark wood are decorated with cheery Mayan woven straw paintings. Peaceful, shallow pool and sun deck. Collection of English paperbacks and guidebooks. Parking available. Check-out noon. Singles and doubles with fans 50 pesos. Triples 70 pesos. Add 10 pesos for A/C.

**Hospedaje Lol-Be,** Calle 69 #542B (tel. 24-25-65), between Calles 56 and 58. Small, clean, pink rooms whose peeling bathrooms lack seats. Double-bed singles 35 pesos. Doubles 40 pesos, with two beds 50 pesos.

**Casa de Huéspedes Peniche,** Calle 62 #507 (tel. 28-55-18), between Calles 63 and 65. The cheapest option near the *zócalo*. Beautiful, disintegrating 250-year-old colonial building with stained-glass windows and wooden doors that don't lock. Unfortunately, communal bathrooms manage to look even older and are in a dreadful state of disrepair. Enormous rooms with 20-foot ceilings and checkered floors have antique furniture and wobbly standing fans. Lock-out 11pm. Check-out noon. Parking available. Singles start at 23 pesos. The one room with private bath goes for 43.70 pesos.

## FOOD

Mérida's inventive specialties make good use of the fruits and grains that flourish in Yucatán's hot, humid climate. Try *sopa de lima* (frothy lime soup with chicken and tortilla bits), *pollo pibil* (chicken with herbs baked in banana leaves), *poc-chuc* (pork steak with onions doused in sour orange juice), *papadzules* (chopped hard-boiled eggs wrapped in corn tortillas served with pumpkin sauce), and *huevos motuleños* (refried beans, fried egg, chopped ham, and cheese on a tortilla garnished with tomato sauce, peas, and fried banana). Those burned by over-seasoned *chiles* will note that, in Mérida, one can safely explore unknown stews and sauces— the local scorcher, *chile habanero,* does not lurk within dishes but instead waits patiently in a garnish bowl.

The cheapest food in town fills the **market** that stretches south from Calle 65, two blocks east of the *zócalo*. For a taste of *horchata* (a rice drink flavored with vanilla, honey, and almond), head for the overflowing fruit and vegetable stands on the main floor. For more substantial nourishment, head to the market's second level off Calle 56 at Calle 67. Over 20 small *puestos* (restaurants), offering a variety of *yucateco* dishes for 5-10 pesos, cram this cavernous area (restaurant complex open Mon.-Sat. 8am-8pm, Sun. 8am-5pm).

**Restaurante Amaro,** Calle 59 #507 (tel. 28-24-51), between Calles 60 and 62. Healthy vegetarian fare served up under thick arboreal shade. Soothing private courtyard and patient service provide welcome change. Delicious vegetable soup 10 pesos. *Chile relleno* (stuffed green pepper) 23 pesos. Open daily 8am-11pm.

**Los Almendros and Los Gran Almendros,** Calle 50 #493 (tel. 28-54-59), between Calles 57 and 59, on Parquet Mejorada, and at Calle 57 #468 (tel. 23-81-35), between Calles 50 and 52, respectively. This trim, air conditioned tourist trap is as atypical a place as you'll find for sampling tasty *típico* dishes. Menus have color pictures—look before you leap and try to find salvation in a warm plate of filling *pollo pibil* (19 pesos), or the house specialty, *Poc-chuc los Almendros* (32 pesos). Somehow this type of food simply tastes better when prepared in a wooden shack. Los Almendros open daily 10am-11pm. Less touristy Gran Almendros open daily 1-5pm.

**El Tucho,** Calle 60 #482 (tel. 24-23-23), between Calles 55 and 57. A loud restaurant/afternoon cabaret popular with both locals and tourists. While singers, musicians, and comedians entertain you, troupes of waiters ferry trays of free *botanas* (tacos and hors d'oeuvres) between customers. As long as you keep drinking, the *botanas* keep on comin'. Real meals 20-30 pesos. Open daily noon-9pm. Credit cards accepted.

**El Louvre,** Calle 62 #499-D (tel. 25-50-73), on the northwest corner of the *zócalo*. Don't be misled by the name of this popular local hang-out (pronounced LOOvray); french fries are all you'll get in that respect. Nevertheless, great sandwiches (8.30-13 pesos) and a central location make this *the* place for a lunch break. The menu confidently announces: "Broken English spoken perfectly"—judge for yourself. If you're not up to brain, tongue, or guts, tacos are 14 pesos. Open 24 hrs.

**Restaurante y Café Express** (tel. 28-16-91), on Calle 60 overlooking Parque Hidalgo, between Calles 59 and 61. Something of an institution among older *muchachos meridaños,* this bustling café is a place to people-watch during breakfast. A foreboding mural of the Governor's Palace at Uxmal dominates the southern wall. If you've forgotten what corn flakes taste like, order *Desayuno No. 2,* which also comes with toast, O.J., and coffee. More substantial *platos regionales* 17-24 pesos. Margaritas a mere 6 pesos. Open daily 7am-11pm.

**Lonchería El Castillo,** Calle 47 at Parque de Santa Ana, between Calles 58 and 60. Ideal evening snack joint on the park if you're staying north of the *zócalo* and want to lose *turistas* altogether. Sizzling *salbutes* and *panuchos* 2 pesos apiece. Open daily 5:30pm-midnight.

## SIGHTS

Mérida's *zócalo* manages to look busy at all hours. During the day it is alive with harried locals and wandering tourists, the latter with necks craned heavenwards to take in the cathedral's twin spires. The pace seems to slow with the setting sun, as couples take over the square to lounge all over *confidenciales* (cozy benches) and each other. The *zócalo* is busiest of all on Sundays, when street vendors cram in dozens of stalls, Yucatecan folk dancers perform in front of the Palacio Municipal, and half the city comes out to people-watch.

While almost all of Mérida's larger historic buildings are within easy walking distance of the *zócalo,* there's no reason to restrict oneself to the downtown area. Pocket-sized parks and fading colonial mansions reward the ambulatory traveler. Public transportation back to *el centro* is easily caught from any main thoroughfare.

The twin towers of the yellow **cathedral** loom over the eastern side of the *zócalo.* The fortress-like presence of the cathedral's Corinthian doors and stark, windowless façade recall the centuries of struggle between Mayans and missionaries. The sturdy stone blocks from which the cathedral was built were stolen from the Mayan temples of T'ho. Built in the austere Herrericano style, the cathedral features rose-colored arched domes and a giant blistering Christ, the second largest crucifix in the world (supposedly open daily 6am-6pm).

On the northern edge of the *zócalo* stands the **Palacio de Gobierno.** Built between 1883 and 1892, it is an amalgamation of two architectural styles—Tuscan (main floor) and Dorian (upper floor). Inside, wonderful, gigantic murals narrate the strife-filled history of the Yucatán peninsula. The stairway painting illustrates the Mayan belief that humanity comes from maize; an image of the Popol Vuh, the central document of Mayan culture, reigns over the next layout (open daily 8am-10pm).

Concerts and classes in *jarana,* the Yucatecan colonial dance, take place under the sheltering balcony of the **Palacio Municipal,** across the *zócalo* from the cathedral. A jail until the 1700s, the building was rebuilt in the colonial style in 1928. During the week, schoolgirls and grandmothers while away their afternoons rhythmically tapping their sturdy white shoes against the tile floor, all the while carefully balancing beer trays on their heads (open Mon.-Sat. 8am-8pm).

On the southern side of the *zócalo,* the **Casa de Montejo,** the oldest colonial structure in Mérida, was constructed in 1549 by order of city founder Francisco de Montejo. Built with stones from the Mayan temple T'ho, the carved façade boasts about the conquest over the Maya. While the expressions on the faces of the soldiers have faded, the anguish of the four Mayan heads on which they stand remains clear. Ironically, the carving follows the Toltec tradition of representing warriors standing on the heads of their conquests. Look for the coats of arms of the King of Spain and of the Montejo family. The building now houses a Bánamex branch (open Mon.-Fri. 9am-5pm).

Mérida's most impressive museum, the **Museo de Antropología,** is housed in a magnificent Italian Renaissance-style building on the corner of Paseo Montejo and

Calle 43. Archaeological finds on display illustrate the *indígena* history of the Yucatán, and extensive anthropological information in Spanish accompanies the artifacts. Geology, horticulture, linguistic history, demography, religion, and daily life are among the topics covered thoroughly. Grimace at the holes drilled in teeth for jewelry stones, stare in awe at the head-flattening devices applied to the craniums of upper-class infants, and envision the quivering heart placed for sacrifice on the *chac mool* (Mayan for "red fingernails") altar. Amazingly clear Mayan murals from minor sites survive also. A prehistoric mammoth tusk and a couple of bones from the caves at Loltún are housed here. The shop downstairs sells comprehensive English-language guidebooks for much less than the price charged at the ruins themselves; pick one up (museum and shop open Mon.-Sat. 8am-8pm, Sun. 8am-2pm; admission 14 pesos, free Sun.).

Celebrating the indigenous crafts and artisans of Mexico, the recently renamed **Museo de la Cultura de los Pueblos Maya** is located six blocks east of the *zócalo* on Calle 59, between Calles 48 and 50, behind the Convento de la Mejorada. The hall upstairs displays a wide array of handiwork, from costumes and masks to pottery, weavings, and *huipile* embroidery mainly from the Yucatán. The room of sculpted skeletons offers a taste of the morbid sense of humor that accompanies the festival "Día de los Muertos" (Day of the Dead). A staffmember guides you around the exhibits, explaining the items on display (open Tues.-Sat. 8am-8pm, Sun. 9am-2pm; free).

On the corner of Calle 59 and Av. Itzáes (Calle 86) lies the **Centenary Park and Zoo.** Any westbound *combi* (1.25 pesos) can drop you off by the PEMEX station on Calle 59, one block east of Itzáes. To reach the zoo, take a five-minute southeasterly stroll through the park and under the snail-paced chairlift (1 peso if you've got nothing better to do). The zoo is home to some stupendously bored lions, tigers, and bears, as well as preening peacocks, flamingos, antelope, hippos, Aztec dogs, and jaguars. A miniature train full of shrieking schoolchildren, whizzing through periodically, fails to rouse the catatonic creatures. On Sundays in the park, however, *meridaños* are much more fun to watch as they turn out in droves of noisy families, infatuated couples, and giggling teenagers. The rare *gringo* species may receive a considerable amount of attention—be prepared (park open Tues.-Sun. and holidays 6am-6pm; zoo open Tues.-Sun. 8am-5pm; admission free).

The **Museo de Historia Natural**, with its main entrance on Calle 59 at Calle 84, one block east of Itzáes, also has a back entrance accessible from the park. Housed in a 19th-century *hacienda*, this small but ambitious collection is concerned with the history of life from the origin of the universe through the emergence of species (open Tues.-Sun. 9am-4pm; admission 10 pesos, free Sun.).

Decaying French-style mansions and local and international boutiques line the **Paseo Montejo,** which, if the traffic would slow down and it were centrally located, would make an elegant Elysian boulevard. Promenades along the Paseo's broad pink sidewalks culminate in the **Monumento a la Patria.** In faux-Mayan style, the stone monument, built in 1956, depicts major figures of Mexican history. An eternal flame and filthy dry fountain stand guard. For an appealing detour from the Paseo, veer left (southwest) onto **Avenida Colón,** a street flanked by closely grouped historic mansions in varying stages of decay; beware the slobbering Rottweilers that guard the houses. A 30-minute walk down Avenida Colón is the **Parque de las Américas,** Calle 20 at Colón, named for its stone monuments to Central and South American states. Note the leafy topiary sculptures of various animals.

Mérida takes special pride in the **Teatro Peón Contreras,** on the corner of Calles 60 and 57. The Italian Renaissance-style building is notable for its rococo interior and its history—starting in 1624, it served as a university for nearly two centuries. The **Universidad Autónoma de Yucatán,** on Calle 57 between Calles 60 and 62, is a Hispano-Moorish complex built in 1938. The ground floor of the complex contains a gallery exhibiting works by local artists and a screening room for films by classic directors (*galería* and *videosala* open Mon.-Fri. 9am-1pm and 4-8pm, Sat. 4-9pm, Sun. 10am-2pm; free).

Many churches, statues, and pocket-sized parks scattered throughout Mérida's *centro* also invite exploration. Much of the Franciscan **Convento de la Mejorada,** on Calle 59, between Calles 48 and 50, has been converted into apartments, but the church still serves its original purpose. The old **Arco** behind the **Parque** and **Iglesia de San Juan de Dios,** located on Calle 64, between Calles 67 and 71, marks the southern limit of the center. The **Iglesia Santiago,** on Calles 59 and 72, is one of the oldest churches in Mexico and has retained its original altarpiece.

## SHOPPING

As the center of the Yucatán shopping universe, Mérida harbors some of Mexico's finest produce, flowers, and handicrafts. Opened in 1909, the **mercado** encompasses four square blocks, its streets paved with bottle tops pounded in by millions of passers-by. The market is a major tourist attraction—expect to receive friendly attention from multi-lingual sandal-sellers and piñata-pushers. For all its variety, the market offers little depth when it comes to *artesanías* and tends toward the kitschy and unclean. Nonetheless, exploring the vast expanse littered with everything from papier-mâché toys to tethered armadillos is an experience even if you don't intend to buy anything.

The main market occupies the block southwest of the Palacio Federal, spreading outward from the corner of Calles 65 and 58. Behind the *palacio,* shops, awnings, and tin-roofed shacks ramble for a good many blocks both east and west. The only border is busy Calle 65 to the north, but even there stands spill over onto the other side of the street and around the small square across from the Palacio Federal.

The second-floor "artisans' market," part of a modern building behind and to the right of the Palacio Federal, sells mainly regional clothing: white *huipiles,* with colorful embroidery skirting the neckline and hem, can be had (with haggling) for 45-60 pesos; *rebozos* (woven shawls) go for 10-15 pesos. *Guayaberas* (men's short-sleeve shirts with distinctive vertical columns of double stitching) fall between 50 and 70 pesos. Bargaining is expected, but those who get carried away are looked upon as scornful of the artisans. Cheaper goods such as *huaraches* (the name given to all types of hand-made leather sandals) are sold on the first floor of the market. Sandal makers (*fabricadores*) will custom-fit the leather on the spot, but be sure to give them a try or two for good measure, as the sandals are sometimes hastily made.

Although jewelry stores line the streets and glut the market, the best prices are at the smaller *prestas* on the streets, in the market, or at the *zócalo* every Sunday. And don't forget: Mérida is the hammock mecca of Mexico and the world. Rather than contend with vendors in the streets and parks who might fleece an unsuspecting *gringo,* step into a hammock *fábrica,* where you can try out hammocks in relative peace. While the fixed prices at **El Aguacate,** Calle 58 #604 (tel. 28-64-29), at Calle 73, may be a little steep, you don't run the risk of being taken for a complete swindle (locals shop here too and pay the same prices). The shop has a huge selection of nylon and cotton hammocks, ranging in size from modest *sencillos* to *especiales* you could trawl the Sea of Córtes with. Prices start at 38 pesos, though you should expect to spend at least 100 pesos anywhere for a good quality item. Wherever you end up shopping, there are two key criteria: a quality hammock is *bien tupida* (tightly woven) so that holes don't readily appear, and it is *ancha,* in fact so wide that you can lie across it with space to spare. El Aguacate's huge, wonderfully soft nylon *matrimoniales* (140 pesos) will last for years, even if your marriage doesn't (open Mon.-Fri. 8am-7pm, Sat. 8am-5pm; MC, Visa, accepted).

## ENTERTAINMENT

Mérida's municipal government provides a never-ending series of free musical and dance events in the city's parks. On Mondays in front of the Palacio Municipal, a *ballet folklórico* is accompanied by the police *vaquería* band at 9pm; the dancing and the dress will take you to the *haciendas* of yore. Big band music of the 40s comes to Santiago Park, Calles 72 and 59, on Tuesday nights at 9pm. Take your steady to the **Mayab Culture House,** on Calle 63 between Calles 64 and 66, which sponsors piano and string instrument concerts on Wednesdays at 9pm. Thursday nights feature a 9pm "Yucatecan Serenade," with romantic music and folk dance in Santa Lucía Park, Calle 60 at 55. On Fridays at 9pm, students perform regional dances at the University of the Yucatán, at the corner of Calles 60 and 57. Mérida's *zócalo* enchants on Sundays, when streets are blocked off at 10:30am for the festive **Mérida en domingo** (Mérida on Sunday). A Yucatecan orchestra performs at 11am, followed by a re-enactment of a *mestizo* wedding at 1pm in front of the Palacio Municipal. Other parks feature *marimba* concerts and *jarana* demonstrations.

When in Mérida, do as *meridaños* do—keep your eyes peeled for announcements of upcoming events glued to walls all over town. The **Teatro Peón Contreras** (tel. 23-73-54), on Calle 60 near Calle 57, hosts special events and frequent concerts. The *ballet folklórico* performs "Roots of Today's Yucatán" every Tuesday night at 9pm. Professional dancers whirl in flamboyant traditional dress under the lights of this marvellous colonial-style theater (tickets 25 pesos at the door). Just around the corner on the Parque de la Madernidad, an excellent, mellow acoustic guitar trio play requests at the **Café Peón Contreras** nightly from 8pm-midnight. The food is expensive, but you can sit on one of the park benches and still hear the band clearly.

For a less high-brow evening, settle in for a beer. Denis Lafoy of the Yucatán Trails travel agency organizes an informal get-together with beer and free food on the first Friday of every month—inquire for further details (see Practical Information). At local establishments, buy a few and you'll get free *botanas* (mini-appetizers). Enjoy comedians and live *marimba* music at **Pancho's** (tel. 23-09-42), Calle 59 between Calles 60 and 62, or **El Tucho** (see Food). Live Latin American music accompanies dinner at **Restaurant Amaro** (see Food) on Thursdays and Saturdays from 8-11pm. Another option is **Tulipanes**, Calle 42 #462-A, between Calles 45 and 47; get ready for non-stop music, *yucateco* dance, and a chilling re-enactment of a Mayan sacrifice. For air-conditioned, panchromatic discos, you'll need to stray far from the center. For the following clubs, a taxi (15 pesos one-way) is the way to go. The patrons of **Bim Bom Bao** (tel. 44-42-90), at Calles 4 and 5 in Mérida's poshest neighborhood, are the city's hip patricians. The gay bar/disco **Kabuki's** on Calle 51, before Calle 50 and 56a, rocks into the wee hours Thursday through Saturday.

# ■ NEAR MÉRIDA: DZIBILCHALTÚN

Some 20km north of Mérida, en route to the Gulf coast at Progreso, lies the archaeological site of Dzibilchaltún (dzib-ill-shahl-TOON). Spread over more than 60 square km of jungle brush, Dzibilchaltún (Place Where There Is Writing on Flat Stones) flourished as a ceremonial and administrative center from approximately 2000 BCE until the Conquest. While Dzibilchaltún's importance and continuous influence on Mayan culture is of great interest to archaeologists and historians, the excavated site now open to tourists is neither as impressive nor as accessible as other ruins near Mérida.

The site's **museum,** at the end of the covered walkway, just beyond the cactus garden, merits a quick visit before you set off. Note the huge, fabulously preserved grimace of Chac, brought here from Kabah. From the museum, follow the path to **sacbé No. I** and turn left.

Farther along this road, Dzibilchaltún's showpiece, the fully restored **Temple of the Seven Dolls,** possesses a rare harmony of proportion and style. The seven clay "dolls" discovered here are believed to represent different illnesses or deformities and are now on display in the museum. The temple also furnishes further proof of the genius of the Maya. Shortly after sunrise, a huge shadow mask of the rain god Chac is said to appear as the sun's rays pierce the temple. The temple is so carefully aligned that it can be used to verify the winter and summer solstices. At 5:30pm on June 21, the sun threads the tiny space between the door jambs on the north side; at 7:30am on December 21 the phenomenon is repeated on the south side.

The other end of sacbé No. 1 leads to a quadrangle, in the center of which stand the incongruent remains of a 16th-century chapel, underscoring the ceremonial value of the site. Just beyond the eastern edge of the quadrangle is the **Cenote Xlacah**, reminiscent of Quintana Roo's oval, saltwater *lagunas*. Xlacah served as a sacrificial well similar to those at Chichén Itzá and as a source of water. Divers have recovered ceremonial artifacts and human bones from the depths of the 44m-deep *cenote*. While the *cenote* is not up to the standard set by those in Valladolid, the water invites a non-sacrificial dip among the water lilies and fish. A path to the south leads past a handful of smaller structures to the site's exit. (Site open daily 8am-5pm. Museum open daily 8am-4pm. Admission 15.60 pesos, free Sun. Wheelchair access. Parking available at the site for 3 pesos.)

**Getting There:** Getting to the ruins is straightforward—it's the return trip that is likely to pose more problems. Conkal-bound *combis* leave the Parque de San Juan in Mérida approximately every 20min. (3 pesos). The *combi* will drop you off at the access road to the ruins, a five-minute walk from the entrance. To get back you'll need to walk back to the Conkal road and pray (like any good Catholic in Mexico) for a *combi* to take you to Rte. 261. Some travelers hitch the 5km to the highway. **Autoprogreso buses** abound on Rte. 261, passing by in both directions every 15min. Early risers should be able to catch a bus to the site, see the ruins, and walk or take a *combi* to the highway by noon to catch a bus to Progreso and the beach.

# ■ ■ ■ PROGRESO

Strategically located on the closest strip of coastline to Mérida, Progreso is a small town in limbo, somewhere between fishing village and commercial center. Intended as an important port for the exportation of Mérida's produce, Progreso did not officially open as such until 1871. Today, the town has combined these two destinies to become the Yucatán's premier commercial fishing port, hauling in shrimp, red snapper, octopus, and tuna. During the summer months and holidays, Progreso's proximity to the capital makes it a popular retreat with *meridaños,* many of whom make the 33km jaunt northward to enjoy the clean, quiet beaches of the Gulf coast. At other times, the town is remarkably tranquil and tourist-free.

The history of Progreso is also tied to *benequén,* a blue-gray plant used to manufacture rope. While the discovery of synthetic fibers has reduced demand for *benequén,* Progreso's stunning old mansions attest to the fabulous ill-gotten profits of the lucrative plant. To see how *benequén* moguls lived, walk east along the *malecón* from the bus station.

**Orientation and Practical Information** Progreso's **Avenida Malecón** (coastal avenue), Calle 19, runs east-west along the beach. Odd-numbered roads run parallel to Malecón, increasing to the south. North-south streets have even numbers and increase to the west. Progreso's *zócalo* is bounded by Calles 78, 80, 31, and 33. The **bus station** (tel. 5-30-24) is on Calle 79 between Calles 80 and 82. **Autoprogreso** buses run to Mérida every 10min. between 5am and 9:45pm (40min., 4.50 pesos one-way, 8 pesos round-trip). Faster *combis* supposedly make the trip in half the time (5.50 pesos one-way, 10 pesos round-trip). To reach the *zócalo* from the terminal, head east on Calle 29 to the end of the block, turn right, and walk two blocks on Calle 80. For the beach, follow Calle 80 in the opposite direction.

The often bored but friendly and helpful people in the **tourist office,** Calle 80 #176 (tel. 5-01-04), just past Calle 37, can provide you with a tourist booklet, including a map (open Mon.-Fri. 9am-2pm and 4-7pm, Sat. 9am-noon; some English spoken). The **police station** (tel. 5-00-26) is in the Palacio Municipal on the *zócalo* at Calle 80, between Calles 31 and 33 (open 24 hrs.). The **post office** is at Calle 31 #150 (tel. 5-05-65), between Calles 78 and 76, just off of the *zócalo*. *Lista de Correos* (open Mon.-Fri. 7am-7pm). **MexPost** (tel. 5-31-00) is next door (open Mon.-Fri. 8am-6pm, Sat. 9am-1pm). **Postal Code:** 97320. In the same building, the **telegram office** (tel. 5-01-28) also offers **fax** service (open Mon.-Fri. 8am-6pm, Sat. 9am-noon). **Long-distance phone calls** can be made from **Tienda El Centenario** (tel. 5-14-10; fax 5-24-54), on Calle 74 between Calles 29 and 31. Calls to the U.S. cost 10 pesos per min., but collect calls are free (for you). The **fax** will cost you a horrendous 35 pesos plus 5 pesos per additional page (open daily 6am-9pm). **Bánamex,** Calle 80 #129 (tel. 5-08-31), is between Calles 27 and 29 (open Mon.-Fri. 9am-1pm). **Lavamática "Progreso,"** Calle 74 #150-A (tel. 5-05-86), between Calles 29 and 31, provides next-day service for 4 pesos per kg (open Mon.-Sat. 8am-1:30pm and 4-7:30pm). The **supermarket San Francisco de Asis** is at Calle 80 #144, between Calles 29 and 31 (open daily 7am-9pm). **Farmacia YZA** is on Calle 78 at Calle 29 (tel. 5-06-84; open 24 hrs.). 24-hr. emergency service is provided by the **Centro Médico Americano** (tel. 5-07-69 or 5-09-51), at Calles 33 and 82.

**Accommodations** Progreso offers a considerable range of budget accommodations; the following establishments are listed in descending order of comfort. The **Hotel Progreso,** Calle 78 #142 (tel. 5-00-30) near Calle 29, has spotless rooms with pin-striped double-beds and mosaic-tiled bathrooms. Check-out 1pm. (Singles with fans 55 pesos. Doubles 65 pesos. Add 30 pesos for A/C. Add 55 pesos for TV and telephone. 15 pesos per additional person.) The **Hotel Miralmar,** Calle 27 #124 (tel. 5-05-52), between Calles 72 and 74, could be more appropriately named Miralcárcel for the cell-like space pods out back. Cozy, pastel-peach rooms with dark wood furniture, TVs, and small, neatly-tiled bathrooms are also available. Check-out noon. (Space pod Singles 40 pesos. Doubles 45 pesos, with two beds 55 pesos. Triples 75 pesos. Upscale singles 55 pesos. Doubles 70 pesos. 15 pesos per extra person.) Clean rooms in ghastly, bright colors are an economical option at the **Posada Juan Carlos,** Calle 74 #148 (tel. 5-10-76), between Calles 29 and 31. Save time by going to the bathroom, taking a shower, and doing your laundry in the sink all at the same time in the incredibly tiny *sencillo* bathrooms (singles 35 pesos; doubles 40 pesos, plus 5 pesos per additional person).

**Food** Owners of Progreso's restaurants, bars, and discos must lead fascinating double lives—many only open their doors in the summer months, when the deluge of beach-bound tourists guarantees big profits. The informal *palapas* along the coastal Av. Malecón stay open all year and all day long. **Carabela,** just east of Calle 72 on Av. Malecón, specializes in scrumptious seafood. *Filete empanizado* 22 pesos (open daily 9am-midnight). Across Calle 72 from Carabela and under a thatched roof, **Restaurant Pelícanos** serves up equally tasty *mariscos* (open 8am-midnight). **El Corobés,** Calle 80 #150 (tel. 5-26-28), at Calle 30, on the *zócalo,* has drawn crowds since 1900. Sandwiches run 4-5 pesos, fish entrees 20-30 pesos, and beer around 5 pesos (open daily 6am-midnight). For a lively high-season scene, **Las Velas Restaurant/Bar** (tel. 5-02-23), on Av. Malecón near Calle 66, has a splendid view of the beach, live Yucatecan music, and a hip, graffiti-covered outdoor dance platform.

**Sights** If you feel like a dip, Progreso's beaches are decent and fairly clean. But a dip is all you'll get, as the shallow water prevents you from being able to swim. The beach fills up with vacationers in July and August, but you'll have the place to yourself the rest of the time. For a more placid spot, head for the beach at **Chelém,** 8km west of town. *Combis* leave for Chelém every 15min. from the parking lot outside of Supermarket San Francisco on Calle 80 (1.50 pesos). If he's not too busy, the custodian of **El Faro** (the lighthouse), at Calle 80 near Calle 25, welcomes visitors during the day. A spiral staircase leads to a monstrous 1000-watt bulb and an array of reflectors. Stepping out on the balcony, you can see the ocean and the miles of marshy river that give the city its distinctive briny scent. The 2km *muelle* (pier) clings tenuously to the sandy beach; in the early morning it's a great spot from which to reel in fish.

# ■■■ MÉRIDA TO CHICHÉN ITZÁ

As Rte. 180 sets off eastwards from Mérida to Chichén Itzá, it first passes near the five private *henequén* (hemp) *haciendas* known as San Pedro, Teya, Ticopó, San Bernardino, and Holactún. Next come the villages, each dominated by a main plaza and an oversized church. First are **Tahmek** and **Hoctún** (47km from Mérida). From Hoctún, **Izamal** is only 24km to the northeast, though buses don't make the detour. A direct bus can be caught from Mérida (see Mérida, Practical Information: Bus Stations on page 498). This tiny town contains the largest church plaza in Mexico, ringed with rows of yellow arches around the church and convent, and some of the earliest Spanish buildings in the region, dating from 1533 and built from the boulders of the Mayan pyramid that they replaced. Since almost all the buildings in Izamal are yellow, the city is sometimes referred to as Ciudad Amarilla ("Yellow City"). Nearby stands the weather-worn pyramid of Kinichkakmó, Maya for "Macaw of Fire," which was plundered by the Spanish for stones to build the church and convent. The ancient *cenote* (freshwater sink-hole) of **Ixcolasc** is only 1km away.

Upon returning to Rte. 180, you arrive at **Kantunil** (68km from Mérida). **Xocchel,** the "Place Where the Chels Read," is an attractive town along Rte. 180 before Kantunil. Next is **Holcá,** and finally, **Libre Unión** (just 24km from Pisté), with a sizeable *cenote.* During squabbles between the territories of Yucatán and Quintana Roo, Libre Unión found itself smack on the border. The town voted to stick together and become part of the state of Yucatán—thus earning its name, "Free Union."

Some travelers hitch or hop buses from one Mayan village to another along the busy road between Mérida and Chichén Itzá. Those who choose to hitch should bring water—the waits can be long, and shade is sparse. Second-class bus drivers stop anywhere if requested, but a new fare is charged for each trip. Slow and irregular second-class bus service limits the number of places you can visit in one day.

# ■■■ CHICHÉN ITZÁ

Chichén Itzá's reputation as prize cultural attraction of the Yucatán is well-deserved. The design and orientation of **El Castillo,** breathtaking from the bottom and harrowing from the top, attests to an incredible level of astronomical understanding. On the walls of the expansive ballcourt, beneath the still-intact rings which were once goals, grisly carvings depict the fate of the ancient game's players. The thousand columns stand wistfully in faultless symmetry, stripped bare of their thatched roofing by the forces of time. The stuccoed annex of the nunnery is covered with intricate representations of the hook-nosed rain god Chac, and the sacrificial *cenote* (natural well) has coughed up enough bones and artifacts to reconstruct the fates of hundreds of human victims. You can't claim to have seen Yucatán without a visit to Chichén Itzá—don't miss it for the world.

Unfortunately, there isn't a travel agency on the peninsula that doesn't hawk Chichén Itzá packages, but these tours usually arrive at midday to massive crowds and scorching sun. Budget travelers should have no problem reaching Chichén Itzá early in the day at a fraction of the cost of traveling with a group. To do so, consider spending the night in Pisté. This allows you to experience the light and sound show the night before (see Sights) and to visit the ruins early the next morning.

## ORIENTATION

The ruins of Chichén Itzá lie 1.5km from **Route 180,** the highway which runs from Mérida (121km west) through Valladolid (43km east) to Cancún (213km east). The town of **Pisté** flanks the highway 2.5km west of the ruins and provides travelers with basic accommodations and services.

Getting to the ruins is easy, as bus companies throughout the Yucatán provide service to Chichén Itzá. Many **buses** leave Mérida for Chichén Itzá (hourly from 5am-8pm, 2hrs., 10 pesos) and first-class buses cruise in from Cancún (8:45am and 2:30pm, 3hrs., 32 pesos). From Valladolid, service is continuous throughout the day (every hr., 40min., 5.50 pesos). From Pisté, flag down any east-bound bus (2-3 pesos) which roll through town approximately every ½hr. As with all Mexican buses, a vigorous, supplicatory wave to the driver is a good idea. Or, you may want to catch a taxi (10 pesos) to make sure you hit the site at exactly eight in the morning (when it first opens). To head back to Pisté or one of the more distant destinations after a day at the ruins, hang out in the bus parking lot until one heading in the right direction swings by. Alternatively, take a taxi to the Pisté bus station (see below), where you can consult the timetable and grab a *refresco* in the shade.

## PRACTICAL INFORMATION

Services at Chichén Itzá are located in the large stone edifice at the site's western entrance. Across from the ticket counter is a small **information booth.** Clear your throat seven times and a Spanish-speaking agent will appear, genie-like, to provide useful information about transportation and lodging. Refer specific questions about the ruins to official guides. The long-distance **telephone** (tel. 6-27-24) is right around the corner from the ticket counter, but it won't let you make international collect calls. **Telephone Code: 985.** The *caseta* stores luggage for free (open daily 8am-5pm). There are also restrooms, a restaurant, an ice cream parlor, a gift shop (which changes U.S. dollars only at a fair rate), a bookstore with guidebooks, an auditorium showing documentaries about the ruins, and a small museum (see Sights). Parking (4 pesos) is available right at the site, from 8am-5pm and ½hr. before each light and sound show.

Pisté manages to provide a few additional services. A single **police** officer sits at a desk in the *comisario* on the eastern side of the *zócalo.* The **post office** is in a small gray building near the *zócalo* across from Abarrotes "El Alba" (open Mon.-Fri. 8:30am-3pm). **Centro Telefónico** (tel. 1-00-89; fax 1-00-88), across from the bus station, charges about 11 pesos per min. for calls to most parts of the U.S. Collect calls 10.45 pesos. Send a **fax** for about 12 pesos per min.; receiving costs 9 pesos per page (open daily 7:30am-9:30pm). Another *caseta* is **Teléfonos de México** (tel. 1-00-58 to -60). Calls to the U.S. 9 pesos per min., collect calls 10 pesos. Copies 45 centavos per page (open daily 7am-9pm). As the town has no bank, the gift shop at the ruins probably offers a better exchange rate than establishments in town.

**Buses** leave from Pisté's bus station (tel. 1-00-52), near the Stardust Inn on the eastern side of town. Buses depart for Mérida (approximately every 1½hrs., 6am-9pm, 1½hrs., 15 pesos), Playa del Carmen (11am, noon, and 3pm, 3½hrs., 36 pesos), and Valladolid and Cancún (hourly from 8am-8pm, 1 and 4hrs. respectively, 6 and 26.50 pesos respectively). **Clínica Promesa,** Calle 14 #50 (tel. 6-31-98, ext. 198), in the blue-green building past the *zócalo* and 100m off Rte. 180, is open 24hrs. for medical emergencies. **Farmacia Isis,** Calle 15 #53, lies a short way past the *zócalo* towards the ruins (open daily 7:30am-9:30pm).

## ACCOMMODATIONS AND CAMPING

Though a few luxury hotels snuggle right up to the ruins, the more economical options are located in Pisté. Pisté's *posadas* are nothing to write home about; the quality of the rooms is directly proportional to the distance you are from the booming trucks barreling down Rte. 180. But Pisté is 10% accommodation, 90% location: your early-morning attack on the ruins is only a 3-minute taxi ride away.

You can pitch a tent in the **RV trailer park** right next to the bus station. Designated spaces have light and power outlets. The 20-peso per person charge includes use of the communal bathrooms and access to the pool. The trailer park is administered by the Stardust Inn (tel. 1-01-22), on the other side of the bus station.

**Posada Olalde,** to the left of Calle 15 (Rte. 180), two blocks down the unmarked dirt road directly across the street from the Carrousel Restaurant. Huge pastel rooms with ceiling fans and private bathrooms. A safe distance from the squawking trucks on Rte. 180. Singles 50 pesos. Doubles 70 pesos. Triples 90 pesos. During high season, extra people can string up hammocks for 10 pesos per person. Haggle during the low season. Traveler's checks accepted.

**Posada Carrousel,** on Calle 15, in central Pisté at the large *palapa* restaurant with the same name. Standard pink rooms with new wood desks. Fans, hot water, and *agua purificada.* Sustain yourself economically by plucking grapes from the vine out back. Singles 40 pesos. Doubles 70 pesos. Triples 80 pesos. Quads 100 pesos. Hammock rental 10 pesos. Prices may rise during high season.

**Hotel El Paso,** Calle 15 #89, a yellow, L-shaped building in the middle of Pisté. Large, lemon-colored second-floor rooms with dandelion windows and buttery bedspreads. Fans, hot water, and gleaming bathrooms. TV in lobby. Check-out 1pm. Singles 50 pesos. Doubles 70 pesos. Triples 80 pesos. Quads 100 pesos. The restaurant's well-priced *menú del día* (17 pesos) includes an appetizer, entree, dessert, and coffee.

**Hotel-Posada Maya,** set back one block from Rte. 180. On the way to the *zócalo*, take a right in front of the big green road sign with directions to Mérida, Espita, and Tizimín. Looks like the owner has decorated the entire building with a bottomless bucket of pink paint. Mystical wooden lampshades adorn tidy rooms, most of which have two double beds. Check-out 1pm. Singles 40 pesos. Doubles 50 pesos. Triples 60 pesos. 15 pesos for hammock space under the *palapa,* 5 pesos more for rental.

## FOOD

The Mayan Empire may well rise again on the profits from Chichén Itzá's restaurants. Once again, stick to Pisté. If you're voraciously hungry at the ruins, consider taking advantage of the cafeteria's all-you-can-eat buffet (35 pesos). An enormous late lunch of *típico* dishes and fresh fruit just might see you through to breakfast. The following listings are located on Calle 15, Pisté's main drag. The restaurants at the larger hotels often allow diners to use their swimming pool even if they buy only a drink. On the sandwich front, El Carrousel bakes cheap, fresh bread every morning—but get there early, as they sell out before noon.

**El Carrousel** (tel. 1-00-78), in central Pisté. Ever-popular with an international crowd, this restaurant serves a wide selection of regional food at reasonable prices. The large thatched *palapa* sways to background *salsa.* 4 chicken tacos 10 pesos, meat entrees around 20 pesos. Open daily 7am-10:30pm.

**Restaurant Sayil,** Calle 15 #55, between El Carrousel and the Stardust Inn. A peaceful place to savor a small selection of local dishes at remarkably low prices. Tables look onto the open family kitchen. *Huevos a la mexicana* 8 pesos. *Pollo pibil* (chicken cooked in banana leaf) 10 pesos. Open daily 7am-10pm.

**El Pollo Mexicano,** a few shops towards the *zócalo* from El Carrousel. Portions include ¼chicken, rice, grilled onions, *salsa,* beans, chicken consommé, and *tortillas* (12 pesos). Eggs (any style) with coffee 8 pesos. Open daily 7am-11pm.

## SIGHTS

As the Mayan name Chichén Itzá ("Mouth of the Well") implies, the area's earliest inhabitants were drawn here by two nearby freshwater *cenotes.* Much of what is known about these sedentary people is based on the pottery shards recovered by archaeologists. Later periods in Chichén Itzá's history are illuminated by the *Chilam Balam,* one of the few pre-Hispanic Mayan texts to survive the early missionaries' book-burnings. The *Chilam Balam* describes the construction of many buildings visible today, focusing on the period between 500 and 800 CE, when construction was purely Mayan.

Chichén was mysteriously abandoned at its height in the 7th century CE, and for the next 300 years it remained a crumbling ghost town. Sometime before 1000 CE, the Toltec tribes of Tula, in what is now Hidalgo state, infiltrated the Yucatán and overcame peaceful Mayan settlements, bringing with them the cult of the plumed serpent Quetzalcóatl (here known as Kukulcán). The Toltecs fortified Chichén and, in the wake of regional imperialism, it became the most important city on the peninsula. Chichén's round buildings and pyramid bear the stamp of Toltec influence,

CHICHÉN ITZÁ

and the images of plumed serpents, warriors, jaguars, and eagles are trademark Toltec images. As the Toltec death cult glorified human sacrifice, the *chac-mool* was the preeminent altar. In 1461, Chichén Itzá was once again abandoned, this time because of war, but religious pilgrims continued to visit the site until well after the Spanish conquest. Today, the relentless flow of the curious ensures that Chichén Itzá will never again stand in solitude.

Before you dart off to the ruins, stop by at the newly opened **Centro Cultural Cecijema** (tel. 1-00-04), the grey building next to the Stardust Inn in Pisté. The center houses a small display of Mayan ceramic replicas and a rotating exhibits. The center's library has a wide selection of English- and Spanish-language books on Mayan art, architecture, and culture. A cafeteria was slated to open in August of 1995 (open daily 8am-5pm; free).

## The Ruins

Pause in the **visitor's complex** at the entrance to Chichén Itzá for an overview of the site. On the terrace, a scale model artfully shrinks the ruins and lays them at your feet. A small **museum** recaps the history of Chichén Itzá and displays a sampling of sculptures and objects removed from the sacred *cenote*. The notice board outside the **auditorium** announces screenings of documentary videos about the ruins in Spanish and in English (museum and auditorium open daily 10am-5pm; free).

If you are mainly interested in the architectural significance of the ruins, hiring a guide at the entrance is unnecessary. If you carry a guidebook (or even just a map) and read the explanatory captions (in Spanish, English, and French) on plaques at each major structure, you can appreciate the ruins inexpensively and at a more leisurely pace. Free maps are available around the corner from the ticket counter, at the telephone *caseta* desk. However, to decipher some of the symbolism of the ruins or to follow the enigmatic recurrence of the number seven throughout the structures, you'll need a guide. The cheapest option is to join one of the Spanish- or English-language guided groups (6-8 people, 1½hrs.) which form at the entrance (30 pesos per person). However, if you can get your own group together, it may be more economical to hire a private guide for a more in-depth tour (150 pesos, 2hrs., up to 20 people). In any case, ask to see identification, which guarantees certification and foreign language ability.

The entire site of Chichén Itzá is open daily from 8am-5pm (admission 21 pesos, free Sun. and for kids 13 and under). From the main parking lot and visitor's center, the first group of ruins is up the gravel path and to the left.

The first sight to meet your eyes is **El Castillo,** Chichén's hallmark. This pyramid, built in honor of Kukulcán, rises in perfect symmetry from the neatly cropped lawn, culminating in a temple supported by pillars in the form of serpents. El Castillo stands as tangible evidence of the astronomical enlightenment of the ancient Maya: the 91 steps on each of the four faces, plus the upper platform, total 365 (the number of days in the non-leap year); the 52 panels on the nine terraced levels equal the number of years in a Mayan calendar cycle; and each face of the nine terraces is divided by a staircase, yielding 18 sections representing the 18 Mayan months.

But that's not all: El Castillo's axes are specifically aligned to produce a biannual optical illusion. At sunrise during the semi-annual equinox, the rounded terraces cast a serpentine shadow on the side of the northern staircase. The sculpted serpent head at the bottom of the staircase completes the illusion. In March, the serpent appears to be sliding down the stairs precisely in the direction of the Sacred Cenote, while in September the motion is reversed. A light-and-shadow lunar serpent-god, identical to that of the equinoxes, creeps up and down the pyramid at the dawn of the full moon following each of the equinoxes. The exact equinox dates and times vary slightly from year to year, but tend to cluster around March 21 and September 21. People from all over the world converge on Chichén to see this incredible phenomenon, crowding accommodations with calendrical precision.

Nestled within El Castillo is an early Toltec temple, the inner chamber of which can be entered through a door at the bottom of the north staircase, behind the serpent's ears. A set of narrow, slippery steps ascends to a ceremonial chamber with a grimacing *chac-mool* sacrificial altar and a rust-red, jaguar-faced throne encrusted with jade stones and flint fangs (open daily 11am-3pm and 4-5pm; free).

West of El Castillo, or to the left of the entrance, lies the **ballcourt.** The enormous "I"-shaped playing field is bounded by two high, parallel walls with a temple at each end. Though this is the largest ballcourt in Mesoamerica, good acoustics make it seem smaller than it is. Voices carry remarkably well along the length of the field. The court also produces an amazing side-to-side echo, which repeats seven times. (Reminds you of long-distance calls from Mexico, no?) The game played here was called *pok-ta-pok.* Players kept the *chicle* ball in constant motion, trying to score by knocking it through stone rings still visible high up on the long walls. Though little more is known about the game (guides tell all sorts of fantastic tales), it appears that one or more players sometimes met their glorious ends here. The famous reliefs at the base of the walls depict two competitors, the one having just decapitated the other. The plumes issuing from the neck of the less fortunate player turn into snakes, representing the soul's passage to the afterlife.

A short distance from the ballcourt toward the grassy open area is the **Tzom-pantli,** Aztec for "Platform of the Skulls." When the Spaniards conquered the Aztecs, they were shocked by the ritualized human sacrifice they found and horrified by the racks in Tenochtitlán designed to display the skulls of the sacrificed. Chichén's Toltec-designed Tzompantli served a similar macabre purpose. Today, eerie rows of skulls in bas-relief decorate the low platform's walls.

Next to the Tzompantli stands the **Platform of Jaguars and Eagles,** named after the military orders who took the names of these ferocious animals and who were charged with obtaining prisoners for human sacrifice. To either side of the feathered serpent heads on the balustrades, reliefs of jaguars and eagles clutch human hearts in their claws. East of the platform is the **Temple of Venus,** where a feathered serpent holds a human head in its mouth. Also visible are reliefs with symbols of the stars and information on their motion.

The dirt path leading directly north from El Castillo, over the ancient Mayan roadway, links the ceremonial plaza with Chichén Itzá's most important religious center, the **Sacred Cenote,** 300m away. The roughly circular sink-hole, perhaps 60m across, induced vertigo in the sacrificial victims perched on the platform before their 25m plunge into the murky depths. The rain-god Chac supposedly dwelt beneath the water's surface and needed frequent gifts to grant good rains. Human remains recovered by divers suggest that children and (presumably valiant) young men were the victims of choice. If they could keep afloat until noon, they were then fished out and forced to tell what they had witnessed during the ordeal.

On the eastern edge of the central plaza, the **Temple of the Warriors** and **Group of the Thousand Columns** present an impressive array of elaborately carved columns which at one time supported a roof of some perishable material. On the temple itself (no longer open to the public), in front of two great feathered serpents and several sculpted animal gods, reclines one of the best-preserved *chac-mools* (reclining figures of messengers to the gods) at Chichén. The ornamentation of this building is largely Toltec; a nearly identical structure stands at Tula, the Toltec capital far to the west.

The Temple of the Warriors marks the end of Chichén's restored monuments and the beginning of an overgrown area extending to the southeast of El Castillo. This corner houses the **Palace of the Sculptured Columns,** the back of which hides a couple of beady-eyed masks of Chac. The rest of the quadrangle is comprised of the **Southeastern Colonnade,** the **market** and its courtyard, and the expansive **Western Colonnade.**

A red dirt path on the south side of El Castillo leads to the less photogenic **South Group** of ruins. Beyond the cafeteria and bathrooms, the first pyramid on the right is the **Ossuary,** or **High Priest's Grave,** its distinctive serpent heads mimicking El Castillo. A natural cave extends from within the pyramid 15m down into the earth.

The human bones and votive offerings found in this cavern are thought to be those of an ancient high priest.

Past the Ossuary, the road forks, presenting two different routes to the second set of ruins in the South Group, often missed by tourists but well worth the visit. The most interesting structure in this group is the **Observatory,** the large circular building on the left-hand side. This ancient planetarium consists of two rectangular platforms with large west-facing staircases and two circular towers. Because of the tower's interior spiral staircase (not open to the public), this structure is often called **El Caracol** ("the Great Conch"). The slits in the dome of the Observatory could be aligned with the important celestial bodies and cardinal directions. El Caracol was built in several stages by Mayan and Toltec architects. Notice the small red handprints on the wall of the building just as you come up the stairs; these were supposedly the hands of the sun god Itzamná. Walking south from El Caracol, toward the Nunnery at the other end of the clearing, you will pass a tiny, ruined sauna and then the **Temple of the Sculptured Wall Panels** behind it. Though difficult to decipher, the panels on the exterior walls contain emblems of Toltec warriors—jaguars, eagles, and serpents—in three rows.

The largest structure in this part of Chichén is the misnamed **Nunnery,** on the south side of the quadrangle. Although it was probably a royal palace to the Maya who built it, its stone rooms reminded Spaniards of a European convent. After several superimpositions and some decay, the building is now almost 20m high on a base 65m long and 35m wide. Above the entrance on the eastern side of the building, you can still see Mayan hieroglyphs. Also on the eastern side, a smaller annex built at an angle is visible. The annex's sculpted masks of Chac and lattice motif are in the Chenes style, usually found only in northeastern Campeche, as at Edzná.

Diagonally across from the nunnery and annex is the religious center, its upper walls encrusted with intricate masks of the hook-nosed Chac. The religious center is remarkable for its fusion of cultural styles: over the doorway are Mayan stone lintels, while the use of wood and inclined edges is evidence of Toltec influence. Above the door are representations of the four *bacabs,* animal deities who hold up the sky.

A poorly maintained path (which is sometimes closed during rainy months) runs about 130m east from the nunnery group, past the chapel to the long **Akab-Dzib.** The oldest parts of this structure are believed to be Chichén's most ancient constructions. The two central rooms were built in the 2nd or 3rd century, while the annexes on either side and to the east were added later. Inside the rooms it is possible to make out the small rose-red hand prints of Itzamná on the ceiling.

The overgrown **Cenote Xtoloc** (Shtoh-LOC) hides in a dip behind the South Group ticket office. To reach it from the office, take the first left 20m into the site. The *cenote* is in the hollow, beyond the small, ruined temple of Xtolob, the lizard god. There is no path down the steep slope through the undergrowth, and swimming is prohibited because of the dangerous underwater currents. In counterpart to the holy waters of the Sacred Cenote, this pool at one time provided all of Chichén with secular drinking water. As the only other waters of note are within the Sacred Cenote, accessed by a dramatic (and final) leap of faith, you may want to hold off on swimming altogether for today. Following **sacbé No. 5,** which becomes a narrow, winding trail, takes you to the back of the observatory.

As if Chichén Itzá couldn't muster enough daytime spectacle, those green panels (whose purpose you've been contemplating all day) pop open for the evening **light and sound show.** The buildings are splashed in red, blue, green, and yellow lights while booming voices detail the history of the site (Spanish version daily at 7pm, 12 pesos; English version daily at 9pm, 18 pesos). To avoid the nighttime walk from Pisté over ruts'n'reptiles, you may want to take a taxi to and from the show (10 pesos each way).

## Chichén Viejo

Beginning about 1km south of the Nunnery, and spreading out southwest of the main site, Chichén Viejo is a collection of unrestored minor ruins scattered throughout the jungle.

The **Group of the Initial Series** and the **Phallic Cluster**, the first set of ruins in Chichén Viejo, are easy enough to find on your own. Follow the dirt path (look for the "Chichén Viejo" sign) to the right of the Nunnery past the intersection of other dirt paths to a covered well. Shortly beyond the well, a right at the T-junction brings you to the cluster, set in a clearing. Chichén Viejo carries the only dated inscriptions at Chichén Itzá, one of which can be clearly seen on the one remaining lintel of the Temple of the Initial Series. This block, upheld by two columns, features a hieroglyphic inscription corresponding to July 30, 878 CE. The rest of the temple stands in ruin. The main features of the appropriately named Phallic Cluster jut proudly from the interior walls of the temple.

The remaining ruins, reached by taking the path to the right of the **House of the Phalli**, following the tracks of the old narrow-gauge *tranvía* (donkey-drawn trolley), and then poking around in the bushes, are best located with the help of a guide. Though official guides will charge you almost as much as for the main site, you can ask some of the merchants at Chichén if they know of someone who would be willing to serve as guide for a fee determined in advance. These unlicensed (and cheap) guides tend to be very knowledgeable, though few speak English. Shrouded by dense jungle, 10 minutes beyond the Phallic Cluster, lie the remains of the **House of the Four Lintels**, carrying another inscription dating to July 13, 881 CE.

This **Principal Group of the Southwest**, where hieroglyphs depict the Mayan practice of compressing the forehead into a conical shape with stone plates, contains a magnificent ruined pyramid, the **Temple of the Three Lintels** (dating to 879 CE), and the **Jaguar Temple**, where a handful of Atlantean columns salute the ancient military order of the Jaguars. Crossed eyes and precious stones embedded in the flesh of the face were also considered signs of beauty.

Turning to the right through the jungle from the Southwest Group, do your best to stumble upon the **Bird Cornice Group**, featuring a strip of carved birds, the **Temple of the Turtle**, where a turtle-shaped stone was found, and the **Temple of the Sculpted Jambs**, whose door jambs are molded into human figures.

# ■ NEAR CHICHÉN ITZÁ

## GRUTAS DE BALANKANCHE

The inner caves of the **Grutas de Balankanche** were only discovered in 1959 when a local amateur speleologist noticed a passageway blocked up with stones. Further exploration opened another 300m of caves which run past stalactites carved to resemble leaves on the ceiling and a huge tree-like column surrounded by dozens of votive vessels with ghoulish masks. Archaeologists have come to believe that the cave was a center for Mayan-Toltec worship of the gods Chac, Tlaloc (the Toltec rain god), and Kukulcán (Quetzalcóatl) during the 10th and 11th centuries. For unknown reasons, subterranean worship in Balankanche stopped at the end of this period, and the offerings of ceramic vessels and stone sculptures rested undisturbed for eight centuries. The impressive stalactites and a strikingly clear underground river definitely merit a visit, but be prepared for an almost incomprehensible Disneyesque tour which dramatizes the cave's history, keeping up with tour groups via a series of hidden speakers. A strangely mute guide, available for questions, paces the group through the chambers along the 1km path. Self-guided tours are not permitted. Tours cost 17 pesos (7 pesos Sun. and holidays). The small museum and garden complex are open daily 9am-4pm. Tours in Spanish begin at 9am, noon, 2, and 4pm; tours in English start at 11am, 1, and 3pm; there is one French tour at 10am.

**Getting There:** Located 6km east of Chichén Itzá and 2km past the Dolores Alba Hotel, the caves are easily reached by hopping on any east-bound bus (3 pesos). Be sure to ask the driver to stop there when you get on.

## YAXUNÁ

**Yaxuná,** 30km southeast of Chichén Itzá, is home to the ruins of yet another ancient Mayan city. The temple at Yaxuná was built by the Maya of Cobá, who were planning to make war on the people of Chichén. A 100km *sacbé,* the longest of the area, linked Yaxuná with Cobá. To keep a close eye on their enemy, the Maya of Cobá aligned their temple with El Castillo.

**Getting There:** Road conditions are poor and few people make it to Yaxuná. In the dry season it is possible, but never easy, to take a drive directly from Pisté to Yaxuná. It's easier to go to Libre Unión and then left to Yaxcabah, a small town 17km down the road and 8km to Yaxuná. There is no public transportation to Yaxuná, but it's possible to hire a truck in Pisté. The charge is about 100 pesos round-trip with a wait and a possible stop at the *cenotes* and caves located between the two sites.

# ■■■ VALLADOLID

In the middle of the Mérida-Cancún route, Valladolid (pop. 100,000) serves as little more than a stopover for a few tourists *en camino* to the more exotic destinations of Chichén Itzá, Río Lagartos, or peaceful Isla Holbox. While most travelers choose to bypass the city, its six churches and mysterious *cenotes* (fresh water sink-holes) merit a quick visit.

In 1543, Francisco de Montejo, the nephew of the eponymous Spanish conquistador, was sent to the Mayan town of Zací to convert the population and to set up a Spanish enclave. After constructing his home with Mayan stone and sweat, he was driven away by Mayan animosity. Another Francisco de Montejo (son of the conquistador) took his place and succeeded where his cousin had failed. In celebration of the souls he had saved, Francisco built the churches that are Valladolid's pride.

Some 250 years later, in 1809, a cabal of Mayan leaders, clergy, and disaffected soldiers devised a revolutionary plot. The scheme was uncovered and thwarted, but the rebellious spirit persisted, and when Mexico resolved itself to independence, a good number of *vallisoletanos* led the fight. Interracial conflict between the elite *ladinos* and oppressed *indígenas* erupted again in the Caste War (1847-48) when machete-wielding Mayan rebels besieged Valladolid for two months. The Maya eventually took the city, sending 10,000 *ladinos* fleeing to Mérida. The caste schism has healed only slowly, but today, *vallisoletanos* are intensely proud of their mixed Hispanic and Mayan heritage of struggle, rebellion, and suffering.

Valladolid has become a noisy, dirty, crowded city. *Indígena* women and eight-year-olds have besieged the *zócalo:* the former dealing colorful *huipiles,* the latter aggressively hawking chewing gum (*¡Chiclets amigo!*). The city bustles with self-importance. Whining mopeds buzz down narrow streets, megaphones broadcast advertisements for local merchants, and careening trucks crush pedestrians' toes at every corner.

## ORIENTATION

Split in half by Rte. 180 as it runs 300km from Mérida to Cancún, Valladolid lies midway between the two cities. The city's even-numbered streets run north-south, increasing westwards. Similarly, odd-numbered streets run east-west, increasing to the south. *El centro* is bordered by Calles 27 and 53 to the north and south and Calles 28 and 60 to the east and west. Except for Cenote X-kekén (see Sights), everything lies within comfortable walking distance from the *zócalo* (circumscribed by Calles 39, 40, 41, and 42). To get to the *zócalo* from the bus station, take a taxi (5 pesos) or walk one block south on Calle 54 to Calle 39. Turn left and follow Calle 39 for six blocks.

## PRACTICAL INFORMATION

**Tourist Information:** In the lobby of the *ayuntamiento* (city hall) on the Calle 40 side of the *zócalo.* Staff can provide you with a city and a state map and answer general questions. Take a quick look upstairs at the four fantastic murals depicting Mayan religiosity, the Hispano-Mayan conflict, and the Mayan uprising during the Caste War. Open Mon.-Fri. 9am-1pm and 4-7pm.

**Police:** (tel. 6-21-00), seven blocks east of the *zócalo* on Calle 41. No English spoken. Open 24 hrs.

**Post Office:** (tel. 6-23-26), on the Calle 40 side of the *zócalo*. Open Mon.-Fri. 8am-3pm. Go next door to **MexPost** (tel. 6-36-75), for priority mail (3 days to the U.S.) and **photocopying** service (0.40 pesos per copy). Open Mon.-Fri. 8am-6pm. **Postal Code:** 97780.

**Telephones:** In a toy shop on Calle 42 (tel. 6-21-04), between Calles 37 and 39, ½ block north of the *zócalo*. Calls to the U.S. 18 pesos per min. Collect or credit card calls 5 pesos. **Fax** available at the same number (19 pesos per min. to send and 6 pesos per page to receive). Open daily 8am-9pm. International calls at the *caseta* at the bus station are also 5 pesos. Open daily 7am-10pm. The public phones on the *zócalo* often swallow money ungratefully. **Telephone Code:** 985.

**Telegrams:** (tel. 6-21-70), on Calle 39, two blocks west of the *zócalo*. Open for telegrams (30-40 pesos to the U.S.) and *giros* Mon.-Fri. 8am-6pm, Sat. 9am-noon.

**Currency Exchange: Bancomer** (tel. 6-21-50), on the Calle 40 side of the *zócalo*, has the best rates. 24-hr Visa **ATM.** Open for exchange Mon.-Fri. 9am-1:30pm.

**Bus Station:** Calle 37 at Calle 54 (tel. 6-34-49). Luggage check 1 peso per piece per day (open 8am-7pm). Many buses arrive *de paso:* they'll take you only if they have room. **Autobuses del Oriente (ADO)** second-class service will take you anywhere you want to go: Cancún (approximately every hr., 1am-9pm, 3hrs., 20.50 pesos), Chichén Itzá and Mérida (approximately every hr., 2am-9pm, 1 and 3hrs. respectively, 5.50 and 20.50 pesos respectively), Tizimín (approximately every hr., 1hr., 7 pesos), and Cobá, Tulum, and Playa del Carmen (4:30am and 1:30pm; 2, 3, and 4hrs. respectively; 16, 22, and 29.50 pesos respectively). If an ADO bus is not leaving for your destination shortly, shop around, though the other bus lines operate less frequently and their second-class service tends to take longer.

**Taxis:** In front of the bus station and in the *zócalo*. 5 pesos through town, 15 pesos to X-kekén. Haggle.

**Bike Rental:** Calle 44 #190, between Calles 39 and 41. The outer *cenote* and the San Bernardino de Siena church are most easily reached by bike. 3 pesos per hr.

**Market:** Bordered by Calles 35, 37, 30, and 32, 5 blocks northeast of the *zócalo*. A good place to come for cheap fruit. Open daily 5am-2pm. Artisans' market occupies the sidewalks near the intersection of Calles 39 and 44. Open Mon.-Sat. 7am-7pm, Sun. 7am-2pm.

**Laundromat: Lavandería Teresita,** Calle 33 and Calle 42 (tel. 6-33-93). Self-service 3.50 pesos wash and dry, full service 5 pesos per kilo. Open daily 7am-7pm.

**Pharmacy: El Descuento,** Calle 42 at Calle 39 (tel. 6-26-44), on the northwest corner of the *zócalo*. You should be able to find one on any block throughout the city, however. No English spoken. Open 24 hrs.

**Medical Services: Hospital S.S.A.** (tel. 6-28-83), two blocks west of the *zócalo* on Calle 41, then five blocks southwest on Calle 41-A. Some of the doctors speak a little English. Open 24 hrs.

## ACCOMMODATIONS

Though it sits on the tourist corridor from Mérida to Cancún and makes a strategic overnight stop for an early-morning jaunt to nearby Chichén Itzá, Valladolid is not much of a tourist destination. A couple of pricey hotels on the *zócalo* are the best the city has to offer. A handful of budget accommodations cluster around the intersection of Calles 44 and 39, one block west of the *zócalo*. With the exception of the Hotel Zací, the hotels listed are an unimpressive but habitable bunch. Wall-mounted loudspeakers on Calle 44, advertising everything from washing detergents to the latest movies, make lounging around in the morning almost impossible; try to get a room far, far from the road.

**Hotel Zací,** Calle 44 #191 (tel. 6-21-67; fax 6-25-94), between Calles 39 and 37. If you're planning to treat yourself once during this trip, this is the place to do it. Rooms are a fantastic value, especially if you can do without A/C. Gorgeous tan-tiled rooms with snug beds are elegantly furnished in dark wood. Good-as-new bathrooms are in tip-top condition. All rooms have ceiling fans and cable TV. Hotel has a restaurant; its courtyard has a neat lawn and pool. Check-out 1pm. Singles 53 pesos. Doubles 79 pesos. Triples 105 pesos. Quads 126 pesos. If you actually want to *use* the A/C in your room, cough up another 21 pesos, or 32 pesos for a quad. To reserve a room during peak times, wire a 50% deposit in advance. Traveler's checks accepted.

**Hotel María Guadalupe,** Calle 44 #198 (tel. 6-20-78), between Calles 39 and 41. Sterile rooms with dark wood decor have enormous closets. Brand new ceiling fans in some rooms look like they were provided by Aeroméxico. Cozy pastel bathrooms. Purified water in the hallway. Check-out 1pm. Singles 47 pesos. Doubles 50 pesos. Three-bed triples 60 pesos. Traveler's checks accepted.

**Nuevo Hotel Mendoza,** Calle 39 #204, 1½ blocks west of the *zócalo* (tel. and fax 6-20-02). Two options available. Regular speckled, avocado-tiled rooms with soft beds and ceiling fans. Singles 40 pesos. Doubles 50 pesos. Incredibly cramped 3-bed triples (60 pesos) could sleep Snow White, the Seven Dwarves, and her five (normal-sized) siblings. Larger suites have better baths and come with extra fans, cable TV, and a fridge. Singles 80 pesos. Doubles 90 pesos. Triples 100 pesos.

**Hotel Lily** (tel. 6-21-63), on Calle 44 between Calles 37 and 39. Clean, bare stucco rooms with ceiling fans are shedding paint. Basic bathrooms in need of a facelift. Some rooms drip during heavy rains. Singles 40 pesos. Doubles 50 pesos. Triples 55 pesos. *Cuartos económicos,* with communal baths, are a better value. Singles 25 pesos. Doubles 35 pesos. Triples 40 pesos. Long distance payphone in the lobby. Squawking loudspeaker next door. Check-out 1pm.

## FOOD

Take advantage of a range of regional specialties served in restaurants throughout the city. Small cuts of pork in tomato sauce go by the name *lomitos de Valladolid.* Hearty and delectable, *escabeche oriental de pavo* is a turkey soup prepared with onions, whole garlics, and spices. *Panuchos* are bite-sized tortillas loaded up with various combinations of chicken, pork, beans, lettuce, tomato, and chili peppers. The bakery next to the Hotel Lily sells fresh loaves every morning, 1 peso apiece.

**El Bazaar,** Calle 39 at Calle 40, on the *zócalo.* Not a restaurant, but a pink open-air courtyard supporting cafés and juice bars under shady arcades. Great for a cheap meal and people-watching. At least one café open daily 6am-midnight. **Milo,** closest to the *zócalo,* sells delicious homemade fruit juices: orange, watermelon, lime, lemon, coco, pineapple, guanábana, mamey, and banana (1 peso). Open daily 8am-2pm and 6-8pm. **La Rancherita** serves all sorts of tacos (2 pesos) and *yucateco* entrees (12 pesos). **Sergio's** prepares good-sized pizzas. Small pizza dripping with cheese 8 pesos. Open daily 5-11:30pm.

**Restaurante Cenote Zací** (tel. 6-21-07), on Calle 36 between Calles 37 and 39, overlooking the *cenote* of the same name. After performing death-defying stunts from the ledge above the water (see Sights), sit back, relax, and marinate in the atmosphere of this lovely domed thatched-roof restaurant. Elegant decor and background music. Excellent liquor selection, including locally produced Xtabentún, a delectable concoction of rum, anise, and honey (4 pesos per cup). Sandwiches 8 pesos. Catch of the day 20 pesos. Open daily 8am-6pm.

**Restaurant San Bernardino de Siena** (better known as **Don Juanito**), Calle 49 #227 (tel. 6-27-20), three blocks east of the church (also known as "San Juan"—hence the restaurant's nickname). Fun murals, a dim interior, and the smell of the thatched roof make for a homey atmosphere. Excellent regional dishes. *Poc-Chuc* (a thin slice of grilled pork) 17.50 pesos. Open daily 7am-10pm.

## SIGHTS

The city's two main *cenotes* (freshwater sink-holes) are its most arresting attractions. **Cenote Zací** (sah-KEY) is only three blocks east of the *zócalo* on Calle 36, between Calles 37 and 39. Well-worn stone stairs lead down into a cavernous hollow studded with plunging stalactites. Bats beat their wings as swans and daring locals dive from terraces into the murky, jade-colored water. Copious quantities of *chinha* (lake lettuce) seem to pad their landing. While admission is four pesos for adults and two pesos for children, the *cenote* can be viewed free (although in the company of colorful butterflies and sunbathing lizards) from the airy *palapa* restaurant at its edge. A small museum to the right of the path is open with the *cenote* daily 8am-6pm. Free parking.

Though farther from the center of town, **Cenote X-kekén** (chay-keh-KEN—also called by its Mayan name, Dzitnup) is more handsome (and free of leaves) than its convenient cousin Zací. A 20-minute bike-ride into the surrounding country (see Practical Information: Bike rental), a 15-peso taxi trip, or an importunate plea to a Mérida-bound bus driver will take you to this idyllic spot. To reach X-kekén by bike take Calle 39 to the highway, then head toward Mérida until you see a sign for Dzitnup. Take a left down this road and continue for 2km until you hit the *cenote*. Take the damp stairway down through a cramped tunnel to the water's edge. Visit before noon, as plunging schoolkids disrupt the deliciously cool, turquoise, glassy surface of the *cenote*'s water in the afternoon. At midday, light pours into the cove through the narrow hole in the roof, refracting into the water and reflecting off the jellyfish-like tree-roots to create an eerie glow. Every 24 hours, a distant spring brings fresh water to the *cenote* (open daily 7am-5pm; admission 5 pesos, children 2.50 pesos).

For holy, rather than secular water, head for Valladolid's stately colonial churches. The Franciscans who settled in the area made themselves many enemies—*indígenas* resented them for imposing Christianity and Spaniards resented their wealth—so they built their churches as stout as fortresses for security's sake.

The most famous church in town is **San Bernardino de Siena,** affiliated with the **Ex-Convento de Sisal,** on Calle 41, four blocks southwest of the intersection of Calles 46 and 41 (Cinco Calles). Built in 1552, these are the oldest ecclesiastical buildings in the Yucatán, and possibly all of Mexico. The monks abandoned the convent in the 18th century, when Mexican religious orders were forced to turn their property over to government authorities. Theft and vandalism during the Caste War left the buildings denuded of much interior decoration. On the altar at the rear of the church is a large image of the Virgin of Guadalupe. Original frescoes are visible behind two side altars. Although remodeled, the confessionals built into the thick walls have been used for centuries. Outside, an impressive colonial irrigation system and 17th-century well draw water from an underground *cenote*, over which part of the complex was constructed. True to form, Spaniards bungled the site's original Mayan name for the site, "Sis-Ha," meaning cold water. The remains of important families and high dignitaries lie in the old cemetery between San Antonio's chapel and the Baptism Chapel (open Tues.-Sun. 8am-2:30pm and 5-8pm).

The **Catedral de San Gervasio,** with its colonial-style twin towers, stands protectress over the *zócalo* on Calle 41. It would rival San Bernardino de Siena for the title

---

### Once Upon a Time, There Was Xtabentún

In the event that Chichén Itzá's ruins and Río Lagartos' National Park have failed to make you swoon, Valladolid's **Xtabentún** is sure to do so. As potent as whiskey, this popular *yucateca* concoction of anise and honey has its origin here. According to legend, Zac-Nicté, a young woman whose beauty had attracted the wicked tribal chief's attention, had fallen for a warrior. For fear of what the chief might do to them, the young lovers sought refuge in the jungle. Coming across a beehive in a *balché* tree, the couple ate their fill of *miel* and left the rest in a hole in the trunk. The next day they discovered that the honey had magically become Xtabentún. When the chief finally caught up with them, he was so impressed with the drink's taste that he let them go and…they lived happily ever after.

You can sample this and other nectars at the Sosa factory outlet on Calle 42, between Calles 47 and 49, four blocks south of the *zócalo*. The Sosa family, who have been making the product for over 100 years (four generations), sell their entire line here at great discounts (Xtabentún 22 pesos per bottle; open daily 10am-1pm and 3-6pm).

of oldest church in the nation, had *vallisoletanos* not violated the sacred right to sanctuary there 250 years ago. According to legend, two alleged criminals who took sanctuary in the church were discovered and brutally murdered by an angry mob. When the bishop learned of the mob's sinful actions, he closed up the church and had it destroyed. When it was rebuilt, the church faced north on Calle 41, instead of west on Calle 42, its original orientation (open daily 5am-noon and 3-9pm).

## ENTERTAINMENT

Valladolid doesn't exactly bend over backwards to entertain visitors. **Cinema Díaz,** just off the *zócalo* at Calles 40 and 41, shows two international films (dubbed into Spanish) daily at 7 and 9pm. Swing by in the early evening to see what's on. If you prefer live entertainment, keep your eyes peeled for occasional functions sponsored by the **Club de Leones** (Lions Club), whose dances, cook-outs, and bake sales are announced in the *zócalo*. The cheapest and perhaps most rewarding hangouts are the **El Bazaar** café complex (see Food) and the *zócalo* itself, where *vallisoletanos* and visitors alike linger until the witching hour. Women should avoid those streets which house *cantinas* at night, as the overflow can become rather unpleasant.

# ■■■ RÍO LAGARTOS

Clinging precariously to an oddly-shaped peninsula 104km north of Valladolid, the small fishing village of Río Lagartos (pop. 3,000) is an idyllic, relatively *gringo*-free *pueblito*. While its secluded sugary beach, sumptuous seafood restaurants, and super-hospitable locals often cause travelers to extend their stays, Río's initial attraction is inevitably the 47,000-hectare **Río Lagartos National Park,** home to some 30,000 pink flamingos and 211 other bird species. With a bit of luck, spider monkeys, white-tailed deer, and alligators, which gave Río its name, can also be spotted.

**Practical Information** Though many travelers come to Río just for the day to visit the national park, the bus transfer in Tizimín can be tricky if you're not coming from Mérida. You won't be able to enter the park first thing and you probably won't have time for the fabulous seafood restaurants and the beach. Your best bet is to arrive in the afternoon, arrange a trip for the next morning, and stay the night. The **Autobuses del Noreste** station in Valladolid is on the corner of Calles 50 and 67. Noreste services Río Lagartos (6:45am, 4:30, and 5:30pm, 3hrs., 40.50 pesos) and Tizimín (8 per day, 2½hrs., 31 pesos).

Unless you take the direct bus from Mérida, the only bus service to Río Lagartos is from **Tizimín,** 48km to the south. From the **Autotransportes de Oriente (ADO)** bus station in Tizimín, walk next door to the **Autobuses del Noreste** terminal. From here, sporadic bus service will take you to Río Lagartos (approximately every 1½hrs., 1¼hrs., 7 pesos). Tizimín is most easily reached from Valladolid (hourly, 1¼hrs.), although you can also catch a bus from Mérida (8 per day, 2½hrs., 31pesos) and Cancún (6 per day, 5am-7pm, 3hrs., 24 pesos). From Mérida it may be quicker to take the Noreste bus to Río Lagartos (6:45am, 4:30, and 5:30pm, 3hrs., 40.50 pesos) or make a three-legged trip via Valladolid rather than wait for the infrequent and slow direct service to Tizimín. Buses return to Tizimín 9 times daily between 9am and 10:15pm. From Tizimín, **ADO** services Cancún (usually via Kantunil Kin; 6 per day, 3:30am-7:30pm, 3hrs., 24 pesos), Mérida (6:30, 8:20am, and 5pm, 2½-3hrs., first class 21 pesos, second class 31 pesos), Valladolid (every hr., 1¼hrs., 7 pesos) and Chetumal (4:30am and 1:30pm, 5-6hrs., 44.50 pesos).

Río's meager services amount to one long-distance **caseta** in the *zócalo* (tel. 3-26-68 or -65) from which establishments are reached by way of extensions. **Telephone Code:** 986. There is neither a post office nor a bank in the village, though an occasional police officer does make a brief appearance in the square.

**Accommodations** The first person you see as you step off the bus is likely to escort you to one of the two accommodations in an amiable, chatty manner unless you insist on going to the other (in which case they'll probably walk you there instead). Both are well-known, and helpful locals will make finding them fairly straightforward.

Camping is not an option as the beach is offshore, across the *laguna.* The only hotel in town is the **María de Fertiti** (tel. 3-26-68, ext. 161), on Calle 14, three blocks southwest of the *zócalo* just past the playground. From the bus station, cut back across Av. Principal (Calle 10) and head west following the sign to the Restaurant "Isla Contoy." Take a right once you hit Calle 14, one block before the waterfront; the hotel is ½ block up on your left. Neat, simple rooms have ceiling fans, hammock hooks, and firm mattresses. Stained bathrooms offer hot water (singles 50 pesos; doubles 70 pesos; triples 80 pesos; quads 100 pesos).

The only other accommodations are the **Cabañas Los Dos Hermanos** (though the sign omits the "Dos"), three blocks further down the road from the bus station and a stone's throw from the harbor. These two *cabañas* (two more are under construction) offer huge double beds with mosquito netting, hammock hooks, TVs, and private bathrooms with hot water for 50 pesos. Some people may be disquieted by the fact that no keys are provided—fret not, the buildings stand in the grounds of the owner's home and nothing has ever been swiped. This apparent security risk is actually an indication of Río's genuine hospitality and the honesty of its inhabitants. As you wander through town you'll notice that doors are left ajar, bikes lean against walls, and high-quality fishing nets are left lying around. As the locals will tell you: ¡*No hay problema!* But as always, use common sense and exercise caution.

**Food** For Río's small size, it is richly endowed with excellent yet economical eateries. For the best in seafood, head to **Restaurant "Isla Contoy,"** Calle 19 #134, on the water at the western side of town. Heading southwest from the *zócalo,* Calle 19 is the first right after the Hotel Fertiti. From the *cabañas,* head west past the bus station to Calle 10. Here, directions to the restaurant send you further west to the intersection of Calles 14 and 19; the restaurant is straight ahead. Assorted ex-marine life hangs from the walls and ceiling. The amiable owner (whose cousin owns the *cabañas*) will proudly show you his prize-winning sunset photos of the harbor. The local specialty, *filete relleno* (breaded fish stuffed with shrimp and *salsa*) is mouthwateringly delicious (24 pesos; open daily 6am-11pm; credit cards accepted). The owner will organize trips to the beach and the national park on request (see Sights).

Equally tasty *típico* dishes are to be had at **La Cueva de Macumba,** also on the waterfront, two blocks north of the *zócalo* near the lighthouse. The delightfully creative owner has decorated the place with a hodge-podge of fishing gear, artfully arranged plumage, and a sea shell chandelier. *Salbutes* (fried *tortillas*) 1.50 pesos apiece. Ask politely and he will let you climb the ladder to his loft/studio, where his latest artistic creation is being born (open daily 6am-1am).

**Sights and Entertainment** The **Río Lagartos National Park** is reached by launches which are easily chartered from fishermen. While Luís and his buddies on the waterfront will charge you a total of 100-150 pesos for the trip, the manager of the "Isla Contoy" Restaurant (see above) will gladly put together a group of travelers to help cut costs (40 pesos per person). The manager also arranges trips to the beach (40 pesos per boat).

A 30-minute meandering cruise along the dead calm waters of the narrow lagoon (the locals stubbornly insist on calling this tidal saltwater inlet *"El Río"*) brings you to a wide and shallow bay, at times filled with the lanky twig-legged pink pals you've come to see. After another half-hour or so of puttering about—your guide will repeatedly cause a ruckus to provide in-flight flamingo photo ops—you can get dropped off on a sand bar near the Las Coloradas salt production facility to wander about on your own and take some more pictures. If you hone your muddy-bottom wading skills and wield a zoom lens, you can get some great shots; however, the birds seem less timid when stalked by boat. Don't get overly preoccupied by the flamingos, though—the pelicans perform acrobatic dives for fish as if trying to convince tourists that they also merit a photo or two. While it's hard to predict when you're likely to see lots of birds (locals often scare the flamingos to remoter parts when they wade about searching for conches), the early morning is your best bet.

The cheerful owner of La Cueva de Macumba (see Food, above) is the resident expert and honorary citizen of **Isla Holbox** (see "Isla Holbox and Chiquilá" on page 527). He can arrange for someone to take you there via *lancha* (infinitely more convenient than via Chiquilá), though the total cost of the stunning two-hour journey along the coast will come to at least 400 pesos.

Consistent with the tranquil and laid back attitude with which this fishing town confronts each new day, Río's nightlife does not get much more exciting than a few satisfying beers after dinner. After dark, the lighthouse keeps watch over the *zócalo* with broad, lazy sweeps of its giant beam. Teenagers crowd the foosball tables in the square while screaming kids provide a cacophony of background noise. Every now and then, an energetic game of basketball draws a small crowd. On Saturday nights, **Restaurant "Los Negritos,"** 100m south of the two plastic flamingos on Principal (Calle 10) near the bus station, turns into a disco. The brightly painted reefscape walls give way to live music and speakers the size of fridges only once a week; at other times this, too, is a fine seafood joint, where lobster goes for only 45 pesos.

# QUINTANA ROO

Decades after much of Mexico had embraced industrialization, Quintana Roo's picturesque coastline and lost ruins were still idylls beneath the Caribbean sun. Indeed, the region did not even achieve statehood until the 1970s. But all this was to change when government bureaucrats hit upon the idea of fashioning an artificial paradise at Cancún. The transformation from tropical paradise to tourist factory was swift: vast sums of money flowed into the area and resorts as awesome as the beaches they swallowed were built almost overnight. Spendthrift *gringos* realized that Quintana Roo was a mere puddle-jump from the southern U.S., and Cancún became the beachhead for what some wryly call "the Second *Conquista.*" Isla Cozumel fell next, with nearby Playa del Carmen to follow. Suddenly, too, the long-sleeping Mayan ruins of **Tulum, Cobá, Xcaret, Xel-Ha,** and **Muyil** were rudely awakened by the flashlights of inquisitive archaeologists. Over the past 20 years, many millions of pesos have been invested in the excavation of these ancient cities, and in the maintenance of the enormous bioreserve of **Sian Ka'an,** a protected jungle and marine habitat for thousands of rare flora and fauna.

In spite of the enormous numbers of tourists who crowd the region, *indígena* communities are still deeply rooted in Quintana Roo. The sun-worshippers who flock south to the state and those who have lived there for hundreds of years have a tangled, sometimes tense relationship. Cultural, economic, and linguistic rifts between *indio, ladino,* and *gringo* sometimes seem like gaping wounds, as deep and sore as the cleft between Club Med and a dirt hut.

# ■■■ CANCÚN

Drunk on the success of Puerto Vallarta and Acapulco, Mexican entrepreneurs began a sweeping search in the late 60s to locate the perfect geographic location to give birth to their enormous ambitions. Cancún (pop. 300,000), blessed with miles of magnificent white beaches bordering steel-blue water, was chosen—with the backing of the Mexican government—as the site for this new tourist nirvana. The government's choice was aesthetically and logistically ideal: connected to the mainland by two bridges, each spanning less than 100 yards, the L-shaped island provides 360° water access and close proximity to the Mayan ruins of Quintana Roo and Yucatán.

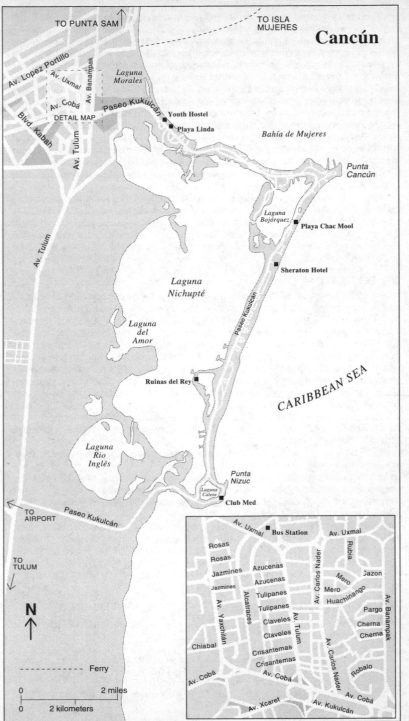

CANCÚN

TO PUNTA SAM

TO ISLA MUJERES

**Cancún**

Av. Lopez Portillo

Av. Uxmal

Av. Banampak

Av. Cobá

Paseo Kukulcán

*Laguna Morales*

Blvd. Kabah

DETAIL MAP

Av. Tulum

Youth Hostel

Playa Linda

*Bahía de Mujeres*

*Punta Cancún*

Av. Tulum

*Laguna Bojórquez*

Playa Chac Mool

Sheraton Hotel

*Laguna Nichupté*

Paseo Kukulcán

*Laguna del Amor*

CARIBBEAN SEA

Ruinas del Rey

*Laguna Rio Inglés*

*Punta Nizuc*

TO AIRPORT

Paseo Kukulcán

*Laguna Caleta*

Club Med

TO TULUM

N

0        2 miles

0        2 kilometers

- - - - - - Ferry

Av. Uxmal        Bus Station        Av. Uxmal

Rosas

Rubia

Rosas

Mero

Cazon

Jazmines        Azucenas

Av. Carlos Nader

Jazmines        Azucenas        Mero

Tulipanes        Huachinango

Av. Yaxchilán

Alcatraces        Tulipanes        Pargo

Claveles        Av. Tulum        Cherna

Chiabal        Claveles        Cherna

Av. Banampak

Crisantemas        Av. Carlos Nader

Crisantemas        Av. Cobá        Robalo

Av. Cobá        Av. Cobá

Av. Xcaret        Av. Kukulcán

Since the first hotel sprung up in 1970, construction has been carefully engineered to best exploit the area's natural resources. The mainland city of Cancún was given space to grow and plenty of housing for hotel workers, and the *Zona Hotelera* (Hotel Zone), located almost exclusively on *Isla Cancún,* was built with almost every conceivable tourist need in mind. The Mexican government installed a water purification system to provide the Hotel Zone with safe tap water, declared all its beaches public spaces, banned begging on the streets, and instituted strict zoning laws to prevent a scourge of skyscrapers. With each multinational hotel chain rushing to erect its representative building on the island, the kaleidoscope of disparate architectural styles left Cancún the randomly assembled (albeit modern) jumble it is today. While wealthy vacationers cruise in taxis to classy restaurants and spring-breakers flit between the downtown discos, hotel employees are packed into lurching diesel buses that ferry them home to humble *colonias* north of the city. Ciudad Cancún grows even more explosively than the *Zona Hotelera,* as thousands arrive looking for work from as far as Mexico City.

Cancún's attractions are obvious. Here, in the middle of the *norteamericano* winter, you can parasail and scuba dive, shop in chic boutiques, snack at McDonald's, and slam tequila at rowdy Tex-Mex bars—all the while speakin' English and spendin' greenbacks. But if you have fewer bills to throw around and are searching for the Yucatán of yore, abandon the mega-resort and seek enjoyment at nearby Tulum or Isla Holbox.

## ORIENTATION

At the easternmost tip of the Yucatán Peninsula, Cancún twinkles 285km east of Mérida via Rte. 180 and 382km north of Chetumal and the Belizean border via Rte. 307. The resort has two sections: **Ciudad Cancún,** center of shopping and services, and **Isla Cancún,** home of the **Zona Hotelera** and the pure white beaches. The cheapest way to reach either section from the airport is to hop into an official *colectivo,* one of the distinctive white Chevrolet jeeps that shuttle new arrivals to their hotels. After purchasing your 30-peso ticket at the desk, you will be squeezed in with six other *gringos* who will invariably get dropped off before you do. Alternatively, a taxi will take you into town for 50 pesos. In Ciudad Cancún, the main drag, **Avenida Tulum** parallels **Yaxchilán** (Yash-chee-YAN), four blocks over. These two streets form a rough parallelogram with **Avenidas Cobá** and **Uxmal.** From the bus station, Tulum and *el centro* stretch to the right of the large white monument in the center of the traffic circle.

Private taxis (white with green stripes) criss-cross Cancún, looking to shuttle tourists from the beaches to the stores and back again in time for sundown (10 pesos and up, depending on how far into the *Zona Hotelera* you are, around 5 pesos for *intra-ciudad;* settle the price before getting in). Buses marked "Hoteles" (3 pesos) run around the clock, linking the *Zona Hotelera's* main drag, **Paseo Kukulcán,** with its counterpart in Ciudad Cancún, Avenida Tulum.

In the city, the abundant pedestrians hinder the pace of traffic. To get off buses in the *Zona Hotelera* try signaling the driver, but don't be shy to follow the example of the locals by pounding hard on the wall: this signals the daredevil drivers to slow down enough so that you break only a few bones when jumping off. Many places rent mopeds, which are useful for exploring the 18 kilometers of beaches which stretch from the Youth Hostel to Punta Nizuc.

## PRACTICAL INFORMATION

Most services are downtown along Av. Tulum, easily accessible from the *Zona Hotelera* by bus.

**Tourist Offices:** Av. Tulum 26 (tel. 84-80-73 or 84-06-72), and other booths all over town. More helpful is the staff of **Cancún Tips** (tel. 84-40-44 or 84-44-43), at Pl. Caracol in the Hotel Zone and at the airport. The firm publishes an English-language magazine (*Cancún Tips*) with invaluable maps and practical information. It also provides discounts at various restaurants and clubs. Try and snag one for free at the airport. Otherwise, it'll cost you US$3 at the main office on the corner of Tulum and Uxmal. English spoken at all offices.

**Police:** (tel. 84-19-13), next to City Hall on Tulum.

**Post Office:** Av. Xel-Ha at Sun Yax Chén (tel. 84-15-24). From Tulum, cut through any side street to Yaxchilán and head up Sun Yax Chén. The post office is 4 blocks farther. Open for stamps and *Lista de Correos* Mon.-Fri. 8am-7pm, Sat. and holidays 9am-1pm. **Fax** Mon.-Fri. 9am-8:30pm, Sat. 9am-4:30pm. **Postal Code:** 77500.

**Telephones:** International collect calls are made in person from *casetas* (8 pesos to the U.S., 12 pesos to Canada). **Caseta M-28** is in Mercado 28 behind the post office. Open daily 7am-9pm. The public phone in Pl. Nautilus near the youth hostel can be used for long distance calls, provided you have a big pile of coins. To make calls within Cancún, prefix the number you are dialing with "8." (The numbers included in this section have already been prefixed with the magic "8.") From **LADATEL** phones, an English-speaking AT&T operator can be reached by dialing 95-800-462-4240. Buy phone cards on Av. Tulum and Tulipanes at La Surtidora, Farmacia Paris, or the *casa de cambio* in front of the **Aquamarina Beach Hotel**, a five-minute walk from the CREA. Open daily 7:30am-8pm. **Telephone information:** 04. **Telephone Code:** 98.

**Telegrams:** (tel. 84-15-29), at the **post office** (see above). Open Mon.-Fri. 9am-8:30pm, Sat. 9am-4:30pm. Allow one day for the message to arrive.

**Consulates: U.S.,** Av. Náder 40 at Uxmal (tel. 84-24-11). Open Mon.-Fri. 9am-2pm and 3-5:30pm. **Canada,** Av. Tulum 200 in Pl. México (tel. 84-37-16). Open Mon.-Fri. 10am-2pm. For emergencies outside of office hours, call the Canadian Embassy in Mexico City (tel. 915-724-7900). **United Kingdom,** in the Hotel Royal Caribbean (*Zona Hotelera;* tel. 85-11-66, ext. 462). Open Mon.-Fri. 9am-5pm. **France,** Av. Xel-Ha 113 (tel. 87-39-50). Open Mon.-Fri. 10:30am-noon and 5-7pm. **Germany,** Punta Conoco 36, in the *centro* (tel. 84-18-98). Open Mon.-Fri. 10am-1pm. **Spain,** Edificio Oasis, Blvd. Kukulcán, in the *Zona Hotelera* (tel. 83-24-66). Open Mon.-Fri. 10am-1pm.

**Currency Exchange:** Of all the banks along Av. Tulum, **Bancomer,** Av. Tulum 20 (tel. 84-44-00), gives the best rate. Open for exchange Mon.-Fri. 9am-1:30pm. Both **Bánamex,** Tulum 19 (tel. 84-54-11), and **Banco Serfín,** Av. Tulum at Cobá (tel. 84-14-24), give cash advances on Visa and MC and have Cirrus **ATMs.** Equally competitive but more convenient is **CUNEX Exchange** (tel. 87-09-01), next to Banco Serfín on the corner of Tulum and Cobá. Open daily 8am-11pm.

**American Express:** On Tulum at Cobá (tel. 84-54-41), next to Hotel América. Personal checks cashed, money wired, and mail held (up to 3 months) for cardholders and traveler's check users. Open Mon.-Fri. 9am-6pm, Sat. 9am-1pm.

**International Airport:** (tel. 86-00-49), on Rte. 307 just south of the city. *Colectivos* 30 pesos, taxis 50 pesos (fixed rates to downtown; buy a ticket at the desk beforehand). Airlines: **Aerocaribe** (tel. 84-20-00), to Cozumel, Mérida, Chetumal, and Villahermosa; **Mexicana** (tel. 87-44-44 or 87-27-69), to Mexico City, Guadalajara, and major U.S. cities; **LACSA** (tel. 87-31-01 or 87-51-01), to Central America; **American** (tel. 86-00-55, 86-01-51, or 86-00-86); **Continental** (tel. 86-00-06 or 86-01-69); **Northwest** (tel. 86-00-44 or 86-00-46); **United** (tel. 86-01-58 or 86-00-25).

**Bus Station:** On Uxmal, at Tulum (tel. 84-13-78). You can stow your luggage here for 3-5 pesos for 24 hrs. There are a number of different bus lines at this difficult-to-navigate station, including **ADO, Caribe, Interplaya,** and **Expresso de Oriente. ADO** provides first-class service to Valladolid (9:15am and 8:45pm, 2hrs., 29 pesos), Chichén Itzá (8:45am and 2:30pm, 3hrs., 32 pesos), Playa del Carmen, Tulum and Chetumal (6:30, 9:15, 11:30am, 4:30pm and 7:24pm, 1hr., 2hrs., and 5hrs. respectively, 11, 21, and 55 pesos), Campeche (11:30am, 6hrs., 103.50 pesos), and Palenque (4:45 and 7pm, 14hrs. overnight, 157 pesos). **Expreso de Oriente** provides the most efficient first-class service to Mérida (every hr. 6am-7pm, 10pm, and midnight-2am, 4hrs., 58 pesos). You can save about 25% by hopping on the second-class buses that leave from the curbside and go as far as Tulum

**CANCÚN**

and Mérida (every ½hr., 5am-10pm). Schedules vary—check at the station for details.

**Ferries:** To Isla Mujeres, take a bus or a van marked "Pto. Juárez" to the two ferry depots north of town (Punta Sam for car ferries, Puerto Juárez for passenger ferries). Passenger ferries (5 pesos or 10 pesos, depending on the boat) shuttle across 15 times from 6am-8:30pm. Ferries to Cozumel (20 or 25 pesos) leave regularly from Playa del Carmen, south of Cancún, accessible by bus from the terminal in town.

**Taxis:** (tel. 83-18-40 or 84-12-77). Throughout *el centro* and the *Zona Hotelera*, taxis are abundant but expensive. In the *Zona* the minimum fare is 15 pesos and a ride into town can run you as much as 40 pesos. Within the *centro*, a taxi ride should run around 10 pesos. Prices are negotiable; be sure to settle the deal before getting in.

**Moped Rental:** The bus system in Cancún has become so extensive that mopeds are an endangered species. Most major hotels rent them, though; try **Hotel Flamingo** (tel. 83-15-44) or **Hotel Las Perlas** (tel. 83-20-22), near CREA. Mopeds go for roughly US$5 per hour, US$35-45 per day.

**English Bookstore: Fama,** Tulum 105 (tel. 84-65-86). International newspapers, magazines, guidebooks, maps, and trashy beach books in English. Open daily 8am-10:30pm.

**Laundromat: Lavandería Automática "Alborada,"** Náder 5 (tel. 84-15-84), next to Suites Alborada and behind the Ayuntamiento Benito Juárez. Claiming to be the finest "Laundry mat" (sic) since 1976, this astute enterprise will do your laundry for 22 pesos. Alternatively, self-service costs…22 pesos! Choose wisely. Self-service hours Mon.-Sat. 8am-6pm. Laundromat open until 7pm.

**Supermarket: Super San Francisco,** Av. Tulum next to Bánamex (tel. 84-11-55). Open Mon.-Sat. 7:30am-10pm, Sun. 7am-9pm. **Super Deli,** a 24-hr. grocery store, is conveniently located near the youth hostel.

**Red Cross:** Av. Yaxchilán 2. For routine medical services, call 84-16-16. Open 24 hrs.

**Pharmacies:** Several along Tulum and Yaxchilán, the largest and most reasonable being **Farmacia Paris,** Yaxchilán 32 (tel. 84-01-64), at the intersection with Calle Rosas. Open 24 hrs.

**Medical Services: Seguro Social,** at Tulum and Cóba (tel. 84-19-19 or 84-23-42). For an ambulance call **Total Assist** at Claveles 5 near Av. Tulum (tel. 84-40-92 or 84-81-16). English spoken. Also try the **Hospital Americano,** Calle Viento 15 (tel. 84-61-33 or 84-63-19 after hours), five blocks south on Tulum after its intersection with Cobá.

**Emergency:** 06.

## ACCOMMODATIONS AND CAMPING

While the Mexican government may have prevented skyscrapers from going up in Cancún, the same, unfortunately, cannot be said for the prices. If you're not careful, this place will suck money out of you faster than you can sign your next traveler's check. Budget travelers either stay at the **CREA Youth Hostel** or avoid the *Zona Hotelera* altogether. Even in Ciudad Cancún, some hotels will charge you upwards of US$20 for a room you wouldn't let your dog sleep in. Campers can pitch a tent cheaply at the CREA (see below), though some sleep on the beach in the *Zona;* ever on the lookout for public drunkenness, police are eager to check campers' blood alcohol levels. Participants in **FAMITEL** (tel. 87-28-29), a partnership between several local families and the state, built clean, bright additional rooms onto their houses (45 pesos for 1 person, 50 pesos for two people; fan, breakfast, and color TV included). If you don't mind the distance from *el centro,* the rooms are the nicest in the city for the price. Most hotels accept credit cards and during high season phone reservations are a good idea. With the exception of the CREA, all hotels listed are within a 10- to 15-minute walk from Av. Tulum.

**CREA Youth Hostel (HI),** Paseo Kukulcán, Km. 2.5, (tel. 83-13-37). 100 single-sex dorm rooms with four bunk beds apiece. Personal lockers provided; lock your valuables when showering. Ceiling fans but no A/C. Bathrooms lack amenities and hot water. Small pool, but the beaches are better for swimming. Basketball court and table-tennis. Maximum stay is 15 days. Lockers, sheets, towels provided. 30 pesos per person, plus a 30-peso deposit. No ID required. 25% discount with a *tarjeta plan joven* and ID, while an HI card is good for a 10% discount. No curfew. Check-out 1pm. You can pitch a tent on the Hostel's front lawn for 15 pesos per person, plus a 30-peso deposit. Locker not included, but you can place your stuff with hostel security.

**Hotel Coral,** Sun Yax Chén (Sun-yash-CHEN) 30 (tel. 84-20-97). Heading west from Av. Yaxchilán, the hotel is two blocks down on the left. Cheerful yellow lobby with TV. Spacious rooms in lively colors with carved dark-wood furniture. Random artwork adorns the walls. Ancient air conditioners get the job done. *Agua purificada* in the hall. Hot water. Courtyard with pool (usually empty). Check-out 1:30pm. Singles 50 pesos, 25 pesos for each additional person. To make reservations, wire payment 10 days in advance.

**Hotel Villa Rossána,** Av. Yaxchilán 25 (tel. 84-19-43). On the right, past Sun Yax Chén, as you come down Yaxchilán. With a new owner, this hotel is in good hands. Huge, plainly furnished rooms include a balcony perfect for sunbathing. All rooms have hot water and ceiling fans. TV and payphone in the lobby. Pleasant courtyard has a pool. Check-out 1pm. Singles 50 pesos. Doubles 70 pesos. Triples 90 pesos. Quads 110 pesos. Add 30 pesos for A/C.

**Hotel Canto,** Sm. 24, Mza. 22 Retorno 5, Av. Yaxchilán (tel. 84-12-67). As you turn off Av. Uxmal, look for the fading pink building on your right. Clean, plain rooms have A/C, color TV, phones, and roomy closets. Spotless, groovy-blue bathrooms with good showers and hot water. *Agua purificada* in the lobby. Check-out 1pm. Singles 80 pesos. Doubles 100 pesos. Triples 110 pesos. Quads 120 pesos.

**Suites Albatros,** Yaxchilán SW-20 (tel. 84-22-42), two blocks south of Cobá. Huge rooms with vividly tiled floors, modern art, and kitchens. Spotlessly clean and bright with hot water, A/C, and fridge. Convenience store and laundromat next door. Manager lives in room #8 and speaks English. Upstairs rooms have balconies. Singles 100 pesos, 20 pesos for each additional person.

## FOOD

In Cancún, the epic battle between Mexican culture and tourism has ended in a glorious triumph for the forces of the latter. As a result, Cancún's food is overpriced and under-spiced. In the *Zona Hotelera,* "cheap" and "restaurant" are mutually exclusive. Don't even think of eating there. However, even most locals avoid eating at the very bottom of the food chain—the road-side booths serving meats of dubious origin—for genuine fear of contracting cholera. You can nevertheless dine well and inexpensively at the many joints along Avs. Cobá, Tulum and Yaxchilán, to name but a few.

If you're looking to avoid tourists altogether (and spend nary a buck in the process), head for **Mercado 28,** behind the post office and circumscribed by Av. Xel-Ha. Numerous budget cafés are located in its western courtyard. Try the hearty *comida corrida* at **Restaurants Margely, Acapulco,** or **La Chaya** (5-25 pesos). All are open daily 7am-6pm. La Chaya, closed on Saturdays, also offers vegetarian meals. Except for Restaurante Río Nizuc all the restaurants listed below are in Ciudad Cancún.

**100% Natural,** Sun Yax Chén 6 (tel. 84-36-17), at Yaxchilán. Not to be confused with the smaller juice shop on Yaxchilán, its beamed, leafy porch and lush tropical garden will sooth sun-dazed spirits. Steer clear of the expensive main dishes and sample the fruits and vegetables in all their forms. Delicious tropical shakes (9-12 pesos) are a terrific side-show. Wheelchair access. Open daily 7am-11pm.

**Chiffer's,** a.k.a. **Café Super San Francisco,** Tulum 18 (tel. 84-11-55), in front of the supermarket of the same name. Resembling a 50s diner and blessed with A/C, Chiffer's is a welcoming oasis for the overheated shopper. Breakfast omelettes 13 pesos. Burgers and sandwiches 14.50-18.50 pesos. Cheesecake 7 pesos. Open daily 7am-11pm.

**Restaurante Río Nizuc,** Paseo Kukulcán, Km. 22. Take the *camión* marked "Hoteles" (3 pesos) to the last stop near the Hotel Regina (Km. 20). Next, hail a taxi (15 pesos) to take you over the *Canal Nizuc,* 2km farther on. Just after the bridge, a pot-holed road on the left leads to a parking lot. Walk down to the canal and follow the boardwalk to the right. A few kilometers west of Punta Nizuc, this mecca of *mariscos* remains as yet undiscovered by the tourist hordes who swarm all over the *Zona Hotelera.* Nevertheless, the crowd of locals gazing wistfully (or quizzically?) at the *gringos* parading by in speedboats attests to the popularity and quality of the food. Sit down in the shade of this open-air, waterfront grill, have a beer (6 pesos), and watch the kids play in the shallow water. Barbecued fish 25 pesos. Seafood platter 30 pesos. Enormous servings. No credit cards. Open daily 11am-6pm.

**El Tacolote,** Av. Cobá 19 (tel. 87-30-45). Look for the sombrero-sporting, taco-gobbling, yellow chicken out front. White and yellow arches bisect this open-grill, family restaurant. Prices start at 11.50 pesos for 6 tasty tacos. Try the *alambre* for 16 pesos. Ice cream 8 pesos. Excellent, friendly service. AmEx, MC, Visa accepted. Open daily 5:30pm-2am.

## SIGHTS

Visitors do not come to Cancún to see Mexico. Most visitors do not even come to Cancún to see Cancún. And even the powdery white sand beaches and glistening blue surf provide only a backdrop for the sight most of the debauched *gringos* have come to see: each other's semi-nude, alcohol-soaked, sunburnt bodies. Cancún's name, meaning "snake nest" in Mayan, has proven to be oddly prophetic.

Progress and culture have been summarily executed and buried in a neon tank top. For those seeking a respite from church and ruin overload, this *norteamericano* outpost, with its glorious beaches, fast-food restaurants, and frenetic nightlife, may be the perfect place to take refuge. Since fun here requires no more than a credit card and a brainstem, your mind won't be doing much wandering. If it does, however, you run the risk of becoming painfully aware of the reality of poverty and inequality upon which the comfortable artifice of Cancún is built.

Even if you stay inland in Ciudad Cancún, you should still take advantage of the well-groomed beaches in front of the luxury hotels in the *Zona Hotelera.* Remember, all beaches are public property, and travelers often discreetly use hotel restrooms, fresh-water showers, and lounge chairs. More peaceful strips of shoreline south of the Sheraton Hotel are accessible by bus.

The beach at the **Sheraton Hotel** is one of the safest and the most pleasant in Cancún. The sand is clean, the water transparent, and the waves active. Organized beach activities include volleyball, beer-drinking, egg-tossing, scuba classes, Mexican-style painting lessons, and bikini contests. To join in the activities, become a visitor of the hotel for the day. Boogie boards rent for 18 pesos for two hours at the small marina on the beach.

Cancún's surf is a whimper to the roar of the rest of the *costa torquesa.* **Playa Chac-Mool,** where waves are about 1 ft. high, is as exciting as it gets. For CREA guests, Cancún's surf is pathetic. **Playa Linda,** a ten-minute walk east, provides the closest decent (but shallow) swimming.

Cancún offers watersport adventures of all types for those with hefty bank accounts. **Marina Agua Ray** (tel. 83-17-73), near Pl. Flamingo, provides wave runners, jet skis, and parasailing, scuba diving, snorkeling, water-skiing, and deep-sea fishing equipment—all at obscenely *gringo*-oriented prices. **Scuba Cancún** (tel. 83-10-11), next to Carlos 'n Charlie's, offers various diving lessons and services at comparatively reasonable prices. The dock to the right of the CREA hostel supports a dive shop which offers two hours of snorkeling for US$20 with equipment.

Consistent with the culturally emaciated façade it presents the world, Cancún's anthropological museum was closed after the 1988 hurricane. It has yet to re-open; no one seems to care. To add insult to injury, Cancún's Mayan ruins have been surrounded and overwhelmed by the torrential Americanization in the form of towering resorts and chilly, overpriced malls. The Sheraton encompasses some small-scale ruins on the highest point in Cancún, affording vivid views in all directions. Other ruins in the immediate vicinity include **El Rey,** between the Sheraton and Club Med. Consisting of a small pyramid and vestiges of Mayan painting, this site, supposedly a regal burying ground, may provide respite from the crispy *gringo* critters who litter the beach (open daily 9am-5pm; admission 5 pesos).

## ENTERTAINMENT

At night, Cancún's laid-back decadence gives way with frightening abruptness to partying so mind-numbingly frenetic that it shames nearby Isla Mujeres and Playa del Carmen. Both in the *Zona* and downtown, discos and bars offer carefree, wallet-emptying nights. Restaurant workers in the *Zona Hotelera* are good at pointing out which spots are hot. Most clubs, with a variety of promotions throughout the week, have a system of cover charges liable to make fellas and feminists fume alike. (Women get in free just about everywhere.)

Near the youth hostel (a 10-minute walk), **La Boom** and **Tequila Boom,** two nightclubs under the same roof, provide multiple levels of laser-lit lechery. While Tequila Boom's starlight ceiling and huge music video screen make for sensory overload, the London Underground sign and compatriot red phonebox are bizarrely out of place. One measly beer will set you back 13-18 pesos (cover US$10; free Mon., but double-check as schedules vary).

On *Isla Cancún*, nighttime attraction centers around **Plaza Caracol.** The premier attraction is **Dady'O** (tel. 83-33-33), although the cave-like entrance makes you feel like you're heading for fiery hell rather than disco heaven. The cave-scape continues through to the multi-tiered dance floor, above which hangs enough technology to power the U.S.S. *Enterprise.* A cafeteria in the club serves snacks (12-25 pesos). Laser show nightly at 11pm (cover US$10; free Tues. and for women on Fri.; open daily 10pm-late). Next door, **Dady Rock** (tel. 83-16-26) has all-you-can-eat/drink deals (US$10-17) several nights a week (open daily 5:30pm-late). In the vicinity, **Tequila Rock** bludgeons eardrums on several different stages. There are various promotions throughout the week, including open bar night on Mondays (male eardrums US$15, female eardrums US$5). Closer to Plaza Caracol and a little easier on the ears, **Cat's Reggae Club** provides perhaps the coolest and coziest dance floor. The reggae beat reverberates around colorful walls decorated with portraits of legendary reggae artists (free Mon. or with *Cancún Tips* card.; other nights about 20 pesos cover). **Christine,** in the Hotel Krystal (tel. 3-11-33), caters to an older, more conservative crowd. Boogeying thirtysomethings look like they've been let loose in an orchestra pit. (50-peso cover for men only. No shorts or sandals. Double-check as schedules vary.)

In Ciudad Cancún, **Risky Time,** above El Tío Bob, on the corner of Tulum and Cobá, has a small dance floor oasis placed amidst ghastly neon palm trees. If you're not into the dance/reggae mix you can play pool in the back behind the bar (no cover). A much bigger dance floor can be found at **Karamba,** a gay disco on Tulipanes, just off Tulum. Its open-air layout and funky pop-art murals are as colorful as the variety of dance music (no cover).

**Bullfights** occur year-round, every Wed. at 3:30pm, in the bullring on Bonampak at Sayil (tel. 84-54-65). Tickets (150 pesos per person, less if you're in a large group) are available at travel agencies on Tulum or at the bullring on a bullfight day. Show includes a performance by the **Ballet Folklórico.** All major credit cards accepted.

# ■■■ ISLA HOLBOX AND CHIQUILÁ

Just off the northeastern tip of the Yucatán Peninsula, Isla Holbox (hol-BOSH, "dark hole" in Mayan) remains safely out of reach of Cancún's tour buses. The 1500 *holboxeños* who inhabit the tiny *pueblo* have a healthy appreciation for fish and tranquility, both of which they enjoy in abundance. The island's small houses are sharply painted and decorated, and dozens of *lanchas* dot the beaches, pointing toward the sea like a flock of single-minded geese. Holbox is the perfect place for a breath of fresh air and a two-day siesta from the feverish pace of the busier tourist attractions. **Chiquilá** is the unfortunate embarkation point for passengers ferrying to the secluded beaches of Isla Holbox. The small settlement will not delay in-transit tourists, but after the last ferry chugs out to sea, late arrivals usually prefer to head back to civilization for a meal and a bed for one simple reason: at dusk the fierce mosquitoes strike fear into even the locals' hearts.

**Orientation and Practical Information** Transportation should be planned carefully and in advance, as buses and boats are infrequent. There is one direct bus that leaves from Cancún at 5pm daily (12 pesos), but doesn't arrive in time for the ferry. The easiest way to arrive on Isla Holblox by nightfall from Cancún is to ask the driver of a Valladolid-bound bus (there are many; buy a ticket to X-Can, 12 pesos) to drop you off at Ideal, beyond the bus station at the crossroads by the big green signpost. Straight ahead is Valladolid; to the right, Chiquilá. A half-dozen taxis lurk here in anticipation of your pesos (30 pesos to Kantunil Kin, 60 pesos all the way to Chiquilá). The **passenger ferry** (*lancha*), with about 30 seats, leaves for Isla Holbox at 8am and 2pm (15 pesos one-way), and returns from the island at 5am and 1pm. Boats may run more frequently on the weekends during the peak season, but don't count on it. The easiest way to navigate this chain of inconvenient schedules is to take the 4am (no, that's not a misprint!) Valladolid-bound bus from Cancún to Ideal, hop a taxi into Kantunil Kin and ride the *Chiquilkan* (local bus, 6 pesos) as far as Chiquilá in time for the 8am crossing. This allows you to be cooling off on Holbox's beach by 9am.

One doesn't need a car to get around the island, but the car ferry can transport passengers. The ferry's schedule is as follows: Chiquilá to Holbox, Tues. and Sat. 9am and 4:30pm, Wed.-Fri. 10am; Holbox to Chiquilá, Tues.-Sat. 6am, Tues. and Sat. 3pm. Try to make the *lancha,* however; its schedule tends to be somewhat more reliable. Returning from Holbox is much easier, since both Valladolid-bound and Cancún-bound buses meet the early boat. Be ready to leap off when the boat strikes the dock, because the buses wait for no man (or woman). If the Cancún bus doesn't show, take the Valladolid-Mérida bus to Kantunil Kin. The Cancún bus swings by here at 6:30am. You can always flag down a Valladolid-Cancún bus at Ideal, though waiting in the sun will be torturous.

Sloshing in an incompletely drained swamp, Chiquilá is neither a pleasant nor an inviting place, worthy of no more than the absolute minimum of time required to get to and away from Holbox. There are only a handful of businesses in this *pueblito*. In striking blue and white and beneath a thatched roof, **Tienda la Estrellita** sells fruit and ice-cold sodas at about 2 pesos apiece (open daily 7am-9pm). Across the way in the corrugated iron shed, **Tienda Rural** provides a slightly larger selection of food and beverages (open daily 8am-1pm, 4-8pm). There are neither accommodations nor eateries in Chiquilá. For those who miss the last ferry to Holbox and find no Holbox-bound fishermen's boats at the dock, the options are to take a *lancha* for around 80 pesos (up to 5 people) or to return to **Kantunil Kin**, 43km south of Chiquilá, on the Chiquilá access road. In Kantunil Kin beds are available at the red-and-white **Casa de Huéspedes "Del Parque"** (tel. 4-68-38, ext. 116), which is on the other side of the basketball court next to the church (singles 50 pesos; doubles 55 pesos; triples 65 pesos).

Holbox's **public telephone** *caseta* is a half-block east of the *zócalo* on Igualdad (open Mon.-Sat. 8am-1pm and 4-8pm; a call costs 2 pesos). The island's **Centro de Salud,** on the right side of Juárez in the blue-and-white building, houses a doctor who may be awakened in case of a serious emergency. The one-man **police** force lounges in his office at the *zócalo* on the corner of Juárez and Díaz (open daily 9am-2pm and 4-8pm, but don't count on it). There is no bank on the island.

**Accommodations and Food** Holbox's modest but growing tourist industry supports a number of hotels. **Posada D'Ingrid** (ext. 168), a few blocks from the beach and west of the *zócalo,* lies closest to the water and proves the most *tran-*

*quila*. Gleaming, salmon-colored rooms provide hot water, clean bathrooms, ceiling fans, and hooks for two hammocks in addition to the double bed (50 pesos). **Posada Los Arcos** (ext. 141) offers a nice view of the beach from under its eponymous arches. Stuccoed rooms are clean and include private bathrooms and fans. Singles and doubles 50 pesos. Triples 70 pesos. Look for *la dueña* in **Tienda Dinora** on the west side of the *zócalo*. Sra. Dinora, nicknamed *"Dinero"* for her entrepreneurial habits, also rents out beachfront *cabañas* with bare interiors, crude bathrooms that lack hot water, standing fans, and mosquito netting for the beds (singles 30 pesos; doubles 40 pesos). Family-size *cabañas,* including a kitchen, go for 70 pesos. Be prepared to be visited by unwelcomed and unexpected cockroaches at night. **Hotel Flamingo** stands close to the dock and features a view of the mainland shaded by coconut palms. Five straightforward rooms with flaky paint and clean bathrooms allow space for up to five people (45 pesos, 15 pesos more during high season). If you want a fan and hot water, you'll pay 25 pesos more for one person, 30 pesos for two, and 35 pesos for three. During high season prices rise by 10 pesos. Check-out noon. To reserve a room (a good idea during Christmas, Feb.-March, and July-Aug.) send a 50% deposit to Hotel Flamingo, Isla Holbox, Q.R. 77310, or call 87-16-68, 87-14-62, or 87-29-83, ext. 52. For a livelier stay, visit **Posada Amapola** (ext. 117). On the edge of the *zócalo,* this small pink house fronts an airy bar. Clean pastel rooms with green-and-white floor tiles. Small bathrooms and ceiling fans, but no hot water (singles and doubles 40 pesos; triples 45 pesos).

Restaurants in Holbox follow the pace of island life, meandering through time without a fixed schedule. Among them is **Zarabanda,** one block south of the *zócalo* and two blocks east of Juárez. Look for the sign on Juárez. In this red brick building with a palm-frond roof, the cooks will prepare excellent fish and meat dishes at very reasonable prices. No menu, no waiters—you just eat what they've got for you. Fried fish 12 pesos (open daily 8am-10pm). **Lonchería El Parque,** off the *zócalo,* two doors down from Dinora's, also serves fresh, cheap seafood dishes, and *antojitos.* Your favorite chicken or beef dish, washed down with an ice-cold beer, will run about 10 pesos (open daily 9am-10pm). **Tienda Dinora** can satisfy any mid-day snack cravings you may experience. Sodas 2.50 pesos. During peak seasons (July-Aug., Dec.-Feb.), Holbox's tranquility is disturbed by the *cuates* (*holboxeño* for foreigners) who sun on the sand or listen to rock, *salsa,* and dance the lambada at **Cariocas Restaurant and Disco,** on Igualdad two blocks east of the *zócalo.* Cariocas serves as a restaurant during the week, with a cover for music on weekends.

**Sights** The island's north shore has a pleasant enough beach, but the main draws, aside from sunning and sleeping, are the boat trips provided by local fishermen. For 150-200 pesos (40-or-so pesos per person if you can get a group together), one of the local fishermen will take you on a four-hour cruise of the surrounding area. First stop is **Isla de Pájaros,** called **Isla Morena** by locals, home to nearly 40 species of birds, including flamingos and pelicans. Next, you'll visit **Ojo de Agua,** an inlet on the mainland fed by a subterranean freshwater spring. Jump in and splash around in the shallow pools. Finally, you'll head across the lagoon which separates Isla Holbox from the mainland (look out for the many dolphins) to **Isla de la Pasión.** This small island caters to day-trippers with its restaurant-bar, live music and volleyball court. On Holbox itself, go exploring on a moped (try **Tienda Dinora** for rental, about 25 pesos per hour) or take a meandering walk along the deserted strips of beach. However, not even a seasoned blood-donor will enjoy bush-whacking through the overgrown, swampy interior, where you can do little more than provide lunch for a half-million hungry mosquitoes.

After the day's (in)activity is over, walk out along one of the piers to enjoy the scarlet sunset. With a bit of luck you may even catch a couple of pelicans gobbling down dinner on one of the disused jetties. After dark, the whole island seems to congregate in the brilliantly lit *zócalo*. Watch a scrappy game of kids' basketball end in a 0-0 tie. No overtime.

ISLA MUJERES

# ■■■ ISLA MUJERES

When in 1517 the Spaniard Francisco Hernández de Córdoba blew into this tiny island (7km by 1km) looking for slaves to work the Cuban mines, he found only women. With the men fishing out at sea, Córdoba saw an island seemingly ruled by the Mayan goddess of fertility, Ixchel. Looking to the deity's numerous female attendants, he dubbed the site "Island of Women." After Córdoba left, the island remained in Spanish hands, existing variously as a private *hacienda*, a haven for pirates, and a home to Caribbean fishermen.

Some present-day inhabitants of the island (pop. 13,500) still fish, but now they also sell goods to the boatloads of daytrippers who arrive each morning from Cancún. But don't discount the independent attitude of this island town: a significant number of shops and restaurants close at mid-day to discreetly avoid the flood of *turistas*. *Isleños* set their own prices, and seem annoyed by potential customers who try to haggle with them. However, most of the street vendors who make their living from *gringo* tourists aren't native islanders—much more aggressive, these vendors expect to be bargained with. In general, *isleños* tend to be more accommodating toward travelers who find lodging on the island. Those who choose to linger on Isla Mujeres will discover beaches of velvety sand, supremely good snorkeling, postcard-perfect azure water, and more breathing room than exists in all of Cancún.

## ORIENTATION

The island lies 11km northeast of the northern coast of Quintana Roo. Passenger ferries (every ½hr., 8am-8pm, 35min., 5 pesos) and speedier cruisers (every ½hr., 6:30am-8:30pm, 15min., 10 pesos) depart from Puerto Juárez, 2km north of Ciudad Cancún, the mainland section of the Cancún resort. Arrive early—ferries are notorious for leaving ahead of schedule if they're full. Puerto Juárez is a 10- to 15-minute ride from Ciudad Cancún on any bus (or van) labeled "Puerto Juárez" (3 pesos), which can be caught along Tulum behind the station. The bus lets you off at the dock; the modern building to your left houses the **tourist office.** Taxis from Ciudad Cancún to Puerto Juárez cost 20 pesos. A car ferry (6 pesos per person, 36 pesos per car) runs to Mujeres from Punta Sam, 5km north of Puerto Juárez.

Vigorous walkers will have no difficulty getting around the bustling *centro*. The town is laid out in a rough grid: six major streets run perpendicular to the dock (**Avenidas López Mateos, Matamoros, Abasolo, Madero, Morelos,** and **Nicolas Bravo,** from north to south). **Avenida Rueda Medina** runs along the coastline and is paralleled by **Avenidas Juárez, Hidalgo, Guerrero,** and **Carlos Lazo,** in that order. Turning left on any of these streets will quickly lead you to **Playa Norte.** Av. Rueda Medina runs the length of the island, past **Playas Paraíso, Lancheros,** and **Indios** and the **Garrafón National Park.** Finally, on the southern tip of the island, beyond a disused lighthouse, are the remains of a Mayan temple. A good source of general information is *Islander,* a local publication available at travel agency shops, the ferry dock at Puerto Juárez, and the tourist office in the *zócalo.* Be sure to pick up a map wherever you get *Islander,* as street names have long since faded from most buildings. Public buses go only as far as Playa Lancheros (3 pesos). Taxis, on the other hand, roam the length of Mujeres; you should have no problem catching one unless you're returning from Garrafón long after the park closes.

## PRACTICAL INFORMATION

**Tourist Office:** Guerrero 8 (tel. 7-03-16), by the *zócalo* basketball court. Helpful with specifics. Most information, including a map of the town, is also available in *Islander, Cancún Tips,* and *Isla Mujeres Tips.* Some English spoken. Open Mon.-Fri. 9am-4pm.

**Police:** Hidalgo at Morelos (tel. 7-00-98), in the Palacio Municipal. Friendly, but little English spoken. Open 24 hrs.

**Post Office:** Guerrero and López Mateos (tel. 7-00-85), at the northwest corner of town, around the corner from the Poc-Na Hostel. Open Mon.-Fri. 8am-7pm, Sat. 9am-1pm. **Postal Code:** 70085.

**Telephones:** Long distance *caseta* in the lobby of **Hotel María Jose** (tel. 7-01-30), on Madero just off Rueda Medina. International collect calls 5 pesos. Open daily 7am-7pm. For by-the-minute calls you'll have to purchase a phone card. **Diego's** general store, on Rueda Medina opposite the dock, charges 15 pesos per minute for **faxes** to the U.S. (fax 7-04-92). Open daily 7am-5pm and 7-11pm. **Telephone Code**: 987.

**Telegrams:** Guerrero 13 (tel. 7-01-13), next to the post office. A/C. Open Mon.-Fri. 9am-3pm. **Fax** (7-01-13).

**Currency Exchange: Banco del Atlántico** (tel. 7-00-05), on Rueda Medina near the ferry dock. Open for exchange Mon.-Fri. 9am-6pm. Better rates are given at exchange booths along Av. Hidalgo.

**Taxis:** (tel. 2-00-66). Lines form near sights and beaches. Rides from town to Playas Paraíso and Lancheros, Garrafón, and the ruins cost 8, 15, and 18 pesos respectively.

**Moped Rental:** Shop around. Although mopeds rent for 20 pesos per hr. almost everywhere, prices for longer periods vary. At **Ciro's**, it'll cost you 50 pesos for three hours, which is plenty of time to see the whole island. MC or Visa required for deposit. Open daily 9am-5pm.

**Laundry Service: Lavandería Tim Phó,** Av. Juárez 94 at Abasolo. 4kg for 10 pesos. 2hr. turnaround. A/C. Open Mon.-Sat. 7am-9pm, Sun 8am-2pm.

**Markets: Super Betino,** Morelos 3, on the *zócalo*. Wide selection of dry goods, wine, beer, and *agua purificada* at non-resort prices. Small deli and pharmacy. Open daily 7am-11pm. For a better selection of fruit and vegetables, try the **fruit stalls** just outside (mangos 3 pesos) or the mini-market **Isla Mujeres,** on Hidalgo between Abasolo and Madero.

**Red Cross:** tel. 7-00-46.

**Pharmacy: Farmacia Lily,** Madero 18 at Hidalgo (tel. 7-01-64). Two blocks from the dock as the crow flies and one block left. Open daily 8:30am-9:30pm.

**Medical Services: Centro de Salud,** Guerrero 5 at Morelos (tel. 7-01-17). White building at the northwest corner of the *zócalo*. Open 24 hrs. Doctors speak English. **Dr. Antonio Torres García** (tel. 7-00-50), Matamoros near Guerrero, speaks a little English. Will make house calls. Can be reached on VHF *canal 69*. Open 24 hrs. Ask for Dr. Zhivago.

## ACCOMMODATIONS AND CAMPING

Isla Mujeres offers numerous options for lodging, but with less variation and far more reasonable prices than nearby Cancún. Some hotels charge the same rates year-round, while others raise prices by 20% or so during peak season. Camping on the beach is not strictly regulated; most people find Playa Indios the most hospitable and unobtrusive spot to sack out. However, it's always wise to sample local opinion before settling in for the night. All hotels listed below are in town, north of the *zócalo*.

**Hotel Marcianito,** centrally located at Abasolo 10 (tel. 7-01-11) between Juárez and Hidalgo. Turquoise floor tiles clash splendidly with navy bed spreads. Try to get one of the upstairs rooms with a balcony where you can people-watch in tranquility. All rooms have ceiling fans, hot water, and purified water supply; some have closets. Check-out noon. Singles 50 pesos. Doubles 60 pesos. Triples 70 pesos. Quads 80 pesos.

**Hotel Carmelina,** Guerrero 6 (tel. 7-00-06), at Madero. Recent construction has left the hotel a patchwork of very different rooms. All are clean and cheerful, with hot water, fans, and mosquito netting. Some have A/C for 15 pesos more. Check-out noon. Singles 40 pesos. Doubles 60 pesos. Triples 70 pesos.

**Hotel Xul-Ha,** Hidalgo 23 (tel. 7-00-75), between Matamoros and López Mateos. Plain, clean bedrooms with sparkling blue bathrooms. All rooms have ceiling fans and hot water. Small lobby with color TV, English paperbacks, and coffee. Quiet location. Check-out 1pm. Singles and doubles 50 pesos. Triples 60 pesos. Prices rise by 10 pesos during peak season. A 10% discount if you stay a week.

**Poc-Na Youth Hostel,** Matamoros 15 (tel. 7-00-59). The modern design of this white stucco hostel provides plenty of space for socializing in the central *palapa*, which serves as a dining hall. Socializing comes at a cost, however, as the Poc-Na's 8-14 person dorms offer little privacy. Bunks are either mixed or single-sex. The hostel's cafeteria serves cheap food from 7am-9pm. Small additional fees for sheets, towels, etc. Prices remain at 18 pesos per person throughout the year, with a deposit of 20 pesos. Check-out 1pm, or 1-6pm for 9 pesos more.

**Hotel Las Palmas,** Guerrero 20 (tel. 7-04-16), across from the post office. Basic pastel rooms with ceiling fans and hanging rails. Bathrooms have hot water. Quiet location. Check-out noon. Singles and doubles 40 pesos. Triples 50 pesos.

## FOOD

The fact that many restaurants on Isla Mujeres aspire to a dash of international chic hasn't completely overwhelmed the *típico* Mexican atmosphere or the low prices. In addition to the ubiquitous *pescado* (fish) and *camarones* (shrimp), such delicacies as *caracol* (conch) and *pulpo* (octopus) tempt you from the murky depths. Here the *ceviche,* Mexico's famous salad appetizer, (seafood marinated in lime juice, cilantro, and other herbs) is at its most tangy. The food market on Guerrero between Matamoros and López Mateos is small and unexciting, but the four *loncherías* in front of it serve cheap and filling meals for around 15 pesos. Seven days a week, the *loncherías* open and close in unison at 7am and 5pm. The youth hostel cafeteria (open daily 7am-9pm) serves a variety of dishes, including breakfast omelettes (12 pesos), sandwiches (6 pesos), and seafood, all for under 20 pesos. If you plan to patronize any of the restaurants listed here, be sure to check the *horario* since many places hibernate from noon 'til sunset while *gringos* are on the loose.

**Chen Huaye,** (meaning "only here" in Mayan) just off the *zócalo* on Av. Bravo. Indeed, only here do you get the impression that you're dining at an advertiser's convention. Immaculate red and white walls remind you: *"¡Siempre Coca-Cola!",* while the chairs are supplied by *Cristal.* Amidst the advertising warfare, the cooked-to-order *típico* dishes are delicious. Try the zesty *pescado a la veracruzana* for 18 pesos. The question is: what do you wash it down with? The answer: chocolate cake (4 pesos). Open every day except Wed. 9am-11pm.

**La Lomita,** two blocks south of Bravo on Juárez. Though only two blocks from the town square, this family restaurant specializing in local cuisine escapes the tourists, who frequent eateries north of the *zócalo.* Seat yourself beneath the blue arches and feast on the *filete isleño* or grilled octopus, both 18 pesos. Alternatively, the *comida del día* will not disappoint. Also open for breakfast. Open daily 9am-11pm.

**El Nopalito,** at the corner of Guerrero and Matamoros (tel. 7-05-55), just down the street from Poc Na. Annexed to a Mesoamerican art and curio store, this small café merits a visit, if only for its fabulous, custom-built Oaxacan batik furniture. No two chairs are alike—pick your favorite animal and sit on it! Heavenly *desayuno tropical* includes yogurt, granola, and fruit salad. Also crepes and waffles, all under 15 pesos. Browse through the Oaxacan and Belizean batiks and Mayan artifacts next door. Open Mon.-Sat. 8am-noon and 6-9pm, Sun. 8am-noon.

**Café Cito,** Matamoros 42, at Juárez. A cool, breezy mix of Mexican, Caribbean, and European cuisine served on hexagonal tables with seashell displays. Choose from a range of dishes, from crepes (8 pesos) and sandwiches (11-14.50 pesos) to the exotic *pez caribeño* (20 pesos). If this divine fare leaves you feeling estranged from your inner self or just plain curious about the future of all humanity, spiritual consultations, muscle tests, tarot, palm, and face readings, and numerology are available—ask for Sabina. Open Mon.-Wed. and Fri.-Sat. 8am-noon and 6-10pm, Thurs. and Sun. 8am-noon.

## SIGHTS

Apparently, even the Maya considered Mujeres's beaches pretty swank; they called it Zacil-Ha, meaning "Sparkling Water." The isle's hot spot is **Playa Norte,** which offers magnificent shallow-water swimming. Two shops do what they can to spoil the mood by renting equipment at Scrooge prices. To get to Playa Norte, follow Guerrero, Carlos Lazo, or Hidalgo away from the *zócalo* to their northern end.

The best way to explore the island for yourself is by moped—the whole trip won't take more than 3 hours, even with a few stops for a swim. **PESCA,** Carretera Sac Bajo, Km. 5, is the first point of interest on a counter-clockwise tour of the southern half of the island. Across the Laguna de Makax from the populated northern half of the island, this biological research station is engaged in a breeding program for two species of sea turtle. Female turtles, captured by PESCA in May, lay their eggs in the safety of the station's beach throughout the summer and are returned to the wild in October. The young are reared for a year before they, too, are released. For 6 pesos a guide will take you on a stroll of the center to see the turtles and their offspring (at various stages of development, depending on the time of year). To support the cause, buy a t-shirt at the gift shop (open daily 9am-5pm).

Nature lovers eager to check out something other than turtle swimming pools should consider a day-trip to nearby **Isla Contoy,** a wildlife sanctuary chock-a-block full of pelicans, cormorants, and about 5,000 other species of birds. **La Isleña** travel agency (tel. 7-05-78), on Morelos half a block from the dock, organizes visits to the island that includes snorkeling, breakfast, and lunch, for 125 pesos (or US$22). The boat leaves at 8:30am, stopping at the **Isla-Che** reef for snorkeling. After puttering around Contoy's shoreline for a while, you get dropped off on the island and can wander to a limited degree before lunch. The boat returns at around 4pm. Stop by the agency to see the video of the trip and to leave a minimal deposit (at least 20 pesos) as a reservation the day before you want to go. Snorkel equipment and free *refrescos* included in the price. Bring sunscreen and a camera. The agency will refund your deposit in the event of fowl weather (open daily 7am-9pm).

Just before the right-hand turnoff to PESCA, about 3km from town, stand the remains of **Hacienda Mundaca.** In the mid-19th century, Fermín Mundaca de Marechaja, a wealthy pirate and slave trader, built these gardens and archways to woo Prisca Gómez, a Spaniard who vacationed on the island. Apparently, he neglected to tell her about his plans and before the *hacienda* was completed she married another *isleño* (whether he was a gentleman or a fisherman depends on who's telling the story). Mundaca went insane, but not before carving his own gravestone (check the Isla Mujeres cemetery) which reads, "As you are, I was; as I am, you will be." Now the site of a reforestation project, the hacienda's overgrown foundation, a well, and an outhouse are all that remain (grounds open Mon.-Fri. 7am-2:30pm, Sat. 7-10am).

Around the corner from the hacienda, **Playa Lanchero** and **Playa Paraíso** are the embarkation points for snorkeling and diving trips to the offshore reefs. While these beaches make pleasant enough sunbathing spots (when reef-bound *gringos* aren't trampling by), the swimming is better at Playa Norte (beaches open daily 7am-5pm). One kilometer further down the road at **Garrafón National Park,** where all the action is under the surface, you can float in champagne-like waters and hob-nob with huge schools of tropical fish only six feet from the beach. It's best to visit early before those diurnal mammals with plastic fins and long, rubber noses start floundering about *en masse.* True snorkel *connoisseurs,* who may be put off by the heavily-touristed park's idiotically tame marine life, should consult the staff of **Bahía Dive Shop** (tel. and fax 7-03-40), on Rueda Medina across from the car ferry dock. For 30 pesos, you can get your hands on a set of mask, snorkel, and fins for the day, along with directions to a more private snorkeling spot. The shop also organizes reef snorkeling trips (US$10) and diving trips (US$25, plus US$15 equipment rental, if needed; open Mon.-Sat. 8am-8pm, Sun. 8am-noon, 2-8pm).

Perched on the southern extremity of the island, a stone's throw past an abandoned lighthouse, stand the remnants of a **Mayan temple.** When a violent storm blew Córdoba to Isla Mujeres all the way from Cuba in 1519, he used the temple to guide him to safe harbor. Before the eastern and southern walls collapsed into the waves, this temple to Ixchel, the goddess of fertility, had slits facing the cardinal directions for astronomical observations. The small figurines of deformed women that once decorated the temple have long since been stolen or destroyed, and the ruined remains were almost totally wiped out by Hurricane Gilbert in 1988. Nevertheless, standing on the building's southern wall, one has to give the Maya credit for choosing such a spectacular location. The panoramic view of sea and sky from this windswept, lonely spot is mind-numbingly beautiful. On a clear day the hotels of Cancún's *Zona Hotelera* are visible 15km to the south. Clamber up the lighthouse's spiral stairway (mind your head) on the way back to the road for an even better view of the whole island.

To complete the tour of the island, continue towards the airport in a counter-clockwise direction. The breezy eastern coastline harbors an endless series of nooks and inlets, ideal for a refreshing dip in the waves.

## ENTERTAINMENT

Isla Mujeres' nightlife is commensurate with its small size and laid-back demeanor. Nevertheless, a handful of locales do what they can to keep peace-loving visitors awake at night. Unless you intend to sleep in the Mayan ruins with your head under a pillow, the deep, throbbing bass will reach you from **Restaurant La Peña,** Guerrero 5 at the *zócalo* (tel. 7-03-09), which becomes a disco once the restaurant closes at 11pm. Colorful crepe paper festoons the lofty *palapa,* swaying above the heads of locals and *foreños* who bop together to popular dance music. If you're not up to dancing, people-watch from one of the groovy swings suspended from the ceiling. **Chimbo's,** on Playa Norte, just about accounts for the rest of Mujeres' nighttime revelers. With a temporary dance floor laid out on the sand and the bulletin-board ceiling decorated with swimsuit models (some lacking swimsuits), this place makes up in energetic tackiness for what it lacks in class. At **Pancho Tequila,** on Matamoros between Hidalgo and Guerrero, the lively mixture of Mexican and international dance music is as refreshing as the air-conditioning. Things usually start up at the bars after 10pm, but as schedules are erratic, it's best to ask around.

# ■■■ PLAYA DEL CARMEN

Smack dab in the middle of Quintana Roo's proverbial *costa torquesa* (Turquoise Coast), Playa del Carmen (pop. 10,000) is a crossroads for archaeologically inclined travelers en route to inland ruins and those heading for the endless beaches of Cozumel and Cancún. While its own serene beaches are cheaper than most tourist-conquered areas, Playa del Carmen is no longer a budget traveler's haven—prices are in hot pursuit of their sky-high Cancún cousins. Though Playa (as locals call it) was founded as a fishing village, the vast majority of its people now earn tourist pesos. As a consequence, the town seems to have lost touch with much of its culture and history, most of which is bundled into one token ruin the size of a beachfront *cabaña.* Focusing on the present rather than the past, Playa's *palapas* and moderately priced seafood restaurants look out onto the breezy pedestrian walkway, where spray-paint artists and hammock vendors hawk their wares.

## ORIENTATION

Playa is centered around its main transportation centers, the ferry dock and the bus stations. The bus drops you off on the main drag, **Avenida Principal** (Juárez), which runs west from the beach to the Cancún-Chetumal Highway 1.5km away. Most services lie along this road. At the bus station/plaza, perpendicular to Avenida Principal, runs **Avenida Quinta,** which encompasses most of the *tiendas* and restaurants. East/west *calles* increase by two in either direction, north-south *avenidas* increase by five. Playa's *playa* lies one block east of Quinta.

## PRACTICAL INFORMATION

**Tourist Office:** A wooden booth on the northwest corner of the plaza, diagonally across Av. Quinta from the bus station. Friendly and helpful English-speaking staff. Brochures and easy-to-read maps. Open Mon.-Sat. 8am-1pm and 5-8pm.

**Police:** (tel. 3-01-63), on Av. Principal two blocks west of the plaza right past the post office. Little English spoken. Open 24 hrs.

**Post Office:** On Av. Principal, three blocks west of the plaza (tel. 3-03-00). *Lista de Correos.* Open Mon.-Sat. 9am-1pm. Stamp dispenser outside. **Postal Code:** 77710.

**Telephones:** Inside **Maya Laundry** (tel. 3-02-72), on Quinta one block north of the plaza. Local calls 3 pesos per min. Calls to the U.S. and Canada 10 pesos per min., to the rest of the world 20 pesos per min. **Faxes** cost 13 pesos per min. to the U.S. and Canada and 23 pesos per min. elsewhere. Collect calls available. Open daily 8am-9pm. **LADATEL** phones are located next to the tourist booth in the plaza. **Telephone Code:** 987.

**Currency Exchange: Banco del Atlántico** (tel. 3-02-72), on the first block west of the plaza on Av. Principal. Happily air conditioned. Credit card cash advances available. Changes U.S. dollars only. Open Mon.-Fri. 8am-1:30pm. **Bancomer,** up the street four blocks on the right (tel. 3-04-00), offers similar rates and has a 24-hr. **ATM.** All currencies exchanged. Visa card cash advances only. Open Mon.-Fri. 9am-1:30pm.

**Bus Station:** All companies share one phone number, tel. 3-01-09. **Autotransportes de Oriente,** in the bus yard on Av. Principal. First-class service to Chetumal (noon and 6pm, 4hrs., 50 pesos) and Escárcega (7am and noon, 7hrs., 94 pesos). For travelers going further afield, **Maya de Oro** buses go to Palenque (8am, 12hrs., 175 pesos) and San Cristóbal (8am, 16hrs., 190 pesos). Hop on a **Grupo Oriente** bus for Chetumal (11 per day, 4hrs., 49 pesos), Mérida (7 per day, 3hrs., 69 pesos), and Valladolid (6 per day, 4hrs., 37 pesos). Second class buses run to Chichén Itzá (5am, 10am, and 5pm, 5hrs., 34.50 pesos) via Ideal and Valladolid. Nine buses run down the coast daily to Chetumal and Tulum (1hr., 8.50 pesos). Listen for drivers bellowing "Cancún!" at the roadside on Av. Principal (every ½hr., 7am-9pm, 1hr., about 10 pesos).

**Laundromat: Maya Laundry** (tel. 3-02-71), on Quinta one block north of the plaza, on the right. Wash and dry 6.50 pesos per kg, socks and underwear 0.50 pesos per pair. Your dirty intimates will be cleaned and plastic-bagged in just 6 hours. Open daily 8am-8pm.

**Pharmacy: Farmacia Paris** (tel. 3-07-44), opposite the bus station on Av. Principal. Everything from postcards to purified water to Pepsi. Open daily 7am-1am.

**Medical Care: Centro de Salud** (tel. 3-03-14), across from the post office on Av. Principal. Some English spoken. Open 24 hrs.

## ACCOMMODATIONS AND CAMPING

Although Playa's hotel industry has been bitten by the infectious tourist bug, there are still several funky and comfortable *posadas* within blocks of the plaza on either of the two main streets. Most accommodations have hot water, but few take traveler's checks or credit cards. Be prepared for frighteningly inflated rates during Playa's increasingly popular high season, when prices are at a maximum (except at the hostel) and quality is generally at a minimum. Bargaining is a good idea, but only during the off-season.

**Hotel Lilly** (tel. 3-01-16), the bright blue building on Av. Principal, one block west of the plaza. Convenient but noisy location near the bus stop. Beware: attempting to climb the flaming pink stairway with a hangover may prove fatal. Superb bathrooms make up for cramped but neat bedrooms and ceiling-fan chatter. Grills on windows afford security, although the manager will take meticulous care of (and responsibility for) your valuables for free. Singles 50 pesos. Doubles 60 pesos. Triples 80 pesos. From Dec.-May, when the hotel is often full, the owner will drive you to the **Hotel Los Dos Hermanos,** three blocks down Av. Principal (open during peak season only), to see if you'd like to stay there.

**Posada Las Flores** (tel. 3-00-85), on Quinta two blocks north of the plaza. Spotless white rooms have firm beds, ceiling fans, and alcove bathrooms. Hammock-filled courtyard perfect for taking that afternoon *siesta.* Hot water: wait and it will come. Check out 11am. Singles 40 pesos. Doubles 50 pesos. Triples 70 pesos. Prices increase during peak season, dude.

**Posada Marinelly** (tel. 3-01-40), on Av. Principal, 2½ blocks from the plaza. Conveniently located. Pleasant, shady courtyard *palapa.* Spankin' white rooms with virginal white concrete beds and ceiling fans. Spirals drawn onto ceiling fans may hypnotize you; be careful not to fall off the balcony. Check-out noon. Singles 50 pesos. Doubles 60 pesos. Triples 70 pesos. Prices rise by 10 pesos during the high season. Reservations can be made by phone.

**CREA Youth Hostel (HI),** a 1km trek from the plaza. Walk 4 blocks on Principal and turn right before Farmacia Lupita. Walk another 4 blocks and turn left after the big concrete IMSS building. The hostel is 100m further on the right. Deserted during the low season. No hot water. No curfew or maximum stay period. Basketball court is a popular hangout with local frogs. (Ribbit.) Bring a lock for your locker. Check-out noon. Single-sex rooms with quaking bunk beds 15 pesos plus 25-peso deposit. *Cabañas* with private bathrooms and charming sci-fi posters 45 pesos. For three people, 65 pesos. 50-peso deposit. 25% discount with *tarjeta plan joven.* 10% discount with HI card.

**Campamento La Ruina,** on the beach 200m north of the ferry dock. With communal bathrooms and cooking facilities, this hostel-style place is popular with Europeans. Plenty of accommodations options. *Cabañas rústicas* with tiny, stiff military-style beds. Ceiling fans but no bathrooms. Singles and doubles 45 pesos. Triples 55 pesos. Quads 65 pesos. You'll pay at least 30 pesos more just for a better view. Hammock-space under the *palapa* will cost you 20 pesos, plus 5 pesos for a hammock rental. Pitch a tent in the sand for 15 pesos, 30 pesos for 2 people, plus 5 pesos for every extra camper. Lockers 5 pesos. Check-out 1pm.

**Mi Casa,** just past Calle 8 on Quinza. Look for the elderly manager perched on his stool under the *palapa* and to the left, opposite Daily Donuts. Mi Casa probably won't look a lot like *tu casa:* cold water runs from the taps in these bare rooms, equipped with ceiling fans and mosquito netting. Owner will let you use hot tap water for coffee or store food in the fridge. Single-bed *cabañas* 35 pesos for one person, 45 pesos for two, 5 pesos for each additional person. Two-bed *cabañas* go for 5 pesos more. Prices rise during peak season.

## FOOD

Higher-end restaurants are becoming increasingly abundant and costly in Playa del Carmen. On the other hand, questionable hygiene conditions plague the cheaper, less centrally located spots. A better bet is to nibble on fruit and snacks along Av. Principal. The following restaurants are located within two blocks of the bus station/plaza area.

**Sabor,** 1½ blocks north on Quinta. Easily missed if you're scurrying for shade on a hot day; look for the flowery, turquoise *parasoles* next to Pez Vela. Coffee, cappucino, and espresso served with a variety of pastries in a small, pleasant shack. Sandwiches made with scrumptiously fresh whole-wheat bread go for 8.50 pesos. Try the refreshing *agua de chaya* with *limón* and *piña* (4 pesos); they say it's good for your kidneys. Open daily 8am-10pm.

**Antojitos El Correo** (tel. 3-03-99). Walk up Principal 2 blocks to the clinic, then go left 1 block. Brand new furniture and carved chairs give the place a Swiss chalet feel—until the palm-frond roof reminds you you're in Mexico. The restaurant's fidgety green parrots, which engage in periodic screeching contests, are on a mission to devour the entire building. Fortunately, they are making slow progress. You have no choice but to try the hearty and ever-changing *menú del día.* For breakfast, try the *huevos a la mexicana* (with tacos, of course) for 6 pesos. Open daily 8:30am-11:30pm.

**Playa Caribe,** on Quinta, a stone's throw from the bus station, on the left. *Sombreros* tacked to the wall hint at the Mexican flavor of the food. Some seafood dishes, such as the *pulpo a la marinera* (25 pesos), are just a tad *picante.* Open daily 6am-11pm.

## SIGHTS AND ENTERTAINMENT

Decorated with an occasional palm tree and fringed by the turquoise waters of the Caribbean, Playa's beach is simply beautiful. Relatively free of seaweed, coral, and most importantly, *turistas,* this is a superb spot to crash and sunbathe. If you're feeling more energetic, 60-100 pesos (depending on the place and your bargaining ability) will buy you an hour's worth of windsurfing. Windsurfers and other gear can be rented from some of the fancier hotels just south of the pier, or from shacks a few hundred meters north. **Albatros** (tel. 3-03-06) offers windsurfing lessons. One km north of town, the beach goes nude. Although Playa has no snorkeling-friendly reefs nearby, there's a decent reef 200m past the Shangri-La Caribe Hotel. The high surf often hinders visibility. After sunning, swimming, and maybe finishing off that novel, there is little to do during the day except wander into the shops on **Av. Quinta.** While the pace of life here is gentle and relaxed, there is one thing the locals do promptly: close shop. As the restaurants close for the day, many people move onto **Karen's Grill,** often embellished with popular local bands (happy hour 7-9pm). If you're looking for a smaller place, hop onto a barside saddle at **La Bamba,** where you can drink and watch music videos until 11pm (or until you fall off the saddle, whichever happens first). The last mumbling *mariachi* swaggers home as the clientele peters out of the bars at around midnight. Only the **Calypso Bar Caribeño,** with its small dance floor lit an iridescent blue, continues to pump out *salsa* until the first signs of dawn brighten the Caribbean horizon (open 10pm-4am).

# ■■■ ISLA COZUMEL

Before the Spaniards overran the island, Ah-Cuzamil-Petin, "place of the swallows," was an important Mayan trading center, in contact with peoples from Veracruz to Honduras. Cozumel was also a sacred ceremonial site, inducing canoe-paddling pilgrims to brave the stormy straits to worship at the shrine of Ixchel, goddess of love and the moon, or at one of more than 40 carvings of smaller deities. Spanish explorer Juan de Grijalva chanced upon the island in 1518, and a year later Cortés stopped here before looting the mainland. The first Catholic mass in Mesoamerica was celebrated here by Grijalva, but neither Cortés nor the Montejos could successfully wrest the coveted island from the Maya until 1545. After 80 years of *conquistador* brutality, it was smallpox which finally annihilated the *indígena* population, leaving the island abandoned by 1600. As the Spanish colony on the Yucatán grew, pirates as infamous as Francis Drake and Jean Lafitte began to use Cozumel's many rocky coves as hideaways. Mayans returned to the island in 1848, seeking refuge from the Caste War.

With strategic insight as acute as its cultural blindness, the U.S. Air Force demolished an entire ancient Mayan city (today called San Miguel) to build a base here during the Second World War. In the 1950s, Jacques Cousteau's exploration of Palancar Reef drew international attention to Cozumel's marine life, and the military airfield became the welcome mat on which armies of tourist invaders wiped their sandy feet.

Today, direct flights from the U.S. and Mexico land daily, ships cruise into port from around the world, and boatloads of passengers stumble in from nearby Playa del Carmen and Puerto Morelos. Cozumel has become home of the package tour: like pink sheep, sunburnt tourists are herded off ferries and onto buses, cheerfully oblivious of local customs and ever trailing cheap *sombreros* bearing the island's name. But Cozumel's 60,000 permanent residents don't seem to mind *gringo* tourism; visitors are greeted heartily, especially those who try to speak Spanish and who show an interest in the island's culture.

## ORIENTATION

The island of Cozumel lies 18km east of the northern Quintana Roo coast, and 85km south of Isla Mujeres. The island is most commonly accessed via ferry from Playa del Carmen to the west or Puerto Morelos to the north. **Ferries** from Puerto Morelos (tel. 2-09-50) transport cars to and from Cozumel twice daily (9am and 1pm), docking in the island's only town, San Miguel de Cozumel (known simply as "Cozumel"), on the west shore. (US$30 per car, US$4.50 per person, 2½hrs.) Tourist vehicles supposedly have priority, but the **car ferry** is inconvenient and unpredictable. The tourist office recommends that you secure a spot in line a full 12 hours in advance.

Two ferry companies shuttle passengers between Playa del Carmen and Cozumel. *Waterjet Mexico* and *Mexico III* (tel. 2-15-88), equipped with A/C and rock videos, make the trip in 25 minutes (30 pesos). The slower boats, *Cozumeleño* and *Xel-Ha* (tel. 2-18-24), lack glitz and take about 40 minutes (25 pesos). The *Cozumeleño* is air-conditioned downstairs, while the *Xel-Ha* is entirely open-air. If you're returning to Playa del Carmen, save money by picking up a round-trip ticket from the *Cozumeleño* booth opposite the bus station on Av. Principal in Playa. A well-haggled fare will be as low as 30 pesos. If you are coming from Cancún, an alternative to the bus-ferry ordeal is the 20-minute **air shuttle** operated by Aerocaribe.

At 53km long and 14km wide, Cozumel is comfortably Mexico's largest Caribbean island. Although public transportation is literally nonexistent, downtown streets are clearly labeled and numbered with stubborn Vulcan logic. If you don't mind occasionally spine-wrenching road conditions, the rest of the island is easily explored by bike or moped. Taxis are everywhere. As is typically the case in the Caribbean, pedestrians usually don't have the right of way.

As you step off the ferry into Cozumel, **Avenida Juárez,** a pedestrian walkway for the first two blocks, is directly in front of you, running east-west through town. *Calles* run parallel to Juárez and are labeled *Sur* and *Norte* (Nte.) with respect to Juárez; numbers increase in both directions moving away from Juárez. North of Juárez, the *calles* increase in even numbers; south of Juárez, they increase in odd numbers. *Avenidas* run north-south, are numbered in multiples of five, and are designated *Norte* if north of Juárez or *Sur* if south. **Avenida Adolfo Rosada Salas** is between Calles 1 and 3 Sur. Juárez becomes the **Carretera Transversal** at the eastern edge of town, extending across the island's midsection to the other shore. The road to the airport forms the city's northern boundary. **Avenida Rafael Melgar** runs along the western edge of town next to the sea and leads north to the luxury hotels and the uninhabited northern coast. The national park at Laguna Chankanaab and the popular beach at San Francisco are south of town on the western shore; off the island's southern tip lie the Palancar Reefs. The nearly deserted eastern coast is dotted by Mayan ruins and supports only a few restaurants and camping spots.

## PRACTICAL INFORMATION

While there are no consulates on Cozumel, Mr. Bryan Wilson (tel. 2-06-54), who works closely with the Mérida U.S. consulate, provides unofficial, free assistance to English-speaking travelers. In an emergency, knock on the door of the white house at Av. 15 and Calle 13 Sur.

**Tourist Office:** (tel. 2-09-66), on the 2nd floor of the "Plaza del Sol," the building to the left of Bancomer. Head up the stairs behind the ground-level shops, and walk around to the front of the building. Friendly employees can provide you with maps and brochures, but offer little in the way of practical information. Get *Cozumel Today* for a decent map. Some English spoken. Open Mon.-Fri. 9am-2pm, although it sometimes closes inexplicably and without warning. Pick up the helpful *Blue Guide to Cozumel* on the dock as you get off the ferry, or at almost any tourist establishment in *el centro*.

**Police:** Calle 11 Sur (tel. 2-00-92), near Rafael Melgar, in the Palacio Municipal. Open 24 hrs. For English service, call 2-04-09 and ask for James García or another bilingual police officer.

**Post Office:** (tel. 2-01-06), off Rafael Melgar along the sea, just south of Calle 7 Sur. *Lista de Correos.* Open Mon.-Fri. 8am-8pm, Sat. 9am-1pm. **MexPost** (tel. 2-50-91) express mail service, on Calle 11 Sur, between Avs. 20 and 25. Open Mon.-Fri. 9am-6pm, Sat. 9am-1pm. **Postal Code:** 77600.

**Telephones:** From the **Calling Station** (tel. 2-14-17), Av. Meglar between Calles 3 and 5 Sur, calls can be made to the U.S. for US$2.15 per minute, and to Canada for US$2.35 per minute. **Fax** service (send/receive: US$1 per page up to 3 pages).

Collect and credit card calls. Coin and **LADATEL** phones located in the plaza. **Telephone Code:** 987. **Telephone Operator:** 09 (English spoken).
**Telegrams:** Next to the post office. 4.50 pesos for the first 10 words, 0.40 pesos for each additional word. Open Mon.-Fri. 8am-6pm, Sat. 9am-1pm.
**Currency Exchange: BanPaís** (tel. 2-16-82), right off the dock, takes a 1% commission for cashing traveler's checks. Changes U.S. dollars only. Open Mon.-Fri. 9am-1:30pm, for exchange 9am-12:30pm. **Bancomer** (tel. 2-05-50), on the plaza, has the same rates but charges a flat fee of US$.50 per check. Cash advances on Visa only. Open Mon.-Fri. 9am-1:30pm, for exchange 10am-1:30pm. **Banco del Atlántico** (tel. 2-01-42), on the SE corner of the plaza, has a 24-hr. **ATM.** Open for exchange Mon.-Fri. 9am-8pm.
**Airport:** (tel. 2-05-03), 2km north of town. Take a taxi (10 pesos for one person, 5 pesos more per person). **Aerocaribe** to Cancún (7 per day, 193 pesos). Also served by **Mexicana** (tel. 2-01-57), **Aerocozumel** (tel. 2-09-28 or 2-08-77), **American** (tel. 2-08-76), and **Continental** (tel. 2-05-76).
**Ferries:** From the dock at the end of Av. Juárez. Arrive ½hr. early as ferries have a nasty habit of leaving before they're supposed to. **Waterjet Mexico** and **Mexico II** to Playa del Carmen (13 per day, 4am-8pm, 25min., 30 pesos). **Cozumeleño** and **Xel-Ha** to Playa del Carmen (12 per day, 4am-7:45pm, 35min., 25 pesos). Schedules change frequently; check at the dock.
**Taxis:** (tel. 2-00-14 or 2-02-36). From the plaza to the airport, 10 pesos; to the Chankanaab park, 30 pesos; to Punta Morena, 50 pesos. Expect to pay more if you cram more people in.
**Car Rental:** You will need to show a driver's license and provide a credit card imprint as a deposit before you can rent. Aptly-named **Budget** (tel. 2-09-03), on Av. 5 between Calles 2 and 4, provides relatively cheap (US$25) rentals. Peak season rates will be a little steeper. Open daily 8am-8pm.
**Moped Rental:** Getting hold of a bike is pretty expensive, though the plain-dealing *muchachos* in the lobby of the Hotel Posada Edem (see Accommodations below) will let you rent one for about 80 pesos. Haggle for all you're worth.
**Bike Rental: Rentadora Cozumel,** Av. 10 at Calle 1 Sur (tel. 2-11-20 or 2-15-03). Bikes rent for 30 pesos per day and must be returned by 6pm. Credit card deposit required. Open daily 8am-8pm.
**Laundromat: Margarita,** Av. 20 Sur 285 (tel. 2-28-65), near Calle 3 Sur. Self-service wash 7 pesos, 10-min. dry 4 pesos. Soap 3 pesos. Open Mon.-Sat. 7am-9pm, Sun. 9am-5pm.
**English Bookstore: Agencia de Publicaciones: Gracia** (tel. 2-00-31), on the east side of the plaza. Pick up last week's *Newsweek* for the price of a decent meal (25-35 pesos).
**Red Cross:** Av. 20 Sur (tel. 2-10-57 or 2-10-58), at Av. Adolfo Salas. 24-hr. emergency service.
**Pharmacy: Farmacia Kiosco** (tel. 2-24-85), on the *zócalo* near Hotel López. Open daily 8am-10pm. 24-hr. pharmacy at the **Medical Center (CEM),** Av. 20 Nte. 425 (tel. 2-29-19 or 2-14-19). From the dock, walk 4 blocks inland and 4½ blocks left. All major credit cards accepted.
**Medical Services:** There are several English-speaking private physicians in Cozumel. For consultations, go to **Dr. M. F. Lewis,** Av. 50 (tel. 2-16-16 or 2-09-12), at Calle 11. 24-hr. tourist medical service. Alternatively, head to the **Medical Center (CEM),** Av. 20 Nte. 425 between Calle 10 Nte. and Calle 8 Nte. (see Pharmacies above). For an ambulance, call 2-06-39.

## ACCOMMODATIONS AND CAMPING

Budget rooms in Cozumel are slightly more expensive than their counterparts in Playa del Carmen, but because of the price of the ferry it makes sense to sleep in Cozumel if you plan to spend more than one day on the island. Most of the tourists stay in fancier hotels on packages deals, but clean, reasonably cheap accommodations are available within blocks of the plaza—resist being roped into a pricey deal when you step off the ferry. Peak-season travelers should expect slightly higher prices, and should hunt down a room before noon.

Campers should encounter no problems with the authorities for short stays, but might want to consult the tourist office (see Practical Information) about longer stays, as well as to find out where camping is permitted. Secluded camping spots are at **Punta Morena** and **Punta Chiqueros,** on the island's Caribbean coast.

**Hotel Posada Edem,** Calle 2 Nte. 4 (tel. 2-11-66). Upon docking, go left 2 blocks, turn right, and go up 2 blocks. Clean rooms with fresh linen, 2 beds, fans, and hot water. Original artwork on the walls. Watch TV in the lobby with the owner. Cute black cat expresses affection by climbing all over you. Check-out 1pm. 50 pesos for up to 3 people. 15 pesos extra for A/C and each additional person. MC, Visa accepted, but with a 6% surcharge.

**Hotel Saolima,** Av. Adolfo Salas 268 (tel. 2-08-86), between Av. 10 Sur and 15 Sur. Big Kermit-colored *cuartos* off a leafy courtyard. Soft beds, ceiling fans, and hot water. Check-out noon. Singles 50 pesos. Doubles 60 pesos. Triples 70 pesos. Rooms with A/C 20 pesos more. No credit cards.

**Hotel Marruang** (tel. 2-16-78 or 2-02-08), on Av. Adolfo Salas, just past Av. 20. Brand spankin' new hotel. Friendly manager goofily ducks under the stairs to get behind the reception desk. Spotless, speckled floors lead to comfy beds, ceiling fans, and fantastic bathrooms. Hot water. Singles and doubles 60 pesos. Triples 75 pesos. No credit cards.

**Cabañas Punta Morena,** Carretera Transversal Km. 17. For more adventurous souls who have their own transportation or are hitchhiking diehards. Flex that thumb all you want, but *Let's Go* still does not recommend hitchhiking. Next to a beachfront seafood restaurant, these *cabañas* have a fabulous view of the windy Eastern seaboard. Accommodations are basic: stone-walled rooms have one double bed and hooks for a hammock. Neat bathrooms lack hot water and toilet seats. Volleyball court on the beach. All rooms 50 pesos. No credit cards.

**Posada Letty** (tel. 2-02-57), Calle 1 Sur past Av. 10. The Posada's business card declares "Cleanliness-Order-Morality," though *Let's Go* is only qualified to vouch for the former. Tidy, pale yellow rooms in a quiet but central location. Hanging rails and ceiling fans. Singles and doubles 60 pesos. Triples 75 pesos.

## FOOD

Food in Cozumel is expensive, and buying it near the beach or the plaza will take an especially large bite out of your peso reserves. Fortunately, there are several moderately priced restaurants a few blocks from the center, as well as some small *típico* cafés hiding on side streets. The **market,** on Av. Adolfo Salas between Av. 20 Sur and 25 Sur, offers the standard items: meat, fish, and fruits. The five small restaurants outside the market do minimal damage to your wallet in exchange for generous portions of regional dishes. For a quick treat, stop by at the **Panificadora Cozumel,** on Calle 2 Nte. between Quinta and Melgar, where pastries and baked goods can be had for pocket change. Fresh *baguettes* 0.70 pesos. Open daily 6am-9:30pm.

**Cedral Beach Restaurant,** opposite the road to the El Cedral ruins on the southwestern tip of the island. This off-the-beaten-path beachfront restaurant specializes in fabulous fresh seafood at very reasonable prices. Check out the resident kittens, born June 1995. Accompany Carlos the chef to the freezer and pick out the fish that you want. Get a few people together and go in for a monstrous red snapper (about 100 pesos—haggle). Lobster, conch, prawns, and other fish also available. All dishes come heftily garnished with nachos, vegetables, and rice. String up a hammock on the beach for that post-feast *siesta*. Open daily 7am-6pm.

**El Abuelo Gerardo** (tel. 2-10-12), on Av. 10 between Juárez and Calle 2 Nte. Soothing music, wooden tables, and paneling transform this garage into a pleasant spot. Grandpa Gerardo dishes up fish filets of every type (22-26 pesos). *Antojitos* 4-18 pesos. A mellow place to grab an ice-cold afternoon beer. Open daily 7:30am-10:30pm.

**Restaurant El Foco** (tel. 2-40-38), Av. 5 Sur 13, 2½ blocks from the plaza. Wooden tables and graffiti-adorned walls give it the nonchalance of a well-loved hangout.

A friendly owner serves up the hearty "foco special" (16 pesos). *Quesadillas* 8 pesos. *Enchiladas* 18 pesos. Open daily noon-1am.

**Cocina Económica Mi Chabelita** (tel. 2-08-96), on Av. 10 Sur near Adolfo Salas. Great budget dining in a bright, coral-colored garage. Ceiling fans are lined up like a row of wind-powered generators. *Comida corrida* with great tacos for less than 20 pesos. Try the fried bananas (5 pesos). Open Mon.-Sat. 8am-9pm.

**Restaurant Casa Denis** (tel. 2-00-67), across from the flea market on the southeast corner of the *zócalo*. Open-air dining under a classy yellow awning. Ancient sketches and the 114 year-old (and aging!) Mamey tree glorify this convenient shack. Also aging is the "business card tablecloth." *Comida regional,* including seafood plates, 15-30 pesos. Fish kebob 22 pesos. Open Mon.-Sat. 7am-10:30pm.

## SIGHTS

Most visitors to Cozumel are here for a specific reason: the beautiful coral reefs around the island, which provide excellent opportunities to snorkel or scuba dive. To get to your favorite snorkeling spot, or to reach the wavy east side, it's best to rent a moped (see Practical Information above). Without the benefit of your own transport, either elevated taxi rates will increase your blood pressure or hitchhiking in the scorching sun will do the same to your body temperature. Be good to yourself, and get some wheels.

As you head south out of town on a counter-clockwise circuit of the island, **Hotel La Ceiba** makes a good stop-off point for snorkeling. You could walk through the hotel restaurant sporting a snorkel, fins, and a g-string and the management still wouldn't care. The hotel has a beach perfect for swimming and a reef and plane wreck offshore waiting to be explored. The **Del Mar Aquatics** dive shop, at the right-hand end of the beach, rents out snorkel equipment for US$5 per day. For US$30 you can jump in with a scuba tank on your back (open daily 7:30am-7:30pm; Visa, MC accepted).

A few more kilometers down the coastal highway is **Chankanaab National Park,** comprising the *laguna,* a botanical garden, museum, restaurant, snorkel area, and a few gift shops. A stroll through the endemic forest in the botanical garden, past the 3-foot beady-eyed sunbathing iguanas, brings you to a few paltry ruins. The perfectly oval natural lagoon, once brimming with reef fish, is now home to the hardy survivors of years of *gringo* sunscreen attrition. Though one can no longer swim in the pool, most fish don't seem to want to either. You do get to jump into the open water, however, where tropical fish come to watch the hundreds of clumsy tourists flounder about. The small museum focuses on the natural (rather than archaeological) resources of the park and houses some fantastic photographs of the underwater caves in the lagoon. (Entrance 25 pesos. Open daily 6am-7pm. For further information, contact the **Fondación de Parques** in town, tel. 2-09-14.)

The best underwater sightseeing is likely to be on the offshore reefs, accessible by boat. Most of the numerous **dive shops** in town are on Calle 3 Sur between Av. Melgar and Av. 10 or on the waterfront. Always consider safety before price, though; look for those shops which have a CADO (Cozumel Association of Dive Operators) insignia on their door. **Blue Bubble Divers,** Av. 5 and Calle 3 Sur (tel. 2-18-65), has a mellow, English-speaking staff (employees continually murmur "Blue bubble...no trouble") and a choice of 20 reefs to visit. Single tank dives cost US$35. Snorkel equipment US$6 for 24 hrs. **Aqua Safari,** Melgar at Calle 5 Sur, equips you for a one-tank scuba dive for US$25. Otherwise, their two-hour snorkeling boat trips run US$10. You can rent snorkeling equipment anywhere on the island, including at Laguna Chankanaab and Playa de San Francisco. The standard rate is US$5-10 plus deposit per 24 hrs.

Between beach hops and reef drops, you may want to hunt down one of several small ruins in Cozumel's overgrown interior. You can visit **El Cedral** and the **Tumba de Caracol** ruins on a bumpy trek to the **Celarain Lighthouse** on the island's southernmost point. The top of the lighthouse offers a thrilling view of the uninhabited interior to the north, while white fishing boats bob like corks in the rough surf to the east.

The route along the eastern coast passes many secluded beaches that would make for good camping spots. (Remember to ask first, though.) While the beaches boast magnificent turquoise waters, the water is turbulent and somewhat dangerous; it should be treated with cautious respect. The coast is dotted with surfside restaurants and bars. Midway along the coast, Carretera Transversal branches west and loops back through the jungle to town. An ominous billboard warns tourists not to head north of the Transversal on the unpaved road which winds toward **Punta Molas** and its lighthouse. **Castillo Real,** a fortress and the largest of the Mayan buildings on the island, can only be reached with the help of four-wheel-drive.

To get to the crumbled stone structures of **San Gervasio,** the only extensively excavated and partially reconstructed ruin on the island, take Juárez out of town. After 8km, a gravel road marked by a "San Gervasio" sign branches to the left. Follow this road for another 8km and you'll be at the ruin site. (Site open daily 8am-4pm. Admission 3 pesos at the gravel road entrance and 10 pesos at the site itself.)

The small, air-conditioned **Museo de la Isla de Cozumel** (tel. 2-14-75 or 2-14-74), on the waterfront between Calles 4 and 6, is filled with photographs and artifacts (open Sun.-Fri. 10am-6pm; admission US$3). Check for other cultural events in the **Centro de Convenciones,** between the Plaza del Sol and Bancomer, or in the plaza itself, where locals gather on Sunday nights for family fun.

---

### Save the Palancar Reef

The Palancar Reef of Cozumel, the second-largest in the world, continually draws legions of scuba fanatics eager to explore its dramatic underwater formations. While the aesthetics are unmistakable, few visitors realize the biological importance of those majestic coral pillars. Coral is to a reef as topsoil is to a rainforest—without it, the basis of all life disappears. If the coral is destroyed, the entire reef's ecosystem disintegrates. International law prohibits the harvesting of coral, but it does not forbid the purchase or exportation of coral-derived jewelry and crafts. Several shops in Cozumel sell goods made from black coral, and by patronizing these establishments, tourists heighten the demand for coral and adversely affect the splendorous reefs they have come to see.

---

## ENTERTAINMENT

Though not as expensive as Cancún, Cozumel's nightlife prices are targeted to the spendthrift *gringos* who jaunt into town from their cruise ships. Cozumel is emptier at night than might be expected for a town of its size, largely because the tour-package herds tend to stay in their hotels after dinner. Obnoxiously boisterous all night long, **Carlos 'n Charlie's** (tel. 2-01-91), on Rafael Melgar just one block north of the dock, entertains *norteamericanos* with crazy drinks, slammer contests, and arm-wrestling matches. Occasional free *tequila* for those willing (and able) to make a fool of themselves in the name of entertainment (*cerveza* 10 pesos; open daily 10am-1:30am). A mellow, more native crowd into reggae music and a swinging 70s scene spends the wee hours at **Joe's Lobster Bar** (tel. 2-32-75), on Av. 10 between Calles 1 and 3 Sur. A live band starts up the action at 10:30pm and the place keeps kicking until 2 or 3am. **La Serpiente Loca,** next to the post office on Rafael Melgar, with its vintage BCs suspended from the rafters, is also a popular hangout (happy hour noon-2pm and 5-7pm). Late at night, those who are still standing head to either of Cozumel's modern, air-conditioned discos: **Scaramouche** (tel. 2-07-99) or **Neptuno.** Both charge a 30-peso cover, and are located on Rafael Melgar, one and five blocks south of the plaza, respectively.

For action and romance without the alcohol, head to **Cinema Cozumel,** on Av. Rafael Melgar between Calles 2 and 4, or **Cine Cecillo Borqucs** on Juárez between

Av. 30 and 35, both of which have nightly showings. Borques' lower prices reflect its more remote location.

# ∎∎∎ TULUM

On the eastern edge of the age-old Etaib (Black Bees) jungle, halfway down the Caribbean coast of the Yucatán, lies the walled Mayan "City of the Dawn." Although the ruins here are less extensive than those at Uxmal and Chichén Itzá, their backdrop is stunning: Tulum's graying temples and nearly intact watchtowers rise above white sand pummeled by the steely-blue Caribbean Sea and tall, wind-bent palm trees. First settled in the fourth century, Tulum was the oldest continuously inhabited city in the New World when the Spanish arrived. It took 50 years of fighting for the Spaniards to conquer the city; three decades later, Tulum was resettled by Mayan refugees from the Caste War. Tulum may well be the ancient city of **Zamá**, a fragment of an impressive civilization glimpsed by Juan de Grijalva on his voyage from Cuba in 1518.

Scattered around the ruins of Tulum are magnificent representations of a figure diving into the water; the images depict the Mayan sunset god, an appropriate symbolic complement to the city of the rising sun. The diving god appears only on the city's western walls, where the depictions are illuminated every evening by the rays of the setting sun. Other stone inscriptions show Tulum to have been the center of a religious fertility cult. Some images, portraying gods surrounded by phalluses and rattlesnakes, are situated so as to be illuminated by the sun during equinoxes.

Today, sun worshippers of a different kind tramp around the 200m-square grounds of the ancient city. Because of their proximity to Playa del Carmen, the ruins are busy even early in the morning, so you'll have to be content to share this beautiful corner of the ancient Maya with others.

## ORIENTATION

Located 42km southeast of Cobá, 63km south of Playa del Carmen, and 127km south of Cancún, Tulum (pop. about 10,000) is the southernmost link in the chain of tourist attractions on the Caribbean coast of Quintana Roo. It also marks the eastern extremity of the major Mayan archaeological sites, stretching all the way from Sayil in Campeche. Although few people live here, Tulum sprawls out over three separate areas: **el crucero** (the crossroads), the beach **cabañas**, and **Pueblo Tulum.** Arriving in Tulum from Cancún on Rte. 307, buses first stop at *el crucero,* a few kilometers before the town and the intersection with Rte. 180 to Mérida. Here, a couple of restaurants, hotels, and minimarts huddle together 800m west of the ruins. The well-paved access road turns south at the ruins, leading to food and lodging at *cabañas* 2km further down the road. Pueblo Tulum, 4km south of *el crucero* on Rte. 307, offers travelers a handful of roadside *típico* restaurants, more minimarts, and some services.

**Buses** provide cheap transportation from Tulum to nearby cities and to the sights and beaches which lie to the north on Rte. 307. Some travelers hitchhike from sight to sight along the highway. *Let's Go* does not recommend hitchhiking. If you're female, drivers may pull over and offer you an unsolicited lift if you start walking, but lone men will have a fairly tough time catching lifts. Taxis congregate at *el crucero* and at the bus stop at Pueblo Tulum's southern end.

## PRACTICAL INFORMATION

The few services available in Pueblo Tulum are along Rte. 307, which serves as the tiny town's main street. There is no tourist office, though a few stands at the ruins can provide sketchy maps. Those desperate to exchange money can do so at the *crucero* or next to the bus office in Pueblo Tulum.

**Police:** (tel. 1-20-55), in the Delegación Municipal, on the left side of Rte. 307 (after the baseball diamond) as you pass through from the north, two blocks past the post office. No English spoken. Open 24 hrs.

**Post Office:** A few hundred meters into town on the left side of Rte. 307 as you pass through from the north. *Lista de Correos.* Open Mon.-Fri. 9am-1pm and 3-6pm. **Postal Code:** 77780.

**Telephones: Caseta de Tulum** (tel. and fax 1-20-01 or -02), on the right side of Rte. 307 just as you enter town from the north. Ask for directions to "GOPI." Calls and faxes to the U.S. are 12 pesos per min. 5 pesos plus 7 pesos per page to receive a **fax.** Open daily 7am-9pm. Another *caseta,* **Savana C.I.** (tel. 1-20-91; fax 1-20-92) is on the left side of Rte. 307, a block past the post office. Calls to the U.S. 12 pesos per min. Collect and credit card calls 10 pesos. There is a public telephone at *el crucero.* **Telephone Code:** 987.

**Buses:** A small waiting room sandwiched between two currency exchange booths opposite the Hotel Maya. **ADO** to Chetumal (5 per day, 3hrs., 39.50 pesos), Escárcega (8am, 8hrs., 70 pesos), and Villahermosa (4:30pm, 11hrs., 110 pesos). **ATS** runs every 45min. to Playa del Carmen (1hr., 9 pesos) and Cancún (2hrs., 18 pesos). **Expreso de Oriente** leaves at 6, 11am, 1, and 6pm to Cobá (45min., 5.50 pesos), Valladolid (2½hrs., 22 pesos), Chichén Itzá (3½hrs., 26.50 pesos) and Mérida (5-6hrs., 40.50 pesos). Buses heading north to Playa del Carmen will stop on request at destinations along the way.

**Taxis:** Available at *el crucero,* in Pueblo Tulum, along Rte. 307, and at various *cabañas.* Unless you are in a group, taxis are an expensive way to travel. From *el crucero* to Pueblo Tulum 10 pesos, to Cabañas Tulum 15 pesos. From Don Armando's Cabañas to Pueblo Tulum 15 pesos.

**Pharmacy: Super Farmacia** (tel. 1-20-52), on the left of Rte. 307 just past the post office. Open daily 8am-9pm. Dr. Arturo F. Ventre speaks English and is available Mon.-Sat. 8am-noon and 4-9pm, Sun. 4-9pm.

## ACCOMMODATIONS AND CAMPING

Tulum offers two kinds of lodging: hotels at the *crucero* or in town, or beachside *cabañas.* Clustered together on the beach 1km from the ruins, the campgrounds and *cabañas* allow you to meet mellow international travelers, perfect your tan on the spectacular beach, and escape the conventional Quintana Roo tourism just a short distance away. Be prepared to give up light, private bathrooms, and a pint of blood (mosquitos are vicious at night) in exchange for a sunset view of El Castillo from the beach. Don't be afraid to ask for help with a hammock if it's (blush!) your first time. Locals will be more than happy to deflower you. (Hint: sleep across, not lengthwise, otherwise tourists will choose to forego the ruins and instead come and see your phenomenal hunchback the next day.) *Let's Go* recommends pouring a bucket of water down the non-flush toilets when you're done using them—Mexican magic does the rest. A taxi to the *cabañas* farthest from Pueblo Tulum is 20 pesos. Hitchhiking is not an option since no cars go that way.

Theft has become a problem at some *cabañas.* Industrious thieves will burrow through the sand and into your *cabaña* (remember, in many cases they have sand floors) if they want your valuables bad enough. So for the sake of your soul and your stuff, be prudent and always exercise caution.

**Don Armando Cabañas** (tel. 45-46-03), on the left, on the paved road 1km south of the ruins. Jocular Don Armando greets guests at the register. Hip international crowd. Cheap restaurant, solid walls, a hammock or cement bed, mosquito netting, decent communal showers, doors with locks—who could ask for more? (Well, maybe flush toilets.) Security guards patrol the premises, as do shy iguanas, chattering birds, and wet young travelers. Volleyball court. To reserve, call and ask for Don Armando's Cabaña. *Cabaña* with 1 bed and 1 hammock for 1 or 2 people 50 pesos. 2-bed *cabañas* 60 pesos. *Cabañas grandes* 70 pesos. Deposit 25 pesos. Camp or hang a hammock for 10 pesos per person.

**Cabañas Santa Fe,** right before Don Armando's as you come from the ruins. With brand spankin' new toilets and showers installed in March '95, these *cabañas*

TULUM

have the edge on Don Armando in the "facilities" department. Volleyball court. Several options to choose from: communal *cabaña*, 10 pesos; bare *cabaña* with hammock 25 pesos; one-bed *cabaña* with sand floor 40 pesos; one-bed *cabaña* with cement floor 45 pesos; and a two-bed *cabaña* 60 pesos. All private *cabañas* include a mosquito net. Hammock rental 10 pesos per night; mosquito net rental 5 pesos per night.

**El Crucero,** on Rte. 307 at the turnoff to the ruins. Holler heartily to get the attention of the staff, who tend to wander. Alternatively, look for them in the restaurant next door. Small, tiled rooms with musty mattresses and rickety fans. Light, private bathrooms and hot water (so they say). Water supply sporadic after dark. Toilets rely on Mexican magic. Check-out 24 hrs. after you arrive. Singles 30 pesos. Doubles 40 pesos. Triples 50 pesos. Quads 70 pesos.

**Hotel Maya,** on the right side of Rte. 307 in the center of Pueblo Tulum. In ancient times, the Maya used the deafening volume of the lobby's TV as a guide when returning home. Spotless, mellow blue rooms all have ceiling fans and shelves. Snow-white bathrooms have hot water; toilets mysteriously parked almost in the showers. Check-out 1pm. Singles 55 pesos. Doubles 75 pesos. Triples 80 pesos.

## FOOD

Tulum's few restaurants serve up decent, authentic-tasting Mexican cuisine. For inexpensive yet satisfying fodder, set sail for El Crucero Restaurant or the *cabañas.* The pueblo has a number of mini-supers and grocery stores ideal for snacks. 50m north of the bus station are a couple of barbecued chicken grills, where you can grab a tasty bite (about 10 pesos) before leaping onto that all-important bus.

**El Crucero Restaurante,** in the hotel of the same name at the crossroads. Tasty foods at reasonable prices enjoyed by a mix of international and local patrons. Feels like a comfortable local pub. Continental breakfast package of fruit salad, orange juice, toast, and coffee is a great start to the day at 15 pesos. Chicken tacos 15.50 pesos. Open daily 7am-9pm.

**Santa Fe Restaurante,** at the campground on the beach. Mellow reggae tunes waft through the newly-reconstructed *palapa.* Fish 15 pesos. *Quesadillas* 10 pesos. Filling portions. Restaurant and bar open daily 6am-11pm.

**El Faisán y El Venado** (tel. 45-11-81), at the crossroads. Serves up a veritable smorgasbord of fairly expensive international eats. For the budget traveler, hamburgers are under 20 pesos and a 4-person pizza is 60 pesos. Don't leave without trying a scoop of the divinely rich coconut ice cream (10 pesos). Friendly staff will change TV channels to suit your desires. Open daily 8am-9pm.

## SIGHTS

### The Ruins

Tulum's ruins lie a brisk 8-minute walk east of Rte. 307 from the *crucero.* For the less mobile (and supremely lazy), a dinky train (5 pesos) covers the distance in a slightly shorter time. Entrance tickets are sold at a booth to the left of the parking lot, where you can also pick up a one-day video camera permit (25 pesos). Having come all this way to learn about the ruins, it's a good idea to get hold of one of the well-informed, multi-lingual guides who are adept at pointing out details, like remains of murals and wall reliefs, which you might miss on your own. Guides charge about 100 pesos for 5 or 6 people or 150 pesos for larger groups. As the cheerful *muchachos* consistently remind uninterested tourists, without a guide the ruins will look like little more than piles of rocks.

Your first glimpse of Tulum will be of the still-impressive dry-laid **wall** that surrounded the city center's three landlocked sides. The wall, made of small rocks wedged together, was originally 3.6m thick and 3m high but has deteriorated over the years. It shielded the city from the aggression of neighboring Mayan city-states and prevented all but the 150 or so priests and governors of Tulum from entering the city for most of the year. After Tulum's defeat at the hands of the Spanish in

1544, the wall fended off English, Dutch, and French pirates, and in 1847 gave rebel Mayans refuge from government forces during the Caste War.

Just inside and to the left of the west gate stand the remains of platforms which once supported huts. Behind these platforms are the **House of the Halach Uinik** (the House of the Ruler), characterized by a traditional Mayan four-column entrance; the **House of the Columns,** the largest residential building in Tulum; and the **Temple of the Frescoes,** a stellar example of post-Classical Mayan architecture. Well-preserved 600-year-old murals inside the temple depict deities intertwined with serpents, as well as fruit, flower, and corn offerings. Masks of Itzamná, the Mayan creator, occupy the northwest and southwest corners of the building.

As with many Mayan structures, four of Tulum's temples were built along astronomical guidelines so that the inner chambers of each are illuminated naturally during one of the two equinoxes or solstices. While priestly rulers sat atop the temples, mentally cranking away at puzzles of astronomy and civil engineering, most Mayans toiled to build what their rulers devised. In contrast to the remarkably precise architectural planning and execution of such earlier cities as Chichén Itzá and Uxmal, Tulum is held together with massive amounts of mortar. The classic Mayan practice of cutting stones to exactly the right dimensions, fitting them together without mortar, and polishing their surfaces was abandoned here.

**El Castillo,** the most prominent structure in Tulum, looms behind the smaller buildings and over the rocky seaside cliff. Serving as a pyramid and temple, it commands a view of the entire walled city. It also served as a lighthouse, allowing returning fishermen to find the only gap in the barrier reef just offshore. Its walls, like those of many buildings in Tulum, slope outward; meanwhile, the doorposts slope inward. The castle was remodeled and rebuilt many times, hence its architectural and structural eccentricities.

In front of the temple is the sacrificial stone where the Maya held battle ceremonies. Once the stars had been consulted and a propitious day determined, a warrior-prisoner was selected for sacrifice. At the climax of the celebration, attendants painted the warrior's body blue—the sacred color of the Maya—and the chief priest cut his heart out and poured the blood over the idols in the temple. The body was given to the soldiers below, who through cannibalism were thought to acquire the strength to overcome their enemies.

To the right of El Castillo on the same plaza is the **Temple of the Initial Series.** Named after a stela found here, the temple bears a date that corresponded to the beginning of the Mayan religious calendar in the year 761 CE. The **Temple of the Descending God,** with a fading relief of a feathered, armed deity diving from the sky, stands on the other side of El Castillo's plaza. Perched on its own precipice on the other side of the beach, the **Temple of the Winds** was acoustically designed to act as a storm-warning system. Surely enough, before Hurricane Gilbert struck the site in 1988, the temple's airways dutifully whistled their alarm (site open daily 8am-5pm; admission 16 pesos, free Sun.).

## The Beach

Hanging out on the beach in *cabañas* is a popular way to end a day at the ruins. Nude bathing is tolerated here, although it usually takes one uninhibited soul to start the ball rolling, so to speak. The ever-vigilant Mexican Navy drops in occasionally to tell everyone to get back in uniform, but once the nudity-patrol is out of sight, the bathing suits make way for the birthday suits once again. *Cabaña* managers complain if you walk through the campgrounds in the buff.

Offshore, you can see the waves mysteriously breaking on Tulum's **barrier reef,** the largest in the Americas; it runs the full length of the Yucatán peninsula, including Belize. Although the water here is not as clear as at Xel-Ha or Akumal (see "Near Tulum" below), the fish are just as plentiful. To enjoy them, you can rent scuba and snorkeling equipment from the dive shop (open daily 8am-3:30pm) at Cabañas Santa Fe. Mask, snorkel, and fins cost 25 pesos per day. The shop plans trips to the reef and a nearby *cenote* for 50 pesos, including rental. Get fins if you snorkel; the 500m swim to the reef is often a struggle against a north-south current.

To escape the beaches, waves, and salty water, rent a bike from Cabañas Santa Fe (50 pesos) and visit one of the *cenotes* in the woods near Pueblo Tulum. Look for a small patch of gravel, large enough for two cars, on the right side of the road as you head toward Chetumal. Follow a rugged path to the serene **Cenote Escondito,** or the smaller **Cenote Kristal** 100m further down the road. A few kilometers south of Tulum on the coast road lies the 1.3-million acre **Sian Ka'an Biosphere Reserve** (entrance free; contact Amigos de Sian Ka'an in Cancún for details, tel. 98/84-95-83).

# ■ NEAR TULUM

## XEL-HA AND AKUMAL

**Xel-Ha** (SHELL-ha), a 6-foot-deep natural aquarium, is a fun (and expensive) place to stop by for a snorkel. Though snorkeling is not permitted in the lagoon for which Xel-Ha is famous, you can splash around all you want in the *caleta* (inlet) nearby—check your sunscreen at the front desk. The steep 60-peso entrance fee (20% discount with any student ID) does not include rental of snorkel equipment, which is available near the inlet for 36 more precious pesos (no discounts this time). Visit before noon, when busloads of tourists from the resorts overrun the place.

The more fragile benthic life has long since been replaced by hardy, soft brown algae which covers all the boulders underwater. Don't bet on seeing any unusual fish life either, though you can find parrot fishes and 3-foot-long barracudas towards the rope which marks the open sea. For relative peace during busy times, cross the inlet and explore the underwater caves, where an altar was once discovered. Be careful and don't go duck-diving under overhangs on your own. Note the bizarre incidence of cool seawater with a warm undercurrent of subterranean fresh water. It is the confluence of these water sources—not suntan lotion—that sometimes impairs underwater visibility. Lockers (6 pesos plus 10-peso deposit) and towels (6 pesos plus 30-peso deposit) are available at the shower area (open daily 8am-5pm).

Xel-Ha also maintains a small archaeological site on the highway 100m south of the entrance to the inlet. **El Templo de Los Pájaros** and **El Palacio,** small Classical and post-Classical ruins, were only recently opened to the public. The former (the ruin farthest into the jungle) overlooks a peaceful, shady *cenote* where swimming is permitted. The jungle at Xel-Ha is rife with mosquitoes, so bring insect repellent (site open daily 8:30am-5pm; admission about 10 pesos).

A few kilometers farther north towards Playa del Carmen lies the bay of **Akumal.** An older, wealthier crowd is drawn to Akumal's underwater attractions: a wealth of snorkel and dive sites. **Snorkeling equipment** rents for US$6 per day, and snorkeling boat trips are US$15 per person. Scuba trips are US$25 per one-tank dive. Cavern-diving courses (US$250) are also available. The **Akumal Dive Shop** (tel. 4-12-59 or 800-5AKUMAL from the U.S.) is open daily 8am-1pm and 2-5pm; MC and Visa are accepted. The **Akumal Dive Center** is open 8am-5pm. Windsurfing equipment can be rented at a beach hut 200m south of the Akumal Dive Center. Inquire for details.

**Getting There:** Xel-Ha lies 15km north of Tulum; in turn, Akumal is 10km past Xel-Ha. Get on any northbound **bus** and ask to be let off at the site of your choice. Hitchhiking is tough here; traffic is fast and waiting can be unnerving. Taxis charge exorbitant rates. Getting back to Tulum at the end of the day can be especially challenging, as buses begin to come less and less frequently. Vigorously wave down a bus on its way to Tulum or Cancún. Locals will usually be able to tell you when the next one is due to pass.

## DOS OJOS CENOTE

For diving of a novel sort, head to **Dos Ojos Cenote,** 1km south of the Xel-Ha archaeological site. Dos Ojos ("two eyes") was originally a dry cave system with beautiful rock formations in shades of amber and massive calcic stalagtites, stalagmites, and columns. More recently, the whole 500m system was flooded, preserving the caves in their new underwater condition. It is now possible to snorkel and dive in the *cenote*, along with the tetras, mollies, and swordfish that you're more used to seeing in your neighborhood pet store.

The trip begins with a bumpy 20-minute ride in an open truck, into which bugs fit for any Indiana Jones movie drop as you fly through the pristine jungle. A complete underwater circuit of the caves, at a depth of 10m, takes about 45 minutes. Meanwhile, snorkelers can explore the larger of the two (hence, *dos* ojos) cave entrances. For divers and snorkelers alike, this is a unique opportunity to explore a spectacular unspoiled cave system which has only been open to the public since 1993. The dive costs US$44 (plus US$15 equipment rental). Snorkelers pay US$30. Three trips depart daily from Xel-Ha at 9:30am, 11am, and 1:30pm. For more information, contact **Divers of the Hidden Worlds** (tel. 74-40-81; open daily 9am-5pm).

# ■■■ COBÁ

Deep within the Yucatán jungle, Cobá receives less attention than her big sisters Chichén Itzá and Tulum. The government has poured less money into the site, leaving an estimated 6,500 buildings unexcavated. And for a change, mosquitoes outnumber tourists; Cobá is a site you can truly explore for yourself. In the jungle which surrounds this ancient city (in its heyday, it is estimated, the city spread out over 10 square kilometers), lizards bask on private pyramids, colorful butterflies flit across the paths, and the ever-fierce *yucateca* mosquito is never far away. Early visitors can explore the site to a cacophony of birds, and just might find themselves alone atop a pyramid looking down on one of Cobá's four lakes. But apart from its relative tranquility, Cobá's appeal lies in its well-preserved stelae and the towering **Castillo**, at 42m the tallest Mayan structure in the northern Yucatán.

**Practical Information** **Expreso de Oriente** buses leave Tulum for Cobá four times daily (6, 11am, 1, and 6pm, 45min., 5.50 pesos). Check for first-class Mérida-bound buses that may be able (and willing) to drop you off at Cobá on the way. Friendly drivers on their way to Cobá (as well as Cobá-bound mega-tour buses) may be waved down at the Cobá *crucero* north of Pueblo Tulum. Otherwise, a taxi from the parking lot at the Tulum ruins will cost you a ghastly 70 pesos one-way. To visit the ruins from Cancún, you'll have to take a bus to Nuevo X-Can (esh-KAN), and connect with a Cobá-bound bus passing through from the west. The two buses which run from Valladolid to Cobá leave at 4:30am and 1pm daily, passing through Nuevo X-Can about one hour later.

Every day, two buses head back to Tulum at 6:30am and 3pm. There are a few more options if you're heading for Valladolid or Mérida (6:30, 11:30am, 1:30, and 6:30pm; 2 and 5hrs. respectively; 17 and 37 pesos respectively). If you're absolutely desperate for a crack at public transportation, walk the 3km to the Valladolid-Tulum road, where buses have no choice but to pass. Travelers without a set schedule often arrange rides with other Cobá visitors or friendly guests at the Hotel Villa Arqueológicas by Lake Cobá, at the opposite end of the road from the ruins.

**Accommodations and Food** The **Hotel Bocadito,** 150m north of the *zócalo*'s basketball court, offers budget accommodations with a cheerful red-and-white motif for overnight visitors. The hotel entrance, teeming with beetles at night, draws bullfrogs (Bud…why…zer) the size of small footballs. Rooms have two beds and ceiling fans. Sinks are in the bedrooms; to flush the seatless toilets, turn the tap. Not all the rooms are identical, so shop around: some have hammock hooks, some fewer beetle carcasses, some less dirt in the bathroom. No hot water. Rooms 40 pesos. AmEx, MC, Visa accepted. Many houses near the ruins also rent rooms.

The restaurant of the same name, adjacent to the hotel, serves up chicken and fish entrees for 23 pesos. For a comprehensive budget feast, order the *menú del día*, which includes soup, nachos, an entree with tacos, bread, dessert, and coffee (28 pesos). Good thing your bed is only a short stagger away. All major credit cards are accepted (open daily 6am-9pm). For breakfast, **Nicté Ha,** on the shore a stone's throw west of the T-junction, is an idyllic spot. Mexican crooners pluck out their heartstrings on the radio. Earlybirds (before 8am or so) may catch a glimpse of an alligator paddling about just offshore. The super-friendly owner will let you browse through her Cobá guidebooks on request. Breakfast eggs (many styles) 10-15 pesos. Dinner entrees 22-26 pesos (open daily 6am-9pm). Although the food at the **Hotel Villa Arqueológicas** is a bit expensive, a salad or drink will buy a dip in their garden-side pool. Restaurant customers can also rent tennis rackets (US$20 deposit) and use the pool tables (10 pesos per hour).

**The Ruins** To get to the ruins, walk south on the main street in town as far as the T-junction at the lake. Here, take a left onto the brilliantly named Av. Voz Suave; the ruins are a 5-minute walk down the road. It's a good idea to find a guide at the entrance, as this will make the visit much more enlightening. Most guides speak English and will take a group of four or five for around 40 pesos per person. If you're not willing to part with that many pesos, or are in a small group, hunt down old Arturo, who will take you on the two-hour tour for less.

Once through the gate, the site's six attractions are laid out before you in a "Y"-formation, the entrance being at the base of the Y. Take an immediate right to the **Grupo Cobá.** To the left looms the impressive **Temple of the Churches,** built over seven 52-year periods, each associated with a new chief priest. Only the front face of the temple has been excavated, revealing a corbel-vaulted passageway (to the left) which you can explore. Climb the 24m to the top for the best view the site has to offer: to the northwest lies the town of Cobá, due west is **Laguna Cobá,** and south, **Laguna Macanxoc** (Ma-kan-SHOK). Rising out of the jungle to the northeast are the grey steps of the ancient city's centerpiece, **El Castillo.** In front of the structure is a stone sacrificial table, upon which animal offerings were made to Chac, the rain god. The stela depicts Chac; another nearby features a kneeling Mayan. Follow a second passageway further south to the **Plaza del Templo,** where assemblies were once held. The red plant dye still visible on the walls of the passageway date from the fifth century CE. A mortar here intimates at the staple food of the ancient (and contemporary) Maya—corn.

Return to the main path for a look at the **ballcourt.** Any two explanations you will hear of the ancient game played here will inevitably differ. Somewhat akin to modern-day soccer, the object was to project a soccer-ball-sized ball of *chicle* through the arches. The only arch which was standing when the site was discovered—it straddled the path—unfortunately came tumbling down when Hurricane Gilbert struck Cobá in 1988. The winning captain's glory was short-lived, however, as he was promptly sacrificed on the altar of the gods. Competitors got suited up for the game in the passageway nearby.

A 1km walk up the "trunk" of the "Y" takes you to four other sites. Branch off to the right and follow this trail for another km to reach a collection of eight stelae in the **Grupo Macanxoc.** On the way, you cross over one of the well-engineered Mayan roads called a *sacbé* (white road). This particular road is 20m wide and raised 4m from the jungle floor. The ornate stone slabs of the Grupo Macanxoc were erected as memorials above the tombs of Mayan royals. Especially impressive and well-preserved is the first, the **Retrato del Rey.** The king is shown standing on the heads of two slaves, bow and arrow in hand, wearing a *quetzal*-feather headdress.

Returning to the central part of the "Y," enter the **Conjunto de las Pinturas** (Assembly of the Paintings). Like the inscriptions on many of the stelae that hide off the side of the road, the murals lining the edges of the temple atop the pyramid have been badly eroded by heat and humidity, twin avatars of the jungle's destructive power. Nonetheless, the short climb to the top brings you tête-à-tête with exquisite carved detail of a few fish and Mayan fishermen's faces. Plant dyes were used here to render the red, orange, and blue colors. The stone slabs at the base of the pyramid are tombs. The small surface area is explained by the fact that the deceased were buried vertically rather than horizontally.

Continue north to the left-hand branch of the "Y." After 200m, follow an unmarked trail on the right to the three stelae of **Chumuc Múl.** The first stela depicts a kneeling Mayan ballplayer. Sure enough, this is the tomb of a victorious captain. You can make out the *chicle* ball in the upper-left-hand corner. The second stela is of a princess, while the third is of a *sacerdote* (priest). His seal is stamped on top of the slab, along with a jaguar's head, a common Mayan symbol of worship. 200m further up this branch of the "Y" you'll run into **sacbé No. 1.** This thoroughfare ran from Chichén Itzá, 101km to the west, all the way to Tulum, 48km to the southeast. Runners were posted every 5km so that messages could be sent between settlements via a series of quick dashes. During the city's height (900-1200 CE), Cobá is believed to have been the major crossroads in a commercial region of 17 cities. Images of the honeybee god around the site are a reminder of this ancient economic hub—the Maya used honey along with coconuts and jade as a medium of exchange.

The tour climaxes with the breathtaking sight of the **Nohoch Múl.** If you believe the legend, which says that each of the nine platforms took 55 years to build, then Mayan slaves labored for almost 500 years (without the wheel, metal tools, or domesticated animals) to complete this *castillo.* Although the view is not as spectacular as that from the Templo de la Iglesia, the 120-step climb *will* make your heart race. The pyramid's nine levels, where Mayan priests once led processions, display carvings of the diving god, a crucial deity in the battle to maintain harmony with the surrounding lakes. Just before the pyramid, Stela No. 20 stands in front of a small ruin. The stela depicts a dignitary of high rank (note the plumed crest and rich clothing) standing on a board supported by two slaves. A deciphered date on the stela reads November 30, 1780.

Regardless of when you arrive at the site, bring a water bottle and wear a hat. And unless you feel like being sacrificed to *Mosca,* the mosquito god, bring plenty of repellent, too. During the high season, 11am-2pm are peak tourist hours (ruins open daily 8am-5pm; admission 14 pesos).

# ■■■ CHETUMAL

Home to more people than all of Belize just minutes to the south, Chetumal (pop. 200,000) sits on the Caribbean coast in Quintana Roo's southeastern corner. Originally known as Playa Obispo, this capital city was established in 1899 to intercept shipments of arms to Mayan rebels and to prevent illegal timber harvesting. The lumber industry still supports area residents, though now it's legal. No beaches or hidden ruins are to be found in Chetumal—just deteriorating brick streets and busy shoppers scoping the forest of duty-free shops. Otherwise, the town serves mainly as a stopover between the Yucatán and Tikal or Belize.

## ORIENTATION

Tucked into the Yucatán's southeastern corner, Chetumal is just north of the Río Hondo, the natural border between Mexico and Belize. There are three principal approaches to the city: Rte. 186 from Escárcega (273km), along the Caribbean coast from Cancún (379km), and from Mérida via Valladolid (458km).

The pointlessly large **bus terminal** at Av. de los Insurgentes and Av. Belice is Chetumal's ground transportation hub. **Autotransportes del Caribe, Batty's, Dorada, ADO, Maya de Oro,** and **Cristóbal Colón** all serve the terminal, although Batty's bus service and **Venus,** with connections to Belize, also run from the Mercado Nuevo four blocks away on Calzada Veracruz and Segundo Circuito. It is also possible to wind up at the **Autotransportes Peninsulares** station, 2km further out of the city, also on Av. de los Insurgentes at Av. Palermo. This station serves Mérida exclusively with mostly first-class buses.

Take a taxi (5 pesos) into town, as it's a long, long way to walk. Chetumal's thriving shopping district lines **Avenida de los Héroes,** starting at Av. Efrain Aguilar at the city's market and extending 1km south to the bay. Along the way, between Aguilar and the bay, Héroes crosses Héroes de Chapultepec, Lázaro Cárdenas, Plutarco

Elías Calles, Ignacio Zaragoza, Obregón, O. Blanco, Carmen Ochoa, and 22 de Enero, in that order. This compact commercial area encompasses most of Chetumal's hotels and restaurants. At the southern terminus of Héroes lies **Boulevard Bahía,** a wide avenue flanked by statues and small plazas that follows the bay for several kilometers. From here you can see part of Belize, the long spit of land stretching out to the right as you face the sea.

## PRACTICAL INFORMATION

**Tourist Office:** The central office seems to be forever relocating—it's currently miles from the center of town up the extension of Belice. The office's **information booth,** on Héroes at Aguilar, is much more accessible. Reasonably helpful staffers provide maps of the city. Open Mon.-Sat. 8am-1pm and 5-9pm, although employees don't stick to these hours very reliably.

**Police:** Insurgentes at Belice (tel. 2-15-00), at the northern end of town next to the bus station. Little English spoken. Open 24 hrs.

**Post Office:** Plutarco Elías Calles 2A (tel. 2-25-78), six blocks south and one block east of the Mercado. Open for stamps and *Lista de Correos* Mon.-Fri. 8am-7pm, Sat. 9am-1pm. **Postal Code:** 77000.

**Telephones:** Long distance *caseta* (tel. 2-45-14; fax 2-98-19) upstairs on Héroes at the Mercado near Aguilar. International collect calls 5 pesos, calls and faxes to the U.S. 10 pesos per min. Open Mon.-Sat. 8am-2pm and 4-9pm, Sun. 8am-1:30pm. Public phones in Chetumal take either the rare 1 peso coins, credit cards, or **LADATEL** phone cards, which can be purchased at Hotel Tulum on Héroes at Aguilar. **Telephone Code:** 983.

**Telegrams:** (tel. 2-06-51), in the same building as the post office, through the door to the left. Open Mon.-Fri. 9am-6pm, Sat. 9am-1pm.

**Consulates: Guatemala,** Chapultepec 354 (tel. 2-85-85), at Cecilio Chi. Will happily help you with your Guatemalan jaunt. For a 90-day tourist visa you'll need your passport and a photocopy of your passport (fee US$5). For a 30-day free tourist visa, you'll need your passport plus photocopy and you'll also have to prove you have sufficient funds for your trip. Open Mon.-Fri. 9am-5pm. **Belize** (tel. 2-28-71), west of Héroes on Obregón, next to Bancomer. Open Mon.-Fri. 9am-2pm and 5-8pm.

**Currency Exchange: Bánamex,** Juárez 51 (tel. 2-47-13), at Obregón, eight blocks south and one block west of the Mercado. Open Mon.-Fri. 9am-2pm. Cirrus ATM open 24 hrs. Across the way, **Bancomer** (tel. 2-70-72) has better rates and smaller lines. **ATM** available. Open Mon.-Fri. 9am-1:30pm.

**Airport:** (tel. 2-04-65), 5km south of the city on Aguilar. **Aviacsa** (tel. 2-77-65) to Mexico City. **Bonanza** (tel. 2-83-06) to Mérida, Cancún, and Isla Cozumel.

**Bus Stations:** At Insurgentes and Belice (tel. 2-78-86). Lockers available for 1 peso per hr. **ADO** (tel. 2-06-39) offers first-class service to Cancún (9 per day, 6hrs., 55 pesos) via Tulum (4hrs., 39.50 pesos) and Playa del Carmen (5hrs., 49 pesos), Campeche (noon, 7hrs., 70.50 pesos), Escárcega (5 per day, 4hrs., 44.50 pesos), Mexico City (11:30am, 4:30, 4:35, and 9pm, 21hrs., 257.50 pesos), Palenque (10:15pm, 7hrs., 79 pesos), Puebla (4:30 and 10pm, 19hrs., 233 pesos), Veracruz (1 and 6:30pm, 13hrs., 173 pesos), and Villahermosa (7 per day, 8hrs., 92.50). **Dorada** (tel. 7-13-57) serves Mérida (7:30am, 1:30, 5, and 11:30pm, 8hrs., 66 pesos). **Cristóbal Colón** runs all the way to Tapachula (9:30pm, 20½hrs., 190 pesos), passing through Escárcega (4hrs., 44 pesos), Palenque (7hrs., 78 pesos), San Cristóbal (11hrs., 112 pesos), Tuxtla Gutiérrez (12½hrs., 118 pesos), and Tonalá (16½hrs., 154 pesos) on the way. **Maya de Oro** sends a luxury bus as far as Tuxtla (midnight, 12½hrs., 130.50 pesos), via Palenque (7hrs., 89 pesos) and San Cristóbal (11hrs., 122 pesos). **Batty's Bus** runs to Belize City (10:45am, 2:15, 3:15, and 5:15pm, 4hrs., 30 pesos). Batty's buses also leave from the Mercado Lázaro Cárdenas (also called Mercado Nuevo) at Calzada Veracruz and Segundo Circuito. Take a taxi (5 pesos) or a bus going to Mercado Nuevo (0.80 pesos) from the *mercado* (9 per day, 4hrs., 35 pesos). **Venus** provides early morning departures leaving at approximately 5, 6, 8, 9, and 10am, as well as throughout the day.

CHETUMAL

**Market:** City market is located on the corner of Aguilar and Héroes, where vendors peddle everything from vibrators to packed cheese. Open daily 6am-3pm. **Super San Francisco de Asis,** next to the bus station.

**Red Cross:** Chapultepec at Independencia (tel. 2-05-71), a block south and 2 blocks west of the bus station, in the back of Hospital Civil Morelos. Open 24 hrs.

**Pharmacies:** Pharmacies are scattered throughout the city. **Farmacia Canto,** Av. Héroes 99 (tel. 2-04-83), is conveniently located at the northern end of the market. Open daily 7am-11pm.

**Hospital: Hospital Civil Morelos,** Aguilar at Juárez (tel. 2-45-98 or 2-19-37).

## ACCOMMODATIONS

While Chetumal's hotels fail to astound, they at least provide a convenient location and inexpensive lodging. For the most part, budget accommodations cluster along or just off Heroés, south of the market. At such low prices, facilities are spartan: don't expect hot water or air conditioning.

**CREA Youth Hostel (HI),** Heróica Escuela Naval at Calzada Veracruz (tel. 2-34-65), at the eastern terminus of Obregón. For once, a youth hostel within manageable walking distance. True to the hostel's claim, clean, modern, single-sex rooms with 2 bunkbeds each provide *bienestar económico.* Check-out noon. Lawn for camping (6 pesos). Bed with sheets, towel, and locker 12.50 pesos. Deposit 20 pesos. 25% off with Plan Joven, 10% with IYH. Breakfast 9.75 pesos, lunch and dinner 12 pesos. Breakfast is always available; other meals only when hostel has several guests. Front desk manned 7am-11pm but you can make arrangements to return later. Fills during July and August, so call to reserve.

**Hotel Brasilia,** Aguilar 186 (tel. 2-09-64), at Héroes, across from the market. Spacious rooms upstairs enjoy a strong breeze from noisy fans. Lobby is as clean as it gets for the price. Private baths with hot water. Check-out noon. Friendly management will store packs. Singles 27 pesos. Doubles 40 pesos. Triples 52 pesos. To make reservations, wire money in advance.

**Hotel Tulum,** Héroes 181 (tel. 2-05-18), just north of Aguilar. Sky-blue rooms with roomy but bare baths. Some lucky guests get a view of a junk-filled roof. Check-out 1pm. Singles 30 pesos. 10 pesos per extra person. U.S. dollars accepted.

**Hotel María Dolores,** Obregón 206 (tel. 2-05-08), half a block west of Héroes. Look for the chirpy image of Donald Duck at the entrance. Lime walls clash with shiny-clean olive bathrooms. No toilet seats, but there are ceiling fans, "hot water," and a restaurant downstairs. Check-out 1pm. Singles 39 pesos. Doubles 44 pesos, with two beds 50 pesos. Triples 60 pesos. U.S. dollars accepted.

**Hotel Doris,** Héroes 49, between Obregón and O. Blanco, 5½ blocks south of the market. Stuffy, uninspired rooms with cement beds and petite but spotless coffee-brown bathrooms with alcove showers. Not to be outdone by the Hotel Tulum, Doris's balconies offer an interesting view of rubble. Check-out noon. Singles 35 pesos. Doubles 40 pesos. 10 pesos per additional person. U.S. dollars are dandy.

**Trailer Park,** in Calderitas 9km northeast of Chetumal, overlooking Chetumal Bay. Well-kept with thin grassy lawn and large coconut palms. Electricity, water hookups, and clean bathrooms. Vehicles, under 40 pesos. Tents or hammock spaces 10 pesos per person. Big bungalows with kitchen about 70 pesos for 1-2 people.

## FOOD

The café-restaurants at the end of Héroes, on 22 de Enero near the bay, are small on atmosphere but even smaller on price. Although somewhat out of the way, they're well worth the trek. Other spots for cheap eats can be found along Obregón, west of Héroes.

**Restaurante Pantoja,** M. Gandhi 181 (tel. 2-39-57), next to Hotel Ucum just north of the market, is an extremely popular family restaurant. The *enchiladas* here are a dream at 12 pesos. Gigantic lemonades 2 pesos. Open Mon.-Sat. 7am-9pm.

**Arcadas Super and Restaurante,** Av. Héroes at Zaragoza (tel. 2-08-84), is an open-air café, bar, and supermarket. "Aztec soup" 8.50 pesos. *Fajitas* and chicken or meat specialties run 21.50-25.50 pesos. Open 24 hrs.

**El Taquito,** Plutarco Elías Calles 220, near Juárez one block west of Héroes, is the only place that makes an attempt at atmosphere. Brace yourself for Belize and come and listen to the fresh beat of Radio Frontera. Prompt service allows plenty of time for gobbling endless *antojitos* under the vast thatched roof. Tacos 2.50 pesos. *Queso fundido* 10 pesos. Open Mon.-Sat. 9am-midnight.

## SIGHTS AND SAND

People come to Chetumal to visit **El Mercado.** Period. Nothing else in town is of much interest to travelers, except the new **Museo de la Cultura Maya,** at Héroes and Mahatma Gandhi, just north of the market, which features replicas of nearby ruins and documents the history of Chetumal (open Tues.-Sun. 9am-7pm; guides available for tours in English or Spanish, and a tip is appreciated; admission 7 pesos). The nearest beach is the *balneario* at **Calderitas,** a 20-minute bus ride from Chetumal. Buses (1 peso) leave every half-hour between 5am and 10pm from Av. Belice between Colón and Gandhi. Although the water is turbid and the shores rocky, the beach looks like a *Where's Waldo* puzzle during summer and school holidays.

Much nicer, both for atmosphere and for swimming, are the three watering-holes near the town of **Bacalar,** 34km away. The local **bus** to Bacalar (5 pesos) leaves every hour between 5:30am and 10:30pm from Chetumal's bus station; *combis* leave every hour from the corner of Hidalgo and Primo de Verdad in front of the public library (30min., 5 pesos). The route passes **Laguna Milagros** and **Cenote Azul** before reaching Bacalar. Quieter than the popular Bacalar, especially during the week, both have bathing areas, dressing rooms, and lakeside restaurants. The huge dining room by Cenote Azul, though expensive, is right on the water.

Past the uninteresting Fuerte de San Felipe in Bacalar lie the docks of the **Laguna de Siete Colores,** named for the hues reflected in its depths. The fresh water is warm, perfectly clear, devoid of plant or animal life, and carpeted by powdery limestone, making it excellent for swimming. Best of all, the laguna is not yet a tourist attraction; schools of bathing *niños* and novice snorkelers populate the waters. Nearby are bathrooms, dressing rooms, fruit vendors, expensive dockside restaurants, and a campground.

Much further afield from Chetumal, the small seaside town of **Xcalac** (200km, 3hrs. from Chetumal), the southernmost center of population on the spit of land extending south from the Sian Ka'an reserve, provides mellow-time bungalows, restaurants, snorkeling, and boat rentals. Nearby off the coast lies the enticing **Banco Chinchorro,** the second-largest shipwreck site in the world, making for a funky deep-sea treasure-hunting dive. Buses to Xcalac and the closer, less service-laden **Mahahval** (150km from Chetumal) depart daily at 7am from Av. 16 de Septiembre at M. Gandhi, 20m from the Restaurante Pantoja (18-21 pesos).

# Index